STATUTORY INSTRUMENTS

1971

PART II
(in two Sections)

SECTION 2

Published by Authority

LONDON
HER MAJESTY'S STATIONERY OFFICE
1971

NOL

PRINTED AND PUBLISHED BY HER MAJESTY'S STATIONERY OFFICE

To be purchased from

49 High Holborn, LONDON, WC1V 6HB
13a Castle Street, EDINBURGH, EH2 3AR   109 St. Mary Street, CARDIFF, CF1 1JW
Brazennose Street, MANCHESTER, M60 8AS   50 Fairfax Street, BRISTOL, BS1 3DE
258 Broad Street, BIRMINGHAM, B1 2HE   80 Chichester Street, BELFAST, BT1 4JY

or through booksellers

1971

Price for the two Sections: £12·75 net

PRINTED IN ENGLAND

SBN 11 840090 8*

Contents of the Volume

PART I, Section 1

PART I, Section 2

PART II, Section 1

PART II, Section 2

PART III

STATUTORY INSTRUMENTS

1971 No. 1023

WAGES COUNCILS

The Wages Regulation (Retail Food) (Scotland)
Order 1971

Made - - - - 21st June 1971

Coming into Operation 9th August 1971

Whereas the Secretary of State has received from the Retail Food Trades
Wages Council (Scotland) the wages regulation proposals set out in the Schedule
hereto;

Now, therefore, the Secretary of State in exercise of his powers under section
11 of the Wages Councils Act 1959(a), and of all other powers enabling him
in that behalf, hereby makes the following Order:—

1. This Order may be cited as the Wages Regulation (Retail Food) (Scotland)
Order 1971.

2.—(1) In this Order the expression "the specified date" means the 9th
August 1971, provided that where, as respects any worker who is paid wages
at intervals not exceeding seven days, that date does not correspond with the
beginning of the period for which the wages are paid, the expression "the
specified date" means, as respects that worker, the beginning of the next such
period following that date.

(2) The Interpretation Act 1889(b) shall apply to the interpretation of this
Order as it applies to the interpretation of an Act of Parliament and as if this
Order and the Orders hereby revoked were Acts of Parliament.

3. The wages regulation proposals set out in the Schedule hereto shall have
effect as from the specified date and as from that date the Wages Regulation
(Retail Food) (Scotland) Order 1970(c) and the Wages Regulation (Retail
Food) (Scotland) (Amendment) Order 1970(d) shall cease to have effect.

Signed by order of the Secretary of State.

21st June 1971.

R. R. D. McIntosh,
Deputy Secretary,
Department of Employment.

(a) 1959 c. 69. (b) 1889 c. 63.
(c) S.I. 1970/428 (1970 I, p. 1473). (d) S.I. 1970/860 (1970 II, p. 2732).

ARRANGEMENT OF SCHEDULE

PART I

STATUTORY MINIMUM REMUNERATION

PART II

ANNUAL HOLIDAY AND HOLIDAY REMUNERATION

PART III

GENERAL

Article 3   SCHEDULE

The following minimum remuneration and provisions as to holidays and holiday remuneration shall be substituted for the statutory minimum remuneration and provisions as to holidays and holiday remuneration set out in the Wages Regulation (Retail Food) (Scotland) Order 1970 (hereinafter referred to as "Order R.F.C.S. (41)") as amended by the Wages Regulation (Retail Food) (Scotland) (Amendment) Order 1970 (Order R.F.C.S. (43)).

PART I

STATUTORY MINIMUM REMUNERATION
APPLICATION

1. Subject to the provisions of paragraphs 2, 7, 8 and 12, the minimum remuneration payable to workers to whom this Schedule applies shall be the remuneration set out in paragraphs 3, 4, 5 and 6.

Any increase in remuneration payable under the provisions of paragraph 5 or 6 shall become effective on the first day of the first full pay week following the date upon which the increase would otherwise become payable under those provisions.

HOURS ON WHICH REMUNERATION IS BASED

2.—(1) The minimum remuneration specified in this Part of this Schedule relates to a week of 42 hours exclusive of overtime, and, except as provided in paragraph 12 (which deals with guaranteed weekly remuneration), is subject to a proportionate reduction according as the number of hours worked is less than 42.

(2) In calculating the remuneration for the purpose of this Schedule recognised breaks for meal times shall, subject to the provisions of paragraph 9 (which relates to waiting time), be excluded.

SHOP MANAGERS AND SHOP MANAGERESSES

3. Subject to the provisions of this paragraph, the minimum remuneration payable to Shop Managers and Shop Manageresses shall be the amount appearing in Column 2 of the following table against the amount of weekly trade shown in Column 1.

Column 1	Column 2	
Weekly Trade	Shop Manageresses All Areas	Shop Managers All Areas
	per week £	per week £
Under £50	12·50	14·05
£50 and under £60	12·65	14·05
£60 „ „ £70	12·80	14·05
£70 „ „ £80	12·90	14·05
£80 „ „ £90	13·05	14·05
£90 „ „ £100	13·15	14·05
£100 „ „ £110	13·55	14·45
£110 „ „ £120	13·70	14·55
£120 „ „ £130	13·80	14·65
£130 „ „ £140	13·90	14·75
£140 „ „ £150	13·95	14·85
£150 „ „ £160	14·00	14·90
£160 „ „ £170	14·05	15·00
£170 „ „ £180	14·15	15·05
£180 „ „ £190	14·20	15·10
£190 „ „ £200	14·25	15·15
£200 „ „ £210	14·40	15·35
£210 „ „ £220	14·50	15·45
£220 „ „ £230	14·55	15·50
£230 „ „ £240	14·60	15·55
£240 „ „ £250	14·65	15·60
£250 „ „ £260	14·70	15·65
£260 „ „ £270	14·75	15·70
£270 „ „ £280	14·80	15·75
£280 „ „ £290	14·85	15·80
£290 „ „ £300	14·90	15·85
£300 „ „ £310	15·15	16·10
£310 „ „ £320	15·20	16·15
£320 „ „ £330	15·25	16·20
£330 „ „ £340	15·30	16·25
£340 „ „ £350	15·35	16·30
£350 „ „ £370	15·40	16·35
£370 „ „ £390	15·45	16·40
£390 „ „ £410	15·50	16·45

Column 1	Column 2	
Weekly Trade	Shop Manageresses All Areas	Shop Managers All Areas
	per week £	per week £
£410 and under £430	15·55	16·50
£430 „ „ £450	15·60	16·55
£450 „ „ £470	15·65	16·60
£470 „ „ £490	15·70	16·65
£490 „ „ £500	15·75	16·70
£500 „ „ £510	15·80	16·75
£510 „ „ £530	15·85	16·80
£530 „ „ £550	15·90	16·85
£550 „ „ £570	15·95	16·90
£570 „ „ £590	16·00	16·95
£590 „ „ £600	16·05	17·00
£600 „ „ £610	16·10	17·05
£610 „ „ £630	16·15	17·10
£630 „ „ £650	16·20	17·15
£650 „ „ £670	16·25	17·20
£670 „ „ £690	16·30	17·25
£690 „ „ £700	16·35	17·30
£700 „ „ £710	16·40	17·35
£710 „ „ £730	16·45	17·40
£730 „ „ £750	16·50	17·45
£750 „ „ £770	16·55	17·50
£770 „ „ £790	16·60	17·55
£790 „ „ £800	16·65	17·60
£800 „ „ £810	16·70	17·65
£810	16·75	17·70
For Shop Managers and Shop Manageresses employed in shops with weekly trade in excess of £810 per week there shall be added to the above amounts of weekly remuneration for Shop Managers and Shop Manageresses employed in shops with a weekly trade of £810, 5p for every additional complete £20 of weekly trade up to and including a weekly trade of £3,100.		
More than £3,100	22·45	23·40

For the purposes of this paragraph, "weekly trade" shall be calculated half-yearly and based on the period of 12 months immediately preceding the commencement of each half-year in the following manner:—

For the 26 pay weeks beginning with the fifth pay week following the last Saturday in February in any year, or for any part thereof, the weekly trade of a shop shall be one fifty-second of the amount of the total receipts for goods sold at that shop during the 52 weeks immediately preceding the last Saturday in February in that year and for the 26 pay weeks in any year immediately following (hereinafter called the "second period"), or for any part thereof, the weekly trade of a shop shall be one fifty-second of the amount of the total receipts in respect of goods sold at that shop during the 52 weeks immediately preceding the last Saturday in August of the same year as that in which the second period begins:

Provided that, so long as a shop has been under management for less than 52 weeks immediately preceding the last Saturday in February in any year or the last Saturday in August in any year, as the case may be, the weekly trade of that shop, for the purpose of calculating the weekly minimum remuneration payable in any pay week under the foregoing table, shall until such period of 52 weeks has elapsed be the amount of the total receipts in respect of goods sold at that shop in the week immediately preceding such pay week and for the purpose of calculating such weekly remuneration as aforesaid payable in respect of each of the first two pay weeks during which a shop is under management the weekly trade of that shop shall be the amount of the total receipts for goods sold thereat in the first week during which the shop is under management.

TEMPORARY SHOP MANAGERS AND TEMPORARY SHOP MANAGERESSES

4.—(1) Subject to the provisions of this paragraph, the minimum remuneration payable to Temporary Shop Managers and Temporary Shop Manageresses during any of the periods of employment in Column 1 shall be at the rate appearing in Column 2 of the following table:—

Column 1	Column 2	
Continuous period of employment as Temporary Shop Manager or Temporary Shop Manageress	Temporary Shop Manageresses All Areas	Temporary Shop Managers All Areas
	per week £	per week £
(a) during the first two weeks	12·25	14·15
(b) during the third and fourth weeks... ...	12·65	14·80
(c) thereafter	the appropriate minimum remuneration for a Shop Manager or Shop Manageress, as the case may be, under the provisions of paragraph 3.	

Provided that where a Temporary Shop Manageress takes charge of a shop managed by a Shop Manager the weekly minimum remuneration payable to the Temporary Shop Manageress during the periods of employment in Column 1 shall be at the rate appearing in Column 2 of the following table:—

Column 1	Column 2
Continuous period of employment as Temporary Shop Manageress	Temporary Shop Manageresses All Areas
	per week £
(i) during the first two weeks	12·50
(ii) during the third and fourth weeks ...	13·00
(iii) thereafter	the appropriate minimum remuneration for a Shop Manageress under the provisions of paragraph 3.

(2) For the purposes of this paragraph where a worker commences a period of employment as a Temporary Shop Manager or Temporary Shop Manageress within six months of the termination of such a period of employment at the same shop, the two periods of employment shall be treated as continuous.

WORKERS OTHER THAN SHOP MANAGERS, SHOP MANAGERESSES, TEMPORARY SHOP MANAGERS, TEMPORARY SHOP MANAGERESSES, CENTRAL TRANSPORT WORKERS AND RETAIL TRANSPORT WORKERS

5. Subject to the provisions of paragraph 1, the minimum remuneration payable to male or female workers of the classes specified in Column 1 of the following table employed in Area 1 or Area 2, as the case may be, shall be the appropriate amount set out in Column 2:—

Column 1	Column 2			
	Male Workers		Female Workers	
	Area 1	Area 2	Area 1	Area 2
	per week £	per week £	per week £	per week £
(1) CLERKS GRADE I other than those referred to in (2) of this paragraph, CLERKS GRADE II, SHOP ASSISTANTS, CENTRAL WAREHOUSE WORKERS, TRANSPORT WORKERS (other than those referred to in paragraph 6) and all other workers being workers aged:—				
15 and under 16 years	7·00	6·75	6·75	6·50
16 „ „ 17 „	7·50	7·25	7·00	6·75
17 „ „ 18 „	8·00	7·75	7·25	7·00
18 „ „ 19 „	9·15	8·85	8·40	8·10
19 „ „ 20 „	9·90	9·50	8·90	8·50
20 „ „ 21 „	10·65	10·15	9·40	8·90
21 „ „ 22 „	12·50	11·90	10·75	10·25
22 years or over	13·50	12·80	11·50	10·95
(2) CLERKS GRADE I aged 23 years or over	13·75	13·00	11·60	11·15

CENTRAL TRANSPORT WORKERS AND RETAIL TRANSPORT WORKERS

6. Subject to the provisions of paragraph 1, the minimum remuneration payable to Central Transport Workers and Retail Transport Workers employed in Area 1 or Area 2, as the case may be, on the types of vehicle described in Column 2 of the following table, shall be the appropriate amount set out in Column 3:—

Column 1	Column 2		Column 3	
	Type of vehicle			
Age of transport worker	Mechanically propelled vehicle with carrying capacity of	Horse drawn vehicle	Area 1	Area 2
(1) CENTRAL TRANSPORT WORKERS			per week £	per week £
21 years or over			13·50	12·80
20 and under 21 years			12·50	11·90
19 „ „ 20 „	1 ton or less	One-horse	10·65	10·15
18 „ „ 19 „			9·90	9·50
Under 18 years			9·15	8·85
	Over 1 ton up to 2 tons	Two-horse	13·65	12·95
All ages	Over 2 tons up to 5 tons	—	13·65	12·95
	Over 5 tons	—	13·85	13·15
(2) RETAIL TRANSPORT WORKERS				
	Over 1½ tons up to 2 tons	Two-horse	13·50	12·80
All ages	Over 2 tons up to 5 tons	—	13·50	12·80
	Over 5 tons	—	13·70	13·00

MINIMUM OVERTIME RATES

7. Subject to the provisions of this paragraph, overtime shall be payable at the following minimum rates:—

(1) For employment on a Sunday—

(a) Where the worker is required to work in connection with the preservation of perishable goods—

(i) where time worked does not exceed 2 hours...   double time for 2 hours

(ii) where time worked exceeds 2 hours—for all time worked ... ...   double time

(b) Where the worker is required to work for any reason other than that referred to in (a) of this sub-paragraph—

(i) where time worked does not exceed 4 hours...   double time for 4 hours

(ii) where time worked exceeds 4 hours—for all time worked ... ...   double time

Provided that where it is, or becomes, the established practice in a Jewish undertaking for the employer to require attendance on Sunday instead of Saturday, the foregoing provisions of this paragraph shall apply in like manner as if in such provisions the word "Saturday" were substituted for "Sunday", except where such substitution is unlawful.

(2) In any week, exclusive of any time

(a) in respect of which a minimum overtime rate is payable under the foregoing provisions of this paragraph;

(b) in respect of which a special time rate is payable under the provisions of paragraph 8;

(c) worked on a customary holiday; or

(d) worked immediately after the closing of the shop to the public not exceeding 15 minutes on any one day or one hour in the aggregate in any week;

for all time worked in excess of 42 hours ...　time-and-a-half:

Provided that in any week which includes one customary holiday the period of 42 hours shall be reduced by 7 hours and, in any week which includes two customary holidays, by 14 hours.

Overtime rates in accordance with the foregoing provisions of this paragraph shall be payable to a Shop Manager or Shop Manageress only if the overtime worked is specifically authorised by the employer or his representative.

SPECIAL TIME

8. The following special time rate shall be payable to a worker who is a shop assistant within the meaning of the Shops Act 1950(a)—

On the worker's weekly half day, where, under section 40 of the Shops Act 1950, the employer is relieved of his obligation to allow the worker a weekly half day—

for all time worked after 1.30 p.m. ...　　... double time.

WAITING TIME

9. A worker shall be entitled to payment of the minimum remuneration specified in this Schedule for all the time during which he is present on the premises of the employer, unless he is present thereon in any of the following circumstances, that is to say—

(1) without the employer's consent, express or implied;

(2) for some purpose unconnected with his work, and other than that of waiting for work to be given to him to perform;

(3) by reason only of the fact that he is resident thereon; or

(4) during normal meal times in a room or place in which no work is being done, and he is not waiting for work to be given to him to perform.

WORKERS WHO ARE NOT REQUIRED TO WORK ON A CUSTOMARY HOLIDAY

10. Where a worker is not required to work on a customary holiday he shall be paid for the customary holiday not less than the amount to which he would have been entitled under the arrangement current immediately prior to the holiday had the day not been a customary holiday and had he worked the number of hours ordinarily worked by him on that day of the week.

(a) 1950 c. 28.

WORKERS WHO WORK ON A CUSTOMARY HOLIDAY

11. Where a worker works on a customary holiday he shall be paid not less than the amount to which he would have been entitled under the arrangement current immediately prior to the holiday had the day not been a customary holiday and had he worked the number of hours ordinarily worked by him on that day of the week, and, in addition

(1) for any time worked not exceeding 2 hours ...   ...   double time for 2 hours

(2) for any time worked in excess of 2 hours but not in
excess of 8 hours   ...   .   hourly rate

(3) for all time worked in excess of 8 hours   ...   ...   double time.

GUARANTEED WEEKLY REMUNERATION PAYABLE TO A FULL-TIME WORKER

12.—(1) Notwithstanding the other provisions of this Schedule, where in any week the total remuneration (including holiday remuneration) payable under those other provisions to a full-time worker is less than the guaranteed weekly remuneration provided under this paragraph, the minimum remuneration payable to that worker for that week shall be that guaranteed weekly remuneration: Provided that the worker throughout his normal working hours in that week (excluding any time allowed to him as a holiday or during which he is absent from work in accordance with sub-paragraph (3) of this paragraph) is capable of and available for work.

(2) The guaranteed weekly remuneration is the remuneration to which the worker would be entitled under paragraph 3, 4, 5 or 6 for 42 hours' work in his usual occupation.

(3) Where in any week a worker at his request and with the written consent of his employer is absent from work during any part of his normal working hours on any day (other than a holiday allowed under Part II of this Schedule or a customary holiday or a holiday allowed to all persons employed in the undertaking or branch of an undertaking in which the worker is employed), the guaranteed weekly remuneration payable in respect of that week shall be reduced in respect of each day on which he is absent as aforesaid by one-sixth where the worker's normal working week is six days or by one-fifth where his normal working week is five days.

Part II

ANNUAL HOLIDAY AND HOLIDAY REMUNERATION
ANNUAL HOLIDAY

13.—(1) Subject to the provisions of paragraph 14, an employer shall, between the date on which this Schedule becomes effective and 31st October 1971, and in each succeeding year between 1st April and 31st October allow a holiday (hereinafter referred to as an "annual holiday") to every worker in his employment to whom this Schedule applies who has been employed by him during the 12 months immediately preceding the commencement of the holiday season for any one of the periods of employment (calculated in accordance with the provisions of paragraph 20) set out in the table below and the duration of the annual holiday shall in the case of each such worker be related to that period as follows:—

Period of employment	Duration of annual holiday
12 months...	12 days
Not less than 11 months but less than 12 months	11 ,,
,, ,, ,, 10 ,, ,, ,, ,, 11 ,, ...	10 ,,
,, ,, ,, 9 ,, ,, ,, ,, 10 ,, ...	9 ,,
,, ,, ,, 8 ,, ,, ,, ,, 9 ,, ...	8 ,,
,, ,, ,, 7 ,, ,, ,, ,, 8 ,, ...	7 ,,
,, ,, ,, 6 ,, ,, ,, ,, 7 ,, ...	6 ,,
,, ,, ,, 5 ,, ,, ,, ,, 6 ,, ...	5 ,,
,, ,, ,, 4 ,, ,, ,, ,, 5 ,, ...	4 ,,
,, ,, ,, 3 ,, ,, ,, ,, 4 ,, ...	3 ,,
,, ,, ,, 2 ,, ,, ,, ,, 3 ,, ...	2 ,,
,, ,, ,, 1 month ,, ,, ,, 2 ,, ...	1 day

(2) Notwithstanding the provisions of the last foregoing sub-paragraph—

(a) the number of days of annual holiday which an employer is required to allow to a worker in any holiday season shall not exceed in the aggregate twice the number of days constituting the worker's normal working week;

(b) where a worker does not wish to take his annual holiday or part thereof during the holiday season in any year and, before the expiration of such holiday season, enters into an agreement in writing with his employer that the annual holiday or part thereof shall be allowed, at a date or dates to be specified in that agreement, after the expiration of the holiday season but before the first day of January in the following year, then any day or days of annual holiday so allowed shall be treated as having been allowed during the holiday season;

(c) the duration of the worker's annual holiday during the holiday season ending on 31st October 1971, shall be reduced by any days of annual holiday duly allowed to him by the employer under the provisions of Order R.F.C.S. (41) between 1st April 1971 and the date on which the provisions of this Schedule become effective.

(3) In this Schedule the expression "holiday season" means, in relation to an annual holiday during the year 1971, the period commencing on 1st April 1971 and ending on 31st October 1971, and, in relation to each subsequent year, the period commencing on 1st April and ending on 31st October in that year.

14. Where at the written request of the worker at any time during the three months immediately preceding the commencement of the holiday season in any year, his employer allows him any day or days of annual holiday and pays him holiday remuneration in respect thereof calculated in accordance with the provisions of paragraphs 17 and 18, then

(1) the annual holiday to be allowed in accordance with paragraph 13 in the holiday season in that year shall be reduced by the day or days of annual holiday so allowed prior to the commencement of that holiday season; and

(2) for the purpose of calculating accrued holiday remuneration under paragraph 19 any day or days of annual holiday deducted in accordance with sub-paragraph (1) hereof shall be treated as if they had been allowed in the holiday season.

15.—(1) Subject to the provisions of this paragraph an annual holiday shall be allowed on consecutive working days, being days on which the worker is normally called upon to work for the employer.

(2) Where the number of days of annual holiday for which a worker has qualified exceeds the number of days constituting his normal working week, the holiday may be allowed in two periods of consecutive working days; so, however, that when a holiday is so allowed, one of the periods shall consist of a number of such days not less than the number of days constituting the worker's normal working week.

(3) For the purposes of this paragraph, days of annual holiday shall be treated as consecutive notwithstanding that a customary holiday on which the worker is not required to work for the employer or a day on which he does not normally work for the employer intervenes.

(4) Where a customary holiday on which the worker is not required to work for the employer immediately precedes a period of annual holiday or occurs during such a period and the total number of days of annual holiday required to be allowed in the period under the foregoing provisions of this paragraph, together with any customary holiday, exceeds the number of days constituting the worker's normal working week, then, notwithstanding the foregoing provisions of this paragraph, the duration of that period of annual holiday may be reduced by one day and in such a case one day of annual holiday may be allowed on a day on which the worker normally works for the employer (not being the worker's weekly short day) in the holiday season or after the holiday season in the circumstances specified in sub-paragraph (2)(b) of paragraph 13.

(5) No day of annual holiday shall be allowed on a customary holiday.

(6) A day of annual holiday under this Schedule may be allowed on a day on which the worker is entitled to a day of holiday (not being a customary holiday) or to a half-holiday under any enactment other than the Wages Councils Act 1959.

16. An employer shall give to a worker not later than the first day of April in each year notice of the commencing date or dates and of the duration of his annual holiday. Such notice may be given individually to the worker or by the posting of a notice in the place where the worker is employed.

REMUNERATION FOR ANNUAL HOLIDAY

17.—(1) Subject to the provisions of paragraph 18, a worker qualified to be allowed an annual holiday under this Schedule shall be paid by his employer, on the last pay day preceding such holiday, one day's holiday pay in respect of each day thereof.

(2) Where an annual holiday is taken in more than one period the holiday remuneration shall be apportioned accordingly.

18. Where any accrued holiday remuneration has been paid by the employer to the worker (in accordance with paragraph 19 of this Schedule or with Order R.F.C.S.

(41) as amended), in respect of employment during either or both of the periods referred to in paragraph 19, the amount of holiday remuneration payable by the employer in respect of any annual holiday for which the worker has qualified by reason of employment during the said period or periods shall be reduced by the amount of the said accrued holiday remuneration, unless that remuneration has been deducted from a previous payment of holiday remuneration made under the provisions of this Schedule or of Order R.F.C.S. (41) as amended.

ACCRUED HOLIDAY REMUNERATION PAYABLE ON TERMINATION OF EMPLOYMENT

19. Where a worker ceases to be employed by an employer after the provisions of this Schedule become effective, the employer shall, immediately on the termination of the employment (hereinafter referred to as the "termination date"), pay to the worker as accrued holiday remuneration:—

(1) in respect of employment occurring in the 12 months up to and including 1st April immediately preceding the termination date, a sum equal to the holiday remuneration for any days of annual holiday for which he has qualified except days of annual holiday which he has been allowed or has become entitled to be allowed before leaving the employment; and

(2) in respect of any employment since 1st April immediately preceding the termination date, a sum equal to the holiday remuneration which would have been payable to him if he could have been allowed an annual holiday in respect of that employment at the time of leaving it:

Provided that—

(a) no worker shall be entitled to the payment by his employer of accrued holiday remuneration if he is dismissed on the grounds of misconduct connected with his employment and is so informed by the employer at the time of dismissal;

(b) where, during the period or periods in respect of which the said accrued holiday remuneration is payable, the worker has at his written request been allowed any day or days of holiday (other than days of holiday allowed by the employer under paragraph 14) for which he had not qualified under the provisions of this Schedule, any accrued holiday remuneration payable as aforesaid may be reduced by the amount of any sum paid by the employer to the worker in respect of such day or days of holiday;

(c) where a worker is employed under a contract of service under which he is required to give not less than one week's notice before terminating his employment and the worker without the consent of his employer terminates his employment:—

(i) without having given not less than one week's notice, or

(ii) before one week has expired from the beginning of such notice, the amount of accrued holiday remuneration payable to the worker shall be the amount payable under the foregoing provisions of this paragraph less an amount equal to one day's holiday pay multiplied in the case of (i) by the number of days constituting the worker's normal working week or, in the case of (ii), by the number of days which at the termination of the employment would complete a normal working week commencing at the beginning of the notice.

CALCULATION OF EMPLOYMENT

20. For the purpose of calculating any period of employment qualifying a worker for an annual holiday or for any accrued holiday remuneration, the worker shall be treated as if he were employed for a month in respect of any month throughout which he has been in the employment of the employer.

PART III

GENERAL

DEFINITIONS

21. For the purposes of this Schedule—

"AREA 1" and "AREA 2" have the meanings respectively assigned to them in paragraph 22.

"CARETAKER" means a worker wholly engaged in guarding the employer's premises for the prevention of theft, fire, damage or trespass.

"CARRYING CAPACITY" means the weight of the maximum load normally carried by the vehicle, and such carrying capacity when so established shall not be affected either by variations in the weight of the load resulting from collections or deliveries or emptying of containers during the course of the journey, or by the fact that on any particular journey a load greater or less than the established carrying capacity is carried.

"CENTRAL TRANSPORT WORKER" means a worker engaged wholly or mainly in driving a mechanically propelled or horse drawn road vehicle for the transport of goods from any receiving point to a Central Warehouse or Depot or from any Central Warehouse or Depot to Shops and on work in connection with the vehicle and its load (if any) while on the road.

"CENTRAL WAREHOUSE WORKER" means a worker wholly or mainly employed in a Central Warehouse, that is to say, a warehouse from which an undertaking in the retail food trades supplies its branch shops.

"CLERK GRADE I" means a worker engaged wholly or mainly on clerical work which includes responsibility for maintaining ledgers or wages books or for preparing financial accounts of the undertaking or of a branch or department thereof.

"CLERK GRADE II" means a worker, other than a Clerk Grade I, engaged wholly or mainly on clerical work.

"CUSTOMARY HOLIDAY" means—

1st and 2nd January (or, if either of these days fall on a Sunday, 3rd January shall be substituted for such day);

the local Spring holiday;

the local Autumn holiday;

Christmas Day (or, if Christmas Day falls on a Sunday, 26th December shall be substituted); and

two other days, observed by local custom as holidays, to be fixed by the employer and notified to the worker; and any day proclaimed as a public holiday throughout Scotland.

"FULL-TIME WORKER" means a worker who normally works for the employer for at least 36 hours in the week on work to which this Schedule applies.

"HOURLY RATE" means the amount obtained by dividing by 42 the weekly minimum remuneration to which the worker is entitled under the provisions of paragraph 3, 4, 5 or 6 and "TIME-AND-A-HALF" and "DOUBLE TIME" mean, respectively, one and a half times and twice that rate.

"MONTH" means "calendar month".

"ONE DAY'S HOLIDAY PAY" means one-sixth of the amount which the worker would be entitled to receive from his employer for a week's work under the arrangement current immediately prior to the annual holiday, or the termination date, as the case may be, if he worked his normal working week and the daily number of hours normally worked by him (exclusive of overtime).

"RETAIL TRANSPORT WORKER" means a worker engaged wholly or mainly in driving a mechanically propelled or horse drawn road vehicle for the transport of goods to the consumer and on work in connection with the vehicle and its load (if any) while on the road.

"SHOP ASSISTANT" means (except in paragraph 8) a worker (other than a Clerk Grade I or a Clerk Grade II) wholly or mainly employed in or about the business of a shop or undertaking engaged—

(1) wholly or mainly in the retail food trades; or

(2) wholly or mainly in the retail food trades and one or more of the groups of retail distributive trades set out in the Appendix to paragraph 23, and to a greater extent in the retail food trades than in any one of those groups.

"SHOP MANAGER", "SHOP MANAGERESS" means the worker, other than a temporary shop manager or temporary shop manageress, who is employed at and is in charge of the shop and who has supervision of other workers (if any) employed at the shop.

"TEMPORARY SHOP MANAGER", "TEMPORARY SHOP MANAGER-ESS" means a worker who, during the temporary absence (for a period of not less than one day) of a shop manager or shop manageress, carries out the duties of the shop manager or shop manageress, whilst the worker is so carrying out the duties of a shop manager or shop manageress.

"WEEK" means the period of six days commencing at midnight on any Sunday and ending at midnight on the following Saturday.

"WEEKLY HALF DAY" means that day in any week on which a worker is, in accordance with the provisions of section 17 of the Shops Act 1950, required not to be employed about the business of a shop after half-past one o'clock in the afternoon.

AREAS

22. In this Schedule—

(1) "AREA 2" means all areas other than those defined in sub-paragraph (2) of this paragraph.

(2) "AREA 1" means—

(a) all Burghs which, according to the Preliminary Report on the Sixteenth Census of Scotland 1961, had a population of ten thousand or more;

(b) the following Special Lighting Districts, the boundaries of which have been defined, namely, Vale of Leven and Renton in the County of Dunbarton; and Larbert and Airth in the County of Stirling;

(c) the following areas the boundaries of which were defined as Special Lighting Districts prior to 10th March 1943, namely Bellshill and Mossend, Blantyre, Cambuslang, Larkhall and Holytown, New Stevenston and Carfin, all in the County of Lanark; and

(d) the following Burghs—

ANGUS COUNTY
  Brechin
ARGYLL COUNTY
  Dunoon
AYR COUNTY
  Ardrossan
  Largs
  Troon
BANFF COUNTY
  Buckie
BUTE COUNTY
  Rothesay
DUNBARTON
  COUNTY
  Helensburgh
  Milngavie
EAST LOTHIAN
  COUNTY
  North Berwick

FIFE COUNTY
  Burntisland
  Leven
  Lochgelly
  St. Andrews
KINCARDINE
  COUNTY
  Stonehaven
LANARK COUNTY
  Lanark
MIDLOTHIAN
  COUNTY
  Dalkeith
ORKNEY COUNTY
  Kirkwall
RENFREW COUNTY
  Gourock

ROSS AND
CROMARTY COUNTY
  Stornoway

STIRLING COUNTY
  Denny and Dunipace
  Kilsyth

WEST LOTHIAN
  COUNTY
  Armadale

WIGTOWN COUNTY
  Stranraer

ZETLAND COUNTY
  Lerwick

WORKERS TO WHOM THIS SCHEDULE APPLIES

23.—(1) (i) Subject to the provisions of sub-paragraph (2) of this paragraph the workers to whom this Schedule applies are all workers employed in Scotland in any undertaking or any branch or department of an undertaking being an undertaking, branch or department engaged—

(a) wholly or mainly in the retail food trades; or

(b) wholly or mainly in the retail food trades and one or more of the groups of retail distributive trades set out in the Appendix hereto, and to a greater extent in the retail food trades than in any one of those groups:

Provided that if a branch or department of an undertaking is not so engaged, this Schedule shall not apply to workers employed in that branch or department (notwithstanding that the undertaking as a whole is so engaged), except in the case of workers as respects their employment in a department of that branch if that department is so engaged.

(ii) For the purposes of this paragraph

(a) in determining the extent to which an undertaking or branch or department of an undertaking is engaged in a group of trades, regard shall be had to the time spent in the undertaking, branch or department on work in that group of trades;

(b) an undertaking or branch or department of an undertaking which is engaged in any operation in a group of trades shall be treated as engaged in that group of trades.

(2) This Schedule does not apply to any of the following workers in respect of their employment in any of the following circumstances, that is to say:—

(i) workers in relation to whom any Wages Council operates (other than the Retail Food Trades Wages Council (Scotland)) in respect of any employment which is for the time being within the field of operation of that Wages Council;

(ii) workers employed on post office business;

(iii) workers for whom minimum rates of wages are fixed by the Scottish Agricultural Wages Board;

(iv) workers employed on the maintenance or repair of buildings, plant, equipment or vehicles (but not including workers employed as cleaners);

(v) workers employed in any ship (which includes every description of vessel used in navigation);

(vi) workers employed as caretakers.

(3) For the purpose of this Schedule the retail food trades do not include the sale by retail of bread, pastry or flour confectionery (other than biscuits or meat pastries) or the sale by retail of meat (other than bacon, ham, pressed beef, sausages, or meat so treated as to be fit for human consumption without further preparation or cooking) or the sale by retail of milk (other than dried or condensed milk) or the sale by retail of ice-cream, aerated waters, chocolate confectionery or sugar confectionery, or the sale of food or drink for immediate consumption, but save as aforesaid consist of the sale by retail of food or drink for human consumption and operations connected therewith including:—

(i) operations in or about the shop or other place where the food or drink aforesaid is sold, being operations carried on for the purpose of such sale or otherwise in connection with such sale;

(ii) operations in connection with the warehousing or storing of such food or drink for the purpose of sale by retail, or otherwise in connection with such sale, where the warehousing or storing takes place at a warehouse or store carried on in conjunction with one or more shops or other places where such food or drink is sold by retail;

(iii) operations in connection with the transport of such food or drink when carried on in conjunction with its sale by retail or with the warehousing or storing operations specified in (ii) of this sub-paragraph; and

(iv) clerical or other office work carried on in conjunction with the sale by retail aforesaid and relating to such sale or to any of the operations in (i) to (iii) of this sub-paragraph;

and for the purpose of this definition "sale by retail" includes any sale of food or drink to a person for use in connection with a catering business carried on by him, when such sale takes place at or in connection with a shop engaged in the retail sale of food or drink to the general public.

APPENDIX TO PARAGRAPH 23
GROUPS OF RETAIL DISTRIBUTIVE TRADES

Group 1. The Retail Furnishing and Allied Trades, that is to say—

(1) the sale by retail of:—

(a) household and office furniture, including garden furniture, mattresses, floor coverings and mirrors, but excluding billiard tables, clocks, pianos, gramophones and pictures;

(b) ironmongery, turnery and hardware of kinds commonly used for household purposes, including gardening implements;

(c) hand tools;

(d) woodware, basketware, glassware, potteryware, chinaware, brassware, plasticware and ceramic goods, being articles or goods of kinds commonly used for household purposes or as household ornaments;

(e) electrical and gas appliances and apparatus, of kinds commonly used for household purposes (excluding clocks), and accessories and component parts thereof;

(f) heating, lighting and cooking appliances and apparatus, of kinds commonly used for household purposes, and accessories and component parts thereof;

(g) radio and television sets and their accessories and component parts;

(h) pedal cycles and their accessories and component parts;

(i) perambulators, push chairs and invalid carriages;

(j) toys, indoor games, requisites for outdoor games, gymnastics and athletics, but excluding billiard tables and sports clothing;

(k) saddlery, leather goods (other than articles of wearing apparel), travel goods and ladies' handbags;

(l) paint, distemper and wallpaper, and oils of kinds commonly used for household purposes (excluding petrol and lubricating oils);

(m) brushes, mops and brooms, used for household purposes, and similar articles;

(n) disinfectants, chemicals, candles, soaps and polishes of kinds commonly used for household purposes;

(2) operations in or about the shop or other place where any of the articles specified in (1) above are sold by retail, being operations carried on for the purpose of such sale or otherwise in connection with such sale;

(3) operations in connection with the warehousing or storing of any of the articles specified in (1) above for the purpose of the sale thereof by retail, or otherwise in connection with such sale, where the warehousing or storing takes place at a warehouse or store carried on in conjunction with one or more shops or other places where the said articles are sold by retail;

(4) operations in connection with the transport of any of the articles specified in (1) above when carried on in conjunction with their sale by retail or with the warehousing or storing operations specified in (3) above; and

(5) clerical or other office work carried on in conjunction with the sale by retail of any of the articles specified in (1) above and relating to such sale or to any of the operations specified in (2) to (4) above;

and for the purpose of this definition the sale by retail of any of the articles specified in (1) above does not include sale by auction (except where the auctioneer sells articles by retail which are his property or the property of his master) but includes the sale of any of the articles therein specified to a person for use in connection with a trade or business carried on by him if such sale takes place at or in connection with a shop engaged in the retail sale to the general public of any of the said articles.

Group 2. The Retail Drapery, Outfitting and Footwear Trades, that is to say—

(1) the sale by retail of:—

(a) wearing apparel of all kinds (including footwear, headwear and handwear) and accessories, trimmings and adornments for wearing apparel (excluding jewellery and imitation jewellery);

(b) haberdashery;

(c) textile fabrics in the piece, leather cloth, plastic cloth and oil cloth (but not including carpets, linoleum and other kinds of floor covering);

(d) knitting, rug, embroidery, crochet and similar wools or yarns;

(e) made-up household textiles (but excluding mattresses and floor coverings);

(f) umbrellas, sunshades, walking sticks, canes and similar articles;

(2) operations in or about the shop or other place where any of the articles included in (1) above are sold by retail, being operations carried on for the purpose of such sale or otherwise in connection with such sale;

(3) operations in connection with the warehousing or storing of any of the articles included in (1) above for the purpose of the sale thereof by retail, or otherwise in connection with such sale, where the warehousing or storing takes place at a warehouse or store carried on in conjunction with one or more shops or other places where the said articles are sold by retail;

(4) operations in connection with the transport of any of the articles included in (1) above when carried on in conjunction with their sale by retail or with the warehousing or storing operations specified in (3) above; and

(5) clerical or other office work carried on in conjunction with the sale by retail of any of the articles included in (1) above and relating to such sale or to any of the operations specified in (2) to (4) above;

and for the purpose of this definition the sale by retail of any of the articles in (1) above includes the sale of that article to a person for use in connection with a trade or business carried on by him if such sale takes place at or in connection with a shop engaged in the retail sale to the general public of any of the articles included in (1) above.

Group 3.   The Retail Bookselling and Stationery Trades, that is to say—

(1) the sale by retail of the following articles:—

　　(a) books (excluding printed music and periodicals);

　　(b) all kinds of stationery including printed forms, note books, diaries and similar articles, and books of kinds used in an office or business for the purpose of record;

　　(c) pens, pencils, ink, blotting paper and similar articles;

　　(d) maps and charts;

　　(e) wrapping and adhesive paper, string, paste and similar articles;

(2) operations in or about the shop or other place where any of the articles specified in (1) above are sold by retail, being operations carried on for the purpose of such sale or otherwise in connection with such sale;

(3) operations in connection with the warehousing or storing of any of the articles specified in (1) above for the purpose of the sale thereof by retail, or otherwise in connection with such sale, where the warehousing or storing takes place at a warehouse or store carried on in conjunction with one or more shops or other places where the said articles are sold by retail;

(4) operations in connection with the transport of any of the articles specified in (1) above when carried on in conjunction with their sale by retail or with the warehousing or storing operations specified in (3) above; and

(5) clerical or other office work carried on in conjunction with the sale by retail of any of the articles specified in (1) above and relating to such sale or to any of the operations specified in (2) to (4) above.

Group 4.   The Retail Newsagency, Tobacco and Confectionery Trades, that is to say—

(1) the sale by retail of the following articles:—

　　(a) newspapers, magazines and other periodicals;

　　(b) tobacco, cigars, cigarettes, snuff and smokers' requisites;

　　(c) articles of sugar confectionery and chocolate confectionery, and ice-cream;

(2) operations in or about the shop or other place where any of the articles specified in (1) above are sold by retail, being operations carried on for the purpose of such sale or otherwise in connection with such sale;

(3) operations in connection with the warehousing or storing of any of the articles specified in (1) above for the purpose of the sale thereof by retail or otherwise in connection with such sale, where the warehousing or storing takes place at a warehouse or store carried on in conjunction with one or more shops or other places where the said articles are sold by retail;

(4) operations in connection with the transport of any of the articles specified in (1) above when carried on in conjunction with their sale by retail or with the warehousing or storing operations specified in (3) above; and

(5) clerical or other office work carried on in conjunction with the sale by retail of any of the articles specified in (1) above and relating to such sale or to any of the operations specified in (2) to (4) above.

EXPLANATORY NOTE

(This Note is not part of the Order.)

This Order, which has effect from 9th August 1971, sets out the statutory minimum remuneration payable and the holidays to be allowed to workers in substitution for the statutory minimum remuneration and holidays set out in the Wages Regulation (Retail Food) (Scotland) Order 1970 (Order R.F.C.S. (41)) as amended by the Wages Regulation (Retail Food) (Scotland) (Amendment) Order 1970 (Order R.F.C.S. (43)), which Orders are revoked.

New provisions are printed in italics.

STATUTORY INSTRUMENTS

1971 No. 1024

INDUSTRIAL TRAINING

The Industrial Training Levy (Hotel and Catering) Order 1971

Made - - -	21*st June* 1971
Laid before Parliament	30*th June* 1971
Coming into Operation	14*th July* 1971

The Secretary of State after approving proposals submitted by the Hotel and Catering Industry Training Board for the imposition of a further levy on employers in the hotel and catering industry and in exercise of his powers under section 4 of the Industrial Training Act 1964(a) and of all other powers enabling him in that behalf hereby makes the following Order :—

Title and commencement

1. This Order may be cited as the Industrial Training Levy (Hotel and Catering) Order 1971 and shall come into operation on 14th July 1971.

Interpretation

2.—(1) In this Order unless the context otherwise requires :—

(*a*) "agriculture" has the same meaning as in section 109(3) of the Agriculture Act 1947(b) or, in relation to Scotland, as in section 86(3) of the Agriculture (Scotland) Act 1948(c) ;

(*b*) "an appeal tribunal" means an industrial tribunal established under section 12 of the Industrial Training Act 1964 ;

(*c*) "assessment" means an assessment of an employer to the levy ;

(*d*) "the Board" means the Hotel and Catering Industry Training Board ;

(*e*) "charity" has the same meaning as in section 360 of the Income and Corporation Taxes Act 1970(d) ;

(*f*) "emoluments" means all emoluments assessable to income tax under Schedule E (other than pensions), being emoluments from which tax under that Schedule is deductible, whether or not tax in fact falls to be deducted from any particular payment thereof ;

(*g*) "employer" means a person who is an employer in the hotel and catering industry at any time in the fifth levy period ;

(*h*) "establishment" (except in sub-paragraphs (*i*) and (*l*) of this paragraph) means an establishment comprising catering activities or a hotel and catering establishment ;

(a) 1964 c. 16.   (b) 1947 c. 48.
(c) 1948 c. 45.   (d) 1970 c. 10.

(*i*) "establishment comprising catering activities" means an establishment in Great Britain at or from which persons were employed in the fifth base period in the supply of food or drink to persons for immediate consumption, but does not include—

(i) a hotel and catering establishment ; or

(ii) an establishment in which the employer supplied for immediate consumption light refreshments to persons employed at or from the same where the employer was not otherwise engaged at or from the establishment in any activities to which paragraph 1 of the Schedule to the industrial training order applies or in the manufacture of any chocolate or flour confectionery so supplied as light refreshments ;

(*j*) "the fifth base period" means the period of twelve months that commenced on 6th April 1970 ;

(*k*) "the fifth levy period" means the period commencing with the day upon which this Order comes into operation and ending on 31st March 1972 ;

(*l*) "hotel and catering establishment" means an establishment in Great Britain that was engaged in the fifth base period wholly or mainly in the hotel and catering industry ;

(*m*) "hotel and catering industry" means any one or more of the activities which, subject to the provisions of paragraph 2 of the Schedule to the industrial training order, are specified in paragraph 1 of that Schedule as the activities of the hotel and catering industry ;

(*n*) "the industrial training order" means the Industrial Training (Hotel and Catering Board) Order 1969(**a**) ;

(*o*) "the levy" means the levy imposed by the Board in respect of the fifth levy period ;

(*p*) "notice" means a notice in writing ;

(*q*) "the supply of food or drink to persons for immediate consumption" means such a supply either by way of business or by a person carrying on a business to persons employed in the business ;

(*r*) other expressions have the same meanings as in the industrial training order.

(2) In the case where an establishment is taken over (whether directly or indirectly) by an employer in succession to, or jointly with, another person, a person employed at any time in the fifth base period at or from the establishment shall be deemed, for the purposes of this Order, to have been so employed by the employer carrying on the said establishment on the day upon which this Order comes into operation, and any reference in this Order to persons employed by an employer in the fifth base period at or from an establishment shall be construed accordingly.

(3) Any reference in this Order to an establishment that ceases to carry on business shall not be taken to apply where the location of the establishment is changed but its business is continued wholly or mainly at or from the new location, or where the suspension of activities is of a temporary or seasonal nature.

(4) The Interpretation Act 1889(**b**) shall apply to the interpretation of this Order as it applies to the interpretation of an Act of Parliament.

(**a**) S.I. 1969/1405 (1969 III, p. 4132).   (**b**) 1889 c. 63.

Imposition of the Levy

3.—(1) The levy to be imposed by the Board on employers in respect of the fifth levy period shall be assessed in accordance with the provisions of this and the next following Article.

(2) Subject to the provisions of the next following Article, the levy shall be assessed by the Board separately in respect of each establishment of an employer (not being an employer who is exempt from the levy by virtue of paragraph (3) of this Article), but in agreement with the employer one assessment may be made in respect of any number of hotel and catering establishments or of establishments comprising catering activities, in which case such establishments shall be deemed for the purposes of the assessment to constitute one establishment.

(3) There shall be exempt from the levy—

    (*a*) an employer in whose case the sum of the emoluments of all the persons employed by him in the fifth base period in the hotel and catering industry at or from the establishment or establishments of the employer was less than £6,000 ;

    (*b*) a charity.

Assessment of the Levy

4.—(1) Subject to the provisions of this Article, the levy assessed in respect of an establishment shall be an amount equal to 1·25 per cent. of the sum of the emoluments of the following persons, being persons employed by the employer at or from the establishment in the fifth base period, that is to say—

    (*a*) in the case of a hotel and catering establishment, all such persons ;

    (*b*) in the case of an establishment comprising catering activities, all such persons employed wholly or mainly in the supply of food or drink to persons for immediate consumption.

(2) In the case of one establishment only of an employer, the sum of the emoluments determined in accordance with the last foregoing paragraph shall be treated for the purpose of the assessment of the levy in respect of that establishment as if that sum were reduced by £2,400.

(3) For the purposes of the application of the provisions of the last foregoing paragraph, the Board shall, if necessary—

    (*a*) select the establishment in relation to which the provisions of the said paragraph are to apply ; or

    (*b*) aggregate the sum total of the emoluments of the persons employed at or from any two or more establishments of the employer (each sum first being determined separately in accordance with paragraph (1) of this Article) in which case the said establishments shall be deemed for the purposes of the assessment thereof to constitute one establishment.

(4) The amount of the levy imposed in respect of an establishment that ceases to carry on business in the fifth levy period shall be in the same proportion to the amount that would otherwise be due under the foregoing provisions of this Article as the number of days between the commencement of the said levy period and the date of cessation of business (both dates inclusive) bears to the number of days in the said levy period.

(5) For the purposes of this Article, no regard shall be had to the emoluments of any person employed as follows—

    (*a*) wholly in the supply (except at or in connection with an hotel, restaurant, café, snack bar, canteen, mess room or similar place of refreshment) of—

        (i) ice cream, chocolate confectionery, sugar confectionery or soft drink ;

        (ii) shellfish or eels ; or

        (iii) food or drink by means of an automatic vending machine ;

    (*b*) wholly in agriculture ;

    (*c*) otherwise than wholly in the supply of food or drink to persons for immediate consumption, where the employment is at or from an establishment engaged mainly in any activities of an industry specified in column 1 of the Schedule to this Order by virtue of the relevant industrial training order specified in column 2 of that Schedule or in any activities of two or more such industries ;

    (*d*) as a member of the crew of an aircraft, or as the master or a member of the crew of a ship or, in the case of a person ordinarily employed as a seaman, in or about a ship in port by the owner or charterer thereof on work of a kind ordinarily done by a seaman on a ship while it is in port ;

    (*e*) by a local authority in any activities mentioned in sub-paragraph (*d*) or (*e*) of paragraph 1 of the Schedule to the industrial training order, not being activities mentioned in head (ii) or head (iv) of paragraph 3(*l*) of that Schedule ; or

    (*f*) in any activities mentioned in sub-paragraph (*b*), (*c*)(ii), (*d*) or (*e*) of paragraph 1 of the Schedule to the industrial training order when carried out by—

        (i) a harbour authority while acting in that capacity ;

        (ii) the Electricity Council, the Central Electricity Generating Board or an Area Electricity Board ;

        (iii) the North of Scotland Hydro-Electric Board or the South of Scotland Electricity Board ;

        (iv) the Gas Council or an Area Gas Board ;

        (v) statutory water undertakers within the meaning of the Water Act 1945(**a**) or regional water boards or water development boards within the meaning of the Water (Scotland) Act 1967(**b**), being the activities of such undertakers or boards in the exercise of their powers or duties as such ;

        (vi) the British Airports Authority, the British European Airways Corporation, the British Overseas Airways Corporation, BEA Helicopters Limited, B.O.A.C. Associated Companies Limited or British Engine Overhaul Limited ;

        (vii) a marketing board ; or

        (viii) the United Kingdom Atomic Energy Authority.

(**a**) 1945 c. 42.   (**b**) 1967 c. 78.

Assessment Notices

5.—(1) The Board shall serve an assessment notice on every employer assessed to the levy, but one notice may comprise two or more assessments.

(2) An assessment notice shall state the Board's address for the service of a notice of appeal or of an application for an extension of time for appealing.

(3) An assessment notice may be served on the person assessed to the levy either by delivering it to him personally or by leaving it, or sending it to him by post, at his last known address or place of business in the United Kingdom or, if that person is a corporation, by leaving it, or sending it by post to the corporation, at such address or place of business or at its registered or principal office.

Payment of the Levy

6.—(1) Subject to the provisions of this Article and of Articles 7 and 8, the amount of each assessment appearing in an assessment notice served by the Board shall be due and payable to the Board one month after the date of the notice.

(2) The amount of an assessment shall not be recoverable by the Board until there has expired the time allowed for appealing against the assessment by Article 8(1) of this Order and any further period or periods of time that the Board or an appeal tribunal may have allowed for appealing under paragraph (2) or (3) of that Article or, where an appeal is brought, until the appeal is decided or withdrawn.

Withdrawal of Assessment

7.—(1) The Board may, by a notice served on the person assessed to the levy in the same manner as an assessment notice, withdraw an assessment if that person has appealed against that assessment under the provisions of Article 8 of this Order and the appeal has not been entered in the Register of Appeals kept under the appropriate Regulations specified in paragraph (5) of that Article, and such withdrawal may be extended by the Board to any other assessment appearing in the assessment notice.

(2) The withdrawal of an assessment shall be without prejudice—

    (*a*) to the power of the Board to serve a further assessment notice in respect of any establishment to which that assessment related ;

    (*b*) to any other assessment included in the original assessment notice and not withdrawn by the Board, and such notice shall thereupon have effect as if any assessment withdrawn by the Board had not been included therein.

Appeals

8.—(1) A person assessed to the levy may appeal to an appeal tribunal against the assessment within one month from the date of the service of the assessment notice or within any further period or periods of time that may be allowed by the Board or an appeal tribunal under the following provisions of this Article.

(2) The Board by notice may for good cause allow a person assessed to the levy to appeal to an appeal tribunal against the assessment at any time within the period of four months from the date of the service of the assessment notice or within such further period or periods as the Board may allow before such time as may then be limited for appealing has expired.

(3) If the Board shall not allow an application for extension of time for appealing, an appeal tribunal shall upon application made to the tribunal by the person assessed to the levy have the like powers as the Board under the last foregoing paragraph.

(4) In the case of an establishment that ceases to carry on business in the fifth levy period on any day after the date of the service of the relevant assessment notice, the foregoing provisions of this Article shall have effect as if for the period of four months from the date of the service of the assessment notice mentioned in paragraph (2) of this Article there were substituted the period of six months from the date of the cessation of business.

(5) An appeal or an application to an appeal tribunal under this Article shall be made in accordance with the Industrial Tribunals (England and Wales) Regulations 1965(a) as amended by the Industrial Tribunals (England and Wales) (Amendment) Regulations 1967(b) except where the establishment to which the relevant assessment relates is wholly in Scotland in which case the appeal or application shall be made in accordance with the Industrial Tribunals (Scotland) Regulations 1965(c) as amended by the Industrial Tribunals (Scotland) (Amendment) Regulations 1967(d).

(6) The powers of an appeal tribunal under paragraph (3) of this Article may be exercised by the President of the Industrial Tribunals (England and Wales) or by the President of the Industrial Tribunals (Scotland) as the case may be.

Evidence

9.—(1) Upon the discharge by a person assessed to the levy of his liability under an assessment the Board shall if so requested issue to him a certificate to that effect.

(2) The production in any proceedings of a document purporting to be certified by the Secretary of the Board to be a true copy of an assessment or other notice issued by the Board or purporting to be a certificate such as is mentioned in the foregoing paragraph of this Article shall, unless the contrary is proved, be sufficient evidence of the document and of the facts stated therein.

Signed by order of the Secretary of State.
21st June 1971.

Paul Bryan,
Minister of State,
Department of Employment.

(a) S.I. 1965/1101 (1965 II, p. 2805). (b) S.I. 1967/301 (1967 I, p. 1040).
(c) S.I. 1965/1157 (1965 II, p. 3266). (d) S.I. 1967/302 (1967 I, p. 1050).

Article 4

SCHEDULE

THE INDUSTRIES REFERRED TO IN ARTICLE 4(5)(*c*) OF THIS ORDER

Column 1	Column 2
The wool, jute and flax industry	The Industrial Training (Wool Industry Board) Order 1964 as amended by the Industrial Training (Wool, Jute and Flax Board) Order 1968(**a**)
The iron and steel industry	The Industrial Training (Iron and Steel Board) Order 1964 as amended by the Industrial Training (Iron and Steel Board) Order 1969(**b**)
The construction industry	The Industrial Training (Construction Board) Order 1964 as amended by the Industrial Training (Construction Board) Order 1967(**c**)
The engineering industry	The Industrial Training (Engineering Board) Order 1964 as amended by the Industrial Training (Engineering Board) Order 1968 and the Industrial Training (Engineering Board) Order 1968 (Amendment) Order 1969(**d**)
The shipbuilding industry	The Industrial Training (Shipbuilding Board) Order 1964 as amended by the Industrial Training (Shipbuilding Board) Order 1968(**e**)
The electricity supply industry	The Industrial Training (Electricity Supply Board) Order 1965(**f**)
The gas industry	The Industrial Training (Gas Industry Board) Order 1965(**g**)
The water supply industry	The Industrial Training (Water Supply Board) Order 1965(**h**)
The ceramics, glass and mineral products industry	The Industrial Training (Ceramics, Glass and Mineral Products Board) Order 1965 as amended by the Industrial Training (Ceramics, Glass and Mineral Products Board) Order 1969(**i**)

(**a**) S.I. 1964/907, 1968/898 (1964 II, p. 1928; 1968 II, p. 2376).
(**b**) S.I. 1964/949, 1969/884 (1964 II, p. 2127; 1969 II, p. 2517).
(**c**) S.I. 1964/1079, 1967/924 (1964 II, p. 2384; 1967 II, p. 2757).
(**d**) S.I. 1964/1086, 1968/1333, 1969/1376 (1964 II, p. 2402; 1968 II, p. 3694; 1969 III, p. 4103).
(**e**) S.I. 1964/1782, 1968/1614 (1964 III, p. 3928; 1968 III, p. 4432).
(**f**) S.I. 1965/1256 (1965 II, p. 3548).
(**g**) S.I. 1965/1257 (1965 II, p. 3552).
(**h**) S.I. 1965/1258 (1965 II, p. 3556).
(**i**) S.I. 1965/1391, 1969/689 (1965 II, p. 4062; 1969 II, p. 1860).

Column 1	Column 2
The furniture and timber industry	The Industrial Training (Furniture and Timber Industry Board) Order 1965 as amended by the Industrial Training (Furniture and Timber Industry Board) Order 1969 and the Industrial Training (Furniture and Timber Industry Board) Order 1969 (Amendment) Order 1970**(a)**
The man-made fibres producing industry	The Industrial Training (Man-made Fibres Producing Industry Board) Order 1966 as amended by the Industrial Training (Man-made Fibres Producing Industry Board) Order 1969**(b)**
The carpet industry	The Industrial Training (Carpet Board) Order 1966 as amended by the Industrial Training (Carpet Board) Order 1968**(c)**
The knitting, lace and net industry	The Industrial Training (Knitting, Lace and Net Industry Board) Order 1966**(d)**
The cotton and allied textiles industry	The Industrial Training (Cotton and Allied Textiles Board) Order 1966**(e)**
The agricultural, horticultural and forestry industry	The Industrial Training (Agricultural, Horticultural and Forestry Board) Order 1966 as amended by the Industrial Training (Agricultural, Horticultural and Forestry Board) Order 1970**(f)**
The road transport industry	The Industrial Training (Road Transport Board) Order 1966 as amended by the Industrial Training (Road Transport Board) Order 1969 and the Industrial Training (Road Transport Board) Order 1969 (Amendment) Order 1969**(g)**
The air transport and travel industry	The Industrial Training (Civil Air Transport Board) Order 1967 as amended by the Industrial Training (Air Transport and Travel Industry Board) Order 1970**(h)**
The petroleum industry	The Industrial Training (Petroleum Board) Order 1967 as amended by the Industrial Training (Petroleum Board) Order 1970**(i)**
The rubber and plastics processing industry	The Industrial Training (Rubber and Plastics Processing Board) Order 1967**(j)**

(a) S.I. 1965/2028, 1969/1290, 1970/1634 (1965 III, p. 5998; 1969 III, p. 3820; 1970 III, p. 5372).
(b) S.I. 1966/143, 1969/1210 (1966 I, p. 257; 1969 II, p. 3545).
(c) S.I. 1966/245, 1968/1882 (1966 I, p. 499; 1968 III, p. 5017).
(d) S.I. 1966/246 (1966 I, p. 506).   (e) S.I. 1966/823 (1966 II, p. 1907).
(f) S.I. 1966/969, 1970/1886 (1966 II, p. 2333; 1970 III, p. 6227).
(g) S.I. 1966/1112, 1969/879, 1871 (1966 III, p. 2712; 1969 II, p. 2495; III, p. 5815).
(h) S.I. 1967/263, 1970/252 (1967 I, p. 968; 1970 I, p. 983).
(i) S.I. 1967/648, 1970/205 (1967 I, p. 2032; 1970 I, p. 926).
(j) S.I. 1967/1062 (1967 II, p. 3151).

Column 1	Column 2
The chemical and allied products industry	The Industrial Training (Chemical and Allied Products Board) Order 1967 as amended by the Industrial Training (Chemical and Allied Products Board) Order 1970(a)
The paper and paper products industry	The Industrial Training (Paper and Paper Products Board) Order 1968(b)
The printing and publishing industry	The Industrial Training (Printing and Publishing Board) Order 1968(c)
The distributive industry	The Industrial Training (Distributive Board) Order 1968 as amended by the Industrial Training (Distributive Board) Order 1970(d)
The food, drink and tobacco industry	The Industrial Training (Food, Drink and Tobacco Board) Order 1968 as amended by the Industrial Training (Food, Drink and Tobacco Board) Order 1971(e)
The footwear, leather and fur skin industry	The Industrial Training (Footwear, Leather and Fur Skin Board) Order 1968(f)
The clothing and allied products industry	The Industrial Training (Clothing and Allied Products Board) Order 1969(g)
The hairdressing and allied services industry	The Industrial Training (Hairdressing and Allied Services Board) Order 1969(h)

EXPLANATORY NOTE

(This Note is not part of the Order.)

This Order gives effect to proposals submitted by the Hotel and Catering Industry Training Board to the Secretary of State for Employment for the imposition of a further levy upon employers in the hotel and catering industry for the purpose of raising money towards the expenses of the Board.

The levy is to be imposed in respect of the fifth levy period commencing with the day upon which this Order comes into operation and ending on 31st March 1972. The levy will be assessed by the Board and there will be a right of appeal against an assessment to an industrial tribunal.

(a) S.I. 1967/1386, 1970/1743 (1967 III, p. 4049; 1970 III, p. 5706).
(b) S.I. 1968/787 (1968 II, p. 2194).   (c) S.I. 1968/786 (1968 II, p. 2185).
(d) S.I. 1968/1032, 1970/1053 (1968 II, p. 2709; 1970 II, p. 3273).
(e) S.I. 1968/1033, 1971/648 (1968 II, p. 2721; 1971 I, p. 1709).
(f) S.I. 1968/1763 (1968 III, p. 4785).
(g) S.I. 1969/1375 (1969 III, p. 4094).   (h) S.I. 1969/1634 (1969 III, p. 5133).

STATUTORY INSTRUMENTS

1971 No. 1025

AGRICULTURE

LIVESTOCK INDUSTRIES

The Beef Cow (England and Wales) (Amendment) Scheme 1971

Made - - - -	*21st June* 1971
Laid before Parliament	*28th June* 1971
Coming into Operation	*29th June* 1971

The Minister of Agriculture, Fisheries and Food and the Secretary of State, acting jointly, in pursuance of section 12 of the Agriculture Act 1967(**a**), as read with the Transfer of Functions (Wales) Order 1969(**b**), and of all their other enabling powers, with the approval of the Treasury, hereby make the following scheme:—

Citation, commencement and interpretation

1.—(1) This scheme, which may be cited as the Beef Cow (England and Wales) (Amendment) Scheme 1971, shall come into operation on 29th June 1971, and shall be construed as one with the principal scheme.

(2) In this scheme, the expression "the principal scheme" means the Beef Cow (England and Wales) Scheme 1967(**c**), as amended (**d**).

Abolition of stocking ratio for the year 1971

2.—(1) In relation to subsidy payments which may be payable for the year 1971, paragraph 4 of the principal scheme (which limits the numbers of eligible cows in respect of which such payments may be made) shall be amended in accordance with the provisions of the following sub-paragraph.

(2) Sub-paragraph (1) of that paragraph shall be amended by the deletion of paragraph (*b*) thereof, together with the word "or", which immediately precedes it, and the words "whichever is the less", which follow it, and sub-paragraph (2) shall be deleted.

Application of scheme to cases where hill cow subsidy is paid

3.—(1) In sub-paragraph (2) of paragraph 6 of the principal scheme (which provides for subsidy payments to be made in respect of eligible cows disqualified from such payments under a hill cattle scheme by reason of the application of a stocking ratio in cases where the land on which the herd is maintained is partly hill land and partly other land), there shall be inserted after the words "partly other land" the words "which is capable of supporting cattle".

(2) In sub-paragraph (3) of that paragraph, the words after "for the purposes of this scheme" to the end of the sub-paragraph shall be deleted.

(**a**) 1967 c. 22.   (**b**) S.I. 1969/388 (1969 I, p. 1070).

(**c**) S.I. 1967/1555 (1967 III, p. 4317).

(**d**) S.I. 1969/693, 1970/2023 (1969 II, p. 1905; 1970 III, p. 6598).

Amendment of paragraph 7 of principal scheme

4. In sub-paragraph (*c*) of paragraph 7 of the principal scheme, the words "or inspection of relevant grass or forage crops," shall be deleted.

Saving for previous years

5. Nothing in this scheme shall affect subsidy payments relating to the prescribed dates in the years 1967 to 1970.

In Witness whereof the Official Seal of the Minister of Agriculture, Fisheries and Food is hereunto affixed on 14th June 1971.

(L.S.)

J.M.L. Prior,
Minister of Agriculture, Fisheries and Food.

Given under my hand on 17th June 1971.

Peter Thomas,
Secretary of State for Wales.

We approve,
21st June 1971.

P. L. Hawkins,
Bernard Weatherill,
Two of the Lords Commissioners
of Her Majesty's Treasury.

EXPLANATORY NOTE

(*This Note is not part of the Scheme.*)

Paragraph 4 of the Beef Cow (England and Wales) Scheme 1967, as amended, restricts the number of cows in respect of which subsidy payments may be made to the number of eligible cows comprised in a herd on a prescribed date in the year in question which satisfy the requirements of the scheme, or to one cow for each two acres of grass and forage crops available for the maintenance of the herd in that year, whichever is the less. The present scheme amends the 1967 scheme by abolishing the stocking ratio altogether in respect of the year 1971, so that subsidy payments will now be made in respect of all eligible cows in a beef herd which qualify.

In paragraph 6(2) of the 1967 scheme, provision is made for beef cow subsidy to be payable in respect of eligible cows in cases where the agricultural unit comprises both hill land, as defined in a hill cattle scheme, and other land, and where the cows in question are disqualified for the purposes of hill cattle subsidy by the application of a stocking ratio. The present scheme provides that, in order to qualify for beef cow subsidy in such circumstances, the agricultural unit on which the herd is maintained must comprise, as well as hill land, land which is capable of supporting cattle.

STATUTORY INSTRUMENTS

1971 No. 1026

AGRICULTURE
LIVESTOCK INDUSTRIES

The Beef Cow Subsidy Payment (England and Wales) (Amendment) Order 1971

Made - - - -	*21st June* 1971
Laid before Parliament	*28th June* 1971
Coming into Operation	*29th June* 1971

The Minister of Agriculture, Fisheries and Food and the Secretary of State, acting jointly, in pursuance of subsections (4) and (7) of section 12 of the Agriculture Act 1967(a), as read with the Transfer of Functions (Wales) Order 1969(b), and of all their other enabling powers, with the approval of the Treasury, hereby make the following order:—

Citation and commencement

1. This order, which may be cited as the Beef Cow Subsidy Payment (England and Wales) (Amendment) Order 1971, shall come into operation on 29th June 1971.

Interpretation

2.—(1) In this order, the expression "the principal order" means the Beef Cow Subsidy Payment (England and Wales) Order 1970(c).

(2) Unless the context otherwise requires, expressions used in this order shall have the same meanings as in the Beef Cow (England and Wales) Scheme 1967(d), as amended(e).

(3) The Interpretation Act 1889(f) shall apply to the interpretation of this order as it applies to the interpretation of an Act of Parliament.

Amendment of principal order

3. In paragraph (*a*) of Article 3 of the principal order, there shall be substituted for the words "final blood test" the words "final diagnostic test".

Increase in subsidy payments

4. Paragraph (*a*) of Article 3 of the principal order (which specifies the amounts of subsidy payment to be made for the years 1970 and 1971 under the Beef Cow (England and Wales) Scheme 1967, as amended, in respect of eligible cows comprised in an accredited herd on the prescribed date in each of those years, or in a herd which subsequently becomes an accredited herd as a result of a final diagnostic test for brucellosis commenced on or before that date) shall have effect in relation to the year 1971 with the substitution of £16 for £12.17s.6d.

(a) 1967 c. 22. (b) S.I. 1969/388 (1969 I, p. 1070).
(c) S.I. 1970/2024 (1970 III, p. 6601). (d) S.I. 1967/1555 (1967 III, p. 4317).
(e) S.I. 1969/693, 1970/2023 (1969 II, p. 1905; 1970 III, p. 6598).
(f) 1889 c. 63.

In Witness whereof the Official Seal of the Minister of Agriculture, Fisheries and Food is hereunto affixed on 14th June 1971.

(L.S.)

J. M. L. Prior,
Ministry of Agriculture, Fisheries and Food.

Given under my hand on 17th June 1971.

Peter Thomas,
Secretary of State for Wales.

We approve,

21st June 1971.

P. L. Hawkins,
Bernard Weatherill,
Two of the Lords Commissioners of
Her Majesty's Treasury.

EXPLANATORY NOTE
(This Note is not part of the Order.)

This order increases the amount of subsidy payable for the year 1971 under the provisions of the Beef Cow (England and Wales) Scheme 1967, as amended, from £12.87½ to £16 in respect of cows comprised in an accredited herd on the prescribed date (normally 31st December), or in a herd which subsequently becomes accredited as a result of a final diagnostic test for brucellosis commenced on or before that date. There is no longer a requirement, as in the previous order, that this must be a blood test.

For other animals comprised in a regular beef herd on the prescribed date, subsidy will continue to be paid at the rate of £11.

STATUTORY   INSTRUMENTS

1971 No. 1027

AGRICULTURE

The Price Stability of Imported Products (Rates of Levy) (Eggs) (No. 13) Order 1971

Made	-	-	-	*21st June* 1971
Coming into Operation				*22nd June* 1971

The Minister of Agriculture, Fisheries and Food, in exercise of the powers conferred upon him by section 1(2), (4), (5), (6) and (7) of the Agriculture and Horticulture Act 1964(a) and of all other powers enabling him in that behalf, hereby makes the following order:—

1. This order may be cited as the Price Stability of Imported Products (Rates of Levy) (Eggs) (No. 13) Order 1971, and shall come into operation on 22nd June 1971.

2.—(1) In this order—

" the Principal Order " means the Price Stability of Imported Products (Levy Arrangements) (Eggs) Order 1970(b) as amended by any subsequent order, and if any such order is replaced by any subsequent order the expression shall be construed as a reference to such subsequent order;

AND other expressions have the same meaning as in the Principal Order.

(2) The Interpretation Act 1889(c) shall apply to the interpretation of this order as it applies to the interpretation of an Act of Parliament and as if this order and the order hereby revoked were Acts of Parliament.

3. In accordance with and subject to the provisions of the Principal Order (which provides for the charging of levies on imports of those eggs and egg products which are specified commodities for the purposes of the Agriculture and Horticulture Act 1964) the rate of general levy for such imports into the United Kingdom of any specified commodity as are described in column 2 of the Schedule to this order in relation to a tariff heading indicated in column 1 of that Schedule shall be the rate set forth in relation thereto in column 3 of that Schedule.

4. The Price Stability of Imported Products (Rates of Levy) (Eggs) (No. 12) Order 1971(d) is hereby revoked.

In Witness whereof the Official Seal of the Minister of Agriculture, Fisheries and Food is hereunto affixed on 21st June 1971.

(L.S.)

G. P. Jupe,
Assistant Secretary.

(a) 1964 c. 28.   (b) S.I. 1970/359 (1970 I, p. 1277).   (c) 1889 c. 63.
(d) S.I. 1971/985 (1971 II, p.2867).

SCHEDULE

1. Tariff Heading	2. Description of Imports	3. Rate of General Levy
04.05	Imports of:—	
	Birds' eggs (in shell or not in shell), fresh, dried or otherwise preserved, sweetened or not, other than egg yolks:	(per 120 eggs)
	A. Eggs in shell:	p
	1. Not exceeding 11 lb. in weight per 120 ..	40
	2. Over 11 lb. but not exceeding 12½ lb. in weight per 120	40
	3. Over 12½ lb. but not exceeding 14 lb. in weight per 120	50
	4. Over 14 lb. but not exceeding 15½ lb. in weight per 120	55
	5. Over 15½ lb. but not exceeding 17 lb. in weight per 120	60
	6. Over 17 lb. in weight per 120	60
	B. Eggs not in shell:	(per ton)
	Whole dried	£110
	Whole frozen or liquid	£60

EXPLANATORY NOTE

(*This Note is not part of the Order.*)

This order, which comes into operation on 22nd June 1971, supersedes the Price Stability of Imported Products (Rates of Levy) (Eggs) (No. 12) Order 1971. It—

(a) reduces the rates of general levy to be charged on imports of eggs in shell in the weight grades numbered 1 and 2 in the Schedule to the order; and

(b) reimposes unchanged the rates of general levy to be charged on imports of shell eggs in the other weight grades and on imports of dried, frozen or liquid whole egg not in shell.

STATUTORY INSTRUMENTS

1971 No. 1028

EXCHANGE CONTROL

The Exchange Control (Authorised Dealers and Depositaries) (Amendment) Order 1971

Made - - - -	21*st June* 1971
Coming into Operation	30*th June* 1971

The Treasury, in exercise of the powers conferred upon them by sections 36(5) and 42(1) of the Exchange Control Act 1947(**a**), hereby make the following Order :—

1.—(1) This Order may be cited as the Exchange Control (Authorised Dealers and Depositaries) (Amendment) Order 1971, and shall come into operation on 30th June 1971.

(2) The Interpretation Act 1889(**b**) shall apply for the interpretation of this Order as it applies for the interpretation of an Act of Parliament.

2. Schedule 2 to the Exchange Control (Authorised Dealers and Depositaries) Order 1971(**c**) shall be amended by inserting the words " United International Bank Ltd." after the words " United Commercial Bank."

3. This Order shall extend to the Channel Islands, and any reference in this Order to the Exchange Control Act 1947 includes a reference to that Act as extended by the Exchange Control (Channel Islands) Order 1947(**d**).

> *Bernard Weatherill,*
> *Walter Clegg,*
> Two of the Lords Commissioners
> of Her Majesty's Treasury.

21st June 1971.

EXPLANATORY NOTE

(*This Note is not part of the Order.*)

This Order amends the list of persons authorised by the Treasury under the Exchange Control Act 1947 to act as dealers in gold and foreign currencies and as depositaries for the purpose of the deposit of securities.

(**a**) 1947 c. 14.   (**b**) 1889 c. 63.   (**c**) S.I. 1971/477 (1971 I, p. 1425).
(**d**) S.R. & O. 1947/2034 (Rev. VI, p. 1001: 1947 I, p. 660).

STATUTORY INSTRUMENTS

1971 No. 1031 (S. 131)

PENSIONS

The Superannuation (Local Government and Approved Employment) Interchange (Scotland) Amendment Rules 1971

Made - - -	17*th June* 1971
Laid before Parliament	29*th June* 1971
Coming into Operation	1*st July* 1971

In exercise of the powers conferred on me by sections 2 and 15 of the Superannuation (Miscellaneous Provisions) Act 1948(**a**), as amended by section 11(6) of the Superannuation (Miscellaneous Provisions) Act 1967(**b**), and of all other powers enabling me in that behalf, I hereby make the following rules :—

Title and commencement

1. These rules may be cited as the Superannuation (Local Government and Approved Employment) Interchange (Scotland) Amendment Rules 1971, and shall come into operation on 1st July 1971.

Interpretation

2.—(1) In these rules "the principal rules" means the Superannuation (Local Government and Approved Employment) Interchange (Scotland) Rules 1970(**c**) ; and words and expressions to which meanings are assigned by the principal rules shall bear the same respective meanings in these rules.

(2) The Interpretation Act 1889(**d**) shall apply for the interpretation of these rules as it applies for the interpretation of an Act of Parliament.

Amendment of principal rules

3.—(1) The principal rules shall be amended as provided in this rule.

(2) In paragraph (1) of rule 2 (interpretation) after the definition of "pension scheme trustees" there shall be inserted—

" "police employment" means employment in which a person is subject to the police pensions regulations ;

"police pensions regulations" means the regulations from time to time in force under the Police Pensions Act 1948(**e**) ;".

(**a**) 1948 c. 33. (**b**) 1967 c. 28.
(**c**) S.I. 1970/1853 (1970 III, p. 6033). (**d**) 1889 c. 63.
(**e**) 1948 c. 24.

(3) At the end of paragraph (2) of rule 2 there shall be inserted the following paragraph :—

"(2A) For the purposes of these rules—

(*a*) references to a police authority shall be construed in the same manner as in the police pensions regulations ;

(*b*) a person in police employment shall be deemed to be in the employment of his police authority ; and

(*c*) a police authority shall be deemed to be pension scheme trustees.".

(4) Schedule 2 ('Fractional' Pension Schemes) shall be amended by adding to the table, beneath the appropriate headings as repeated herein, the following entry :—

Approved body	*Approved pension scheme*	*Prescribed date for rule 5*	*Prescribed date for rule 9*	*Adjustment of service*
(1)	(2)	(3)	(4)	(5)
"Police Authority	The scheme embodied in the police pensions regulations	4th February 1948	4th February 1948	Add $33\frac{1}{3}\%$"

(5) In paragraph 5 of schedule 2 (Computation of transfer value), at the beginning there shall be inserted the words "(1) Except as sub-paragraph (2) below provides", and at the end there shall be added the following sub-paragraph :—

"(2) The transfer value receivable under these rules in respect of a person who leaves police employment shall be such transfer value as is payable in respect of him under the police pensions regulations ; and any such transfer value which has not been reduced by reason of the provisions for flat-rate retirement pension in the National Insurance Act 1965(**a**) shall be treated as unreduced for the purposes of rule 14.".

(6) After paragraph 6 of schedule 2 there shall be added the following paragraph :—

"Police employment : returned contributions

7. In relation to a person leaving police employment, rule 10(*a*)(iii) shall have effect as if it provided as follows :—

"(iii) pay to the fund authority an amount equal to any award paid to him by way of return of contributions or gratuity on or after leaving that employment ; but where under the police pensions regulations he had paid pension contributions at a rate related to 6·25% of his pensionable pay, or had paid additional contributions, within the meaning of those regulations, the payment shall be of an amount equal to so much of the award as would have been payable had he paid such pension contributions at a rate related to 5% of his pensionable pay and had not paid such additional contributions, and".".

(a) 1965 c. 51.

Adjustment of certain references to dates

4. In relation to any person who becomes eligible, subject to compliance with conditions, for the application of Part II or III of the principal rules by virtue of rule 3 above, the principal rules shall have effect as if—

(*a*) any references therein to 1st January 1970 were references to 1st July 1970 and

(*b*) any references therein, however expressed, to 1st January 1971 were references to 1st July 1971.

Gordon Campbell,
One of Her Majesty's Principal
Secretaries of State.

St. Andrew's House,
Edinburgh.
17th June 1971.

EXPLANATORY NOTE

(This Note is not part of the Rules.)

These Rules amend the Superannuation (Local Government and Approved Employment) Interchange (Scotland) Rules 1970 so as to provide for the interchange of superannuation rights where a person transfers from employment in local government in Scotland to service as a policeman and vice versa.

The Rules can have retrospective effect to a limited extent under the express powers of, and subject to the safeguards required by, section 2(5) of the Superannuation (Miscellaneous Provisions) Act 1948.

STATUTORY INSTRUMENTS

1971 No. 1032 (S.132)

BUILDING AND BUILDINGS

The Building Standards (Scotland) Amendment No. 2 (Metrication) Regulations 1971

Made - - -	18*th June* 1971
Laid before Parliament	8*th July* 1971
Coming into Operation	1*st January* 1972

In exercise of the powers conferred on me by subsections (1), (2), (3), (4) and (5) of section 3 of the Building (Scotland) Act 1959(**a**) and of all other powers enabling me in that behalf, and having complied with the provisions of subsection (6) of section 3 of that Act, as substituted by section 1 of the Building (Scotland) Act 1970(**b**), that is to say—

(*a*) having consulted the Building Standards Advisory Committee, and

(*b*) having consulted such other bodies as appear to me to be representative of the interests concerned,

I hereby make the following regulations :—

1.—(1) These regulations may be cited as the Building Standards (Scotland) Amendment No. 2 (Metrication) Regulations 1971, and the Building Standards (Scotland) (Consolidation) Regulations 1970(**c**), the Building Standards (Scotland) Amendment Regulations 1971(**d**) and these regulations may be cited together as the Building Standards (Scotland) Regulations 1970 to 1971.

(2) These regulations shall come into operation on 1st January 1972.

2.—(1) In these regulations, unless the context otherwise requires—

(*a*) "the building standards regulations" means the Building Standards (Scotland) (Consolidation) Regulations 1970 and the Building Standards (Scotland) Amendment Regulations 1971, and other words and expressions have the same meanings as in the building standards regulations ;

(*b*) any reference to a Part, regulation or Schedule shall be construed as a reference to a Part or regulation of, or Schedule to, the building standards regulations and any reference to a numbered Table shall be construed as a reference to a Table in Schedule 9 to the building standards regulations.

(2) References in these regulations to any enactment shall be construed as a reference to that enactment as amended by any subsequent enactment, including any enactment in these regulations.

(**a**) 1959 c. 24.   (**b**) 1970 c. 38.
(**c**) S.I. 1970/1137 (1970 II, p. 3635).   (**d**) S.I. 1971/748 (1971 II, p. 2153).

(3) The Interpretation Act 1889(a) shall apply for the interpretation of these regulations as it applies for the interpretation of an Act of Parliament.

Amendments set out in the Schedules to these regulations

3. The metric measures specified in column (3) of the First Schedule to these regulations shall, as from the date of coming into operation of these regulations, be substituted for the imperial measures specified in column (2) and shown opposite column (3) with reference to the regulations of the building standards regulations specified in column (1) thereof.

4. The tables relating to regulations D22, F27, Q14 and Q15 of the building standards regulations set out in the Second Schedule to these regulations shall, as from the date of coming into operation of these regulations, be substituted for the corresponding tables incorporated in regulations D22, F27, Q14 and Q15 of the building standards regulations.

5. The metric measures specified in column (3) of the Third Schedule to these regulations shall, as from the date of coming into operation of these regulations, be substituted for the imperial measures specified in column (2) and shown opposite column (3) with reference to the Schedule of the building standards regulations specified in column (1) thereof.

6. The metric measures specified in column (6) of the Fourth Schedule to these regulations shall, as from the date of coming into operation of these regulations, be substituted for the imperial measures specified either in column (3) or in column (5) and shown opposite column (6) with reference to the provisions of Schedule 10 to the building standards regulations which are identified in column (1) and either in column (2) or in column (4) of the said Fourth Schedule.

7. The tables numbered 2, 4, 5, 7, 9, 10, 13, 15, 16 and 18 and set out in the Fifth Schedule to these regulations shall, as from the date of coming into operation of these regulations, be substituted respectively for Tables 2, 4, 5, 7, 9, 10, 13, 15, 16 and 18 set out in Schedule 9 to the building standards regulations.

8. The provisions contained in the Sixth Schedule to these regulations shall, as from the date of coming into operation of these regulations, be substituted for the provisions of Part B of Schedule 10 to the building standards regulations with reference to regulation M21(1) of the building standards regulations.

Specific amendments to the Building Standards Regulations

9. In the titles of Tables 10 and 15 within Schedule 9, in the Arrangement of Regulations set out at the beginning of the building standards regulations, for the word "feet" there shall be substituted the word "metres".

10. In regulation E5, in paragraph (3)—

    (*a*) in sub-paragraph (*b*)(i), for the figure "24" there shall be substituted the figure "2·23" ;

    (*b*) in sub-paragraph (*b*)(ii), for the figure "3" there shall be substituted the figure "0·3".

(a) 1889 c. 63.

11. In regulation E8—

(*a*) in paragraph (3)(*a*), for the words "the number obtained by dividing by 42 the aggregate in inches" there shall be substituted the words "the aggregate in metres" ;

(*b*) in paragraph (3)(*b*), for the words "3 the area in square feet" there shall be substituted the words "0·3 the area in square metres".

12. In regulation E10, in paragraph (4)(*b*), for the words "one square inch for one square foot of floor area" there shall be substituted the words "0·7 per cent. of the floor area".

13. In regulation J2—

(*a*) for the definition of "surface heat transfer coefficient" there shall be substituted—

' "surface heat transfer coefficient", in relation to a surface, means the rate of heat transfers in watts between each square metre of the surface and the ambient air when there is a difference in temperature of one degree Celsius between the surface and the ambient air ;' ;

(*b*) for the definition of "thermal transmittance coefficient" there shall be substituted—

' "thermal transmittance coefficient", in relation to any structure, being a roof, wall or floor, means the rate of heat transfers in watts through one square metre of the structure when there is a difference in temperature of one degree Celsius between the air on the internal and external surfaces of the structure.'.

14. In regulation J3, in paragraph (1), for the figures "0·85" and "0·20" there shall be substituted the figures "0·15" and "1·1" respectively.

15. For regulation J4 there shall be substituted—

"**Walls*

J4.—(1) Every part of external wall of a building of occupancy sub-group A1, A2, A3 or A4, which does not comprise a window or other glazed opening, shall be so constructed that the thermal transmittance coefficient thereof is not more than 1·7.

(2) The external walls of a building of occupancy sub-group A1 or A2, being a wholly detached house, or of occupancy sub-group A3 or A4, shall be so constructed that the average thermal transmittance coefficient over the area of all such walls is not more than 2·4.

(3) The average thermal transmittance coefficient over the area of all the external walls of a building of occupancy sub-group A1 or A2, other than a wholly detached house, shall be not more than—

(*a*) 2·4 where the area of the external walls exceeds 125 per cent of the total area of any internal separating walls ;

(*b*) 2·7 where the area of the external walls is between 75 per cent and 125 per cent of the total area of any internal separating walls ;

(*c*) 3·3 where the area of the external walls is less than 75 per cent of the total area of any internal separating walls.

(3A) For the purposes of paragraphs (2) and (3) of this regulation the area of any external wall shall include the area of any windows or other glazed openings therein.

(4) In calculating the average thermal transmittance coefficient for the purposes of this regulation—

(*a*) the thermal transmittance coefficient of any single glazing shall be taken as 5·7 and of any double glazing as 2·8, and

(*b*) where the average thermal transmittance coefficient over all the windows and other glazed openings in the external walls of the house or building of occupancy sub-group A3 or A4 is 4·3 or more, the average thermal transmittance coefficient over the remaining parts of the walls shall be taken to be not less than 1·1, and

(*c*) where the average thermal transmittance coefficient over all the windows and other glazed openings in the external walls of the house or building of occupancy sub-group A3 or A4 is less than 4·3 the average thermal transmittance coefficient over the remaining parts of the walls shall be taken to be not less than 0·6.

(5) For the purposes of this regulation, "wall" shall include any internal or external surface finishes thereon and in any calculation for the purposes of this regulation the sum of the surface resistance of the internal and external surfaces shall be taken as 0·18.".

16. In regulation J5, in paragraph (2), for the figures "1·00" and "0·20" there shall be substituted the figures "0·18" and "1·1" respectively.

17. In regulation K7—

(*a*) in paragraph (1)(*a*)(ii), for the words "75 square inches for every 750 cubic feet of the room" there shall be substituted the words "2250 square millimetres for each cubic metre of the room so, however, that in no case shall an opening area be less than 48 000 square millimetres" ;

(*b*) in paragraph (2)(*e*)(i)(B), for the words "10 square inches for every 750 cubic feet of the room" there shall be substituted the words "300 square millimetres for each cubic metre of the room so, however, that in no case shall an opening area be less than 6500 square millimetres".

18. In regulation K8(*a*)(ii), for the words "10 square inches for every 750 cubic feet of the garage" there shall be substituted the words "300 square millimetres for each cubic metre of the garage so, however, that in no case shall an opening area be less than 6500 square millimetres".

19. In regulation K10(2)(i), for the words "10 square inches for every 750 cubic feet of the room" there shall be substituted the words "300 square millimetres for each cubic metre of the room so, however, that in no case shall an opening area be less than 6500 square millimetres".

20. In regulation K10, in paragraph (4), for sub-paragraph (*c*) there shall be substituted—

"(*c*) where the cubic space per occupant exceeds 21 cubic metres—

(i) (A) direct to the external air by a window, roof-light or ventilator having an opening area of one-twentieth of the floor area of the room, and

(B) by a permanent ventilator having a minimum cross-sectional area per occupant as set forth in column (2) of the table annexed to this regulation, or

(ii) by mechanical means to provide a fresh air supply at the rates set out in Table 13.

Table referred to in paragraph (4)(c)(i)(B) of this regulation

Cubic space per occupant (cubic metres) (1)	Minimum cross-sectional area per occupant (square millimetres) (2)
Exceeding 21 but not exceeding 28	6500
Exceeding 28 but not exceeding 35	5850
Exceeding 35 but not exceeding 42	5200
Exceeding 42 but not exceeding 49	4550
Exceeding 49 but not exceeding 56	3900
Exceeding 56 but not exceeding 63	3250
Exceeding 63 but not exceeding 70	2600
Exceeding 70 but not exceeding 77	1950
Exceeding 77 but not exceeding 84	1300
Exceeding 84	650

""

21. In regulation K13(i), for the words "10 square inches for every 750 cubic feet of that part of the access" there shall be substituted the words "300 square millimetres for each cubic metre of that part of the access so, however, that in no case shall an opening area be less than 6500 square millimetres".

22. In Part A of Schedule 10, in paragraph 5, the words ' "B.t.u." means British thermal units' and the words ' "S.W.G." means Standard Wire Gauge' shall be deleted.

23. In Part B of Schedule 10—

(a) in specification (6)(b)(ii) to regulation G8, for the words "22 S.W.G." there shall be substituted the words "0·7 millimetre thickness" ;

(b) in the specification relating to regulation J4(2), in the column headings (3), (4) and (5) of the table, for the mean U-values of "0·42", "0·48" and "0·58" there shall be substituted the values "2·4", "2·7" and "3·3" respectively.

Gordon Campbell,
One of Her Majesty's Principal
Secretaries of State.

St. Andrew's House,
Edinburgh.
18th June 1971.

FIRST SCHEDULE

Regulation 3

Regulation (1)	Imperial Measure (2)	Metric Measure (3)
PART A		
A3(1) in the definition of "permanent ventilator"	4 feet	2 metres
A7(1)(b)	square feet	square metres
PART D		
D2(1) in the definition of "opening"	1/32 inch	1 millimetre
D3(2)	50 feet	15 metres
D3(2)(a)	50 feet	15 metres
D3(2)(b)	30 feet	9 metres
D3(2)(c)	20 feet	6 metres
D4 Proviso	400 square feet	40 square metres
D6(d)	3 feet 6 inches	1 metre
D7(3)	15 inches	375 millimetres
D7(3) Proviso (i)	45 feet	14 metres
	5 feet	1·5 metres
D7(3) Proviso (ii)	40 feet	12·5 metres
D7(3) Proviso (iii)	5 feet	1·5 metres
D7(3) Proviso (iv)	40 feet	12·5 metres
	5 feet	1·5 metres
D7(3) Proviso (v)	40 feet	12·5 metres
	5 feet	1·5 metres
D7(6) Proviso (ii)	4 square feet	0·4 square metre
D10(3)(a)(i)	1 inch	25 millimetres
D10(3)(a)(ii)	6 inches	150 millimetres
D12 Proviso (2)(c)(iii)(A)	100 feet	30 metres
D12 Proviso (2)(c)(iii)(B)	40 feet	12·5 metres
D15	⅜ inch	9 millimetres
D15 Proviso (i)	150 square inches	0·1 square metre
	5 feet	1·5 metres
D15 Proviso (ii)	40 feet	12·5 metres
D17(2)	0·3 calories per square centimetre per second (66 British thermal units per square foot per minute)	12·6 kilowatts per square metre
D17(2)(a)	4 calories per square centimetre per second (884 British thermal units per square foot per minute)	168 kilowatts per square metre

First Schedule—*continued*

Regulation (1)	Imperial Measure (2)	Metric Measure (3)
D17(2)(b)	2 calories per square centimetre per second (442 British thermal units per square foot per minute)	84 kilowatts per square metre
D17(3)	1/32 inch	1 millimetre
D17(4)(a)	150 square inches	0·1 square metre
	5 feet	1·5 metres
D17(4)(c)(i)	10 square feet	0·9 square metre
D17(4)(c)(ii)	12 feet	3·6 metres
D17(4)(d)	50 feet	15 metres
D17(5)	3 feet 6 inches	1 metre
D17(6)(b)	80 feet	24 metres
D17(6)(b)(i)	60 square feet	5·6 square metres
	3 feet 6 inches	1 metre
D17(6)(b)(ii)	160 square feet	15 square metres
	8 feet	2·4 metres
D17(6)(b)(iii)	160 square feet	15 square metres
	20 feet	6 metres
	40 feet	12·5 metres
	16 feet	4·9 metres
D17(7)(c)(iii)	1/32 inch	1 millimetre
D18(2)(a)	20 feet	6 metres
D18(2)(b)(i)	30 square feet	3 square metres
	5 feet	1·5 metres
	20 feet	6 metres
D18(2)(b)(ii)	40 feet	12 metres
D18(2)(c)(i)	75 feet	22 metres
D18(2)(c)(ii)	5 feet	1·5 metres
D18(2)(c)(iii)	30 square feet	3 square metres
D18(3)(a)	40,000 cubic feet	1130 cubic metres
D18(4)(a)	40 feet	12 metres
D18(4) Proviso (i)	30 square feet	3 square metres
D18(4) Proviso (ii)	5 feet	1·5 metres
D18(4) Proviso	20 feet	6 metres
D18(7)(i)	20 feet	6 metres
D18(7)(ii)	400 square feet	40 square metres
D20(1)	200 square feet	19 square metres
D22(1)	20 gallons	90 litres
D22(2)(b)	275 gallons	1250 litres
D22(2) Proviso (ii)	275 gallons	1250 litres
	750 gallons	3400 litres
D22(3)(c)(i)	275 gallons	1250 litres
D22(3)(c)(ii)	275 gallons	1250 litres
	750 gallons	3400 litres
D22(3)(c)(iii)	750 gallons	3400 litres
D22(5)(a)(i)	750 gallons	3400 litres
D22(5)(b)	9 inches	225 millimetres
D22(5)(b)(i)(A)	750 gallons	3400 litres
	3 feet	900 millimetres
D22(5)(b)(i)(B)	1 foot	300 millimetres

First Schedule—*continued*

Regulation (1)	Imperial Measure (2)	Metric Measure (3)
D22(5)(b)(ii)(A)	750 gallons	3400 litres
	3 feet	900 millimetres
D22(5)(b)(ii)(B)	1 foot	300 millimetres
D22(5)(b)(iii)(A)	750 gallons	3400 litres
D22(5)(c)(i)	750 gallons	3400 litres
	20 feet	6 metres
D22(5)(c)(ii)	6 feet	1·8 metres
PART E		
E2(3)(d)	$\frac{1}{2}$ inch	13 millimetres
E5(1)(a)(i)	10 feet	3 metres
	60 feet per minute	18 metres per minute
E5(1)(a)(ii)	40 feet per minute	12·5 metres per minute
E5(3)(b)	square feet	square metres
E6(3)(ab)	10 feet	3 metres
E6(3)(b)	3 feet 6 inches	1·1 metres
E9(3)	10 feet	3 metres
E9(3)(a)	10 feet	3 metres
E9(3)(b)	10 feet	3 metres
E9(4) Proviso	4 square feet	0·4 square metre
E10(1)	80 feet	24 metres
E10(1)(a)	10,000 square feet	900 square metres
	80 feet	24 metres
E10(3)	30 square feet	2·8 square metres
E10(4)(a)(i)	120 square feet	11 square metres
E10(4)(a)(ii)	30 square feet	2·8 square metres
E10(5)(b)	10 square feet	0·9 square metre
E10(5)(c)	10 feet	3 metres
E12(2)	3 feet 3 inches	900 millimetres
E12(3)(a)	7 feet	2·1 metres
E12(3)(b)	4 feet	1·2 metres
E13(2)(b)	3 feet	900 millimetres
E15(1)	35 feet	11 metres
E15(2)	4 feet 6 inches	1·4 metres
E15(3)	Centigrade (80·6° Fahrenheit)	Celsius
E16(3)(a)	1/32 inch	1 millimetre
E16(3)(b)	$\frac{1}{8}$ inch	3 millimetres
E17(1)	80 feet	24 metres
E17(3)(a)	3 feet 6 inches	1·1 metres
E17(3)(b)	2 feet 9 inches	850 millimetres
	1 foot 9 inches	550 millimetres
E17(4)	6 feet	1·8 metres
E17(4)(a)	35 feet	11 metres

FIRST SCHEDULE—*continued*

Regulation (1)	Imperial Measure (2)	Metric Measure (3)
E17(4)(a)(i)	15 feet	4·5 metres
	30 feet	9 metres
	5 feet	1·5 metres
E17(4)(a)(ii)	8 feet 6 inches	2·6 metres
	11 feet 6 inches	3·5 metres
E17(4)(b)	35 feet	11 metres
E17(4)(b)(i)	8 tons	8 tonnes
E17(4)(b)(ii)	10 feet	3 metres
	43 feet	13 metres
	16 feet	4·9 metres
E17(4)(b)(iii)	10 feet	3 metres
	11 feet 6 inches	3·5 metres
	27 feet	8·3 metres
E18(b)(i)	100,000 cubic feet	2800 cubic metres
	8 feet	2·4 metres
	1,000 square feet	90 square metres
E18(b)(ii)	10 feet	3 metres
E18(c)(i)	8 tons	8 tonnes
E18(c)(ii)	10 feet	3 metres
	43 feet	13 metres
	16 feet	4·9 metres
E18(c)(iii)	8 tons	8 tonnes
	10 feet	3 metres
	11 feet 6 inches	3·5 metres
	27 feet	8·3 metres
E18 Proviso	400 square feet	37 square metres
E19(1)(a)	35 feet	11 metres
E19(1)(b)(i)	2,500 square feet	230 square metres
E19(1)(b)(ii)	10,000 square feet	900 square metres
E19(2)(a)	2,500 square feet	230 square metres
E19(2)(b)	10,000 square feet	900 square metres
	200 feet	61 metres
E19(2) Proviso (i)(B)	15 feet	4·5 metres
E19(3)	4 inches	100 millimetres
E19(5)(a)	200 feet	61 metres
E19(6)	15 feet	4·5 metres
E19(8)(a)	60 feet	18 metres
E19(8)(b)	40 feet	12·5 metres
E19(9)	4 inches	100 millimetres
E20(1)	80 feet	24 metres
E20(1) Proviso (ii)(C)	15 feet	4·5 metres
E20(3)	15½ square feet	1·4 square metres
	1,200 pounds	550 kilogrammes
E20(5)(d)(i)	15 feet	4·5 metres
E20(5)(d)(ii)	50 feet	15 metres
PART F		
F1(1)(a)(i)	150,000 British thermal units per hour	45 kilowatts

FIRST SCHEDULE—*continued*

Regulation (1)	Imperial Measure (2)	Metric Measure (3)
F1(1)(a)(ii)	1 cubic foot	0·03 cubic metre
	3 cubic feet	0·08 cubic metre
F1(2)(a)(i)	150,000 British thermal units per hour	45 kilowatts
F1(2)(a)(ii)	1 cubic foot	0·03 cubic metre
F1(3)(a)(i)	150,000 British thermal units per hour	45 kilowatts
F1(3)(a)(ii)	150,000 British thermal units per hour	45 kilowatts
F1(3)(a)(iii)	3 cubic feet	0·08 cubic metre
F2(2)(a)	100 pounds per cubic foot	1600 kilogrammes per cubic metre
F2(3)(a)(i)	Centigrade (1,832° Fahrenheit)	Celsius
F2(3)(b)	Centigrade (248° Fahrenheit)	Celsius
F4(1)(a)(i)	$\frac{3}{16}$ inch	4·75 millimetres
F4(1) Proviso (i)	6 feet	1·8 metres
F4(1) Proviso (ii)	1 foot 6 inches	460 millimetres
	No. 16 Standard Wire Gauge	1·6 millimetres
F4(3)(b)	8 inches	200 millimetres
	12 inches	300 millimetres
F4(4)(a)	6 inches	150 millimetres
F4(4)(b)	1 inch	25 millimetres
F4(4)(c)(i)(B)	1 inch	25 millimetres
F4(4)(c)(ii)(A)	$7\frac{1}{2}$ inches	190 millimetres
F4(4)(c)(ii)(B)	$4\frac{1}{2}$ inches	100 millimetres
F4(5) Proviso (iii)	$\frac{1}{2}$ inch	12·5 millimetres
F4(6) Proviso (iii)	$\frac{1}{2}$ inch	12·5 millimetres
F4(7)	8 inches	200 millimetres
F4(8)(a)	8 inches	200 millimetres
F4(8)(b)	12 inches	300 millimetres
F5(2)	7 feet 6 inches	2·3 metres
F5(3)	40 feet	12 metres
F5(4)(a)	2 feet	600 millimetres
	5 feet	1·5 metres
F5(4)(b)	3 feet	1 metre
	7 feet 6 inches	2·3 metres
F5(4)(c)	3 feet	1 metre
	7 feet 6 inches	2·3 metres
F6(1)	8 inches	200 millimetres
F6(1) Proviso (i)	8 inches	200 millimetres
	6 inches	150 millimetres
F6(2)	$1\frac{1}{2}$ inches	38 millimetres

FIRST SCHEDULE—*continued*

Regulation (1)	Imperial Measure (2)	Metric Measure (3)	
F7	2 inches	50	millimetres
F8	8 inches	200	millimetres
	¼ inch	7	millimetres
F9(2)(b)(i)	4 inches	100	millimetres
F9(2)(b)(ii)	6 inches	150	millimetres
F9(3)(a)	8 inches	200	millimetres
F9(3)(b)	12 inches	300	millimetres
F9(3) Proviso (i)	4 inches	100	millimetres
F9(3) Proviso (ii)	6 inches	150	millimetres
F13(2)(a)	8 inches	200	millimetres
F13(2)(b)	12 inches	300	millimetres
F13(3)(a)(i)	4 inches	100	millimetres
F13(3)(a)(ii)	6 inches	150	millimetres
F13(3)(b)(i)	8 inches	200	millimetres
F13(3)(b)(ii)	12 inches	300	millimetres
F13(3) Proviso	8 inches	200	millimetres
F13(3) Proviso (i)	4 inches	100	millimetres
F13(3) Proviso (ii)	6 inches	150	millimetres
F13(5)	1½ inches	38	millimetres
F13(5) Proviso	1½ inches	38	millimetres
F14	12 inches	300	millimetres
F14(a)	4 inches	100	millimetres
	12 inches	300	millimetres
F15(2)(c)	6 inches	150	millimetres
	33 inches	840	millimetres
F15(2)(d)	20 inches	500	millimetres
F15(3)	5 inches	125	millimetres
F15(3) Proviso	4 inches	100	millimetres
F15(5)(a)(i)	2 inches	50	millimetres
F15(5)(a)(ii)	4 inches	100	millimetres
F15(5)(a)(iv)	9 inches	225	millimetres
F15(5)(a)(v)	2 inches	50	millimetres
F16(2)	5 inches	125	millimetres
F16(4)	2 feet 9 inches	840	millimetres
F17	2 inches	50	millimetres
F17 Proviso (i)	10 inches	250	millimetres
F20(2)(b)	1⅞ inches	48	millimetres
F20(3)(a)(i)	12 inches	300	millimetres
F20(3)(a)(ii)	8 inches	200	millimetres
F20(3)(b)	6 inches	150	millimetres
F20(3)(c)	6 inches	150	millimetres
F20(4)	6 inches	150	millimetres
F22(3)	1 inch	25	millimetres
F22(4)(b)	1 inch	25	millimetres

FIRST SCHEDULE—*continued*

Regulation (1)	Imperial Measure (2)	Metric Measure (3)
F24	1 inch	25 millimetres
F25	1 inch	25 millimetres
F27(2)(b)	64 square inches	40 000 square millimetres
F27(2)(c)(i)	2 feet	600 millimetres
F27(2)(c)(ii)	11 feet	3·4 metres
F27(2)(c)(ii)(A)	5 feet	1·5 metres
	2 feet	600 millimetres
F27(2)(c)(ii)(B)	5 feet	1·5 metres
	11 feet	3·4 metres
F27(2)(f)	6 feet	1·8 metres
F27(2)(h)	24 inches	600 millimetres
F27(2)(i)	20 feet	6 metres
F27(2)(j)(i)	96 square inches	62 000 square millimetres
F27(3)(a)	2½ inches	63 millimetres
F28	1 inch	25 millimetres
	3 inches	75 millimetres
F28 Proviso	Centigrade (212° Fahrenheit)	Celsius
F29	½ inch	12·5 millimetres
F29(a)(i)	6 inches	150 millimetres
F29(b)	9 inches	225 millimetres
F29 Proviso (i)	9 inches	225 millimetres
F29 Proviso (ii)	Centigrade (212° Fahrenheit)	Celsius
F32	15 feet	4·5 metres
PART K		
K3(2)	one square foot	0·1 square metre
K5(1)	40 square feet	3·7 square metres
K5(1)(a)(ii)(A)	10 square inches	6500 square millimetres
K5(1)(a)(ii)(B)	10 square inches	6500 square millimetres
K5(1) Proviso (ii)	30 square inches	19 000 square millimetres
K5(3)(a)	15 square inches	9500 square millimetres
K5(3)(b)	15 square inches	9500 square millimetres
K6(a)(ii)	one square foot	0·1 square metre
K7(2)(e)	40 square feet	3·7 square metres
K8	4,000 square feet	370 square metres
K8(a)(i)	400 square feet	40 square metres
	10 square inches	6500 square millimetres
K8 Proviso	400 square feet	40 square metres
K9(3)(c)	9 inches	200 millimetres
K9(5)(b)	2,000 square feet	190 square metres
K9(5)(c)	two feet	600 millimetres

FIRST SCHEDULE—*continued*

Regulation (1)	Imperial Measure (2)	Metric Measure (3)
K10(4)(a)	100 cubic feet	2·8 cubic metres
K10(4)(b)	100 cubic feet	2·8 cubic metres
	750 cubic feet	21 cubic metres
K11(2) Proviso (i)	1,500 cubic feet	42 cubic metres
K11(2) Proviso (i)(B)	30 square inches	19 000 square millimetres
K11(3)	525 cubic feet	14·9 cubic metres
K12(2)	400 cubic feet	11·3 cubic metres
K12(2)(a)	5 square inches	3250 square millimetres
K12(2)(b)	15 square inches	9500 square millimetres
K12(3)	400 cubic feet	11·3 cubic metres
	750 cubic feet	21 cubic metres
	5 square inches	3250 square millimetres
K14(1)(a)	100 square inches	65 000 square millimetres
K14(2)	10 square inches	6500 square millimetres
K15	6 feet 6 inches	2 metres
K15 Proviso (i)	5 feet 6 inches	1·7 metres
K15 Proviso (ii)	2 feet	600 millimetres
K16(1)(b)	10 feet	3 metres
K16(6)(a)	3 feet 6 inches	1 metre
K16(6)(b)	10 feet	3 metres
PART L		
L2(1) in the definition of "working plane"	2 feet 9 inches	850 millimetres
L4(1)(a)	50 square feet	4·5 square metres
L7(3)	2 feet 9 inches	840 millimetres
L8(3)(a)(i)	9 feet 6 inches	2·9 metres
L8(3)(a)(ii)	9 feet 6 inches	2·9 metres
L8(3)(b)(ii)	40 feet	12·5 metres
L8(3)(c)(iii)(B)(I)	40 feet	12·5 metres
L10(1) Proviso	40 feet	12 metres
L10(1) Proviso (i)	7 feet 3 inches	2·2 metres
L10(1) Proviso (ii)	2 feet 8 inches	800 millimetres
L10(2)(a)	6 feet (where it twice occurs)	1·8 metres
PART M		
M3(2) Proviso	100 yards	90 metres
M3(2) Proviso (ii)(A)	50 feet	15 metres
M4(3)(c)	3 inches	75 millimetres
M4(5)(b)	40 feet	12·5 metres
M4(5)(c)	50 yards	45 metres
M4(6) Proviso	24 inches	600 millimetres

FIRST SCHEDULE—*continued*

Regulation (1)	Imperial Measure (2)	Metric Measure (3)	
M5(2)	4 feet	1·2	metres
M6(1)(b)	six inches	150	millimetres
M6(1) Proviso	3 feet	1	metre
M6(2)	30 feet	9	metres
M9	20 feet	6	metres
M10	2 inches	50	millimetres
M12(1)	Centigrade (113° Fahrenheit)		Celsius
M15(1)	3 inches	75	millimetres
M15(4)(b)	2½ inches	63	millimetres
M16(2) Proviso	15 feet	5	metres
M17(2)	2 inches	50	millimetres
PART Q			
Q2(2)(a)	150 feet (where it twice occurs)	46	metres
Q2(2)(b)	30 feet	9	metres
	150 feet	46	metres
Q2(2)	10 feet	3	metres
	5 tons	5	tonnes
Q2(3)(a)(i)	3 feet	900	millimetres
Q2(3)(a)(ii)	4 feet	1·2	metres
Q2(3)(a)(iii)	6 feet	1·8	metres
Q2(3)(b)(i)	3 feet	900	millimetres
Q2(3)(b)(ii)	3 feet 6 inches	1	metre
Q2(3)(c)(i)	3 feet	900	millimetres
Q2(3)(c)(ii)	4 feet	1·2	metres
Q2(7)	3 feet 6 inches	1·1	metres
	4 feet	1·2	metres
Q2(8)	4 inches	100	millimetres
Q6(1)(b)	31 feet	9	metres
Q6(2)(b)(ii)(B)	62 feet	19	metres
Q6(5)(a)	100 feet per minute	0·5	metre per second
Q6(5)(b)	150 feet per minute	0·75	metre per second
Q6(5)(c)	200 feet per minute	1	metre per second
Q6(5)(d)	300 feet per minute	1·5	metres per second
Q7(2)(a)	75 square feet	7	square metres
Q7(3)(i)	120 square feet	11	square metres
	10 square feet	0·9	square metre
Q7(3)(ii)	5 square feet	0·5	square metre

FIRST SCHEDULE—*continued*

Regulation (1)	Imperial Measure (2)	Metric Measure (3)
Q8(1)(a)	7 feet 6 inches	2·3 metres
Q8(1)(b)	6 feet 9 inches	2·06 metres
Q8(2)(a)	7 feet 6 inches	2·3 metres
	7 feet	2·1 metres
Q8(2)(b)(i)	525 cubic feet	14·9 cubic metres
Q8(2)(b)(ii)	7 feet 6 inches	2·3 metres
	6 feet 3 inches	1·9 metres
Q8(2)(c)	7 feet 6 inches	2·3 metres
	5 feet	1·5 metres
Q8(2)(d)	7 feet 6 inches	2·3 metres
	5 feet	1·5 metres
Q8(2)(e)	6 feet 9 inches	2·06 metres
	5 feet	1·5 metres
Q9(1)(a)(i)	5 feet	1·5 metres
Q9(1)(a)(iii)	3 feet 6 inches	1 metre
	2 feet 3 inches	685 millimetres
	2 feet	600 millimetres
	1 foot 9 inches	530 millimetres
Q9(2)(a)(ii)	5¼ square feet	0·49 square metres
	2 feet	600 millimetres
	2 feet 2 inches	660 millimetres
Q9(2)(b)(iii)	3½ inches	90 millimetres
Q10(2)(b)	3 square feet	0·28 square metre
Q11(2)	12 cubic feet	0·34 cubic metre
Q11(2) Proviso	6 cubic feet	0·17 cubic metre
Q11(3)(a)	5 square inches	3250 square millimetres
Q11(5)	18 inches	460 millimetres
Q12(b)	40 cubic feet	1·13 cubic metres
Q12(c)	4 inches	100 millimetres
	3 inches	75 millimetres
Q12 Proviso (i)	40 cubic feet	1·13 cubic metres
Q14(1) Proviso (ii)(B)	450 square feet	42 square metres
Q15(2)(a)(iii)	9 feet	2·7 metres
Q15(2)(c)(ii)	12 pounds	5·4 kilogrammes
Q16(2)	12 inches	300 millimetres
Q17(3)	6,000 British thermal units per hour	2 kilowatts
Q18(2)	20 square feet	1·9 square metres
Q19(2) Table footnote (b)	110 square feet	10 square metres
Q20(1)(b)	31 feet	9 metres

First Schedule—*continued*

Regulation (1)	Imperial Measure (2)	Metric Measure (3)
PART R		
R1(b)	20 feet	6 metres
R1(e)	3 inches	75 millimetres
R2(b)	60 feet	18 metres

Regulation 4   SECOND SCHEDULE

New Table to be substituted for Table in Regulation D22(4) of the Building Standards Regulations

Capacity of tank (litres) (1)	Minimum distance of tank from building containing appliance (2)	Conditions (3)	Minimum distance of tank from boundary (4)	Conditions (5)
Exceeding 90 but not exceeding 1250	1·8 metres	(a) The tank is underground, or (b) there is a screen wall, or (c) the external wall of the building is protected.	760 millimetres	(a) The tank is underground, or (b) there is a screen wall.
Exceeding 1250 but not exceeding 3400	1·8 metres	(a) The tank is underground, or (b) there is a screen wall, or (c) the external wall of the building is protected.	760 millimetres	(a) The tank is underground, or (b) there is a screen wall.
Exceeding 3400	6 metres	(a) The tank is underground, or (b) there is a screen wall, or (c) the external wall of the building is protected.	6 metres	(a) The tank is underground, or (b) there is a screen wall.

SECOND SCHEDULE—*continued*

NEW TABLE TO BE SUBSTITUTED FOR TABLE IN REGULATION F27(2) OF THE BUILDING
STANDARDS REGULATIONS

Appliance (1)	No. of appliances (2)	Maximum total input rating (kilo-watts) (3)	No. of appliances (4)	Maximum total input rating (kilo-watts) (5)
Convector gas fire with controlled flue flow (42–70 cubic metres) ...	5	30	7	45
Instantaneous water heater	10	300	10	450
Storage water heater, circulator or air heater	10	120	10	180

NEW TABLE TO BE SUBSTITUTED FOR TABLE IN REGULATION Q14(2) OF THE BUILDING
STANDARDS REGULATIONS

Appliance	Capable of dealing in one operation with dry weight of washing	Scale—number of houses to each appliance not more than—

(A)
  (i) Combined washing and rinsing machines powered by electricity and heated by gas, electricity or steam
     and
	(*a*) 4 kilogrammes
	or
	(*b*) 9 kilogrammes
		(*a*) 15
		or
		(*b*) 30

(ii) Tubs and	—	15
(iii) Hydro-extractors powered by electricity, or wringers	(*a*) 4 kilogrammes or (*b*) 6 kilogrammes	(*a*) 30 or (*b*) 60

(B)
  (i) Combined washing, boiling, rinsing and spin-drying machines powered by electricity and heated by gas, electricity or steam
     and
	4 kilogrammes	15

(ii) Tubs	—	15

SECOND SCHEDULE—*continued*

NEW TABLE TO BE SUBSTITUTED FOR TABLE IN REGULATION Q15(1) OF THE BUILDING STANDARDS REGULATIONS

Description of house (1)	Head Drying facilities (2) (3)	Sited (4)
Not in blocks of flats ...	(1) Drying area of not less than 4·2† square metres.	On ground adjacent to house or building.
In block of flats of less than 5 storeys ...	(2) Individual drying area not less than 4·2† square metres or communal drying area on scale of not less than 4·2† square metres per house.	On ground adjacent to building.
In a block of flats ...	(3) Individual drying area not less than 4·2† square metres or communal drying area on scale of not less than 4·2† square metres per house.	On a balcony or On a flat roof or In a room or other part of the block set aside for the purpose.
	(4)(a) Individual drying cabinet or tumbler dryer and	(a) Within house.
	(b) Individual drying area not less than 2·8 square metres or communal drying area on scale of not less than 2·8 square metres per house.	(b) On a balcony or On a flat roof or In a room or other part of the block set aside for the purpose.
	(5) Individual drying cabinet or tumbler dryer and Hydro-extractor capable of dealing with 2·7 kilogrammes dry weight of washing in one operation and powered by electricity.	Within house.
	(6)(a) Communal heated drying cabinets or tumbler dryers and	(a) In the block.
	(b) Individual drying area not less than 2·8 square metres or communal drying area on scale of not less than 2·8 square metres per house.	(b) On a balcony or On a flat roof or In a room or other part of the block set aside for the purpose.
In a block of flats in respect of which there is provided communal laundry facilities such as are mentioned in regulation Q14(2)(a)...	(7) Communal heated drying cabinets or tumbler dryers.	In the block.

†*Note:* This area shall be 2·8 square metres in relation to a house in a block of flats comprising—
    (i) one or two apartments, or
    (ii) three apartments, two of which have a floor area of less than 10 square metres.

THIRD SCHEDULE   Regulation 5

Schedule (1)	Imperial Measure (2)	Metric Measure (3)
SCHEDULE 1		
Paragraph (11) Proviso (i)(B)	5 feet	1·5 metres
(D)	3 feet	900 millimetres
Paragraph (14) Proviso (i)	5 feet	1·5 metres
(ii)	7 feet 6 inches	2·3 metres
(iii)	10 feet	3 metres
(iv)	20 feet	6 metres
SCHEDULE 3		
Class 1—Description	one acre	0·4 hectare
(c)	7 feet	2·1 metres
Limitations (i)(A)	40,000 cubic feet	1130 cubic metres
(B)	42 feet	13 metres
(ii)	4 feet	1·2 metres
Class 2—Description (c)	7 feet	2·1 metres
Limitations (i)(A)	40,000 cubic feet	1130 cubic metres
(B)	42 feet	13 metres
(ii)	4 feet	1·2 metres
Class 3—Limitations (A)	42 feet	13 metres
(B)	42 feet	13 metres
Class 4—Limitation	3 feet 6 inches	1 metre
Class 7—Limitations (i)	100 square feet	9 square metres
(ii)	20 feet	6 metres
Class 16—Description (a)	7 feet	2·1 metres
(b)	4 feet	1·2 metres
SCHEDULE 5		
Paragraph (5)	500 square feet	46 square metres
Proviso (i)	2 inches	50 millimetres
(7) (a)	100 square inches	65 000 square millimetres
(b)	100 square inches	65 000 square millimetres
	100 square feet	9 square metres
SCHEDULE 6		
Paragraph (2)(a)	5 feet	1·5 metres
(b)	5 feet	1·5 metres
(3)(a)	5 feet	1·5 metres
(4)	5 feet	1·5 metres
(5)	5 feet	1·5 metres
(6)(c)	1/32 inch	1 millimetre

THIRD SCHEDULE—*continued*

Schedule (1)	Imperial Measure (2)	Metric Measure (3)
SCHEDULE 7		
Part I paragraph (4)(c)(i)	2 feet 9 inches	850 millimetres
Part II Heading	40 feet	12·5 metres
paragraph 5	40 feet	12·5 metres
	1 foot	300 millimetres
Part IV Heading	40 feet	12·5 metres
paragraph 10	40 feet	12·5 metres
Part V paragraph 11 diagram	100 ft.	30 metres
	90	27
	80	24
	70	21
	60	18
	50	15
	40	12
	30	9
	20	6
	10	3
Table: (a)	214 feet	64 metres
	274 feet	82 metres
	374 feet	112 meters
	568 feet	170 metres
(b)	107 feet	32 metres
	137 feet	41 metres
	187 feet	56 metres
	284 feet	86 metres
SCHEDULE 8		
Part I Heading	24 inches	600 millimetres
Test 1	2 feet	600 millimetres
	3·4 pounds per square inch	234 millibars
	8 feet	2·4 metres
	2 feet	600 millimetres
Test 2	2 inches	50 millimetres
	1½ inches	38 millimetres
Part II Test 3	5 feet	1·5 metres
	3·4 pounds per square inch	234 millibars
	8 feet	2·4 metres
	5 feet	1·5 metres
Test 4	2 inches	50 millimetres
	1½ inches	38 millimetres
Part III Test 5	2 inches	50 millimetres
SCHEDULE 9		
TABLE 1		
Column 2 : Heading	110 square feet	10 square metres
Column 3 : (i)	110 square feet	10 square metres
(ii)	110 square feet	10 square metres

THIRD SCHEDULE—*continued*

Schedule (1)	Imperial Measure (2)	Metric Measure (3)	
SCHEDULE 9—*continued*			
TABLE 6			
Walls Column 2	3 feet 6 inches	1	metre
TABLE 11			
A2 Part I Head 1	35 feet	11	metres
2(b)	3 feet	900	millimetres
Part II Head 1(a)	35 feet	11	metres
2(b)	80 feet	24	metres
3(d)	80 feet	24	metres
4(c)	80 feet	24	metres
Part IV Head 1(c)(ii)	15 feet	4·5	metres
(iii)	50 feet	15	metres
2(c)(ii)	15 feet	4·5	metres
(iii)	50 feet	15	metres
3(c)(ii)	15 feet	4·5	metres
(iii)	50 feet	15	metres
4(b)	35 feet	11	metres
5(b)	80 feet	24	metres
A3 8(a)	35 feet	11	metres
B1 11(a)	35 feet	11	metres
(c)	4,000 square feet	370	square metres
B2 12(a)	15 feet	4·5	metres
(b)	40 feet	12·5	metres
C2 15(a)	15 feet	4·5	metres
(c)	4,000 square feet	370	square metres
D and E 18(a)	15 feet	4·5	metres
(c)	4,000 square feet	370	square metres
Part V Head 1(b)	10 feet	3	metres
Footnote—ventilated lobby, etc.	15 square feet	1·4	square metres
TABLE 12			
Part I Heading to first column	cycles/second	hertz	
Part II Heading to first column	cycles/second	hertz	
SCHEDULE 11			
Part I			
Column (1) Heading	6 inches	150	millimetres
Column (2) Head 4(b)	twenty feet	6	metres
8(a)	110 pounds per cubic foot	1760	kilogrammes per cubic metre
8(b)	110 pounds per cubic foot	1760	kilogrammes per cubic metre
	$\frac{3}{4}$-inch	19	millimetres
	$\frac{3}{8}$-inch	10	millimetres

THIRD SCHEDULE—*continued*

Schedule (1)	Imperial Measure (2)	Metric Measure (3)
SCHEDULE 11—*continued*		
Column (2) Head 9(B)(b)(i)	0·01 inch	0·3 millimetre
	12 inches	300 millimetres
9(B)(b)(iii)	4 inches	100 millimetres
	3 feet	900 millimetres
9(B)(c)	¾-inch	19 millimetres
Part II		
Column (1) Heading	6 inches	150 millimetres
Part III		
General notes on mixes specified for mortar and rendering in this schedule		
8(b)	⅝-inch	15 millimetres
	⅜-inch	10 millimetres
8(c)	¼-inch	7 millimetres

Regulation 6

FOURTH SCHEDULE

Relevant provision of the building standards regulations (1)	Specification number(s) applying to the relevant entry in the third column of Part B of Schedule 10 (2)	Imperial measure in the third column of Part B of Schedule 10 (3)	Relevant entry in the fourth column of Part B of Schedule 10 (4)	Imperial measure in the fourth column of Part B of Schedule 10 (5)	Metric measure (6)
D20(2)	—	10 feet	—	—	3 metres
			Table	14 feet	4·3 metres
				16 feet	4·9 metres
				18 feet	5·5 metres
				19 feet	5·8 metres
F22(1)	—	—	(3)(a)	10 feet	3 metres
			(4)(a)	10 feet	3 metres
			(5)(a)	20 feet	6 metres
			(6)(a)	20 feet	6 metres
			(7)(a)	30 feet	9 metres
			(8)(a)	30 feet	9 metres
			(9)(a)	40 feet	12 metres
			(10)(a)	40 feet	12 metres
			(14)	¼-inch	7 millimetres
				⅝-inch	15 millimetres
			(15)(a)	10 feet	3 metres
			(16)(a)	20 feet	6 meres
			(17)(a)	30 feet	9 metres
			(18)(a)	40 feet	12 metres
G6	—	—	(1)(b)	4 inches	100 millimetres

BUILDING AND BUILDINGS

FOURTH SCHEDULE—continued

(1) Relevant provision of the building standards regulations	(2) Specification number(s) applying to the relevant entry in the third column of Part B of Schedule 10	(3) Imperial measure in the third column of Part B of Schedule 10	(4) Relevant entry in the fourth column of Part B of Schedule 10	(5) Imperial measure in the fourth column of Part B of Schedule 10	(6) Metric measure
G7	—	—	(1)(b)(i)	7 gallons	31 litres
	—	—	(1)(b)(ii)	1 hundredweight	50 kilogrammes
	—	—		3½ inches	90 millimetres
	—	—		3 inches	75 millimetres
	—	—	(2)(b)(i)	2 inches	50 millimetres
	—	—	(2)(c)	6 inches	150 millimetres
	—	—		1½ square inches	3000 square millimetres
	—	—		foot	metre
	—	—	(4)	6 inches	150 millimetres
	—	—	(5)	6 inches	150 millimetres
	—	—	(6)(a)	6 inches	150 millimetres
	—	—	(6)(a)(i)	6½ gallons	29 litres
	—	—		1 hundredweight	50 kilogrammes
	—	—	(6)(c)(ii)	6 inches	150 millimetres
	—	—	(6)(d)	6 inches	150 millimetres
	—	—	(7)(a)	6 inches	150 millimetres
G8	—	—	(1)(a)(i)	10 inches	250 millimetres
	—	—	(1)(a)(ii)	13½ inches	340 millimetres
	—	—	(1)(e)(i)	¾-inch	19 millimetres
	—	—	(2)(a)(i)	8 inches	200 millimetres
	—	—	(2)(a)(ii)	9 inches	225 millimetres
	—	—	(3)(a)	3 inches	75 millimetres
	—	—		2 inches	50 millimetres
	—	—	(4)(a)(i)	10 inches	250 millimetres
	—	—	(4)(a)(ii)	12 inches	300 millimetres
	—	—	(4)(d)(i)	½-inch	12·5 millimetres
	—	—		$\frac{13}{16}$-inch	21 millimetres
	—	—	(5)(b)(i)	4 inches	100 millimetres

Provision	For	Provision	For		Substitute
—	—	(5)(b)(ii)	6 inches		150 millimetres
—	—	—	13/16-inch		21 millimetres
—	—	(6)(d)(ii)	6 inches		150 millimetres
(6)	9 inches (where it twice occurs)	—	—		225 millimetres
—	—	(8)(a)	6 inches		150 millimetres
—	—	(9)(b)(ii)	12 inches		300 millimetres
(7)	9 inches	—	—		225 millimetres
—	—	(11)(g)(i)	6 inches		150 millimetres
—	—	—	6 inches		150 millimetres
(10)	2 feet 6 inches	—	—		760 millimetres
(11)	2 feet 6 inches	—	—		760 millimetres
—	—	(22)(c)	6 inches		150 millimetres
—	—	—	12 inches		300 millimetres
—	—	(22)(d)	3¾ inches		95 millimetres
—	—	(22)(e)	8½ inches		216 millimetres
—	—	—	4½ inches		120 millimetres
—	—	—	1 inch		25 millimetres
—	—	—	¾-inch		19 millimetres
—	—	—	1¼ inches		30 millimetres
—	—	—	13 S.W.G.		2·3 millimetres diameter
—	—	—	6 S.W.G.		4·8 millimetres diameter
—	—	—	1¼ inches		30 millimetres
—	—	—	15 S.W.G.		1·8 millimetres diameter
—	—	—	6 S.W.G.		4·8 millimetres diameter
—	—	(22)(f)	¾-inch		19 millimetres
—	—	—	1 inch		25 millimetres
—	—	—	2 inches		50 millimetres
—	—	(23)(c)	5 inches		125 millimetres
—	—	—	6 inches		150 millimetres
—	—	—	1 inch		25 millimetres
H2(1)					
(1) to (5)	1 foot 6 inches	—	—		460 millimetres
—	2 feet 3 inches (where it twice occurs)	—	—		690 millimetres
—	—	(1)	9 inches		225 millimetres
—	—	—	½-inch		12·5 millimetres
—	—	(2)	100 pounds per square foot		490 kilogrammes per square metre
—	—	—	14 inches		360 millimetres
—	—	—	½-inch		12·5 millimetres

FOURTH SCHEDULE—continued

Relevant provision of the building standards regulations (1)	Specification number(s) applying to the relevant entry in the third column of Part B of Schedule 10 (2)	Imperial measure in the third column of Part B of Schedule 10 (3)	Relevant entry in the fourth column of Part B of Schedule 10 (4)	Imperial measure in the fourth column of Part B of Schedule 10 (5)	Metric measure (6)
H2(1)—cont'd	—	—	(3)	7 inches ½-inch	175 millimetres 12·5 millimetres
	—	—	(4)	95 pounds per square foot 8 inches ½-inch	460 kilogrammes per square metre 200 millimetres 12·5 millimetres
	—	—	(5)	95 pounds per square foot 10 inches ½-inch	460 kilogrammes per square metre 250 millimetres 12·5 millimetres
	—	—	(6)	90 pounds per square foot 4 inches 2 inches ½-inch	440 kilogrammes per square metre 100 millimetres 50 millimetres 12·5 millimetres
	—	—	(7)	100 pounds per square foot 4 inches 2 inches ½-inch	490 kilogrammes per square metre 100 millimetres 50 millimetres 12·5 millimetres
	—	—	(8)	95 pounds per square foot 3 inches 95 pounds per cubic foot 3 inches ½-inch	460 kilogrammes per square metre 75 millimetres 1520 kilogrammes per cubic metre 75 millimetres 12·5 millimetres
	—	—	(9)	50 pounds per square foot 6 inches ½-inch	250 kilogrammes per square metre 150 millimetres 12·5 millimetres
	—	—	(10)	85 pounds per square foot 14 inches	415 kilogrammes per square metre 360 millimetres

Regulation	Paragraph	Additional measurement	Item	Imperial measurement	Metric equivalent
H2(1) and H2(2)	(1) to (3)	—	(11)	3 inches	75 millimetres
		—		95 pounds per cubic foot	1520 kilogrammes per cubic metre
		—		2 inches	50 millimetres
		—		½-inch	12·5 millimetres
		—		50 pounds per square foot	250 kilogrammes per square metre
		—	(12)	4 inches	100 millimetres
		—		60 pounds per cubic foot	960 kilogrammes per cubic metre
		—		3 inches	75 millimetres
		—		½-inch	12·5 millimetres
		—		50 pounds per square foot	250 kilogrammes per square metre
		2 feet	(1)	—	600 millimetres
		—		3/16-inch	4·5 millimetres
		—	(2)(a)	6 inches	150 millimetres
		—	(2)(b)	75 pounds per square foot	365 kilogrammes per square metre
		—	(2)(c)	4 inches	100 millimetres
		—	(2)(d)	45 pounds per square foot	220 kilogrammes per square metre
		—	(3)(a)	45 pounds per square foot	220 kilogrammes per square metre
		—	(3)(b)	45 pounds per square foot	220 kilogrammes per square metre
		—	(3)(c)	45 pounds per square foot	220 kilogrammes per square metre
		—	(3)(d)	4 inches	100 millimetres
		—	(4)(a)	45 pounds per square foot	220 kilogrammes per square metre
		—		45 pounds per square foot	220 kilogrammes per square metre
		—		45 pounds per square foot	220 kilogrammes per square metre
		—		45 pounds per square foot	220 kilogrammes per square metre
		—	(4)(c)	9 inches (where it twice occurs)	225 millimetres
		—		17 pounds per square foot	80 kilogrammes per square metre
		—	(4)(d)	½-inch	12·5 millimetres
		—		¾-inch	19 millimetres
J3(1)	(1) to (4)	½-inch	(1)(a)	—	12·5 millimetres
		⅝-inch	(1)(b)	—	16 millimetres
		⅜-inch	(1)(c)	—	9·5 millimetres
		—	(1)(e)	1 inch	25 millimetres
		—		1 inch	25 millimetres
		—		1 inch	25 millimetres
		—		¾-inch	19 millimetres
		—		5 pounds per cubic foot	80 kilogrammes per cubic metre

FOURTH SCHEDULE—*continued*

Relevant provision of the building standards regulations (1)	Specification number(s) applying to the relevant entry in the third column of Part B of Schedule 10 (2)	Imperial measure in the third column of Part B of Schedule 10 (3)	Relevant entry in the fourth column of Part B of Schedule 10 (4)	Imperial measure in the fourth column of Part B of Schedule 10 (5)	Metric measure (6)
J3(1)—cont'd	—	—	(2)(a)	1 inch	25 millimetres
	—	—	(2)(c)	½-inch	12·5 millimetres
	—	—		5 pounds per cubic foot	80 kilogrammes per cubic metre
	—	—	(4)(a)	1½ inches	38 millimetres
	—	—	(4)(b)	2 inches	50 millimetres
	—	—	(4)(c)	1 inch	25 millimetres
	—	—	(4)(d)	¾-inch	19 millimetres
	—	—	(4)(e)	¾-inch	19 millimetres
	—	—		5 pounds per cubic foot	80 kilogrammes per cubic metre
	—	—	(5)	30 pounds per 12 square yards	13 kilogrammes per 10 square metres
	—	—		⅜-inch	9·5 millimetres
	—	—	(5)(a)	¾-inch	19 millimetres
	—	—	(5)(b)	¾-inch	19 millimetres
	—	—		5 pounds per cubic foot	80 kilogrammes per cubic metre
	—	—	(5)(c)	¾-inch	19 millimetres
	—	—	(5)(d)	¾-inch	19 millimetres
	—	—	(5)(e)	2 inches	50 millimetres
	(6)	¾-inch	—	—	19 millimetres
	—	—	(6)(a)	1½ inches	38 millimetres
	—	—	(6)(b)	2½ inches	63 millimetres
	—	—	(6)(c)	2½ inches	63 millimetres
	—	—		40 pounds per cubic foot	640 kilogrammes per cubic metre
	—	—	(6)(d)	4 inches	100 millimetres
	—	—	(7)	5 inches	125 millimetres
	—	—		45 pounds per cubic foot	720 kilogrammes per cubic metre
	(8)	¾-inch	—	—	19 millimetres
	—	—	(8)(a)	¾-inch	19 millimetres

J4(1)	(1) to (17)	3 inches (where it occurs three times)	—	75 millimetres
		2 inches (where it occurs three times)	—	50 millimetres
		(1)(a)	150 pounds per cubic foot	2400 kilogrammes per cubic metre
		(1)(b)(i)	4 inches	100 millimetres
			150 pounds per cubic foot	2400 kilogrammes per cubic metre
		(1)(b)(ii)	4 inches	100 millimetres
			90 pounds per cubic foot	1440 kilogrammes per cubic metre
			3 inches	75 millimetres
		(1)(c)	½-inch	12·5 millimetres
		(2)(a)(i)	5 inches	125 millimetres
		(2)(a)(ii)	10 inches	250 millimetres
		(2)(b)(i)	150 pounds per cubic foot	2400 kilogrammes per cubic metre
			4 inches	100 millimetres
		(2)(b)(ii)	90 pounds per cubic foot	1440 kilogrammes per cubic metre
			3 inches	75 millimetres
		(2)(c)	½-inch	12·5 millimetres
		(3)(b)(i)	90 pounds per cubic foot	1440 kilogrammes per cubic metre
			4 inches	100 millimetres
		(3)(b)(ii)	70 pounds per cubic foot	1120 kilogrammes per cubic metre
			3 inches	75 millimetres
		(3)(c)	½-inch	12·5 millimetres
		(4)(b)	150 pounds per cubic foot	2400 kilogrammes per cubic metre
			4 inches	100 millimetres
		(4)(c)	⅜-inch	10 millimetres
			¾-inch	19 millimetres
		(5)(b)(i)	70 pounds per cubic foot	1120 kilogrammes per cubic metre
			4 inches	100 millimetres
		(5)(b)(ii)	50 pounds per cubic foot	800 kilogrammes per cubic metre
			3 inches	75 millimetres
		(5)(c)	½-inch	12·5 millimetres
		(6)(c)(i)	⅜-inch	10 millimetres
			¾-inch	19 millimetres
		(6)(c)(ii)	½-inch	12·5 millimetres
		(7)(c)(i)	25 pounds per cubic foot	400 kilogrammes per cubic metre
			¾-inch	19 millimetres
			1 inch	25 millimetres
			25 pounds per cubic foot	400 kilogrammes per cubic metre
			¾-inch	19 millimetres

FOURTH SCHEDULE—continued

(1) Relevant provision of the building standards regulations	(2) Specification number(s) applying to the relevant entry in the third column of Part B of Schedule 10	(3) Imperial measure in the third column of Part B of Schedule 10	(4) Relevant entry in the fourth column of Part B of Schedule 10	(5) Imperial measure in the fourth column of Part B of Schedule 10	(6) Metric measure
J4(1)-cont'd					
	—	—	(7)(c)(ii)	½-inch	12·5 millimetres
				25 pounds per cubic foot	400 kilogrammes per cubic metre
				¾-inch	19 millimetres
	—	—	(8)(b)	50 pounds per cubic foot	800 kilogrammes per cubic metre
				5 inches	125 millimetres
	—	—	(8)(c)	½-inch	12·5 millimetres
	—	—	(9)(b)(i)	50 pounds per cubic foot	800 kilogrammes per cubic metre
				4 inches	100 millimetres
	—	—	(9)(b)(ii)	70 pounds per cubic foot	1120 kilogrammes per cubic metre
				5 inches	125 millimetres
	—	—	(9)(c)(i)	⅜-inch	10 millimetres
				¾-inch	19 millimetres
	—	—	(9)(c)(ii)	½-inch	12·5 millimetres
				25 pounds per cubic foot	400 kilogrammes per cubic metre
				¾-inch	19 millimetres
	—	—	(10)(b)	50 pounds per cubic foot	800 kilogrammes per cubic metre
				4 inches	100 millimetres
	—	—	(10)(c)(i)	⅜-inch	10 millimetres
				¾-inch	19 millimetres
	—	—	(10)(c)(ii)	1 inch	25 millimetres
				25 pounds per cubic foot	400 kilogrammes per cubic metre
				¾-inch	19 millimetres
	—	—	(11)(b)	40 pounds per cubic foot	640 kilogrammes per cubic metre
				8 inches	200 millimetres
	—	—	(11)(c)	½-inch	12·5 millimetres
	—	—	(12)(a)	90 pounds per cubic foot	1440 kilogrammes per cubic metre
				3 inches	75 millimetres
	—	—	(12)(b)	90 pounds per cubic foot	1440 kilogrammes per cubic metre
				3 inches	75 millimetres

Provision	Imperial	Metric
(12)(c)	½-inch	12·5 millimetres
(13)(b)	70 pounds per cubic foot	1120 kilogrammes per cubic metre
(13)(c)	3 inches	75 millimetres
(14)(c)	½-inch	12·5 millimetres
(15)(c)	⅜-inch	10 millimetres
	¾-inch	19 millimetres
	¾-inch	19 millimetres
(16)(a)	50 pounds per cubic foot	800 kilogrammes per cubic metre
	4 inches	100 millimetres
(16)(b)	50 pounds per cubic foot	800 kilogrammes per cubic metre
	4 inches	100 millimetres
(16)(c)	½-inch	12·5 millimetres
	⅜-inch	10 millimetres
(17)(c)	¾-inch	19 millimetres
—		100 millimetres
		50 millimetres
(18)(a)	13/16-inch	21 millimetres
(18)(b)(i)	⅜-inch	10 millimetres
(18)(b)(ii)	½-inch	12·5 millimetres
	3/16-inch	5 millimetres
—		38 millimetres
(19)(a)	13/16-inch	21 millimetres
(19)(b)	⅜-inch	10 millimetres
(19)(c)	⅜-inch	10 millimetres
(20)(c)	⅜-inch	10 millimetres
(21)(a)(i)	10 inches	250 millimetres
(21)(a)(ii)	110 pounds per cubic foot	1760 kilogrammes per cubic metre
	12 inches	300 millimetres
	110 pounds per cubic foot	1760 kilogrammes per cubic metre
(21)(b)	¾-inch	19 millimetres
(21)(c)	½-inch	12·5 millimetres
(22)(a)(i)	150 pounds per cubic foot	2400 kilogrammes per cubic metre
	13 inches	330 millimetres
(22)(a)(ii)	10 inches	250 millimetres
(22)(a)(iii)	18 inches	460 millimetres
(22)(b)	⅜-inch	10 millimetres
	¾-inch	19 millimetres
(23)(b)(i)	⅜-inch	10 millimetres
	¾-inch	19 millimetres

Auxiliary columns:

(18)	(19) and (20)
4 inches	1½ inches
2 inches	

FOURTH SCHEDULE—*continued*

Relevant provision of the building standards regulations (1)	Specification number(s) applying to the relevant entry in the third column of Part B of Schedule 10 (2)	Imperial measure in the third column of Part B of Schedule 10 (3)	Relevant entry in the fourth column of Part B of Schedule 10 (4)	Imperial measure in the fourth column of Part B of Schedule 10 (5)	Metric measure (6)
J4(1)-cont'd	—	—	(23)(b)(ii)	½-inch	12·5 millimetres
	—	—		25 pounds per cubic foot	400 kilogrammes per cubic metre
	—	—		¾-inch	19 millimetres
	—	—	(24)(a)	8 inches	200 millimetres
	—	—		50 pounds per cubic foot	800 kilogrammes per cubic metre
	—	—	(25)(a)	10 inches	250 millimetres
	—	—		50 pounds per cubic foot	800 kilogrammes per cubic metre
	—	—	(26)(a)	8 inches	200 millimetres
	—	—		40 pounds per cubic foot	640 kilogrammes per cubic metre
J5(2)	—	—	(1)	2 inches	50 millimetres
	—	—	(2)	2 inches	50 millimetres
	—	—	(3)	¾-inch	19 millimetres
	—	—	(4)	½-inch	12·5 millimetres
	—	—		5 pounds per cubic foot	80 kilogrammes per cubic metre
	—	—	(5)	1 inch	25 millimetres
	—	—	(8)	1½ inches	38 millimetres
	—	—	(9)	2 inches	50 millimetres
	—	—	(10)	4 inches	100 millimetres
	—	—		35 pounds per cubic foot	560 kilogrammes per cubic metre
	—	—	(11)	5 inches	125 millimetres
	—	—		45 pounds per cubic foot	720 kilogrammes per cubic metre
M8(1)(b)	(2)	3 feet	—	—	900 millimetres
	—	—	(2)(a)	4½ inches	112·5 millimetres
	—	—	(2)(b)	4 inches	100 millimetres
M8(2)	—	—	(2)	12 inches	300 millimetres

Reference			Sub-ref	Imperial	Metric
M14(1)(b)	—	—	(1)	1½ inches	38 millimetres
	—	—	(5)(a)	2½ inches	63 millimetres
	—	—	(5)(c)	2½ inches	63 millimetres
	—	—	(6)(b)	2½ inches	63 millimetres
	—	—	(7)(b)	2½ inches	63 millimetres
	—	—	(8)	2½ inches	63 millimetres
M14(2)(a)	—	—	(1)	2 feet	600 millimetres
	—	—		6 feet	1·8 metres
	—	—	(1)(b)	3 feet	900 millimetres
	—	—	(2)	6 feet	1·8 metres
Q2(2)	—	—	(1)(b)(i)	2½ inches	63 millimetres
	—	—	(1)(b)(ii)	6 inches	150 millimetres
	—	—	(1)(b)(iii)	2 inches	50 millimetres
	—	—	(2)(b)	5 inches	125 millimetres
	—	—		3½ pounds per square yard	1·9 kilogrammes per square metre
	—	—	(2)(c)	4,000 pounds per square inch	28 newtons per square millimetre
Q2(4)	—	—	(1)(b)	2 inch	50 millimetres
	—	—	(2)(b)(i)	4 inches	100 millimetres
	—	—	(2)(b)(ii)	1¼ inches	32 millimetres
Q9(2)	—	—	(b)	½-inch	12·5 millimetres

Regulation 7   FIFTH SCHEDULE

NEW TABLE TO BE SUBSTITUTED FOR TABLE 2 OF SCHEDULE 9 TO THE BUILDING STANDARDS REGULATIONS

SCHEDULE 9—*continued*

TABLE 2—OCCUPANT LOAD FACTORS   Regulation A7

Description of Room or Storey (1)	Occupant Load Factor‡ (2)
Assembly halls (moveable or no seating)	0·5
Bars (including public and lounge bars)	0·5
Bedrooms (in buildings other than those classified A1 or A2)	4·6
Bowling alleys and Billiard rooms	9·3
Canteens	1·1
Clubs	0·5
Common rooms	1·1
Concourses	0·7
Conference rooms and Committee rooms	1·1
Crush halls and Queuing lobbies	0·7
Dance halls	0·7
Dining rooms	1·1
Dormitories	4·6
Enquiry rooms	3·7
Factory shop floors—workrooms and storage...	4·6
Grandstands (without fixed seating)	0·5
Kitchens	9·3
Libraries, Museums, Art Galleries	4·6
Lounges	1·9
Messrooms	1·1
Offices (a) for storeys not divided into rooms	5·1
(b) for individual rooms	3·7
Reading rooms	1·9
Restaurants, Cafes	1·1
Shops trading in the common type of consumer goods (including Standard Industrial Classification 820/1, 820/2, 821/1, 821/2, 821/3 and 821/5 and including shops trading in chemists' wares, fancy goods, toys, games and sports goods)†	
(a) basement storeys	1·4*
(b) ground and upper storeys	1·9*
Shops specialising in more expensive or exclusive trades ... ... (including Standard Industrial Classification 821/4 and including shops trading in furniture and carpets)†	7·0*
Shops for personal services including hairdressing	1·9
Stadia (without fixed seating)	0·5
Staff rooms	1·1
Studios (radio, film, television, recording)	1·4
Warehouses	27·9
Writing rooms	1·9

*The factors are to be applied to the gross sales floor area.

†These references to numbered heads of classification of industry are references to the heads set forth in the third edition of the Standard Industrial Classification issued by the Central Statistical Office in September 1968.

‡Where any room or storey is used or is likely to be used for a variety of purposes the more or, as the case may be, the most onerous occupant load factor shall be applied.

FIFTH SCHEDULE—*continued*

NEW TABLE TO BE SUBSTITUTED FOR TABLE 4 OF SCHEDULE 9 TO THE BUILDING STANDARDS REGULATIONS

Regulation D2

TABLE 4—NOTIONAL PERIODS OF FIRE RESISTANCE

In this Table—

(*a*) "Class 1 aggregate" means foamed slag, pumice, blast furnace slag, pelleted fly ash, crushed brick and burnt clay products including expanded clay, well-burnt clinker and crushed limestone.

"Class 2 aggregate" means flint-gravel, granite, and all crushed natural stones other than limestones.

(*b*) Any reference to plaster means—

   (i) in the case of an external wall 1 metre or more from the boundary, plaster applied on the internal face only;

   (ii) in the case of any other wall, plaster applied to both faces;

   (iii) if to plaster of a given thickness on the external face of a wall, except in the case of a reference to vermiculite-gypsum or perlite-gypsum plaster, a reference to rendering on the external face of the same thickness;

   (iv) if to vermiculite-gypsum plaster, shall be construed as a reference to vermiculite-gypsum plaster of a mix within the range of 1½ to 2:1 by volume.

(*c*) Any reference to sprayed asbestos means sprayed asbestos conforming to B.S. 3590:1963.

(*d*) The imposed load is assumed to be shared by both leaves for periods of fire resistance in excess of 2 hours.

FIFTH SCHEDULE—continued

SCHEDULE 9—continued

TABLE 4—continued

Part I: Walls

A. Masonry construction

Minimum thickness in millimetres (excluding plaster) for a period of fire resistance of

Materials and construction	Loadbearing						Non-loadbearing					
	4 hours	3 hours	2 hours	1½ hours	1 hour	½ hour	4 hours	3 hours	2 hours	1½ hours	1 hour	½ hour
1. Reinforced concrete, minimum concrete cover to main reinforcement of 25 millimetres—												
(a) unplastered	180	150	100	100	75	75						
(b) 12·5 millimetres cement-sand plaster	180	150	100	100	75	75						
(c) 12·5 millimetres gypsum-sand plaster	180	150	100	100	75	75						
(d) 12·5 millimetres vermiculite-gypsum plaster	125	100	75	75	63	63						
2. No-fines concrete of Class 2 aggregate—												
(a) 12·5 millimetres concrete-sand plaster							150					
(b) 12·5 millimetres gypsum-sand plaster							150					
(c) 12·5 millimetres vermiculite-gypsum plaster							150					
3. Brickwork of clay, concrete or sand-lime bricks unreinforced—												
(a) unplastered	200	200	100	100	100	100	170	170	100	100	75	75
(b) 12·5 millimetres cement-sand plaster	200	200	100	100	100	100	170	170	100	100	75	75
(c) 12·5 millimetres gypsum-sand plaster	200	200	100	100	100	100	170	170	100	100	75	75
(d) 12·5 millimetres vermiculite-gypsum or perlite-gypsum plaster	100	100	100	100	100	100	100	100	100	100	75	75

	1	2	3	4	5	6	7	8	9	10	11	12
4. Blockwork of solid concrete blocks of Class 1 aggregate—												
(a) unplastered	150	150	100	100	100	100	150	130	75	75	75	50
(b) 12·5 millimetres cement-sand plaster	150	150	100	100	100	100	100	100	75	75	75	50
(c) 12·5 millimetres gypsum-sand plaster	150	150	100	100	100	100	100	100	75	75	75	50
(d) 12·5 millimetres vermiculite-gypsum plaster	100	100	100	100	100	100	75	75	75	62	50	50
5. Blockwork of solid concrete blocks of Class 2 aggregate—												
(a) unplastered	100	150	100	100	100	100	150	150	100	100	75	50
(b) 12·5 millimetres cement-sand plaster		150	100	100	100	100	150	100	100	100	75	50
(c) 12·5 millimetres gypsum-sand plaster		150	100	100	100	100	150	100	100	100	75	50
(d) 12·5 millimetres vermiculite-gypsum plaster		100	100	100	100	100	100	100	75	75	75	50
6. Blockwork of solid autoclaved aerated concrete blocks unplastered, density 475-1200 kilogrammes per cubic metre	180	150	100	100	100	100	100	75	62	62	50	50
7. Blockwork of hollow concrete blocks of Class 1 aggregate—												
(a) unplastered			100	100	100	100	150	150	100	100	100	75
(b) 12·5 millimetres cement-sand plaster			100	100	100	100	150	150	100	75	75	75
(c) 12·5 millimetres gypsum-sand plaster			100	100	100	100	150	150	100	75	75	75
(d) 12·5 millimetres vermiculite-gypsum plaster			100	100	100	100	100	100	75	75	62	62
8. Blockwork of hollow concrete blocks of Class 2 aggregate—												
(a) unplastered							150	150	150	125	125	125
(b) 12·5 millimetres cement-sand plaster							150	150	150	125	125	100
(c) 12·5 millimetres gypsum-sand plaster							150	150	150	125	125	100
(d) 12·5 millimetres vermiculite-gypsum plaster							125	125	100	100	100	75

FIFTH SCHEDULE—continued

SCHEDULE 9—continued

TABLE 4—continued

Part I: Walls—continued

Minimum thickness in millimetres (excluding plaster) for period of fire resistance of

Materials and construction	Loadbearing						Non-loadbearing					
	½ hour	1 hour	1½ hours	2 hours	3 hours	4 hours	½ hour	1 hour	1½ hours	2 hours	3 hours	4 hours
9. Blockwork of cellular clay blocks—												
(a) one cell not less than 50 per cent. solid, 12·5 millimetres cement-sand or gypsum-sand plaster												
(b) one cell not less than 30 per cent. solid, 12·5 millimetres cement-sand or gypsum-sand plaster							75	100				
(c) two cells not less than 70 per cent. solid, 12·5 millimetres cement-sand or gypsum-sand plaster	100	100	100	100			150	150				
(d) two cells not less than 45 per cent. solid, 12·5 millimetres cement-sand or gypsum-sand plaster							75	100	230	230		
(e) three cells not less than 70 per cent. solid, 12·5 millimetres cement-sand or gypsum-sand plaster	150	150	150	150	150	150	150	150	150	150	150	150

10. Cavity wall with outer leaf of brickwork or blockwork of clay, composition, concrete, or sand-lime bricks or blocks minimum 100 millimetres thick and—												
(a) inner leaf of solid brickwork or blockwork of clay, composition, concrete or sand-lime bricks or blocks other than those specified below … … … …	100	100	100	100	100	100	100	75	75	75	75	75
(b) inner leaf of solid concrete blockwork of blocks of Class 1 aggregate … …	100	100	100	100	100	100	100	75	75	75	75	50
(c) inner leaf of hollow concrete blockwork of blocks of Class 1 aggregate … …	100	100	100	100	100	100	100	100	75	75	75	62
(d) inner leaf of solid concrete blockwork of blocks of Class 2 aggregate … …				100	100	100	100	75	75	75	75	50
(e) inner leaf of blockwork of aerated concrete blocks, including autoclaved aerated concrete blocks, density 475-1200 kilogrammes per cubic metre … … …	150	150	100	100	100	100	75	75	62	62	50	50

FIFTH SCHEDULE—*continued*
SCHEDULE 9—*continued*
TABLE 4—*continued*
Part I: Walls—*continued*

B. *Framed and composite construction*

Materials of construction	Period of fire resistance in hours

1. Steel frame with external cladding of 16 millimetres rendering on metal lathing and internal lining of autoclaved aerated concrete blocks, density 480–1120 kilogrammes per cubic metre of thickness of—

50 millimetres	2
62 millimetres	3
75 millimetres	4

2. Steel frame with external cladding of 100 millimetres concrete blocks and internal lining of 16 millimetres gypsum plaster on metal lathing ... — 4

3. Steel frame with external cladding of bricks of clay, concrete or sand-lime 100 millimetres thick and internal lining of asbestos insulation board of thickness of—

9 millimetres	3

4. Steel frame with external cladding of 16 millimetres rendering on metal lathing and internal lining of—

9 millimetres asbestos insulation board	$\frac{1}{2}$
16 millimetres gypsum plaster on metal lathing...	1

5. Steel or timber frame with facings on each side of—

(*a*) metal lathing with cement-sand or gypsum plaster of thickness of:

19 millimetres	1
12·5 millimetres	$\frac{1}{2}$

(*b*) metal lathing with vermiculite-gypsum or perlite-gypsum plaster of thickness of:

25 millimetres	2
19 millimetres	$1\frac{1}{2}$
12·5 millimetres	1

(*c*) 9·5 millimetres plasterboard with gypsum plaster of thickness of:

5 millimetres	$\frac{1}{2}$

(*d*) 9·5 millimetres plasterboard with vermiculite-gypsum plaster of thickness of:

25 millimetres	2
16 millimetres	$1\frac{1}{2}$
10 millimetres	1
5 millimetres	$\frac{1}{2}$

(*e*) 12·5 millimetres plasterboard with gypsum plaster of thickness of:

12·5 millimetres	1
nil	$\frac{1}{2}$

(*f*) 12·5 millimetres plasterboard with vermiculite-gypsum plaster of thickness of:

25 millimetres	2
16 millimetres	$1\frac{1}{2}$
10 millimetres	1

(*g*) 19 millimetres plasterboard (or 2 layers of 9·5 millimetres) fixed to break joint without finish ... ... | 1

FIFTH SCHEDULE—*continued*
SCHEDULE 9—*continued*
TABLE 4—*continued*
Part I: Walls—continued

Materials of construction	Period of fire resistance in hours
(*h*) 19 millimetres plasterboard (or 2 layers of 9·5 millimetres) with vermiculite-gypsum plaster of thickness of:	
16 millimetres	2
10 millimetres	$1\frac{1}{2}$
(*i*) 12·5 millimetres fibre insulation board with gypsum plaster of thickness of:	
12·5 millimetres	$\frac{1}{2}$
(*j*) (i) 9 millimetres asbestos insulation board fixed to 9 millimetres asbestos insulation board fillets planted on face of studs ...	$\frac{1}{2}$
(ii) 12 millimetres asbestos insulation board...	$\frac{1}{2}$
(*k*) 25 millimetres woodwool slabs with gypsum plaster of thickness of:	
12·5 millimetres	1
6. Compressed straw slabs in timber frames finished on both faces with gypsum plaster of thickness of—	
5 millimetres	1
7. Plasterboard 9·5 millimetres thick on each side of cellular core—	
(*a*) unplastered	$\frac{1}{2}$
(*b*) 12·5 millimetres gypsum plaster	$\frac{1}{2}$
(*c*) 22 millimetres vermiculite-gypsum plaster	2
8. Plasterboard 12·5 millimetres thick on each side of cellular core—	
(*a*) unplastered	$\frac{1}{2}$
(*b*) 12·5 millimetres gypsum plaster	1
(*c*) 16 millimetres vermiculite-gypsum plaster	2
9. Plasterboard 19 millimetres finished on both faces with 16 millimetres gypsum plaster...	1
10. Plasterboard 12·5 millimetres bonded with neat gypsum plaster to each side of 19 millimetres plasterboard	$1\frac{1}{2}$
11. 3 layers of 19 millimetres plasterboard bonded with gypsum plaster ...	2
12. Woodwool slab with 12·5 millimetres render or plaster of thickness of—	
75 millimetres	2
50 millimetres	1
13. Compressed straw slabs with 75 millimetres by 12·5 millimetres wood cover strips to joints, of thickness of—	
50 millimetres	$\frac{1}{2}$
C. *External walls not on the boundary*	
1. Steel frame with external cladding of non-combustible sheets with internal lining of—	
(*a*) asbestos insulation board of thickness of 9 millimetres	4
(*b*) metal lathing with cement-sand or gypsum plaster of thickness of 12·5 millimetres	4
(*c*) sprayed asbestos of thickness of 12·5 millimetres	4
(*d*) 2 layers of 9·5 millimetres plasterboard	$\frac{1}{2}$
(*e*) 9·5 millimetres plasterboard finished with gypsum plaster of thickness of 12·5 millimetres	$\frac{1}{2}$

FIFTH SCHEDULE—*continued*

SCHEDULE 9—*continued*

TABLE 4—*continued*

Part I: Walls—continued

Materials of construction	Period of fire resistance in hours
(*f*) 12·5 millimetres plasterboard finished with 5 millimetres gypsum plaster	½
(*g*) 50 millimetres compressed straw slabs	½
(*h*) 50 millimetres compressed straw slabs finished with 5 millimetres gypsum plaster	1
†2. Timber frame with external cladding of 10 millimetres cement-sand or cement-lime rendering and internal cladding of—	
(*a*) 9 millimetres asbestos insulation board	1
(*b*) 16 millimetres gypsum plaster on metal lathing	1
(*c*) 9·5 millimetres plasterboard finished with 12·5 millimetres gypsum plaster	1
(*d*) 12·5 millimetres plasterboard finished with 5 millimetres gypsum plaster	1
(*e*) 50 millimetres compressed straw slabs	1
(*f*) aerated concrete blocks:	
50 millimetres	3
62 millimetres	4
75 millimetres	4
100 millimetres	4
3. Timber frame with external cladding of 100 millimetres clay, concrete or sand-lime bricks or blocks, finished internally with—	
(*a*) asbestos insulation board	4
(*b*) 16 millimetres gypsum plaster on metal lathing	4
†4. Timber frame with external cladding of weather boarding or 9·5 millimetres exterior grade plywood and internal lining of—	
(*a*) 9 millimetres asbestos insulation board	½
(*b*) 16 millimetres gypsum plaster on metal lathing	½
(*c*) 9·5 millimetres plasterboard finished with 12·5 millimetres gypsum plaster	½
(*d*) 12·5 millimetres plasterboard finished with 5 millimetres gypsum plaster	½
(*e*) 50 millimetres compressed straw slabs	½
(*f*) 75 millimetres woodwool slabs faced each side with asbestos cement	2
(*g*) aerated concrete blocks:	
50 millimetres	3
62 millimetres	4
75 millimetres	4
100 millimetres	4

†The presence of a combustible vapour barrier within the thickness of these constructions will not affect these periods of fire resistance.

Part II: *Reinforced concrete columns*

Construction and materials	Minimum dimension§ of concrete column without finish (in millimetres) for a fire resistance in accordance with Table 6 for a period of—					
	4 hours	3 hours	2 hours	1½ hours	1 hour	½ hour
1.—(a) without plaster	450	400	300	250	200	150
(b) finished with 12·5 millimetres encasement of vermiculite-gypsum plaster	275	225	200	150	120	120
(c) with 12·5 millimetres cement-sand or gypsum-sand plaster on mesh reinforcement fixed round column	300	275	225	150	150	150
(d) with hard drawn steel wire fabric 2·5 millimetres of maximum 150 millimetres pitch in each direction placed in concrete cover to main reinforcement	300	275	225	200	150	150
(e) with limestone or lightweight aggregate as coarse aggregate	300	275	225	200	200	150
2. Built into† a separating wall, fire division wall, external wall on the boundary or other external walls‡—						
(a) without plaster	180	150	100	100	75	75
(b) finished with 12·5 millimetres vermiculite-gypsum plaster	125	100	75	75	63	63

†No part of column projecting beyond either face of wall.
‡Extending to its full height and not less than 600 millimetres on each side of column.
§The minimum dimension of a circular column is the diameter.

Part III: *Reinforced concrete beams*

Construction and materials	Minimum concrete cover (in millimetres) (without finish) to main reinforcement for a fire resistance in accordance with Table 6 for a period of—					
	4 hours	3 hours	2 hours	1½ hours	1 hour	½ hour
(a) without plaster	63	55	45	35	25	12·5
(b) finished with 12·5 millimetres vermiculite-gypsum plaster	25	12·5	12·5	12·5	12·5	12·5
(c) with 12·5 millimetres cement-sand or gypsum-sand plaster, on mesh reinforcement fixed round beam	50	40	30	20	12·5	12·5

FIFTH SCHEDULE—*continued*

SCHEDULE 9—*continued*

TABLE 4—*continued*

Part IV: Prestressed concrete beams

Additional protection	Minimum average thickness† of concrete cover (in millimetres) for a fire resistance in accordance with Table 6 for a period of—					
	4 hours	3 hours	2 hours	1½ hours	1 hour	½ hour
1. No additional protection...	100‡	83‡	63‡	50‡	38	25
2. Vermiculite concrete slabs, as permanent shuttering, 12·5 millimetres thick	75‡	63	45	32	25	12·5
3. Vermiculite concrete slabs, as permanent shuttering, 25 millimetres thick	63	50	38	25	12·5	12·5
4. Gypsum plaster on mesh reinforcement fixed around beams, 12·5 millimetres thick	90‡	70	50	38	25	12·5
5. Vermiculite-gypsum plaster 12·5 millimetres thick or sprayed asbestos 12·5 millimetres thick	75‡	63	45	32	25	12·5
6. Vermiculite-gypsum plaster 25 millimetres thick or sprayed asbestos 25 millimetres thick ...	50	45	32	20	12·5	12·5

†This part of the Table gives minimum average thicknesses which shall be assessed as the arithmetic mean distance of each element of prestressing steel in the member from the nearest outside concrete face which may be exposed to fire.

‡Mesh reinforcement or continuous arrangement of stirrups must be incorporated in the beams to retain the concrete in position around the prestressing steel. This reinforcement should have a concrete cover of minimum average thickness of 25 millimetres.

Part V: Prestressed concrete slabs

Additional protection	Minimum average thickness† of concrete cover (in millimetres) for a fire resistance in accordance with Table 6 for a period of—					
	4 hours	3 hours	2 hours	1½ hours	1 hour	½ hour
1. No additional protection...	63‡	50‡	38	32	25	12·5
2. Gypsum plaster on metal lath as a jointless suspended ceiling with non-combustible fixing, 12·5 millimetres thick	38	25	12·5	12·5	12·5	12·5
3. Vermiculite-gypsum plaster or sprayed asbestos applied direct to soffit, 12·5 millimetres thick ...	38	25	12·5	12·5	12·5	12·5

†This part of the Table gives minimum average thicknesses which shall be assessed as the arithmetic mean distance of each element of prestressing steel in the member from the nearest outside concrete face which may be exposed to fire.

‡Mesh reinforcement must be incorporated in the slab in the soffit to retain the concrete in position around the prestressing steel. This reinforcement should have a concrete cover of minimum average thickness of 25 millimetres.

FIFTH SCHEDULE—*continued*
SCHEDULE 9—*continued*
TABLE 4—*continued*
Part VI:　Structural steel

(1) *Encased steel stanchions (Weight of steel not less than 45 kilogrammes per metre)*

Construction and materials	Minimum thickness (in millimetres) of protection for a fire resistance in accordance with Table 6 for a period of—					
	4 hours	3 hours	2 hours	1½ hours	1 hour	½ hour
A. *Solid protection†* (*unplastered*)						
1. Reinforced concrete not leaner than 1:2:4 mix with natural aggregates—						
(*a*) concrete not assumed to be loadbearing ...	50	38	25	25	25	25
(*b*) concrete assumed to be loadbearing in accordance with B.S.449:1959	75	50	50	50	50	50
2. Solid bricks of clay composition or sand-lime...	75	50	50	50	50	50
3. Solid blocks of foamed slag or pumice concrete reinforced‡ in every horizontal joint	62	62	50	50	50	50
4. Sprayed asbestos—140 to 240 kilogrammes per cubic metre	44	32	19	15	10	10
5. Sprayed vermiculite-cement			38	32	19	12·5
B. *Hollow protection§*						
1. Solid bricks of clay composition or sand-lime reinforced in every horizontal joint, unplastered	100	75	50	50	50	50
2. Solid blocks of foamed slag or pumice concrete reinforced‡ in every horizontal joint, unplastered	75	62	50	50	50	50
3. Metal lath with gypsum or cement-lime plaster of thickness of			38‖	25	19	12·5
4. (*a*) Metal lath with vermiculite-gypsum or perlite-gypsum plaster of thickness of ...	50‖	35‖	19	16	12·5	12·5
(*b*) metal lath spaced 25 millimetres from flanges with vermiculite-gypsum or perlite-gypsum plaster of thickness of	44	32	19	12·5	12·5	12·5
5. Gypsum plasterboard with 1·6 millimetres wire binding at 100 millimetres pitch—						
(*a*) 9·5 millimetres plasterboard with gypsum plaster of thickness of					12·5	12·5
(*b*) 19 millimetres plasterboard with gypsum plaster of thickness of			12·5	10	7	7
6. Gypsum plasterboard with 1·6 millimetres wire binding at 100 millimetres pitch—						
(*a*) 9·5 millimetres plasterboard with vermiculite-gypsum plaster of thickness of			16	12·5	10	7
(*b*) 19 millimetres plasterboard with vermiculite-gypsum plaster of thickness of	32‖	19	10	10	7	7
7. Metal lath with sprayed asbestos of thickness of	44	32	19	15	10	10
8. Vermiculite-cement slabs of 4:1 mix reinforced with wire mesh and finished with plaster skim. Slabs of thickness of	63	44	25	25	25	25
9. Asbestos insulation boards of density 510 to 880 kilogrammes per cubic metre (screwed to 25 millimetres thick asbestos battens for ½-hour and 1 hour periods)			25	19	12	9

†Solid protection means a casing which is bedded close up to the steel without intervening cavities and with all joints in that casing made full and solid.

‡Reinforcement. Where reinforcement is required in this Table, that reinforcement shall consist of steel binding wire not less than 2·3 millimetres in thickness, or a steel mesh weighing not less than 0·48 kilogrammes per square metre. In concrete protection the spacing of that reinforcement shall not exceed 150 millimetres in any direction.

§Hollow protection means that there is a void between the protective material and the steel. All hollow protection to columns shall be effectively sealed at each floor level.

‖Light mesh reinforcement required 12·5 to 19 millimetres below surface unless special corner beads are used.

FIFTH SCHEDULE—*continued*

SCHEDULE 9—*continued*

TABLE 4—*continued*

Part VI: *Structural steel—continued*

(2) *Encased steel beams (Weight of steel not less than 30 kilogrammes per metre)*

Construction and materials	Minimum thickness (in millimetres) of protection for a fire resistance in accordance with Table 6 for a period of—					
	4 hours	3 hours	2 hours	1½ hours	1 hour	½ hour
A. *Solid protection† (unplastered)*						
1. Reinforced concrete not leaner than 1:2:4 mix with natural aggregates—						
(*a*) concrete not assumed to be loadbearing ...	63	50	25	25	25	25
(*b*) concrete assumed to be loadbearing in accordance with B.S.449:1959	75	50	50	50	50	50
2. Sprayed asbestos—140 to 240 kilogrammes per cubic metre	44	32	19	15	10	10
3. Sprayed vermiculite-cement			38	32	19	12·5
B. *Hollow protection‡*						
1. Metal lathing						
(*a*) with cement-lime plaster of thickness of ...			38	25	19	12·5
(*b*) with gypsum plaster of thickness of... ...			22	19	16	12·5
(*c*) with vermiculite-gypsum or perlite-gypsum plaster of thickness of	32	19	12·5	12·5	12·5	12·5
2. Gypsum plasterboard with 1·6 millimetres wire binding at 100 millimetres pitch—						
(*a*) 9·5 millimetres plasterboard with gypsum plaster of thickness of					12·5	12·5
(*b*) 19 millimetres plasterboard with gypsum plaster of thickness of			12·5	10	7	7
3. Plasterboard with 1·6 millimetres wire binding at 100 millimetres pitch—						
(*a*) 9·5 millimetres plasterboard nailed to wooden brackets finished with gypsum plaster of thickness of						12·5
(*b*) 9·5 millimetres plasterboard with vermiculite-gypsum plaster of thickness of			16	12·5	10	7
(*c*) 19 millimetres plasterboard with vermiculite-gypsum plaster of thickness of	32§	19	10	10	7	7
(*d*) 19 millimetres plasterboard with gypsum plaster of thickness of			12·5			
4. Metal lathing with sprayed asbestos—140 to 240 kilogrammes per cubic metre of thickness of ...	44	32	19	15	10	10
5. Asbestos insulation boards of density 510 to 880 kilogrammes per cubic metre (screwed to 25 millimetres thick asbestos battens for ½-hour and 1 hour periods)			25	19	12	9
6. Vermiculite-cement slabs of 4:1 mix reinforced with wire mesh and finished with plaster skim. Slabs of thickness of	63	44	25	25	25	25
7. Gypsum-sand plaster 12·5 millimetres thick applied to heavy duty (Type B) woodwool slabs of thickness of			50	38	38	38

†Solid protection means a casing which is bedded close up to the steel without intervening cavities and with all joints in that casing made full and solid.

‡Hollow protection means that there is a void between the protective material and the steel. All hollow protection to columns shall be effectively sealed at each floor level.

§Light mesh reinforcement required 12·5 to 19 millimetres below surface unless special corner beads are used.

FIFTH SCHEDULE—*continued*

SCHEDULE 9—*continued*

TABLE 4—*continued*

Part VII: Structural aluminium

Encased aluminium alloy stanchions and beams

Construction and materials	Minimum thickness (in millimetres) of protection for a fire resistance in accordance with Table 6 for a period of—					
	4 hours	3 hours	2 hours	1½ hours	1 hour	½ hour
A. *Solid protection†*						
1. Sprayed asbestos—140 to 240 kilogrammes per cubic metre			48	32	19	10
2. Sprayed vermiculite-cement					44	19
B. *Hollow protection‡*						
1. Metal lath with vermiculite-gypsum or perlite-gypsum plaster of thickness of			50	32	22	16	12·5
2. Metal lath finished with neat gypsum plaster of thickness of					19	12·5
3. Gypsum plasterboard 19 millimetres thick with 1·6 millimetres wire binding at 100 millimetres pitch finished with gypsum-vermiculite plaster of thickness of			38	22	16	10	10
4. Asbestos insulation board of density 510 to 880 kilogrammes per cubic metre (screwed to 25 millimetres thick asbestos battens for the ½-hour period)					34	21	9

†Solid protection means a casing which is bedded close up to the alloy without intervening cavities and with all joints in that casing made full and solid.

‡Hollow protection means that there is a void between the protective material and the alloy. All hollow protection to columns shall be effectively sealed at each floor level.

3060 BUILDING AND BUILDINGS

FIFTH SCHEDULE—continued
SCHEDULE 9—continued
TABLE 4—continued
Part VIII: Timber floors

A. All floors other than compartment and separating floors except floors in flats up to four storeys (Sub-group A2)

Minimum width of joist (millimetres) (1)	Minimum thickness of tongued and grooved boarding (millimetres)† (2)	Ceiling base (3)	Ceiling finish for a fire resistance in accordance with the requirements set out in Table 6 for a period of— (4)			
			2 hours	1½ hours	1 hour	½ hour
37‡	16	2 layers plasterboard of total thickness of 19 millimetres				nil
		9 millimetres asbestos insulation board				nil
		12 millimetres asbestos insulation board			25 millimetres glass fibre or mineral wool on top	nil
		9·5 millimetres plaster-board			12·5 millimetres vermiculite-gypsum plaster	12·5 millimetres gypsum plaster
		12·5 millimetres plaster-board				5 millimetres gypsum plaster
		19 millimetres plaster-board				nil
		metal lathing fixed direct to joists			22 millimetres gypsum plaster or 12·5 millimetres vermiculite-gypsum plaster	15 millimetres gypsum plaster or 12·5 millimetres vermiculite-gypsum plaster

49‡	16 as floating floor on 25 millimetres glass fibre or mineral wool quilt	25 millimetres wood-wool slabs			10 millimetres vermiculite-gypsum plaster	5 millimetres gypsum plaster
		12·5 millimetres plasterboard with metal lath or brandering			19 millimetres gypsum plaster	12·5 millimetres gypsum plaster
21		6 millimetres asbestos insulation board				nil
		12·5 millimetres fibre insulation board†				5 millimetres gypsum plaster
		metal lathing fixed direct to joists	38 millimetres sprayed asbestos§	30 millimetres sprayed asbestos§	19 millimetres sprayed asbestos§	12·5 millimetres sprayed asbestos§
		metal lath			19 millimetres sprayed asbestos§	15 millimetres gypsum plaster or 12·5 millimetres sprayed asbestos§
49		19 millimetres plasterboard			12·5 millimetres vermiculite-gypsum plaster	12·5 millimetres gypsum plaster
		12·5 millimetres plasterboard				5 millimetres gypsum plaster
		19 millimetres plasterboard in two layers laid to break bond				nil

FIFTH SCHEDULE—*continued*

SCHEDULE 9—*continued*

TABLE 4—*continued*

Part VIII: Timber floors—continued

A. *All floors other than compartment and separating floors except floors in flats up to four storeys (Sub-group A2)—continued*

Minimum width of joist (millimetres) (1)	Minimum thickness of tongued and grooved boarding (millimetres)† (2)	Ceiling base (3)	Ceiling finish for a fire resistance in accordance with the requirements set out in Table 6 for a period of— (4)			
			2 hours	1½ hours	1 hour	½ hour
49	21	12·5 millimetres fibre insulation board				12·5 millimetres gypsum plaster
		6 millimetres asbestos insulation board				nil
		25 millimetres wood-wool slabs			10 millimetres vermiculite-gypsum plaster	5 millimetres gypsum plaster

B. *For a floor above the lowest in a small house (Sub-group A1)*

Minimum width of joist (millimetres) (1)	Minimum thickness of tongued and grooved boarding (millimetres)† (2)	Ceiling base (3)	Ceiling finish for a fire resistance in accordance with the requirements set out in Table 6 (4)
37‡	16	9·5 millimetres plasterboard	nil
		12·5 millimetres plasterboard	nil
		12·5 millimetres fibre insulation board†	12·5 millimetres gypsum plaster
49	21	12·5 millimetres fibre insulation board†	nil

†Or an equal thickness of wood chipboard.

‡All forms of ceiling protection for 38 millimetres joists are suitable for 50 millimetres joists.

§Sprayed asbestos in accordance with B.S. 3590:1963.

FIFTH SCHEDULE—*continued*

SCHEDULE 9—*continued*

TABLE 4—*continued*

Part IX: Concrete floors

Construction (1)	Minimum thickness of solid substance including screed (millimetres) (2)	Ceiling finish (in millimetres) for a fire resistance in accordance with the requirements set out in Table 6 for a period of— (3)					
		4 hours	3 hours	2 hours	1½ hours	1 hour	½ hour
Solid flat slab or filler joist floor. Units of channel or T section	90	25V or 25A	19V or 19A	10V or 12·5A	10V or 12·5A	7V or 10A	nil
	100	19V or 19A	12·5V	7V	7V	nil	nil
	125	10V or 12·5A	7V	nil	nil	nil	nil
	150	nil	nil	nil	nil	nil	nil
Solid flat slab or filler joist floor with 25 millimetres wood-wool slab ceiling base	90	12·5G	12·5G	nil	12·5G	nil	nil
	100	nil	nil	nil	nil	nil	nil
	125		nil	nil	nil	nil	nil
	150			nil	nil	nil	nil
Units of inverted U section with minimum thickness at crown	63	nil	nil	nil	nil	nil	nil
	75			nil	nil	nil	nil
	100					nil	nil
	150					nil	nil

Construction	Thickness						
Hollow block construction or units of box or I section	63 75 90 125	nil		nil	nil	nil nil	nil nil nil
Cellular steel with concrete topping	63	12·5V suspended on metal lathing or 12·5A (direct)	12·5V suspended on metal lathing or 12·5A	12·5G suspended on metal lathing	12·5G suspended on metal lathing	12·5G suspended on metal lathing	nil

"A"—sprayed asbestos in accordance with B.S. 3590:1963

"V"—vermiculite-gypsum plaster

"G"—gypsum plaster

FIFTH SCHEDULE—*continued*

NEW TABLE TO BE SUBSTITUTED FOR TABLE 5 OF SCHEDULE 9 TO THE BUILDING STANDARDS REGULATIONS

SCHEDULE 9—*continued*

TABLE 5—LIMITS OF CUBIC CAPACITY OF BUILDING   Regulation D3
AND AREA OF STOREY IN RELATION TO STRUCTURAL FIRE PRECAUTIONS

Occupancy		Number of storeys	Maximum cubic capacity of building, division or compartment (cubic metres)	Maximum area of storey in the building or within division (square metres)
Group	Sub-group			
(1)	(2)	(3)	(4)	(5)
A (Residential)	1	Not more than two storeys ...	N.L.	230
	2	One or more storeys	N.L.	460
	3	One or more storeys	14 000	1 900
	4	One or more storeys	8 500	1 400
B (Commercial)	1	One or more storeys	28 000	4 600
	2	One or more storeys	7 100†	2 800†
C (Assembly)	1	One or more storeys	N.L.	N.L.
	2	One or more storeys	21 000	1 900
	3	One or more storeys	N.L.	1 900
D (Industrial)	1	One storey	N.L.	93 000
		More than one storey	84 000	7 400
	2	One storey	N.L.	33 000
		More than one storey	28 000	2 800
	3	One storey	N.L.	9 000
		More than one storey	8 500	900
E (Storage)	1	One storey	N.L.	14 000
		More than one storey	21 000	2 800
	2	One storey	N.L.	900
		More than one storey	4 200	460

N.L. No upper limit is imposed.

†In the case of a shop in occupancy sub-group B2 the maximum cubic capacity stated in column (4) shall be doubled, and the maximum area stated in column (5) shall be increased to 3700 square metres if the building, division or compartment, or storey in the building or within the division, as the case may be, is fitted throughout, save in protected zones as defined in regulation E2, with an automatic sprinkler system complying with the recommendations of CP 402.201: 1952 as read with Amendment No. 1 (PD 2998, March 1958) and Amendment No. 2 (PD 4054, January 1961).

FIFTH SCHEDULE—*continued*

NEW TABLE TO BE SUBSTITUTED FOR TABLE 7 OF SCHEDULE 9 TO THE BUILDING STANDARDS REGULATIONS

SCHEDULE 9—*continued*

TABLE 7—PERIODS OF FIRE RESISTANCE　　　Regulation D5

Part I: Periods of fire resistance according to height and cubic capacity of all buildings of occupancy groups A, B and C

Occupancy		The following are not exceeded:—		Specified period of fire resistance†	
Group (1)	Sub-group (2)	Height of building or division (metres) (3)	Capacity of undivided building or of division or of compartment (cubic metres) (4)	hours (5)	hours (6)
A (Residential)	1	Not more than two storeys	N.L.	½	1
	2	15 24 N.L.	N.L. N.L. N.L.	½ 1 1½	1 1 1½
	3	9 24 N.L.	4 200 8 500 14 000	½ 1 1½	1 1 1½
	4	9 24 N.L.	2 800 5 700 8 500	½ 1 1½	1 1 1½
B (Commercial)	1	6 12 24 N.L.	1 130 4 200 14 000 28 000	Nil‡ ½ 1 1½	1 1 1 1½
	2	6 12 24 N.L.	708 2 120 4 200 7 100	½ 1 2 3	1 1½ 2 3
C (Assembly)	1	N.L.	N.L.	½	½
	2	7·5 18 30 N.L.	4 200 8 500 14 000 21 000	Nil‡ ½ 1 1½	1 1 1 1½
	3	6 12 24 N.L.	566 2 800 14 000 N.L.	Nil‡ ½ 1 2	1 1 1 2

†If more than one period specified for any element, higher or highest to apply (see regulation D5(3)).

‡A minimum of ½-hour for external walls (see Table 6).

N.L.　No upper limit is imposed.

FIFTH SCHEDULE—*continued*

SCHEDULE 9—*continued*

TABLE 7—*continued*

Part II: Periods of fire resistance according to floor area of single storey buildings of occupancy groups D and E

Occupancy		Floor area of undivided building or of division not exceeding:—	Specified period of fire resistance†	
Group	Sub-group			
(1)	(2)	(square metres) (3)	hours (5)	hours (6)
D (Industrial)	1	9 000 93 000	$\frac{1}{2}$ 1	$\frac{1}{2}$ 1
	2	1 400 7 000 33 000	$\frac{1}{2}$ 1 $1\frac{1}{2}$	1 1 $1\frac{1}{2}$
	3	460 900 2 300 9 000	$\frac{1}{2}$ 1 $1\frac{1}{2}$ 2	1 $1\frac{1}{2}$ $1\frac{1}{2}$ 2
E (Storage)	1	900 2 300 14 000	$\frac{1}{2}$ 1 2	1 1 2
	2	90 190 280 460 900	$\frac{1}{2}$ 1 $1\frac{1}{2}$ 3 4	$1\frac{1}{2}$ $1\frac{1}{2}$ 2 3 4

†If more than one period specified for any element, higher or highest to apply (see regulation D5(3)).

FIFTH SCHEDULE—*continued*

SCHEDULE 9—*continued*

TABLE 7—*continued*

Part III: Periods of fire resistance according to height and cubic capacity of buildings of more than one storey of occupancy groups D and E

Occupancy		The following are not exceeded:—		Specified period of fire resistance†	
Group (1)	Sub-group (2)	Height of undivided building or division (metres) (3)	Capacity of undivided building or of division or of compartment (cubic metres) (4)	hours (5)	hours (6)
D (Industrial)	1	9 15 N.L.	8 500 28 000 84 000	Nil‡ $\frac{1}{2}$ 1	$\frac{1}{2}$ $\frac{1}{2}$ 1
	2	9 12 15 24 N.L.	1 700 4 200 8 500 17 000 28 000	Nil‡ $\frac{1}{2}$ 1 $1\frac{1}{2}$ 2	1 1 1 $1\frac{1}{2}$ 2
	3	9 12 15 24 N.L.	708 1 410 2 800 4 200 8 500	$\frac{1}{2}$ 1 $1\frac{1}{2}$ 2 3	1 $1\frac{1}{2}$ $1\frac{1}{2}$ 2 3
E (Storage)	1	9 12 15 24 N.L.	850 1 410 2 800 8 500 21 000	Nil‡ $\frac{1}{2}$ 1 2 3	1 1 1 2 3
	2	9 12 15 24 N.L.	425 850 1 410 2 120 4 200	$\frac{1}{2}$ 1 $1\frac{1}{2}$ 3 4	$1\frac{1}{2}$ $1\frac{1}{2}$ 2 3 4

†If more than one period specified for any element, higher or highest to apply (see regulation D5(3)).

‡A minimum of $\frac{1}{2}$-hour for external walls (see Table 6).

N.L.   No upper limit is imposed.

FIFTH SCHEDULE—*continued*

NEW TABLE TO BE SUBSTITUTED FOR TABLE 9 OF SCHEDULE 9 TO THE BUILDING STANDARDS REGULATIONS

SCHEDULE 9—*continued*

Regulation D17 and Schedule 6

TABLE 9—STRUCTURAL FIRE PRECAUTIONS—MINIMUM DISTANCE BETWEEN ENCLOSING RECTANGLE OF OPENINGS IN THE SIDE OF A BUILDING AND THE BOUNDARY

Part I: *Buildings of occupancy sub-group B2, C3, D2 or D3 or occupancy group E*

Height (in metres) of enclosing rectangle not exceeding	Width (in metres) of enclosing rectangle not exceeding	Percentage of openings not exceeding—								
		20	30	40	50	60	70	80	90	100
		Distance (in metres) from boundary								
3	3	1·1	1·5	1·8	2·0	2·3	2·5	2·7	2·9	3·0
3	6	1·5	2·0	2·4	2·8	3·2	3·4	3·7	4·0	4·2
3	9	1·7	2·3	2·8	3·3	3·8	4·1	4·5	4·8	5·0
3	12	1·8	2·5	3·1	3·7	4·2	4·7	5·0	5·4	5·6
3	15	1·8	2·6	3·3	3·9	4·5	5·0	5·4	5·9	6·2
3	18	1·8	2·7	3·5	4·2	4·8	5·2	5·8	6·3	6·7
3	21	1·8	2·8	3·6	4·3	5·0	5·5	6·0	6·6	7·1
3	24	1·8	2·8	3·7	4·5	5·1	5·7	6·2	6·9	7·4
3	27	1·8	2·9	3·8	4·6	5·3	5·9	6·5	7·1	7·7
3	30	1·8	2·9	3·8	4·7	5·4	6·0	6·7	7·4	7·9
3	40	1·8	2·9	3·9	4·8	5·7	6·4	7·2	7·8	8·6
3	50	1·8	2·9	3·9	4·9	5·8	6·7	7·5	8·2	9·0
3	60	1·8	2·9	3·9	5·0	5·9	6·8	7·7	8·5	9·3
3	80	1·8	2·9	3·9	5·0	6·0	7·0	7·9	8·9	9·7
3	100	1·8	2·9	3·9	5·0	6·0	7·0	7·9	9·0	10·0
3	N.L.	1·8	2·9	3·9	5·0	6·0	7·0	7·9	9·0	10·0
6	3	1·5	2·0	2·4	2·8	3·2	3·4	3·7	4·0	4·2
6	6	2·2	2·9	3·5	4·0	4·5	4·9	5·3	5·7	6·0
6	9	2·6	3·5	4·3	4·9	5·5	6·0	6·5	6·9	7·2
6	12	3·0	4·0	4·8	5·5	6·3	6·8	7·4	7·9	8·3
6	15	3·2	4·3	5·3	6·2	7·0	7·5	8·2	8·8	9·1
6	18	3·3	4·5	5·7	6·6	7·5	8·2	8·9	9·5	10·0
6	21	3·4	4·8	6·0	7·0	8·0	8·8	9·5	10·2	10·6
6	24	3·5	5·0	6·2	7·2	8·4	9·3	10·0	10·7	11·2
6	27	3·5	5·1	6·4	7·6	8·7	9·7	10·4	11·2	11·8
6	30	3·6	5·2	6·7	7·8	9·0	10·0	11·0	11·8	12·5
6	40	3·6	5·5	7·1	8·5	10·0	11·0	12·0	13·0	14·0
6	50	3·7	5·7	7·4	9·0	10·5	11·5	12·8	14·0	15·0
6	60	3·7	5·7	7·5	9·3	11·0	12·0	13·5	15·0	16·0
6	80	3·7	5·9	7·7	9·7	11·3	13·0	14·3	15·8	17·3
6	100	3·7	5·9	7·8	10·0	11·8	13·3	15·0	16·5	18·0
6	120	3·7	5·9	7·8	10·0	11·8	13·8	15·3	17·0	18·8
6	140	3·7	5·9	7·8	10·0	12·0	14·0	16·0	18·0	19·0
6	160	3·7	5·9	7·8	10·0	12·0	14·0	16·0	18·0	20·0
6	N.L.	3·7	5·9	7·8	10·0	12·0	14·0	16·0	18·0	20·0

N.L. No upper limit is imposed.

FIFTH SCHEDULE—*continued*

SCHEDULE 9—*continued*

TABLE 9—*continued*

Part I—*continued*

Height (in metres) of enclosing rectangle not exceeding	Width (in metres) of enclosing rectangle not exceeding	Percentage of openings not exceeding—								
		20	30	40	50	60	70	80	90	100
		Distance (in metres) from boundary								
9	3	1·7	2·3	2·8	3·3	3·8	4·1	4·5	4·8	5·0
9	6	2·6	3·5	4·3	4·9	5·5	6·0	6·5	6·9	7·2
9	9	3·3	4·4	5·3	6·0	6·7	7·3	8·0	8·5	9·0
9	12	3·7	5·0	6·0	6·9	7·7	8·4	9·2	9·7	10·5
9	15	4·1	5·5	6·7	7·7	8·5	9·3	10·2	11·0	11·5
9	18	4·4	6·0	7·2	8·4	9·4	10·2	11·0	12·0	12·5
9	21	4·7	6·3	7·7	9·0	10·2	11·0	12·0	12·8	13·5
9	24	4·8	6·6	8·0	9·5	10·8	11·8	12·8	13·5	14·3
9	27	5·0	6·8	8·5	10·0	11·3	12·3	13·3	14·3	15·0
9	30	5·1	7·0	8·8	10·3	11·8	13·0	14·0	15·0	15·8
9	40	5·3	7·5	9·5	11·3	13·0	14·3	15·5	16·8	17·5
9	50	5·5	7·9	10·2	12·3	14·0	15·5	16·8	18·3	19·5
9	60	5·5	8·2	10·8	12·8	14·8	16·5	18·0	19·5	20·8
9	80	5·5	8·5	11·3	13·5	15·8	17·5	19·5	21·3	22·8
9	100	5·6	8·6	11·5	14·3	16·5	18·5	20·8	22·5	24·5
9	120	5·6	8·6	11·5	14·5	17·0	19·3	21·5	23·5	25·8
9	140	5·6	8·6	11·5	14·8	17·3	19·8	22·3	24·3	26·8
9	160	5·6	8·6	11·8	15·0	18·0	20·0	23·0	25·0	28·0
9	180	5·6	8·6	11·8	15·0	18·0	21·0	23·0	26·0	28·0
9	200	5·6	8·6	11·8	15·0	18·0	21·0	24·0	26·0	29·0
9	240	5·6	8·6	11·8	15·0	18·0	21·0	24·0	26·0	29·0
9	280	5·6	8·6	11·8	15·0	18·0	21·0	24·0	26·0	30·0
9	320	5·6	8·6	11·8	15·0	18·0	21·0	24·0	26·0	30·0
9	N.L.	5·6	8·6	11·8	15·0	18·0	21·0	24·0	26·0	30·0
12	3	1·8	2·5	3·1	3·7	4·2	4·7	5·0	5·4	5·6
12	6	3·0	4·0	4·8	5·5	6·3	6·8	7·4	7·9	8·3
12	9	3·7	5·0	6·0	6·9	7·7	8·4	9·2	9·7	10·5
12	12	4·3	5·8	7·0	8·0	9·0	9·7	10·8	11·5	12·0
12	15	4·8	6·4	7·8	9·0	10·0	11·0	12·0	12·8	13·3
12	18	5·2	7·0	8·5	9·8	11·0	12·0	13·0	13·8	14·5
12	21	5·6	7·5	9·2	10·5	12·0	12·8	14·0	15·0	15·8
12	24	5·8	7·9	9·7	11·3	12·5	13·8	14·8	15·8	16·5
12	27	6·2	8·2	10·3	11·8	13·3	14·5	15·8	16·8	17·5
12	30	6·3	8·5	10·5	12·3	14·0	15·0	16·5	17·5	18·3
12	40	6·7	9·4	11·8	13·8	15·5	17·3	18·5	20·0	21·0
12	50	7·0	9·9	12·8	14·8	17·0	18·8	20·3	22·8	23·0
12	60	7·1	10·5	13·3	15·8	18·0	20·0	21·5	23·5	24·8
12	80	7·2	11·0	14·3	17·0	19·5	21·5	23·5	25·8	27·5
12	100	7·4	11·3	14·8	18·0	20·8	23·0	25·5	27·8	29·8
12	120	7·5	11·5	15·0	18·5	21·8	24·0	26·8	29·5	31·5
12	140	7·5	11·8	15·3	19·0	22·3	25·0	27·8	30·5	34·0
12	160	7·5	11·8	15·5	20·0	23·0	26·0	29·0	32·0	35·0
12	180	7·5	11·8	15·5	20·0	23·0	26·0	30·0	33·0	36·0
12	200	7·5	11·8	15·5	20·0	23·0	27·0	31·0	33·0	37·0
12	240	7·5	11·8	15·5	20·0	24·0	27·0	32·0	34·0	38·0
12	280	7·5	11·8	15·5	20·0	24·0	28·0	32·0	35·0	38·0
12	320	7·5	11·8	15·5	20·0	24·0	28·0	32·0	36·0	39·0
12	360	7·5	11·8	15·5	20·0	24·0	28·0	32·0	36·0	39·0
12	400	7·5	11·8	15·5	20·0	24·0	28·0	32·0	36·0	40·0
12	N.L.	7·5	11·8	15·5	20·0	24·0	28·0	32·0	36·0	40·0

N.L.   No upper limit is imposed.

FIFTH SCHEDULE—*continued*

SCHEDULE 9—*continued*

TABLE 9—*continued*

Part I—*continued*

Height (in metres) of enclosing rectangle not exceeding	Width (in metres) of enclosing rectangle not exceeding	Percentage of openings not exceeding—								
		20	30	40	50	60	70	80	90	100
		Distance (in metres) from boundary								
15	3	1·8	2·6	3·3	3·9	4·5	5·0	5·4	5·9	6·2
15	6	3·2	4·3	5·3	6·2	7·0	7·5	8·2	8·8	9·1
15	9	4·1	5·5	6·7	7·7	8·5	9·3	10·2	11·0	11·5
15	12	4·8	6·4	7·8	9·0	10·0	11·0	12·0	12·8	13·3
15	15	5·5	7·2	8·8	10·0	11·3	12·3	13·3	14·3	15·0
15	18	5·9	7·9	9·6	11·0	12·3	13·3	14·5	15·5	16·3
15	21	6·3	8·5	10·5	12·0	13·3	14·3	15·8	16·5	17·5
15	24	6·7	9·0	11·0	12·8	14·3	15·3	16·8	17·8	18·8
15	27	7·0	9·4	11·5	13·3	15·0	16·3	17·8	18·8	19·8
15	30	7·3	10·0	12·0	14·0	15·8	17·0	18·5	19·8	20·8
15	40	8·0	11·0	13·5	15·8	18·0	19·5	21·0	22·5	23·5
15	50	8·4	11·8	14·8	17·3	19·5	21·5	23·0	24·8	26·0
15	60	8·7	12·5	15·5	18·0	20·8	23·3	25·0	26·8	28·0
15	80	8·9	13·3	16·8	20·0	23·0	25·5	27·8	30·0	31·5
15	100	9·0	13·8	17·8	21·3	24·5	27·3	29·8	32·5	34·5
15	120	9·1	14·0	18·5	22·3	25·5	28·5	31·3	34·3	36·8
15	140	9·1	14·5	19·0	23·0	27·0	30·0	34·0	36·0	39·0
15	160	9·1	14·5	19·0	24·0	28·0	31·0	35·0	38·0	41·0
15	180	9·1	14·5	19·0	24·0	28·0	32·0	35·0	39·0	42·0
15	200	9·1	14·5	19·5	24·8	29·0	32·0	36·0	40·0	43·0
15	240	9·1	14·5	19·5	24·8	29·0	33·0	37·0	41·0	45·0
15	280	9·1	14·5	19·5	24·8	30·0	34·0	38·0	42·0	46·0
15	320	9·1	14·5	19·5	24·8	30·0	34·0	39·0	43·0	47·0
15	360	9·1	14·5	19·5	24·8	30·0	35·0	39·0	44·0	48·0
15	400	9·1	14·5	19·5	24·8	30·0	35·0	40·0	45·0	48·0
15	460	9·1	14·5	19·5	24·8	30·0	35·0	40·0	45·0	49·0
15	520	9·1	14·5	19·5	24·8	30·0	35·0	40·0	45·0	50·0
15	N.L.	9·1	14·5	19·5	24·8	30·0	35·0	40·0	45·0	50·0

N.L.   No upper limit is imposed.

FIFTH SCHEDULE—*continued*

SCHEDULE 9—*continued*

TABLE 9—*continued*

Part II: Buildings of occupancy group A or occupancy sub-group B1, C1, C2 or D1

Height (in metres) of enclosing rectangle not exceeding	Width (in metres) of enclosing rectangle not exceeding	Percentage of openings not exceeding—								
		20	30	40	50	60	70	80	90	100
		Distance (in metres) from boundary								
3	3	1·0	1·0	1·1	1·3	1·5	1·6	1·8	1·9	2·0
3	6	1·0	1·2	1·5	1·8	2·0	2·2	2·4	2·7	2·8
3	9	1·0	1·2	1·7	2·0	2·3	2·6	2·8	3·1	3·3
3	12	1·0	1·3	1·8	2·2	2·5	2·8	3·1	3·4	3·7
3	15	1·0	1·3	1·8	2·3	2·6	3·0	3·3	3·7	3·9
3	18	1·0	1·3	1·8	2·3	2·7	3·1	3·5	3·8	4·2
3	21	1·0	1·3	1·8	2·4	2·8	3·2	3·6	3·9	4·3
3	24	1·0	1·3	1·8	2·4	2·8	3·3	3·7	4·1	4·5
3	27	1·0	1·3	1·8	2·4	2·9	3·3	3·8	4·1	4·6
3	30	1·0	1·3	1·8	2·4	2·9	3·4	3·8	4·2	4·7
3	40	1·0	1·3	1·8	2·4	2·9	3·4	3·9	4·2	4·8
3	60	1·0	1·3	1·8	2·4	2·9	3·5	3·9	4·2	5·0
3	N.L.	1·0	1·3	1·8	2·4	2·9	3·5	3·9	4·2	5·0
6	3	1·0	1·2	1·5	1·8	2·0	2·2	2·4	2·7	2·8
6	6	1·0	1·7	2·2	2·6	2·9	3·2	3·5	4·0	4·0
6	9	1·1	2·0	2·6	3·1	3·5	4·0	4·3	4·7	4·9
6	12	1·3	2·3	3·0	3·5	4·0	4·5	4·8	5·2	5·5
6	15	1·3	2·4	3·2	3·8	4·3	5·0	5·3	5·7	6·2
6	18	1·3	2·4	3·3	4·0	4·5	5·2	5·7	6·2	6·6
6	21	1·3	2·5	3·4	4·2	4·8	5·4	6·0	6·6	7·0
6	24	1·3	2·5	3·5	4·3	5·0	5·6	6·2	6·8	7·2
6	27	1·4	2·5	3·5	4·4	5·1	5·8	6·4	7·1	7·6
6	30	1·4	2·6	3·6	4·4	5·2	5·9	6·7	7·2	7·8
6	40	1·4	2·6	3·6	4·6	5·5	6·3	7·1	7·8	8·5
6	50	1·4	2·6	3·7	4·7	5·7	6·6	7·4	8·1	9·0
6	60	1·4	2·6	3·7	4·8	5·7	6·7	7·5	8·4	9·3
6	80	1·4	2·6	3·7	4·8	5·9	6·8	7·7	8·6	9·7
6	100	1·4	2·6	3·7	4·8	5·9	6·9	7·8	8·6	10·0
6	N.L.	1·4	2·6	3·7	4·8	5·9	6·9	7·8	8·6	10·0
9	3	1·0	1·2	1·7	2·0	2·3	2·6	2·8	3·1	3·3
9	6	1·1	2·0	2·6	3·1	3·5	4·0	4·3	4·7	4·9
9	9	1·3	2·5	3·3	3·9	4·4	4·8	5·3	5·7	6·0
9	12	1·5	2·9	3·7	4·4	5·0	5·5	6·0	6·5	6·9
9	15	1·8	3·2	4·1	4·9	5·5	6·1	6·7	7·2	7·7
9	18	1·9	3·4	4·4	5·2	6·0	6·6	7·2	7·9	8·4
9	21	1·9	3·5	4·7	5·5	6·3	7·0	7·7	8·4	9·0
9	24	1·9	3·6	4·8	5·7	6·6	7·4	8·0	8·8	9·5
9	27	2·0	3·6	5·0	5·9	6·8	7·7	8·5	9·3	10·0
9	30	2·0	3·7	5·1	6·2	7·0	8·0	8·8	9·7	10·3
9	40	2·0	3·7	5·3	6·5	7·5	8·6	9·5	10·6	11·3
9	50	2·0	3·8	5·5	6·7	7·9	9·1	10·2	11·3	12·3
9	60	2·0	3·8	5·5	6·8	8·2	9·5	10·8	11·7	12·8
9	80	2·0	3·9	5·5	7·1	8·5	9·9	11·3	12·3	13·5
9	100	2·0	3·9	5·6	7·1	8·6	10·2	11·5	12·6	14·3
9	120	2·0	3·9	5·6	7·2	8·6	10·3	11·8	12·6	15·0
9	N.L.	2·0	3·9	5·6	7·2	8·6	10·3	11·8	12·6	15·0

N.L. No upper limit is imposed.

FIFTH SCHEDULE—*continued*

SCHEDULE 9—*continued*

TABLE 9—*continued*

Part II—continued

Height (in metres) of enclosing rectangle not exceeding	Width (in metres) of enclosing rectangle not exceeding	Percentage of openings not exceeding—								
		20	30	40	50	60	70	80	90	100
		Distance (in metres) from boundary								
12	3	1·0	1·3	1·8	2·2	2·5	2·8	3·1	3·4	3·7
12	6	1·3	2·3	3·0	3·5	4·0	4·5	4·8	5·2	5·5
12	9	1·5	2·9	3·7	4·4	5·0	5·5	6·0	6·5	6·9
12	12	1·7	3·3	4·3	5·1	5·8	6·3	7·0	7·6	8·0
12	15	2·0	3·7	4·8	5·7	6·4	7·1	7·8	8·5	9·0
12	18	2·3	4·0	5·2	6·2	7·0	7·7	8·5	9·1	9·8
12	21	2·4	4·2	5·6	6·5	7·5	8·3	9·2	9·8	10·5
12	24	2·5	4·5	5·8	7·0	7·9	8·7	9·7	10·5	11·3
12	27	2·5	4·6	6·2	7·2	8·2	9·2	10·3	11·0	11·8
12	30	2·6	4·7	6·3	7·5	8·5	9·6	10·5	11·5	12·3
12	40	2·6	4·9	6·7	8·2	9·4	10·6	11·8	13·0	13·8
12	50	2·7	5·0	7·0	8·6	9·9	11·1	12·8	13·8	14·8
12	60	2·7	5·1	7·1	8·9	10·5	11·8	13·3	14·5	15·8
12	80	2·7	5·1	7·2	9·2	11·0	12·8	14·3	15·8	17·0
12	100	2·7	5·2	7·4	9·4	11·3	13·3	14·8	16·3	18·0
12	120	2·7	5·2	7·5	9·5	11·5	13·5	15·0	16·8	18·5
12	140	2·7	5·2	7·5	9·6	11·8	13·8	15·3	17·0	19·0
12	160	2·7	5·2	7·5	9·6	11·8	13·8	15·5	17·0	20·0
12	N.L.	2·7	5·2	7·5	9·6	11·8	13·8	15·5	17·0	20·0
15	3	1·0	1·3	1·8	2·3	2·6	3·0	3·3	3·7	3·9
15	6	1·3	2·4	3·2	3·8	4·3	5·0	5·3	5·7	6·2
15	9	1·8	3·2	4·1	4·9	5·5	6·1	6·7	7·2	7·7
15	12	2·0	3·7	4·8	5·7	6·4	7·1	7·8	8·5	9·0
15	15	2·1	4·1	5·5	6·4	7·2	7·9	8·8	9·5	10·0
15	18	2·4	4·5	5·9	7·0	7·9	8·7	9·6	10·3	11·0
15	21	2·7	4·9	6·3	7·5	8·5	9·3	10·5	11·1	12·0
15	24	2·9	5·2	6·7	7·9	9·0	10·0	11·0	11·8	12·8
15	27	3·0	5·3	7·0	8·3	9·4	10·5	11·5	12·5	13·3
15	30	3·1	5·6	7·3	8·7	10·0	10·9	12·0	13·3	14·0
15	40	3·2	6·0	8·0	9·5	11·0	12·3	13·5	14·8	15·8
15	50	3·3	6·1	8·4	10·2	11·8	13·3	14·8	16·3	17·3
15	60	3·3	6·3	8·7	10·7	12·5	14·0	15·5	17·0	18·0
15	80	3·3	6·4	8·9	11·2	13·3	15·0	16·8	18·5	20·0
15	100	3·4	6·4	9·0	11·5	13·8	16·0	17·8	19·5	21·3
15	120	3·4	6·5	9·1	11·7	14·0	16·5	18·5	20·3	22·3
15	140	3·4	6·5	9·1	11·8	14·5	17·0	19·0	20·8	23·0
15	160	3·4	6·5	9·1	11·9	14·5	17·3	19·0	21·0	24·0
15	180	3·4	6·5	9·1	12·0	14·5	17·3	19·0	21·0	24·0
15	200	3·4	6·5	9·1	12·0	14·5	17·3	19·5	21·0	24·8
15	N.L.	3·4	6·5	9·1	12·0	14·5	17·3	19·5	21·0	24·8

N.L.   No upper limit is imposed.

FIFTH SCHEDULE—*continued*

NEW TABLE TO BE SUBSTITUTED FOR TABLE 10 OF SCHEDULE 9 TO THE BUILDING STANDARDS REGULATIONS

SCHEDULE 9—*continued*

Regulation D17 and Schedule 6

TABLE 10—STRUCTURAL FIRE PRECAUTIONS—LIMITING DISTANCE (IN METRES) IN RESPECT OF A RECESS HAVING OPENINGS ONLY IN THE BACK WALL

Part I: *For a reduction in percentage effective opening of 10 per cent.*

Depth of recess (in metres) exceeding	Percentage of openings not exceeding—								
	15	20	25	30	40	50	60	80	100
1	1·0	1·2	1·7	2·2	3·2	4·2	5·2	7·2	9·2
3	2·0	3·6	5·1	6·6	9·6	12·6	15·7	21·6	27·6
5	3·4	6·0	8·5	11·0	16·0	21·1	26·2	36·1	46·1
7	4·7	8·4	12·0	15·5	22·5	29·5	36·5	50·5	—
9	6·1	10·8	15·4	20·0	29·0	38·0	47·0	—	—
15	10·2	18·0	25·7	33·2	48·0	—	—	—	—
30	20·4	36·0	51·5	—	—	—	—	—	—

Part II: *For a reduction in percentage effective opening of 20 per cent.*

Depth of recess (in metres) exceeding	Percentage of openings not exceeding—					
	30	40	50	60	80	100
1	1·0	1·2	1·7	2·2	3·2	4·2
3	2·0	3·6	5·1	6·6	9·6	12·6
5	3·4	6·0	8·5	11·0	16·0	21·1
7	4·7	8·4	12·0	15·5	22·5	29·5
9	6·1	10·8	15·4	20·0	29·0	38·0
15	10·2	18·0	25·7	33·2	48·0	—
30	20·4	36·0	51·5	—	—	—

FIFTH SCHEDULE—*continued*

NEW TABLE TO BE SUBSTITUTED FOR TABLE 13 OF SCHEDULE 9 TO THE BUILDING STANDARDS REGULATIONS

SCHEDULE 9—*continued*

Regulations K3–K7, K9–K11. and K13   TABLE 13—MECHANICAL VENTILATION OF BUILDINGS—RATE OF FRESH AIR SUPPLY

	Minimum rate of supply in cubic metres of fresh air per hour per person		Minimum rate of supply in no. of air changes per hour
A. *Room or apartment (excluding kitchen) with cubic space per occupant—*		Laboratory	4
		Changing room	3
		Gymnasium	3
exceeding 0·25 cubic metre but not exceeding 8	28	Swimming bath	4
		Shower bath	10
exceeding 8 cubic metres but not exceeding 11	20	Anaesthetic room ... ...⎫ Sterilising room ... ... ⎬ Operating theatre ... ...⎭	10
exceeding 11 cubic metres but not exceeding 14	17	X-ray room ... ...⎫ First-aid room... ... ...⎬ Recovery room ... ...⎭	3
exceeding 14 cubic metres ...	12		
	Minimum rate of supply in no. of air changes per hour	Drying room	10
		Cloakroom	2
		Stairway or access way —in building of occupancy sub-group A1 or A2	1
		—in any other building ...	2
B. *Room with no occupant capacity (including kitchen)—*			
Watercloset ... ...⎫ Bathroom with W.C. pan ...⎬	3	Storage room	1
Bathroom without W.C. pan ...⎫ Washroom ... ...⎬	2	Building for car parking ...	8
Kitchen—in building of occupancy sub-group A1 or A2...	6	Garage —for repair of vehicles ...	6
—in any other building	20	—for commercial or public service vehicles... ...	4
Pantry ⎱(exceeding 1·5 cubic Larder ⎰ metres)	2	Lift machine room	3
Servery ⎱ ... ... Scullery ⎰	2	Any other room	1
Laundry	10		
Boiler room	10		

Fifth Schedule—*continued*

New Table to be substituted for Table 15 of Schedule 9 to the Building Standards Regulations

Table 15—Minimum distance (in metres) between window openings

Regulation L10

Angle† at window of house to be erected not more than—

	90°	80°	70°	60°	50°	40°	30°	20°	10°	0°
90°	18	18	18	18	13	9	6	4	3	2
80°	18	18	18	13	9	6	4	3	2	
70°	18	18	13	9	6	4	3	2		
60°	18	13	9	6	4	3	2			
50°	13	9	6	4	3	2				
40°	9	6	4	3	2					
30°	6	4	3	2						
20°	4	3	2							
10°	3	2								
0°	2									

Angle† at window of any other house not more than— (row labels, left column)

Distances shall be interpolated for intermediate angles

†That is, the horizontal angle included between—

(i) the shortest line joining any part of one window opening to any part of the other, and

(ii) the vertical plane of the opening of the window (see regulation L10).

FIFTH SCHEDULE—continued

NEW TABLE TO BE SUBSTITUTED FOR TABLE 16 OF SCHEDULE 9 TO THE BUILDING STANDARDS REGULATIONS

SCHEDULE 9—continued

Regulations L4 and L8 and Schedule 7

TABLE 16—DAYLIGHTING—MINIMUM WIDTH OF WINDOW OPENINGS (ROOMS WITH ONE WINDOW SITUATED IN THE MIDDLE OF THE EXTERNAL WALL)

Part I: Living rooms

Height of head of window opening above floor†		Floor area of room		Minimum width of window opening (metres) — Width of room measured parallel to window, exceeding (metres)												
Exceeding (metres)	Not exceeding (metres)	Exceeding (square metres)	Not exceeding (square metres)	2·7	3·0	3·3	3·6	3·9	4·2	4·5	4·8	5·1	5·4	5·7	6·0	6·3
(1)	(2)	(3)	(4)	(5)												
2·4	2·5	23	24	—	—	—	3·25	2·65	2·30	2·07	1·92	1·83	1·80	1·80	1·80	1·80
		22	23	—	—	—	2·80	2·40	2·10	1·85	1·75	1·72	1·71	1·71	1·71	1·71
		21	22	—	—	2·67	2·57	2·12	1·90	1·67	1·64	1·62	1·62	1·62	1·62	1·62
		20	21	—	2·55	2·45	2·22	2·00	1·67	1·59	1·55	1·53	1·53	1·53	1·53	1·53
		19	20	—	2·27	2·05	2·00	1·65	1·55	1·48	1·44	1·44	1·44	1·44	1·44	1·44
		18	19	2·45	1·96	1·75	1·70	1·52	1·42	1·38	1·35	1·35	1·35	1·35	1·35	1·35
		17	18	2·07	1·72	1·57	1·52	1·35	1·29	1·26	1·26	1·26	1·26	1·26	1·26	1·26
		16	17	1·85	1·47	1·42	1·40	1·22	1·20	1·19	1·18	1·18	1·18	1·18	1·18	1·18
		15	16	1·52	1·22	1·17	1·20	1·15	1·12	1·10	1·10	1·10	1·10	1·10	1·10	1·10
		14	15	1·30	1·10	1·05	1·10	1·05	1·02	1·02	1·02	1·02	1·02	1·02	1·02	1·02
		13	14	1·10	0·94	0·88	0·97	0·94	0·93	0·93	0·93	0·93	0·93	0·93	0·93	0·93
		—	13				0·85	0·85	0·85	0·85	0·85	0·85	0·85	0·85	0·85	0·85

2·3	2·4	23	24	—	—	—	—	3·37	2·77	2·45	2·20	2·10	2·07	2·05	2·05	2·05
		22	23	—	—	—	—	2·87	2·55	2·17	2·02	1·98	1·95	1·95	1·95	1·95
		21	22	—	—	—	3·22	2·60	2·20	2·00	1·95	1·88	1·85	1·85	1·85	1·85
		20	21	—	—	—	2·75	2·35	1·97	1·82	1·78	1·75	1·75	1·75	1·75	1·75
		19	20	—	—	3·10	2·45	2·00	1·85	1·72	1·65	1·65	1·65	1·65	1·65	1·65
		18	19	—	2·75	2·52	2·02	1·87	1·62	1·57	1·54	1·54	1·54	1·54	1·54	1·54
		17	18	—	2·40	2·27	1·85	1·60	1·52	1·46	1·44	1·44	1·44	1·44	1·44	1·44
		16	17	—	2·07	1·87	1·62	1·42	1·37	1·34	1·34	1·34	1·34	1·34	1·34	1·34
		15	16	2·30	1·80	1·65	1·42	1·32	1·26	1·24	1·24	1·24	1·24	1·24	1·24	1·24
		14	15	1·85	1·45	1·33	1·23	1·14	1·14	1·14	1·14	1·14	1·14	1·14	1·14	1·14
		13	14	1·55	1·27	1·18	1·08	1·05	1·05	1·05	1·05	1·05	1·05	1·05	1·05	1·05
		—	13	1·30	1·10	1·05	1·00	0·97	0·97	0·97	0·97	0·97	0·97	0·97	0·97	0·97
2·2	2·3	23	24	—	—	—	—	—	3·60	2·92	2·67	2·52	2·44	2·40	2·37	2·37
		22	23	—	—	—	—	3·70	3·15	2·75	2·52	2·34	2·27	2·25	2·25	2·25
		21	22	—	—	—	—	3·37	2·72	2·40	2·22	2·16	2·13	2·13	2·13	2·13
		20	21	—	—	—	—	2·82	2·50	2·15	2·07	2·03	2·02	2·02	2·02	2·02
		19	20	—	—	—	3·15	2·55	2·22	1·97	1·92	1·90	1·90	1·90	1·90	1·90
		18	19	—	—	—	2·57	2·30	1·92	1·85	1·82	1·78	1·78	1·78	1·78	1·78
		17	18	—	—	2·80	2·35	1·87	1·75	1·69	1·65	1·65	1·65	1·65	1·65	1·65
		16	17	—	2·60	2·37	1·92	1·72	1·62	1·55	1·52	1·52	1·52	1·52	1·52	1·52
		15	16	—	2·25	1·95	1·72	1·53	1·47	1·42	1·40	1·40	1·40	1·40	1·40	1·40
		14	15	2·32	1·80	1·70	1·50	1·40	1·35	1·32	1·30	1·30	1·30	1·30	1·30	1·30
		13	14	1·90	1·52	1·42	1·27	1·25	1·23	1·21	1·21	1·21	1·21	1·21	1·21	1·21
		—	13	1·62	1·30	1·25	1·19	1·14	1·12	1·12	1·12	1·12	1·12	1·12	1·12	1·12
2·1	2·2	23	24	—	—	—	—	—	—	3·95	3·47	3·05	2·86	2·80	2·80	2·80
		22	23	—	—	—	—	—	—	3·62	3·07	2·80	2·68	2·65	2·65	2·65
		21	22	—	—	—	—	—	3·65	3·05	2·72	2·60	2·55	2·50	2·50	2·50
		20	21	—	—	—	—	—	3·35	2·72	2·55	2·45	2·40	2·35	2·35	2·35
		19	20	—	—	—	—	3·40	2·72	2·42	2·30	2·24	2·20	2·20	2·20	2·20
		18	19	—	—	—	—	2·77	2·45	2·27	2·15	2·07	2·05	2·05	2·05	2·05
		17	18	—	—	—	2·97	2·47	2·17	2·02	1·91	1·91	1·91	1·91	1·91	1·91
		16	17	—	—	—	2·50	2·07	1·90	1·83	1·78	1·78	1·78	1·78	1·78	1·78
		15	16	—	—	2·52	2·25	1·87	1·75	1·70	1·67	1·67	1·67	1·67	1·67	1·67
		14	15	—	2·35	2·20	1·80	1·66	1·59	1·55	1·55	1·55	1·55	1·55	1·55	1·55
		13	14	2·42	1·92	1·72	1·57	1·50	1·45	1·42	1·42	1·42	1·42	1·42	1·42	1·42
		—	13	2·12	1·57	1·52	1·35	1·30	1·27	1·27	1·27	1·27	1·27	1·27	1·27	1·27

†(a) Height of foot of glazed portion of opening not exceeding 1·15 metres.
(b) The table gives minimum widths for ground floor windows on a level site; the height of window head may be reduced by up to 0·30 metre on floors above the ground floor.

FIFTH SCHEDULE—continued

SCHEDULE 9—continued

TABLE 16—continued

Part I: Living rooms—continued

Height of head of window opening above floor† Exceeding (metres) (1)	Not exceeding (metres) (2)	Floor area of room Exceeding (square metres) (3)	Not exceeding (square metres) (4)	Minimum width of window opening (metres) — Width of room measured parallel to window, exceeding (metres) (5)												
				2·7	3·0	3·3	3·6	3·9	4·2	4·5	4·8	5·1	5·4	5·7	6·0	6·3
2·0	2·1	23	24	—	—	—	—	—	—	—	—	4·05	3·68	3·45	3·37	3·37
		22	23	—	—	—	—	—	—	—	4·17	3·70	3·42	3·21	3·15	3·15
		21	22	—	—	—	—	—	—	4·22	3·60	3·27	3·12	3·02	2·96	2·96
		20	21	—	—	—	—	—	—	3·77	3·17	2·87	2·80	2·80	2·80	2·80
		19	20	—	—	—	—	—	3·75	3·27	2·87	2·70	2·65	2·65	2·65	2·65
		18	19	—	—	—	—	—	3·37	2·77	2·61	2·49	2·49	2·49	2·49	2·49
		17	18	—	—	—	—	3·45	2·67	2·52	2·38	2·32	2·32	2·32	2·32	2·32
		16	17	—	—	—	—	2·75	2·37	2·27	2·18	2·14	2·14	2·14	2·14	2·14
		15	16	—	—	—	2·97	2·37	2·15	2·05	1·97	1·97	1·97	1·97	1·97	1·97
		14	15	—	—	—	2·30	2·00	1·88	1·82	1·82	1·82	1·82	1·82	1·82	1·82
		13	14	—	2·52	2·32	2·05	1·75	1·70	1·67	1·67	1·67	1·67	1·67	1·67	1·67
		—	13	—	2·12	2·07	1·67	1·57	1·52	1·52	1·52	1·52	1·52	1·52	1·52	1·52
—	2·0	23	24	—	—	—	—	—	—	—	—	—	5·02	4·55	4·45	4·40
		22	23	—	—	—	—	—	—	—	—	4·57	4·52	4·35	3·98	3·95
		21	22	—	—	—	—	—	—	—	4·60	4·12	4·22	3·77	3·67	3·65
		20	21	—	—	—	—	—	—	—	4·07	3·65	3·65	3·44	3·41	3·41
		19	20	—	—	—	—	—	—	—	4·07	3·65	3·36	3·18	3·18	3·18
		18	19	—	—	—	—	—	—	4·05	3·50	3·20	2·95	2·95	2·95	2·95
		17	18	—	—	—	—	—	—	3·60	3·02	2·82	2·75	2·75	2·75	2·75

16	17	—	—	—	—	2·55	2·55	2·55	2·55	2·55	2·65	2·87	3·70	—
15	16	—	—	—	3·57	2·37	2·37	2·37	2·37	2·37	2·42	2·47	2·82	3·57
14	15	—	—	2·77	2·70	2·22	2·22	2·22	2·22	2·22	2·22	2·27	2·37	2·70
13	14	—	2·75	2·77	2·30	2·07	2·07	2·07	2·07	2·07	2·07	2·09	2·15	2·30
—	13	—	2·20	—	2·07	1·92	1·92	1·92	1·92	1·92	1·92	1·92	1·97	2·07

†(a) Height of foot of glazed portion of opening not exceeding 1·15 metres.

(b) The table gives minimum widths for ground floor windows on a level site; the height of window head may be reduced by up to 0·30 metre on floors above the ground floor.

FIFTH SCHEDULE—continued

SCHEDULE 9—continued

TABLE 16—continued

Part II: Kitchens

Height of head of window opening above floor†		Floor area of room		Width of room measured parallel to window, exceeding (metres)									
Exceeding (metres)	Not Exceeding (metres)	Exceeding (square metres)	Not exceeding (square metres)	Minimum width of window opening (metres)									
(1)	(2)	(3)	(4)	1·2	1·5	1·8	2·1	2·4	2·7	3·0	3·3	3·6	3·9
									(5)				
2·4	2·5	16	17	—	—	—	1·84	1·33	1·14	1·10	1·10	1·10	1·10
		15	16	—	—	—	1·82	1·33	1·14	1·10	1·10	1·10	1·10
		14	15	—	—	—	1·81	1·33	1·14	1·09	1·09	1·09	1·09
		13	14	—	—	—	1·79	1·32	1·13	1·09	1·09	1·09	1·09
		12	13	—	—	—	1·78	1·32	1·13	1·08	1·08	1·08	1·08
		11	12	—	—	—	1·76	1·32	1·13	1·08	1·08	1·08	1·08
		10	11	—	—	—	1·74	1·31	1·12	1·07	1·07	1·07	1·07
		9	10	—	—	—	1·70	1·30	1·10	1·06	1·06	1·06	1·06
		8	9	—	—	1·65	1·59	1·23	1·07	1·03	1·03	1·03	1·03
		7	8	—	—	1·20	1·20	1·00	0·93	0·91	0·91	0·91	0·91
		6	7	—	—	0·88	0·92	0·81	0·79	0·79	0·79	0·79	0·79
		5	6	—	1·10	0·63	0·74	0·69	0·68	0·68	0·68	0·68	0·68
		4	5	1·15	0·72	0·47	0·59	0·57	0·57	0·57	0·57	0·57	0·57
		3	4	0·72	0·49	0·35	0·46	0·46	0·46	0·46	0·46	0·46	0·46
		—	3	0·44	0·35	0·35	0·35	0·35	0·35	0·35	0·35	0·35	0·35
2·3	2·4	16	17	—	—	—	—	1·55	1·32	1·24	1·24	1·24	1·24
		15	16	—	—	—	—	1·55	1·31	1·24	1·24	1·24	1·24
		14	15	—	—	—	—	1·54	1·30	1·23	1·23	1·23	1·23
		13	14	—	—	—	—	1·54	1·29	1·23	1·23	1·23	1·23

Group 2·2

Floor	A	B	C	D	E	F	G (×4)
13	—	—	—	—	1·53	1·29	1·22
12	—	—	—	2·08	1·53	1·28	1·22
11	—	—	—	2·05	1·52	1·27	1·21
10	—	—	—	2·00	1·51	1·26	1·21
9	—	—	—	1·90	1·41	1·22	1·17
8	—	—	—	1·38	1·12	1·04	1·02
7	—	—	1·40	1·05	0·92	0·89	0·89
6	—	1·27	1·00	0·80	0·77	0·76	0·76
5	—	0·82	0·70	0·65	0·63	0·63	0·63
4	0·82	0·55	0·53	0·51	0·50	0·50	0·50
3	0·48	0·39	0·38	0·38	0·38	0·38	0·38

Group 2·3

Floor	V	U	T	S	P	Q	R (×4)
17	—	—	—	—	1·87	1·50	—
16	—	—	—	—	1·87	1·50	1·37
15	—	—	—	—	1·86	1·50	1·37
14	—	—	—	—	1·86	1·49	1·37
13	—	—	—	—	1·85	1·49	1·37
12	—	—	—	—	1·84	1·48	1·36
11	—	—	—	—	1·83	1·47	1·36
10	—	—	—	—	1·79	1·46	1·36
9	—	—	—	—	1·68	1·40	1·31
8	—	—	—	1·67	1·29	1·16	1·13
7	—	—	1·68	1·20	1·00	0·97	0·97
6	—	—	1·17	0·93	0·84	0·82	0·82
5	—	0·95	0·79	0·71	0·68	0·68	0·68
4	0·95	0·60	0·57	0·55	0·55	0·55	0·55
3	0·52	0·42	0·42	0·42	0·42	0·42	0·42

Group 2·2 / 2·1

Floor	a	b	c	d	P	Q	R (×4)
17	—	—	—	—	2·35	1·78	—
16	—	—	—	—	2·34	1·78	1·57
15	—	—	—	—	2·34	1·77	1·57
14	—	—	—	—	2·33	1·77	1·57
13	—	—	—	—	2·32	1·76	1·56
12	—	—	—	—	2·31	1·76	1·56
11	—	—	—	—	2·28	1·75	1·55
10	—	—	—	—	2·22	1·75	1·55
9	—	—	—	—	2·12	1·65	1·49
8	—	—	—	—	1·54	1·36	1·30
7	—	—	—	1·44	1·18	1·13	1·11
6	—	—	1·39	1·09	0·96	0·93	0·93
5	—	1·14	0·92	0·79	0·76	0·76	0·76
4	1·14	0·70	0·64	0·60	0·59	0·59	0·59
3	0·59	0·46	0·46	0·46	0·46	0·46	0·46

†(a) Height of foot of glazed portion of opening not exceeding 1·15 metres.
(b) The table gives minimum widths for ground floor windows on a level site; the height of window head may be reduced by up to 0·30 metre on floors above the ground floor.

FIFTH SCHEDULE—continued

SCHEDULE 9—continued

TABLE 16—continued

Part II: Kitchens—continued

Height of head of window opening above floor†		Floor area of room		Width of room measured parallel to window, exceeding (metres)									
Exceeding (metres)	Not exceeding (metres)	Exceeding (square metres)	Not exceeding (square metres)	1·2	1·5	1·8	2·1	2·4	2·7	3·0	3·3	3·6	3·9
(1)	(2)	(3)	(4)	Minimum width of window opening (metres) (5)									
2·0	2·1	16	17		—	—	—	—	2·22	1·86	1·84	1·83	1·83
		15	16		—	—	—	—	2·22	1·86	1·84	1·83	1·83
		14	15		—	—	—	—	2·21	1·86	1·84	1·83	1·83
		13	14		—	—	—	—	2·21	1·85	1·83	1·82	1·82
		12	13		—	—	—	—	2·20	1·85	1·83	1·82	1·82
		11	12		—	—	—	—	2·19	1·84	1·82	1·81	1·81
		10	11		—	—	—	—	2·17	1·84	1·82	1·81	1·81
		9	10		—	—	—	—	2·14	1·83	1·82	1·81	1·81
		8	9		—	—	—	—	2·00	1·78	1·73	1·73	1·73
		7	8		—	—	—	1·92	1·55	1·49	1·49	1·49	1·49
		6	7		—	—	1·85	1·43	1·29	1·27	1·27	1·27	1·27
		5	6		—	1·78	1·28	1·11	1·07	1·07	1·07	1·07	1·07
		4	5		1·42	1·10	0·93	0·87	0·87	0·87	0·87	0·87	0·87
		3	4		0·85	0·75	0·71	0·69	0·69	0·69	0·69	0·69	0·69
		—	3	0·69	0·52	0·52	0·52	0·52	0·52	0·52	0·52	0·52	0·52

2·0													
—	16	17	—	—	—	—	—	—	2·35	2·33	2·25	2·20
	15	16	—	—	—	—	—	—	2·35	2·32	2·24	2·19
	14	15	—	—	—	—	—	—	2·34	2·30	2·23	2·18
	13	14	—	—	—	—	—	—	2·34	2·28	2·22	2·17
	12	13	—	—	—	—	—	—	2·33	2·26	2·20	2·16
	11	12	—	—	—	—	—	—	2·32	2·23	2·18	2·15
	10	11	—	—	—	—	—	—	2·31	2·20	2·16	2·13
	9	10	—	—	—	—	—	—	2·30	2·18	2·11	2·11
	8	9	—	—	—	—	—	2·01	2·18	2·08	2·03	2·03
	7	8	—	—	—	—	1·84	1·56	1·75	1·75	1·75	1·75
	6	7	—	—	—	1·62	1·34	1·26	1·50	1·50	1·50	1·50
	5	6	—	—	1·44	1·10	1·04	1·03	1·26	1·26	1·26	1·26
	4	5	—	1·08	0·88	0·84	0·81	0·81	1·03	1·03	1·03	1·03
	3	4	0·85	0·63	0·62	0·62	0·62	0·62	0·81	0·81	0·81	0·81
	—	3							0·62	0·62	0·62	0·62

†(a) Height of foot of glazed portion of opening not exceeding 1·15 metres.

(b) The table gives minimum widths for ground floor windows on a level site; the height of window head may be reduced by up to 0·30 metre on floors above the ground floor.

FIFTH SCHEDULE—continued

SCHEDULE 9—continued

TABLE 16—continued

Part III: *Apartments other than living rooms*

Height of head of window opening above floor Exceeding (metres) (1)	Not exceeding (metres) (2)	Floor area of room Exceeding (square metres) (3)	Not exceeding (square metres) (4)	Width of room measured parallel to window, exceeding (metres) Minimum width of window opening (metres) (5)										
				1·8	2·1	2·4	2·7	3·0	3·3	3·6	3·9	4·2	4·5	4·8
2·4	2·5	16	17	—	—	1·40	1·02	0·87	0·78	0·70	0·65	0·62	0·62	0·62
		15	16	—	1·65	1·20	0·92	0·72	0·65	0·60	0·57	0·57	0·57	0·57
		14	15	—	1·37	0·97	0·75	0·63	0·57	0·54	0·52	0·52	0·52	0·52
		13	14	—	1·12	0·83	0·65	0·55	0·52	0·49	0·47	0·47	0·47	0·47
		12	13	1·47	0·97	0·70	0·55	0·47	0·44	0·42	0·42	0·42	0·42	0·42
		11	12	1·10	0·82	0·57	0·45	0·42	0·39	0·38	0·38	0·38	0·38	0·38
		10	11	0·90	0·67	0·47	0·40	0·36	0·35	0·35	0·35	0·35	0·35	0·35
		9	10	0·70	0·52	0·40	0·35	0·32	0·32	0·32	0·32	0·32	0·32	0·32
		8	9	0·55	0·40	0·34	0·30	0·28	0·28	0·28	0·28	0·28	0·28	0·28
		7	8	0·42	0·32	0·28	0·25	0·25	0·25	0·25	0·25	0·25	0·25	0·25
		6	7	0·32	0·25	0·22	0·22	0·22	0·22	0·22	0·22	0·22	0·22	0·22
		5	6	0·22	0·20	0·18	0·18	0·18	0·18	0·18	0·18	0·18	0·18	0·18
		—	5	0·17	0·15	0·15	0·15	0·15	0·15	0·15	0·15	0·15	0·15	0·15
2·3	2·4	16	17	—	—	1·75	1·25	1·05	0·95	0·82	0·75	0·70	0·70	0·70
		15	16	—	—	1·45	1·12	0·88	0·82	0·72	0·68	0·65	0·65	0·65
		14	15	—	1·67	1·17	0·90	0·74	0·69	0·65	0·62	0·60	0·60	0·60
		13	14	—	1·37	1·07	0·77	0·66	0·61	0·57	0·55	0·55	0·55	0·55
		12	13	1·32	1·15	0·82	0·65	0·55	0·52	0·50	0·50	0·50	0·50	0·50
		11	12		0·92	0·67	0·54	0·50	0·47	0·45	0·45	0·45	0·45	0·45

The following table is printed sideways on the page. It gives minimum widths (in metres) against two left-hand index columns. The column headings (heights of window head) are not shown on this page. Three index groups are present, labelled 2·2, 2·3 and 2·1 (with an additional 2·2 marking).

Group 2·2

idx	idx											
11	10	0·40	0·40	0·40	0·40	0·40	0·40	0·40	0·45	0·55	0·80	1·07
10	9	0·35	0·35	0·35	0·35	0·35	0·35	0·35	0·37	0·47	0·60	0·82
9	8	0·30	0·30	0·30	0·30	0·30	0·30	0·30	0·32	0·35	0·47	0·65
8	7	0·27	0·27	0·27	0·27	0·27	0·27	0·27	0·28	0·32	0·35	0·50
7	6	0·24	0·24	0·24	0·24	0·24	0·24	0·24	0·24	0·24	0·27	0·37
6	5	0·20	0·20	0·20	0·20	0·20	0·20	0·20	0·20	0·20	0·22	0·25
5	—	0·17	0·17	0·17	0·17	0·17	0·17	0·17	0·17	0·17	0·17	0·20

Group 2·3

idx	idx											
17	16	0·85	0·85	0·85	0·87	1·00	1·15	1·27	1·57	—	—	—
16	15	0·77	0·77	0·77	0·82	0·87	1·00	1·10	1·39	1·85	—	—
15	14	0·70	0·70	0·70	0·72	0·76	0·82	0·90	1·12	1·47	1·75	—
14	13	0·64	0·64	0·64	0·65	0·67	0·71	0·77	0·95	1·35	1·42	—
13	12	0·58	0·58	0·58	0·58	0·58	0·61	0·65	0·80	1·05	1·15	1·32
12	11	0·52	0·52	0·52	0·52	0·52	0·52	0·56	0·62	0·82	0·97	1·00
11	10	0·47	0·47	0·47	0·47	0·47	0·47	0·49	0·55	0·67	0·75	0·77
10	9	0·41	0·41	0·41	0·41	0·41	0·41	0·41	0·46	0·57	0·55	0·60
9	8	0·36	0·36	0·36	0·36	0·36	0·36	0·36	0·38	0·40	0·42	0·45
8	7	0·32	0·32	0·32	0·32	0·32	0·32	0·32	0·33	0·36	0·34	0·30
7	6	0·27	0·27	0·27	0·27	0·27	0·27	0·27	0·27	0·30	0·25	0·20
6	5	0·23	0·23	0·23	0·23	0·23	0·23	0·23	0·23	0·23	0·20	—
5	—	0·20	0·20	0·20	0·20	0·20	0·20	0·20	0·20	0·20	—	—

Group 2·1 (with 2·2 marking)

idx	idx											
17	16	0·95	0·98	1·02	1·10	1·22	1·52	1·67	2·10	—	—	—
16	15	0·88	0·88	0·88	0·94	1·07	1·25	1·45	1·92	1·95	—	—
15	14	0·82	0·82	0·82	0·84	0·92	1·01	1·15	1·50	1·82	1·87	—
14	13	0·75	0·75	0·75	0·75	0·79	0·84	0·95	1·20	1·37	1·47	—
13	12	0·69	0·69	0·69	0·69	0·72	0·76	0·80	1·02	1·05	1·27	1·30
12	11	0·62	0·62	0·62	0·62	0·62	0·67	0·70	0·80	0·82	0·95	0·97
11	10	0·55	0·55	0·55	0·55	0·55	0·55	0·58	0·67	0·70	0·70	0·72
10	9	0·48	0·48	0·48	0·48	0·48	0·48	0·50	0·52	0·53	0·52	0·52
9	8	0·42	0·42	0·42	0·42	0·42	0·42	0·42	0·44	0·40	0·37	0·35
8	7	0·35	0·35	0·35	0·35	0·35	0·35	0·35	0·37	0·32	0·30	0·25
7	6	0·30	0·30	0·30	0·30	0·30	0·30	0·30	0·30	0·27	0·22	—
6	5	0·25	0·25	0·25	0·25	0·25	0·25	0·25	0·25	0·20	—	—
5	—	0·20	0·20	0·20	0·20	0·20	0·20	0·20	0·20	—	—	—

†(a) Height of foot of glazed portion of opening not exceeding 1·15 metres.

(b) The table gives minimum widths for ground floor windows on a level site; the height of window head may be reduced by up to 0·30 metre on floors above the ground floor.

FIFTH SCHEDULE—continued

SCHEDULE 9—continued

TABLE 16—continued

Part III: Apartments other than living rooms—continued

Height of head of window opening above floor†		Floor area of room		Width of room measured parallel to window, exceeding (metres)										
Exceeding (metres)	Not exceeding (metres)	Exceeding (square metres)	Not exceeding (square metres)	1·8	2·1	2·4	2·7	3·0	3·3	3·6	3·9	4·2	4·5	4·8
(1)	(2)	(3)	(4)	Minimum width of window opening (metres) (5)										
2·0	2·1	16	17	—	—	—	—	2·35	2·20	1·70	1·37	1·25	1·22	1·20
		15	16	—	—	—	—	1·90	1·70	1·52	1·22	1·14	1·10	1·10
		14	15	—	—	—	2·12	1·57	1·47	1·17	1·07	1·02	1·00	1·00
		13	14	—	—	—	1·68	1·25	1·12	1·05	0·94	0·91	0·91	0·91
		12	13	—	—	1·95	1·42	1·02	0·94	0·83	0·82	0·82	0·82	0·82
		11	12	—	—	1·42	1·05	0·82	0·77	0·74	0·74	0·74	0·74	0·74
		10	11	—	1·80	1·10	0·85	0·68	0·67	0·67	0·67	0·67	0·67	0·67
		9	10	—	1·30	0·92	0·65	0·60	0·60	0·60	0·60	0·60	0·60	0·60
		8	9	1·30	0·90	0·65	0·54	0·52	0·52	0·52	0·52	0·52	0·52	0·52
		7	8	0·95	0·65	0·49	0·45	0·45	0·45	0·45	0·45	0·45	0·45	0·45
		6	7	0·67	0·45	0·40	0·37	0·37	0·37	0·37	0·37	0·37	0·37	0·37
		5	6	0·42	0·35	0·32	0·30	0·30	0·30	0·30	0·30	0·30	0·30	0·30
		—	5	0·30	0·25	0·22	0·22	0·22	0·22	0·22	0·22	0·22	0·22	0·22

2·0												
1·60	1·62	1·70	1·97	2·60	—	—	—	—	—	—	17	16
1·37	1·40	1·47	1·72	2·10	2·60	2·75	—	—	—	—	16	15
1·25	1·27	1·32	1·45	1·65	2·16	2·45	2·45	—	—	—	15	14
1·13	1·13	1·15	1·24	1·42	1·65	1·80	2·22	2·17	—	—	14	13
1·02	1·02	1·02	1·07	1·15	1·45	1·50	1·52	1·55	—	—	13	12
0·92	0·92	0·92	0·92	0·95	1·07	1·14	1·15	1·22	1·32	1·32	12	11
0·82	0·82	0·82	0·72	0·83	0·88	0·95	0·92	0·90	0·90	0·92	11	10
0·72	0·72	0·72	0·63	0·72	0·72	0·76	0·67	0·65	0·60	0·57	10	9
0·63	0·63	0·63	0·54	0·63	0·63	0·64	0·57	0·52	0·42	0·37	9	8
0·54	0·54	0·54	0·45	0·54	0·54	0·54	0·47	0·38	0·32		8	7
0·45	0·45	0·45	0·36	0·45	0·45	0·45	0·36	0·27			7	6
0·36	0·36	0·36	0·27	0·36	0·36	0·36	0·27				6	5
0·27	0·27	0·27		0·27	0·27	0·27					5	—
—												

†(a) Height of foot of glazed portion of opening not exceeding 1·15 metres.
(b) The table gives minimum widths for ground floor windows on a level site; the height of window head may be reduced by up to 0·30 metre on floors above the ground floor.

FIFTH SCHEDULE—*continued*

NEW TABLE TO BE SUBSTITUTED FOR TABLE 18 OF SCHEDULE 9 TO THE BUILDING STANDARDS REGULATIONS

Regulations Q7, Q8, Q10 and Q13

TABLE 18—STANDARDS OF HOUSING ACCOMMODATION

Size of house (1)	Number of apartments (other than living room) less than 10 square metres (2)	Minimum area in square metres of—			Minimum capacity in cubic metres of—	
		Aggregate area of living room and kitchen‡ (3)	Kitchen (4)	Aggregate area of apartments other than living room (5)	Larder and dry goods store (6)	Linen and general storage (7)
One apartment	—	†23	4·2	†	0·68	4·8
Two apartments	Nil	20	4·6	11	0·85	5·0
	One	16	2·8	8·8	0·68	4·8
Three apartments	Nil	25	7·0	22	1·25	9·3
	One	23	6·5	18	1·25	9·3
	Two	20	4·6	16	0·85	5·0
Four apartments	Nil	28	7·0	33	1·70	9·5
	One	28	7·0	29	1·42	9·5
	Two	25	7·0	25	1·25	9·3
	Three	23	6·5	21	1·25	9·3
Five apartments	Nil	28	7·0	45	1·70	9·6
	One	28	7·0	40	1·70	9·6
	Two	28	7·0	36	1·70	9·5
	Three	28	7·0	32	1·42	9·5
	Four	25	7·0	28	1·25	9·3
Six or more apartments	—	28	7·0	Four of the apartments shall have a minimum area equal to the appropriate area for a five apartment house	1·70	9·6

†In the case of a one apartment house the figure given in column (3) includes sleeping accommodation.

‡The area specified in this column includes any part of a living room or kitchen reserved for dining.

Regulation 8

SIXTH SCHEDULE

New Provisions to be substituted for Provisions of Part B of Schedule 10 to the Building Standards Regulations with reference to Regulation M21 of the Building Standards Regulations

Provision of regulation deemed to be satisfied	Element of structure or fitting	Case dealt with or relevant conditions	Specification
M21(1)(a)—as to the suitability and strength of materials	Gutter	Cast iron gutter	(1) The gutter, fittings and accessories conform to B.S. 460:1964.
		Asbestos cement gutter	(2) The gutter, fittings and accessories conform to B.S. 569.
		Aluminium and aluminium alloy gutter ...	(3) The gutter, fittings and accessories conform to B.S. 2997.
		Pressed steel gutter ...	(4) The gutter, fittings and accessories conform to B.S. 1091.
		Wrought copper and wrought zinc gutter ...	(5) The gutter, fittings and accessories conform to B.S. 1431.
M21(1)(b)—as to size		Half-round eaves gutter	(a) The gutter is one of the sizes specified in column (1) of the following table;
			(b) the flow capacity specified in the appropriate columns (2) to (4) of the said table is not less than the flow load from the roof;
			(c) the flow load from the roof for the purposes of this Specification shall be taken to be the number of litres per second obtained by multiplying the area of the roof draining to the gutter (in square metres) by—
			(i) where the pitch of the roof does not exceed 50 degrees, a factor of 0·021,
			(ii) where the pitch of the roof exceeds 50 degrees, a factor of the aggregate of 0·021 plus 0·012 x Tangent A (where A is the angle of the pitch of the roof)—

SIXTH SCHEDULE—*continued*

Provision of regulation deemed to be satisfied	Element of structure or fitting	Case dealt with or relevant conditions	Specification
M21(1)(b)—as to size—cont'd.	Gutter—cont'd.	Half-round eaves gutter—cont'd.	TABLE

TABLE

Flow capacities †*(in litres per second) for half-round gutters with outlet at one end*

Gutter size (millimetres) (1)	Slope of less than 1 in 600 (2)		Slope 1 in 600 and over, and longer than 6 metres (3)		Slope 1 in 600 and over, and length 6 metres or less (4)	
	True‡	Nominal§	True‡	Nominal§	True‡	Nominal§
75	0·4	0·3	0·6	0·5	0·5	0·4
100	0·8	0·7	1·1	0·9	1·1	0·8
115	1·1	0·8	1·6	1·2	1·4	1·1
125	1·5	1·1	2·1	1·5	1·9	1·4
150	2·3	1·8	3·3	2·5	3·0	2·3
†*Note:* Where there is a bend these flow capacities shall be reduced by the percentage shown—						
(a) if bend within 1·8 metres of outlet						
(i) sharp bend ...	20%		25%		25%	
(ii) round bend ...	10%		25%		25%	
(b) bend between 1·8 metres and 3·6 metres of outlet						
(i) sharp bend ...	10%		12½%		12½%	
(ii) round bend ...	5%		12½%		12½%	

‡"True" means a true half-round gutter (i.e. pressed steel to B.S. 1091 or asbestos cement to B.S. 569).

§"Nominal" means a nominally half-round gutter (i.e. aluminium to B.S. 2997 or cast iron to B.S. 460:1964).

M21(1)(e)—as to adequacy of outlet

(a) The gutter is of one of the sizes specified in column (1) of the following table;
(b) the outlet is of the appropriate size specified in column (3) or (4) of the said table—

TABLE

Half-round gutter outlet sizes (diameter in millimetres)

Half-round gutter size (millimetres) (1)	Sharp (S.C.) or round-cornered (R.C.) outlet (2)	Outlet at one end of gutter (3)	Outlet not at one end of gutter (4)
75	S.C. R.C.	50 50	50 50
100	S.C. R.C.	63 50	63 50
115	S.C. R.C.	63 50	75 63
125	S.C. R.C.	75 63	90 75

EXPLANATORY NOTE

(This Note is not part of the Regulations.)

These Regulations amend the Building Standards (Scotland) Regulations 1970 and 1971 by substituting metric measures for imperial measures with effect from 1st January 1972.

STATUTORY INSTRUMENTS

1971 No. 1033

AGRICULTURE

The Price Stabilisation Levies (Supplementary Provisions) Regulations 1971

Made - - - -		*22nd June* 1971
Laid before Parliament		*30th June* 1971
Coming into Operation		*3rd July* 1971

The Commissioners of Customs and Excise, by virtue of the powers conferred on them by section 1(9) of and paragraph 1(4) of the Schedule to the Agriculture and Horticulture Act 1964(a), and of all other powers enabling them in that behalf, hereby make the following Regulations:—

1.—(1) These Regulations may be cited as the Price Stabilisation Levies (Supplementary Provisions) Regulations 1971 and shall come into operation on 3rd July 1971.

(2) The Interpretation Act 1889(b) shall apply for the interpretation of these Regulations as it applies for the interpretation of an Act of Parliament.

2. For Regulation 5 of the Price Stabilisation Levies (Supplementary Provisions) Regulations 1964(c) there shall be substituted the following Regulation:—

"5. In these Regulations "specified commodities" means commodities, other than fresh, chilled or frozen beef and veal, specified for the purposes of section 1(1) of the Agriculture and Horticulture Act 1964."

3. In its application by virtue of paragraph 1 of the Schedule to the Agriculture and Horticulture Act 1964, section 88(4) of the Customs and Excise Act 1952(d) shall have effect as if the words "fresh, chilled or frozen beef and veal" were inserted after the words "hydrocarbon oils".

22nd June 1971.

C. T. Cross,
Commissioner of Customs and Excise.

King's Beam House
Mark Lane
London EC3R 7HE.

(a) 1964 c. 28.
(c) S.I. 1964/814 (1964 II, p. 1717).
(b) 1889 c. 63.
(d) 1952 c. 44.

EXPLANATORY NOTE

(This Note is not part of the Regulations.)

These Regulations exclude fresh, chilled or frozen beef and veal from the provisions of the Price Stabilisation Levies (Supplementary Provisions) Regulations 1964, and therefore enable fresh, chilled or frozen beef and veal subject to such levy to be warehoused without payment of levy if intended for home consumption as well as if intended for exportation and use as ship's stores.

The Regulations also enable the proprietor of warehoused fresh, chilled or frozen beef and veal to pay levy by reference to the quantity ascertained at the time of delivery for home use.

STATUTORY INSTRUMENTS

1971 No. 1034

INDUSTRIAL TRAINING

The Industrial Training Levy (Water Supply) Order 1971

Made - - -		*22nd June* 1971
Laid before Parliament		*1st July* 1971
Coming into Operation		*14th July* 1971

The Secretary of State after approving proposals submitted by the Water Supply Industry Training Board for the imposition of a further levy on employers in the water supply industry and in exercise of his powers under section 4 of the Industrial Training Act 1964(a) and of all other powers enabling him in that behalf hereby makes the following Order : —

Title and commencement

1. This Order may be cited as the Industrial Training Levy (Water Supply) Order 1971 and shall come into operation on 14th July 1971.

Interpretation

2.—(1) In this Order unless the context otherwise requires : —

(*a*) "activities of the water supply industry" means any activities (not being agriculture) which, subject to the provisions of paragraph 2 of Schedule 1 to the industrial training order, are specified in paragraph 1 of that Schedule as activities of the water supply industry ;

(*b*) "agriculture" has the same meaning as in section 109(3) of the Agriculture Act 1947(b) or, in relation to Scotland, as in section 86(3) of the Agriculture (Scotland) Act 1948(c) ;

(*c*) "an appeal tribunal" means an industrial tribunal established under section 12 of the Industrial Training Act 1964 ;

(*d*) "assessment" means an assessment of an employer to the levy ;

(*e*) "emoluments" means all emoluments assessable to income tax under Schedule E (other than pensions), being emoluments from which tax under that Schedule is deductible, whether or not tax in fact falls to be deducted from any particular payment thereof ;

(*f*) "employer" means an employer in the water supply industry, being on the day upon which this Order comes into operation statutory water undertakers or a regional water board ;

(*g*) "the Industrial Training Board" means the Water Supply Industry Training Board ;

(a) 1964 c. 16.   (b) 1947 c. 48.
(c) 1948 c. 45.

(*h*) "the industrial training order" means the Industrial Training (Water Supply Board) Order 1965(**a**) ;

(*i*) "the levy" means the levy imposed by the Board in respect of the sixth levy period ;

(*j*) "notice" means a notice in writing ;

(*k*) "regional water board" means a regional water board within the meaning of the Water (Scotland) Act 1967(**b**) ;

(*l*) "the sixth base period" means the period of twelve months that commenced on 6th April 1970 ;

(*m*) "the sixth levy period" means the period commencing with the day upon which this Order comes into operation and ending on 31st March 1972 ;

(*n*) "statutory water undertakers" means any statutory water undertakers within the meaning of the Water Act 1945(**c**).

(2) The Interpretation Act 1889(**d**) shall apply to the interpretation of this Order as it applies to the interpretation of an Act of Parliament.

Imposition of the Levy

3.—(1) The levy to be imposed by the Industrial Training Board on employers in respect of the sixth levy period shall be assessed in accordance with the provisions of this Article.

(2) The levy shall be assessed by the Industrial Training Board in respect of each employer.

(3) The amount of the levy imposed on an employer shall be a sum equal to 1·6 per cent. of the emoluments of the persons following—

(*a*) in the case of statutory water undertakers, all persons employed by the employer in the sixth base period in activities of the water supply industry and any other persons employed at any time in that period in a water undertaking or part of a water undertaking that on the day upon which this Order comes into operation forms part of the water undertaking of the employer ;

(*b*) in the case of a regional water board, all persons employed by the board in activities of the water supply industry in the sixth base period.

(4) For the purposes of this Article no regard shall be had to persons wholly engaged in agriculture or in the supply of food or drink for immediate consumption.

Assessment Notice

4.—(1) The Industrial Training Board shall serve an assessment notice on every employer.

(2) An assessment notice shall state the address of the said Board for the service of a notice of appeal or of an application for an extension of time for appealing.

(3) An assessment notice may be served on an employer by sending it by post to the employer's registered or principal office.

(**a**) S.I. 1965/1258 (1965 II, p. 3556).   (**b**) 1967 c. 78.
(**c**) 1945 c. 42.   (**d**) 1889 c. 63.

Payment of the Levy

5.—(1) Subject to the provisions of this Article and of Articles 6 and 7, the amount of an assessment appearing in an assessment notice served by the Industrial Training Board shall be payable to the Board in two instalments determined in accordance with the provisions of the next following paragraph, and the said instalments shall be due respectively one month and five months after the date of the assessment notice.

(2) The first of the said instalments shall be equal to 1·0 per cent. of the emoluments by reference to which the amount of the said levy has been assessed in accordance with the provisions of Article 3 of this Order, and the second instalment shall be equal to the balance of the amount payable under the assessment notice.

(3) An instalment of an assessment shall not be recoverable by the Industrial Training Board until there has expired the time allowed for appealing against the assessment by Article 7(1) of this Order and any further period or periods of time that the said Board or an appeal tribunal may have allowed for appealing under paragraph (2) or (3) of that Article or, where an appeal is brought, until the appeal is decided or withdrawn.

Withdrawal of Assessment

6.—(1) The Industrial Training Board may, by a notice served on the person assessed to the levy in the same manner as an assessment notice, withdraw an assessment if that person has appealed against that assessment under the provisions of Article 7 of this Order and the appeal has not been entered in the Register of Appeals kept under the appropriate Regulations specified in paragraph (4) of that Article.

(2) The withdrawal of an assessment shall be without prejudice to the power of the Industrial Training Board to serve a further assessment notice on the person assessed to the levy.

Appeals

7.—(1) A person assessed to the levy may appeal to an appeal tribunal against the assessment within one month from the date of the service of the assessment notice or within any further period or periods of time that may be allowed by the Industrial Training Board or an appeal tribunal under the following provisions of this Article.

(2) The Industrial Training Board by notice may for good cause allow a person assessed to the levy to appeal to an appeal tribunal against the assessment at any time within the period of four months from the date of the service of the assessment notice or within such further period or periods as the Board may allow before such time as may then be limited for appealing has expired.

(3) If the Industrial Training Board shall not allow an application for extension of time for appealing, an appeal tribunal shall upon application made to the tribunal by the person assessed to the levy have the like powers as the Board under the last foregoing paragraph.

(4) An appeal or an application to an appeal tribunal under this Article shall be made in accordance with the Industrial Tribunals (England and

Wales) Regulations 1965(a) as amended by the Industrial Tribunals (England and Wales) (Amendment) Regulations 1967(b) except in the case of a regional water board when the appeal or application shall be made in accordance with the Industrial Tribunals (Scotland) Regulations 1965(c) as amended by the Industrial Tribunals (Scotland) (Amendment) Regulations 1967(d).

(5) The powers of an appeal tribunal under paragraph (3) of this Article may be exercised by the President of the Industrial Tribunals (England and Wales) or by the President of the Industrial Tribunals (Scotland) as the case may be.

Evidence

8.—(1) Upon the discharge by a person assessed to the levy of his liability under an assessment the Industrial Training Board shall if so requested issue to him a certificate to that effect.

(2) The production in any proceedings of a document purporting to be certified by the Secretary of the Industrial Training Board to be a true copy of an assessment or other notice issued by the Board or purporting to be a certificate such as is mentioned in the foregoing paragraph of this Article shall, unless the contrary is proved, be sufficient evidence of the document and of the facts stated therein.

Signed by order of the Secretary of State.
22nd June 1971.

Paul Bryan,
Minister of State,
Department of Employment.

EXPLANATORY NOTE

(This Note is not part of the Order.)

This Order gives effect to proposals submitted by the Water Supply Industry Training Board to the Secretary of State for Employment for the imposition of a further levy on employers in the water supply industry for the purpose of raising money towards the expenses of the Board.

The levy is to be imposed in respect of the sixth levy period commencing with the date on which this Order comes into operation and ending on 31st March 1972. The levy will be assessed by the Industrial Training Board and there will be a right of appeal against an assessment to an industrial tribunal.

(a) S.I. 1965/1101 (1965 II, p. 2805).   (b) S.I. 1967/301 (1967 I, p. 1040).
(c) S.I. 1965/1157 (1965 II, p. 3266).   (d) S.I. 1967/302 (1967 I, p. 1050).

1971 No. 1035

INCOME TAX

The Mineral Royalties (Tax) Regulations 1971

Made - - - -	*23rd June* 1971
Laid before the House of Commons - -	*30th June* 1971
Coming into Operation	*1st July* 1971

The Commissioners of Inland Revenue, in exercise of the powers conferred upon them by section 29(6) of the Finance Act 1970(a), hereby make the following Regulations:—

1.—(1) These Regulations may be cited as the Mineral Royalties (Tax) Regulations 1971, and shall come into operation on 1st July 1971.

(2) The Interpretation Act 1889(b) shall apply for the interpretation of these Regulations as it applies for the interpretation of an Act of Parliament.

(3) In these Regulations:—

the "principal section" means section 29 of the Finance Act 1970;

"agreement" means a mineral lease or agreement, as defined in the principal section;

"specified operations" means the winning and working, grading, washing, grinding and crushing of minerals, but in relation to any particular agreement, includes only such of those operations as are in fact authorised by the agreement;

"rights" includes liberties.

2. Subject to Regulation 3 below, where a payment is made on or after 6th April 1970 in respect of a sum receivable on or after that date under an agreement which relates both to the winning and working of minerals and to other matters, then, notwithstanding any allocation of the payment under the terms of the agreement, so much but no more of the payment is to be treated for the purposes of the principal section as mineral royalties as might reasonably have been expected to be provided for by the agreement if—

(*a*) it conferred only the right to carry out specified operations in relation to minerals in or under the land to which the agreement relates; and

(*b*) any buildings, structures, roads, shafts, adits or other works existing on the land at the time when the agreement was granted or made were not in existence.

Provided that no such payments are to be treated as mineral royalties unless minerals in or under the land are being or have been won and worked pursuant to rights conferred by or under the agreement, or there is reasonable prospect of their being so won and worked.

(a) 1970 c. 24.   (b) 52 & 53 Vict. c. 63.

3. The whole of a payment under an agreement shall for the purposes of the principal section be treated as a mineral royalty if under Regulation 2 above nine-tenths or more of it would be so treated.

4. Nothing in these Regulations applies to any periodical payments such as are referred to in subsection (9)(*b*) of the principal section (payments made under certain statutes in Northern Ireland).

By Order of the Commissioners of Inland Revenue,

23rd June 1971.

Alan Lord,
Secretary.

EXPLANATORY NOTE

(*This Note is not part of the Regulations.*)

Section 29, Finance Act 1970 governs the taxation of royalties receivable on or after 6th April 1970 under a mineral lease or agreement, and empowers the Commissioners of Inland Revenue to make provision by regulations as to the extent to which payments under a mineral lease or agreement are to be treated for this purpose as royalties if they relate to other matters besides the winning and working of minerals. These regulations make such provision.

STATUTORY INSTRUMENTS

1971 No. 1036

POULTRY

The Live Poultry (Restrictions) Amendment Order 1971

Made - - -		*22nd June* 1971
Coming into Operation		*24th June* 1971

The Minister of Agriculture, Fisheries and Food and the Secretary of State, acting jointly, in exercise of the powers vested in them under sections 1, 20, 45, 84 and 85 of the Diseases of Animals Act 1950(**a**) as read with the Transfer of Functions (Animal Health) Order 1955(**b**) and of all other powers enabling them in that behalf, hereby order as follows :—

Citation, interpretation and commencement

1. This order, which may be cited as the Live Poultry (Restrictions) Amendment Order 1971, shall be construed as one with the Live Poultry (Restrictions) Order 1971(**c**) (in this order referred to as "the principal order"), and shall come into operation on 24th June 1971.

Extension of application of Part I of principal order to Scotland

2. The principal order shall be amended by substituting for the words "England and Wales" in Article 3 thereof the words "the whole of Great Britain".

Removal of prohibition on certain movements of poultry

3. The principal order shall be amended by the deletion of Article 11 and Schedules 3 and 4 thereof.

IN WITNESS WHEREOF the Official Seal of the Minister of Agriculture, Fisheries and Food is hereunto affixed on 16th June 1971.

(L.S.)   *J. M. L. Prior,*
Minister of Agriculture, Fisheries and Food.

Given under the Seal of the Secretary of State for Scotland on 22nd June 1971.

(L.S.)   *Gordon Campbell,*
Secretary of State for Scotland.

(**a**) 1950 c. 36. For change of title of the Minister see S.I. 1955/554 (1955 I, p. 1200).
(**b**) S.I. 1955/958 (1955 I, p. 1184).   (**c**) S.I. 1971/311 (1971 I, p. 1046).

EXPLANATORY NOTE

(This Note is not part of the Order.)

This Order amends the Live Poultry (Restrictions) Order 1971 so as to make Articles 4, 5, 6, 7 and 8 applicable to Scotland as well as to England and Wales, and so as to remove the prohibition imposed by that order upon the movement of poultry into certain specified areas of England and Wales.

1971 No. 1037

FOOD AND DRUGS

MILK AND DAIRIES

The Milk (Northern Ireland) Order 1971

Made - - -		*22nd June* 1971
Laid before Parliament		*30th June* 1971
Coming into Operation		*4th July* 1971

The Minister of Agriculture, Fisheries and Food, in exercise of the powers conferred on him by sections 6, 7 and 22(3) of the Emergency Laws (Re-enactments and Repeals) Act 1964(a) and of all other powers enabling him in that behalf, hereby makes the following order :—

Citation, commencement and extent

1.—(1) This order may be cited as the Milk (Northern Ireland) Order 1971, and shall come into operation on 4th July 1971.

(2) This order shall apply only to Northern Ireland.

Interpretation

2. In this order—

"catering business" means the business or undertaking of an inn, public-house, hotel, restaurant, café, tea-shop, buffet, coffee-stall or any place of refreshment open to the public, or of a club, boarding house, apartment house, refreshment contractor, staff dining room or canteen, or of any school feeding centre, school premises or other educational establishment where milk is provided for pupils ; and "caterer" shall be construed accordingly ;

"farm bottled milk" and "pasteurised milk" have the meaning respectively assigned to them under sections 1 and 3 of the Milk Act (Northern Ireland 1950(b) as amended by the Milk (Amendment) Act (Northern Ireland) 1963(c) ;

"milk" means liquid cow's milk but does not include separated milk, skimmed milk, condensed milk or evaporated milk ;

"the Ministry" means the Ministry of Agriculture for Northern Ireland ;

"sell" includes offer or agree to sell or expose for sale.

(a) 1964 c. 60.　　(b) 1950 c. 31 (N.I.).　　(c) 1963 c. 11 (N.I.).

Maximum prices and exemptions

3.—(1) No person shall sell any milk at a price exceeding the maximum price specified in relation thereto in the Schedule to this order :

Provided that where any milk is sold in a quantity of one-third of a pint or half a pint and, in either case, the maximum price therefor in accordance with the foregoing provisions of this article would include an odd fraction of a new penny, other than one-half of a new penny, that maximum price shall be increased to the next higher half of a new penny if the said fraction is less than one-half or to the next higher whole new penny if the said fraction is greater than one-half.

(2) No person shall in connection with the sale or disposition or proposed sale or disposition of any milk in relation to which a maximum price applies enter or offer to enter into any artificial transaction or make or demand any unreasonable charge.

(3) The provisions of this article shall not apply as respects any supply of milk (*a*) by a caterer in the course of his catering business, or (*b*) from any automatic vending machine.

Licences or authorisations

4.—(1) The provisions of this order are subject to any licence or authorisation which may be granted under this order by the Ministry.

(2) Every person holding a licence or authorisation granted under this order shall comply with every condition imposed by such licence or authorisation.

(3) Every licence or authorisation granted under this order is and shall remain the property of the Ministry ; and the licensee or any person in possession of any such licence or authorisation shall, if requested to do so by or on behalf of the Ministry, produce or deliver it to such person or to a person of such class or description, and within such time, as may be specified in the request.

Revocation

5. The Milk (Northern Ireland) Order 1965(**a**), the Milk (Northern Ireland) (Amendment) Order 1969(**b**), and the Milk (Northern Ireland) (Amendment) Order 1970(**c**) are hereby revoked :

Provided that unless any contrary intention appears any licence or authorisation granted under the Milk (Northern Ireland) Order 1965, as amended, or having effect by virtue thereof, and subsisting immediately before the coming into operation of this order, shall continue to have effect as though granted by the Ministry under the corresponding provision of this order.

In Witness whereof the Official Seal of the Minister of Agriculture, Fisheries and Food is hereunto affixed on 22nd June 1971.

(L.S.)

J. M. L. Prior,
Minister of Agriculture, Fisheries and Food.

(a) S.I. 1965/1412 (1965 II, p. 4176).   (b) S.I. 1969/973 (1969 II, p. 2859).
(c) S.I. 1970/1079 (1970 II, p. 3341).

SCHEDULE   Article 3(1)

MAXIMUM PRICES OF MILK

Milk	Maximum Price (Rate per Pint)
	p
Farm bottled milk	$5\frac{1}{2}$
Pasteurised milk	$5\frac{1}{2}$

EXPLANATORY NOTE

(*This Note is not part of the Order.*)

This order, which comes into operation on 4th July 1971,—

(a) supersedes the Milk (Northern Ireland) Order 1965 as amended ;

(b) prescribes a new maximum price for Pasteurised milk on sales in Northern Ireland ;

(c) extends the definition of "catering business" to cover school premises or other educational establishments where milk is provided for pupils ;

(d) permits the maximum price of one-third of a pint of milk to be rounded up to the nearest new halfpenny or new penny, as the case may be, if that maximum price would otherwise include an odd fraction of a new penny other than a new halfpenny.

STATUTORY INSTRUMENTS

1971 No. 1038

FOOD AND DRUGS

MILK AND DAIRIES

The Milk (Great Britain) Order 1971

Made - - -	*22nd June* 1971
Laid before Parliament	*30th June* 1971
Coming into Operation	*4th July* 1971

The Minister of Agriculture, Fisheries and Food and the Secretary of State, acting jointly in exercise of the powers conferred on them by sections 6 and 7 of the Emergency Laws (Re-enactments and Repeals) Act 1964(a) and of all other powers enabling them in that behalf, hereby make the following order:—

Citation, commencement and extent

1.—(1) This order may be cited as the Milk (Great Britain) Order 1971, and shall come into operation on 4th July 1971.

(2) This order shall not extend to Northern Ireland.

Interpretation

2.—(1) In this order—

"catering business" means the business or undertaking of an inn, public-house, hotel, restaurant, café, tea-shop, buffet, coffee-stall or any place of refreshment open to the public, or of a club, boarding house, apartment house, refreshment contractor, staff dining room or canteen, or of any school feeding centre, school premises or other educational establishment where milk is provided for pupils; and "caterer" shall be construed accordingly;

"Channel Islands milk" means—

> (*a*) as respects England and Wales, milk which is produced from cows of the Channel Islands breeds and which is labelled "Channel Islands milk", "Jersey milk" or "Guernsey milk" when sold in a container;

> (*b*) as respects Scotland, milk which is lawfully sold as Channel Islands milk pursuant to the Milk and Dairies (Channel Islands and South Devon Milk) (Scotland) Regulations 1967(b);

(a) 1964 c. 60. (b) S.I. 1967/81 (1967 I, p. 178).

"Homogenised milk" means milk which (i) has been treated by heat (ii) has been so processed as to break up the globules of butterfat and cause them to remain uniformly distributed throughout the milk instead of rising to the surface and (iii) when sold in a container is labelled "Homogenised milk" ;

"milk" means liquid cow's milk but does not include separated milk, skimmed milk, condensed milk or evaporated milk ;

"the Ministers" means the Minister of Agriculture, Fisheries and Food and the Secretary of State acting jointly ;

"Pasteurised milk" means milk in respect of which the special designation "Pasteurised" is lawfully used, in relation to England and Wales, pursuant to the Milk (Special Designation) Regulations 1963(a), as amended (b), and, in relation to Scotland, pursuant to the Milk (Special Designations) (Scotland) Order 1965(c), as amended (d) ;

"Premium milk" means milk in respect of which the special designation "Premium" is lawfully used pursuant to the Milk (Special Designations) (Scotland) Order 1965, as amended ;

"sell" includes offer or agree to sell or expose for sale ;

"South Devon milk" means—

(a) as respects England and Wales, milk which is produced from cows of the South Devon breed and which is labelled "South Devon milk" when sold in a container ;

(b) as respects Scotland, milk which is lawfully sold as South Devon milk pursuant to the Milk and Dairies (Channel Islands and South Devon Milk) (Scotland) Regulations 1967 ;

"Standard milk" means milk in respect of which the special designation "Standard" is lawfully used pursuant to the Milk (Special Designations) (Scotland) Order 1965, as amended ;

"Sterilised milk" means milk in respect of which the special designation "Sterilised" is lawfully used, in relation to England and Wales, pursuant to the Milk (Special Designation) Regulations 1963, as amended, and, in relation to Scotland, pursuant to the Milk (Special Designations) (Scotland) Order 1965, as amended ;

"Ultra Heat Treated milk" means milk in respect of which the special designation "Ultra Heat Treated" is lawfully used, in relation to England and Wales, pursuant to the Milk (Special Designation) Regulations 1963, as amended, and, in relation to Scotland, pursuant to the Milk (Special Designations) (Scotland) Order 1965, as amended ;

"Untreated milk" means milk in respect of which the special designation "Untreated" is lawfully used pursuant to the Milk (Special Designation) Regulations 1963, as amended ;

"Untreated Milk Farm Bottled" means untreated milk which has been bottled at the place of production and in respect of which the description "Untreated Milk Farm Bottled" is lawfully used pursuant to the Milk (Special Designation) Regulations 1963, as amended.

(a) S.I. 1963/1571 (1963 III, p. 2937). (b) S.I. 1965/1555 (1965 II, p. 4543).
(c) S.I. 1965/253 (1965 I, p. 617). (d) S.I. 1966/1573 (1966 III, p. 4850).

(2) Any reference in this order to any regulations or other order shall be construed as a reference to such regulations or order as amended by any subsequent regulations or order.

Maximum prices and exemptions

3.—(1) No person shall sell any milk—

(a) on a sale in England and Wales, at a price exceeding the maximum price applicable in accordance with the provisions of Schedule 1 to this order ;

(b) on a sale in Scotland, excluding the islands other than the islands of Islay, Coll and Gigha in the County of Argyll and those in the Counties of Bute and Orkney, at a price exceeding the maximum price applicable in accordance with the provisions of Schedule 2 to this order:

Provided that where any milk is sold in a quantity of one-third of a pint or half a pint and, in either case, the maximum price therefor in accordance with the foregoing provisions of this article would include an odd fraction of a new penny, other than one-half of a new penny, that maximum price shall be increased to the next higher half of a new penny if the said fraction is less than one-half or to the next higher whole new penny if the said fraction is greater than one-half.

(2) No person shall in connection with the sale or disposition or proposed sale or disposition of any milk, in any area to which the provisions of paragraph (1) of this article apply, enter or offer to enter into any artificial transaction or make or demand any unreasonable charge.

(3) The provisions of this article shall not apply as respects any supply of milk (a) by a caterer in the course of his catering business, (b) by a retailer for consumption on his retail premises, or (c) from an automatic vending machine.

Licences or authorisations

4.—(1) The provisions of this order are subject to any licence or authorisation which may be granted under this order by or on behalf of the Ministers.

(2) Every person holding a licence or authorisation granted under this order shall comply with every condition imposed by such licence or authorisation.

(3) Every licence or authorisation granted under this order is and shall remain the property of the Ministers ; and the licensee or any person in possession of any such licence or authorisation shall, if requested to do so by or on behalf of the Ministers, produce or deliver it to such person or to a person of such class or description, and within such time, as may be specified in the request.

Revocations

5. The Milk (Great Britain) Order 1967(a), the Milk (Great Britain) (Amendment) Order 1969(b) and the Milk (Great Britain) (Amendment) Order 1970(c) are hereby revoked :

(a) S.I. 1967/455 (1967 I, p. 1398).   (b) S.I. 1969/972 (1969 II, p. 2855).
(c) S.I. 1970/1078 (1970 II, p. 3338).

Provided that unless any contrary intention appears any licence or authorisation granted under the Milk (Great Britain) Order 1967, as amended, or having effect by virtue thereof, and subsisting immediately before the coming into operation of this order, shall continue to have effect as though granted by the Ministers under the corresponding provision of this order.

In Witness whereof the Official Seal of the Minister of Agriculture, Fisheries and Food is hereunto affixed on 22nd June 1971.

(L.S.)   *J. M. L. Prior,*

Minister of Agriculture, Fisheries and Food.

Gordon Campbell,

22nd June 1971.   Secretary of State for Scotland.

Article 3(1)(*a*)

SCHEDULE 1

Maximum Prices of Milk in England and Wales

1. Subject to the provisions of this Schedule, the maximum price of milk on a sale in England and Wales shall be a price in accordance with the following table:—

Milk	Maximum Price (Rate per Pint)
	p
Channel Islands milk	6½
South Devon milk	6½
Untreated Milk Farm Bottled	6¼
Ultra Heat Treated milk	6
Sterilised milk	6
Homogenised milk	6
Untreated milk	5½
Pasteurised milk	5½
Milk other than the above mentioned...	5½

2. A reasonable charge may be made by the seller in addition to the appropriate maximum price specified in the above table for milk sold by him as Kosher milk or Kedassia milk if—

   (a) such milk is sold in a container distinctly labelled "Kosher" or "Kedassia", as the case may be; and

   (b) such milk has been prepared for consumption in accordance with the appropriate Jewish practice relating thereto.

Article 3(1)(b)

SCHEDULE 2

MAXIMUM PRICES OF MILK IN SCOTLAND

1. Subject to the provisions of this Schedule, the maximum price of milk on a sale in Scotland, excluding the islands other than the islands of Islay, Coll and Gigha in the County of Argyll and those in the Counties of Bute and Orkney, shall be a price in accordance with the following table:—

Milk	Maximum Price (Rate per Pint)
	p
Channel Islands milk	6½
South Devon milk	6½
Premium milk	6½
Ultra Heat Treated milk	6
Sterilised milk	6
Homogenised milk	6
Standard milk	5½
Pasteurised milk	5½
Milk other than the above mentioned...	5½

2. A reasonable charge may be made by the seller in addition to the appropriate maximum price specified in the above table for milk sold by him as Kosher milk or Kedassia milk if—

   (a) such milk is sold in a container distinctly labelled "Kosher" or "Kedassia", as the case may be; and

   (b) such milk has been prepared for consumption in accordance with the appropriate Jewish practice relating thereto.

EXPLANATORY NOTE

(This Note is not part of the Order.)

This order, which comes into operation on 4th July 1971,—

(a) supersedes the Milk (Great Britain) Order 1967 as amended ;

(b) prescribes new maximum prices for milk on sales in Great Britain ;

(c) extends the definition of "catering business" to cover school premises or other educational establishments where milk is provided for pupils ;

(d) permits the maximum price of one-third of a pint of milk to be rounded up to the nearest new halfpenny or new penny, as the case may be, if that maximum price would otherwise include an odd fraction of a new penny other than a new halfpenny.

STATUTORY INSTRUMENTS

1971 No. 1039

JUDGMENTS

The Reciprocal Enforcement of Foreign Judgments (Israel) Order 1971

Made - - - -	*23rd June* 1971
Coming into Operation	*26th July* 1971

At the Court at Buckingham Palace, the 23rd day of June 1971

Present,

The Queen's Most Excellent Majesty in Council

Whereas by section 1 of the Foreign Judgments (Reciprocal Enforcement) Act 1933(a) Her Majesty, if She is satisfied that, in the event of the benefits conferred by Part I of the said Act being extended to judgments given in the superior courts of any foreign country, substantial reciprocity of treatment will be assured as respects the enforcement in that foreign country of judgments given in the superior courts of the United Kingdom, is empowered to direct by Order in Council that Part I of the said Act shall extend to that foreign country and that such courts of that foreign country as are specified in the Order shall be deemed to be superior courts of that country for the purposes of the said Part I:

And whereas by section 3 of the said Act it is provided that rules of court made for the purposes of that Act shall have effect subject to any such provisions contained in Orders in Council made under section 1 of the said Act as are declared by the said Orders to be necessary for giving effect to agreements made between Her Majesty and foreign countries in relation to matters with respect to which there is power to make rules for the purposes of that Act:

And whereas a Convention, a copy whereof is set out in the Schedule to this Order, relating to the Reciprocal Recognition and Enforcement of Judgments in Civil Matters, signed at London on 28th October 1970, has been ratified by the Government of the United Kingdom of Great Britain and Northern Ireland and the Government of Israel:

And whereas Her Majesty is satisfied that, in the event of Part I of the said Act being extended to judgments given in the superior courts of Israel, substantial reciprocity of treatment will, under the terms of the said Convention, be assured as respects the enforcement in Israel of judgments given in the superior courts of the United Kingdom ; and is accordingly minded to direct that Part I of the said Act shall extend to Israel:

(a) 1933 c. 13.

And whereas it is expedient to specify the Courts in Israel which are, for the purposes of that Act, to be deemed to be superior courts, and necessary, in order to give effect to the said Convention, to make certain provisions in relation to matters with respect to which there is power to make rules of court for the purposes of the said Act:

Now, therefore, Her Majesty, by virtue and in exercise of Her powers under the said Act, and of all other powers enabling Her in that behalf, is pleased, by and with the advice of Her Privy Council, to order, and it is hereby ordered, as follows: —

1. This Order may be cited as the Reciprocal Enforcement of Foreign Judgments (Israel) Order 1971 and shall come into operation on 26th July 1971.

2. Part I of the Foreign Judgments (Reciprocal Enforcement) Act 1933 shall extend to Israel.

3. The following courts of Israel shall be deemed superior courts of Israel for the purposes of Part I of the Foreign Judgments (Reciprocal Enforcement) Act 1933, that is to say: —

The Supreme Court ;
The District Courts ;
Rabbinical Courts ;
Moslem Religious Courts ;
Christian Religious Courts ;
Druze Religious Courts.

4. No security for costs shall be required to be given by any person making application for the registration of a judgment of a superior court of Israel.

5. A judgment of a superior court of Israel shall, in the absence of proof to the contrary, be deemed to be capable of execution in Israel if a certified copy of the judgment is produced authenticated by the court stamp and accompanied by a certificate issued by an officer of the original court that it is capable of execution in Israel.

6. The rate of interest due under the law of Israel upon the sum in respect of which a judgment of a superior court of Israel is given shall be deemed to be that specified in the judgment or any certificate of the original court accompanying the judgment and, if no rate is so specified, no interest shall be deemed to be due thereon under the law of Israel.

7. A translation of the judgment of a superior court of Israel or of any other document accompanying an application for registration of such a judgment shall, if certified by a notary or by a diplomatic or consular officer of either the United Kingdom or Israel, be accepted without further authentication.

W. G. Agnew.

SCHEDULE

CONVENTION
BETWEEN THE GOVERNMENT OF THE UNITED KINGDOM OF GREAT BRITAIN AND NORTHERN IRELAND AND THE GOVERNMENT OF ISRAEL PROVIDING FOR THE RECIPROCAL RECOGNITION AND ENFORCEMENT OF JUDGMENTS IN CIVIL MATTERS

The Government of the United Kingdom of Great Britain and Northern Ireland and the Government of Israel ;

Desiring to provide on the basis of reciprocity for the recognition and enforcement of judgments in civil matters ;

Have agreed as follows:

General

ARTICLE 1

For the purposes of this Convention:

(a) " territory " shall be interpreted in accordance with the provisions of Article 10 ;

(b) " judgment " means any decision of a court, however described (judgment, order or the like), by which the rights of the parties are determined and which cannot be altered by that court. It includes judgments against which an appeal may be pending or which may still be subject to appeal in the courts of the country of the original court. If the amount of the costs or interest to be paid under a judgment is not fixed by the judgment itself but by a separate court order, such order shall be deemed to be part of the judgment for the purposes of this Convention ;

(c) " original court " means in relation to any judgment the court by which such judgment was given ; and " court applied to " the court in which it is sought to obtain recognition of a judgment or to which an application for the registration of a judgment or for the grant of an enforcement declaration is made ;

(d) " judgment debtor " means the person against whom the judgment was given in the original court and includes, where necessary, any person against whom such judgment is enforceable under the law of the country of the original court ;

(e) " judgment creditor " means the person in whose favour the judgment was given and includes, where necessary, any other person in whom the rights under the judgment have become vested under the law of the country of the original court ;

(f) " appeal " includes any proceeding by way of discharging or setting aside a judgment or an application for a new trial or a stay of execution.

ARTICLE 2

(1) Subject to the provisions of paragraph (2) of this Article, this Convention shall apply to judgments in any civil proceedings, and to judgments in any criminal proceedings for the payment of a sum of money in respect of compensation or damages to an injured party, given after the date of the entry into force of this Convention by the following courts:

(a) in the case of the United Kingdom, the House of Lords; for England and Wales, the Supreme Court of Judicature (Court of Appeal and High Court of Justice) and the Courts of Chancery of the Counties Palatine of Lancaster and Durham; for Scotland, the Court of Session and the Sheriff Court; and for Northern Ireland, the Supreme Court of Judicature; and

(b) in the case of Israel, the Supreme Court, the District Courts, Rabbinical Courts, Moslem Religious Courts, Christian Religious Courts and Druze Religious Courts.

(2) This Convention shall not apply to:

(a) judgments given on appeal from courts not referred to in paragraph (1) of this Article;

(b) judgments given in proceedings for the recovery of taxes or other charges of a like nature or for the recovery of a fine or other penalty;

(c) judgments given in proceedings arising out of injury or damage falling within the definition of " nuclear damage " in the Vienna Convention of the 21st of May, 1963 on Civil Liability for Nuclear Damage(a).

(3) This Convention shall not preclude the recognition and enforcement in the territory of one Contracting Party, in accordance with the municipal law for the time being in force in the country concerned, of judgments given by any court in the territory of the other Contracting Party, being judgments to which this Convention does not apply or judgments given in circumstances where the provisions of this Convention do not require such recognition or enforcement.

Recognition of judgments

ARTICLE 3

(1) For the purposes of this Convention, the recognition of a judgment means that the judgment shall be treated as conclusive as to the matter thereby adjudicated upon in any further action as between the same parties (judgment creditor and judgment debtor).

(2) Judgments given in the territory of one Contracting Party shall be recognised in the territory of the other subject to the provisions of paragraphs (3), (4) and (5)

(a) Comd. 2333

of this Article and where no objection to the judgment can be established on any of the following grounds:

(a) in the case in question, the jurisdiction of the original court is not recognised under the provisions of Article 4 ;

(b) the judgment debtor, being the defendant in the proceedings in the original court, did not, notwithstanding that process may have been duly served on him in accordance with the law of the country of the original court, receive notice of those proceedings in sufficient time to enable him to defend the proceedings and did not appear, or if it is proved to the court applied to that he was not afforded a reasonable opportunity to present his arguments and to produce his evidence ;

(c) the judgment was, in the opinion of the court applied to, obtained by fraud ;

(d) the recognition of the judgment is likely to prejudice the sovereignty or safety of the State or would be contrary to public policy ;

(e) the judgment debtor, being a defendant in the original proceedings, was a person who, under the rules of public international law, was entitled to immunity from the jurisdiction of the courts of the country of the original court and did not submit to the jurisdiction of that court ;

(f) the judgment is sought to be enforced against a person who, under the rules of public international law, is entitled to immunity from the jurisdiction of the court applied to.

(3) Where the court applied to is satisfied that proceedings by way of appeal have been instituted against the judgment in the country of the original court, or that such proceedings have not been actually instituted, but the time for appeal has not elapsed under the law of that country, the court applied to may, in so far as the law of its country permits, recognise the judgment, refuse to recognise the judgment or adjourn its decision on the recognition of the judgment so as to allow the judgment debtor an opportunity of completing or of instituting such proceedings.

(4) Where the court applied to is satisfied that the matter in dispute in the proceedings in the original court had, previously to the date of the judgment in the original court, been the subject of a judgment by a court having jurisdiction in the matter, the court applied to may refuse to recognise the judgment of the original court.

(5) Where the court applied to is satisfied that, at the time when proceedings were instituted in the original court in the matter in dispute, proceedings as to the same matter between the same parties were pending before any court or tribunal of the country of the court applied to, the latter may refuse to recognise the judgment of the original court.

ARTICLE 4

(1) For the purposes of sub-paragraph (a) of paragraph (2) of Article 3, the courts of the country of the original court shall, subject to the provisions of

paragraphs (2) to (5) of this Article, be recognised as possessing jurisdiction in all cases :

(a) if the judgment debtor, being a defendant in the proceedings in the original court, submitted to the jurisdiction of that court by voluntarily appearing in the proceedings otherwise than for the purpose of protecting, or obtaining the release of, property seized, or threatened with seizure, in the proceedings or of contesting the jurisdiction of that court ; or

(b) if the judgment debtor was plaintiff or counter-claimant in the proceedings in the original court ; or

(c) if the judgment debtor, being a defendant in the proceedings in the original court, had before the commencement of the proceedings agreed, in respect of the subject matter of the proceedings, to submit to the jurisdiction of that court or of the courts of the country of that court ; or

(d) if the judgment debtor, being a defendant in the original court, was, at the time when the proceedings were instituted, resident, or being a body corporate had its principal place of business, in the country of that court ; or

(e) if the judgment debtor, being a defendant in the original court, had an office or place of business in the country of that court and the proceedings in that court were in respect of a transaction effected through or at that office or place.

(2) The provisions of paragraph (1) of this Article shall not apply to judgments where the subject matter of the proceedings was immovable property, unless such property was situated in the country of the original court.

(3) The provisions of paragraph (1) of this Article shall not apply to judgments given in actions of which the subject matter was ships, aircraft or their cargo, if, according to the law of either Contracting Party, they are conclusive not only against the parties to the proceedings but also against any other person claiming an interest in such ships, aircraft or their cargo inconsistent with the judgment. The jurisdiction of the original court shall, however, be recognised if such ships, aircraft or their cargo were situated in the country of the original court at the time of the commencement of the proceedings in that court.

(4) The jurisdiction of the original court need not be recognised in the cases specified in sub-paragraphs (d) and (e) of paragraph (1) and in paragraphs (2) and (3) of this Article, if the bringing of the proceedings in the original court was contrary to an agreement under which the dispute in question was to be settled otherwise than by proceedings in the courts of the country of the original court.

(5) The provisions of paragraph (1) of this Article shall not apply to judgments in any proceedings concerning matrimonial matters, administration of the estates of deceased persons, bankruptcy, winding up of companies, lunacy, guardianship

of infants or paternity. However, in the case of such judgments, the jurisdiction of the courts of the country of the original court shall be recognised where such recognition is in accordance with the law of the country of the court applied to.

Enforcement of judgments

ARTICLE 5

(1) Subject to the provisions of paragraph (2) of this Article, judgments given in the territory of one Contracting Party shall be enforced by execution in the territory of the other in the manner provided in Articles 6 to 8 of this Convention, provided that the following conditions are fulfilled:

(a) they are enforceable by execution in the country of the original court ;

(b) there is payable thereunder a sum of money ;

(c) the judgment debt has not been wholly satisfied ;

(d) they are recognised by the court applied to under the provisions of Article 3.

(2) Where the court applied to is satisfied that proceedings by way of appeal have been instituted against the judgment in the country of the original court, or that such proceedings have not been actually instituted, but the time for appeal has not elapsed under the law of that country, the court applied to may, in so far as the law of its country permits, enforce the judgment, refuse to enforce the judgment or adjourn its decision on the enforcement of the judgment so as to allow the judgment debtor an opportunity of completing or of instituting such proceedings.

ARTICLE 6

(1) In order that a judgment given in the courts of Israel may be enforced in the territory within the jurisdiction of the courts of the United Kingdom, an application by a judgment creditor for its registration should, in accordance with the procedure of the court applied to, be made:

(a) in England and Wales, to the High Court of Justice ;

(b) in Scotland, to the Court of Session ; and

(c) in Northern Ireland, to the Supreme Court of Judicature.

(2) The application for registration should be accompanied by:

(a) a certified copy of the complete judgment authenticated by the court stamp and accompanied by a certificate issued by an officer of the original court that it is capable of execution in the country of that court ;

(b) an affidavit of the facts required by the rules of the court applied to ;

(c) a translation into English of any document required by this paragraph certified by a notary or by a diplomatic or consular officer of either Contracting Party.

(3) The documents enumerated in paragraph (2) shall require no further authentication.

(4) If an application is made in accordance with paragraphs (1) and (2) of this Article in respect of a judgment fulfilling the conditions laid down in Article 5, registration shall be granted.

ARTICLE 7

(1) In order that a judgment given in the courts of the United Kingdom may be enforced in the territory within the jurisdiction of the courts of Israel, an application by a judgment creditor for the grant of an enforcement declaration should, in accordance with the procedure of the court applied to, be made to the District Court of Jerusalem.

(2) The application for the grant of an enforcement declaration should be accompanied by:

(a) a certified copy of the judgment authenticated by the court seal, or in the case of judgments of the Sheriff Court, authenticated by the signature of the Sheriff Clerk;

(b) an affidavit of the facts required by the rules of the court applied to;

(c) a certificate issued by the original court giving particulars of the proceedings and a statement of the grounds on which the judgment was based, and specifying whether at the date of the issue of the certificate the time for appeal has elapsed without any proceedings by way of appeal having been instituted against the judgment in the United Kingdom;

(d) a translation into Hebrew of any document required by this paragraph certified by a sworn translator or by a diplomatic or consular officer of either Contracting Party.

(3) The documents enumerated in paragraph (2) shall require no further authentication.

(4) If an application is made in accordance with paragraphs (1) and (2) of this Article in respect of a judgment fulfilling the conditions laid down in Article 5, an enforcement declaration shall be granted.

ARTICLE 8

(1) From the date on which it is granted registration under Article 6 or an enforcement declaration under Article 7 a judgment shall, for the purpose of its execution by virtue of that grant, have effect in the country of the court applied to as if it were a judgment originally given in that country on that date.

(2) The procedure for the registration of a judgment under Article 6 and the procedure for the grant of an enforcement declaration of a judgment under Article 7 shall be as simple and rapid as possible, and no security for costs shall be required of any person making application for such registration or for the grant of an enforcement declaration.

(3) A period of not less than six years, running from the date of the judgment of the original court if no appeal has been brought to a higher court in the country of the original court or from the date of the judgment given in the last instance if such an appeal has been brought, shall be allowed by the court applied to for the purpose of making any application for registration or for a grant of an enforcement declaration.

(4) if it is found by the court applied to that the judgment of the original court is in respect of different matters and that one or more, but not all, of the provisions of the judgment are such that, if those provisions had been contained in separate judgments, those judgments could properly have been registered or could have been granted an enforcement declaration, the judgment may be registered or granted an enforcement declaration in respect only of the provisions aforesaid.

(5) If it is found by the court applied to that the judgment has been, at the date of the application, partly but not wholly satisfied by payment, the judgment shall be registered or an enforcement declaration shall be granted in respect of the balance remaining payable at that date, provided that the judgment is otherwise one which would be enforceable under the provisions of this Convention.

(6) If under a judgment a sum of money is payable which is expressed in a currency other than that of the country of the court applied to, the law of the country of the court applied to shall determine if, and if so in what manner and in what conditions, the amount payable under the judgment may or shall be converted into the currency of the country of the court applied to for the purposes of the satisfaction or enforcement of the judgment debt.

(7) When granting registration or an enforcement declaration, the court applied to shall, if so requested by the judgment creditor, include the costs of an incidental to registration or the grant of an enforcement declaration.

(8) Where a judgment is granted registration or an enforcement declaration it shall carry, in respect of the period up to the date of the grant, interest at the rate, if any, specified in the judgment or in any certificate of the original court accompanying the judgment. As from the date of the grant, interest shall be allowed at 4 per cent. per annum on the total sum (principal and interest) in respect of which the registration or the enforcement declaration is granted.

Final provisions

ARTICLE 9

Any difficulties which may arise in connexion with the interpretation or application of this Convention shall be settled through the diplomatic channel.

ARTICLE 10

(1) This Convention shall apply in the case of the Government of the United Kingdom of Great Britain and Northern Ireland to the territory within the jurisdiction of the courts of England and Wales, Scotland and Northern Ireland, and in the case of the Government of Israel, to the territory within the jurisdiction of the courts of Israel.

(2) The Government of the United Kingdom may, by a notification given through the diplomatic channel, at any time while this Convention is in force, and provided that an agreement has been concluded by an Exchange of Notes on the points mentioned in paragraph (3) of this Article, extend the operation of this Convention to any territory for whose international relations the Government of the United Kingdom are responsible.

(3) Prior to any notification of extension in respect of any territory under the preceding paragraph, an agreement shall be concluded between the Contracting Parties by an Exchange of Notes as to the courts of the territory concerned which shall be courts to whose judgments this Convention shall apply, and the courts to which application for the registration of any judgment shall be made.

(4) The date of the coming into force of any extension under this Article shall be three months from the date of the notification given under paragraph (2) of this Article.

(5) Either of the Contracting Parties may, at any time after the expiry of three years from the coming into force of an extension of this Convention to any of the territories referred to in paragraph (2) of this Article, terminate such extension on giving six months' notice of termination through the diplomatic channel.

(6) The termination of this Convention under Article 11 shall, unless otherwise expressly agreed by both Contracting Parties, also terminate it in respect of any territory to which it has been extended under paragraph (2) of this Article.

ARTICLE 11

This Convention shall be subject to ratification. Instruments of ratification shall be exchanged as soon as possible. The Convention shall come into force three months after the date on which the instruments of ratification are exchanged and shall remain in force for three years after the date of its coming into force. If neither of the Contracting Parties shall have given notice through the diplomatic channel to the other, not less than six months before the expiration of the said period of three years, of intention to terminate the Convention, it shall remain in force until the expiration of six months from the date on which either of the Contracting Parties shall have given notice to terminate it.

In witness whereof the undersigned, being duly authorised thereto by their respective Governments, have signed this Convention.

Done in duplicate at London this 28th day of October, 1970, corresponding to the 28th day of Tishri, 5731, in the English and Hebrew languages, both texts being equally authoritative.

For the Government of the United
  Kingdom of Great Britain and
  Northern Ireland:

For the Government of Israel:

JOSEPH GODBER

MICHAEL COMAY

EXPLANATORY NOTE

(This Note is not part of the Order.)

This Order extends Part I of the Foreign Judgments (Reciprocal Enforcement) Act 1933 to the judgments of the superior courts of Israel and makes certain provisions regarding the registration and enforcement of such judgments.

Relevant judgments given on or after the 26th July 1971 will be enforceable in the United Kingdom upon registration in the High Court, the Court of Session or the Supreme Court of Judicature in Northern Ireland.

STATUTORY INSTRUMENTS

1971 No. 1040

PETROLEUM

The Petroleum (Inflammable Liquids) Order 1971

Made - - -	*23rd June* 1971
Coming into Operation	*1st July* 1971

At the Court at Buckingham Palace, the 23rd day of June 1971

Present,

The Queen's Most Excellent Majesty in Council

Her Majesty, in exercise of the powers conferred on Her by section 19 of the Petroleum (Consolidation) Act 1928(a), is pleased, by and with the advice of Her Privy Council, to order, and it is hereby ordered, as follows :—

1.—(1) This Order may be cited as the Petroleum (Inflammable Liquids) Order 1971 and shall come into operation on 1st July 1971, except that for the purpose of making any regulations under section 6 of the Petroleum (Consolidation) Act 1928 as applied by this Order to come into operation on or after the said date this Order shall come into operation forthwith.

(2) The Petroleum (Inflammable Liquids) Order 1968(b) is hereby revoked.

(3) The Interpretation Act 1889(c) shall apply to the interpretation of this Order as it applies to the interpretation of an Act of Parliament, and as if this Order and the Order revoked by this Order were Acts of Parliament.

2.—(1) Sections 6, 13(2) and (3), 14, 15, 16 and 18 of the Petroleum (Consolidation) Act 1928 shall apply to such of the following substances, solutions and mixtures as give off an inflammable vapour at a temperature below 23 degrees Centigrade (73 degrees Fahrenheit), that is to say—

(a) the substances specified in the first column in Part I of the Schedule to this Order, being substances which are known also by the name or names (if any) mentioned in the second column ;

(b) any solution or mixture (not being a mixture of petroleum as defined in the Schedule to the Petroleum (Mixtures) Order 1929(d)) which contains any of the said substances ; and

(c) any solution specified in Part II of the Schedule to this Order.

(a) 1928 c. 32.   (b) S.I. 1968/570 (1968 I, p. 1300).
(c) 1889 c. 63.
(d) S.R. & O. 1929/993 (Rev. XVIII, p. 7: 1929, p. 1143).

(2) For the purposes of this Article a substance, solution or mixture shall be regarded as giving off an inflammable vapour at a temperature below 23 degrees Centigrade (73 degrees Fahrenheit) if it does so when tested as if it were petroleum-spirit in the manner set forth in Part II of Schedule 2 to the said Act of 1928.

3. Nothing in this Order shall render invalid any order, notice, direction or warrant made, given or issued, or other thing done, under any provision of the Petroleum (Consolidation) Act 1928 as applied by the Petroleum (Inflammable Liquids) Order 1968, and any such order, notice, direction, warrant or thing which could have been made, given, issued or done under any such provision as applied by this Order and in force or having effect at the date when this Order comes into operation shall be deemed to have been made, given, issued or done under that provision as applied by this Order.

W. G. Agnew.

SCHEDULE

PART I

Name of substance	Alternative name or names
Acetaldehyde	Ethanal
Acetaldehyde oxime	Acetaldoxime
Acetone	Dimethyl ketone Propanone
Acrylaldehyde	Acraldehyde Acrolein Allyl aldehyde Propenal
Acrylonitrile	Propenenitrile Vinyl cyanide
Allyl acetate	
Allyl alcohol	Prop-2-en-l-ol 2-Propen-l-ol
Allylamine	2-Propenylamine
Allyl bromide	3-Bromopropene
Allyl chloride	3-Chloropropene
Allyl ethyl ether	3-Ethoxypropene
Allyl formate	2-Propenyl methanoate
Benzenethiol	Thiophenol
Benzotrifluoride	Trifluoromethylbenzene
Bicycloheptadiene	
Boron trifluoride diethyl etherate	
2-Bromobutane	*sec*Butyl bromide
1-Bromo-2, 3-epoxypropane	Epibromohydrin
2-Bromoethyl ethyl ether	

SCHEDULE—*continued*

PART I—*continued*

Name of substance	*Alternative name or names*
1-Bromo-3-methylbutane	*iso*Amyl bromide
1-Bromo-2-methylpropane	*iso*Butyl bromide
2-Bromo-2-methylpropane	*tert*Butyl bromide
2-Bromopentane	*sec*Amyl bromide
1-Bromopropane	Propyl bromide
2-Bromopropane	*iso*Propyl bromide
3-Bromopropyne	Propargyl bromide
Butanedione	Diacetyl
Butane-1-thiol	{ n-Butane thiol { Butyl mercaptan
Butan-2-ol	{ *sec*Butanol { *sec*Butyl alcohol
Butanone	{ Ethyl methyl ketone { Methyl ethyl ketone
But-3-en-2-one	{ 3-Butene-2-one { Methyl vinyl ketone
*iso*Butyl acetate	
*sec*Butyl acetate	2-Butanol acetate
Butylamine	1-Aminobutane
*iso*Butylamine	1-Amino-2-methylpropane
*sec*Butylamine	2-Aminobutane
*tert*Butylamine	{ 2-Amino-2-methylpropane { 2-Amino *iso*butane
Butyl ethyl ether	1-Ethoxybutane
Butyl formate	Butyl methanoate
*iso*Butyl formate	
Butyl methyl ether	1-Methoxybutane
Butyl nitrite	
*iso*Butyl propionate	
Butyl vinyl ether	
*iso*Butyl vinyl ether	
But-2-yne	{ 2-Butine { Crotonylene { Dimethyl acetylene
Butyraldehyde	Butanal
*iso*Butyraldehyde	2-Methylpropanal
Butyronitrile	Propyl cyanide
Butyryl chloride	Butanoyl chloride
*iso*Butyryl chloride	*iso*Butanoyl chloride
1-Chlorobutane	Butyl chloride
2-Chlorobutane	*sec*Butyl chloride
1-Chloro-3-methylbutane	*iso*Amyl chloride
2-Chloro-2-methylbutane	*tert*Amyl chloride
Chloromethyl ethyl ether	
Chloromethyl methyl ether	{ Chlorodimethyl ether { Chloromethoxy methane
1-Chloro-2-methylpropane	*iso*Butyl chloride
2-Chloro-2-methylpropane	*tert*Butyl chloride
3-Chloro-2-methylprop-l-ene	
1-Chloropentane	Amyl chloride

SCHEDULE—*continued*

PART I—*continued*

Name of substance	*Alternative name or names*
1-Chloropropane	Propyl chloride
2-Chloropropane	*iso*Propyl chloride
Crotonaldehyde	{ 2-Butenal *β*-Methyl acrolein Propyl aldehyde Propylene aldehyde
Cycloheptatriene	
Cyclohexene	Tetrahydrobenzine
Cyclohexylamine	Aminocyclohexane
Cyclo-octatetraene	
Diacetone alcohol	{ Diacetone, technical 4-Hydroxy-2-keto-4-methylpentane 4-Hydroxy-4-methylpentan-2-one
Diallylamine	Di-2-propenylamine
Diallyl ether	
Di*iso*butene	Di*iso*butylene
Di*iso*butylamine	
1,1-Dichloroethane	Ethylidene chloride
1,2-Dichloroethane	Ethylene dichloride
1,1-Dichloroethylene	Vinylidene chloride
1,2-Dichloroethylene	Acetylene dichloride
1,2-Dichloropropane	{ Propylene chloride Propylene dichloride
1,2-Di (dimethylamino) ethane	Tetramethyl ethylene diamine
1,1-Diethoxyethane	{ Acetal Diethyl acetal Ethylidene diethyl ether
Diethoxymethane	{ Diethyl formal Ethylal methylene diethyl ether Formaldehyde diethyl acetal
3,3-Diethoxypropene	Acrolein acetal
Diethylamine	
Diethyl ether	{ Diethyl oxide Ethoxyethane Ethyl ether
Diethyl sulphide	
2,3-Dihydropyran	
1,1-Dimethoxyethane	{ Dimethyl acetal Ethylidene dimethyl ether
Dimethoxymethane	{ Methylal Methylene dimethyl ether
2-Dimethylaminoacetonitrile	2-Dimethylaminoethyl cyanide
1,3-Dimethylbutylamine	2-Amino-4-methylpentane
Dimethyl carbonate	Methyl carbonate
Dimethyldichlorosilane	
Dimethyldiethoxysilane	
Dimethyl disulphide	
NN-Dimethylhydrazine	1,1-Dimethylhydrazine
NN'-Dimethylhydrazine	1,2-Dimethylhydrazine

SCHEDULE—*continued*

PART I—*continued*

Name of substance	*Alternative name or names*
Dimethyl sulphide	{ Methanthiomethane { Methyl sulphide
1,4-Dioxan	{ 1,4-Diethylene dioxide { Dioxan { Dioxyethylene ether
Dioxolane	
Dipropylamine	
Di*iso*propylamine	
Dipropyl ether	
Di*iso*propyl ether	{ 2-*iso*Propoxypropane { *iso*Propyl ether
Divinyl ether	Vinyl ether
Ethane thiol	Ethyl mercaptan
Ethanol	Ethyl alcohol
Ethyl acetate	
Ethyl acrylate	Ethyl propenoate
2-Ethylbutyraldehyde	Diethyl acetaldehyde
Ethyl *iso*butyrate	{ *iso*Butyric ether { Ethyl 2-methylpropanoate
Ethyl chloroformate	Ethyl chlorocarbonate
Ethyl crotonate	
Ethyldichlorosilane	
Ethyleneimine	{ Aziridene { Dimethyleneimine
Ethyl formate	Ethyl methanoate
Ethyl nitrite	
1-Ethylpiperidine	N-Ethylpiperidine
Ethyl propionate	
Ethyltrichlorosilane	
Ethyl vinyl ether	
Flurobenzene	
2-Fluorotoluene	o-Fluorotoluene
3-Fluorotoluene	m-Fluorotoluene
Furan	
Fusel oil	
2-Iodobutane	*sec*Butyl iodide
1-Iodo-2-methylpropane	*iso*Butyl iodide
2-Iodo-2-methylpropane	*tert*Butyl iodide
1-Iodopropane	Propyl iodide
2-Iodopropane	*iso*Propyl iodide
Iron carbonyl	Iron pentacarbonyl
Isoprene monomer	2-Methyl-1,3-butadiene
Methacraldehyde	{ *a*-Methacrolein { 2-Methylpropenal
Methanol	Methyl alcohol
Methyl acetate	
Methyl acetone	
Methyl acrylate	
Methylated spirit	

SCHEDULE—*continued*

PART I—*continued*

Name of substance	*Alternative name or names*
3-Methylbutane-1-thiol	Amyl mercaptan Pentanethiol
2-Methylbutan-2-ol	*tert*Amyl alcohol Ethyl dimethyl carbinol 2-Methyl-2-butanol
3-Methylbutan-1-ol	*iso*Amyl alcohol
3-Methylbutan-2-one	3-Methyl-2-butanone Methyl *iso*propyl ketone
Methyl *tert*butyl ether	
Methyl butyrate	
Methyl chloroformate	Methyl chlorocarbonate
Methyldichlorosilane	Methylhydrogendichlorosilane
N-Methylformamide	Form-methylamide
Methyl formate	
Methylhydrazine	
Methyl methacrylate, monomer	
2-Methylpentan-2-ol	
4-Methylpentan-2-one	*iso*Butyl methyl ketone Hexone Methyl *iso*butyl ketone 4-Methyl-2-pentanone
1-Methylpiperidine	N-Methyl piperidine
2-Methylpropan-2-ol	*tert*Butanol *tert*Butyl alcohol 2-Methyl-2-propanol Trimethyl carbinol
Methyl propionate	
Methyltrichlorosilane	
2-Methylvaleraldehyde	*a*-Methylvaleraldehyde
Methyl *iso*valerate	
Nickel carbonyl	Nickel tetracarbonyl
Paraldehyde	
Pentan-2-ol	*sec*Amyl alcohol Methyl propyl carbinol 2-Pentanol
Pentan-2-one	Ethyl acetone Methyl propyl ketone 2-Pentanone
Pentan-3-one	Diethyl ketone Ethyl propionyl Metacetone Propione
*iso*Pentyl acetate	*iso*Amyl acetate
Pentylamine	1-Aminopentane n-Amylamine
*iso*Pentylamine	*iso*Amylamine
Pentyl nitrite	n-Amyl nitrite

SCHEDULE—*continued*

Part I—*continued*

Name of substance	*Alternative name or names*
*iso*Pentyl nitrite	*iso*Amyl nitrite
1-Phenylpropane-1,2-dione	
Piperidine	
Propane-1-thiol	Propyl mercaptan
Propane-2-thiol	*iso*Propyl mercaptan

Propan-1-ol
$\begin{cases} \text{1-Propanol} \\ \text{Propyl alcohol} \end{cases}$

Propan-2-ol
$\begin{cases} \text{Dimethyl carbinol} \\ \text{2-Propanol} \\ iso\text{Propanol} \\ iso\text{Propyl alcohol} \\ sec\text{Propyl alcohol} \end{cases}$

*iso*Propenyl acetate	
Propionaldehyde	
Propionitrile	Ethyl cyanide
Propyl acetate	
*iso*Propyl acetate	
Propylamine	
*iso*Propylamine	
*iso*Propyl butyrate	
*iso*Propyl *iso*butyrate	
*iso*Propyl chloroformate	
Propyleneimine	

Propylene oxide
$\begin{cases} \text{1,2-Epoxy propane} \\ \text{Methyloxiran} \\ \text{Propene oxide} \end{cases}$

Propyl formate	
*iso*Propyl formate	
Propyl nitrate	
*iso*Propyl nitrate	
*iso*Propyl propionate	
Pyridine	
Pyrrolidine	
Tetrahydrofuran	
1,2,3,6-Tetrahydropyridine	
Tetrahydrothiophen	Tetramethylene sulphide
Tetrapropyl orthotitanate	
Thioacetic acid	
Thiophen	
Triethylamine	

Triethyl borate
$\begin{cases} \text{Ethylborate} \\ \text{Triethoxyboron} \end{cases}$

Trimethyl borate	Trimethoxyborine
Trimethylchlorosilane	

*iso*Valeraldehyde
$\begin{cases} iso\text{Amyl aldehyde} \\ \text{3-Methyl butanal} \\ \beta\text{-Methyl valeraldehyde} \end{cases}$

Vinyl acetate	
Vinyltrichlorosilane	

PART II

Dimethylamine solution in alcohol or water.

Ethylamine solution in alcohol or water.

Glyceryl trinitrate (otherwise known as nitroglycerine) solution in alcohol, not exceeding 5 per cent. of glyceryl trinitrate.

Methylamine solution in alcohol or water.

Trimethylamine solution in alcohol or water.

EXPLANATORY NOTE

(*This Note is not part of the Order.*)

This Order revokes and reproduces with amendments the Petroleum (Inflammable Liquids) Order 1968. In the list of substances to which specified provisions of the Petroleum (Consolidation) Act 1928 are applied by the Order, certain substances are added and certain substances are omitted. The exclusion of substances which do not give off an inflammable vapour at a temperature below 23° Centigrade (73° Fahrenheit) is extended to all substances mentioned in the list (not only, as at present, to certain specified solutions), and for the purpose of determining whether they do so the manner of testing provided by Schedule 2 to the Act for petroleum-spirit is applied. Changes are made in the alternative names set out in the second column of the list and in nomenclature generally.

STATUTORY INSTRUMENTS

1971 No. 1048

CUSTOMS AND EXCISE

The Anti-Dumping Duty (No. 3) Order 1971

Made - - - -	*23rd June* 1971
Laid before the *House of Commons*	*25th June* 1971
Coming into Operation	*30th June* 1971

Whereas by the Anti-Dumping (Provisional Charge to Duty) (No. 2) Order 1971(a), which came into operation on 1st April 1971, goods of the description set out in the Schedule hereto were made subject to a provisional charge in respect of an anti-dumping duty of £5 per ton:

And whereas the said Order remains in force:

Now, therefore, the Secretary of State in exercise of his powers under Sections 1, 2, 8(1) and 15(4) of the Customs Duties (Dumping and Subsidies) Act 1969(b) hereby makes the following Order:—

1.—(1) This Order may be cited as the Anti-Dumping Duty (No. 3) Order 1971 and shall come into operation on 30th June 1971.

(2) The Interpretation Act 1889(c) shall apply to the interpretation of this Order as it applies to the interpretation of an Act of Parliament and as if this Order and the Order hereby revoked were Acts of Parliament.

2. There shall be charged on the import into the United Kingdom on a date not earlier than 1st April 1971 nor later than 22nd June 1971 of any goods of the description set out in the Schedule hereto (being goods classified in the Customs Tariff 1959(d) under the heading mentioned in the first column of that Schedule) a duty of customs at the rate mentioned in the third column.

3. Section 2 of the Customs Duties (Dumping and Subsidies) Act 1969 shall apply to the duty imposed by this Order.

4. The Anti-Dumping (Provisional Charge to Duty) (No. 2) Order 1971 is hereby revoked.

Michael Noble,
Minister for Trade,
Department of Trade and Industry.

23rd June 1971.

(a) S.I. 1971/519 (1971 I, p. 1521).   (b) 1969 c. 16.   (c) 1889 c. 63.
(d) See S.I. 1970/1522 (1970 III, p. 4935).

SCHEDULE

Relevant Tariff Heading	Description of Goods	Rate of Duty
31.02(B)	Ammonium nitrate originating in Rumania ...	£3·39 per ton

EXPLANATORY NOTE

(This Note is not part of the Order.)

This Order imposes an anti-dumping duty of £3·39 per ton on Rumanian ammonium nitrate. The duty is imposed retrospectively in relation to a period beginning on the 1st April 1971 (when such goods became subject to a provisional charge to duty of £5 per ton), and ending on the 22nd June 1971.

The Order applies to the duty Section 2 of the Customs Duties (Dumping and Subsidies) Act 1969, which enables relief to be granted where particular goods have not been dumped or the margin of dumping is less than the amount of the duty.

The Order also revokes the Anti-Dumping (Provisional Charge to Duty) (No. 2) Order 1971 which imposed the provisional charge mentioned above together with a distinct charge upon calcium ammonium nitrate originating in Rumania. The additional £1·61 per ton of any provisional charge paid in respect of Rumanian ammonium nitrate and the whole of any charge paid in respect of Rumanian calcium ammonium nitrate are now refundable.

STATUTORY INSTRUMENTS

1971 No. 1049

INDUSTRIAL TRAINING

The Industrial Training Levy (Road Transport) Order 1971

Made - - -	*23rd June* 1971
Laid before Parliament	*1st July* 1971
Coming into Operation	*14th July* 1971

The Secretary of State after approving proposals submitted by the Road Transport Industry Training Board for the imposition of a further levy on employers in the road transport industry and in exercise of his powers under section 4 of the Industrial Training Act 1964(a) and of all other powers enabling him in that behalf hereby makes the following Order :—

Title and commencement

1. This Order may be cited as the Industrial Training Levy (Road Transport) Order 1971 and shall come into operation on 14th July 1971.

Interpretation

2.—(1) In this Order unless the context otherwise requires :—

(*a*) "agriculture" has the same meaning as in section 109(3) of the Agriculture Act 1947(b) or, in relation to Scotland, as in section 86(3) of the Agriculture (Scotland) Act 1948(c) ;

(*b*) "an appeal tribunal" means an industrial tribunal established under section 12 of the Industrial Training Act 1964 ;

(*c*) "assessment" means an assessment of an employer to the levy ;

(*d*) "the Board" means the Road Transport Industry Training Board ;

(*e*) "business" means any activities of industry or commerce ;

(*f*) "charity" has the same meaning as in section 360 of the Income and Corporation Taxes Act 1970(d) ;

(*g*) "emoluments" means all emoluments assessable to income tax under Schedule E (other than pensions), being emoluments from which tax under that Schedule is deductible, whether or not tax in fact falls to be deducted from any particular payment thereof ;

(*h*) "employer" means a person who is an employer in the road transport industry at any time in the fifth levy period ;

(a) 1964 c. 16.   (b) 1947 c. 48.
(c) 1948 c. 45.   (d) 1970 c. 10.

(*i*) "the fifth base period" means the period of twelve months that commenced on 6th April 1970 ;

(*j*) "the fifth levy period" means the period commencing with the day upon which this Order comes into operation and ending on 5th April 1972 ;

(*k*) "the industrial training order" means the Industrial Training (Road Transport Board) Order 1969(**a**) as amended by the Industrial Training (Road Transport Board) Order 1969 (Amendment) Order 1969(**b**);

(*l*) "the levy" means the levy imposed by the Board in respect of the fifth levy period ;

(*m*) "notice" means a notice in writing ;

(*n*) "road transport establishment" means an establishment in Great Britain engaged in the fifth base period wholly or mainly in the road transport industry for a total of twenty-seven or more weeks or, being an establishment that commenced to carry on business in the fifth base period, for a total number of weeks exceeding one half of the number of weeks in the part of the said period commencing with the day on which business was commenced and ending on the last day thereof ;

(*o*) "the road transport industry" means any one or more of the activities which, subject to the provisions of paragraph 2 of the Schedule to the industrial training order, are specified in paragraph 1 of that Schedule as the activities of the road transport industry ;

(*p*) other expressions have the same meaning as in the industrial training order.

(2) Any reference in this Order to persons employed at or from a road transport establishment shall in any case where the employer is a company be construed as including a reference to any director of the company (or any person occupying the position of director by whatever name he is called) who devotes substantially the whole of his time to the service of the company.

(3) In the case where a road transport establishment is taken over (whether directly or indirectly) by an employer in succession to, or jointly with, another person, a person employed at any time in the fifth base period at or from the establishment shall be deemed, for the purposes of this Order, to have been so employed by the employer carrying on the said establishment on the day upon which this Order comes into operation, and any reference in this Order to persons employed by the employer at or from a road transport establishment in the fifth base period shall be construed accordingly.

(4) Any reference in this Order to an establishment that commences to carry on business or that ceases to carry on business shall not be taken to apply where the location of the establishment is changed but its business is continued wholly or mainly at or from the new location, or where the suspension of activities is of a temporary or seasonal nature.

(5) The Interpretation Act 1889(**c**) shall apply to the interpretation of this Order as it applies to the interpretation of an Act of Parliament.

(a) S.I. 1969/879 (1969 II, p. 2495). (b) S.I. 1969/1871 (1969 III, p. 5815).
(c) 1889 c. 63.

Imposition of the levy

3.—(1) The levy to be imposed by the Board on employers in respect of the fifth levy period shall be assessed in accordance with the provisions of this Article.

(2) The levy shall be assessed by the Board in respect of each employer, not being an employer who is exempt from the levy by virtue of paragraph (5) of this Article, and, subject to the provisions of this Article, the amount thereof shall be the following percentage of the sum of the emoluments of all the persons employed by the employer in the fifth base period at or from his road transport establishment or establishments (being an establishment or establishments carrying on business in the fifth levy period), that is to say—

(*a*) where the said sum exceeded £5,000, but was less than £30,000, 1·5 per cent.;

(*b*) where the said sum was £30,000 or more, 2·2 per cent..

(3) Where any persons whose emoluments are taken into account for the purposes of paragraph (2) of this Article were employed at or from an establishment that ceases to carry on business in the fifth levy period, the sum of the emoluments of those persons shall, for the purposes of the assessment, be reduced in the same proportion as the number of days between the commencement of the said levy period and the date of cessation of business (both dates inclusive) bears to the number of days in the said levy period, but the appropriate percentage shall be determined in accordance with the provisions of the said paragraph as if the provisions of this paragraph did not apply.

(4) For the purposes of this Article no regard shall be had to the emoluments of any person employed as follows :—

(*a*) by the London Transport Executive wholly in any activities to which paragraph 1(*o*) of the Schedule to the industrial training order applies, not being activities that are specified in head (ii) (v) or (vi) of paragraph 3(*p*) of that Schedule and are incidental or ancillary to principal activities of the road transport industry ;

(*b*) by a local authority or a joint board or joint committee of such authorities in any activities, not being activities carried out for the purposes of a passenger road transport service provided by the authority, board or committee ;

(*c*) wholly in agriculture ;

(*d*) wholly as a registered dock worker on dock work ; or

(*e*) wholly in the supply of food or drink for immediate consumption.

(5) There shall be exempt from the levy—

(*a*) an employer in whose case the sum of the emoluments of all the persons employed by him in the fifth base period at or from the road transport establishment or establishments of the employer was £5,000 or less ;

(*b*) a charity.

Assessment Notices

4.—(1) The Board shall serve an assessment notice on every employer assessed to the levy.

(2) The amount payable under an assessment notice shall be rounded down to the nearest £1.

(3) An assessment notice shall state the Board's address for the service of a notice of appeal or of an application for an extension of time for appealing.

(4) An assessment notice may be served on the person assessed to the levy either by delivering it to him personally or by leaving it, or sending it to him by post, at his last known address or place of business in the United Kingdom or, if that person is a corporation, by leaving it, or sending it by post to the corporation, at such address or place of business or at its registered or principal office.

Payment of levy

5.—(1) Subject to the provisions of this Article and of Articles 6 and 7, the amount of the levy payable under an assessment notice served by the Board shall be payable to the Board as follows—

> (a) where paragraph 2(a) of Article 3 of this Order applies, by one payment due one month after the date of the assessment notice ; or

> (b) where paragraph 2(b) of the said Article applies, by two instalments, the first of which shall be equal to 1·5% of the sum of the emoluments by reference to which the amount of the said levy has been assessed in accordance with the provisions of the said Article, and the second equal to the balance of the amount payable under the assessment notice. The first of the said instalments shall be due one month after the date of the assessment notice and the second on 1st March 1972.

(2) No part of an assessment shall be recoverable by the Board until there has expired the time allowed for appealing against the assessment by Article 7(1) of this Order and any further period or periods of time that the Board or an appeal tribunal may have allowed for appealing under paragraph (2) or (3) of that Article or, where an appeal is brought, until the appeal is decided or withdrawn.

Withdrawal of assessment

6.—(1) The Board may, by a notice served on the person assessed to the levy in the same manner as an assessment notice, withdraw an assessment if that person has appealed against that assessment under the provisions of Article 7 of this Order and the appeal has not been entered in the Register of Appeals kept under the appropriate Regulations specified in paragraph (5) of that Article.

(2) The withdrawal of an assessment shall be without prejudice to the power of the Board to serve a further assessment notice on the employer, and where the withdrawal is made by reason of the fact that an establishment has ceased to carry on business in the fifth levy period, the said notice may provide that the whole amount payable thereunder shall be due one month after the date of the notice.

Appeals

7.—(1) A person assessed to the levy may appeal to an appeal tribunal against the assessment within one month from the date of the service of the assessment notice or within any further period or periods of time that may be allowed by the Board or an appeal tribunal under the following provisions of this Article.

(2) The Board by notice may for good cause allow a person assessed to the levy to appeal to an appeal tribunal against the assessment at any time within the period of four months from the date of the service of the assessment notice or within such further period or periods as the Board may allow before such time as may then be limited for appealing has expired.

(3) If the Board shall not allow an application for extension of time for appealing, an appeal tribunal shall upon application made to the tribunal by the person assessed to the levy have the like powers as the Board under the last foregoing paragraph.

(4) In the case of an assessment that has reference to an establishment that ceases to carry on business in the fifth levy period on any day after the date of the service of the assessment notice, the foregoing provisions of this Article shall have effect as if for the period of four months from the date of the service of the assessment notice mentioned in paragraph (2) of this Article there were substituted the period of six months from the date of the cessation of business.

(5) An appeal or an application to an appeal tribunal under this Article shall be made in accordance with the Industrial Tribunals (England and Wales) Regulations 1965(**a**) as amended by the Industrial Tribunals (England and Wales) (Amendment) Regulations 1967(**b**) except where the assessment relates to persons employed at or from one or more establishments which are wholly in Scotland and to no other persons in which case the appeal or application shall be made in accordance with the Industrial Tribunals (Scotland) Regulations 1965(**c**) as amended by the Industrial Tribunals (Scotland) (Amendment) Regulations 1967(**d**).

(6) The powers of an appeal tribunal under paragraph (3) of this Article may be exercised by the President of the Industrial Tribunals (England and Wales) or by the President of the Industrial Tribunals (Scotland) as the case may be.

Evidence

8.—(1) Upon the discharge by a person assessed to the levy of his liability under an assessment the Board shall if so requested issue to him a certificate to that effect.

(2) The production in any proceedings of a document purporting to be certified by the Secretary of the Board to be a true copy of an assessment or other notice issued by the Board or purporting to be a certificate such as is mentioned in the foregoing paragraph of this Article shall, unless the contrary is proved, be sufficient evidence of the document and of the facts stated therein.

Signed by order of the Secretary of State.
23rd June 1971.

Paul Bryan,
Minister of State,
Department of Employment.

(**a**) S.I. 1965/1101 (1965 II, p. 2805). (**b**) S.I. 1967/301 (1967 I, p. 1040).
(**c**) S.I. 1965/1157 (1965 II, p. 3266). (**d**) S.I. 1967/302 (1967 I, p. 1050).

EXPLANATORY NOTE

(This Note is not part of the Order.)

This Order gives effect to proposals submitted by the Road Transport Industry Training Board to the Secretary of State for Employment for the imposition of a further levy upon employers in the road transport industry for the purpose of raising money towards the expenses of the Board.

The levy is to be imposed in respect of the fifth levy period commencing with the day upon which this Order comes into operation and ending on 5th April 1972. The levy will be assessed by the Board and there will be a right of appeal against an assessment to an industrial tribunal.

STATUTORY INSTRUMENTS

1971 No. 1054

SOCIAL SECURITY

The Supplementary Benefit (Determination of Requirements) Regulations 1971

Laid before Parliament in draft

Made - - - - *22nd June* 1971

Coming into Operation-

> *Regulations* 1, 2 *20th September* 1971
>
> *Regulation* 3 *6th December* 1971

Whereas a draft of the following regulations was laid before Parliament and approved by resolution of each House of Parliament:

Now, therefore, the Secretary of State for Social Services, with the consent of the Treasury, in exercise of the powers conferred by section 5 of the Ministry of Social Security Act 1966(a), and of all other powers enabling him in that behalf, hereby makes the following regulations:—

Citation, commencement and interpretation

1.—(1) These regulations may be cited as the Supplementary Benefit (Determination of Requirements) Regulations 1971 and shall come into operation in the case of regulations 1 and 2 on 20th September 1971, and in the case of regulation 3 on 6th December 1971.

(2) In these regulations, unless the context otherwise requires, "the Act" means the Ministry of Social Security Act 1966(a) and other expressions have the same meaning as in the Act.

(3) The rules for the construction of Acts of Parliament contained in the Interpretation Act 1889(b) shall apply for the purpose of the interpretation of these regulations as they apply for the purpose of the interpretation of an Act of Parliament.

Amendment of provisions for calculating requirements

2.—(1) Part II (calculation of requirements) of Schedule 2 to the Act (provisions for determining right to and amount of benefit) shall be varied in accordance with the following provisions of this regulation.

(a) 1966 c. 20.   (b) 1889 c. 63.

(2) For paragraph 9 (normal requirements) and paragraph 10 (blind persons' requirements), as varied(a), there shall be substituted the following paragraphs—

"*Normal requirements*

9. Requirements of persons other than blind persons—

	£
(*a*) husband and wife or other persons falling within paragraph 3(1) of this Schedule	9·45
(*b*) person living alone or householder not falling within sub-paragraph (*a*) of this paragraph who is directly responsible for household necessities and rent (if any)	5·80

(*c*) any other person aged—

(i) not less than 21 years	4·60
(ii) less than 21 but not less than 18 years	4·05
(iii) less than 18 but not less than 16 years	3·60
(iv) less than 16 but not less than 13 years	3·00
(v) less than 13 but not less than 11 years	2·45
(vi) less than 11 but not less than 5 years	2·00
(vii) less than 5 years	1·70

Blind persons

10. Requirements of persons who are or include blind persons—

(*a*) husband and wife or other persons falling within paragraph 3(1) of this Schedule—

	£
(i) if one of them is blind	10·70
(ii) if both of them are blind	11·50

(*b*) any other blind person aged—

(i) not less than 21 years	7·05
(ii) less than 21 but not less than 18 years	5·05
(iii) less than 18 but not less than 16 years	4·40
(iv) less than 16 but not less than 13 years	3·00
(v) less than 13 but not less than 11 years	2·45
(vi) less than 11 but not less than 5 years	2·00
(vii) less than 5 years	1·70 "

(3) For paragraph 11 (persons in receipt of supplementary pension), as varied (**b**), there shall be substituted the following—

"*Persons in receipt of supplementary pension*

11. Additional requirements of person eligible for supplementary pension—

(*a*) where he or a person whose requirements are aggregated with his under paragraph 3 of this Schedule is aged not less than 80 years	£0·75
(*b*) in any other case	£0·50"

(4) In paragraph 13(1)(*b*) (increase on account of rent of the amount specified for requirements where the beneficiary is a non-householder aged 18 or over), as varied(a), for "£0·60" there shall be substituted "£0·65".

(a) S.I. 1970/816, 1784 (1970 II, p. 2657; III, p. 5793).
(b) S.I. 1968/1118, 1970/1784 (1968 II, p. 3076; 1970 III, p. 5793).

Additional provisions relating to attendance requirements

3.—(1) The said Part II of Schedule 2 to the Act shall be further varied in accordance with the following provisions of this regulation.

(2) Immediately after paragraph 12 there shall be inserted the following paragraph—

"*Attendance requirements*

12A.—(1) The amounts applicable under the preceding paragraphs shall be increased by £4·80 in respect of the attendance requirements of a severely disabled person who either—

(*a*) is entitled to attendance allowance in respect of his own disablement at the rate of £4·80 a week, or

(*b*) is a child in respect of whose disablement some other person, being the person claiming or in receipt of benefit under this Act or a person whose requirements are aggregated with his under paragraph 3 of this Schedule, is entitled to attendance allowance at the rate of £4·80 a week.

(2) In this paragraph—

(*a*) "attendance allowance" means an attendance allowance under the National Insurance Act 1965;

(*b*) "attendance requirements" in relation to a disabled person means that person's requirements, by reason of the severity of his physical or mental disablement, for such attention or supervision from another person as is referred to in sub-section (2) of section 4 of the National Insurance (Old persons' and widows' pensions and attendance allowance) Act 1970 or, in relation to a disabled child, that sub-section as modified by regulations made under sub-section (5) of that section.

(3) For the purposes of this paragraph the provisions of regulations under the National Insurance Act 1965 relating to overlapping benefits shall not be treated as affecting the rate of attendance allowance to which a person is entitled."

(3) In paragraph 14(1) (trade disputes), for the reference to paragraph 13 there shall be substituted a reference to paragraphs 12A and 13.

(4) In paragraph 17 (persons paying for board and lodging), for the reference to paragraphs 9 to 12 there shall be substituted a reference to paragraphs 9 to 12A.

Keith Joseph,
Secretary of State for Social Services.

18th June 1971.

We consent.

V. H. Goodhew,
Walter Clegg,
Two of the Lords Commissioners
of Her Majesty's Treasury.

22nd June 1971.

EXPLANATORY NOTE

(This Note is not part of the Regulations.)

These Regulations vary the provisions of Part II (requirements) of Schedule 2 to the Ministry of Social Security Act 1966 (determination of entitlement to and amount of benefit under the Act). Regulation 1 is formal. Regulation 2 increases the weekly amounts allowed for normal requirements and blind persons' requirements, the requirements of persons receiving supplementary pension where the recipient (or a person whose resources are aggregated with his) is aged 80 years or more, and for the requirements of non-householders where paragraph 13 of the Schedule (rent) specifies an amount of money ; these provisions come into operation on 20th September 1971. Regulation 3, which comes into operation on 6th December 1971, provides for an increase of amounts applicable in cases of severe disablement where a person has title or underlying title to attendance allowance, a benefit under the National Insurance Act 1965 (1965 c.51) introduced by the National Insurance (Old persons' and widows' pensions and attendance allowance) Act 1970 (1970 c.51).

1971 No. 1056

CUSTOMS AND EXCISE

The Import Duties (General) (No. 5) Order 1971

Made - - - -	25th June 1971
Laid before the House of Commons - -	30th June 1971
Coming into Operation -	1st July 1971

The Lords Commissioners of Her Majesty's Treasury, by virtue of the powers conferred on them by sections 1, 2 and 13 of the Import Duties Act 1958(a) and of all other powers enabling them in that behalf, on the recommendation of the Secretary of State hereby make the following Order:—

1.—(1) This Order may be cited as the Import Duties (General) (No. 5) Order 1971.

(2) The Interpretation Act 1889(b) shall apply for the interpretation of this Order as it applies for the interpretation of an Act of Parliament.

(3) This Order shall come into operation on 1st July 1971.

2. Grain sorghum shall cease to be included among the goods chargeable with import duty under heading 10.07 of the Customs Tariff 1959, and accordingly Schedule 1 to the Import Duties (General) (No. 7) Order 1970(c) (which by reference to the Tariff sets out the import duties chargeable under the Import Duties Act 1958) shall be amended by omitting the rates of duty specified in columns 2 and 3 of that Schedule in relation to heading 10.07 and by inserting the following subheadings immediately below heading 10.07:—

" (A) Grain sorghum	—	—
(B) Other	10%	C —
		E 10%"

P. L. Hawkins,
Bernard Weatherill,
Two of the Lords Commissioners
of Her Majesty's Treasury.

25th June 1971.

EXPLANATORY NOTE

(*This Note is not part of the Order.*)

This Order removes the import duty from grain sorghum.

(a) 1958 c. 6.   (b) 1889 c. 63.   (c) S.I. 1970/1522 (1970 III, p. 4935).

STATUTORY INSTRUMENTS

1971 No. 1057

POST OFFICE

The Postal Packets (Customs and Excise) Regulations 1971

Made - - -		*25th June* 1971
Coming into Operation		*1st July* 1971

The Lords Commissioners of Her Majesty's Treasury, by virtue of the powers conferred on them by section 16(2) of the Post Office Act 1953(a), as amended by section 76 of, and paragraph 2(4) of Schedule 4 to, the Post Office Act 1969(b), and of all other powers enabling them in that behalf, and on the recommendation of the Commissioners of Customs and Excise and, after consultation with the Post Office, of the Minister of Posts and Telecommunications, hereby make the following Regulations :—

1. These Regulations may be cited as the Postal Packets (Customs and Excise) Regulations 1971, and shall come into force on the 1st July 1971.

2.—(1) In these Regulations—

"Post Office" has the meaning assigned to those words by the Post Office Act 1969 ;

"Commissioners" means Commissioners of Customs and Excise ;

"dutiable goods" has the meaning assigned to those words by section 307(1) of the Customs and Excise Act 1952(c) but includes goods chargeable with purchase tax ;

"duty" and "duty of customs or excise" include purchase tax ;

"importer" has the meaning assigned to it by section 307(1) of the Customs and Excise Act 1952 ;

"inland post" means the post for the transmission of those postal packets to which the Inland Post Regulations 1968(d) apply ;

"letter packet" means a packet transmitted at the letter rate of postage and containing goods ;

"datapost packet" means a postal packet containing goods which is posted in the United Kingdom as a datapost packet for transmission to a place outside the United Kingdom in accordance with the terms of a contract entered into between the Post Office and the sender of the packet ; or which is received at a Post Office in the United Kingdom from a place outside the United Kingdom for transmission and delivery in the United Kingdom as a datapost packet ;

(a) 1953 c. 36.
(c) 1952 c. 44.

(b) 1969 c. 48.
(d) S.I. 1968/1253 (1968 II, p. 3383).

"prescribed" means prescribed by the provisions of the Universal Postal Convention and Detailed Regulations made thereunder which are for the time being in force ;

"proper" in relation to an officer means appointed or authorised by the Commissioners or the Post Office to perform any duty in relation to a postal packet.

(2) In these Regulations (except in relation to the inland post) the expressions "insured box", "printed packet" and "small packet" have the same meanings as in the Post Office Overseas Letter Post Scheme 1971(a), and "parcel" has the same meaning as in the Post Office Overseas Parcel Post Scheme 1971(b).

(3) In these Regulations, in relation to the inland post, the expression "parcel" has the same meaning as in the Inland Post Regulations 1968, and references to insured boxes, printed packets, small packets and datapost packets shall, in relation to the inland post, be deemed to be omitted.

(4) Any reference in these Regulations to the provisions of any enactment or regulation or Post Office Scheme shall be construed, unless the context otherwise requires, as a reference to those provisions as amended, re-enacted or replaced by any subsequent enactment or regulation or scheme.

(5) The Interpretation Act 1889(c) shall apply for the interpretation of these Regulations as it applies for the interpretation of an Act of Parliament and as if these Regulations and the Regulations hereby revoked were Acts of Parliament.

3. The Postal Packets (Customs and Excise) Regulations 1969(d) are hereby revoked.

4. Section 16 of the Post Office Act 1953 as amended by section 87 of the Post Office Act 1969 and Article 9 of the Postal Services (Channel Islands Consequential Provisions) Order 1969(e) shall apply to all postal packets, other than postcards and telegrams, which are posted in the United Kingdom for transmission to any place outside it or which are brought by post into the United Kingdom.

5. In their application to goods contained in such postal packets, the following provisions of the Customs and Excise Act 1952 shall be subject to the following modifications and exceptions :—

(a) Section 28 shall apply only in any case, or class of cases, in which the Commissioners require an entry to be made in accordance with that section, and proviso (ii) to subsection (2) thereof shall apply with the modification that any direction made by the Commissioners as to goods not permitted to be entered for warehousing may be restricted to goods of any description specified in the direction which are brought by post into the United Kingdom.

(b) Section 31 shall apply only where the Commissioners have required entry to be made, and, where they have so required, shall apply only to the extent, and with the modification, set out in Regulation 14 of these Regulations.

(a) PO Scheme P7/1971. (b) PO Scheme P8/1971.
(c) 1889 c. 63. (d) S.I. 1969/1399 (1969 III, p. 4125).
(e) S.I. 1969/1368 (1969 III, p. 4082).

(c) In the application of section 34, subsection (1) shall not apply, and paragraph (c) of subsection (2) shall apply with the substitution, for the words "at the time of their importation", of the words "at the time when, the packet containing the goods having been presented to the proper officer of Customs and Excise, the amount of duty appearing to be due is assessed by him".

(d) In the application of section 44, paragraph (a) of that section shall be omitted.

(e) Section 47 shall apply with the modification that for references in that section to "shipped for exportation" and "shipping" there shall be substituted references to "posted (or, as the context may require, posting) in the United Kingdom for transmission to any place outside it".

(f) Section 49 shall apply only in any case, or class of cases, in which the Commissioners require a specification to be delivered.

(g) Section 65(1) shall apply to goods brought by post into the United Kingdom, or posted in the United Kingdom for transmission to any place outside it, if an entry or specification is required of such goods when they are imported or exported otherwise than by post.

(h) In the application of section 79 the proviso to subsection (2) shall be omitted and subsection (3) shall apply with the modification that the time of exportation of goods shall be the time when they are posted (or re-directed) in the United Kingdom for transmission to a place outside it.

(ij) Section 91 shall apply to any goods deposited in a Queen's Warehouse under Regulation 14 of these Regulations as it applies to goods so deposited under or by virtue of any provision of the Customs and Excise Act 1952.

(k) Neither section 135 nor section 143 shall apply.

(l) In the application of section 173, subsections (1) and (4) shall be omitted.

(m) In the application of paragraph 1(1) of Schedule 6 the words in brackets shall be omitted, and in the case of goods which are not entered for home use the time of sale contemplated in that sub-paragraph shall be taken to be, in the case of goods entered for any purpose other than home use, the time when they are entered for such other purpose and, in the case of goods which are not entered for any purpose, the time when, the packet containing them having been presented to the proper officer of Customs and Excise, the amount of duty appearing to be due is assessed by him.

(n) Paragraph 1 of Schedule 7 shall, in the case of a thing brought by post into the United Kingdom, apply with the substitution, for the words "to any person who to their knowledge was at the time of seizure the owner or one of the owners thereof", of the words "to the person to whom the postal packet containing the thing is addressed", and paragraph 10(1) of the said Schedule shall not apply.

6. Dutiable goods shall not be brought by post into the United Kingdom from a place situated outside the United Kingdom and the Isle of Man for delivery in the United Kingdom or the Isle of Man, except:

(*a*) in a parcel, an insured box, a letter packet, a small packet or a datapost packet; or

(*b*) in a printed packet, provided that the goods are of such a description as to be transmissible in such a packet under paragraph 22 of the Post Office Overseas Letter Post Scheme 1971.

7.—(1) This Regulation relates to:—

(*a*) parcels brought by post into the United Kingdom;

(*b*) insured boxes brought by post into the United Kingdom;

(*c*) packets brought by post into the United Kingdom, being printed packets containing or consisting of dutiable goods, small packets, letter packets or datapost packets, where the value of any such packet exceeds £40;

(*d*) packets brought by post into the United Kingdom, being printed packets containing or consisting of dutiable goods, small packets, letter packets or datapost packets, where the value of any such packet does not exceed £40.

(2) Every parcel referred to in paragraph (1)(*a*) of this Regulation shall have affixed to it, or be accompanied by, a customs declaration fully and correctly stating the nature, quantity and value of the goods which it contains or of which it consists, and such other particulars as the Commissioners or the Post Office may require.

(3) Every insured box referred to in paragraph (1)(*b*) of this Regulation shall have attached to, or enclosed in, it a full and correct customs declaration of the kind described in paragraph (2) of this Regulation and, in addition, shall bear on the outside the top portion of a green label in the prescribed form.

(4) Every packet referred to in paragraph (1)(*c*) of this Regulation shall have attached to it a full and correct customs declaration of the kind described in paragraph (2) of this Regulation and, in addition, shall bear on the outside the top portion of a green label in the prescribed form:

Provided that any packet referred to in this paragraph, being a registered letter packet containing any article of value, may have the customs declaration referred to in this paragraph enclosed in it.

(5) Every packet referred to in paragraph (1)(*d*) of this Regulation shall either—

(*a*) bear on the outside a green label in the prescribed form, in which the declaration as to the description, net weight and value of the contents shall be fully and correctly completed; or

(*b*) bear on the outside the top portion of a green label in the prescribed form and, in addition, have attached to it a full and correct customs declaration of the kind described in paragraph (2) of this Regulation:

Provided that any packet referred to in this paragraph, being a registered letter packet containing any article of value, may have the customs declaration referred to in sub-paragraph (*b*) of this paragraph enclosed in it.

8.—(1) This Regulation relates to:—

(*a*) parcels posted in the United Kingdom for transmission to any place outside it;

(*b*) insured boxes posted in the United Kingdom for transmission to any place outside it;

(*c*) packets posted in the United Kingdom for transmission to any place outside it, being printed packets containing or consisting of goods which are dutiable in the country of destination, small packets, letter packets or datapost packets, where the value of any such packet exceeds £40;

(*d*) packets posted in the United Kingdom for transmission to any place outside it, being printed packets containing or consisting of goods which are dutiable in the country of destination, small packets, letter packets or datapost packets, where the value of any such packet does not exceed £40.

(2) Every parcel referred to in paragraph (1)(*a*) of this Regulation shall have affixed to it, or be accompanied by, a customs declaration fully and correctly stating the nature, quantity and value of the goods which it contains or of which it consists, and such other particulars as the Commissioners or the Post Office may require.

(3) Every insured box referred to in paragraph (1)(*b*) of this Regulation shall bear on the outside the top portion of a green label in the prescribed form and, in addition, shall have attached to it or, if the postal administration of the country of destination so requires, or the sender so prefers, enclosed in it, a full and correct customs declaration of the kind described in paragraph (2) of this Regulation.

(4) Every packet referred to in paragraph (1)(*c*) of this Regulation shall bear on the outside the top portion of a green label in the prescribed form and, in addition, shall have attached to it, or, if the postal administration of the country of destination so requires, enclosed in it, a full and correct customs declaration of the kind described in paragraph (2) of this Regulation:

Provided that any packet referred to in this paragraph, being a registered letter packet containing any article of value, may have the customs declaration referred to in this paragraph enclosed in it if the sender so prefers.

(5) Every packet referred to in paragraph (1)(*d*) of this Regulation shall either—
(*a*) bear on the outside a green label in the prescribed form, in which the declaration as to the description, net weight and value of the contents shall be fully and correctly completed; or, if the sender so prefers,

(*b*) bear on the outside the top portion of a green label in the prescribed form and, in addition, have attached to it or, if the postal administration of the country of destination so requires, enclosed in it, a full and correct customs declaration of the kind described in paragraph (2) of this Regulation:

Provided that any packet referred to in this paragraph, being a registered letter packet containing any article of value, may have the customs declaration referred to in sub-paragraph (*b*) of this paragraph enclosed in it if the sender so prefers.

9.—(1) Without prejudice to the application of Regulations 7(1)(*c*) and (*d*), (4) and (5), and 8(1)(*c*) and (*d*), (4) and (5) of these Regulations to any printed packet contained in it, every mail bag containing printed packets containing or consisting of goods which are dutiable in the country of destination, brought by post into the United Kingdom or posted in the United Kingdom for transmission to any place outside it under the provisions of paragraph 30 of the Post Office Overseas Letter Post Scheme 1971, shall have affixed to the bag label a green label in the prescribed form.

(2) Regulations 7 and 8 of these Regulations and this Regulation shall not apply to a postal packet or mail bag which, having been posted in the Isle of Man, is brought by post to the United Kingdom for delivery there, or which is posted in the United Kingdom for delivery in the Isle of Man, or which is posted in a place situated outside the United Kindom and the Isle of Man for delivery in a place so situated.

10. Without prejudice to the provisions of Regulations 7, 8 and 9 of these Regulations, every postal packet containing goods to be exported by post without payment of any duty of customs or excise to which they are subject, or on drawback or repayment of such duty, shall on its removal to the post office—

(*a*) be accompanied by such shipping bill, declaration or other document containing such particulars as the Commissioners may require,

and

(*b*) have affixed to its outer cover in the form and manner so required a label having printed thereon the words "Exported under Revenue control by Post", or be distinguished in such other manner as may be so required.

11. The proper officer of the Post Office is hereby authorised to perform in relation to any postal packet or the goods which it contains such of the duties required by virtue of the customs enactments to be performed by the importer or exporter of goods as the Commissioners may require.

12. In such cases or classes of case as the Commissioners may so require, the proper officer of the Post Office shall produce to the proper officer of Customs and Excise postal packets arriving in the United Kingdom or about to be despatched from the United Kingdom, and, if the proper officer of Customs and Excise so requires, shall open for customs examination any packet so produced.

13. The proper officer of the Post Office accepting any outgoing packet in respect of which the requirements of paragraph (*b*) of Regulation 10 of these Regulations have been duly complied with shall endorse a certificate of the posting of the packet on the appropriate document and shall give it to the sender.

14.—(1) If goods are brought by post into the United Kingdom, and an officer of Customs and Excise sends to the addressee of the packet in which they are contained, or to any other person who is for the time being the importer of the goods, a notice requiring entry to be made of them or requiring a full and accurate account of them to be delivered to the proper officer but entry is not made or such account is not delivered within 28 days of the date of such notice or within such longer period as the Commissioners may allow, then unless the Commissioners have required the packet to be delivered to them under Regulation 17 of these Regulations the Post Office shall—

(a) return the goods to the sender of the packet in which they were contained, or otherwise export them from the United Kingdom in accordance with any request or indication appearing on the packet; or

(b) deliver the goods to the proper officer of Customs and Excise; or

(c) with the permission of the Commissioners, and under the supervision of the proper officer of Customs and Excise, destroy them.

(2) Where goods have been delivered to him in accordance with paragraph 1(b) of this Regulation, the proper officer of Customs and Excise may cause the goods to be deposited in a Queen's Warehouse, and section 31(3) of the Customs and Excise Act 1952 shall apply to the goods as it applies to goods so deposited under the said section 31.

15.—(1) On delivering a postal packet the proper officer of the Post Office may demand payment of any duty or other sum due to the Commissioners in respect of it, and any sum so received shall be paid over to the Commissioners by the Post Office.

(2) If payment is not made of any duty so demanded, then, subject to paragraph (3) of this Regulation, the Post Office may, with the agreement of the Commissioners, dispose of the goods contained in the packet as it sees fit.

(3) If any amount demanded in accordance with paragraph (1) of this Regulation, but not paid, is an amount other than duty, the Post Office shall deliver the packet to the proper officer of Customs and Excise.

16. If dutiable goods are brought by post into the United Kingdom in any postal packet contrary to Regulation 6 of these Regulations, or if any postal packet or mail bag to which Regulations 7, 8 and 9 of these Regulations or any of them apply does not contain, does not have affixed or attached to it, or is not accompanied by, the declaration, or does not bear the green label, required by those Regulations or any of them, or if the contents of any postal packet do not agree with the green label or customs declaration affixed or attached to the packet, or by which it is accompanied, or if the other requirements of those Regulations or any of them are not complied with in every material respect, then in every such case the packet or mail bag and all its contents shall be liable to forfeiture.

17. If the Commissioners require any postal packet to be delivered to them on the ground that any goods contained in it are liable to forfeiture under the customs enactments (including these Regulations) or under the Exchange Control Act 1947(a), then the proper officer of the Post Office shall deliver the packet to the proper officer of Customs and Excise.

18. Nothing in these Regulations shall authorise the sending or bringing of any article out of or into the United Kingdom by post contrary to any provisions of the Post Office Overseas Parcel Post Scheme 1971, the Post Office Overseas Letter Post Scheme 1971 or the Inland Post Regulations 1968, as amended, which are applicable thereto.

Bernard Weatherill,
Walter Clegg,
Two of the Lords Commissioners of
Her Majesty's Treasury.

25th June 1971.

(a) 1947 c. 14.

EXPLANATORY NOTE

(This Note is not part of the Regulations.)

These Regulations, which set out the customs requirements relating to incoming and outgoing postal packets and to goods contained in them, supersede the Postal Packets (Customs and Excise) Regulations 1969. Changes in the 1969 Regulations are necessitated by amendments to the provisions of the Acts of the Universal Postal Union on which certain of the 1969 Regulations were based; some minor and drafting amendments have also been made.

The principal changes in the Regulations are as follows:

(*a*) References to Phonopost packets have been deleted, in consequence of the abolition of this category of postal packet in the international posts.

(*b*) The distinction, so far as customs requirements are concerned, between certain packets brought by letter post to the United Kingdom by way of trade and such packets brought by post to the United Kingdom otherwise than by way of trade has been replaced by a distinction between packets valued in excess of £40 and packets of which the value is £40 or less. Completion of a separate customs declaration is not obligatory in the case of packets of a value of £40 or less, provided that the packet bears on the outside an international customs green label in the prescribed form, in which the declaration as to the description, net weight and value of the contents has been fully and correctly completed.

(*c*) The changed requirements described in (*b*) above also apply generally to outgoing packets sent by letter post.

(*d*) In addition to being accompanied by a separate customs declaration all insured boxes must now bear on the outside the top portion of an international customs green label in the prescribed form. The separate customs declaration in respect of goods sent from the United Kingdom by the insured box post may, instead of being attached to the outside, now be enclosed in the insured box at the request of the postal administration of the country of destination or if the sender so prefers.

(*e*) The separate customs declaration in respect of goods sent to the United Kingdom by letter post (as distinct from parcel or insured box post) may, in the case of registered letter packets containing articles of value, be enclosed in the packet (which must, in addition, bear on the outside the top portion of an international customs green label in the prescribed form).

(*f*) The separate customs declaration in respect of goods sent from the United Kingdom by letter post to any place outside it may be enclosed in the packet if the postal administration of the country of destination so requires or, in the case of registered letter packets containing articles of value, if the sender so prefers. In all such cases the packet must, in addition, bear on the outside the top portion of an international customs green label in the prescribed form.

(*g*) Datapost packets have been brought within the scope of these Regulations.

STATUTORY INSTRUMENTS

1971 No. 1058

WAGES COUNCILS

The Wages Regulation (Retail Bread and Flour Confectionery) (England and Wales) Order 1971

Made - - -		24*th June* 1971
Coming into Operation		30*th August* 1971

Whereas the Secretary of State has received from the Retail Bread and Flour Confectionery Trade Wages Council (England and Wales) the wages regulation proposals set out in the Schedule hereto ;

Now, therefore, the Secretary of State in exercise of his powers under section 11 of the Wages Councils Act 1959(a), and of all other powers enabling him in that behalf, hereby makes the following Order :—

1. This Order may be cited as the Wages Regulation (Retail Bread and Flour Confectionery) (England and Wales) Order 1971.

2.—(1) In this Order the expression "the specified date" means the 30th August 1971, provided that where, as respects any worker who is paid wages at intervals not exceeding seven days, that date does not correspond with the beginning of the period for which the wages are paid, the expression "the specified date" means, as respects that worker, the beginning of the next such period following that date.

(2) The Interpretation Act 1889(b) shall apply to the interpretation of this Order as it applies to the interpretation of an Act of Parliament and as if this Order and the Orders hereby revoked were Acts of Parliament.

3. The wages regulation proposals set out in the Schedule hereto shall have effect as from the specified date and as from that date the Wages Regulation (Retail Bread and Flour Confectionery) (England and Wales) Order 1970(c) and the Wages Regulation (Retail Bread and Flour Confectionery) (England and Wales) (Amendment) Order 1970(d) shall cease to have effect.

Signed by order of the Secretary of State.

24th June 1971.

R. R. D. McIntosh,

Deputy Secretary,
Department of Employment.

(a) 1959 c. 69.
(c) S.I. 1970/573 (1970 I, p. 1820).
(b) 1889 c. 63.
(d) S.I. 1970/1301 (1970 III, p. 4332).

ARRANGEMENT OF SCHEDULE

PART I

STATUTORY MINIMUM REMUNERATION

PART II

ANNUAL HOLIDAY AND HOLIDAY REMUNERATION

PART III

GENERAL

SCHEDULE   Article 3

The following minimum remuneration and provisions as to holidays and holiday remuneration shall be substituted for the statutory minimum remuneration and the provisions as to holidays and holiday remuneration fixed by the Wages Regulation (Retail Bread and Flour Confectionery) (England and Wales) Order 1970 (hereinafter referred to as "Order B.F.C. (28)") as amended by the Wages Regulation (Retail Bread and Flour Confectionery) (England and Wales) (Amendment) Order 1970 (Order B.F.C. (30)).

PART I

STATUTORY MINIMUM REMUNERATION

APPLICATION

1. Subject to the provisions of paragraphs 2, 2A, 10, 11, 11A, 16 and 16A, the minimum remuneration for workers to whom this Schedule applies shall be the remuneration set out in paragraphs 3, 4, 5, 6, 7 and 8.

Any increase in remuneration payable under the provisions of paragraph 5, 6, 7 or 8 shall become effective on the first day of the first full pay week following the date upon which the increase would otherwise become payable under those provisions.

HOURS ON WHICH REMUNERATION IS BASED

2.—(1) *Up to and including 29th August 1972* the minimum remuneration specified in paragraphs 3, 5, 6, 7 and 8 relates to a week of *41 hours* exclusive of overtime, and, except as provided in paragraph 16, is subject to a proportionate reduction according as the number of hours worked is less than *41*.

(2) In calculating the remuneration for the purpose of this Schedule recognised breaks for meal times shall, subject to the provisions of paragraph 13, be excluded.

2A.—(1) *On and after 30th August 1972* the minimum remuneration specified in paragraphs 3, 5, 6, 7 and 8 relates to a week of *40 hours* exclusive of overtime, and, except as provided in paragraph 16A, is subject to a proportionate reduction according as the number of hours worked is less than *40*.

(2) In calculating the remuneration for the purpose of this Schedule recognised breaks for meal times shall, subject to the provisions of paragraph 13, be excluded.

MANAGERS AND MANAGERESSES

3. Subject to the provisions of this paragraph, the minimum remuneration for Managers and Manageresses employed in the areas specified in Column 2 of the next following table shall be the amount appearing in the said Column 2 against the amount of weekly trade shown in Column 1 of the said table:—

Column 1	Column 2					
	Per week					
WEEKLY TRADE	London Area		Provincial A Area		Provincial B Area	
	Male	Female	Male	Female	Male	Female
	£	£	£	£	£	£
Under £130..	14·65	13·80	14·35	13·50	13·75	12·95
£130 and under £140	14·75	13·90	14·45	13·60	13·85	13·05
£140 „ „ £150	14·85	14·00	14·55	13·70	13·95	13·15
£150 „ „ £160	14·95	14·10	14·65	13·80	14·05	13·25
£160 „ „ £170	15·00	14·15	14·70	13·85	14·10	13·30
£170 „ „ £180	15·05	14·20	14·75	13·90	14·15	13·35
£180 „ „ £190	15·10	14·25	14·80	13·95	14·20	13·40
£190 „ „ £200	15·15	14·30	14·85	14·00	14·25	13·45
£200 „ „ £210	15·20	14·35	14·90	14·05	14·30	13·50
£210 „ „ £220	15·25	14·40	14·95	14·10	14·35	13·55
£220 „ „ £230	15·30	14·45	15·00	14·15	14·40	13·60
£230 „ „ £240	15·35	14·50	15·05	14·20	14·45	13·65
£240 „ „ £250	15·40	14·55	15·10	14·25	14·50	13·70
£250 „ „ £260	15·45	14·60	15·15	14·30	14·55	13·75
£260 „ „ £270	15·50	14·65	15·20	14·35	14·60	13·80
£270 „ „ £280	15·55	14·70	15·25	14·40	14·65	13·85
£280 „ „ £290	15·60	14·75	15·30	14·45	14·70	13·90
£290 „ „ £300	15·65	14·80	15·35	14·50	14·75	13·95
£300 „ „ £310	15·80	14·95	15·50	14·65	14·90	14·10
£310 up to and including £730 ..	The appropriate amount specified in this table for a worker employed at a shop where the weekly trade is £300 and in addition 5p for every complete £10 of weekly trade in excess of that sum					
More than £730 ..	17·95	17·10	17·65	16·80	17·05	16·25

For the purposes of this paragraph, "weekly trade" shall be calculated half-yearly and based on the period of 12 months immediately preceding the commencement of each half-year in the following manner:—

For the period of 26 weeks beginning (a) with the fifth week or (b) with the 31st week following the accounting date in any year, the weekly trade of a shop shall be 1/52nd of the amount of the total receipts for goods sold at that shop during the 52 weeks immediately preceding the accounting date (in the case of (a) hereof) or immediately preceding the 26th week following the accounting date (in the case of (b) hereof).

Except as provided as aforesaid, the weekly trade in respect of any week shall be the amount of the total receipts for goods sold at the shop in the preceding week.

In this paragraph the expression "accounting date" means that date in each year on which the books of accounts of a shop are closed for the purpose of preparing the annual accounts in respect of that shop, or, in the absence of any such date, the 5th April in any year.

TEMPORARY MANAGERS AND TEMPORARY MANAGERESSES

4.—(1) Subject to the provisions of this paragraph, the minimum remuneration for Temporary Managers and Temporary Manageresses, for each continuous period of employment as Temporary Manager or Temporary Manageress (reckoned in accordance with the provisions of sub-paragraph (2) of this paragraph), shall be the appropriate minimum remuneration for a Manager or Manageress, as the case may be, under the provisions of paragraph 3.

(2) In reckoning any continuous period of employment as Temporary Manager or Temporary Manageress, for the purposes of this paragraph, no account shall be taken of any—

(a) period of employment which does not exceed two consecutive working days in duration ; or

(b) day of employment on which the Manager or Manageress, as the case may be, is allowed a day of holiday (whether in pursuance of this Schedule or not) other than a day included in a period of employment mentioned in (a) of this sub-paragraph:

Provided that the total number of days of which no account shall be taken as aforesaid by virtue of (b) of this sub-paragraph shall not exceed 12 in any one calendar year.

(3) The minimum remuneration payable to a Temporary Manager or a Temporary Manageress for any period or day of employment mentioned in (a) or (b) of sub-paragraph (2) of this paragraph shall be not less than the minimum remuneration appropriate to the worker under paragraph 5.

WORKERS OTHER THAN MANAGERS, MANAGERESSES, TEMPORARY MANAGERS, TEMPORARY MANAGERESSES, ROUNDSWORKERS AND TRANSPORT WORKERS

5.—(1) Subject to the provisions of this Schedule, the minimum remuneration for male or female workers of the classes specified in Column 1 of the next following table employed in the London Area, Provincial A Area or Provincial B Area, as the case may be, shall be the appropriate amount set out in Column 2 of the said table : —

Column 1	Column 2					
	Per week					
(a) FIRST ASSISTANTS	The minimum remuneration which would be payable to the worker under (b) of this sub-paragraph increased by 25p					
	London Area		Provincial A Area		Provincial B Area	
	Male	Female	Male	Female	Male	Female
	£	£	£	£	£	£
(b) ALL OTHER INDOOR WORKERS						
Aged 22 years or over.. ..	13·30	11·55	13·00	11·25	12·40	10·75
„ 21 and under 22 years	12·65	10·95	12·35	10·70	11·80	10·20
„ 20 „ „ 21 „	11·95	10·40	11·70	10·15	11·15	9·70
„ 19 „ „ 20 „	11·30	9·80	11·05	9·55	10·55	9·15
„ 18 „ „ 19 „	10·65	9·25	10·40	9·00	9·90	8·60
„ 17 „ „ 18 „	8·65	7·50	8·45	7·30	8·05	7·00
„ 16 „ „ 17 „	8·00	6·95	7·80	6·75	7·45	6·45
„ under 16 years	7·30	6·35	7·15	6·20	6·80	5·90

(2) Notwithstanding the foregoing provisions of this paragraph, the minimum remuneration payable under the provisions of this paragraph during his or her first six months of employment in the retail bread and flour confectionery trade to a male or female worker who enters, or has entered, that trade for the first time at or over the age of 20 years shall be the appropriate minimum remuneration specified at (b) of the foregoing table reduced—

(a) during the first three months of the employment by 50p, and

(b) during the second three months of the employment by 25p.

ROUNDSWORKERS

6. Subject to the provisions of this Schedule, the minimum remuneration for Roundsworkers employed in the London Area, Provincial A Area or Provincial B Area, as the case may be, shall be the appropriate amount set out in Column 2 of the next following table:—

Column 1	Column 2		
	Per week		
	London Area	Provincial A Area	Provincial B Area
	£	£	£
Workers aged 21 years or over	14·80	14·50	13·90
„ „ 20 and under 21 years	13·30	13·05	12·50
„ „ 19 „ „ 20 „	12·60	12·35	11·80
„ „ 18 „ „ 19 „	11·85	11·60	11·10
„ „ 17 „ „ 18 „	9·60	9·45	9·05
„ „ 16 „ „ 17 „	8·90	8·70	8·35
„ „ under 16 years	8·15	8·00	7·65

ASSISTANT ROUNDSWORKERS

7. Subject to the provisions of this Schedule, the minimum remuneration for Assistant Roundsworkers employed in the London Area, Provincial A Area or Provincial B Area, as the case may be, shall be the appropriate amount set out in Column 2 of the next following table:—

Column 1	Column 2 Per week					
	London Area		Provincial A Area		Provincial B Area	
	Male	Female	Male	Female	Male	Female
	£	£	£	£	£	£
Workers aged 21 years or over ..	13·80	11·90	13·50	11·60	12·90	11·15
„ „ 20 and under 21 years	12·40	10·70	12·15	10·45	11·60	10·05
„ „ 19 and under 20 years	11·75	10·10	11·50	9·85	10·95	9·50
„ „ 18 and under 19 years	11·05	9·50	10·80	9·30	10·30	8·90
„ „ 17 and under 18 years	8·95	7·75	8·80	7·55	8·40	7·25
„ „ 16 and under 17 years	8·30	7·15	8·10	6·95	7·75	6·70
„ „ under 16 years ..	7·60	6·55	7·45	6·40	7·10	6·15

TRANSPORT WORKERS

8. Subject to the provisions of this Schedule, the minimum remuneration for Transport Workers employed in the London Area, Provincial A Area or Provincial B Area, as the case may be, shall be the appropriate amount set out in Column 3 of the next following table:—

Column 1	Column 2		Column 3 Per week		
Age of Transport Worker	Mechanically propelled vehicle with carrying capacity of	Horse drawn vehicle	London Area	Provincial A Area	Provincial B Area
			£	£	£
21 years or over			15·30	15·00	14·40
20 and under 21 years ..		One-	13·75	13·50	12·95
19 „ „ 20 „ ..	1 ton or less	horse	13·00	12·75	12·25
18 „ „ 19 „ ..			12·25	12·00	11·50
under 18 years			9·95	9·75	9·35
All ages	Over 1 ton and up to 5 tons	Two-horse	15·80	15·50	14·90
	Over 5 tons	—	16·30	16·00	15·40

WORKERS WHO WORK IN TWO OR MORE AREAS

9. The minimum remuneration applicable to a Roundsworker, Assistant Roundsworker or Transport Worker in any week in which he works in the London Area, Provincial A Area and Provincial B Area or in any two of those areas is the remuneration which would be applicable if the worker worked solely at the bakery or depot from which he operates.

NIGHT WORK

10. For any time worked between 9 p.m. and 5 a.m. a worker shall be paid, in addition to the minimum remuneration to which he is entitled under the other provisions of this Schedule, *4p* for each hour (or part of an hour) so worked.

MINIMUM OVERTIME RATES

11. *Up to and including 29th August 1972* overtime rates shall be payable to workers to whom this Schedule applies as follows:—

(1) To any worker for work on a Sunday—

    (a) where time worked does not exceed 4½ hours   double time for 4½ hours

    (b) where time worked exceeds 4½ hours but does
       not exceed 8 hours   ...   .   double time for 8 hours

    (c) where time worked exceeds 8 hours—
       for all time worked   ...   .   double time

(2) To any worker other than a roundsworker, assistant roundsworker or a transport worker—

    (a) on the weekly short day in any week during which, under sub-section (3) of section 40 of the Shops Act 1950**(a)**, the employer is relieved of his obligation to allow the worker a weekly half-holiday—

       for all time worked after 1.30 p.m. ...   ...   double time

    (b) on the weekly short day (not being a weekly short day to which (a) of this sub-paragraph applies)—

       for all time worked after 1.30 p.m.   ...   time-and-a-half

    (c) on any day other than a weekly short day, a Sunday or a customary holiday—

       (i) for the first 4 hours worked in excess of 9   time-and-a-quarter

       (ii) thereafter   ...   .   time-and-a-half

Provided that where the employer normally requires the worker's attendance on five days only in the week the said minimum overtime rates of time-and-a-quarter and time-and-a-half shall be payable after 9½ hours' and 13½ hours' work respectively;

    (d) in any week exclusive of any time worked on a customary holiday and of any time for which a minimum overtime rate is payable under the other provisions of this paragraph—

       (i) for the first 4 hours worked in excess of *41*   time-and-a-quarter

       (ii) thereafter   ...   .   time-and-a-half

(a) 1950 c. 28.

(3) To a roundsworker or an assistant roundsworker in any week exclusive of any time worked on a Sunday or a customary holiday—

    (*a*) for the first 6 hours worked in excess of *41* ...   time-and-a-quarter

    (*b*) thereafter   ...   .   time-and-a-half

(4) To a transport worker in any week exclusive of any time worked on a Sunday or a customary holiday whichever of the following amounts is the greater:—

    (*a*) for all time worked in excess of 8 hours on any day on five days in the week and in excess of 10 hours on one day to be specified by the employer or where none is specified the last day of the week—

        (i) for the first 4 hours so worked   ...   ...   time-and-a-quarter

        (ii) thereafter   ...   .   time-and-a-half

  or (*b*) for all time worked in excess of *41 hours*—

        (i) for the first 4 hours...   ...   ...   time-and-a-quarter

        (ii) thereafter   ...   .   time-and-a-half

Provided that—

    (i) overtime rates under this paragraph shall be payable to a manager or manageress only if the overtime worked is specifically authorised by the employer or his representative;

    (ii) where a worker is employed in a shop which is registered under section 53 of the Shops Act 1950 (which relates to persons observing the Jewish Sabbath), the provisions of this paragraph shall apply as if for the word "Sunday" there were substituted the word "Saturday";

    (iii) in any week which includes one customary holiday "35 hours" shall be substituted for "*41 hours*" where it occurs in the foregoing provisions of this paragraph and in any week which includes two customary holidays "28 hours" shall be substituted for the said "*41 hours*".

11A. *On and after 30th August 1972* overtime rates shall be payable to workers to whom this Schedule applies as follows:—

(1) To any worker for work on a Sunday—

    (*a*) where time worked does not exceed 4½ hours   double time for 4½ hours

    (*b*) where time worked exceeds 4½ hours but does not exceed 8 hours   ...   .   double time for 8 hours

    (*c*) where time worked exceeds 8 hours—

      for all time worked   ...   .   double time

(2) To any worker other than a roundsworker, assistant roundsworker or a transport worker—

    (*a*) on the weekly short day in any week during which, under sub-section (3) of section 40 of the Shops Act 1950, the employer is relieved of his obligation to allow the worker a weekly half-holiday—

      for all time worked after 1.30 p.m....   ...   double time

(b) on the weekly short day (not being a weekly short day to which (a) of this sub-paragraph applies)—

for all time worked after 1.30 p.m....   ... time-and-a-half

(c) on any day other than a weekly short day, a Sunday or a customary holiday—

(i) for the first 4 hours worked in excess of 9   time-and-a-quarter

(ii) thereafter ...   . time-and-a-half

Provided that where the employer normally requires the worker's attendance on five days only in the week the said minimum overtime rates of time-and-a-quarter and time-and-a-half shall be payable after 9½ hours' and 13½ hours' work respectively;

(d) in any week exclusive of any time worked on a customary holiday and of any time for which a minimum overtime rate is payable under the other provisions of this paragraph—

(i) for the first 4 hours worked in excess of 40   time-and-a-quarter

(ii) thereafter ...   . time-and-a-half

(3) To a roundsworker or an assistant roundsworker in any week exclusive of any time worked on a Sunday or a customary holiday—

(a) for the first 6 hours worked in excess of 40 ...   time-and-a-quarter

(b) thereafter   ...   . time-and-a-half

(4) To a transport worker in any week exclusive of any time worked on a Sunday or a customary holiday whichever of the following amounts is the greater:—

(a) for all time worked in excess of 8 hours on any day on five days in the week and in excess of 10 hours on one day to be specified by the employer or where none is specified the last day of the week—

(i) for the first 4 hours so worked   ...   ... time-and-a-quarter

(ii) thereafter ...   . time-and-a-half

or (b) for all time worked in excess of 40 hours—

(i) for the first 4 hours   ...   . time-and-a-quarter

(ii) thereafter ...   . time-and-a-half

Provided that—

(i) overtime rates under this paragraph shall be payable to a manager or manageress only if the overtime worked is specifically authorised by the employer or his representative ;

(ii) where a worker is employed in a shop which is registered under section 53 of the Shops Act 1950 (which relates to persons observing the Jewish Sabbath), the provisions of this paragraph shall apply as if for the word "Sunday" there were substituted the word "Saturday" ;

(iii) in any week which includes one customary holiday '35 hours' shall be substituted for "40 hours" where it occurs in the foregoing provisions of this paragraph and in any week which includes two customary holidays "28 hours" shall be substituted for the said "40 hours".

BENEFITS OR ADVANTAGES

12.—(1) The benefits or advantages set out in this sub-paragraph being benefits or advantages provided, in pursuance of the terms and conditions of the employment of a worker to whom this Schedule applies, by the employer or by some other person under arrangements with the employer, are authorised to be reckoned as payment of wages by the employer in lieu of payment in cash in the following manner:—

(a) Dinner of good and sufficient quality and quantity provided on each day on which the worker normally works in the week, other than the weekly short day, as an amount of 50p per week.

(b) Tea of good and sufficient quality and quantity provided on each day on which the worker normally works in the week, other than the weekly short day, as an amount of *20p* per week.

(2) Nothing in this paragraph shall be construed as authorising the making of any deduction or the giving of remuneration in any manner which is illegal by virtue of the Truck Acts 1831 to 1940(a), or of any other enactment.

WAITING TIME

13. A worker shall be entitled to payment of the minimum remuneration specified in this Part of this Schedule for all the time during which he is present on the premises of the employer, unless he is present thereon in any of the following circumstances, that is to say—

(1) without the employer's consent, express or implied ;

(2) for some purpose unconnected with his work and other than that of waiting for work to be given to him to perform ;

(3) by reason only of the fact that he is resident thereon ; or

(4) during normal meal times and he is not waiting for work to be given to him to perform.

WORKERS WHO ARE REQUIRED TO WORK ON A CUSTOMARY HOLIDAY

14.—(1) Subject to the provisions of sub-paragraph (2) of this paragraph where a worker is required to work on a customary holiday he shall be paid not less than the amount to which he would have been entitled under the other provisions of this Schedule had the day not been a customary holiday and had he worked the number of hours ordinarily worked by him on that day of the week and, in addition thereto—

(a) where time worked does not exceed 4½ hours ... time-and-a-half for 4½ hours

(b) where time worked exceeds 4½ hours but does not exceed 8 hours ... ... time-and-a-half for 8 hours

(c) where time worked exceeds 8 hours— for all time worked ... ... time-and-a-half

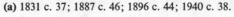

(a) 1831 c. 37; 1887 c. 46; 1896 c. 44; 1940 c. 38.

(2) Where the customary holiday on which a worker is required to work is a day fixed by the employer, being a day on which the worker would normally work during the period commencing on 24th December and ending on the next following 15th January, the worker shall not be entitled to the additional payment under this paragraph unless—

(a) he normally works for the employer for more than nine hours in a week ; and

(b) he has been in the employment of the employer throughout the period of four weeks ending on 23rd December immediately preceding the customary holiday.

WORKERS WHO ARE NOT REQUIRED TO WORK ON A CUSTOMARY HOLIDAY

15.—(1) Subject to the provisions of sub-paragraph (2) and sub-paragraph (3) of this paragraph, a worker who is not required to work on a customary holiday shall be paid for that holiday the amount to which he would have been entitled under the foregoing provisions of this Schedule had the day not been a customary holiday and had he worked the number of hours ordinarily worked by him on that day of the week:

Provided that where, in the case of a worker who normally works for the employer on six days in the week, a customary holiday falls on his weekly short day, the worker shall be paid, in addition to any amount to which he is entitled under this paragraph, an amount equal to the statutory minimum remuneration to which he would be entitled for 4 hours' work, unless he has not been employed after 1.30 p.m. on another week day in the week in which the customary holiday occurs or in the week next following that week on a day other than his weekly short day being in neither case a day of customary holiday or a day of annual holiday.

(2) A worker shall not be entitled to any payment under this paragraph unless he—

(a) works for the employer throughout the last working day on which work was available for him preceding the holiday ; and

(b) presents himself for employment at the usual starting time on the first working day after the holiday:

Provided that (a) or (b), as the case may be, of this sub-paragraph shall be deemed to be complied with where the worker is excused by his employer or is prevented by his proved illness or injury from working or presenting himself for employment as aforesaid.

(3) A worker shall not be entitled to any payment under this paragraph in respect of a customary holiday which is a day fixed by the employer, being a day on which the worker would normally work during the period commencing on 24th December and ending on the next following 15th January unless—

(a) he is a worker who normally works for the employer for more than nine hours in a week ; and

(b) he has been in the employment of the employer throughout the period of four weeks ending on 23rd December immediately preceding the customary holiday.

GUARANTEED WEEKLY REMUNERATION PAYABLE TO A
FULL-TIME WORKER

16.—(1) *Up to and including 29th August 1972* notwithstanding the other provisions of this Schedule, where in any week the total remuneration (including holiday remuneration but excluding the amount specified in sub-paragraph (2) of this paragraph) payable under those other provisions to a full-time worker is less than the guaranteed weekly remuneration provided under this paragraph, the minimum remuneration payable to that worker for that week shall be that guaranteed weekly remuneration with the addition of any amount which may be payable in respect of remuneration excluded from the total remuneration referred to in this sub-paragraph.

(2) The amount to be excluded from the total remuneration referred to in the foregoing sub-paragraph is the whole of the remuneration payable in respect of overtime for work on a Sunday or on the weekly short day and one half of the remuneration payable in respect of work on a customary holiday.

(3) The guaranteed weekly remuneration payable in respect of any week to a full-time worker is the remuneration to which he would be entitled under paragraph 3, 4, 5, 6, 7 or 8 for *41 hours'* work in his normal occupation:

Provided that—

(*a*) where the worker normally works for the employer on work to which this Schedule applies for less than *41 hours* in the week by reason only of the fact that he does not hold himself out as normally available for work for more than the number of hours he normally works in the week, and the worker has informed the employer in writing that he does not so hold himself out, the guaranteed weekly remuneration shall be the remuneration to which the worker would be entitled (calculated as in paragraph 2) for the number of hours in the week normally worked by the worker for the employer on work to which this Schedule applies ;

(*b*) where in any week a worker at his request and with the consent of his employer is absent from work during any part of his normal working hours on any day (other than a day of annual holiday allowed under Part II of this Schedule or a customary holiday or a holiday allowed to all persons in the undertaking or branch of an undertaking in which the worker is employed), the guaranteed weekly remuneration payable in respect of that week shall be reduced in respect of each day on which he is absent as aforesaid by one-sixth where the worker's normal working week is six days or by one-fifth where his normal working week is five days.

(4) Guaranteed weekly remuneration is not payable in respect of any week unless the worker throughout his normal working hours in that week (excluding any time allowed to him as a holiday or during which he is absent from work in accordance with the second proviso to sub-paragraph (3) of this paragraph) is

(*a*) capable of and available for work ; and

(*b*) willing to perform such duties outside his normal occupation as the employer may reasonably require if his normal work is not available in the establishment in which he is employed.

(5) Guaranteed weekly remuneration is not payable in respect of any week if the worker's employment is terminated before the end of that week.

(6) If the employer is unable to provide the worker with work by reason of a strike or other circumstances beyond his control and gives the worker four clear days' notice to that effect, guaranteed weekly remuneration shall not be payable after the expiry of such notice in respect of any week during which or during part of which the employer continues to be unable to provide work as aforesaid:

Provided that in respect of the week in which the said notice expires there shall be paid to the worker, in addition to any remuneration payable in respect of time worked in that week, any remuneration that would have been payable if the worker had worked his normal hours of work on every day in the week prior to the expiry of the notice.

16A.—(1) On and after 30th August 1972 notwithstanding the other provisions of this Schedule, where in any week the total remuneration (including holiday remuneration but excluding the amount specified in sub-paragraph (2) of this paragraph) payable under those other provisions to a full-time worker is less than the guaranteed weekly remuneration provided under this paragraph, the minimum remuneration payable to that worker for that week shall be that guaranteed weekly remuneration with the addition of any amount which may be payable in respect of remuneration excluded from the total remuneration referred to in this sub-paragraph.

(2) The amount to be excluded from the total remuneration referred to in the foregoing sub-paragraph is the whole of the remuneration payable in respect of overtime for work on a Sunday or on the weekly short day and one half of the remuneration payable in respect of work on a customary holiday.

(3) The guaranteed weekly remuneration payable in respect of any week to a full-time worker is the remuneration to which he would be entitled under paragraph 3, 4, 5, 6, 7 or 8 for *40 hours'* work in his normal occupation:

Provided that—

(a) where the worker normally works for the employer on work to which this Schedule applies for less than *40 hours* in the week by reason only of the fact that he does not hold himself out as normally available for work for more than the number of hours he normally works in the week, and the worker has informed the employer in writing that he does not so hold himself out, the guaranteed weekly remuneration shall be the remuneration to which the worker would be entitled (calculated as in paragraph 2A) for the number of hours in the week normally worked by the worker for the employer on work to which this Schedule applies;

(b) where in any week a worker at his request and with the consent of his employer is absent from work during any part of his normal working hours on any day (other than a day of annual holiday allowed under Part II of this Schedule or a customary holiday or a holiday allowed to all persons in the undertaking or branch of an undertaking in which the worker is employed), the guaranteed weekly remuneration payable in respect of that week shall be reduced in respect of each day on which he is absent as aforesaid by one-sixth where the worker's normal working week is six days or by one-fifth where his normal working week is five days.

(4) Guaranteed weekly remuneration is not payable in respect of any week unless the worker throughout his normal working hours in that week (excluding any time allowed to him as a holiday or during which he is absent from work in accordance with the second proviso to sub-paragraph (3) of this paragraph) is

(a) capable of and available for work; and

(b) willing to perform such duties outside his normal occupation as the employer may reasonably require if his normal work is not available in the establishment in which is is employed.

(5) Guaranteed weekly remuneraticn is not payable in respect of any week if the worker's employment is terminated before the end of that week.

(6) If the employer is unable to provide the worker with work by reason of a strike or other circumstances beyond his control and gives the worker four clear days' notice to that effect, guaranteed weekly remuneration shall not be payable after the expiry of such notice in respect of any week during which or during part of which the employer continues to be unable to provide work as aforesaid:

Provided that in respect of the week in which the said notice expires there shall be paid to the worker, in addition to any remuneration payable in respect of time worked in that week, any remuneration that would have been payable if the worker had worked his normal hours of work on every day in the week prior to the expiry of the notice.

PART II

ANNUAL HOLIDAY AND HOLIDAY REMUNERATION

ANNUAL HOLIDAY

17.—(1) An employer shall, between the date on which this Schedule becomes effective and 31st October 1971 and in each succeeding year between 6th April and 31st October allow a holiday (hereinafter referred to as an "annual holiday") to every worker in his employment to whom this Schedule applies who has been employed by him during the 12 months immediately preceding the commencement of the holiday season for any one of the periods of employment (calculated in accordance with the provisions of paragraph 23) set out in the first column of the table below and the duration of the annual holiday shall in the case of each such worker be related to that period as follows:—

Period of employment	Duration of annual holiday for workers with a normal working week of			
	Six days	Five days	Four days	Three days or less
12 months	12 days	10 days	8 days	6 days
At least 11 months	11 „	9 „	7 „	5 „
„ „ 10 „	10 „	8 „	7 „	5 „
„ „ 9 „	9 „	7 „	6 „	4 „
„ „ 8 „	8 „	7 „	5 „	4 „
„ „ 7 „	7 „	6 „	5 „	3 „
„ „ 6 „	6 „	5 „	4 „	3 „
„ „ 5 „	5 „	4 „	3 „	2 „
„ „ 4 „	4 „	3 „	3 „	2 „
„ „ 3 „	3 „	2 „	2 „	1 day
„ „ 2 „	2 „	2 „	1 day	1 „
„ „ 1 month	1 day	1 day	1 „	—

(2) Notwithstanding the provisions of the last foregoing sub-paragraph—

(a) the number of days of annual holiday which an employer is required to allow to a worker in any holiday season shall not exceed in the aggregate twice the number of days constituting the worker's normal working week ;

(b) where before the expiration of any holiday season a worker enters into an agreement in writing with his employer that the annual holiday or part thereof shall be allowed on a specified date or dates after the expiration of the holiday season but before the commencement of the next following holiday season, then any day or days of annual holiday so allowed shall for the purposes of this Schedule be treated as having been allowed during the holiday season ;

(c) where a worker has, on 1st August in any year, been in the employment of the employer for not less than six months, the duration of his annual holiday in that year shall be not less than the number of days constituting his normal working week ;

(d) the duration of the worker's annual holiday during the holiday season ending on 31st October 1971, shall be reduced by any days of annual holiday duly allowed to him by the employer under the provisions of Order B.F.C. (28) as amended between 6th April 1971, and the date on which the provisions of this Schedule become effective.

(3) In this Schedule the expression "holiday season" means in relation to the year 1971 the period between 6th April 1971 and 31st October 1971 and, in each succeeding year, the period between 6th April and 31st October of the same year.

18.—(1) Subject to the provisions of this paragraph, an annual holiday shall be allowed on consecutive working days, being days on which the worker is normally called upon to work for the employer.

(2) Where the number of days of annual holiday for which a worker has qualified exceeds the number of days constituting his normal working week, the holiday may by agreement between the employer and the worker be allowed in two periods of consecutive working days ; so however that when a holiday is so allowed, one of the periods shall consist of a number of such days not less than the number of days constituting the worker's normal working week.

(3) For the purposes of this paragraph, days of annual holiday shall be treated as consecutive notwithstanding that a customary holiday on which the worker is not required to work for the employer or a day on which he does not normally work for the employer intervenes.

(4) Where a customary holiday on which the worker is not required to work for the employer immediately precedes a period of annual holiday or occurs during such a period and the total number of days of annual holiday required to be allowed in the period under the foregoing provisions of this paragraph, together with any customary holiday, exceeds the number of days constituting the worker's normal working week then, notwithstanding the foregoing provisions of this paragraph, the duration of that period of annual holiday may be reduced by one day and in such a case one day of annual holiday may be allowed on a day on which the worker normally works for the employer (not being the worker's weekly short day) in the holiday season.

(5) No day of annual holiday shall be allowed on a customary holiday.

(6) A day of annual holiday under this Schedule may be allowed on a day on which the worker is entitled to a day of holiday (not being a customary holiday) or to a half-holiday under any enactment other than the Wages Councils Act 1959.

19. An employer shall give to a worker reasonable notice of the commencing date or dates and of the duration of his annual holiday. Such notice may be given individually to a worker or by the posting of a notice in the place where the worker is employed.

HOLIDAY REMUNERATION

20.—(1) Subject to the provisions of paragraph 21, a worker qualified to be allowed an annual holiday under this Schedule shall be paid by his employer, on the last pay day preceding such holiday, one day's holiday pay in respect of each day thereof.

(2) Where an annual holiday is taken in more than one period, the holiday remuneration shall be apportioned accordingly.

21. Where any accrued holiday remuneration has been paid by the employer to the worker (in accordance with paragraph 22 of this Schedule or with Order B.F.C. (28) as amended), in respect of employment during the periods referred to in paragraph 22, the amount of holiday remuneration payable by the employer in respect of any annual holiday for which the worker has qualified by reason of employment during the said period shall be reduced by the amount of the said accrued holiday remuneration unless that remuneration has been deducted from a previous payment of holiday remuneration made under the provisions of this Schedule or of Order B.F.C. (28) as amended.

ACCRUED HOLIDAY REMUNERATION PAYABLE ON TERMINATION OF EMPLOYMENT

22. Where a worker ceases to be employed by an employer after the provisions of the Schedule become effective the employer shall, immediately on the termination of the employment (hereafter in this Schedule referred to as "the termination date"), pay to the worker as accrued holiday remuneration: —

(1) in respect of employment in the 12 months up to and including 5th April immediately preceding the termination date, a sum equal to the holiday remuneration for any days of annual holiday for which he has qualified except days of annual holiday which he has been allowed or has become entitled to be allowed before leaving the employment; and

(2) in respect of any employment since 5th April immediately preceding the termination date, a sum equal to the holiday remuneration which would have been payable to him if he could have been allowed an annual holiday in respect of that employment at the time of leaving it:

Provided that—

(a) no worker shall be entitled to the payment by his employer of accrued holiday remuneration if he is dismissed on the grounds of misconduct and is so informed by the employer at the time of dismissal;

(b) where, during the period or periods in respect of which the said accrued holiday remuneration is payable, the worker—

(i) has at his written request been allowed any day or days of holiday for which he has not qualified under the provisions of this Schedule, any accrued holiday remuneration payable as aforesaid may be reduced by the amount of any sum paid by the employer to the worker in respect of such day or days of holiday; or

(ii) has been allowed an annual holiday in accordance with (c) of sub-paragraph (2) of paragraph 17 of this Schedule or Order B.F.C. (28) as amended, any accrued holiday remuneration payable as aforesaid may be reduced by one day's holiday pay in respect of each day by which the said holiday exceeded the number of days of annual holiday to which he would have been entitled under the provisions of sub-paragraph (1) of the said paragraph 17 or Order B.F.C. (28) as amended ;

(c) where a worker is employed under a contract of service under which he is required to give not less than one week's notice before terminating his employment and the worker without the consent of his employer terminates his employment without having given such notice or before one week has expired from the beginning of such notice, the amount of accrued holiday remuneration payable to the worker shall be the amount payable under the foregoing provisions of this paragraph less an amount—

(i) in the case of a worker who left without giving notice, equal to the statutory minimum remuneration which would be payable to him at the termination date for one week's work if working his normal working week and the normal number of daily hours worked by him ; and

(ii) in the case of a worker who left without working the full period of his week's notice, equal to one day's holiday pay for each day during the said period on which he failed to work.

CALCULATION OF EMPLOYMENT

23. For the purposes of calculating any period of employment qualifying a worker for an annual holiday or for any accrued holiday remuneration under this Schedule, the worker shall be treated as if he were employed for a month in respect of any month throughout which he has been in the employment of the employer.

PART III

GENERAL

DEFINITIONS

24. In this Schedule, unless the context otherwise requires, the following expressions have the meanings hereby respectively assigned to them, that is to say : —

"CARRYING CAPACITY" means the weight of the maximum load normally carried by the vehicle, and such carrying capacity when so established shall not be affected either by variations in the weight of the load resulting from collections or deliveries or emptying of containers during the course of the journey, or by the fact that on any particular journey a load greater or less than the established carrying capacity is carried.

"CLEANER" means a worker engaged wholly or mainly in cleaning premises.

"CUSTOMARY HOLIDAY" means

(1) Christmas Day (or, if Christmas Day falls on a Sunday, such week day as may be appointed by national proclamation, or if none is so appointed, the next following Tuesday), Boxing Day, Good Friday, Easter Monday, Whit Monday (or where another day is substituted therefor by national proclamation, that day), August Bank Holiday and any day proclaimed as an additional Bank Holiday or a general holiday ; or, in the case of each of the said days, such week day (other than a weekly short day) as may be substituted therefor, being a day—

    (a) on which the worker normally works for the employer, and

    (b) which is by local custom recognised as a day of holiday ; and

(2) one other day, being a day on which the worker would normally work during the period commencing on 24th December and ending on the next following 15th January, to be fixed by the employer and notified to the worker not less than three weeks before the holiday.

"FIRST ASSISTANT" means—

(1) in a shop where a manager or manageress and not less than five other workers (excluding part-time workers employed as cleaners) are employed, such one of those other workers as may be designated by the employer as "first assistant" for the purposes of this Schedule or, if no worker is so designated, the worker who has been longest employed in the shop ;

(2) in a shop where no manager or manageress is employed—

    (a) where two or more workers (excluding part-time workers employed as cleaners) are employed, such one of those workers as may be designated by the employer as "first assistant" for the purposes of this Schedule or, if no worker is so designated, the worker who has been longest employed in the shop ;

    (b) where only one worker is employed, that worker ;

provided that a worker shall not be deemed to be a first assistant by virtue of (2) of this definition, except during a period when the employer is absent from the shop and the period of absence is of not less than one day's duration.

"FULL-TIME WORKER" means a worker who normally works for the employer for at least 36 hours in the week on work to which this Schedule applies.

"LONDON AREA", "PROVINCIAL A AREA" and "PROVINCIAL B AREA" have the meanings respectively assigned to them in paragraph 25.

"MANAGER", "MANAGERESS" means a worker who is employed at, and is normally immediately in charge of the operation of, a shop and who has immediate control of—

(1) one or more other workers being full-time workers, or

(2) two or more part-time workers (excluding part-time workers employed as cleaners) ;

and for the purpose of this definition a worker shall not be deemed not to be immediately in charge of the operation of a shop by reason only of being subject to the supervision of the employer or some person acting on his behalf, being in either case a person who is not normally, during the hours when the shop is open to the public, wholly or mainly engaged in work at the shop.

"MONTH" means the period commencing on a date of any number in one month and ending on the day before the date of the same number in the next month or, if the commencing date is the 29th, 30th or 31st day of a month and there is no date of the same number in the next month, then on the last day of that month.

"NORMAL WORKING WEEK" means the number of days on which it has been usual for the worker to work in a week while in the employment of the employer during the 12 months immediately preceding the commencement of the holiday season or, where accrued holiday remuneration is payable under (2) of paragraph 22 on the termination of the employment, during the 12 months immediately preceding the date of the termination of the employment:

Provided that—

(1) part of a day shall count as a day ;

(2) no account shall be taken of any week in which the worker did not perform any work for which statutory minimum remuneration has been fixed.

"ONE DAY'S HOLIDAY PAY" means the appropriate proportion of the remuneration which the worker would be entitled to receive from his employer at the date of the annual holiday (or, where the holiday is taken in more than one period, at the date of the first period) or at the termination date, as the case may be, for one week's work, if working his normal working week and the number of daily hours normally worked by him (exclusive of overtime), and if paid at the appropriate rate of statutory minimum remuneration for work for which statutory minimum remuneration is payable and at the same rate for any work for the same employer for which such remuneration is not payable, and in this definition "appropriate proportion" means—

where the worker's normal working week is six days	...	...	one-sixth
„	„	„	„	„	„	five „	... ...	one-fifth
„	„	„	„	„	„	four „	... ...	one-quarter
„	„	„	„	„	„	three „	... ...	one-third
„	„	„	„	„	„	two „	... ...	one-half
„	„	„	„	„	„	one day	... ...	the whole.

"ROUNDSWORKER" means a worker wholly or mainly employed as a salesman on a definite or established route and responsible for keeping account of retail sales to customers and of any cash or tokens received in payment and who is not accompanied, save in exceptional circumstances, by any other person who exercises control or supervision.

"ROUNDSWORKER, ASSISTANT" means a worker wholly or mainly employed in assisting any person carrying out the duties normally performed by a roundsworker, whether or not such person is a roundsworker as defined in this Schedule.

"TEMPORARY MANAGER", "TEMPORARY MANAGERESS", means a worker who, in the absence of the Manager or Manageress, as the case may be, is employed at and is temporarily immediately in charge of the operation of a shop, whilst the worker is so in charge ; and for the purpose of this definition a worker shall not be deemed not to be immediately in charge of the operation of a shop by reason only of being subject to the supervision of the employer or some person acting on his behalf, being in either case a person who is not normally, during the hours when the shop is open to the public, wholly or mainly engaged in work at the shop.

"TIME-AND-A-QUARTER", "TIME-AND-A-HALF" and "DOUBLE TIME" mean, respectively, one and a quarter times, one and a half times and twice the hourly rate obtained by dividing the minimum weekly remuneration to which the worker is entitled under the provisions of paragraph 3, 4, 5, 6, 7 or 8—

(a) by 41 up to and including 29th August 1972
(b) by 40 on and after 30th August 1972.

"TRANSPORT WORKER" means a worker (other than a roundsworker or assistant roundsworker) engaged wholly or mainly in driving a mechanically propelled or horse drawn road vehicle for the transport of goods and on work in connection with the vehicle and its load (if any) while on the road.

"WEEK" means "pay week".

"WEEKLY SHORT DAY" means that day in any week on which the worker is, in accordance with the provisions of section 17 of the Shops Act 1950, required not to be employed about the business of a shop after half past one o'clock in the afternoon or, where there is no such day, a working day in the week fixed by the employer and notified to the worker not later than the Saturday preceding the week during which it is to have effect or, failing such notification, the last working day in the week.

AREAS

25. In this Schedule—

(1) "LONDON AREA" means the Metropolitan Police District, as defined in the London Government Act 1963(a), the City of London, the Inner Temple and the Middle Temple ;

(2) "PROVINCIAL B AREA" comprises all areas other than those specified in sub-paragraphs (1) and (3) of this paragraph ;

(3) "PROVINCIAL A AREA" comprises—

(a) all areas other than the London Area which according to the Registrar General's Preliminary Report on the Census of England and Wales 1961, were administered by County Borough, Municipal Borough or Urban District Councils and which had a population of ten thousand or more, and,

(b) the areas administered by the following Municipal Boroughs and Urban District Councils : —

BEDFORDSHIRE—
Biggleswade
Kempston

BRECONSHIRE—
Brecknock
Brynmawr

BUCKKINGHAM-
SHIRE—
Eton

CAERNARVON-
SHIRE—
Caernarvon

CARMARTHEN-
SHIRE—
Ammanford
Burry Port

CHESHIRE—
Alderley Edge
Bollington
Bowdon
Knutsford
Lymm
Middlewich
Sandbach

CORNWALL—
St. Ives
Saltash

CUMBERLAND—
Cockermouth
Keswick

DENBIGHSHIRE—
Abergele
Denbigh

DERBYSHIRE—
Ashbourne
Clay Cross
New Mills

DEVON—
Dawlish
Ilfracombe

DORSET—
Bridport
Swanage

ELY, ISLE OF—
Ely
Whittlesey

ESSEX—
Epping
Frinton and Walton

(a) 1963 c. 33.

ESSEX *cont.*
Halstead
Witham

FLINTSHIRE—
Connah's Quay
Holywell

GLOUCESTERSHIRE—
Charlton Kings

GLAMORGAN—
Glyncorrwg

HAMPSHIRE—
Alton
Fleet
Petersfield
Romsey

HEREFORDSHIRE—
Leominster
Ross-on-Wye

HERTFORDSHIRE—
Tring
Ware

KENT—
Southborough
Swanscombe

LANCASHIRE—
Abram
Adlington
Aspull
Barrowford
Billinge-and-Winstanley
Blackrod
Brierfield
Church
Clayton-le-Moors
Kirkham
Lees
Little Lever
Longridge
Milnrow
Mossley
Padiham
Preesall
Rainford

LANCASHIRE *cont.*
Rishton
Skelmersdale
Standish-with-Langtree
Tottington
Trawden
Up Holland
Wardle
Whitworth
Withnell

LEICESTERSHIRE—
Ashby de la Zouch
Ashby Woulds
Shepshed

LINCOLNSHIRE—
Sleaford

MERIONETHSHIRE—
Ffestiniog

MONMOUTHSHIRE—
Abergavenny
Blaenavon
Monmouth
Rhymney

NORFOLK—
East Dereham

**NORTHAMPTON-
SHIRE—**
Daventry
Desborough
Irthlingborough
Raunds
Rothwell

**NORTHUMBER-
LAND—**
Hexham
Prudhoe

OXFORDSHIRE—
Henley-on-Thames
Witney

PEMBROKESHIRE—
Haverfordwest

SHROPSHIRE—
Bridgnorth
Dawley
Ludlow
Whitchurch

SOMERSET—
Burnham-on-Sea
Minehead
Wells

STAFFORDSHIRE—
Amblecote
Stone
Uttoxeter

SUSSEX—
Newhaven

WESTMORLAND—
Windermere

WIGHT, ISLE OF—
Ventnor

WILTSHIRE—
Devizes
Warminster

YORKSHIRE—
Cudworth
Darfield
Denby Dale
Denholme
Dodworth
Driffield
Earby
Filey
Hebden Royd
Heckmondwike
Horbury
Knaresborough
Loftus
Meltham
Northallerton
Penistone
Queensbury and Shelf
Ripponden
Royston
Scalby
Selby
Silsden

WORKERS TO WHOM THIS SCHEDULE APPLIES

26.—(1) Subject to the provisions of sub-paragraph (2) of this paragraph, the workers to whom this Schedule applies are all workers employed in England and Wales in any undertaking or any branch or department of an undertaking, being an undertaking, branch or department, wholly or mainly engaged in the retail bread and flour confectionery trade:

Provided that if a branch or department of an undertaking is not so engaged, this Schedule shall not apply to workers employed in that branch or department (notwithstanding that the undertaking as a whole is so engaged) except as respects their employment in a department of that branch if that department is so engaged.

(2) This Schedule does not apply to any of the following workers in respect of their employment in any of the following circumstances, that is to say: —

    (i) workers in relation to whom any of the following wages councils operates in respect of any employment which is for the time being within the field of operation of that wages council, that is to say: —

        (a) the Baking Wages Council (England and Wales);

        (b) the Milk Distributive Wages Council (England and Wales);

        (c) the Road Haulage Wages Council;

    (ii) workers in relation to whom any Wages Council (which was immediately before 30th May 1959 a Wages Board established under the Catering Wages Act 1943(a)) operates in respect of any employment which is for the time being within the field of operation of that Wages Council;

    (iii) workers (other than workers employed as cleaners) employed in the maintenance or repair of buildings, plant, equipment or vehicles;

    (iv) workers employed in any ship (which includes every description of vessel used in navigation);

    (v) workers employed on post office business.

(3) For the purposes of this Schedule the retail bread and flour confectionery trade does not include the sale of biscuits or meat pastries or any sale for immediate consumption on the premises at which the sale is effected, but save as aforesaid consists of the sale by retail of bread (including rolls) or flour confectionery (including pastry) and operations connected with any such sale, including: —

    (i) operations in or about a shop or other place where the bread or flour confectionery is sold, being operations carried on for the purpose of or in connection with such sale;

    (ii) operations in connection with the transport of bread or flour confectionery when carried on in conjunction with its sale by retail;

    (iii) clerical or other office work carried on in conjunction with the sale by retail as aforesaid and relating to such sale or to any of the operations specified in (i) or (ii) of this sub-paragraph;

and for the purposes of this definition "sale by retail" includes any sale to a person for use in connection with a catering business carried on by him, when such sale takes place at or in connection with a shop engaged in the retail sale of bread or flour confectionery to the general public.

EXPLANATORY NOTE

(This Note is not part of the Order.)

This Order, which has effect from 30th August 1971, sets out the statutory minimum remuneration payable and the holidays to be allowed in substitution for the statutory minimum remuneration and holidays set out in the Wages Regulation (Retail Bread and Flour Confectionery) (England and Wales) Order 1970 (Order B.F.C. (28)), as amended by the Wages Regulation (Retail Bread and Flour Confectionery) (England and Wales) (Amendment) Order 1970 (Order B.F.C. (30)), which Orders are revoked.

New provisions are printed in italics.

STATUTORY INSTRUMENTS

1971 No. 1060

FACTORIES

The Fees of Appointed Factory Doctors Order 1971

Made - - -	*28th June* 1971
Coming into Operation	*8th July* 1971

The Secretary of State by virtue of his powers under section 152 of the Factories Act 1961(a) and of all other powers enabling him in that behalf, hereby makes the following Order :—

Citation and commencement

1. This Order may be cited as the Fees of Appointed Factory Doctors Order 1971 and shall come into operation on 8th July 1971.

Revocation

2. The Fees of Appointed Factory Doctors Order 1969(b) is hereby revoked.

Interpretation

3.—(1) The Interpretation Act 1889(c) shall apply to the interpretation of this Order as it applies to the interpretation of an Act of Parliament, and as if this Order and the Order hereby revoked were Acts of Parliament.

(2) For the purposes of this Order, unless the context otherwise requires, the following expressions have the meanings hereby assigned to them respectively, that is to say :—

"the appointed factory doctor's central point" means a place fixed by the Chief Inspector for the purpose of calculating the mileage or, where no place is so fixed, the residence of the appointed factory doctor ;

"the principal Act" means the Factories Act 1961 as amended by or under any other Act ;

"section" means section of the principal Act.

(3) The references in Article 4(3) of this Order to the first examination of any person for the purposes of specified Regulations are references to the examination which is for the appointed factory doctor who carries it out the first examination by him of a particular person for the purposes of the Regulations under which the examination is carried out.

(a) 1961 c. 34.   (b) S.I. 1969/1633 (1969 III, p. 5129).   (c) 1889 c. 63.

Fees of Appointed Factory Doctors

4.—(1) Subject to the provisions of Article 5 of this Order, the Secretary of State hereby determines that the fees payable by occupiers of factories to appointed factory doctors for the carrying out of such of their duties under the principal Act as are specified in paragraphs (2), (3), (4) and (5) of this Article shall be of the amounts respectively so specified.

(2) For examinations of young persons under section 99(4) or under section 118, or after the service by an inspector on the occupier of a notice under section 119 as to the employment of a young person in a factory, the fees shall be as follows, that is to say :—

(*a*) when the examination is at the factory—£1·05 for the first and 60p for each other person examined on the occasion of any one visit to the factory, and in addition, if the distance (measured by the shortest route by which the appointed factory doctor can travel by road) between the appointed factory doctor's central point and the factory exceeds two miles, 10p for each complete mile by which that distance exceeds two miles ;

(*b*) when the examination is not at the factory but at the residence of the appointed factory doctor or at some other place appointed by him for the purpose and approved by the Chief Inspector—60p for each person examined.

(3) For examinations of persons for the purposes of the undermentioned Regulations the fees shall (wherever the examinations take place) be as follows, that is to say :—

(*a*) in the case of the Work in Compressed Air Special Regulations 1958(a), £2·55 for the first examination of any person for the purposes of those Regulations and 85p for any other examination of that person for the purposes of those Regulations ;

(*b*) in the case of the Diving Operations Special Regulations 1960(b), £3·45 for the first examination of any person for the purposes of those Regulations and £1·75 for any other examination of that person for the purposes of those Regulations ;

(*c*) in the case of the Carcinogenic Substances Regulations 1967(c), £1·60 for the first examination of any person for the purposes of those Regulations and 80p for any other examination of that person for the purposes of those Regulations ;

(*d*) in the case of the Ionising Radiations (Unsealed Radioactive Substances) Regulations 1968(d), £3·45 for the first examination of any person for the purposes of those Regulations and £1·75 for any other examination of that person for the purposes of those Regulations ; and

(*e*) in the case of the Ionising Radiations (Sealed Sources) Regulations 1969(e), £3·45 for the first examination of any person for the purposes of those Regulations and £1·75 for any other examination of that person for the purposes of those Regulations ;

and in addition, if the distance (measured as aforesaid) between the appointed factory doctor's central point and the place of the examination exceeds two miles, 10p for each complete mile by which that distance exceeds two miles.

(a) S.I. 1958/61 (1958 I, p. 1115).   (b) S.I. 1960/688 (1960 II, p. 1410).
(c) S.I. 1967/879 (1967 II, p. 2619).   (d) S.I. 1968/780 (1968 II, p. 2153).
(e) S.I. 1969/808 (1969 II, p. 2296).

(4) For examinations of employed persons for the purposes of section 75 or of any Regulations under section 76 (other than the Regulations specified in paragraph (3) of this Article), the fees shall be as follows, that is to say :—

(a) when the examination is at the factory or other place of employment— £1·05 for the first and 35p for each other person examined on the occasion of any one visit to the factory or place, and in addition, if the distance (measured as aforesaid) between the appointed factory doctor's central point and the factory exceeds two miles, 10p for each complete mile by which that distance exceeds two miles ;

(b) when the examination is not at the factory or other place of employment but at the residence of the appointed factory doctor or at some other place appointed by him for the purpose and approved by the Chief Inspector—35p for each person examined.

(5) For an examination or part of an examination consisting, in either case, of a haemoglobin estimation made in pursuance of the Lead Processes (Medical Examinations) Regulations 1964(a), the fees shall be as follows, that is to say :—

(a) in respect of the first or only person examined on any one occasion— £1·10 ;

(b) in respect of the second to the tenth person examined on any one occasion—55p for each person ; and

(c) in respect of the eleventh and each subsequent person examined on any one occasion—35p for each person.

Inclusions and exclusions

5. The fees specified in this Order—

(a) are subject to any agreement between the appointed factory doctor and the occupier of a factory ;

(b) include payment for the making of entries in registers, the issuing or refusal of certificates and the carrying out of other duties as may be required in connection with the examinations ;

(c) do not cover, in the case of the fees specified in Article 4(2) and (4) of this Order, any special examinations of the blood, microscopical examinations of urine, X-ray examinations, serological tests or other special investigations undertaken in connection with examinations of employed persons on particular occasions or in particular instances (and this Order shall be without prejudice to the making of arrangements between the appointed factory doctor and the occupier of a factory for the carrying out of such special investigations) ; and

(d) do not cover, in the case of the fees specified in Article 4(3) of this Order, any examination of the blood or any other special examination required in pursuance of Regulation 29(1) of the Ionising Radiations (Sealed Sources) Regulations 1969 or Regulation 32(1) of the Ionising Radiations (Unsealed Radioactive Substances) Regulations 1968, or

---

(a) S.I. 1964/1728 (1964 III, p. 3846).

any chest examination by radiography required in pursuance of Regulation 9 of the Diving Operations Special Regulations 1960.

Signed by order of the Secretary of State.
28th June 1971.

K. Barnes,
Deputy Secretary,
Department of Employment.

EXPLANATORY NOTE

(This Note is not part of the Order.)

This Order determines the amount of fees payable by occupiers of factories to appointed factory doctors for various services required under the Factories Act 1961. It increases the fees determined by the Fees of Appointed Factory Doctors Order 1969 which is revoked. The fees determined by this Order can be varied by agreement between the appointed factory doctor and the occupier of a factory.

STATUTORY INSTRUMENTS

1971 No. 1061

PETROLEUM

The Inflammable Liquids (Conveyance by Road) Regulations 1971

Made - - -	*28th June* 1971
Laid before Parliament	*8th July* 1971
Coming into Operation	*9th July* 1971

In exercise of the powers conferred by section 6 of the Petroleum (Consolidation) Act 1928(a), as applied by the Petroleum (Inflammable Liquids) Order 1971(b), I hereby make the following Regulations :—

1.—(1) These Regulations may be cited as the Inflammable Liquids (Conveyance by Road) Regulations 1971 and shall come into operation on 9th July 1971.

(2) The Inflammable Liquids (Conveyance by Road) Regulations 1968(c) are hereby revoked.

2.—(1) In these Regulations—

"conveyance" means conveyance by road, and "conveyed" and "conveying" shall be construed accordingly ;

"inflammable liquid" means any substance, solution or mixture to which section 6 of the Petroleum (Consolidation) Act 1928 was applied by Article 2 of the Petroleum (Inflammable Liquids) Order 1971 ;

"owner", in relation to a vehicle which is the subject of a hiring agreement or hire-purchase agreement, means the person in possession of the vehicle under that agreement ;

"vehicle" includes a trailer which does not form part of an articulated vehicle.

(2) For the purposes of these Regulations an articulated vehicle shall be treated as one vehicle.

(3) The Interpretation Act 1889(d) shall apply to the interpretation of these Regulations as it applies to the interpretation of an Act of Parliament, and as if these Regulations and the Regulations revoked by these Regulations were Acts of Parliament.

(a) 1928 c. 32.
(c) S.I. 1968/927 (1968 II, p. 2421).
(b) S.I. 1971/1040 (1971 II, p.3125).
(d) 1889 c. 63.

3. Subject to Regulation 9 below, every person engaged in the conveyance, or the loading or unloading in connection with conveyance, of any inflammable liquid shall secure so far as is reasonably possible that none of the inflammable liquid is spilt.

4. Subject to Regulation 9 below, no person engaged in the conveyance, or the loading or unloading in connection with conveyance, of any inflammable liquid shall smoke or carry any naked flame.

5. Subject to Regulation 9 below, no portable light capable of igniting inflammable vapour, no explosive substance and no substance or article capable of causing fire or explosion by spontaneous decomposition shall be carried on any vehicle conveying any inflammable liquid.

6. Subject to Regulation 9 below, a suitable and efficient fire extinguisher shall be carried in an easily accessible position on any vehicle conveying any inflammable liquid.

7. Subject to Regulation 9 below, the owner of a vehicle used for the conveyance of any inflammable liquid who employs any person in connection with the conveyance shall furnish a copy of these Regulations to, or affix a copy thereof in some place where it can conveniently be read by, that person and shall take all other measures necessary to ensure that that person is acquainted with and carries out the provisions of these Regulations.

8.—(1) It shall be the duty of a local authority empowered under the Petroleum (Consolidation) Act 1928 to grant petroleum-spirit licences to enforce within their district the provisions of these Regulations, and the owner of a vehicle used for the conveyance of any inflammable liquid and any person employed in connection with the conveyance shall provide all reasonable facilities to a duly authorised officer of the local authority for the purpose of his ascertaining whether the provisions of these Regulations are being duly observed.

(2) Any such local authority as aforesaid in England or Wales may institute proceedings for any offence against these Regulations committed in the area of that authority.

9. Regulations 3 to 7 of these Regulations shall not apply in relation to the conveyance of any inflammable liquid (other than acetaldehyde) in a vehicle, if—

(a) all the inflammable liquid in the vehicle is contained in receptacles which comply with the provisions of the Schedule to these Regulations ; or

(b) in the case of conveyance otherwise than in a tank wagon or tank trailer, the total quantity of inflammable liquid in the vehicle does not exceed 500 kilograms (1,102·5 pounds).

R. Maudling,
One of Her Majesty's Principal
Secretaries of State.

Home Office,
  Whitehall.
28th June 1971.

SCHEDULE Regulation 9

CONDITIONS AS TO RECEPTACLES

1. The receptacle must be made of metal, glass, porcelain, stoneware or suitable plastic material.

2. The receptacle must not contain more than 1 kilogram (2·2 pounds) of the liquid.

3. The receptacle must be so constructed and closed that none of the contents can, under normal conditions, escape from it.

4. The receptacle must be so constructed that no part of its interior surface can, under normal conditions, be so affected by contact with the contents as to make the use of that receptacle dangerous.

5.—(1) Subject to sub-paragraph (2) below, the receptacle must be enclosed in a protective package made of metal, wood or fibre-board and, where that package encloses several receptacles, it must not contain, in all, more than 30 kilograms (66·2 pounds) of inflammable liquid.

(2) This paragraph shall not apply in the case of a metal aerosol receptacle enclosed in polyethylene film by a process of shrinking and sealing by heat.

6. The receptacle, if made of glass, porcelain or stoneware, must be secured inside the protective package referred to in paragraph 5 above by suitable cushioning material.

EXPLANATORY NOTE

(This Note is not part of the Regulations.)

These Regulations revoke and replace the Inflammable Liquids (Conveyance by Road) Regulations 1968 consequent on the Petroleum (Inflammable Liquids) Order 1971. The provisions of the 1968 Regulations are repeated with the following amendments :—

(a) the quantity of inflammable liquid (other than acetaldehyde) which may be conveyed in a vehicle (other than a tank wagon or tank trailer) without compliance with the Regulations is raised from 250 to 500 kilograms (Regulation 9) ;

(b) the requirements of the Regulations are relaxed in the case of certain aerosol containers (Schedule, paragraph 5).

STATUTORY INSTRUMENTS

1971 No. 1062

PETROLEUM

The Inflammable Substances (Conveyance by Road) (Labelling) Regulations 1971

Made - - -	*28th June* 1971
Laid before Parliament	*8th July* 1971
Coming into Operation	*9th July* 1971

In exercise of the powers conferred by section 6 of the Petroleum (Consolidation) Act 1928(a), both as enacted and as applied by the Petroleum (Mixtures) Order 1929(b), the Petroleum (Carbon Disulphide) Order 1958(c), as amended (d) and the Petroleum (Inflammable Liquids) Order 1971(e), I hereby make the following Regulations :—

1.—(1) These Regulations may be cited as the Inflammable Substances (Conveyance by Road) (Labelling) Regulations 1971 and shall come into operation on 9th July 1971.

(2) The Inflammable Substances (Conveyance by Road) (Labelling) Regulations 1968(f) are hereby revoked.

2.—(1) In these Regulations—

"carrying tank" means the tank or, if there is more than one, tanks on a tank wagon or tank trailer designed for the conveyance of liquid, but does not include a fuel tank ;

"conveyance" means conveyance by road, and "conveyed" shall be construed accordingly ;

"container" (subject to paragraph (4) below) means any vessel, can, drum, barrel or other receptacle, but does not include the carrying tank of a tank wagon or tank trailer, a freight container or a fuel tank ;

"freight container" means a receptacle having an internal capacity of not less than 14·5 cubic metres (512·1 cubic feet), so constructed as to be suitable for repeated use in the conveyance of freight by one or more means of transport without intermediate reloading of the contents, but does not include a carrying tank ;

"fuel tank" means a tank which forms part of a vehicle and is designed for carrying fuel for use only in the propulsion of that vehicle ;

(a) 1928 c. 32.   (b) S.R. & O. 1929/993 (Rev. XVIII, p. 7: 1929 p. 1143).
(c) S.I. 1958/257 (1958 II, p. 1888).
(d) The amending Order is not relevant to the subject matter of these Regulations.
(e) S.I. 1971/1040 (1971 II, p. 3125). (f) S.I. 1968/928 (1968 II, p. 2424).

"inflammable substance" has the meaning assigned to it by Regulation 3 below ;

"owner", in relation to a vehicle which is the subject of a hiring agreement or hire-purchase agreement, means the person in possession of the vehicle under that agreement ;

"petroleum-spirit" means—

(a) petroleum-spirit as defined in section 23 of the Petroleum (Consolidation) Act 1928, as enacted, or

(b) mixtures of petroleum as defined in the Petroleum (Mixtures) Order 1929 (being certain substances to which the said Act is, with modifications and exceptions, applied by the said Order),

and does not include any substance, other than the said mixtures, to which the said Act is applied by any Order made, or having effect as if made, under the said section 19 ;

"potable spirit" means any spirit intended for human consumption ;

"vehicle" includes a trailer which does not form part of an articulated vehicle.

(2) For the purposes of these Regulations an articulated vehicle shall be treated as one vehicle.

(3) For the purposes of these Regulations a freight container conveyed on a vehicle shall be treated as forming part of the vehicle.

(4) In these Regulations, the expression "container" does not include a container which is itself contained in another container or which is wholly enveloped in a covering of whatever nature, but that expression does include that other container or covering (unless it is itself so contained or enveloped).

(5) In these Regulations any reference to the prescribed notice is a reference to a notice which complies with the provisions of Schedule 1 to these Regulations.

(6) The Interpretation Act 1889(a) shall apply to the interpretation of these Regulations as it applies to the interpretation of an Act of Parliament, and as if these Regulations and the Regulations revoked by these Regulations were Acts of Parliament.

3. These Regulations apply to any inflammable substance (that is to say, petroleum-spirit, carbon disulphide or any substance, solution or mixture to which section 6 of the Petroleum (Consolidation) Act 1928 was applied by Article 2 of the Petroleum (Inflammable Liquids) Order 1971) :

Provided that they do not apply to petroleum-spirit or carbon disulphide which is conveyed in such circumstances that the Petroleum-Spirit (Conveyance by Road) Regulations 1957(b) as amended (c) or, as the case may be, the Carbon Disulphide (Conveyance by Road) Regulations 1958(d) as amended (e) do not apply in relation to its conveyance.

4.—(1) Subject to Regulation 7 below, the provisions of Part I of Schedule 2 to these Regulations shall be complied with in the case of any vehicle engaged in the conveyance of any inflammable substance to which these Regulations apply.

(a) 1889 c. 63.　　　　　　　　　(b) S.I. 1957/191 (1957 II, p. 1853).
(c) The amending Regulations are not relevant to the subject matter of these Regulations.
(d) S.I. 1958/313 (1958 II, p. 1889).　　(e) S.I. 1962/2527 (1962 III, p. 3401).

(2) The provisions of Part II of the said Schedule 2 shall be complied with (in addition to those of Part I of that Schedule) in the case of a tank wagon or tank trailer engaged in the conveyance of any inflammable substance to which these Regulations apply other than petroleum-spirit.

5.—(1) Subject to Regulation 8 below, the provisions of Schedule 3 to these Regulations shall be complied with in relation to the marking of a container containing any quantity of acetaldehyde or carbon disulphide to which these Regulations apply, or more than 1 kilogram (2·2 pounds) of any other inflammable substance other than petroleum-spirit.

(2) Subject to Regulation 8 below, the provisions of paragraph 3 of the said Schedule 3 shall be complied with in relation to the marking of a container containing more than 1 kilogram (2·2 pounds) of petroleum-spirit to which these Regulations apply.

6. The owner of a vehicle used for the conveyance of any inflammable substance to which these Regulations apply who employs any person in connection with the conveyance shall furnish a copy of these Regulations to, or affix a copy thereof in some place where it can conveniently be read by, that person and shall take all other measures necessary to ensure that that person is acquainted with and carries out the provisions of these Regulations :

Provided that the provisions of this Regulation need not be complied with in relation to a vehicle which satisfies the requirements of paragraph (1) or (2) of Regulation 7 below.

7.—(1) The provisions of Part I of Schedule 2 to these Regulations need not be complied with in the case of any vehicle (other than a tank wagon or tank trailer) which is not engaged in the conveyance of acetaldehyde or carbon disulphide to which these Regulations apply, if—

(a) the total quantity of all the inflammable substances to which these Regulations apply conveyed in the vehicle does not exceed 500 kilograms (1,102·5 pounds) ;

(b) in the case of every container such as is mentioned in Regulation 5(1) above which is conveyed in the vehicle, the provisions of Schedule 3 to these Regulations are complied with (except in so far as the container is exempted from those provisions or any of them under Regulation 8 below) ; and

(c) in the case of every container such as is mentioned in Regulation 5(2) above which is conveyed in the vehicle, the provisions of paragraph 3 of the said Schedule 3 are complied with.

(2) The provisions of Part I of the said Schedule 2 need not be complied with, in the case of a vehicle which is not engaged in the conveyance of acetaldehyde or carbon disulphide to which these Regulations apply, if all the inflammable substances to which these Regulations apply conveyed in the vehicle are in receptacles which comply with the provisions of Schedule 4 to these Regulations.

8.—(1) In the case of a container which does not contain any acetaldehyde or carbon disulphide—

(a) none of the provisions of the said Schedule 3 need be complied with, if that container is itself a receptacle which complies with the provisions of the said Schedule 4 or all the inflammable substances in that container are contained in one or more receptacles which comply with those provisions ;

(b) the provisions of paragraph 1 of the said Schedule 3 need not be complied with if—

    (i) that container is itself a receptacle which does not contain more than 2·5 litres (4·4 pints) of an inflammable substance and complies with the provisions of the said Schedule 4, other than paragraph 2 thereof ; or

    (ii) all the inflammable substances in that container are contained in not more than 6 receptacles, and each of them contains not more than 2·5 litres (4·4 pints) of the substance and complies with the provisions of the said Schedule 4, other than paragraph 2 thereof.

(2) None of the provisions of the said Schedule 3 need be complied with in the case of a metal container containing not more than 5 litres (1·1 gallons) of a substance, solution or mixture to which section 6 of the Petroleum (Consolidation) Act 1928 was applied by Article 2 of the Petroleum (Inflammable Liquids) Order 1971, other than acetaldehyde, and not containing any other inflammable substance.

(3) The provisions of paragraph 3 of the said Schedule 3 need not be complied with in the case of—

    (a) a metal container containing not more than 5 litres (1·1 gallons) of petroleum-spirit and not containing any other inflammable substance ; or

    (b) a container (whether or not of metal) containing any quantity of a potable spirit and not containing any other inflammable substance.

9.—(1) Where any vehicle or container conveying or containing any of the substances to which this Regulation applies (being substances which are corrosive as well as inflammable) is required by these Regulations to display a prescribed notice, it shall also display a notice which complies with the provisions of Schedule 1 to the Corrosive Substances (Conveyance by Road) Regulations 1971(a).

(2) For the purposes of this Regulation—

    (a) Part I of Schedule 2 and paragraph 3 of Schedule 3 to these Regulations shall have effect as if, after the words "prescribed notice" wherever they occur, there were inserted the words "and the notice required by Regulation 9 above" ; and

    (b) paragraph 3 of the said Schedule 2 shall have effect as if, after the word "INFLAMMABLE", there were inserted the words "or "CORROSIVE" as the case may be".

(3) The substances to which this Regulation applies are as follows, that is to say :—

          Dimethyldichlorosilane
          Ethyldichlorosilane
          Ethyltrichlorosilane
          Methyldichlorosilane
          Methyltrichlorosilane
          Trimethylchlorosilane
          Vinyltrichlorosilane

(a) S.I. 1971/618 (1971 I, p. 1611).

10.—(1) It shall be the duty of a local authority empowered under the Petroleum (Consolidation) Act 1928 to grant petroleum-spirit licences to enforce within their district the provisions of these Regulations, and the owner of a vehicle used for the conveyance of an inflammable substance to which these Regulations apply and any person employed in connection with the conveyance shall provide all reasonable facilities to a duly authorised officer of the local authority for the purpose of his ascertaining whether the provisions of these Regulations are being duly observed.

(2) Any such local authority as aforesaid in England or Wales may institute proceedings for any offence against these Regulations committed in the area of that authority.

R. Maudling,
One of Her Majesty's Principal
Secretaries of State.

Home Office,
Whitehall.

28th June 1971.

SCHEDULE 1 Regulation 2(5)

PRESCRIBED NOTICE

1. The notice shall be in the form set out below, except that the word "LIQUID" may, if appropriate, be inserted in the notice after the word "INFLAMMABLE" and such other information as may be appropriate may be inserted therein.

2. The dimensions of the notice shall be not less than—

   (a) 20 centimetres (7·9 inches) square, in the case of a notice displayed on a vehicle in accordance with Schedule 2 to these Regulations;

   (b) 10 centimetres (3·9 inches) square, in the case of a notice displayed on a container in accordance with Schedule 3 to these Regulations.

3. The letters in the notice shall be not less than—

   (a) 2·5 centimetres (1 inch) high, in the case of a notice displayed on a vehicle as aforesaid;

   (b) 1·25 centimetres (0·5 inch) high, in the case of a notice displayed on a container as aforesaid.

4. The flame symbol and letters in the notice shall be black and the background shall be bright red.

Regulations 4, 7 and 9   SCHEDULE 2

PART I

MARKING OF VEHICLES

1. The prescribed notice shall be clearly displayed at the front and at the rear of the vehicle.

2. The prescribed notice shall be painted or otherwise indelibly marked on the vehicle or on a notice board or adhesive label securely fixed to the vehicle, and shall be kept clean and in good repair.

3. The prescribed notice shall—

    (a) be so placed on the vehicle that it is clearly visible from the front or, as the case may be, the rear of the vehicle with the letters of the word "INFLAMMABLE" in a vertical plane and arranged horizontally ; and

    (b) subject to sub-paragraph (a) of this paragraph, be placed at the highest practicable point on the vehicle and as near as possible to the centre thereof.

4. A notice board or label used for the purposes of paragraph 2 of this Schedule shall be made of durable material.

PART II

ADDITIONAL MARKING OF TANK WAGONS AND TANK TRAILERS

5.—(1) On each side of the carrying tank or, if the carrying tank is divided into compartments containing inflammable substances of different sorts, on each side of each such compartment there shall be displayed a notice clearly indicating the substance contained therein in accordance with the following provisions of this paragraph.

(2) In the case of a substance falling within Article 2(1)(a) of the Petroleum (Inflammable Liquids) Order 1971, the notices required by sub-paragraph (1) of this paragraph to be displayed shall indicate the name of the substance (being a name by which the substance is described in either column in the Table in Part I of the Schedule to the said Order).

(3) In the case of a solution or mixture falling within Article 2(1)(b) of the said Order, the notices so required to be displayed shall indicate the name of the inflammable substance contained therein in the largest proportion (being a name by which the substance is described in either column in the said Table) followed by the word "Solution" or "Mixture" as the case may be:

Provided that—

    · (a) in the case of a potable spirit, the said notices may indicate the name by which the spirit is commonly known ; and

    (b) in the case of a solution or mixture intended for disposal as waste, the said notices may bear the words "Disposable Waste".

(4) In the case of a solution falling within Article 2(1)(c) of the said Order, the notices so required to be displayed shall indicate the name of the substance dissolved therein (being the name by which the substance is described in Part II of the said Schedule) followed by the word "Solution".

6. Each such notice shall be painted or otherwise indelibly marked on the carrying tank or on a notice board or adhesive label complying with the requirements of paragraph 4 of this Schedule and securely fixed to the carrying tank.

7. The letters in each such notice shall be red and—

(a) in the case of a carrying tank divided into compartments for the conveyance of inflammable substances of different sorts shall be not less than 5 centimetres (2 inches) high ; and

(b) otherwise shall be not less than 10 centimetres (3·9 inches) high.

8. The background of each such notice shall be white.

Regulations 5, 7, 8 and 9   SCHEDULE 3

MARKING OF CONTAINERS

1.—(1) On the outside of the container there shall be displayed a notice clearly indicating the substance contained therein in accordance with the following provisions of this paragraph.

(2) In the case of a substance falling within Article 2(1)(a) of the Petroleum (Inflammable Liquids) Order 1971, the notice required by sub-paragraph (1) of this paragraph to be displayed shall indicate the name of the substance (being a name by which the substance is described in either column in the Table in Part I of the Schedule to the said Order).

(3) In the case of a solution or mixture falling within Article 2(1)(b) of the said Order, the notice so required to be displayed shall indicate the name of the inflammable substance contained therein in the largest proportion (being a name by which the substance is described in either column in the said Table) followed by the word "Solution" or "Mixture" as the case may be:

Provided that—

(a) in the case of a potable spirit, the said notices may indicate the name by which the spirit is commonly known ; and

(b) in the case of a solution or mixture intended for disposal as waste, the said notices may bear the words "Disposable Waste".

(4) In the case of a solution falling within Article 2(1)(c) of the said Order, the notice so required to be displayed shall indicate the name of the substance dissolved therein (being the name by which the substance is described in Part II of the said Schedule) followed by the word "Solution".

2. Each such notice shall be painted or otherwise indelibly marked on the container or on a label securely fixed thereto.

3. The prescribed notice shall be painted or otherwise indelibly marked on the outside of the container or on a label securely fixed thereto.

Regulations 7 and 8   SCHEDULE 4

CONDITIONS AS TO RECEPTACLES

1. The receptacle must be made of metal, glass, porcelain, stoneware or suitable plastic material.

2. The receptacle must not contain more than 1 kilogram (2·2 pounds) of an inflammable substance.

3. The receptacle must be so constructed and closed that none of the contents can, under normal conditions of conveyance, escape from it.

4. The receptacle must be so constructed that no part of its interior surface can, under normal conditions of conveyance, be so affected by contact with the contents as to make the use of that receptacle dangerous.

5.—(1) Subject to sub-paragraph (2) below, the receptacle must be enclosed in a protective package made of metal, wood or fibre-board and, where that package encloses several receptacles, it must not contain, in all, more than 30 kilograms (66·2 pounds) of inflammable substances.

(2) This paragraph shall not apply in the case of a metal aerosol receptacle enclosed in polyethylene film by a process of shrinking and sealing by heat.

6. The receptacle, if made of glass, porcelain or stoneware, must be secured inside the protective package referred to in paragraph 5 above by suitable cushioning material.

EXPLANATORY NOTE

(*This Note is not part of the Regulations.*)

These Regulations revoke and replace the Inflammable Substances (Conveyance by Road) (Labelling) Regulations 1968, consequent on the Petroleum (Inflammable Liquids) Order 1971. The provisions of the 1968 Regulations are repeated with amendments, the principal changes being as follows :—

. (a) the quantity of inflammable substances which may in certain circumstances be conveyed in a vehicle (other than a tank wagon or tank trailer) which is not carrying acetaldehyde or carbon disulphide without displaying the prescribed notice on the vehicle is raised from 250 to 500 kilograms (Regulation 7(1)(a)) ;

(b) a metal container containing not more than 5 litres of any inflammable liquid mentioned in the Petroleum (Inflammable Liquids) Order 1971 other than acetaldehyde will no longer be required to display the name of the liquid or the prescribed notice (Regulation 8(2)) ;

(c) a metal container containing not more than 5 litres of petroleum-spirit, and any type of container containing potable spirits, will no longer be required to display the prescribed notice (Regulation 8(3));

(d) in the case of substances which are corrosive as well as inflammable, notices to that effect are required to be displayed on vehicles and containers (Regulation 9);

(e) the marking requirements are relaxed in the case of certain aerosol containers (Schedule 4, paragraph 5).

STATUTORY INSTRUMENTS

1971 No. 1065

LANDLORD AND TENANT

The Rent Assessment Committees (England and Wales) Regulations 1971

Made - - -	*29th June* 1971
Laid before Parliament	*7th July* 1971
Coming into Operation	*2nd August* 1971

The Secretary of State for the Environment (as respects England, except Monmouthshire) and the Secretary of State for Wales (as respects Wales and Monmouthshire) in exercise of their powers under section 50(1) (as read with section 114(1)) of the Rent Act 1968(a), section 56(1) of the Housing Act 1969(b) and section 6(3) of the Rent (Control of Increases) Act 1969(c), and of all other powers enabling them in that behalf, and after consultation with the Council on Tribunals, hereby make the following regulations—

Citation and commencement

1. These regulations may be cited as the Rent Assessment Committees (England and Wales) Regulations 1971 and shall come into operation on 2nd August 1971.

Interpretation

2.—(1) The Interpretation Act 1889(d) shall apply for the interpretation of these regulations as it applies for the interpretation of an Act of Parliament.

(2) In these regulations, unless the context otherwise requires—

"chairman" means the chairman of a committee ;

"committee" means a rent assessment committee, constituted under Schedule 5 to the Rent Act 1968, to which a reference is made ;

"hearing" means the meeting or meetings of a committee to hear oral representations made in relation to a reference ;

"party" means, in the case where a reference is subject to a hearing, any person who is entitled under regulation 3(3) of these regulations to receive notice of the hearing and, in the case where a reference is not to be subject to a hearing, any person who is entitled to make representations in writing to the committee ;

"reference" means a matter or an application, as the case may be, which is referred by a rent officer to a rent assessment committee under Schedule 6 or Schedule 7 to the Rent Act 1968, or Part II of Schedule 2 to the Housing Act 1969.

(3) For the purpose of any of these regulations relating to procedure at a hearing, any reference to a party shall be construed as including a reference to a person authorised by a party to make oral representations on his behalf pursuant to paragraph 8, or paragraph 12(1), of Schedule 6, or paragraph 7(3) of Schedule 7, to the Rent Act 1968, or paragraph 13 of Schedule 2 to the Housing Act 1969, as the case may be.

(a) 1968 c. 23.   (b) 1969 c. 33.   (c) 1969 c. 62.   (d) 1889 c. 63.

Hearings

3.—(1) A hearing by a committee shall be in public unless, for special reasons, the committee decide otherwise; but nothing in these regulations shall prevent a member of the Council on Tribunals in that capacity from attending any hearing.

(2) Such hearing shall be on such date and at such time and place as the committee shall appoint.

(3) Notices of such date, time and place shall be given by the committee, not less than 10 days before the said date—

(*a*) where the reference is an application for a certificate of fair rent referred pursuant to paragraph 2 or paragraph 6 of Schedule 7 to the Rent Act 1968, to the applicant and, in a case to which paragraph 9 of the said Schedule applies, to the tenant ;

(*b*) where the reference is an application supported by a certificate of fair rent referred pursuant to paragraph 11 of Schedule 6 to the Rent Act 1968, to the applicant ; and

(*c*) in every other case, to the landlord and to the tenant.

4. At the hearing—

(*a*) the parties shall be heard in such order, and, subject to the provisions of these regulations, the procedure shall be such as the committee shall determine ;

(*b*) a party may call witnesses, give evidence on his own behalf and cross-examine any witnesses called by the other party.

Documents, etc.

5.—(1) The committee shall, where the reference is to be subject to a hearing, take all reasonable steps to ensure that there is supplied to each of the parties before the date of the hearing—

(*a*) a copy of, or sufficient extracts from or particulars of, any document relevant to the reference which has been received from the rent officer or from a party (other than a document which is in the possession of such party, or of which he has previously been supplied with a copy by the rent officer) ; and

(*b*) a copy of any document which embodies the results of any enquiries made by or for the committee for the purposes of that reference, or which contains relevant information in relation to fair rents previously determined for other dwelling-houses and which has been prepared for the committee for the purposes of that reference.

(2) Where at any hearing—

(i) any document relevant to the reference is not in the possession of a party present at that hearing ; and

(ii) that party has not been supplied with a copy of, or sufficient extracts from or particulars of, that document by the rent officer or by the committee in accordance with the provisions of paragraph (1) of this regulation,

then unless—

(*a*) that party consents to the continuation of the hearing ; or

(*b*) the committee consider that that party has a sufficient opportunity of dealing with that document without an adjournment of the hearing,

2h

the committee shall adjourn the hearing for a period which they consider will afford that party a sufficient opportunity of dealing with that document.

6. Where a reference is not to be subject to a hearing, the committee shall supply to each of the parties a copy of, or sufficient extracts from or particulars of, any such document as is mentioned in paragraph (1)(*a*) of regulation 5 of these regulations (other than a document excepted from that paragraph) and a copy of any such document as is mentioned in paragraph (1)(*b*) of that regulation, and they shall not reach their decision until they are satisfied that each party has been given a sufficient opportunity of commenting upon any document of which a copy, or from which extracts or of which particulars, has or have been so supplied, and upon the other's case.

Inspection of dwelling-house

7.—(1) The committee may of their own motion, and shall at the request of one of the parties (subject in either case to any necessary consent being obtained) inspect the dwelling-house which is the subject of the reference.

(2) An inspection may be made before, during or after the close of the hearing, or at such stage in relation to the consideration of the representations in writing, as the committee shall decide, and the committee shall give to the parties and their representatives an opportunity to attend.

(3) Notice of an inspection shall be given as though it were notice of a hearing, save that the requirements for such notice may be dispensed with or relaxed in so far as the committee are satisfied that the parties have received sufficient notice.

(4) Where an inspection is made after the close of a hearing, the committee shall, if they consider that it is expedient to do so on account of any matter arising from the inspection, reopen the hearing ; and if the hearing is to be reopened paragraph (3) of regulation 3 of these regulations shall apply as it applied to the original hearing, save in so far as its requirements may be dispensed with or relaxed with the consent of the parties.

Adjournment

8. The committee at their discretion may of their own motion, or at the request of the parties, or one of them, at any time and from time to time postpone or adjourn a hearing ; but they shall not do so at the request of one party only unless, having regard to the grounds on which and the time at which such request is made and to the convenience of the parties, they deem it reasonable to do so. Such notice of any postponed or adjourned hearing as is reasonable in the circumstances shall be given to the parties by the committee.

Non-appearance

9. If a party does not appear at a hearing the committee, on being satisfied that the requirements of these regulations regarding the giving of notice of hearings have been duly complied with, may proceed to deal with the reference upon the representations of any party present and upon the documents and information which they may properly consider.

Decisions

10.—(1) The decision of the committee upon a reference shall be recorded in a document signed by the chairman (or in the event of his absence or incapacity, by another member of the committee) which shall contain the reasons for the decision, but shall contain no reference to the decision being by a majority (if that be the case) or to any opinion of a minority.

(2) The chairman (or in the event of his absence or incapacity, either of the other members of the committee) shall have power, by certificate under his hand, to correct any clerical or accidental error or omission in the said document.

(3) A copy of the said document and of any such correction shall be sent by the committee to the parties and to the rent officer.

Giving of notices, etc.

11. Where any notice or other written matter is required under the provisions of these regulations to be given or supplied by the committee (including any such matter to be supplied to a party for the purposes of a reference to which regulation 6 of these regulations applies) it shall be sufficient compliance with the regulations if such notice or matter is sent by post in a prepaid letter and addressed to the party for whom it is intended at his usual or last known address, or if that party has appointed an agent to act on his behalf in relation to the reference, to that agent at the address of the agent supplied to the committee.

Peter Walker,
Secretary of State for the Environment.

29th June 1971.

Peter Thomas,
Secretary of State for Wales.

29th June 1971.

EXPLANATORY NOTE

(This Note is not part of the Regulations.)

These regulations, which apply in England and Wales, regulate the procedure to be followed by rent assessment committees appointed under Part IV of the Rent Act 1968. They supplement the provisions regulating the procedure to be followed by those committees which are contained in Schedules 6 and 7 to the Rent Act 1968 (which relate to applications for the registration of rents and to applications for certificates of fair rent) and in Part II of Schedule 2 to the Housing Act 1969 (which relates to applications for the registration of a rent where that registration will be the first after a tenancy has been converted from control to regulation under Part III of the Housing Act).

STATUTORY INSTRUMENTS

1971 No. 1067

BUILDING SOCIETIES

The Building Societies (Special Advances) Order 1971

Laid before Parliament in draft

Made - - - -	1st *July* 1971
Coming into Operation	1st *July* 1971

Whereas a draft of the following Order has been approved by a resolution of each House of Parliament as required by section 21(6) of the Building Societies Act 1962(a) :

Now, therefore, the Chief Registrar, with the consent of the Treasury, pursuant to the powers conferred upon him by subsections (4) and (5) of section 21 of the Building Societies Act 1962, and to all other powers enabling him in that behalf, hereby makes the following Order :—

1.—(1) This Order may be cited as the Building Societies (Special Advances) Order 1971, and shall come into operation on the day on which it is made.

(2) The Interpretation Act 1889(b) shall apply to the interpretation of this Order as it applies to the interpretation of an Act of Parliament.

2. The sum prescribed under section 21 of the Building Societies Act 1962 shall, in relation to advances made by building societies in any financial year beginning on or after the date of the coming into operation of this Order, be thirteen thousand pounds.

3. The Building Societies (Special Advances) Order 1967(c) is hereby revoked but not so as to affect its operation in relation to advances made by a building society in its financial year beginning before and current at the date of the coming into operation of this Order.

Dated 1st July 1971.

S. D. Musson,
Chief Registrar of Friendly Societies.

We consent to this Order,

P L. Hawkins,
H. S. P. Monro,
Two of the Lords Commissioners of
Her Majesty's Treasury.

Dated 1st July 1971.

(a) 1962 c. 37.   (b) 1889 c. 63.   (c) S.I. 1967/1861 (1967 III, p. 5000)

EXPLANATORY NOTE

(This Note is not part of the Order.)

This Order enables a building society to advance to an individual person £13,000 instead of £10,000 without the advance being treated as a Special Advance under the Building Societies Act 1962. It supersedes the Building Societies (Special Advances) Order 1967.

STATUTORY INSTRUMENTS

1971 No. 1069

AGRICULTURE

The Price Stability of Imported Products (Rates of Levy) (Cereals) (No. 1) Order 1971

Made - - - - 30th June 1971

Coming into Operation 1st July 1971

The Minister of Agriculture, Fisheries and Food, in exercise of the powers conferred upon him by section 1(2), (4), (5) and (6) of the Agriculture and Horticulture Act 1964(a) and of all other powers enabling him in that behalf, hereby makes the following order:—

1. This order may be cited as the Price Stability of Imported Products (Rates of Levy) (Cereals) (No. 1) Order 1971, and shall come into operation on 1st July 1971.

2.—(1) In this order—

" the Principal Order " means the Price Stability of Imported Products (Levy Arrangements) (Cereals) Order 1971(b), as amended by any subsequent order and if any such order is replaced by any subsequent order the expression shall be construed as a reference to such subsequent order;

AND other expressions have the same meaning as in the Principal Order.

(2) The Interpretation Act 1889(c) shall apply to the interpretation of this order as it applies to the interpretation of an Act of Parliament.

3. In accordance with and subject to the provisions of Part II of the Principal Order (which provides for the charging of levies on imports of certain specified commodities) the rate of levy for such imports into the United Kingdom of any specified commodity as are described in column 2 of the Schedule to this order in relation to a tariff heading indicated in column 1 of that Schedule shall be the rate set forth in relation thereto in column 3 of that Schedule.

In Witness whereof the Official Seal of the Minister of Agriculture, Fisheries and Food is hereunto affixed on 30th June 1971.

(L.S.)

M. E. Johnston,
Authorised by the Minister.

(a) 1964 c. 28. (b) S.I. 1971/631 (1971 I, p. 1660). (c) 1889 c. 63.

SCHEDULE

1. Tariff Heading	2. Description of Imports	3. Rate of Levy
	Imports of:—	per ton £
10.01	Wheat (other than denatured wheat)..	2·50
11.01	Wheat flours not containing chalk and containing not more than 1 per cent. by weight of fibre at the prescribed standard moisture content	4·25

EXPLANATORY NOTE

(This Note is not part of the Order.)

This order, which comes into operation on 1st July 1971, fixes rates of levy at £2·50 per ton on imports of wheat (other than denatured wheat) and £4·25 per ton on imports of certain wheat flours not containing chalk.

STATUTORY INSTRUMENTS

1971 No. 1070

INDUSTRIAL TRAINING

The Industrial Training Levy (Knitting, Lace and Net) Order 1971 (Amendment) Order 1971

Made - - -	30*th June* 1971
Laid before Parliament	9*th July* 1971
Coming into Operation	21*st July* 1971

The Secretary of State after approving proposals submitted by the Knitting, Lace and Net Industry Training Board for the amendment of the Industrial Training Levy (Knitting, Lace and Net) Order 1971(a) (which Order, hereinafter referred to as the "principal Order", makes provision as to the levy to be imposed by the Board on employers in the knitting, lace and net industry in respect of the fifth levy period) and in exercise of his powers under section 4 of the Industrial Training Act 1964(b) and of all other powers enabling him in that behalf hereby makes the following Order :—

Title and commencement

1.—(1) This Order may be cited as the Industrial Training Levy (Knitting, Lace and Net) Order 1971 (Amendment) Order 1971 and shall come into operation on 21st July 1971.

(2) The Interpretation Act 1889(c) shall apply to the interpretation of this Order as it applies to the interpretation of an Act of Parliament and as if this Order and the principal Order were Acts of Parliament.

Amendment of principal Order

2.—(1) For paragraph (3) of Article 3 of the principal Order there shall be substituted the following paragraph :—

"(3) Subject to the provisions of this Article, the levy assessed in respect of a knitting, lace and net establishment of an employer shall be an amount equal to 0·75 per cent. of the sum of the emoluments of all the persons employed in the fifth base period by the employer at or from that establishment.".

(2) For paragraph (7) of the said Article 3 there shall be substituted the following paragraph :—

"(7) There shall be exempt from the levy—

(*a*) an employer in whose case the sum of the emoluments of all the persons employed by him in the fifth base period at or from the knitting, lace and net establishment or establishments of the employer was less than £8,834 ;

(a) S.I. 1971/460 (1971 I. p. 1371).   (b) 1964 c. 16.
(c) 1889 c. 63.

(*b*) a charity.".

3. For paragraph (1) of Article 5 of the principal Order there shall be substituted the following paragraph :—

"(1) Subject to the provisions of this Article and of Articles 6 and 7, the amount of each assessment appearing in an assessment notice served by the Board shall be payable to the Board in two equal instalments, and the said instalments shall be due respectively one month and five months after the date of the notice.".

Signed by order of the Secretary of State.

Paul Bryan,
Minister of State,
30th June 1971. Department of Employment.

EXPLANATORY NOTE
(*This Note is not part of the Order.*)

This Order gives effect to proposals submitted by the Knitting, Lace and Net Industry Training Board to the Secretary of State for Employment for the amendment of the Industrial Training Levy (Knitting, Lace and Net) Order 1971, which provides for the imposition of a levy on employers in the industry in respect of the fifth levy period, commencing on 7th April and ending on 31st December 1971.

The amendments are as follows :—

(*a*) the levy is reduced from 0·85 per cent. to 0·75 per cent. of the emoluments of persons employed in the fifth base period ;

(*b*) an employer is exempt from the levy where the emoluments of his employees in the fifth base period were less than £8,834 (instead of £8,677) ;

(*c*) the second instalment of the levy becomes due five months (instead of seven months) after the date of the assessment notice.

STATUTORY INSTRUMENTS

1971 No. 1072 (S.135)

ANIMALS

The Brucellosis (Payments for Cows in Accredited Herds) (Variation) (Scotland) Scheme 1971

Made - - -	23rd *June* 1971
Laid before Parliament	7th *July* 1971
Coming into Operation	9th *July* 1971

In exercise of the powers conferred upon me by section 106(1), (9) and (10) of the Agriculture Act 1970(a) and of all other powers enabling me in that behalf, and with the consent of the Treasury, I hereby make the following scheme :—

Citation, extent, commencement and interpretation

1.—(1) This scheme may be cited as the Brucellosis (Payments for Cows in Accredited Herds) (Variation) (Scotland) Scheme 1971, shall apply to Scotland only and shall come into operation on 9th July 1971.

(2) This scheme shall be construed as one with the Brucellosis (Payments for Cows in Accredited Herds) (Scotland) Scheme 1970(b) (hereinafter referred to as "the principal scheme").

Variation of the principal scheme

2. The principal scheme shall be varied as follows :—

(a) By substituting in paragraph 2(1) thereof for the definition of "accredited herd" the following definition :—

" 'Accredited herd' means a herd of cattle which, to the satisfaction of the Secretary of State or the Minister of Agriculture, Fisheries and Food either—

(a) has been found to be free from brucellosis by means of a series of diagnostic tests carried out by him or on his behalf and has been, since the date of commencement of such tests, the subject of adequate precautions against the introduction or reintroduction and consequent spreading of brucellosis ; or

(b) has been wholly constituted by the transfer of animals from other accredited herds in Great Britain or from such similar herds outside Great Britain as the Secretary of State in relation to herds in Scotland or the Minister of Agriculture, Fisheries and Food in relation to herds in England and Wales may either generally or in any special case allow, and has been, since being so constituted, the subject of such precautions as aforesaid ;" ;

(a) 1970 c. 40.   (b) S.I. 1970/1459 (1970 III, p. 4789).

(b) by omitting in paragraph 3 thereof the words "or any subsequent year" and by inserting in that paragraph immediately after "£4" the words "and in respect of the year 1971 or any subsequent year a payment of £6·50";

(c) by substituting in paragraph 4(2)(a) thereof for the figure "5" the figure "6";

(d) by substituting in paragraph 4(2)(b) thereof for the date "31st March 1975" the date "31st March 1976";

(e) by adding at the end of paragraph 4(3)(a) thereof the words "or the period from the date last mentioned until 31st March 1976, whichever is the longer";

(f) by adding at the end of paragraph 4(3)(b) thereof the words "or until 31st March 1976, whichever is the later".

Gordon Campbell,
One of Her Majesty's Principal
Secretaries of State.

St. Andrew's House,
Edinburgh.
17th June 1971.

We consent.

V. H. Goodhew,
Walter Clegg,
Two of the Lords Commissioners of
Her Majesty's Treasury.

23rd June 1971.

EXPLANATORY NOTE

(This Note is not part of the Scheme.)

This Scheme increases from £4 to £6·50 the payment made by the Secretary of State, under The Brucellosis (Payments for Cows in Accredited Herds) (Scotland) Scheme 1970, in respect of cows kept for dairy purposes and comprised in accredited herds, the milk from which is neither sold under the provisions of a milk marketing scheme by a registered producer nor deemed for the purpose of any payments under such a scheme to have been produced from such cows. The higher rate will apply only to cows which are comprised in an eligible herd on the qualifying day in relation to the year 1971 or any subsequent year.

The scheme provides for payments for an additional year in the case of certain herds.

The definition of "accredited herd" has been amended to include herds constituted from animals transferred from other accredited herds in Great Britain or from similar herds outside Great Britain provided that the herds have been the subject of adequate precautions against the introduction or reintroduction and consequent spreading of the disease.

STATUTORY INSTRUMENTS

1971 No. 1075

CUSTOMS AND EXCISE

The Anti-Dumping (Provisional Charge to Duty) (No. 3) Order 1971

Made - - - -	1st July 1971
Laid before the House of Commons - -	7th July 1971
Coming into Operation	8th July 1971

The Secretary of State, in exercise of the powers conferred upon him by sections 1, 2, 8 and 9(3) of the Customs Duties (Dumping and Subsidies) Act 1969(a), hereby makes the following Order:—

1. This Order may be cited as the Anti-Dumping (Provisional Charge to Duty) (No. 3) Order 1971 and shall come into operation on 8th July 1971.

2. Goods of the description set out in the Schedule hereto (being goods classified in the Customs Tariff 1959(b) under the heading mentioned in the first column of that Schedule) shall be subject to a provisional charge to duty in respect of a duty of customs at the rate set out in the third column of that Schedule.

3. Section 2 of the Customs Duties (Dumping and Subsidies) Act 1969 (which allows relief to be given where goods are shown not to have been dumped or where the margin of dumping is less than the provisional charge) shall apply to the provisional charge imposed by this Order.

Anthony Grant,
Parliamentary Under Secretary of State,
Department of Trade and Industry.

1st July 1971.

(a) 1969 c. 16.   (b) See S.I. 1970/1522 (1970 III, p. 4935).

SCHEDULE

Relevant Tariff Heading	Description of Goods	Relevant Rate
Ex 44.18 (B)	Wood chipboard without surface lamination—	
	(a) originating in Norway and being a product of A/L Orkla Skogindustri, Namdal Skogindustri A/S or A/S Saga Skogindustri;	£3·00 per cubic metre
	(b) originating in Sweden and being a product of Ry Aktiebolag;	£2·00 per cubic metre
	(c) originating in Sweden and being a product of Skogsägarnas Industri Ab;	£0·50 per cubic metre
	(d) originating in Finland and being a product of Osuuskunta Metsäliitto Levymyynti, Oulu Osakeyhtiö, Suomen Osuuskauppojen Keskuskunta, Oy Wilh. Schauman Ab or Tiwi Oy;	£2·00 per cubic metre
	(e) originating in Finland and being a product of Pellos Oy;	£1·48 per cubic metre
	(f) originating in the Republic of Ireland and being a product of Munster Chipboard Co. Ltd. or Chipboard Ltd.	£1·25 per cubic metre

EXPLANATORY NOTE

(This Note is not part of the Order.)

This Order imposes a provisional charge in respect of an anti-dumping duty on imports of unfaced wood chipboard which originates in Norway, Sweden, Finland or the Irish Republic and is produced by certain firms in those countries (named in the Schedule to the Order).

The making of the Order enables the Commssioners of Customs and Excise to require security for the payment of any anti-dumping duty which may be imposed retrospectively on such imports under section 8(1) of the Customs Duties (Dumping and Subsidies) Act 1969. If any duty is imposed retrospectively, it may only be so imposed on goods imported while the Order is in force, and its rate may not exceed the rate mentioned in the Schedule to the Order.

The Order expires automatically after three months unless previously revoked or extended (for not more than three months) by a further Order.

STATUTORY INSTRUMENTS

1971 No. 1076 (S.136)

AGRICULTURE

AGRICULTURAL GRANTS, GOODS AND SERVICES

The Farm Capital Grant (Variation) (Scotland) Scheme 1971

Made - - -	*30th June* 1971
Laid before Parliament	*8th July* 1971
Coming into Operation	*1st September* 1971

In exercise of the powers conferred on me by sections 28 and 29 of the Agriculture Act 1970(a) and of all other powers enabling me in that behalf, with the approval of the Treasury, I hereby make the following scheme :—

Citation, commencement, extent and interpretation

1.—(1) This scheme, which may be cited as the Farm Capital Grant (Variation) (Scotland) Scheme 1971, shall come into operation on 1st September 1971 and shall apply to Scotland only.

(2) The Interpretation Act 1889(b) shall apply for the interpretation of this scheme as it applies for the interpretation of an Act of Parliament.

Variation of the principal scheme

2. The Farm Capital Grant (Scotland) Scheme 1970(c) shall be varied as follows—

(a) by inserting in paragraph 5 thereof immediately after the words "qualify for" the words "consideration for a" ;

(b) by inserting at the end of Schedule 2 thereto the following paragraph :—

"**6.**—(1) Notwithstanding the provisions of paragraph 1 of this Schedule insofar as they relate to orchard grubbing, the amount of any grant payable under this scheme towards expenditure in respect of the grubbing of an orchard, or any part of an orchard—

(a) in which all the trees are apple trees or pear trees, or

(b) in which apple trees or pear trees are interspersed throughout with other trees and are in number not less than half of all the trees in that orchard or part of an orchard,

may, if application for approval of that expenditure for the purposes of a grant under this scheme is made before 1st April 1973, be equal to the amount fixed for the time being by the Secretary of State for the purposes of paragraph 5 of this Schedule as representing the standard cost of that work.

(a) 1970 c. 40.   (b) 1889 c. 63.   (c) S.I. 1970/1805 (1970 III, p. 5869).

(2) Without prejudice to any other conditions which may be imposed by or under this scheme, the making of any such grant, being a grant the amount of which is calculated in accordance with this paragraph, shall be subject to the condition that during the period beginning with the day of making the application for approval of the expenditure towards which the grant is made and ending with the expiration of 5 years after the completion of the work in respect of which the grant is made the aggregate area of land (being land which is occupied at the beginning of that period for the purposes of the agricultural business for the purposes of which, or in connection with which, the expenditure has been or is to be incurred) on which apple trees or pear trees, not being trees in respect of the grubbing of which the said expenditure has been or is to be incurred, are grown at any time during that period shall not increase."

Gordon Campbell,
One of Her Majesty's Principal
Secretaries of State.

St. Andrew's House,
Edinburgh.
30th June 1971.

We approve.

V. H. Goodhew,
Walter Clegg,
Two of the Lords Commissioners of
Her Majesty's Treasury.

30th June 1971.

EXPLANATORY NOTE

(This Note is not part of the Scheme.)

This varying Scheme, which applies to Scotland only, provides for an additional and higher rate of grant under the Farm Capital Grant (Scotland) Scheme 1970 towards approved expenditure on the grubbing of an orchard, or part of an orchard, containing apple trees or pear trees if application for approval of the expenditure is made before 1st April 1973. The grant is equal in amount to the standard cost fixed for the work and grant made at this higher rate is subject to a specified condition restricting replanting.

STATUTORY INSTRUMENTS

1971 No. 1077

AGRICULTURE

AGRICULTURAL GRANTS, GOODS AND SERVICES

The Farm Capital Grant (Variation) Scheme 1971

Made - - -	*1st July* 1971
Laid before Parliament	*8th July* 1971
Coming into Operation	*1st September* 1971

The Minister of Agriculture, Fisheries and Food and the Secretary of State for Wales, acting jointly, in exercise of the powers conferred on them by sections 28, 29 and 51(1) of the Agriculture Act 1970(a) and of all other powers enabling them in that behalf, with the approval of the Treasury, hereby make the following scheme :—

Citation, commencement, extent and interpretation

1.—(1) This scheme, which may be cited as the Farm Capital Grant (Variation) Scheme 1971, shall come into operation on 1st September 1971 and shall apply to England and Wales and Northern Ireland.

(2) The Interpretation Act 1889(b) shall apply to the interpretation of this scheme as it applies to the interpretation of an Act of Parliament.

Variation of the principal scheme

2. The Farm Capital Grant Scheme 1970(c) shall be varied as follows :—

   (*a*) by inserting in paragraph 5(1) thereof immediately after the words "qualify for" the words "consideration for a" ;

   (*b*) by inserting at the end of Schedule 3 thereto the following paragraph : —

      "6.—(1) Notwithstanding the provisions of paragraph 1 of this Schedule insofar as they relate to orchard grubbing, the amount of any grant payable under this scheme towards expenditure in respect of the grubbing of an orchard, or any part of an orchard—

      (*a*) in which all the trees are apple trees or pear trees to which this paragraph applies, or

      (*b*) in which apple trees or pear trees to which this paragraph applies are interspersed throughout with other trees and are in number not less than half of all the trees in that orchard or part of an orchard,

---

(a) 1970 c. 40.   (b) 1889 c. 63.   (c) S.I. 1970/1759 (1970 III, p. 5741).

may, if application for approval of that expenditure for the purposes of a grant under this scheme is made before 1st April 1973, be equal to the amount fixed for the time being by the appropriate Minister for the purposes of paragraph 5 of this Schedule as representing the standard cost of that work.

(2) Without prejudice to any other conditions which may be imposed by or under this scheme, the making of any such grant, being a grant the amount of which is calculated in accordance with this paragraph, shall be subject to the condition that during the period beginning with the day of making the application for approval of the expenditure towards which the grant is made and ending with the expiration of 5 years after the completion of the work in respect of which the grant is made the aggregate area of land (being land which is occupied at the beginning of that period for the purposes of the agricultural business for the purposes of which, or in connection with which, the expenditure has been or is to be incurred) on which apple trees or pear trees to which this paragraph applies, not being trees in respect of the grubbing of which the said expenditure has been or is to be incurred, are grown at any time during that period shall not increase.

(3) The apple trees and pear trees to which this paragraph applies are any plants capable of bearing in season, respectively, apples other than cider apples and pears other than perry pears and in this paragraph the expressions "cider apples" and "perry pears" have the meanings assigned to them by article 2(1) of, and Schedule 3 to, the Apple and Pear Development Council Order 1966(a).".

In Witness whereof the Official Seal of the Minister of Agriculture, Fisheries and Food is hereunto affixed on 29th June 1971.

(L.S.)

J. M. L. Prior,
Minister of Agriculture, Fisheries
and Food.

Given under my hand on 1st July 1971.

Peter Thomas,
Secretary of State for Wales.

We approve.
1st July 1971.

H. S. P. Monro,
P. L. Hawkins,
Two of the Lords Commissioners of
Her Majesty's Treasury.

(a) S.I. 1966/1579 (1966 III, p. 4883).

EXPLANATORY NOTE

(This Note is not part of the Scheme.)

This varying scheme, which applies to England and Wales and Northern Ireland, provides for an additional and higher rate of grant under the Farm Capital Grant Scheme 1970 towards approved expenditure on the grubbing of an orchard, or part of an orchard, containing apple trees or pear trees (excluding cider apple trees and perry pear trees) if application for approval of the expenditure is made before 1st April 1973. The grant is equal in amount to the standard cost fixed for the work and grant made at this higher rate is subject to a specified condition restricting replanting.

STATUTORY INSTRUMENTS

1971 No. 1078

PURCHASE TAX

The Purchase Tax (No. 3) Order 1971

Made - - - -	*5th July* 1971
Laid before the House of Commons - - -	*9th July* 1971
Coming into Operation -	*12th July* 1971

The Lords Commissioners of Her Majesty's Treasury, by virtue of the powers conferred on them by section 2(3) of the Purchase Tax Act 1963(a), and of all other powers enabling them in that behalf, hereby make the following Order:—

1.—(1) This Order may be cited as the Purchase Tax (No. 3) Order 1971.

(2) The Interpretation Act 1889(b) shall apply for the interpretation of this Order as it applies for the interpretation of an Act of Parliament.

(3) This Order shall come into operation on 12th July 1971.

2. In Group 11 of Part I of Schedule 1 to the Purchase Tax Act 1963, after paragraph (2)(v) of the heading " Exempt " there shall be inserted the following sub-paragraph:—

(vi) electrically or mechanically adjustable beds, specially designed for invalids.

3. Group 12 of Part I of Schedule 1 to the Purchase Tax Act 1963 shall be amended as follows:—

(*a*) at the end of paragraph (*b*) there shall be added the words " including parts of and accessories for waste disposal units "; and

(*b*) after paragraph (8) of the heading " Exempt " there shall be inserted the following paragraph:—

(9) Appliances and apparatus specially designed for invalids, the following—

(i) chair lifts and stair lifts for use with invalid chairs;

(ii) hoists and lifters.

Bernard Weatherill,

H. S. P. Monro,

Two of the Lords Commissioners
of Her Majesty's Treasury.

5th July 1971.

(a) 1963 c. 9.   (b) 1889 c. 63.

EXPLANATORY NOTE

(This Note is not part of the Order.)

This Order extends the tax to parts of and accessories for waste disposal units. It relieves from the tax certain aids, appliances and apparatus for invalids.

STATUTORY INSTRUMENTS

1971 No. 1079 (S.137)

EDUCATION, SCOTLAND
The Schools (Scotland) Code (Amendment No. 1) Regulations 1971

Made - - -	*2nd July* 1971
Laid before Parliament	*9th July* 1971
Coming into Operation	*1st August* 1971

In exercise of the powers conferred upon me by section 2 of the Education (Scotland) Act 1962(a) as set out in section 1(1) of the Education (Scotland) Act 1969(b), and by section 144 of the said Act of 1962, as amended by the said Act of 1969, and of all other powers enabling me in that behalf, I hereby make the following regulations:—

Citation, construction and commencement

1. These regulations, which may be cited as the Schools (Scotland) Code (Amendment No. 1) Regulations 1971, shall be construed as one with the Schools (Scotland) Code 1956(c) as amended (d) (hereinafter referred to as the "principal regulations"), and shall come into operation on 1st August 1971.

Amendment of regulation 4 of the principal regulations

2. In regulation 4 of the principal regulations for paragraph (4) there shall be substituted the following paragraph—

"(4) Where a registered or a conditionally registered teacher cannot be obtained to fill a teaching post in a special school or in a secondary school or department, the authority may appoint some other person temporarily to fill the post for a period not exceeding 12 months, provided that—

(*a*) the authority have received the prior approval of the reference panel to the appointment; and

(*b*) the authority shall continue to take all practical steps to obtain a registered or a conditionally registered teacher to fill the post."

Gordon Campbell,
One of Her Majesty's
Principal Secretaries of State.

St. Andrew's House,
Edinburgh.
2nd July1971.

(a) 1962 c. 47.   (b) 1969 c. 49.   (c) S.I. 1956/894 (1956 I, p. 735).
(d) The relevant amending instruments are S.I. 1967/1162, 1968/1055 (1967 II, p. 3396: 1968 II, p. 2849).

EXPLANATORY NOTE

(This Note is not part of the Regulations.)

This amendment to the Code requires an education authority to secure the approval of the reference panel before making an appointment of an unqualified teacher to fill a post in either a special school or a secondary school on a temporary basis.

1971 No. 1081 (L.25)

COUNTY COURTS

The County Court Districts (Miscellaneous) Order 1971

Made	- - -	28*th June* 1971
Coming into Operation		26*th July* 1971

The Lord Chancellor, in exercise of the powers conferred on him by section 2 of the County Courts Act 1959(a) and, so far as is required by subsection (2) of that section, with the consent of the Chancellor of the Duchy of Lancaster, hereby makes the following Order:—

1.—(1) This Order may be cited as the County Court Districts (Miscellaneous) Order 1971 and shall come into operation on 26th July 1971.

(2) In this Order "the principal Order" means the County Court Districts Order 1970(b), as amended (c).

(3) The Interpretation Act 1889(d) shall apply to the interpretation of this Order as it applies to the interpretation of an Act of Parliament.

2. The amendments set out in columns 2 and 3 of the schedule to this Order shall be made in their proper alphabetical position in the corresponding columns of schedule 1 to the principal Order opposite the names of the courts mentioned in column 1 of the schedule to this Order:

Provided that nothing in this Order shall affect the jurisdiction of the Lambeth County Court or the Preston County Court to hear and determine any proceedings pending therein on the coming into operation of this Order.

Dated 16th June 1971.

Hailsham of St. Marylebone, C.

This Order, so far as it relates to any county court held for a Duchy of Lancaster district, is made with my consent.

Dated 28th June 1971.

Geoffrey Rippon,
Chancellor of the Duchy of Lancaster.

(a) 1959 c. 22. (b) S.I. 1970/16 (1970 I, p. 17).
(c) The relevant amending instruments are S.I. 1970/904, 2031, (1970 II, p. 2833;III, p. 6621). (d) 1889 c. 63.

SCHEDULE

Column 1	Column 2	Column 3
BANBURY	In the entry relating to Banbury Rural District:—	
		Delete "East Adderbury" and "West Adderbury" and insert "Adderbury"
BLACKBURN	In the entry relating to Bowland Rural District:—	
	Delete the words "(part). *Other part* in Preston County Court District".	Insert "Bowland Forest High"
CHIPPENHAM	In the entry relating to Calne and Chippenham Rural District:—	
		Insert "Seagry"
LAMBETH	For the entry relating to the London Borough of Southwark substitute the following:—	
		"That part of the Borough to the south and west of a line drawn from the point where the Borough boundary crosses Lambeth Road, eastward along the middle of Lambeth Road and St. George's Road, southward along the middle of Elephant and Castle to the Walworth Road, then to the east of the buildings fronting the Walworth Road and Camberwell Road to its junction with Camberwell Church Street and eastward to the north of the buildings fronting Camberwell Church Street, Peckham Road, Peckham High Street and Queen's Road to the Borough boundary."
NORTH-ALLERTON	In the entry relating to Bedale Rural District:—	
	For "*Other part* in Ripon County Court District." substitute "*Other part* in Harrogate County Court District."	
OXFORD	In the entry relating to Abingdon Rural District:—	
		Delete "Draycott Moor" and for the words "Kingston Bagpuize" substitute "Kingston Bagpuize with Southmoor".
PRESTON	Delete "Bowland Rural District (part). *Other part* in Blackburn County Court District."	Delete "Bowland Forest High".

SCHEDULE—*continued*

Column 1	Column 2	Column 3
SOUTHWARK	For the entry relating to the London Borough of Southwark substitute the following:—	
		"That part of the Borough to the north and east of a line drawn from the point where the Borough boundary crosses Lambeth Road eastward along the middle of Lambeth Road and St. George's Road, southward along the middle of the Elephant and Castle to the Walworth Road, then to the east of the buildings fronting Walworth Road and Camberwell Road to its junction with Camberwell Church Street and eastward to the north of the buildings fronting Camberwell Church Street, Peckham Road, Peckham High Street and Queen's Road to the Borough boundary."
WITNEY	In the entry relating to Witney Rural District:—	
		Delete "Blackbourton" and insert "Carterton with Black Bourton".
YORK	In the entry relating to Nidderdale Rural District:—	
	For "*Other parts* in Harrogate and Ripon County Court Districts" substitute "*Other part* in Harrogate County Court District".	

EXPLANATORY NOTE

(This Note is not part of the Order.)

This Order amends the County Court Districts Order 1970 to reflect recent alterations in the local authority areas situated within the districts of the Banbury, Chippenham, Oxford and Witney County Courts resulting from Orders made by the Secretary of State for the Environment under section 142 of the Local Government Act 1933 (c.51).

The present Order also transfers one parish from the district of the Preston County Court to the district of the Blackburn County Court and part of the London Borough of Southwark is transferred from the district of the Lambeth County Court to the district of the Southwark County Court. Minor consequential amendments of a formal nature are made in the references to the local authority areas for the county courts at Northallerton and York. None of the foregoing amendments affects the sittings or offices of the courts.

STATUTORY INSTRUMENTS

1971 No. 1082

LAND REGISTRATION

The Land Registration Fee Order 1971

Made - - - -	*28th June* 1971
Coming into Operation	*1st August* 1971

The Lord Chancellor, with the advice and assistance of the Rule Committee appointed in pursuance of section 144 of the Land Registration Act 1925(a) and with the concurrence of the Treasury, in exercise of the powers conferred on him by section 145 of that Act, hereby makes the following Order:—

1.—(1) This Order may be cited as the Land Registration Fee Order 1971 and shall come into operation on 1st August 1971.

(2) The Interpretation Act 1889(b) shall apply to the interpretation of this Order as it applies to the interpretation of an Act of Parliament.

2. For paragraph 14 of the Land Registration Fee Order 1970(c) there shall be substituted the following paragraph :—

" 14(1) A charge to secure further advances, where the total amount of the advances or of the money to be owing at any one time is in any way limited, shall be treated as a charge to secure the amount so limited.

(2) A charge to secure further advances, where the total amount of the advances or of the money to be owing at any one time is in no way limited, shall be treated as a charge to secure the amount of principal owing at the date of the application for registration of the charge together with the amount of any further advances which the lender is obliged to make thereunder; and, as evidence of the amount of principal so owing and of any further obligatory advances, the Registrar may require a statement in writing, signed by the applicant or his solicitor or by any other person who in the Registrar's opinion is competent to make such a statement."

3. At the end of paragraph VI in the Schedule to the Land Registration Fee Order 1970 there shall be inserted the following proviso:—

" Provided that upon an application for registration of a transfer to give effect to an appointment or discharge of a trustee, the fee payable shall not exceed £2 for each title affected with a maximum fee of £50 upon any one application."

Dated 25th June 1971.

Hailsham of St. Marylebone, C.

We concur,

Dated 28th June 1971.

Walter Clegg,
H. S. P. Monro,
Two of the Lords Commissioners
of Her Majesty's Treasury.

(a) 1925 c. 21.   (b) 1889 c. 63.   (c) S.I. 1970/557 (1970 I, p. 1779).

EXPLANATORY NOTE
(This Note is not part of the Order.)

This Order, which amends the Land Registration Fee Order 1970, requires the registration fee on a charge securing unlimited amounts to be calculated by reference to the principal owing and future obligatory advances instead of by reference to stamp duty. The Order also reduces from £250 to £2 per title and £50 for several titles the maximum transfer fee payable on the appointment or discharge of trustees.

STATUTORY INSTRUMENTS

1971 No. 1083 (L.26)

COUNTY COURTS

FEES

The County Court Fees (Amendment) Order 1971

Made - - -	24*th June* 1971
Laid before Parliament	12*th July* 1971
Coming into Operation	2*nd August* 1971

The Lord Chancellor and the Treasury, in exercise of the powers conferred on them by section 177 of the County Courts Act 1959(**a**) and section 2 of the Public Offices Fees Act 1879(**b**), hereby make and concur in the following Order :—

1.—(1) This Order may be cited as the County Court Fees (Amendment) Order 1971 and shall come into operation on 2nd August 1971.

(2) In this Order a fee referred to by number means the fee so numbered in the Table of Fees contained in the Schedule to the County Court Fees Order 1959(**c**), as amended (**d**).

(3) The Interpretation Act 1889(**e**) shall apply to the interpretation of this Order as it applies to the interpretation of an Act of Parliament.

2. After Fee No. 22 there shall be inserted the following fee :—

"The Attachment of Earnings Act 1971(**f**)

22A	(i) On an application for an attachment of earnings order to secure maintenance payments	50p

(ii) On an application for an attachment of earnings order (other than a consolidated attachment order) to secure payment of a judgment debt which—

	does not exceed £10 ...			£1
exceeds £10 „ „ „	£20 ...			£2
„ £20 „ „ „	£30 ...			£3
„ £30 „ „ „	£50 ...			£4
„ £50 „ „ „	£100 ...			£5
exceeds £100				£6

(**a**) 1959 c. 22. (**b**) 1879 c. 58.
(**c**) S.I. 1959/1262 (1959 I, p. 803).
(**d**) The relevant amending instruments are S.I. 1961/355, 1965/395, 1966/243, 1971/101 (1961 I, p. 565; 1965 I, p. 1099; 1966 I, p. 496; 1971 I, p. 188).
(**e**) 1889 c. 63. (**f**) 1971 c. 32.

Fee No. 22A(i) *or* (ii) *is not payable where an attachment of earnings order is made on the hearing of a judgment summons.*

Where a judgment summons has been issued in respect of the same judgment debt or part thereof but, in consequence of section 11 of the Administration of Justice Act 1970(**a**), *no order has been made on the judgment summons, credit shall be given for Fee No.* 50 *in calculating Fee No.* 22A(ii).

(iii) On a consolidated attachment order under Order 25, Rule 90	The same fee as would be payable if the order were an administration order."
This fee is payable out of the money paid into court.	

3. Fee No. 28(iii) shall be omitted.

4. In Fee No. 63 after the words "the Act" there shall be inserted the words "or section 4 of the Attachment of Earnings Act 1971".

5. After Fee No. 72 there shall be inserted the following fee :—

	"Register of attachment of earnings orders	
73	On a request for a search under Order 25, Rule 78(3)	25p
	This fee includes the issue of a certificate of the result of the search."	

Dated 21st June 1971.

Hailsham of St. Marylebone. C.

Dated 24th June 1971.

Walter Clegg,
V. H. Goodhew,
Two of the Lords Commissioners
of Her Majesty's Treasury.

(**a**) 1970 c. 31.

EXPLANATORY NOTE

(This Note is not part of the Order.)

This Order provides for the fees to be paid in county courts in proceedings under the Attachment of Earnings Act 1971. It will come into force with the Act on 2nd August 1971.

STATUTORY INSTRUMENTS

1971 No. 1087

ROAD TRAFFIC

SPECIAL ROADS

The Motorways Traffic (England and Wales) (Amendment) Regulations 1971

Made - - -	*1st July* 1971
Laid before Parliament	*13th July* 1971
Coming into Operation	*20th July* 1971

The Secretary of State for the Environment (as respects England excluding Monmouthshire) and the Secretary of State for Wales (as respects Wales and Monmouthshire) in exercise of their powers under section 13 of the Road Traffic Regulation Act 1967(a) and all other enabling powers, and after consultation with representative organisations in accordance with the provisions of section 107(2) of that Act, hereby make the following Regulations :—

1. These Regulations shall come into operation on 20th July 1971 and may be cited as the Motorways Traffic (England and Wales) (Amendment) Regulations 1971.

2. The Interpretation Act 1889(b) shall apply for the interpretation of these Regulations as it applies for the interpretation of an Act of Parliament, and as if for the purposes of section 38 of that Act these Regulations were an Act of Parliament and the Regulations revoked by Regulation 3 below were an Act of Parliament thereby repealed.

3. The Motorways Traffic (England) (Amendment) Regulations 1966(c) are hereby revoked.

4. The Motorways Traffic Regulations 1959(d) shall have effect as though after Regulation 11 there were inserted the following Regulation :—

"Restriction on use of right-hand or off side lane

    11(A)—(1) This Regulation applies to—

        (*a*) a motor vehicle other than—

            (i) a motor car with an unladen weight not exceeding 3 tons,

            (ii) a heavy motor car constructed solely for the carriage of passengers and their effects and not adapted or used for any other purpose, or

            (iii) a motor cycle ; and

        (*b*) a motor vehicle drawing a trailer.

(**a**) 1967 c. 76.   (**b**) 1889 c. 63.
(**c**) S.I. 1966/530 (1966 II, p. 1108).   (**d**) S.I. 1959/1147 (1959 II, p. 2507).

(2) Subject to paragraphs (3) and (4) below, no vehicle to which this Regulation applies shall be driven, or moved or stop or remain at rest on the right-hand or off side lane of a length of carriageway which has three traffic lanes at any place where all three lanes are open for use by traffic proceeding in the same direction.

(3) Where, in relation to a length of carriageway which has four traffic lanes, there is a traffic sign (being a sign which bears, inter-alia, the legend "crawler lane") indicating that the left-hand or near side lane comprised in that length is intended primarily for use by slow moving traffic, paragraph (2) above shall apply in relation to that length as if the said traffic lane and the traffic lane immediately next to it comprised a single traffic lane and, accordingly, as if the said length of carriageway were a length having three traffic lanes.

(4) The prohibition contained in paragraph (2) above shall not apply to a vehicle while it is being driven on any right-hand or off side lane such as is mentioned in that paragraph in so far as it is necessary for the vehicle to be so driven to enable it to pass another vehicle which is carrying or drawing a load of exceptional width.".

Signed by authority of the Secretary of State for the Environment.

Dated 1st July 1971.

John Peyton,
Minister for Transport Industries,
Department of the Environment.

Dated 1st July 1971.

Peter Thomas,
Secretary of State for Wales.

EXPLANATORY NOTE

(This Note is not part of the Regulations.)

Regulation 11(A) of the Motorways Traffic Regulations 1959 (as inserted by the Motorways Traffic (England) (Amendment) Regulations 1966) imposes a restriction on certain vehicles (in general, goods vehicles having an unladen weight exceeding 3 tons and vehicles drawing a trailer) from using the right-hand or off-side lane of a length of carriageway of a motorway which has three traffic lanes. These Regulations, which apply in relation to England and Wales, re-enact Regulation 11(A) amended so as to apply that restriction to a length of carriageway which has four traffic lanes where the left-hand or near side lane is intended primarily for slow moving traffic.

STATUTORY INSTRUMENTS

1971 No. 1088

WAGES COUNCILS

The Wages Regulation (Stamped or Pressed Metal-Wares) Order 1971

Made - - -	*5th July* 1971
Coming into Operation	*26th July* 1971

Whereas the Secretary of State has received from the Stamped or Pressed Metal-Wares Wages Council (Great Britain) the wages regulation proposals set out in the Schedule hereto ;

Now, therefore, the Secretary of State in exercise of his powers under section 11 of the Wages Councils Act 1959(a), and of all other powers enabling him in that behalf, hereby makes the following Order :—

1. This Order may be cited as the Wages Regulation (Stamped or Pressed Metal-Wares) Order 1971.

2.—(1) In this Order the expression "the specified date" means the 26th July 1971, provided that where, as respects any worker who is paid wages at intervals not exceeding seven days, that date does not correspond with the beginning of the period for which the wages are paid, the expression "the specified date" means, as respects that worker, the beginning of the next such period following that date.

(2) The Interpretation Act 1889(b) shall apply to the interpretation of this Order as it applies to the interpretation of an Act of Parliament and as if this Order and the Order hereby revoked were Acts of Parliament.

3. The wages regulation proposals set out in the Schedule hereto shall have effect as from the specified date and as from that date the Wages Regulation (Stamped or Pressed Metal-Wares) Order 1970(c) shall cease to have effect.

Signed by order of the Secretary of State.
5th July 1971.

J. R. Lloyd Davies,
. Assistant Secretary,
Department of Employment.

(a) 1959 c. 69.   (b) 1889 c. 63.
(c) S.I. 1970/296 (1970 I, p. 1093).

Article 3 SCHEDULE

The following minimum remuneration shall be substituted for the statutory minimum remuneration fixed by the Wages Regulation (Stamped or Pressed Metal-Wares) Order 1970 (Order Q. (102)).

STATUTORY MINIMUM REMUNERATION

PART I

GENERAL

1.—(1) The minimum remuneration payable to a worker to whom this Schedule applies (except in any week for which guaranteed weekly remuneration is payable under paragraph 7) is as follows, that is to say:—

(a) for all work except work to which a minimum overtime rate applies under Part IV of this Schedule—

(i) in the case of a time worker, the hourly general minimum time rate applicable to the worker,

(ii) in the case of a worker employed on piece work, piece rates each of which would yield, in the circumstances of the case, to an ordinary worker, at least the same amount of money as the hourly piece work basis time rate applicable to the worker ;

(b) for all work to which a minimum overtime rate applies under Part IV of this Schedule, that rate.

(2) In this Schedule, the expressions "hourly general minimum time rate" and "hourly piece work basis time rate" mean respectively the weekly general minimum time rate and the weekly piece work basis time rate applicable to the worker under Part II or Part III of this Schedule divided, in either case, by 40.

Part II

MALE WORKERS

GENERAL MINIMUM TIME RATES AND PIECE WORK BASIS TIME RATES

2. The general minimum time rates and piece work basis time rates applicable to male workers are:—

(1) Workers aged 21 years or over employed as POLISHERS, BRAZIERS, BURNISHERS, DROP-STAMPERS, DIPPERS who are also BRONZERS, DIPPERS or ANNEALERS, as follows:—

	General minimum time rates Per week of 40 hours	Piece work basis time rates Per week of 40 hours
	£	£
(a) Polishers:—		
Grade I	14·85	15·75
Grade II	15·30	16·25
Grade III	16·30	17·30
(b) Braziers, burnishers, drop-stampers or dippers who are also bronzers:—		
Grade I	14·85	15·75
Grade II	15·20	16·15
Grade III	16·20	17·20
(c) Dippers or annealers	14·85	15·75

Provided that where a worker is employed on work of more than one grade the rate applicable in respect of all such work shall be that applicable to the highest grade upon which he is employed.

(2) Workers aged 21 years or over other than the workers specified in sub-paragraph (1) of this paragraph, as follows:—

General minimum time rates Per week of 40 hours	Piece work basis time rates Per week of 40 hours
£	£
13·70	14·50

(3) All male workers under 21 years of age, as follows:—

	General minimum time rates Per week of 40 hours	Piece work basis time rates Per week of 40 hours
	£	£
Aged 20 and under 21 years	11·45	12·15
„ 19 „ „ 20 „	9·90	10·50
„ 18 „ „ 19 „	8·60	9·10
„ 17 „ „ 18 „	6·95	7·35
„ 16 „ „ 17 „	5·65	6·00
„ under 16 years	4·45	4·70

PART III

FEMALE WORKERS

GENERAL MINIMUM TIME RATES AND PIECE WORK BASIS TIME RATES

3. The general minimum time rates and piece work basis time rates applicable to female workers are:—

(1) Workers employed as POLISHERS or DROP-STAMPERS, as follows:—

	General minimum time rates Per week of 40 hours		Piece work basis time rates Per week of 40 hours	
	up to and including 5th December 1971	on and after 6th December 1971	up to and including 5th December 1971	on and after 6th December 1971
	£	£	£	£
Aged 21 years or over ...	12·60	12·85	13·35	13·60
„ 20 and under 21 years	11·70	11·95	12·40	12·65
„ 19 „ „ 20 „	11·35	11·55	12·00	12·25
„ 18 „ „ 19 „	11·05	11·25	11·70	11·95
„ 17 „ „ 18 „	8·35	8·55	8·90	9·05
„ 16 „ „ 17 „	6·80	6·95	7·25	7·40
„ under 16 years ...	5·40	5·55	5·75	5·85

(2) Workers—who are employed as HAND BRUSH JAPANNERS capable of finishing all classes of work (or, in the case of workers aged under 18 years, are training to qualify as such) ; or

who are employed as HAND BRUSH LACQUERERS capable of finishing all classes of work (or, in the case of workers aged under 18 years, are training to qualify as such) ; or

who are employed as BLOW PIPE BRAZIERS using hard solder ; or

who are employed as SOLDERERS using ordinary hand iron or blow pipe with bar, strip or wire solder ; or

who are employed as DIPPERS engaged wholly or partially in dipping articles into any of the following acids:—aqua fortis, hydrochloric acid or sulphuric acid ;

as follows:—

	General minimum time rates Per week of 40 hours		Piece work basis time rates Per week of 40 hours	
	up to and including 5th December 1971	on and after 6th December 1971	up to and including 5th December 1971	on and after 6th December 1971
	£	£	£	£
Aged 21 years or over ...	12·35	12·60	13·10	13·35
„ 20 and under 21 years	11·45	11·70	12·15	12·40
„ 19 „ „ 20 „	11·05	11·30	11·75	11·95
„ 18 „ „ 19 „	10·80	11·00	11·40	11·65
„ 17 „ „ 18 „	8·15	8·30	8·65	8·80
„ 16 „ „ 17 „	6·65	6·80	7·05	7·20
„ under 16 years ...	5·15	5·25	5·45	5·55

(3) All female workers other than the workers specified in sub-paragraph (1) or (2) of this paragraph, as follows:—

	General minimum time rates Per week of 40 hours		Piece work basis time rates Per week of 40 hours	
	up to and including 5th December 1971	on and after 6th December 1971	up to and including 5th December 1971	on and after 6th December 1971
	£	£	£	£
Aged 21 years or over ...	12·25	12·50	13·00	13·25
„ 20 and under 21 years	11·30	11·55	12·00	12·25
„ 19 „ „ 20 „	10·95	11·15	11·60	11·85
„ 18 „ „ 19 „	10·70	10·90	11·35	11·55
„ 17 „ „ 18 „	7·90	8·10	8·40	8·55
„ 16 „ „ 17 „	6·45	6·60	6·85	7·00
„ under 16 years ...	5·05	5·15	5·35	5·45

PART IV

OVERTIME AND WAITING TIME

MINIMUM OVERTIME RATES

4. Subject to the provisions of this Schedule, minimum overtime rates are payable to any worker as follows:—

(1) on a Sunday—for all time worked   ...   .   double time

(2) in England and Wales—

    (a) on a customary holiday other than a day of customary holiday fixed by the employer—for all time worked ...   .   double time

    (b) on a day of customary holiday fixed by the employer—for all time worked   ...   .   the hourly general minimum time rate

(3) in Scotland—

    (a) on a customary holiday other than either of the last two days of customary holiday in each year fixed by the employer—for all time worked   double time

    (b) on each of the last two days of customary holiday in each year fixed by the employer—for all time worked ...   .   the hourly general minimum time rate

(4) on a Saturday, not being a customary holiday—for all time worked in excess of 4 hours...   ...   .   time-and-a-half

(5) in any week, exclusive of any time in respect of which a minimum overtime rate is payable under the preceding provisions of this paragraph—

    (a) for the first two hours worked in excess of 40   ...   time-and-a-quarter

    (b) thereafter   ...   .   time-and-a-half

5. In this Part of this Schedule:—

(1) the expressions "time-and-a-quarter", "time-and-a-half" and "double time" mean respectively—

(*a*) in the case of a time worker, one and a quarter times, one and a half times and twice the hourly general minimum time rate otherwise applicable to the worker ;

(*b*) in the case of a worker employed on piece work,

(i) a time rate equal respectively to one quarter, one half and the whole of the hourly general minimum time rate which would be payable to the worker if he were a time worker and a minimum overtime rate did not apply and, in addition thereto,

(ii) piece rates each of which would yield, in the circumstances of the case, to an ordinary worker, at least the same amount of money as the hourly piece work basis time rate applicable to the worker.

(2) The expression "customary holiday" means:—

(*a*) (i) In England and Wales—

Christmas Day (or, if Christmas Day falls on a Sunday, such week day as may be appointed by national proclamation, or, if none is so appointed, the next following Tuesday), Boxing Day, Good Friday, Easter Monday, Whit Monday (or where another day is substituted therefor by national proclamation, that day), August Bank Holiday, and two other days (being days of the week on which the worker normally works for the employer) in the course of a calendar year to be fixed by the employer and notified to the worker not less than three weeks before the holiday ;

(ii) In Scotland—

New Year's Day (or, if New Year's Day falls on a Sunday, the following Monday) ;
the local Spring holiday ;
the local Autumn holiday ; and
five other days (being days of the week on which the worker normally works for the employer) in the course of a calendar year to be fixed by the employer and notified to the worker not less than three weeks before the holiday ;

or (*b*) in the case of each of the said days (other than a day fixed by the employer in Scotland and notified to the worker as aforesaid) such weekday as may be substituted therefor, being a day recognised by local custom as a day of holiday in substitution for the said day or a day agreed between the employer and the worker or his representative.

WAITING TIME

6.—(1) A worker is entitled to payment of the minimum remuneration specified in this Schedule for all time during which he is present on the premises of his employer, unless he is present thereon in any of the following circumstances :—

(*a*) without the employer's consent, express or implied ;

(*b*) for some purpose unconnected with his work and other than that of waiting for work to be given to him to perform ;

(*c*) by reason only of the fact that he is resident thereon ;

(*d*) during normal meal times in a room or place in which no work is being done, and he is not waiting for work to be given to him to perform.

(2) The minimum remuneration payable under sub-paragraph (1) of this paragraph to a piece worker when not engaged on piece work is that which would be applicable if he were a time worker.

PART V

GUARANTEED WEEKLY REMUNERATION

7.—(1) Subject to the provisions of this paragraph, a worker who ordinarily works for the employer at least 34 hours weekly on work to which this Schedule applies shall be paid the guaranteed weekly remuneration in respect of any week in which he is in the employment of the employer, and either performs no work to which this Schedule applies or works for less than 34 hours on such work.

(2) The guaranteed weekly remuneration is 34 hours' pay calculated at the general minimum time rate ordinarily applicable to the worker:

Provided that where in any week a worker is absent from work by reason of a recognised holiday allowed by his employer, not being a holiday allowed to the worker under the provisions of the Wages Councils Act 1959, the worker's guaranteed weekly remuneration in that week shall be reduced by an amount which is in the same proportion to 34 hours' pay, calculated as aforesaid, as the number of hours for which the worker is absent from work in that week by reason of the recognised holiday is to the number of hours ordinarily worked in a week by him for the employer on work to which this Schedule applies ; and for the purposes of this proviso the expression "recognised holiday" means—

(a) a customary holiday as defined in paragraph 5 ; and

(b) during the twelve months commencing on 1st May in each year, one period of not more than fifteen consecutive days or two periods of consecutive days aggregating not more than sixteen days being the period or periods during which the establishment at which the worker ordinarily works is closed for the purpose of giving persons there employed an annual holiday.

(3) The guaranteed weekly remuneration in any week shall be reduced by the amount of any holiday remuneration paid, or payable, by the employer to the worker in respect of any holiday allowed to, and taken by, the worker in that week under the provisions of the Wages Councils Act 1959.

(4) In calculating the number of hours worked in any week for the purposes of this paragraph, the worker shall be treated as though he had worked on any holiday allowed to, and taken by, him in that week under the provisions of the Wages Councils Act 1959, the number of hours ordinarily worked by him on that day of the week, provided that the worker shall not be treated as having worked in any week throughout which he is on holiday.

(5) Payment of the guaranteed weekly remuneration in any week is subject to the condition that the worker throughout the period of his ordinary employment in that week, excluding any day allowed to him as a holiday, (whether under the Wages Councils Act 1959, or because the day is, or forms part of, a recognised holiday, as defined in the proviso to sub-paragraph (2) of this paragraph) is—

(a) capable of and available for work ; and

(b) willing to perform such duties outside his normal occupation as the employer may reasonably require if his normal work is not available to him in the establishment in which he is employed.

(6) The guaranteed weekly remuneration shall not be payable to a worker for any week—

(a) in which work is not available for him by reason of a strike or lockout ; or

(b) in which the worker has been dismissed on the grounds of serious misconduct ; or

(c) if at any time in the week the worker is absent from work by reason of sickness ; or (*d*) if at any time in the week or during the preceding four weeks the worker has been absent from work without the leave of his employer ; or

(*e*) in which the amount of remuneration payable to the worker, calculated in accordance with the preceding paragraphs of this Schedule, exceeds the amount of the remuneration which would be payable to him under the provisions of this paragraph.

(7) The guaranteed weekly remuneration applicable to a piece worker shall be the sum to which he would be entitled if he were a time worker.

PART VI

INTERPRETATION

8. In this Schedule the expressions "Grade I", "Grade II" and "Grade III" have the following meanings—

(1) in the case of a POLISHER

"Grade I" means a worker employed in polishing who is not of Grade II or Grade III ;

"Grade II" means a worker who has had not less than six years' experience as a polisher, is employed in any process of any class of common work and bobs or mops ;

"Grade III" means a worker who, in addition to fulfilling the conditions of Grade II, is also an expert in all processes of both common and best work or is a charge hand responsible for all work and order in the shop ;

(2) in the case of a BRAZIER

"Grade I" means a worker employed in brazing who is not of Grade II or Grade III ;

"Grade II" means a worker who has had not less than six years' experience as a brazier, and is employed in brazing all classes of metal except aluminium ;

"Grade III" means a worker who, in addition to fulfilling the conditions of Grade II, is also employed in brazing aluminium or is a charge hand responsible for all work and order in the shop ;

(3) in the case of a BURNISHER

"Grade I" means a worker employed in burnishing who is not of Grade II or Grade III ;

"Grade II" means a worker who has had not less than six years' experience as a burnisher, is employed as a hook and straight burnisher at the vice and satisfactorily burnishes deep thin shell work at the lathe;

"Grade III" means a worker who, in addition to fulfilling the conditions of Grade II, is an expert in speed and quality in all classes of work or is a charge hand responsible for all work and order in the shop ;

(4) in the case of a DROP-STAMPER

"Grade I" means a worker employed in drop-stamping who is not of Grade II or Grade III ;

"Grade II" means a worker who has had not less than six years' experience as a drop-stamper and is employed in all classes of deep or shallow work ;

"Grade III" means a worker who, in addition to fulfilling the conditions of Grade II, is an expert in all classes of work or is a charge hand responsible for all work and order in the shop ;

(5) in the case of a DIPPER WHO IS ALSO A BRONZER

"Grade I" means a worker employed in dipping and bronzing who is not of Grade II or Grade III ;

"Grade II" means a worker who has had not less than six years' experience as a dipper and bronzer and is employed in dipping or bronzing, or on art bronzing and colouring, or electro-plating ;

"Grade III" means a worker who, in addition to fulfilling the conditions of Grade II, has also an expert knowledge of art bronzing or metal colouring or electro depositing and solutions or is a charge hand responsible for all work and order in the shop.

APPLICABILITY OF STATUTORY MINIMUM REMUNERATION

9. This Schedule does not apply to workers who are persons registered as handicapped by disablement in pursuance of the Disabled Persons (Employment) Acts 1944 and 1958(a), in respect of their employment by Remploy Limited, but save as aforesaid applies to workers in relation to whom the Stamped or Pressed Metal-Wares Wages Council (Great Britain) operates, that is to say, workers employed in Great Britain in the trade specified in the Schedule to the Trade Boards (Stamped or Pressed Metal-Wares Trade, Great Britain) (Constitution and Proceedings) Regulations 1924(b), namely :—

(1) the manufacture from metal in sheet or strip form by cold stamping or cold pressing of articles known in the trade as metal small wares ;

(2) the cutting, shearing, annealing and hardening of metal in an establishment in which the metal is used for such manufacture ;

(3) the covering of corset steels prior to capping or tipping in an establishment in which the steels are capped or tipped ;

(4) finishing (including dipping, nickelling, plating, tinning, japanning, stove-enamelling, lacquering, bronzing, colouring, painting, varnishing, barrelling, burnishing, grinding, planishing, polishing, and the capping, counting, lopping, studding, or tipping of corset busks or steels) and similar operations when done in conjunction with such manufacture ;

(5) viewing, inspecting, testing, sorting, boxing, carding, carrying, delivering, despatching, labelling, packeting, packing, portering, warehousing, weighing and similar processes or operations when done in conjunction with such manufacture ;

(6) the assembling of the above-mentioned wares or parts thereof, whether the things assembled are made inside or outside Great Britain ; and

(7) any process or operation which is included in the Button-making Trade, as defined for the purposes of the Trade Boards Acts, when carried on in an establishment mainly engaged in any of the processes or operations defined in the preceding sub-paragraphs hereof ;

excluding:

(i) the production by the processes and operations defined in sub-paragraphs (1) to (6) above of any article or part of any article in an establishment in which such article or part is incorporated with or fitted to any other article made in that establishment or part of any other article made in that establishment, unless

(a) such other article or part is wholly or mainly made by the processes or operations specified in sub-paragraphs (1) to (4) and (6) above, or

(b) the establishment is mainly engaged in the processes or operations specified in sub-paragraphs (1) to (7) above ;

(a) 1944 c. 10 and 1958 c. 33.   (b) S.R. & O. 1924/1485 (1924, p. 1776).

(ii) any processes or operations included in the following Orders or any amendments or variations thereof : —

the Trade Boards (Coffin Furniture and Cerement-making) Order 1919(a) ;

the Trade Board (Hollow-ware) Order 1913(b) ;

the Trade Boards (Perambulator and Invalid Carriage) Order 1919(c) ;

the Trade Boards (Pin, Hook and Eye, and Snap Fastener) Order 1919(d) ;

the Trade Boards (Toy) Order 1920(e) ;

(iii) (a) the manufacture of articles known in the trade as real or imitation jewellery, and (b) the manufacture of any article or part of any article in an establishment mainly engaged in the manufacture of such jewellery ;

(iv) (a) the manufacture of steel and base metal pens and loose leaf metals, and (b) the manufacture of any article or part of any article in an establishment mainly engaged in the manufacture of such pens or metals ;

(v) (a) the manufacture of locks and latches (other than locks which are parts of fittings of bags or cases), and (b) the manufacture of any article or part of any article in an establishment mainly engaged in the manufacture of such locks or latches ;

(vi) the manufacture of any article or part of any article in an establishment mainly engaged in the manufacture of any electrical machinery appliances, apparatus or accessories other than small electric light fittings ;

(vii) the manufacture of any article or part of any article in an establishment mainly engaged in the manufacture of cast iron hollow-ware ;

(viii) any operation done in an establishment mainly engaged in work known in the trade as the work of an establishment of an outplater to the trade ;

(ix) (a) the manufacture of the component parts of cycles, motor cars or motor cycles, and (b) the manufacture of any article or part of any article when made in an establishment mainly engaged in the manufacture of cycles, motor cars or motor cycles, or of component parts of cycles, motor cars or motor cycles ;

(x) the manufacture of accessories or parts thereof primarily intended for use on motor cars ;

(xi) the manufacture of any article or part of any article known in the trade as electro-plate and articles of similar character if manufactured of Britannia metal or nickel or similar white alloys ;

(xii) the manufacture of any article or part of any article from precious metals, or base metals covered when in sheet or strip form wholly or partially by any process or operation with precious metals ;

(xiii) the manufacture of any article or part of any article from wire, either round, flat or shaped ;

(xiv) the manufacture of lamps, medals, iron and steel hinges, harness furniture, driving chains, ammunition, domestic kitchen utensils or parts of such articles ;

(xv) processes or operations specified in sub-paragraphs (1) to (6) above, when performed in an establishment mainly engaged in any process or operation which is included in the Button-making Trade as defined for the purposes of the Trade Boards Acts.

(a) S.R. & O. 1919/1839 (1919 II, p. 508).   (b) Confirmed by 3 & 4 Geo. 5. c. clxii.
(c) S.R. & O. 1919/1796 (1919 II, p. 521).   (d) S.R. & O. 1919/1840 (1919 II, p. 523).
(e) S.R. & O. 1920/470 (1920 II, p. 792).

EXPLANATORY NOTE

(This Note is not part of the Order.)

This Order, which has effect from 26th July 1971, sets out the statutory minimum remuneration payable in substitution for that fixed by the Wages Regulation (Stamped or Pressed Metal-Wares) Order 1970 (Order Q. (102)), which Order is revoked.

New provisions are printed in italics.

STATUTORY INSTRUMENTS

1971 No. 1089

WAGES COUNCILS

The Wages Regulation (Stamped or Pressed Metal-Wares) (Holidays) Order 1971

Made - - -	*5th July* 1971
Coming into Operation	*26th July* 1971

Whereas the Secretary of State has received from the Stamped or Pressed Metal-Wares Wages Council (Great Britain) the wages regulation proposals set out in the Schedule hereto :

Now, therefore, the Secretary of State in exercise of his powers under section 11 of the Wages Councils Act 1959(a), and of all other powers enabling him in that behalf, hereby makes the following Order :—

1. This Order may be cited as the Wages Regulation (Stamped or Pressed Metal-Wares) (Holidays) Order 1971.

2.—(1) In this Order the expression "the specified date" means the 26th July 1971, provided that where, as respects any worker who is paid wages at intervals not exceeding seven days, that date does not correspond with the beginning of the period for which the wages are paid, the expression "the specified date" means, as respects that worker, the beginning of the next such period following that date.

(2) The Interpretation Act 1889(b) shall apply to the interpretation of this Order as it applies to the interpretation of an Act of Parliament and as if this Order and the Order hereby revoked were Acts of Parliament.

3. The wages regulation proposals set out in the Schedule hereto shall have effect as from the specified date and as from that date the Wages Regulation (Stamped or Pressed Metal-Wares) (Holidays) Order 1965(c) shall cease to have effect.

Signed by order of the Secretary of State.
5th July 1971.

J. R. Lloyd Davies,
Assistant Secretary,
Department of Employment.

(a) 1959 c. 69. (b) 1889 c. 63.
(c) S.I. 1965/1343 (1965 II, p. 3837).

SCHEDULE

The following provisions as to holidays and holiday remuneration shall be substituted for the provisions as to holidays and holiday remuneration set out in the Wages Regulation (Stamped or Pressed Metal-Wares) (Holidays) Order 1965 (hereinafter referred to as "Order Q. (99) "), as amended by Schedule 2 to the Wages Regulation (Stamped or Pressed Metal-Wares) Order 1970 (Order Q. (102)).

PART I

APPLICATION

1. This Schedule applies to every worker for whom statutory minimum remuneration has been fixed.

PART II

CUSTOMARY HOLIDAYS

2.—(1) An employer shall allow to every worker to whom this Schedule applies a holiday (hereinafter referred to as a "customary holiday") in each year on the days specified in the following sub-paragraph, provided that the worker has been in his employment for a period of not less than four weeks immediately preceding the customary holiday and has worked for the employer during the whole or part of that period and (unless excused by the employer or absent by reason of the proved illness of the worker) has worked for the employer throughout the last seven working days on which work was available to him immediately prior to the customary holiday.

(2) The said customary holidays are:—

(a) (i) In England and Wales—

Christmas Day (or, if Christmas Day falls on a Sunday, such week day as may be appointed by national proclamation, or, if none is so appointed, the next following Tuesday), Boxing Day, Good Friday, Easter Monday, Whit Monday (or where another day is substituted therefor by national proclamation, that day), August Bank Holiday, and two other days (being days of the week on which the worker normally works for the employer) in the course of a calendar year to be fixed by the employer and notified to the worker not less than three weeks before the holiday ;

(ii) In Scotland—

New Year's Day (or, if New Year's Day falls on a Sunday, the following Monday) ;

the local Spring holiday ;

the local Autumn holiday ; and

five other days (being days of the week on which the worker normally works for the employer) in the course of a calendar year to be fixed by the employer and notified to the worker not less than three weeks before the holiday ;

or (b) in the case of each of the said days (other than a day fixed by the employer in Scotland and notified to the worker as aforesaid) such weekday as may be substituted therefor, being a day recognised by local custom as a day of holiday in substitution for the said day or a day agreed between the employer and the worker or his representative.

2

(3) Notwithstanding the preceding provisions of this paragraph, an employer may (except where in the case of a woman or young person such a requirement would be unlawful) require a worker who is otherwise entitled to any customary holiday under the foregoing provisions of this Schedule to work thereon, and, in lieu of any customary holiday on which he so works, the worker shall be entitled to be allowed a day's holiday (hereinafter referred to as a "holiday in lieu of a customary holiday") on a week day on which he would normally work for the employer within the period of four weeks next ensuing.

(4) A worker who is required to work on a customary holiday shall be paid:—

(a) for all time worked thereon, the statutory minimum remuneration then appropriate to the worker for work on a customary holiday ; and

(b) in respect of the holiday in lieu of the customary holiday, holiday remuneration in accordance with paragraph 6.

PART III

ANNUAL HOLIDAY

3.—(1) Subject to the provisions of paragraph 4, in addition to the holidays specified in Part II of this Schedule an employer shall, between the date on which the provisions of this Schedule become effective and 30th September 1971, and in each succeeding year between 1st May and 30th September, allow a holiday (hereinafter referred to as an "annual holiday") to every worker in his employment to whom this Schedule applies who has been employed by him during the 12 months immediately preceding the commencement of the holiday season for any of the periods set out in the table below and the duration of the annual holiday shall, in the case of each such worker, be related to his period of employment during that 12 months as follows:—

Period of employment	Duration of annual holiday for workers with a normal working week of—			
	Six days	Five days	Four days	Three days or less
At least 48 weeks	12 days	10 days	8 days	6 days
„ „ 44 „	11 „	9 „	7 „	6 „
„ „ 40 „	10 „	8 „	6 „	5 „
„ „ 36 „	9 „	7 „	6 „	5 „
„ „ 32 „	8 „	6 „	5 „	4 „
„ „ 28 „	7 „	5 „	4 „	4 „
„ „ 24 „	6 „	5 „	4 „	3 „
„ „ 20 „	5 „	4 „	3 „	3 „
„ „ 16 „	4 „	3 „	2 „	2 „
„ „ 12 „	3 „	2 „	2 „	1 day
„ „ 8 „	2 „	1 day	1 day	1 „
„ „ 4 „	1 day	1 „	—	—

(2) Notwithstanding the provisions of the last foregoing sub-paragraph—

(a) the number of days of annual holiday which an employer is required to allow to a worker in any holiday season shall not exceed in the aggregate twice the number of days constituting the worker's normal working week.

(*b*) the duration of the worker's annual holiday during the holiday season ending on 30th September 1971, shall be reduced by any days of annual holiday duly allowed to him by the employer under the provisions of Order Q.(99), as amended, between 1st May 1971 and the date on which this Schedule becomes effective.

(3) In this Schedule the expression "holiday season" means in relation to an annual holiday during the year 1971, the period commencing on 1st May 1971, and ending on 30th September 1971, and in relation to each subsequent year, the period commencing on 1st May and ending on 30th September in that year.

4.—(1) An annual holiday under this Schedule shall be allowed on consecutive working days, being days on which the worker is normally called upon to work for the employer, and days of annual holiday shall be treated as consecutive notwithstanding that a Sunday, a customary holiday on which the worker is not required to work for the employer or a holiday in lieu of a customary holiday intervenes:

Provided that—

(i) Where the duration of an annual holiday which an employer is required to allow to a worker exceeds the number of days constituting the worker's normal working week the said holiday may be allowed in two separate periods of such consecutive working days, and in that event, notwithstanding the foregoing provisions of this Schedule, the annual holiday shall be allowed as follows:—

(*a*) as to one period, not being less than the number of days constituting the worker's normal working week, during the holiday season, and

(*b*) as to the other period, during the holiday season or within the period ending on 30th April immediately following the holiday season.

(ii) One day of the annual holiday may be allowed on a non-consecutive working day (other than the worker's weekly short day) falling within the holiday season (or after the holiday season in the circumstances specified in sub-paragraph (1)(i)(*b*) of this paragraph) where the annual holiday or, as the case may be, such separate period, is allowed immediately after a customary holiday on which the worker is not required to work or so that such a holiday intervenes.

(2) Subject to the provisions of sub-paragraph (1) of this paragraph, any day of annual holiday under this Schedule may be allowed on a day on which the worker is entitled to a day of holiday or to a half-holiday under any enactment other than the Wages Councils Act 1959.

5. An employer shall give to a worker reasonable notice of the commencing date or dates and duration of the period or periods of his annual holiday. Such notice may be given individually to the worker or by the posting of a notice in the place where the worker is employed.

PART IV

HOLIDAY REMUNERATION

A—CUSTOMARY HOLIDAYS AND HOLIDAYS IN LIEU OF CUSTOMARY HOLIDAYS

6.—(1) Subject to the provisions of this paragraph, for each day of holiday to which a worker is entitled under Part II of this Schedule he shall be paid by the employer holiday remuneration equal to the amount, calculated at the appropriate rate of statutory minimum remuneration, to which he would have been entitled if the day had not been a day of holiday and he had worked on that day on work for which statutory minimum remuneration is payable for the time usually worked by him on that day of the week:

Provided, however, that payment of the said holiday remuneration is subject to the condition that the worker presents himself for employment at the usual starting hour on the first working day following the holiday and works throughout his normal working hours on that day or, if he fails to do so, failure is by reason of the proved illness of the worker or with the consent of the employer.

(2) The holiday remuneration in respect of any customary holiday shall be paid by the employer to the worker not later than the pay day on which the wages are paid for the pay week including the first working day following the customary holiday.

(3) The holiday remuneration in respect of any holiday in lieu of a customary holiday shall be paid not later than the pay day on which the wages are paid for the pay week including the first working day following the holiday in lieu of a customary holiday: Provided that the said payment shall be made immediately upon the termination of the worker's employment in the case where he ceases to be employed before being allowed a holiday in lieu of a customary holiday to which he is entitled, and in that case the proviso to sub-paragraph (1) of this paragraph shall not apply.

B—ANNUAL HOLIDAY

7.—(1) Subject to the provisions of paragraph 8, a worker qualified to be allowed an annual holiday under this Schedule shall be paid by his employer in respect thereof, on the last pay day preceding such annual holiday, one day's holiday pay (as defined in paragraph 11) in respect of each day thereof.

(2) Where under the provisions of paragraph 4 an annual holiday is allowed in more than one period, the holiday remuneration shall be apportioned accordingly.

8. Where any accrued holiday remuneration has been paid by the employer to the worker in accordance with paragraph 9 of this Schedule, or in accordance with Order Q. (99) as amended, in respect of employment during any of the periods referred to in that paragraph or that Order respectively, the amount of holiday remuneration payable by the employer in respect of any annual holiday for which the worker has qualified by reason of employment during the said period shall be reduced by the amount of the said accrued holiday remuneration unless that remuneration has been deducted from a previous payment of holiday remuneration made under the provisions of this Schedule or of Order Q. (99) as amended.

ACCRUED HOLIDAY REMUNERATION PAYABLE ON
TERMINATION OF EMPLOYMENT

9. Where a worker ceases to be employed by an employer after the provisions of this Schedule become effective the employer shall, immediately on the termination of the employment, pay to the worker as accrued holiday remuneration:—

(1) in respect of employment in the 12 months up to the 30th day of the preceding April, a sum equal to the holiday remuneration for any days of annual holiday for which he has qualified, except days of annual holiday which he has been allowed or has become entitled to be allowed before leaving the employment; and

(2) in respect of any employment since the 30th day of the preceding April, a sum equal to the holiday remuneration which would have been payable to him if he could have been allowed an annual holiday in respect of that employment at the time of leaving it.

Part V

GENERAL

10. For the purposes of calculating any period of employment qualifying a worker for an annual holiday or for any accrued holiday remuneration under this Schedule, the worker shall be treated :—

(1) as if he were employed for a week in respect of any week in which—

(a) he has worked for the employer for not less than *10* hours and has performed some work for which statutory minimum remuneration is payable ;

(b) he has been absent throughout the week solely by reason of the proved illness of, or accident to, the worker, provided that the number of weeks which may be treated as weeks of employment for such reason shall not exceed six in the aggregate in the period of 12 months immediately preceding the commencement of the holiday season ;

(c) he is absent from work throughout the week owing to suspension due to shortage of work, provided that the number of weeks which may be treated as weeks of employment for such reason shall not exceed four in the aggregate in any such period as aforesaid, and

(2) as if he were employed on any day of holiday allowed under the provisions of this Schedule or of Order Q. (99), as amended, and for the purposes of the provisions of sub-paragraph (1) of this paragraph, a worker who is absent on such a holiday shall be treated as having worked thereon for the employer for the number of hours ordinarily worked by him on that day of the week on work for which statutory minimum remuneration is payable.

11. In this Schedule, unless the context otherwise requires, the following expressions have the meanings hereby respectively assigned to them, that is to say :—

"appropriate rate of statutory minimum remuneration" means—

(a) in the case of a time worker, the rate or rates of statutory minimum remuneration applicable to the worker, and

(b) in the case of a piece worker, the rate or rates of statutory minimum remuneration which would be applicable to the worker if he were a time worker.

"normal working week" means the number of days on which it has been usual for the worker to work in a week in the employment of the employer during the 12 months immediately preceding the commencement of the holiday season or, where under paragraph 9 accrued holiday remuneration is payable on the termination of the employment, during the 12 months immediately preceding the date of the termination of the employment:

Provided that—

(i) part of a day shall count as a day ;

(ii) no account shall be taken of any week in which the worker did not perform any work for which statutory minimum remuneration has been fixed.

"one day's holiday pay" means the appropriate proportion of the remuneration which the worker would be entitled to receive from his employer at the date of the annual holiday (or where the holiday is allowed in more than one period at the date of the first period) or at the termination of the employment, as the case may require, for one week's work if working his normal working week and the number of daily hours normally worked by him (exclusive of overtime), and if paid at the appropriate rate of statutory minimum remuneration for work for which statutory minimum remuneration is payable and at the same rate for any work for which such remuneration is not payable, and in this definition "appropriate proportion" means—

> where the worker's normal working week is six days ... one-sixth
> where the worker's normal working week is five days ... one-fifth
> where the worker's normal working week is four days ... one-quarter
> where the worker's normal working week is three days
>   or less ... ... one-third

"statutory minimum remuneration" means statutory minimum remuneration (other than holiday remuneration) fixed by a wages regulation order made by the Secretary of State to give effect to proposals submitted to him by the Stamped or Pressed Metal-Wares Wages Council (Great Britain).

"week" in paragraphs 3 and 10 means "pay week".

12. The provisions of this Schedule are without prejudice to any agreement for the allowance of any further holidays with pay or for the payment of additional holiday remuneration.

EXPLANATORY NOTE

(This Note is not part of the Order.)

This Order, which has effect from 26th July 1971, sets out the holidays which an employer is required to allow to workers and the remuneration to be paid to such workers for those holidays, in substitution for the holidays and holiday remuneration fixed by the Wages Regulation (Stamped or Pressed Metal-Wares) (Holidays) Order 1965 (Order Q.(99)), as amended, which Order is revoked.

New provisions are printed in italics.

STATUTORY INSTRUMENTS

1971 No. 1090

PLANT BREEDERS' RIGHTS

The Plant Breeders' Rights (Lettuces) Scheme 1971

Made - - -	6th *July* 1971
Laid before Parliament	14th *July* 1971
Coming into Operation	15th *July* 1971

The Minister of Agriculture, Fisheries and Food, the Secretary of State for Scotland and the Secretary of State for the Home Department (being the Secretary of State concerned with agriculture in Northern Ireland), acting jointly, in exercise of the powers conferred on them by sections 1 and 3 of the Plant Varieties and Seeds Act 1964(a) (extended to Northern Ireland by the Plant Varieties and Seeds (Northern Ireland) Order 1964(b) and to the Isle of Man by the Plant Varieties and Seeds (Isle of Man) Order 1969(c)), and of all other powers enabling them in that behalf, after consultation with the Controller of Plant Variety Rights and with representatives of such interests as appear to them to be concerned, hereby make the following Scheme:—

Citation and Commencement

1. This Scheme may be cited as the Plant Breeders' Rights (Lettuces) Scheme 1971 and shall come into operation on 15th July 1971.

Interpretation

2.—(1) In this Scheme, unless the context otherwise requires—

"the Act" means the Plant Varieties and Seeds Act 1964 ;

"plant breeders' rights" means rights which may be granted in accordance with Part I of the Act ;

"plant variety" means any clone, line, hybrid or genetic variant.

(2) The Interpretation Act 1889(d) shall apply to the interpretation of this Scheme as it applies to the interpretation of an Act of Parliament.

Plant Varieties for which Plant Breeders' Rights may be Granted

3. There are prescribed for the purposes of the grant of plant breeders' rights all plant varieties of lettuces which conform with the characteristics of cultivated plant varieties of the species *Lactuca sativa* L.

(a) 1964 c. 14.   (b) S.I. 1964/1574 (1964 III, p. 3543).
(c) S.I. 1969/1829 (1969 III, p. 5701).   (d) 1889 c. 63.

Period for which Rights are Exercisable

4. The period for which plant breeders' rights shall be exercisable in respect of the plant varieties referred to in the last preceding paragraph shall be 15 years.

In Witness whereof the official seal of the Minister of Agriculture, Fisheries and Food is hereunto affixed on 28th June 1971.

(L.S.)
J. M. L. Prior,
Minister of Agriculture, Fisheries and Food.

Gordon Campbell,
2nd July 1971.
Secretary of State for Scotland.

R. Maudling,
6th July 1971.
Secretary of State for the Home Department.

EXPLANATORY NOTE

(*This Note is not part of the Scheme.*)

This Scheme, made under the Plant Varieties and Seeds Act 1964, prescribes the varieties of lettuces in respect of which grants of plant breeders' rights may be made and also prescribes the period of 15 years as that during which the rights may be exercised.

STATUTORY INSTRUMENTS

1971 No. 1091

PLANT BREEDERS' RIGHTS
The Plant Breeders' Rights (Runner Beans) Scheme 1971

Made - - -	*6th July* 1971
Laid before Parliament	*14th July* 1971
Coming into Operation	*15th July* 1971

The Minister of Agriculture, Fisheries and Food, the Secretary of State for Scotland and the Secretary of State for the Home Department (being the Secretary of State concerned with agriculture in Northern Ireland), acting jointly, in exercise of the powers conferred on them by sections 1, 3, 5 and 7 of the Plant Varieties and Seeds Act 1964(a) (extended to Northern Ireland by the Plant Varieties and Seeds (Northern Ireland) Order 1964(b) and to the Isle of Man by the Plant Varieties and Seeds (Isle of Man) Order 1969(c)), and of all other powers enabling them in that behalf, after consultation with the Controller of Plant Variety Rights and with representatives of such interests as appear to them to be concerned, hereby make the following Scheme :—

Citation and Commencement

1. This Scheme may be cited as the Plant Breeders' Rights (Runner Beans) Scheme 1971 and shall come into operation on 15th July 1971.·

Interpretation

2.—(1) In this Scheme, unless the context otherwise requires—

"the Act" means the Plant Varieties and Seeds Act 1964 ;

"the Controller" means the Controller of Plant Variety Rights ;

"plant breeders' rights" means rights which may be granted in accordance with Part I of the Act ;

"plant variety" means any clone, line, hybrid or genetic variant.

(2) The Interpretation Act 1889(d) shall apply to the interpretation of this Scheme as it applies to the interpretation of an Act of Parliament.

Plant Varieties for which Plant Breeders' Rights may be Granted

3. There are prescribed for the purposes of the grant of plant breeders' rights all plant varieties of runner beans which conform with the characteristics of cultivated plant varieties of the species *Phaseolus coccineus* L.

Period for which Rights are Exercisable

4. The period for which plant breeders' rights shall be exercisable in respect of the plant varieties referred to in the last preceding paragraph shall be 15 years.

(a) 1964 c. 14.
(c) S.I. 1969/1829 (1969 III, p. 5701).

(b) S.I. 1964/1574 (1964 III, p. 3543).
(d) 1889 c. 63.

Class of Plant Varieties for the Purposes of Section 5(7) of the Act

5. In relation to the plant varieties referred to in paragraph 3 of this Scheme, the class of plant varieties prescribed for the purposes of section 5(7) of the Act (which enables a class of plant varieties to be prescribed in connection with the use of names likely to deceive or cause confusion) consists of all varieties of runner beans and French beans.

Period Prescribed for the Purposes of Section 7(2) of the Act

6. In relation to the plant varieties referred to in paragraph 3 of this Scheme, the period prescribed for the purposes of section 7(2) of the Act (which enables a provision to be made whereby a compulsory licence granted by the Controller as respects a plant variety of a species or group specified in a scheme shall not have effect for a prescribed period after the grant of rights in that plant variety) shall be 3 years.

In Witness whereof the official seal of the Minister of Agriculture, Fisheries and Food is hereunto affixed on 28th June 1971.

(L.S.)

J. M. L. Prior,
Minister of Agriculture, Fisheries and Food.

Gordon Campbell,
2nd July 1971.　　　　Secretary of State for Scotland.

R. Maudling,
6th July 1971.　　　　Secretary of State for the Home Department.

EXPLANATORY NOTE
(*This Note is not part of the Scheme.*)

This Scheme, made under the Plant Varieties and Seeds Act 1964, prescribes the varieties of runner beans in respect of which grants of plant breeders' rights may be made and also prescribes the period of 15 years as that during which the rights may be exercised.

The aforesaid Act, as read with this Scheme, provides that infringements of the rights in the registered name of a variety of runner bean may be the subject of legal proceedings when committed in connection with any other variety of runner bean or any variety of French bean.

This Scheme also provides that a compulsory licence granted by the Controller of Plant Variety Rights in respect of a variety of runner bean shall not have effect during a period of 3 years from the date of the grant of rights in that variety.

STATUTORY INSTRUMENTS

1971 No. 1092

PLANT BREEDERS' RIGHTS
The Plant Breeders' Rights (Cymbidiums) Scheme 1971

Made - - -	*6th July* 1971
Laid before Parliament	*14th July* 1971
Coming into Operation	*15th July* 1971

The Minister of Agriculture, Fisheries and Food, the Secretary of State for Scotland and the Secretary of State for the Home Department (being the Secretary of State concerned with agriculture in Northern Ireland), acting jointly, in exercise of the powers conferred on them by sections 1 and 3 of, and paragraph 1 of Schedule 3 to, the Plant Varieties and Seeds Act 1964(a) (extended to Northern Ireland by the Plant Varieties and Seeds (Northern Ireland) Order 1964(b) and to the Isle of Man by the Plant Varieties and Seeds (Isle of Man) Order 1969(c)) and of all other powers enabling them in that behalf, after consultation with the Controller of Plant Variety Rights and with representatives of such interests as appear to them to be concerned, hereby make the following Scheme :—

Citation and Commencement

1. This Scheme may be cited as the Plant Breeders' Rights (Cymbidiums) Scheme 1971 and shall come into operation on 15th July 1971.

Interpretation

2.—(1) In this Scheme, unless the context otherwise requires,—

"the Act" means the Plant Varieties and Seeds Act 1964 ;

"plant breeders' rights" means rights which may be granted in accordance with Part I of the Act ;

"plant variety" means any clone, line, hybrid or genetic variant.

(2) The Interpretation Act 1889(d) shall apply to the interpretation of this Scheme as it applies to the interpretation of an Act of Parliament.

Plant Varieties for which Plant Breeders' Rights may be Granted

3. There are prescribed for the purposes of the grant of plant breeders' rights all plant varieties of cymbidiums which conform with the characteristics of cultivated plant varieties of the genus *Cymbidium* Sw.

Period for which Rights are Exercisable

4. The period for which plant breeders' rights shall be exercisable in respect of the plant varieties referred to in the last preceding paragraph shall be 15 years.

(a) 1964 c. 14.
(c) S.I. 1969/1829 (1961 III, p. 5701).
(b) S.I. 1964/1574 (1964 III, p. 3543).
(d) 1889 c. 63.

Additional Rights

5. Plant breeders' rights exercisable in respect of the plant varieties referred to in paragraph 3 of this Scheme shall include the exclusive right to produce or propagate and to authorise others to produce or propagate any such plant variety for the purpose of selling cut blooms of that variety.

In Witness whereof the official seal of the Minister of Agriculture, Fisheries and Food is hereunto affixed on 28th June 1971.

(L.S.)

J. M. L. Prior,
Minister of Agriculture, Fisheries and Food.

Gordon Campbell,
2nd July 1971. Secretary of State for Scotland.

R. Maudling,
6th July 1971. Secretary of State for the Home Department.

EXPLANATORY NOTE
(This Note is not part of the Scheme.)

This Scheme, made under the Plant Varieties and Seeds Act 1964, prescribes the varieties of cymbidiums in respect of which grants of plant breeders' rights may be made and also prescribes the period of 15 years as that during which the rights may be exercised.

Plant breeders' rights in respect of any variety of cymbidium to which the Scheme applies are extended to the production and propagation of the variety for the purpose of selling cut blooms.

STATUTORY INSTRUMENTS

1971 No. 1093

PLANT BREEDERS' RIGHTS

The Plant Breeders' Rights (Trees, Shrubs and Woody Climbers) (Amendment) Scheme 1971

Made - - -	6th *July* 1971
Laid before Parliament	14th *July* 1971
Coming into Operation	15th *July* 1971

The Minister of Agriculture, Fisheries and Food, the Secretary of State for Scotland and the Secretary of State for the Home Department (being the Secretary of State concerned with agriculture in Northern Ireland), acting jointly, in exercise of the powers conferred on them by sections 1, 3, 5 and 7 of, and paragraph 1 of Schedule 3 to, the Plant Varieties and Seeds Act 1964(a) (extended to Northern Ireland by the Plant Varieties and Seeds (Northern Ireland) Order 1964(b), and to the Isle of Man by the Plant Varieties and Seeds (Isle of Man) Order 1969(c)) and of all other powers enabling them in that behalf, after consultation with the Controller of Plant Variety Rights and with representatives of such interests as appear to them to be concerned, hereby make the following Scheme:—

Citation, Commencement and Interpretation

1.—(1) This Scheme may be cited as the Plant Breeders' Rights (Trees, Shrubs and Woody Climbers) (Amendment) Scheme 1971 and shall come into operation on 15th July 1971.

(2) The Interpretation Act 1889(d) shall apply to the interpretation of this Scheme as it applies to the interpretation of an Act of Parliament.

Amendment of Principal Scheme

2. The Plant Breeders' Rights (Trees, Shrubs and Woody Climbers) Scheme 1969(e) (hereinafter referred to as "the principal Scheme") is hereby amended by substituting for the several items relating to the genera *Prunus* L., *Pyrus* L., *Ribes* L., *Rubus* L. and *Vaccinium* L. set out in Columns 1 to 5, inclusive of the

---

(a) 1964 c. 14.   (b) S.I. 1964/1574 (1964 III, p. 3543).
(c) S.I. 1969/1829 (1969 III, p .5701).   (d) 1889 c. 63.
(e) S.I. 1969/1024 (1969 II, p. 3011).

Schedule to the principal Scheme the following items (the headings of the respective columns being here included for reference only)—

Column 1 Genus or species	Column 2 Period of years for which rights are exercisable	Column 3 Classes of plant varieties prescribed for purposes of section 5(7)	Column 4 Period of years prescribed for purposes of section 7(2)	Column 5 Additional rights
Prunus L. (decorative varieties only) other than varieties of the *Prunus* species expressly referred to elsewhere in this Column.	25	*Prunus*	3	Included
Pyrus L. (decorative varieties only)	25	*Pyrus*	3	
Ribes L. (decorative varieties only)	15	*Ribes*	2	
Rubus L. (decorative varieties only)	15	*Rubus*	2	
Vaccinium L. (decorative varieties only)	25	*Vaccinium*	5	

In Witness whereof the Official Seal of the Minister of Agriculture, Fisheries and Food is hereunto affixed on 28th June 1971.

(L.S.)

J. M. L. Prior,
Minister of Agriculture, Fisheries and Food.

2nd July 1971.

Gordon Campbell,
Secretary of State for Scotland.

6th July 1971.

R. Maudling,
Secretary of State for the Home Department.

EXPLANATORY NOTE

(This Note is not part of the Scheme.)

This Scheme amends the Plant Breeders' Rights (Trees, Shrubs and Woody Climbers) Scheme 1969 (S.I. 1969/1024) by restricting the inclusion in that Scheme of certain genera of plant varieties to decorative varieties of those genera.

STATUTORY INSTRUMENTS

1971 No. 1094

PLANT BREEDERS' RIGHTS

The Plant Breeders' Rights (Amendment) Regulations 1971

Made - - -	*6th July* 1971
Laid before Parliament	*14th July* 1971
Coming into Operation	*15th July* 1971

The Minister of Agriculture, Fisheries and Food, the Secretary of State for Scotland and the Secretary of State for the Home Department (being the Secretary of State concerned with agriculture in Northern Ireland) acting jointly, in exercise of the powers vested in them by sections 9, 10 and 36 of the Plant Varieties and Seeds Act 1964(a) (extended to Northern Ireland by the Plant Varieties and Seeds (Northern Ireland) Order 1964(b) and to the Isle of Man by the Plant Varieties and Seeds (Isle of Man) Order 1969(c)) and of all other powers enabling them in that behalf, after consultation with the Council on Tribunals in accordance with section 8 of the Tribunals and Inquiries Act 1958(d) as applied to the Controller of Plant Variety Rights and any officer authorised to exercise the functions of the said Controller under section 11(5) of the Plant Varieties and Seeds Act 1964 and to the Plant Variety Rights Tribunal by section 12 of the last mentioned Act, hereby make the following Regulations :—

Citation and Commencement

1.—(1) These Regulations may be cited as the Plant Breeders' Rights (Amendment) Regulations 1971 and shall come into operation on 15th July 1971.

(2) These Regulations shall be read as one with the Plant Breeders' Rights Regulations 1969(e) (hereinafter referred to as "the principal Regulations").

Amendment of Principal Regulations

2. The principal Regulations are hereby amended as follows :

(*a*) In Regulation 12(1) at the end of sub-paragraph (iii), the word "and" shall be omitted.

(*b*) In Regulation 12(1)(ii), after the word "Controller" where it first appears, there shall be inserted the words "or produce to him for examination, as may be required,"

(*c*) In each of the following places, namely,
Regulations 13(8), 14(1), 22(1) and 22(2), paragraphs 2 and 7, the heading of paragraph 8 and the paragraph headed "To be completed by

---

(a) 1964 c. 14.
(c) S.I. 1969/1829 (1969 III, p. 5701).
(e) S.I. 1969/1021 (1969 II, p. 2976).
(b) S.I. 1964/1574 (1964 III, p. 3543).
(d) 1958 c. 66.

applicants requiring a Protective Direction" of Schedule 2, immediately after the words "United Kingdom" there shall be added the words "or the Isle of Man".

(d) In Regulation 16(1) the words "or on behalf of" shall be omitted.

(e) In Regulation 20(1) the words "to be prepared" shall be omitted and for the words "which shall" there shall be substituted the word "to".

(f) In Regulation 20(2) for the words "he has caused to be" there shall be substituted the words "have been".

(g) In Schedule 3, Part II, in paragraph 1(1), for the reference to 250 seed tubers there shall be substituted a reference to 170 seed tubers.

(h) In Schedule 3, Part V, in paragraph 1(1), for the reference to 200 grams there shall be substituted a reference to 150 grams.

(i) In Schedule 3, Part VI, in paragraph 1(1), for the reference to 200 grams there shall be substituted a reference to 120 grams.

(j) At the end of Schedule 3 there shall be added three further Parts as follows:

PART XXIX

Lettuces

Quantity

1.—(1) During the year beginning with the making of the application ½ oz. of seed shall be delivered.

(2) During each of the immediately succeeding years until the completion of the tests and trials there shall be delivered such reproductive and other plant material in such quantity and of such description and quality as shall appear to the Controller to be necessary or desirable for the proper completion of the tests and trials.

Packing

2. The seed shall be packed in a suitable container of sufficient strength to withstand mechanical damage during transit.

Quality

3.—(1) *Health*
The seed shall be free from serious seed-borne diseases.

(2) *Purity and germination*

The seed shall be accompanied by a report of a test made at an official seed testing station established under the Seeds Act 1920(a) or a seed testing station licensed under that Act and made within 3 months immediately preceding the delivery of the seed stating that in a sample of 1 oz.:—

(a) the percentage of purity was not less than 98, and

(b) the percentage of germination was not less than 70.

(a) 1920 c. 54.

Dressings and Treatments

4. The seed shall not have been subjected to any fungicidal or insecticidal treatment.

PART XXX

Runner Beans

Quantity

1.—(1) During the year beginning with the making of the application 9 lb. of seed shall be delivered.

(2) During each of the immediately succeeding years until the completion of the tests and trials there shall be delivered such reproductive and other plant material in such quantity and of such description and quality as shall appear to the Controller to be necessary or desirable for the proper completion of the tests and trials.

Packing

2. The seed shall be packed in a suitable container of sufficient strength to withstand mechanical damage during transit.

Quality

3.—(1) *Health*
The seed shall be free from serious seed-borne diseases.

(2) *Purity and germination*

The seed shall be accompanied by a report of a test made at an official seed testing station established under the Seeds Act 1920 or a seed testing station licensed under that Act and made within the 3 months immediately preceding the delivery of the seed stating that in a sample of 8 oz.:—

(*a*) the percentage of purity was not less than 99, and

(*b*) the percentage of germination was not less than 60.

Dressings and Treatments

4. The seed shall not have been subjected to any fungicidal treatment.

PART XXXI

Cymbidiums

One plant of the variety, bearing at least one flowering spike with at least two thirds of its flowers open, shall be produced for examination.

In Witness whereof the official seal of the Minister of Agriculture, Fisheries and Food is hereunto affixed on 28th June 1971.

(L.S.)   *J. M. L. Prior,*
                          Minister of Agriculture, Fisheries and Food.

                                   Gordon Campbell,
2nd July 1971.   Secretary of State for Scotland.

                                   R. Maudling,
6th July 1971.   Secretary of State for the Home Department.

EXPLANATORY NOTE

(This Note is not part of the Regulations.)

These Regulations amend the Plant Breeders' Rights Regulations 1969 (S.I. 1969/1021). Schemes having been made to enable plant breeders' rights to be granted in respect of lettuces, runner beans and cymbidiums, the Regulations specify the reproductive and other plant material to be delivered or produced for examination when an application is made for a grant of plant breeders' rights in respect of plant varieties of those kinds. These Regulations also amend the principal Regulations in minor respects.

1971 No. 1095 (L.27)

COUNTY COURTS

PROCEDURE

The Administration Order Rules 1971

Made - - -	*5th July* 1971
Laid before Parliament	*16th July* 1971
Coming into Operation	*2nd August* 1971

The Lord Chancellor, in exercise of the power conferred on him by section 156 of the County Courts Act 1959(a), hereby makes the following Rules :—

Citation, commencement and interpretation

1.—(1) These Rules may be cited as the Administration Order Rules 1971 and shall come into operation on 2nd August 1971.

(2) In these Rules, unless the context otherwise requires—

"the Act of 1959" means the County Courts Act 1959 ;

"the Act of 1971" means the Attachment of Earnings Act 1971(b) ;

"the County Court Rules" means the rules for the time being in force under section 102 of the Act of 1959 ;

a rule referred to by number means the rule so numbered in these Rules, and a form referred to by number means the form so numbered in the Appendix to these Rules ;

expressions used in the Act of 1971 have the same meaning as in that Act.

(3) The Interpretation Act 1889(c) shall apply to the interpretation of these Rules as it applies to the interpretation of an Act of Parliament.

Application of County Court Rules and powers of registrar

2.—(1) Subject to the provisions of these Rules and of any enactment, the County Court Rules shall apply with the necessary modifications to proceedings relating to administration orders.

(2) For the purposes of paragraph (1) any provision of these Rules authorising or requiring anything to be done shall be treated as if it were a provision of the County Court Rules.

(3) Any power conferred on the court by any provision of Part VII of the Act of 1959, the Act of 1971 or these Rules may be exercised by the registrar.

(a) 1959 c. 22.   (b) 1971 c. 32.   (c) 1889 c. 63.

Request under the Act of 1959

3. A debtor who desires to obtain an administration order under section 148 of the Act of 1959 shall file in the court office a request in Form 1.

List under the Act of 1971

4. A list furnished by a debtor pursuant to an order under section 4(1)(*b*) of the Act of 1971 shall be in Form 2.

Affidavit

5. The debtor shall verify the statements in Form 1 or 2 by affidavit.

Transfer of proceedings under section 148(2) *of the Act of* 1959

6.—(1) The court to which a request is made for an administration order may give notice to the debtor to show cause why a certificate of the judgment obtained against him should not be forwarded to another court as provided in section 148(2) of the Act of 1959.

(2) For the purposes of the said section 148(2) the fact that a court has made an attachment of earnings order to secure the payment of a judgment debt shall be evidence in proceedings in another court on a request by the judgment debtor for an administration order that it would be more convenient for the first-mentioned court to administer the debtor's estate.

(3) If the court to which a request is made for an administration order causes a certificate of the judgment obtained against the debtor in that court to be forwarded to another court under the said section 148(2), the registrar of the first-mentioned court shall send notice thereof to the debtor.

Notice of hearing

7.—(1) On the filing of a request in Form 1, the receipt of a certificate of judgment forwarded in accordance with section 148(2) of the Act of 1959, or the receipt of a list in Form 2, the registrar shall appoint a day for the hearing at which the making of an administration order is to be considered and shall give not less than 10 clear days' notice thereof to the debtor and to each creditor mentioned in Form 1 or 2.

(2) The notice to the debtor shall be in Form 3 and the notice to the creditors in Form 4.

Objection to debts

8.—(1) Any creditor to whom notice has been sent under rule 7 and who objects to any debt included in Form 1 or 2 shall not less than 5 clear days before the day appointed for the hearing give notice of his objection to the registrar, to the debtor and to the creditor to whose debt he objects and shall state in the notice the grounds of his objection.

(2) By leave of the court an objection to a debt may be considered although notice of the objection has not been given.

Application of money received in proceedings stayed under section 150 *of the Act of* 1959

9. Where proceedings against the debtor are stayed under section 150(2) of the Act of 1959, any money paid into court shall—

(*a*) if the administration order was made by the court in which such proceedings are pending, be dealt with as that court directs ; and

(*b*) if the administration order was made by another court, shall be paid by the registrar of the court in which the proceedings are pending to the registrar of the other court and dealt with as that court directs.

Course of proceedings

10. On the day appointed pursuant to rule 7(1)—

(1) any creditor, whether or not he has received notice in Form 4, may attend and prove his debt and, subject to the provisions of rule 8, object to any debt which the debtor has included in Form 1 or 2 ;

(2) every debt included by the debtor in Form 1 or Form 2 shall be taken to be proved unless it is objected to by a creditor, or disallowed by the court, or required by the court to be supported by evidence ;

(3) any creditor whose debt is objected to by either the debtor or any other creditor or is required by the court to be supported by evidence, shall prove his debt ;

(4) the court may adjourn the proof of any debt and, if it does so, may either adjourn consideration of the question whether an administration order should be made or proceed to determine the question, in which case, if an administration order is made, the debt, when proved, shall be added to the debts scheduled to the order ;

(5) any creditor whose debt is admitted or proved, and, by leave of the court, any creditor the proof of whose debt has been adjourned, shall be entitled to be heard and to adduce evidence.

Circumstances in which administration order need not be made

11. Where any facts are proved on proof of which a court exercising jurisdiction in bankruptcy would be required either to refuse, suspend or attach conditions to the debtor's discharge if he were adjudged bankrupt, the court may decline to make an administration order.

Duration of administration order

12. No administration order shall be made under which the payment of instalments, if kept up without default, would extend over a period of more than 10 years from the date of the order.

Proceedings when order made

13.—(1) An administration order shall be in Form 5 and a copy thereof shall be sent to the debtor.

(2) Notice in Form 6 of the order having been made shall be sent to each creditor whose name has been included by the debtor in Form 1 or 2 or who has proved his debt.

(3) Notice of the order having been made shall also be sent in the same form (with the necessary modifications) to every other court in which, to the knowledge of the registrar, judgment has been obtained or proceedings are pending against the debtor in respect of any debt scheduled to the order.

Objections

14.—(1) After an administration order has been made, any creditor who has not received notice in Form 4 and who desires to object to any debt scheduled to the order, or to the manner in which payment is directed to be made, shall give notice to the registrar of his objection and of the grounds thereof.

(2) On receipt of the notice the court shall consider the objection and may—

    (*a*) allow it ;

    (*b*) dismiss it ; or

    (*c*) adjourn it for hearing on notice being given to such persons and on such terms as to security for costs or otherwise as the court thinks fit.

(3) Without prejudice to the generality of paragraph (2), the court may dismiss an objection if it is not satisfied that the creditor gave notice of it within a reasonable time of his becoming aware of the administration order.

Proof by creditor omitted, or of subsequent debt

15.—(1) Any creditor in respect of a debt due before the making of an administration order and not scheduled thereto who desires to prove his debt, or any person who after the date of the order becomes a creditor of the debtor and desires to prove his debt under section 149(*d*) of the Act of 1959, shall send particulars of his claim to the registrar who shall thereupon send notice to the debtor in Form 7.

(2) If the debtor does not within the period allowed by the notice give notice that he disputes the claim, the claim shall, unless required by the court to be supported by evidence, be deemed to be proved and shall be added to the schedule to the order accordingly, and notice of the addition shall be sent to the creditor in Form 8.

(3) If the debtor within the period allowed gives notice of his objection in Form 7 or the court requires the claim to be supported by evidence, the registrar shall fix a day for consideration of the matter and give notice thereof to both parties in Form 9 ; and on the hearing the court may either disallow the claim, or allow it in whole or in part, in which latter case the debt allowed shall be added to the schedule.

Application for leave to bring or join in bankruptcy proceedings

16. An application by a creditor under section 20(3) of the Administration of Justice Act 1965(a) for leave to present or join in a bankruptcy petition shall be made on notice to the debtor in accordance with Order 13, Rule 1, of the County Court Rules and the court may, if it thinks fit, order that notice shall also be given to the other creditors.

Conduct of administration order

17.—(1) The court shall appoint a person to have the conduct of the administration order and may at any time remove him and appoint another person in his place.

(a) 1965 c. 2.

(2) It shall be the duty of the person so appointed to take all proper proceedings for enforcing the order ; but in case of his neglect to proceed, or of urgency, any creditor scheduled to the order may, by leave of the court, take such proceedings.

(3) The person so appointed may apply to the court to exercise its powers under rule 21.

(4) If any facts become known to the person so appointed on which the order might be revoked under rule 18 or on which an attachment of earnings order might be made to secure the payments under the administration order, he shall bring such facts to the attention of the court which may thereupon direct notice in Form 10 to be given to the debtor or make such other order as it thinks fit.

Revocation of order

18.—(1) An administration order may at any time be revoked by the court in any of the following cases :—

(a) where two or more of the instalments ordered to be paid are in arrear ;

(b) where the debtor has wilfully inserted in Form 1 or 2 the wrong name or address of any creditor or the wrong particulars of any debt ;

(c) where the debtor after the date of the order has obtained credit to the extent of £10 or upwards without informing the creditor that the order is in force ;

(d) where the order has been obtained by fraud or misrepresentation ;

(e) where a receiving order has since the date of the administration order been made against the debtor ;

(f) where an attachment of earnings order has been made to secure the payment of a debt payable by the debtor under a judgment given after the making of the administration order.

(2) An order revoking an administration order shall be in Form 11.

(3) An application to revoke an administration order may be made on the application of any person entitled to take proceedings under rule 17, any creditor scheduled to the order or any creditor not so scheduled but whose debt has been notified to the court under rule 15 ; and notice in Form 10 of the application shall be given to the debtor, except where the application is made on the ground of a receiving order having been made against him.

Order on application for revocation

19. Where notice is given to the debtor in Form 10 or an application is made to revoke an administration order, the court may—

(a) revoke the order pursuant to rule 18 ; or

(b) suspend the order or make a new order for payment by instalments under rule 21 ; or

(c) make an order in Form 12 directing that the order shall be revoked unless the debtor pays the sum in payment of which he has made default, either within a specified time, or by instalments to be specified in the order ; or

(d) make an attachment of earnings order to secure payments under the administration order ; or

(e) discharge or vary any attachment of earnings order made to secure the payments under the administration order.

Effect of revocation

20.—(1) A copy of an order in Form 11 shall be sent by the registrar to—

(a) the debtor ;

(b) every creditor named in the schedule to the order ;

(c) every creditor not so named whose debt has been notified to the court ;

(d) every other court in which, to the knowledge of the registrar, judgment has been obtained or proceedings were pending against the debtor at the time the order was made in respect of a debt of any such creditor.

(2) Where an administration order is revoked, any attachment of earnings order made to secure the payments required by the administration order shall be discharged.

Suspension of order

21. If at any time it appears to the court that the debtor is unable from any cause to pay any instalment, the court may suspend the operation of the order for such time and on such terms as it thinks fit or vary the instalments ordered to be paid and may make any consequential variation in any attachment of earnings order made to secure the payments under the administration order or discharge the said attachment of earnings order.

Calculation of arrears

22. In calculating the amount in arrear under an administration order, any instalments accruing due during a period for which such order has been suspended shall not be reckoned in that amount.

Proportionate payment of debts scheduled under section 149(d) of the Act of 1959

23. All creditors scheduled under section 149(d) of the Act of 1959 before the administration order is superseded under section 155 of that Act shall rank equally in proportion to the amount of their debts subject to the priority given by the said paragraph (d) to those scheduled as having been creditors before the date of the order, but no payment made to any creditor by way of dividend or otherwise shall be disturbed by reason of any subsequent proof by any other creditor under the said paragraph (d).

Dividends

24.—(1) Dividends shall from time to time be declared and distributed among the creditors entitled thereto.

(2) When a dividend is declared, notice in Form 13 shall be sent to each such creditor.

Change of debtor's residence

25.—(1) A debtor who changes his residence shall forthwith inform the court of his new address.

(2) Where the debtor becomes resident in the district of another court, the court in which the administration order is being conducted may transfer the proceedings to that other court.

Use of forms

26. The forms in the Appendix to these Rules shall be used in the cases to which they are applicable with such variations as circumstances require.

Revocation

27. The Administration Order Rules 1936(**a**), the Administration Order (Amendment) Rules 1949(**b**) and the Administration Order (Amendment) Rules 1965(**c**) shall be revoked.

Dated 5th July 1971.

Hailsham of St. Marylebone, C.

(a) S. R. & O. 1936/1317 (Rev. V, p. 164: 1936 I, p. 661).
(b) S.I. 1949/2275 (1949 I, p. 1200).   (c) S.I. 1965/901 (1965 I, p. 2385).

APPENDIX

FORMS

Rule 3   Form 1

REQUEST FOR ADMINISTRATION ORDER

In the   County Court

Request No.

Plaint No.

BETWEEN   Plaintiff

and   Defendant

I,

of

the above-named defendant, state that a judgment was obtained against me in this action on the   day of   19   , for the sum of £ and that I am unable to pay the amount forthwith.

I owe the persons mentioned in the list below, including the plaintiff in this action, the sums given opposite their names, which do not total more than £500. To the best of my knowledge I am not indebted to any other person whatsoever.

I request that an order be made for the administration of my estate under section 148 of the County Courts Act 1959, providing for the payment of my debts in full [*or* to the extent of   pence in the pound] by instalments of £ for every month.

LIST OF CREDITORS

Name of creditor (and plaint number in the case of a judgment debt)	Address of creditor	Description	Amount of debt £	Name & address of any other person liable for the debt	Particulars and estimated value of any security given in respect of the debt
		TOTAL £			

NOTE: The plaintiff's judgment debt must be inserted as well as all other debts. If any of the above creditors, in addition to the plaintiff, has sued the defendant in any court, the summons or order in each case must be produced to the registrar.

(Form 1 continued)

Answer *all* the following questions.   Do not leave blanks.

Particulars of Defendant's Resources and Needs

1. EMPLOYMENT

    (*a*) What is your age?

    (*b*) By whom are you employed? (BLOCK CAPITALS) (If you have more than one employer give answers in respect of each of them)

    (*c*) Where are you employed?
        (FULL ADDRESS)

    (*d*) In what capacity are you employed?

    (*e*) What is the address of your employer's Head Office if different from (*c*) above?

    (*f*) What is your works number?
                pay reference?

2. PAY AND INCOME

    (*a*) What is your basic pay before deductions?   £............per week/month

    (*b*) What overtime, bonuses, fees, allowances or commission do you receive?

    (*c*) What deductions are normally made from your pay?   £............per week/month for

    (*d*) What is your usual take-home pay?   £............per week/month

    (*e*) Do you receive a pension or any other income?   Please give details

3. LIABILITIES

    (*a*) What persons, if any, are financially dependent on you? Please give details (including the ages of any dependent children) and mention any contribution they make to your household expenses.

    (*b*) What rent or mortgage instalments do you have to pay?   £............per week/month for

    (*c*) What rates, if any, do you have to pay?   £............per week/month

    (*d*) Do you have to pay under any other court orders?   Please give details.

    (*e*) What other regular payments have you to make?

    (*f*) Have you any other liabilities which you would like the court to take into account? Please give details.

I,..aforesaid make oath and say that, to the best of my knowledge, the names of all my creditors, and the debts due from me to them, are truly set forth in the above list of creditors, and that the particulars contained in my request and the above statements are true.

Sworn at   in the   of
            this   day of   19   }..

                                       Before me...........................
officer of a court, appointed by the Judge to take affidavits.

Rule 4   Form 2

                                        In the   County Court
                                            Plaint No.
                            [or Attachment Application No.   ]
BETWEEN   Plaintiff
and   Defendant
I,
of

the above-named defendant, state that I owe the persons mentioned in the list below,
including the plaintiff in this action, the sums given opposite their names, which do
not total more than £500.   To the best of my knowledge I am not indebted to any
other person whatsoever.

If an order is made for the administration of my estate, I request that it may provide
for the payment of my debts in full [or to the extent of   pence in the
pound] by instalments of £   for every month.

LIST OF CREDITORS

Name of creditor (and plaint number in the case of a judgment debt)	Address of creditor	Description	Amount of debt £	Name & address of any other person liable for the debt	Particulars and estimated value of any security given in respect of the debt
		TOTAL £			

NOTE: The plaintiff's judgment debt must be inserted as well as all other debts.   If any
of the above creditors, in addition to the plaintiff, has sued the defendant in any
court, the summons or order in each case must be produced to the registrar.

I,..aforesaid make oath and say that, to the best
of my knowledge, the names of all my creditors, and the debts due from me to them,
are truly set forth in the above list of my creditors, and that the above particulars and
statements are true.

Sworn at   in the   of   ⎫
            this   day of   19   ⎬..
                                                       ⎭

                                        Before me...........................
                                        officer of a court, appointed by
                                        the Judge to take affidavits.

Form 3 Rule 7(2)

NOTICE TO DEBTOR

In the County Court

Request No.

[*or* Attachment Application No.]

IN THE MATTER of [*insert name of debtor*]

Debtor

TAKE NOTICE that the question of making an Administration Order in this matter [which has been transferred to this court from the County Court] will be heard at [*insert address of Court House*]
on the day of 19 , at o'clock.

AND FURTHER TAKE NOTICE that you must bring with you to the court all your books of account, invoices, papers, summonses, or other documents relating to any debts owing by you.

Dated 19

Registrar.

To

of

Rule 7(2)   Form 4

In the   County Court

Request No.

[*or* Attachment Application No.   ]

Seal

IN THE MATTER of [*insert name of debtor*]

Debtor

The above-named debtor has filed a request for an Administration Order under section 148 of the County Courts Act 1959 [and the request has been forwarded to this court from the   County Court].

[*or* An application has been made to the court for an attachment of earnings order against the above-named debtor and the court has asked him to furnish a list of his creditors with a view to making an Administration Order.]

AND the debtor has proposed that if an Administration Order is made it should provide for the payment of his debts in full [*or* to the extent of   pence in the pound] to be paid by instalments of £   for every month.

TAKE NOTICE that the court will proceed to hear this matter at [*insert address of Court House*]
on   the   day of   19   , at   o'clock.

The debtor has notified the court that you are a creditor of his and states that he owes you the sum of £   . Particulars of the debtor's means are attached to this notice.

A copy of the list of creditors filed by the debtor, with the amounts stated to be owing to them, is attached to this notice.

If you wish to object to the debt of any creditor named in the list, or to [the amount of the composition or] the instalments which the debtor proposes to pay, you must give written notice to the Registrar of the court and to the debtor and, in the case of objection to a debt, to the creditor whose debt is objected to, not less than five clear days before the day mentioned above, stating the grounds of your objection.

If you claim more than the amount stated to be due to you, you should bring with you to the court on the day mentioned above any witnesses, books etc., necessary to prove your claim.

The debtor's proposal mentioned above does not prejudice the power of the court to make an order providing for the payment of his debts [to a greater or less extent, or] by greater or smaller instalments as appears practicable to the court in the circumstances of the case.

Dated   19   .

Registrar.

To

of

Form 5 Rule 13(1)

ADMINISTRATION ORDER

In the County Court

Administration Order No.

IN THE MATTER of an Administration Order against

Debtor

IT IS ORDERED that the above-named debtor do pay the debts in the schedule to this order, and all other debts now due and afterwards proved under this order, in full [*or* to the extent of pence in the pound], by instalments of £ for every month until this order is complied with.

[AND IT IS ORDERED that the said debtor do pay the said instalments to the Registrar of the court, the first of such payments to be made on the day of 19 .]

AND IT IS DIRECTED that of have the conduct of this order.

Dated 19

Registrar.

This order may at any time be revoked in any of the following cases:—

(1) Where two or more of the instalments ordered to be paid are in arrear.

(2) Where the debtor has wilfully inserted in the list of creditors given by him the wrong name or address of any creditor, or the wrong particulars of any debt.

(3) Where the debtor after the date of this order has obtained credit to the extent of £10 or upwards, without informing the creditor that an administration order is in force.

(4) Where the order has been obtained by fraud or misrepresentation.

(5) Where a receiving order has been made against the debtor since the date of this order.

(6) Where an attachment of earnings order has been made to secure the payment of a debt payable by the debtor under a judgment given after the making of this order.

SCHEDULE OF DEBTS

Name of creditor	Amount £
TOTAL £	

TO THE DEBTOR: Take notice that if you change your address you must at once give notice to the Registrar of your new address.

Rule 13(2)   Form 6

NOTICE TO CREDITORS OF MAKING OF ADMINISTRATION ORDER

                              In the   County Court

                              Administration Order No.

IN THE MATTER of an Administration Order against

                                                    Debtor

   TAKE NOTICE that the court has this day made an Administration Order providing
for the payment of the debts of the above-named debtor in full [*or* to the extent of
                 pence in the pound], and £   the costs of these proceedings,
by instalments of £   every month, and has directed that
of   shall have the conduct of the order.

   [Your claim against the debtor has been [allowed and scheduled at the sum of
£   ] [*or* disallowed].

   TO CREDITOR: Please bring this notice with you if you attend at the court office
                 for any purpose connected with the order.]
[*Where notice of the order is sent to another court substitute this paragraph:*—
   The debts scheduled to the order include a debt of £   due to
                          in respect of which a judgment has been obtained or
proceedings (Plaint No.   ) are pending in the
County Court [*or as the case may be*].]

                              Dated   19   .

                                                    Registrar.

   To

        of

Form 7   Rule 15(1)

NOTICE TO DEBTOR OF CREDITOR'S CLAIM

In the   County Court

Administration Order No.

Seal

IN THE MATTER of an Administration Order against

Debtor

TAKE NOTICE that

of

states that you owe him the sum of £   for

and claims to be scheduled to the Administration Order made against you as a creditor for that sum.

AND FURTHER TAKE NOTICE that if you wish to dispute his claim, you must within seven days complete the notice below and return it to the Registrar of the court. If you do not do so, the claim may be taken to be admitted by you and may be added to the schedule accordingly.

Dated   19

Registrar.

To the debtor

NOTICE

Administration Order No.

TAKE NOTICE that I object to the claim of

of

made against me, because [*state reasons*].

Dated   19

(*Signed*)   *Debtor.*

To the Registrar of the County Court

Rule 15(2) Form 8

NOTICE TO CREDITOR OF INCLUSION OF HIS DEBT IN SCHEDULE

In the County Court

Administration Order No.

IN THE MATTER of an Administration Order against

Debtor

TAKE NOTICE that your claim has been added to the schedule of debts in the order.

Dated 19 .

Registrar.

To

of

Please bring this notice with you if you attend at the court office for any purpose connected with the order.

Rule 15(3) Form 9

NOTICE OF HEARING OF OBJECTION TO CLAIM

In the County Court

Administration Order No.

IN THE MATTER of an Administration Order against

Debtor

Notice having been given by you [*or* the debtor] of your [*or* his] intention to dispute [the claim of
of against you] [*or* your claim against him],

TAKE NOTICE that the objection will be heard at
County Court [*insert address of Court House*]
on the day of 19 , at o'clock.

You should bring with you to the court on the day mentioned above any witnesses, books etc., necessary to defeat [*or* prove] the claim.

Dated 19 .

Registrar.

To

of

Form 10   Rule 17(4)

NOTICE TO DEBTOR TO SHOW CAUSE WHY ADMINISTRATION ORDER SHOULD
NOT BE REVOKED

In the   County Court

Administration Order No.

IN THE MATTER of an Administration Order against

Debtor

TAKE NOTICE that you are hereby required to attend personally in this court, at
[*insert address of Court House*]
on   the   day of   19   , at
       o'clock, to show cause [why the Administration Order made against you
in this court on the   day of   19   , should not be revoked
on the following grounds [*set out grounds alleged for revocation*]] [*or as the case may
be*].

Dated   19

Registrar.

To the debtor

Form 11   Rules 18(2)
                                  & 20(1)

ORDER REVOKING ADMINISTRATION ORDER

In the   County Court

Administration Order No.

IN THE MATTER of an Administration Order against

Debtor

IT IS HEREBY ORDERED that the Administration Order made against the above-
named debtor in this court on the   day of
         19   , be revoked on the following grounds:—
[*state grounds*].

Dated   19

Registrar.

Rule 19(1)   Form 12

ORDER CONDITIONALLY REVOKING ADMINISTRATION ORDER

In the   County Court

Administration Order No.

IN THE MATTER of an Administration Order against

Debtor

IT IS HEREBY ORDERED that the Administration Order made against the above-named debtor in this court on the   day of   19 ,
be revoked unless the sum of £   in payment of which the debtor has
made default be paid on or before the   day of   19   [or by
instalments of £   for every month, the first on the   day of
       19   ].

Dated   19   .

Registrar.

Rule 24(2)   Form 13

NOTICE OF DIVIDEND

In the   County Court

Administration Order No.

IN THE MATTER of an Administration Order against

Debtor

TAKE NOTICE that a sum has been paid into court in this matter sufficient to
provide for payment of a dividend of   pence in the pound.

The amount of the dividend on the debt of £   scheduled as due to [*insert
name of creditor*] is £   .   A cheque for this amount is enclosed.

Dated   19   .

Registrar.

To

EXPLANATORY NOTE

(This Note is not part of the Rules.)

These Rules, which replace the existing Rules regarding administration orders, regulate the procedure consequent on an application for an administration order under Part VII of the County Courts Act 1959 or an order requiring a debtor to furnish a list of his creditors under section 4 of the Attachment of Earnings Act 1971.

STATUTORY INSTRUMENTS

1971 No. 1101 (S. 138)

LANDLORD AND TENANT

RENT CONTROL, ETC. (SCOTLAND)

The Rent Assessment Committees (Scotland) Regulations 1971

Made - - - -	*2nd July* 1971
Laid before Parliament	*14th July* 1971
Coming into Operation	*2nd August* 1971

In exercise of the powers conferred upon me by section 46 of the Rent Act 1965(a) and that section as extended by section 56(1) of the Housing (Scotland) Act 1969(b) and by section 6(4) of the Rent (Control of Increases) Act 1969(c) and of all other powers enabling me in that behalf and after consultation with the Council on Tribunals, I hereby make the following regulations:—

Citation and commencement

1. These regulations may be cited as the Rent Assessment Committees (Scotland) Regulations 1971 and shall come into operation on 2nd August 1971.

Interpretation

2.—(1) The Interpretation Act 1889(d) shall apply for the interpretation of these regulations as it applies for the interpretation of an Act of Parliament.

(2) In these regulations unless the context otherwise requires,

"chairman" means the chairman of a committee;

"committee" means a rent assessment committee, constituted in accordance with the provisions of Schedule 2 to the Rent Act 1965 to which a reference is made;

"hearing" means the meeting or meetings of a committee to hear oral representations made in relation to a reference;

"party" means, in the case where a reference is subject to a hearing, any person who is entitled under regulation 3(2) of these regulations to receive notice of the date, time and place of the hearing and, in the case where a reference is not to be subject to a hearing, any person who is entitled to make representations in writing to the committee;

"reference" means a matter which is referred by a rent officer to a committee under paragraphs 9 or 16 of Schedule 3 to the Rent Act 1965 or paragraph 11 of Schedule 3 to the Housing (Scotland) Act 1969, or an application for a certificate of fair rent which is referred by a rent officer to a committee under paragraphs 4 or 8 of Schedule 4 to the Rent Act 1965 or under these paragraphs of the said Schedule 4 as applied by paragraph 4 of Schedule 3 to the Housing (Scotland) Act 1969.

(3) For the purpose of any of these regulations relating to procedure at a hearing, any reference to a party shall be construed as including a reference to a person authorised by that party to be heard on his behalf whether or not that person is an advocate or a solicitor pursuant to paragraph 11 or paragraph 16(4)

(a) 1965 c. 75.	(b) 1969 c. 34.
(c) 1969 c. 62.	(d) 1889 c. 63.

of Schedule 3 to the Rent Act 1965 or paragraph 13 of Schedule 3 to the Housing (Scotland) Act 1969 or paragraph 11 of Schedule 4 to the Rent Act 1965 or that last paragraph as applied by paragraph 4 of Schedule 3 to the Housing (Scotland) Act 1969, as the case may be.

Hearings

3.—(1) Where a reference is to be subject to a hearing, the committee shall appoint a date, time and place for a hearing.

(2) A committee shall give not less than ten days' notice in writing of the date, time and place so appointed for a hearing—

(*a*) to the landlord and the tenant where the reference is a matter referred to the committee under paragraph 9 of Schedule 3 to the Rent Act 1965 or under paragraph 11 of Schedule 3 to the Housing (Scotland) Act 1969; or

(*b*) to the applicant where the reference is a matter relating to an application for the registration of a rent for a dwellinghouse in accordance with a certificate of fair rent referred to the committee under paragraph 16 of Schedule 3 to the Rent Act 1965; or

(*c*) to the applicant where the reference is an application for a certificate of fair rent referred to the committee under paragraphs 4 or 8 of Schedule 4 to the Rent Act 1965 and, in a case to which paragraph 13 of that Schedule applies, to the tenant; or

(*d*) to the applicant and tenant where the reference is an application for a certificate of fair rent referred to the committee under paragraphs 4 or 8 of Schedule 4 to the Rent Act 1965 as applied by paragraph 4 of Schedule 3 to the Housing (Scotland) Act 1969.

(3) A hearing shall be in public unless for special reasons the committee otherwise decide, but nothing in these regulations shall prevent a member of the Council on Tribunals or of its Scottish Committee in that capacity from attending any hearing.

(4) At a hearing—

(*a*) the parties shall be heard in such order and, subject to the provisions of these regulations, the procedure shall be such as the committee shall determine; and

(*b*) a party may call witnesses, give evidence on his own behalf and cross-examine any witnesses called by the other party.

(5) The committee at their discretion may on their own motion, or at the request of the parties or one of them, at any time and from time to time postpone or adjourn a hearing; but they shall not do so at the request of one party only unless, having regard to the grounds upon which and the time at which such request is made and to the convenience of the parties, they deem it reasonable to do so. The committee shall give to the parties such notice of any postponed or adjourned hearing as they deem to be reasonable in the circumstances.

(6) If a party does not appear at a hearing, the committee, on being satisfied that the requirements of this regulation regarding the giving of notice of a hearing have been duly complied with, may proceed to deal with the reference upon the representations of any party present and upon the documents and information which they may properly consider.

Documents

4.—(1) Where the reference is to be subject to a hearing, the committee shall take all reasonable steps to ensure that there is supplied to each of the parties before the date of the hearing—

(a) a copy of, or sufficient extracts from, or particulars of, any document relevant to the reference which has been received from the rent officer or from a party (other than a document which is in the possession of such party or of which that party has previously been supplied with a copy by the rent officer); and

(b) a copy of any document which embodies results of any enquiries made by or for the committee for the purposes of that reference, or which contains relevant information in relation to fair rents previously determined for other dwellinghouses and which has been prepared for the committee for the purposes of that reference.

(2) At any hearing where—

(i) any document relevant to the reference is not in the possession of a party present at such hearing; and

(ii) such party has not been supplied with a copy of, or relevant extracts from, or particulars of, such document by the rent officer or by the committee in accordance with the provisions of paragraph (1) of this regulation,

then unless—

(a) such party consents to the continuation of the hearing; or

(b) the committee consider that such party has a sufficient opportunity of dealing with such document without an adjournment of the hearing,

the committee shall not consider such document until after they have adjourned the hearing for a period which they consider will afford such party a sufficient opportunity of dealing with such document.

(3) Where a reference is not to be subject to a hearing the committee shall supply to each of the parties a copy of, or sufficient extracts from, or particulars of, any such document as is mentioned in paragraph (1)(a) of this regulation (other than a document excepted from that paragraph) and a copy of any such document as is mentioned in paragraph (1)(b) of this regulation, and they shall not reach their decision until they are satisfied that each party has been given a sufficient opportunity of commenting upon any document of which a copy or from which extracts or of which particulars has or have been so supplied, and upon the other party's case.

Inspection of dwellinghouse

5.—(1) The committee may on their own motion and shall at the request of one of the parties (subject in either case to any necessary consent being obtained) inspect the dwellinghouse which is the subject of the reference.

(2) An inspection may be made before, during or after the close of the hearing, or at such stage in relation to the consideration of the representations in writing as the committee shall determine.

(3) The committee shall give such notice in writing as they deem sufficient of an inspection to the party or parties and shall allow each party and his representative to attend any such inspection.

(4) Where an inspection is made after the close of a hearing the committee may, if they consider that it is expedient to do so on account of any matter arising from the inspection, re-open the hearing; and if the hearing is to be re-opened paragraph (2) of regulation 3 of these regulations shall apply as it applied to the original hearing, save in so far as its requirements may be dispensed with or relaxed with the consent of the parties.

Decisions

6.—(1) The decision of the committee upon a reference shall be recorded in a document signed by the chairman (or in the event of his absence or incapacity, by another member of the committee) which shall contain the reasons for the decision but shall contain no reference to the decision being a majority (if that be the case) or to any opinion of a minority.

(2) The chairman (or in the event of his absence or incapacity, another member of the committee) shall have power, by a certificate under his hand, to correct any clerical or accidental error or omission in the said document.

(3) A copy of the said document and of any such correction shall be sent by the committee to the party or parties and to the rent officer.

Giving of notices etc.

7. Where any notice or other written matter is required under the provisions of these regulations to be given or supplied by the committee to a party or parties, it shall be sufficient compliance with the regulations if such notice or matter is sent by post in a pre-paid letter addressed to the party for whom it is intended at his usual or last known address or if that party has appointed an agent to act on his behalf in relation to the reference, to that agent at the address of the agent supplied to the Committee.

Gordon Campbell,
One of Her Majesty's Principal
Secretaries of State.

St. Andrew's House,
Edinburgh.
2nd July 1971.

EXPLANATORY NOTE

(This Note is not part of the Regulations.)

These Regulations regulate the procedure to be followed by Rent Assessment Committees in Scotland, and supplement the provisions regarding the procedure to be followed by such Committees which are contained in Schedules 3 and 4 to the Rent Act 1965 and Schedule 3 to the Housing (Scotland) Act 1969.

STATUTORY INSTRUMENTS

1971 No. 1102

PLANT BREEDERS' RIGHTS

The Plant Breeders' Rights (Fees) (Amendment) Regulations 1971

Made - - -	*8th July* 1971
Laid before Parliament	*14th July* 1971
Coming into Operation	*15th July* 1971

The Minister of Agriculture, Fisheries and Food, the Secretary of State for Scotland and the Secretary of State for the Home Department (being the Secretary of State concerned with agriculture in Northern Ireland), acting jointly, in exercise of the powers vested in them by sections 9 and 36 of the Plant Varieties and Seeds Act 1964(a) (extended to Northern Ireland by the Plant Varieties and Seeds (Northern Ireland) Order 1964(b) and to the Isle of Man by the Plant Varieties and Seeds (Isle of Man) Order 1969(c)) and of all other powers enabling them in that behalf, with the approval of the Treasury, hereby make the following Regulations :—

Citation and Commencement

1. These Regulations may be cited as the Plant Breeders' Rights (Fees) (Amendment) Regulations 1971 and shall come into operation on 15th July 1971.

Amendment of Principal Regulations

2. The Plant Breeders' Rights (Fees) Regulations 1968(d), as amended (e), are hereby further amended—

    (*a*) by substituting in the third column of Schedule 2, opposite the item "(*c*) a rose variety", for the figures "20 0 0" the figures "30·00" ;

    (*b*) by adding in the second column of Schedule 2, at the end of the entry numbered 20, the following further items—

        "(*y*) a lettuce variety

        (*z*) a runner bean variety"

    and in the fourth column of the said Schedule opposite each of the items so added, the figures "40·00".

(a) 1964 c. 14.
(b) S.I. 1964/1574 (1964 III, p. 3543).
(c) S.I. 1969/1829 (1969 III, p. 5701).
(d) S.I. 1968/619 (1968 I, p. 1444).
(e) The relevant amending instrument is S.I. 1970/454 (1970 I, p. 1530).

(c) by inserting in Schedule 2, following the entry numbered 20, a further entry as follows (the heading of the columns in the said Schedule being repeated below for reference only)—

No.	Matter	When Payable	Amount
			£ p
"20A	The examination of a cymbidium variety which is the subject of an application for a grant of plant breeders' rights.	Within 14 days of demand made by the Controller	20·00 "

In Witness whereof the official seal of the Minister of Agriculture, Fisheries and Food is hereunto affixed on 28th June 1971.

(L.S.)

J. M. L. Prior,
Minister of Agriculture, Fisheries and Food.

2nd July 1971.

Gordon Campbell,
Secretary of State for Scotland.

6th July 1971.

R. Maudling,
Secretary of State for the Home Department.

V. H. Goodhew,
P. L. Hawkins,
Two of the Lords Commissioners of
Approved on 8th July 1971.   Her Majesty's Treasury.

EXPLANATORY NOTE

(This Note is not part of the Regulations.)

These Regulations further amend the Plant Breeders' Rights (Fees) Regulations 1968 by prescribing the fees payable for trials or examination of three further classes of plant varieties for which plant breeders' rights may be granted. They also provide for an increase in the fee payable for the trials of a rose variety.

STATUTORY INSTRUMENTS

1971 No. 1103

SEA FISHERIES

The Foreign Sea-Fishery Officers (International Commission for the Northwest Atlantic Fisheries Scheme) Order 1971

Made - - - -	*7th July* 1971
Laid before Parliament	*15th July* 1971
Coming into Operation	*1st August* 1971

The Minister of Agriculture, Fisheries and Food and the Secretaries of State for Scotland and the Home Department (being the Secretaries of State respectively concerned with the sea-fishing industry in Scotland and Northern Ireland) in exercise of the powers conferred on them by section 7(4) of the Sea Fisheries Act 1968(a) and of all other powers enabling them in that behalf, hereby make the following Order:—

Citation and Commencement

1. This Order may be cited as the Foreign Sea-Fishery Officers (International Commission for the Northwest Atlantic Fisheries Scheme) Order 1971 and shall come into operation on 1st August 1971.

Interpretation

2.—(1) in this Order:—

"the Act" means the Sea Fisheries Act 1968;

"the Commission" means the International Commission for the Northwest Atlantic Fisheries established under the Convention;

"the Convention" means the International Convention for the Northwest Atlantic Fisheries signed in Washington on 8th February 1949(b);

"the Convention area" means the area to which the Convention applies comprising the waters described in Part II of Schedule 1 to this Order;

"the Scheme" means the Scheme of Joint Enforcement of the Commission which is set out in Part I of Schedule 1 to this Order, being a Recommendation which has been adopted as a proposal by the Commission and which takes effect as an international arrangement by virtue of the agreement thereto of the member states of the Commission, subject to the Reservations mentioned in the said Part I of Schedule 1;

"subarea" means an area, being one of the five subareas into which the Convention Area is divided, the boundaries of which are as defined in the Annex to the Convention;

(a) 1968 c. 77.   (b) Cmd. 8071.

(2) The Interpretation Act 1889(a) shall apply for the interpretation of this Order as it applies for the interpretation of an Act of Parliament.

Foreign Sea-Fishery Officers

3. In relation to the Scheme there are hereby specified as foreign sea-fishery officers, entitled to exercise in relation to British fishing boats anywhere within the Convention area outside the fishery limits of the British Islands, the powers referred to in section 9 of the Act, officers of the countries referred to in Schedule 2 to this Order, who are duly appointed by the government of their respective countries as inspectors under the terms of the Scheme and who hold a document of identity in the form approved under the Scheme.

In witness whereof the Official Seal of the Minister of Agriculture, Fisheries and Food is hereunto affixed on 5th July 1971.

(L.S.)   *J. M. L. Prior,*
                        Minister of Agriculture, Fisheries and Food.

                                        Gordon Campbell,
6th July 1971.   Secretary of State for Scotland.

Given under the Hand of the Secretary of State for the Home Department on 7th July 1971.

                                        R. Maudling,
                    Secretary of State for the Home Department.

SCHEDULE 1

PART I

SCHEME OF JOINT ENFORCEMENT

Recommendation

That, pursuant to paragraph 5 of Article VIII of the Convention, the following arrangements be established, as from 1st July 1971, for international control outside national fishery limits for the purpose of ensuring the application of the Convention and the measures in force thereunder:—

(1) Control shall be carried out by inspectors of the fishery control services of Contracting Governments. The names of the inspectors appointed for that purpose by their respective governments shall be notified to the Commission.

(2) Ships carrying inspectors shall fly a special flag or pennant approved by the Commission to indicate that the inspector is carrying out international inspection duties. The names of the ships so used for the time being, which may be either special inspection vessels or fishing vessels, shall be notified to the Commission.

(a) 1889 c. 63

(3) Each inspector shall carry a document of identity supplied by the authorities of the flag state in a form approved by the Commission and given him on appointment stating that he has authority to act under the arrangements approved by the Commission.

(4) Subject to the arrangements agreed under paragraph (9), a vessel employed for the time being in fishing for sea fish or in the treatment of sea fish in the Convention area shall stop when given the appropriate signal in the International Code of Signals by a ship carrying an inspector unless actually fishing, shooting or hauling, in which case it shall stop immediately it has finished hauling. The master of the vessel shall permit the inspector, who may be accompanied by a witness, to board it. The master shall enable the inspector to make such examination of catch, nets or other gear and any relevant documents as the inspector deems necessary to verify the observance of the Commission's recommendations in force in relation to the flag state of the vessel concerned and the inspector may ask for any explanations that he deems necessary.

(5) On boarding the vessel an inspector shall produce the document described in (3) above. Inspections shall be made so that the vessel suffers the minimum interference and inconvenience. An inspector shall limit his enquiries to the ascertainment of the facts in relation to the observance of the Commission's recommendations in force in relation to the flag state of the vessel concerned. In making his examination an inspector may ask the master for any assistance he may require. He shall draw up a report of his inspection in a form approved by the Commission. He shall sign the report in the presence of the master of the vessel who shall be entitled to add or have added to the report any observations which he may think suitable and must sign such observations. Copies of the report shall be given to the master of the vessel and to the Inspector's Government who shall transmit copies to the appropriate authorities of the flag state of the vessel and to the Commission. Where any infringement of the recommendations is discovered the inspector should where possible also inform the competent authorities of the flag state, as notified to the Commission, and any inspection ship of the flag state known to be in the vicinity.

(6) Resistance to an inspector or failure to comply with his directions shall be treated by the flag state of the vessel as if the inspector were an inspector of that state.

(7) Inspectors shall carry out their duties under these arrangements in accordance with the rules set out in this recommendation but they shall remain under the operational control of their national authorities and shall be responsible to them.

(8) Contracting Governments shall consider and act on reports of foreign inspectors under these arrangements on the same basis as reports of national inspectors. The provisions of this paragraph shall not impose any obligation on a Contracting Government to give the report of a foreign inspector a higher evidential value than it would possess in the inspector's own country. Contracting Governments shall collaborate in order to facilitate judicial or other proceedings arising from a report of an inspector under these arrangements.

(9) (i) Contracting Governments shall inform the Commission by 1st March each year of their provisional plans for participation in these arrangements in the following year and the Commission may make suggestions to Contracting Governments for the co-ordination of national operations in this field including the number of inspectors and ships carrying inspectors.

(ii) The arrangements set out in this Recommendation and the plans for participation shall apply between Contracting Goverments unless otherwise agreed between them; and such agreement shall be notified to the Commission.

Provided, however, that implementation of the scheme shall be suspended between any two Contracting Governments if either of them has notified the Commission to that effect, pending completion of an agreement.

(10) (i) Nets shall be inspected in accordance with the regulations in force for the subarea in which the inspection takes place. The number of undersized meshes and the width of each mesh examined shall be entered in the inspector's report, together with the average width of the meshes examined.

(ii) Inspectors shall have authority to inspect all nets.

(11) The inspector shall affix an identification mark approved by the Commission, to any net which appears to have been used in contravention of the Commission's recommendations in force in relation to the flag state of the vessel concerned and shall record this fact in his report.

(12) The inspector may photograph the net in such a way that the identification mark and the measurement of the net is visible, in which case the subjects photographed should be listed in the report and copies of the photographs should be attached to the copy of the report to the flag state.

(13) The inspector shall have authority, subject to any limitations imposed by the Commission, to carry out such examination and measurement of the catch as he deems necessary to establish whether the Commission's recommendations are being complied with.   He shall report his findings to the authorities of the flag state of the inspected vessel as soon as possible.

RESERVATIONS

(a) as between the Union of Soviet Socialist Republics and other Contracting Governments the provisions of the Scheme relating to inspection of gear below deck and of catch do not apply;

(b) as between Poland and other Contracting Governments the provisions of the Scheme relating to inspection of gear or catch below deck do not apply; and

(c) as between Romania and other Contracting Governments the provisions of the Scheme relating to inspection of gear below deck and of catch do not apply.

PART II

CONVENTION AREA

All waters, except territorial waters, bounded by a line beginning at a point on the coast of Rhode Island in 71° 40′ west longitude; thence due south to 39° north latitude; thence due east to 42° west longitude; thence due north to 59° north latitude; thence due west to 44° west longitude; thence due north to the coast of Greenland; thence along the west coast of Greenland to 78° 10′ north latitude; thence southwards to a point in 75° north latitude and 73° 30′ west longitude; thence along a rhumb line to a point in 69° north latitude and 59° west longitude; thence due south to 61° north latitude; thence due west to 64° 30′ west longitude; thence due south to the coast of Labrador; thence in a southerly direction along the coast of Labrador to the southern terminus of its boundary with Quebec; thence in a westerly direction along the coast of Quebec, and in an easterly and southerly direction along the coasts of New Brunswick, Nova Scotia, and Cape Breton Island to Cabot Strait, thence along the coasts of Cape Breton Island, Nova Scotia, New Brunswick, Maine, New Hampshire, Massachusetts, and Rhode Island to the point of beginning.

SCHEDULE 2

Foreign Countries which are parties to the Scheme

1.   Denmark

2.   France

3.   Iceland

4.   Italy

5. Japan
6. Norway
7. Poland
8. Portugal
9. Romania
10. Spain
11. Union of Soviet Socialist Republics
12. United States of America

EXPLANATORY NOTE

(This Note is not part of the Order.)

This Order specifies the class of persons who are to be foreign sea-fishery officers for the purposes of the Scheme of Joint Enforcement of the Northwest Altantic Fisheries Commission.

STATUTORY INSTRUMENTS

1971 No. 1105

CIVIL AVIATION

The Air Navigation (Fees) (Second Amendment) Regulations 1971

Made - - -	*7th July* 1971
Coming into Operation	1*st August* 1971

The Secretary of State with the consent of the Treasury and in exercise of his powers under Article 78 of the Air Navigation Order 1970(a), as amended (b), and of all other powers enabling him in that behalf, hereby makes the following Regulations:—

1. These Regulations may be cited as the Air Navigation (Fees) (Second Amendment) Regulations 1971 and shall come into operation on 1st August 1971.

2. The Interpretation Act 1889(c) shall apply for the purpose of the interpretation of these Regulations as it applies for the purpose of the interpretation of an Act of Parliament.

3. The Schedule to the Air Navigation (Fees) Regulations 1970(d), as amended (e), shall be further amended as follows:—

(1) In paragraph 1 after "The fee to be paid" there shall be inserted "on application";

(2) In paragraph 4 for sub-paragraph (1)(*c*) of the proviso there shall be substituted the following:—

"(c) in any other case in respect of each 1,000 lb. or part thereof of the maximum total weight of the aircraft .. £9·00";

(3) In paragraph 5(b) for "10 0" there shall be substituted "£0·50";

(4) In paragraph 6:—

(*a*) after "where the maximum total weight authorised of the glider does not exceed 2,000 lb.," there shall be inserted "and £5·00 where the maximum total weight authorised of the glider exceeds 2,000 lb.,";

(*b*) for the words and figures after "in any other case shall be" there shall be substituted "£9·00 in respect of each 1,000 lb. or part thereof of the maximum total weight authorised of the aircraft.";

(a) S.I. 1970/954 (1970 II, p. 2964).　　(b) There is no relevant amending instrument.
(c) 1889 c. 63.　　(d) S.I. 1970/1085 (1970 II, p. 3426).
(e) S.I. 1971/468 (1971 I, p. 1387).

(5) In paragraph 17 after "The fee to be paid" there shall be inserted "on application".

Robert Burns,
A Deputy Secretary,
Department of Trade and Industry.

7th July 1971.

We consent to the making of these Regulations.

V. H. Goodhew,
P. L. Hawkins,
Lords Commissioners of
Her Majesty's Treasury.

7th July 1971.

EXPLANATORY NOTE

(This Note is not part of the Regulations.)

These Regulations further amend the Schedule to the Air Navigation (Fees) Regulations 1970, as amended. In addition to a minor drafting amendment, these Regulations make the following changes:—

(1) The fees to be paid for certificates of registration and copies of documents are required to be paid on application.

(2) The fee for the first issue of a certificate of airworthiness in respect of an aircraft (other than a glider) which conforms to a prototype aircraft or to a modification of such a prototype aircraft is increased in all cases to £9·00 per 1,000 lb. of the maximum total weight, and the reduced fee for such aircraft when the maximum total weight does not exceed 2,000 lb. is abolished.

(3) The reduced fees for the second or subsequent issue, or renewal, of a certificate of airworthiness in respect of an aircraft (other than a glider) when its maximum total weight authorised does not exceed 5,000 lb. are abolished and replaced by a fee at the rate of £9·00 per 1,000 lb. which already applies to such aircraft when their maximum total weight authorised exceeds 5,000 lb. A fee is included for gliders whose maximum total weight authorised exceeds 2,000 lb.

STATUTORY INSTRUMENTS

1971 No. 1108 (C.25)

TOWN AND COUNTRY PLANNING, ENGLAND AND WALES

The Town and Country Planning Act 1968 (Commencement No. 6) (Teesside etc.) Order 1971

Made - - - *12th July* 1971

The Secretary of State for the Environment in exercise of the power conferred on him by section 105 of the Town and Country Planning Act 1968(a) hereby makes the following Order :—

1.—(1) This Order may be cited as the Town and Country Planning Act 1968 (Commencement No. 6) (Teesside etc.) Order 1971.

(2) In this Order :—

"the Act" means the Town and Country Planning Act 1968 ;

"the principal Act" means the Town and Country Planning Act 1962(b) ; and

"the Order area" means the area described in Schedule 1 to this Order.

2. The provisions of the Act specified in the first column of Schedule 2 hereto (which relate to the matters specified in the second column of the said Schedule) shall come into operation in the Order area on 6th August 1971.

3. The bringing into operation of paragraph 5 of Schedule 9 to the Act shall not prejudice the continued operation of any reference in the principal Act to the carrying out of a survey or the preparation, approval, making or amendment of a development plan under Part II of that Act, or to a plan or amendment approved or made under the said Part II, until the repeal of the said Part II as respects the Order area.

SCHEDULE 1

THE ORDER AREA

The county borough of Teesside.

In the administrative county of the North Riding of Yorkshire, the urban districts of Guisborough, Loftus, Saltburn and Marske-by-the-Sea and Skelton and Brotton and the rural district of Stokesley.

(a) 1968 c. 72.   (b) 1962 c. 38.

In the administrative county of Durham, in the rural district of Stockton, the whole of the following parishes:—

> Newsham
> Aislaby
> Egglescliffe
> Longnewton
> Preston-on-Tees
> Elton
> Redmarshall
> Carlton
> Whitton
> Grindon
> Wolviston
> Newton Bewley
> Greatham

and that part of the parish of Elwick Hall which is to the south or west of Close Beck.

SCHEDULE 2

PROVISIONS COMING INTO OPERATION IN THE ORDER AREA ON 6TH AUGUST 1971

Provisions of the Act	Subject matter of provisions
Part I, except sections 13 and 14, and except so far as it enables any matter or thing to be prescribed.	New provisions as to development plans.
In Schedule 9, paragraph 5.	Adaptation of provisions in the principal Act as to surveys and development plans.
In Schedule 9, paragraph 54.	Adaptation of provisions of paragraph 5 of Schedule 2 to the principal Act as to joint advisory committees for development plans, to structure plans and local plans.
In Schedule 11, the entry relating to the principal Act section 210.	Repeal consequential on the bringing into operation of the above-mentioned provisions.

Peter Walker
Secretary of State for the Environment

12th July 1971

EXPLANATORY NOTE

(This Note is not part of the Order.)

This Order brings into force for the county borough of Teesside and certain adjacent areas in the administrative counties of Durham and the North Riding of Yorkshire as described in Schedule 1 to the Order the provisions of the Town and Country Planning Act 1968 which are set out in Schedule 2, subject to the transitional provision contained in Article 3. The provisions which are brought into force are the new substantive provisions as to development plans in Part 1 of the Act and certain provisions in Schedules 9 and 11 to the Act which are consequential on the operation of those provisions.

STATUTORY INSTRUMENTS

1971 No. 1109

TOWN AND COUNTRY PLANNING, ENGLAND AND WALES

The Town and Country Planning (Structure and Local Plans) Regulations 1971

Made - - - -	*12th July* 1971
Laid before Parliament	*15th July* 1971
Coming into Operation	*6th August* 1971

ARRANGEMENT OF REGULATIONS

PART I

APPLICATION, CITATION, COMMENCEMENT AND INTERPRETATION

PART II

PUBLICITY IN CONNECTION WITH THE PREPARATION OF STRUCTURE OR LOCAL PLANS: SALE OF DOCUMENTS AND PRESCRIBED PERIOD FOR MAKING REPRESENTATIONS

PART III

CONSULTATION

PART IV

FORM AND CONTENT OF STRUCTURE PLANS

PART X

PREPARATION AND MAKING, ETC., OF STRUCTURE OR LOCAL PLANS
BY THE SECRETARY OF STATE

45. Preparation and making, etc., of structure or local plans by the Secretary of State.

PART XI

STRUCTURE AND LOCAL PLANS: RECONCILIATION OF CONTRADICTIONS

46. Reconciliation of contradictions in structure plans.
47. Reconciliation of contradictions in local plans.
48. Reconciliation of contradictions between local plans.

SCHEDULE I

STRUCTURE PLANS

PART I.　Matters to which policy is required to relate by regulation 9(1).

PART II.　Matters required by regulation 10 to be contained in written statement.

SCHEDULE 2

LOCAL PLANS

PART I.　Matters to which proposals are required to relate by regulation 16(1).

PART II.　Matters required by regulation 17 to be contained in written statement.

SCHEDULE 3

FORMS OF NOTICES

The Secretary of State for the Environment (as respects England, except Monmouthshire) and the Secretary of State for Wales (as respects Wales and Monmouthshire) in exercise of their powers under section 2(3) and (6), 3 (1) (2) and (3), 4 (3) (a), 6(3) (5) and (9), 7(1) (2) and (3), and 13(1) and (2) of the Town and Country Planning Act 1968(a), and section 217 of the Town and Country Planning Act 1962(b), and all other powers enabling them in that behalf hereby make the following regulations:—

PART I

APPLICATION, CITATION, COMMENCEMENT AND INTERPRETATION

Application

1. These regulations shall apply to England (except Greater London) and Wales.

Citation and commencement

2. These regulations may be cited as the Town and Country Planning (Structure and Local Plans) Regulations 1971, and shall come into operation on 6th August 1971.

Interpretation

3.—(1) In these regulations—

"the Act" means the Town and Country Planning Act 1968;

(a) 1968 c. 72.　　　　　　　　(b) 1962 c. 38.

"action area" has the meaning assigned to it by section 2(5) of the Act;

"an area of town development" means an area (comprising one or more parts defined on one occasion) in the whole of which town development within the meaning of the Town Development Act 1952(a) is to be carried out;

"certified copy" means a copy certified by the clerk of the local planning authority as being a true copy;

"county" means an administrative county;

"document" includes a map, diagram, illustration or other descriptive matter in any form, and also includes, where appropriate, a copy of a document;

"duly made", in relation to objections, means duly made in accordance with a notice given or served under these regulations;

"local plan" means a local plan mentioned in section 6 of the Act;

"notice by advertisement" means a notice published in the London Gazette and in each of two successive weeks in at least one local newspaper circulating in the locality in which the land to which the notice relates is situated;

"structure plan" means a structure plan mentioned in section 2 of the Act;

"written statement" means, as respects a structure plan, the written statement required by section 2(3) of the Act, and, as respects a local plan, the written statement required by section 6(3) of the Act.

(2) A regulation or schedule referred to in these regulations only by number means the regulation or schedule so numbered in these regulations.

(3) The Interpretation Act 1889(b) shall apply for the interpretation of these regulations as it applies for the interpretation of an Act of Parliament.

PART II

PUBLICITY IN CONNECTION WITH THE PREPARATION OF STRUCTURE OR LOCAL PLANS: SALE OF DOCUMENTS AND PRESCRIBED PERIOD FOR MAKING REPRESENTATIONS

Sale of copies of documents made public for the purpose mentioned in section 3(1)(a) or 7(1)(a) of the Act

4. The local planning authority shall, in such particular cases as the Secretary of State may direct, provide persons making a request in that behalf with copies of any plan or other document which has been made public for the purpose mentioned in section 3(1)(a) or 7(1)(a) of the Act, subject to the payment of a reasonable charge therefor.

Prescribed period for making representations

5. The local planning authority shall consider any representations mentioned in section 3(1) or 7(1) of the Act which are made to them within such period (not being less than six weeks) as the authority shall specify when giving publicity under the said section 3(1) or 7(1) to the matters proposed to be included in a structure or local plan.

PART III

CONSULTATION

Consultation

6.—(1) Before finally determining the content of a structure or local plan, the

---

(a) 1952 c. 54.　　　　　　　　　(b) 1889 c. 63.

local planning authority shall consult with respect to the matters they propose to include in the plan the following authorities or bodies, namely:—

(a) where the plan relates to any land in a county district, the council of that district;

(b) such other authorities or bodies as the local planning authority think appropriate or the Secretary of State may direct.

(2) The local planning authority shall give to any authority or body whom they consult under paragraph (1) above an adequate opportunity of expressing views with respect to the matters proposed to be included in the plan and shall consider any such views before finally determining the content of the plan.

PART IV

FORM AND CONTENT OF STRUCTURE PLANS

Title

7. A structure plan shall be given a title which shall include the name of the local planning authority, and, where the plan relates to part only of the authority's area, an indication of the part to which it relates; and each document contained in or accompanying a structure plan shall bear the title of the plan.

Treatment of certain urban or proposed urban areas

8.—(1) As respects any part of the area to which a structure plan (other than a structure plan for the whole or any part of a county borough) relates, being a part which is, or which it is proposed should become, urban or predominantly urban, the local planning authority may with the consent of the Secretary of State, and shall, if the Secretary of State so directs, as well as formulating their policy and general proposals for that part as part of the whole area to which the plan relates, formulate policy and general proposals for that part in a separate part of the plan.

(2) A separate part of a structure plan prepared under paragraph (1) above shall be prepared as if it were itself a structure plan.

Policy and general proposals

9.—(1) The policy formulated in a structure plan written statement shall relate to such of the matters specified in Part I of Schedule 1 as the local planning authority may think appropriate.

(2) The policy and general proposals formulated in a structure plan written statement shall be set out so as to be readily distinguishable from the other contents thereof.

(3) A structure plan written statement shall include a reasoned justification of the policy and general proposals formulated therein.

Matters to be contained in written statement

10. In addition to the other matters required to be contained therein by the Act and by these regulations, a structure plan written statement shall contain the following matters, namely, such indications as the local planning authority may think appropriate of the items set out in Part II of Schedule 1.

Action areas: prescribed period

11. The prescribed period for the purposes of section 2(5) of the Act (indication of an action area in the general proposals in a structure plan) shall be ten years from the date on which the particular structure plan is submitted to the Secretary of State.

Diagrams and insets

12.—(1) A structure plan shall contain or be accompanied by a diagram, called the key diagram, showing, so far as the local planning authority may think practicable, the policy and general proposals formulated in the written statement:

Provided that the policy and general proposals for any part of the area to which a structure plan relates, may, instead of being shown on the key diagram, be shown on an inset; and the location of any inset shall be shown on the key diagram.

(2) No diagram or inset contained in, or accompanying, a structure plan shall be on a map base.

Explanation of notation on diagrams

13. Any diagram contained in, or accompanying, a structure plan shall include an explanation of the notation used thereon.

PART V

FORM AND CONTENT OF LOCAL PLANS

Title

14. A local plan shall be given a title which shall include the name of the local planning authority, the name given to the particular plan by or under regulation 15, and an indication of the area to which the plan relates; and each document contained in or accompanying a local plan shall bear the title of the plan.

District, action area and subject plans

15.—(1) A local plan based on a comprehensive consideration of matters affecting the development and other use of land in the area to which it relates shall, unless it is a local plan for an action area, be called a district plan.

(2) A local plan for an action area shall be called an action area plan.

(3) A local plan which is based on a consideration of a particular description or descriptions of development or other use of land in the area to which it relates shall be called by the name of the subject or subjects to which it relates.

Proposals

16.—(1) The proposals formulated in a local plan written statement shall relate to such of the matters specified in Part I of Schedule 2 as the local planning authority may think appropriate.

(2) The proposals formulated in a local plan written statement shall be set out so as to be readily distinguishable from the other contents thereof.

(3) A local plan written statement shall contain a reasoned justification of the proposals formulated therein.

Matters to be contained in written statement

17. In addition to the other matters required to be contained therein by the Act and by these regulations, a local plan written statement shall contain the following matters, namely, such indications as the local planning authority may think appropriate of the items set out in Part II of Schedule 2.

Maps, insets and diagrams

18.—(1) The map comprised in a local plan in compliance with section 6(3) of the Act shall be called the proposals map, and shall—

(*a*) be prepared on a map base reproduced from, or based on, the Ordnance Survey map, and showing National Grid lines and numbers;

(*b*) subject as hereinafter mentioned, be prepared to such scale as the local planning authority may think appropriate, or the Secretary of State may direct:

Provided that the proposals for any part of the area to which a local plan relates may be shown to a larger scale on an inset prepared in accordance with sub-paragraph (*a*) above; and the proposals shown on an inset may be shown on the proposals map by showing thereon the boundary of the inset.

(2) A proposals map or inset which defines land as the site of a proposed road for the purposes of section 21 of the Highways Act 1959(**a**), or which defines land as the site of a proposed road or as land required for the widening of an existing road and designates that land as land to which section 206 of the Highways Act 1959 applies, shall be to a scale of not less than 1/2500.

(3) Any map forming part of a local plan shall show the scale to which it has been prepared; and any map or diagram contained in, or accompanying, a local plan shall include such explanation as the local planning authority may think necessary of the notation used thereon.

(4) In addition to the other matters shown thereon, a proposals map shall show the boundary of any area of town development.

Part VI

Procedure for the Approval or Rejection of Structure Plans

Submission of structure plan to the Secretary of State

19. A structure plan shall be prepared in duplicate. One duplicate shall be submitted to the Secretary of State, together with two certified copies thereof and a statement giving particulars of the matters specified in section 3(3)(*a*) and (*b*) of the Act.

Notice of submission of structure plan

20. On the submission of a structure plan to the Secretary of State the local planning authority shall give notice by advertisement in the appropriate form (Form 1) specified in Schedule 3, or a form substantially to the like effect.

Notice of return of structure plan

21. Where, under section 3(4) of the Act, the Secretary of State returns a structure plan to the local planning authority, the authority shall give notice by advertisement in the appropriate form (Form 2) specified in Schedule 3, or a form substantially to the like effect.

(**a**) 1959 c. 25.

Notice of resubmission of structure plan

22. On the resubmission of a structure plan to the Secretary of State the local planning authority shall give notice by advertisement in the appropriate form (Form 3) specified in Schedule 3, or a form substantially to the like effect, and shall serve a notice in the same terms on any person who made objections to the plan to the Secretary of State when it was originally submitted to him.

Local inquiry to be a public local inquiry

23. A local inquiry held for the purpose of considering objections made to a structure plan shall be a public local inquiry.

Notice of local inquiry or other hearing

24. Where the Secretary of State causes a local inquiry to be held for the purpose of considering objections made to a structure plan, he shall, at least six weeks before the date of the inquiry, give notice by advertisement in the appropriate form (Form 4) specified in Schedule 3, or a form substantially to the like effect, and shall serve a notice in the same terms on any person whose objections have been duly made and are not withdrawn and on such other persons as he thinks fit; and where the Secretary of State causes a hearing (other than a local inquiry) to be held for the said purpose, he shall, at least six weeks before the date of the hearing, serve a notice in the appropriate form (Form 4) specified in Schedule 3, or a form substantially to the like effect, on any person whose objections have been duly made and are not withdrawn and on such other persons as he thinks fit.

Proposed modifications

25. Where the Secretary of State proposes to modify a structure plan he shall, except as respects any modification which he is satisfied will not materially affect the content of the plan,—

> (*a*) notify the local planning authority of the proposed modifications, and the authority shall give notice by advertisement in the appropriate form (Form 5) specified in Schedule 3, or a form substantially to the like effect, and shall serve a notice in the same terms on such persons as the Secretary of State may direct;
>
> (*b*) consider any objections duly made to the proposed modifications;
>
> (*c*) decide whether or not to afford to persons whose objections so made are not withdrawn, or to any of them, an opportunity of appearing before, and being heard by, a person appointed by him for the purpose; and
>
> (*d*) if a local inquiry or other hearing is held, also afford the like opportunity to the local planning authority and to such other persons as he thinks fit:

Provided that the Secretary of State shall not be obliged to cause a local inquiry or other hearing to be held for the purpose of considering objections made to proposed modifications; but if a local inquiry is held it shall be a public local inquiry.

Notification of the Secretary of State's decision

26. The Secretary of State shall notify the local planning authority in writing of his decision on a structure plan and the authority shall forthwith give notice by advertisement in the appropriate form (Form 6) specified in Schedule 3, or a form substantially to the like effect, and shall serve a notice in the same terms on any person who, in accordance with a notice given or served under this part

of these regulations, has requested the authority to notify him of the decision
on the plan and on such other persons as the Secretary of State may direct.

Copies of notices and certificates as to notices to be sent to the Secretary of State

27. On first giving notice by advertisement in accordance with any provision
in this part of these regulations, the local planning authority shall send the
Secretary of State a certified copy of the notice; and, after complying with the
requirements of any provision in this part of these regulations relating to the
giving or giving and serving of notices, the authority shall send the Secretary of
State a certificate to that effect.

PART VII

PROCEDURE FOR THE ADOPTION, ABANDONMENT, APPROVAL OR
REJECTION OF LOCAL PLANS

Preparation of local plan

28. A local plan shall be prepared in duplicate.

Notice of preparation of local plan

29. A local planning authority who have prepared a local plan shall give notice
by advertisement in the appropriate form (Form 7) specified in Schedule 3,
or a form substantially to the like effect.

Notice of withdrawal of copies of local plan and subsequent action

30.—(1) A local planning authority who are given directions by the Secretary
of State under section 7(4) of the Act and who, in accordance with section 7(5)(*a*)
of the Act, withdraw the copies of a local plan made available for inspection as
required by section 7(2) of the Act, shall give notice by advertisement in the
appropriate form (Form 8) specified in Schedule 3, or a form substantially to
the like effect, and, for the purpose of complying with section 7(5)(*b*) of the Act,
shall serve a notice in the same terms on any person by whom objections to the
plan have been made to the authority.

(2) After satisfying the Secretary of State as mentioned in section 7(4) of the
Act and before taking any further steps for the adoption of the plan, the authority
shall again make copies of the plan available for inspection at the places where
they were previously available for inspection, and shall give notice by advertisement in the appropriate form (Form 9) specified in Schedule 3, or a form
substantially to the like effect, and shall serve a notice in the same terms on any
person who made objections to the plan to the authority when copies were
previously available for inspection.

Local inquiry to be a public local inquiry

31. A local inquiry held for the purpose of considering objections made to a
local plan shall be a public local inquiry.

Notice of local inquiry or other hearing

32. Where a local planning authority cause a local inquiry to be held for the
purpose of considering objections made to a local plan, they shall, at least six
weeks before the date of the inquiry, give notice by advertisement in the appropriate form (Form 10) specified in Schedule 3, or a form substantially to the like
effect, and shall serve a notice in the same terms on any person whose objections
have been duly made and are not withdrawn and on such other persons as they
think fit; and, where the authority cause a hearing (other than a local inquiry)
to be held for the said purpose, they shall, at least six weeks before the date of
the hearing, serve a notice in the appropriate form (Form 10) specified in Schedule

3, or a form substantially to the like effect, on any person whose objections have been duly made and are not withdrawn and on such other persons as they think fit.

Report of local inquiry or other hearing

33.—(1) Where, for the purpose of considering objections made to a local plan, a local inquiry or other hearing is held, the local planning authority shall, as part of the consideration of those objections, consider the report of the person appointed to hold the inquiry or other hearing and decide whether or not to take any action as respects the plan in the light of the report and each recommendation, if any, contained therein; and the authority shall prepare a statement of their decisions, giving their reasons therefor.

(2) The authority shall make certified copies of the report, and of the statement prepared under paragraph (1) above, available for inspection not later than the date on which notice is first given under regulation 35.

Proposed modifications

34.—(1) Where the local planning authority propose to modify a local plan, they shall—

(*a*) prepare a list of the proposed modifications, giving their reasons for proposing them;

(*b*) give notice by advertisement in the appropriate form (Form 11) specified in Schedule 3, or a form substantially to the like effect, and shall serve a notice in the same terms on any person whose objections to the plan have been duly made and are not withdrawn and on such other persons as they think fit;

(*c*) consider any objections duly made to the proposed modifications;

(*d*) decide whether or not to afford to persons whose objections so made are not withdrawn, or to any of them, an opportunity of appearing before, and being heard by, a person appointed by the Secretary of State for the purpose; and

(*e*) if a local inquiry or other hearing is held, also afford the like opportunity to such other persons as they think fit;

Provided that, unless the Secretary of State directs them to do so, the authority shall not be obliged to cause a local inquiry or other hearing to be held for the purpose of considering objections made to proposed modifications; but, if a local inquiry is held, it shall be a public local inquiry.

(2) Regulations 32 and 33 shall apply in relation to proposed modifications as they apply in relation to a local plan.

Action following decision to adopt local plan

35.—(1) Where a local planning authority decide to adopt a local plan, they shall, before adopting the plan, give notice by advertisement in the appropriate form (Form 12) specified in Schedule 3, or a form substantially to the like effect, and shall serve a notice in the same terms on any person whose objections to the plan have been duly made and are not withdrawn, and on such other persons as they think fit.

(2) After complying with paragraph (1) above, the authority shall send the Secretary of State by recorded delivery service a certificate that they have complied therewith; and, subject as mentioned in section 9(3) of the Act, the authority shall not adopt the plan until the expiration of twenty-eight days from the date on which the certificate is sent:

Provided that, if, before the plan is adopted, the Secretary of State directs the authority not to adopt the plan until he notifies them that he has decided not to give a direction under section 9(3) of the Act, the authority shall not adopt the plan until they receive such notification.

Notice of adoption or abandonment of local plan

36. Where the local planning authority adopt or abandon a local plan, they shall give notice by advertisement in the appropriate form (Form 13) specified in Schedule 3, or a form substantially to the like effect, and shall serve a notice in the same terms on any person who, in accordance with a notice given or served under this part of these regulations, has requested the authority to notify him of the adoption, abandonment, approval or rejection of the plan, and on such other persons as they think fit.

Documents to be sent to the Secretary of State

37. In addition to the document mentioned in regulation 35(2), the local planning authority shall send the Secretary of State—

(a) not later than the date on which notice is first given under regulation 29, two certified copies of the local plan prepared by them and a statement giving particulars of the matters specified in section 7(3)(a) and (b) of the Act;

(b) not later than the date on which notice of the adoption of a local plan is first given under regulation 36, two certified copies of the plan adopted;

(c) not later than the date on which notice is first given or served under any provision in this part of these regulations, a copy of each document (other than a document mentioned in paragraph (a) or (b) above) referred to in the notice as having been deposited;

(d) on first giving or serving notice under any provision in this part of these regulations, a certified copy of the notice; and

(e) any other relevant document the Secretary of State may at any time require.

Approval or rejection of local plan by the Secretary of State

38. Where a local planning authority are required by section 9(4) of the Act to submit a local plan to the Secretary of State for his approval, regulations 23 to 27 shall apply in relation to the plan as they apply in relation to a structure plan.

PART VIII

STRUCTURE AND LOCAL PLANS: AVAILABILITY AND SALE OF DOCUMENTS, REGISTER AND INDEX MAP

Availability of documents referred to in notices

39.—(1) Where a notice given or served under these regulations refers to a deposited document, the local planning authority shall make the document available for inspection at their office, at a place in each county district wholly or partly comprised in the area to which the relevant plan relates, and at such other places as the authority think convenient to the public having regard to the area to which the plan relates.

(2) Any document made available for inspection under paragraph (1) above shall, unless it is withdrawn in accordance with section 3(6) or 7(5)(a) of the Act, or unless the relevant plan is rejected or abandoned, be available for inspection free of charge at all reasonable hours from a date not later than the date on which the notice is given or served until the expiration of six weeks from the date of the publication of the first notice of the approval or adoption of the plan required by these regulations.

Availability of operative structure and local plans

40.—(1) The local planning authority shall make any operative structure or local plan available for inspection at their office, and shall make certified copies of any such plan available for inspection at a place in each county district wholly or partly comprised in the area to which the plan relates and at such other places as the authority think convenient to the public having regard to the area to which the plan relates.

(2) Any document made available for inspection under paragraph (1) above shall be accompanied by a statement setting out the provisions of section 178(1) and (2) of the Town and Country Planning Act 1962, as amended by section 106 and paragraph 37 of Schedule 9 to the Town and Country Planning Act 1968.

(3) Any document made available for inspection under this regulation shall be available for inspection free of charge at all reasonable hours.

Sale of documents

41.—(1) The local planning authority shall provide persons making a request in that behalf with copies of any plan or other document which has been made available for inspection under section 3(2) or 7(2) of the Act, subject to the payment of a reasonable charge therefor.

(2) As soon as possible after a structure or local plan becomes operative the local planning authority shall arrange for the printing of the plan, and thereafter, at such times as the authority think fit, or the Secretary of State may direct, shall arrange for the reprinting of the plan; and printed copies of the plan shall be made available for sale to the public at a reasonable charge:

Provided that, unless the Secretary of State otherwise directs, it shall suffice in relation to the application of this paragraph to any operative alteration, repeal or replacement of a structure or local plan, if the alteration, repeal or replacement is taken into account when the plan is next reprinted.

Register and index map

42.—(1) The local planning authority shall prepare and keep up-to-date a register containing the following information in respect of their area, namely,—

(a) brief particulars of any structure or local plan copies of which have been made available for inspection under section 3(2) or 7(2) of the Act, and of any action taken in connection with any such plan, including, in the case of an operative plan, the date on which the plan became operative and a reference to the boundary of the plan as shown on the index map prepared under paragraph (2) below;

(b) brief particulars of any proposals for the alteration, repeal or replacement of any structure or local plan copies of which have been made available for inspection under section 3(2) or 7(2) of the Act, as applied, and of any action taken in connection with any such proposals, including, in the case of an operative alteration, repeal or replacement, the date on which it became operative.

(2) The authority shall also prepare and keep up-to-date an index map for their area showing the boundary of any operative structure or local plan, together with a reference to the appropriate entry in the register prepared under paragraph (1) above.

(3) The authority shall make the register and index map available for inspection with any operative structure or local plan made available for inspection under regulation 40, and shall make certified copies of the register and index

map available for inspection with copies of any structure or local plan made available for inspection under the provisions of the Act or of these regulations; and documents made available for inspection under this paragraph shall be available for inspection free of charge at all reasonable hours.

PART IX

ALTERATION OF STRUCTURE PLANS AND ALTERATION, REPEAL OR REPLACEMENT OF LOCAL PLANS.

Alteration of structure plans

43. The provisions of these regulations relating to structure plans shall apply, with any necessary modifications, in relation to proposals for alterations to a structure plan as they apply in relation to a structure plan.

Alteration, repeal or replacement of local plans

44. The provisions of these regulations relating to local plans shall apply, with any necessary modifications, in relation to proposals for the alteration, repeal or replacement of a local plan as they apply in relation to a local plan.

PART X

PREPARATION AND MAKING, ETC., OF STRUCTURE OR LOCAL PLANS BY THE SECRETARY OF STATE

Preparation and making, etc., of structure or local plans by the Secretary of State

45. The provisions of these regulations shall apply, with any necessary modifications, in relation to the preparation and making of a structure plan or local plan or, as the case may be, the alteration, repeal or replacement of a structure or local plan, by the Secretary of State under section 12 of the Act:

Provided that the local planning authority shall, unless the Secretary of State otherwise directs, give and serve such notices as are required by these regulations and comply with Part VIII hereof.

PART XI

STRUCTURE AND LOCAL PLANS: RECONCILIATION OF CONTRADICTIONS

Reconciliation of contradictions in structure plans

46.—(1) In the case of any contradiction in a structure plan between a separate part prepared under regulation 8 and the rest of the plan, the provisions of the separate part shall prevail.

(2) Subject to paragraph (1) above, in the case of any contradiction in a structure plan between the written statement and any other document forming part of the plan, the provisions of the written statement shall prevail.

Reconciliation of contradictions in local plans

47. In the case of any contradiction between the written statement and any other document forming part of a local plan, the provisions of the written statement shall prevail.

Reconciliation of contradictions between local plans

48. In the case of any contradiction between local plans for the same part of any area, the provisions which are more recently adopted, approved or made shall prevail.

SCHEDULE 1

STRUCTURE PLANS

PART I

MATTERS TO WHICH POLICY IS REQUIRED TO RELATE BY REGULATION 9(1)

The matters to which the policy formulated in a structure plan written statement is required to relate by regulation 9(1) are such of the following matters as the local planning authority may think appropriate:

    (i) Population.

    (ii) Employment.

    (iii) Housing.

    (iv) Industry and commerce.

    (v) Transportation.

    (vi) Shopping.

    (vii) Education.

    (viii) Other social and community services.

    (ix) Recreation and leisure.

    (x) Conservation, townscape and landscape.

    (xi) Utility services.

    (xii) Any other relevant matters.

PART II

MATTERS REQUIRED BY REGULATION 10 TO BE CONTAINED IN WRITTEN STATEMENT

The matters required by regulation 10 to be contained in a structure plan written statement are such indications as the local planning authority may think appropriate of the following:

    (i) The existing structure of the area to which the plan relates and the present needs and opportunities for change.

    (ii) Any changes already projected, or likely to occur, which may materially affect matters dealt with in the plan, and the effect those changes are likely to have.

    (iii) The extent (if any) to which the area to which the plan relates is affected by an order or proposal to make an order under section 1 of the New Towns Act 1946 or 1965 (designation of sites of new towns).

    (iv) The extent (if any) to which town development within the meaning of the Town Development Act 1952 is being, or is to be, carried out in the area to which the plan relates.

    (v) The size, composition and distribution of population, and the state of employment and industry (and the assumptions on which estimates are based) in the area to which the plan relates, both at the time the plan is prepared and at such future times as the local planning authority think appropriate for the purposes of the plan.

    (vi) The regard the local planning authority have had to the current policies with respect to the economic planning and development of the region as a whole.

    (vii) The regard the local planning authority have had to social policies and considerations.

    (viii) The regard the local planning authority have had to the resources likely to be available for carrying out the policy and general proposals formulated in the plan.

(ix) The broad criteria to be applied as respects the control of development in the area, or any part of the area, to which the plan relates.

(x) The extent and nature of the relationship between the policies formulated in the plan.

(xi) The considerations underlying any major items of policy formulated in the plan as respects matters of common interest to the local planning authority by whom the plan is prepared and the local planning authorities for neighbouring areas, and the extent to which those major items have been agreed by the authorities concerned.

(xii) Any other relevant matters.

SCHEDULE 2

LOCAL PLANS

PART I

MATTERS TO WHICH PROPOSALS ARE REQUIRED TO RELATE BY REGULATION 16(1)

The matters to which the proposals formulated in a local plan written statement are required to relate by regulation 16(1) are such of the following matters as the local planning authority may think appropriate:

(i) Population.

(ii) Employment.

(iii) Housing.

(iv) Industry and commerce.

(v) Transportation.

(vi) Shopping.

(vii) Education.

(viii) Other social and community services.

(ix) Recreation and leisure.

(x) Conservation, townscape and landscape.

(xi) Utility services.

(xii) Any other relevant matters.

PART II

MATTERS REQUIRED BY REGULATION 17 TO BE CONTAINED IN WRITTEN STATEMENT

The matters required by regulation 17 to be contained in a local plan written statement are such indications as the local planning authority may think appropriate of the following:

(i) The character, pattern and function of the existing development and other use of land in the area to which the plan relates and the present needs and opportunities for change.

(ii) Any changes already projected, or likely to occur, which may materially affect matters dealt with in the plan, and the effect those changes are likely to have.

(iii) The regard the local planning authority have had to social policies and considerations.

(iv) The regard the local planning authority have had to the resources likely to be available for carrying out the proposals formulated in the plan.

(v) The criteria to be applied as respects the control of development in the area, or any part of the area, to which the plan relates.

(vi) The extent and nature of the relationship between the proposals formulated in the plan.

(vii) Any other relevant matters.

SCHEDULE 3

Regulation 20   FORMS OF NOTICES

Form 1: Form of notice of submission of structure plan

NOTICE OF SUBMISSION OF STRUCTURE PLAN

Town and Country Planning Act 1968
(Title of structure plan)

(1) submitted the above-named structure plan to the [Secretary of State for the Environment] [Secretary of State for Wales] (2) on   19   for his approval.   [The plan relates to land in the following county district(s): (3)] (2)

Certified copies of the plan, of the report of survey and of the statement mentioned in section 3(3) of the Act have been deposited at (4).

The deposited documents are available for inspection free of charge (5).

Objections to the plan should be sent in writing to the Secretary, [Department of the Environment, 2 Marsham Street, London, SW1] [Welsh Office, Summit House, Windsor Place, Cardiff, CF1 3BX] (2) before (6).   Objections should state the matters to which they relate and the grounds on which they are made*.   A person making objections may send a written request (stating his name and the address to which notice is to be sent) to (7) to be notified of the decision on the plan.

19 .

(Signature)

*Forms for making objections are obtainable at the places where documents have been deposited.

Regulation 21

Form 2: Form of notice of return of structure plan

NOTICE OF RETURN OF STRUCTURE PLAN

Town and Country Planning Act 1968
(Title of structure plan)

The above-named structure plan has been returned to (1) by the [Secretary of State for the Environment] [Secretary of State for Wales] (2) and the council have been directed to take certain further action as respects publicity in connection with the plan, and, after doing so, to resubmit the plan to the Secretary of State with such modifications, if any, as the authority then consider appropriate [within (8)] (2).

When the plan is resubmitted objections made to the plan as originally submitted will be considered, and there will be an opportunity to make objections to the plan as resubmitted.

19 .

(Signature)

Regulation 22

Form 3: Form of notice of resubmission of structure plan

NOTICE OF RESUBMISSION OF STRUCTURE PLAN

Town and Country Planning Act 1968
(Title of structure plan)

[To:] (9)

(1) resubmitted the above-named structure plan [with modifications] [without modification] (2) to the [Secretary of State for the Environment] [Secretary of State for Wales] (2) on   19   for his approval.   [The plan relates to land in the following county district(s): (3)] (2).

Certified copies of the plan, of the report of survey and of the statement mentioned in section 3(3) of the Act have been deposited at (4).

The deposited documents are available for inspection free of charge (5).

Objections to the plan should be sent in writing to the Secretary, [Department of the Environment, 2 Marsham Street, London SW1] [Welsh Office, Summit House, Windsor Place, Cardiff, CF1 3BX] (2) before (6).   Objections should state the matters to which they relate and the grounds on which they are made*.   A person making objections may send a written request (stating his name and the address to which notice is to be sent) to (7) to be notified of the decision on the plan.   Objections made to the plan when it was originally submitted to the Secretary of State will be considered by him.

19   .

(Signature)

*Forms for making objections are obtainable at the places where documents have been deposited.

Regulation 24

Form 4: Form of notice of local inquiry or other hearing

NOTICE OF [PUBLIC LOCAL INQUIRY] [HEARING] (2)

Town and Country Planning Act 1968
(Title of structure plan)

[To:] (9)

(10) WILL HOLD A [PUBLIC LOCAL INQUIRY] [HEARING] (2) AT (11) INTO OBJECTIONS MADE TO THE ABOVE-NAMED STRUCTURE PLAN

19   .

(Signature)

Regulation 25

Form 5: Form of notice of proposed modifications to structure plan

NOTICE OF PROPOSED MODIFICATIONS TO STRUCTURE PLAN

Town and Country Planning Act 1968
(Title of structure plan)

[To:] (9)

The [Secretary of State for the Environment] [Secretary of State for Wales] (2) proposes to modify the above-named structure plan.

Certified copies of the plan and of the list of proposed modifications (other than modifications which the Secretary of State is satisfied will not materially affect the content of the plan) have been deposited at (4).

The deposited documents are available for inspection free of charge (5).

Objections to the proposed modifications should be sent in writing to the Secretary, [Department of the Environment, 2 Marsham Street, London SW1] [Welsh Office, Summit House, Windsor Place, Cardiff CF1 3BX] (2) before (6). Objections should state the matters to which they relate and the grounds on which they are made*. A person making objections may send a written request (stating his name and the address to which notice is to be sent) to (7) to be notified of the decision on the plan.

19 .

(Signature)

*Forms for making objections are obtainable at the places where documents have been deposited.

Regulation 26

Form 6: Form of notice of approval or rejection of structure plan

NOTICE OF [APPROVAL] [REJECTION] (2) OF STRUCTURE PLAN

Town and Country Planning Acts 1962 and 1968
(Title of structure plan)

[To:] (9)

On   19   the [Secretary of State for the Environment] [Secretary of State for Wales] [approved] [rejected](2) the above-named structure plan [so far as it relates to (12)] [with modifications] [and] [with reservations] (2).

Certified copies of the plan and of the Secretary of State's letter notifying his decision have been deposited at (4).

The deposited documents are available for inspection free of charge (5).

[The plan became operative on (13), but if any person aggrieved by the plan desires to question its validity on the ground that it is not within the powers conferred by Part I of the Town and Country Planning Act 1968, or that any requirement of the said Part I or of any regulations made thereunder has not been complied with in relation to the approval of the plan, he may, within six weeks from (14) make an application to the High Court under section 178(1) of the Town and Country Planning Act 1962, as amended by paragraph 37 of Schedule 9 to the Town and Country Planning Act 1968] (15).

19 .

(Signature)

Footnotes to forms 1 *to* 6

1. Insert name of local planning authority.
2. Insert as or where appropriate.
3. Insert name(s) of county district(s).
4. Insert address of local planning authority's office and addresses of other places at which documents deposited.
5. Specify days and hours during which deposited documents are available for inspection.
6. Specify date not less than six weeks after date on which notice first published in local newspaper.
7. State appropriate officer and name and address of local planning authority.
8. State period specified in directions.
9. Insert, together with name and address of addressee, in personal notice.
10. State name of person appointed to hold local inquiry or hearing.
11. State time and date of local inquiry or other hearing and address at which it is to be held.
12. Give indication of area.
13. Insert date appointed in Secretary of State's letter.
14. Insert date of first publication of the notice.
15. Insert paragraph only if the plan is approved.

Regulation 29

Form 7: *Form of notice of preparation of local plan*

NOTICE OF PREPARATION OF LOCAL PLAN

Town and Country Planning Act 1968
(Title of local plan)

(1) have prepared the above-named local plan. [The plan relates to land in the following county district (s):—(2)] (3).

Certified copies of the plan, of the report of survey and of the statement mentioned in section 7(3) of the Act have been deposited at (4).

The deposited documents are available for inspection free of charge (5).

Objections to the plan should be sent in writing to (6) before (7). Objections should state the matters to which they relate and the grounds on which they are made,* and may include a request (stating the address to which notice is to be sent) to be notified of the decision on the plan.

19 .

(Signature)

*Forms for making objections are obtainable at the places where documents have been deposited.

Regulation 30(1)

Form 8: Form of notice of withdrawal of copies of local plan

NOTICE OF WITHDRAWAL OF COPIES OF LOCAL PLAN

Town and Country Planning Act 1968
(Title of local plan)

[To:] (8)

The [Secretary of State for the Environment] [Secretary of State for Wales] (3) has directed (1) not to take any further steps for the adoption of the above-named local plan without taking certain further action as respects publicity in connection with the plan and satisfying him that they have done so.

The copies of the plan made available for inspection have been withdrawn. Before (1) take further steps for the adoption of the plan, copies of the plan will again be made available fori nspection at the places where they were previously available for inspection. Objections made to the plan when copies were previously available for inspection will be considered, and there will be a further opportunity to make objections to the plan.

19 .

(Signature)

Regulation 30(2)

Form 9: Form of notice of re-deposit of copies of local plan

NOTICE OF RE-DEPOSIT OF COPIES OF LOCAL PLAN

Town and Country Planning Act 1968
(Title of local plan)

[To:] (8)

(1) have decided to take further steps for the adoption of the above-named local plan. [The plan relates to land in the following county district(s):—(2)] (3).

Certified copies of the plan, of the report of survey and of the statement mentioned in section 7(3) of the Act have been deposited at (4).

The deposited documents are available for inspection free of charge (5).

Objections to the plan should be sent in writing to (6) before (7). Objections should state the matters to which they relate and the grounds on which they are made*, and may include a request (stating the address to which notice is to be sent) to be notified of the decision on the plan. Objections made to the plan when copies were previously available for inspection will be considered.

19 .

(Signature)

*Forms for making objections are obtainable at the places where documents have been deposited.

Regulation 32

Form 10: Form of notice of local inquiry or other hearing

NOTICE OF [PUBLIC LOCAL INQUIRY] [HEARING] (3)

Town and Country Planning Act 1968
(Title of local plan)

(9) WILL HOLD A [PUBLIC LOCAL INQUIRY] [HEARING] (3) AT (10) INTO OBJECTIONS MADE [TO PROPOSED MODIFICATIONS] (3) TO THE ABOVE-NAMED LOCAL PLAN.

19 .

(Signature)

Regulation 34

Form 11: Form of notice of proposal to modify local plan

NOTICE OF PROPOSAL TO MODIFY LOCAL PLAN

Town and Country Planning Act 1968
(Title of local plan)

[To:] (8)

(1) propose to modify the above-named local plan.

Certified copies of the plan, of the report of the [inquiry into] [hearing of] (3) objections, of the council's statement prepared following the consideration of the report and of the list of proposed modifications have been deposited at (4).

The deposited documents are available for inspection free of charge (5).

Objections to the proposed modifications should be sent in writing to (6) before (7). Objections should state the matters to which they relate and the grounds on which they are made*, and may include a request (stating the address to which notice is to be sent) to be notified of the decision on the plan.

19 .

(Signature)

*Forms for making objections are obtainable at the places where documents have been deposited.

Regulation 35

Form 12: Form of notice of decision to adopt local plan

NOTICE OF DECISION TO ADOPT LOCAL PLAN

Town and Country Planning Act 1968
(Title of local plan)

[To:] (8)

(1) have decided to adopt the above-named local plan [as modified by them] (3) on or after (11), unless, before the plan has been adopted, the [Secretary of State for the Environment] [Secretary of State for Wales] (3) directs that the plan shall not be adopted until further notice or shall not have effect unless approved by him.

Certified copies of the plan [together with certified copies of the reports of all local inquiries or other hearings held and of the council's statements prepared following the consideration of such reports] (12) have been deposited at (4).

The deposited documents are available for inspection free of charge (5).

19 .

(Signature)

Regulation 36
Form 13: Form of notice of adoption or abandonment of local plan

NOTICE OF [ADOPTION] [ABANDONMENT] (3) OF LOCAL PLAN

Town and Country Planning Acts 1962 and 1968
(Title of local plan)

[To:] (8)

On   19   (1) by resolution [adopted] [abandoned] (3) the above-named
local plan [as modified by the council] (3).

Certified copies of the plan and of the resolution [together with certified copies of the
reports of all local inquiries or other hearings held and of the council's statements
prepared following the consideration of such reports] (12) have been deposited at (4).

The deposited documents are available for inspection free of charge (5).

[The plan became operative on (13), but if any person aggrieved by the plan desires
to. question its validity on the ground that it is not within the powers conferred by
Part I of the Town and Country Planning Act 1968, or that any requirement of the
said Part I or of any regulations made thereunder has not been complied with in
relation to the adoption of the plan, he may, within six weeks from (14), make an
application to the High Court under section 178(1) of the Town and Country Planning
Act 1962, as amended by paragraph 37 of Schedule 9 to the Town and Country
Planning Act 1968.] (15).

        19 .

                                                        (Signature)

Footnotes to forms 7 to 13

1. Insert name of local planning authority.
2. Insert name(s) of county district(s).
3. Insert as or where appropriate.
4. Insert address of local planning authority's office and addresses of other places
   at which documents deposited.
5. Specify days and hours during which deposited documents are available for inspection by public.
6. State appropriate officer and name and address of local planning authority.
7. Specify date not less than six weeks after date on which notice first published in
   local newspaper.
8. Insert, together with name and address of addressee, in personal notice.
9. Insert name of person appointed to hold local inquiry or hearing.
10. State time and date of local inquiry or other hearing and address at which it is
    to be held.
11. Specify date taking account of the period of 28 days specified in regulation 35(2).
12. Modify as necessary or omit where inappropriate.
13. Insert date appointed in the resolution.
14. Insert date of first publication of the notice.
15. Insert paragraph only if plan is adopted.

Peter Walker,
Secretary of State for the Environment.

12th July 1971.

Peter Thomas,
Secretary of State for Wales.

12th July 1971.

EXPLANATORY NOTE

(*This Note is not part of the Regulations.*)

These regulations make provision with respect to the form and content of structure and local plans prepared under Part I of the Town and Country Planning Act 1968, and with respect to the procedure to be followed in connection with the preparation, submission, withdrawal, approval, adoption, making, alteration, repeal and replacement of such plans.

STATUTORY INSTRUMENTS

1971 No. 1116 (C.26)

INSURANCE

The Employers' Liability (Compulsory Insurance) Act 1969 (Commencement) Order 1971

Made - - - *9th July* 1971

The Secretary of State, in exercise of his powers under section 7(3) of the Employers' Liability (Compulsory Insurance) Act 1969(a) and of all other powers enabling him in that behalf, hereby makes the following Order :—

1. The Employers' Liability (Compulsory Insurance) Act 1969 shall come into operation on 1st January 1972.

2. This Order may be cited as the Employers' Liability (Compulsory Insurance) Act 1969 (Commencement) Order 1971.

Signed by order of the Secretary of State.
9th July 1971.

K. Barnes,
Deputy Secretary,
Department of Employment.

EXPLANATORY NOTE

(*This Note is not part of the Order.*)

This Order brings into operation on 1st January 1972 the Employers' Liability (Compulsory Insurance) Act 1969.

(a) 1969 c. 57.

STATUTORY INSTRUMENTS

1971 No. 1117

INSURANCE

The Employers' Liability (Compulsory Insurance) General Regulations 1971

Made - - -	*9th July* 1971
Laid before Parliament	*20th July* 1971
Coming into Operation	
All Regulations except 6 and 7	1*st January* 1972
Regulations 6 and 7	1*st January* 1973

The Secretary of State, in exercise of his powers under sections 1(2) and (3)(*a*), 2(2), 4(1) and (2) and 6 of the Employers' Liability (Compulsory Insurance) Act 1969(**a**) (hereinafter referred to as "the Act") and of all other powers enabling him in that behalf, hereby makes the following Regulations:—

Commencement, citation and interpretation

1.—(1) These Regulations may be cited as the Employers' Liability (Compulsory Insurance) General Regulations 1971 and shall come into operation on 1st January 1972, with the exception of Regulations 6 and 7 which shall come into operation on 1st January 1973.

(2) The Interpretation Act 1889(**b**) shall apply to the interpretation of these Regulations as it applies to the interpretation of an Act of Parliament.

Prohibition of certain conditions in policies of insurance

2.—(1) Any condition in a policy of insurance issued or renewed in accordance with the requirements of the Act after the coming into operation of this Regulation which provides (in whatever terms) that no liability (either generally or in respect of a particular claim) shall arise under the policy, or that any such liability so arising shall cease—

(*a*) in the event of some specified thing being done or omitted to be done after the happening of the event giving rise to a claim under the policy;

(*b*) unless the policy holder takes reasonable care to protect his employees against the risk of bodily injury or disease in the course of their employment;

(*c*) unless the policy holder complies with the requirements of any enactment for the protection of employees against the risk of bodily injury or disease in the course of their employment; and

(*d*) unless the policy holder keeps specified records or provides the insurer with or makes available to him information therefrom,

is hereby prohibited for the purposes of the Act.

(**a**) 1969 c. 57.   (**b**) 1889 c. 63.

(2) Nothing in this Regulation shall be taken as prejudicing any provision in a policy requiring the policy holder to pay to the insurer any sums which the latter may have become liable to pay under the policy and which have been applied to the satisfaction of claims in respect of employees or any costs and expenses incurred in relation to such claims.

Limit of amount of compulsory insurance

3. The amount for which an employer is required by the Act to insure and maintain insurance shall be two million pounds in respect of claims relating to any one or more of his employees arising out of any one occurrence.

Employees not ordinarily resident in Great Britain

4. The requirements of the Act and regulations thereunder shall apply in respect of employees not ordinarily resident in Great Britain who are present in Great Britain in the course of employment there for a continuous period of not less than fourteen days, as they apply in respect of employees ordinarily resident in Great Britain.

Issue of certificates of insurance

5.—(1) Every employer entering into a contract of insurance in accordance with the requirements of the Act shall be issued by the insurer with whom he contracts, in respect of the policy of insurance expressing the contract, with a certificate of insurance in the form and containing the particulars specified in the Schedule to these Regulations.

(2) Every such certificate of insurance shall be issued not later than thirty days after the date on which the insurance commences or is renewed.

Display of copies of certificates of insurance

6.—(1) Where a certificate of insurance has been issued to an employer in accordance with Regulation 5 he shall display a copy or copies of that certificate at his place of business or, where he has more than one place of business, at each place of business at which he employs any person whose claims may be the subject of indemnity under the policy of insurance to which that certificate relates.

(2) Copies of any certificate of insurance issued in accordance with Regulation 5 shall be displayed in such numbers and characters and in such positions as to be easily seen and read by every person employed whose claims may be the subject of indemnity under the policy of insurance to which the certificate relates and, where displayed in the open, shall be protected from the weather.

(3) Copies of any certificate of insurance issued in accordance with Regulation 5 shall be kept displayed until the expiration of the period of insurance stated in the certificate or if the policy of insurance to which the certificate relates is cancelled before that time, until the policy is cancelled and, in either case, shall not be displayed thereafter.

Production of certificates of insurance

7. Where an employer is served with a notice issued on behalf of the Secretary of State requiring him to do so, he shall produce or send to any officer of the Department of Employment specified in the notice, at the address and within the time specified therein, the original or a copy of every certificate of insurance issued to him in accordance with Regulation 5, which relates to a period of insurance current at the date of the notice.

Inspection of policies of insurance

8. An employer who has entered into a contract of insurance in accordance with the requirements of the Act shall during the currency of the insurance permit the policy of insurance expressing the contract or a copy of the policy to be inspected by any inspector duly authorised by the Secretary of State for the purposes of the Act either (in the case of a company) at the registered office or (in any case) at a place of business of the employer as the inspector requires and at a time when the inspector requires it to be produced for inspection, being a time of which reasonable notice has been given.

Production by inspectors of evidence of authority

9. Any inspector duly authorised by the Secretary of State for the purposes of the Act shall, if so required when visiting any premises for those purposes, produce to an employer or his agent some duly authenticated document showing that he is so authorised.

9th July 1971.

Robert Carr,
Secretary of State for Employment.

SCHEDULE Regulation 5

CERTIFICATE OF INSURANCE

EMPLOYERS' LIABILITY (COMPULSORY INSURANCE) ACT 1969

(A copy or copies of this certificate must be displayed at each place of business at which the policy holder employs persons covered by the policy.)

Policy No................

1. Name of policy holder.

2. Date of commencement of insurance.

3. Date of expiry of insurance.

We hereby certify that the policy to which this certificate relates is issued in accordance with the requirements of the Employers' Liability (Compulsory Insurance) Act 1969 and regulations thereunder.

Signed on behalf of.....................................(Authorised Insurer)

.... (Signature)

EXPLANATORY NOTE
(This Note is not part of the Regulations.)

These Regulations prohibit for the purposes of the Employers' Liability (Compulsory Insurance) Act 1969 certain conditions in policies of insurance which would entitle insurers to deny liability under the policy. They limit the amount for which an employer is required by the Act to insure to two million pounds in respect of any one occurrence giving rise to liability. They apply the statutory requirements in respect of certain persons employed in Great Britain who are not ordinarily resident here.

The Regulations also require insurers entering into contracts of insurance with employers in accordance with the requirements of the Act to issue certificates of insurance in a prescribed form and require employers to display copies of the certificates for the information of their employees. The Regulations make provision for the production of the certificates or a copy of the certificates for inspection and require employers to permit inspectors authorised by the Secretary of State to inspect the policy of insurance or a copy thereof.

STATUTORY INSTRUMENTS

1971 No. 1119

MAGISTRATES' COURTS
The Justices of the Peace Act 1949 (Compensation) (Amendment) Regulations 1971

Made - - - -	8*th July* 1971
Coming into Operation	10*th August* 1971

In exercise of the powers conferred on me by section 42 of the Justices of the Peace Act 1949(a) as extended by section 32 of the Administration of Justice Act 1964(b), I hereby make the following Regulations:—

1. These Regulations may be cited as the Justices of the Peace Act 1949 (Compensation) (Amendment) Regulations 1971 and shall come into operation on 10th August 1971.

2. In these Regulations any reference to the principal Regulations is a reference to the Justices of the Peace Act 1949 (Compensation) Regulations 1965(c).

3.—(1) Nothing in Regulation 4 of these Regulations shall affect the entitlement of any person to compensation under the principal Regulations where that entitlement has been determined before the date of the coming into operation of these Regulations.

(2) Notwithstanding anything contained in the principal Regulations, Regulations 5, 6, 7, 8 and 9 of these Regulations shall apply with effect from the date of the coming into operation of these Regulations in relation to any compensation under the principal Regulations awarded before that date.

4. After Regulation 2(1) of the principal Regulations (interpretation) there shall be inserted the following provision:—

"(1A) Except as provided in Regulations 6(2) and 12(2) of these Regulations, the expression "relevant employment" shall not include service in the armed forces of the Crown.".

5. For Regulation 8(1)(*a*) of the principal Regulations (deductions to be made in calculating resettlement compensation) there shall be substituted the following provision:—

"(*a*) unemployment, sickness or injury benefit under any Act relating to national insurance claimable by him in respect of such week (excluding any amount claimable by him in respect of any dependant);".

6. In Regulation 18(1)(i) of the principal Regulations (payment of retirement compensation to a pensionable officer on his becoming incapacitated or reaching minimum pensionable age) the words "or accrued incapacity retiring allowance" shall be omitted.

(a) 1949 c. 101.   (b) 1964 c. 42.
(c) S.I. 1965/283 (1965 I, p.720).

7. After Regulation 33 of the principal Regulations (reduction of compensation) there shall be inserted the following Regulation:—

"*Deduction in respect of national insurance benefit*

33A.—(1) Where in any week a person is entitled to long-term compensation for loss or diminution of emoluments and is also entitled to unemployment, sickness or injury benefit under any Act relating to national insurance, other than a benefit claimable by him in respect of a dependant, there shall be deducted from the long-term compensation payable for that week a sum equal to the amount by which the aggregate of such national insurance benefits claimable in respect of that week, the weekly rate at which the long-term compensation would be payable but for this Regulation, and the weekly rate of any superannuation benefit taken into account for the purpose of Regulation 15(4) of these Regulations, exceeds two-thirds of the weekly rate of the net emoluments of the employment which he has lost or in which the emoluments have been diminished:

Provided that this paragraph shall not apply in relation to any such sickness or injury benefit insofar as an equivalent sum is deducted from the emoluments of his current employment and such deduction from those emoluments has not occasioned an increase in his long-term compensation.

(2) For the purposes of paragraph (1) of this Regulation the expression "weekly rate" means seven three hundred and sixty-fifths of the relevant annual rate.".

8. In Regulation 34 of the principal Regulations (certain changes in circumstances to be notified to the compensating authority) there shall be inserted after sub-paragraph (*c*) the following provision:—

"or

> (*d*) a person entitled to long-term compensation is receiving or starts to receive any benefit, any increase in benefit or any further benefit under any Act relating to national insurance,".

9. In Regulation 35(7) (review of awards of compensation) for the words "Regulation 32 or 33" there shall be substituted the words "Regulation 32, 33 or 33A".

R. Maudling,
One of Her Majesty's Principal
Secretaries of State.

Home Office,
 Whitehall.
8th July 1971.

EXPLANATORY NOTE

(This Note is not part of the Regulations.)

These Regulations amend the Justices of the Peace Act 1949 (Compensation) Regulations 1965 (the principal Regulations) as follows:—

(i) the expression "relevant employment" (which is defined in Regulation 2(1) of the principal Regulations and which affects qualification for compensation and calculation of the amount) is not to include service in the armed forces of the Crown other than certain national service which is expressly made relevant employment for determining whether a person is qualified to claim compensation (Regulation 4);

(ii) all national insurance benefits (other than benefits payable in respect of dependants) are to be taken into account in assessing resettlement compensation and not only, as at present, benefits at the flat rate applicable to a single person (Regulation 5);

(iii) a textual error in Regulation 18(1) of the principal Regulations is corrected (Regulation 6);

(iv) national insurance benefits (other than benefits payable in respect of dependants) are to be deducted from long-term compensation to such extent as is necessary to ensure that the total of benefits and compensation received in any week does not exceed two-thirds of the emoluments for the loss or reduction of which compensation is payable. This was until recently secured by Regulations under the National Insurance Acts (Regulations 7 and 9);

(v) a person entitled to long-term compensation is required to inform the compensating authority about national insurance benefits received by him (Regulation 8).

The provisions mentioned in (ii) to (v) above apply to compensation in payment at the date of commencement of these Regulations as well as compensation awarded after that date (Regulation 3).

STATUTORY INSTRUMENTS

1971 No. 1120

LOCAL GOVERNMENT, ENGLAND AND WALES
LONDON GOVERNMENT

The Probation (Compensation) (Amendment) Regulations 1971

Made - - - -	*8th July* 1971
Laid before Parliament	*21st July* 1971
Coming into Operation	*10th August* 1971

Whereas the Minister for the Civil Service has determined under section 60(2) of the Local Government Act 1958(a) (read with Article 2(1) of the Minister for the Civil Service Order 1968(b)) that the Secretary of State is the appropriate Minister to make Regulations thereunder in relation to the persons to whom these Regulations relate:

And whereas the Secretary of State is the appropriate Minister for the purposes of section 85(4) of the London Government Act 1963(c) as applied by section 35 of the Administration of Justice Act 1964(d) in relation to those persons:

Now, therefore, in exercise of the powers conferred on me by the said section 60(2) and the said section 85(4) as so applied, I hereby make the following Regulations:—

1. These Regulations may be cited as the Probation (Compensation) (Amendment) Regulations 1971 and shall come into operation on 10th August 1971.

2. In these Regulations any reference to the principal Regulations is a reference to the Probation (Compensation) Regulations 1965(e).

3.—(1) Nothing in Regulation 4 of these Regulations shall affect the entitlement of any person to compensation under the principal Regulations where that entitlement has been determined before the date of the coming into operation of these Regulations.

(2) Notwithstanding anything contained in the principal Regulations, Regulations 5, 6, 7 and 8 of these Regulations shall apply with effect from the date of the coming into operation of these Regulations in relation to any compensation under the principal Regulations awarded before that date.

4. After Regulation 2(1) of the principal Regulations (interpretation) there shall be inserted the following provision:—

"(1A) Except as provided in Regulations 6(2) and 12(2) of these Regulations, the expression "relevant employment" shall not include service in the armed forces of the Crown.".

(a) 1958 c. 55. (b) S.I. 1968/1656 (1968 III, p. 4485).
(c) 1963 c. 33. (d) 1964 c. 42.
(e) S.I. 1965/620 (1965 I, p. 1940).

5. For Regulation 8(1)(*a*) of the principal Regulations (deductions to be made in calculating resettlement compensation) there shall be substituted the following provision:—

> "(*a*) unemployment, sickness or injury benefit under any Act relating to national insurance claimable by him in respect of such week (excluding any amount claimable by him in respect of any dependant);".

6. After Regulation 33 of the principal Regulations (reduction of compensation) there shall be inserted the following Regulation:—

"Deduction in respect of national insurance benefit

33A.—(1) Where in any week a person is entitled to long-term compensation for loss or diminution of emoluments and is also entitled to unemployment, sickness or injury benefit under any Act relating to national insurance, other than a benefit claimable by him in respect of a dependant, there shall be deducted from the long-term compensation payable for that week a sum equal to the amount by which the aggregate of such national insurance benefits claimable in respect of that week, the weekly rate at which the long-term compensation would be payable but for this Regulation, and the weekly rate of any superannuation benefit taken into account for the purpose of Regulation 15(4) of these Regulations, exceeds two-thirds of the weekly rate of the net emoluments of the employment which he has lost or in which the emoluments have been diminished:

Provided that this paragraph shall not apply in relation to any such sickness or injury benefit insofar as an equivalent sum is deducted from the emoluments of his current employment and such deduction from those emoluments has not occasioned an increase in his long-term compensation.

(2) For the purposes of paragraph (1) of this Regulation the expression "weekly rate" means seven three hundred and sixty-fifths of the relevant annual rate.".

7. In Regulation 34 of the principal Regulations (certain changes in circumstances to be notified to the compensating authority) there shall be inserted after sub-paragraph (*c*) the following provision:—

> "or
>
> (*d*) a person entitled to long-term compensation is receiving or starts to receive any benefit, any increase in benefit or any further benefit under any Act relating to national insurance,".

8. In Regulation 35(7) (review of awards of compensation) for the words "Regulation 32 or 33" there shall be substituted the words "Regulation 32, 33 or 33A".

R. Maudling,
One of Her Majesty's Principal
Secretaries of State.

Home Office,
  Whitehall.
8th July 1971.

EXPLANATORY NOTE

(This Note is not part of the Regulations.)

These Regulations amend the Probation (Compensation) Regulations 1965 (the principal Regulations) as follows:—

(i) the expression "relevant employment" (which is defined in Regulation 2(1) of the principal Regulations and which affects qualification for compensation and calculation of the amount) is not to include service in the armed forces of the Crown other than certain national service which is expressly made relevant employment for determining whether a person is qualified to claim compensation (Regulation 4);

(ii) all national insurance benefits (other than benefits payable in respect of dependants) are to be taken into account in assessing resettlement compensation and not only, as at present, benefits at the flat rate applicable to a single person (Regulation 5);

(iii) national insurance benefits (other than benefits payable in respect of dependants) are to be deducted from long-term compensation to such extent as is necessary to ensure that the total of benefits and compensation received in any week does not exceed two-thirds of the emoluments for the loss or reduction of which compensation is payable. This was until recently secured by Regulations under the National Insurance Acts (Regulations 6 and 8);

(iv) a person entitled to long-term compensation is required to inform the compensating authority about national insurance benefits received by him (Regulation 7).

The provisions mentioned in (ii) to (iv) above apply to compensation in payment at the date of commencement of these Regulations as well as compensation awarded after that date (Regulation 3).

STATUTORY INSTRUMENTS

1971 No. 1121

LOCAL GOVERNMENT, ENGLAND AND WALES

LONDON GOVERNMENT

The Fire Services (Compensation) (Amendment) Regulations 1971

Made - - -	*8th July* 1971
Laid before Parliament	*21st July* 1971
Coming into Operation	*10th August* 1971

Whereas the Minister for the Civil Service has determined under section 60(2) of the Local Government Act 1958(a) (read with Article 2(1) of the Minister for the Civil Service Order 1968(b)) that the Secretary of State is the appropriate Minister in relation to members of fire brigades of a class prescribed by the Firemen's Pension Scheme for the purposes of section 2 of the Fire Services Act 1951(c):

Now, therefore, in exercise of the powers conferred on me by the said section 60(2) and section 85(4) of the London Government Act 1963(d), I hereby make the following Regulations:—

1. These Regulations may be cited as the Fire Services (Compensation) (Amendment) Regulations 1971 and shall come into operation on 10th August 1971.

2. In these Regulations any reference to the principal Regulations is a reference to the Fire Services (Compensation) Regulations 1965(e).

3.—(1) Notwithstanding anything contained in the principal Regulations, Regulations 4, 5 and 6 of these Regulations shall apply with effect from the date of the coming into operation of these Regulations in relation to any compensation under the principal Regulations awarded before that date.

(2) Nothing in Regulation 7 of these Regulations shall affect the entitlement of any person to compensation under the principal Regulations where that entitlement has been determined before the date of the coming into operation of these Regulations.

(a) 1958 c. 55.	(b) S.I. 1968/1656 (1968 III, p. 4485).
(c) 1951 c. 27.	(d) 1963 c. 33.
(e) S.I. 1965/563 (1965 I, p. 1726).	

4. For Regulation 6(1)(*a*) of the principal Regulations (deductions to be made in calculating resettlement compensation) there shall be substituted the following provision :—

"(*a*) unemployment, sickness or injury benefit under any Act relating to national insurance claimable by him in respect of such week (excluding any amount claimable by him in respect of any dependant) ;".

5. After Regulation 26 of the principal Regulations (adjustment of compensation) there shall be inserted the following Regulation :—

"Deduction in respect of national insurance benefit

26A.—(1) Where in any week a person is entitled to long-term compensation for loss or diminution of emoluments and is also entitled to unemployment, sickness or injury benefit under any Act relating to national insurance, other than a benefit claimable by him in respect of a dependant, there shall be deducted from the long-term compensation payable for that week a sum equal to the amount by which the aggregate of such national insurance benefits claimable in respect of that week, the weekly rate at which the long-term compensation would be payable but for this Regulation, and the weekly rate of any superannuation benefit taken into account for the purpose of Regulation 13(4) of these Regulations, exceeds two-thirds of the weekly rate of the net emoluments of the employment which he has lost or in which the emoluments have been diminished :

Provided that this paragraph shall not apply in relation to any such sickness or injury benefit in so far as an equivalent sum is deducted from the emoluments of his current employment and such deduction from those emoluments has not occasioned an increase in his long-term compensation.

(2) For the purposes of paragraph (1) of this Regulation the expression "weekly rate" means seven three hundred and sixty-fifths of the relevant annual rate.".

6. In Regulation 27 of the principal Regulations (certain changes in circumstances to be notified to the compensating authority) there shall be inserted after sub-paragraph (*c*) the following provision :—

"or,

(*d*) a person entitled to long-term compensation is receiving or starts to receive any benefit, any increase in benefit or any further benefit under any Act relating to national insurance,".

7. After Regulation 37(2) of the principal Regulations (interpretation) there shall be inserted the following provision :—

"(2A) Except as provided in Regulations 4(2) and 10(2) of these Regulations, the expression "relevant employment" shall not include service in the armed forces of the Crown.".

R. Maudling,
One of Her Majesty's Principal
Secretaries of State.

Home Office,
Whitehall.
8th July 1971.

EXPLANATORY NOTE

(This Note is not part of the Regulations.)

These Regulations amend the Fire Services (Compensation) Regulations 1965 (the principal Regulations) as follows :—

    (i) all national insurance benefits (other than benefits payable in respect of dependants) are to be taken into account in assessing resettlement compensation and not only, as at present, benefits at the flat rate applicable to a single person (Regulation 4) ;

    (ii) national insurance benefits (other than benefits payable in respect of dependants) are to be deducted from long-term compensation to such extent as is necessary to ensure that the total of benefits and compensation received in any week does not exceed two-thirds of the emoluments for the loss or reduction of which compensation is payable. This was until recently secured by Regulations under the National Insurance Acts (Regulation 5) ;

    (iii) a person entitled to long-term compensation is required to inform the compensating authority about national insurance benefits received by him (Regulation 6) ;

    (iv) the expression "relevant employment" (which is defined in Regulation 38(1) of the principal Regulations and which affects qualification for compensation and calculation of the amount) is not to include service in the armed forces of the Crown other than certain national service which is expressly made relevant employment for determining whether a person is qualified to claim compensation (Regulation 7).

The provisions mentioned in (i) to (iii) above apply to compensation in payment at the date of commencement of these Regulations as well as compensation awarded after that date (Regulation 3).

STATUTORY INSTRUMENTS

1971 No. 1122

LOCAL GOVERNMENT, ENGLAND AND WALES

LONDON GOVERNMENT

The Clerks of the Peace and Justices' Clerks (Compensation) (Amendment) Regulations 1971

Made - - -	*8th July* 1971
Laid before Parliament	*21st July* 1971
Coming into Operation	*10th August* 1971

Whereas the Minister for the Civil Service has determined under section 60(2) of the Local Government Act 1958(**a**), both as originally enacted and as applied by section 29(6) of the Administration of Justice Act 1964(**b**), and as read with Article 2(1) of the Minister for the Civil Service Order 1968(**c**), that the Secretary of State is the appropriate Minister to make Regulations thereunder in relation to the persons to whom these Regulations relate :

And whereas the Secretary of State is the appropriate Minister for the purposes of section 85(4) of the London Government Act 1963(**d**) as applied by section 35 of the Administration of Justice Act 1964 in relation to those persons :

Now, therefore, in exercise of the powers conferred on me by the said section 60(2), both as originally enacted and so applied, and the said section 85(4) as so applied, I hereby make the following Regulations :—

1. These Regulations may be cited as the Clerks of the Peace and Justices' Clerks (Compensation) (Amendment) Regulations 1971 and shall come into operation on 10th August 1971.

2. In these Regulations any reference to the principal Regulations is a reference to the Clerks of the Peace and Justices' Clerks (Compensation) Regulations 1965(**e**).

3.—(1) Nothing in Regulation 4 of these Regulations shall affect the entitlement of any person to compensation under the principal Regulations where that entitlement has been determined before the date of the coming into operation of these Regulations.

(2) Notwithstanding anything contained in the principal Regulations, Regulations 5, 6, 7, 8 and 9 of these Regulations shall apply with effect from the date of the coming into operation of these Regulations in relation to any compensation under the principal Regulations awarded before that date.

(**a**) 1958 c. 55.   (**b**) 1964 c. 42.
(**c**) S.I. 1968/1656 (1968 III, p. 4485).   (**d**) 1963 c. 33.
(**e**) S.I. 1965/517 (1965 I, p. 1350).

4. After Regulation 2(1) of the principal Regulations (interpretation) there shall be inserted the following provision :—

"(1A) Except as provided in Regulations 6(2) and 12(2) of these Regulations, the expression "relevant employment" shall not include service in the armed forces of the Crown.".

5. For Regulation 8(1)(*a*) of the principal Regulations (deductions to be made in calculating resettlement compensation) there shall be substituted the following provision :—

"(*a*) unemployment, sickness or injury benefit under any Act relating to national insurance claimable by him in respect of such week (excluding any amount claimable by him in respect of any dependant) ;".

6. In Regulation 18(1)(i) of the principal Regulations (payment of retirement compensation to a pensionable officer on his becoming incapacitated or reaching minimum pensionable age) the words "or accrued incapacity retiring allowance" shall be omitted.

7. After Regulation 33 of the principal Regulations (reduction of compensation) there shall be inserted the following Regulation :—

"Deduction in respect of national insurance benefit

33A.—(1) Where in any week a person is entitled to long-term compensation for loss or diminution of emoluments and is also entitled to unemployment, sickness or injury benefit under any Act relating to national insurance, other than a benefit claimable by him in respect of a dependant, there shall be deducted from the long-term compensation payable for that week a sum equal to the amount by which the aggregate of such national insurance benefits claimable in respect of that week, the weekly rate at which the long-term compensation would be payable but for this Regulation, and the weekly rate of any superannuation benefit taken into account for the purpose of Regulation 15(4) of these Regulations, exceeds two-thirds of the weekly rate of the net emoluments of the employment which he has lost or in which the emoluments have been diminished :

Provided that this paragraph shall not apply in relation to any such sickness or injury benefit insofar as an equivalent sum is deducted from the emoluments of his current employment and such deduction from those emoluments has not occasioned an increase in his long-term compensation.

(2) For the purposes of paragraph (1) of this Regulation the expression "weekly rate" means seven three hundred and sixty-fifths of the relevant annual rate.".

8. In Regulation 34 of the principal Regulations (certain changes in circumstances to be notified to the compensating authority) there shall be inserted after sub-paragraph (*c*) the following provision :—

"or

(*d*) a person entitled to long-term compensation is receiving or starts to receive any benefit, any increase in benefit or any further benefit under any Act relating to national insurance,".

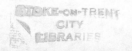

9. In Regulation 35(7) (review of awards of compensation) for the words "Regulation 32 or 33" there shall be substituted the words "Regulation 32, 33 or 33A".

R. *Maudling*,
One of Her Majesty's Principal
Secretaries of State.

Home Office,
   Whitehall.
8th July 1971.

EXPLANATORY NOTE

(*This Note is not part of the Regulations.*)

These Regulations amend the Clerks of the Peace and Justices' Clerks (Compensation) Regulations 1965 (the principal Regulations) as follows :—

   (i) the expression "relevant employment" (which is defined in Regulation 2(1) of the principal Regulations and which affects qualification for compensation and calculation of the amount) is not to include service in the armed forces of the Crown other than certain national service which is expressly made relevant employment for determining whether a person is qualified to claim compensation (Regulation 4) ;

   (ii) all national insurance benefits (other than benefits payable in respect of dependants) are to be taken into account in assessing resettlement compensation and not only, as at present, benefits at the flat rate applicable to a single person (Regulation 5) ;

   (iii) a textual error in Regulation 18(1) of the principal Regulations is corrected (Regulation 6) ;

   (iv) national insurance benefits (other than benefits payable in respect of dependants) are to be deducted from long-term compensation to such extent as is necessary to ensure that the total of benefits and compensation received in any week does not exceed two-thirds of the emoluments for the loss or reduction of which compensation is payable. This was until recently secured by Regulations under the National Insurance Acts (Regulations 7 and 9) ;

   (v) a person entitled to long-term compensation is required to inform the compensating authority about national insurance benefits received by him (Regulation 8).

The provisions mentioned in (ii) to (v) above apply to compensation in payment at the date of commencement of these Regulations as well as compensation awarded after that date (Regulation 3).

STATUTORY INSTRUMENTS

1971 No. 1123

DECIMAL CURRENCY

The Decimal Currency (End of Transitional Period) Order 1971

Made - - -	13*th July* 1971
Laid before Parliament	15*th July* 1971
Coming into Operation	31*st August* 1971

The Treasury, in exercise of the powers conferred on them by section 16(1) of the Decimal Currency Act 1969(a) and of all other powers enabling them in that behalf, hereby make the following Order :—

1. This Order may be cited as the Decimal Currency (End of Transitional Period) Order 1971, and shall come into operation on 31st August 1971.

2. The Interpretation Act 1889(b) shall apply for the interpretation of this Order as it applies for the interpretation of an Act of Parliament.

3. The transitional period, as defined in section 16(1) of the Decimal Currency Act 1969, shall end with 31st August 1971.

Bernard Weatherill,
P. L. Hawkins,
Two of the Lords Commissioners
of Her Majesty's Treasury.

13th July 1971.

EXPLANATORY NOTE

(*This Note is not part of the Order.*)

This Order brings to an end on 31st August 1971 the transitional period under the Decimal Currency Act 1969. After the end of the transitional period all payments have to be made in the new currency, and the threepence and penny of the old currency cease to be legal tender.

(a) 1969 c. 19.   (b) 1889 c. 63.

STATUTORY INSTRUMENTS

1971 No. 1124

AGRICULTURE

The Price Stability of Imported Products (Specified Commodities) (Poultry Meat) Order 1971

Made - - -	13*th July* 1971
Laid before Parliament	20*th July* 1971
Coming into Operation	21*st July* 1971

The Minister of Agriculture, Fisheries and Food and the Secretaries of State respectively concerned with agriculture in Scotland and Northern Ireland, acting jointly in exercise of the powers conferred upon them by section 1(1) of the Agriculture and Horticulture Act 1964(**a**) and of all other powers enabling them in that behalf, hereby make the following order :—

1. This order may be cited as the Price Stability of Imported Products (Specified Commodities) (Poultry Meat) Order 1971, and shall come into operation on 21st July 1971.

2.—(1) In this order—

"the Act" means the Agriculture and Horticulture Act 1964 ;

"produce" and "related product" have the meaning respectively assigned to them by section 1(10) of the Act ;

"tariff heading" means a heading of the Customs Tariff 1959 (as provided under section 1(4) of the Import Duties Act 1958(**b**)) and the four figure reference "02.02" in the Schedule to this order is a reference to such a tariff heading.

(2) In interpreting and applying this order any description of commodities specified in column 2 of the Schedule to this order in relation to a tariff heading indicated in column 1 of the Schedule is to be taken to comprise all produce and related products which would be classified under the same description in that tariff heading.

(3) The Interpretation Act 1889(**c**) shall apply to the interpretation of this order as it applies to the interpretation of an Act of Parliament.

(**a**) 1964 c. 28.　　　　　　　　　　　　　(**b**) 6 & 7 Eliz. 2 c. 6.
(**c**) 1889 c. 63.

3. Commodities of any description specified in column 2 of the Schedule to this order in relation to a tariff heading indicated in column 1 of the Schedule shall be commodities in relation to which the powers conferred by section 1(2) of the Act may be exercised.

In Witness whereof the Official Seal of the Minister of Agriculture, Fisheries and Food is hereunto affixed on 8th July 1971.

(L.S.)   *J. M. L. Prior,*
                      Minister of Agriculture, Fisheries and Food.

                                          Gordon Campbell,
8th July 1971.   Secretary of State for Scotland.

Given under the hand of the Secretary of State for the Home Department on 13th July 1971.

                                          R. Maudling,
                      Secretary of State for the Home Department.

SCHEDULE

SPECIFIED COMMODITIES

1 Tariff heading	2 Description
02.02	Dead poultry (that is to say fowls, ducks, geese, turkeys and guinea fowls), fresh, chilled or frozen, including cuts but excluding offals.

EXPLANATORY NOTE

(This Note is not part of the Order.)

This order specifies dead poultry (that is to say fowls, ducks, geese, turkeys and guinea fowls), fresh, chilled or frozen, as commodities in relation to which the Ministers may exercise powers conferred by section 1(2) of the Agriculture and Horticulture Act 1964 to make orders prescribing minimum price levels for imports into the United Kingdom and charging levies on imports in support thereof.

STATUTORY INSTRUMENTS

1971 No. 1128

TRANSPORT

PENSIONS AND COMPENSATION

The British Transport (Pensions of Employees) Order 1971

Made - - - -	*9th July* 1971
Laid before Parliament	*21st July* 1971
Coming into Operation	*22nd July* 1971

The Secretary of State for the Environment and the Secretary of State for Scotland, acting jointly, make this Order in exercise of their powers under section 74 of the Transport Act 1962(**a**), as read with section 136 of the Transport Act 1968(**b**), and of all other enabling powers: —

Commencement, citation and interpretation

1.—(1) This Order shall come into operation on the 22nd July 1971, and may be cited as the British Transport (Pensions of Employees) Order 1971.

(2) In this Order—

"national transport authority" means any of the following—
the British Railways Board,
the British Transport Docks Board,
the British Waterways Board,
the Transport Holding Company,
the National Freight Corporation,
the National Bus Company,
the Scottish Transport Group,
a subsidiary of any of the above bodies;

"term", in relation to a pension scheme, includes any rule or provision of the scheme, or of any statutory provision relating to the scheme, or of any deed or other instrument made for the purposes of the scheme.

(3) The Interpretation Act 1889(**c**) shall apply for the interpretation of this Order as it applies for the interpretation of an Act of Parliament.

Removal of requirement for Ministerial consent in connection with pension schemes of national transport authorities

2.—(1) Article 17 of the British Transport Reorganisation (Pensions of Employees) (No. 3) Order 1962 (**d**) and Article 12 of the British Transport (Pensions of Employees) (No. 1) Order 1968(**e**) (which prohibit national transport authorities from paying pensions or entering into obligations under pension schemes without the consent of the Secretary of State) are hereby revoked.

(**a**) 1962 c. 46.   (**b**) 1968 c. 73.   (**c**) 1889 c. 63.   (**d**) S.I. 1962/2758 (1962 III, p.3866).
(**e**) S.I. 1968/2011 (1968 III, p. 5450)

(2) Where the terms of a pension scheme, the participants in which include employees of a national transport authority, provide for the making of changes in that scheme with the consent or approval of the Secretary of State or of a Minister of the Crown whose functions are now vested in the Secretary of State, or prohibit the making of such changes without such consent or approval, the requirement of those terms (howsoever expressed) for such consent or approval to the making of such changes shall cease to have effect.

Signed by authority of the Secretary of State for the Environment 9th July 1971.

John Peyton,
Minister for Transport Industries
Department of the Environment.

Given under the Seal of the Secretary of State for Scotland 9th July 1971.

(L.S.)

Gordon Campbell,
Secretary of State for Scotland.

EXPLANATORY NOTE
(*This Note is not part of the Order.*)

This Order revokes the provisions of the British Transport Reorganisation (Pensions of Employees) (No. 3) Order 1962 and the British Transport (Pensions of Employees) (No. 1) Order 1968 which require national transport authorities to obtain the consent of the Secretary of State before paying pensions or entering into obligations under pension schemes. The Order also sets aside specific provisions to the same effect appearing in existing pension schemes of national transport authorities.

STATUTORY INSTRUMENTS

1971 No. 1130

ECCLESIASTICAL LAW

The Legal Officers Fees Order 1971

Made (*Approved by the General Synod*)	13th *July* 1971
Laid before Parliament	20th *July* 1971
Coming into Operation	1st *September* 1971

We, the Fees Committee constituted in accordance with the provisions of section 1 of the Ecclesiastical Fees Measure 1962(a), in the exercise of the powers conferred by that section, do hereby order as follows :—

1. The Tables of Fees set forth in the Schedule to this Order are hereby established and contain particulars of the fees which are to be demanded taken and received by the respective legal officers named in the Schedule for the performance by them after the commencement of this Order of the duties of their offices in relation to the respective matters specified in the Schedule.

2. The following fees shall no longer be payable :—

    (i) In the Table of Fees in the Schedule to the Ecclesiastical Officers Remuneration Order No. 2 1953(b) the fees payable in connection with the Reorganisation Areas Measure 1944(c).

    (ii) In Table 1 in the Schedule to the Legal Officers Fees Order 1964(d) items 5 and 18 and items 6 and 7 in so far as they relate to perpetual curacies ;

    (iii) In Table IV in the Schedule to the Legal Officers Fees Order 1964 fees payable under the Union of Benefices Measure 1923(e), the New Parishes Measure 1943(f), the Pastoral Reorganisation Measure 1949(g), the Benefices (Suspension of Presentation) Measure 1953(h) and the Representation of the Laity Measure 1956(i).

3. This Order may be cited as the Legal Officers Fees Order 1971 and shall come into operation on the first day of September 1971.

Dated the twelfth day of May 1971.

> *Conolly H. Gage,*
> *J. R. Cumming Bruce,*
> *H. Montgomery-Campbell,*

Approved by the General Synod the thirteenth day of July 1971.

> *John Guillum Scott,*
> Secretary.

(a) 10 & 11 Eliz. 2. No. 1.   (b) S.I. 1953/1709 (1953 I, p. 598).   (c) 7 & 8 Geo. 6. No. 1.
(d) S.I. 1964/1033 (1964 II, p. 2269).   (e) 14 & 15 Geo. 5. No. 2.   (f) 6 & 7 Geo. 6. No. 1.
(g) 12, 13 & 14 Geo. 6. No. 3.   (h) 1 & 2 Eliz. 2. No. 5.   (i) 4 & 5 Eliz. 2. No. 2.

THE SCHEDULE

TABLE I

FEES UNDER THE PASTORAL MEASURE 1968(a)

Matter		Fee £.
1.	Registration of Order in Council or order under section 9(3), payable to Diocesan Registrar	0·75
2.	Preparing or approving instrument constituting a joint pastoral committee under section 12(1), payable to:—	
	Diocesan Registrar ..	1·05
	Secretary to Bishop ..	7·35
3.	Preparing or approving instrument revoking or varying such instrument under section 12(3) or dissolving joint pastoral committee under section 12(6), payable to:—	
	Diocesan Registrar ..	1·05
	Secretary to Bishop ..	4·20
4.	Notice of termination of plurality by bishop to patron or parochial church council under section 17(2)	0·75
5.	Admission to office of rector for term of years payable to:—	
	Diocesan Registrar ..	3·15
	Secretary to Bishop ..	6·30
6.	Licence of vicar in a team ministry	5·25
7.	Licence extending term of years of rector or vicar in a team ministry	2·10
8.	Instrument designating a building a parish centre of worship or revoking such designation under section 29 payable to:—	
	Diocesan Registrar ..	1·05
	Secretary to Bishop ..	5·25
9.	Order relating to a redundant chapel belonging to a charity under section 55	Fee based on Schedule II to the Solicitors Remuneration Order.
10.	Suspension of presentation under section 67(1)	8·40
11.	Notice under section 67(3)(a)	8·40
12.	Notice of extension under section 67(4)	8·40
13.	Registration of copy of notice under section 67(5), payable to Diocesan Registrar	0·75
14.	Direction as to services under section 74(3)	1·05
15.	Direction by bishop as to banns and marriages under Schedule 3, paragraph 14(3)	2·10

Provisions relating to Table 1:—

1. In this Table "section" refers to that section of the Pastoral Measure 1968.

2. Unless otherwise stated the fees are payable to the Secretary to the Bishop.

3. Items 5, 6 and 7 are the liability of the Bishop and section 5 of the Ecclesiastical Fees Measure 1962 applies to them. Items 10, 11, 12 and 13 are the liability of the sequestrators. The remaining fees are the liability of the Diocesan Pastoral Account.

(a) 1968 No. 1.

TABLE II

MISCELLANEOUS FEES

Matter		Fee £.
1.	Licence of curate in charge of a parish	5·25
2.	Dispensation under section 2 of the Prayer Book (Miscellaneous Provisions) Measure 1965(a)	1·05
3.	Direction by the bishop as to banns and marriages under section 23 of the Marriage Act 1949(b)	2·10
4.	Advising Bishop as to exercise of powers under Synodical Government Measure 1969(c), Schedule 3, Rule 43	1·50
5.	Application to Bishop under the Synodical Government Measure 1969, Schedule 3, Appendix II, paragraph 17 ..	1·50

Provisions relating to Table II:—

1. Unless otherwise stated the fees are payable to the Secretary to the Bishop.

2. Item 1 is the liability of the Bishop and section 5 of the Ecclesiastical Fees Measure 1962 applies to it. Items 2 and 3 are the liability of the Diocesan Pastoral Account. Items 4 and 5 are the liability of the party applying to the Bishop.

EXPLANATORY NOTE

(*This Note is not part of the Order.*)

This Order establishes tables of Fees for ecclesiastical legal officers. Most fees arise in consequence of the coming into operation of the Pastoral Measure 1968 and the Synodical Government Measure 1969 and of these some replace fees established by the Ecclesiastical Officers Remuneration Order No. 2 1953 and the Legal Officers Fees Order 1964.

(a) 1965 No. 3.   (b) 12, 13 & 14 Geo. 6. c. 76.   (c) 1969 No. 2.

STATUTORY   INSTRUMENTS

1971 No. 1132 (L. 28)

SUPREME COURT OF JUDICATURE, ENGLAND

PROCEDURE

The Rules of the Supreme Court (Amendment No. 3) 1971

Made - - - -	12*th July* 1971
Laid before Parliament	20*th July* 1971
Coming into Operation	2*nd August* 1971

We, the Rule Committee of the Supreme Court, being the authority having for the time being power under section 99(4) of the Supreme Court of Judicature (Consolidation) Act 1925(a) to make, amend or revoke rules regulating the practice and procedure of the Supreme Court of Judicature, hereby exercise those powers and all other powers enabling us in that behalf as follows:—

1.—(1) These Rules may be cited as the Rules of the Supreme Court (Amendment No. 3) 1971 and shall come into operation on 2nd August 1971.

(2) In these Rules an Order referred to by number means the Order so numbered in the Rules of the Supreme Court 1965(b), as amended (c).

(3) The Interpretation Act 1889(d) shall apply to the interpretation of these Rules as it applies to the interpretation of an Act of Parliament.

2. Order 80, rule 14, shall be revoked.

3.—(1) Order 110 shall be amended as follows:—

(*a*) In rule 1(1) after the words " section 1 " there shall be inserted the words " or subsection (2) or (3) of section 3 ".

(*b*) In rule 1(3) after the words " section 2 " there shall be inserted the words " or, as the case may be, section 3A ".

(*c*) In rule 2(1) after the words " section 1 " there shall be inserted the words " or subsection (2) or (3) of the said section 3 ".

(*d*) In rule 2(3)—
   (i) after the words " section 2(1) " there shall be inserted the words " or section 3A(1) ", and

---

(a) 1925 c. 49.
(c) There are no relevant amending instruments.
(b) S.I. 1965/1776 (1965 III, p. 4995).
(d) 1889 c. 63.

(ii) after the words " section 1 " there shall be inserted the words " or subsection (2) of section 3 ".

(*e*) In rule 3 after the words " section 1 " there shall be inserted the words " or subsection (2) or (3) of the said section 3 ".

(2) In its application to an action pending at the commencement of the Law Reform (Miscellaneous Provisions) Act 1971(**a**), paragraph (1)(*d*)(ii) of this rule shall have effect as if the words to be inserted in Order 110, rule 2(3), after " section 1 " were " or subsection (2) or (3) of section 3 ".

Dated 12th July 1971.

Hailsham of St. Marylebone, C.
Widgery, C.J.
Denning, M.R.
George Baker, P.
Cyril Salmon, L.J.
John Pennycuick, V-C.
John R. Willis, J.
Nigel Bridge, J.
James Fox-Andrews.
Oliver Lodge.
W. O. Carter.
H. Montgomery-Campbell.

EXPLANATORY NOTE

(This Note is not part of the Rules.)

These Rules amend the Rules of the Supreme Court so as to take account of the relevant provisions of the Law Reform (Miscellaneous Provisions) Act 1971.

(**a**) 1971 c. 43.

STATUTORY INSTRUMENTS

1971 No. 1133 (C.27)

CIVIL AVIATION

The Civil Aviation Act 1968 (Commencement) Order 1971

Made - - - *13th July* 1971

The Secretary of State, in exercise of his powers under sections 13(2) and 14(13) of the Civil Aviation Act 1968(a), and of all other powers enabling him in that behalf, hereby makes the following Order :—

1. This Order may be cited as the Civil Aviation Act 1968 (Commencement) Order 1971.

2. Section 13(2) and subsections (1) to (12) of section 14 of the Civil Aviation Act 1968 shall come into force on 13th July 1971.

Michael Noble,
Minister for Trade,
Department of Trade and Industry.

13th July 1971.

EXPLANATORY NOTE

(This Note is not part of the Order.)

This Order brings into force section 13(2) of the Civil Aviation Act 1968 (which repeals specified provisions of the Civil Aviation Act 1949 (c. 67) relating to aerodromes in Northern Ireland) and subsections (1) to (12) of section 14 of the Civil Aviation Act 1968 (which make provision for the detention and sale of aircraft for unpaid airport charges). The other provisions of the Act are already in force. By virtue of section 28(6) of the Civil Aviation Act 1968, section 14 of that Act will cease to extend to Northern Ireland on the coming into force of section 13(2).

(a) 1968 c. 61.

STATUTORY INSTRUMENTS

1971 No. 1134

CIVIL AVIATION

The Civil Aviation (Airport Charges) (Sale of Detained Aircraft) Regulations 1971

Made - - -	13*th July* 1971
Coming into Operation	30*th July* 1971

The Secretary of State, in exercise of his powers under section 14(4) of the Civil Aviation Act 1968(a), and of all other powers enabling him in that behalf, hereby makes the following Regulations.

Citation and operation

1. These Regulations may be cited as the Civil Aviation (Airport Charges) (Sale of Detained Aircraft) Regulations 1971 and shall come into operation on 30th July 1971.

Interpretation

2.—(1) In these Regulations—

"the Act" means the Civil Aviation Act 1968 ;

"an authority" means an aerodrome authority which has detained an aircraft under section 14 of the Act ;

"operator" in relation to an aircraft, means the person who, at the relevant time, has the management of that aircraft.

(2) The Interpretation Act 1889(b) applies for the purpose of the interpretation of these Regulations as it applies for the purpose of the interpretation of an Act of Parliament.

Steps to be taken to bring proposed application to court to notice of interested persons and afford them an opportunity of becoming a party to the proceedings.

3. An authority proposing to apply to the court for leave to sell an aircraft under section 14 of the Act shall take such of the following steps for bringing the proposed application to the notice of persons whose interests may be affected by the determination of the court thereon and for affording to any such person an opportunity of becoming a party to the proceedings on the application as are applicable to the aircraft :

(1) At least 21 days before applying to the court, the authority shall publish :

(i) in the London Gazette and also, if the aircraft is detained in Scotland, in the Edinburgh Gazette ; and

---

(a) 1968 c. 61.   (b) 1889 c. 63.

(ii) in one or more local newspapers circulating in the locality in which the aircraft is detained

such a notice as is prescribed by Regulation 4 of these Regulations, and shall also, unless in that case it is impracticable to do so, serve such a notice, in the manner so prescribed, on each of the following persons :

(a) the person in whose name the aircraft is registered ;

(b) the person, if any, who appears to the authority to be the owner of the aircraft ;

(c) any person who appears to the authority to be a charterer of the aircraft whether or not by demise ;

(d) any person who appears to the authority to be the operator of the aircraft ;

(e) H P Information Ltd being a company incorporated under the Companies Act 1948(a) ;

(f) any person who is registered as a mortgagee of the aircraft under an Order in Council made under section 16 of the Act or who appears to the authority to be a mortgagee of the aircraft under the law of any country other than the United Kingdom ;

(g) any other person who appears to the authority to have a proprietary interest in the aircraft.

(2) If any person who has been served with a notice in accordance with paragraph (1) of this Regulation informs the authority in writing within 14 days of the service of the notice of his desire to become a party to the proceedings the authority shall make that person a defendant to the application.

Content and service of the notice under Regulation 3

4.—(1) A notice under Regulation 3 of these Regulations shall—

(a) state the nationality and registration marks of the aircraft ;

(b) state the type of aircraft ;

(c) state that, by reason of default in the payment of a sum due to the authority for airport charges, the authority, on a date which shall be specified in the notice, detained the aircraft under section 14 of the Act, and, unless payment of the sum so due is made within a period of 56 days from the date when the detention began, or within 21 days of the date of service of the notice, whichever shall be the later, will apply to the court for leave to sell the aircraft ;

(d) invite the person to whom the notice is given to inform the authority in writing within 14 days of the service of the notice if he wishes to become a party to the proceedings on the application.

(2) A notice under Regulation 3 of these Regulations shall be served—

(a) by delivering it to the person to whom it is to be sent ; or

(b) by leaving it at his usual or last known place of business or abode ; or

(c) by sending it by post in a prepaid registered letter, or by the recorded delivery service, addressed to him at his usual or last known place of business or abode ; or

---

(a) 1948 c. 38.

(d) if the person to whom it is to be sent is an incorporated company or body, by delivering it to the secretary, clerk or other appropriate officer of the company or body at their registered or principal office, or sending it by post in a prepaid registered letter, or by the recorded delivery service, addressed to the secretary, clerk or other officer of the company or body at that office.

(3) Any notice which is sent by post in accordance with the preceding paragraph, to a place outside the United Kingdom shall be sent by air mail or by some other equally expeditious means.

Michael Noble,
Minister for Trade,
Department of Trade and Industry.

13th July 1971.

EXPLANATORY NOTE

(This Note is not part of the Regulations.)

These Regulations prescribe the steps to be taken by an aerodrome authority which has detained an aircraft in Great Britain under section 14 of the Civil Aviation Act 1968 for non-payment of airport charges, before applying to the court for leave to sell the aircraft under that section. By virtue of section 28(6) of the Civil Aviation Act 1968, section 14 of that Act ceased to extend to Northern Ireland on 13th July 1971, the date appointed under section 13(2) of that Act, by the Civil Aviation Act 1968 (Commencement) Order 1971 (S.I. 1971/1133 (C. 27)) for the repeal of specified provisions of the Civil Aviation Act 1968 relating to aerodromes in Northern Ireland.

STATUTORY INSTRUMENTS

1971 No. 1135

CIVIL AVIATION

The Civil Aviation (Navigation Services Charges) Regulations 1971

Made - - - -	*13th July* 1971
Laid before Parliament	*22nd July* 1971
Coming into Operation	*30th July* 1971

The Secretary of State in exercise of his powers under sections 4 and 7 of the Civil Aviation (Eurocontrol) Act 1962(a) and section 15(4) of the Civil Aviation Act 1968(b) and of all other powers enabling him in that behalf, and with the consent of the Treasury in respect of Regulations 5, 6 and 7 hereby makes the following Regulations:

Citation and Operation

1. These Regulations may be cited as the Civil Aviation (Navigation Services Charges) Regulations 1971 and shall come into operation on 30th July 1971.

Interpretation

2.—(1) In these Regulations:

"aircraft documents", in relation to any aircraft, means any certificate of registration, maintenance or airworthiness of that aircraft, any log book relating to the use of that aircraft or its equipment and any similar document;

"airport charges" means charges payable to a person owning or managing an aerodrome in the United Kingdom to which section 14 of the Civil Aviation Act 1968 or any enactment of the Parliament of Northern Ireland containing provisions corresponding to that section for the time being applies for the use of, or for services provided at, the aerodrome but does not include charges payable by virtue of these Regulations;

"operator", in relation to an aircraft, means the person who, at the relevant time, has the management of that aircraft;

"the 1962 Act" means the Civil Aviation (Eurocontrol) Act 1962;

"the court" means, as respects England and Wales, the High Court, as respects Scotland, the Court of Session; and, as respects Northern Ireland, the High Court of Justice in Northern Ireland;

(a) 1962 c. 8.　　　　　　　　　(b) 1968 c. 61.

"maximum total weight authorised" means, in relation to an aircraft, the maximum total weight of the aircraft and its contents at which the aircraft may take off in the United Kingdom in the most favourable circumstances in accordance with the certificate of airworthiness for the time being in force in respect of the aircraft; however, if that certificate indicates a maximum total weight at which the aircraft may taxi, that weight shall be taken to be the maximum total weight authorised;

"the specified amount" means, in relation to a landing or take-off, the additional cost incurred by the Secretary of State in providing navigation services by reason of the landing or take-off, as the case may be, being made outside hours;

"the standard charge" means—

(a) in the case of an aircraft other than a helicopter, for each complete 1,000 lb. of the maximum total weight authorised of the aircraft in respect of which the charge is made, and for each fraction of 1,000 lb. not being less than 500 lb., a charge

(i) for services provided in connection with the use of Heathrow—London, Gatwick—London, Stansted—London or Prestwick aerodromes, of 15 new pence;

(ii) for services provided in connection with the use of any of the other aerodromes referred to in Regulation 4, of $22\frac{1}{2}$ new pence;

(b) in the case of a helicopter, a charge equal to one half of the amount which, in the circumstances, would be the standard charge in the case of an aircraft other than a helicopter;

"within hours" means within the notified hours of watch of the air traffic control unit at the aerodrome, and "outside hours" shall be construed accordingly.

(2) Expressions used in these Regulations shall unless the context otherwise requires have the same respective meanings as in the Air Navigation Order 1970(a) as amended (b).

(3) The Interpretation Act 1889(c) shall apply for the purpose of the interpretation of these Regulations as it applies for the purpose of the interpretation of an Act of Parliament.

Revocation

3.—(1) Subject to paragraph (2) of this Regulation, the Civil Aviation (Navigation Services Charges) Regulations 1964(d), the Civil Aviation (Navigation Services Charges) (Amendment) Regulations 1966(e), the Civil Aviation (Navigation Services Charges) (Second Amendment) Regulations 1968(f) and the Civil Aviation (Navigation Services Charges) (Third Amendment) Regulations 1969(g) are hereby revoked.

(2) Section 38(2) of the Interpretation Act 1889 (which relates to the effect of repeals) shall apply to these Regulations as if these Regulations were an Act of Parliament and as if the Regulations revoked by paragraph (1) of this Regulation were Acts of Parliament thereby repealed.

(a) S.I. 1970/954 (1970 II, p. 2964).
(c) 1889 c. 63.
(e) S.I. 1966/465 (1966 I, p. 982).
(g) S.I. 1969/510 (1969 I, p. 1414).

(b) There is no relevant amending instrument.
(d) S.I. 1964/1071 (1964 II, p. 2367).
(f) S.I. 1968/423 (1968 I, p. 1109).

Aerodromes in respect of which charges are payable

4. The charges imposed by these Regulations shall be payable in respect of services provided at the following aerodromes, namely, Heathrow—London, Gatwick—London, Stansted—London, Prestwick, Aberdeen (Dyce), Belfast (Aldergrove), Birmingham, Bournemouth (Hurn), Edinburgh, Glamorgan (Rhoose), Glasgow, Liverpool and Manchester.

Charges for navigation services

5.—(1) Subject to the provisions of these Regulations, the operator of every aircraft for which navigation services are provided by the Secretary of State in connection with the use of an aerodrome referred to in Regulation 4 of these Regulations (whether or not the services are actually used or could be used with the equipment installed in the aircraft) shall pay to the Secretary of State for those services on the occasion specified in the first column of the following table the charges specified in relation to those occasions in the second column thereof:—

TABLE

(*a*) Upon each landing of the aircraft at that aerodrome within hours ...	the standard charge
(*b*) Upon each landing of the aircraft at that aerodrome outside hours ...	the standard charge surcharged by 75%, (in the case of a helicopter by 150%) or by the specified amount, whichever is the greater.
(*c*) Upon each take-off of the aircraft at that aerodrome outside hours, being either	
(i) a take-off which does not take place within 1 hour of landing or	
(ii) a take-off which takes place within 1 hour of a landing made within hours	the specified amount or 75% of the standard charge (in the case of a helicopter 150%) whichever is the greater.

(2) Where on the occasion of any landing or take-off (as the case may be) the shortest distance in the case of a landing between the aerodrome of departure and the aerodrome of landing and in the case of a take-off between the aerodrome of departure and the aerodrome of intended landing does not exceed 115 miles measured along the great circle, for the references to "the standard charge" in the Table in paragraph (1) of this Regulation there shall be substituted references to "half the standard charge".

(3) Where the flight of an aircraft taking off or landing, as the case may be, is a flight to or from a place outside the United Kingdom, Channel Islands and the Isle of Man, or a flight which is part of a through journey of the aircraft to or from a place outside those countries, for the references to "the standard charge" in paragraphs (1) and (2) of this Regulation there shall be substituted references to "112½% of the standard charge".

Services provided outside hours where the intention to land or take-off is not carried out

6. Whenever, by reason of his having received from the operator or commander of an aircraft notice of intention to make use outside hours of an aerodrome referred to in Regulation 4 of these Regulations for landing or take-off or as an alternate aerodrome, the Secretary of State provides navigation services outside hours but the aircraft does not land or take-off there on the occasion specified in the notice, the operator of the aircraft shall pay, in respect of each such aerodrome—

(*a*) in the case of an intended landing or intended use of the aerodrome as an alternate aerodrome, an amount equal to the surcharge payable under Regulation 5 of these Regulations on the landing of the aircraft outside hours;

(*b*) in the case of an intended take-off, an amount equal to the charge, if any, which would have been payable under Regulation 5 of these Regulations if the aircraft had actually taken off outside hours at the intended time;

Provided that a charge shall not be payable under this Regulation if the notice of intention is cancelled not less than 30 minutes before the end of the last period of watch within hours before the time specified in the notice for landing or for the intended use of the aerodrome as an alternate aerodrome or for take-off, as the case may be.

Dispensations

7. The Secretary of State may dispense wholly or in part with any charge payable under Regulations 5 and 6 of these Regulations, if he determines that it is proper to do so, having regard to all the circumstances of the case.

Detention and sale of aircraft for unpaid charges

8. Where default is made in the payment of charges incurred in respect of any aircraft under these Regulations, the Secretary of State or an authorised person may, subject to the provisions of this and the following Regulations take such steps as are necessary to detain, pending payment, either—

(*a*) the aircraft in respect of which the charges were incurred (whether or not they were incurred by the person who is the operator of the aircraft at the time when the detention begins); or

(*b*) any other aircraft of which the person in default is the operator at the time when the detention begins;

and if the charges are not paid within 56 days of the date when the detention begins, the Secretary of State may sell the aircraft in order to satisfy the charges.

9. The Secretary of State or the authorised person concerned shall not detain, or continue to detain, an aircraft under these Regulations by reason of any alleged default in the payment of charges payable under these Regulations if the operator of the aircraft or any other person claiming an interest therein—

(*a*) disputes that the charges, or any of them, are due or, if the aircraft is detained under Regulation 8(*a*) of these Regulations, that the charges in question were incurred in respect of that aircraft; and

(*b*) gives to the Secretary of State, pending the determination of the dispute, sufficient security for the payment of the charges which are alleged to be due.

10. The Secretary of State shall not sell an aircraft under these Regulations without the leave of the court; and the court shall not give leave except on proof that a sum is due to the Secretary of State for charges under these Regulations, that default has been made in the payment thereof and that the aircraft which the Secretary of State seeks leave to sell is liable to sale under these Regulations by reason of the default.

11. The Secretary of State shall, before applying to the court for leave to sell an aircraft under these Regulations, take such steps for bringing the proposed application to the notice of interested persons and for affording them an opportunity of becoming a party to the proceedings as are set forth in the Schedule to these Regulations. If such leave is given, the Secretary of State shall secure that the aircraft is sold for the best price that can reasonably be obtained; but failure to comply with any requirement of this Regulation or of the said Schedule in respect of any sale, while actionable as against the Secretary of State at the suit of any person suffering loss in consequence thereof, shall not, after the sale has taken place, be a ground for impugning its validity.

12. The proceeds of any sale under these Regulations shall be applied as follows, and in the following order, that is to say:—

(*a*) in payment of any customs duty or purchase tax which is due in consequence of the aircraft having been brought into the United Kingdom;

(*b*) in payment of the expenses incurred by the Secretary of State in detaining, keeping and selling the aircraft, including his expenses in connection with the application to the court;

(*c*) in payment of any airport charges incurred in respect of any aircraft which are due from the operator of the aircraft to the person owning or managing the aerodrome at which the aircraft was detained under these Regulations;

(*d*) in payment of any charge in respect of the aircraft which is due by virtue of these or any other Regulations under section 4 of the 1962 Act

and the surplus, if any, shall be paid to or among the person or persons whose interests in the aircraft have been divested by reason of the sale.

13. The power of detention and sale conferred by these Regulations in respect of an aircraft extends to the equipment of the aircraft and any stores for use in connection with its operation (being equipment and stores carried in the aircraft) whether or not the property of the person who is its operator, and references to the aircraft in Regulations 9 to 12 of these Regulations include, except where the context otherwise requires, references to any such equipment and stores.

14. The power of detention conferred by these Regulations in respect of an aircraft extends to any aircraft documents carried in it, and any such documents may, if the aircraft is sold under these Regulations, be transferred by the Secretary of State to the purchaser.

15. The power conferred by these Regulations to detain an aircraft in respect of which charges have been incurred may be exercised on the occasion on which the charges have been incurred or on any subsequent occasion when the aircraft is on the aerodrome in respect of which those charges were incurred or on any other aerodrome owned or managed by the Secretary of State or on which the Secretary of State provides the navigation services.

16. Nothing in these Regulations shall prejudice any right of the Secretary of State to recover any charges, or any part thereof, by action.

Michael Noble,
Minister for Trade,
13th July 1971. Department of Trade and Industry.

We consent to the making of these Regulations.

Bernard Weatherill,
P. L. Hawkins,
Lords Commissioners of Her
13th July 1971. Majesty's Treasury.

SCHEDULE

Steps to be taken to bring proposed application to court to notice of interested persons and afford them an opportunity of becoming a party to the proceedings.

1. The Secretary of State, if he proposes to apply to the court for leave to sell an aircraft under these Regulations, shall take such of the following steps for bringing the proposed application to the notice of persons whose interests may be affected by the determination of the court thereon and for affording to any such person an opportunity of becoming a party to the proceedings on the application as are applicable to the aircraft:

(1) At least 21 days before applying to the court, the Secretary of State shall publish:

    (i) in the London Gazette and also, if the aircraft is detained in Scotland, in the Edinburgh Gazette, or, if it is detained in Northern Ireland, in the Belfast Gazette; and

    (ii) in one or more local newspapers circulating in the locality in which the aircraft is detained;

such a notice as is prescribed by paragraph 2 of this Schedule, and shall also, unless in that case it is impracticable to do so, serve such a notice, in the manner so prescribed, on each of the following persons:

    (*a*) the person in whose name the aircraft is registered;

    (*b*) the person, if any, who appears to the Secretary of State to be the owner of the aircraft;

    (*c*) any person who appears to the Secretary of State to be a charterer of the aircraft whether or not by demise;

    (*d*) any person who appears to the Secretary of State to be the operator of the aircraft;

    (*e*) H P Information Ltd., being a company incorporated under the Companies Act 1948(a);

(a) 1948 c. 38.

(*f*) any person who is registered as a mortgagee of the aircraft under an Order in Council made under section 16 of the Civil Aviation Act 1968 or who appears to the Secretary of State to be a mortgagee of the aircraft under the law of any country other than the United Kingdom;

(*g*) any other person who appears to the Secretary of State to have a proprietary interest in the aircraft.

(2) If any person who has been served with a notice in accordance with sub-paragraph (1) of this paragraph informs the Secretary of State in writing within 14 days of the service of the notice of his desire to become a party to the proceedings the Secretary of State shall make that person a defendant to the application.

2. *Content and service of the notice under paragraph 1*

(1) A notice under paragraph 1 of this Schedule shall—

(*a*) state the nationality and registration marks of the aircraft;

(*b*) state the type of aircraft;

(*c*) state that by reason of default in the payment of a sum due to the Secretary of State for charges imposed by these Regulations, the Secretary of State, on a date which shall be specified in the notice, detained the aircraft under these Regulations and, unless payment of the sum so due is made within a period of 56 days from the date when the detention began, or within 21 days of the date of service of the notice, whichever shall be the later, will apply to the court for leave to sell the aircraft;

(*d*) invite the person to whom the notice is given to inform the Secretary of State within 14 days of the service of the notice if he wishes to become a party to the proceedings on the application.

(2) A notice under paragraph 1 of this Schedule shall be served—

(*a*) by delivering it to the person to whom it is to be sent; or

(*b*) by leaving it at his usual or last known place of business or abode; or

(*c*) by sending it by post in a prepaid registered letter, or by the recorded delivery service, addressed to him at his usual or last known place of business or abode; or

(*d*) if the person to whom it is to be sent is an incorporated company or body, by delivering it to the secretary, clerk or other appropriate officer of the company or body at their registered or principal office, or sending it by post in a prepaid registered letter, or by the recorded delivery service, addressed to the secretary, clerk or officer of the company or body at that office.

(3) Any notice which is sent by post in accordance with the preceding paragraph to a place outside the United Kingdom shall be sent by air mail or by some other equally expeditious means.

CIVIL AVIATION

EXPLANATORY NOTE

(This Note is not part of the Regulations.)

These Regulations revoke the Civil Aviation (Navigation Services Charges) Regulations 1964, as amended. They reproduce with minor and drafting amendments the substance of Regulations 1 to 7 of the 1964 Regulations as amended, and include, in relation to aircraft detained for non-payment of charges, provisions corresponding to those in section 14 of the Civil Aviation Act 1968 and the Regulations made thereunder.

The main new provisions are as follows:—

(1) Power is conferred on the Secretary of State to sell the aircraft if the charges are not paid within 56 days of the date when the detention begins (Regulation 8).

(2) The Secretary of State is precluded from detaining the aircraft if the charges are disputed and sufficient security is given to him (Regulation 9).

(3) The Secretary of State is prohibited from selling an aircraft without the leave of the court (Regulation 10) and is required, before applying to the court for leave to sell an aircraft, to take specified steps for bringing the proposed application to the notice of interested persons and for affording such persons an opportunity of becoming a party to the proceedings (Regulation 11).

(4) The Secretary of State is required to secure that the aircraft is sold for the best price that can reasonably be obtained (Regulation 11), and to apply the proceeds of sale in a prescribed manner (Regulation 12).

STATUTORY INSTRUMENTS

1971 No. 1136

WAGES COUNCILS
The Wages Regulation (Hairdressing) Order 1971

Made - - -	13*th July* 1971
Coming into Operation	13*th September* 1971

Whereas the Secretary of State has received from the Hairdressing Undertakings Wages Council (Great Britain) (hereafter in this Order referred to as the "Wages Council") the wages regulation proposals set out in the Schedule hereto ;

Now, therefore, the Secretary of State in exercise of his powers under section 11 of the Wages Councils Act 1959(**a**), and of all other powers enabling him in that behalf, hereby makes the following Order :—

1. This Order may be cited as the Wages Regulation (Hairdressing) Order 1971.

2.—(1) In this Order the expression "the specified date" means the 13th September 1971, provided that where, as respects any worker who is paid wages at intervals not exceeding seven days, that date does not correspond with the beginning of the period for which the wages are paid, the expression "the specified date" means, as respects that worker, the beginning of the next such period following that date.

(2) The Interpretation Act 1889(**b**) shall apply to the interpretation of this Order as it applies to the interpretation of an Act of Parliament and as if this Order and the Order hereby revoked were Acts of Parliament.

3. The wages regulation proposals set out in the Schedule hereto shall have effect as from the specified date and as from that date the Wages Regulation (Hairdressing) Order 1970(**c**) shall cease to have effect.

Signed by order of the Secretary of State.

13th July 1971.

J. R. Lloyd Davies,
Assistant Secretary,
Department of Employment.

(**a**) 1959 c. 69.　　　　(**b**) 1889 c. 63.
(**c**) S.I. 1970/283 (1970 I, p. 1027).

ARRANGEMENT OF SCHEDULE

PART I

STATUTORY MINIMUM REMUNERATION

PART II

HOLIDAYS AND HOLIDAY REMUNERATION

PART III

GENERAL

Article 3

SCHEDULE

The following minimum remuneration and provisions as to holidays and holiday remuneration shall be substituted for the statutory minimum remuneration and provisions as to holidays and holiday remuneration fixed by the Wages Regulation (Hairdressing) Order 1970 (Order H.U. (42)).

PART I

STATUTORY MINIMUM REMUNERATION
APPLICATION

1. Subject to the provisions of paragraphs 2, 8 and 10, the minimum remuneration payable to workers to whom this Schedule applies shall be the remuneration set out in paragraphs 3, 4 and 6.

Any increase in remuneration payable under the provisions of paragraph 3 or 6 shall become effective on the first day of the first full pay week following the date upon which the increase would otherwise become payable under those provisions.

HOURS ON WHICH REMUNERATION IS BASED

2.—(1) The minimum remuneration specified in this Part of this Schedule relates to a week of 42 hours exclusive of overtime and, except as provided in paragraph 10 (which relates to guaranteed weekly remuneration), is subject to a proportionate reduction according as the number of hours worked is less than 42.

(2) In calculating the remuneration for the purpose of this Schedule recognised breaks for meal times shall, subject to the provisions of paragraph 9, be excluded.

APPRENTICE, OPERATIVE HAIRDRESSER

3. Subject to the provisions of paragraph 1, the minimum remuneration payable to an apprentice (whose employment complies with the conditions specified in paragraph 7) or operative hairdresser employed in the London Area, Provincial A Area or Provincial B Area, as the case may be, during the period of employment specified in Column 1 of the next following table shall be the appropriate amount set out in Column 2.

Column 1	Column 2	
	London Area	Provincial A Area and Provincial B Area
	Per week	Per week
(1) Apprentice (employed in a ladies' or gentlemen's saloon)—	£	£
First six months of employment as an apprentice	4·00	3·75
Second six months of employment as an apprentice	4·40	4·00
Third six months of employment as an apprentice	5·25	4·95
Fourth six months of employment as an apprentice	5·60	5·25
Fifth six months of employment as an apprentice	6·50	6·20
Sixth six months of employment as an apprentice	6·80	6·50

	Worker employed in a			
	Ladies' Saloon		Gentlemen's Saloon	
(2) Operative hairdresser—	London Area	Provincial A Area and Provincial B Area	London Area	Provincial A Area and Provincial B Area
	Per week	Per week	Per week	Per week
	£	£	£	£
First year of employment as an operative hairdresser— Male	9·40	9·10	11·05	10·75
Female	8·70	8·40	11·05	10·75
Second year of employment as an operative hairdresser— Male	11·45	11·00	13·75	13·30
Female	10·75	10·25	13·75	13·30
After two years of employment as an operative hairdresser— Male	13·75	13·30	13·75	13·30
Female	12·10	11·70	13·75	13·30

Provided that where under the terms of his employment a worker may at any time be required to do hairdressing for both ladies and gentlemen the rate applicable, in whichever saloon he is employed, shall be the rate appropriate to the worker when employed in either a ladies' or a gentlemen's saloon, whichever is the higher.

2m

MANAGER, MANAGERESS, CHARGEHAND

4. Subject to the provisions of paragraph 1, the minimum remuneration payable to a worker specified in Column 1 of the next following table employed in the London Area, Provincial A Area or Provincial B Area, as the case may be, shall be the appropriate amount set out in Column 2.

Column 1		Column 2 Worker employed in a			
		Ladies' Saloon		Gentlemen's Saloon	
		London Area	Provincial A Area and Provincial B Area	London Area	Provincial A Area and Provincial B Area
		Per week	Per week	Per week	Per week
		£	£	£	£
Chargehand—	Male	15·00	14·70	14·85	14·50
	Female	13·50	13·15	14·85	14·50
Manager		16·35	16·00	16·15	15·80
Manageress		14·80	14·45	16·15	15·80

Provided that where the worker is responsible for both a ladies' saloon and a gentlemen's saloon, the rate applicable shall be the rate appropriate to the worker when employed in either a ladies' saloon or a gentlemen's saloon, whichever is the higher.

EXPERIENCE UNDER THE GOVERNMENT VOCATIONAL TRAINING SCHEME

5. Where any worker has completed the period of training in hairdressing in respect of which training allowances are payable under the Government Vocational Training Scheme, such period of training shall, for the purposes of this Schedule, be treated as though it were a period of two years' employment as an operative hairdresser.

WORKERS OTHER THAN THOSE TO WHOM PARAGRAPH 3 OR PARAGRAPH 4 APPLIES

6. Subject to the provisions of paragraph 1, the minimum remuneration payable to male or female workers (other than workers to whom paragraph 3 or 4 applies) of the classes specified in Column 1 of the next following table employed in the London Area, Provincial A Area or Provincial B Area, as the case may be, shall be the appropriate amount set out in Column 2.

Column 1	Column 2					
	London Area Per week		Provincial A Area Per week		Provincial B Area Per week	
	Male	Female	Male	Female	Male	Female
	£	£	£	£	£	£
(1) Clerk, receptionist, manicurist, sales assistant, cashier, clerical assistant:—						
Aged 22 years or over	13·60	10·80	13·30	10·50	12·90	10·00
„ 21 and under 22 years	12·70	9·95	12·25	9·60	11·80	9·10
„ 20 „ „ 21 „	10·35	8·30	10·00	8·00	9·60	7·70
„ 19 „ „ 20 „	9·65	7·90	9·30	7·60	8·90	7·25
„ 18 „ „ 19 „	8·90	7·40	8·60	7·10	8·15	6·75
„ 17 „ „ 18 „	7·25	6·10	6·95	5·80	6·60	5·50
„ 16 „ „ 17 „	6·80	5·75	6·45	5·45	6·20	5·15
„ under 16 years	6·45	5·45	6·10	5·15	5·85	4·85
(2) All other workers:—						
Aged 22 years or over	13·00	10·40	12·75	10·10	12·55	9·65
„ 21 and under 22 years	12·50	9·75	12·10	9·45	11·60	8·95
„ 20 „ „ 21 „	10·30	8·25	9·95	7·95	9·45	7·60
„ 19 „ „ 20 „	9·60	7·90	9·25	7·50	8·80	7·15
„ 18 „ „ 19 „	8·80	7·30	8·50	7·05	8·10	6·65
„ 17 „ „ 18 „	7·20	6·05	6·85	5·70	6·55	5·45
„ 16 „ „ 17 „	6·75	5·70	6·40	5·35	6·10	5·10
„ under 16 years	6·35	5·35	6·05	5·10	5·80	4·80

APPRENTICES

CONDITIONS AS TO RATES FOR APPRENTICES

7.—(1) For the purposes of this Schedule "APPRENTICE" means any worker during the first three years of his apprenticeship during which the following conditions are satisfied, in respect of that worker, that is to say:—

(a) the worker shall be employed during the whole of his time under a written contract of apprenticeship which has been duly executed and which contains the following provisions or provisions substantially to the same effect and no provisions contrary thereto:—

(i) the worker of his own free will, and if he is under the age of 18 years with the consent of his guardian, binds himself to serve the employer as his apprentice in his trade of hairdressing for the term of not less than three years;

(ii) the employer will employ the worker as his apprentice during the said term and to the best of his power, skill and knowledge instruct the worker or cause him to be instructed in either ladies' or gentlemen's hairdressing or both;

(iii) the employer will keep the worker under his own supervision or place him under the supervision of one or more operative hairdressers;

(b) the total number of workers employed at any time at the establishment at which the worker works in respect of whom the conditions contained in (a) of this sub-paragraph are fulfilled or who are prospective apprentices to whom sub-paragraph (4) of this paragraph relates, shall not exceed one for each qualified operative hairdresser.

(2) For the purposes of this paragraph a person shall not be a qualified operative hairdresser unless:—

(i) he is wholly or mainly engaged in hairdressing and has completed not less than three years' service under a contract of apprenticeship which satisfies the conditions in sub-paragraph (1)(a) of this paragraph, or

(ii) he is wholly or mainly engaged in hairdressing and has completed a course of not less than two years' full-time training in hairdressing at a technical college or other similar institution approved by the Wages Council, or

(iii) he is wholly or mainly engaged in hairdressing and has been so engaged for not less than two years under a contract of employment other than a contract of apprenticeship in an undertaking to which this Schedule applies, or

(iv) if an employer or a manager he has had not less than three years' experience as a hairdresser.

(3) For the purposes of this paragraph:—

(i) no account shall be taken of a qualified operative hairdresser who is not employed in the branch or branches of hairdressing in which the worker is bound to serve;

(ii) no account shall be taken of a qualified operative hairdresser who does not normally work for the employer for at least 24 hours a week as a worker to whom this Schedule applies;

(iii) no account shall be taken of a temporary absence of a qualified operative hairdresser or a casual vacancy for a short period in the number of qualified operative hairdressers employed.

(4) Notwithstanding the foregoing provisions of this paragraph, where an employer employs a worker as a prospective apprentice for a probationary period not exceeding three months (or such extended period as is hereinafter mentioned) and the condition specified at (b) of sub-paragraph (1) of this paragraph is satisfied in the case of that worker, the minimum remuneration applicable to that worker during the probationary period shall be that applicable to an apprentice employed in accordance with the conditions specified in the provisions of sub-paragraph (1) of this paragraph, and, in the event of the worker being continued thereafter at his employment as an apprentice, the said probationary period shall, for the purposes of this Schedule, be treated as part of the period of apprenticeship, whether or not it is included therein. Where, before the expiration of three months from the commencement of employment as a prospective apprentice as aforesaid, the Wages Council has received and acknowledged in writing written notification of such employment, the said probationary period may be extended as the Wages Council may consider necessary or desirable:

Provided that such written notification shall be signed by both employer and worker and shall include a statement to the effect that—

(i) the signatories intend to enter into a written contract of apprenticeship, and that an extension of the probationary period is required for the drawing up and execution of such written contract, or

(ii) the worker has been absent from work for a stated reason on a stated number of days during the probationary period, or

(iii) the employer or worker is doubtful, on stated medical grounds supported by medical evidence, whether to enter into such written contract.

(5) A worker who, after attaining the age of 15 years, undergoes a full-time course of instruction in hairdressing of not less than two years' duration at any school or institution approved by the Wages Council, shall, at the end of the course of instruction, be deemed for the purposes of this paragraph to have served a period of three years' apprenticeship during which the conditions specified in sub-paragraph (1) of this paragraph were satisfied.

MINIMUM OVERTIME RATES

8. Overtime shall be payable to any worker at the following minimum rates:—

(1) On a Sunday or customary holiday—

for all time worked ... ,.. ... ... double time

Provided that where it is, or becomes, the established practice in a Jewish undertaking for the employer to require attendance on Sunday instead of Saturday, the foregoing provisions of this paragraph shall apply in like manner as if in such provisions the word "Saturday" were substituted for "Sunday", except where such substitution is unlawful.

(2) (a) On the weekly short day (not being the weekly short day to which (b) applies)—

for all time worked after 1.30 p.m. ... ... time-and-a-half

(b) On the weekly short day in any week during which, under section 40 of the Shops Act 1950(a), the employer is relieved of his obligation to allow the worker a weekly half-holiday—

for all time worked after 1.30 p.m. ... ... double time

(3) In any week, exclusive of any time in respect of which an overtime rate is payable under the provisions of (1) and (2) of this paragraph:

(a) for the first four hours worked in excess of 42... time-and-a-quarter

(b) thereafter ... ... time-and-a-half

Provided that in any week which includes one customary holiday "35 hours" shall be substituted for "42 hours" and in any week which includes two customary holidays "28 hours" shall be substituted for the said "42 hours".

WAITING TIME

9. A worker shall be entitled to payment of the minimum remuneration specified in this Schedule for all the time during which he is present on the premises of the employer, unless he is present thereon in any of the following circumstances, that is to say—

(1) without the employer's consent, express or implied ;

(2) for some purpose unconnected with his work, and other than that of waiting for work to be given to him to perform ;

(3) by reason only of the fact that he is resident thereon ; or

(4) during normal meal times in a room or place in which no work is being done, and he is not waiting for work to be given to him to perform.

GUARANTEED WEEKLY REMUNERATION PAYABLE TO A FULL-TIME WORKER

10.—(1) Notwithstanding the other provisions of this Schedule, where in any week the total remuneration (including holiday remuneration but excluding the amount specified in sub-paragraph (2) of this paragraph) payable under those

(a) 1950 c. 28.

other provisions to a full-time worker is less than the guaranteed weekly remuneration provided under this paragraph, the minimum remuneration payable to that worker for that week shall be that guaranteed weekly remuneration with the addition of any amount excluded as aforesaid.

(2) The amount to be excluded from the total remuneration referred to in the foregoing sub-paragraph is the whole of the remuneration payable in respect of overtime for work on a Sunday or on the weekly short day and one half of the remuneration payable in respect of overtime for work on a customary holiday.

(3) The guaranteed weekly remuneration is the remuneration to which the worker would be entitled under paragraph 3, 4 or 6 for 42 hours' work in his normal occupation:

Provided that

(a) where the worker normally works for the employer on work to which this Schedule applies for less than 42 hours in the week by reason only of the fact that he does not hold himself out as normally available for work for more than the number of hours he normally works in the week, and the worker has informed his employer in writing that he does not so hold himself out, the guaranteed weekly remuneration shall be the remuneration to which the worker would be entitled (calculated in accordance with paragraph 2) for the number of hours in the week normally worked by the worker for the employer on work to which this Schedule applies ;

(b) where in any week a worker at his request and with the written consent of his employer is absent from work during any part of his normal working hours on any day (other than a holiday allowed under Part II of this Schedule or a holiday allowed to all persons employed in the undertaking or branch of an undertaking in which the worker is employed), the guaranteed weekly remuneration payable in respect of that week shall be reduced in respect of each day on which he is absent as aforesaid by one-sixth where the worker's normal working week is six days or by one-fifth where his normal working week is five days.

(4) Guaranteed weekly remuneration is not payable in respect of any week unless the worker throughout his normal working hours in that week (excluding any time allowed to him as a holiday or during which he is absent from work in accordance with proviso (b) to sub-paragraph (3) of this paragraph) is

(a) capable of and available for work ; and

(b) willing to perform such duties outside his normal occupation as the employer may reasonably require if his normal work is not available in the establishment in which he is employed.

(5) Guaranteed weekly remuneration is not payable in respect of any week if the worker's employment is terminated before the end of that week.

(6) If the employer is unable to provide the worker with work by reason of a strike or other circumstances beyond his control and gives the worker four clear days' notice to that effect, guaranteed weekly remuneration shall not be payable after the expiry of such notice in respect of any week during which or during part of which the employer continues to be unable to provide work as aforesaid:

Provided that in respect of the week in which the said notice expires there shall be paid to the worker, in addition to any remuneration payable in respect of time worked in that week, any remuneration that would have been payable if the worker had worked his normal hours of work on every day in the week prior to the expiry of the notice.

Part II

HOLIDAYS AND HOLIDAY REMUNERATION
CUSTOMARY HOLIDAYS

11.—(1) An employer shall allow to every worker in his employment to whom this Schedule applies a holiday (in this Schedule referred to as a "customary holiday") in each year on the days specified in the next following sub-paragraph, provided that the worker has been in his employment for a period of not less than four weeks immediately preceding the customary holiday, and has worked for the employer during the whole or part of that period, and (unless excused by the employer or absent by reason of the proved illness of, or accident to, the worker) has worked for the employer throughout the last working day on which work was available to him immediately prior to the customary holiday.

(2) The said customary holidays are:—

(a) (i) In England and Wales—

Christmas Day (or, if Christmas Day falls on a Sunday, such week-day as may be appointed by national proclamation, or, if none is so appointed, the next following Tuesday), Boxing Day, Good Friday, Easter Monday, Whit Monday (or where another day is substituted therefor by national proclamation, that day) and August Bank Holiday;

(ii) In Scotland—

New Year's Day (or, if New Year's Day falls on a Sunday, the following Monday);

the local Spring holiday;

the local Autumn holiday;

Christmas Day (or, if Christmas Day falls on a Sunday, the following Monday); and

two other days observed by local custom as holidays to be fixed by the employer and notified to the worker;

or (b) in the case of each of the said days (other than a day fixed by the employer in Scotland and notified to the worker as aforesaid) a day substituted by the employer therefor, being a day recognised by local custom as a day of holiday.

(3) Notwithstanding the preceding provisions of this paragraph, an employer may (except where in the case of a woman or young person such a requirement would be unlawful) require a worker who is otherwise entitled to any customary holiday under the foregoing provisions of this Schedule to work thereon, and, in lieu of any such customary holiday on which he so works, the worker shall be allowed a day's holiday (hereinafter referred to as a "holiday in lieu of a customary holiday") on a week-day on which he would normally work within the period of 21 days next ensuing.

(4) A worker who is required to work on a customary holiday shall be paid:—

(a) for all time worked thereon, in accordance with paragraph 8; and

(b) in respect of the holiday in lieu of the customary holiday, holiday remuneration in accordance with paragraph 15.

ANNUAL HOLIDAY

12.—(1) In addition to the holidays specified in paragraph 11, an employer shall, between the date on which the provisions of this Schedule become effective and 31st October 1971, and in each succeeding year between 1st April and 31st October, allow a holiday (hereinafter referred to as an "annual holiday") to every worker in his employment to whom this Schedule applies who has been employed by him during the 12 months immediately preceding the commencement of the holiday season for any one of the periods of employment (calculated in accordance with the provisions of paragraph 19) set out in the table below and the duration of the annual holiday shall in the case of each such worker be related to that period as follows:—

Period of employment	Duration of annual holiday where the worker's normal working week is			
	Six days	Five days	Four days	Three days or less
12 months	12 days	10 days	8 days	6 days
Not less than 11 months but less than 12 months	11 ,,	9 ,,	7 ,,	5 ,,
,, ,, ,, 10 ,, ,, ,, ,, 11 ,,	10 ,,	8 ,,	7 ,,	5 ,,
,, ,, ,, 9 ,, ,, ,, ,, 10 ,,	9 ,,	7 ,,	6 ,,	4 ,,
,, ,, ,, 8 ,, ,, ,, ,, 9 ,,	8 ,,	7 ,,	5 ,,	4 ,,
,, ,, ,, 7 ,, ,, ,, ,, 8 ,,	7 ,,	6 ,,	5 ,,	3 ,,
,, ,, ,, 6 ,, ,, ,, ,, 7 ,,	6 ,,	5 ,,	4 ,,	3 ,,
,, ,, ,, 5 ,, ,, ,, ,, 6 ,,	5 ,,	4 ,,	3 ,,	2 ,,
,, ,, ,, 4 ,, ,, ,, ,, 5 ,,	4 ,,	3 ,,	3 ,,	2 ,,
,, ,, ,, 3 ,, ,, ,, ,, 4 ,,	3 ,,	2 ,,	2 ,,	1 day
,, ,, ,, 2 ,, ,, ,, ,, 3 ,,	2 ,,	2 ,,	1 day	1 ,,
,, ,, ,, 1 month ,, ,, ,, 2 ,,	1 day	1 day	1 ,,	nil

(2) Notwithstanding the provisions of the last foregoing sub-paragraph—

(a) the number of days of annual holiday which an employer is required to allow to a worker in any holiday season shall not exceed in the aggregate twice the number of days constituting the worker's normal working week;

(b) where a worker does not wish to take his annual holiday or part thereof during the holiday season in any year and, before the expiration of such holiday season, enters into an agreement in writing with his employer that the annual holiday or part thereof shall be allowed, at a date or dates to be specified in that agreement, after the expiration of the holiday season but before the commencement of the next following holiday season, then any day or days of annual holiday so allowed shall be treated as having been allowed during the holiday season.

(c) the duration of the worker's annual holiday during the holiday season ending on 31st October 1971, shall be reduced by any days of annual holiday duly allowed to him by the employer under the provisions of Order H.U. (42) between 1st April 1971 and the date on which the provisions of this Schedule become effective.

(3) In this Schedule the expression "holiday season" means in relation to the year 1971 the period commencing on 1st April 1971 and ending on 31st October 1971 and, in each succeeding year, the period commencing on 1st April and ending on 31st October of the same year.

13.—(1) Subject to the provisions of this paragraph, an annual holiday shall be allowed on consecutive working days, being days on which the worker is normally called upon to work for the employer.

(2) Where the number of days of annual holiday for which a worker has qualified exceeds the number of days constituting his normal working week, the holiday may be allowed in two periods of consecutive working days; so, however, that when a holiday is so allowed, one of the periods shall consist of a number of such days not less than the number of days constituting the worker's normal working week.

(3) For the purposes of this paragraph, days of annual holiday shall be treated as consecutive notwithstanding that a holiday allowed to a worker under paragraph 11 or a day on which he does not normally work for the employer intervenes.

(4) Where a holiday allowed to a worker under paragraph 11 immediately precedes a period of annual holiday or occurs during such a period and the total number of days of annual holiday required to be allowed in the period under the foregoing provisions of this paragraph, together with any such holiday, exceeds the number of days constituting the worker's normal working week, then, notwithstanding the foregoing provisions of this paragraph, the duration of that period of annual holiday may be reduced by one day and in such a case one day of annual holiday may be allowed on a day on which the worker normally works for the employer (not being the worker's weekly short day) in the holiday season or after the holiday season in the circumstances specified in sub-paragraph (2)(*b*) of paragraph 12.

(5) A day of annual holiday under this Schedule may be allowed on a day on which the worker is entitled to a day of holiday (not being a customary holiday) or to a half-holiday under any enactment other than the Wages Councils Act 1959: Provided that where the total number of days of annual holiday allowed to a worker under this Schedule is less than the number of days in his normal working week, the said annual holiday shall be in addition to the said day of holiday or the said half-holiday.

14. An employer shall give to a worker reasonable notice of the commencing date or dates and of the duration of his annual holiday. Such notice may be given individually to the worker or by the posting of a notice in the place where the worker is employed.

REMUNERATION FOR CUSTOMARY HOLIDAYS

15.—(1) Subject to the provisions of this paragraph, for each day of holiday to which a worker is entitled under paragraph 11 he shall be paid by the employer holiday remuneration equal to the statutory minimum remuneration to which he would have been entitled if the day had not been a day of holiday and he had been employed on work for which statutory minimum remuneration is payable for the time usually worked by him on that day of the week:

Provided, however, that payment of the said holiday remuneration is subject to the condition that the worker (unless excused by the employer or absent by reason of the proved illness of, or accident to, the worker) presents himself for employment at the usual starting hour on the first working day following the holiday.

(2) The holiday remuneration in respect of any customary holiday shall be paid by the employer to the worker on the day on which the wages for the first working day following the holiday are paid.

(3) The holiday remuneration in respect of any holiday in lieu of a customary holiday shall be paid on the day on which the wages are paid for the first working day following the holiday in lieu: Provided that the said payment shall be made immediately upon the termination of the worker's employment in the case where he ceases to be employed before being allowed a holiday in lieu of a customary holiday to which he is entitled, and in that case the condition specified in sub-paragraph (1) of this paragraph shall not apply.

REMUNERATION FOR ANNUAL HOLIDAY

16.—(1) Subject to the provisions of paragraph 17, a worker qualified to be allowed an annual holiday under this Schedule shall be paid by his employer, on the last pay-day preceding such holiday, one day's holiday pay in respect of each day thereof.

(2) Where an annual holiday is taken in more than one period the holiday remuneration shall be apportioned accordingly.

17. Where any accrued holiday remuneration has been paid by the employer to the worker (in accordance with paragraph 18 of this Schedule or with Order H.U. (42)) in respect of employment during either or both of the periods referred to in paragraph 18, the amount of holiday remuneration payable by the employer

in respect of any annual holiday for which the worker has qualified by reason of employment during the said period or periods, shall be reduced by the amount of the said accrued holiday remuneration unless that remuneration has been deducted from a previous payment of holiday remuneration made under the provisions of this Schedule or of Order H.U. (42).

ACCRUED HOLIDAY REMUNERATION PAYABLE ON TERMINATION OF EMPLOYMENT

18. Where a worker ceases to be employed by an employer after the provisions of this Schedule become effective the employer shall, immediately on the termination of the employment (hereinafter referred to as the "termination date"), pay to the worker as accrued holiday remuneration:—

(1) in respect of employment in the 12 months up to 1st April immediately preceding the termination date, a sum equal to the holiday remuneration for any days of annual holiday for which he has qualified except days of annual holiday which he has been allowed or has become entitled to be allowed before leaving the employment; and

(2) in respect of any employment since 1st April immediately preceding the termination date, a sum equal to the holiday remuneration which would have been payable to him if he could have been allowed an annual holiday in respect of that employment at the time of leaving it:
Provided that—

    (a) no worker shall be entitled to the payment by his employer of accrued holiday remuneration if he is dismissed on the grounds of misconduct and is so informed by the employer at the time of dismissal;

    (b) where a worker is employed under a contract of service under which he is required to give not less than one week's notice before terminating his employment and the worker, without the consent of his employer, terminates his employment without having given not less than one week's notice or before one week has expired from the beginning of such notice, the amount of accrued holiday remuneration payable to the worker shall be the amount payable under the foregoing provision of this paragraph less an amount equal to the statutory minimum remuneration which would be payable to him at the termination date for one week's work if working his normal working week and the normal number of daily hours worked by him.

CALCULATION OF EMPLOYMENT

19. For the purposes of calculating any period of employment qualifying a worker for an annual holiday or for any accrued holiday remuneration, the worker shall be treated as if he were employed for a month in respect of any month throughout which he has been in the employment of the employer.

PART III

GENERAL

DEFINITIONS

20. In this Schedule "APPRENTICE" has the meaning assigned to it in paragraph 7 and the following expressions have the meanings hereby assigned to them—

"CHARGEHAND" means an operative hairdresser responsible to a manager or manageress, or to an employer performing the duties of a manager or a manageress, for the control and supervision of staff.

"CLERK" or "RECEPTIONIST" means a worker who is wholly or mainly engaged in one or more of the following activities:—clerical work which includes responsibility for maintaining ledgers or wages books or for preparing financial accounts of a hairdressing undertaking or of a branch or department thereof ; receiving customers or arranging customer's appointments.

"FULL-TIME WORKER" means a worker who normally works for the employer for at least 36 hours in the week on work to which this Schedule applies.

"HAIRDRESSING" and "HAIRDRESSING UNDERTAKING" have the meanings respectively assigned to them in paragraph 22.

"LONDON AREA", "PROVINCIAL A AREA" and "PROVINCIAL B AREA" have the meanings respectively assigned to them in paragraph 21.

"MANAGER" or "MANAGERESS" means a worker responsible to the employer for the conduct of a hairdressing undertaking, including supervision and training of staff, control of cash and records and care of equipment and premises.

"MANICURIST" means a worker who is wholly or mainly engaged in manicuring.

"MONTH" means the period commencing on a date of any number in one month and ending on the day before the date of the same number in the next month, or, if the commencing date is the 29th, 30th or 31st day of a month and there is no date of the same number in the next month, then on the last day of that month.

"NORMAL WORKING WEEK" means the number of days on which it has been usual for the worker to work in a week while in the employment of the employer during the 12 months immediately preceding the commencement of the holiday season, or, where accrued holiday remuneration is payable under (2) of paragraph 18 on the termination of the employment, during the 12 months immediately preceding the termination date:

Provided that—

(1) part of a day shall count as a day ;

(2) no account shall be taken of any week in which the worker did not perform any work for which statutory minimum remuneration has been fixed.

"ONE DAY'S HOLIDAY PAY" means the appropriate proportion of the remuneration which the worker would be entitled to receive from his employer at the date of the annual holiday (or, where the annual holiday is taken in more than one period, at the date of the first period) or at the termination date, as the case may be, for one week's work if working his normal working week and the number of daily hours normally worked by him (exclusive of overtime), and if paid at the appropriate rate of statutory minimum remuneration for work for which statutory minimum remuneration is payable and at the same rate for any work for the same employer for which such remuneration is not payable, that is to say:—

where the worker's normal working week is six days						...	...	one-sixth
„	„	„	„	„	„	„ five „	...	...	one-fifth
„	„	„	„	„	„	„ four „	...	...	one-quarter
„	„	„	„	„	„	„ three „	...	...	one-third
„	„	„	„	„	„	„ two „	...	...	one-half
„	„	„	„	„	„	„ one day	...	...	the whole.

"OPERATIVE HAIRDRESSER" means a worker, other than an apprentice, a manager or manageress, who is wholly or mainly engaged in hairdressing.

"SALES ASSISTANT", "CASHIER" or "CLERICAL ASSISTANT" means a worker (other than a clerk or receptionist) who is wholly or mainly engaged in one or more of the following activities:—the serving of customers making retail purchases of goods, receiving cash or giving change, clerical work.

"TIME-AND-A-QUARTER", "TIME-AND-A-HALF" and "DOUBLE TIME" mean, respectively, one and a quarter times, one and a half times and twice the hourly rate obtained by dividing by 42 the minimum weekly remuneration to which the worker is entitled under the provisions of paragraph 3, 4 or 6.

"WEEK" means pay week.

"WEEKLY SHORT DAY" means that day in any week on which the worker is, in accordance with the provisions of section 17 of the Shops Act 1950, required not to be employed about the business of a shop after half-past one o'clock in the afternoon, or—

(1) where the day falls on a customary holiday, a working day not being a customary holiday within the period of 21 days next ensuing, to be fixed by the employer and notified to the worker not later than the Saturday preceding the week during which it is to have effect ; or, failing such notification, the last working day in the said period of 21 days not being a customary holiday ;

(2) where there is no such day, a working day in the week, not being a customary holiday, fixed by the employer and notified to the worker not later than the Saturday preceding the week during which it is to have effect ; or, failing such notification, the last working day in the week not being a customary holiday.

AREAS

21. In this Schedule:—

(1) "LONDON AREA" means the Metropolitan Police District, as defined in the London Government Act 1963(**a**), the City of London, the Inner Temple and the Middle Temple.

(2) "PROVINCIAL A AREA" means
   (*a*) In Scotland,
     (i) the following burghs:—

ABERDEEN COUNTY
Aberdeen (including part in Kincardine County)
Fraserburgh
Peterhead

ANGUS COUNTY
Arbroath
Brechin
Dundee
Forfar
Montrose

ARGYLL COUNTY
Dunoon

AYR COUNTY
Ardrossan
Ayr
Irvine
Kilmarnock
Largs
Prestwick
Saltcoats
Stevenston
Troon

BANFF COUNTY
Buckie

BUTE COUNTY
Rothesay

CLACKMANNAN COUNTY
Alloa

DUMFRIES COUNTY
Dumfries

DUNBARTON COUNTY
Bearsden
Clydebank
Dumbarton
Helensburgh
Kirkintilloch
Milngavie

EAST LOTHIAN COUNTY
North Berwick

FIFE COUNTY
Buckhaven and Methil
Burntisland
Cowdenbeath
Dunfermline
Kirkcaldy
Leven
Lochgelly
St. Andrews

INVERNESS COUNTY
Inverness

KINCARDINE COUNTY
Stonehaven

LANARK COUNTY
Airdrie
Coatbridge
Glasgow
Hamilton
Lanark
Motherwell and Wishaw
Rutherglen

MIDLOTHIAN COUNTY
Dalkeith
Edinburgh
Musselburgh

MORAY COUNTY
Elgin

ORKNEY COUNTY
Kirkwall

PERTH COUNTY
Perth

RENFREW COUNTY
Barrhead
Gourock
Greenock
Johnstone
Paisley
Port Glasgow
Renfrew

ROSS AND CROMARTY COUNTY
Stornoway

ROXBURGH COUNTY
Hawick

SELKIRK COUNTY
Galashiels

STIRLING COUNTY
Denny and Dunipace
Falkirk
Grangemouth
Kilsyth
Stirling

WEST LOTHIAN COUNTY
Armadale
Bathgate
Bo'ness

WIGTOWN COUNTY
Stranraer

ZETLAND COUNTY
Lerwick

     (ii) The following Special Lighting Districts, the boundaries of which have been defined, namely, Vale of Leven and Renton in the County of Dunbarton ; and Larbert and Airth in the County of Stirling ; and

(**a**) 1963 c. 33.

(iii) The following areas, the boundaries of which were defined as Special Lighting Districts prior to 10th March 1943, namely:—Bellshill and Mossend, Blantyre, Cambuslang, Larkhall and Holytown, New Stevenston and Carfin, all in the County of Lanark.

(b) In England and Wales, the areas administered by County Borough, Municipal Borough or Urban District Councils, except where they are included in the London area or are listed in (3)(b) of this paragraph.

(3) "PROVINCIAL B AREA" means

(a) In Scotland, all areas other than those listed in (2)(a) of this paragraph ;

(b) In England and Wales, all areas not included in the London area administered by Rural District Councils, and the areas administered by the following Municipal Borough and Urban District Councils:—

ENGLAND (excluding Monmouthshire)

BEDFORDSHIRE
Ampthill
Sandy

BERKSHIRE
Wallingford
Wantage

BUCKINGHAMSHIRE
Buckingham
Linslade
Marlow
Newport Pagnell

CHESHIRE
Alsager
Longdendale

CORNWALL
Bodmin
Bude Stratton
Fowey
Helston
Launceston
Liskeard
Looe
Lostwithiel
Padstow
Penryn.
St. Just
Torpoint

DERBYSHIRE
Bakewell
Whaley Bridge
Wirksworth

DEVON
Ashburton
Buckfastleigh
Budleigh Salterton
Crediton

DEVON—contd.
Dartmouth
Great Torrington
Holsworthy
Honiton
Kingsbridge
Lynton
Northam
Okehampton
Ottery St. Mary
Salcombe
Seaton
South Molton
Tavistock
Totnes

DORSET
Blandford Forum
Lyme Regis
Shaftesbury
Sherborne
Wareham
Wimborne Minster

DURHAM
Barnard Castle
Tow Law

ELY, ISLE OF
Chatteris

ESSEX
Brightlingsea
Burnham-on-Crouch
Saffron Walden
West Mersea
Wivenhoe

GLOUCESTERSHIRE
Nailsworth
Tewkesbury

HEREFORDSHIRE
Bromyard
Kington
Ledbury

HERTFORDSHIRE
Baldock
Chorleywood
Royston
Sawbridgeworth

HUNTINGDONSHIRE
Huntingdon and
   Godmanchester
Ramsey
St. Ives
St. Neots

KENT
Lydd
New Romney
Queenborough
Sandwich
Tenterden

LANCASHIRE
Carnforth
Grange

LINCOLNSHIRE
Alford
Barton-upon-Humber
Bourne
Brigg
Horncastle
Mablethorpe and Sutton
Market Rasen
Woodhall Spa

ENGLAND (excluding Monmouthshire)—*contd.*

NORFOLK
Cromer
Diss
Downham Market
Hunstanton
North Walsham
Sheringham
Swaffham
Thetford
Wells-next-the-Sea
Wymondham

NORTHAMPTON-
SHIRE
Brackley
Burton Latimer
Higham Ferrers
Oundle

NORTHUMBERLAND
Alnwick
Amble

OXFORDSHIRE
Bicester
Chipping Norton
Thame
Woodstock

RUTLAND
Oakham

SHROPSHIRE
Bishop's Castle
Church Stretton
Ellesmere
Market Drayton
Newport
Wem

SOMERSET
Chard
Crewkerne
Glastonbury
Ilminster
Portishead
Shepton Mallet
Street
Watchet
Wellington

SUFFOLK
Aldeburgh
Beccles
Bungay
Eye
Hadleigh
Halesworth
Haverhill
Leiston-cum-Sizewell
Saxmundham
Southwold
Sudbury
Stowmarket
Woodbridge

SUSSEX
Arundel
Rye

WESTMORLAND
Appleby
Lakes

WILTSHIRE
Bradford-on-Avon
Calne
Malmesbury
Marlborough
Melksham
Westbury
Wilton

WORCESTERSHIRE
Bewdley
Droitwich

YORKSHIRE
Hedon
Hornsea
Malton
Norton
Pickering
Richmond
Tickhill
Withernsea

WALES AND MONMOUTHSHIRE

ANGLESEY
Almwch
Beaumaris
Llangefni
Menai Bridge

BRECKONSHIRE
Builth Wells
Hay
Llanwrtyd Wells

CAERNARVONSHIRE
Bethesda
Betws-y-Coed
Criccieth
Llanfairfechan
Penmaenmawr
Portmadoc
Pwllheli

CARDIGANSHIRE
Aberayron
Cardigan
Lampeter
New Quay

CARMARTHENSHIRE
Cwmamman
Kidwelly
Llandeilo
Llandovery
Newcastle Emlyn

DENBIGHSHIRE
Llangollen
Llanrwst
Ruthin

FLINTSHIRE
Buckley
Mold

GLAMORGAN
Cowbridge

MERIONETHSHIRE
Bala
Barmouth
Dolgellau
Towyn

MONMOUTHSHIRE
Caerleon
Chepstow
Usk

MONTGOMERYSHIRE
Llanfyllin
Llanidloes
Machynlleth
Montgomery
Newtown and
    Llanllwchaiarn
Welshpool

PEMBROKESHIRE
Fishguard and
    Goodwick
Narberth
Neyland
Tenby

RADNORSHIRE
Knighton
Llandrindod Wells
Presteigne

(4) Any reference to a local government area shall be construed as a reference to that area as it was on 23rd April 1961, unless otherwise stated.

WORKERS TO WHOM THIS SCHEDULE APPLIES

22.—(1) Subject to the provisions of this paragraph and of paragraph 23, this Schedule applies to the workers in relation to whom the Hairdressing Undertakings Wages Council (Great Britain) operates, that is to say, workers specified in the Schedule to the Wages Council (Hairdressing Undertakings, Great Britain) Order 1947(a), namely:—

all workers employed in Great Britain in a hairdressing undertaking in respect of their employment in such undertaking.

(2) This Schedule does not apply to any of the following workers in respect of their employment in any of the following circumstances, that is to say

(a) workers who are employed exclusively as chiropodists ;

(b) workers employed in a department of a hairdressing undertaking being a department which is wholly or mainly engaged in the retail sale of goods (other than hairdressers' sundries) ;

(c) workers employed by an employer engaged in the production of cinematograph films on work in connection with such production ;

(d) registered members of the Institute of Trichologists (Incorporated) employed exclusively in their professional capacity as trichologists ;

(e) workers employed by a Regional Hospital Board or Board of Governors of a Teaching Hospital, while so employed.

(3) In this Schedule the following expressions have the meanings hereby assigned to them:—

"hairdressing undertaking" means an undertaking or any part of an undertaking which is wholly or mainly engaged in hairdressing, including operations incidental or ancillary thereto ;

"hairdressing" includes the following operations performed on hair growing on the head, face or neck of a male or female person, that is to say, lathering, shaving, cutting, singeing, shampooing, waving, setting, dressing, tinting, dyeing, bleaching and similar operations.

TRAINING UNDER THE GOVERNMENT VOCATIONAL TRAINING SCHEME

23. Notwithstanding anything hereinbefore contained, this Schedule does not apply to trainees during any period in respect of which they are in receipt of allowances as provided under the Government Vocational Training Scheme for resettlement training if they are trainees who have been placed by the Department of Employment with the employer for a period of approved training and if the requirements of the said Scheme are duly complied with.

EXPLANATORY NOTE
(This Note is not part of the Order.)

This Order, which has effect from 13th September 1971, sets out the statutory minimum remuneration payable and the holidays to be allowed in substitution for the statutory minimum remuneration and holidays set out in the Wages Regulation (Hairdressing) Order 1970 (Order H.U. (42)) which Order is revoked.

New provisions are printed in italics.

(a) S.R. & O. 1947/1879 (Rev. XXIII, p. 437: 1947 I, p. 2474).

STATUTORY INSTRUMENTS

1971 No. 1137

ANIMALS

DISEASES OF ANIMALS

The Equine Animals (Importation) Amendment Order 1971

Made - - -	14*th July* 1971
Laid before Parliament	14*th July* 1971
Coming into Operation	15*th July* 1971

The Minister of Agriculture, Fisheries and Food and the Secretary of State, acting jointly, in exercise of the powers vested in them under sections 1(1), 24(1), 33(1)(xii), 84(3)(a) and 85(1) of the Diseases of Animals Act 1950(a), (as extended by the Diseases of Animals (Extension of Definitions) Order 1952(b), as adapted to air transport by section 11(1) of the Agriculture (Miscellaneous Provisions) Act 1954(c), and read with the Transfer of Functions (Animal Health) Order 1955(d) and as amended by section 105(1) of the Agriculture Act 1970(e)) and all other powers enabling them in that behalf, hereby order as follows :—

Citation, interpretation and commencement

1. This order, which may be cited as the Equine Animals (Importation) Amendment Order 1971, shall be construed as one with the Equine Animals (Importation) Order 1969(f) (in this order referred to as "the principal order"), and shall come into operation on 15th July 1971.

Amendment of Principal Order

2. Article 4 of the principal order (which contains provisions regulating the importation of equine animals into Great Britain) shall be amended as follows :—

(a) by the deletion of paragraph (2) thereof and the substitution therefor of the following paragraph—

"(2) The landing or unloading in Great Britain of any equine animal brought from any country (not being a specified country) outside Great Britain, except Northern Ireland, the Republic of

---

(a) 1950 c. 36.   For change of title of the Minister see S.I. 1955/554 (1955 I, p. 1200).
(b) S.I. 1952/1236 (1952 I, p. 128).   (c) 1954 c. 39.
(d) S.I. 1955/958 (1955 I, p. 1184).   (e) 1970 c. 40.
(f) S.I. 1969/915 (1969 II, p. 2791).

Ireland, the Channel Islands or the Isle of Man, is hereby prohibited unless—

(a) in the case of an equine animal brought from any country in Europe, it is accompanied by a certificate as mentioned in article 5 below of a veterinary surgeon duly authorised by the government of the country from which the equine animal was brought, or

(b) in the case of an equine animal brought from any country outside Europe, it is landed or unloaded under the authority and in accordance with the provisions of a licence issued by the Minister".

(b) by the insertion of the following paragraphs immediately following paragraph (3) thereof —

"(4) A licence referred to in paragraph (2)(b) of this Article (which may be either general or specific and in either case conditional or unconditional) may be issued by the Minister, in the case of a general licence by publication of the terms of such licence to an extent which appears sufficient in the opinion of the Minister to bring the licence to the attention of interested persons, or in the case of a specific licence, which shall be in writing, by delivery of such licence to the licensee to whom it is granted.

(5) Failure to comply with any condition of a licence issued under this order shall be an offence against the Act.

(6) In this article the expression "the Minister" in the application of this order to England and Wales means the Minister of Agriculture, Fisheries and Food and in its corresponding application to Scotland means the Secretary of State."

In Witness whereof the Official Seal of the Minister of Agriculture, Fisheries and Food is hereunto affixed on 13th July 1971.

(L.S.) *J. M. L. Prior,*
Minister of Agriculture, Fisheries and Food.

Gordon Campbell,
14th July 1971. Secretary of State for Scotland.

EXPLANATORY NOTE
(*This Note is not part of the Order.*)

This order amends the Equine Animals (Importation) Order 1969 by providing that equine animals from countries outside Europe (other than countries from which importation is altogether forbidden by the principal order) can no longer be imported into Great Britain without restriction if accompanied by an appropriate veterinary certificate but must now have their importation authorised by a licence issued by the Minister.

STATUTORY INSTRUMENTS

1971 No. 1141

POLICE

The Police (Amendment) (No. 2) Regulations 1971

Made - - -	*15th July* 1971
Laid before Parliament	*23rd July* 1971
Coming into Operation	*1st August* 1971

In exercise of the powers conferred on me by section 33 of the Police Act 1964(**a**), and after consulting the Police Council for the United Kingdom in accordance with section 4(4) of the Police Act 1969(**b**), I hereby make the following Regulations :—

PART I

CITATION, OPERATION ETC.

1. These Regulations may be cited as the Police (Amendment) (No. 2) Regulations 1971.

2. These Regulations shall come into operation on 1st August 1971 and shall have effect—

(*a*) for the purposes of Part II thereof, as from that date ;

(*b*) for the purposes of Part III thereof, as from 1st September 1971.

3. In these Regulations any reference to the principal Regulations is a reference to the Police Regulations 1971(**c**), as amended (**d**).

PART II

AMENDMENTS TAKING EFFECT AS FROM 1ST AUGUST 1971

4. For Regulation 33 of the principal Regulations (reckoning of previous service) there shall be substituted the following Regulation :—

"*Reckoning of previous service*

33.—(1) A member of a police force of the rank of constable who, on or after 10th May 1948, rejoined or joined that force, having previously resigned from that or some other force, shall be entitled to reckon for the purposes of the scale of pay for the rank of constable the service which was so reckonable immediately before he previously resigned.

(2) For the purposes of the foregoing provisions of this Part of these Regulations, where a member of a police force has transferred thereto from some other force, his service in those two forces shall be treated as if it

---

(**a**) 1964 c. 48. (**b**) 1969 c. 63.
(**c**) S.I. 1971/156 (1971 I, p. 439).
(**d**) The amending Regulations are not relevant to the subject matter of these Regulations.

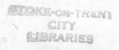

were service in the same police force ; but for the purposes hereof Regulation 32(2) shall have effect as if the words "on temporary promotion thereto" were omitted in each place where they occur :

Provided that in the case of a member of a police force of a rank higher than that of inspector who voluntarily transferred thereto from some other force, this paragraph shall have effect subject to any contrary agreement.".

5. For Regulation 36(4) of the principal Regulations (certified service in the British South Africa Police) there shall be substituted the following provision :—

"(4) The reference in paragraph (1) to certified service in the British South Africa Police is a reference to continuous service as a member thereof, for a period which included 11th November 1965, up to such time, on or after that date, as the person concerned ceased to perform duties therein, subject to his having ceased to perform those duties before 2nd March 1970 and subject to it having been certified by or on behalf of the Secretary of State that he approves the application of this Regulation in the case of the person concerned ; and a certificate given (or having effect as if it had been given) for the purposes of this paragraph as originally made shall be deemed to be such a certificate.".

6. After Regulation 49 of the principal Regulations there shall be inserted the following Regulation :—

"Women's stockings allowance

49A. A woman member of a police force who is not supplied with stockings or tights by the police authority shall be paid in lieu an allowance at the rate of £9 a year unless she is being paid either a uniform allowance under Regulation 48 or a plain clothes allowance under Regulation 50(1).".

7. In Regulation 51(2) of the principal Regulations (detective expenses allowance) for the rate "£0·50 a week" there shall be substituted the rate "£1 a week".

8.—(1) In Schedule 11 to the principal Regulations (issue of uniform and equipment) the entry relating to stockings shall be omitted from the second Table in paragraph 1.

(2) After paragraph 3 of the said Schedule 11 there shall be inserted the following paragraph :—

"3A. Where, in the case of women members, stockings or tights are provided by the police authority for the purposes of duty the issue shall be at the rate of 18 pairs annually.".

PART III

AMENDMENT TAKING EFFECT AS FROM 1ST SEPTEMBER 1971

9. In Regulation 37(2) of the principal Regulations (deductions from pay of sickness or injury benefits) for the words "and, for the purposes thereof" to the end there shall be substituted the following words :—

"and, for the purposes thereof, a policewoman who, as a married woman or a widow, is excepted from liability to pay contributions under section 3 of the National Insurance Act 1965(a) shall be deemed to be entitled to any sickness benefit, together with any supplement thereto payable under section 2 of the National Insurance Act 1966(b), to which she would have been entitled had she not been so excepted.".

R. Maudling,
One of Her Majesty's Principal
Secretaries of State.

Home Office,
Whitehall.
15th July 1971.

EXPLANATORY NOTE

(*This Note is not part of the Regulations.*)

These Regulations amend the Police Regulations 1971.

Regulations 4 and 5 amend provisions governing the reckoning of previous service for the purposes of pay by extending the provisions applicable in the case of persons who transfer between home police forces and by making fresh provision for the certification of previous service in the British South Africa Police.

Regulations 6 and 8 provide that a policewoman who is issued with stockings (or tights) shall receive 18 instead of 12 pairs annually but that she may, instead, be paid an allowance.

Regulation 7 increases the rate of a detective expenses allowance.

Regulation 9 relates to the deduction from pay of national insurance sickness benefit and provides that a married or widowed policewoman who does not receive such benefit because she is excepted from the liability to pay national insurance contributions shall be liable to the like deduction as would fall to be made if she paid contributions and received such benefit.

(a) 1965 c. 51.   (b) 1966 c. 6.

STATUTORY INSTRUMENTS

1971 No. 1142

ROAD TRAFFIC

The Public Service Vehicles (Definition of Express Carriage) Regulations 1971

Made - - -	16*th July* 1971
Laid before Parliament	26*th July* 1971
Coming into Operation	9*th August* 1971

The Secretary of State for the Environment, in exercise of his powers under sections 117(3) and 160(1) of the Road Traffic Act 1960(a) and of all other enabling powers, and after consultation with representative organisations in accordance with section 260(2) of that Act, hereby makes the following Regulations:—

1. These Regulations may be cited as the Public Service Vehicles (Definition of Express Carriage) Regulations 1971 and shall come into operation on 9th August 1971.

2. The Interpretation Act 1889(b) shall apply for the interpretation of these Regulations as it applies for the interpretation of an Act of Parliament.

3. In subsection (3) of section 117 of the Road Traffic Act 1960 (which provides that for the purposes of that Act an express carriage is a public service vehicle carrying passengers at separate fares none of which is less than one shilling or such greater sum as may be prescribed) the sum of 11 new pence shall be the greater sum for that purpose.

Signed by authority of the Secretary of State 16th July 1971.

John Peyton,
Minister for Transport Industries,
Department of the Environment.

EXPLANATORY NOTE

(This Note is not part of the Regulations.)

Section 117(3) of the Road Traffic Act 1960 defines an express carriage as a public service vehicle carrying passengers at separate fares of which the minimum is one shilling (5 new pence). These Regulations prescribe that the minimum fare for this purpose shall be 11 new pence.

(a) 1960 c. 16.   (b) 1889 c. 63.

STATUTORY INSTRUMENTS

1971 No. 1144

IRON AND STEEL

The Iron and Steel (Borrowing Powers) Order 1971

Laid before the House of Commons in draft

Made - - - - 16th July 1971

Coming into Operation 9th August 1971

The Secretary of State in exercise of his powers under section 3(1) of the Iron and Steel Act 1969(a) and all other powers him enabling hereby makes the following Order, a draft of which has been approved by a resolution of the Commons House of Parliament in accordance with subsection (2) of the said section 3 :—

1. This Order may be cited as the Iron and Steel (Borrowing Powers) Order 1971 and shall come into operation on 9th August 1971.

2. The aggregate of the amounts outstanding in respect of any borrowing by the British Steel Corporation and the publicly-owned companies and of any sums paid to the British Steel Corporation by the Secretary of State, mentioned in the said section 3(1), shall not exceed the sum of £650 million.

Dated 16th July 1971.

John Davies,
Secretary of State for Trade and Industry.

EXPLANATORY NOTE

(This Note is not part of the Order.)

Section 3 of the Iron and Steel Act 1969 sets an overall limit on borrowing by the British Steel Corporation and the publicly-owned companies and investment by the Secretary of State in the British Steel Corporation of £500 million or such greater sum not exceeding £650 million as may be specified by the Secretary of State by Order.

This Order specifies the maximum permissible limit as £650 million.

(a) 1969 c. 45.

STATUTORY INSTRUMENTS

1971 No. 1145

PURCHASE TAX

The Purchase Tax (No. 4) Order 1971

Made - - - -	19*th July* 1971
Laid before the House of Commons - - -	19*th July* 1971
Coming into Operation -	20*th July* 1971

The Lords Commissioners of Her Majesty's Treasury, by virtue of the powers conferred on them by section 2(3) of the Purchase Tax Act 1963(**a**), and of all other powers enabling them in that behalf, hereby make the following Order:—

1.—(1) This Order may be cited as the Purchase Tax (No. 4) Order 1971.

(2) The Interpretation Act 1889(**b**) shall apply for the interpretation of this Order as it applies for the interpretation of an Act of Parliament.

(3) This Order shall come into operation on 20th July 1971.

2. Part I of Schedule 1 to the Purchase Tax Act 1963, as amended by section 1(4) of the Finance Act 1969(**c**), shall have effect with the substitution—

(*a*) for any reference to $13\frac{3}{4}$ per cent. of a reference to $11\frac{1}{4}$ per cent.;

(*b*) for any reference to 22 per cent. of a reference to 18 per cent.;

(*c*) for any reference to $36\frac{2}{3}$ per cent. of a reference to 30 per cent.; and

(*d*) for any reference to 55 per cent. of a reference to 45 per cent.

Edward Heath,

Anthony Barber,

Two of the Lords Commissioners of Her Majesty's Treasury.

19th July 1971.

EXPLANATORY NOTE

(*This Note is not part of the Order.*)

This Order reduces to $11\frac{1}{4}$ per cent., 18 per cent., 30 per cent. and 45 per cent. the rates of purchase tax on the classes of goods heretofore taxable respectively at $13\frac{3}{4}$ per cent., 22 per cent., $36\frac{2}{3}$ per cent. and 55 per cent.

(**a**) 1963 c. 9. (**b**) 1889 c. 63. (**c**) 1969 c. 32.

STATUTORY INSTRUMENTS

1971 No. 1146

HIRE PURCHASE

The Control of Hiring (Revocation) Order 1971

Made - - - -	19*th July* 1971
Laid before Parliament -	19*th July* 1971
Coming into Operation	20*th July* 1971

The Secretary of State in exercise of his powers under sections 1 and 7 of the Emergency Laws (Re-enactment and Repeals) Act 1964(a) hereby orders as follows:—

1. This Order may be cited as the Control of Hiring (Revocation) Order 1971 and shall come into operation on 20th July 1971.

2. The Control of Hiring Order 1969(b) is hereby revoked.

John Davies,

Secretary of State for Trade and Industry.

19th July 1971.

(a) 1964 c. 60.   (b) S.I. 1969/1307 (1969 III, p. 3888).

STATUTORY INSTRUMENTS

1971 No. 1147

HIRE PURCHASE

The Hire-Purchase and Credit Sale Agreements (Control) (Revocation) Order 1971

Made - - -	19th July 1971
Laid before Parliament	19th July 1971
Coming into Operation	20th July 1971

The Secretary of State in exercise of his powers under sections 1 and 7 of the Emergency Laws (Re-enactments and Repeals) Act 1964(a) hereby orders as follows:—

1. This Order may be cited as the Hire-Purchase and Credit Sale Agreements (Control) (Revocation) Order 1971 and shall come into operation on 20th July 1971.

2. The Hire-Purchase and Credit Sale Agreements (Control) Order 1969(b) is hereby revoked.

John Davies,

Secretary of State for Trade and Industry.

19th July 1971.

(a) 1964 c. 60.   (b) S.I. 1969/1308 (1969 III, p. 3899).

STATUTORY INSTRUMENTS

1971 No. 1149 (C.28)

SOCIAL SECURITY

The National Insurance Act 1971 (Commencement No. 1) Order 1971

Made - - -	16*th July* 1971	
Laid before Parliament	23*rd July* 1971	
Coming into Operation	26*th July* 1971	

The Secretary of State for Social Services, in conjunction with the Treasury, and in exercise of powers conferred by section 16(3) of and paragraph 1 of Schedule 6 to the National Insurance Act 1971(a) and of all other powers enabling him in that behalf, hereby makes the following Order :—

Citation and commencement

1. This Order may be cited as the National Insurance Act 1971 (Commencement No. 1) Order 1971 and shall come into operation on 26th July 1971.

Appointed days

2.—(1) Subject to the following provisions of this Order, the day appointed for the coming into force of any provision of the National Insurance Act 1971 specified in column 1 of the Schedule to this Order, so far as that provision relates to any subject matter specified in column 2 of that Schedule, shall be the date specified in column 3 of that Schedule in relation to that subject matter.

(2) As respects the period beginning with 20th September 1971 and ending with 22nd September 1971, the rate of a person's unemployment or sickness benefit for any day in that period by virtue of section 19(3) of the National Insurance Act 1965(b) (which relates to unemployment and sickness benefit for persons over pensionable age and regulates the rate of benefit in such cases by reference to the rate of retirement pension) shall be determined as if the day appointed for the coming into force of the provisions of the said Act of 1971 relating to higher rates of retirement pension under the said Act of 1965 were 23rd September 1971.

(3) In the case of a person to whom injury benefit under the National Insurance (Industrial Injuries) Act 1965(c) is payable for 22nd September 1971 at a reduced weekly rate by virtue of the provisions of section 29(1) of that Act (which relates to adjustments for successive accidents), the rate of that injury benefit and of any sickness benefit payable under the National Insurance Act 1965 shall be determined as if the day appointed for the coming into force of the provisions of the said Act of 1971 relating to higher rates of those

(a) 1971 c. 50.   (b) 1965 c. 51.   (c) 1965 c. 52.

benefits were 22nd September 1971 and, where appropriate, as if the reference to 23rd September 1971 in the last preceding paragraph were a reference to 22nd September 1971.

Keith Joseph,
Secretary of State for Social Services.

15th July 1971.

Bernard Weatherill,
Walter Clegg,
Two of the Lords Commissioners of Her Majesty's Treasury.

16th July 1971.

Article 2   SCHEDULE

Provisions of the National Insurance Act 1971	Subject Matter	Appointed Day
Section 1(1) and (2) and Schedule 1	Higher rates of flat-rate contributions under the National Insurance Act 1965	20th September 1971
Section 1(3)	Higher aggregate graduated contributions under the National Insurance Act 1965	21st September 1971
Section 1(4) (in relation only to the following provision)	Higher income limit for exception from liability to pay contributions	20th September 1971
Section 1(4) (in relation only to the following provision)	Relaxation of restrictions on crediting of contributions to persons excepted from liability on grounds of small income	6th September 1971
Section 1(5)	Payments to the National Insurance Fund out of money provided by Parliament in addition to Exchequer supplements	20th September 1971
Section 2(1) and Schedule 2	Rates of benefit under the National Insurance Act 1965 in the case of— (*a*) unemployment, sickness and invalidity benefit (*b*) maternity allowance (*c*) widow's benefit, guardian's allowance, retirement pension, age addition and child's special allowance (*d*) attendance allowance	23rd September 1971 20th September 1971 20th September 1971 6th December 1971
Section 2(2)	Earnings rule for retirement pensions	20th September 1971
Section 2(3)	Increase of retirement pension in respect of contributions paid after pensionable age	20th September 1971
Section 3	Invalidity benefit for chronic sick	23rd September 1971

SCHEDULE—(*continued*)

Provisions of the National Insurance Act 1971	Subject Matter	Appointed Day
Section 4	Increase for adult dependants in the case of— (*a*) retirement pension (*b*) invalidity pension	20th September 1971 23rd September 1971
Section 5	Retirement pension and age addition for persons over 80	20th September 1971
Section 6(1) and (3)	Calculation of earnings-related supplement and widow's supplementary allowance	20th September 1971
Section 6(2)	Application of earnings-related supplement where injury benefit is payable under the National Insurance (Industrial Injuries) Act 1965	23rd September 1971
Section 7 and Schedule 3	Higher rates of contributions under the National Insurance (Industrial Injuries) Act 1965	20th September 1971
Section 8(1) and Schedule 4	Higher rates and amounts of benefit under the National Insurance (Industrial Injuries) Act 1965 in the case of— (*a*) injury benefit (including increases thereof) and increases of disablement pension in respect of children and adult dependants in the case of a beneficiary receiving, as an in-patient in a hospital or similar institution, medical treatment for the relevant injury or loss of faculty (*b*) disablement benefit (including increases of disablement pension other than those mentioned in the preceding sub-paragraph) (*c*) widow's pension under s. 19 and widower's pension under s.20 (*d*) allowance in respect of children of deceased's family under s.21 (*e*) maximum under s. 29(1)(*a*) of aggregate of weekly benefits payable for successive accidents (*f*) maximum disablement gratuity under s. 12(3)	23rd September 1971 22nd September 1971 20th September 1971 20th September 1971 22nd September 1971 22nd September 1971
Section 8(2)	Death benefit in respect of a person formerly entitled to an increase of disablement pension because of the need for constant attendance	26th July 1971
Section 8(3)	Increases of disablement benefit for adult dependants—reduction in respect of dependant's earnings	22nd September 1971
Section 8(4)	Higher rate of pension under the National Insurance (Industrial Injuries) Act 1965 for certain widows	20th September 1971
Section 9	Increase of unemployability supplement	22nd September 1971

SCHEDULE—(*continued*)

Provisions of the National Insurance Act 1971	Subject Matter	Appointed Day
Section 10(1)	Adjustment of benefit payable under the National Insurance (Industrial Injuries) Act 1965 to or in respect of hospital in-patients	26th July 1971
Section 10(2)	Proviso to s.15(2) of the National Insurance (Industrial Injuries) Act 1965 to cease to have effect	8th December 1971
Section 11	Higher rate of benefit under the Industrial Injuries and Diseases (Old Cases) Act 1967(a)	22nd September 1971
Section 13	Expenses	20th September 1971
Section 14 and Schedule 5	Minor and consequential amendments to the Law Reform (Personal Injuries) Act 1948(b) the National Insurance Act 1965, the Ministry of Social Security Act 1966(c), the National Insurance Act 1969(d) and the National Insurance (Old persons' and widows' pensions and attendance allowance) Act 1970(e) in the case of—	
	(*a*) unemployment, sickness and invalidity benefit	23rd September 1971
	(*b*) maternity allowance	20th September 1971
	(*c*) widow's benefit, guardian's allowance retirement pension, age addition and child's special allowance	20th September 1971
	Minor and consequential amendments to the National Insurance (Industrial Injuries) Act 1965 in the case of—	
	(*a*) injury benefit (including increases thereof) and increases of disablement pension in respect of children and adult dependants in the case of a beneficiary receiving, as an in-patient in a hospital or similar institution, medical treatment for the relevant injury or loss of faculty	23rd September 1971
	(*b*) disablement benefit (including increases of disablement pension other than those mentioned in the preceding paragraph)	22nd September 1971
	(*c*) adjustments under s. 29(2) for successive accidents	22nd September 1971
	Minor and consequential amendments to the National Insurance Act 1966(f) specified in—	
	(*a*) paragraph 8(1) of Schedule 5 to the National Insurance Act 1971	8th December 1971
	(*b*) paragraph 8(2) of that Schedule	22nd September 1971
	Minor amendments to the Industrial Injuries and Diseases (Old Cases) Act 1967	26th July 1971
	Payment of benefit to third party	26th July 1971

(a) 1967 c. 34.	(b) 1948 c. 41.	(c) 1966 c. 20.
(d) 1969 c. 44.	(e) 1970 c. 51.	(f) 1966 c. 6.

SCHEDULE—(*continued*)

Provisions of the National Insurance Act 1971	Subject Matter	Appointed Day
Section 15	Interpretation	26th July 1971
Section 16(1) (other than paragraphs (*a*) and (*b*)), (2) and (4)	Citation, extent, etc.	26th July 1971
Section 16(3) and Schedule 6	Commencement Regulations and schemes: temporary exclusion of certain requirements	26th July 1971
	Transitory provisions relating to— section 2(3)	20th September 1971
	section 6(2)	23rd September 1971
	section 8(2) section 9	26th July 1971 22nd September 1971
Section 16(3) and Schedule 7	Repeals affecting— the National Insurance Act 1965— section 43(1), (4) and (5)	20th September 1971
	the National Insurance (Industrial Injuries) Act 1965— section 15(2)	8th December 1971
	the National Insurance Act 1967(a)— section 1(1)(*d*)	20th September 1971
	the National Insurance Act 1969— section 1(1) and (4) and Schedule 1 section 2(1) and Schedule 2 in the case of—	20th September 1971
	(*a*) unemployment and sickness benefit (*b*) maternity allowance	23rd September 1971 20th September 1971
	(*c*) widow's benefit, guardian's allowance, retirement pension and child's special allowance section 3(1) and (2) section 5 and Schedule 4 section 6 and Schedule 5 in the case of—	20th September 1971 20th September 1971 20th September 1971
	(*a*) injury benefit (including increases thereof) and increases of disablement pension in respect of children and adult dependants in the case of a beneficiary receiving as an in-patient in a hospital or similar institution, medical treatment for the relevant injury or loss of faculty	23rd September 1971
	(*b*) disablement benefit (including increases of disablement pension other than those mentioned in the preceding sub-paragraph)	22nd September 1971
	(*c*) widow's pension and widower's pension	20th September 1971
	(*d*) allowance in respect of children of deceased's family	20th September 1971

(a) 1967 c. 73.

SCHEDULE—(*continued*)

Provisions of the National Insurance Act 1971	Subject Matter	Appointed Day
Section 16(3) and Schedule 7 (contd.)	the National Insurance (Old persons' and widows' pensions and attendance allowance) Act 1970—	
	section 1(2)(*b*)	20th September 1971
	section 7(1)	20th September 1971
	Schedule 2,	
	paragraph 11	8th December 1971

STATUTORY INSTRUMENTS

1971 No. 1151 (C.29)

SUPREME COURT OF JUDICATURE, ENGLAND

CRIMINAL PROCEDURE, ENGLAND AND WALES

The Courts Act 1971 (Commencement) Order 1971

Made - - -	14*th July* 1971
Laid before Parliament	27*th July* 1971
Coming into Operation	1*st October* 1971

The Lord Chancellor, in exercise of the power conferred on him by section 59(2) of the Courts Act 1971(a), hereby makes the following Order :—

1.—(1) This Order may be cited as the Courts Act 1971 (Commencement) Order 1971 and shall come into operation on 1st October 1971.

(2) In this Order "the Act" means the Courts Act 1971.

(3) The Interpretation Act 1889(b) shall apply to this Order as it applies to an Act of Parliament.

2.—(1) The Act, except the provisions mentioned in sub-paragraph (2) below, shall come into force on 1st January 1972.

(2) The following provisions of the Act, that is to say—

section 20(3), so far as it relates to judges of the Court of Appeal and of the High Court ;

section 39 ;

section 46 ;

section 56(1) and (4), so far as it relates to the provisions of schedule 8 and schedule 11 referred to below ;

sections 58 and 59 ;

schedule 8, paragraphs 18(3), 34(2) and 46 ;

schedule 11, Part I, so far as it relates to section 96(3) of the County Courts Act 1959(c) and Part IV, so far as it relates to section 1(4) of the Magistrates' Courts Act 1952(d) and to section 1(3) of the Criminal Appeal Act 1966(e) ;

shall come into force on 1st October 1971.

Dated 14th July 1971.

Hailsham of St. Marylebone, C.

(a) 1971 c. 23.	(b) 1889 c. 63.	(c) 1959 c. 22.
(d) 1952 c. 55.	(e) 1966 c. 31.	

EXPLANATORY NOTE

(This Note is not part of the Order.)

This Order brings the Courts Act 1971 into operation on 1st January 1972, with the exception of the provisions listed in article 2(2) which are brought into force on 1st October 1971.

STATUTORY INSTRUMENTS

1971 No. 1152 (L.29)

COUNTY COURTS

The County Courts (Admiralty Jurisdiction) Order 1971

Made - - - -	16*th July* 1971
Coming into Operation	16*th August* 1971

The Lord Chancellor, in exercise of the powers conferred on him by section 55 of the County Courts Act 1959(a), hereby makes the following Order:—

1.—(1) This Order may be cited as the County Courts (Admiralty Jurisdiction) Order 1971 and shall come into operation on 16th August 1971.

(2) The Interpretation Act 1889(b) shall apply to the interpretation of this Order as it applies to the interpretation of an Act of Parliament.

2. The courts mentioned in column 1 of the Schedule to this Order shall have Admiralty jurisdiction and the districts of those courts for the purpose of such jurisdiction shall, in addition to their existing districts, include the districts of the courts mentioned opposite thereto in column 2 of the Schedule.

3. The County Courts (Admiralty Jurisdiction) Order 1966(c) is hereby revoked.

Dated 16th July 1971.

Hailsham of St. Marylebone, **C.**

(a) 1959 c. 22.   (b) 1889 c. 63.
(c) S.I. 1966/1547 (1966 III, p. 4382).

SCHEDULE

Column 1 Courts having Admiralty jurisdiction	Column 2 Courts whose districts are assigned to courts in column 1 for Admiralty purposes
Aberystwyth	Dolgellau Machynlleth
Bangor	Caernarvon Conway, Llandudno and Colwyn Bay Llangefni and Holyhead Portmadoc
Barnstaple	Bideford
Barrow in Furness and Ulverston	Kendal
Blackpool	—
Boston	Spalding Skegness and Spilsby
Bridgwater	Minehead Weston super Mare
Brighton	Chichester Eastbourne Hastings Lewes Worthing
Bristol	Thornbury
Cardiff	Barry Bridgend
Carmarthen	Ammanford Cardigan
Chester	Holywell Mold Rhyl
Colchester and Clacton	Harwich Maldon
Dover	Ashford Folkestone
Exeter	Axminster and Chard
Gloucester	Stroud
Great Grimsby	Louth Scunthorpe
Great Yarmouth	Norwich
Hartlepool	—
Haverfordwest	—

Column 1 Courts having Admiralty jurisdiction	Column 2 Courts whose districts are assigned to courts in column 1 for Admiralty purposes
Ipswich	Halesworth Woodbridge
Kingston upon Hull	Beverley Bridlington Goole Scarborough Whitby
King's Lynn	Wisbech
Liverpool	Birkenhead Ellesmere Port Runcorn St. Helens Southport Warrington
Lowestoft	—
Manchester	Altrincham Salford
Mayor's & City of London Court	Bow Brentford Dartford Gravesend Grays Thurrock Ilford Kingston upon Thames Lambeth Shoreditch Southend Southwark Wandsworth West London Westminster Woolwich
Middlesbrough	—
Newcastle upon Tyne	Alnwick Berwick on Tweed Blyth Gateshead Hexham Morpeth North Shields South Shields
Newport, Isle of Wight	—
Newport (Mon.)	Chepstow Monmouth Pontypool & Abergavenny

Column 1 Courts having Admiralty jurisdiction	Column 2 Courts whose districts are assigned to courts in column 1 for Admiralty purposes
Plymouth	Kingsbridge Liskeard
Poole	Bournemouth
Portsmouth	—
Preston	Chorley Lancaster
Ramsgate	Canterbury Deal Margate
Rochester	Sheerness Sittingbourne
Southampton	Lymington
Stockton on Tees	—
Sunderland	—
Swansea	Llanelli Neath and Port Talbot
Torquay	Newton Abbot
Truro and Falmouth	Bodmin Launceston Penzance Redruth St. Austell
West Hartlepool	—
Weymouth	Dorchester
Whitehaven	Carlisle Workington

EXPLANATORY NOTE
(This Note is not part of the Order.)

This Order replaces the County Courts (Admiralty Jurisdiction) Order 1966 and takes account of the large number of changes in county court districts and names which have occurred since 1966. It also removes the restrictions imposed by previous Orders on the places at which Admiralty jurisdiction may be exercised in the case of courts held at more than one place.

STATUTORY INSTRUMENTS

1971 No. 1153

MEDICINES

The Medicines (First Appointed Day) Order 1971

Made - - - *17th July* 1971

The Secretaries of State respectively concerned with health in England and in Wales, the Secretary of State concerned with health and with agriculture in Scotland, the Minister of Health and Social Services for Northern Ireland, the Minister of Agriculture, Fisheries and Food and the Minister of Agriculture for Northern Ireland, acting jointly, in exercise of their powers under section 16(1) of the Medicines Act 1968(a), as having effect subject to the provisions of article 2(2) of, and Schedule 1 to, the Transfer of Functions (Wales) Order 1969(b), and of all other powers enabling them in that behalf, after consulting such organisations as appear to them to be representative of interests likely to be substantially affected by this order, hereby make the following order:—

1. The appointed day for the purposes of section 16(1) of the Medicines Act 1968 (in that Act referred to as "the first appointed day") shall be 1st September 1971.

2. This order may be cited as the Medicines (First Appointed Day) Order 1971.

Keith Joseph,
Secretary of State for Social Services.

14th July 1971.

Peter Thomas,
Secretary of State for Wales.

14th July 1971.

Gordon Campbell,
Secretary of State for Scotland.

14th July 1971.

W. K. Fitzsimmons,
Minister of Health and Social Services
for Northern Ireland.

15th July 1971.

(a) 1968 c. 67. (b) S.I. 1969/388 (1969 I, p. 1070).

In witness whereof the official seal of the Minister of Agriculture, Fisheries and Food is hereunto affixed on 16th July 1971.

(L.S.) *J. M. L. Prior,*
Minister of Agriculture, Fisheries and Food.

H. W. West,
Minister of Agriculture for Northern Ireland.
17th July 1971.

EXPLANATORY NOTE

(This Note is not part of the Order.)

This Order appoints the 1st September 1971 (known as "the first appointed day") as the day from which the licensing restrictions contained in sections 7 and 8 of the Medicines Act 1968 shall apply to the manufacture, wholesale dealing in, and marketing of medicinal products, subject to certain transitional exemptions specified in section 16 of the Act. The exemptions relate to medicinal products on the market and to businesses carried on in the United Kingdom for a specified period before the appointed day. The first appointed day is also the day from which the restrictions imposed by sections 31, 32, 34 and 40 of the Act operate. These relate to clinical trials and medicinal tests on animals, to restrictions as to animals on which medicinal tests have been carried out, and to medicated animal feeding stuffs, and they are similarly subject to transitional provisions. It is also the day on which the provisions contained in section 96 of the Act, which relate to advertisements and representations directed to practitioners, come into operation, and again there are transitional provisions.

STATUTORY INSTRUMENTS

1971 No. 1156

HIGHWAYS, ENGLAND AND WALES

The Special Roads (Classes of Traffic) Order 1971

Made - - -	*15th June* 1971
Laid before Parliament	*22nd June* 1971
Coming into Operation	*26th July* 1971

The Secretary of State for the Environment, in exercise of his powers under sections 12(3) and 286(2) and (3) of the Highways Act 1959(a) and of all other enabling powers, hereby makes the following Order :—

1.—(1) This Order may be cited as the Special Roads (Classes of Traffic) Order 1971, and shall come into operation on the tenth day following the day it is approved by Parliament.

(2) The Interpretation Act 1889(b) shall apply for the interpretation of this Order as it applies for the interpretation of an Act of Parliament, and as if for the purposes of section 38 of that Act this Order were an Act of Parliament and the Orders revoked by Article 4 of this Order were Acts of Parliament thereby repealed.

2. Schedule 4 to the Highways Act 1959 shall be amended so as to have effect as set out in the Schedule to this Order.

3. In schemes under section 11 of the Highways Act 1959 made before the 30th June 1961, references to traffic in Class VII set out in Schedule 4 to the said Act of 1959 shall be construed as including references to traffic in Classes X and XI set out in that Schedule.

4. The Special Roads (Classes of Traffic) Order 1961(c) and the Special Roads (Classes of Traffic) (England and Wales) Order 1968(d) are hereby revoked.

Signed by authority of the Secretary of State 15th June 1971.

John Peyton,
Minister for Transport Industries,
Department of the Environment.

(a) 1959 c. 25.
(c) S.I. 1961/1210 (1961 II, p. 2408).

(b) 1889 c. 63.
(d) S.I. 1968/1966 (1968 III, p. 5372).

SCHEDULE

CLASSES OF TRAFFIC FOR PURPOSES OF SPECIAL ROADS

CLASS I:

Heavy and light locomotives, motor tractors, heavy motor cars, motor cars and motor cycles whereof the cylinder capacity of the engine is not less than 50 cubic centimetres, and trailers drawn thereby, which comply with general regulations as to construction and use made under section 64 of the Road Traffic Act 1960(a) and in the case of which the following conditions are satisfied, that is to say:—

(i) that the whole weight of the vehicle is transmitted to the road surface by means of wheels;

(ii) that all wheels of the vehicle are equipped with pneumatic tyres;

(iii) that the vehicle is not controlled by a pedestrian;

(iv) that the vehicle is not a vehicle chargeable with duty under paragraph 2 of Part I of Schedule 3 to the Vehicles (Excise) Act 1971(b); and

(v) in the case of a motor vehicle it is so constructed as to be capable of attaining a speed of twenty-five miles per hour on the level under its own power, when unladen and not drawing a trailer.

CLASS II:

Motor vehicles and trailers the use of which for or in connection with the conveyance of abnormal indivisible loads is authorised by order made by the Secretary of State for the Environment under section 64(4) of the Road Traffic Act 1960.

Motor vehicles and trailers constructed for naval, military, air force or other defence purposes, the use of which is authorised by order made by the said Secretary of State under section 64(4) of the Road Traffic Act 1960.

Motor vehicles and trailers, to which any of the following Articles of the Motor Vehicles (Authorisation of Special Types) General Order 1969(c), as amended (d), namely, Article 16 (which relates to vehicles for moving excavated material), Article 17 (which relates inter alia to vehicles constructed for use outside the United Kingdom) and Article 21 (which relates to engineering plant) relate and which are authorised to be used by any of those Articles of the said Order or by any other Order under section 64(4) of the Road Traffic Act 1960, the said motor vehicles being vehicles in respect of which the following condition is satisfied, that is to say, that the vehicle is so constructed as to be capable of attaining a speed of twenty-five miles per hour on the level under its own power, when unladen and not drawing a trailer.

CLASS III:

Motor vehicles controlled by pedestrians.

CLASS IV:

All motor vehicles (other than invalid carriages and motor cycles whereof the cylinder capacity of the engine is less than 50 cubic centimetres) not comprised in Class I, Class II or Class III.

(a) 1960 c. 16.   (b) 1971 c. 10.
(c) S.I. 1969/344 (1969 I, p. 947).
(d) The relevant amending instrument is S.I. 1971/980 (1971 II, p. 2848).

Class V:

Vehicles drawn by animals.

Class VI:

Vehicles (other than pedal cycles, perambulators, push-chairs and other forms of baby carriages) drawn or propelled by pedestrians.

Class VII:

Pedal cycles.

Class VIII:

Animals ridden, led or driven.

Class IX:

Pedestrians, perambulators, push-chairs and other forms of baby carriages and dogs held on a lead.

Class X:

Motor cycles whereof the cylinder capacity of the engine is less than 50 cubic centimetres.

Class XI:

Invalid carriages.

In this Schedule any expression defined for the purposes of the Road Traffic Act 1960 has the same meaning as in that Act and the expression "abnormal indivisible load" has the same meaning as in the Motor Vehicles (Authorisation of Special Types) General Order 1969.

EXPLANATORY NOTE

(*This Note is not part of the Order.*)

Schedule 4 to the Highways Act 1959, as amended by the Special Roads (Classes of Traffic) Order 1961 and the Special Roads (Classes of Traffic) (England and Wales) Order 1968, specifies classes of traffic for the purposes of special roads.

This Order revokes the above mentioned Orders of 1961 and 1968 and provides for Schedule 4 to be amended so to have effect as set out in the Schedule to the Order. The principal changes made by this Order to Schedule 4 are :—

1. Heavy and light locomotives are added to the composition of Class I specified in Schedule 4, subject, inter alia, to these vehicles being

capable of attaining a speed of 25 miles per hour on the level under their own power when unladen and not drawing a trailer ;

2.　Motor vehicles and trailers authorised to be used on roads under either Article 16, 17 or 21 of the Motor Vehicles (Authorisation of Special Types) General Order 1969, as amended, which Articles relate respectively to vehicles for moving excavated material, vehicles constructed for use outside the United Kingdom and vehicles being engineering plant, are added to the composition of Class II specified in Schedule 4, subject in the case of the motor vehicles to their being capable of attaining a speed of 25 miles per hour on the level under their own power when unladen and not drawing a trailer.

STATUTORY   INSTRUMENTS

1971 No. 1157

AGRICULTURE

The Price Stability of Imported Products (Rates of Levy) (Eggs) (No. 14) Order 1971

Made - - - -   19th July 1971

Coming into Operation   20th July 1971

The Minister of Agriculture, Fisheries and Food, in exercise of the powers conferred upon him by section 1(2), (4), (5), (6) and (7) of the Agriculture and Horticulture Act 1964(a) and of all other powers enabling him in that behalf, hereby makes the following order:—

1. This order may be cited as the Price Stability of Imported Products (Rates of Levy) (Eggs) (No. 14) Order 1971, and shall come into operation on 20th July 1971.

2.—(1) In this order—

" the Principal Order " means the Price Stability of Imported Products (Levy Arrangements) (Eggs) Order 1970(b) as amended by any subsequent order, and if any such order is replaced by any subsequent order the expression shall be construed as a reference to such subsequent order;

AND other expressions have the same meaning as in the Principal Order.

(2) The Interpretation Act 1889(c) shall apply to the interpretation of this order as it applies to the interpretation of an Act of Parliament and as if this order and the order hereby revoked were Acts of Parliament.

3. In accordance with and subject to the provisions of the Principal Order (which provides for the charging of levies on imports of those eggs and egg products which are specified commodities for the purposes of the Agriculture and Horticulture Act 1964) the rate of general levy for such imports into the United Kingdom of any specified commodity as are described in column 2 of the Schedule to this order in relation to a tariff heading indicated in column 1 of that Schedule shall be the rate set forth in relation thereto in column 3 of that Schedule.

4. The Price Stability of Imported Products (Rates of Levy) (Eggs) (No. 13) Order 1971(d) is hereby revoked.

In Witness whereof the Official Seal of the Minister of Agriculture, Fisheries and Food is hereunto affixed on 19th July 1971.

(L.S.)

G. P. Jupe,
Assistant Secretary.

(a) 1964 c. 28.   (b) S.I. 1970/359 (1970 I, p. 1277).   (c) 1889 c. 63.
(d) S.I. 1971/1027 (1971 II, p. 3007).

SCHEDULE

1. Tariff Heading	2. Description of Imports	3. Rate of General Levy
04.05	Imports of:—	
	Birds' eggs (in shell or not in shell), fresh, dried or otherwise preserved, sweetened or not, other than egg yolks:	(per 120 eggs)
	A. Eggs in shell:	p
	1. Not exceeding 11 lb. in weight per 120 ..	45
	2. Over 11 lb. but not exceeding 12½ lb. in weight per 120	50
	3. Over 12½ lb. but not exceeding 14 lb. in weight per 120	70
	4. Over 14 lb. but not exceeding 15½ lb. in weight per 120	75
	5. Over 15½ lb. but not exceeding 17 lb. in weight per 120	60
	6. Over 17 lb. in weight per 120	60
	B. Eggs not in shell:	(per ton)
	Whole dried	£110
	Whole frozen or liquid	£60

EXPLANATORY NOTE

(*This Note is not part of the Order.*)

This order, which comes into operation on 20th July 1971, supersedes the Price Stability of Imported Products (Rates of Levy) (Eggs) (No. 13) Order 1971. It—

(*a*) increases the rates of general levy to be charged on imports of eggs in shell in the weight grades numbered 1 to 4 in the Schedule to the order; and

(*b*) reimposes unchanged the rates of general levy to be charged on imports of shell eggs in the other weight grades and on imports of dried, frozen or liquid whole egg not in shell.

1971 No. 1158 (S.140)

REGISTRATION OF BIRTHS, DEATHS, MARRIAGES, ETC.

The Registration of Births, Still-births, Deaths and Marriages (Prescription of Forms) (Scotland) Amendment Regulations 1971

Made - - - *15th July* 1971

Coming into Operation *1st January* 1972

In exercise of the powers conferred upon me by section 54(1)(*b*) of the Registration of Births, Deaths and Marriages (Scotland) Act 1965(a), and of all other powers enabling me in that behalf and with the approval of the Secretary of State for Scotland, I hereby make the following regulations :—

Citation and Commencement

1.—(1) These regulations may be cited as the Registration of Births, Still-births, Deaths and Marriages (Prescription of Forms) (Scotland) Amendment Regulations 1971 and shall come into operation on 1st January 1972.

(2) These regulations and the Registration of Births, Still-births, Deaths and Marriages (Prescription of Forms) (Scotland) Regulations 1965(b) shall be construed as one and may be cited together as the Registration of Births, Still-births, Deaths and Marriages (Prescription of Forms) (Scotland) Regulations 1965 and 1971.

Interpretation

2.—(1) The Interpretation Act 1889(c) shall apply for the interpretation of these regulations as it applies for the interpretation of an Act of Parliament.

(2) In these regulations, "the principal regulations" means the Registration of Births, Still-births, Deaths and Marriages (Prescription of Forms) (Scotland) Regulations 1965.

Amendment of Principal Regulations

3. For Schedule 1 to the principal regulations there shall be substituted Schedule 1 to these regulations.

4. For Schedule 2 to the principal regulations there shall be substituted Schedule 2 to these regulations.

5. For Schedule 5 to the principal regulations there shall be substituted Schedule 3 to these regulations.

(a) 1965 c. 49.   (b) S.I. 1965/1839 (1965 III, p. 5535).
(c) 1889 c. 63.

6. For Schedule 10 to the principal regulations there shall be substituted Schedule 4 to these regulations.

7. For Schedule 16 to the principal regulations there shall be substituted Schedule 5 to these regulations.

8. For Schedule 17 to the principal regulations there shall be substituted Schedule 6 to these regulations.

9. For Schedule 18 to the principal regulations there shall be substituted Schedule 7 to these regulations.

10. For Schedule 27 to the principal regulations there shall be substituted Schedule 8 to these regulations.

A. L. Rennie,
Registrar General
for Scotland.

New Register House,
Edinburgh.
14th July 1971.

I approve,

Gordon Campbell,
One of Her Majesty's
Principal Secretaries of State.

St. Andrew's House,
Edinburgh.
15th July 1971.

SCHEDULE 1

BIRTH	District no.	Year	Entry no.	N.H.S. no.						

Registered in the District of

1 Surname	2 Sex
Name(s)	

3 When born 19............	4 Where born
............hours	

5 Mother's name(s) and surname	6 Maiden surname

7 Mother's usual residence (if different from 4 above)

8 Father's name(s) and surname

9 Occupation

10 Date and place of parents' marriage	Year	Month	Day	Place

11 Informant's signature and qualification

....

12 When registered	Year 19...	Month	Day	13
				.... *Registrar*

14	

SCHEDULE 2

STILL-BIRTH	District no.	Year	Entry no.

REGISTERED IN THE DISTRICT OF

1 When born 19............	2 Where born	3 Sex

............*hours*

4 Mother's name(s) and surname	5 Maiden surname

6 Mother's usual residence (if different from 2 above)

7 Father's name(s) and surname

8 Occupation

9 Date and place of parents' marriage	Year	Month	Day	Place

10 Cause or probable cause of death
I (*a*)

(*b*)

(*c*)

II

Certifying registered medical practitioner
or midwife

11 Informant's signature and qualification

....

12 When registered	Year 19...	Month	Day	13

Registrar

14

SCHEDULE 3

ABBREVIATED CERTIFICATE OF BIRTH

REGISTRATION OF BIRTHS, DEATHS AND MARRIAGES (SCOTLAND) ACT 1965, Ss. 19 AND 40

BIRTH	District no.	Year	Entry no.	N.H.S. no.					

REGISTERED IN THE DISTRICT OF

1 Surname	2 Sex
Name(s)	

3 When born	4 Where born

I HEREBY CERTIFY that the above particulars are extracted from a Register of Births in my custody.

Given under my hand this ....day of................................19...

....Registrar

District of...................................

REGISTRATION OF BIRTHS, DEATHS, MARRIAGES, ETC.

SCHEDULE 4

DEATH	District no.		Year		Entry no.

REGISTERED IN THE DISTRICT OF

1 Surname	2 Sex
Name(s)	

3 Occupation

4 Marital status	5 Date of birth	Year	Month	Day	6 Age

7 Name(s), surname and occupation of spouse(s)

8 When and where died
                19............

9 Usual residence (if different from 8 above)

10 Name(s), surname and occupation of father	11 Name(s), surname(s) and maiden surname of mother

12 Cause of death
I   (a)

     (b)

     (c)

II

Certifying registered medical practitioner

13 Informant's signature, qualification and address   ....

14 When registered	Year 19...	Month	Day	15 .... *Registrar*

16

SCHEDULE 5

ABBREVIATED CERTIFICATE OF BIRTH

REGISTRATION OF BIRTHS, DEATHS AND MARRIAGES (SCOTLAND) ACT 1965, S.40

Vol.	Entry no.	Year	N.H.S. no.					

1 Surname	2 Sex
Name(s)	

3 When born	4 Country of birth
	....

IT IS HEREBY CERTIFIED that the above particulars are extracted from a register kept in the General Register Office.

Given under the Seal of the General Register Office, New Register House, Edinburgh

on the....................................day of....................................19 ......

SCHEDULE 6

MARRIAGE	District no.		Year		Entry no.

IN THE DISTRICT OF

1 When and where married
19.............

2 Surname	BRIDEGROOM		BRIDE	
Name(s)				
	(*Signed*)		(*Signed*)	

3 Occupation		

4 Marital status	5 Date of birth	Year	Month	Day	4		5 Year	Month	Day

6 Birthplace		

7 Usual residence		

8 Father's name(s), surname and occupation		
Mother's name(s), surname(s), and maiden surname		

9 Person solemnizing the marriage	(*Signed*)	Designation
Witnesses	(*Signed*)	
with		
	(*Signed*)	
addresses		

Schedule 6 cont.

10 When registered	Year 19...	Month	Day	11
				....
				Registrar
12				

SCHEDULE 7
SCHEDULE OF MARRIAGE

1 When and where married 19............		
2 Surname Name(s) (*Signature*)	**BRIDEGROOM** (*Signature*)	**BRIDE**
3 Occupation		
4 Marital status	**5** Date of birth Year Month Day	**4** **5** Year Month Day
6 Birth place		
7 Usual residence		
8 Father's name(s), surname and occupation		
Mother's name(s) surname(s) and maiden surname		
9 Person solemnizing the marriage	* *Designation*	
Witnesses with addresses	† *Witness*	
	† *Witness*	

*Signature and designation of person solemnizing marriage
†Signatures and addresses of two witnesses

	Year	Month	Day	
DATE OF REGISTRATION	19			

....
Registrar's signature

SCHEDULE 8

Registration District { No.   R.C.E.

Name

REGISTER OF CORRECTIONS ETC.

Register of   District   Year   Entry no.

Annotation of the entry

Annotate   of the above-noted entry as follows:—   R.C.E.

Issue of extracts, special-purpose certificates, abbreviated certificates and short special-purpose certificates of the entry

(*a*) Extracts and special-purpose certificates:

(*b*) Abbreviated certificates and short special-purpose certificates:

General Register Office, Edinburgh. 19 ,

This page is to be placed in the binder provided and carefully preserved.

EXPLANATORY NOTE

(*This Note is not part of the Regulations.*)

These Regulations amend the Registration of Births, Deaths and Marriages (Prescription of Forms) (Scotland) Regulations 1965 by substituting eight revised forms for the corresponding forms prescribed by the 1965 regulations.

STATUTORY INSTRUMENTS

1971 No. 1159 (S.141)

REGISTRATION OF BIRTHS, DEATHS, MARRIAGES, ETC.

SCOTLAND

The Registration of Births, Deaths and Marriages (Civil Marriage Schedule) (Scotland) Regulations 1971

Made - - -	*15th July* 1971
Laid before Parliament	*27th July* 1971
Coming into Operation	*1st January* 1972

In exercise of the powers conferred upon me by section 54(1)(c) of the Registration of Births, Deaths and Marriages (Scotland) Act 1965(a), and with the approval of the Secretary of State for Scotland, I hereby make the following regulations :—

Citation, Commencement and Interpretation

1.—(1) These regulations may be cited as the Registration of Births, Deaths and Marriages (Civil Marriage Schedule) (Scotland) Regulations 1971 and shall come into operation on 1st January 1972.

(2) The Interpretation Act 1889(b) shall apply for the interpretation of these regulations as it applies for the interpretation of an Act of Parliament.

Marriage Schedule

2. For the Schedule of Marriage set out in Schedule 1 to the Marriage (Scotland) Act 1939(c) there shall be substituted the Schedule of Marriage set out in the Schedule to these regulations.

Revocation

3. The Registration of Births, Deaths and Marriages (Civil Marriage Schedule) (Scotland) Regulations 1965(d) are hereby revoked.

A. L. Rennie,
Registrar General
for Scotland.

New Register House,
Edinburgh.
14th July 1971.

I approve,

Gordon Campbell,
One of Her Majesty's
Principal Secretaries of State.

St. Andrew's House,
Edinburgh.
15th July 1971.

(a) 1965 c. 49.
(c) 1939 c. 34.
(b) 1889 c. 63.
(d) S.I. 1965/1843 (1965 III, p. 5571).

SCHEDULE

SCHEDULE OF MARRIAGE

1 When and where married 19............		
2 Surname	**BRIDEGROOM**	**BRIDE**
Name(s)		
	(*Signature*)	(*Signature*)
3 Occupation		
4 Marital status	**5** Date of birth · Year : Month : Day	**4** · **5** Year : Month : Day
6 Birthplace		
7 Usual residence		
8 Father's name(s), surname and occupation		
Mother's name(s), surname(s) and maiden surname		

SCHEDULE—*cont.*

SCHEDULE OF MARRIAGE—*cont.*

9 Person solemnizing the marriage	*	*Designation*
Witnesses with addresses	†	*Witness*
	†	*Witness*

*Signature and designation of person solemnizing marriage

†Signatures and addresses of two witnesses

	Year	Month	Day	
DATE OF REGISTRATION	19			.... Registrar's signature

EXPLANATORY NOTE

(This Note is not part of the Regulations.)

These Regulations provide a new form of Schedule of Marriage for the purposes of section 1(1) of the Marriage (Scotland) Act 1939 in substitution for the form prescribed by the Registration of Births, Deaths and Marriages (Civil Marriage Schedule) (Scotland) Regulations 1965.

STATUTORY INSTRUMENTS

1971 No. 1160 (S.142)

REGISTRATION OF BIRTHS, DEATHS, MARRIAGES, ETC.

The Registration of Births, Deaths and Marriages (Adopted Children Register) (Scotland) Regulations 1971

Made - - -	15th July 1971
Laid before Parliament	27th July 1971
Coming into Operation	1st January 1972

In exercise of the powers conferred upon me by section 54(1)(*d*) of the Registration of Births, Deaths and Marriages (Scotland) Act 1965(**a**), and with the approval of the Secretary of State for Scotland, I hereby make the following regulations :—

Citation, Commencement and Interpretation

1.—(1) These regulations may be cited as the Registration of Births, Deaths and Marriages (Adopted Children Register) (Scotland) Regulations 1971 and shall come into operation on 1st January 1972.

(2) The Interpretation Act 1889(**b**) shall apply for the interpretation of these regulations as it applies for the interpretation of an Act of Parliament.

Form of Entry in Adopted Children Register

2. For the form of entry set out in Schedule 2 to the Adoption Act 1958(**c**), there shall be substituted the form of entry set out in the Schedule to these regulations.

Revocation

3. The Registration of Births, Deaths and Marriages (Adopted Children Register) (Scotland) Regulations 1965(**d**) are hereby revoked.

A. L. Rennie,
Registrar General
for Scotland.

New Register House,
Edinburgh.
14th July 1971.

(**a**) 1965 c. 49.   (**b**) 1889 c. 63.
(**c**) 7 & 8 Eliz. 2. c. 5.   (**d**) S.I. 1965/1841 (1965 III, p. 5567).

I approve,

Gordon Campbell,
One of Her Majesty's
Principal Secretaries of State.

St. Andrew's House,
Edinburgh.

15th July 1971.

SCHEDULE
ADOPTED CHILDREN REGISTER

Vol:	Entry no.	Year	N.H.S. no.					

1 Surname

Name(s)

2 Sex

3 When born

4 Country of birth

5 Name(s), surname, occupation and address of adopter(s)

6 ADOPTION ORDER

Date

Made by

7 Date of registration

....
Registrar General

EXPLANATORY NOTE

(This Note is not part of the Regulations.)

These Regulations provide a new form of entry in the Adopted Children Register for the purposes of section 23 of the Adoption Act 1958 in substitution for the form prescribed by the Registration of Births, Deaths and Marriages (Adopted Children Register) (Scotland) Regulations 1965.

1971 No. 1161 (S.143)

COURT OF SESSION, SCOTLAND

Act of Sederunt (Rules of Court Amendment No. 5) 1971

Made	-	-	-	16*th July* 1971
Coming into Operation		16*th August* 1971

The Lords of Council and Session, under and by virtue of the powers conferred upon them by section 16 of the Administration of Justice (Scotland) Act 1933(a) and of all other powers competent to them in that behalf, do hereby enact and declare as follows :

1. Rule 347 of the Rules of Court (b) is hereby amended by the deletion of the Chapter IV which was substituted by the Act of Sederunt (Rules of Court Amendment No. 5 1970) (Alteration of Fees to Shorthand Writers) 1971(c), and by the further substitution of a new Chapter IV as follows :

"CHAPTER IV

TABLE OF FEES TO SHORTHAND WRITERS

"1. Attending trials, proofs and commissions, per hour, with a minimum fee of £5 per day ...   .   £1·70

The above fees will be paid by the Exchequer.   No fee will be paid where intimation of postponement or settlement is made by 4 p.m. on the previous day.

2. Extending Notes, except when these are transcribed daily, per sheet of 250 words ...   .   £0·50

Extending Notes, when these are transcribed daily, per sheet of 250 words ...   .   £0·60

3. Transcripts of Notes of Evidence will only be made on directions from the Court, and the cost thereof in defended cases will in the first instance be payable by the solicitors for the parties in equal shares. The daily transcript of Notes of Evidence shall be made only if all compearing parties shall consent thereto.   Where an undefended case is continued, or where for other reasons the Court considers it necessary that the Notes should be extended for the use of the Court and so directs, the cost will be borne by the pursuer's solicitor in the first instance.   In any case where the Notes of Evidence have not been extended, but are required for a reclaiming motion, the solicitor for the reclaimer may request the shorthand writer to extend the Notes, and the transcript thereof will thereupon be lodged in process, the cost being payable in the first instance by the reclaimer's solicitor.

4. In any case where the Court on a motion enrolled for that purpose certifies that there is reasonable ground for reclaiming and that the re-

(a) 1933 c. 41.
(c) S.I. 1971/198 (1971 I, p. 585).

(b) S.I. 1965/321 (1965 I, p. 803).

claimer is unable, for financial reasons, to meet the cost of the necessary transcript from which copies for the use of the Inner House are made, the cost of such transcript will be paid out of public funds.

5. Carbon Copies—

Where Notes of Evidence have been directed to be supplied for the use of the Court, carbon or duplicate copies may be made available to parties at a cost of £0·08 per sheet payable to the shorthand writer by the solicitor for the parties obtaining the said copies."

2. This Act of Sederunt may be cited as the Act of Sederunt (Rules of Court Amendment No. 5) 1971, and shall come into operation on 16th August 1971.

And the Lords appoint this Act of Sederunt to be inserted in the Books of Sederunt.

William Grant,
I. P. D.

Edinburgh,
16th July 1971.

EXPLANATORY NOTE

(This Note is not part of the Act of Sederunt.)

This Act of Sederunt amends the Rules of Court by prescribing a new table of fees payable to Shorthand Writers in the Court of Session.

STATUTORY INSTRUMENTS

1971 No. 1162 (S. 144)

COURT OF SESSION, SCOTLAND

Act of Sederunt (Rules of Court Amendment No. 6) 1971

Made - - -		*16th July* 1971
Coming into Operation		*16th August* 1971

The Lords of Council and Session, under and by virtue of the powers conferred upon them by section 16 of the Administration of Justice (Scotland) Act 1933(a), section 11 of the Adoption Act 1958(b), and all other powers competent to them in that behalf do hereby enact and declare as follows:—

1. Paragraph (*c*) of Rule 230 of the Rules of Court(c) is hereby amended by the deletion therefrom of the word "forty" and the substitution for the said word "forty" of the words "one hundred".

2. This Act of Sederunt may be cited as the Act of Sederunt (Rules of Court Amendment No. 6) 1971 and shall come into operation on 16th August 1971.

And the Lords appoint this Act of Sederunt to be inserted in the Books of Sederunt.

William Grant,
I.P.D.

Edinburgh.
16th July 1971.

EXPLANATORY NOTE

(This Note is not part of the Act of Sederunt.)

This Act of Sederunt increases from 40 years to 100 years the period during which an adoption petition process shall not normally be made accessible to any person after the date of the adoption order.

(a) 1933 c. 41. (b) 7 & 8 Eliz. 2. c. 5. (c) S.I. 1965/321 (1965 I, p. 803).

STATUTORY INSTRUMENTS

1971 No. 1163 (S. 145)

SHERIFF COURT, SCOTLAND

Act of Sederunt (Adoption of Children Amendment) 1971

Made - - -	16*th July* 1971
Coming into Operation	16*th August* 1971

The Lords of Council and Session, under and by virtue of the powers conferred upon them by section 34 of the Administration of Justice (Scotland) Act 1933(a), section 11 of the Adoption Act 1958(b), and all other powers competent to them in that behalf do hereby enact and declare as follows:—

1. Paragraph 15 of the Act of Sederunt (Adoption of Children) 1959(c) is hereby amended by the deletion therefrom of the figure "40" and the substitution for the said figure "40" of the words "one hundred".

2. This Act of Sederunt may be cited as the Act of Sederunt (Adoption of Children Amendment) 1971, and shall come into operation on 16th August 1971.

And the Lords appoint this Act of Sederunt to be inserted in the Books of Sederunt.

William Grant,
I.P.D.

Edinburgh.
16th July 1971.

EXPLANATORY NOTE

(This Note is not part of the Act of Sederunt.)

This Act of Sederunt increases from 40 years to 100 years the period during which an adoption petition process shall not normally be made accessible to any person after the date of the adoption order.

(a) 1933 c. 41.   (b) 7 & 8 Eliz. 2. c. 5.   (c) S.I. 1959/763 (1959 I, p. 649).

STATUTORY INSTRUMENTS

1971 No. 1164 (S.146)

SHERIFF COURT, SCOTLAND

Act of Sederunt (Confirmation of Executors Amendment) 1971

Made - - -	16*th July* 1971
Coming into Operation	1*st January* 1972

The Lords of Council and Session, under and by virtue of the powers conferred upon them by section 18 of the Confirmation of Executors (Scotland) Act 1858(a), section 16 of the Sheriff Courts and Legal Officers (Scotland) Act 1927(b), section 34 of the Administration of Justice (Scotland) Act 1933(c), section 22 of the Succession (Scotland) Act 1964(d), and of all other powers competent to them in that behalf, do hereby enact and declare as follows :—

The Act of Sederunt anent certain Forms of Procedure in the Sheriff's Ordinary and Small Debt Courts and for the Confirmation of Executors, dated 3rd February 1933(e), is hereby amended as follows :—

(1) The last paragraph of Section 5 of the said Act of Sederunt, being the paragraph commencing "Where" and ending "is.", is hereby deleted.

(2) The Schedule appended hereto is substituted for Schedule D appended to the said Act of Sederunt.

(3) This Act of Sederunt may be cited as the Act of Sederunt (Confirmation of Executors Amendment) 1971, and shall come into operation on 1st January 1972.

And the Lords appoint this Act of Sederunt to be inserted in the Books of Sederunt.

William Grant,
I. P. D.

Edinburgh,
16th July 1971.

(a) 21 & 22 Vict. c. 56.   (b) 17 & 18 Geo. 5 c. 35.
(c) 23 & 24 Geo. 5 c. 41.   (d) 1964 c. 41.
(e) S.R. & O. 1933/48 (Rev. XX, p. 829:1933 p. 1784).

SCHEDULE D

SHERIFF COURT OF...............

at..........................

Confirmation was issued from the Commissariot of
on   19   in favour of (*here describe executors*) as Executors

> (NOTE.—*Insert any qualification in the appointment of Executors, e.g. executor-nominate, executor-dative,* sine qua non *or that a majority is a quorum.*)

of A. B.

> (*here describe deceased*)

who died on 19   , DOMICILED IN SCOTLAND

It is hereby certified that the said Confirmation contained, *inter alia,* the following item of estate situated in (*insert Scotland, England and Wales, or Northern Ireland as appropriate*)

> (*Here state in each Certificate such item as may be desired by the person requesting the Certificate.*)

Given under the Seal of Office of the Commissariot of
and signed by the Clerk of Court at
        the   day of   Nineteen hundred
and

Sheriff Clerk of

NOTE.—*Where issued from the Commissariot of Edinburgh the form may be varied or adapted as required.*

EXPLANATORY NOTE

(*This Note is not part of the Act of Sederunt.*)

This Act of Sederunt makes provision for the form of certificates of Confirmation issued, when the domicile of the deceased is in Scotland, for items of estate in England and Wales or Northern Ireland. It also deletes from the Act of Sederunt of 1933 the clause authorising the certification of an English extract or Act of Record.

STATUTORY INSTRUMENTS

1971 No. 1165 (S.147)

COURT OF SESSION, SCOTLAND

SHERIFF COURT, SCOTLAND

Act of Sederunt (Edictal Citations, Commissary Petitions and Petitions of Service) 1971

Made - - -	*16th July* 1971	
Coming into Operation	*16th August* 1971	

The Lords of Council and Session, by virtue of the powers conferred upon them by sections 16 and 34 of the Administration of Justice (Scotland) Act 1933(a) and section 22 of the Succession (Scotland) Act 1964(b) and of all other powers competent to them in that behalf, do hereby enact and declare as follows :

1.—(1) The provisions of section 51 and 52 of the Court of Session Act 1825(c), in so far as they prescribe procedure for and in connection with edictal citations, charges, publications, citations and services sometime made at the Market Cross of Edinburgh, pier and shore of Leith, as against persons furth of Scotland, shall no longer apply.

(2) All such edictal citations, charges, publications, citations and services shall be done and performed by service of a copy thereof at the office of the Keeper of Edictal Citations of the Court of Session, in the manner now practised in cases of citation or charge at the dwelling house of a party not personally apprehended ; and the Keeper of Edictal Citations or his clerk shall record on each such copy delivered to him the date of receipt by his office.

(3) Each such copy as is referred to in the last foregoing sub-paragraph shall be preserved for three years from the date of the receipt recorded thereon, and it shall at all times be available for inspection at the office of the Keeper of Edictal Citations during that period.

2.—(1) The provisions of section 4 of the Confirmation and Probate Act 1858(d), in so far as they prescribe procedure in petitions for the appointment of an executor, shall no longer apply.

(2) Every petition for the appointment of an executor shall be intimated by the Sheriff Clerk affixing a full copy of the petition on the door of the Sheriff Court house or in some conspicuous place of the Court or of the office of the Sheriff Clerk, in such manner as the Sheriff shall direct.

(a) 1933 c. 41.　　　　　　　　　　(b) 1964 c. 41.
(c) 1825 c. 120.　　　　　　　　　　(d) 1158 c. 56.

3.—(1) The provisions of Section 30 of the Titles to Land Consolidation (Scotland) Act 1868(**a**), as saved by Section 37 of the Succession (Scotland) Act 1964(**b**), in so far as they prescribe procedure in petitions of service, shall no longer apply.

(2) A petition presented to the Sheriff of Chancery for general service, where the domicile of the deceased is known and was within Scotland, shall not proceed until the Sheriff Clerk of Chancery shall have received official notice from the Sheriff Clerk of the county of the domicile of the person deceased that publication has been made in such county, and such publication shall be effected by affixing an abstract of the petition on the door of the Sheriff Court house or in some conspicuous place of the Court or of the office of the Sheriff Clerk, in such manner as the Sheriff of the county shall direct.

(3) A petition presented to the Sheriff of Chancery for Special Service or a petition presented to the Sheriff of Chancery under section 10 of the Conveyancing (Scotland) Act 1874(**c**), shall not proceed until the Sheriff Clerk of Chancery shall have received official notice (i) from the Sheriff Clerk of the county or of each of the counties in which the lands are situated that publication has been made in such county or in each such county as the case may be, and either (ii) where the domicile of the deceased is known and was within Scotland, from the Sheriff Clerk of the county of the domicile of the person deceased that publication has been made in such county, or (iii) where the domicile of the deceased is furth of Scotland or is unknown, from the Sheriff Clerk of the Lothians and Peebles at Edinburgh that publication has been made at Edinburgh ; and each such publication shall be effected by affixing an abstract of the petition on the door of the Sheriff Court house or in some conspicuous place of the Court or of the office of the Sheriff Clerk, in such manner as the Sheriff of the county or counties shall direct.

(4) A petition presented to the Sheriff of Chancery for General Service, where the domicile of the deceased was furth of Scotland or where such domicile is unknown and the person deceased died more than ten years prior to the presentation of the petition, shall not proceed until the Sheriff Clerk of Chancery shall have received official notice from the Sheriff Clerk of the Lothians and Peebles at Edinburgh that publication has been made at Edinburgh, and such publication shall be effected by affixing an abstract of the petition on the door of the Sheriff Court house or in some conspicuous place of the Court or of the office of the Sheriff Clerk, in such manner as the Sheriff of the Lothians and Peebles shall direct.

(5) In each such petition as aforesaid, no further publication shall be necessary.

4. This Act of Sederunt may be cited as the Act of Sederunt (Edictal Citations, Commissary Petitions and Petitions of Service) 1971, and shall come into operation on 16th August 1971.

And the Lords appoint this Act of Sederunt to be inserted in the Books of Sederunt.

Edinburgh,
16th July 1971.

William Grant,
I. P. D.

(**a**) 1964 c. 41.   (**b**) 1868 c. 101.   (**c**) 1874 c. 49.

EXPLANATORY NOTE

(This Note is not part of the Act of Sederunt.)

This Act of Sederunt makes new provision for the execution of edictal citations, for the publication of petitions for appointment of executors, and for the publication of petitions of service of heirs.

STATUTORY INSTRUMENTS

1971 No. 1166

PURCHASE TAX

The Purchase Tax (No. 5) Order 1971

Made - - - -	*20th July* 1971
Laid before the House of	
Commons - - - -	*28th July* 1971
Coming into Operation -	*29th July* 1971

The Lords Commissioners of Her Majesty's Treasury, by virtue of the powers conferred on them by section 2(3) of the Purchase Tax Act 1963(a), and of all other powers enabling them in that behalf, hereby make the following Order:—

1.—(1) This Order may be cited as the Purchase Tax (No. 5) Order 1971.

(2) The Interpretation Act 1889(b) shall apply for the interpretation of this Order as it applies for the interpretation of an Act of Parliament.

(3) This Order shall come into operation on 29th July 1971.

2. Drugs and medicines, manufactured or prepared (except toilet preparations) of any of the classes specified in the Schedule to this Order shall not be included in any class of goods which are chargeable goods within the meaning of the Purchase Tax Act 1963.

3.—(1) In Group 33 of Part I of Schedule 1 to the Purchase Tax Act 1963, in paragraph (2) of the heading " Exempt ", for the words following " Schedule to " there shall be substituted the words " the Purchase Tax (No. 5) Order 1971 ".

(2) The Purchase Tax (No. 1) Order 1970 (c) is hereby revoked.

Walter Clegg,
V. H. Goodhew,
Two of the Lords Commissioners
of Her Majesty's Treasury.

20th July 1971.

(a) 1963 c. 9.   (b) 1889 c. 63.   (c) S.I. 1970/364 (1970 I, p. 1287).

SCHEDULE

HEAD I

Acetarsol, salts thereof and preparations containing not less than 6 per cent. by weight of acetarsol or the equivalent thereof.

Aerosol sprays prepared for application to the skin as a counter-irritant and analgesic, whose active ingredients consist solely of one or more chlorofluoro-hydrocarbons.

Aqueous solutions of dimethyl sulphoxide prepared solely for veterinary purposes.

Bromethol.

Chlorhexidine, and salts thereof, and solutions, creams and pessaries which contain not less than 1 per cent. of any one of those substances as sole active ingredient and are prepared for veterinary use or for use in obstetrics.

Cyclopropane.

Ethyl chloride (whether perfumed or not).

Halothane.

Hexachlorophane pastes prepared solely for internal administration for veterinary purposes which contain not less than 26 per cent. (by weight) of hexachlorophane as the sole active ingredient.

Hexachlorophane solutions in oil prepared solely for internal administration for veterinary purposes which contain not less than 5 per cent. (by weight) of hexachlorophane as the sole active ingredient.

Hypertonic solutions, sterilised and pyrogen-free designed solely for peritoneal dialysis.

Iodised oil.

Nitrous oxide.

Oxygen.

Penicillinases.

Solutions of 1-(3,4,-dimethoxyphenyl)-1-dimethylamino-4-phenylbutane hydrochloride, prepared for veterinary purposes.

Sterilised aqueous fluids designed solely for irrigation in surgical procedures.

Vaporising fluids containing not less than 85 per cent. by volume of cresols, for use, undiluted, as inhalants.

Any one of the following substances, prepared for use by injection:—

Antihaemophilic globulin of human or animal origin;

Aqueous solutions of amino acids with vitamins and mineral salts, whether with or without one or more of the following substances, that is to say, sorbitol, casein hydrolysate, glucose and ethanol;

Aqueous solutions of dextrose, sodium acetate and the chlorides of calcium, magnesium, potassium and sodium, whether containing a preservative or not, prepared solely for veterinary purposes;

Aqueous solutions of glucose, of sodium chloride, or glucose with sodium chloride, whether with or without salts of calcium and whether containing a preservative or not;

Aqueous solutions of glucose containing dicobaltic edetate;

Aqueous solutions containing one or more of the following substances:—inorganic electrolytes, sodium citrate, sodium lactate, dextrose and laevulose, whether containing a preservative or not;

Aqueous solutions of sorbitol, whether with or without L-arginine and L-arginine hydrochloride;

Bismuth, and compounds thereof;

Calcium gluconate;

Calcium glucono-galacto-gluconate;

Compounds of iron;

Cottonseed oil emulsified with soya lecithin;

Mercury, and salts thereof;

Organic compounds of copper, whether containing an analgesic or not;

Plasma substitutes;

Protein desensitising solutions;

Protein hydrolysates, whether or not containing one or more of the following, that is to say, ethanol, sugars and flavouring agents;

Soya bean oil, emulsified with egg lecithin;

Urea.

Any one of the following substances prepared for use in dental surgery:—

Diamminosilver nitrate;

Germicidal cements and fillings;

Lignocaine, and salts thereof, with cetrimide.

HEAD II

Any one of the substances and preparations described under this head with or without one or more of the following things, namely, an excipient, vehicle, base or preservative:—

Acetazolamide, and salts thereof;

Acetohexamide;

Acinitrazole;

Activated magnesium aluminium silicates mixed with calcium chloride, magnesium chloride, potassium acetate, sodium acetate and sodium chloride, prepared for veterinary use;

Activated magnesium aluminium silicates mixed with neomycin sulphate;

Activated magnesium aluminium silicates with pectin, whether or not mixed with one of the following, that is to say, a mixture of bismuth carbonate and kanamycin sulphate, or neomycin sulphate;

Activated magnesium aluminium silicates with streptomycin sulphate, whether or not mixed with phthalylsulphathiazole and sulphadiazine;

Alcuronium chloride;

Allopurinol;

Allylisopropylacetylurea;

Aloxiprin;

Aluminium dimagnesium trisilicate, whether or not mixed with hyoscyamine, hyoscine, apoatropine and belladonnine;

Aluminium glycinate, whether or not mixed with either or both of the following substances, that is to say, magnesium carbonate and magnesium trisilicate;

Aluminium hydroxide, whether or not mixed with ambutonium bromide, secbutobarbitone and magnesium hydroxide;

Aluminium phosphate;

Aluminium sodium silicate mixed with an extract of belladonna, whether or not also mixed with amylobarbitone and ascorbic acid;

Amantadine hydrochloride;

Amicarbalide, and salts thereof;

Amiloride hydrochloride whether or not mixed with hydrochlorothiazide;

Aminacrine hydrochloride mixed with domiphen bromide, lignocaine hydrochloride, and 2-(dodecyloxypolyethoxy)ethanol;

Amino acids obtained by the hydrolysis of proteins or such acids prepared synthetically, and combinations of two or more of those acids;

Aminometradine;

Aminonitrothiazole;

Amiphenazole, and salts thereof;

Amisometradine;

Ancrod;

Arachis oil extract of crude coal tar when mixed with liquid paraffin, tar, cade oil and coal tar, prepared for medicinal use;

Arecoline hydrobromide;

Ascaridole;

Atropine sulphate, mixed with hyoscine hydrobromide, hyoscyamine sulphate, kaolin and pectin, whether or not also mixed with one of the following substances, that is to say, neomycin sulphate, phenobarbitone or powdered opium;

Batyl alcohol;
Benperidol;
Benzhexol, and salts thereof;
Benzonatate;
Benzoyl peroxide, whether or not mixed with sulphur;
Bephenium embonate, bephenium hydroxynaphthoate and mixtures of these substances;
Betahistine dihydrochloride;
Biperiden hydrochloride;
Bisacodyl;
NN'-Bis[1-methyl-3-(2,2,6-trimethylcyclohexyl)propyl]-*NN'*-bis(dimethyl)-1, 6-hexanediammonium salts, whether or not mixed with hydrocortisone;
Bothrops jararaca venom, prepared for use as a haemostatic;
Bromhexine hydrochloride;
Bromvaletone;
Bunamidine hydrochloride;
Buphenine hydrochloride;
Bupivacaine, and salts thereof, whether or not mixed with adrenaline, and salts thereof;
Busulphan;
Butyl aminobenzoate combined with dibromopropamidine embonate and chlorphenoctium amsonate;
n-Butyl *N*-phenyldithiocarbamate;

Calcium borogluconate, whether or not mixed with one or more of the following substances, that is to say, dextrose, salts of calcium and salts of magnesium;
Captodiame, and its hydrochloride;
Carbarsone, and salts thereof, prepared for veterinary use;
Carbinoxamine maleate, mixed with ephedrine hydrochloride and pholcodine;
Carbinoxamine maleate mixed with either pseudo-ephedrine or pseudo-ephedrine hydrochloride, whether or not also mixed with noscapine;
Cetyldimethylbenzylammonium chloride mixed with one of the following substances, that is to say, amethocaine hydrochloride, benzocaine or choline salicylate;
Cetylpyridinium chloride combined with either or both of the following substances, that is to say, sodium propionate and benzocaine;
Chiniofon;
Chlophedianol hydrochloride;
The molecular compound of chloral hydrate with paracetamol;
Chlorambucil;
Chlorhexadol;
Chlormethiazole edisylate;
2-*o*-Chlorobenzyl-thio-4-dimethylamino-5-methylpyrimidine hydrochloride;
7-Chloro-2, 3-dihydro-1-methyl-5-phenyl-1*H*-1, 4-benzodiazepine, and its hydrochloride;
Chlorotrianisene;
Chlorphenesin, whether or not mixed with one or more of the following substances, that is to say, boric acid, hexachlorophane and zinc oxide;
Chlorpropamide;
Chlorquinaldol;
Chlorthenoxazin mixed with phenacetin;
Choline chloride;
Choline salicylate complexed with magnesium sulphate;
Clioquinol, mixed with 5-(*p*-aminobenzenesulphonamido)-3-methyl-1-phenylpyrazole, N'-(6-chloro-3-pyridazinyl) sulphanilamide and ethinyloestradiol prepared for veterinary use;
Clofazimine;
Clomiphene citrate;
Clomipramine hydrochloride;
Clonidine hydrochloride;
Clopamide, whether or not mixed with potassium salts;
Clorexolone, whether or not mixed with potassium salts;

Colaspase;
Colchicum alkaloids, and salts thereof;
Crufomate;
Cyclandelate;
Cyclocoumarol;
Cyclophosphamide;
Cytarabine, whether or not mixed with benzyl alcohol;

Danthron, mixed with poloxalkol;
Debrisoquine sulphate;
Deglycyrrhizinised block liquorice (containing not more than 3 per cent. glycyrrhi-
    zinic acid) when mixed with bismuth subnitrate, aluminium hydroxide gel, light
    magnesium carbonate, sodium bicarbonate and powdered frangula bark;
Dehydrocholic acid, and its sodium salt;
Deptropine citrate, whether or not mixed with isoprenaline hydrochloride;
Dequalinium salts, 1-alkyl-4-aminoquinaldinium salts, and mixtures of these
    substances, whether or not mixed with benzocaine;
Dextromoramide, and salts thereof;
Di-(2-aminoethyl)disulphide, and salts thereof;
Diamthazole dihydrochloride;
Diazoxide;
Dibenzepin hydrochloride;
1, 4-Di(3-bromopropionyl)piperazine;
2-4-Dichlorobenzyl alcohol with amyl-*m*-cresol;
Dichlorophen;
Di-(2-chloropropyl)-2-naphthylamine with urethane;
Dichlorphenamide;
Dichlorvos, prepared for veterinary use;
Dicoumarol;
The diethylamide of 3,5-dimethylisooxazol-4-carboxylic acid;
2-Diethylaminoethyl diphenylacetate and 2-diethylaminoethyl α-cyclohexylphenyl-
    acetate, their salts, and any combination thereof with phenobarbitone;
2-(2-Diethylaminoethoxy)ethyl 1-phenylcyclopentane-1-carboxylate citrate, whether
    or not mixed with menthol;
Diethylcarbamazine, and salts thereof;
Dihydrocodeine hydrogen tartrate mixed with one of the following, that is to say,
    acetylsalicylic acid or paracetamol;
Dihydroxyaluminium sodium carbonate, whether or not mixed with calcium
    carbonate and polyhydroxyaluminium sodium carbonate complexes, whether or
    not mixed with one of the following substances, that is to say, calcium carbonate
    and magnesium trisilicate;
3,5-Di-iodo-3'-chloro-4'-(*p*-chlorophenoxy)salicylanilide prepared for veterinary
    use;
(3,5-Di-iodo-4-hydroxy)phenyl-α-aminopropionic acid;
Dimercaprol;
Dimethindene maleate;
Dimethothiazine mesylate;
2,3-Dimethyl-4-nicotinamido-1-phenylpyrazol-5-one;
3,5-Dinitro-*N*-(5-nitrofurfurylideneamino)salicylamide mixed with polysorbate 80;
Dioctyl sodium sulphosuccinate, whether or not mixed with one of the following
    substances, that is to say, bisacodyl, danthron or oxyphenisatin diacetate;
Disodium *p*-[di(carboxymethylmercapto)arseno]benzamide prepared for veterinary
    use;
Distigmine bromide;
Dithiazanine iodide;
Dithranol;
Ditophal;
Dothiepin;
Doxepin hydrochloride;
Droperidol;
Dyflos;

Edetic acid, and salts thereof;
Edrophonium salts;
Emepronium bromide;
Ethambutol, and salts thereof;
Ethinamate;
Ethinyl oestradiol with formaldehyde-sulphathiazole, penicillin and streptomycin, prepared for veterinary use;
Etholglucid;
Ethyl biscoumacetate;
N-Ethyl-di-(3-phenylpropyl)amine, and salts thereof;
1-Ethyl-2-methyl-7-methoxytetrahydrophenanthrene-2-carboxylic acid;
Ethyl pyrophosphate;

Fenchlorphos;
Fenfluramine hydrochloride;
Fentanyl, and salts thereof, whether or not mixed with fluanisone or droperidol;
Fenticlor mixed with triamcinolone acetonide;
Flavoxate hydrochloride;
Flufenamic acid;
Fluocortolone, mixed with its hexanoate and with the hexachlorophane complex with clemizole;
4'-Fluoro-4-(4-pyrid-2-yl)piperazin-1-ylbutyrophenone;
Fluphenazine decanoate;
Fluphenazine enanthate;

4-O-β-D-Galactopyranosyl-D-fructose;
Gefarnate;
Gentisic acid, and salts thereof;
Glibenclamide;
Glyceryl trinitrate;
Guaiphenesin, mixed with brompheniramine maleate, phenylephrine hydrochloride and phenylpropanolamine hydrochloride, whether or not also mixed with codeine phosphate;
Guaiphenesin, mixed with codeine phosphate and pheniramine maleate;
Guaiphenesin, mixed with dextromethorphan hydrobromide, eucalyptol and menthol;
Guaiphenesin, mixed with ephedrine hydrochloride, theophylline and phenobarbitone;
Guaiphenesin, whether or not mixed with N-methylephedrine hydrochloride;
Guaiphenesin, mixed with phenylpropanolamine hydrochloride;
Guanoclor sulphate;
Guanoxan sulphate;

Halethazole, and salts thereof;
Halquinol, whether or not mixed with one or more of the following substances, that is to say, benzoyl peroxide, coal tar, eugenol, menthol, methyl salicylate and triamcinoline acetonide;
Hexamine mixed with camphoric acid;
Hexazole;
Hydroxyurea;

Ibufenac;
Ibuprofen;
Inproquone, and the 3,6-dimethoxyethoxy analogue;
Insulin and compounds thereof with one or more proteins or with zinc, or both with one or more proteins and with zinc;
Iodinated casein, prepared for stimulating milk production in cattle and pigs;
Ion-exchange resins;
Iprindole hydrochloride;
Isoetharine hydrochloride;
Isoxsuprine hydrochloride;
Isoxsuprine lactate, prepared for veterinary use;

Ketamine hydrochloride;

Levodopa;
Liothyronine, and salts thereof;
Lucanthone, and salts thereof;

Mannomustine, and salts thereof;
Mebeverine hydrochloride;
Mebutamate;
Mefenamic acid;
Mefruside;
Melphalan;
Mepacrine, and salts thereof;
Mepenzolate bromide, whether or not mixed with neomycin sulphate;
β-Mercaptoethylamine, and salts thereof;
Mercaptopurine;
Metformin;
Methallenoestril;
Methallibure, prepared for veterinary use;
Methanthelinium bromide;
Methocarbamol mixed with acetylsalicylic acid;
4-(4-Methoxy-1-naphthyl)-4-oxobutyric acid, and salts thereof;
Methsuximide;
1-Methylaminomethyl-dibenzo[b.e]bicyclo[2.2.2]octadiene hydrochloride;
17α-Methylandrost-5-en-3β.17β-diol;
N-Methyl-N-(β-picolyl)tropamide, and salts thereof;
Methyl prednisolone, mixed with neomycin sulphate, pentahydroxochloro-
   dialuminium and sulphur;
Metoclopramide hydrochloride;
Metronidazole;
Mexenone;
Mitobronitol;
Monosulfiram and disulfiram;
Mustine, and salts thereof;

Nalidixic acid mixed with kaolin;
Naphthalophos;
Niclofolan, prepared for veterinary use;
Niclosamide;
Nicoumalone;
Nifuratel;
Niridazole;
Nitrazepam;
Nitroxynil, and salts thereof;
Norethynodrel mixed with mestranol;
Noxythiolin, whether or not mixed with amethocaine hydrochloride or lignocaine
   hydrochloride;

Opipramol hydrochloride;
Oxazepam;
Oxeladin, and salts thereof, whether or not mixed with menthol;
Oxethazaine, whether or not mixed with aluminium hydroxide gel and magnesium
   hydroxide;
Oxprenolol hydrochloride;
Oxymetazoline hydrochloride;
Oxypertine;
Oxyphenisatin, and its diacetate;
Oxyphenonium bromide;

Paracetamol, whether or not mixed with ambucetamide;
Parbendazole, prepared for veterinary use;
Pargyline hydrochloride;
Paromomycin, mixed with pectin and kaolin;

Penicillamine;
Pentazocine;
Penthienate methobromide;
Pericyazine;
Phanquone, whether or not mixed with clioquinol;
Phenamidine isethionate;
Pheneturide;
Phenformin;
Phenglutarimide, and salts thereof;
Phenindione;
Phenoperidine hydrochloride;
Phenprocoumon;
Phenylpropanolamine hydrochloride mixed with paracetamol;
Pimozide;
Pipenzolate bromide, whether or not mixed with activated dimethicone;
Piperazine phosphate, mixed with thiabendazole, prepared for anthelmintic use;
Piperidolate hydrochloride;
Polyhexanide mixed with cetrimide prepared for veterinary use;
Polysorbate 80;
Potassium gluconate;
Potassium hydroxyquinoline sulphate mixed with benzoyl peroxide;
Povidone-iodine, prepared for surgical or medical use;
Practolol;
Pralidoxime, and salts thereof;
Preparations comprising the dried, defatted pancreas of the pig, together with cellulase and ox bile extract;
Procarbazine hydrochloride;
Procyclidine hydrochloride;
Propanidid;
Prothionamide;
Protriptyline hydrochloride;
Pyrantel tartrate;

Quaternary cationic detergents with bactericidal activity and mixtures of two or more of such substances;
Quinuronium sulphate;

Russell's viper venom, prepared for use as a haemostatic;

Salbutamol and salts thereof;
Salicylamide mixed with paracetamol;
Selenium sulphide;
Silver, whether or not mixed with benzoyl peroxide, prepared for veterinary use;
Sodium antimonylgluconate;
Sodium glucaldrate;
Sodium phytate;
Sodium tetradecyl sulphate prepared for injection as a sclerosant;
Sorbide nitrate;
Spironolactone;
Steroids used as androgenic, oestrogenic or progestational agents, or anabolic agents, having the carbon-ring structure of gonane, with any degree of unsaturation, but without additional rings;
Stibophen;
Stilboestrol, hexoestrol, dienoestrol, and esters of any of those substances, whether or not mixed with sulphatolamide;
Stilboestrol with either streptomycin and polymyxin B or organo-mercury compounds, prepared for veterinary use;
Sulisobenzone, prepared for the treatment of photoaesthesia;
Sulphadimidine, mixed with 1,1'-dimethyl-4,4'-bipyridylium dichloride, prepared for veterinary use;
Suramin;

Temazepam;
Tetracosactrin, and its hexa-acetate;
Tetramisole hydrochloride;
Thenium closylate, whether or not mixed with piperazine phosphate;
Thiabendazole;
Thiabendazole, mixed with 3,5-diiodo-3'-chloro-4'(p-chlorophenoxy)salicylanilide, prepared for veterinary use;
Thiocarlide;
Thiotepa;
Thiothixene;
Thurfyl nicotinate;
Thyroxine;
L-Thyroxine sodium, whether or not mixed with liothyronine sodium;
Titanium dioxide, when mixed with titanium peroxide, titanium salicylate and titanium tannate;
Tolazamide;
Tolbutamide;
Tolnaftate;
Tranylcypromine sulphate, whether or not mixed with trifluoperazine hydrochloride;
Tretamine;
Triaziquone;
Triethanolamine polypeptide oleate condensate;
2,4,6-Tribromo-3-hydroxytoluene, mixed with salicyclic acid, prepared for veterinary use;
Triclofos, and salts thereof;
Trifluoperidol hydrochloride;
Trimeprazine tartrate mixed with citric acid, guaiphenesin, ipecacuanha liquid extract, menthol, phenylpropanolamine hydrochloride and sodium citrate;
Trimetaphan (+)-camsylate;
Trimetazidine hydrochloride;
Trimethoprim mixed with sulphamethoxazole;
Trimipramine, and salts thereof;
Trimustine, and salts thereof;
Triphenylchloroethylene;
Trometamol mixed with sodium chloride and potassium chloride;
Tybamate;

Uramustine;
Urokinase;

Vinblastine sulphate;
Vincristine sulphate;

Warfarin sodium;

Xylazine, prepared for veterinary use;

Yellow bone marrow concentrate;

The acid phosphate of the 3-diethylamino-2,2-dimethylpropanol ester of tropic acid;

Compounds obtained by coupling p-aminobenzoyl histamine to despeciated horse serum globulin by means of the diazo reaction;

Preparations obtained from bovine plasma containing the haemostatic enzyme known as thrombin;

Preparations containing the haemostatic enzyme known as thrombokinase;

Compounds whereof the sole constituents are procaine, or a salt thereof, and gliadin or amyloprolamin, whether with strychnine sulphate or not;

The whole small intestine of the pig, cleansed, defatted, dried and powdered, and preparations derived from it.

HEAD III

The substances described under this head, and preparations consisting only of one of those substances and one or more of the following things, namely, an excipient, vehicle, base or preservative, or of two or more of those substances whether with one or more of the following things, namely, an excipient, vehicle, base or preservative, or not:—

Acepifylline;

Acepromazine maleate;

Acetylcholine, methacholine, and salts thereof;

N^4-Acetyl-4'-nitrophenylsulphanilamide with dibutyltin dilaurate and with N,N'-di-(3-nitrobenzenesulphonyl) ethylenediamine prepared for veterinary use;

Adrenaline, and salts thereof;

Alkaloids of Veratrum species;

Aluminium sulphate mixed with an organo-phosphorous compound, prepared for veterinary use;

Aminoacridine flavines, whether or not mixed with 8-hydroxyquinoline and gamma benzene hexachloride;

p-Aminobenzenesulphonamide, salts of p-aminobenzenesulphonamide, derivatives of p-aminobenzenesulphonamide having any of the hydrogen atoms of the p-amino group or of the sulphonamide group substituted by another radical, salts of such derivatives and preparations of those substances with pectin and kaolin;

Aminocaproic acid;

p-Aminosalicylic acid, and salts thereof, derivatives of p-aminosalicylic acid, and salts of such derivatives;

Amitriptyline, and salts thereof;

Amodiaquine, and salts thereof;

Amphetamine, and salts thereof, derivatives of amphetamine, and salts of such derivatives;

Amprolium, and salts thereof;

Anileridine, and salts thereof;

Arsanilic acid, and its sodium salt, prepared for veterinary use;

Arsphenamine, derivatives of arsphenamine, and salts of such derivatives;

Atropine, and salts and derivatives thereof;

Azacyclonol hydrochloride;

Azapetine, and salts thereof;

Azathioprine;

Bamethan, and salts thereof;

Bamipine, and salts thereof;

Barbituric acid and thiobarbituric acid, derivatives and salts thereof, whether or not mixed with one or more of the following substances, that is to say, aluminium acetylsalicylate, amidopyrine, bromvaletone, phenacetin, phenyl-dimethylisopropylpyrazolone, and sodium dihydroxyaluminium glycinate;

Beclamide;

Bemegride, and its sodium derivatives;

Benactyzine, and salts thereof;

Benzilonium bromide;

Benzocaine;

Benztropine, and salts thereof;

Benzyl benzoate, and preparations containing not less than 10 per cent of benzyl benzoate;

1-Benzyl-3-(dimethylcarbamoyloxy)pyridinium bromide;

Betaine, and salts thereof, whether or not combined with pepsin;

Bethanidine sulphate;

Bismuth glycollylarsanilate;

Bismuth tryparsamide;

Bretylium salts;

Butanilicaine, and salts thereof;

4'-n-Butoxyphenyl 3-morpholinopropyl ether hydrochloride;

4′-Butoxy-3-piperidinopropiophenone, and salts thereof;
Butyl aminobenzoate, and salts thereof;

Caffeine, caffeine citrate, caffeine and sodium benzoate, caffeine and sodium iodide, and caffeine and sodium salicylate;
Caramiphen, and salts thereof;
Carbachol;
Carbamazepine;
Carbamoyl-β-methylcholine chloride;
Carbenoxolone, and salts thereof;
Carbimazole;
4′-Carboxyphenylmethanesulphonanilide;
Carisoprodol;
Chloral betaine;
Chlorcyclizine hydrochloride;
Chlordiazepoxide, and salts thereof, whether or not mixed with clidinium bromide;
Chloroform (anaesthetic);
2-Chloro-4-nitrobenzamide;
2-Chloropropane;
Chloroquine, and salts thereof;
Chlorothiazide and other derivatives of bendrofluazide, whether or not mixed with potassium salts;
Chlorphentermine, and salts thereof;
Chlorproguanil, and salts thereof;
Chlorpromazine, and salts thereof;
Chlorprothixene, and salts thereof;
Chlorthalidone;
Chorionic gonadotrophin and serum gonadotrophin;
Cinchocaine, and salts thereof;
Cinchona alkaloids, and salts thereof;
Clioquinol, whether or not mixed with flumethasone pivalate and titanium dioxide;
Clofibrate, whether or not mixed with androsterone;
Cocaine, and salts thereof;
Cortisone and analogous steroid hormones, and esters thereof whether or not mixed with one or more of the following substances, that is to say, chlorhexidine, and salts thereof, acetylsalicylic acid, aluminium hydroxide, dequalinium chloride, domiphen bromide, gamma benzene hexachloride, hexachlorophane, magnesium trisilicate, bismuth subgallate, bismuth oxide anhydrous, balsam Peru, resorcinol and zinc oxide;
Cropropamide mixed with crotethamide;
Crotamiton;
Cyacetazide, whether or not combined with piperazine, prepared for veterinary use;
Cyclizine, and salts thereof;
Cyclopentamine hydrochloride, whether or not mixed with pyrrobutamine;
Cyclopentolate, and salts thereof;
Cyprenorphine;

Dapsone, and derivatives thereof;
Decoquinate;
Dehydroemetine, and salts thereof;
Demecarium bromide;
Desferrioxamine, and salts thereof;
Desipramine, and its hydrochloride;
Dextromethorphan, and salts thereof, whether or not mixed with one or more of the following substances, that is to say, ammonium chloride, extract of ipecacuanha, menthol and syrup of tolu;
Dextropropoxyphene, and salts thereof, whether or not mixed with one or more of the following substances, that is to say, acetylsalicylic acid, paracetamol and phenacetin;
N-(Dialkylaminoalkyl)phenothiazine, and salts thereof;
pp′-Diaminophenylpyridylsulphone, and derivatives thereof;
Diaveridine, whether or not mixed with sulphaquinoxaline;

Diazepam, and salts thereof;
Dichloralphenazone;
1,3-Di(p-chlorobenzylideneamino)guanidine hydrochloride;
Dicyclomine hydrochloride;
2-Diethylaminoethyl-4-amino-1-naphthoate, and salts thereof;
Diethylaminoethyltheophylline camsylate;
3,3-Diethyl-2,4-diketotetrahydropyridine;
Diethylpropion hydrochloride;
Diethylthiambutene hydrochloride;
Dihydrocodeine, and salts thereof, whether or not mixed with one or more of the
   following substances, that is to say, ammonium salicylate and liquid extract of
   thyme;
Dihydrocodeinone, and salts thereof;
3,4-Dihydroxy-1-(α-hydroxy-β-aminopropyl)benzene hydrochloride;
Di-iodohydroxyquinoline, whether or not mixed with boric acid, dextrose or lactose;
Diloxanide, and its furoic acid ester;
Dimethisoquin hydrochloride;
Dimethoxanate, and salts thereof;
N-(α-Dimethylaminopropionyl)phenothiazine methobromide;
Dimetridazole;
Dinitolmide;
4, 4'Dinitrocarbanilide and 2-hydroxy-4, 6-dimethylpyrimidine molecular complex;
Diphemanil methylsulphate;
Diphenoxylate hydrochloride mixed with atropine sulphate;
Dipipanone hydrochloride;
Diprenorphine;
Diprophylline;
Dipyrone, whether or not mixed with methindizate hydrochloride;
Disodium cromoglycate;
Disulphamide, whether or not mixed with potassium salts;

Ecothiopate iodide;
Emetine and bismuth iodide;
Emetine, and salts thereof;
Emylcamate;
Ephedrine, and salts thereof;
Ergot, and alkaloids thereof, derivatives of such alkaloids, and salts of such
   alkaloids or of their derivatives;
Esters of amino alcohols with benzoic acid (whether substituted or not), and salts
   thereof, whether or not combined with benzyl alcohol;
Ethacrynic acid, and salts thereof;
Ethamsylate;
Ethchlorvynol;
Ethebenecid;
Ethenyl-p-diethoxydiphenylamidine hydrochloride;
Ethers for general inhalation anaesthesia, and mixtures thereof;
Ethionamide;
Ethoheptazine citrate, whether or not mixed with acetylsalicylic acid or paracetamol;
Ethosalamide, whether or not mixed with phenacetin;
Ethosuximide;
Ethylenediamine dihydroiodide;
N-Ethyl-N'-(5-nitro-2-thiazolyl)urea;
Ethyleneglycol monophenylether;
Etorphine;

Ferrous fumarate anhydrous;
Ferrous succinate with or without succinic acid;
Fluopromazine, and salts thereof;
Fluorouracil;
Fluphenazine, and salts thereof;
Folic acid or derivatives thereof, whether or not combined with a salt of iron;
Forminitrazole;

Frusemide;
Furazolidone, and its 5-morpholinomethyl derivative;

Ganglionic or neuromuscular blocking agents and their antidotes containing at
least two quaternary ammonium groups terminal to a polymethylene chain or
chains;
Preparations of the following glands: parathyroid, thyroid, pituitary, suprarenal,
ovary, testis, spleen, corpus luteum, prostate, pancreas;
Glutethimide;
Glycopyrronium bromide;
The glycoside formed by the combination of 5,7,3',4'-tetrahydroxy-flavanol with
glucose and rhamnose;
Glycosides of digitalis;
Gold, and salts and compounds thereof;
Guanethidine sulphate;

Haloperidol;
Haloxon, and mixtures thereof with the inorganic compounds of both cobalt and
copper;
Hexachloroethane;
Hexetidine;
Hexocyclium methylsulphate;
Homatropine, and salts thereof;
Homatropine methobromide suitably prepared for sustained action by controlled
release;
Hormones produced by the anterior lobe of the pituitary gland;
Hydantoin derivatives, and salts thereof;
Hydrallazine, and salts thereof; dihydrallazine, and salts thereof;
Hydromorphone, and salts thereof;
Hydroxychloroquine sulphate;
Hydroxydione sodium succinate;
4-Hydroxy-3-nitrophenylarsonic acid;
1-(4-Hydroxyphenyl)-2-methylaminoethanol, and salts thereof;
Hydroxyzine, and salts thereof, whether or not mixed with menthol;
Hyoscine, and salts thereof, quaternary derivatives of hyoscine, and salts of such
derivatives;
Hyoscyamine, and salts thereof;

Idoxuridine;
Iminazole-4,5-dicarboxyamide;
Imipramine, and salts thereof;
Indomethacin;
Inositol nicotinate;
The intrinsic factor derived from the gastro-intestinal tract of animals;
Iodine, complexed with one or more surface active agents, prepared for veterinary
or surgical use;
Iron complexed with one or more of the amino acids obtained by the hydrolysis of
proteins or such acids prepared synthetically, whether or not mixed with sorbitol
powder;
Isoaminile, and salts thereof;
Isocarboxazid, and salts thereof;
Isoniazid, and salts thereof, derivatives of isoniazid, and salts of such derivatives;
Isopropamide iodide;

Khellin;

Lachesine salts;
Leptazol;
Levallorphan, and salts thereof;
Lignocaine, and salts thereof, whether or not mixed with cetyl pyridinium chloride,
eucalyptol and menthol;
Liver extracts and haemopoietic principles of liver, whether or not combined with
one or more of the following substances, that is to say, yeast, yeast concentrates,
compounds of iron and salts of manganese or of copper;

Lobeline, and salts thereof;
Lysergide tartrate;
Lypressin;

Mafenide, and salts thereof;
Malic acid, partly or wholly esterified with propylene glycol, mixed with benzoic acid, malic acid and salicylic acid;
Mecamylamine hydrochloride;
Mephenesin, whether or not mixed with paracetamol; mephenesin carbamate;
Mephentermine, and salts thereof;
Meprobamate, whether or not mixed with acetylsalicylic acid or with tridihexethyl chloride;
Mepyramine, and salts thereof, mixed with paracetamol;
Metaraminol, and salts thereof;
Methadone, and salts thereof;
Methaqualone, and salts thereof;
Methdilazine, and salts thereof;
Methimazole;
Methixene hydrochloride;
Methocarbamol;
Methorphinan, and salts thereof;
Methoserpidine;
Methotrimeprazine, and salts thereof;
Methoxamine hydrochloride;
Methoxyphenamine hydrochloride, with or without sodium citrate;
Methyl benzoquate;
Methyldopa, and salts of the ethyl ester of methyldopa;
l-N-Methylephedrine, and salts thereof;
N-Methyl-5-methylazadecylamine methobromide, in a polymerised form;
Methyl ($\pm$)-1-(α-methylbenzyl)imidazole-5-carboxylate hydrochloride, prepared for veterinary use;
Methylpentynol; methylpentynol carbamate;
Methylphenidate hydrochloride;
N-Methylpipecolin-2,6-xylidide hydrochloride;
Methyprylone;
Methyridine;
Metriphonate;
Metyrapone;
Morantel tartrate and diethylcarbamazine prepared as an anthelmintic for veterinary use;
Morphine, esters of morphine, ethers of morphine, and salts of any of those substances;

Nalidixic acid;
Nalorphine, and salts thereof;
Naphazoline, and salts thereof;
β-Naphthoxyethanol;
Neostigmine salts and neostigmine alkyl salts;
Nicotinyl alcohol, and salts thereof;
Nikethamide, whether or not combined with either or both of the following substances, that is to say, adenosine and calcium thiocyanate;
Nitrofurazone;
Noradrenaline, and salts thereof;
Nortriptyline, and salts thereof;
Noscapine, and salts thereof, whether or not mixed with paracetamol and terpin hydrate;

Octaverine;
Orciprenaline, and salts thereof;
Organo-mercury compounds;
Orthocaine;
Oxophenarsine, and salts thereof;

Oxyclozanide, whether or not mixed with tetramisole hydrochloride;
Oxymorphone hydrochloride;
Oxyphenbutazone;
Oxytocin;

Pamaquin;
Papaveretum;
Papaverine, and salts thereof;
Pecazine, and salts thereof;
Pempidine, and salts thereof;
Pentaerythritol tetranitrate, whether or not mixed with glyceryl trinitrate;
Penthrichloral;
Pentose nucleotide, and salts thereof;
Perphenazine, and salts thereof;
Pethidine hydrochloride;
Phenacemide;
Phenactropinium salts;
Phenadoxone, and salts thereof;
Phenazocine, and salts thereof;
Phenbutrazate hydrochloride mixed with phenmetrazine theoclate;
Phencyclidine hydrochloride;
Phenelzine, and salts thereof;
Phenmetrazine hydrochloride;
Pheniprazine, and salts thereof;
Phenothiazine, and mixtures thereof with one or more of the following substances,
    that is to say hexachlorophane, lead arsenate, organo-phosphorous compounds,
    2-phenylbenzimidazole, and the inorganic compounds of cobalt, of copper, of
    iron and of manganese;
Phenoxybenzamine hydrochloride;
Phensuximide;
Phentolamine, and salts thereof;
Phenylbutazone;
Phenylephrine bitartrate;
Phenylephrine hydrochloride, whether or not mixed with isoetharine mesylate and
    thenyldiamine hydrochloride;
Pholedrine, and salts thereof;
Physostigmine, and salts thereof;
Pilocarpine, and salts thereof;
Pipamazine, and salts thereof;
Pipazethate, and salts thereof;
Piperazine adipate and piperazine citrate;
Piperazine, and salts thereof, prepared for anthelmintic use;
Piperazine-1-carbodithioic betaine, whether or not mixed with thiabendazole;
Pipradrol hydrochloride;
Pivazide hydrochloride;
Poldine methylsulphate;
Polypeptides of 8 to 10 amino acid residues with pressor action;
Prilocaine;
Primaquine, and salts thereof;
Primidone;
Probenecid;
Procainamide;
Prochlorperazine, and salts thereof;
Proguanil, and salts thereof;
Pronethalol hydrochloride;
Propantheline bromide;
Propiomazine maleate;
Propranolol hydrochloride;
Propylhexedrine, and salts thereof;
Protamines, and salts thereof;
Prothipendyl, and salts thereof;
Proxyphylline;

Pseudo-ephedrine, and salts thereof;
Pyrazinamide;
Pyridostigmine salts;
Pyrimethamine;

Quinethazone;

Rauwolfia species, and alkaloids thereof;

Salicylamide;
Sennosides A and B, and salts thereof; preparations of senna fruit standardised in
    terms of sennosides A and B;
Sodium p-glycollylarsanilate;
Sodium propionate with or without one or more of the following substances, that
    is to say, cobalt sulphate, potassium chloride, sodium phosphate and terpineol;
Sparteine, and salts thereof;
Stanozolol;
Stilbamidine and other diamidines of diphenyl or diphenoxy derivatives of aliphatic
    hydrocarbons whether substituted or not, and salts thereof;
Strychnine, and salts thereof;
Sulphinpyrazone;
Sulthiame;
Suxamethonium salts;

Tetrabenazine;
Tetradeca- or hexadeca-methylene bisquinolinium salts; tetradeca- or hexadeca-
    methylene bisisoquinolinium salts;
Tetraethylammonium halides;
Tetrahydrozoline hydrochloride;
Thalidomide, and salts thereof, whether or not mixed with acetylsalicylic acid and
    phenacetin;
Thenalidine, and salts thereof, whether or not combined with calcium salts;
Theobromine;
Theobromine calcium combined with one or more of the following substances,
    that is to say, calcium salicylate and potassium iodide;
Theophylline, whether or not combined with one or more of the following substances,
    that is to say, choline, ethylenediamine, meglumine, mono-ethanolamine and
    sodium glycinate;
Thevetin;
Thiambutosine;
Thiethylperazine, and salts thereof;
Thiopropazate dihydrochloride;
Thioproperazine, and salts thereof;
Thioridazine, and salts thereof;
Thiosemicarbazones and isothiosemicarbazones;
Thiouracil, and derivatives thereof;
Thymoxamine hydrochloride, whether or not mixed with dried extract of belladonna
    root;
Tolazoline, and salts thereof;
Tolpropamine, and salts and derivatives thereof;
Triamterene;
3,4′,5-Tribromosalicylanilide, whether or not mixed with 4′,5-dibromosalicylanilide,
    prepared for veterinary use;
Trichloroethylene, whether with or without a stabiliser or a colouring agent;
Tricyclamol chloride;
Trifluoperazine, and salts thereof;
Trimethoprim;
Triprolidine hydrochloride;
Trolnitrate phosphate;
Troxidone, and other oxazolidine diones;
Tryparsamide;
Tuaminoheptane, and salts thereof;

Tubocurarine, and salts thereof;

Tyloxapol, and mixtures thereof with both sodium bicarbonate and glycerin;

Undecenoic acid, and the zinc salt thereof;

Vanilloyldiethylamine;

Viprynium embonate;

Vitamins, vitamin complexes and provitamins, whether or not combined with one or more of the following substances, that is to say, iodine, sodium chloride, and oxides, hydroxides and salts of any metal other than sodium;

Xylometazoline hydrochloride;

Zinc sulphate mixed with an organo-phosphorous compound, prepared for veterinary use;

Any antimicrobial substance being:

    (a) a substance synthesized by bacteria, fungi or protozoa; or

    (b) a substance the chemical properties of which are identical with, or similar to any substance within paragraph (a) above; or

    (c) a salt or derivative or a salt of a derivative of any substance within paragraphs (a) and (b) above; or

    (d) any substance within paragraph (a), (b) or (c) above mixed with one or more of the following substances, that is to say, cobalt salts, NN'-di-(4-amino-2-methyl-6-quinolyl)urea hydrochloride, p-hydroxybenzoic esters, kaolin, quaternary ammonium bactericides, salicyl alcohol, cloponone and myralact;

Preparations of stomach containing the haemopoietic principle thereof in a therapeutic concentration, and preparations consisting only of any such preparation of stomach as aforesaid and a salt of iron or dried yeast;

Preparations of the substances known as streptokinase or streptokinase-streptodornase which are produced from a suitable strain of haemolytic streptococcus;

The following substances and salts thereof, derivatives of these substances and salts of such derivatives:

Antazoline;

Anti-histamine substances, being tetra-substituted N derivatives of ethylene diamine;

Bromodiphenhydramine;
Buclizine;

Cinnarizine;
Clemizole;
Cyproheptadine;

3-Dibutylaminomethyl-4,5,6-trihydroxy phthalide;
Diphenhydramine;
Diphenylpyraline;
Doxylamine;

Isoprenaline;
Isothipendyl;

Mebhydrolin;
Meclozine;
Mepyramine;

Phenindamine;
Pheniramine;
Phenyltoloxamine.

Head IV

Such of the therapeutic substances commonly known as vaccines, sera, toxins, antitoxins and antigens, and such preparations of the said substances, as are described under this head:—

Any one of the said substances prepared for use by injection or by application to the scarified skin; any preparation so prepared consisting only of two or more of the said substances;

The following, prepared for oral administration:—

The vaccine prepared from the irradiated larvae of Dictyocaulus viviparus;

Vaccines prepared from attenuated strains of poliomyelitis virus.

EXPLANATORY NOTE

(This Note is not part of the Order.)

This Order consolidates the list of drugs and medicines which were free of purchase tax at the date of the making of this Order. The list supersedes the existing list shown in the Purchase Tax (No. 1) Order 1970 and includes the items subsequently exempted from tax by directions of the Commissioners of Customs and Excise under section 17(3) of the Purchase Tax Act 1963.

The Order does not exempt any additional substance or cancel any existing exemption, but some items previously listed under their chemical names now appear under the names approved by the British Pharmacopoeia Commission.

STATUTORY INSTRUMENTS

1971 No. 1171

SEA FISHERIES

BOATS AND METHODS OF FISHING

The Fishing Nets (North-East Atlantic) Order 1971

Made - - - -	19*th July* 1971
Laid before Parliament	27*th July* 1971
Coming into Operation	1*st August* 1971

The Minister of Agriculture, Fisheries and Food and the Secretaries of State for Scotland and the Home Department (being the Secretaries of State respectively concerned with the sea-fishing industry in Scotland and Northern Ireland) in exercise of the powers conferred upon them by sections 3 and 15 of the Sea Fish (Conservation) Act 1967(a) as the latter section is amended by section 22(1) of, and sub-paragraph (3) of paragraph 38 of Part II of Schedule 1 to, the Sea Fisheries Act 1968(b) and of all other powers enabling them in that behalf hereby make the following Order:—

Citation and Commencement

1. This Order may be cited as the Fishing Nets (North-East Atlantic) Order 1971 and shall come into operation on 1st August 1971.

Interpretation

2.—(1) In this Order—

"the area dividing line" means a line drawn east from the meridian of 44° west longitude along the parallel of 59° north latitude to the meridian of 42° west longitude, thence south to the parallel of 48° north latitude, thence east to the meridian of 18° west longitude, thence north to the parallel of 60° north latitude, thence east to the meridian of 15° west longitude, thence north to the parallel of 62° north latitude, thence east to the meridian of 10° west longitude, thence north to the parallel of 63° north latitude, thence east to the meridian of 4° west longitude, thence north to the parallel of 64° north latitude, thence east to the meridian of 51° east longitude;

"British sea-fishery officer" means any person who is for the time being a British sea-fishery officer by virtue of section 7 of the Sea Fisheries Act 1968;

"the Faroes Area" means the area bounded by a line drawn east from the meridian of 15° west longitude along the parallel of 60° north latitude to the meridian of 5° west longitude, thence north to the parallel of 60° 30' north latitude, thence east to the meridian of 4° west longitude, thence north to the parallel of 63° north latitude, thence west to the meridian of 10° west longitude, thence south to the parallel of 62° north latitude, thence west to the meridian of 15° west longitude, thence south to the parallel of 60° north latitude;

(a) 1967 c. 84.   (b) 1968 c. 77.

"foreign fishing boat" has the meaning assigned to it by the Fishery Limits Act 1964(a);

"fishing boat" means a vessel of whatever size and in whatever way propelled which is for the time being employed in sea-fishing or in the sea-fishing service;

"the Irish Sea" means the area bounded on the north by the parallel of 54° 38′ north latitude, on the east by the western coasts of England and Wales, on the south by the parallel of 51° north latitude and on the west by the meridian of 7° west longitude and the eastern coasts of the Republic of Ireland and Northern Ireland;

"net" means any net (not being a purse-seine net or a ring-net) constructed to take fish whilst being towed or hauled through the sea, whether on or near the bottom of the sea or otherwise, by or from a fishing boat;

"topside chafer" means a piece of netting attached to the upperside of the cod-end of a net for the purpose of preventing or reducing wear and tear.

(2) The Interpretation Act 1889(b) shall apply for the interpretation of this Order as it applies for the interpretation of an Act of Parliament, and as if this Order and the Order hereby revoked were Acts of Parliament.

Revocation of Previous Orders

3. The Fishing Nets (North-East Atlantic) Order 1969(c) is hereby revoked.

Areas in relation to which this Order has application

4. This Order has application in relation to those areas of the Atlantic and Arctic Oceans and seas adjacent to those oceans which lie north of the parallel of 36° north latitude, between the meridians of 42° west longitude and 51° east longitude and north of 59° north latitude between 44° west longitude and 42° west longitude (but excluding the Mediterranean and Baltic Seas and Belts lying to the south and east of lines drawn from Hasenore Head, Denmark, to Gniben Point, Denmark, from Korshage, Denmark, to Spodsbierg, Denmark, and from Gilbierg Head, Denmark, to Kullen, Sweden).

Sizes of Mesh of Nets

5.—(1) Except as hereinafter provided there shall not be carried, in any British fishing boat registered in the United Kingdom for the purpose of fishing for sea-fish in any of the waters referred to in the first column of Schedule 1 to this Order, any net or part of a net of a type specified in the second column of Schedule 1 opposite the reference to the said waters unless it has in all its parts meshes of such dimensions that when any mesh is stretched diagonally lengthwise of the net a flat gauge 2 millimetres thick, and of a width specified in the third column of Schedule 1 opposite the reference to that type of net, will pass easily through the mesh whether the net is wet or dry.

(2) Except as hereinafter provided, there shall not be carried, by any foreign fishing boat within the fishery limits of the British Islands adjacent to the United Kingdom for the purpose of fishing for sea-fish in any of the waters in relation to which this Order has application, any net or part of a net of a type specified in

(a) 1964 c. 72. (b) 1889 c. 63.
(c) S.I. 1969/1823 (1969 III, p. 5660).

the first column of Schedule 2 to this Order unless it has in all its parts meshes of such dimensations that when any mesh is stretched diagonally lengthwise of the net a flat gauge 2 milllimetres thick, and of a width specified in the second column of Schedule 2 opposite the reference to that type of net, will pass easily through the mesh whether the net is wet or dry.

Obstruction of nets

6.—(1) Except as hereinafter provided, there shall not be carried in

(*a*) any British fishing boat registered in the United Kingdom, or

(*b*) any foreign fishing boat in any waters adjacent to the United Kingdom, and within the fishery limits of the British Islands

for the purposes of fishing for sea-fish in any waters to which this Order has application, any net having a covering of canvas or other material attached to it, or in respect of which any artifice may have been employed in such a manner that the mesh in any part of the net is obstructed or otherwise diminished in effect.

(2) Nothing in this Order shall be deemed to prohibit the attachment to the underside of the cod-end of a net of any canvas, netting or other material for the purpose of preventing or reducing wear and tear.

Topside Chafers

7.—(1) There shall not be carried in any British fishing boat registered in the United Kingdom any net to which a topside chafer is attached unless the net in question is a trawl net, the attachment is made for the purpose of fishing in waters north of the area dividing line, and the chafer complies with one of the following specifications:—

(*a*) a piece of netting, rectangular in shape, having in all its parts meshes the dimensions of which are not less than those of the meshes of the cod-end whether the netting and the cod-end respectively be wet or dry; being in width at least one and a half times the width of the part of the cod-end which is covered by it, (such widths being measured at right angles to the long axis of the cod-end); and fastened to the cod-end only along the forward and lateral edges of the piece of netting in such a way that—

(i) if there is a splitting strop, the piece of netting begins at a distance of not more than four of the meshes to which it is attached forward of the splitting strop and ends at a distance of not less than four of such meshes forward of the cod-line mesh; or

(ii) if there is no splitting strop, the piece of netting extends for not more than one-third of the length of the cod-end and ends at a distance of not less than four of the meshes of the net to which it is attached forward of the cod-line mesh; or

(*b*) pieces of netting having in all their parts meshes the dimensions of which are not less than those of the meshes of the cod-end whether the netting and the cod-end respectively be wet or dry; each piece being

(i) fastened by its forward edge only across the cod-end at right angles to the long axis of the cod-end;

(ii) of a width of at least the width of the cod-end (such width being measured at right angles to the long axis of the cod-end at the point of attachment) and

(iii) of not more than ten meshes long;

and the said pieces having an aggregate length when so attached not exceeding two-thirds of the length of the cod-end; or

(c) a piece of netting made of the same material as the cod-end, having in all its parts meshes whereof the dimensions are twice the dimensions of the meshes of the cod-end, whether the netting and the cod-end respectively be wet or dry, and fastened to the cod-end along the forward, lateral and rear edges only of the netting, in such a way that each mesh of the piece of netting coincides with four meshes of the cod-end.

(2) The provisions of this Article shall be without prejudice to the provisions of Article 7 of the Fishing Nets (Northwest Atlantic) Order 1969(a) and the carrying of any net to which a topside chafer is attached in accordance with the provisions of that Article shall be deemed not to be a contravention of the provisions of this Article.

Defences—British Fishing Boats

8. In any proceedings in respect of a contravention of Article 5 (1) of this Order it shall be a sufficient defence to prove that the net to which the proceedings relate:—

(1) was being carried solely for the purpose of fishing in waters situated north of the area dividing line for mackerel, clupeoid fish, sand-eels (Ammodytes), Norway pout (Gadus esmarkii), smelts, eels, great weevers (Trachinus draco), capelin (Mallotos villosus), blue whiting (Gadus poutassou), horse mackerel (Trachurus trachurus), Polar cod (Boreogadus saida), saury (Scomberesox saurus), shrimps, prawns, nephrops or molluscs other than squid; or

(2) had in no part of its cod-end meshes of such dimensions that when any mesh was stretched diagonally lengthwise of the net a flat gauge of 50 mm. broad and 2 mm. thick would pass easily through it whether the net was wet or dry and was being carried solely for the purpose of fishing:—

(a) for mackerel, clupeoid fish, sand-eels (Ammodytes), Norway pout (Gadus esmarkii), smelts, eels, great weevers (Trachinus draco), capelin (Mallotus villosus), Polar cod (Boreogadus saida), saury (Scomberesox saurus), shrimps, prawns or molluscs other than squids in waters south of the area dividing line, or

(b) for horse mackerel (Trachurus trachurus) in waters south of the area dividing line and north of the parallel of 48° north latitude, or

(c) for blue whiting (Gadus poutassou) in waters south of the area dividing line and north of the parallel of 48° north latitude other than such part of those waters as lies between the parallels of 52° 30′ north latitude and 48° north latitude and between the meridians of 7° west longitude and 18° west longitude, or

(d) for Nephrops norvegicus (commonly known as Norway lobster or Dublin Bay prawn) in the Irish Sea, and that none of the sea-fish taken in the course of the voyage on which the net to which the proceedings relate was carried, was landed, or was to be landed, at a place other than one bordering upon the Irish Sea; or

(a) S.I. 1969/628 (1969 I, p. 1734).

(3)(a) had in all its parts meshes of such dimensions that when any mesh was stretched diagonally lengthwise of the net a flat gauge 60 mm. broad and 2 mm. thick would pass easily through it whether the net was wet or dry, and

(b) was carried solely in that part of the Irish Sea which lies between the parallels of 53° and 54° 30' north latitude and west of the meridian of 5° 15' west longitude for the purpose of fishing for whiting, and

(c) was carried in a fishing boat operating from and landing its catch at a port or place bordering upon the said part of the Irish Sea.

Defences—Foreign Fishing Boats

9. In any proceedings in respect of a contravention of Article 5(2) of this Order it shall be a sufficient defence to prove that the net to which the proceedings relate:—

(a) had in no part of its cod-end meshes of such dimensions that when any mesh was stretched diagonally lengthwise of the net a flat guage 50 mm. broad and 2 mm. thick would pass easily through it whether the net was wet or dry, and that it was being carried solely for the purpose of fishing for mackerel, clupeoid fish, sand-eels (Ammodytes), Norway pout (Gadus esmarkii), smelts, eels, great weevers (Trachinus draco), capelin (Mallotus villosus), horse mackerel (Trachurus trachurus), blue whiting (Gadus poutassou), Polar cod, (Boreogadus saida), saury (Scomberesox saurus), shrimps, prawns, nephrops or molluscs, or

(b) being a net of a type specified in the first column of Schedule 3, had in all its parts meshes of such dimensions that when any mesh was stretched diagonally lengthwise of the net a flat guage 2mm. thick and of a width specified in the second column of Schedule 3 opposite the reference to that type of net would pass easily through the mesh whether the net was wet or dry, and that it was being carried solely for the purpose of fishing south of the parallel of 48° north latitude.

Powers of British Sea-Fishery Officers

10. For the purpose of the enforcement of the provisions of this Order there are hereby conferred on every British sea-fishery officer the powers of a British Sea-Fishery Officer under Section 8(2) to (4) of the Sea Fisheries Act 1968(a).

In witness whereof the Official Seal of the Minister of Agriculture, Fisheries and Food is hereunto affixed on 14th July 1971.

L.S.

J. M. L. Prior,
Minister of Agriculture, Fisheries & Food.

16th July 1971.

Gordon Campbell,
Secretary of State for Scotland.

19th July 1971.

R. Maudling,
Secretary of State for the Home Department.

(a) 1968 c. 77.

Article 5(1)

SCHEDULE 1

Column 1	Column 2	Column 3
Waters	Net	Appropriate width of gauge
(a) Waters of the areas north of the area dividing line	(1) Seine net	110 millimetres
	(2) Such part of any trawl net as is made of cotton hemp, polyamide fibres or poly-ester fibres	120 millimetres
	(3) Such part of any trawl net as is made of any other material	130 millimetres
(b) Waters of the Faroes area	(1) Seine net	105 millimetres
	(2) Such part of any trawl net as is made of manila or sisal	110 millimetres
	(3) Such part of any trawl net as is made of any other material	105 millimetres
(c) All other waters of the areas in relation to which this Order has effect	(1) Seine net, or such part of any trawl net as is made of single twine and contains no manila or sisal	70 millimetres
	(2) Such part of any trawl net as is made of double twine and contains no manila or sisal	75 millimetres
	(3) Such part of any trawl net as is made of manila or sisal	80 millimetres

Article 5(2)

SCHEDULE 2

Column 1	Column 2
Net	Appropriate width of gauge
(1) Seine net, or such part of any trawl net as is made of single twine and contains no manila or sisal	70 millimetres
(2) Such part of any trawl net as is made of double twine and contains no manila or sisal	75 millimetres
(3) Such part of any trawl net as is made of manila or sisal	80 millimetres

Article 9

SCHEDULE 3

Column 1	Column 2
Net	Appropriate width of guage
(1) Such part of any net as is made of single twine synthetic fibre	60 millimetres
(2) Such part of any net as is made of double twine synthetic fibre	65 millimetres
(3) Such part of any net as is made of manila or sisal	70 millimetres

EXPLANATORY NOTE

(This Note is not part of the Order.)

This Order supersedes the Fishing Nets (North-East Atlantic) Order 1969. It prescribes minimum sizes of mesh for the fishing nets carried by registered British fishing boats for fishing in areas specified in the Order and by foreign fishing boats within the fishery limits of the British Islands adjacent to the United Kingdom.

The principal changes are:—

1. The Order now applies to all nets with the exception of purse-seine nets and ring nets, constructed to take fish while being towed or hauled through the sea by or from a fishing boat.

2. The area dividing line has been extended further to the north at its eastern end.

STATUTORY INSTRUMENTS

1971 No. 1172

SEA FISHERIES

BOATS AND METHODS OF FISHING

The Fishing Nets (Northwest Atlantic) Order 1971

Made - - - -	*20th July* 1971
Laid before Parliament	*27th July* 1971
Coming into Operation	*1st August* 1971

The Minister of Agriculture, Fisheries and Food and the Secretaries of State for Scotland and the Home Department (being the Secretaries of State respectively concerned with the sea fishing industry in Scotland and Northern Ireland) in exercise of the powers conferred upon them by sections 3 and 15 of the Sea Fish (Conservation) Act 1967(a) as the latter section is amended by section 22(1) of, and sub-paragraph (3) of paragraph 38 of Part II of Schedule 1 to, the Sea Fisheries Act 1968(b) and all other powers enabling them in that behalf, hereby make the following Order:—

Citation and commencement

1. This Order may be cited as the Fishing Nets (Northwest Atlantic) Order and shall come into operation on 1st August 1971.

Interpretation

2.—(1) In this Order—

"British sea-fishery officer" means any person who is for the time being a British sea-fishery officer by virtue of section 7 of the Sea Fisheries Act 1968;

"fishing boat" means a vessel of whatever size, and in whatever way propelled, which is for the time being employed in sea fishing or the sea fishing service;

"net" means any net constructed to take fish whilst being towed or hauled at or near the bottom of the sea by or from a fishing boat;

"subarea 1" means that area forming part of the waters in relation to which this Order has application which lies to the north and east of a rhumb line from a point in 75° north latitude and 73° 30′ west longitude to a point in 69° north latitude and 59° west longitude; east of 59° west longitude; and to the north and east of a rhumb line from a point in 61° north latitude and 59° west longitude to a point in 52° 15′ north latitude and 42° west longitude;

(a) 1967 c, 84,   (b) 1968 c, 77,

"subarea 2" means that area forming part of the waters in relation to which this Order has application which lies to the south and west of subarea 1 and to the north of the parallel of 52° 15′ north latitude;

"subarea 3" means that area forming part of the waters in relation to which this Order has application lying south of the parallel of 52° 15′ north latitude and to the east of a line extending due north from Cape Bauld on the north coast of Newfoundland to a point in 52° 15′ north latitude; to the north of the parallel 39° north latitude and to the east and north of a rhumb line extending in a northwesterly direction which passes through a point in 43° 30′ north latitude, 55° west longitude, in the direction of a point in 47° 50′ north latitude, 60° west longitude, until it intersects a straight line connecting Cape Ray on the coast of Newfoundland with Cape North on Cape Breton Island; thence in a northeasterly direction along the said line to Cape Ray;

"division 3 N/P" means those waters forming part of subarea 3 which lie south of the Newfoundland coast, west of a line from Cape St. Mary to a point in 46° north latitude, 54° 30′ west longitude, south of a line drawn eastwards along the parallel 46° north latitude to meet the meridian 46° 30′ west longitude; and west of a line due south to meet the parallel 39° north latitude;

"subarea 4" means that area forming part of the waters in relation to which this Order has application lying to the west of subarea 3 and to the east of a line described as follows:— beginning at the terminus of the international boundary between the United States of America and Canada in Grand Manan Channel, at a point in 44° 46′ 35·34″ north latitude, 66° 54′ 11·23″ west longitude, thence due south to the parallel of 43° 50′ north latitude; thence due west to the meridian of 67° 40′ west longitude; thence due south to the parallel of 42° 20′ north latitude; thence due east to a point in 66° west longitude; thence along a rhumb line in a south easterly direction to a point in 42° north latitude, 65° 40′ west longitude; thence due south to the parallel of 39° north latitude;

"subarea 5" means that area forming part of the waters in relation to which this Order has application lying to the west of the western boundary of subarea 4;

(2) The Interpretation Act 1889(a) shall apply for the interpretation of this Order as it applies for the interpretation of an Act of Parliament, and as if this Order and the Order hereby revoked were Acts of Parliament.

Revocation of previous Order

3. The Fishing Nets (Northwest Atlantic) Order 1969(b) is hereby revoked.

Waters in relation to which this Order has application

4. This Order has application in relation to those waters, except territorial waters, bounded by a line drawn due south from the coast of Rhode Island along 71° 40′ west longitude to 39° north latitude; thence due east to 42° west longitude; thence due north to 59° north latitude; thence due west to 44° west longitude; thence due north to the coast of Greenland; thence along the west coast of Greenland to 78° 10′ north latitude; thence southward to a point in 75° north latitude and 73° 30′ west longitude; thence along a rhumb line to a

---

(a) 1889 c. 63. (b) S.I. 1969/628 (1969 I, p. 1734).

point in 69° north latitude and 59° west longitude; thence due south to 61° north latitude; thence due west to 64° 30′ west longitude; thence due south to the coast of Labrador; thence in a southerly direction along the coast of Labrador to the southern terminus of its boundary with Quebec; thence in a westerly direction along the coast of Quebec, and in an easterly and southerly direction along the coasts of New Brunswick, Nova Scotia, and Cape Breton Island to Cabot Strait; thence along the coasts of Cape Breton Island, Nova Scotia, New Brunswick, Maine, New Hampshire, Massachusetts, and Rhode Island to the point of beginning; and which waters comprise the subareas 1 to 5 as defined for the purposes of this Order.

Sizes of Mesh of Nets

5.—(1) Except as hereinafter provided, there shall not be carried in any British fishing boat registered in the United Kingdom any net or part of a net of a description specified in Column 2 of Schedule 1 to this Order for the purpose of fishing in any of the subareas forming part of the waters to which this Order has application and specified in Column 1 of the Schedule for fish of a description specified in relation to that subarea unless it has in all its parts meshes of such a size that when any mesh is stretched diagonally lengthwise of the net a flat gauge 2 mm. thick and of the width specified in Column 3 of the said Schedule 1 opposite to the reference to that description of net and that subarea, will pass easily through the mesh whether the net is wet or dry.

(2) For the purposes of the last foregoing paragraph the reference to fish of a description specified in relation to any subarea shall be construed as a reference to fish of a description specified in relation to that subarea in Schedule 2 to this Order.

Obstruction of Nets

6.—(1) Except as hereinafter provided, there shall not be carried in any British fishing boat registered in the United Kingdom for the purpose of fishing in any of the subareas forming part of the waters to which this Order has application for fish of any description specified in Schedule 2 to this Order in relation to that subarea any net or part of a net having a covering of canvas or any other material attached to it or in respect of which any artifice may have been employed in such manner that the mesh in any part of the net is obstructed or otherwise diminished in effect.

(2) Nothing in this Order shall be deemed to prohibit the attachment to the underside of the cod-end of any net, of canvas, netting or other material for the purpose of preventing or reducing wear and tear.

Topside Chafers

7.—(1) There shall not be carried in any British fishing boat registered in the United Kingdom any net to which a topside chafer is attached unless the net is a trawl net, the attachment is made for the purpose of fishing in waters in relation to which this Order has application and the chafer complies with one of the following specifications:—

(a) a piece of netting, rectangular in shape, having in all its parts meshes the dimensions of which are not less than those of the meshes of the cod-end whether the netting and the cod-end respectively be wet or dry; being in width at least one and a half times the width of the part of the cod-end which is covered by it, (such widths being measured at right angles to the long axis of the cod-end); and fastened to the cod-end only along the forward and lateral edges of the piece of netting in such a way that—

(i) if there is a splitting strop, the piece of netting begins at a distance of not more than four of the meshes to which it is attached forward of the splitting strop and ends at a distance of not less than four of such meshes forward of the cod-line mesh, or

(ii) if there is no splitting strop, the piece of netting extends for not more than one-third of the length of the cod-end and ends at a distance of not less than four of the meshes of the net to which it is attached forward of the cod-line mesh; or

(b) pieces of netting having in all their parts meshes the dimensions of which are not less than those of the meshes of the cod-end whether the netting and the cod-end respectively be wet or dry; each piece being—

(i) fastened by its forward edge only across the cod-end at right angles to the long axis of the cod-end;

(ii) of a width of at least the width of the cod-end (such width being measured at right angles to the long axis of the cod-end at the point of attachment), and

(iii) of not more than ten meshes long; and the said pieces having an aggregate length when so attached not exceeding two-thirds of the length of the cod-end; or

(c) a piece of netting made of the same material as the cod-end, having in all its parts meshes whereof the dimensions are twice the dimensions of the meshes of the cod-end, whether the netting and the cod-end respectively be wet or dry, and fastened to the cod-end along the forward, lateral and rear edges only of the netting, in such a way that each mesh of the piece of netting coincides with four meshes of the cod-end.

(2) In this Article "topside chafer" means a piece of netting attached to the upperside of the cod-end of a net for the purpose of preventing or reducing wear and tear.

(3) The provisions of this Article shall be without prejudice to the provisions of Article 7 of the Fishing Nets (North-East Atlantic) Order 1971(a) and the carrying of any net to which a topside chafer is attached in accordance with the provisions of that Article shall be deemed not to be a contravention of the provisions of this Article.

Defences

8.—(1) In any proceedings in respect of a contravention of Article 5 of this Order it shall be a sufficient defence to prove in relation to any net to which the proceedings relate being a net carried for the purpose of fishing in subarea 3 that the net was being carried on a voyage undertaken solely for the purpose of fishing in division 3 N/P primarily for redfish (Sebastes):

(a) S.I. 1971/1171 (1971 II, p. 3446).

Provided that the provisions of this paragraph shall not apply in any case where the fishing boat on which the net was carried has on board during the voyage a quantity of—

(a) cod (Gadus morhua); or

(b) haddock (Melanogrammus aeglefinus); or

(c) sea fish of any other description specified in relation to subarea 3 in said Schedule 2 (excluding redfish (Sebastes))

any of which exceeds 5,000 lbs. (2,268 Kgs.) or one-tenth of the total weight of all fish on board whichever is the greater.

(2) In any proceedings in respect of a contravention of Article 5 of this Order it shall be a sufficient defence to prove in relation to any net to which the proceedings relate being a net carried for the purpose of fishing in subarea 4 that the net was being carried on a voyage undertaken solely for the purpose of fishing in subarea 4 primarily for sea fish of a description other than the descriptions of sea fish specified in relation to subarea 4 in Schedule 2 to this Order:

Provided that the provisions of this paragraph shall not apply in any case where the fishing boat on which the net was carried has on board during the voyage a quantity of—

(a) cod (Gadus morhua); or

(b) haddock (Melanogrammus aeglefinus); or

(c) sea fish of any other description specified in relation to subarea 4 in said Schedule 2

any of which exceeds 5,000 lbs. (2,268 Kgs.) or one-tenth of the total weight of all the fish on board whichever is the greater.

(3) In any proceedings in respect of a contravention of Article 5 of this Order it shall be a sufficient defence to prove in relation to any net to which the proceedings relate being a net carried for the purpose of fishing in subarea 5 that the net was being carried on a voyage undertaken solely for the purpose of fishing in subarea 5 primarily for any description of sea fish other than cod (Gadus morhua) or haddock (Melanogrammus aeglefinus):

Provided that the provisions of this paragraph shall not apply in any case where the fishing boat on which the net was carried has on board during the voyage a quantity of such cod or of such haddock exceeding in either case 5,000 lbs. (2,268 Kgs.) or one-tenth in weight of the total weight of all fish on board whichever is the greater.

Enforcement

9. For the purpose of the enforcement of the provisions of this Order there are hereby conferred on every British sea-fishery officer the powers of a British sea-fishery officer under section 8(2) and (3) of the Sea Fisheries Act 1968(a).

(a) 1968 c. 77.

In witness whereof the Official Seal of the Minister of Agriculture, Fisheries and Food is hereunto affixed on 14th July 1971.

(L.S.)
J. M. L. Prior,
Minister of Agriculture, Fisheries and Food.

16th July 1971.
Gordon Campbell,
Secretary of State for Scotland.

20th July 1971.
R. Maudling,
Secretary of State for the Home Department.

Article 5

SCHEDULE 1

PRESCRIPTION OF SIZE OF MESH

Column 1	Column 2	Column 3
Subarea	Description of Net	Width of flat gauge
1.	(1) Seine net	110 millimetres
2.	(2) Such part of any trawl net as is made of cotton, hemp, polyamide fibres or polyester fibres	120 millimetres
3.	(3) Such part of any trawl net as is made of manila or any other material not mentioned in (2) above	130 millimetres
4.	(1) Seine net	100 millimetres
	(2) Such part of any trawl net as is made of cotton, hemp, polyamide fibres or polyester fibres	105 millimetres
5.	(3) Such part of any trawl net as is made of manila or any other material not mentioned in (2) above	114 millimetres

Articles 5 and 6

SCHEDULE 2

SPECIFICATIONS OF DESCRIPTIONS OF FISH IN RELATION TO SUBAREAS

Subarea 1	Subarea 2	Subarea 3	Subarea 4	Subarea 5
cod (Gadus morhua)	cod (Gadus morhua)	cod (Gadus morhua)	cod (Gadus morhua)	cod (Gadus morhua)
haddock (Melanogrammus aeglefinus)	haddock (Melanogrammus aeglefinus)	haddock (Melanogrammus aeglefinus)	haddock (Melanogrammus aeglefinus)	haddock (Melanogrammus aeglefinus)
redfish (Sebastes)	redfish (Sebastes)	redfish (Sebastes)	witch (Glyptocephalus cynoglossus)	yellowtail flounder (Limanda ferruginea)
halibut (Hippoglossus hippoglossus)	halibut (Hippoglossus hippoglossus)	halibut (Hippoglossus hippoglossus)	yellowtail flounder (Limanda ferruginea)	
witch (Glyptocephalus cynoglossus)	witch (Glyptocephalus cynoglossus)	witch (Glyptocephalus cynoglossus)	winter flounder (Pseudopleuronectes americanus)	
American plaice (Hippoglossoides platessoides)	American plaice (Hippoglossoides platessoides)	yellowtail flounder (Limanda ferruginea)	American plaice (Hippoglossoides platessoides)	
Greenland halibut (Reinhardtius hippoglossoides)	Greenland halibut (Reinhardtius hippoglossoides)	American plaice (Hippoglossoides platessoides)		
		Greenland halibut (Reinhardtius hippoglossoides)		
		pollock (Pollachius virens)		
		white hake (Urophycis tenuis)		

EXPLANATORY NOTE

(This Note is not part of the Order.)

This Order regulates the sizes of mesh of seine and trawl nets carried by registered British fishing boats for the purpose of fishing in five defined areas of the Northwest Atlantic for sea fish specified in the Order. The Order, which supersedes the Fishing Nets (Northwest Atlantic) Order 1969, increases the minimum mesh sizes for subareas 2 and 3 and has been extended to include yellowtail flounder in relation to subarea 5.

STATUTORY INSTRUMENTS

1971 No. 1175

DECIMAL CURRENCY

The Decimal Currency Board (Dissolution) Order 1971

Laid before Parliament in draft

Made   - - -   *20th July* 1971

Coming into Operation   *30th September* 1971

The Treasury, in exercise of the powers conferred on them by section 6 of the Decimal Currency Act 1967(a) and of all other powers enabling them in that behalf, hereby make the following Order :—

1. This Order may be cited as the Decimal Currency Board (Dissolution) Order 1971, and shall come into operation on 30th September 1971.

2. The Interpretation Act 1889(b) shall apply for the interpretation of this Order as it applies for the interpretation of an Act of Parliament.

3.—(1) The Decimal Currency Board (in this Order referred to as "the Board") is hereby dissolved.

(2) All the property, rights, liabilities and obligations to which the Board was entitled or subject immediately before the coming into operation of this Order are hereby transferred to the Treasury.

4. This Order shall not affect the validity of anything done by the Board before the coming into operation of this Order ; and anything which, at the time of the coming into operation of this Order, is in process of being done by or in relation to the Board (including, in particular, any legal proceedings to which the Board is a party) may, if it relates to any property, rights, liabilities or obligations transferred by this Order, be continued by or in relation to the Treasury.

5. Section 4(2) of the Decimal Currency Act 1967 and the words "The Decimal Currency Board" thereby inserted in Part II of Schedule 1 to the House of Commons Disqualification Act 1957(c) are hereby repealed.

(a) 1967 c. 47.   (b) 1889 c. 63.
(c) 1957 c. 20.

H. S. P. Monro,

V. H. Goodhew,

Two of the Lords Commissioners
of Her Majesty's Treasury.

20th July 1971.

EXPLANATORY NOTE

(This Note is not part of the Order.)

This Order dissolves the Decimal Currency Board on 30th September 1971 and transfers to the Treasury the Board's assets and liabilities.

STATUTORY INSTRUMENTS

1971 No. 1176

INDUSTRIAL TRAINING

The Industrial Training Levy (Shipbuilding) Order 1971

Made - - -	*20th July* 1971
Laid before Parliament	*28th July* 1971
Coming into Operation	*4th August* 1971

The Secretary of State after approving proposals submitted by the Shipbuilding Industry Training Board for the imposition of a further levy on employers in the shipbuilding industry and in exercise of his powers under section 4 of the Industrial Training Act 1964(**a**) and of all other powers enabling him in that behalf hereby makes the following Order :—

Title and commencement

1. This Order may be cited as the Industrial Training Levy (Shipbuilding) Order 1971 and shall come into operation on 4th August 1971.

Interpretation

2.—(1) In this Order unless the context otherwise requires :—

(*a*) "agriculture" has the same meaning as in section 109(3) of the Agriculture Act 1947(**b**) or, in relation to Scotland, as in section 86(3) of the Agriculture (Scotland) Act 1948(**c**) ;

(*b*) "an appeal tribunal" means an industrial tribunal established under section 12 of the Industrial Training Act 1964 ;

(*c*) "assessment" means an assessment of an employer to the levy ;

(*d*) "the Board" means the Shipbuilding Industry Training Board ;

(*e*) "business" means any activities of industry or commerce ;

(*f*) "charity" has the same meaning as in section 360 of the Income and Corporation Taxes Act 1970(**d**) ;

(*g*) "emoluments" means all emoluments assessable to income tax under Schedule E (other than pensions), being emoluments from which tax under that Schedule is deductible, whether or not tax in fact falls to be deducted from any particular payment thereof ;

(*h*) "employer" means a person who is an employer in the shipbuilding industry at any time in the seventh levy period ;

(*i*) "the industrial training order" means the Industrial Training (Shipbuilding Board) Order 1968(**e**) ;

(*j*) "the levy" means the levy imposed by the Board in respect of the seventh levy period ;

(*k*) "notice" means a notice in writing ;

(**a**) 1964 c. 16. (**b**) 1947 c. 48.
(**c**) 1948 c. 45. (**d**) 1970 c. 10.
(**e**) S.I. 1968/1614 (1968 III, p. 4432).

(*l*) "shipbuilding establishment" means an establishment in Great Britain engaged in the seventh base period wholly or mainly in the shipbuilding industry for a total of twenty-seven or more weeks or, being an establishment that commenced to carry on business in the seventh base period, for a total number of weeks exceeding one-half of the number of weeks in the part of the said period commencing with the day on which business was commenced and ending on the last day thereof ;

(*m*) "the shipbuilding industry" means any one or more of the activities which, subject to the provisions of paragraph 2 of the Schedule to the industrial training order, are specified in paragraph 1 of that Schedule as the activities of the shipbuilding industry ;

(*n*) "the seventh base period" means the period of twelve months that commenced on 6th April 1970 ;

(*o*) "the seventh levy period" means the period commencing with the day upon which this Order comes into operation and ending on 31st July 1972.

(2) Any reference in this Order to an establishment that commences to carry on business or that ceases to carry on business shall not be taken to apply where the location of the establishment is changed but its business is continued wholly or mainly at or from the new location, or where the suspension of activities is of a temporary or seasonal nature.

(3) The Interpretation Act 1889(**a**) shall apply to the interpretation of this Order as it applies to the interpretation of an Act of Parliament.

Imposition of the Levy

3.—(1) The levy to be imposed by the Board on employers in respect of the seventh levy period shall be assessed in accordance with the provisions of this Article.

(2) The levy shall be assessed by the Board separately in respect of each shipbuilding establishment of an employer, not being an employer who is exempt from the levy by virtue of paragraph (6) of this Article.

(3) Subject to the provisions of this Article, the levy assessed in respect of a shipbuilding establishment of an employer shall be an amount equal to 1·7 per cent. of the sum (less £5,000) of the emoluments of all the persons following, that is to say—

(*a*) any persons employed by the employer at or from that establishment in the seventh base period ;

(*b*) any persons deemed to have been so employed under the provisions of the next following paragraph.

(4) In the case where a shipbuilding establishment is taken over (whether directly or indirectly) by an employer in succession to, or jointly with, another person, a person employed at any time in the seventh base period at or from the establishment shall be deemed, for the purposes of this Article, to have been so employed by the employer carrying on the said establishment on the day upon which this Order comes into operation.

(5) The amount of the levy imposed in respect of a shipbuilding establishment that ceases to carry on business in the seventh levy period shall be in

the same proportion to the amount that would otherwise be due under paragraph (3) of this Article as the number of days between the commencement of the said levy period and the date of cessation of business (both dates inclusive) bears to the number of days in the said levy period.

(6) There shall be exempt from the levy—

    (*a*) an employer in respect of whom the sum of the emoluments of all the persons employed by him in the seventh base period at or from a shipbuilding establishment in no case exceeds £5,058 ;

    (*b*) a charity.

(7) For the purposes of this Article no regard shall be had to the emoluments of any person—

    (*a*) employed as the master or a member of the crew of a ship or any person ordinarily employed in or about a ship in port on work of a kind ordinarily done by a seaman on a ship while it is in port ;

    (*b*) engaged wholly in any operations mentioned in paragraph 1(*a*) or 1(*b*) of the Schedule to the industrial training order being a person undergoing a course of training as a sea-going officer or rating (otherwise than in the sea-fishing service) under an agreement in writing with an employer in the shipping industry or with any organisation of employers in that industry or any association of such organisations ;

    (*c*) engaged wholly in agriculture ; or

    (*d*) engaged wholly in the supply of food or drink for immediate consumption.

Assessment Notices

4.—(1) The Board shall serve an assessment notice on every employer assessed to the levy, but one notice may comprise two or more assessments.

(2) The amount of any assessment payable under an assessment notice shall be rounded down to the nearest £1.

(3) An assessment notice shall state the Board's address for the service of a notice of appeal or of an application for an extension of time for appealing.

(4) An assessment notice may be served on the person assessed to the levy either by delivering it to him personally or by leaving it, or sending it to him by post, at his last known address or place of business in the United Kingdom or, if that person is a corporation, by leaving it, or sending it by post to the corporation, at such address or place of business or at its registered or principal office.

Payment of the Levy

5.—(1) Subject to the provisions of this Article and of Articles 6 and 7, the amount of each assessment appearing in an assessment notice served by the Board shall be payable to the Board in three equal instalments, and the said instalments shall be due respectively one month, four months and seven months after the date of the notice.

(2) An instalment of an assessment shall not be recoverable by the Board until there has expired the time allowed for appealing against the assessment by Article 7(1) of this Order and any further period or periods of time that the Board or an appeal tribunal may have allowed for appealing under paragraph (2) or (3) of that Article or, where an appeal is brought, until the appeal is decided or withdrawn.

Withdrawal of Assessment

6.—(1) The Board may, by a notice served on the person assessed to the levy in the same manner as an assessment notice, withdraw an assessment if that person has appealed against that assessment under the provisions of Article 7 of this Order and the appeal has not been entered in the Register of Appeals kept under the appropriate Regulations specified in paragraph (5) of that Article.

(2) The withdrawal of an assessment shall be without prejudice to the power of the Board to serve a further assessment notice in respect of any establishment to which that assessment related and, where the withdrawal is made by reason of the fact that an establishment has ceased to carry on business in the seventh levy period, the said notice may provide that the whole amount payable thereunder in respect of the establishment shall be due one month after the date of the notice.

Appeals

7.—(1) A person assessed to the levy may appeal to an appeal tribunal against the assessment within one month from the date of the service of the assessment notice or within any further period or periods of time that may be allowed by the Board or an appeal tribunal under the following provisions of this Article.

(2) The Board by notice may for good cause allow a person assessed to the levy to appeal to an appeal tribunal against the assessment at any time within the period of four months from the date of the service of the assessment notice or within such further period or periods as the Board may allow before such time as may then be limited for appealing has expired.

(3) If the Board shall not allow an application for extension of time for appealing, an appeal tribunal shall upon application made to the tribunal by the person assessed to the levy have the like powers as the Board under the last foregoing paragraph.

(4) In the case of an establishment that ceases to carry on business in the seventh levy period on any day after the date of the service of the relevant assessment notice the foregoing provisions of this Article shall have effect as if for the period of four months from the date of the service of the assessment notice mentioned in paragraph (2) of this Article there were substituted the period of six months from the date of the cessation of business.

(5) An appeal or an application to an appeal tribunal under this Article shall be made in accordance with the Industrial Tribunals (England and Wales) Regulations 1965(a) as amended by the Industrial Tribunals (England and Wales) (Amendment) Regulations 1967(b), except where the establishment to which the relevant assessment relates is wholly in Scotland, in which case the appeal or application shall be made in accordance with the Industrial Tribunals (Scotland) Regulations 1965(c) as amended by the Industrial Tribunals (Scotland) (Amendment) Regulations 1967(d).

(6) The powers of an appeal tribunal under paragraph (3) of this Article may be exercised by the President of the Industrial Tribunals (England and Wales) or by the President of the Industrial Tribunals (Scotland) as the case may be.

(a) S.I. 1965/1101 (1965 II, p. 2805). (b) S.I. 1967/301 (1967 I, p. 1040).
(c) S.I. 1965/1157 (1965 II, p. 3266). (d) S.I. 1967/302 (1967 I, p. 1050).

Evidence

8.—(1) Upon the discharge by a person assessed to the levy of his liability under an assessment the Board shall if so requested issue to him a certificate to that effect.

(2) The production in any proceedings of a document purporting to be certified by the Secretary to the Board to be a true copy of an assessment or other notice issued by the Board or purporting to be a certificate such as is mentioned in the foregoing paragraph of this Article shall, unless the contrary is proved, be sufficient evidence of the document and of the facts stated therein.

Signed by order of the Secretary of State.

20th July 1971.

Paul Bryan,
Minister of State,
Department of Employment.

EXPLANATORY NOTE
(This Note is not part of the Order.)

This Order gives effect to proposals submitted by the Shipbuilding Industry Training Board to the Secretary of State for Employment for the imposition of a further levy on employers in the shipbuilding industry for the purpose of raising money towards the expenses of the Board.

The levy is to be imposed in respect of the seventh levy period commencing with the day on which this Order comes into operation and ending on 31st July 1972. The levy will be assessed by the Board, and there will be a right of appeal against an assessment to an industrial tribunal.

STATUTORY INSTRUMENTS

1971 No. 1178

PENSIONS

The Personal Injuries (Civilians) (Amendment) Scheme 1971

Made - - -	*20th July* 1971
Laid before Parliament	*28th July* 1971
Coming into Operation —	
Article 3	*1st October* 1971
Remainder	*20th September* 1971

The Secretary of State for Social Services, with the consent of the Treasury, in exercise of the powers conferred upon him by section 2 of the Personal Injuries (Emergency Provisions) Act 1939(a), and of all other powers enabling him in that behalf, hereby makes the following Scheme :—

Citation, interpretation and commencement

1.—(1) This Scheme, which may be cited as the Personal Injuries (Civilians) (Amendment) Scheme 1971, amends the Personal Injuries (Civilians) Scheme 1964(b), as amended (c), (hereinafter referred to as "the principal Scheme").

(2) Subject to the provisions of the next following paragraph, this Scheme shall come into operation on 20th September 1971 so, however, that in relation to any award payable weekly the foregoing reference to 20th September 1971, where this is not the normal weekly pay day for that award, shall be construed as a reference to the first normal weekly pay day for that award following 20th September 1971.

(3) Article 3 of this Scheme shall come into operation on 1st October 1971.

Higher rates of pensions and allowances under the principal Scheme

2. For the rates of pension and allowances set out in paragraphs 1, 2, 3, 3A, 4, 6, 7, 8, 9, 10 and 11 of Schedule 3 to the principal Scheme (rates of pension and allowances, other than rates of allowance for wear and tear of clothing, payable in respect of disablement) there shall be substituted the rates set out in paragraphs 1, 2, 3, 3A, 4, 6, 6A, 7, 8, 9, 10 and 11 of Part I of the Schedule hereto.

3. For the rates of allowance for wear and tear of clothing set out in paragraph 5 of Schedule 3 to the principal Scheme there shall be substituted the rates set out in Part II of the Schedule hereto.

4. For the rates of pensions and allowances set out in paragraphs 1 to 12 of Schedule 4 to the principal Scheme (rates of pensions and allowances payable in respect of death) there shall be substituted the rates set out in the corresponding paragraphs of Part III of the Schedule hereto.

(a) 2 & 3 Geo. 6. c. 82.   (b) S.I. 1964/2077 (1964 III, p. 5187).
(c) S.I. 1966/163, 648, 935, 1967/1250, 1968/176, 1206, 1969/1035, 1970/143 (1966 I, p. 299; II, pp. 1454, 2269; 1967 II, p. 3167; 1968 I, p. 425; II, p. 3228; 1969 II, p. 3055; 1970 I, p. 625).

Amendment of Articles of the principal Scheme

5. In Articles 17 (unemployability allowances), 21 (treatment allowances), 29 and 49 (allowance to elderly widows), and 66 (forfeiture of pensions) of the principal Scheme there shall be made the amendments set out in Part IV of the Schedule hereto.

Article added to the principal Scheme, and consequential amendments

6. After Article 17 of the principal Scheme there shall be added the Article set out in paragraph 1 of Part V of the Schedule hereto, and in Article 17 and Article 23 (allowance for part-time treatment) there shall be made the amendments set out in paragraphs 2 and 3 of the said Part respectively.

Keith Joseph,
Secretary of State for Social Services.

19th July 1971.

We consent.

V. H. Goodhew,
H. S. P. Munro,
Two of the Lords Commissioners of
Her Majesty's Treasury.

20th July 1971.

SCHEDULE

Part I

Rates of pension and allowances (other than rates of allowance for wear and tear of clothing) to be substituted in Schedule 3 to the principal Scheme

Description of Pension or Allowance	Rate
1. Pension for 100 per cent disablement under Article 11.	£10·00 per week
2. Education allowance under Article 13.	£120·00 per annum (maximum)
3. Constant attendance allowance—	
(a) under the proviso to Article 14	£8·00 per week (maximum)
(b) in any other case under that Article	£4·00 per week (maximum)
3A. Exceptionally severe disablement allowance under Article 14A.	£4·00 per week
4. Severe disablement occupational allowance under Article 15.	£2·00 per week
6. Unemployability allowances—	
(a) personal allowance under Article 17(1) (i)	£6·55 per week
(b) additional allowances for dependants by way of—	
(i) increase or further increase of allowance in respect of a wife or dependent husband under Article 17(4)(c)	£3·20 per week (maximum)
(ii) allowance in respect of an adult dependant under Article 17(4)(d)	£3·70 per week (maximum)
(iii) increased allowance under Article 17(4)(f)—	
(a) in respect of the child, or the elder or eldest of the children, of a disabled person	£2·95 per week
(b) in respect of the second child of a disabled person	£2·05 per week
(c) in respect of each other child of a disabled person	£1·95 per week
6A. Invalidity allowance payable under Article 17A—	
(a) if on the relevant date the disabled person was under the age of 35 or if that date fell before 5th July 1948	£1·00 per week
(b) if head (a) does not apply and on the relevant date the disabled person was under the age of 45	£0·60 per week
(c) if heads (a) and (b) do not apply and on the relevant date the disabled person was a man under the age of 60 or a woman under the age of 55	£0·30 per week

Description of Pension or Allowance	Rate

7. Comforts allowance—
   (a) under Article 18(1)(a)   £1·70 per week
   (b) under Article 18(1)(b) or 44(1)   £0·85 per week

8. Allowance for lowered standard of occupation under Article 19.   £4·00 per week (maximum)

9. Age allowance under Article 20 where the degree of pensioned disablement is—
   (a) 40 or 50 per cent.   £0·50 per week
   (b) 60 or 70 per cent.   £0·70 per week
   (c) 80 or 90 per cent.   £1·00 per week
   (d) 100 per cent.   £1·40 per week

10. Treatment allowances—
   (a) increase of personal allowance under Article 21(2)   £1·40 per week (maximum)

   (b) increase of personal allowance under Article 21(3)—
     (i) under sub-paragraph (a)   £6·00 per week
     (ii) under sub-paragraph (c)—
       (a) if on the relevant date the disabled person was under the age of 35 or if that date fell before 5th July 1948   £1·00 per week
       (b) if head (a) does not apply and on the relevant date the disabled person was under the age of 45   £0·60 per week
       (c) if heads (a) and (b) do not apply and on the relevant date the disabled person was a man under the age of 60 or a woman under the age of 55.   £0·30 per week

   (c) increased additional allowance under Article 21(4) proviso (a)   £3·70 per week

   (d) increased additional allowance under Article 21(4) proviso (b)—
     (i) in respect of the child, or the elder or eldest of the children, of a disabled person   £1·85 per week
     (ii) in respect of the second child of a disabled person   £0·95 per week
     (iii) in respect of each other child of a disabled person   £0·85 per week

   (e) higher rate of additional allowance under Article 21(4A)—
     (i) in respect of the child, or the elder or eldest of the children, of a disabled person   £2·95 per week
     (ii) in respect of the second child of a disabled person   £2·05 per week
     (iii) in respect of each other child of a disabled person   £1·95 per week

   (f) additional allowance under Article 21(5)   £3·70 per week

11. Part-time treatment allowance under Article 23   £4·00 a day (maximum)

PART II

Rates of allowance for wear and tear of clothing to be substituted in paragragh 5 of Schedule 3 to the principal Scheme

Description of allowance	Rate
Allowance for wear and tear of clothing—	
(*a*) under Article 16(1)(*a*)	£12·00 per annum
(*b*) under Article 16(1)(*b*) and 16(2)	£19·00 per annum

PART III

Rates of pension and allowances to be substituted in Schedule 4 to the principal Scheme

Description of Pension or Allowance	Rate
1. Pension to widow—	
(*a*) under Article 26(1)(*a*)	£7·80 per week
(*b*) under Article 26(1)(*b*)	£1·80 per week
2. Rent allowance under Article 28	£3·00 per week (maximum)
3. Allowance under Article 29 or 49 to an elderly widow—	
(*a*) if age 65 but under age 70	£0·50 per week
(*b*) if age 70 or over	£1·00 per week
4. Pension under Article 30 to unmarried dependant who lived as wife	£1·00 per week (maximum)
5. Pension to dependent widower under Article 32	£7·80 per week (maximum)
6. Allowances under Article 33 in respect of children under the age of 15—	
(*a*) in respect of the child, or the elder or eldest of the children, of a deceased person	£3·15 per week
(*b*) in respect of each other child of a deceased person—	
(i) where the child qualifies for a family allowance under the Family Allowances Act 1965 or under any legislation in Northern Ireland or the Isle of Man corresponding to that Act	£2·65 per week
(ii) where the child does not so qualify	£3·00 per week
7. Pensions under Article 34(1) to motherless or fatherless children under the age of 15—	
(*a*) in respect of the child, or the elder or eldest of the children, of a deceased person, and in respect of each other	

Description of Pension or Allowance	Rate
child of a deceased person who does not qualify for a family allowance as aforesaid	£3·15 per week
(b) in respect of each other child of a deceased person who qualifies for a family allowance as aforesaid	£2·65 per week

8. Pension or allowance under Article 35(3) to or in respect of a child over the age of 15—
    (a) where the child has attained the age of 18 and is incapable of self-support by reason of an infirmity which arose before he attained the age of 15   £6·00 per week (maximum)
    (b) any other case   £4·65 per week (maximum)

9. Education allowance under Article 36   £120·00 per annum (maximum)

10. Pensions to parents—
    (a) minimum rate under Article 38(4)   £0·25 per week
    (b) maximum rate under Article 38(4)—
        (i) where there is only one eligible parent   £1·00 per week
        (ii) where there is more than one eligible parent   £1·38 per week
    (c) increase under the proviso to Article 38(4)
        (i) where there is only one eligible parent —£0·38 per week (maximum)
        (ii) where there is more than one eligible parent—£0·62 per week (maximum)

11. Pensions to other dependants—
    (a) for each juvenile dependant under Article 39(4)   £0·30 per week (maximum)
    (b) aggregate rate under Article 39(4)   £1·00 per week (maximum)
    (c) under Article 39(5)   £1·00 per week (maximum)

12. Funeral Grant under Article 40(1)   £30·00 (maximum)

PART IV

Amendments of Articles of the principal Scheme

1. In Article 17 (unemployability allowances) the following amendments shall be made:—

(1) For paragraph (3) there shall be substituted the following paragraph—

"(3) A disabled person shall not be eligible for any award under this Article if he is in receipt of a retirement pension (not being contributory old age pension or age addition) or graduated retirement benefit under the National Insurance Acts 1965 to 1971, or under any legislation in Northern Ireland corresponding to those Acts."

(2) In paragraph (4) the following amendments shall be made:—

    (i) In sub-paragraph (c) for the words "by the appropriate amount" there shall be substituted the words "by an amount not exceeding the appropriate amount".

    (ii) In sub-paragraph (d) for the words "at the appropriate rate" there shall be substituted the words "at a rate not exceeding the appropriate rate".

2. In Article 21 (treatment allowances) the following amendments shall be made:—

(1) For sub-paragraph (*b*) of the proviso to paragraph (1) there shall be substituted the following sub-paragraph—

"(*b*) Where a disabled person is in receipt of a treatment allowance under this Article in respect of any period, no payment shall be made in respect of that period of any other award under the foregoing provisions of this Part of this Scheme except—

(i) an award under Article 13, 14A, 16, 17(1)(i), 17A or 18 ; or

(ii) an award under Article 14 but, in the case of treatment in a hospital or similar institution the whole or part of the cost of which is paid out of public funds, for the first four weeks thereof only ; or

(iii) where the disabled person is not in receipt of an increase of his personal allowance under paragraph (3) of this Article, an award under Article 15."

(2) For paragraph (3) there shall be substituted the following paragraph—

"(3) Except where a disabled person is in receipt of an allowance under Article 17(1)(i) or is receiving treatment in a hospital or similar institution and is not entitled to an additional allowance in respect of a dependant under the following provisions of this Article, he may be awarded an increase of his personal allowance—

(*a*) if he is not eligible for any such benefit as is mentioned in paragraph (6) of this Article, at the appropriate rate specified in Schedule 3 paragraph 10(*b*)(i) ;

(*b*) if he is eligible for such benefit at a rate lower than the appropriate rate specified in the said paragraph 10(*b*)(i), at a rate equal to the difference between the lower rate and the rate so specified ;

(*c*) if he is not eligible for invalidity pension and allowance solely by reason of his failure to satisfy the contribution conditions of the National Insurance Acts 1965 to 1971, at the appropriate rate specified in Schedule 3 paragraph 10(*b*)(ii) ;

(*d*) for the purpose of determining the appropriate rate in paragraph 10(*b*)(ii) the relevant date shall be such date as would have been the qualifying date had he been eligible for invalidity pension and allowance."

(3) After paragraph (4) there shall be inserted the following new paragraph—

"(4A) The rate of an additional allowance awarded under paragraph (4) of this Article in respect of a child or children of a disabled person who is in receipt of an increase of his personal allowance under paragraph (3)(*c*) of this Article may be further increased to the appropriate rate specified in Schedule 3 paragraph 10(*e*)."

(4) In paragraph (5) for the words "Schedule 3 paragraph 10(*e*)" there shall be substituted the words "Schedule 3 paragraph 10(*f*)".

(5) In paragraph (6) for the words from "National Insurance (Industrial Injuries) Acts" to "National Insurance Acts 1946 to 1964" there shall be substituted the words—

"National Insurance (Industrial Injuries) Acts 1965 to 1971, sickness benefit, retirement pension, invalidity pension and allowance or contributory old age pension under the National Insurance Acts 1965 to 1971".

3. In Articles 29 and 49 (allowance to elderly widows) for the words from "has attained the age of 70 years" to the end of the Article there shall be substituted the words—

"has attained the age of 65 years or the age of 70 years, as the case may be, she may be awarded an allowance at whichever of the rates specified in Schedule 4, paragraph 3 is appropriate."

4. In Article 66 (forfeiture of pensions) in paragraph (1)(*a*) there shall be substituted for the words "approved school or remand home" the words "or Young Offenders Institution."

PART V

Article to be added to the principal Scheme, and consequential amendments

1. After Article 17 there shall be inserted the following Article:—

"*Invalidity allowance*

17A.—(1) Where a disabled person is awarded an allowance under Article 17(1)(i) in respect of unemployability and has not on the relevant date (whether before or after the coming into operation of this Article) attained the age of 60 or, in the case of a woman, the age of 55, he may be awarded an additional allowance at the appropriate rate specified in Schedule 3 paragraph 6A.

(2) Subject to the following provisions of this Article the relevant date for the purposes of paragraph (1) of this Article shall be the commencing date of the period in respect of which an allowance under Article 17(1)(i) is awarded and, if there have been two or more such periods, the commencing date of the latter or last of them.

(3) For the purposes of paragraph (2) of this Article where a break between two periods in respect of which an allowance under Article 17(1)(i) has been awarded does not exceed 13 weeks those periods shall not be treated as separate periods.

(4) If the unemployability in respect of which an allowance is awarded forms part of a period of interruption of employment for the purposes of the National Insurance Acts 1965 to 1971 which has continued without a break from a date earlier than the date fixed under paragraphs (2) and (3) of this Article, the relevant date shall be the first day of incapacity for work for those purposes in that period.

(5) Notwithstanding anything in the foregoing provisions of this Article, the relevant date may be such other date as the Secretary of State may determine if in his opinion the circumstances of any particular case so require.

(6) This Article shall not apply if on the date on which it comes into operation the disabled person is a man over the age of 65 or a woman over the age of 60.

(7) The provisions of paragraph (5) of Article 17, in so far as they provide for taking into account any benefit payable out of public funds under the law of any place outside the United Kingdom, shall apply to an allowance awarded under this Article as they apply to a personal allowance awarded under that Article."

2. In paragraph (5) of Article 17 for the reference to the National Insurance Act 1946 there shall be substituted a reference to the National Insurance Act 1965, and for the reference to the National Insurance Acts 1946 to 1964 there shall be substituted a reference to the National Insurance Acts 1965 to 1971.

3. In Article 23 (allowance for part-time treatment) for the words in the proviso "Article 13, 14, 14A, 15, 16, 17(1)(i), 18 or 20" there shall be substituted the words "Article 13, 14, 14A, 15, 16, 17(1)(i), 17A, 18 or 20".

EXPLANATORY NOTE
(This Note is not part of the Scheme.)

1. This Scheme further amends the Personal Injuries (Civilians) Scheme 1964, which provides for compensation to or in respect of civilians injured or killed in the 1939-45 War.

2. Articles 2, 3 and 4 make amendments relating to the rates of pensions or allowances in the principal Scheme which are increased as follows :—

(a) the rates of pensions in respect of 100 per cent disablement from £8·40 a week to £10·00 a week with proportionate increases where the degree of disablement is less than 100 per cent ;

(b) the rates of pensions for certain widows from £6·50 a week to £7·80 a week, and for dependent widowers from a maximum of £6·50 a week to a maximum of £7·80 a week ;

(c) the normal maximum rate of an allowance payable for constant attendance from £3·30 a week to £4·00 a week and the maximum rate for exceptional cases of very severe disablement from £6·60 a week to £8·00 a week ;

(d) the exceptionally severe disablement allowance from £3·00 a week to £4·00 a week ;

(e) the severe disablement occupational allowance from £1·00 a week to £2·00 a week ;

(f) the allowance for unemployable pensioners from £5·45 a week to £6·55 a week ;

(g) the total additional allowance payable in respect of the wife or adult dependant of an unemployable pensioner and of a pensioner receiving treatment as defined in Article 21(8) from £3·10 a week to £3·70 a week ;

(h) the allowances payable in respect of children of unemployable pensioners in respect of the first or only child from £1·55 a week to £2·95 a week, in respect of the second child from £0·65 a week to £2·05 a week, and in respect of any other child from £0·55 a week to £1·95 a week ;

(i) the allowances for comforts from £1·25 a week and £0·63 a week to £1·70 a week and £0·85 a week respectively ;

(j) the maximum allowance for lowered standard of occupation from £3·35 a week to £4·00 a week ;

(k) the allowances payable in respect of children of pensioners receiving treatment as defined in Article 21(8) in respect of the first or only child from £1·55 a week to £1·85 a week, in respect of the second child from £0·65 a week to £0·95 a week, and in respect of any other child from £0·55 a week to £0·85 a week ;

(l) the allowances payable to pensioners who have attained the age of 65 and whose pensioned disablement is assessed at 40 per cent or over from between £0·38 a week and £1·00 a week to between £0·50 a week and £1·40 a week respectively ;

(m) the maximum of the additional personal treatment allowance payable to a pensioner who is not entitled to full sickness benefit or invalidity pension and allowance under national insurance provisions from £5·00 a week to £6·00 a week ;

(n) the allowances for wear and tear of clothing from £9·00 a year and £14·00 a year to £12·00 a year and £19·00 a year respectively ;

(*o*) the allowance for elderly widows age 70 or over from £0·75 a week to £1·00 a week ;

(*p*) the maximum rent allowance payable to certain widows from £2·50 a week to £3·00 a week ;

(*q*) the allowances payable in respect of children in the care of widows in respect of the first or only child from £2·65 a week to £3·15 a week, and in respect of each other child from £2·15 a week to £2·65 a week where the child qualifies for a family allowance, and from £2·50 a week to £3·00 a week where the child does not so qualify ;

(*r*) the rates of pensions and allowances payable for motherless or fatherless children in respect of the first or only child or any other child who does not qualify for a family allowance from £2·65 a week or a maximum of £3·90 a week to £3·15 a week or a maximum of £4·65 a week according to the age of the child, and in respect of each other child under the age of 15 who qualifies for a family allowance from £2·15 a week to £2·65 a week ;

(*s*) the maximum rates of pensions payable to motherless or fatherless children who, having attained the age of 18 years, are incapable of self-support by reason of infirmity which arose before they became 15 years of age, from £5·00 a week to £6·00 a week.

Article 5 makes amendments, the effects of which are :—

(*a*) to prevent a disabled person being rendered ineligible for unemployability allowance by the receipt of national insurance age addition, and to make the rate of increase of a wife's allowance payable with unemployability allowance adjustable to her financial circumstances ;

(*b*) to enable constant attendance allowance to be paid for the first four weeks of treatment in a hospital or similar institution the cost of which is payable wholly or partly out of public funds, to provide for an increase of treatment allowance to be awarded to a disabled person who is not eligible for national insurance invalidity pension and allowance, at a rate appropriate to his age, and to increase the rate of additional allowance payable for his children in these circumstances ;

(*c*) to provide for an allowance to be made to elderly widows, at the age of 65 ;

(*d*) to modify the provisions for forfeiture to take account of changes in the law relating to children.

Article 6 brings into force provisions granting a new invalidity allowance to be paid with unemployability allowances, and makes consequential amendments.

STATUTORY INSTRUMENTS

1971 No. 1179

FOOD AND DRUGS

FOOD HYGIENE

The Meat Inspection (Amendment) Regulations 1971

Made - - -	*20th July* 1971
Laid before Parliament	*28th July* 1971
Coming into Operation	*16th August* 1971

The Minister of Agriculture, Fisheries and Food and the Secretary of State for Social Services, acting jointly, in exercise of the powers conferred on them by sections 13 and 123 of the Food and Drugs Act 1955(a), as read with the Secretary of State for Social Services Order 1968(b), and of all other powers enabling them in that behalf, hereby make the following regulations after consultation with such organisations as appear to them to be representative of interests substantially affected by the regulations and reference to the Food Hygiene Advisory Council under section 82 of the said Act:—

Citation, commencement and interpretation

1.—(1) These regulations may be cited as the Meat Inspection (Amendment) Regulations 1971, and shall come into operation on 16th August 1971.

(2) The Interpretation Act 1889(c) shall apply to the interpretation of these regulations as it applies to the interpretation of an Act of Parliament.

Amendment of principal regulations

2. The Meat Inspection Regulations 1963(d), as amended (e), shall be further amended by substituting for paragraph (3) of regulation 12 thereof the following paragraph:—

"(3) No such charge determined by a local authority shall exceed—

(*a*) in the case of each horse or bovine animal other than a calf, eighteen new pence;

(*b*) in the case of each calf or pig, five new pence;

(*c*) in the case of each sheep, lamb or goat, four new pence."

In witness whereof the Official Seal of the Minister of Agriculture, Fisheries and Food is hereunto affixed on 13th July 1971.

(L.S.)

J. M. L. Prior,
Minister of Agriculture, Fisheries and Food.

Keith Joseph,
20th July 1971.
Secretary of State for Social Services.

(a) 4 & 5 Eliz. 2. c. 16.
(b) S.I. 1968/1699 (1968 III, p. 4585).
(c) 1889 c. 63.
(d) S.I. 1963/1229 (1963 II, p. 2041).
(e) S.I. 1965/1497, 1966/915 (1965 II, p. 4342; 1966 II, p. 2196).

EXPLANATORY NOTE

(This Note is not part of the Regulations.)

These amending regulations, which come into operation on 16th August 1971, raise the maximum charges which can be determined by a local authority for inspections of carcases carried out in pursuance of regulation 3 of the principal regulations.

STATUTORY INSTRUMENTS

1971 No. 1186

CUSTOMS AND EXCISE

The Import Duty Drawbacks (No. 2) Order 1971

Made - - - -	*22nd July* 1971
Laid before the	
House of Commons	*29th July* 1971
Coming into Operation	*3rd August* 1971

The Lords Commissioners of Her Majesty's Treasury, by virtue of the powers conferred on them by sections 9 and 13 of, and Schedule 5 to, the Import Duties Act 1958(a) and section 2(5) of the Finance Act 1965(b), and of all other powers enabling them in that behalf, on the recommendation of the Secretary of State hereby make the following Order:—

1.—(1) This Order may be cited as the Import Duty Drawbacks (No. 2) Order 1971.

(2) The Interpretation Act 1889(c) shall apply for the interpretation of this Order as it applies for the interpretation of an Act of Parliament.

(3) In this Order " the principal Order " means the Import Duty Drawbacks (No. 1) Order 1971(d).

(4) This Order shall come into operation on 3rd August 1971.

2. There shall be omitted from Schedule 1 to the principal Order (which relates to the drawbacks to be allowed on the exportation of imported articles or goods incorporating them) so much of the entries relating to the tariff headings specified in column 1 of Schedule 1 to this Order as is specified in column 2 of that Schedule.

3.—(1) In Schedule 1 to the principal Order there shall be inserted, under the heading " Vegetable products " and in the appropriate places in numerical order, the entries set out in Schedule 2 to this Order.

(2) In the said Schedule 1, for column 2 of the entry relating to heading 08.02 (citrus fruit) there shall be substituted the following—

> "Allowable for fresh grapefruit, fresh oranges, lemons and limes; but, except for fresh grapefruit, allowable only on their exportation in the packages in which they were imported.".

4. There shall be omitted from Schedule 2 to the principal Order (which relates to the drawbacks to be allowed on the exportation of goods produced or manufactured from imported articles) so much of the entries, column 1 of

---

(a) 1958 c. 6. (b) 1965 c. 25. (c) 1889 c. 63.
(d) S.I. 1971/274 (1971 I, p. 939).

which (exported goods) begins with or consists of the words specified in column 1 of Schedule 3 to this Order, as is specified in column 2 of the said Schedule 3.

5. In Schedule 2 to the principal Order, for column 1 of the entry beginning " Methacrylates " there shall be substituted the following:—

" Methacrylates:

1. Methacrylates falling within heading 29.14 of the Customs Tariff 1959, the following—butyl methacrylate, hexyl methacrylate, lauryl methacrylate and stearyl methacrylate.

2. Methacrylates falling within heading 38.19 of the Customs Tariff 1959, the following—decyl-octyl methacrylate."

P. L. Hawkins,
Bernard Weatherill,
Two of the Lords Commissioners
of Her Majesty's Treasury.

22nd July 1971.

SCHEDULE 1

DELETIONS FROM SCHEDULE 1 TO THE PRINCIPAL ORDER

Tariff heading to which entry relates	Extent of omission
39.07	In column 2, paragraph (*n*).
40.14	In column 2, paragraph (*b*).
73.15	The whole entry.
73.32	In column 2, the words from "and for bolts" onwards.
73.35	In column 2, the words from "and for springs" onwards.
73.40	In column 2, paragraph (*f*).
74.04	The whole entry.
76.04	The whole entry.
76.16	In column 2, paragraph (*e*).
79.03	The whole entry.
79.04 and 79.06	In column 2, the words from "and for articles" onwards.

SCHEDULE 2

ENTRIES TO BE INSERTED IN SCHEDULE 1 TO THE PRINCIPAL ORDER

Tariff headings comprising imported articles for which drawback is allowable	*Restrictions on drawback*
07.01 (vegetables, fresh or chilled).	Allowable for aubergines and capsicums, but only on their exportation in the packages in which they were imported.

Tariff headings comprising imported articles for which drawback is allowable	Restrictions on drawback
08.01 (dates, bananas etc. fresh or dried).	Allowable for the following fresh fruit, namely, bananas, avocados, mangoes, and pineapples, but only on their exportation in the packages in which they were imported.
08.03 (figs, fresh or dried)...	Allowable for fresh figs, but only on their exportation in the packages in which they were imported.
08.07 (stone fruit, fresh) ...	Allowable for apricots and litchis, but only on their exportation in the packages in which they were imported.
08.08 (berries, fresh) ...	Allowable for cranberries and Chinese gooseberries, but only on their exportation in the packages in which they were imported.
08.09 (other fruit, fresh) ...	Allowable for melons and pomegranates, but only on their exportation in the packages in which they were imported.

SCHEDULE 3

DELETIONS FROM SCHEDULE 2 TO THE PRINCIPAL ORDER

Column 1 of entry	Extent of omission
Cuprammonium products	All 3 columns relating to items 2 and 4.
Heat-absorbing glass	The whole entry.
Linseed oil	All 3 columns relating to item 1.
Quebracho extract	All 3 columns relating to items 3 and 4.
Shuttlecocks and shuttlecock skirts ...	The whole entry.

EXPLANATORY NOTE
(This Note is not part of the Order.)

This Order—

(1) provides for the allowance of drawback of import duty on certain fresh fruit and vegetables exported in the packages in which they were imported;

(2) provides for the allowance of drawback of import duty on decyl-octyl methacrylate manufactured from imported acetone cyanohydrin;

(3) revokes the provisions for drawback of import duty in respect of:—

(a) parts of hand-operated appliances used for making labels or name plates from plastic or metal strip and certain tapes for use with such appliances;

(b) heat-absorbing glass manufactured from imported glass;

(c) certain warp-knitted fabrics manufactured from imported cuprammonium yarn;

(d) ground soluble quebracho extract manufactured from imported solid soluble quebracho extract and blends of quebracho extract manufactured from imported solid insoluble quebracho extract;

(e) linseed oil, with or without driers, manufactured from imported linseed; and

(f) certain shuttlecocks and shuttlecock skirts.

STATUTORY INSTRUMENTS

1971 No. 1187 (S.148)

AGRICULTURE

HILL LANDS

The Hill Cattle (Scotland) (Amendment) Scheme 1971

Made - - -	*19th July* 1971
Laid before Parliament	*29th July* 1971
Coming into Operation	*30th July* 1971

In exercise of the powers conferred on me by sections 13, 15 and 17 of the Hill Farming Act 1946(a), as extended by section 43 of the Agriculture Act 1967(b), and of all other powers enabling me in that behalf, and with the approval of the Treasury, I hereby make the following scheme :—

Citation, commencement and interpretation

1.—(1) This scheme may be cited as the Hill Cattle (Scotland) (Amendment) Scheme 1971 and shall come into operation on 30th July 1971.

(2) This scheme shall be construed as one with the Hill Cattle (Scotland) Scheme 1968(c) as amended by the Hill Cattle (Scotland) (Amendment) Scheme 1970(d).

Amendment of definition of accredited herd

2. For the definition of the expression "accredited herd" contained in paragraph 2(2) of the Hill Cattle (Scotland) (Amendment) Scheme 1970, there shall be substituted the following definition :—

" 'accredited herd' means a herd which to the satisfaction of the Secretary of State for Scotland or the Minister of Agriculture, Fisheries and Food either—

(a) has been found to be free from brucellosis by means of a series of diagnostic tests carried out by him or on his behalf and has been, since the date of commencement of such tests, the subject of adequate precautions against the introduction or re-introduction and consequent spreading of brucellosis, or

(b) has been wholly constituted by the transfer of animals from other accredited herds in Great Britain or from such similar herds outside Great Britain as the Secretary of State for Scotland, in relation to herds in Scotland, or the Minister of Agriculture, Fisheries and Food,

---

(a) 1946 c. 73.
(c) S.I. 1968/981 (1968 II, p. 2590).

(b) 1967 c. 22.
(d) S.I. 1970/1648 (1970 III, p. 5423).

in relation to herds in England and Wales, may either generally or in any special case allow, and has been, since being so constituted, the subject of such precautions as aforesaid".

Gordon Campbell,
One of Her Majesty's Principal
Secretaries of State.

St. Andrew's House,
Edinburgh.
14th July 1971.

We approve.

Walter Clegg,
V. H. Goodhew,
Two of the Lords Commissioners
of Her Majesty's Treasury.

19th July 1971.

EXPLANATORY NOTE

(This Note is not part of the Scheme.)

This Scheme amends the definition of "accredited herd" in the Hill Cattle (Scotland) (Amendment) Scheme 1970. As a result of the amendment, a herd will be regarded as "accredited" for the purposes of the hill cattle subsidy (a) if it has been found to be free from brucellosis by means of a series of diagnostic tests carried out by or on behalf of the Secretary of State for Scotland or the Minister of Agriculture, Fisheries and Food, or (b) has been wholly constituted by the transfer of cattle from other accredited herds in Great Britain or, where this is allowed, from similar herds outside Great Britain, and in any of the cases aforesaid has subsequently been the subject of adequate precautions against the introduction or re-introduction and consequent spreading of the disease.

STATUTORY INSTRUMENTS

1971 No. 1188 (S.149)

AGRICULTURE

HILL LANDS

The Hill Cattle Subsidy Payment (Scotland) Order 1971

Made - - -	19*th July* 1971
Laid before Parliament	29*th July* 1971
Coming into Operation	30*th July* 1971

In exercise of the powers conferred upon me by sections 14(3) and 17 of the Hill Farming Act 1946(**a**), as amended by section 8 of the Livestock Rearing Act 1951(**b**), and of all other powers enabling me in that behalf, and with the approval of the Treasury, I hereby make the following order :—

Citation and commencement

1. This order may be cited as the Hill Cattle Subsidy Payment (Scotland) Order 1971 and shall come into operation on 30th July 1971.

Interpretation

2.—(1) Unless the context otherwise requires, expressions used in this order shall have the same meaning as in the Hill Cattle (Scotland) Scheme 1968(**c**) and the Hill Cattle (Scotland) (Amendment) Scheme 1970(**d**) as amended by the Hill Cattle (Scotland) (Amendment) Scheme 1971(**e**).

(2) The Interpretation Act 1889(**f**) shall apply for the interpretation of this order as it applies for the interpretation of an Act of Parliament.

Amounts of subsidy payments

3. Subject to the provisions of the Hill Cattle (Scotland) Scheme 1968 as amended by the said schemes of 1970 and 1971, the amount which may be paid in respect of each of the years 1971 and 1972 by way of subsidy payment under that scheme in respect of any breeding cow shall be :—

(*a*) in the case of a cow comprised in a herd which is an accredited herd on the qualifying day or which subsequently becomes such a herd as a result of a final diagnostic test for brucellosis commenced on or before that day, £28·75 ;

(*b*) in the case of any other cow, £23·75.

(**a**) 1946 c. 73.

(**b**) 1951 c. 18.

(**c**) S.I. 1968/981 (1968 II, p. 2590).

(**d**) S.I. 1970/1648 (1970 III, p. 5423).

(**e**) S.I. 1971/1187. (1971 II, 3483).

(**f**) 1889 c. 63.

Existing order not to apply

4. The Hill Cattle Subsidy Payment (Scotland) Order 1970(a) shall cease to apply to subsidy payments in respect of the years 1971 and 1972.

Gordon Campbell,
One of Her Majesty's Principal
Secretaries of State.

St. Andrew's House,
Edinburgh.
14th July 1971.

We approve.

Walter Clegg,
V. H. Goodhew,
Two of the Lords Commissioners
of Her Majesty's Treasury.

19th July 1971.

EXPLANATORY NOTE

(This Note is not part of the Order.)

This Order increases the amount of subsidy payable for the years 1971 and 1972 under the provisions of the Hill Cattle (Scotland) Scheme 1968, as amended, from £25·62½ (£25 12s. 6d.) to £28·75 (£28 15s.) in respect of a breeding cow comprised in an accredited herd on the qualifying day in either of those years, or in a herd which subsequently becomes an accredited herd as a result of a final diagnostic test for brucellosis commenced on or before that day.

For other cows to which the scheme applies, subsidy will continue to be paid at the rate of £23·75 (£23 15s.).

(a) S.I. 1970/1649 (1970 III, p. 5426).

STATUTORY INSTRUMENTS

1971 No. 1189 (S.150)

AGRICULTURE

LIVESTOCK INDUSTRIES

The Beef Cow (Scotland) (Amendment) Scheme 1971

Made - - -	*19th July* 1971
Laid before Parliament	*29th July* 1971
Coming into Operation	*30th July* 1971

In exercise of the powers conferred on me by section 12 of the Agriculture Act 1967(**a**) and of all other powers enabling me in that behalf, and with the approval of the Treasury, I hereby make the following scheme :—

Citation, commencement and interpretation

1.—(1) This scheme may be cited as the Beef Cow (Scotland) (Amendment) Scheme 1971 and shall come into operation on 30th July 1971.

(2) This scheme shall be construed as one with the Beef Cow (Scotland) Scheme 1967(**b**) as amended by the Beef Cow (Scotland) (Amendment) Scheme 1970(**c**).

Amendment of definition of accredited herd

2. For the definition of the expression "accredited herd" contained in paragraph 2(2) of the Beef Cow (Scotland) (Amendment) Scheme 1970, there shall be substituted the following definition:—

" 'accredited herd' means a herd which to the satisfaction of the Secretary of State for Scotland or the Minister of Agriculture, Fisheries and Food either—

    (*a*) has been found to be free from brucellosis by means of a series of diagnostic tests carried out by him or on his behalf and has been, since the date of commencement of such tests, the subject of adequate precautions against the introduction or re-introduction and consequent spreading of brucellosis, or

    (*b*) has been wholly constituted by the transfer of animals from other accredited herds in Great Britain or from such similar herds outside Great Britain as the Secretary of State for Scotland, in relation to herds in Scotland, or the Minister of Agriculture, Fisheries and Food,

---

(**a**) 1967 c. 22.   (**b**) S.I. 1967/1560 (1967 III, p. 4328).

(**c**) S.I. 1970/1650 (1970 III, p. 5428).

in relation to herds in England and Wales, may either generally or in any special case allow, and has been, since being so constituted, the subject of such precautions as aforesaid".

Gordon Campbell,
One of Her Majesty's Principal
Secretaries of State.

St. Andrew's House,
Edinburgh.
14th July 1971.

We approve.

Walter Clegg,
V. H. Goodhew,
Two of the Lords Commissioners
of Her Majesty's Treasury.

19th July 1971.

EXPLANATORY NOTE

(This Note is not part of the Scheme.)

This Scheme amends the definition of "accredited herd" in the Beef Cow (Scotland) (Amendment) Scheme 1970. As a result of the amendment, a herd will be regarded as "accredited" for the purposes of the beef cow subsidy (a) if it has been found to be free from brucellosis by means of a series of diagnostic tests carried out by or on behalf of the Secretary of State for Scotland or the Minister of Agriculture, Fisheries and Food, or (b) has been wholly constituted by the transfer of animals from other accredited herds in Great Britain or, where this is allowed, from similar herds outside Great Britain, and in any of the cases aforesaid has subsequently been the subject of adequate precautions against the introduction or re-introduction and consequent spreading of the disease.

STATUTORY INSTRUMENTS

1971 No. 1190 (S.151)

AGRICULTURE

LIVESTOCK INDUSTRIES

The Beef Cow Subsidy Payment (Scotland) Order 1971

Made - - -	19*th July* 1971
Laid before Parliament	29*th July* 1971
Coming into Operation	30*th July* 1971

In exercise of the powers conferred on me by section 12(4) and (7) of the Agriculture Act 1967(**a**) and of all other powers enabling me in that behalf, and with the approval of the Treasury, I hereby make the following order :—

Citation and commencement

1. This order may be cited as the Beef Cow Subsidy Payment (Scotland) Order 1971 and shall come into operation on 30th July 1971.

Interpretation

2.—(1) Unless the context otherwise requires, expressions used in this order shall have the same meaning as in the Beef Cow (Scotland) Scheme 1967(**b**) and the Beef Cow (Scotland) (Amendment) Scheme 1970(**c**) as amended by the Beef Cow (Scotland) (Amendment) Scheme 1971(**d**).

(2) The Interpretation Act 1889(**e**) shall apply for the interpretation of this order as it applies for the interpretation of an Act of Parliament.

Amounts of subsidy payments

3. Subject to the provisions of the Beef Cow (Scotland) Scheme 1967 as amended by the said schemes of 1970 and 1971, the amount which may be paid by way of subsidy payment under that scheme in respect of any cow which on the prescribed date in the year 1971 is comprised in a herd shall be—

    (*a*) in the case of a cow comprised in a herd which is an accredited herd on the prescribed date or which subsequently becomes such a herd as a result of a final diagnostic test for brucellosis commenced on or before that date, £16 ;

    (*b*) in the case of any other cow, £11.

(**a**) 1967 c. 22.

(**b**) S.I. 1967/1560 (1967 III, p. 4328).

(**c**) S.I. 1970/1650 (1970 III, p. 5428).

(**d**) S.I. 1971/1189. (1971 II, p. 3487).

(**e**) 1889 c. 63.

Existing order not to apply

4. The Beef Cow Subsidy Payment (Scotland) Order 1970(a) shall cease to apply to subsidy payments in respect of the year 1971.

Gordon Campbell,
One of Her Majesty's Principal
Secretaries of State.

St. Andrew's House,
Edinburgh.
14th July 1971.

We approve.

Walter Clegg,
V. H. Goodhew,
Two of the Lords Commissioners
of Her Majesty's Treasury.

19th July 1971.

EXPLANATORY NOTE

(This Note is not part of the Order.)

This Order increases the amount of subsidy payable for the year 1971 under the provisions of the Beef Cow (Scotland) Scheme 1967, as amended, from £12·87$\frac{1}{2}$ (£12 17s. 6d.) to £16 in respect of a cow comprised in an accredited herd on the prescribed date in that year, or in a herd which subsequently becomes an accredited herd as a result of a final diagnostic test for brucellosis commenced on or before that date.

For other cows to which the scheme applies, subsidy will continue to be paid at the rate of £11.

(a) S.I. 1970/1651 (1970 III, p. 5430).

STATUTORY INSTRUMENTS

1971 No. 1194

INDUSTRIAL TRAINING

The Industrial Training Levy (Distributive Board) Order 1971

Made - - -	*22nd July* 1971	
Laid before Parliament	*2nd August* 1971	
Coming into Operation	*5th August* 1971	

The Secretary of State after approving proposals submitted by the Distributive Industry Training Board for the imposition of a further levy on employers in the distributive industry and in exercise of his powers under section 4 of the Industrial Training Act 1964(a) and of all other powers enabling him in that behalf hereby makes the following Order :—

Title and Commencement

1. This Order may be cited as the Industrial Training Levy (Distributive Board) Order 1971 and shall come into operation on 5th August 1971.

Interpretation

2.—(1) In this Order unless the context otherwise requires :—

(a) "an appeal tribunal" means an industrial tribunal established under section 12 of the Industrial Training Act 1964 ;

(b) "assessment" means an assessment of an employer to the levy ;

(c) "the Board" means the Distributive Industry Training Board ;

(d) "business" means any activities of industry or commerce ;

(e) "distributive establishment" means an establishment in Great Britain engaged in the third base period wholly or mainly in the distributive industry for a total of twenty-seven or more weeks or, being an establishment that commenced to carry on business in the third base period, for a total number of weeks exceeding one half of the number of weeks in the part of the said period commencing with the day on which business was commenced and ending on the last day thereof ;

(f) "the distributive industry" means any one or more of the activities which, subject to the provisions of paragraph 2 of the Schedule to the industrial training order, are specified in paragraph 1 of that Schedule as the activities of the distributive industry ;

(a) 1964 c. 16.

(g) "emoluments" means all emoluments assessable to income tax under Schedule E (other than pensions), being emoluments from which tax under that Schedule is deductible, whether or not tax in fact falls to be deducted from any particular payment thereof ;

(h) "employer" means a person who is an employer in the distributive industry at any time in the third levy period ;

(i) "the industrial training order" means the Industrial Training (Distributive Board) Order 1970(a) ;

(j) "the levy" means the levy imposed by the Board in respect of the third levy period ;

(k) "notice" means a notice in writing ;

(l) "the third base period" means the period of twelve months that commenced on 6th April 1970 ;

(m) "the third levy period" means the period commencing with the day upon which this Order comes into operation and ending on 31st March 1972 ;

(n) other expressions have the same meanings as in the industrial training order.

(2) Any reference in this Order to an establishment that commences to carry on business or that ceases to carry on business shall not be taken to apply where the location of the establishment is changed but its business is continued wholly or mainly at or from the new location, or where the suspension of activities is of a temporary or seasonal nature.

(3) In the case where a distributive establishment is taken over (whether directly or indirectly) by an employer in succession to, or jointly with, another person, a person employed at any time in the third base period at or from the establishment shall be deemed for the purposes of this Order to have been so employed by the employer carrying on the said establishment on the day upon which this Order comes into operation, and any reference in this Order to persons employed by the employer at or from a distributive establishment in the third base period shall be construed accordingly.

(4) The Interpretation Act 1889(b) shall apply to the interpretation of this Order as it applies to the interpretation of an Act of Parliament.

Imposition of the Levy

3.—(1) The levy to be imposed by the Board on employers in respect of the third levy period shall be assessed in accordance with the provisions of this Article.

(2) Subject to the provisions of this Article, the levy shall be assessed by the Board in respect of each employer and the amount thereof shall be equal to 0·7 per cent. of the sum (less £3,000) of the emoluments of all the persons employed by the employer at or from the distributive establishment or establishments of the employer in the third base period.

(3) Where the sum of the emoluments of the persons mentioned in the last foregoing paragraph is less than £6,000 the employer shall be exempt from the levy.

(a) S.I. 1970/1053 (1970 II, p. 3273). (b) 1889 c. 63.

(4) Where any persons whose emoluments are taken into account for the purposes of this Article were employed at or from an establishment that ceases to carry on business in the third levy period, the sum of the emoluments of those persons shall be reduced in the same proportion as the number of days between the commencement of the said levy period and the date of cessation of business (both dates inclusive) bears to the number of days in the said levy period.

(5) For the purposes of this Article no regard shall be had to the emoluments of—

(a) any person who, being a registered pharmacist or a registered optician, is employed wholly or mainly in activities undertaken by him personally in the exercise of his profession ;

(b) any person employed as a member of the crew of an aircraft or as the master or member of the crew of a ship or any person ordinarily employed in or about a ship in port on work of a kind ordinarily done by a seaman on a ship while it is in port ;

(c) a registered dock worker employed on dock work ;

(d) any person wholly employed in agriculture ;

(e) any person wholly employed in the supply of food or drink to persons being a supply—

(i) for immediate consumption ;

(ii) of hot fried fish or hot chipped potatoes ; or

(iii) by means of an automatic vending machine at or in connection with an hotel, restaurant, café, snack bar, canteen, mess room or similar place of refreshment ; or

(f) any person employed in an establishment that is engaged in selling by retail any of the goods specified in the categories following : —

(i) bread, flour, flour confectionery and yeast ;

(ii) milk, ice cream and any commodity similar to ice cream ;

(iii) meat ;

(iv) bacon ;

(v) fish ;

(vi) horticultural produce ;

where the sale of goods comprised in any one or in any two of such categories constitutes the sole or main activity of the establishment.

Assessment Notices

4.—(1) The Board shall serve an assessment notice on every employer assessed to the levy.

(2) The amount of an assessment shall be rounded down, where necessary, to the nearest £1.

(3) An assessment notice shall state the Board's address for the service of a notice of appeal or of an application for an extension of time for appealing.

(4) An assessment notice may be served on the person assessed to the levy either by delivering it to him personally or by leaving it, or sending it to him

by post, at his last known address or place of business in the United Kingdom or, if that person is a corporation, by leaving it, or sending it by post to the corporation, at such address or place of business or at its registered or principal office.

Payment of the Levy

5.—(1) Subject to the provisions of this Article and of Articles 6 and 7, the amount of the assessment payable under an assessment notice served by the Board shall be payable to the Board in two instalments equal to one-fifth and four-fifths of the said amount respectively, and the said instalments shall be due respectively one month and four months after the date of the notice.

(2) The amount of an instalment mentioned in the last foregoing paragraph may be rounded up or down by the Board to a convenient figure, but so that the aggregate amount of both instalments shall be equal to the amount of the assessment.

(3) An instalment of an assessment shall not be recoverable by the Board until there has expired the time allowed for appealing against the assessment by Article 7(1) of this Order and any further period or periods of time that the Board or an appeal tribunal may have allowed for appealing under paragraph (2) or (3) of that Article or, where an appeal is brought, until the appeal is decided or withdrawn.

Withdrawal of Assessment

6.—(1) The Board may, by a notice served on the person assessed to the levy in the same manner as an assessment notice, withdraw an assessment if that person has appealed against that assessment under the provisions of Article 7 of this Order and the appeal has not been entered in the Register of Appeals kept under the appropriate Regulations specified in paragraph (5) of that Article.

(2) The withdrawal of an assessment shall be without prejudice to the power of the Board to serve a further assessment notice on the employer.

Appeals

7.—(1) A person assessed to the levy may appeal to an appeal tribunal against the assessment within one month from the date of the service of the assessment notice or within any further period or periods of time that may be allowed by the Board or an appeal tribunal under the following provisions of this Article.

(2) The Board by notice may for good cause allow a person assessed to the levy to appeal to an appeal tribunal against the assessment at any time within the period of four months from the date of the service of the assessment notice or within such further period or periods as the Board may allow before such time as may then be limited for appealing has expired.

(3) If the Board shall not allow an application for extension of time for appealing, an appeal tribunal shall upon application made to the tribunal by the person assessed to the levy have the like powers as the Board under the last foregoing paragraph.

(4) In the case of an assessment that has reference to an establishment that ceases to carry on business in the third levy period on any day after the date of the service of the assessment notice, the foregoing provisions of this Article shall have effect as if for the period of four months from the date of the service of the assessment notice mentioned in paragraph (2) of this Article there were substituted the period of six months from the date of the cessation of business.

(5) An appeal or an application to an appeal tribunal under this Article shall be made in accordance with the Industrial Tribunals (England and Wales) Regulations 1965(a) as amended by the Industrial Tribunals (England and Wales) (Amendment) Regulations 1967(b) except where the assessment has reference to persons employed at or from one or more establishments that are wholly in Scotland and to no other persons, in which case the appeal or application shall be made in accordance with the Industrial Tribunals (Scotland) Regulations 1965(c) as amended by the Industrial Tribunals (Scotland) (Amendment) Regulations 1967(d).

(6) The powers of an appeal tribunal under paragraph (3) of this Article may be exercised by the President of the Industrial Tribunals (England and Wales) or by the President of the Industrial Tribunals (Scotland) as the case may be.

Evidence

8.—(1) Upon the discharge by a person assessed to the levy of his liability under an assessment the Board shall if so requested issue to him a certificate to that effect.

(2) The production in any proceedings of a document purporting to be certified by the Secretary of the Board to be a true copy of an assessment or other notice issued by the Board or purporting to be a certificate such as is mentioned in the foregoing paragraph of this Article shall, unless the contrary is proved, be sufficient evidence of the document and of the facts stated therein.

Signed by order of the Secretary of State.
22nd July 1971.

Paul Bryan,
Minister of State,
Department of Employment.

EXPLANATORY NOTE

(This Note is not part of the Order.)

This Order gives effect to proposals submitted by the Distributive Industry Training Board to the Secretary of State for Employment for the imposition of a further levy on employers in the distributive industry for the purpose of raising money towards the expenses of the Board.

The levy is to be imposed in respect of the third levy period commencing with the date upon which this Order comes into operation and ending on 31st March 1972. The levy will be assessed by the Board and there will be a right of appeal against an assessment to an industrial tribunal.

(a) S.I. 1965/1101 (1965 II, p. 2805).   (b) S.I. 1967/301 (1967 I, p. 1040).
(c) S.I. 1965/1157 (1965 II, p. 3266).   (d) S.I. 1967/302 (1967 I, p. 1050).

STATUTORY INSTRUMENTS

1971 No. 1195 (S.152)

ELECTRICITY

The Electricity (Borrowing Powers) (Scotland) Order 1971

Laid before the House of Commons in draft

Made - - -		19*th July* 1971
Coming into Operation		2*nd August* 1971

In exercise of the powers conferred upon me by section 47(7) of the Electricity Act 1947(**a**) as set out in Schedule 3 to the Electricity and Gas Act 1963(**b**) and as amended and extended by section 1 of the Electricity (Scotland) Act 1969(**c**) and of all other powers enabling me in that behalf, I hereby make the following order a draft of which has been laid before the Commons House of Parliament and has been approved by Resolution of that House in accordance with section 1(3) of the said Electricity (Scotland) Act 1969 :—

1. This order may be cited as the Electricity (Borrowing Powers) (Scotland) Order 1971, and shall come into operation on the day beginning fourteen days after it is made.

2. The aggregate of the amounts outstanding in respect of any borrowing mentioned in the said section 47(7) (as set out and as amended as aforesaid) or in section 3 of the Gas and Electricity Act 1968(**d**), shall not exceed the sum of £800 million.

Gordon Campbell,
One of Her Majesty's Principal
Secretaries of State.

St. Andrew's House,
Edinburgh.
19th July 1971.

(**a**) 1947 c. 54.	(**b**) 1963 c. 59.
(**c**) 1969 c. 1.	(**d**) 1968 c. 39.

EXPLANATORY NOTE

(This Note is not part of the Order.)

Under section 47(7) of the Electricity Act 1947, as set out in Schedule 3 to the Electricity and Gas Act 1963 and as amended by section 1 of the Electricity (Scotland) Act 1969, the aggregate outstanding borrowing (including the borrowing of foreign currency under section 3 of the Gas and Electricity Act 1968) by the Scottish Electricity Boards is limited to £700 million or such greater sum, not exceeding £800 million, as the Secretary of State may by order specify.

This Order specifies that the aggregate outstanding borrowing shall not exceed £800 million.

STATUTORY INSTRUMENTS

1971 No. 1196 (S.153)

FOOD AND DRUGS

FOOD HYGIENE

The Food (Meat Inspection) (Scotland) Amendment Regulations 1971

Made - - -	17*th July* 1971
Laid before Parliament	28*th July* 1971
Coming into Operation	16*th August* 1971

In exercise of the powers conferred upon me by sections 13 and 56 of the Food and Drugs (Scotland) Act 1956(**a**), and of all other powers enabling me in that behalf, having consulted with such organisations as appear to me to be representative of interests substantially affected by these regulations and after reference to the Scottish Food Hygiene Council under section 25 of that Act, I hereby make the following regulations :—

1.—(1) These regulations may be cited as the Food (Meat Inspection) (Scotland) Amendment Regulations 1971, and shall come into operation on 16th August 1971.

(2) The Interpretation Act 1889(**b**) shall apply for the interpretation of these regulations as it applies for the interpretation of an Act of Parliament.

2. The Food (Meat Inspection) (Scotland) Regulations 1961(**c**), as amended (**d**), shall be further amended as follows :—

> (*a*) by substituting for the words "two shillings and sixpence" in sub-paragraph (*a*) of regulation 22(3) thereof the words "eighteen new pence" ;
>
> (*b*) by substituting for the words "ninepence" in sub-paragraph (*b*) of the said regulation the words "five new pence" ;
>
> (*c*) by substituting for the word "sixpence" in sub-paragraph (*c*) of the said regulation the words "four new pence".

Gordon Campbell,
One of Her Majesty's Principal
Secretaries of State.

St. Andrew's House,
Edinburgh.

17th July 1971.

(**a**) 1956 c. 30.　(**b**) 1889 c. 63.
(**c**) S.I. 1961/243 (1961 I, p. 395).　(**d**) S.I. 1963/1231 (1963 II, p. 2055).

EXPLANATORY NOTE

(This Note is not part of the Regulations.)

These amending regulations raise the maximum charge for meat inspection permitted by regulation 22(3) of the Food (Meat Inspection) (Scotland) Regulations 1961, as read with the Food (Meat Inspection) (Scotland) Amendment Regulations 1963. Local authorities may increase their charges up to the new maxima subject to the provisions of regulation 22 of these regulations.

STATUTORY INSTRUMENTS

1971 No. 1197

LAND REGISTRATION

The Land Registration (Powers of Attorney) Rules 1971

Made - - -	22*nd July* 1971
Laid before Parliament	2*nd August* 1971
Coming into Operation	1*st October* 1971

The Lord Chancellor, with the advice and assistance of the Rule Committee appointed in pursuance of section 144 of the Land Registration Act 1925(a), in exercise of the powers conferred on him by that section, hereby makes the following Rules :—

1.—(1) These Rules may be cited as the Land Registration (Powers of Attorney) Rules 1971 and shall come into operation on 1st October 1971.

(2) The Interpretation Act 1889(b) shall apply to the interpretation of these Rules as it applies to the interpretation of an Act of Parliament.

2. The following rule shall be substituted for Rule 82 of the Land Registration Rules 1925(c) :—

"Instruments executed by attorney

82.—(1) If any instrument executed by an attorney is delivered at the Registry, there shall be furnished to the Registrar either the instrument creating the power of attorney, or a copy by means of which its contents may be proved under section 3 of the Powers of Attorney Act 1971(d) or a document which complies with section 4 of the Evidence and Powers of Attorney Act 1940(e).

(2) The Registrar may retain any instrument creating a power of attorney or any copy or document produced pursuant to this rule.

(3) If any transaction between the donee of a power of attorney and the person dealing with him is not completed within twelve months of the date on which the power came into operation, evidence shall be produced to the Registrar to satisfy him that the power had not been revoked at the time of the transaction.

(a) 1925 c. 21. (b) 1889 c. 63.
(c) S.R. & O. 1925/1093 (Rev. XII, p. 81: 1925, p. 717).
(d) 1971 c. 27. (e) 1940 c. 28.

(4) Unless the Registrar otherwise directs, the evidence that the power had not been revoked shall consist of a statutory declaration by the person dealing with the donee that, at the time of the completion of the transaction, the declarant did not know of the revocation of the power and did not know of the occurrence of any event (such as the death, bankruptcy or other incapacity of the donor) which had the effect of revoking the power :

Provided that where the power is expressed in the instrument creating it to be irrevocable and to be given by way of security, the statutory declaration shall be to the effect that, at the time of the completion of the transaction, the declarant did not know that the power was not in fact given by way of security and did not know that the power had been revoked by the donor acting with the consent of the donee."

Dated 22nd July 1971.

Hailsham of St. Marylebone, C.

EXPLANATORY NOTE

(This Note is not part of the Rules.)

These Rules, which amend the Land Registration Rules 1925 to take account of the Powers of Attorney Act 1971, prescribe new requirements in the Land Registry as to the production and proof of powers of attorney.

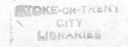

STATUTORY INSTRUMENTS

1971 No. 1198

MEDICINES

The Medicines (Exportation of Specified Products for Human Use) Order 1971

Made - - -	*22nd July* 1971
Laid before Parliament	*2nd August* 1971
Coming into Operation	*31st August* 1971

Whereas it appears to the Secretaries of State respectively concerned with health in England, in Wales and in Scotland, and to the Minister of Health and Social Services for Northern Ireland (hereinafter called "the Ministers") to be requisite for securing that any exemption conferred by section 48(1) of the Medicines Act 1968(a) does not apply to medicinal products consisting wholly or partly of substances the purity or potency of which cannot, in their opinion, be adequately tested by chemical means, that the following Order shall be made: Now, therefore, the Ministers acting jointly in exercise of their powers under section 49 of the Medicines Act 1968, as having effect subject to the provisions of article 2(2) of and Schedule 1 to the Transfer of Functions (Wales) Order 1969(b), and of all other powers enabling them in that behalf, after consulting such organisations as appear to them to be representative of interests likely to be substantially affected by the following Order, hereby order as follows:—

Citation and commencement

1. This order may be cited as the Medicines (Exportation of Specified Products for Human Use) Order 1971 and shall come into operation on 31st August 1971.

Interpretation

2.—(1) In this order unless the context otherwise requires—

"the Act" means the Medicines Act 1968;

"antigens" are substances which on administration to a human being or animal are capable of eliciting a specific immunological response;

"antisera" are substances which consist wholly or partly of sera derived from animals which have been immunised against one or more micro-organisms, viruses or other antigens;

"antitoxins" are substances which consist wholly or partly of immuno-globulins of antisera derived from animals which have been immunised against one or more toxins, whether detoxified or not;

"sera" means the fluid element of coagulated blood;

"toxins" are substances used in the diagnosis, prevention or treatment of disease and consisting wholly or partly of poisonous substances derived from specific micro-organisms, plants or animals;

"vaccines" are substances which consist wholly or partly of

(*a*) any micro-organisms, viruses or other organisms in any state,

(*b*) any toxins of microbial origin which have been detoxified, or

---

(a) 1968 c. 67.   (b) S.I. 1969/388 (1969 I, p. 1070).

(c) any extracts or derivatives of any micro-organisms or of any viruses, being substances which, when administered to human beings or animals, are used for the prevention or treatment of specific diseases;

and other expressions have the same meaning as in the Act.

(2) The Interpretation Act 1889(a) shall apply to the interpretation of this order as it applies to the interpretation of an Act of Parliament.

Provisions in respect of the exporting of certain classes of medicinal products

3. There are hereby specified the following classes of medicinal products in relation to which nothing in section 48(1) of the Act shall affect the operation of any of the provisions of sections 7 to 47 of the Act, that is to say:—

medicinal products for use for human beings which consist wholly or partly of antigens, antitoxins, sera, antisera, toxins or vaccines.

Keith Joseph,
Secretary of State for Social Services.

22nd July 1971.

Peter Thomas,
Secretary of State for Wales.

21st July 1971.

Gordon Campbell,
Secretary of State for Scotland.

22nd July 1971.

W. K. Fitzsimmons,
Minister of Health and Social Services
for Northern Ireland.

22nd July 1971.

EXPLANATORY NOTE
(*This Note is not part of the Order.*)

This Order excepts certain classes of medicinal products for human use from the postponement of the operation of sections 7 to 47 of the Medicines Act 1968, granted by section 48(1) of the Act. The classes of medicinal products excepted are those of which the purity or potency cannot, in the opinion of the Health Ministers, be adequately tested by chemical means.

(a) 1889 c. 63.

STATUTORY INSTRUMENTS

1971 No. 1199

CLEAN AIR

The Smoke Control Areas (Authorised Fuels) (No. 2) Regulations 1971

Made - - -	*22nd July* 1971
Laid before Parliament	*30th July* 1971
Coming into Operation	*4th August* 1971

The Secretary of State for the Environment, in exercise of his powers under section 34(1) of the Clean Air Act 1956(a), and of all other powers enabling him in that behalf, hereby makes the following regulations :—

Title and commencement

1. These regulations may be cited as the Smoke Control Areas (Authorised Fuels) (No. 2) Regulations 1971 and shall come into operation on 4th August 1971.

Interpretation

2. The Interpretation Act 1889(b) shall apply for the interpretation of these regulations as it applies for the interpretation of an Act of Parliament.

Authorised fuels for the purposes of the Clean Air Act 1956

3. The following fuels are hereby declared to be authorised fuels for the purposes of the Clean Air Act 1956 :—

(*a*) "XL" Briquettes, which have been manufactured by Taylor Brothers (Dundee) Limited and which—

    (i) comprise "Coalite" breeze (or "Homefire" char) and Welsh anthracite duff (as to approximately 97 per cent. of total weight) and borax and starch (as to the remaining weight) and

    (ii) have been subjected to a mild heat treatment process ;

(*b*) "Anthracine" ovoids which have been manufactured by Les Houilleries du Nord-Pas-de-Calais and which—

    (i) comprise French anthracite (as to approximately 92 per cent. of total weight and pitch (as to the remaining weight) and

---

(a) 1956 c. 52.   (b) 1889 c. 63.

(ii) have been subjected to a mild heat treatment process.

Peter Walker,
Secretary of State for the Environment
22nd July 1971.

EXPLANATORY NOTE

(This Note is not part of the Regulations.)

Section 11 of the Clean Air Act 1956 makes it an offence to emit smoke from a chimney of a building within a smoke control area unless it can be shown that the emission of smoke arose solely from use of an authorised fuel. These Regulations declare "XL" briquettes and "Anthracine" ovoids to be authorised fuels.

STATUTORY INSTRUMENTS

1971 No. 1200

MEDICINES

The Medicines (Control of Substances for Manufacture) Order 1971

Made - - -		*23rd July* 1971
Laid before Parliament		*3rd August* 1971
Coming into Operation		*1st September* 1971

The Secretaries of State respectively concerned with health in England and in Wales, the Secretary of State concerned with health and with agriculture in Scotland, the Minister of Health and Social Services for Northern Ireland, the Minister of Agriculture, Fisheries and Food and the Minister of Agriculture for Northern Ireland, acting jointly, in exercise of their powers under section 105(1)(*a*) of the Medicines Act 1968(a), as having effect subject to the provisions of article 2(2) of and Schedule 1 to the Transfer of Functions (Wales) Order 1969(b) and of all other powers enabling them in that behalf, after consulting such organisations as appear to them to be representative of interests likely to be substantially affected by this order and after taking into account the advice of the Committee on Safety of Medicines and the advice of the Veterinary Products Committee, hereby order as follows:—

Citation and commencement

1. This order may be cited as the Medicines (Control of Substances for Manufacture) Order 1971 and shall come into operation on 1st September 1971.

Interpretation

2.—(1) In this order unless the context otherwise requires:—

"the Act" means the Medicines Act 1968;

"Committee on Safety of Medicines" means the Committee established by the Medicines (Committee on Safety of Medicines) Order 1970(c);

"Veterinary Products Committee" means the Committee established by the Medicines (Veterinary Products Committee) Order 1970(d).

(2) The expressions used in Schedule 1 to this order have the meanings given to them in Schedule 2 to this order and other expressions have the same meaning as in the Act.

(3) The Interpretation Act 1889(e) shall apply to the interpretation of this order as it applies to the interpretation of an Act of Parliament.

(a) 1968 c. 67.   (b) S.I. 1969/388 (1969 I, p. 1070).
(c) S.I. 1970/1257 (1970 II, p. 4098).   (d) S.I. 1970/1304 (1970 III, p. 4335).
                          (e) 1889 c. 63.

Application of specified provisions of the Act to specified ingredients used in the manufacture of medicinal products

3. There are hereby specified the substances set out in numbered paragraphs in Column 1 of Schedule 1 to this order, as being substances which when not manufactured, sold, supplied, imported or exported for use for a medicinal purpose wholly or mainly in either or both of the ways specified in section 130(1) of the Act appear to the Ministers to be substances which are not in themselves medicinal products but are used as ingredients in the manufacture of medicinal products, and it is hereby directed that the provisions contained in Part II, sections 62, 66 and 67 of Part III of the Act, and the provisions contained in Parts V and VIII of the Act shall have effect in relation to each of those substances in the circumstances set out in the corresponding paragraph of Column 2 of the said Schedule, as those provisions have effect in relation to medicinal products.

Keith Joseph,
Secretary of State for Social Services.

22nd July 1971.

Peter Thomas,
Secretary of State for Wales.

21st July 1971.

Gordon Campbell,
Secretary of State for Scotland.

22nd July 1971.

W. K. Fitzsimmons,
Minister of Health and Social Services
for Northern Ireland.

22nd July 1971.

In Witness whereof the official seal of the Minister of Agriculture, Fisheries and Food is hereunto affixed on 22nd July 1971.

(L.S.)

J. M. L. Prior,
Minister of Agriculture,
Fisheries and Food.

H. W. West,
Minister of Agriculture
for Northern Ireland.

23rd July 1971.

Article 2(2) and Article 3

SCHEDULE 1

Column 1	Column 2
Substances appearing to the Ministers to be substances which, as described in article 3 of this order, are not themselves medicinal products but which are used as ingredients in the manufacture of medicinal products	Circumstances in which the order applies to the substances referred to in Column 1
1. Amphotericin B	When manufactured, assembled, sold, supplied, imported or exported for use as an ingredient in a medicinal product for parenteral injection into human beings or animals.
2. Bacitracin	
3. Capreomycin	
4. Colistin	,, ,,
5. Erythromycin	,, ,,
6. Gentamicin	,, ,,
7. Heparin	,, ,,
8. Hyaluronidase	,, ,,
9. Kanamycin	,, ,,
10. Neomycin	,, ,,
11. Penicillin	,, ,,
12. Polymyxin B	,, ,,
13. Preparations of the pituitary ... (posterior lobe)	,, ,,
14. Streptomycin	,, ,,
15. The lincomycins	,, ,,
16. The rifamycins	,, ,,
17. The tetracyclines	,, ,,
18. Vancomycin	,, ,,
19. Viomycin	,, ,,
20. Oxytetracycline	When manufactured, assembled, sold, supplied, imported or exported for use as an ingredient in a medicinal product which is to be administered to human beings or animals by means other than parenteral injection.
21. Tetracycline	

SCHEDULE 1 *continued*

Column 1	Column 2
Substances appearing to the Ministers to be substances which, as described in article 3 of this order, are not themselves medicinal products but which are used as ingredients in the manufacture of medicinal products	Circumstances in which the order applies to the substances referred to in Column 1
22. Dextrans	When manufactured, assembled, sold, supplied, imported or exported for use as ingredients of dextran injections for human or animal use.
23. Antigens	When manufactured, assembled, sold, supplied, imported or exported for use as an ingredient in a medicinal product for human or animal use.
24. Antisera	
25. Antitoxins	,, ,,
26. Chorionic gonadotrophin ...	,, ,,
27. Corticotrophin	,, ,,
28. Follicle-stimulating hormone ...	,, ,,
29. Insulin	,, ,,
30. Sera...	,, ,,
31. Streptodornase	,, ,,
32. Streptokinase	,, ,,
33. Toxins	,, ,,
34. Vaccines	,, ,,
35. Preparations of blood	When manufactured, assembled, sold, supplied, imported or exported for use as an ingredient in a medicinal product for human use.
36. Plasma	When manufactured, assembled, sold, supplied, imported or exported for use as an ingredient in a medicinal product for administration to animals.
37. Any substances wholly or partly derived from animals not being substances specifically mentioned in any of the above paragraphs of this column.	

Article 2(2)

SCHEDULE 2

"Amphotericin B" is any antimicrobial substance or mixture of such substances produced by *Streptomyces nodosus*. The expression includes any salt or derivative, or salt of a derivative, of amphotericin B and any substance the chemical and biological properties of which are identical with or similar to those of amphotericin B but which is produced by other means.

"Antigens" are substances which on administration to a human being or animal are capable of eliciting a specific immunological response.

"Antisera" are substances which consist wholly or partly of sera derived from animals which have been immunised against one or more micro-organisms, viruses or other antigens.

"Antitoxins" are substances which consist wholly or partly of immunoglobulins of antisera derived from animals which have been immunised against one or more toxins whether detoxified or not.

"Bacitracin" is any antimicrobial polypeptide produced by strains of *Bacillus licheniformis* and of *Bacillus subtilis* (var. *Tracey*), which yields on hydrolysis with mineral acids the amino acids L-cysteine, D-glutamic acid, L-histidine, L-isoleucine, L-leucine, L-lysine, D-ornithine, D-phenylalanine and DL-aspartic acid. The expression includes any salt or derivative, or salt of a derivative, of bacitracin and any substance the chemical and biological properties of which are identical with or similar to those of bacitracin but which is produced by other means.

"Capreomycin" is any antimicrobial polypeptide or mixture of such polypeptides produced by the strain of *Streptomyces capreolus* which on 1st September 1967 was numbered NRRL 2773 in the culture collection of the Northern Utilisation Research and Development Branch of the United States Department of Agriculture, and which yields on hydrolysis with mineral acids the amino acids α,β-diaminopropionic acids and α-(2-iminohexahydro-4-pyrimidyl)glycine together with serine, alanine and β-lysine. The expression includes any salt or derivative, or salt of a derivative, of capreomycin and any substance the chemical and biological properties of which are identical with or similar to capreomycin but which is produced by other means.

"Chorionic gonadotrophin" is a dry, sterile preparation of the gonad stimulating substance obtained from the urine of pregnant women.

"Colistin" is any antimicrobial polypeptide or mixture of such polypeptides produced by strains of *Bacillus polymyxa* (var. *colistinus*) which yields on hydrolysis with mineral acids only the amino acids leucine, threonine and α,γ-diaminobutyric acid together with 6-methylheptanoic acid and 6-methyloctanoic acid. The expression includes any salt or derivative, or any salt of a derivative, of colistin and any substance the chemical and biological properties of which are identical with or similar to those of colistin but which is produced by other means.

"Corticotrophin" is a substance obtained from the anterior lobe of the pituitary gland and which contains the peptide hormone that increases the rate at which corticoid hormones are secreted by the adrenal gland.

"Dextrans" are the substances produced by the fermentation of sucrose by means of strains of *Leuconostoc mesenteroides*, or by means of purified enzymes derived from such strains being polymers of glucose in which the linkages between the glucose units are almost entirely of the α-1,6 type.

"Dextran injections" are preparations of solutions of dextrans in physiological saline or other vehicle suitable for intravenous injection of dextrans.

"Erythromycin" is any antimicrobial weakly basic substance or mixture of such substances produced by *Streptomyces erythreus* (Waksman) which has the following characteristics—

(a) it forms a dihydrate which has a melting point of about 135°C.;

(b) on mild acid hydrolysis it yields the base erythralosamine with a melting point of about 206°C.

The expression includes any salt or derivative, or salt of a derivative, of erythromycin and any substance the chemical and biological properties of which are identical with or similar to those of erythromycin but which is produced by other means.

"Follicle-stimulating hormone" is an extract of post-menopausal urine containing that hormone which has the property of stimulating growth and maturation of germinal follicles in the ovary. Such extract may contain substances with interstitial cell stimulating hormone activity.

"Gentamicin" is any antimicrobial basic substance or mixture of such substances produced by the strain of *Micromonospora purpurea* which on 1st September 1967 was numbered NRRL 2953 in the culture collection of the Northern Utilisation Research and Development Branch of the United States Department of Agriculture. The expression includes any salt or derivative, or salt of a derivative, of gentamicin and any substance the chemical and biological properties of which are identical with or similar to those of gentamicin but which is produced by other means.

"Heparin" is a substance containing the sodium salt of a sulphated polysaccharide obtained from mammalian tissues which has the property of prolonging the clotting time of blood in human beings or animals.

"Hyaluronidase" is a substance prepared from mammalian testicles or sperm or from other sources of the enzymes which diminish the viscosity of the hyaluronic acid present in mammalian tissues.

"Insulin" is a preparation of the specific antidiabetic principle of the pancreas.

"Kanamycin" is any antimicrobial substance or mixture of such substances produced by *Streptomyces kanamyceticus*. The expression includes any salt or derivative, or salt of a derivative, of kanamycin and any substance the chemical and biological properties of which are identical with or similar to those of kanamycin but which is produced by other means.

"The lincomycins" are the antimicrobial substances produced by *Streptomyces lincolnensis* (var. *lincolnensis*). These substances are the basic amides of hygric acid or of a substituted hygric acid with 6-amino-6,8-dideoxy-1-thiogalacto-octopyranose or with substituted 6-amino-6,8-dideoxy-1-thiogalacto-octopyranose. The expression includes any salt or derivative, or salt of a derivative, of any lincomycin and any substance the chemical and biological properties of which are identical with or similar to those of any lincomycin but which is produced by other means.

"Lincomycin" is one of the lincomycins which incorporates *trans*-L-4-propylhygric acid and a methylthio group in the pyranose ring.

"Neomycin" is any antimicrobial substance or mixture of such substances produced by *Streptomyces fradiae* which are complex organic bases and which yield on hydrolysis with mineral acids the base neamine. The expression includes any salt or derivative, or salt of a derivative, of neomycin and any substance the chemical and biological properties of which are identical with or similar to those of neomycin but which is produced by other means.

"Oxytetracycline" is 4-dimethylamino-1,4,4a,5,5a,6,11,12a-octahydro-3,5,6,10,12, 12a-hexahydroxy-6-methyl-1,11-dioxonaphthacene-2-carboxamide. The expression includes any salt of oxytetracycline.

"Parenteral injection" in relation to any substance includes any administration of the substance by insertion into the body by any route other than that of the gastro-intestinal tract but does not include any application of the substance to the skin.

"Penicillin" is any antimicrobial acid, any salt thereof, or any derivative which is obtained therefrom which contains in its structure a fused thiazolidine β-lactam nucleus.

"Plasma" means the fluid element of uncoagulated blood.

"Polymyxin B" is any antimicrobial polypeptide or mixture of such polypeptides produced by strains of *Bacillus polymyxa* which yields on hydrolysis with mineral acids only the amino acids leucine, phenylalanine, threonine and α,γ-diaminobutyric acid together with 6-methylheptanoic acid and 6-methyloctanoic acid. The expression includes any salt or derivative, or salt of a derivative, of polymyxin B and any substance the chemical and biological properties of which are identical with or similar to those of polymyxin B but which is produced by other means.

"Preparations of blood" include whole blood from human beings or animals, serum or plasma made from such blood, any protein or other substance separated from such blood and any dried product prepared from any such serum, plasma, protein or other substance.

"Preparations of the pituitary (posterior lobe)" include the active principles thereof (whether obtained by fractionation of the gland or by synthesis) and derivatives of those principles with the same specific biological action.

"The rifamycins" are a group of related antimicrobial macrolactams produced by the growth of *Streptomyces mediterranei* and containing the chemical structure of 11-acetoxy-7,9,15-trihydroxy-13-methoxy-2,6,8,10,12-pentamethylpentadeca-2,4, 14-trienoic acid amide, attached by the nitrogen atom and by the oxygen atom in the 15-position respectively to the 7- and 2-positions of a 5,6,9-trioxygenated 2, 4-dimethyl-1-oxonaphtho[2,1-*b*] furan. The expression includes any salt or derivative, or salt of a derivative, of any rifamycin and any substance the chemical and biological properties of which are identical with or similar to those of any rifamycin but which is produced by other means.

"Rifamide" is an antimicrobial base produced from a rifamycin known as rifamycin B and has the chemical structure of 11-acetoxy-7,9,15-trihydroxy-13-methoxy-2,6,8, 10,12-pentamethylpentadeca-2,4,14-trienoic acid amide, attached by the nitrogen atom and by the oxygen atom in the 15-position respectively to the 7- and 2-positions of 5,6-dihydroxy-2,4-dimethyl-1-oxonaphtho[2,1-*b*] furan-9-oxyacetic acid diethylamide.

"Sera" means the fluid element of coagulated blood.

"Streptodornase" is the substance produced by strains of streptococcus which catalyzes the depolymerisation of deoxyribonucleic acid.

"Streptokinase" is the substance produced by strains of streptococcus which activates an inactive precursor of a fibrinolytic enzyme present in plasma.

"Streptomycin" is any antimicrobial complex organic base or mixture of such bases produced by *Streptomyces griseus* which—
  (a) yields on hydrolysis with mineral acids the base streptidine (*meso*-1: 3-diguanidocyclohexane-2,4,5,6-tetraol); and
  (b) yields on hydrolysis by a 4 per cent solution of sodium hydroxide the substance maltol (3-hydroxy-2-methyl-γ-pyrone).

The expression includes any salt or derivative, or salt of a derivative, of streptomycin and any substance the chemical and biological properties of which are identical with or similar to those of streptomycin but which is produced by other means.

"The tetracyclines" are the antimicrobial bases which contain the chemical structure naphthacene-2-carboxamide, hydrogenated to any extent, and having each of the positions 1,3,10,11,12 and 12a substituted by an hydroxyl or an oxo group.

"Tetracycline" is 4-diamethylamino-1,4,4a,5,5a,6,11,12a-octahydro-3,6,10,12, 12a-pentahydroxy-6-methyl-1,11-dioxonaphthacene-2-carboxamide. The expression includes any salt of tetracycline.

"Toxins" are substances used in the diagnosis, prevention or treatment of disease and consisting wholly or partly of poisonous substances derived from specific micro-organisms, plants or animals.

"Vaccines" are substances which consist wholly or partly of—

(a) any micro-organisms, viruses or other organisms in any state,

(b) any toxins of microbial origin which have been detoxified, or

(c) any extracts or derivatives of any micro-organisms or of any viruses,

being substances which, when administered to human beings or animals, are used for the prevention or treatment of specific diseases.

"Vancomycin" is any mixture of antimicrobial substances produced by *Streptomyces orientalis*. The expression includes any salt or derivative, or salt of a derivative, of vancomycin and any substance the chemical and biological properties of which are identical with or similar to those of vancomycin but which is produced by other means.

"Viomycin" is any antimicrobial organic base produced by the growth of *Streptomyces griseus* (var. *purpureus*), which yields on hydrolysis with mineral acids urea, L-serine, α,β-diaminopropionic acid and 3,6-diaminohexanoic acid. The expression includes any salt or derivative, or salt of a derivative, of viomycin and any substance the chemical and biological properties of which are identical with or similar to those of viomycin but which is produced by other means.

EXPLANATORY NOTE

(This Note is not part of the Order.)

This Order extends certain specified provisions of the Medicines Act 1968, concerning, in relation to medicinal products, the holding of licences and certificates, the regulation of dealings, offences and penalties, labelling, leaflets and containers, and certain miscellaneous matters, so that those provisions will also relate to the substances described in Schedule 1 to this order in the circumstances there specified.

STATUTORY INSTRUMENTS

1971 No. 1201

SOCIAL SECURITY

The National Insurance (Industrial Injuries) (Increase of Benefit and Miscellaneous Provisions) Regulations 1971

Made - - - -	*26th July* 1971
Laid before Parliament	*4th August* 1971
Coming into Operation—	
Regulation 4(7)	*8th December* 1971
Remainder	*5th August* 1971

The Industrial Injuries Joint Authority and the Secretary of State for Social Services, in exercise of the powers conferred by the provisions of the National Insurance Acts and the National Insurance (Industrial Injuries) Act 1965(a) set out respectively in Parts I and II of Schedule 1 to this instrument, and of all other powers enabling them in that behalf, hereby make the following regulations, which contain no provisions other than such as are made in consequence of the National Insurance Act 1971(b) and which accordingly, by virtue of section 16 of and paragraph 2(1)(*a*) of Schedule 6 to that Act, are exempt from the requirements of section 62(2) of the said Act of 1965 (reference to Industrial Injuries Advisory Council):—

Citation, commencement and interpretation

1.—(1) These regulations may be cited as the National Insurance (Industrial Injuries) (Increase of Benefit and Miscellaneous Provisions) Regulations 1971 and shall come into operation, in the case of regulation 4(7), on 8th December 1971 and in the case of the remainder of the regulations on 5th August 1971.

(2) In these regulations, unless the context otherwise requires—

"the principal Act" means the National Insurance (Industrial Injuries) Act 1965;

"the Act of 1971" means the National Insurance Act 1971;

"the Benefit Regulations" means the National Insurance (Industrial Injuries) (Benefit) Regulations 1964(c), as amended(d);

"the Claims and Payments Regulations" means the National Insurance (Industrial Injuries) (Claims and Payments) Regulations 1964(e);

and other expressions have the same meaning as in the principal Act.

(3) References in these regulations to any enactment or regulation shall, except in so far as the context otherwise requires, include references to such enactment or regulation as amended or extended by or under any subsequent enactment, order or regulation.

(4) The rules for the construction of Acts of Parliament contained in the Interpretation Act 1889(f) shall apply for the purpose of the interpretation of

---

(a) 1965 c. 52. (b) 1971 c. 50.
(c) S.I. 1964/504 (1964 I, p. 833).
(d) The relevant amending instruments are S.I. 1967/832, 1969/1168, 1970/46 (1967 II, p.2482; 1969 II, p. 3432; 1970 I, p. 243).
(e) S.I. 1964/73 (1964 I, p. 115). (f) 1889 c. 63.

these Regulations as they apply for the purpose of the interpretation of an Act of Parliament.

Increase in rates and amounts of benefit payable under regulations

2.—(1) The rates and amounts of benefit of the several descriptions specified in Schedule 2 to these regulations shall be increased as from the dates respectively specified in paragraph (2) of this regulation, and accordingly the provisions of the Benefit Regulations set out in column 1 of that Schedule (which provisions relate to the said rates and amounts of benefit) shall be amended as from the appropriate date by substituting for the rates and amounts set out in column 3 of that Schedule the corresponding rates and amounts set out in column 4 thereof.

(2) The said increases shall operate, in so far as they relate to injury benefit, as from 23rd September 1971, in so far as they relate to widow's pension as from 20th September 1971, and in so far as they relate to any other benefit as from 22nd September 1971:

Provided that the increased amount of a disablement gratuity shall be payable only where the period taken into account by the assessment of the extent of disablement in respect of which the gratuity is awarded begins on or after 22nd September 1971, but nevertheless the amendment made by this regulation to Schedule 4 of the Benefit Regulations (which Schedule, as applied by regulations 6 and 8 of those regulations, prescribes, in relation to awards of disablement gratuity, the weekly rate of pension payable in lieu thereof and the weekly amount by which increase of benefit during hospital treatment is reduced) shall have effect as from 22nd September 1971, whether the period taken into account by the assessment began before or after that date.

Conditions relating to payment of additional benefit under awards made before the appointed or prescribed day

3. Where an award of any benefit under the principal Act has been made before the day appointed or prescribed for the payment of benefit of the description to which the award relates at a higher weekly rate by virtue of the Act of 1971 or of these regulations, paragraph 3(1) of Schedule 6 to the National Insurance Act 1969 (which relates to the effect of any such award) shall, if the period to which the award relates has not ended before that day, have effect subject to the condition that if the award has not been made in accordance with the provisions of sub-paragraph (2) of that paragraph (which sub-paragraph authorises the making of such an award providing for the payment of the benefit at the higher weekly rate as from that day) and a question arises as to—

    (*a*) the weekly rate at which the benefit is payable by virtue of the Act of 1971 or of these regulations, or

    (*b*) whether the conditions for the receipt of the benefit at the higher weekly rate are satisfied,

the benefit shall be or continue to be payable at the weekly rate specified in the award until the said question shall have been determined in accordance with the provisions of the principal Act.

Amendments to the Benefit Regulations

4.—(1) In regulation 9(1) of the Benefit Regulations (increase of benefit in respect of a wife, and computation of earnings), after the word "beneficiary" there shall be inserted the words "(not being a beneficiary who is entitled to an unemployability supplement and is residing with his wife)".

(2) In the said regulation 9, after paragraph (1) there shall be inserted the following paragraph:—

"(1A) For the purpose of section 18(3A) of the Act (beneficiary entitled to unemployability supplement and residing with his wife), the earnings of the wife of a beneficiary shall be calculated or estimated in accordance with the provisions of the said National Insurance (Computation of Earnings) Regulations as if the manner and basis of the calculation or estimate were for the purposes of the National Insurance Act and of any regulations made thereunder.".

(3) In regulation 10(2)(a) of the Benefit Regulations (earnings condition for increase of benefit for dependent relatives), after the words "(calculated or estimated in such manner and on such basis as is prescribed by" there shall be inserted the words "paragraphs (1) and (2) of".

(4) In regulation 11(2) of the Benefit Regulations (earnings condition for increase of benefit for female person having care of child), immediately before the beginning thereof there shall be inserted the words "Subject to paragraph (2A) of this regulation," and for the words "(calculated or estimated in such manner and on such basis as is prescribed as aforesaid for the purpose of the said section 18)" there shall be substituted the words "(calculated or estimated in such manner and on such basis as is prescribed by regulation 9(1) and (2) for the purpose of the said section 18 in relation to the earnings of a wife)".

(5) In the said regulation 11, after paragraph (2) there shall be inserted the following paragraphs:—

"(2A) Where a beneficiary is entitled to unemployability supplement and any such female person is residing with him and the earnings of such female person (other than her earnings from any employment by the beneficiary in caring for a child or children of the beneficiary's family) for the calendar week ending last before any week for which he is entitled to benefit under the said section 18 in respect of such female person exceeded £9·50, the weekly rate of benefit under the said section 18 shall for the last-mentioned week be reduced—

    (a) where the excess is less than £2·00, by 5 new pence for each complete 10 new pence of the excess, and

    (b) where the excess is not less than £2·00, by 5 new pence for each complete 10 new pence of the excess up to £2·00 and by 5 new pence for each complete 5 new pence of any further excess.

(2B) For the purpose of the last preceding paragraph of this regulation, the weekly earnings of a female person who is residing with a beneficiary entitled to unemployability supplement shall be calculated or estimated in such manner and on such basis as is prescribed by regulation 9(1A) and (2) for the purposes of the said section 18 in relation to the earnings of a wife.".

(6) In regulation 18(b) of the Benefit Regulations (higher rate of pension payable to widows during a limited period following death of husband), for the words "£1·50" there shall be substituted the words "£1·80".

(7) For regulation 26 of the Benefit Regulations (provisions relating to medical treatment as an in-patient) there shall be substituted the following regulations:—

"Condition for receipt of increase of disablement pension for constant attendance under section 15 of the Act while receiving medical treatment as an in-patient

26.—(1) For the purposes of section 15 of the Act (increase of disablement pension in respect of the need of constant attendance), subject to paragraph (2) of this regulation it shall be a condition for the receipt of an increase of disablement pension under the said section 15 for any period in respect of any person that during that period he is not receiving, or has not received, free in-patient treatment, and for this purpose a person shall be regarded as receiving or having received free in-patient treatment if he would be so regarded for the purposes of the National Insurance (Hospital In-Patients) Regulations 1949(a), as amended(b).

(2) Where a person was entitled to an increase of disablement pension under the said section 15 in respect of the period immediately before he commenced to undergo any treatment mentioned in paragraph (1) of this regulation, that paragraph shall not apply in respect of the first 4 weeks of any continuous period during which he is undergoing such treatment.

(3) For the purpose of paragraph (2) of this regulation, 2 or more distinct periods separated by an interval not exceeding 28 days, or by 2 or more such intervals, shall be treated as a continuous period equal in duration to the total of such distinct periods and ending on the last day of the later or last such period.

Treatment of distinct periods of hospital in-patient treatment as continuous for the purposes of section 16 of the Act

26A. For the purposes of section 16 of the Act (increase of disablement benefit during hospital treatment) a person who receives medical treatment as an in-patient for 2 or more distinct periods separated by an interval of less than a week in each case shall be treated as receiving such treatment continuously from the beginning of the first period until the end of the last.".

(8) In regulation 39(2)(*b*) of the Benefit Regulations (adjustment of dependency benefit under the principal Act where personal benefit is payable), for the words "(not being home confinement grant, maternity grant or death grant)" there shall be substituted the words "(not being maternity grant, death grant or age addition)".

(9) In regulation 42 of the Benefit Regulations (payments by way of unemployability supplement etc. to persons entitled to workmen's compensation), after paragraph (2) there shall be added the following paragraph:—

"(3) For the purposes of this regulation, the meaning in section 13A(2) of the principal Act (increase of unemployability supplement by reference to beneficiary's age on qualifying date) of 'the qualifying date' shall, subject to the provisions of subsections (3), (4) and (5) of that section, be the beginning of the first week for which the said person qualified for a payment by way of unemployability supplement under this regulation.".

(10) In regulation 44 of the Benefit Regulations (payments by way of unemployability supplement etc. to certain former constables and firemen), in the proviso to paragraph (2) the words "payment under this paragraph shall be adjusted by reference to the said injury pension so as to be payable at a weekly rate of £5, and" shall be deleted, and after paragraph (2) there shall be inserted the following paragraph:—

"(2A) For the purposes of this regulation, the meaning in section 13A(2) of the principal Act (increase of unemployability supplement by reference to beneficiary's age on qualifying date) of 'the qualifying date' shall be the same as that prescribed by regulation 42(3) in relation to persons entitled to payments by way of unemployability supplement.".

(a) S.I. 1949/1461 (1949 I, p. 2718).
(b) The relevant amending instrument is S.I. 1960/1283 (1960 II, p. 2163).

Amendment to the Claims and Payments Regulations

5. After regulation 24 of the Claims and Payments Regulations there shall be inserted the following regulation:—

"*Payment of benefit to a third party*

24A. For any period during which benefit is payable to a beneficiary in respect of another person only if the beneficiary is contributing at not less than a certain weekly rate to the maintenance of, or to the cost of providing for, that other person, then if it appears to the Secretary of State to be necessary for protecting the interests of the beneficiary or of the other person, or if the beneficiary so requests the Secretary of State, the Secretary of State may direct that the whole or part of the benefit payable to the beneficiary (whether or not benefit payable in respect of the other person) shall be paid to another person on behalf of the beneficiary.".

Given under the official seal of the Industrial Injuries Joint Authority.

(L.S.)

D. G. Kelly,
Secretary,
Industrial Injuries Joint Authority.

26th July 1971.

Signed by authority of the Secretary of State for Social Services.

Paul Dean,
Parliamentary Under Secretary of State,
Department of Health and Social Security.

26th July 1971.

SCHEDULE 1

PROVISIONS CONFERRING POWERS EXERCISED IN MAKING THESE REGULATIONS

PART I

Provisions conferring powers exercised by the Industrial Injuries Joint Authority

Enactment	Relevant Provisions	Relevant Amending Enactments
The National Insurance (Industrial Injuries) Act 1965(a)	Section 12(3)	—
	Section 14(7)	—
	Section 15(1)	—
	Section 18(1)(*d*) and (3)	—
	Section 18(3B)	The National Insurance Act 1971 (b), Section 8(3).
	Section 19(4)	—
	Section 30	—
	Section 33(2)	—
	Section 78(2)	—
	Section 81	—

PART II

Provisions conferring powers exercised by the Secretary of State for Social Services

Enactment	Relevant Provisions	Relevant Amending Enactments
The National Insurance (Industrial Injuries) Act 1965	Section 16	—
	Section 30A	The National Insurance Act 1971, Section 10(1)
The National Insurance Act 1969(c)	Schedule 6, paragraph 3 and 4	—
The National Insurance Act 1971	Schedule 5, paragraph 13(1)	—

(a) 1965 c. 52.   (b) 1971 c. 50.
(c) 1969 c. 44.

Regulation 2

SCHEDULE 2

AMENDMENT OF PROVISIONS OF THE BENEFIT REGULATIONS
RELATING TO RATES AND AMOUNTS OF BENEFIT

1	2	3	4
Amended provision	Description of rates and amounts of benefit	Existing rate or amount	New rate or amount
Regulation 4(2)	Weekly rates of injury benefit in respect of children under the upper limit of compulsory school age:—		
	(a) where the employment or employments amounted to full-time or substantially full-time employment;	£4·50	£5·50
	(b) in any other case	£1·55	£1·85
Regulation 7	Weekly rates of allowance in respect of constant attendance:—		
	(a) where to a substantial extent dependent on such attendance;	£3·30	£4·00
	(b) maximum payable where so dependent and attendance required is greater by reason of exceptionally severe disablement; ...	£4·95	£6·00
	(c) where entirely or almost entirely dependent on such attendance...	£6·60	£8·00
Regulation 18(b)	Higher rate of widow's pension payable for first 26 weeks	£7·00	£8·40
Schedule 3 (applied by Regulation 3)	Amount of gratuities for degrees of disablement of:—		
	1 per cent	£55·00	£66·00
	2 per cent	£82·50	£99·00
	3 per cent	£110·00	£132·00
	4 per cent	£137·50	£165·00
	5 per cent	£165·00	£198·00
	6 per cent	£192·50	£231·00
	7 per cent	£220·00	£264·00
	8 per cent	£247·50	£297·00
	9 per cent	£275·00	£330·00
	10 per cent	£302·50	£363·00
	11 per cent	£330·00	£396·00
	12 per cent	£357·50	£429·00
	13 per cent	£385·00	£462·00
	14 per cent	£412·50	£495·00
	15 per cent	£440·00	£528·00
	16 per cent	£467·50	£561·00
	17 per cent	£495·00	£594·00
	18 per cent	£522·50	£627·00
	19 per cent	£550·00	£660·00
Schedule 4 (applied by Regulations 6 and 8)	Weekly rate of disablement pension payable in lieu of disablement gratuity for degree of disablement of:—		
	less than 20 per cent but not less than 16 per cent;	£1·70	£2·00
	less than 16 per cent but not less than 11 per cent;	£1·28	£1·50
	less than 11 per cent but not less than 6 per cent;	£0·85	£1·00
	less than 6 per cent	£0·43	£0·50

EXPLANATORY NOTE

(This Note is not part of the Regulations.)

These Regulations increase the rates of certain benefits payable under regulations made under the National Insurance (Industrial Injuries) Act 1965 in order to bring them into conformity with the higher rates of benefit payable directly under that Act by virtue of the Act of 1971, and contain consequential and transitional provisions following upon the passing of the last-mentioned Act.

These Regulations amend the National Insurance (Industrial Injuries) (Benefit) Regulations 1964 to vary the conditions relating to the earnings of a female person residing with a beneficiary entitled to unemployability supplement and having care of his children, and to make minor consequential amendments. They also provide that a beneficiary shall not be entitled to constant attendance allowance after the first four weeks in hospital if he is receiving free in-patient treatment.

The National Insurance (Industrial Injuries) (Claims and Payments) Regulations 1964 are also amended by these Regulations to provide that where a beneficiary is entitled to benefit in respect of a dependant the Secretary of State may direct that the whole or part of the benefit payable to the beneficiary shall be paid to another person on his behalf.

These Regulations are made in consequence of the National Insurance Act 1971 and in accordance with Schedule 6, paragraph 2(1), to that Act have not been referred to the Industrial Injuries Advisory Council.

STATUTORY INSTRUMENTS

1971 No. 1202

SOCIAL SECURITY

The National Insurance (Assessment of Graduated Contributions) Amendment Regulations 1971

Made - - - -	26th July 1971
Laid before Parliament	2nd August, 1971
Coming into Operation	21st September 1971

The Secretary of State for Social Services, in exercise of powers under section 4(4), (6) and (7) of the National Insurance Act 1965(a), and of all other powers enabling him in that behalf, hereby makes the following regulations which contain no provisions other than such as are made in consequence of the National Insurance Act 1971(b) and which accordingly, by virtue of section 16(3) of, and paragraph 2 of Schedule 6 to, the last mentioned Act, are exempt from the requirements of section 108 of the said Act of 1965 (reference to the National Insurance Advisory Committee):—

Citation, commencement and interpretation

1. These regulations, which may be cited as the National Insurance (Assessment of Graduated Contributions) Amendment Regulations 1971, shall be read as one with the National Insurance (Assessment of Graduated Contributions) Regulations 1967(c), as amended(d), (hereinafter referred to as "the principal regulations") and shall come into operation on the 21st September 1971.

Amendment of regulation 2 of the principal regulations

2. In regulation 2 of the principal regulations (equivalent amounts) for the sum of £12 in paragraph 2(a) there shall be substituted the sum of £24 and for the sum of £52 in paragraph 2(c) there shall be substituted the sum of £104.

Amendment of regulation 3 of, and Schedules 4 and 5 to, the principal regulations

3.—(1) Regulation 3 of, and Schedules 4 and 5 to, the principal regulations (calculation of graduated contributions) shall be amended in accordance with the following provisions of this regulation.

(2) In the proviso to paragraph (3) of the said regulation 3 for the proportions "4¾ per cent., 4¼ per cent., 3¼ per cent., 2¾ per cent., and ½ per cent." there shall be substituted the proportions "4·75 per cent., 4·35 per cent., 4·25 per cent., 3·85 per cent., 3·25 per cent., 2·75 per cent., 1·6 per cent., 1·1 per cent., 0·5 per cent., and 0·4 per cent." and for the words "as amended by section 1(2) of the National Insurance Act 1969" there shall be substituted the words "as from time to time in force".

(a) 1965 c. 51.   (b) 1971 c. 50   (c) S.I. 1967/844 (1967 II, p. 2513).
(d) S.I. 1969/1133, 1970/46 (1969 II, p. 3363; 1970 I, p. 243).

(3) After the said proviso there shall be added the following proviso:—

"And provided that under paragraph (3) of this regulation no amount shall be payable which is in excess of the maximum weekly or, as the case might be, monthly amount specified in the second column of the appropriate Schedule, or, where the graduated contribution period is a multiple of a week or a month, of a sum equal to the same multiple of the said maximum amount."

(4) For the provisions of Schedules 4 and 5 to the principal regulations there shall be substituted the provisions set out in the Schedule to these regulations.

Amendment of regulation 9 of the principal regulations

4. In regulation 9 of the principal regulations (annual maximum) for the words "any income tax year ending on or after" in paragraph (*f*) there shall be substituted the words "the income tax year ending on" and after the said paragraph (*f*) there shall be added the following paragraphs:—

"(*g*) in respect of the income tax year ending on 5th April 1972 shall, if the graduated contributions so paid in that year amount to £62·81 or more, be £62·31 ;

(*h*) in respect of any income tax year ending on or after 5th April 1973 shall, if the graduated contributions so paid in that year amount to £78·41 or more, be £77·91.".

Signed by authority of the Secretary of State for Social Services.

Paul Dean,
Parliamentary Under-Secretary of State,
Department of Health and Social Security.

26th July 1971.

Regulation 3   SCHEDULE

1. Provisions to be substituted in Schedule 4 to the principal regulations:—
EMPLOYMENT WHICH IS NOT A NON-PARTICIPATING EMPLOYMENT

PART I WEEKLY SCALE		PART II MONTHLY SCALE	
Amount of payment	Amount of contribution	Amount of payment	Amount of contribution
£	£	£	£
9 ·01	0 ·01	39 ·02	0 ·02
9 ·25	0 ·02	40 ·00	0 ·09
9 ·50	0 ·04	42 ·00	0 ·19
10 ·00	0 ·06	44 ·00	0 ·28
10 ·50	0 ·08	46 ·00	0 ·38
		48 ·00	0 ·47
11 ·00	0 ·11	50 ·00	0 ·57
11 ·50	0 ·13	52 ·00	0 ·66
12 ·00	0 ·15		
12 ·50	0 ·18	54 ·00	0 ·76
13 ·00	0 ·20	56 ·00	0 ·85
		58 ·00	0 ·95
13 ·50	0 ·23	60 ·00	1 ·04
14 ·00	0 ·25	62 ·00	1 ·14
14 ·50	0 ·27	64 ·00	1 ·23
15 ·00	0 ·30	66 ·00	1 ·33
15 ·50	0 ·32	68 ·00	1 ·42
16 ·00	0 ·34		
		70 ·00	1 ·52
16 ·50	0 ·37	72 ·00	1 ·61
17 ·00	0 ·39	74 ·00	1 ·71
17 ·50	0 ·42	76 ·00	1 ·80
18 ·00	0 ·45	78 ·00	1 ·94
19 ·00	0 ·49	82 ·00	2 ·11
		86 ·00	2 ·29
20 ·00	0 ·54	90 ·00	2 ·46
21 ·00	0 ·58		
22 ·00	0 ·62	94 ·00	2 ·64
23 ·00	0 ·67	98 ·00	2 ·81
24 ·00	0 ·71	102 ·00	2 ·98
		106 ·00	3 ·16
25 ·00	0 ·75	110 ·00	3 ·33
26 ·00	0 ·80	114 ·00	3 ·51
27 ·00	0 ·84	118 ·00	3 ·68
28 ·00	0 ·88	122 ·00	3 ·85
29 ·00	0 ·93		
		126 ·00	4 ·03
30 ·00	0 ·97	130 ·00	4 ·20
31 ·00	1 ·01	134 ·00	4 ·38
32 ·00	1 ·06	138 ·00	4 ·55
33 ·00	1 ·10	142 ·00	4 ·72
34 ·00	1 ·15	146 ·00	4 ·90
		150 ·00	5 ·07
35 ·00	1 ·19	154 ·00	5 ·25
36 ·00	1 ·23		
37 ·00	1 ·28	158 ·00	5 ·42
38 ·00	1 ·32	162 ·00	5 ·59
39 ·00	1 ·36	166 ·00	5 ·77
		170 ·00	5 ·94
40 ·00	1 ·41	174 ·00	6 ·12
41 ·00	1 ·45	178 ·00	6 ·29
42 ·00	1 ·47	182 ·00	6 ·38
or more		or more	

2. Provisions to be substituted in Schedule 5 to the principal regulations:—

NON-PARTICIPATING EMPLOYMENT

| PART I | | PART II | |
| WEEKLY SCALE | | MONTHLY SCALE | |
Amount of payment	Amount of contribution	Amount of payment	Amount of contribution
£	£	£	£
9 ·01	0 ·01	39 ·01	0 ·01
12 ·00	0 ·02	40 ·00	0 ·03
15 ·00	0 ·04	50 ·00	0 ·08
18 ·00	0 ·07		
19 ·00	0 ·11	60 ·00	0 ·13
		70 ·00	0 ·17
20 ·00	0 ·15	78 ·00	0 ·28
21 ·00	0 ·20	82 ·00	0 ·46
22 ·00	0 ·24	86 ·00	0 ·63
23 ·00	0 ·28		
24 ·00	0 ·33	90 ·00	0 ·80
		94 ·00	0 ·98
25 ·00	0 ·37	98 ·00	1 ·15
26 ·00	0 ·41	102 ·00	1 ·33
27 ·00	0 ·46	106 ·00	1 ·50
28 ·00	0 ·50		
29 ·00	0 ·55	110 ·00	1 ·67
		114 ·00	1 ·85
30 ·00	0 ·59	118 ·00	2 ·02
31 ·00	0 ·63	122 ·00	2 ·20
32 ·00	0 ·68	126 ·00	2 ·37
33 ·00	0 ·72		
34 ·00	0 ·76	130 ·00	2 ·54
		134 ·00	2 ·72
35 ·00	0 ·81	138 ·00	2 ·89
36 ·00	0 ·85	142 ·00	3 ·07
37 ·00	0 ·89	146 ·00	3 ·24
38 ·00	0 ·94		
39 ·00	0 ·98	150 ·00	3 ·41
		154 ·00	3 ·59
40 ·00	1 ·02	158 ·00	3 ·76
41 ·00	1 ·07	162 ·00	3 ·94
42 ·00	1 ·08	166 ·00	4 ·11
or more			
		170 ·00	4 ·28
		174 ·00	4 ·46
		178 ·00	4 ·63
		182 ·00	4 ·72
		or more	

EXPLANATORY NOTE

(This Note is not part of the Regulations.)

These Regulations contain no provisions other than such as are made in consequence of the National Insurance Act 1971 and accordingly they are, by virtue of section 16(3) of, and paragraph 2 of Schedule 6 to, that Act, exempt from reference to the National Insurance Advisory Committee, and no such reference has been made. The Regulations amend the provisions of the National Insurance (Assessment of Graduated Contributions) Regulations 1967 relating to the determination of graduated contributions payable where remuneration is not paid weekly, to the manner in which graduated contributions are to be calculated, and to the annual maximum of graduated contributions payable by a person in respect of remuneration from two or more employments.

STATUTORY INSTRUMENTS

1971 No. 1203 (S.154)

POLICE

The Police (Scotland) Amendment (No. 3) Regulations 1971

Made - - -	23rd July 1971
Laid before Parliament	30th July 1971
Coming into Operation	1st August 1971

In exercise of the powers conferred on me by section 26 of the Police (Scotland) Act 1967(a), and of all other powers enabling me in that behalf, and after consulting the Police Council for the United Kingdom in accordance with section 4(4) of the Police Act 1969(b), I hereby make the following regulations :—

PART I

CITATION, COMMENCEMENT AND INTERPRETATION

1. These regulations may be cited as the Police (Scotland) Amendment (No. 3) Regulations 1971.

2. These regulations shall come into operation on 1st August 1971 and shall have effect as follows, that is to say—

(a) for the purposes of Part II thereof, as from 1st August 1971 ; and

(b) for the purposes of Part III thereof, as from 1st September 1971.

3. In these regulations any reference to the principal regulations is a reference to the Police (Scotland) Regulations 1968(c), as amended (d).

4. The Interpretation Act 1889(e) shall apply for the interpretation of these regulations as it applies for the interpretation of an Act of Parliament.

PART II

PROVISIONS TAKING EFFECT AS FROM 1ST AUGUST 1971

5. For Regulation 29 of the principal regulations (reckoning of previous service) there shall be substituted the following regulation :—

"Reckoning of previous service

29.—(1) A constable of a police force of the rank of constable who, on or after 28th June 1948, rejoined or joined that force, having previously resigned from that or some other force, shall be entitled to reckon, for the purposes of the scale of pay for the rank of constable, the service which was so reckonable immediately before he previously resigned.

(2) A constable of the rank of constable shall be entitled to reckon, for the purposes of the scale of pay for the rank of constable, any period of

(a) 1967 c. 77.   (b) 1969 c.63.
(c) S.I. 1968/716 (1968 II, p. 2024).
(d) The relevant amending instrument is S.I. 1971/196 (1971 I, p. 574).
(e) 1889 c. 63.

service in Her Majesty's forces following a period of service as defined in regulation 30.

(3) For the purposes of the foregoing provisions of this Part of these regulations, where a constable of a police force has transferred thereto from some other force, his service in those two forces shall be treated as if it were service in the same police force ; but for the purposes hereof regulation 28(2) shall have effect as if the words "on temporary promotion thereto" were omitted in each place where they occur :

Provided that in the case of a constable of a police force of a rank higher than that of inspector who voluntarily transferred thereto from some other force, this paragraph shall have effect subject to any contrary agreement.".

6. After regulation 44 of the principal regulations there shall be inserted the following regulation :—

"Women's stockings allowance

44A. A woman constable who is not supplied with stockings or tights by the police authority shall be paid in lieu an allowance at the rate of £9 a year unless she is being paid a plain clothes allowance under regulation 45(1).".

7. In regulation 46(2) of the principal regulations (detective expenses allowance) for the rate "£0·500 a week" there shall be substituted the rate "£1 a week".

8.—(1) In Schedule 9 to the principal regulations (issue of uniform and equipment) the entry relating to stockings shall be omitted from the second Table in paragraph 1.

(2) In paragraph 3 of the said Schedule 9 the words "12 pairs of stockings" shall be omitted.

(3) After paragraph 5 of the said Schedule 9 there shall be inserted the following paragraph :—
"5A. Where, in the case of women constables, stockings or tights are provided by the police authority for the purposes of duty the issue shall be at the rate of 18 pairs annually.".

PART III

PROVISIONS TAKING EFFECT AS FROM 1ST SEPTEMBER 1971

9. In regulation 32(2) of the principal regulations (deductions from pay of sickness or injury benefits) for the words "and, for the purposes thereof" to the end there shall be substituted the following words :—
"and, for the purposes thereof, a woman constable who, as a married woman or a widow, is excepted from liability to pay contributions under section 3 of the National Insurance Act 1965 shall be deemed to be entitled to any sickness benefit, together with any supplement thereto payable under section 2 of the National Insurance Act 1966, to which she would have been entitled had she not been so excepted.".

Gordon Campbell,
One of Her Majesty's Principal
Secretaries of State.

St. Andrew's House,
Edinburgh.
23rd July 1971.

EXPLANATORY NOTE

(This Note is not part of the Regulations.)

These Regulations amend the Police (Scotland) Regulations 1968.

Part II relates to the reckoning for pay purposes of service in a higher rank following a voluntary transfer to another force ; the scale of issue of stockings and tights, or payment of an allowance in lieu, to women constables ; and detective expenses allowance. It will have effect as from 1st August 1971.

Part III relates to the deduction from pay of sickness or injury benefits in the case of women constables who are married or are widows. It will have effect as from 1st September 1971.

1971 No. 1206

CINEMATOGRAPHS AND CINEMATOGRAPH FILMS

BRITISH FILMS (FINANCE)

The Cinematograph Films (Collection of Levy) (Amendment No. 2) Regulations 1971

Laid before Parliament in draft
Made - - - 26th July 1971
Coming into Operation 3rd October 1971

Whereas a draft of these Regulations has been laid before Parliament and approved by Resolution of each House pursuant to section 2(7) of the Cinematograph Films Act 1957(a), as amended and extended by the Films Act 1970(b) :

Now, therefore, the Secretary of State in exercise of his powers under section 2 of the said Act of 1957, as so amended and extended, and after consultation with the Cinematograph Films Council, hereby makes the following Regulations :—

1. These Regulations may be cited as the Cinematograph Films (Collection of Levy) (Amendment No. 2) Regulations 1971 and shall come into operation on 3rd October 1971.

2. The Interpretation Act 1889(c) shall apply to the interpretation of these Regulations as it applies to the interpretation of an Act of Parliament.

3. The Cinematograph Films (Collection of Levy) Regulations 1968(d), as amended (e), shall have effect as if in Regulation 3, for the figure "£400" in the two places in which it occurs there were substituted the figure "£500".

26th July 1971.

Nicholas Ridley,
Parliamentary Under Secretary of State,
Department of Trade and Industry.

(a) 1957 c. 21.   (b) 1970 c. 26.   (c) 1889 c. 63.
(d) S.I. 1968/1077 (1968 II, p. 2905).
(e) The amending Regulations do not expressly relate to the subject matter of these Regulations.

EXPLANATORY NOTE

(This Note is not part of the Regulations.)

These Regulations further amend the Cinematograph Films (Collection of Levy) Regulations 1968 under which total or partial exemption from payment of levy is allowed in respect of cinemas at which takings or average takings are small. These Regulations increase from £400 to £500 the amount by reference to which such exemption is allowed.

STATUTORY INSTRUMENTS

1971 No. 1209

PENSIONS

The Injury Warrant 1971

Made - - -	26*th July* 1971
Laid before Parliament	2*nd August* 1971
Coming into Operation	20th *September* 1971

The Minister for the Civil Service, in exercise of the powers conferred on him by section 18 of the Superannuation Act 1965(a), as amended by section 1 of the Superannuation (Miscellaneous Provisions) Act 1967(b), and as extended by section 6 of the Ministerial Salaries Consolidation Act 1965(c), and of all other powers enabling him in that behalf, hereby directs as follows :—

1.—(1) This Warrant may be cited as the Injury Warrant 1971, and the Injury Warrants 1952 to 1967(d) and this Warrant may be cited together as the Injury Warrants 1952 to 1971.

(2) This Warrant shall come into operation on 20th September 1971.

2.—(1) Any reference in this Warrant to the provisions of any enactment shall be construed, unless the context otherwise requires, as a reference to those provisions as amended by any subsequent enactment.

(2) The Interpretation Act 1889(e) shall apply for the interpretation of this Warrant as it applies for the interpretation of an Act of Parliament.

3. The Injury Warrant 1952, as amended, shall be further amended by substituting for paragraph 16 thereof the following paragraph :—

"**16.**—(1) Subject to the following provisions of this paragraph, where a person to whom this Warrant applies sustains an injury, the amount of any gratuity or annual allowance which may be granted under the foregoing provisions of this Warrant shall be reduced by the value, or, as may be appropriate, the annuity value or the annual value, of any rights which have accrued or probably will accrue to him from that injury in respect of industrial injury benefit, industrial disablement benefit, sickness benefit or invalidity pension.

(2) For the purposes of this paragraph the value of any such right shall be the amount which the Minister for the Civil Service may determine to be either its value or, as the case may be, its annuity value or annual value.

(a) 1965 c. 74. (b) 1967 c. 28. (c) 1965 c. 58.
(d) S.I. 1952/60, 1957/1354, 1965/1024, 1967/876 (1952 II, p. 2400; 1957 II, p. 1758; 1965 I, p. 2496; 1967 II, p. 2614). (e) 1889 c. 63.

(3) For the purposes of this paragraph no account shall be taken of—

(a) so much of a disablement pension as represents an increase payable under section 15 of the National Insurance (Industrial Injuries) Act 1965(**a**) (increase of disablement pension where constant attendance needed) or under section 6 of the National Insurance Act 1966(**b**) (increase of disablement pension in cases of exceptionally severe disablement) ; or

(b) so much of an unemployability supplement as represents an increase payable under section 13A of the National Insurance (Industrial Injuries) Act 1965 (early onset of incapacity for work).

(4) In this paragraph—

(a) "industrial injury benefit", "industrial disablement benefit", "disablement pension" and "unemployability supplement" have the same meanings as in the National Insurance (Industrial Injuries) Act 1965;

(b) "sickness benefit" has the same meaning as in the National Insurance Act 1965(**c**) ; and

(c) "invalidity pension" has the same meaning as in section 3 of the National Insurance Act 1971(**d**)."

4. Paragraph 1(d) of the Injury Warrant 1967 is hereby revoked.

Given under the official seal of the Minister for the Civil Service on 26th July 1971.

(L.S.)

K. H. McNeill,
Authorised by the Minister
for the Civil Service.

EXPLANATORY NOTE

(This Note is not part of the Warrant.)

This Warrant amends the Injury Warrant 1952 which, together with the Injury Warrants 1957, 1965 and 1967, provides for the grant of allowances or gratuities to Ministers, civil servants and other persons employed by the Government in a civil capacity who are injured in the discharge of their duties.

The Warrant of 1952 provides for allowances and gratuities to be reduced by the value of any industrial injury benefit, industrial disablement benefit or sickness benefit to which the injured person may be entitled under the National Insurance Acts. This Warrant adds to these benefits the invalidity pension provided for in section 3 of the National Insurance Act 1971.

The Warrant also provides that the increase in unemployability supplement provided for in s.9 of the National Insurance Act 1971 in cases of early onset of incapacity for work shall be disregarded when reducing an allowance or gratuity on account of industrial disablement benefit.

(**a**) 1965 c. 52. (**b**) 1966 c. 6.
(**c**) 1965 c. 51. (**d**) 1971 c. 50.

STATUTORY INSTRUMENTS

1971 No. 1210 (S.155)

RATING AND VALUATION

The Valuation (Post Office Telecommunication Services) (Scotland) Order 1971

Made	-	-	-	21st *July* 1971
Laid before Parliament				3rd *August* 1971
Coming into Operation				4th *August* 1971

In exercise of the powers conferred on me by section 53(1), (2), (3) and (4) of the Post Office Act 1969(a) and of all other powers enabling me in that behalf, and after consultation with the Post Office and such associations of local authorities and such local authorities as I consider appropriate, I hereby make the following order :—

Citation and commencement

1. This order may be cited as the Valuation (Post Office Telecommunication Services) (Scotland) Order 1971 and shall come into operation on 4th August 1971.

Interpretation

2.—(1) "Article" means an Article of this order.

(2) The Interpretation Act 1889(b) shall apply for the interpretation of this order as it applies for the interpretation of an Act of Parliament.

Determination of aggregate amount of rateable values

3. For the purposes of the valuation roll for the year 1971-72 the aggregate amount of the rateable values of all lands and heritages occupied by the Post Office by any such property as follows, namely, posts, wires, underground cables and ducts, telephone kiosks and other equipment not within a building, being property used for the purposes of telecommunication services, shall be £421,000.

Re-determination of aggregate amount of rateable values

4. For the purposes of the valuation roll for each of the years specified in column (1) of the Schedule to this order the aggregate amount determined in Article 3 shall be re-determined by the addition of the percentage shown in relation to each year in column (2) of the Schedule.

Apportionment of aggregate amount of rateable values

5.—(1) The aggregate amount determined in Article 3 or under Article 4, as the case may be, shall be apportioned by the Assessor of Public Undertakings (Scotland) in the valuation roll made up by him among rating areas as follows :—

(a) 1969 c. 48.   (b) 1889 c. 63.

(a) for the year 1971-72, in the proportion which the aggregate of the rateable values of all lands and heritages other than the lands and heritages described in Article 3 in the rating area of each rating authority as at 16th May in that year bears to the aggregate of the rateable values of all lands and heritages other than the lands and heritages described in Article 3 in the rating areas of all rating authorities as at 16th May in that year ;

(b) for each year specified in column (1) of the Schedule to this order, in the proportion which the aggregate of the rateable values of all lands and heritages other than the lands and heritages described in Article 3 in the rating area of each rating authority as at 16th May in the preceding year bears to the aggregate of the rateable values of all lands and heritages other than the lands and heritages described in Article 3 in the rating areas of all rating authorities as at 16th May in the preceding year.

(2) For the purposes of this Article, the aggregate of the rateable values of all lands and heritages other than the lands and heritages described in Article 3 in the rating area of each rating authority or of all rating authorities, as the case may be, shall be taken to be such sum as the Secretary of State shall estimate to be the amount thereof from the best information available to him at the time at which the apportionment is required to be made.

Gordon Campbell,
One of Her Majesty's Principal
Secretaries of State.

St. Andrew's House,
Edinburgh.
21st July 1971.

SCHEDULE

COLUMN (1)	COLUMN (2)
1972-73	7½ per cent.
1973-74	15 per cent.
1974-75	22½ per cent.
1975-76	30 per cent.

EXPLANATORY NOTE

(This Note is not part of the Order.)

This Order determines for the year 1971-72 the aggregate amount of the rateable values of the posts, wires, underground cables and ducts, telephone kiosks and other equipment not within a building used by the Post Office for telecommunication services. It also determines the manner in which the aggregate rateable values for the years 1972-73 to 1975-76, inclusive, are to be determined ; and how the aggregate rateable values for each of the years covered by the Order are to be apportioned among rating areas.

STATUTORY INSTRUMENTS

1971 No. 1211 (S.156)

ROADS AND BRIDGES, SCOTLAND
The Special Roads (Classes of Traffic) (Scotland) Order 1971

Made - - -	*22nd June* 1971
Laid before Parliament	*24th June* 1971
Coming into Operation	*26th July* 1971

In exercise of the powers conferred on me by sections 2(3) and 17(1) of the Special Roads Act 1949(a) as read with the Transfer of Functions (Roads, Bridges and Ferries) Order 1955(b) and of all other powers enabling me on that behalf, I hereby make the following order :—

1. This order may be cited as the Special Roads (Classes of Traffic) (Scotland) Order 1971, and shall come into operation on the tenth day following the day on which it is approved by Parliament.

2. The Interpretation Act 1889(c) shall apply for the interpretation of this order as it applies for the interpretation of an Act of Parliament, and as if this order and the orders hereby revoked were Acts of Parliament.

3. The Special Roads (Classes of Traffic) (Scotland) Order 1964(d) and the Special Roads (Classes of Traffic) (Scotland) Order 1968(e) are hereby revoked.

4. The composition of the classes of traffic specified in Schedule 2 to the Special Roads Act 1949 shall be varied so as to have effect as set out in the Schedule to this order.

Gordon Campbell,
One of Her Majesty's Principal
Secretaries of State.

St. Andrew's House,
Edinburgh.
22nd June 1971.

(a) 1949 c. 32.   (b) S.I. 1955/1955 (1955 I, p. 1205).
(c) 1889 c. 63.   (d) S.I. 1964/1084 (1964 II, p. 2398).
(e) S.I. 1968/1982 (1968 III, p. 5396).

SCHEDULE

CLASSES OF TRAFFIC FOR PURPOSES OF SPECIAL ROADS

CLASS   I: Heavy and light locomotives, motor tractors, heavy motor cars, motor cars and motor cycles whereof the cylinder capacity of the engine is not less than 50 cubic centimetres, and trailers drawn thereby, which comply with general regulations as to construction and use made under section 64 of the Road Traffic Act 1960(a) and in the case of which the following conditions are satisfied, that is to say:—

(i) that the whole weight of the vehicle is transmitted to the road surface by means of wheels ;

(ii) that all wheels of the vehicle are equipped with pneumatic tyres ;

(iii) that the vehicle is not controlled by a pedestrian ;

(iv) that the vehicle is not a vehicle chargeable with duty under Paragraph 2 of Part I of Schedule 3 to the Vehicles (Excise) Act 1971(b) ; and

(v) in the case of a motor vehicle it is so constructed as to be capable of attaining a speed of twenty-five miles per hour on the level under its own power, when unladen and not drawing a trailer.

CLASS   II: Motor vehicles and trailers the use of which for or in connection with the conveyance of abnormal indivisible loads is authorised by order made by the Secretary of State for the Environment under section 64(4) of the Road Traffic Act 1960.

Motor vehicles and trailers constructed for naval, military, air force or other defence purposes, the use of which is authorised by order made by the said Secretary of State under section 64(4) of the Road Traffic Act 1960.

Motor vehicles and trailers, to which the following Articles of the Motor Vehicles (Authorisation of Special Types) General Order 1969(c), as amended (d), relate, namely, Article 16 (which relates to vehicles for moving excavated material), Article 17 (which relates inter alia to vehicles constructed for use outside the United Kingdom) and Article 21 (which relates to engineering plant) and which are authorised to be used by those Articles of the said Order or by any other Order under section 64(4) of the Road Traffic Act 1960, the said motor vehicles being vehicles in respect of which the following condition is satisfied, that is to say, that the vehicle is so constructed as to be capable of attaining a speed of twenty-five miles per hour on the level under its own power, when unladen and not drawing a trailer.

CLASS   III: Motor vehicles controlled by pedestrians.

CLASS   IV: All motor vehicles (other than invalid carriages and motor cycles whereof the cylinder capacity of the engine is less than 50 cubic centimetres) not comprised in Class I, Class II or Class III.

CLASS   V: Vehicles drawn by animals.

CLASS   VI: Vehicles (other than pedal cycles, perambulators, push-chairs and other forms of baby carriages) drawn or propelled by pedestrians.

CLASS   VII: Pedal cycles, motor cycles whereof the cylinder capacity of the engine is less than 50 cubic centimetres and invalid carriages.

(a) 1960 c. 16.   (b) 1971 c. 10.
(c) S.I. 1969/344 (1969 I, p. 947).
(d) The relevant amending instrument is S.I. 1971/980 (1971 II, p. 2848).

CLASS VIII: Animals ridden, led or driven (other than dogs held on a lead).

CLASS IX: Pedestrians, perambulators, push-chairs and other forms of baby carriages and dogs held on a lead.

In this Schedule any expression defined for the purposes of the Road Traffic Act 1960 has the same meaning as in that Act and the expression "abnormal indivisible load" has the same meaning as in the Motor Vehicles (Authorisation of Special Types) General Order 1969.

EXPLANATORY NOTE

(This Note is not part of the Order.)

Schedule 2 to the Special Roads Act 1949, as amended by the Special Roads (Classes of Traffic) (Scotland) Order 1964 and the Special Roads (Classes of Traffic) (Scotland) Order 1968, specifies classes of traffic for the purposes of special roads.

This Order revokes the above mentioned Orders of 1964 and 1968 and provides for Schedule 2 to be amended so as to have effect as set out in the Schedule to the Order. The principal changes made by this Order to Schedule 2 are :—

1. Heavy and light locomotives are added to the composition of Class I specified in Schedule 2, subject, inter alia, to these vehicles being capable of attaining a speed of 25 miles per hour on the level under their own power when unladen and not drawing a trailer ;

2. Motor vehicles and trailers authorised to be used on roads under either Article 16, 17 or 21 of the Motor Vehicles (Authorisation of Special Types) General Order 1969, as amended, which Articles relate respectively to vehicles for moving excavated material, vehicles constructed for use outside the United Kingdom and vehicles being engineering plant, are added to the composition of Class II specified in Schedule 2, subject in the case of the motor vehicles to their being capable of attaining a speed of 25 miles per hour on the level under their own power when unladen and not drawing a trailer.

STATUTORY INSTRUMENTS

1971 No. 1212 (S.157)

RATING AND VALUATION

The Valuation (Water Undertakings) (Scotland) (Adjustment) Order 1971

Made - - -	*8th July* 1971
Laid before the Commons House of Parliament	*12th July* 1971
Coming into Operation	*22nd July* 1971

In exercise of the powers conferred on me by paragraph 3 of Schedule 2 to the Local Government (Scotland) Act 1966(a), and of all other powers enabling me in that behalf, and after consultation with such associations of local authorities and other bodies and associations as appear to me to be concerned, I hereby make the following order :—

1.—(1) This order may be cited as the Valuation (Water Undertakings) (Scotland) (Adjustment) Order 1971 and shall come into operation on the day following the day on which it is approved by a resolution of the Commons House of Parliament.

(2) The Interpretation Act 1889(b) shall apply for the interpretation of this order as it applies for the interpretation of an Act of Parliament.

2. For the purposes of determining the cumulo rateable value of lands and heritages occupied for the purposes of a water undertaking for the year 1971-72 and subsequent years the national average rateable value per unit per day shall be the amount determined under the provisions of paragraph 3 of the Valuation (Water Undertakings) (Scotland) (No. 1) Order 1967(c) increased by 75 per cent.

Gordon Campbell,
One of Her Majesty's
Principal Secretaries of State.

St. Andrew's House,
Edinburgh.
8th July 1971.

(a) 1966 c. 51.   (b) 1889 c. 63.   (c) S.I. 1967/601 (1967 I, p. 1808).

EXPLANATORY NOTE

(This Note is not part of the Order.)

This Order adjusts the provisions for determining the norm (the national average rateable value per thousand gallons of water per day) which is to be used in calculating the cumulo rateable values of water undertakings for 1971-72 and subsequent years. The adjustment has regard to the general change in rateable values arising from the revaluation in 1971 and its effect is to increase the norm from £5·568 to £9·744.

STATUTORY INSTRUMENTS

1971 No. 1213 (S.158)

RATING AND VALUATION

The Valuation (Scottish Gas Board) (Scotland) Order 1971

Made - - -	*8th July* 1971
Laid before the Commons	
House of Parliament	*12th July* 1971
Coming into Operation	*22nd July* 1971

In exercise of the powers conferred on me by section 12(2) of the Local Government (Financial Provisions) (Scotland) Act 1963(a), and of all other powers enabling me in that behalf, and after consultation with the Scottish Gas Board, the Scottish Valuation Advisory Council and such associations of local authorities as appear to me to be concerned, I hereby make the following order :—

1.—(1) This order may be cited as the Valuation (Scottish Gas Board) (Scotland) Order 1971 and shall come into operation on the day following the day on which it is approved by a resolution of the Commons House of Parliament.

(2) The Interpretation Act 1889(b) shall apply for the interpretation of this order as it applies for the interpretation of an Act of Parliament.

2. For the purpose of Schedule 4 to the Valuation and Rating (Scotland) Act 1956(c) (which relates to the valuation and rating of Gas Boards) the basic rateable valuation of the Scottish Gas Board for the year 1971-72 and subsequent years shall be £1,281,860.

3. The Valuation (Scottish Gas Board) (Scotland) Order 1967(d) in its application to years subsequent to the year 1970-71 is hereby revoked.

Gordon Campbell,
One of Her Majesty's
Principal Secretaries of State.

St. Andrew's House,
Edinburgh.
8th July 1971.

(a) 1963 c. 12.
(c) 1956 c. 60.

(b) 1889 c. 63.
(d) S.I. 1967/1164 (1967 II, p. 3407).

EXPLANATORY NOTE

(This Note is not part of the Order.)

This Order, which revokes the Valuation (Scottish Gas Board) (Scotland) Order 1967, provides for an increase in the basic rateable valuation of the Scottish Gas Board to take account of the general increase in valuations arising from the revaluation in 1971.

1971 No. 1214 (S.159)

SHERIFF COURT, SCOTLAND

Act of Sederunt (Sheriff Court Procedure Amendment) 1971

Made - - -		*23rd July* 1971
Coming into Operation		*23rd August* 1971

The Lords of Council and Session, under and by virtue of the powers conferred upon them by section 34 of the Administration of Justice (Scotland) Act 1933(a) and of all other powers competent to them in that behalf do hereby enact and declare as follows :

1. The Sheriff Courts (Scotland) Act 1907(b)(hereinafter referred to as "the Act") shall be amended as follows :

(1) At the end of Rule 5 of the First Schedule to the Act there shall be added the words: "provided that the *induciae* for the citation (other than edictal citation) of a defender under Rule 15B, where the defender is resident in a country outside Europe, shall be three weeks if the citation is personal and six weeks if the citation is postal."

(2) There shall be added after Rule 15A of the First Schedule to the Act, a new Rule as follows:

"15B. (*a*) In any action in which the sheriff shall have jurisdiction over a defender furth of Scotland in proceedings founded on delict, service of the initial writ against such defender may be effected, in addition to any method of citation competent apart from this Rule, either personally, or by posting separately in Scotland and in the country in which the defender is resident a registered or recorded delivery letter or the nearest equivalent thereof which the available postal services permit, addressed to the defender at his residence or place of business enclosing a full copy of the initial writ with relative citation.

(*b*) In the case of edictal citation in an action to which this Rule relates, where the defender has a known solicitor in Scotland or has a known residence or place of business the solicitor for the pursuer shall post a copy of the initial writ with relative citation either to the defender's known solicitor in Scotland or to the defender himself at his residence or place of business.

(*c*) For the purposes of this Rule, personal service shall include service in accordance with the rules for personal service under the domestic law of any part of the United Kingdom so far as such rules permit the service thereby of such initial writ ; service by the British Consul or his duly authorised depute or assistant in the country of residence of the defender ; and service in accordance with any Convention or service abroad or judicial documents in

---

(a) 1933 c. 41. (b) 1907 c. 51.

civil matters, to which the United Kingdom and the country of residence of the defender are signatories.

(*d*) Posting in Scotland for the purposes of this Rule shall be effected by a solicitor entitled to practice in the sheriff court. The forms for citation and execution of citation appropriate for citation of a defender within Scotland shall be used, *mutatis mutandis,* for the purposes of this Rule provided that a translation of the citation, in a language of the country of the defender's residence, may be attached if appropriate.

(*e*) On the face of the envelope used for postal service under this Rule there shall be written or printed a notice, with a translation where appropriate in a language of the country of the defender's residence, in the same or similar terms as that which is required in the case of ordinary service by registered letter, and the execution to be returned by the solicitor shall be accompanied by the relative receipt or receipts by the postal authorities receiving the letter or letters."

2. This Act of Sederunt may be cited as the Act of Sederunt (Sheriff Court Procedure Amendment) 1971 and shall come into operation on 23rd August 1971.

And the Lords appoint this Act of Sederunt to be inserted in the Books of Sederunt.

Edinburgh.
23rd July 1971.

William Grant,
I.P.D.

EXPLANATORY NOTE
(This Note is not part of the Act of Sederunt.)

This Act of Sederunt amends the sheriff court rules by making new provision for the service of an initial writ upon a defender furth of Scotland in an action founded on delict.

1971 No. 1215 (S.160)

COURT OF SESSION, SCOTLAND
Act of Sederunt (Rules of Court Amendment No. 7) 1971

Made - - -	*23rd July* 1971
Coming into Operation	*23rd August* 1971

The Lords of Council and Session, under and by virtue of the powers conferred upon them by section 16 of the Administration of Justice (Scotland) Act 1933(a) and of all other powers competent to them in that behalf do hereby enact and declare as follows :

1. The Rules of Court (b) are hereby amended as follows :

(1) By adding at the end of Rule 72 a new paragraph as follows :

"(c) The induciae for the citation of a defender under Rule 75A, where the defender is resident in a country outside Europe, shall be three weeks if the citation is personal and six weeks if the citation is postal."

(2) By deleting paragraph (a) of Rule 75 and by substituting therefor a new paragraph (a) as follows:

"(a) Subject to the povisions of Rule 75A hereof, all citations against persons furth of Scotland shall be made at the office of the Extractor of the Court of Session on an *induciae* of fourteen days. The citation shall, as nearly as may be, be in the form shown in Form 4."

(3) By deleting from paragraph (d) of Rule 75 the figure "155" and by substituting "160".

(4) By adding between Rule 75 and Rule 76 a new Rule as follows:

"75A. *Citation in actions founded on delict.*

"(a) In any action in which the Court of Session shall have jurisdiction over a defender furth of Scotland in proceedings founded on delict, service of the summons against such defender may be effected, in addition to any method of citation competent apart from this Rule, either personally, or by posting separately in Edinburgh and in the country in which the defender is resident a registered or recorded delivery letter or the nearest equivalent thereof which the available postal services permit, addressed to the defender at his residence or place of business enclosing a full copy of the summons with relative citation.

"(b) For the purposes of this Rule, personal service shall include service in accordance with the rules for personal service under the domestic law of any part of the United Kingdom so far as such rules permit the service thereby of such summons ; service by the British Consul or his duly authorised depute or assistant in the country of residence of the defender ; and service in accordance with any

---

(a) 1933 c. 41.   (b) S.I. 1965/321 (1965 I, p. 803).

Convention on service abroad of judicial documents in civil matters, to which the United Kingdom and the country of residence of the defender are signatories.

"(c) Posting in Edinburgh for the purposes of this Rule shall be effected by a solicitor entitled to practice in the Court of Session. The forms shown in Form 3 shall be used, *mutatis mutandis,* in the case of postal citation under this Rule, provided that a translation of the citation, in a language of the country of the defender's residence, may be attached if appropriate.

"(d) On the face of the envelope used for postal service under this Rule there shall be written or printed a notice, with a translation where appropriate in a language of the defender's residence, in the same or similar terms as that which is required in the case of ordinary service by registered letter, and the execution to be returned by the solicitor shall be accompanied by the relative receipt or receipts by the postal authorities receiving the letter or letters."

2. This Act of Sederunt may be cited as the Act of Sederunt (Rules of Court Amendment No. 7) 1971 and shall come into operation on 23rd August 1971.

And the Lords appoint this Act of Sederunt to be inserted in the Books of Sederunt.

Edinburgh.
23rd July 1971.

William Grant,
I.P.D.

EXPLANATORY NOTE
(This Note is not part of the Act of Sederunt.)

This Act of Sederunt amends the Rules of Court by making new provision for the service of a summons upon a defender furth of Scotland in an action founded on delict.

STATUTORY INSTRUMENTS

1971 No. 1216
MARRIAGE

REGISTRATION OF BIRTHS, DEATHS, MARRIAGES, ETC.

The Marriage (Authorised Persons) (Amendment) Regulations 1971

Made - - -		*27th July* 1971
Coming into Operation		*1st August* 1971

The Registrar General, in exercise of the powers conferred on him by section 74 of the Marriage Act 1949(**a**) and of all other powers enabling him in that behalf, with the approval of the Secretary of State for Social Services, hereby makes the following regulations :—

Commencement, citation and interpretation

1.—(1) These regulations shall come into operation on 1st August 1971 and may be cited as the Marriage (Authorised Persons) (Amendment) Regulations 1971.

(2) The Interpretation Act 1889(**b**) shall apply to the interpretation of these regulations as it applies to the interpretation of an Act of Parliament.

Manner of registration of marital condition

2.—(1) After paragraph (*a*) of regulation 17 of the Marriage (Authorised Persons) Regulations 1952(**c**) (manner of registration), there shall be inserted the following paragraph :—

"(*b*) in the case of a party whose previous marriage was annulled on the ground that the marriage was voidable, he shall enter the words "Previous marriage annulled".

(2) Paragraphs (*b*) and (*c*) of the said regulation shall be re-lettered "(*c*)" and "(*d*)" respectively.

Given under my hand on 23rd July 1971.

Michael Reed,
Registrar General.

I approve.

Keith Joseph,
Secretary of State for Social Services.

27th July 1971.

(**a**) 1949 c. 76.   (**b**) 1889 c. 63.
(**c**) S.I. 1952/1869 (1952 II, p. 1691).

EXPLANATORY NOTE

(This Note is not part of the Regulations.)

These regulations make a minor amendment to the Marriage (Authorised Persons) Regulations 1952 which prescribe the manner in which the marital condition of the parties to a marriage is to be described in marriage registers kept by authorised persons, who register marriages which take place, without the presence of a registrar, in buildings registered for the solemnization of marriages. The amendment is made to accord with section 5 of the Nullity of Marriage Act 1971 (c.44). The regulations prescribe the manner in which the condition of a party to a marriage is to be described where the previous marriage of such a party was annulled on the ground that the marriage was voidable.

1971 No. 1217

REGISTRATION OF BIRTHS, DEATHS, MARRIAGES ETC.

ENGLAND AND WALES

The Registration of Marriages (Welsh Language) (Amendment) Regulations 1971

Made - - - -	26th July 1971
Coming into Operation	1st August 1971

The Registrar General, in exercise of the powers conferred on him by sections 55 and 74 of the Marriage Act 1949(a), section 20 of the Registration Service Act 1953(b) as extended by sections 2(2) and 3 of the Welsh Language Act 1967(c) and of all other powers enabling him in that behalf, with the approval of the Secretary of State for Wales, hereby makes the following regulations :—

Commencement, citation and interpretation

1.—(1) These regulations shall come into operation on 1st August 1971 and may be cited as the Registration of Marriages (Welsh Language) (Amendment) Regulations 1971.

(2) The Interpretation Act 1889(d) shall apply to the interpretation of these regulations as it applies to the interpretation of an Act of Parliament.

Welsh version

2. In schedule 2 to the Registration of Marriages (Welsh Language) Regulations 1971(e) (English and Welsh versions of the form of words required to be used in completing an entry in a marriage register) there shall be added after the last entry in column (1) the words " Previous marriage annulled " and after the last entry in column (2) the words " Priodas flaenorol wedi'i dirymu ".

Given under my hand on 23rd July 1971.

Michael Reed,
Registrar General.

I approve,

Peter Thomas,
Secretary of State for Wales.

26th July 1971.

(a) 1949 c. 76.   (b) 1953 c. 37.   (c) 1967 c. 66.   (d) 1889 c. 63.
(e) S.I. 1971/129 (1971 I, p. 246).

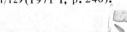

EXPLANATORY NOTE

(This Note is not part of the Regulations.)

These regulations make a minor amendment to the Registration of Marriages (Welsh Language) Regulations 1971 which provide for Welsh as well as English to be used under certain conditions in the registration of marriages in Wales or Monmouthshire. The amendment is made to accord with section 5 of the Nullity of Marriage Act 1971 (c. 44).

The regulations prescribe the Welsh version of the form of words to be used in marriage registers to describe the marital condition of a party to a marriage where the previous marriage of such a party was annulled on the ground that the marriage was voidable.

STATUTORY INSTRUMENTS

1971 No. 1218

REGISTRATION OF BIRTHS, DEATHS, MARRIAGES, ETC.

ENGLAND AND WALES

The Registration of Births, Deaths and Marriages (Amendment) Regulations 1971

Made - - -	*27th July* 1971
Coming into Operation	1*st August* 1971

The Registrar General, in exercise of the powers conferred on him by sections 55 and 74 of the Marriage Act 1949(**a**), section 20 of the Registration Service Act 1953(**b**) and of all other powers enabling him in that behalf, with the approval of the Secretary of State for Social Services, hereby makes the following regulations :—

Commencement, citation and interpretation

1.—(1) These regulations shall come into operation on 1st August 1971 and may be cited as the Registration of Births, Deaths and Marriages (Amendment) Regulations 1971.

(2) The Interpretation Act 1889(**c**) shall apply to the interpretation of these regulations as it applies to the interpretation of an Act of Parliament.

Manner of registration of marital condition

2.—(1) After paragraph (*a*) of regulation 68(2) of the Registration of Births, Deaths and Marriages Regulations 1968(**d**) (manner of registration), there shall be inserted the following paragraph :—

"(*b*) if a party's previous marriage was annulled on the ground that the marriage was voidable, he shall enter the words "Previous marriage annulled"."

(2) Paragraphs (*b*) and (*c*) of the said regulation shall be re-lettered "(*c*)" and "(*d*)" respectively.

Given under my hand on 23rd July 1971.

Michael Reed,
Registrar General.

I approve.

Keith Joseph,
Secretary of State for Social Services.

27th July 1971.

(**a**) 1949 c. 76.   (**b**) 1953 c. 37.
(**c**) 1889 c. 63.   (**d**) S.I. 1968/2049 (1968 III, p. 5522).

EXPLANATORY NOTE

(This Note is not part of the Regulations.)

These regulations make a minor amendment to the Registration of Births, Deaths and Marriages Regulations 1968 which prescribe the manner in which registrars are to record in marriage registers the marital condition of the parties to a marriage. The amendment is made to accord with section 5 of the Nullity of Marriage Act 1971 (c.44). The regulations prescribe the manner in which the condition of a party to a marriage is to be described where the previous marriage of such a party was annulled on the ground that the marriage was voidable.

STATUTORY INSTRUMENTS

1971 No. 1219

SOCIAL SECURITY

The National Insurance (Age Addition) Regulations 1971

Made - - -	*26th July* 1971
Laid before Parliament	*5th August* 1971
Coming into Operation	*20th September* 1971

The Secretary of State for Social Services in exercise of his powers under section 52 of the National Insurance Act 1965(**a**) and section 5(2) and (3) of the National Insurance Act 1971(**b**), and of all other powers enabling him in that behalf, and in conjunction with the Treasury so far as relates to matters with regard to which they have so directed, hereby makes the following regulations which contain no provisions other than such as are made in consequence of the said Act of 1971 and which accordingly by virtue of section 16(3) and paragraph 2(1)(*a*) of Schedule 6 to that Act are exempt from the requirements of section 108 of the said Act of 1965 (reference to the National Insurance Advisory Committee) :—

Citation, commencement and interpretation

1.—(1) These regulations may be cited as the National Insurance (Age Addition) Regulations 1971 and shall come into operation on 20th September 1971.

(2) In these regulations, unless the context otherwise requires—
"the principal Act" means the National Insurance Act 1965,
and other expressions have the same meaning as in the principal Act.

(3) References in these regulations to any enactment or regulation shall, except in so far as the context otherwise requires, be construed as references to that enactment or regulation as amended or extended by or under any other enactment, order or regulation.

(4) The rules for the construction of Acts of Parliament contained in the Interpretation Act 1889(**c**) shall apply for the purposes of the interpretation of these regulations as they apply for the purposes of the interpretation of an Act of Parliament.

Conditions for entitlement to age addition

2. The conditions for entitlement to age addition, where the person concerned is not entitled to a retirement pension, shall be—

    (*a*) that he is in receipt of a payment by reference to which the amount of a retirement pension, if it were otherwise payable to him, would, by virtue of the National Insurance (Overlapping Benefits) Regulations 1948(**d**), as amended (**e**), be extinguished ; and

---

(**a**) 1965 c. 51.   (**b**) 1971 c. 50.   (**c**) 1889 c. 63.
(**d**) S.I. 1948/2711 (Rev. XVI, p. 196: 1948 I, p. 2657).
(**e**) S.I. 1952/526, 1957/1889, 2077, 1961/557, 1962/12, 1966/970 (1952 II, p. 2196; 1957 I, pp. 1603, 1556; 1961 I, p. 1228; 1962 I, p. 10; 1966 II, p. 2340).

(b) either—

    (i) that the contribution conditions for a retirement pension under section 30 or 32 of, or regulations made under paragraph 17 of Schedule 11 to, the principal Act are satisfied in his case ; or

    (ii) that had he made a claim for it he would have been entitled to a retirement pension by virtue of section 1(1) of the National Insurance (Old persons' and widows' pensions and attendance allowance) Act 1970(a) or any regulations made thereunder ; or

    (iii) that had he made a claim for it he would have been entitled to a retirement pension by virtue of section 5(1) of the National Insurance Act 1971(b).

Claims for age addition

3. In all cases age addition may be paid without a claim being made for it.

Amendment of the National Insurance (Claims and Payments) Regulations 1971

4. In the National Insurance (Claims and Payments) Regulations 1971(c), after regulation 10 the following regulation shall be inserted—

"*Time and manner of payment of age addition*

10A.—(1) Subject to the provisions of these regulations, age addition shall be paid weekly in advance.

(2) Where the person to whom an age addition is payable is a pensioner it shall be payable on the day of the week on which the pension payable to him for that week is payable and in the same manner as that pension.

(3) Where the person to whom an age addition is payable is not a pensioner, it shall be payable on such day of the week and in such manner as the Secretary of State may in any particular case or class of cases determine.

(4) The provisions of paragraphs (5), (6), (8), (9) and (10) of regulation 10 of these regulations shall apply in relation to age addition as they apply in relation to a pension and as if the expression 'pension order' wherever it appears in those paragraphs included an order for the payment of age addition and as if the reference to a pensioner were a reference to a person entitled to age addition".

Signed by authority of the Secretary of State for Social Services.

Paul Dean,
Parliamentary Under Secretary of State,
Department of Health and Social Security.

26th July 1971.

Walter Clegg,
Bernard Weatherill,
Two of the Lords Commissioners
of Her Majesty's Treasury.

26th July 1971.

(a) 1970 c. 51.   (b) 1971 c. 50.
(c) S.I. 1971/707 (1971 I, p. 1908).

EXPLANATORY NOTE
(This Note is not part of the Regulations.)

These Regulations set out the conditions which a person who is not entitled to a retirement pension must satisfy in order to be entitled to age addition (which was introduced by the National Insurance Act 1971 and is payable to persons who have attained the age of 80). Provision is also made relating to claims for and payment of age addition.

STATUTORY INSTRUMENTS

1971 No. 1220

SOCIAL SECURITY

The National Insurance (Increase of Benefit and Miscellaneous Provisions) Regulations 1971

Made - - -	*26th July* 1971
Laid before Parliament	*5th August* 1971
Coming into Operation	*20th September* 1971

The National Insurance Joint Authority, in exercise of powers conferred by sections 45, 50 and 99 of the National Insurance Act 1965(a), and the Secretary of State for Social Services, in exercise of his powers under sections 10, 31 and 49 of and paragraphs 17 and 18 of Schedule 11 to that Act, paragraph 5 of Schedule 7 to the National Insurance Act 1967(b), paragraph 3 of Schedule 6 to the National Insurance Act 1969(c), section 1 of the National Insurance (Old persons' and widows' pensions and attendance allowance) Act 1970(d) and paragraph 4 of Schedule 6 to the National Insurance Act 1971(e), and of all other powers enabling them in that behalf, and in conjunction with the Treasury so far as relates to matters with regard to which the Treasury have so directed, hereby make the following regulations, which contain no provisions other than such as are made in consequence of the said Act of 1971 and which accordingly, by virtue of section 16(3) of and paragraph 2(1)(*a*) of Schedule 6 to that Act, are exempt from the requirements of section 108 of the National Insurance Act 1965 (reference to the National Insurance Advisory Committee) :—

Citation, commencement and interpretation

1.—(1) These regulations may be cited as the National Insurance (Increase of Benefit and Miscellaneous Provisions) Regulations 1971, and shall come into operation on 20th September 1971.

(2) In these regulations, unless the context otherwise requires—

"the principal Act" means the National Insurance Act 1965 ;

"the Act of 1971" means the National Insurance Act 1971 ;
and other expressions have the same meanings as in the principal Act.

(3) References in these Regulations to any enactment or regulation shall, except in so far as the context otherwise requires, be construed as references to that enactment or regulation as amended or extended by or under any other enactment, order or regulation.

(4) The rules for the construction of Acts of Parliament contained in the Interpretation Act 1889(f) shall apply for the purpose of the interpretation of these regulations as they apply for the purpose of the interpretation of an Act of Parliament.

(a) 1965 c. 51.	(b) 1967 c. 73.
(c) 1969 c. 44.	(d) 1970 c. 51.
(e) 1971 c. 50.	(f) 1889 c. 63.

Higher rates and amounts of benefit payable under regulations

2. Subject to the provisions of regulations 5 and 7(1) of these regulations, as from the dates specified in column 1 of Schedule A to these regulations there shall be substituted for each of the Tables mentioned in column 2 thereof the Table mentioned in the Schedule set opposite thereto in column 3.

Miscellaneous amendments relating to benefit and to contributions

3.—(1) As from the dates specified in column 1 of Schedule J to these regulations, there shall in the regulations mentioned in column 2 thereof be made the amendments specified against those regulations mentioned in columns 3 and 4 thereof.

(2) As from 20th September 1971, Schedule 2 to the National Insurance (New Entrants Transitional) Regulations 1949(a), as amended (b) (amounts payable, by way of refund of contributions, to persons entering insurance too late to be able to satisfy contribution conditions for widow's benefit or retirement pension), shall be amended by the addition thereto, at the end, of the provisions set out in Schedule K to these regulations.

Conditions relating to payment of additional benefit under awards made before the appointed or prescribed day

4. Where an award of any benefit under the principal Act has been made before the day appointed or prescribed for the payment of benefit of the description to which the award relates at a higher weekly rate by virtue of the Act of 1971 or of these regulations, paragraphs 2 and 3 of Schedule 6 to the National Insurance Act 1969 (effect of any such award) shall, if the period to which the award relates has not ended before that day, have effect subject to the condition that, if the award has not been made in accordance with the provisions of sub-paragraph (2) of the said paragraph 3 (which sub-paragraph authorises the making of such an award providing for the payment of the benefit at the higher weekly rate as from that day) and a question arises as to—

(a) the weekly rate at which the benefit is payable by virtue of the Act of 1971 or of these regulations, or

(b) whether the conditions for the receipt of the benefit at the higher weekly rate are satisfied,

the benefit shall be or continue to be payable at the weekly rate specified in the award until the said question shall have been determined in accordance with the provisions of the principal Act.

Persons not ordinarily resident in Great Britain

5.—(1) Notwithstanding the provisions of these or any other regulations, but subject to the provisions of this regulation, a person who is not ordinarily resident in Great Britain immediately before 20th September 1971 (in this regulation referred to as "the said date") shall, unless and until that person becomes ordinarily resident in Great Britain, be disqualified for receiving—

(a) in the·case of a woman who immediately before the said date is a married woman and had not retired from regular employment, any additional retirement pension by virtue of her husband's insurance, if the husband before the said date had retired from regular employment and was not ordinarily resident in Great Britain ;

(a) S.I. 1949/352 (1949 I, p. 2737).
(b) As last amended by S.I. 1969/1361 (1969 III, p. 4048).

(b) in the case of a woman who immediately before the said date is a widow, any additional retirement pension by virtue of her husband's insurance, if her husband had died before the said date ;

(c) in any other case, any additional retirement pension (not being additional retirement pension to which either of the two foregoing subparagraphs applies) if that person had retired from regular employment before the said date ;

(d) any additional widow's benefit if her husband had died or retired before the said date ;

(e) any additional child's special allowance if her former husband had died before the said date.

(2) Notwithstanding as aforesaid, if immediately before the said date a person is not ordinarily resident in Great Britain but that person has, or would, but for the absence of any child from Great Britain, have in his family immediately before the said date a child in relation to whom the conditions for guardian's allowance specified in section 29 of the principal Act are satisfied, that person and any other person who would otherwise be entitled to any additional guardian's allowance in respect of that child shall be disqualified for receiving any additional guardian's allowance in respect of that child unless and until the child becomes (or is) included in the family of a person who is ordinarily resident in Great Britain.

(3) The disqualifications for the receipt of additional benefit contained in this regulation shall not apply to a person for any period during which he is in Great Britain.

(4) For the purposes of this regulation references to additional benefit of any description are to be construed as referring to additional benefit of that description by virtue (either directly or indirectly) of any provision of the Act of 1971 (other than section 2(3) thereof) or of these regulations (other than regulation 7(2)).

(5) A widow who—

(a) is not ordinarily resident in Great Britain immediately before the said date, and was entitled to widow's benefit immediately before attaining pensionable age, or who would, but for any provision of the principal Act disqualifying her for the receipt of such benefit, have been so entitled ; and

(b) is or becomes entitled to a retirement pension by virtue of her own insurance the right to which is calculated by taking into account under section 33 of the principal Act her husband's contributions ;

shall be disqualified for receiving any additional retirement pension the right to which is so calculated unless and until she becomes ordinarily resident in Great Britain if either—

(i) her husband died before the said date ; or

(ii) before the said date he had retired from regular employment and was not ordinarily resident in Great Britain.

(6) The provisions of paragraph 3(1) of Part II of Schedule 6 to the National Insurance Act 1969(a) shall apply where, notwithstanding the foregoing provisions of this regulation, benefit of an amount higher than the amount awarded to a person has in fact been paid to him.

(a) 1969 c. 44.

(7) The disqualification for the receipt of additional retirement pension contained in paragraph (1)(c) of this regulation shall not apply to a woman in relation to a retirement pension by virtue of her husband's insurance, if that husband had not retired from regular employment before the said date and either—

(i) he was her husband immediately before that date ; or

(ii) she married him on or after that date.

Amendment to the National Insurance (Old Persons' Pensions) Regulations 1970

6. As from 20th September 1971, there shall be substituted for paragraph (1) of regulation 7 of the National Insurance (Old Persons' Pensions) Regulations 1970(a), as amended (b) (rates of benefit for or in respect of persons over pensionable age on 5th July 1948), the following paragraph :—

"(1) Subject to paragraphs (3) and (4) of this regulation, the weekly rate of benefit to which a woman is entitled by virtue of regulation 3, 4, 5 or 6 of these regulations shall be £3·60."

Transitory provisions

7.—(1) As respects the period beginning on 20th September 1971 and ending on 22nd September 1971, the rate of a person's unemployment or sickness benefit for any day in the said period payable by virtue of section 19(3) of the principal Act (unemployment and sickness benefit for persons over pensionable age) shall be determined as if the day from which higher rates of retirement pension are payable by virtue of the foregoing provisions of these regulations were 23rd September 1971.

(2) As from 20th September 1971, for the purposes of sections 31(1) and 34(1) of the principal Act (increase of retirement pension and woman's retirement pension in certain cases for contributions paid after pensionable age), as amended by section 1(1)(e) of the National Insurance Act 1967(c), by paragraphs (4) and (5) respectively of regulation 4 of the Family Allowances, National Insurance, Industrial Injuries and Miscellaneous Provisions (Decimalisation of the Currency) Regulations 1970(d), and by section 2(3) of the Act of 1971, where—

(a) at least one relevant contribution has been paid for a contribution week beginning on or after 30th October 1967, and

(b) at least one relevant contribution has been paid for a contribution week beginning before 20th September 1971 which cannot be applied for the purposes of the operation of the said section 31(1) or 34(1) with respect to contribution weeks beginning before 20th September 1971 because a set of 9, 12 or a multiple of 9 or 12 (as the case may be) contributions had not been completed,

the contributions which have for that reason not been so applied may be treated as having been paid—

(i) if they are fewer than 9, for contribution weeks beginning on or after 20th September 1971 ;

(ii) if they are more than 9, 9 for contribution weeks beginning on or after 30th October 1967 but before 20th September 1971, and the remainder for contribution weeks beginning on or after 20th September 1971.

(a) S.I. 1970/1280 (1970 II, p. 4168).   (b) S.I. 1970/1580 (1970 III, p. 5325).
(c) 1967 c. 73.   (d) S.I. 1970/46 (1970 I, p. 243).

(3) Regulation 7(2) of the National Insurance (Increase of Benefit and Miscellaneous Provisions) Regulations 1967(a) shall be amended by the insertion, after the words "30th October 1967", of the words "but before 20th September 1971".

Signed by authority of the Secretary of State for Social Services.

Paul Dean,
Parliamentary Under Secretary of State,
Department of Health and Social Security.
26th July 1971.

Given under the Official Seal of the National Insurance Joint Authority.

(L.S.)

D. G. Kelly,
Secretary,
National Insurance Joint Authority.
26th July 1971.

Walter Clegg,
Bernard Weatherill,
Two of the Lords Commissioners
of Her Majesty's Treasury.
26th July 1971.

(a) S.I. 1967/1265 (1967 II, p. 3673).

SCHEDULE A   Regulation 2

Date of operation	Existing table	Schedule containing substituted table
1	2	3
23rd September 1971	The National Insurance (Unemployment and Sickness Benefit) Regulations 1967(a) Table contained in Schedule 2 as amended(b)	Schedule B
20th September 1971	The National Insurance (Maternity Benefit and Miscellaneous Provisions) Regulations 1954(c) Table contained in regulation 13 as amended(d)	Schedule C
20th September 1971	The National Insurance (Widow's Benefit and Retirement Pensions) Regulations 1948(e) Table contained in the Schedule as amended(f)	Schedule D
20th September 1971	The National Insurance (Pensions, Existing Beneficiaries and Other Persons) (Transitional) Regulations 1948(g) Table contained in Schedule 1 as amended (h)	Schedule E
	Table contained in Schedule 2 as amended (i)	Schedule F
	Table contained in Schedule 3 as amended (j)	Schedule G
20th September 1971	The National Insurance (Pensions, Existing Contributors) (Transitional) Regulations 1948(k) Table contained in Schedule 2 as amended(l)	Schedule H
	Tables contained in Schedule 5 Part III as amended (m)	Schedule I

(a) S.I. 1967/330 (1967 I, p. 113 1).
(b) As amended by reg. 2 of and Schedules A and B to S.I. 1969/1361 (1969 III, p. 4048), and by reg. 7(2) of and Schedule 5 to S.I. 1970/46 (1970 I, p. 243).
(c) S.I. 1954/189 (1954 I, p. 1387).
(d) As last amended by reg. 2 of and Schedules A and C to S.I. 1969/1361 (1969 III, p. 4048), and by reg. 11(1) of S.I. 1970/46 (1970 I, p. 243).
(e) S.I. 1948/1261 (Rev. XVI, p. 207: 1948 I, p. 2704).
(f) As last amended by reg. 2 of and Schedules A and D to S.I. 1969/1361 (1969 III, p. 4048), and by reg. 6(2) of and Schedule 4 to S.I. 1970/46 (1970 I, p. 243).
(g) S.I. 1948/55 Rev. XVI, p. 36: 1948 I, p. 2822).
(h) As last amended by reg. 2 of and Schedules A and E to S.I. 1969/1361 (1969 III, p. 4048), and by reg. 15(3) of and Schedule 13 to S.I. 1970/46 (1970 I, p. 243).
(i) As last amended by reg. 2 of and Schedules A and F to S.I. 1969/1361 (1969 III, p. 4048), and by reg. 15(3) of and Schedule 14 to S.I. 1970/46 (1970 I, p. 243).
(j) As last amended by reg. 2 of and Schedules A and G to S.I. 1969/1361 (1969 III, p. 4048), and by reg. 15(3) of and Schedule 15 to S.I. 1970/46 (1970/I, p. 243).
(k) S.I. 1948/612 (Rev. XVI, p. 18: 1948 I, p. 2834).
(l) As last amended by reg. 2 of and Schedules A and H to S.I. 1969/1361 (1969 III, p. 4048), and by reg. 16(3) of and Schedule 16 to S.I. 1970/46 (1970 I, p. 243).
(m) As last amended by reg. 2 of and Schedules A and I to S.I. 1969/1361 (1969 III, p. 4048), and by reg. 16(4) of and Schedule 17 to S.I. 1970/46 (1970 I, p. 243).

Regulation 2   SCHEDULE B

1	2	3	4	5
Number of contributions paid or credited in the relevant contribution year	Full weekly rate of benefit applicable under Schedule 3 to the Act			
	£ 6·00	£ 4·20	£ 3·70	£ 3·30
	Reduced rate at which benefit is payable			
	£	£	£	£
48—49	5·76	4·14	3·57	3·18
46—47	5·52	4·02	3·44	3·06
43—45	5·28	3·78	3·27	2·94
40—42	4·84	3·54	3·04	2·75
37—39	4·39	3·18	2·81	2·52
34—36	3·94	2·84	2·50	2·30
30—33	3·47	2·52	2·19	2·04
26—29	3·00	2·10	1·85	1·65

Regulation 2   SCHEDULE C

Numbers including the number of contributions paid or credited in respect of the relevant period	Weekly rate	
	Of maternity allowance without increase	Of increase in respect of adult dependant
1	2	3
	£	£
48—49	5·76	3·57
46—47	5·52	3·44
43—45	5·28	3·27
40—42	4·84	3·04
37—39	4·39	2·81
34—36	3·94	2·50
30—33	3·47	2·19
26—29	3·00	1·85

SCHEDULE D   Regulation 2

1	2	3	4
	Full weekly rate of benefit applicable under Schedule 3 to the National Insurance Act 1965		
Yearly average of contributions paid or credited	£ 8·40	£ 6·00	£ 3·70
	Reduced rate at which benefit payable		
	£	£	£
48—49	8·05	5·76	3·57
46—47	7·70	5·52	3·44
43—45	7·30	5·28	3·27
40—42	6·78	4·84	3·04
37—39	6·16	4·39	2·81
34—36	5·52	3·94	2·50
30—33	4·86	3·47	2·19
26—29	4·20	3·00	1·85
22—25	3·56	2·56	1·55
18—21	2·92	2·09	1·27
13—17	2·24	1·68	1·07

SCHEDULE E   Regulation 2

Rate of widow's basic pension or contributory old age pension by virtue of husband's insurance and rate (apart from additional allowance or increase) of widow's pension immediately before the appointed day	Corresponding rate of widowed mother's allowance, widow's pension or retirement pension for a widow by virtue of husband's insurance	Corresponding increased rate of widow's basic pension or of contributory old age pension by virtue of husband's insurance
1	2	3
s. d.	£	£
9 0	5·40	1·66
8 0	4·79	1·45
7 0	4·20	1·25
6 0	3·60	1·04
5 0	3·00	0·90
4 0	—	0·77
3 0	—	0·56
2 0	—	0·40

Regulation 2 SCHEDULE F

Rate of retirement pension	Corresponding rate of increase in respect of an adult dependant or of retirement pension for a wife
1	2
£	£
5·40	3·34
4·96	3·04
4·79	2·98
4·39	2·66
4·20	2·60
3·94	2·45
3·60	2·19
3·47	2·14
3·28	2·09
3·00	1·85
2·70	1·77
2·56	1·59
2·40	1·55
2·26	1·47
2·09	1·35
2·02	1·17
1·80	1·13
1·68	1·07
1·50	0·95
1·42	0·84
1·20	0·72
1·08	0·72
0·90	0·63
0·82	0·45
0·66	0·45
0·54	0·42
0·52	0·36

SCHEDULE G   Regulation 2

Rate at which an old age or widow's pension would, apart from the Increase of Pensions Regulations and but for the repeal of the Contributory Pensions Acts, have been payable	Rate of retirement pension (except in a case where column 4 applies) being the rate at which an old age or widow's pension would, but for the repeal of the Contributory Pensions Acts, have been payable	Corresponding increased rate of retirement pension	Rate of retirement pension for wife by virtue of husband's insurance, where he is alive, being the rate at which an old age pension would, but for the repeal of the Contributory Pensions Acts, have been payable	Corresponding increased rate of retirement pension
1	2	3	4	5
s. d.	£ s. d.	£	s. d.	£
9 0	1 3 0	5·40	14 0	3·34
8 3	1 1 0	4·96	12 6	3·04
8 0	1 0 0	4·79	12 0	2·98
7 3	18 6	4·39	11 0	2·66
7 0	18 0	4·20	11 0	2·60
6 6	16 6	3·94	10 0	2·45
6 0	15 0	3·60	9 0	2·19
5 9	14 6	3·47	9 0	2·14
5 6	14 0	3·28	8 6	2·09
5 0	13 0	3·00	8 0	1·85
4 6	11 6	2·70	7 0	1·77
4 3	11 0	2·56	6 6	1·59
4 0	10 0	2·40	6 0	1·55
3 9	9 6	2·26	6 0	1·47
3 6	9 0	2·09	5 6	1·35
3 3	8 6	2·02	5 0	1·17
3 0	8 0	1·80	5 0	1·13
2 9	7 0	1·68	4 6	1·07
2 6	6 6	1·50	4 0	0·95
2 3	6 0	1·42	3 6	0·84
2 0	5 0	1·20	3 0	0·72
1 9	4 6	1·08	3 0	0·72
1 6	4 0	0·90	2 6	0·63
1 3	3 6	0·82	2 0	0·45
1 0	3 0	0·66	2 0	0·45
9	2 0	0·54	1 6	0·42
6	1 6	0·52	1 0	0·36

Regulation 2   SCHEDULE H

Yearly average of contributions paid or credited 1	Reduced rate at which pension is payable 2
	£
48—49	1·73
46—47	1·66
43—45	1·58
40—42	1·45
37—39	1·32
34—36	1·18
30—33	1·04
26—29	0·90
22—25	0·77
18—21	0·63
13—17	0·50

SCHEDULE I

Regulation 2   TABLE 1

Rate at which an old age pension would, but for the repeal of the Contributory Pensions Acts, have been payable 1	Corresponding rate of retirement pension where pensionable age attained during period:—				
	From 5 July 1948 to 4 July 1949 2	From 5 July 1949 to 4 July 1950 3	From 5 July 1950 to 4 July 1951 4	From 5 July 1951 to 4 July 1952 5	From 5 July 1952 to 4 July 1953 6
£ s. d.	£	£	£	£	£
1 3 0	5·52	5·52	5·76	5·76	5·76
1 0 0	4·96	5·14	5·40	5·52	5·76
18 0	4·44	4·79	5·14	5·52	5·76
15 0	3·72	4·20	4·96	5·40	5·76
13 0	3·28	4·00	4·79	5·14	5·76
10 0	2·92	3·60	4·20	4·96	5·52
8 0	2·40	3·00	4·00	4·96	5·52
5 0	1·68	2·56	3·72	4·79	5·52
3 0	1·20	2·40	3·60	4·44	5·52
— —	0·66	1·80	3·00	4·20	5·40

TABLE 2

Yearly average of contributions paid or credited	£ 0·66	£ 1·20	£ 1·68	£ 1·80	£ 2·40	£ 2·56	£ 2·92	£ 3·00	£ 3·28	£ 3·60	£ 3·72	£ 4·00	£ 4·20	£ 4·44	£ 4·79	£ 4·96	£ 5·14	£ 5·40	£ 5·52	£ 5·76
Corresponding Rates of Retirement Pensions																				
1	2	3	4	5	6	7	8	9	10	11	12	13	14	15	16	17	18	19	20	21
	£	£	£	£	£	£	£	£	£	£	£	£	£	£	£	£	£	£	£	£
48—49	0·64	1·08	1·50	1·72	2·26	2·44	2·70	2·94	3·22	3·47	3·64	3·94	4·14	4·39	4·50	4·79	4·96	5·14	5·40	5·52
46—47	0·64	1·08	1·50	1·72	2·09	2·40	2·56	2·92	3·00	3·28	3·60	3·72	4·00	4·20	4·44	4·50	4·79	4·96	5·14	5·40
43—45	0·64	1·08	1·42	1·68	2·02	2·26	2·44	2·70	2·94	3·22	3·28	3·60	3·72	4·00	4·20	4·39	4·50	4·79	4·96	5·14
40—42	0·64	0·90	1·24	1·50	1·80	2·09	2·40	2·44	2·70	2·94	3·00	3·22	3·47	3·64	3·94	4·00	4·20	4·39	4·44	4·79
37—39	0·54	0·82	1·20	1·42	1·72	1·80	2·09	2·26	2·44	2·70	2·92	2·94	3·00	3·28	3·60	3·64	3·94	4·00	4·14	4·39
34—36	0·54	0·82	1·08	1·20	1·50	1·68	1·80	2·02	2·26	2·44	2·56	2·70	2·92	2·94	3·22	3·28	3·47	3·60	3·64	3·94
30—33	0·52	0·66	0·90	1·08	1·42	1·50	1·68	1·72	1·80	2·09	2·26	2·40	2·44	2·56	2·92	2·94	3·00	3·22	3·28	3·47
26—29	0·52	0·64	0·82	0·90	1·20	1·24	1·42	1·50	1·68	1·72	1·80	2·02	2·09	2·26	2·40	2·44	2·56	2·70	2·92	2·94
22—25	0·52	0·54	0·66	0·82	0·90	1·08	1·20	1·24	1·42	1·42	1·50	1·68	1·72	1·80	2·02	2·09	2·26	2·26	2·40	2·44
18—21	0·36	0·52	0·64	0·66	0·82	0·90	0·90	1·08	1·20	1·20	1·24	1·42	1·42	1·50	1·68	1·72	1·80	1·80	2·02	2·02
13—17	0·36	0·52	0·54	0·54	0·64	0·66	0·66	0·82	0·90	0·90	1·08	1·20	1·20	1·20	1·24	1·24	1·42	1·42	1·50	1·50

TABLE 3

Rate of retirement pension	Corresponding rate of increase in respect of an adult dependant or of retirement pension for a wife	Rate of retirement pension	Corresponding rate of increase in respect of an adult dependant or of retirement pension for a wife
1	2	3	4
£	£	£	£
5·76	3·57	2·70	1·77
5·52	3·39	2·56	1·59
5·40	3·34	2·44	1·59
5·14	3·22	2·40	1·55
4·96	3·04	2·26	1·47
4·79	2·98	2·09	1·35
4·50	2·81	2·02	1·17
4·44	2·75	1·80	1·13
4·39	2·66	1·72	1·07
4·20	2·60	1·68	1·07
4·14	2·50	1·50	0·95
4·00	2·45	1·42	0·84
3·94	2·45	1·24	0·84
3·72	2·24	1·20	0·72
3·64	2·24	1·08	0·72
3·60	2·19	0·90	0·63
3·47	2·14	0·82	0·45
3·28	2·09	0·66	0·45
3·22	1·91	0·64	0·42
3·00	1·85	0·54	0·42
2·94	1·80	0·52	0·36
2·92	1·80	0·36	0·30

SCHEDULE J

Regulation 3(1)

Date of operation	Regulations amended	Amendments	
		There shall be substituted for the expressions specified in column 3 (wherever they occur) the expressions specified in column 4	
1	2	3	4
1. 20th September 1971	The National Insurance (Pensions, Existing Beneficiaries and Other Persons) (Transitional) Regulations 1948 regulations 9 and 10 as amended(a) (Rates of converted pensions for existing beneficiaries, of increase of retirement pension in respect of adult dependants, and of retirement pension for wives of certain existing beneficiaries)		
	Regulation 9(1A)	£1·50	30 per cent of the amount specified in paragraph 8 of Part I of Schedule 3 to the National Insurance Act 1965(b)
	Regulation 9(2)	the rate of £1·50 a week	the rate per week of 30 per cent of the amount specified in paragraph 8 of Part I of Schedule 3 to the National Insurance Act 1965
	Regulation 9(3) proviso	3rd November 1969	20th September 1971
		£5·00 £3·10	£6·00 £3·70
	Regulation 10(1)	£ s. d. 5 0 0	£6·00
	Regulation 10(2) proviso(a)	3rd November 1969	20th September 1971

(a) The relevant amending instruments are S.I. 1951/1232, 1957/1950, 1965/35, 40, 1969/1361, 1970/46 (1951 I, p. 1457; 1957 I, p. 1704; 1965 I, pp. 34, 47; 1969 III, p. 4048; 1970 I, p. 243).
(b) 1965 c. 51.

SCHEDULE J—(*continued*)

Date of operation	Regulations amended	Amendments	
		There shall be substituted for the expressions specified in column 3 (wherever they occur) the expressions specified in column 4	
1	2	3	4
2. 20th September 1971	The National Insurance (Pensions, Existing Contributors) (Transitional) Regulations 1948		
	(Rates of benefit for certain widows)		
	Regulation 6(2) as amended (a)	the rate of £1·50 a week	the rate per week of 30 per cent of the amount specified in paragraph 8 of Part I of Schedule 3 to the National Insurance Act 1965(b)
	Regulation 11(4)(a) as amended (c)	£ s. d. 5 0 0	£6·00
3. 20th September 1971	The National Insurance (Widow's Benefit and Retirement Pensions) Regulations 1948 (d) as amended (e)		
	(Contributions to be disregarded in computing increase of retirement pension)		
	Regulation 12(2)(a) as amended(f)	a rate not exceeding £1·50 a week	a rate per week not exceeding 30 per cent of the amount specified in paragraph 8 of Part I of Schedule 3 to the National Insurance Act 1965(b)

(a) The relevant amending instruments are S.I. 1965/35, 1970/46 (1965 I, p. 34; 1970 I, p. 243).
(b) 1965 c. 51.
(c) As last amended by reg. 4(1) and Schedule J of S.I. 1969/1361 (1969 III, p. 4048).
(d) S.I. 1948/1261 (Rev. XVI, p. 207: 1948 I, p. 2704).
(e) The relevant amending instruments are S.I. 1964/2001, 1970/46 (1964 III, p. 5061; 1970 I, p. 243).
(f) S.I. 1970/46 (1970 I, p. 243).

SCHEDULE J—(continued)

Date of operation	Regulations amended	Amendments	
		There shall be substituted for the expressions specified in column 3 (wherever they occur) the expressions specified in column 4	
1	2	3	4
4. The date in re-relation to any benefit under the principal Act as from which the weekly rate of that benefit is increased by virtue of the Act of 1971 or of these Regulations	The National Insurance (Hospital In-Patients) Regulations 1949(a) regulations 3, 4, 5 as amended (b) and regulation 6 as amended(c) (Reduction in certain circumstances of weekly rates of benefit in the case of hospital in-patients)		
	Regulation 3(4)	£1·25 £1·00	£1·45 £1·20
	Regulation 4	£1·00 £2·00	£1·20 £2·40
	Regulation 5(1)	£1·25 £1·00	£1·45 £1·20
	Regulation 5(2)	£2·25 £2·00 £1·00	£2·65 £2·40 £1·20
	Regulation 5(3)(a)	£2·00	£2·40
	Regulation 5(3)(b)	£3·25 £3·00	£3·85 £3·60
	Regulation 5(4)(c)	£1·25 £1·00	£1·45 £1·20
	Regulation 5(4)(d)	£2·90	£3·50
	Regulation 6(3) and (4)	£1·00 £1·25 £2·25 £2·00	£1·20 £1·45 £2·65 £2·40

(a) S.I. 1949/1461 (1949 I, p. 2718).
(b) The relevant amending instruments are S.I. 1957/1849, 2077, 1969/1361, 1970/46 (1957 I, pp. 1546, 1556; 1969 III, p. 4048; 1970 I, p. 243).
(c) The relevant amending instruments are S.I. 1957/1849, 1969/1361, 1970/46 (1957 I, p. 1546; 1969 III, p. 4048; 1970 I, p. 243).

SCHEDULE J—(continued)

Date of operation	Regulations amended	Amendments	
		There shall be substituted for the expressions specified in column 3 (wherever they occur) the expressions specified in column 4	
1	2	3	4
20th September 1971	The National Insurance (Hospital In-Patients) Regulations 1949		
	(Benefit payable on discharge from a hospital or similar institution)		
	Regulation 6A(2) as amended(a)	£7·00	£9·00
5. 20th September 1971	The National Insurance (New Entrants Transitional) Regulations 1949(b)		
	(Modification of provisions of the Act relating to retirement pensions in the case of certain widows)		
	Regulation 5(2)(a) as amended(c)	£ s. d. 5 0 0	£6·00

(a) The relevant amending instruments are S.I. 1960/1283, 1969/1361, 1970/46 (1960 II, p. 2163; 1969 III, p. 4048; 1970 I, p. 243).
(b) S.I. 1949/352 (1949 I, p. 2737).
(c) As last amended by reg. 4(1) and Schedule J of S.I. 1969/1361 (1969 III, p. 4048).

SCHEDULE K

Regulation 3(2)

PROVISIONS TO BE ADDED TO SCHEDULE 2 TO THE NATIONAL INSURANCE (NEW ENTRANTS TRANSITIONAL) REGULATIONS 1949

9. Applicable (in substitution for the provisions of paragraph 8 of this Schedule) to contributions in respect of contribution weeks commencing on or after 20th September 1971.

MEN

Age of man at expiration of period of currency of contribution card on which contribution was paid	Employed	Self-employed	Non-employed
	Portion of contribution to be refunded		
(1)	new pence (2)	new pence (3)	new pence (4)
	47	94	94
	Total number of new pence to be refunded (including interest) in respect of each contribution		
65 and over	48	95	95
64	49	97	97
63	50	99	99
62	51	102	102
61	53	104	104
60	54	107	107
59	55	109	109

WOMEN

Age of woman at expiration of period of currency of contribution card on which contribution was paid	Employed	Self-employed	Non-employed
	Portion of contribution to be refunded		
(5)	new pence (6)	new pence (7)	new pence (8)
	41	72	70
	Total number of new pence to be refunded (including interest) in respect of each contribution		
60 and over	41	73	71
59	42	74	72
58	43	75	73
57	44	77	75
56	45	79	77
55	46	81	79
54	47	83	81

EXPLANATORY NOTE

(This Note is not part of the Regulations.)

These Regulations are, by virtue of paragraph 2(1) of Schedule 6 to the National Insurance Act 1971, exempt from reference to the National Insurance Advisory Committee and no such reference has been made.

The regulations increase the rates of benefit payable under certain regulations made under the National Insurance Acts 1965 to 1970, or deemed by virtue of section 117 of the National Insurance Act 1965 to have been made under that Act, in order to bring them into conformity with the higher rates of benefit payable under that Act by virtue of the Act of 1971, and contain other provisions of a minor or consequential character.

1971 No. 1221 (C.31)

LOCAL AUTHORITY SOCIAL SERVICES

The Local Authority Social Services Act 1970 (Commencement No. 3) Order 1971

Made - - - - 26th July 1971

The Secretary of State for Social Services, in exercise of his powers under section 15(4) of the Local Authority Social Services Act 1970(a) and of all other powers enabling him in that behalf, hereby orders as follows:—

1. This Order may be cited as the Local Authority Social Services Act 1970 (Commencement No. 3) Order 1971.

2. The appointed day for the coming into force of section 11 of the Local Authority Social Services Act 1970 (which relates to the amendment of the Health Visiting and Social Work (Training) Act 1962(b)) shall be 1st October 1971.

Keith Joseph,
Secretary of State for Social Services.

26th July 1971.

EXPLANATORY NOTE

(This Note is not part of the Order.)

This Order brings into force in the United Kingdom on 1st October 1971 section 11 of the Local Authority Social Services Act 1970, which amends certain provisions of the Health Visiting and Social Work (Training) Act 1962 in relation to the naming and composition of the Councils constituted under that Act.

(a) 1970 c. 42.   (b) 1962 c. 33.

STATUTORY INSTRUMENTS

1971 No. 1222

SOCIAL SECURITY

WORKMEN'S COMPENSATION

The Pneumoconiosis, Byssinosis and Miscellaneous Diseases Benefit (Amendment) Scheme 1971

Made	- - -	26th July 1971
Laid before Parliament		5th August 1971
Coming into Operation		22nd September 1971

The Secretary of State for Social Services, with the consent of the Treasury, in exercise of his powers under sections 5 and 7 of the Industrial Injuries and Diseases (Old Cases) Act 1967(a), as amended by section 11(1), (2) and (3) of and Schedule 5, paragraph 13(2), to the National Insurance Act 1971(b), and of all other powers enabling him in that behalf, hereby makes, in consequence of the said Act of 1971, the following Scheme :—

Citation, interpretation and commencement

1. This Scheme, which may be cited as the Pneumoconiosis, Byssinosis and Miscellaneous Diseases Benefit (Amendment) Scheme 1971, shall be read as one with the Pneumoconiosis, Byssinosis and Miscellaneous Diseases Benefit Scheme 1966(c), as amended (d) (hereinafter referred to as "the principal Scheme"), and shall come into operation on 22nd September 1971.

Amendment of Article 4 of the principal Scheme

2. In paragraph 1(*a*)(ii) of Article 4 of the principal Scheme (allowance for partial disablement), for the sum "£3·05" there shall be substituted the sum "£3·65".

Amendment of Article 5 of the principal Scheme

3. At the end of paragraph (1) of Article 5 of the principal Scheme (increase of allowance in respect of a wife) there shall be added the following proviso :—

"Provided that where a person is also entitled to an increase of allowance under the provisons of Article 7(1) of this Scheme, and is residing with his wife, the provisions of paragraph 1(*b*) of Schedule 2 hereto shall

---

(a) 1967 c. 34.   (b) 1971 c. 50.
(c) S.I. 1966/164 (1966 I, p. 303).
(d) The relevant amending instruments are S.I. 1969/1196, 1970/46 (1969 II, p. 3531; 1970 I, p. 243).

not have effect, but where the earnings of his wife for the calendar week ending last before any week for which he is entitled to any such increase of allowance exceeded the amount first stated in section 18(3A) of the Industrial Injuries Act, the increase of allowance under this Article shall be reduced in the manner provided by the said section 18(3A), and for these purposes the earnings of his wife shall be calculated in accordance with the provisions of Regulation 9(1A) and (2) of the Benefit Regulations.".

Amendment of Article 6 of the principal Scheme

4. For Article 6 of the principal Scheme, and the proviso thereto, there shall be substituted the following Article :—

"Increase of allowance in respect of children

6. For any period during which a person has a family which includes a child or children within the meaning of section 17 of the Industrial Injuries Act, the weekly rate of the allowance payable to that person shall be increased by an amount equal to the increase (if any) which would be payable to him in respect of that child or those children under the said section 17—

(*a*) if, in the case of a person entitled to an allowance in respect of total disablement but not to an increase of allowance under the provisions of Article 7(1) of this Scheme, he were entitled to injury benefit ;

(*b*) if, in the case of a person entitled to an increase of allowance under the provisions of Article 7(1) of this Scheme, he were entitled to a disablement pension plus unemployability supplement :

Provided that where, for any period, the conditions for the receipt by a person of an increase of allowance under this Article are satisfied, such increase of allowance shall be adjusted by reference to the weekly rate at which an allowance or an increase of benefit in respect of that child or those children is payable for that period under the Industrial Injuries Act or the National Insurance Act 1965 so as to be payable (if at all) for that period at a weekly rate arrived at by deducting from the weekly rate at which the increase of allowance under this Article would otherwise have been payable the said weekly rate of any allowance or increase of benefit payable under the above-mentioned Acts.".

Amendment of Article 7 of the principal Scheme

5.—(1) In paragraph (1) of Article 7 of the principal Scheme (increase of allowance on account of unemployability), after the words "the said section 13" there shall be inserted the words "or, as the case may be, the said section 13 and section 13A of the said Act".

(2) After paragraph (1) of the said Article, there shall be inserted the following paragraph :—

"(1A) For the purposes of this Article, the reference in section 13A(2) of the Industrial Injuries Act (increase of unemployability supplement by reference to beneficiary's age on qualifying date) to 'the qualifying date' shall, subject to the provisions of subsections (3), (4) and (5) of that section, mean the beginning of the first week for which a person qualified for an increase of allowance under this Article.".

(3) For paragraph (4) of the said Article, there shall be substituted the following paragraph :—

"(4) Where a person is entitled to an allowance in respect of partial disablement and is also entitled to an increase of that allowance under this Article, the provisions of Article 5 shall apply to him for any period during which he is entitled to such increase as they apply to a person entitled to an allowance in respect of total disablement and an increase of that allowance under this Article.".

Amendment of Schedule 2 to the principal Scheme

6. In Schedule 2 to the principal Scheme (conditions relating to increase of allowance in respect of a wife), for sub-paragraph 1(*b*) and the proviso thereto there shall be substituted the following sub-paragraph :—

"(*b*) Regulation 9(1) of the Benefit Regulations (which regulation provides that an increase of benefit in respect of a wife shall not be payable where her weekly earnings exceed the amount therein specified), and for the purpose of this sub-paragraph the weekly earnings of a wife shall be ascertained in the manner specified in paragraphs (1) and (2) of the said regulation.".

Amendment of Schedule 3 to the principal Scheme

7. Schedule 3 to the principal Scheme (provisions of the Industrial Injuries Act and of regulations made thereunder applicable (with the necessary modifications) to claims for and payment of allowances) shall be amended by the insertion after the entry relating to Regulation 24 in the first and second columns thereof respectively of the words "Regulation 24A" and "Payment of benefit to a third party".

Signed by authority of the Secretary of State for Social Services.

Paul Dean,
Parliamentary Under Secretary of State,
Department of Health and Social Security.

26th July 1971.

We consent,

Walter Clegg,
Bernard Weatherill,
Two of the Lords Commissioners of
Her Majesty's Treasury.

26th July 1971.

EXPLANATORY NOTE

(This Note is not part of the Scheme.)

This Scheme amends the Pneumoconiosis, Byssinosis and Miscellaneous Diseases Benefit Scheme 1966 so as to give effect to section 11(1), (2) and (3) of and Schedule 5, paragraph 13(2), to the National Insurance Act 1971 by increasing the rate of allowance in respect of partial disablement, varying the conditions relating to a wife's earnings where she is residing with a person entitled to an increase of allowance on account of unemployability under the provisions of Article 7, increasing the allowance in respect of children where a person is entitled to such an increase of allowance, extending the Scheme to provide for a further increase of allowance under the said Article 7 by reference to a person's age corresponding to the increase of unemployability supplement under section 13A of the Industrial Injuries Act, and by making provision for payment of allowance to a third party. Minor consequential amendments are also made.

This Scheme is made in consequence of the National Insurance Act 1971, and accordingly, by virtue of Schedule 6, paragraph 2(2), of that Act, no draft of the Scheme has been laid before Parliament.

STATUTORY INSTRUMENTS

1971 No. 1223

SOCIAL SECURITY

The Workmen's Compensation (Supplementation) Amendment Scheme 1971

Made - - -	26th July 1971
Laid before Parliament	5th August 1971
Coming into Operation	22nd September 1971

The Secretary of State for Social Services, with the consent of the Treasury, in exercise of his powers under section 2 of the Industrial Injuries and Diseases (Old Cases) Act 1967(a), as amended by section 11(1) of the National Insurance Act 1971(b), and of all other powers enabling him in that behalf, hereby makes, in consequence of the said Act of 1971, the following Scheme :—

Citation, interpretation and commencement

1. This Scheme, which may be cited as the Workmen's Compensation (Supplementation) Amendment Scheme 1971, shall be read as one with the Workmen's Compensation (Supplementation) Scheme 1966(c), as amended (d) (hereinafter referred to as "the principal Scheme"), and shall come into operation on 22nd September 1971.

Amendment of Article 7 of the principal Scheme

2.—(1) In paragraph (1) of Article 7 of the principal Scheme (computation of loss of earnings), for the words "31st October 1969" there shall be substituted the words "18th September 1971".

(2) For the proviso to paragraph (1) of the said Article 7 there shall be substituted the following proviso :—

"Provided that—

(*a*) in assessing, in relation to any person, the standard of remuneration in any class of employment, regard shall be had to that person's reasonable prospects of advancement and the class of employment in which he was employed at the time when the accident happened shall be treated, for this purpose, as extending to and including employment in the capacities to which persons so employed are, in the normal

---

(a) 1967 c. 34.   (b) 1971 c. 50.
(c) S.I. 1966/165 (1966 I, p. 325).
(d) The relevant amending instruments are S.I. 1969/1195, 1970/46 (1969 II, p. 3529; 1970 I, p. 243).

course, advanced and to which if he had continued to be so employed, without the accident having happened, he would have had at least the normal prospects of advancement ;

(b) where the amount representing a person's loss of earnings has been ascertained in accordance with this Article, but by reference to a period earlier than that now specified herein, and the Board is satisfied that it is unlikely that there has been any material change in that amount, if the Board in their discretion so direct, such amount shall continue to represent that person's loss of earnings determined in accordance with this Article notwithstanding that it has not been ascertained by reference to the period now specified.".

Amendment of Article 10 of the principal Scheme

3. In paragraph (1)(*a*)(iii) of Article 10 of the principal Scheme (allowances in respect of two or more different injuries or diseases) for the sum "£3·05" there shall be substituted the sum "£3·65".

Amendment of Schedule 1 to the principal Scheme

4. For the provisions set out in Schedule 1 to the principal Scheme (calculation of amount of lesser incapacity allowances under Scheme), there shall be substituted the provisions set out in the Schedule to this Scheme.

Transitional provision

5. Where a lesser incapacity allowance has been awarded to a person under the principal Scheme before 22nd September 1971 and a question arises as to the weekly rate of that allowance payable in consequence of this Scheme, the case shall be reviewed by the Board in the light of the amendments made by this Scheme and the allowance shall continue to be payable at the weekly rate specified in the award until the question shall have been determined in accordance with the provisions of the principal Scheme.

Signed by authority of the Secretary of State for Social Services.

Paul Dean,
Parliamentary Under Secretary of State,
Department of Health and Social Security.

26th July 1971.

We consent.

Walter Clegg,
Bernard Weatherill,
Two of the Lords Commissioners of
Her Majesty's Treasury.

26th July 1971.

Article 4 **SCHEDULE**

Schedule substituted for Schedule 1
to the principal Scheme

Article 5 **SCHEDULE 1**

Loss of earnings	Rate of lesser incapacity allowance
£	£
0·49½	0·15
0·99½	0·30
1·74½	0·45
2·49½	0·60
3·24½	0·85
3·99½	1·10
4·74½	1·35
5·49½	1·75
6·24½	2·15
6·99½	2·55
7·74½	2·95
8·49½	3·35
8·50	3·65

EXPLANATORY NOTE

(*This Note is not part of the Scheme.*)

This Scheme amends the Workmen's Compensation (Supplementation) Scheme 1966 so as to give effect to section 11(1) of the National Insurance Act 1971 by increasing the weekly rate of lesser incapacity allowance payable in certain circumstances. Consequent upon the increase, adjustments have been made to the intermediate rates of lesser incapacity allowance and the provisions in the Scheme for determining a person's loss of earnings have been modified where those have previously been ascertained and the Board is satisfied that it is unlikely that there has been any material change therein.

This Scheme is made in consequence of the Act of 1971 and accordingly, by virtue of Schedule 6, paragraph 2(2), of that Act, no draft of the Scheme has been laid before Parliament.

STATUTORY INSTRUMENTS

1971 No. 1233

CUSTOMS AND EXCISE

The Hydrocarbon Oil Duties (Drawback) (No. 1) Order 1971

Made - - - -	28*th July* 1971
Laid before the House of Commons - - -	3*rd August* 1971
Coming into Operation	4*th August* 1971

The Lords Commissioners of Her Majesty's Treasury, by virtue of the powers conferred on them by section 13 of the Hydrocarbon Oil (Customs and Excise) Act 1971(**a**), and of all other powers enabling them in that behalf, hereby make the following Order:—

1.—(1) This Order may be cited as the Hydrocarbon Oil Duties (Drawback) (No. 1) Order 1971.

(2) The Interpretation Act 1889(**b**) shall apply for the interpretation of this Order as it applies for the interpretation of an Act of Parliament.

(3) This Order shall come into operation on 4th August 1971.

2. The Hydrocarbon Oil Duties (Drawback) (No. 1) Order 1967(**c**) is hereby revoked.

Bernard Weatherill,
V. H. Goodhew,
Two of the Lords Commissioners of
Her Majesty's Treasury.

28th July 1971.

EXPLANATORY NOTE

(This Note is not part of the Order.)

This Order revokes a Drawback Order which has become superfluous as the result of the relief from hydrocarbon oil duty granted by section 7 of the Hydrocarbon Oil (Customs and Excise) Act 1971 in respect of oil used in the manufacture or preparation of certain articles.

(**a**) 1971 c. 12.   (**b**) 1888 c. 63.   (**c**) 1967/1022 (1967 II, p. 3108).

1971 No. 1234

ANTHRAX
The Anthrax Prevention Order 1971

Made - - - - 28*th July* 1971

Coming into Operation 1*st September* 1971

At the Court at Buckingham Palace, the 28th day of July 1971

Present,

The Queen's Most Excellent Majesty in Council

Her Majesty, in pursuance of section 1 of the Anthrax Prevention Act 1919(a) and of all other powers enabling Her in that behalf, is pleased, by and with the advice of Her Privy Council, to order, and it is hereby ordered, as follows:—

Citation, commencement and revocation

1.—(1) This Order may be cited as the Anthrax Prevention Order 1971 and shall come into operation on 1st September 1971.

(2) The Order in Council dated 9th March 1921(b) regulating the importation of certain goods likely to be infected with anthrax, in so far as it relates to Great Britain, and the Anthrax Prevention (Goat Hair and Shaving Brushes) Order 1961(c) are hereby revoked.

Interpretation

2.—(1) The Interpretation Act 1889(d) shall apply for the interpretation of this Order as it applies for the interpretation of an Act of Parliament, and as if this Order and the Orders hereby revoked were Acts of Parliament.

(2) In this Order, unless the context otherwise requires:—

"approved" means approved in writing for the time being for the purposes of this Order by the Secretary of State;

"China cashmere" includes cashmere produced in the Mongolian People's Republic;

"freight container" means a container in which goods may be transported, having fittings by which it can be moved by a lifting machine or appliance and having an internal volume of not less than 7 cubic metres;

"goat hair" includes goat wool and noils and other by-products in the production of tops and yarns made wholly or partly of goat hair;

"proper officer" means the proper officer within the meaning of the Customs and Excise Act 1952(e); and

"tops and yarns" includes sliver and rovings and other intermediate products.

(3) References in this Order to an enactment shall be construed as references to that enactment as amended by or under any other enactment.

(a) 1919 c. 23.
(c) S.I. 1961/2040 (1961 III, p. 3727).
(e) 1952 c. 44.

(b) S.R. & O. 1921/352 (1921 p. 38).
(d) 1889 c. 63.

Declaration of infection with anthrax

3. It is hereby declared that—

(*a*) goat hair of whatever origin and all goods mixed therewith and tops and yarns made wholly or partly of goat hair; and

(*b*) wool and animal hair produced in or exported from or through the United Arab Republic or the Sudan and all goods mixed therewith,

are, with the exceptions specified in the Schedule to this Order, goods likely to be infected with anthrax.

Prohibition of the importation of tops and yarns

4.—(1) Except as provided in paragraph (2) of this Article, the importation into Great Britain, otherwise than merely for re-exportation by way of transhipment, or in the same ship, to a destination outside the United Kingdom, of tops and yarns made wholly or partly of goat hair is hereby prohibited.

(2) Paragraph (1) of this Article does not apply to goods of any kind specified in the Schedule to this Order.

Conditions of the importation of certain goods

5.—(1) Except as provided in paragraph (4) of this Article, the importation into Great Britain of goat hair, or of goods mixed therewith, and of wool or animal hair produced in or exported from or through the United Arab Republic or the Sudan, or of goods mixed therewith, is hereby prohibited—

(*a*) except at the ports of Liverpool, Hull, Harwich, Felixstowe and Dover;

(*b*) unless, in the case of goods imported at Harwich, Felixstowe and Dover, the packages containing the goods are inside freight containers; and

(*c*) unless, in all cases, the condition or conditions specified respectively in paragraph (2) or (3) of this Article are complied with.

(2) The said condition is, in the case of goods which are imported solely for re-exportation by means of transhipment, or in the same ship, to a destination outside the United Kingdom, that they shall be so re-exported.

(3) The said conditions in any other case are the following—

(*a*) that the goods shall be completely enclosed in packings or wrappings so as to reduce as far as practicable the risk of infection from anthrax;

(*b*) that all packages containing any such goods (other than packages inside freight containers) shall, when landed, be placed together and shall not be mixed with any other goods;

(*c*) that the goods shall be consigned to a factory in Great Britain which is approved for the disinfection of goods of the kinds specified in paragraph (1) of this Article;

(*d*) that the importer shall, if so required by the proper officer, give such security by bond or otherwise for the due removal of the goods to the said factory as the officer may require; and

(*e*) that all packages containing wool or animal hair produced in or exported from or through the United Arab Republic or the Sudan, or goods mixed therewith, shall be prominently and legibly marked with the words "UNITED ARAB REPUBLIC" or "SUDAN" as the case may be.

(4) This Article does not apply to goods of any kind specified in the Schedule to this Order or to samples of goods completely enclosed in packings or wrappings so as to reduce as far as practicable the risk of infection from anthrax.

W. G. Agnew.

Articles 3, 4(2) and 5(4) SCHEDULE

GOODS TO WHICH THE PROHIBITIONS AND RESTRICTIONS ON IMPORTATION DO NOT APPLY

1. Cashmere yarns which have been bleached and dyed.

2. Mohair yarns.

3. Mohair tops originating from the United States of America or the Republic of South Africa which are imported in unbroken bales as originally shipped from the country of origin and which—

(a) if shipped from the country of origin to Great Britain, are shipped direct or, if transhipped at an intermediate port, are shipped on a through bill of lading which is produced to the proper officer; or

(b) if shipped to Great Britain from a port other than a port in the country of origin, are proved to the satisfaction of the Secretary of State or some person authorised by the Secretary of State in that behalf to be mohair tops originating from the United States of America or the Republic of South Africa (as the case may be).

4. China cashmere (other than dehaired China cashmere to which paragraph 5 of this Schedule applies) which is imported in unbroken bales as originally shipped from the People's Republic of China and which—

(a) if shipped from a port in the People's Republic of China to Great Britain, is shipped direct or, if transhipped at an intermediate port, is shipped on a through bill of lading which is produced to the proper officer; or

(b) if shipped to Great Britain from a port other than a port in the People's Republic of China, is proved to the satisfaction of the Secretary of State or some person authorised by the Secretary of State in that behalf to be China cashmere and to have been shipped from the People's Republic of China.

5. Dehaired China cashmere which is accompanied by an approved certificate to show that it is China cashmere.

6. Mohair (other than Van mohair) which is imported in unbroken bales as originally shipped from the country of origin and which—

(a) if shipped from the country of origin to Great Britain, is shipped direct or, if transhipped at an intermediate port, is shipped on a through bill of lading which is produced to the proper officer; or

(b) if shipped to Great Britain from a port other than a port in the country of origin, is proved to the satisfaction of the Secretary of State or some person authorised by the Secretary of State in that behalf not to be Van mohair.

7. Material of a kind mentioned in Article 5(1) which is accompanied by an approved certificate to show that it has been disinfected abroad in an approved manner and of which a sample has under approved arrangements been tested and found to be free from anthrax.

EXPLANATORY NOTE
(This Note is not part of the Order.)

This Order prohibits the importation into Great Britain, with specified exceptions, of tops and yarns made wholly or partly of goat hair.

The Order also prohibits the importation into Great Britain, with specified exceptions, of goat hair and goods mixed therewith and of any wool or animal hair produced in or exported from or through the United Arab Republic or the Sudan and goods mixed therewith, unless specified conditions are complied with, including a condition that the goods shall be consigned to a factory in Great Britain approved by the Secretary of State for the disinfection of such goods.

This Order supersedes the Order in Council dated 9th March 1921 regulating the importation of certain goods likely to be infected with anthrax and the Anthrax Prevention (Goat Hair and Shaving Brushes) Order 1961. The 1961 Order, which relates only to Great Britain, is revoked and the 1921 Order is revoked in so far as it relates to Great Britain.

STATUTORY INSTRUMENTS

1971 No. 1235

ASSOCIATED STATES

The Anguilla (Administration) Order 1971

Made - - - - 28th July 1971
Coming into Operation 4th August 1971

At the Court at Buckingham Palace, the 28th day of July 1971

Present,

The Queen's Most Excellent Majesty in Council

Her Majesty in exercise of the powers conferred upon Her by section 1(1) of the Anguilla Act 1971(a) is pleased, by and with the advice of Her Privy Council, to order, and it is hereby ordered, as follows: —

Citation, commencement, revocation and termination

1.—(1) This Order may be cited as the Anguilla (Administration) Order 1971.

(2) This Order shall come into operation on 4th August 1971, and the Anguilla (Temporary Provision) Order 1969(b) is revoked with effect from that date.

(3) This Order shall cease to have effect on such date as a Secretary of State may by order appoint.

Interpretation

2.—(1) In this Order—

" the Commissioner " means such person as Her Majesty may appoint by instrument under Her Sign Manual and Signet to be Her Majesty's Commissioner in Anguilla for the purposes of this Order and includes any person appointed by Her Majesty by instructions given through a Secretary of State to act in that office and, to the extent to which a deputy appointed under section 3 of this Order is authorised to act, that deputy ;

" the Constitution " means the Constitution of the Associated State(c) ; and

" the Courts Order " means the West Indies Associated States Supreme Court Order 1967(d).

(2) The Interpretation Act 1889(e) shall apply, with the necessary adaptations, for the purpose of interpreting this Order and otherwise in relation thereto as it applies for the purpose of interpreting and in relation to Acts of the United Kingdom Parliament.

(a) 1971 c. 63. (b) S.I. 1969/371 (1969 I, p. 1016). (c) Schedule 2 to S.I. 1967/228
(1967 I, p. 594). (d) S.I. 1967/223 (1967 I, p. 364). (e) 1889 c. 63.

Commissioner's deputy

3.—(1) Whenever the Commissioner

(a) has occasion to be absent from Anguilla for a period that he has reason to believe will be of short duration ; or

(b) is suffering from an illness that he has reason to believe will be of short duration

he may, by writing under his hand, appoint any person in Anguilla to be his deputy during such absence or illness and in that capacity to perform on his behalf such of the functions of the office of Commissioner as may be specified in the writing.

(2) The powers and authority of the Commissioner shall not be abridged, altered or in any way affected by the appointment of a deputy under this section, and a deputy shall conform to and observe all instructions that the Commissioner may from time to time address to him:

Provided that the question whether or not a deputy has complied with any such instructions shall not be enquired into in any court of law.

(3) A person appointed as a deputy under this section shall hold that appointment for such period as may be specified in the instrument by which he is appointed, and his appointment may be revoked at any time by Her Majesty by instructions given through a Secretary of State or by the Commissioner.

Functions of Commissioner

4.—(1) The Commissioner shall have such powers and other functions as may be conferred upon him by this Order or by or under any other law for the time being in force in Anguilla.

(2) Her Majesty may by instructions given to the Commissioner through a Secretary of State confer upon the Commissioner powers and other functions additional to those conferred upon him by this Order or by or under any other law ; and, unless it is otherwise provided therein, any such instructions shall have the force of law and in that case shall be published in Anguilla in such manner as the Commissioner may direct.

(3) In the exercise of the functions conferred upon him by this Order or by or under any other law the Commissioner shall act in accordance with such instructions as may from time to time be given to him by Her Majesty through a Secretary of State.

(4) The question whether the Commissioner has complied with any such instructions as to the exercise of any of his functions shall not be enquired into in any court of law.

Power to make ordinances

5.—(1) The Commissioner, acting after consultation with the Anguilla Council, may by ordinance make provision for securing and maintaining public safety and public order in Anguilla and generally for securing and maintaining good government within Anguilla.

(2) Any ordinance made under this section shall be published in Anguilla in such manner as the Commissioner may direct.

(3) (a) Any ordinance made under this section may be disallowed by Her Majesty through a Secretary of State.

(b) Whenever an ordinance has been disallowed by Her Majesty notice of the disallowance shall, as soon as is practicable, be published in Anguilla in such manner as the Commissioner may direct and the ordinance shall be annulled with effect from the date of publication of the notice.

(c) The provisions of section 38(2) of the Interpretation Act 1889 shall apply to the annulment of any ordinance under this section as they apply to the repeal of an Act of Parliament, save that any law repealed or amended by or in pursuance of that ordinance shall have effect as from the date of the annulment as if that ordinance had not been made.

Exercise of certain functions by Commissioner

6. So long as this Order is in operation and subject to any ordinances made under section 5 of this Order, all laws for the time being in force in Anguilla (except the Constitution and the Courts Order) shall have effect as if any function conferred thereby upon the Governor, the Cabinet, any Minister or any public officer of the Associated State were exercisable by the Commissioner to such extent as he may consider necessary for the purposes mentioned in that section.

Anguilla Council

7.—(1) There shall be a Council for Anguilla, which shall be called the Anguilla Council.

(2) The Council shall consist of not less than seven members, who shall be elected in accordance with provision made by ordinance under section 5 of this Order, and such number of other members, not exceeding six, as may be appointed by the Commissioner, after consultation with the Council, by writing under his hand.

Qualifications for membership of Council

8. A person shall be qualified for election or appointment as a member of the Council if, but only if, that person—

(a) is a British subject of the age of twenty-one years or upwards ;

(b) is a person who is not disqualified for election or appointment as such by any such ordinances as may be made in that behalf under section 5 of this Order ; and

(c) in the case of an elected member

(i) was born in Anguilla and is domiciled there at the date of his nomination for election ; or

(ii) has resided in Anguilla for a period of not less than three years immediately before the date of his nomination for election and is domiciled there at that date, and is the son or daughter of parents at least one of whom was born in Anguilla.

Oath by members of Anguilla Council

9. Before assuming the functions of his office a member of the Anguilla Council shall make before the Commissioner or some other person authorised in that behalf by the Commissioner an oath of allegiance and an oath for the due execution of his office in the forms set out in the Schedule to this Order.

Dissolution of Council

10.—(1) The Commissioner, acting after consultation with the Anguilla Council, may at any time dissolve the Council.

(2) Unless sooner dissolved the Council shall continue for four years from the date of its first sitting after any general election of members and shall then stand dissolved.

(3) In the exercise of the powers conferred upon him by this section the Commissioner shall act in accordance with the advice of the Council unless in any particular case he is directed by a Secretary of State to act otherwise.

Tenure of office of members of Council

11.—(1) The seat of a member of the Anguilla Council shall become vacant—

(a) at the next dissolution of the Council after his election or appointment ;

(b) if any circumstances arise that, if he were not a member of the Council, would cause him to be disqualified for election or appointment as such ; or

(c) in the case of an appointed member, at the expiration of such time, or upon the occurrence of any such event, as may be specified in the instrument by which he is appointed.

(2) A member of the Council may resign his seat therein by writing under his hand addressed to the Commissioner and his seat shall become vacant when the writing is received by the Commissioner.

Presiding in Council

12. There shall preside at each meeting of the Anguilla Council—

(a) the Commissioner ; or

(b) in the absence of the Commissioner, such member of the Council as the Commissioner may have designated in that behalf.

Proceedings of Council

13.—(1) The Anguilla Council shall not be summoned except by authority of the Commissioner:

Provided that the Commissioner shall summon the Council if so requested in writing by four or more members of the Council.

(2) The Commissioner shall determine what business shall be transacted at each meeting of the Council:

Provided that, if the Commissioner is requested in writing by four or more members of the Council to cause any particular item of business to be placed before the Council, he shall cause that item to be placed before a meeting of the Council.

(3) No business shall be transacted in the Council if objection is taken by any member present that there are less than four members of the Council present besides any member presiding.

(4) Subject to the last foregoing subsection, the Council shall not be disqualified for the transaction of business by reason of any vacancy in the membership of the Council (including any vacancy when the Council is first constituted or is reconstituted at any time) ; and any proceedings in the Council shall be valid notwithstanding that some person who was not entitled to do so took part in those proceedings.

(5) (a) When the Commissioner or other person presiding in the Council considers that the business before the Council makes it desirable, he may summon any person to a meeting of the Council, notwithstanding that the person is not a member of the Council.

(b) Any person so summoned shall be entitled to take part, as if he were an appointed member of the Council, in the proceedings of the Council relating to the matter in respect of which he was summoned.

(6) (a) Where it is desirable to determine the opinion of the Council on any matter by voting, the opinion of the majority of the elected members present and voting shall be regarded as the opinion of the Council.

(b) If on any question the votes of the elected members are equally divided, the Commissioner may give a casting vote.

(7) The Commissioner, acting after consultation with the Council, may make rules regulating the procedure of the Council and the orderly conduct of its proceedings.

Consultation with Council

14.—(1) Subject to the provisions of this section, the Commissioner shall act in co-operation with the Anguilla Council and accordingly shall consult with the Council in the formulation of policy and in the exercise of the powers vested in him by any law other than this Order.

(2) The Commissioner shall not be obliged to consult with the Council in the exercise of any power conferred upon him by any law other than this Order that he is empowered or directed by that or any other law to exercise without consulting the Council.

(3) The Commissioner shall not be obliged by subsection (1) of this section to consult with the Council in any case in which in his judgment—

(a) the matters to be decided are too unimportant to require consultation with the Council thereon ;

(b) such consultation would involve material prejudice to Her Majesty's service ; or

(c) the matters to be decided are too urgent to admit of such consultation by the time within which it may be necessary for him to act:

Provided that in any case falling within paragraph (c) the Commissioner shall report the action he has taken to the Council at the first convenient opportunity.

(4) In every case in which the Commissioner is required by section 5(1), 7(2) or 13(7) of this Order or by subsection (1) of this section to consult with the Council, he shall act in accordance with the advice of the Council unless in any particular case he has first obtained the approval of a Secretary of State for acting otherwise:

Provided that, if in his judgment the matter is too urgent to admit of his obtaining such approval within the time in which it may be necessary for him to act in any particular case, he may act in that case without such approval, in which event he shall forthwith report the matter to a Secretary of State with the reasons for his action.

(5) Whenever the Commissioner acts against the advice of the Council, any member of the Council may require that there shall be recorded in the minutes any advice or opinion he may give upon the question at issue and his reasons ; and if he does so the Commissioner shall forthwith transmit copies of the minutes to a Secretary of State.

Existing laws

15.—(1) It is hereby declared, for the avoidance of doubts, that, subject to the provisions of this Order, all laws for the time being in force in the Associated State have full force and effect in Anguilla :

Provided that so long as this Order is in operation no law enacted by the Legislature of the Associated State after the commencement of this Order shall extend to Anguilla unless it is provided in any ordinance made under section 5 of this Order that it shall so extend.

(2) Ordinances made under section 5 of this Order may provide that any law of the Associated State for the time being in force (except the Constitution and the Courts Order) shall have effect in relation to Anguilla with such amendments for the purposes mentioned in that section as may be specified in such ordinances :

Provided that no provision making amendments to any law of the Associated State shall be brought into effect without the approval of a Secretary of State.

Discharge of magistrate's functions

16.—(1) The Commissioner may appoint any fit and proper person to exercise within Anguilla any powers, duties or jurisdiction conferred upon any magistrate or justice of the peace by any law for the time being in force in Anguilla and, subject to the provisions of any instructions given to the Commissioner by Her Majesty through a Secretary of State concerning the tenure of office of any such person, may terminate any such appointment.

(2) Persons appointed under the preceding subsection shall, for the purposes of any law for the time being in force in Anguilla, be regarded as holding offices constituted for Anguilla.

Discharge of functions of Supreme Court

17.—(1) The Commissioner, acting in pursuance of instructions given by Her Majesty through a Secretary of State, may appoint fit and proper persons to exercise in or in relation to Anguilla any powers, duties or jurisdiction conferred upon the Court of Appeal or, as the case may be, the High Court established by the Courts Order or upon the Chief Justice or any other judge of either of those courts, or upon any officer of either of those courts, by any law for the time being in force in, or having effect in relation to, Anguilla and, subject to the provisions of any such instructions concerning the tenure of office of any such person, may terminate any such appointment.

(2) Any powers, duties or jurisdiction exercisable in or in relation to Anguilla by any person or persons appointed under the preceding subsection shall, to the extent that it is so provided in any instructions given to the Commissioner by Her Majesty through a Secretary of State, be so exercisable by that person or those persons, as the case may be, to the exclusion of any other person or persons.

(3) Any reference in any law for the time being in force in, or having effect in relation to, Anguilla to the Court of Appeal or, as the case may be, the High Court established by the Courts Order or to the Chief Justice or any other judge of either of those courts or to any officer of either of those courts shall, to the extent that any person or persons appointed under subsection (1) of this section are authorised to exercise in or in relation to Anguilla any powers, duties or jurisdiction, have effect in relation to such powers, duties or jurisdiction as if that reference included a reference to that person or, as the case may be, those persons.

(4) Persons appointed under subsection (1) of this section shall, for the purposes of any law for the time being in force in Anguilla, be regarded as holding offices constituted for Anguilla.

Transitional provisions

18.—(1) The person who immediately before the commencement of this Order holds office as Her Majesty's Commissioner in Anguilla shall be deemed to have been appointed as such for the purposes of this Order.

(2) Any regulation made for the purposes of the Anguilla (Temporary Provision) Order 1969 and in force immediately before the commencement of this Order shall, with effect from such commencement, have effect as if it were an ordinance made under section 5 of this Order and may be amended or revoked accordingly.

(3) The persons who, immediately before the commencement of this Order, were members of the existing Anguilla Council shall be deemed to be members of the Council established by section 7 of this Order until the next dissolution thereof ; and the provisions of section 11 of this Order shall apply in relation to such persons.

W. G. Agnew.

SCHEDULE Section 9

FORMS OF OATHS AND AFFIRMATIONS

1. *Oath of Allegiance*

I, ..., do swear that I will be faithful and bear true allegiance to Her Majesty Queen Elizabeth the Second, Her Heirs and Successors, according to law. So help me God.

2. *Affirmation of Allegiance*

I, ..., do solemnly and sincerely affirm and declare that I will be faithful and bear true allegiance to Her Majesty Queen Elizabeth the Second, Her Heirs and Successors, according to law.

3. *Oath for due execution of office*

I, ..., do swear that I will well and truly serve Her Majesty Queen Elizabeth the Second, Her Heirs and Successors, in the office of a member of the Anguilla Council. So help me God.

4. *Affirmation for due execution of office*

I, ..., do solemnly and sincerely affirm and declare that I will well and truly serve Her Majesty Queen Elizabeth the Second, Her Heirs and Successors, in the office of a member of the Anguilla Council.

EXPLANATORY NOTE

(This Note is not part of the Order.)

This Order revokes the Anguilla (Temporary Provision) Order 1969, and makes new provision with respect to the functions of Her Majesty's Commissioner in Anguilla, including provision conferring upon him power to make ordinances. The Order also establishes a Council for Anguilla and provides for the Commissioner to act in co-operation with the Council.

STATUTORY INSTRUMENTS

1971 No. 1236

ANTARCTICA

The Antarctic Treaty (Specially Protected Area) Order 1971

Made - - - -	28th July 1971
Laid before Parliament	3rd August 1971
Coming into Operation	4th August 1971

At the Court at Buckingham Palace, the 28th day of July 1971

Present,

The Queen's Most Excellent Majesty in Council

Her Majesty, in exercise of the powers conferred upon Her by section 7(2)(*b*) of the Antarctic Treaty Act 1967(a), is pleased, by and with the advice of Her Privy Council, to order, and it is hereby ordered, as follows :—

1. This Order may be cited as the Antarctic Treaty (Specially Protected Area) Order 1971 and shall come into operation on 4th August 1971.

2. For the purposes of the Antarctic Treaty Act 1967, the following area, being an area which has been recommended for inclusion in Annex B to Schedule 2 to the said Act, is designated as a Specially Protected Area :

SPECIALLY PROTECTED AREA No. 16

COPPERMINE PENINSULA, ROBERT ISLAND,

SOUTH SHETLAND ISLANDS

Lat. 62° 23'S., Long. 59° 42'W.

This area, the location of which is shown on the map in the Schedule hereto, comprises all the land west of a line drawn from north to south across the Peninsula, 100 metres west of the two shelters found on the isthmus.

W. G. Agnew.

(a) 1967 c. 65.

SCHEDULE

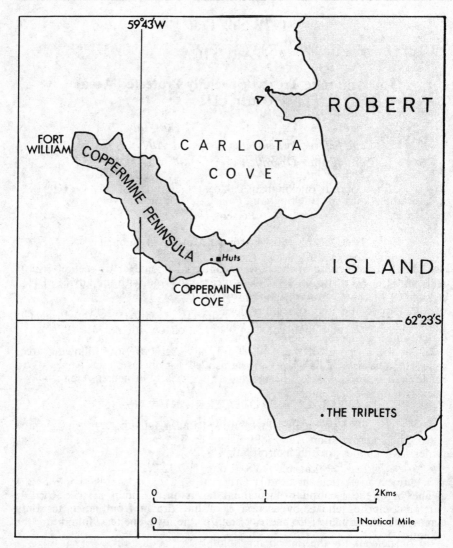

EXPLANATORY NOTE

(This Note is not part of the Order.)

This Order designates as a Specially Protected Area for the purposes of the Antarctic Treaty Act 1967 a further area in the Antarctic which has been recommended for inclusion in Annex B to the Agreed Measures for the Conservation of Antarctic Fauna and Flora (Schedule 2 to the Act) in pursuance of Article IX(1) of the Antarctic Treaty.

STATUTORY INSTRUMENTS

1971 No. 1237

DIPLOMATIC AND INTERNATIONAL IMMUNITIES AND PRIVILEGES

The Commonwealth Countries and Republic of Ireland (Immunities and Privileges) Order 1971

Made - - - - 28th July 1971
Laid before Parliament 3rd August 1971
Coming into Operation 1st September 1971

At the Court at Buckingham Palace, the 28th day of July 1971

Present,

The Queen's Most Excellent Majesty in Council

Her Majesty, by virtue and in exercise of the powers conferred on Her by section 12 of the Consular Relations Act 1968(a), as amended by section 4 of the Diplomatic and other Privileges Act 1971(b), or otherwise in Her Majesty vested, is pleased, by and with the advice of Her Privy Council, to order, and it is hereby ordered, as follows:—

1. This Order may be cited as the Commonwealth Countries and Republic of Ireland (Immunities and Privileges) Order 1971 and shall come into operation on 1st September 1971.

2.—(1) In this Order "the Act" means the Consular Relations Act 1968. (2) The Interpretation Act 1889(c) shall apply for the interpretation of this Order as it applies for the interpretation of an Act of Parliament.

3. Subject to Article 11 of this Order, the like privileges and immunities as are conferred on consular officers and on members of their families forming part of their households by section 1 of the Act read with Section II of Chapter II in Schedule 1 to the Act shall be conferred

(a) on persons for the time being holding any of the offices or an office in any of the classes of office specified in Schedule 1 to this Order, and on members of their families forming part of their households, and

(b) on members of the staff of any such officer as is mentioned in paragraph (a) of this Article who appear to the Secretary of State to perform duties substantially corresponding to duties which, in the case of a foreign sovereign Power, would be performed by a consular officer, and on members of their families forming part of their households.

4. Subject to Article 11 of this Order, the like privileges and immunities as are conferred on consular employees and on members of their families forming part of their households by section 1 of the Act read with Section II

(a) 1968 c. 18.   (b) 1971 c. 64.   (c) 1889 c. 63.

of Chapter II in Schedule 1 to the Act shall be conferred on members of the staff of any such officer as is mentioned in Article 3(*a*) of this Order who appear to the Secretary of State to perform duties substantially corresponding to those which, in the case of a foreign sovereign Power, would be performed by a consular employee, and on members of their families forming part of their households.

5. Subject to Article 11 of this Order, the like privileges and immunities as are conferred on members of the service staff of a consular post and on members of their families forming part of their households by section 1 of the Act read with Section II of Chapter II in Schedule 1 to the Act shall be conferred on members of the staff of any such officer as is mentioned in Article 3(*a*) of this Order who appear to the Secretary of State to perform duties substantially corresponding to those which, in the case of a consular post of a foreign sovereign Power, would be performed by a member of the service staff, and on members of their families forming part of their households.

6. The like privilege as is conferred on members of the private staff of members of a consular post by section 1 of the Act read with paragraph 2 of Article 48 in Schedule 1 to the Act shall be conferred on members of the private staff of any such officer, or of any member of the staff of such officer, as is mentioned in Articles 3, 4 or 5 of this Order.

7. The like privileges and immunities as are conferred on a consular post by Section I of Chapter II in Schedule 1 to the Act shall be conferred on a post which is headed by any such officer as is mentioned in Article 3(*a*) of this Order.

8. The like exemption from dues and taxes as is accorded under Article 32 in Schedule 1 to the Act to the residence of the career head of a consular post shall be extended to the residence of any such officer as is mentioned in Article 3(*a*) of this Order and to the residence of any such member of his staff as is mentioned in Articles 3(*b*) or 4 of this Order, provided that, in either case, the residence is owned or leased by the country which employs the officer concerned or by any person acting on its behalf.

9.—(1) Subject to Article 11 of this Order, the like privileges and immunities as are conferred on honorary consular officers by section 1 of the Act read with Chapter III in Schedule 1 to the Act shall be conferred on such officers as are mentioned in paragraph (2) of this Article.

(2) The officers referred to in paragraph (1) of this Article are persons for the time being holding any of the offices specified in Schedule 2 to this Order.

10. The like privileges and immunities as are conferred on a post headed by an honorary consular officer by Chapter III in Schedule 1 to the Act shall be conferred on a post which is headed by any such person as is mentioned in Article 9(2) of this Order.

11.—(1) Any such officer or member of the staff as is mentioned in Article 3 or Article 9(2) of this Order who is comprised within the definition of " national of the receiving State " in section 1(2) of the Act and is not also a citizen of the country by which he is employed or who is permanently resident in the United Kingdom shall enjoy only immunity from jurisdiction and personal inviolability in respect of official acts performed in the exercise of his functions, and the privilege provided in paragraph 3 of Article 44 in

Schedule 1 to the Act. Privileges and immunities shall not be conferred under this Order on any member of the family of such an officer.

(2) Privileges and immunities shall not be conferred under this Order on any such member of the staff of an officer as is mentioned in Articles 4 or 5 of this Order or on any member of the family of such a member of the staff if the member of staff is comprised within the definition of "national of the receiving State" in section 1(2) of the Act and is not also a citizen of the country by which he is employed, or is permanently resident in the United Kingdom.

(3) Privileges and immunities shall not be conferred under this Order on any member of the family of any such officer as is mentioned in Article 3(a) of this Order or on any member of the family of any member of the staff of any such officer if the member of the family is comprised within the definition of "national of the receiving State" in section 1(2) of the Act or is permanently resident in the United Kingdom.

(4) The privilege referred to in Article 6 of this Order shall not be conferred on any member of a private staff who is comprised within the definition of "national of the receiving State" in section 1(2) of the Act and is not also a citizen of the country by which his employer is employed, or who is permanently resident in the United Kingdom.

12. The Orders referred to in Schedule 3 to this Order are hereby revoked.

W. G. Agnew.

SCHEDULE 1
OFFICES

The Associated States
   The Commissioner for the Eastern Caribbean, London
Malawi
   The Chief Agent, London
Nauru
   The Representative in the United Kingdom, London
Republic of Ireland
   The Trade Inspector, Liverpool

Classes of Office

Trade Commissioners and Assistant Trade Commissioners for any independent country within the Commonwealth.
   Migration Officers for the Commonwealth of Australia.
   Immigration Officers for Canada.
   Assistant Commissioners for India.
   Regional Welfare Officers for Jamaica.
   Agents General for the States of Australia.
   Agents General for the Provinces of Canada.

SCHEDULE 2
OFFICES

Cyprus
   The Honorary Commissioner, Glasgow

SCHEDULE 3

Orders revoked	References
The Commonwealth Countries and Republic of Ireland (Immunities) (No. 2) Order 1967	S.I. 1967/815 (1967 II, p. 2431).
The Commonwealth Countries and Republic of Ireland (Immunities) (Amendment) Order 1968	S.I. 1968/464 (1968 I, p. 1180).
The Commonwealth Countries and Republic of Ireland (Immunities) (Amendment) (No. 2) Order 1968	S.I. 1968/1374 (1968 II, p. 3813).
The Commonwealth Countries and Republic of Ireland (Immunities) (Amendment) Order 1969	S.I. 1969/142 (1969 I. p. 383).

EXPLANATORY NOTE

(This Note is not part of the Order.)

This Order, which is made under the Consular Relations Act 1968, as amended by the Diplomatic and other Privileges Act 1971, supersedes the Orders listed in Schedule 3, which are revoked. It confers

(i) on the persons holding offices specified in Schedules 1 and 2 to the Order, and on members of their families forming part of their households,

(ii) on posts which are headed by such persons,

(iii) on members of their staffs, and on members of their families forming part of their households,

the like privileges and immunities as are conferred by section 1 read with Schedule 1 of the Consular Relations Act 1968 on a consular post and on persons connected with a consular post of a foreign sovereign Power.

In addition it accords relief from rates and taxes for the residences of officers whose offices are specified in Schedule 1 to the Order and certain members of their staffs.

STATUTORY   INSTRUMENTS

1971 No. 1238
ADMINISTRATION OF ESTATES
The Consular Conventions (Polish People's Republic) Order 1971

Made - - - -	28th July 1971
Laid before Parliament	3rd August 1971
Coming into Operation	13th August 1971

At the Court at Buckingham Palace, the 28th day of July 1971

Present,

The Queen's Most Excellent Majesty in Council

Whereas by section 6(1) of the Consular Conventions Act 1949(a) (hereinafter referred to as "the Act") it is enacted that Her Majesty may by Order in Council direct that sections 1 and 2 of the Act (which provide for the exercise by consular officers of certain powers in relation to the property of deceased persons) shall apply to any foreign State specified in the Order, being a State with which a Consular Convention providing for matters for which provision is made by those sections has been concluded by Her Majesty:

And whereas such a Consular Convention between Her Majesty in respect of the United Kingdom of Great Britain and Northern Ireland and the Council of State of the Polish People's Republic was signed at London on 23rd February 1967(b) and will enter into force on 13th August 1971 :

Now, therefore, Her Majesty, by virtue and in exercise of the powers in that behalf by the Act or otherwise in Her Majesty vested, is pleased, by and with the advice of Her Privy Council, to order, and it is hereby ordered, as follows:

1. This Order may be cited as the Consular Conventions (Polish People's Republic) Order 1971 and shall come into operation on 13th August 1971.

2. Sections 1 and 2 of the Act shall apply to the Polish People's Republic.

W. G. Agnew.

EXPLANATORY NOTE

(This Note is not part of the Order.)

This Order provides for the application of sections 1 and 2 of the Consular Conventions Act 1949 to Poland and enables Her Majesty to give effect to the provisions relating to administration of estates in the Consular Convention between the United Kingdom and Poland which was signed at London on 23rd February 1967.

The purport of sections 1 and 2 of the Act is stated in the preamble to this Order. Section 1 relates to England and, with the modifications contained in section 7 of the Act, to Northern Ireland ; section 2 relates to Scotland.

(a) 1949 c. 29.	(b) Cmnd. 3307.

STATUTORY INSTRUMENTS

1971 No. 1239

JUDICIAL COMMITTEE

The Hong Kong (Appeal to Privy Council) (Amendment) Order 1971

Made - - - - 28*th July* 1971

Coming into Operation 4*th August* 1971

At the Court at Buckingham Palace, the 28th day of July 1971

Present,

The Queen's Most Excellent Majesty in Council

Her Majesty, in exercise of the powers conferred on Her by section 24 of the Judicial Committee Act 1833(**a**) and of all other powers enabling Her in that behalf, is pleased, by and with the advice of Her Privy Council, to order, and it is hereby ordered, as follows: —

1.—(1) This Order may be cited as the Hong Kong (Appeal to Privy Council) (Amendment) Order 1971 and shall be construed as one with the Hong Kong (Appeal to Privy Council) Order in Council 1909(**b**), which Order, as amended by the Hong Kong (Appeal to Privy Council) (Amendment) Order in Council 1957(**c**), is hereinafter referred to as "the principal Order".

(2) This Order, the Hong Kong (Appeal to Privy Council) Order in Council 1909 and the Hong Kong (Appeal to Privy Council) (Amendment) Order in Council 1957 may be cited together as the Hong Kong (Appeal to Privy Council) Orders 1909 to 1971.

(3) This Order shall come into operation on 4th August 1971.

2. Paragraph (*a*) of Rule 2 of the Rules contained in the principal Order is hereby amended by the substitution for the reference to $5,000, in both places where it occurs, of a reference to $50,000.

3. Paragraph (*a*) of Rule 4 of the Rules contained in the principal Crder is hereby amended by the substitution for the reference to $15,000 of a reference to $30,000.

W. G. Agnew.

(a) 1833 c. 41. (b) S. R. & O. (Rev. XI, p. 374: 1909, p. 805).
(c) S.I. 1957/2059 (1957 I, p. 1203).

EXPLANATORY NOTE
(This Note is not part of the Order.)

The Rules regulating appeals from Hong Kong to the Privy Council confer a right of appeal from any final judgment where the matter in dispute or claim amounts to $5,000 or upwards. This Order increases that amount to $50,000. It also increases the maximum security that may be required from an appellant for the due prosecution of an appeal, and for any costs awarded against him, from $15,000 to $30,000.

STATUTORY INSTRUMENTS

1971 No. 1240

CARIBBEAN AND NORTH ATLANTIC TERRITORIES

The Virgin Islands Constitution (Amendment) Order 1971

Made - - - -	28*th July* 1971
Laid before Parliament	3*rd August* 1971
Coming into Operation	4*th August* 1971

At the Court at Buckingham Palace, the 28th day of July 1971

Present,

The Queen's Most Excellent Majesty in Council

Her Majesty, by virtue and in exercise of the powers vested in Her by sections 5 and 7 of the West Indies Act 1962(**a**) and of all other powers enabling Her in that behalf, is pleased, by and with the advice of Her Privy Council, to order, and it is hereby ordered, as follows:—

1.—(1) This Order may be cited as the Virgin Islands Constitution (Amendment) Order 1971.

(2) This Order shall be construed as one with the Virgin Islands Constitution Orders 1967 to 1970(**b**) and those Orders and this Order may be cited together as the Virgin Islands Constitution Orders 1967 to 1971.

(3) This Order shall come into operation on 4th August 1971.

2.—(1) Section 3 of the Virgin Islands (Constitution) Order 1967 is amended by the deletion of paragraph (1) and the substitution of the following:—

"(1) There shall be a Governor of the Virgin Islands who shall be appointed by Her Majesty by Commission under Her Sign Manual and Signet and shall hold office during Her Majesty's pleasure".

(2) Any reference in the Virgin Islands Constitution Orders 1967 to 1970 to the Administrator shall be construed as a reference to the Governor.

3.—(1) Any reference to the Administrator in any existing law in force or otherwise having effect in, or in relation to, the Virgin Islands immediately before the commencement of this Order shall, in respect of any period commencing on or after the commencement of this Order, be construed as a reference to the Governor.

(2) For the purposes of this Order, the expression "existing law" means any Order in Council, ordinance, law, rule, regulation or other instrument made or having effect as part of the law of the Virgin Islands, but does not include any Act of the Parliament of the United Kingdom so having effect.

W. G. Agnew.

(**a**) 1962 c. 19.   (**b**) S.I. 1967/471, 1969/1065, 1970/1942 (1967 I, p. 1418; 1969 II, p. 3122; 1970 III, p. 6341).

EXPLANATORY NOTE

(This Note is not part of the Order.)

This Order changes the title of the Administrator of the Virgin Islands to that of Governor and replaces references to the Administrator by references to the Governor in the Virgin Islands Constitution Orders 1967 to 1970, and in other laws in force in the Virgin Islands.

STATUTORY INSTRUMENTS

1971 No. 1241

HEALTH VISITING AND SOCIAL WORK

The Central Council for Education and Training in Social Work Order 1971

Made - - -	*28th July* 1971
Laid before Parliament	*3rd August* 1971
Coming into Operation	*1st October* 1971

At the Court at Buckingham Palace, the 28th day of July 1971.

Present,

The Queen's Most Excellent Majesty in Council

Her Majesty, in exercise of the powers conferred upon Her by section 3(3) of the Health Visiting and Social Work (Training) Act 1962(a), as amended by section 11 of the Local Authority Social Services Act 1970(b), and of all other powers enabling Her in that behalf, is pleased, by and with the advice of Her Privy Council, to order, and it is hereby ordered, as follows:—

Citation and Commencement

1. This Order may be cited as the Central Council for Education and Training in Social Work Order 1971, and shall come into operation on 1st October 1971.

Interpretation

2.—(1) In this Order, unless the context otherwise requires:—

"The Act of 1962" means the Health Visiting and Social Work (Training) Act 1962;

"the Act of 1968" means the Social Work (Scotland) Act 1968(c);

"the Council" means the Central Council for Education and Training in Social Work.

(2) The Interpretation Act 1889(d) shall apply to the interpretation of this Order as it applies to the interpretation of an Act of Parliament.

Conferment on the Council of functions in relation to other social work

3. The functions of the Council as set out in section 3(1) and (2) of the Act of 1962 (functions of the Central Council for Education and Training in Social Work) shall be extended to include such social work as is required in the services provided under the enactments set out in Schedule 1 to this Order or any corresponding enactments in force in Northern Ireland, or similar services provided by a voluntary organisation.

Modification of the constitution of the Council

4. The First Schedule to the Act of 1962 (Constitution, etc., of Councils) shall be modified in accordance with the provisions set out in Schedule 2 to this Order.

W. G. Agnew.

(a) 1962 c. 33.   (b) 1970 c. 42.   (c) 1968 c. 49.   (d) 1889 c. 63.

Article 3
SCHEDULE 1

1. Services provided under enactments applying to England and Wales

Enactment	Nature of functions
(a) Enactments specified in the Local Authority Social Services Act 1970 (c. 42). Schedule 1.	Services assigned to the social services committee in so far as such services are not included in section 3(5) of the Act of 1962.
(b) Sections 1, 2 and 9 of the Children and Young Persons Act 1969 (c. 54) in so far as they are not included in (a) above.	Function of a local authority in its capacity as a local education authority.
(c) Criminal Justice Act 1948 (11 and 12 Geo. 6. c. 58). Sections 45 and 46; 5th Schedule.	Probation and after care services.
(d) Education Acts 1944-1970 (7 and 8 Geo. 6. c. 31: 9 and 10 Geo. 6. c. 50; 11 and 12 Geo. 6 c. 40; 1 and 2 Eliz. 2. c. 33; 7 and 8 Eliz. 2. c. 60; 10 and 11 Eliz. 2. c. 12; 1964 c. 82; 1965 c. 3; 1967 c. 3; 1968 c. 17; 1968 c. 37; 1970 c. 14; 1970 c. 52).	Functions of a local authority in their capacity as a local education authority.
(e) National Health Service Act 1946 (as amended) (9 and 10 Geo. 6. c. 81).	Services provided under Part II of the Act and administered by Regional Hospital Boards and Boards of Governors of Teaching Hospitals.

2. Services provided under enactments applying to Scotland

Services provided under the Act of 1968 in so far as such services are not included in section 3(5) of the Act of 1962 or under sections 3 and 12 of the National Health Service (Scotland) Act 1947 (c. 27).

Article 4
SCHEDULE 2

Modification of the Constitution of the Council

1. In paragraph 1 of the First Schedule to the Act of 1962 for the words "thirty-two" there shall be substituted the words "fifty-three".

2. For paragraph 4 of the First Schedule to the Act of 1962 there shall be substituted the following paragraph:—

"4. The other members of the Central Council for Education and Training in Social Work shall be appointed as follows:—

(a) Nine by the Ministers of whom—

(i) not fewer than three shall be appointed after consultation with such voluntary organisations providing services similar to any service provided under any of the enactments specified in section 3(5) or in any Order in Council made under section 3(3) of this Act as the Ministers think fit,

(ii) not fewer than one shall be appointed from England or Wales and not fewer than one from Scotland after consultation with such bodies concerned with, or representing organisations of persons concerned with the provision of education and training in social work as the Ministers think fit, but other than those separately represented on the Council, and

(iii) not fewer than two shall be appointed after consultation with such organisations as are considered by the Ministers to represent social workers but other than those separately represented on the Council.

(b) One by the Governor of Northern Ireland.

(c) Three by the Association of Municipal Corporations.

(d) Three by the County Councils Association.

(e) Two by the Scottish local authority associations.

(f) One by the Central Council of Probation and After-Care Committees.

(g) One by the Inner London Education Authority.

(h) One by the Regional Hospital Boards.

(i) Two by the Committee of Vice-Chancellors and Principals of the Universities of the United Kingdom.

(j) One by the Council for National Academic Awards.

(k) One by the Committee of Directors of Polytechnics.

(l) One by the Association of Principals of Technical Institutions jointly with the Association of Colleges for Further and Higher Education.

(m) One by the Association of Teachers in Technical Institutions.

(n) One by the Joint University Council for Social and Public Administration.

(o) Two by the Association of Social Work Teachers.

(p) One by the Local Government Training Board.

(q) One by the National Institute for Social Work Training.

(r) Eight by the British Association of Social Workers.

(s) Two after consultation with such organisations as are considered by the Ministers to represent Directors of Social Services in England and Wales.

(t) One by the Association of Directors of Social Work (in Scotland).

(u) One by the Conference of Principal Probation Officers.

(v) Two by the National Association of Probation Officers.

(w) One by the Residential Child Care Association.

(x) One by the British Medical Association.

(y) One by the Society of Medical Officers of Health.

(z) One by the Joint Committee of the Royal Colleges, the Royal Scottish Corporations and the Central Consultants and Specialists Committee (known as the Joint Consultants Committee).

(z) (i) One by a proposed advisory council for the personal social services in England and Wales.

(z) (ii) One by the Advisory Council for Probation and After-Care.

(z) (iii) One by the Advisory Council on Social Work (in Scotland).

3. In place of paragraph 11 of the First Schedule to the Act of 1962 there shall be substituted the following paragraph:—

"11. The Ministers shall ensure that at least three members of the Central Council for Education and Training in Social Work are persons who at the time of their appointment are ordinarily resident in Wales; the Health Ministers and the Secretary of State for Education and Science shall ensure that at least one member of the Council for the Education and Training of Health Visitors is a person who at the time of his appointment is ordinarily resident in Wales; and shall, if necessary, make their appointments accordingly.".

4. Paragraphs 7 and 8 of the First Schedule to the Act of 1962 shall be repealed.

5. In paragraph 10 of the First Schedule to the Act of 1962 for the words "each Council" there shall be substituted the words, "the Council for the Education and Training of Health Visitors".

6. After paragraph 20 of the First Schedule to the Act of 1962 there shall be inserted the following paragraph:—

"*Interpretation*

21. In this Schedule "The Ministers" means the Secretaries of State respectively for Social Services, the Home Department, Education and Science, Scotland and Wales, the Minister of Health and Social Services for Northern Ireland and the Minister of Home Affairs for Northern Ireland.".

EXPLANATORY NOTE

(This Note is not part of the Order.)

This Order, made under section 3(3) of the Health Visiting and Social Work (Training) Act 1962, extends the functions of the Central Council for Education and Training in Social Work to include social work required in the services provided under the enactments set out in Schedule 1 or any corresponding enactments in force in Northern Ireland or similar services provided by a voluntary organisation.

The Order also, by Schedule 2, makes modifications to the constitution of the Central Council for Education and Training in Social Work.

STATUTORY INSTRUMENTS

1971 No. 1242

FUGITIVE CRIMINAL

The Fugitive Offenders (Designated Commonwealth Countries) Order 1971

Made - - -	*28th July* 1971
Laid before Parliament	*3rd August* 1971
Coming into Operation	*16th August* 1971

At the Court at Buckingham Palace, the 28th day of July 1971

Present,

The Queen's Most Excellent Majesty in Council

Her Majesty, in exercise of the powers conferred on Her by section 2(1) of the Fugitive Offenders Act 1967(a), is pleased, by and with the advice of Her Privy Council, to order, and it is hereby ordered, as follows :—

1. This Order may be cited as the Fugitive Offenders (Designated Commonwealth Countries) Order 1971 and shall come into operation on 16th August 1971.

2. Nauru is hereby designated for the purposes of section 1 of the Fugitive Offenders Act 1967.

W. G. Agnew.

EXPLANATORY NOTE

(This Note is not part of the Order.)

Section 2(1) of the Fugitive Offenders Act 1967 enables any country within the Commonwealth to be designated by Order in Council for the purposes of section 1 of the Act (so that the provisions of the Act relating to the return of offenders to the independent Commonwealth countries will apply). This Order designates Nauru for those purposes.

(a) 1967 c. 68.

STATUTORY INSTRUMENTS

1971 No. 1243

MINISTERS OF THE CROWN

The Transfer of Functions (Development Fund) Order 1971

Made - - - -	28*th July* 1971
Laid before Parliament	3*rd August* 1971
Coming into Operation	4*th August* 1971

At the Court at Buckingham Palace, the 28th day of July 1971

Present,

The Queen's Most Excellent Majesty in Council.

Her Majesty, in pursuance of section 1 of the Ministers of the Crown (Transfer of Functions) Act 1946(a), is pleased, by and with the advice of Her Privy Council, to order, and it is hereby ordered, as follows:—

Citation, interpretation and commencement

1.—(1) This Order may be cited as the Transfer of Functions (Development Fund) Order 1971.

(2) The Interpretation Act 1889(b) applies for the interpretation of this Order as it applies for the interpretation of an Act of Parliament.

(3) In this Order " instrument ", without prejudice to the generality of that expression, includes in particular Royal Warrants, Orders in Council, orders, regulations, schemes, memoranda and articles of association, agreements and other documents; and any reference in this Order to an enactment is a reference to it as amended by or under any other enactment.

(4) This Order shall come into operation on 4th August 1971.

Transfer of functions from Treasury to Secretary of State

2. There are hereby transferred to the Secretary of State the functions conferred on the Treasury by Part I and section 18 of the Development and Road Improvement Funds Act 1909(c) (which relate to the Development Commissioners and the development fund) except the functions conferred on the Treasury by section 2(5) of that Act (which provides for the management of the development fund to be regulated by Treasury minute).

Supplemental

3.—(1) There are hereby transferred to the Secretary of State—

(a) the development fund and all other property to which the Treasury were entitled immediately before the coming into operation of this Order in connection with any functions transferred by this Order; and

(b) all rights and liabilities to which the Treasury were then entitled or subject in connection with any such functions.

(2) Any enactment or instrument passed or made before the coming into operation of this Order shall have effect, so far as may be necessary for the

---

(a) 1946 c. 31.	(b) 1889 c. 63.	(c) 1909 c. 47.

purpose or in consequence of any transfer effected by this Order, as if for any reference to the Treasury or an officer of the Treasury there were substituted a reference to, or to an officer of, the Secretary of State.

(3) This Order shall not affect the validity of anything done by or in relation to the Treasury before the coming into operation of this Order; and anything which, at the time of the coming into operation of this Order, is in process of being done by or in relation to the Treasury (including in particular any legal proceedings then pending to which the Treasury are a party) may, if it relates to any functions, property, rights or liabilities transferred by this Order, be continued by or in relation to the Secretary of State.

(4) Any approval, conditions, direction, regulations or terms given or made or other thing whatsover done by the Treasury in the exercise of any function transferred by this Order shall, if in force at the coming into operation of this Order, continue in force and have effect as if given, made or done by the Secretary of State; and any application made to the Treasury under Part I of the said Act of 1909 and pending immediately before the coming into operation of this Order shall have effect as if made to the Secretary of State.

W. G. Agnew.

EXPLANATORY NOTE

(This Note is not part of the Order.)

This Order transfers to the Secretary of State the functions of the Treasury relating to the development fund except the function of regulating the management of the fund by Treasury minute. The Order does not transfer any of the Development Commissioners' functions.

STATUTORY INSTRUMENTS

1971 No. 1244 (C.32)

SUPREME COURT OF JUDICATURE, ENGLAND
MAGISTRATES' COURTS
The Administration of Justice Act 1970 (Commencement No. 5) Order 1971

Made - - - 26*th July* 1971

The Lord Chancellor, in exercise of the powers conferred on him by section 54(4) of the Administration of Justice Act 1970(a), hereby makes the following Order :—

1.—(1) This Order may be cited as the Administration of Justice Act 1970 (Commencement No. 5) Order 1971.

(2) In this Order "the Act" means the Administration of Justice Act 1970.

(3) The Interpretation Act 1889(b) shall apply to this Order as it applies to an Act of Parliament.

2. The provisions of the Act specified in the Schedule to this Order shall come into operation on 1st October 1971.

Dated 26th July 1971.

Hailsham of St. Marylebone, C.

(a) 1970 c. 31.   (b) 1889 c. 63.

SCHEDULE

Provisions of the Act	Subject matter of provisions
Section 1	Redistribution of business among divisions of the High Court.
Section 2	Admiralty Court.
Section 3	Commercial Court.
Section 4	Power of judges of Commercial Court to take arbitrations.
Section 50	Proof of age before magistrates.
Section 54(3) so far as it relates to the provisions of Schedule 11 mentioned in the last item of this Schedule.	Repeals.
Schedule 1	High Court business assigned to Family Division.
Schedule 2	Amendment of enactments consequential on section 1 of the Act.
Schedule 3	Application of Arbitration Act 1950(a) to judge-arbitrators.
Schedule 11 so far as it relates to sections 6, 9 and 10 of the Guardianship of Infants Act 1886(b), the Administration of Estates Act 1925(c) and sections 5(1), 58 and 225 of the Supreme Court of Judicature (Consolidation) Act 1925(d).	Enactments repealed.

EXPLANATORY NOTE

(This Note is not part of the Order.)

This Order brings into operation on 1st October 1971 the provisions of the Administration of Justice Act 1970 relating to the reorganisation of the High Court, the power of Commercial Court judges to take arbitrations and the proof of age in magistrates' courts. These are the only provisions of the Act which have not previously been brought into force.

(a) 1950 c. 27.   (b) 1886 c. 27.

(c) 1925 c. 23.   (d) 1925 c. 49.

STATUTORY INSTRUMENTS

1971 No. 1245 (L.30)

SUPREME COURT OF JUDICATURE, ENGLAND

FEES AND STAMPS

The Supreme Court Fees (Amendment) Order 1971

Made - - -		*27th July* 1971
Coming into Operation		*1st October* 1971

The Lord Chancellor, the Judges of the Supreme Court and the Treasury, in exercise of the powers and authorities vested in them respectively by section 213 of the Supreme Court of Judicature (Consolidation) Act 1925(a) and sections 2 and 3 of the Public Offices Fees Act 1879(b), do hereby, according as the provisions of the said enactments respectively authorise and require them, make, advise, consent to and concur in the following Order :—

1.—(1) This Order may be cited as the Supreme Court Fees (Amendment) Order 1971 and shall come into operation on 1st October 1971.

(2) The Interpretation Act 1889(c) shall apply to the interpretation of this Order as it applies to the interpretation of an Act of Parliament.

2. The Supreme Court Fees Order 1970(d) shall be amended as follows :—

(1) In Article 5, the figure "(1)" shall be inserted at the beginning, and the following sub-paragraph shall be added at the end :—

"(2) Where Fee No. 94 has been paid on the appointment of a judge of the Commercial Court as an arbitrator or umpire but the arbitration does not proceed to a hearing or an award, the fee shall be refunded."

(2) The following fee shall be inserted at the end of section 11 of the Schedule :—

(a) 1925 c. 49.　　　　　　　　(b) 1879 c. 58.
(c) 1889 c. 63.　　　　　　　　(d) S.I. 1970/1870 (1970 III, p. 6135).

Column 1	Column 2		Column 3
Item	Fee		Document to be Marked
	A	B	
	£　s.　d.	£	
"Judge sitting as arbitrator 94. On the appointment of a judge of the Commercial Court as an arbitrator or umpire under section 4 of the Administration of Justice Act 1970(a).	250　0　0	250·00	The arbitration agreement or other document produced to the judge as constituting the submission to arbitration.
95. For every two days or part thereof (after the first two days) of the hearing of the reference before a judge so appointed an arbitrator or umpire.	250　0　0	250·00	None (fee to be paid before award is taken up.)".

Dated 26th July 1971.

Hailsham of St. Marylebone, C.

Widgery, C. J.
Denning, M. R.
George Baker, P.

Dated 27th July 1971.

Walter Clegg,
Bernard Weatherill,
Two of the Lords Commissioners
of Her Majesty's Treasury.

EXPLANATORY NOTE
(This Note is not part of the Order.)

This Order adds a new provision to the Supreme Court Fees Order 1970 prescribing £250 as the fee payable by the parties to a Commercial Judge appointed as sole arbitrator or umpire under section 4 of the Administration of Justice Act 1970, with an additional £250 for every two days or part thereof, after the first two days, of the hearing of the reference before the judge so appointed.

(a) 1970 c. 31.

STATUTORY INSTRUMENTS

1971 No. 1253 (L.31)

CRIMINAL PROCEDURE, ENGLAND AND WALES

The Indictment Rules 1971

Made - - -	23rd *July* 1971
Laid before Parliament	6th *August* 1971
Coming into Operation	1st *October* 1971

We, the Rule Committee of the Supreme Court, in exercise of the powers conferred on us by section 19 of the Criminal Justice Administration Act 1956(a), hereby make the following rules under the Indictments Act 1915(b) :—

1. These Rules may be cited as the Indictment Rules 1971 and shall come into operation on 1st October 1971.

2.—(1) The rules contained in Schedule 2 to these Rules are hereby revoked.

(2) Any reference in any statutory instrument to a rule contained in the rules revoked by these Rules shall, if there is a corresponding rule in these Rules, be construed as a reference to that corresponding rule.

3. The Interpretation Act 1889(c) shall apply to the interpretation of these Rules as it applies to the interpretation of an Act of Parliament.

4.—(1) An indictment shall be in the form in Schedule 1 to these Rules or in a form substantially to the like effect.

(2) Where more than one offence is charged in an indictment, the statement and particulars of each offence shall be set out in a separate paragraph called a count, and rules 5 and 6 of these Rules shall apply to each count in the indictment as they apply to an indictment where one offence is charged.

(3) The counts shall be numbered consecutively.

5.—(1) Subject only to the provisions of rule 6 of these Rules, every indictment shall contain, and shall be sufficient if it contains, a statement of the specific offence with which the accused person is charged describing the offence shortly, together with such particulars as may be necessary for giving reasonable information as to the nature of the charge.

(2) An indictment for a specific offence shall not be open to objection in respect of its form if it is framed in accordance with a form of indictment for that offence for the time being approved by the Lord Chief Justice.

(a) 1956 c. 34.   (b) 1915 c. 90.   (c) 1889 c. 63.

6. Where the specific offence with which an accused person is charged in an indictment is one created by or under an enactment, then (without prejudice to the generality of rule 5 of these Rules)—

(a) the statement of offence shall contain a reference to—

(i) the section of, or the paragraph of the Schedule to, the Act creating the offence in the case of an offence created by a provision of an Act ;

(ii) the provision creating the offence in the case of an offence created by a provision of a subordinate instrument ;

(b) the particulars shall disclose the essential elements of the offence:

Provided that an essential element need not be disclosed if the accused person is not prejudiced or embarrassed in his defence by the failure to disclose it ;

(c) it shall not be necessary to specify or negative an exception, exemption, proviso, excuse or qualification.

7. Where an offence created by or under an enactment states the offence to be the doing or the omission to do any one of any different acts in the alternative, or the doing or the omission to do any act in any one of any different capacities, or with any one of any different intentions, or states any part of the offence in the alternative, the acts, omissions, capacities or intentions, or other matters stated in the alternative in the enactment or subordinate instrument may be stated in the alternative in an indictment charging the offence.

8. It shall be sufficient in an indictment to describe a person whose name is not known as a person unknown.

9. Charges for any offences may be joined in the same indictment if those charges are founded on the same facts, or form or are a part of a series of offences of the same or a similar character.

10.—(1) A person charged on indictment shall, if he so requests, be supplied by the proper officer of the court of trial with a copy of the indictment free of charge.

(2) The cost of supplying a person charged on indictment with a copy of the indictment shall be treated as part of the costs of the prosecution for the purpose of section 1 of the Costs in Criminal Cases Act 1952(a).

Dated 23rd July 1971.

Hailsham of St. Marylebone, C.
Widgery, C. J.
Denning, M. R.
George Baker, P.
Cyril Salmon, L. J.
John Pennycuick, V.-C.
James Fox-Andrews.
J. H. Buzzard.
Oliver Lodge.
Glanville Davies.
H. Montgomery-Campbell.

(a) 1952 c. 48.

SCHEDULE 1 Rule 4(1)

INDICTMENT

COURT OF TRIAL ....

THE QUEEN V. ....

charged as follows:—

STATEMENT OF OFFENCE

PARTICULARS OF OFFENCE

Date......................   ....
                                                  Appropriate officer of the court

SCHEDULE 2 Rule 2

RULES REVOKED

Rules	References
The Indictment Rules 1915	Scheduled to the Indictments Act 1915 (c.90).
The Indictment Rules 1916	S.R. & O. 1916/282 (Rev. V, p. 331: 1916 I, p. 130).
The Indictment (Criminal Informations and Inquisitions) Rules 1916	S.R. & O. 1916/323 (Rev. V, p. 335: 1916 I, p. 134).
The Indictment Rules 1923	S.R. & O. 1923/1364 (Rev. V, p. 336: 1923, p. 193).
The Indictment Rules 1957	S.I. 1957/669 (1957 I, p. 533).

EXPLANATORY NOTE

(*This Note is not part of the Rules.*)

These Rules revoke and replace the Indictment Rules 1915 as amended. The forms of indictment set out in the Appendix to the rules of 1915 have not been reproduced. Instead a standard form of indictment has been prescribed and provision has been made in rule 5(2) of these Rules for specimen forms of indictment to be approved by the Lord Chief Justice. The substance of the rules of 1915 have been reproduced though unnecessary matter has been omitted.

1971 No. 1254

TRANSPORT

The Transport Holding Company (Transfer of Assets) Order 1971

Made - - - -	*29th July* 1971
Laid before Parliament	*5th August* 1971
Coming into Operation	*1st December* 1971

The Secretary of State for the Environment makes this Order in exercise of his powers under section 53(1) of the Transport Act 1968(a) and of all other enabling powers:—

Commencement, citation, interpretation

1.—(1) This Order shall come into operation on the 1st December 1971, and may be cited as the Transport Holding Company (Transfer of Assets) Order 1971.

(2) In this Order the expression "the transfer date" means the 1st January 1972.

(3) The Interpretation Act 1889(b) shall apply for the interpretation of this Order as it applies for the interpretation of an Act of Parliament.

Transfer of property etc to the National Freight Corporation

2. On the transfer date there shall be transferred to the National Freight Corporation from the Transport Holding Company the following property, rights and liabilities of the Transport Holding Company;—

(*a*) the securities of Pickfords Travel Service Limited, so far as beneficially owned on that date by the Transport Holding Company,

(*b*) any rights and liabilities on that date of the Transport Holding Company regarding those securities,

(*c*) the right to any money owed on that date by Pickfords Travel Service Limited to the Transport Holding Company,

(*d*) the liability represented by any money owed on that date by the Transport Holding Company to Pickfords Travel Service Limited, and

(*e*) any actual or contingent liability of the Transport Holding Company on that date under any guarantee or indemnity given by the Transport Holding Company before that date in respect of any liabilities of Pickfords Travel Service Limited or otherwise in relation to that company.

(a) 1968 c. 73.   (b) 1889 c. 63.

Conferment of powers

3. On and after the transfer date the National Freight Corporation shall have, in addition to their existing powers, such additional powers as are necessary to ensure the continued carrying on by Pickfords Travel Service Limited of any activities carried on by that company before the transfer date which would otherwise fall by virtue of section 25 of the Transport Act 1962(a) to be discontinued after the transfer.

Signed by authority of the Secretary of State 29th July 1971.

John Peyton,
Minister for Transport Industries,
Department of the Environment.

EXPLANATORY NOTE

(This Note is not part of the Order.)

This Order transfers Pickfords Travel Service Ltd from the Transport Holding Company to the National Freight Corporation, and confers on the National Freight Corporation the powers necessary to ensure the continued carrying on, of the current activities of Pickfords Travel Service Ltd.

(a) 1962 c. 46.

STATUTORY INSTRUMENTS

1971 No. 1257

DEFENCE

The Board of Inquiry (Army) (Amendment) Rules 1971

Made - - -	*30th July* 1971
Laid before Parliament	*6th August* 1971
Coming into Operation	*1st September* 1971

The Secretary of State, in exercise of the powers conferred upon him by section 135 of the Army Act 1955(a), as amended by section 26 of the Army and Air Force Act 1961(b) and of all other powers enabling him in that behalf hereby makes the following rules:—

Citation, Interpretation and Commencement

1.—(1) These Rules may be cited as the Board of Inquiry (Army) (Amendment) Rules 1971.

(2) The Interpretation Act 1889(c), shall apply to the interpretation of these Rules as it applies to the interpretation of an Act of Parliament.

(3) These Rules shall come into operation on the 1st day of September 1971.

Amendment of Rule 7 of the Principal Rules

2. Rule 7 of the Board of Inquiry (Army) Rules 1956(d), as amended (e), shall be further amended as follows:—

(1) For paragraph (2) there shall be substituted the following:—

"(2) One of the members of the board may be a warrant officer or (in the case where a board is convened with reference to such absence and deficiency (if any) as are mentioned in sub-paragraph (*a*) of paragraph (1) of Rule 4) a non-commissioned officer of the Royal Marines not below the rank of quarter-master-sergeant."

(2) In paragraph (3) for the words "(in the case of a board referred to in paragraph (2) of this Rule) a warrant officer or" there shall be substituted the words "a warrant officer or (in the case mentioned in paragraph (2) of this Rule)."

Dated this 30th day of July 1971.

Carrington,
One of Her Majesty's
Principal Secretaries of State

(a) 1955 c. 18.	**(b)** 1961 c. 52.
(c) 1889 c. 63.	**(d)** S.I. 1956/630 (1956 I, p. 207).
(e) The relevant amending instrument is S.I. 1961/2469 (1961 III, p. 4536).	

EXPLANATORY NOTE

(This Note is not part of the Rules.)

These Rules amend the Board of Inquiry (Army) Rules 1956, as amended, so as to enable a Warrant Officer to be a member of any Board of Inquiry and not merely a member of a Board convened under Rule 4(1)(*a*) of the Rules.

STATUTORY INSTRUMENTS

1971 No. 1259

CRIMINAL PROCEDURE, ENGLAND AND WALES

COSTS AND EXPENSES

The Witnesses' Allowances (Amendment) Regulations 1971

Made - - -	28*th July* 1971
Coming into Operation	1*st September* 1971

In exercise of the powers conferred upon me by section 12 of the Costs in Criminal Cases Act 1952(**a**), as amended by section 52 of, and Schedule 5 to, the Criminal Appeal Act 1968(**b**), I hereby make the following Regulations :—

1. These Regulations may be cited as the Witnesses' Allowances (Amendment) Regulations 1971 and shall come into operation on 1st September 1971.

2. Regulation 5 of the Witnesses' Allowances Regulations 1971(**c**) shall be amended by the substitution of the words "£12" and "£6" for the words "£10" and "£5" respectively.

3. Regulation 15 of the said Regulations shall be amended as follows :—

(*a*) in paragraph (1)(*a*) the words "£6" and "£5·16" shall be substituted for the words "£5" and "£4·30" respectively ;

(*b*) in paragraph (1)(*b*) the words "£6·24", "£9·60" and "£3·44" shall be substituted for the words "£5·20", "£8" and "£2·87" respectively.

R. Maudling,
One of Her Majesty's Principal
Secretaries of State.

Home Office,
Whitehall.
28th July 1971.

EXPLANATORY NOTE

(This Note is not part of the Regulations.)

These Regulations provide for an increase in allowances to lawyers, doctors, dentists and veterinary surgeons called as professional witnesses and to medical practitioners for written reports to a court.

(**a**) 1952 c. 48. (**b**) 1968 c. 19. (**c**) S.I. 1971/107 (1971 I, p. 195).

1971 No. 1260
CORONERS
EXPENSES

The Coroners (Fees and Allowances) (Amendment) Rules 1971

Made	- - -	28*th July* 1971
Coming into Operation		1*st September* 1971

In exercise of the powers conferred upon me by section 1(1) of the Coroners Act 1954(a), I hereby make the following Rules :—

1. These Rules may be cited as the Coroners (Fees and Allowances) (Amendment) Rules 1971 and shall come into operation on 1st September 1971.

2. Rule 4 of the Coroners (Fees and Allowances) Rules 1971(b) shall be amended as follows :—

(*a*) in paragraph (1) the words "£7·50" shall be substituted for the words "£6·25" ;

(*b*) in paragraph (2) the words "£12" and "£6" shall be substituted for the words "£10" and "£5" respectively ;

(*c*) in the proviso to paragraph (2) the words "£7·50" and "£6" shall be substituted for the words "£6·25" and "£5" respectively ;

(*d*) in paragraph (4) the words "£6" and "£3·72" shall be substituted for the words "£5" and "£3·10" respectively.

3. Rule 5 of the said Rules shall be amended by substituting the words "£12" and "£6" for the words "£10" and "£5" respectively.

R. Maudling,
One of Her Majesty's Principal
Secretaries of State.

Home Office,
 Whitehall.
28th July 1971.

EXPLANATORY NOTE
(This Note is not part of the Rules.)

These Rules provide for increases in the fees paid to medical practitioners for performing post-mortem examinations and to lawyers, doctors, dentists and veterinary surgeons for appearance as witnesses at inquests.

(a) 1954 c. 31.   (b) S.I. 1971/108 (1971 I, p. 200).

STATUTORY INSTRUMENTS

1971 No. 1263

SOCIAL SECURITY

The National Insurance (Industrial Injuries) (Colliery Workers Supplementary Scheme) Amendment Order 1971

Made - - -	*30th July* 1971
Laid before Parliament	*10th August* 1971
Coming into Operation	*23rd September* 1971

Whereas the National Committee for the time being constituted in accordance with the Supplementary Scheme set out in Schedule 1 to the National Insurance (Industrial Injuries) (Colliery Workers Supplementary Scheme) Amendment and Consolidation Order 1970(a) is the body charged with the administration of that Scheme and has requested the Secretary of State to vary and amend the provisions of the said Supplementary Scheme in manner set out in the following Order :—

Now, therefore, the Secretary of State, in exercise of his powers under section 47(1)(*a*)(ii) of the National Insurance Act 1965(b), as applied by section 82(2) of the National Insurance (Industrial Injuries) Act 1965(c), and of all other powers enabling him in that behalf, hereby makes, in consequence of the National Insurance Act 1971(d), the following Order :—

Citation, commencement and interpretation

1.—(1) This Order, which may be cited as the National Insurance (Industrial Injuries) (Colliery Workers Supplementary Scheme) Amendment Order 1971, shall come into operation on 23rd September 1971.

(2) In this Order, "the Scheme" means the Supplementary Scheme set out in Schedule 1 to the National Insurance (Industrial Injuries) (Colliery Workers Supplementary Scheme) Amendment and Consolidation Order 1970 as varied and amended(e).

Amendment of Article 7 of the Scheme

2. In Article 7(1)(*c*) of the Scheme (limitation of supplementary benefit), after the words "sickness benefit" there shall be inserted the words ", invalidity benefit".

Signed by authority of the Secretary of State for Social Services.

Paul Dean,
Parliamentary Under-Secretary of State,
Department of Health and Social Security.

30th July 1971.

(a) S.I. 1970/376 (1970 I, p. 1316).   (b) 1965 c. 51.
(c) 1965 c. 52.   (d) 1971 c. 50.
(e) S.I. 1970/1879 (1970 III, p. 6167).

EXPLANATORY NOTE

(This Note is not part of the Order.)

This Order amends the provisions of the National Insurance (Industrial Injuries) Colliery Workers Supplementary Scheme to provide that invalidity benefit, introduced by the National Insurance Act 1971, be included in the benefits taken into account when determining under the provisions of the Scheme the rate of supplement payable.

This Order is made in consequence of the National Insurance Act 1971 and, in accordance with Schedule 6, paragraph 2(2), to that Act, no draft of the Order has been laid before Parliament.

STATUTORY INSTRUMENTS

1971 No. 1264

AGRICULTURE

The Price Stability of Imported Products (Rates of Levy) (Cereals) (No. 2) Order 1971

Made - - - - 30th July 1971

Coming into Operation 2nd August 1971

The Minister of Agriculture, Fisheries and Food, in exercise of the powers conferred upon him by section 1(2), (4), (5), (6) and 7 of the Agriculture and Horticulture Act 1964(a) and of all other powers enabling him in that behalf, hereby makes the following order:—

1. This order may be cited as the Price Stability of Imported Products (Rates of Levy) (Cereals) (No. 2) Order 1971, and shall come into operation on 2nd August 1971.

2.—(1) In this order—

" the Principal Order " means the Price Stability of Imported Products (Levy Arrangements) (Cereals) Order 1971(b), as amended by any subsequent order and if any such order is replaced by any subsequent order the expression shall be construed as a reference to such subsequent order;

AND other expressions have the same meaning as in the Principal Order.

(2) The Interpretation Act 1889(c) shall apply to the interpretation of this order as it applies to the interpretation of an Act of Parliament.

3. In accordance with and subject to the provisions of Part II of the Principal Order (which provides for the charging of levies on imports of certain specified commodities) the rate of levy for such imports into the United Kingdom of any specified commodity as are described in column 2 of the Schedule to this order in relation to a tariff heading indicated in column 1 of that Schedule shall be the rate set forth in relation thereto in column 3 of that Schedule.

4. The Price Stability of Imported Products (Rates of Levy) (Cereals) (No. 1) Order 1971(d) is hereby revoked.

In Witness whereof the Official Seal of the Minister of Agriculture, Fisheries and Food is hereunto affixed on 30th July 1971.

(L.S.)

K. W. Wilkes,
Assistant Secretary.

(a) 1964 c. 28.   (b) S.I. 1971/631 (1971 I, p. 1660).   (c) 1889 c. 63.
(d) S.I. 1971/1069 (1971 II, p. 3200).

1. Tariff Heading	2. Description of Imports	3. Rate of Levy
	Imports of:—	per ton £
10.01	Wheat (other than denatured wheat)..	2·25
11.01	Wheat flours not containing chalk and containing not more than 1 per cent. by weight of fibre at the prescribed standard moisture content	4·25

EXPLANATORY NOTE

(This Note is not part of the Order.)

This order, which comes into operation on 2nd August 1971, supersedes the Price Stability of Imported Products (Rates of Levy) (Cereals) (No. 1) Order 1971. It—

(a) reduces to £2·25 per ton the rate of levy on imports of wheat (other than denatured wheat); and

(b) reimposes unchanged the rate of levy in force immediately before the commencement of the order in relation to certain specified wheat flours.

STATUTORY INSTRUMENTS

1971 No. 1265

CLEAN AIR

The Smoke Control Areas (Exempted Fireplaces) Order 1971

Made - - -	*30th July* 1971
Laid before Parliament	*10th August* 1971
Coming into Operation	*24th August* 1971

The Secretary of State for the Environment, in exercise of his powers under section 11(4) of the Clean Air Act 1956(a) and of all other powers enabling him in that behalf, hereby orders as follows:—

Title and commencement

1. This order may be cited as the Smoke Control Areas (Exempted Fireplaces) Order 1971 and shall come into operation on 24th August 1971.

Interpretation

2. The Interpretation Act 1889(b) shall apply for the interpretation of this order as it applies for the interpretation of an Act of Parliament.

Class of fireplace exempted from section 11 of the Clean Air Act 1956

3. The class of fireplace described in column (1) of the schedule hereto shall, subject to the conditions specified in column (2), be exempted from the provisions of section 11 of the Clean Air Act 1956 (which empowers a local authority to declare the whole or any part of their district to be a smoke control area).

SCHEDULE

(1) Class of Fireplace	(2) Conditions
The fireplace known as the Rayburn CB 34 and manufactured by Glynwed Foundries Limited	The fireplace shall be installed, maintained and operated so as to minimise the emission of smoke and in accordance with the manufacturer's instructions. No fuel shall be used other than selected washed coal singles.

Peter Walker,
Secretary of State for the Environment.

30th July 1971.

(a) 1956 c. 52.   (b) 1889 c. 63.

EXPLANATORY NOTE

(This Note is not part of the Order.)

Section 11 of the Clean Air Act 1956 empowers local authorities to declare the whole or any part of their district to be a smoke control area in which the emission of smoke is, generally, prohibited. This Order exempts the Rayburn CB 34 from the provisions of that section, upon certain conditions as to proper operation.

STATUTORY INSTRUMENTS

1971 No. 1267

MEDICINES

The Medicines (Surgical Materials) Order 1971

Laid before Parliament in draft

Made - - -		*30th July* 1971
Coming into Operation		*1st September* 1971

The Secretaries of State respectively concerned with health in England and in Wales, the Secretary of State concerned with health in Scotland, and the Minister of Health and Social Services for Northern Ireland, (hereinafter referred to as "the Health Ministers") acting jointly, in exercise of their powers under section 104(1) of the Medicines Act 1968(a), as having effect subject to the provisions of article 2(2) of and Schedule 1 to, the Transfer of Functions (Wales) Order 1969(b), and of all other powers enabling them in that behalf, after consulting such organisations as appear to them to be representative of interests likely to be substantially affected by the following order and after having taken into account the advice of the Medicines Commission, hereby make the following order, a draft of which has been laid before Parliament and has been approved by resolution of each House of Parliament.

Citation and commencement

1. This order may be cited as the Medicines (Surgical Materials) Order 1971 and shall come into operation on 1st September 1971.

Interpretation

2.—(1) In this order unless the context otherwise requires—
"the Act" means the Medicines Act 1968 ;
and other expressions have the same meaning as in the Act.

(2) The Interpretation Act 1889(c) shall apply to the interpretation of this order as it applies to the interpretation of an Act of Parliament.

Application of specified provisions of the Act to certain surgical materials

3. The articles or substances described in the Schedule to this order are hereby specified as being articles or substances appearing to the Health Ministers to be articles or substances which are not medicinal products but are manufactured, sold, supplied, imported or exported for use wholly or partly for a medicinal purpose, and it is hereby directed that the provisions contained in Parts I and II of the Act, sections 62, 64, 65 and 67 of Part III of the Act, and the provisions contained in Parts V, VI and VIII of the Act

---

(a) 1968 c. 67.
(c) 1889 c. 63.

(b) S.I. 1969/388 (1969 I, p. 1070).

shall have effect in relation to the said articles or substances described in the Schedule to this order, as those provisions have effect in relation to medicinal products.

Keith Joseph,
Secretary of State for Social Services.

29th July 1971.

Given under my hand on 29th July 1971.

Peter Thomas,
Secretary of State for Wales.

Given under my hand on 30th July 1971.

Gordon Campbell,
Secretary of State for Scotland.

Given under my hand on 30th July 1971.

W. K. Fitzsimmons,
Minister of Health and Social Services
for Northern Ireland.

SCHEDULE

SURGICAL MATERIALS

1. Any surgical ligature and surgical suture prepared from the gut or any tissue of an animal, or any form of binding material prepared from the gut or any tissue of an animal, which is manufactured, sold, supplied, imported or exported wholly or partly for use in surgical operations upon the human body.

2. Any other surgical ligature or surgical suture prepared from any source, which is manufactured, sold, supplied, imported or exported wholly or partly for use in surgical operations upon the human body and is capable of being absorbed by body tissues.

3. Any absorbent or protective material manufactured, sold, supplied, imported or exported wholly or partly for use in surgical operations upon the human body and capable of being absorbed by body tissues.

EXPLANATORY NOTE

(*This Note is not part of the Order.*)

This Order, made under section 104(1) of the Medicines Act 1968, extends the application of specified provisions of the Act to certain surgical materials which are articles or substances which are not medicinal products but which are manufactured, sold, supplied, imported or exported for use wholly or partly for a medicinal purpose.

STATUTORY INSTRUMENTS

1971 No. 1269 (L.32)

SUPREME COURT OF JUDICATURE, ENGLAND

PROCEDURE

The Rules of the Supreme Court (Amendment No. 4) 1971

Made - - -	*23rd July* 1971
Laid before Parliament	*10th August* 1971

Coming into Operation-
Parts I, III *and rules* 45, 46 *and* 48   *31st August* 1971
Remainder   *1st October* 1971

We, the Rule Committee of the Supreme Court, being the authority having for the time being power under section 99(4) of the Supreme Court of Judicature (Consolidation) Act 1925(a) to make, amend or revoke rules regulating the practice and procedure of the Supreme Court of Judicature, hereby exercise those powers and all other powers enabling us in that behalf as follows :—

PART I

CITATION, COMMENCEMENT AND INTERPRETATION

1.—(1) These Rules may be cited as the Rules of the Supreme Court (Amendment No. 4) 1971.

(2) Parts I and III of these Rules and rules 45, 46 and 48 shall come into operation on 31st August 1971, and the remainder shall come into operation on 1st October 1971.

(3) In these Rules an Order referred to by number means the Order so numbered in the Rules of the Supreme Court 1965(b), as amended (c).

(4) The Interpretation Act 1889(d) shall apply to the interpretation of these Rules as it applies to the interpretation of an Act of Parliament.

(a) 1925 c. 49.   (b) S.I. 1965/1776 (1965 III, p. 4995).
(c) The relevant amending instruments are S.I. 1966/1055, 1514, 1967/829, 1809, 1968/1244, 1969/1105, 1970/944, 1208, 1861, 1971/354, 835 (1966 II, p. 2588; III, p. 4196; 1967 II, p. 2476; III, p. 4832; 1968 II, p. 3360; 1969 II, p. 3228; 1970 II, pp. 2932, 4001; III, p. 6081; 1971 I, p. 1144; II, p. 2388).
(d) 1889 c. 63.

PART II

AMENDMENTS CONSEQUENTIAL ON THE RECONSTITUTION OF THE HIGH COURT

2. Order 1 shall be amended as follows :—

(1) In rule 4(2), for the words "registrar of the Probate, Divorce and Admiralty Division" there shall be substituted the words "the Admiralty Registrar or any registrar of the Family Division".

(2) The following rule shall be inserted after rule 4 :—

"Construction of references to proceedings in Queen's Bench Division, etc.

4A. In these Rules, unless the context otherwise requires—

(*a*) any reference to proceedings in the Queen's Bench Division shall be construed as including a reference to proceedings in the Commercial Court but not to proceedings in the Admiralty Court ; and

(*b*) any reference to a master, if it relates only to a master of the Queen's Bench Division, shall in relation to any Admiralty cause or matter be construed as including the Admiralty Registrar."

3. In Order 4, rule 9, for paragraph (2) there shall be substituted the following paragraph :—

"(2) Paragraph (1) shall apply in relation to registrars of the Family Division, and as between masters of the Queen's Bench Division and the Admiralty Registrar, as it applies in relation to masters."

4. In Order 11, rule 1, the following sub-paragraph shall be inserted after sub-paragraph (*l*) :—

"(*m*) if the action is a probate action within the meaning of Order 76."

5. Order 12 shall be amended as follows :—

(1) In rule 8, for paragraph (2) there shall be substituted the following paragraph :—

"(2) An application under this rule must be made—

(*a*) in an action in the Queen's Bench Division, by summons ;

(*b*) in any other action, by summons or motion."

(2) In rule 9, the following paragraph shall be inserted after paragraph (3) :—

"(3A) Where an originating summons to which an appearance is required is issued out of the principal registry of the Family Division, the appropriate office for entering an appearance is in all cases that registry ; and where an originating summons by which proceedings assigned to the Family Division are begun is issued out of a district registry, the appropriate office for entering an appearance is in all cases the district registry."

6. Order 28 shall be amended as follows :—

(1) In rule 2, the following sub-paragraph shall be inserted at the end of paragraph (1) :—

"(c) of the principal registry of the Family Division, where the cause or matter is assigned to the Family Division."

(2) In rule 9(3), after the words "Queen's Bench Division" there shall be inserted the words "or the Family Division".

7. Order 32 shall be amended as follows :—

(1) In rule 8(1), after the word "masters" there shall be inserted the words "the Admiralty Registrar".

(2) In rule 10, after the word "master" there shall be inserted the words "or to the Admiralty Registrar".

8. Order 34 shall be amended as follows :—

(1) In rule 3, sub-paragraph (e) of paragraph (5) shall be deleted.

(2) In rule 4, the word "or" shall be inserted at the end of sub-paragraph (a) ; in sub-paragraph (b), for the words "the senior judge of the Chancery Division" there shall be substituted the words "the Vice-Chancellor" and the word "or" shall be deleted ; and sub-paragraph (c) shall be deleted.

9. Order 35 shall be amended as follows :—

(1) In rule 10, after the word "Division" where it first occurs there shall be inserted the word "and", and the words "and of any probate action so tried" shall be deleted.

(2) In rule 12, after the word "action" there shall be inserted the words "in the Queen's Bench Division".

10. Order 37 shall be amended as follows :—

(1) In rule 1(1), after the words "assessed by a master" there shall be inserted the words "or, in an Admiralty cause or matter, by the Admiralty Registrar."

(2) In rule 2(b), there shall be inserted at the end the words "except in an Admiralty cause or matter, when the certificate shall be filed in the Admiralty Registry."

11. In Order 43, the following rule shall be added after rule 8 :—

"Guardian's accounts

9. The accounts of a person appointed guardian of a minor's estate must be verified and passed in the same manner as that provided by Order 30 in relation to a receiver's account or in such other manner as the Court may direct."

12. In Order 46, rule 6(6)(b), for sub-paragraph (b) there shall be substituted the following sub-paragraph :—

"(b) where that cause or matter is proceeding in the principal registry of the Family Division, that registry ;".

13. In Order 50, rule 9, after the words "a master" there shall be inserted the words "and the Admiralty Registrar".

14. In Order 51, rule 2, after the words "a master" there shall be inserted the words "and the Admiralty Registrar".

15. Order 54 shall be amended as follows :—

(1) In rule 1(1), there shall be inserted at the beginning the words "Subject to rule 11".

(2) The following rule shall be inserted at the end :—

"Applications relative to the custody etc., of minors

11. An application by a parent or guardian of a minor for a writ of habeas corpus ad subjiciendum relative to the custody, care or control of the minor must be made in the Family Division, and this Order shall accordingly apply to such applications with the appropriate modifications."

16. Order 56 shall be amended as follows :—

(1) In rule 1(1), there shall be inserted at the beginning the words "Except where they relate to affiliation proceedings".

(2) The following rule shall be inserted after rule 4 :—

"Appeals relating to affiliation proceedings

4A. Appeals from a court of quarter sessions by case stated which relate to affiliation proceedings shall be heard and determined by a Divisional Court of the Family Division, and the foregoing provisions of this Order shall accordingly apply to such appeals with the substitution of references to the principal registry of the Family Division for references to the Crown Office and such other modifications as may be appropriate."

(3) For rule 5 there shall be substituted the following rule :—

"Appeal from magistrates' court by case stated

5.—(1) Except as provided by paragraph (2), all appeals from a magistrates' court by case stated shall be heard and determined by a Divisional Court of the Queen's Bench Division.

(2) An appeal by way of case stated against an order or determination of a magistrates' court shall be heard and determined by a Divisional Court of the Family Division if the order or determination appealed against was made or given in affiliation proceedings, or on an application under section 14 of the Matrimonial Proceedings and Property Act 1970(a), or if it relates to the enforcement of—

(a) an order for the payment of money made by virtue of the Matrimonial Proceedings (Magistrates' Courts) Act 1960(b), or

---

(a) 1970 c. 45.   (b) 1960 c. 48.

(b) an order for the payment of money to a wife for her maintenance or for her maintenance and that of any child or children of hers, registered in a court in England or Wales under Part II of the Maintenance Orders Act 1950(a) or the Maintenance Orders (Facilities for Enforcement) Act 1920(b) or confirmed by such a court under the last-mentioned Act, or

(c) an order for alimony, maintenance or other payments made or having effect as if made under Part II or III of the Matrimonial Causes Act 1965(c) or Part I of the Matrimonial Proceedings and Property Act 1970 and registered in a magistrates' court under the Maintenance Orders Act 1958(d)."

17. Order 57 shall be amended as follows :—

(1) In rule 2(3), there shall be inserted at the beginning the words "Except where it relates to proceedings in the Admiralty Court".

(2) The words "or the Admiralty Registry, as the circumstances of the case require" shall be deleted from rules 2(4)(c) and 3(a) and inserted in rules 2(4)(a), 3(b), 4(1) and (2) and 6 after the words "the Crown Office".

(3) In rule 2(4), after the words "Queen's Bench Division" there shall be inserted the words "(including the Admiralty Court)".

(4) In rule 5, after the words "the Crown Office" there shall be inserted the words "or the principal registry of the Family Division, as the circumstances of the case require".

18. Order 58 shall be amended as follows :—

(1) In rule 1(1), after the words "master of the Queen's Bench Division" there shall be inserted the words "the Admiralty Registrar or a".

(2) In rule 2(1), the words from "including" to "1882" in sub-paragraph (a) shall be omitted ; and at the end there shall be inserted the following paragraph :—

"In this paragraph "master of the Queen's Bench Division" does not include the Admiralty Registrar."

(3) In rule 2(2), the words from the beginning to "1882" shall be omitted, and for the words "any such registrar" there shall be substituted the words "a registrar of the Family Division" ; and in sub-paragraph (a), for the words "the said section 17", there shall be substituted the words "section 17 of the Married Women's Property Act 1882(e)".

(4) In rule 7(1), after the words "Queen's Bench Division" there shall be inserted the words "(including the Admiralty Court)".

19. In Order 59, rule 5(5)(c), the words "in a probate cause or" shall be omitted.

20. In Order 61, rule 2, the following paragraph shall be added at the end :—

"(6) In this rule, references to a tribunal other than the Lands Tribunal include references to a judge of the Commercial Court acting as an arbitrator or umpire under section 4 of the Administration of Justice Act 1970(f).'

(a) 1950 c. 37.	(b) 1920 c. 33.	(c) 1965 c. 72.
(d) 1958 c. 39.	(e) 1882 c. 75.	(f) 1970 c. 31.

21. In Order 62, rule 1(1), in the fifth definition, the words "or Admiralty proceedings (as so defined)" shall be deleted ; and for the definition of "registrar" there shall be substituted the following definition :—

" "registrar" (except where the context otherwise requires) means the Admiralty Registrar or a registrar of the Family Division ;".

22. In Order 68, rule 1(1), after the words in brackets, there shall be inserted the words "and in every cause or matter taken in the Admiralty Court".

23. Order 72 shall be amended as follows :—

(1) In the title, the words "in the Queen's Bench Division" shall be omitted.

(2) In rule 2(1), for the words after "provisions of this Order" there shall be substituted the words "for trial in the Commercial Court, and one of the Commercial Judges shall be in charge of that list."

(3) In rule 4(1), for the words " "Commercial List" " there shall be substituted the words " "Commercial Court" ".

(4) In rule 5(3), for the words "commercial list" there shall be substituted the words "Commercial Court" ; and for the words "that list" where they first appear there shall be substituted the words "the commercial list."

24. Order 74 shall be amended as follows :—

(1) In the title, for the date "1965" there shall be substituted the date "1970".

(2) In rule 1(1), for the words "1965 shall be assigned to the Probate, Divorce and Admiralty Division" there shall be substituted the words "1970 shall be assigned to the Queen's Bench Division and taken by the Admiralty Court".

(3) In rule 1(2), the words from "and proceedings" to the end shall be deleted.

(4) In rule 2(1), for the words "Probate, Divorce and Admiralty Division" there shall be substituted the words "Queen's Bench Division constituted so far as practicable of Admiralty Judges".

25. Order 75 shall be amended as follows :—

(1) In rule 1(2), in the definition of "limitation action", for the date "1960" there shall be substituted the date "1970".

(2) In rule 2(1), for the words "section 56(3)" there shall be substituted the words "section 56(2)" ; for the words "Probate, Divorce and Admiralty Division" there shall be substituted the words "Queen's Bench Division" ; and at the end there shall be added the words "and taken by the Admiralty Court".

(3) In rule 22(7), rule 24(2), rule 25(5) and rule 35(1), for the words "the judge in person" there shall be substituted the words "a judge in person" ; and in rule 35(1), for the words "the judge" where they first appear there shall be substituted the words "a judge".

(4) In rule 26(3) and rule 30(6), for the words "President of the Probate, Divorce and Admiralty Division" there shall be substituted the words "Lord Chief Justice".

(5) Rule 29 shall be omitted.

(6) In rule 33(1), for the words "Probate, Divorce and Admiralty Division and" there shall be substituted the words "Queen's Bench Division and taken by the Admiralty Court, and shall".

(7) In rule 36(3), the words "as it applies in relation to Queen's Bench proceedings so begun but" shall be omitted.

(8) In rule 42(3), the words after "or in such other manner as may be agreed upon" shall be omitted.

26. For Order 76 there shall be substituted the following Order :—

"ORDER 76

CONTENTIOUS PROBATE PROCEEDINGS

Application and interpretation

1.—(1) This Order applies to probate causes and matters, and the other provisions of these Rules apply to those causes and matters subject to the provisions of this Order.

(2) In these Rules "probate action" means an action for the grant of probate of the will, or letters of administration of the estate, of a deceased person or for the revocation of such a grant or for a decree pronouncing for or against the validity of an alleged will, not being an action which is non-contentious or common form probate business.

(3) In this Order, "will" includes a codicil.

Requirements in connection with issue of writ

2.—(1) A probate action must be begun by writ, and the writ must be issued out of the Central Office.

(2) Before a writ beginning a probate action is issued it must be indorsed with—

    (a) a statement of the nature of the interest of plaintiff and of the defendant in the estate of the deceased to which the action relates ; and

    (b) a memorandum signed by a master of the Chancery Division showing that the writ has been produced to him for examination and that two copies of it have been lodged with him.

Parties to action for revocation of grant

3. Every person who is entitled or claims to be entitled to administer the estate of a deceased person under or by virtue of an unrevoked grant of probate of his will or letters of administration of his estate shall be made a party to any action for revocation of the grant.

Lodgment of grant in action for revocation

4.—(1) Where, at the commencement of an action for the revocation of a grant of probate of the will or letters of administration of the estate of a deceased person, the probate or letters of administration, as the case may be, have not been lodged in court, then—

    (*a*) if the action is commenced by a person to whom the grant was made, he shall lodge the probate or letters of administration in the office of the Chief Master within 7 days after the issue of the writ ;

    (*b*) if any defendant to the action has the probate or letters of administration in his possession or under his control, he shall lodge it or them in the office of the Chief Master within 14 days after the service of the writ upon him.

In this paragraph "court" includes the principal registry of the Family Division or a district probate registry.

(2) Any person who fails to comply with paragraph (1) may, on the application of any party to the action, be ordered by the Court to lodge the probate or letters of administration in the office of the Chief Master within a specified time ; and any person against whom such an order is made shall not be entitled to take any step in the action without the leave of the Court until he has complied with the order.

Affidavit of testamentary scripts

5.—(1) Unless the Court otherwise directs, the plaintiff and every defendant who has entered an appearance in a probate action must swear an affidavit—

    (*a*) describing any testamentary script of the deceased person, whose estate is the subject of the action, of which he has any knowledge or, if such be the case, stating that he knows of no such script, and

    (*b*) if any such script of which he has knowledge is not in his possession or under his control, giving the name and address of the person in whose possession or under whose control it is or, if such be the case, stating that he does not know the name or address of that person.

(2) Any affidavit required by this rule must be filed, and an office copy thereof and any testamentary script referred to therein which is in the possession or under the control of the deponent, must be lodged in the judge's chambers within 14 days after the entry of appearance by a defendant to the action or, if no defendant enters an appearance therein and the Court does not otherwise direct, before an order is made for the trial of the action.

(3) Where any testamentary script required by this rule to be lodged in the judge's chambers or any part thereof is written in pencil, then, unless the Court otherwise directs, a facsimile copy of that script, or of the page or pages thereof containing the part written in pencil, must also be lodged in the judge's chambers and the words which appear in pencil in the original must be underlined in red ink in the copy.

(4) Except with the leave of the Court, a party to a probate action shall not be allowed to inspect an affidavit filed, ar any testamentary script lodged, by any other party to the action under this rule, unless and until an affidavit sworn by him containing the information referred to in paragraph (1) has been filed.

(5) In this rule "testamentary script" means a will or draft thereof, written instructions for a will made by or at the request or under the instructions of the testator and any document purporting to be evidence of the contents, or to be a copy, of a will which is alleged to have been lost or destroyed.

Default of appearance

6.—(1) Order 13 shall not apply in relation to a probate action.

(2) Where any of several defendants to a probate action fails to enter an appearance, the plaintiff, upon filing an affidavit proving due service of the writ, or notice of the writ, on that defendant may, after the time limited for appearing, proceed with the action as if that defendant had entered an appearance.

(3) Where the defendant, or all the defendants, to a probate action, fails or fail to enter an appearance, then, unless on the application of the plantiff the Court orders the action to be discontinued, the plaintiff may after the time limited for appearing by the defendant apply to the Court for an order for trial of the action.

(4) Before applying for an order under paragraph (3) the plaintiff must file an affidavit proving due service of the writ, or notice of the writ, on the defendant and, if no statement of claim is indorsed on the writ, he must lodge a statement of claim in the judge's chambers.

(5) Where the Court grants an order under paragraph (3), it may direct the action to be tried on affidavit evidence.

Service of statement of claim

7. The plaintiff in a probate action must, unless the Court gives leave to the contrary or unless a statement of claim is indorsed on the writ, serve a statement of claim on every defendant who enters an appearance in the action and must do so before the expiration of 6 weeks after entry of appearance by that defendant or of 8 days after the filing by that defendant of an affidavit under rule 5, whichever is the later.

Counterclaim

8.—(1) Notwithstanding anything in Order 15, rule 2(1), a defendant to a probate action who alleges that he has any claim or is entitled to any relief or remedy in respect of any matter relating to the grant of probate of the will, or letters of administration of the estate, of the deceased person which is the subject of the action must add to his defence a counterclaim in respect of that matter.

(2) If the plaintiff fails to serve a statement of claim, any such defendant may, with the leave of the Court, serve a counterclaim and the action shall then proceed as if the counterclaim were the statement of claim.

Contents of pleadings

9.—(1) Where the plaintiff in a probate action disputes the interest of a defendant he must allege in his statement of claim that he denies the interest of that defendant.

(2) In a probate action in which the interest by virtue of which a party claims to be entitled to a grant of letters of administration is disputed, the party disputing that interest must show in his pleading that if the allegations made therein are proved he would be entitled to an interest in the estate.

(3) Without prejudice to Order 18, rule 7, any party who pleads that at the time when a will, the subject of the action, was alleged to have been executed the testator did not know and approve of its contents must specify the nature of the case on which he intends to rely, and no allegation in support of that plea which would be relevant in support of any of the following other pleas, that is to say :—

(*a*) that the will was not duly executed,

(*b*) that at the time of the execution of the will the testator was not of sound mind, memory and understanding, and

(*c*) that the execution of the will was obtained by undue influence or fraud,

shall be made by that party unless that other plea is also pleaded.

Default of pleadings

10.—(1) Order 19 shall not apply in relation to a probate action.

(2) Where any party to a probate action fails to serve on any other party a pleading which he is required by these Rules to serve on that other party, then, unless the Court orders the action to be discontinued or dismissed, that other party may, after the expiration of the period fixed by or under these Rules for service of the pleading in question, apply to the Court for an order for trial of the action ; and if an order is made the Court may direct the action to be tried on affidavit evidence.

Discontinuance and dismissal

11.—(1) Order 21 shall not apply in relation to a probate action.

(2) At any stage of the proceedings in a probate action the Court may, on the application of the plaintiff or of any party to the action who has entered an appearance therein, order the action to be discontinued or dismissed on such terms as to costs or otherwise as it thinks just, and may further order that a grant of probate of the will, or letters of administration of the estate, of the deceased person, as the case may be, which is the subject of the action, be made to the person entitled thereto.

(3) An application for an order under this rule may be made by motion or summons or by notice under Order 25, rule 7.

Compromise of action: trial on affidavit evidence

12. Where, whether before or after the service of the defence in a probate action, the parties to the action agree to a compromise, the Court may order the trial of the action on affidavit evidence.

Transmission of documents and orders between Family Registry and Chancery Chambers

13.—(1) If after a probate action has been commenced a master of the Chancery Division so requests, the principal registrar of the Family Division shall send him any documents in the custody of the principal registry of the Family Division, or of any district probate registry, which are relevant to that action.

(2) Immediately after an order for the grant or revocation of probate or administration has been drawn up and entered, the chief registrar of the Chancery Division shall send an office copy of the order to the principal registry of the Family Division, together with any document of which probate or administration with the will annexed is to be granted.

Application for order to bring in will, etc.

14.—(1) Any application in a probate action for an order under section 26 of the Court of Probate Act 1857(a) shall be for an order requiring a person to bring a will or other testamentary paper into the office of the Chief Master or to attend in court for examination.

(2) An application under paragraph (1) shall be made by summons in the action, which must be served on the person against whom the order is sought.

(3) Any application in a probate action for the issue of a subpoena under section 23 of the Court of Probate Act 1858(b) shall be for the issue of a subpoena requiring a person to bring into the office of the Chief Master a will or other testamentary paper.

(4) An application under paragraph (3) may be made ex parte and must be supported by an affidavit setting out the grounds of the application.

(5) An application under paragraph (3) shall be made to a master who may, if the application is granted, authorise the issue of a subpoena accordingly.

(6) Any person against whom a subpoena is issued under the said section 23 and who denies that the will or other testamentary paper referred to in the subpoena is in his possession or under his control may file an affidavit to that effect.

Administration pendente lite

15.—(1) An application under section 163 of the Act for an order for the grant of administration may be made by summons issued in the Chancery Division.

(2) Where an order for a grant of administration is made under the said section 163, Order 30, rules 2, 4 and 6 and (subject to sub-section (2) of the said section) rule 3, shall apply as if the administrator were a receiver appointed by the Court ; and every application relating to the conduct of the administration shall be made in the Chancery Division."

27. In Order 80, paragraph (1) of rule 3, and rules 4 and 5, shall be omitted.

(a) 1857 c. 77.   (b) 1858 c. 95.

28. In Order 81, rule 10(2), for the words "or district registrar" there shall be substituted the words "or the Admiralty Registrar or a district registrar".

29. Order 89, rule 1, shall be amended as follows :—

(1) In paragraph (1), for the words from the beginning to "by which they" there shall be substituted the words "the originating summons by which proceedings under section 17 of the Married Women's Property Act 1882".

(2) In paragraph (2), the words from the beginning to "a master" shall be omitted.

(3) In paragraph (3), the words "a master and" shall be omitted.

30. Order 91 shall be omitted, and Order 90 shall be re-numbered as Order 91 ; and the following Order shall be inserted after Order 89 :—

"ORDER 90

Miscellaneous Proceedings in the Family Division

I. General

Interpretation

1. In this Order, "principal registry" means the principal registry of the Family Division, and "registrar" means a registrar of that Division.

Assignment and commencement of proceedings

2. All proceedings to which this Order relates shall be assigned to the Family Division and, except as provided by rules 3 and 5, shall be begun in the principal registry.

II. Proceedings Concerning Minors

Application to make minor a ward of court

3.—(1) An application to make a minor a ward of court must be made by originating summons issued out of the principal registry or out of a district registry as defined by the matrimonial causes rules.

(2) Where there is no person other than the minor who is a suitable defendant, an application may be made ex parte to a registrar for leave to issue either an ex parte originating summons or an originating summons with the minor as defendant thereto ; and, except where such leave is granted, the minor shall not be made a defendant to an originating summons under this rule in the first instance.

(3) Particulars of any summons under this rule issued in a district registry shall be sent by the district registrar to the principal registry for recording in the register of wards.

When minor ceases to be a ward of court

4.—(1) A minor who, by virtue of section 9(2) of the Law Reform (Miscellaneous Provisions) Act 1949(**a**), becomes a ward of court on the issue of a summons under rule 3 shall cease to be a ward of court—

(*a*) if an application for an appointment for the hearing of the summons is not made within the period of 21 days after the issue of the summons, at the expiration of that period ;

(*b*) if an application for such an appointment is made within that period, on the determination of the application made by the summons unless the Court hearing it orders that the minor be made a ward of court.

(2) Nothing in paragraph (1) shall be taken as affecting the power of the Court under section 9(3) of the said Act to order that any minor who is for the time being a ward of court shall cease to be a ward of court.

(3) If no application for an appointment for the hearing of a summons under rule 3 is made within the period of 21 days after the issue of the summons, a notice stating whether the applicant intends to proceed with the application made by the summons must be left at the registry in which the matter is proceeding immediately after the expiration of that period.

Applications under Guardianship of Minors Act 1971

5. Where there is pending any proceeding by reason of which a minor is a ward of court, any application under the Guardianship of Minors Act 1971(**b**) (hereafter in this Part of this Order referred to as "the Act of 1971") with respect to that minor may be made by summons in that proceeding, but except in that case any such application must be made by originating summons issued out of the principal registry or out of a district registry as defined by the matrimonial causes rules.

Defendants to guardianship summons

6.—(1) Where the minor with respect to whom an application under the Act of 1971 is made is not the plaintiff, he shall not, unless the Court otherwise directs, be made a defendant to the summons or, if the application is made by ordinary summons, be served with the summons, but, subject to paragraph (2) any other person appearing to be interested in, or affected by, the application shall be made a defendant or be served with the summons, as the case may be, including, where the application is made under section 5 of the Act of 1971 with respect to a minor who has been received into the care of a local authority under section 1 of the Children Act 1948(**c**), that authority.

(2) The Court may dispense with service of the summons (whether originating or ordinary) on any person and may order it to be served on any person not originally served.

Guardianship proceedings may be in chambers

7. Applications under the Act of 1971 may be disposed of in chambers.

(a) 1949 c. 100.	(b) 1971 c. 3.	(c) 1948 c. 43.

Applications for consent to marriage

8.—(1) Subject to paragraph (2), the provisions of this Order relating to applications under the Act of 1971 shall apply with the necessary modifications to applications under section 3 of the Marriage Act 1949(a) for obtaining the Court's consent to the marriage of a minor.

(2) Where an application under the said section 3 is made in consequence of a refusal to give consent to a marriage every person who has refused consent shall be made a defendant to the summons and rule 6(1) shall not apply.

Appeals and applications affecting minors

9.—(1) Every appeal to the High Court—

(a) under section 16(2) or (3) of the Act of 1971 from a county court or magistrates' court, or

(b) under section 10 of the Adoption Act 1958(b) from a magistrates' court,

shall be heard and determined by a Divisional Court of the Family Division.

(2) Order 55, rule 4(2), shall apply to any appeal under this rule, and subject thereto, rule 16 of this Order (except paragraph (2) thereof) shall apply with the necessary modifications to any such appeal as it applies to appeals under the Matrimonial Proceedings (Magistrates' Courts) Act 1960.

(3) After entry of an appeal from a county court or magistrates' court under the Act of 1971 the Divisional Court may, on an application made ex parte or otherwise, make any order with respect to the custody or maintenance of the minor in question pending the appeal or otherwise as it thinks proper.

Removal of guardianship proceedings from a county court

10.—(1) An application for an order under section 16(1) of the Act of 1971 for the removal of an application from a county court into the High Court shall be made by an originating summons issued out of the principal registry and, unless the Court otherwise directs, the summons need not be served on any person.

(2) The application may be heard by a registrar, but, if an order is made for the removal to the High Court of an application to the county court, that application shall be heard by a single judge of the Family Division.

(3) Where an order is made under the said section 16(1), the plaintiff must send a copy of the order to the registrar of the county court from which the proceedings are ordered to be removed.

(4) On receipt by the proper officer of the documents referred to in Order 16, rule 19, of the County Court Rules 1936(c), that officer must forthwith file the said documents and give notice to all parties that the application removed is proceeding in the High Court.

(a) 1949 c. 76.   (b) 1958 c. 5.
(c) S.R. & O. 1936/626 (1936 I, p. 282).

(5) The application so removed shall proceed in the High Court as if it had been made by originating summons issued out of the principal registry.

Drawing up and service of orders

11. The provisions of the matrimonial causes rules relating to the drawing up and service of orders shall apply to proceedings under this Part of this Order as if they were proceedings under those rules.

Jurisdiction of registrars

12.—(1) In proceedings to which this Part of this Order applies a registrar may transact all such business and exercise all such authority and jurisdiction as may be transacted and exercised by a judge in chambers.

(2) Paragraph (1) is without prejudice to the power of the judges to reserve to themselves the transaction of any such business or the exercise of any such authority or jurisdiction.

III. OTHER PROCEEDINGS

Application for declaration affecting matrimonial status

13.—(1) Where, apart from costs, the only relief sought in any proceedings is a declaration with respect to the matrimonial status of any person, the proceedings shall be begun by petition.

(2) The petition shall state—

(*a*) the names of the parties and the residential address of each of them at the date of presentation of the petition ;

(*b*) the place and date of any ceremony of marriage to which the application relates ;

(*c*) whether there have been any previous proceedings between the parties with reference to the marriage or the ceremony of marriage to which the application relates or with respect to the matrimonial status of either of them and, if so, the nature of those proceedings ;

(*d*) all other material facts alleged by the petitioner to justify the making of the declaration and the grounds on which he alleges that the Court has jurisdiction to make it ;

and shall conclude with a prayer setting out the declaration sought and any claim for costs.

(3) Nothing in the foregoing provisions shall be construed—

(*a*) as conferring any jurisdiction to make a declaration in circumstances in which the Court could not otherwise make it, or

(*b*) as affecting the power of the Court to refuse to make a declaration notwithstanding that it has jurisdiction to make it.

(4) This rule does not apply to proceedings to which rule 14 applies.

Application under section 39 of Matrimonial Causes Act 1965

14.—(1) A petition under section 39 of the Matrimonial Causes Act 1965 shall, in addition to stating the grounds on which the petitioner relies, set out the date and place of birth of the petitioner and the maiden name of his mother, and, if the petitioner is known by a name other than that which appears in the certificate of his birth, that fact shall be stated in the petition and in any decree made thereon.

(2) The petition shall be supported by an affidavit by the petitioner verifying the petition and giving particulars of every person whose interest may be affected by the proceedings and his relationship to the petitioner :

Provided that if the petitioner is under 16, the affidavit shall, unless otherwise directed, be made by his next friend.

(3) An affidavit for the purposes of paragraph (2) may contain statements of information or belief with the sources and grounds thereof.

(4) On filing the petition, the petitioner shall issue and serve on the Attorney-General a summons for directions as to the persons, other than the Attorney-General, who are to be made respondents to the petition.

(5) It shall not be necessary to serve the petition on the Attorney-General otherwise than by delivering a copy of it to him in accordance with subsection (6) of the said section 39.

(6) The Attorney-General may file an answer to the petition within 21 days after directions have been given under paragraph (4) and no directions for trial shall be given until that period has expired.

(7) A respondent who files an answer shall at the same time lodge in the divorce registry as many copies of the answer as there are other parties to the proceedings and a registrar shall send one of the copies to each of those parties.

Further proceedings on petition under rule 13 or 14

15.—(1) Unless a judge otherwise directs, all proceedings on any petition to which rule 13 or 14 relates shall take place in London.

(2) Subject to rules 2, 13 and 14 and paragraph (1) of this rule, the matrimonial causes rules shall apply with the necessary modifications to the petition as if it were a petition in a matrimonial cause.

Appeals under the Matrimonial Proceedings (Magistrates' Courts) Act 1960

16.—(1) Every appeal to the High Court under the Matrimonial Proceedings (Magistrates' Courts) Act 1960 shall be entered by lodging two copies of the notice of motion in the principal registry.

(2) Order 55, rule 4(2), shall apply to the appeal as if for the period of 28 days therein specified there were substituted a period of 6 weeks.

(3) Notwithstanding anything in Order 10, rule 5, notice of the motion need not be served personally.

(4) On entering the appeal or as soon as practicable thereafter, the appellant shall, unless otherwise directed, lodge in the principal registry—

(*a*) two certified copies of the summons and of the order appealed against,

(*b*) two copies of the clerk's notes of the evidence,

(*c*) two copies of the justices' reasons for their decision,

(*d*) a certificate that notice of the motion has been duly served on the clerk and on every party affected by the appeal, and

(*e*) where the notice of the motion includes an application to extend the time for bringing the appeal, a certificate (and a copy thereof) by the appellant's solicitor, or the appellant if he is acting in person, setting out the reasons for the delay and the relevant dates.

(5) If the clerk's notes of the evidence are not produced, the Court may hear and determine the appeal on any other evidence or statement of what occurred in the proceedings before the magistrates' court as appears to the Court to be sufficient.

(6) The Court shall not be bound to allow the appeal on the ground merely of misdirection or improper reception or rejection of evidence unless, in the opinion of the Court, substantial wrong or miscarriage of justice has been thereby occasioned.

(7) A registrar may dismiss an appeal to which this rule applies for want of prosecution or, with the consent of the parties, may dismiss the appeal or give leave for it to be withdrawn, and may deal with any question of costs arising out of the dismissal or withdrawal."

31. Order 104 shall be amended as follows :—

(1) In rule 1, the definitions of "the Act of 1925" and "the chief registrar" shall be deleted ; and for the definition of "the divorce registry" there shall be substituted :—

" "the principal registry" means the principal registry of the Family Division ;".

(2) In rules 1, 2, 4, 5 and 6, for the words "the divorce registry" wherever they appear there shall be substituted the words "the principal registry".

(3) In rule 2, paragraph (7) shall be omitted.

(4) In rule 3, the definition of "guardianship order" shall be deleted.

(5) In rule 4(1), for the words from the beginning to "together, in either case, with" there shall be substituted the words "An application for the registration of an English order may be made by lodging with a registrar of the Family Division a certified copy of the order, together with".

(6) In rule 4, for paragraph (3) there shall be substituted the following paragraph :—

"(3) The prescribed officer for the purposes of the Act of 1950 shall be the senior registrar."

(7) In rule 4(4), the words "the chief registrar or" and the words "as the case may be" shall be deleted.

(8) In rule 4, for paragraph (5) there shall be substituted the following paragraph :—

"(5) The fact that the order has been registered in the Court of Session or the Supreme Court of Northern Ireland shall be noted in the court minutes."

(9) In rule 4(6), the words "other than a guardianship order" shall be deleted.

(10) In rule 4(8), for the words "the appropriate registrar shall give notice of the discharge or variation" there shall be substituted the words "the registrar or district registrar by whom the discharge or variation was ordered shall give notice thereof" ; and the second sentence shall be deleted.

(11) In rule 4, for paragraph (9) there shall be substituted the following paragraph :—

"(9) Where the registration of an English order registered in the Court of Session or the Supreme Court of Northern Ireland is cancelled under section 24(1) of the Act of 1950, the prescribed officer to whom notice of the cancellation is to be sent under section 24(3) of that Act shall be the senior registrar ; and on receipt of such notice he shall cause particulars of it to be entered in Part I of the register."

(12) In rule 5, for paragraph (1) there shall be substituted the following paragraph :—

"(1) In relation to a Scottish or Northern Irish order the prescribed officer for the purposes of section 17(2) of the Act of 1950 shall be the senior registrar."

(13) In rule 5(2), for the words "the chief registrar or the senior registrar, as the case may be" there shall be substituted the words "the senior registrar".

(14) In rule 5(4), for the words "the registrar to whom a certified copy of the order was sent for registration" there shall be substituted the words "the senior registrar".

(15) In rule 5(3) and (5), for the words "the chief master in the case of a guardianship order and before a registrar of the divorce registry in any other case", wherever they appear, there shall be substituted the words "a registrar of the principal registry".

(16) In rule 5(6), the words "(other than a guardianship order)" shall be deleted.

(17) In rule 6, the number "(1)" at the beginning shall be deleted, and for the words "the registrar" where they first appear there shall be substituted the words "a registrar of the principal registry" ; and paragraph (2) shall be omitted.

(18) In rule 7, for the definition of "proper officer" there shall be substituted the following definition :—

" "proper officer" means—

(a) in the case of an order registered in the High Court under the Maintenance Orders (Facilities for Enforcement) Act 1920 or Part II of the Act of 1950, the senior registrar ;

(b) in the case of an order made by a magistrates' court which is to be or has been registered in the High Court under Part I of the Act of 1958, the senior registrar or the district registrar to whom a certified copy of the order has been sent pursuant to section 2(4)(c) of that Act ; and

(c) in any other case, the senior registrar or, where the order was made in a cause or matter proceeding in a district registry, the registrar of that registry."

(19) In rule 8(1)(b) and (2), the words "and, in the case of an order made under section 3(2), 5(4) or 6 of the Act of 1925, the duplicate order" wherever they appear shall be deleted.

(20) In rule 8(5), for sub-paragraphs (a) and (b) there shall be substituted the words "enter particulars of the registration in the court minutes".

(21) For rule 11 there shall be substituted the following rule :—

"Appeal from variation etc., of order by magistrates' court

11. An appeal to the High Court under section 4(7) of the Act of 1958 shall be heard and determined by a Divisional Court of the Family Division, and Order 90, rule 9, shall apply as it apples in relation to an appeal from a magistrates' court under the Guardianship of Minors Act 1971."

(22) In rule 17(1), the words from "if the related maintenance order" to "in any other case" shall be deleted.

32. In Order 107, rule 1(1), for the words "registrar of the Probate, Divorce and Admiralty Division" there shall be substituted the words "the Admiralty Registrar or any registrar of the Family Division".

33. In Order 109, rule 2, for paragraph (2) there shall be substituted the following paragraph :—

"(2) An appeal under the said section 13 from an order or decision of a magistrates' court under section 54(3) of the Magistrates' Courts Act 1952(a) shall be heard and determined by a Divisional Court of the Family Division."

34. Order 112 shall be omitted.

35. Appendix A shall be amended as follows :—

(1) In Form No. 4 (General form of writ of summons for use in probate action)—

(a) in the heading, for the words "Probate, Divorce and Admiralty Division (Probate)" there shall be substituted the words "Chancery Division (Probate)" ;

_____

(a) 1952 c. 55.

(*b*) the paragraph headed "DIRECTIONS FOR ENTERING APPEARANCE" shall be deleted, and the following paragraph shall be inserted in its place :—

"DIRECTIONS FOR ENTERING APPEARANCE

The defendant may enter an appearance in person or by a solicitor either (1) by handing in the appropriate forms, duly completed, at the Central Office, Royal Courts of Justice, Strand, London, WC2A 2LL or (2) by sending them to that Office by post. The appropriate forms may be obtained by sending a postal order for [*insert current price*] with an addressed envelope, foolscap size, to the Clerk of Accounts, Vote Office, Royal Courts of Justice, Strand, London WC2A 2LL."

(2) In Form No. 14 (Memorandum of Appearance), in the paragraph beginning "To be completed in duplicate", for the words "(probate action)" there shall be substituted the words "(Family Division proceedings)".

(3) In Form No. 87 (Notice of motion for writ of habeas corpus ad subjiciendum), Form No. 88 (Notice directed by Court of adjourned application for writ of habeas corpus), Form No. 89 (Writ of habeas corpus ad subjiciendum) and Form No. 90 (Notice to be served with writ of habeas corpus ad subjiciendum), after the words "Queen's Bench Division" wherever they appear there shall be inserted the words "[*or* Family Division *as the case may be*]".

(4) In Form No. 104 (Attachment of earnings order under the Maintenance Orders Act 1958), for the word "Division" in the heading there shall be substituted the words "Family Division".

36. In Appendix B, Form No. 1 (Writ of summons in action in rem issued out of Admiralty Registry) and Form No. 2 (Writ of summons in action in rem issued out of district registry) for the words "Probate, Divorce and Admiralty Division" there shall be substituted the words :—

"Queen's Bench Division
Admiralty Court".

37.—(1) Where on the date when section 1 of the Administration of Justice Act 1970 comes into force any proceedings are pending in one Division which, if begun after that date, would have been required by that section to be assigned to another Division, the power conferred on the Court by Order 4, rule 3, to transfer the proceedings to that other Division may at any time be exercised by the Court of its own motion.

(2) Unless the Court has already exercised its power under paragraph (1), it shall, on the first application in any such proceedings after the coming into force of the said section 1, consider whether or not to exercise that power.

(3) Where by virtue of paragraph (1) the Court makes an order under Order 4, rule 3, of its own motion, the order need not be drawn up ; but the Court shall give notice thereof to the parties to the proceedings.

(4) On the coming into force of the said section 1, all proceedings which involve the exercise of the High Court's Admiralty jurisdiction or its jurisdiction as a prize court, shall be treated as having been assigned to the Queen's Bench Division.

38. In the Rules of the Supreme Court, for—

(*a*) the references to the Probate, Divorce and Admiralty Division specified in the first column of the schedule to these Rules ;

(*b*) the references to the principal probate registry (or, as the case may be, divorce registry), specified in the second column of the said schedule ; and

(*c*) the references to the principal (or, as the case may be, senior) probate registrar specified in the third column of the said schedule,

there shall be substituted references to the Family Division, the principal registry of the Family Division and the principal registrar of the Family Division respectively.

39. The Arrangement of Orders at the beginning of the Rules of the Supreme Court 1965 shall be amended as follows :—

(1) In the title of Order 72, the words "in the Queen's Bench Division" shall be omitted.

(2) In the title of Order 74, for the date "1965" there shall be substituted the date "1970".

(3) For the title of Order 76 there shall be substituted the title "Contentious Probate Proceedings".

(4) For the title of Order 90 there shall be substituted the title "Miscellaneous Proceedings in the Family Division".

(5) For the title of Order 91 there shall be substituted the title "Revenue Proceedings in Chancery Division".

(6) The entry relating to Order 112 shall be omitted.

PART III

DISCOVERY AND RELATED PROCEDURES

40. The following rule shall be inserted in Order 24 after rule 7 :—

"Application under section 31 or 32(1) of Administration of Justice Act 1970

7A.—(1) An application for an order under section 31 of the Administration of Justice Act 1970 for the disclosure of documents before the commencement of proceedings shall be made by originating summons and the person against whom the order is sought shall be made defendant to the summons.

(2) An application after the commencement of proceedings for an order under section 32(1) of the said Act for the disclosure of documents by a person who is not a party to the proceedings shall be made by summons, which must be served on that person personally and on every party to the proceedings other than the applicant.

(3) A summons under paragraph (1) or (2) shall be supported by an affidavit which must—

(*a*) in the case of a summons under paragraph (1), state the grounds on which it is alleged that the applicant and the person against whom the order is sought are likely to be parties to subsequent proceedings in the High Court in which a claim for personal injuries is likely to be made ;

(*b*) in any case, specify or describe the documents in respect of which the order is sought and show, if practicable by reference to any pleading served or intended to be served in the proceedings, that the documents are relevant to an issue arising or likely to arise out of a claim for personal injuries made or likely to be made in the proceedings and that the person against whom the order is sought is likely to have or have had them in his possession, custody or power.

(4) A copy of the supporting affidavit shall be served with the summons on every person on whom the summons is required to be served.

(5) An order under the said section 31 or 32(1) for the disclosure of documents may be made conditional on the applicant's giving security for the costs of the person against whom it is made or on such other terms, if any, as the Court thinks just, and shall require the person against whom the order is made to make an affidavit stating whether any documents specified or described in the order are, or at any time have been, in his possession, custody or power and, if not then in his possession, custody or power, when he parted with them and what has become of them.

(6) No person shall be compelled by virtue of such an order to produce any documents which he could not be compelled to produce—

(*a*) in the case of a summons under paragraph (1), if the subsequent proceedings had already been begun, or

(*b*) in the case of a summons under paragraph (2), if he had been served with a writ of subpoena duces tecum to produce the documents at the trial.

(7) In this rule "a claim for personal injuries" means a claim in respect of personal injuries to a person (including any disease contracted by him and any impairment of his physical or mental condition) or in respect of a person's death.

(8) For the purposes of rules 10 and 11 an application for an order under the said section 31 or 32(1) shall be treated as a cause or matter between the applicant and the person against whom the order is sought."

41. In Order 24, rule 8, for the words "rule 3 or rule 7" there shall be substituted the words "rule 3, 7 or 7A".

42. The following rule shall be inserted in Order 29 after rule 7 :—

"Inspection etc. of property under section 21 of Administration of Justice Act 1969 or section 32(2) of Administration of Justice Act 1970

7A.—(1) The power conferred by section 21(1) of the Administration of Justice Act 1969(**a**) to make an order in respect of property pending the commencement of proceedings in the High Court shall be exercisable only

---

(a) 1969 c. 58.

in respect of property as to which it appears to the Court that it may become the subject matter of subsequent proceedings involving a claim for personal injuries.

(2) An application for an order under the said section 21(1) shall be made by originating summons and the person against whom the order is sought shall be made defendant to the summons.

(3) An application after the commencement of proceedings for an order under section 32(2) of the Administration of Justice Act 1970 in respect of property which is not the property of or in the possession of any party to the proceedings shall be made by summons, which must be served on the person against whom the order is sought personally and on every party to the proceedings other than the applicant.

(4) A summons under paragraph (2) or (3) shall be supported by an affidavit which must—

> (*a*) in the case of a summons under paragraph (2), state the grounds on which it is alleged that the applicant and the person against whom the order is sought are likely to be parties to subsequent proceedings in the High Court in which a claim for personal injuries is likely to be made ;

> (*b*) in any case, specify or describe the property in respect of which the order is sought and show, if practicable by reference to any pleading served or intended to be served in the proceedings, that it is or may become the subject matter of the proceedings or that it is property as to which any question arises in the proceedings.

(5) A copy of the supporting affidavit shall be served with the summons on every person on whom the summons is required to be served.

(6) An order made under the said section 21 or 32(2) may be made conditional on the applicant's giving security for the costs of the person against whom it is made or on such other terms, if any, as the Court thinks just.

(7) No such order shall be made if it appears to the Court—

> (*a*) that compliance with the order, if made, would result in the disclosure of information relating to a secret process, discovery or invention not in issue in the proceedings, and

> (*b*) that the application would have been refused on that ground if—

>> (i) in the case of a summons under paragraph (2), the subsequent proceedings had already been begun, or

>> (ii) in the case of a summons under paragraph (3), the person against whom the order is sought were a party to the proceedings.

(8) In this rule "a claim for personal injuries" means a claim in respect of personal injuries to a person (including any disease contracted by him and any impairment of his physical or mental condition) or in respect of a person's death."

43. The following paragraph shall be added to Order 62, rule 3 :—

"(12) Where an application is made in accordance with Order 24, rule 7A, or Order 29, rule 7A, for an order under section 21 of the Administration of Justice Act 1969 or section 31 or 32 of the Administration of Justice Act 1970, the person against whom the order is sought shall be entitled, unless the Court otherwise directs, to his costs of and incidental to the application and of complying with any order made thereon and he may, after giving the applicant 7 days' notice of his intention to do so, tax such costs and, if they are not paid within 4 days after taxation, sign judgment for them."

44. The following paragraph shall be added to Appendix 1 to Order 62:—

"6. Where a party is entitled by virtue of rule 3(12) to require any costs to be taxed, the requisite document for the purposes of rule 21 is a copy of the notice given by him pursuant to rule 3(12)."

PART IV

MISCELLANEOUS AMENDMENTS

45. Order 15, rule 6, shall be amended as follows :—

(1) For paragraph (2)(*b*) there shall be substituted the following paragraph :—

"(*b*) order any of the following persons to be added as a party, namely—

(i) any person who ought to have been joined as a party or whose presence before the Court is necessary to ensure that all matters in dispute in the cause or matter may be effectually and completely determined and adjudicated upon, or

(ii) any person between whom and any party to the cause or matter there may exist a question or issue arising out of or relating to or connected with any relief or remedy claimed in the cause or matter which in the opinion of the Court it would be just and convenient to determine as between him and that party as well as between the parties to the cause or matter."

(2) In paragraph (3) for the word "defendant" there shall be substituted the word "party" and at the end there shall be added the following words :—

"or, as the case may be, the question or issue to be determined as between him and any party to the cause or matter."

46. Order 62 shall be amended as follows :—

(1) In rule 13(1)—

(*a*) for the words from the beginning to "(Taxing Office)" there shall be substituted the words "A principal clerk of the Supreme Court (Taxing Office) authorised in that behalf by the Lord Chancellor"; and

(*b*) in sub-paragraph (*a*) the words from "if the amount" to "£350" shall be omitted

(2) In Appendix 3, Part III, paragraph 7, for the figures "£4 10s. (£4·50)" there shall be substituted the figures "£6 10s. (£6·50)".

47. In Order 63, rules 6, 7 and 8 shall be revoked except in relation to any instrument creating a power of attorney, or any copy of such an instrument, filed or deposited in the Central Office before 1st October 1971.

48. The following rule shall be inserted in Order 77 after rule 8 :—

"Joinder of Commissioners of Inland Revenue under Order 15, *rule* 6(2)(*b*)(ii)

8A. Nothing in Order 15, rule 6(2)(*b*)(ii),shall be construed as enabling the Commissioners of Inland Revenue to be added as a party to any cause or matter except with their consent signified in writing or in such manner as may be authorised."

Dated 23rd July 1971.

Hailsham of St. Marylebone, C.
Widgery, C. J.
Denning, M. R.
George Baker, P.
Cyril Salmon, L. J.
John Pennycuick, V-C.
James Fox-Andrews.
Oliver Lodge.
H. Mongomery-Campbell.

SCHEDULE

Rule 38

AMENDMENT OF REFERENCES IN CONSEQUENCE OF THE RE-NAMING OF THE PROBATE, DIVORCE AND ADMIRALTY DIVISION AS THE FAMILY DIVISION

1. *References to Probate, Divorce and Admiralty Division*	2. *References to principal probate registry*	3. *References to principal (or senior) probate registrar*
Order 17, rule 4.	Order 1, rule 4(1).	Order 59, rule 5(5)(*c*).
Order 30, rule 4(4).	Order 4, rule 6(1).	Order 104, rule 1.
Order 32, rules 7(2), 8(1), 10, 11(1), 12, 23 and 24(1).	Order 30, rule 2(4).	Appendix A, Form No. 37.
	Order 32, rules 2(3)(*c*) and 7(1).	
Order 50, rule 9.		
	Order 41, rule 9(3).	
Order 51, rule 2.		
	Order 56, rule 6(1)(*a*).	
Order 56, rule 6(1)(*a*).		
	Order 57, rules 2(4)(*c*) and 3(*a*).	
Order 57, rules 2(4)(*c*) and 3(*a*).		
	Order 59, rules 5(5)(*c*) and 16(2A) and (6).	
Order 58, rules 1(1), 2(2) and 7(2).	Order 62, rules 7(6), 12(1) and (7), 21(5)(*a*), 22(4)(*a*), 34(1) and (5), 35(7).	
Order 62, rules 1(1), 2(2), 12(7), 21(1), (3)(*a*), and (4), 22(1) and (2), 23(4), 24(1), Appendix 1, paragraph 1 and Appendix 2, items 4 and 37.	Order 67, rule 1(2), Table (*e*).	
	Order 89, rule 1(1).	
	Order 99, rule 6(2).	
Order 64, rules 2(1) and 7(1)(*c*).	Appendix A, Forms No. 6 and 14.	
Order 80, rule 13(2)(*b*).		
Order 89, rule 1(2).		
Order 106, rule 2(2).		

EXPLANATORY NOTE

(This Note is not part of the Rules.)

These Rules amend the Rules of the Supreme Court in a number of respects.

Part II makes changes consequential on the reconstitution of the Divisions of the High Court by sections 1—4 of the Administration of Justice Act 1970. These sections rename the Probate, Divorce and Admiralty Division as the Family Division, and concentrate in it the family and domestic business of the High Court, including wardship, guardianship and adoption cases ; transfer Admiralty and prize business to the Queen's Bench Division, where the Admiralty Court is established for the purpose ; transfer contentious probate cases to the Chancery Division ; establish the Commercial Court within the Queen's Bench Division to take the commercial list ; and empower judges of the Commercial Court in certain circumstances to sit as arbitrators. A large number of rules are amended as a result of these provisions. Order 76 (probate actions) is re-written (rule 26), and Orders 91 and 112 are merged into a new Order 90 entitled "Miscellaneous Proceedings in the Family Division" (rule 30). Provision is made for the transfer of pending proceedings to other Divisions in consequence of the reorganization of business (rule 37) and for the alteration of references to the Probate, Divorce and Admiralty Division generally (rule 38 and Schedule).

Part III provides for the disclosure of documents and the inspection etc. of property under section 21 of the Administration of Justice Act 1969 and sections 31 and 32 of the Administration of Justice Act 1970. Part IV extends the power of the Court to order the joinder of parties ; makes fresh provision for the taxation of costs by principal clerks of the Supreme Court Taxing Office ; increases the fixed costs allowed on the issue of writs of execution, and revokes the rules dealing with the filing of powers of attorney in consequence of the coming into operation of the Powers of Attorney Act 1971 (c.27).

STATUTORY INSTRUMENTS

1971 No. 1271

AGRICULTURE

The Price Stability of Imported Products (Rates of Levy) (Eggs) (No. 15) Order 1971

Made - - - -	2nd August 1971
Coming into Operation	3rd August 1971

The Minister of Agriculture, Fisheries and Food, in exercise of the powers conferred upon him by section 1(2), (4), (5), (6) and (7) of the Agriculture and Horticulture Act 1964(a) and of all other powers enabling him in that behalf, hereby makes the following order:—

1. This order may be cited as the Price Stability of Imported Products (Rates of Levy) (Eggs) (No. 15) Order 1971, and shall come into operation on 3rd August 1971.

2.—(1) In this order—

" the Principal Order " means the Price Stability of Imported Products (Levy Arrangements) (Eggs) Order 1970(b) as amended by any subsequent order, and if any such order is replaced by any subsequent order the expression shall be construed as a reference to such subsequent order;

AND other expressions have the same meaning as in the Principal Order.

(2) The Interpretation Act 1889(c) shall apply to the interpretation of this order as it applies to the interpretation of an Act of Parliament and as if this order and the order hereby revoked were Acts of Parliament.

3. In accordance with and subject to the provisions of the Principal Order (which provides for the charging of levies on imports of those eggs and egg products which are specified commodities for the purposes of the Agriculture and Horticulture Act 1964) the rate of general levy for such imports into the United Kingdom of any specified commodity as are described in column 2 of the Schedule to this order in relation to a tariff heading indicated in column 1 of that Schedule shall be the rate set forth in relation thereto in column 3 of that Schedule.

4. The Price Stability of Imported Products (Rates of Levy) (Eggs) (No. 14) Order 1971(d) is hereby revoked.

In Witness whereof the Official Seal of the Minister of Agriculture, Fisheries and Food is hereunto affixed on 2nd August 1971.

(L.S.)

G. P. Jupe,
Assistant Secretary.

(a) 1964 c. 28.　　(b) S.I. 1970/359 (1970 I, p. 1277).　　(c) 1889 c. 63.
(d) S.I. 1971/1157 (1971 II, p. 3399).

SCHEDULE

1. Tariff Heading	2. Description of Imports	3. Rate of General Levy
04.05	Imports of:—	
	Birds' eggs (in shell or not in shell), fresh, dried or otherwise preserved, sweetened or not, other than egg yolks:	(per 120 eggs)
	A. Eggs in shell:	p
	1. Not exceeding 11 lb. in weight per 120 ..	40
	2. Over 11 lb. but not exceeding 12½ lb. in weight per 120	45
	3. Over 12½ lb. but not exceeding 14 lb. in weight per 120	65
	4. Over 14 lb. but not exceeding 15½ lb. in weight per 120	65
	5. Over 15½ lb. but not exceeding 17 lb. in weight per 120	55
	6. Over 17 lb. in weight per 120	55
	B. Eggs not in shell:	(per ton)
	Whole dried	£110
	Whole frozen or liquid	£60

EXPLANATORY NOTE

(*This Note is not part of the Order.*)

This order, which comes into operation on 3rd August 1971, supersedes the Price Stability of Imported Products (Rates of Levy) (Eggs) (No. 14) Order 1971. It—

(*a*) reduces the rates of general levy to be charged on imports of eggs in shell in the weight grades numbered 1 to 6 in the Schedule to the order; and

(*b*) reimposes unchanged the rates of general levy to be charged on imports of dried, frozen or liquid whole egg not in shell.

STATUTORY INSTRUMENTS

1971 No. 1272

HOUSING, ENGLAND AND WALES

The Housing Subsidies (Representative Rates of Interest) Order 1971

Laid before the House of Commons in draft

Made - - - *2nd August* 1971

Coming into Operation 10th *August* 1971

The Secretary of State for the Environment, in exercise of his powers under sections 2(2), 2(5) and 21(1) of the Housing Subsidies Act 1967(a) and of all other powers enabling him in that behalf and after consultation with such recipient authorities, and such bodies representative of recipient authorities, as appear to him to be appropriate, hereby makes the following order in the terms of a draft approved by resolution of the Commons House of Parliament :—

Citation, commencement and interpretation

1.—(1) This order may be cited as the Housing Subsidies (Representative Rates of Interest) Order 1971 and shall come into operation on 10th August 1971.

(2) The Interpretation Act 1889(b) applies for the interpretation of this order as it applies for the interpretation of an Act of Parliament.

Representative rates of interest

2. The rates of interest to be specified for the purposes of section 2(2) of the Housing Subsidies Act 1967 in respect of approved dwellings provided in England and Wales shall be as follows :—

(*a*) in relation to all local authorities and all housing associations, in respect of the financial year commencing on 1st April 1971 ... ...   8·32 per cent.

(*b*) in relation to all development corporations and the Commission for the New Towns, in respect of the financial year commencing on 1st April 1971 ...   9·22 per cent.

Peter Walker,
2nd August 1971. Secretary of State for the Environment

(a) 1967 c. 29. (b) 1889 c. 63.

EXPLANATORY NOTE

(This Note is not part of the Order.)

This Order specifies representative borrowing rates for the year 1971/72 for the several bodies who receive housing subsidies under the Housing Subsidies Act 1967. The main subsidy will meet the difference between the loan charges on the aggregate approved cost of dwellings completed in that year at the borrowing rates specified in the Order, and the loan charges which would have been incurred at a fixed borrowing rate of 4 per cent.

STATUTORY INSTRUMENTS

1971 No. 1275

INDUSTRIAL DEVELOPMENT

INVESTMENT GRANTS

Investment Grants Termination (No. 1) Order 1971

Made - - -	3rd *August* 1971
Laid before Parliament	12th *August* 1971
Coming into Operation	16th *August* 1971

The Secretary of State in exercise of his powers under section 1(6) of the Investment and Building Grants Act 1971(a), and all other powers in that behalf enabling him, hereby orders as follows :—

Citation, commencement and interpretation

1.—(1) This Order may be cited as the Investment Grants Termination (No. 1) Order 1971 and shall come into force on 16th August 1971.

(2) The Interpretation Act 1889(b) shall apply to the interpretation of this Order as it applies to the interpretation of an Act of Parliament.

Dates before which certain applications for grant are to be made

2.—(1) Applications for grant under Part I of the Industrial Development Act 1966(c) in respect of expenditure incurred before 1st January 1969 are to be made before 1st January 1972.

(2) Such applications in respect of expenditure incurred during the period 1st January 1969 to 31st March 1969 (both dates inclusive) are to be made before 1st April 1972.

(3) Such applications in respect of expenditure incurred during the period 1st April 1969 to 30th June 1969 (both dates inclusive) are to be made before 1st July 1972.

(4) Such applications in respect of expenditure incurred during the period 1st July 1969 to 30th September 1969 (both dates inclusive) are to be made before 1st October 1972.

Form and manner of applications

3. The applications for grant to which this Order applies are to be made in such form and manner, and to contain such particulars and be accompanied by such documents, as the Secretary of State may direct.

3rd August 1971.

Anthony Grant,
Parliamentary Under Secretary of State,
Department of Trade and Industry.

(a) 1971 c. 51.	(b) 1889 c. 63.	(c) 1966 c. 34.

EXPLANATORY NOTE

(This Note is not part of the Order.)

This Order specifies certain dates by which applications for investment grant in respect of expenditure incurred before a related date or in related periods, must be made and provides for the making of directions as to the form of such applications, the particulars they must contain and the documents to accompany them.

STATUTORY INSTRUMENTS

1971 No. 1280

WAGES COUNCILS

The Wages Regulation (Made-up Textiles) Order 1971

Made - - - *4th August* 1971

Coming into Operation 1*st September* 1971

Whereas the Secretary of State has received from the Made-up Textiles Wages Council (Great Britain) the wages regulation proposals set out in the Schedule hereto ;

Now, therefore, the Secretary of State in exercise of his powers under section 11 of the Wages Councils Act 1959(a), and of all other powers enabling him in that behalf, hereby makes the following Order :—

1. This Order may be cited as the Wages Regulation (Made-up Textiles) Order 1971.

2.—(1) In this Order the expression "the specified date" means the 1st September 1971, provided that where, as respects any worker who is paid wages at intervals not exceeding seven days, that date does not correspond with the beginning of the period for which the wages are paid, the expression "the specified date" means, as respects that worker, the beginning of the next such period following that date.

(2) The Interpretation Act 1889(b) shall apply to the interpretation of this Order as it applies to the interpretation of an Act of Parliament and as if this Order and the Order hereby revoked were Acts of Parliament.

3. The wages regulation proposals set out in the Schedule hereto shall have effect as from the specified date and as from that date the Wages Regulation (Made-up Textiles) Order 1970(c) shall cease to have effect.

Signed by order of the Secretary of State.

4th August 1971.

J. R. Lloyd Davies,

Assistant Secretary,
Department of Employment.

(a) 1959 c. 69.　　(b) 1889 c. 63.　　(c) S.I. 1970/1227 (1970 II, p. 4055).

Article 3

SCHEDULE

The following minimum remuneration shall be substituted for the statutory minimum remuneration fixed by the Wages Regulation (Made-up Textiles) Order 1970 (Order M.T. (66)).

STATUTORY MINIMUM REMUNERATION

PART I

GENERAL

1. The minimum remuneration payable to a worker to whom this Schedule applies for all work except work to which a minimum overtime rate applies under Part IV of this Schedule is:—

(1) in the case of a time worker, the general minimum time rate payable to the worker under Part II or Part III of this Schedule ;

(2) in the case of a worker employed on piece work, piece rates each of which would yield, in the circumstances of the case, to an ordinary worker at least the same amount of money as the piece work basis time rate applicable to the worker under Part II or Part III of this Schedule.

PART II

MALE WORKERS

GENERAL MINIMUM TIME RATES

2. The general minimum time rates payable to male workers are as follows:—

	Per hour p
(1) Workers aged 21 years or over and employed as awl and needle stitchers (leather and canvas), cutters, letter writers (other than stencillers), machinists (sewing), mixers, palm and needle hands, ropers of tents and coal sacks, or splicers of ropes over $1\frac{1}{2}$ in. in circumference	34

(2) All other workers, being aged—

		Per hour p
21 years or over	$31\frac{1}{2}$
20 and under 21 years	27
19 „ „ 20 „	$25\frac{1}{2}$
18 „ „ 19 „	$24\frac{1}{2}$
17 „ „ 18 „	21
16 „ „ 17 „	$17\frac{1}{2}$
under 16 years	$14\frac{1}{2}$

Provided that the general minimum time rate payable during his first six months' employment in the trade to a worker who enters, or has entered, the trade for the first time at or over the age of 18 years shall be $\frac{1}{2}p$ per hour less than the rate otherwise payable under sub-paragraph (1) or (2) of this paragraph.

PIECE WORK BASIS TIME RATES

3. The piece work basis time rates applicable to male workers employed on piece work are as follows:—

	Per hour p
(1) Workers employed as awl and needle stitchers (leather and canvas), cutters, letter writers (other than stencillers), machinists (sewing), mixers, palm and needle hands, ropers of tents and coal sacks, or splicers of ropes over 1½ in. in circumference	39
(2) All other workers	36

PART III

FEMALE WORKERS

GENERAL MINIMUM TIME RATES

4. The general minimum time rates payable to female workers are as follows:—

	Per hour p
(1) Workers aged 18 years or over and employed as awl and needle stitchers (leather and canvas), cutters, letter writers (other than stencillers), machinists (sewing), mixers, palm and needle hands, ropers of tents and coal sacks, or splicers of ropes over 1½ in. in circumference	27

(2) All other workers, being aged—

	Per hour p
18 years or over	25½
17 and under 18 years	22½
16 „ „ 17 „	18½
under 16 years	15½

Provided that the general minimum time rate payable during her first six months' employment in the trade to a worker who enters, or has entered, the trade for the first time at or over the age of 16 years shall be ½p per hour less than the minimum rate otherwise payable under sub-paragraph (1) or (2) of this paragraph.

PIECE WORK BASIS TIME RATES

5. The piece work basis time rates applicable to female workers employed on piece work are as follows:—

	Per hour p
(1) Workers employed as awl and needle stitchers (leather and canvas), cutters, letter writers (other than stencillers), machinists (sewing), mixers, palm and needle hands, ropers of tents and coal sacks, or splicers of ropes over 1½ in. in circumference	30½
(2) All other workers	29

PART IV

OVERTIME AND WAITING TIME

MINIMUM OVERTIME RATES

6. Minimum overtime rates are payable to a worker to whom this Schedule applies as follows:—

(1) on any day except a Saturday, Sunday or customary holiday—

  (*a*) for the first 2 hours worked in excess of 8 hours   time-and-a-quarter

  (*b*) thereafter   ...   .   time-and-a-half

 Provided that where it is, or may become, the established practice of the employer to require the worker's attendance on five days only in the week the said minimum overtime rates of time-and-a-quarter and time-and-a-half shall be payable after 8¾ and 10¾ hours' work respectively;

(2) on a Saturday, not being a customary holiday—

  (*a*) for the first 2 hours worked in excess of 3 hours   time-and-a-quarter

  (*b*) thereafter   ...   .   time-and-a-half

 Provided that where it is, or may become, the established practice of the employer to require the worker's attendance on five days only in the week, minimum overtime rates shall be payable to the worker for all time worked on a Saturday as follows:—

  (i) for the first 2 hours   ...   .   time-and-a-quarter

  (ii) thereafter   ...   .   time-and-a-half

(3) on a Sunday or a customary holiday for all time worked   double time

(4) in any week exclusive of any time for which a minimum overtime rate is payable under the foregoing provisions of this paragraph, for all time worked in excess of 40 hours   ...   .   time-and-a-quarter.

7. In this Part of this Schedule—

(1) the expression "customary holiday" means—

  (*a*) (i) in England and Wales—

     Christmas Day (or, if Christmas Day falls on a Sunday, such week day as may be appointed by national proclamation, or, if none is so appointed, the next following Tuesday), Boxing Day, Good Friday, Easter Monday, Whit Monday (or where another day is substituted therefor by national proclamation, that day) and August Bank Holiday;

(ii) in Scotland—

New Year's Day and the following day:

Provided that if New Year's Day falls on a Sunday the holidays shall be the following Monday and Tuesday and if New Year's Day falls on a Saturday the holidays shall be New Year's Day and the following Monday ;

the local Spring Holiday ;

the local Autumn Holiday ;

two other days (being normal working days for the workers concerned) in the course of a calendar year, to be fixed by the employer and notified to the workers not less than three weeks before the holiday ; or

(b) in the case of each of the said days such week day as may be substituted therefor, being either—

(i) a day which is by local custom recognised as a day of holiday, or

(ii) a day which falls within three weeks of the day for which it is substituted, and is mutually agreed between the employer and the worker.

(2) the expressions "time-and-a-quarter", "time-and-a-half" and "double time" mean respectively—

(a) in the case of a time worker, one and a quarter times, one and a half times and twice the general minimum time rate otherwise applicable to the worker under Part II or Part III of this Schedule ;

(b) in the case of a worker employed on piece work—

(i) a time rate equal respectively to one quarter, one half and the whole of the piece work basis time rate otherwise applicable to the worker under Part II or Part III of this Schedule and, in addition thereto,

(ii) the piece rates otherwise applicable to the worker under paragraph 1(2).

WAITING TIME

8.—(1) A worker is entitled to payment of the minimum remuneration specified in this Schedule for all time during which he is present on the premises of his employer unless he is present thereon in any of the following circumstances—

(a) without the employer's consent, express or implied,

(b) for some purpose unconnected with his work and other than that of waiting for work to be given to him to perform,

(c) by reason only of the fact that he is resident thereon,

(d) during normal meal times in a room or place in which no work is being done, and he is not waiting for work to be given to him to perform.

(2) The minimum remuneration payable under sub-paragraph (1) of this paragraph to a piece worker when not engaged on piece work is that which would be applicable if he were a time worker.

PART V

APPLICABILITY OF STATUTORY MINIMUM REMUNERATION

9. This Schedule does not apply to workers who are persons registered as handicapped by disablement in pursuance of the Disabled Persons (Employment) Acts 1944 and 1958(a), in respect of their employment by Remploy Limited but, save as aforesaid, applies to workers in relation to whom the Made-up Textiles Wages Council (Great Britain) operates, that is to say, workers employed in Great Britain in the trade specified in the Schedule to the Trade Boards (Made-up Textiles Trade, Great Britain) (Constitution and Proceedings) Regulations 1932(b), that is to say: —

(1) The making from woven fabrics of any of the following articles, or the repairing thereof: —

tarpaulins ; tents ; marquees ; rick, cart or wagon covers ; nose-bags, oilskin clothing or headgear or linings therefor ; flags made of more than one piece ; baths, basins, buckets, beds, cots, hammocks, ground sheets or similar articles ; girths and articles known in the trade as horse-clothing.

(2) The making of any of the following articles from fabrics of the kind specified in sub-paragraph (1) above, or the repairing thereof, when carried on in association with or in conjunction with the making or repairing of any of the articles mentioned in the said sub-paragraph: —

rope-bound coal and coke sacks ; haversacks or knapsacks ; outside and inside blinds or awnings ; flags made of one piece ; bunting decorations ;

including: —

(A) the following operations when carried on in association with or in conjunction with the operations specified in sub-paragraphs (1) and (2) above, viz., operations known in the trade as—

(i) the dyeing, oiling, tarring, chemically treating, or otherwise proofing of the fabrics mentioned in sub-paragraph (1) and the preparation of dressings therefor ;

(ii) cutting, sewing, finishing, stencilling or branding by hand or machine ;

(B) the following or similar operations performed by hand or machine when incidental to and carried on in association with or in conjunction with the operations specified in sub-paragraphs (1) and (2) above: —

(i) the splicing or braiding of rope, cord or twine ;

(ii) the making of fittings of leather or webbing, including the assembling of metal or other parts ;

(a) 1944 c. 10 and 1958 c. 33.
(b) S.R. & O. 1932/805 (Rev. XXIII, p. 480: 1932, p. 1706).

(iii) the sewing or attaching to any of the articles mentioned in sub-paragraph (1) or (2) above of:—

(*a*) rope, cord or twine ;

(*b*) leather, webbing or metal or fittings made thereof ;

(C) the warehousing of, the packing of, and similar operations in regard to any of the articles mentioned in sub-paragraphs (1) and (2) above, when carried on in association with or in conjunction with the operations specified in the said sub-paragraphs ;

(D) the warehousing of, the packing of, and similar operations in regard to any other articles when carried on in or in association with or in conjunction with any business, establishment, branch or department mainly engaged in any of the operations mentioned in sub-paragraph (C) above ;

but excluding:—

(i) the making of haversacks and knapsacks when made in association with or in conjunction with the making of and as part of military web equipment ;

(ii) the making of folding or deck chairs ;

(iii) the making or repairing of horse-clothing, girths and nose-bags when carried on in association with or in conjunction with the making or repairing of leather saddlery or harness ;

(iv) the making or repairing of rubberised articles ;

(v) the making or repairing of tarpaulins or of rope-bound coal and coke sacks in an establishment, business, branch or department in which the making of sails is the main or principal business of the establishment, business, branch or department ;

(vi) the printing by hand or machine of flags or parts thereof ;

(vii) the operations mentioned in sub-paragraph (C) above, when carried on in or in association with or in conjunction with any business, establishment, branch or department mainly engaged in the warehousing of, the packing of, and similar operations in regard to corn sacks, flour sacks, coal sacks, sugar sacks, cement bags, sand bags, nail bags, potato bags, seed bags and similar sacks or bags ;

(viii) operations performed by workers directly employed by railway companies ;

(ix) operations included in the Trade Boards (Hat, Cap and Millinery) Order 1919(**a**) ;

(x) operations included in the Trade Boards (Linen and Cotton Handkerchief and Household Goods and Linen Piece Goods) Order 1920(**b**) ;

(xi) operations included in the Trade Boards (Rope, Twine and Net) Order 1919(**c**), but not specifically mentioned in the Trade Boards (Made-up Textiles) Order 1920(**d**).

(**a**) S.R. & O. 1919/1262 (1919 II, p. 515).   (**b**) S.R. & O. 1920/103 (1920 II, p. 780).
(**c**) S.R. & O. 1919/930 (1919 II, p. 524).   (**d**) S.R. & O. 1920/1901 (1920 II, p. 782).

EXPLANATORY NOTE

(This Note is not part of the Order.)

This Order, which has effect from 1st September 1971, sets out the statutory minimum remuneration payable in substitution for that fixed by the Wages Regulation (Made-up Textiles) Order 1970 (Order M.T. (66)), which Order is revoked.

New provisions are printed in italics.

STATUTORY INSTRUMENTS

1971 No. 1281 (S. 164)

CLEAN AIR

The Smoke Control Areas (Exempted Fireplaces) (Scotland) Order 1971

Made - - -	3rd *August* 1971
Laid before Parliament	10th *August* 1971
Coming into Operation	24th *August* 1971

In exercise of the powers conferred on me by section 11(4) of the Clean Air Act 1956(a), and of all other powers enabling me in that behalf, and being satisfied that fireplaces of the class described can be used for burning fuel other than authorised fuels without producing a substantial quantity of smoke, I hereby make the following order:—

Citation and commencement

1. This order may be cited as the Smoke Control Areas (Exempted Fireplaces) (Scotland) Order 1971 and shall come into operation on 24th August 1971.

Interpretation

2. The Interpretation Act 1889(b) shall apply for the interpretation of this order as it applies for the interpretation of an Act of Parliament.

Class of fireplace exempted from section 11 of the Clean Air Act 1956

3. In Scotland the class of fireplace described in column (1) of the Schedule hereto shall, subject to the conditions specified in column (2), be exempted from the provisions of section 11 of the Clean Air Act 1956 (which empowers a local authority to declare the whole or any part of their district to be a smoke control area).

Gordon Campbell,
One of Her Majesty's Principal
Secretaries of State.

St. Andrew's House,
Edinburgh.
3rd August 1971.

(a) 1956 c. 52.   (b) 1889 c. 63.

Article 3

Column 1 Classes of Fireplace	Column 2 Conditions
The fireplace known as the Rayburn CB 34 and manufactured by Glynwed Foundries Limited	The fireplace shall be installed, maintained and operated so as to minimise the emission of smoke and in accordance with the manufacturers instructions. No fuel shall be used other than selected washed coal singles.

EXPLANATORY NOTE

(This Note is not part of the Order.)

Section 11 of the Clean Air Act 1956 empowers local authorities to declare the whole or any part of their district to be a smoke control area in which the emission of smoke is, generally, prohibited. This Order exempts the Rayburn CB34 fireplace from the provisions of that section, upon certain conditions as to proper operation.

STATUTORY INSTRUMENTS

1971 No. 1284

ROAD TRAFFIC

The Road Vehicles (Excise) (Prescribed Particulars) (Amendment) Regulations 1971

Made - - - -	*5th August* 1971
Laid before Parliament	*5th August* 1971
Coming into Operation	*Immediately after being laid before Parliament*

The Secretary of State for the Environment, in exercise of his powers under section 12 of the Vehicles (Excise) Act 1971(a) and section 23 of that Act as modified by section 39(1) thereof and paragraph 20 of Part I of Schedule 7 thereto and as extended by section 7 of the Finance Act 1971(b), and of all other enabling powers, hereby makes the following Regulations:—

1. These Regulations shall come into operation immediately after being laid before Parliament and may be cited as the Road Vehicles (Excise) (Prescribed Particulars) (Amendment) Regulations 1971.

2. The Road Vehicles (Excise) (Prescribed Particulars) Regulations 1966(c) as amended (d) shall have effect as though—

(*a*) in Regulation 8 (invalid vehicles) after the words "disabled persons)" there were inserted the words "or section 7 of the Finance Act 1971 (which also relates to vehicles adapted for disabled persons)"; and

(*b*) in the form VE.1/4 as set out in Schedule 2 to the Regulations, at the end of the Declaration there were added the following words:—

"(Further declaration by a person too disabled to drive himself) I FURTHER DECLARE that the following extensive, conspicuous and permanent adaptations have been carried out on the vehicle to make it suitable for the transport, of me as a disabled person, by a full-time constant attendant as driver (state here adaptations).".

Signed by authority of the Secretary of State.

C. P. Scott-Malden,
A Deputy Secretary in the
Department of the Environment.

5th August 1971.

(a) 1971 c. 10.   (b) 1971 c. 68.
(c) S.I. 1966/224 (1966 I, p. 435).
(d) The amending Regulations are not relevant to the subject matter of these Regulations.

EXPLANATORY NOTE

(This Note is not part of the Regulations.)

These Regulations amend the Road Vehicles (Excise) (Prescribed Particulars) Regulations 1966 to provide for the declaration to be made and the particulars to be furnished by a disabled person in relation to a vehicle exempted from duty under the Vehicles (Excise) Act 1971 by virtue of section 7 of the Finance Act 1971.

STATUTORY INSTRUMENTS

1971 No. 1285

ROAD TRAFFIC

The Road Vehicles (Registration and Licensing) (Amendment) Regulations 1971

Made - - -	*5th August* 1971
Laid before Parliament	*5th August* 1971
Coming into Operation	*Immediately after being laid before Parliament*

The Secretary of State for the Environment, in exercise of his powers under section 23 of the Vehicles (Excise) Act 1971(a), as modified by section 39(1) of, and paragraph 20 of Part I of Schedule 7 to, that Act and as extended by section 7 of the Finance Act 1971(b), and of all other enabling powers, hereby makes the following Regulations :—

1. These Regulations shall come into operation immediately after being laid before Parliament and may be cited as the Road Vehicles (Registration and Licensing) (Amendment) Regulations 1971.

2. Regulation 26 of the Road Vehicles (Registration and Licensing) Regulations 1971(c) (which provides for the declaration to be made and the particulars to be furnished in relation to certain vehicles exempted from duty under the Vehicles (Excise) Act 1971) shall have effect as if—

(*a*) in paragraph (1), for the words "fitted with controls" onwards there were substituted the words "which are exempted from duty by virtue of the provisions of section 7(2) of the Act or section 7 of the Finance Act 1971." ; and

(*b*) in paragraph (2)—

   (i) after the words "the said section 7(2)" there shall be inserted the words "or the said section 7", and

   (ii) for the words "stating that" onwards there shall be substituted the words "stating—

      (*a*) in a case to which the said section 7(2) applies, that he obtained a grant paid by either Secretary of State out of moneys provided by Parliament in respect of the cost of fitting controls to the vehicle enabling it to be driven by him as having a particular disability or that he has a disability of a kind such that grants in respect of the fitting of such controls are so paid ; or

---

(a) 1971 c. 10.   (b) 1971 c. 68.
(c) S.I. 1971/450 (1971 I, p. 1305).

(b) in a case to which the said section 7 applies, that—

    (i) he has a particular disability that so incapacitates him in the use of his limbs that he has to be driven and cared for by a full-time constant attendant, and

    (ii) he is sufficiently disabled to be eligible under the Health Services and Public Health Act 1968(a), for an invalid tricycle if he were not too disabled to drive it.".

Signed by authority of the Secretary of State.

5th August 1971.

C. P. Scott-Malden,
A Deputy Secretary in the
Department of the Environment.

EXPLANATORY NOTE

(This Note is not part of the Regulations.)

Regulation 26 of the Road Vehicles (Registration and Licensing) Regulations 1971 provides for the declaration to be made and the particulars to be furnished with respect to certain vehicles exempted from duty under the Vehicles (Excise) Act 1971. These Regulations amend Regulation 26 so as to make similar provision with respect to vehicles exempted from such duty by virtue of section 7 of the Finance Act 1971.

(a) 1968 c. 46.

STATUTORY INSTRUMENTS

1971 No. 1287

ANIMALS
POULTRY

The Diseases of Animals (Approved Disinfectants) (Amendment) Order 1971

Made - - - -   *3rd August* 1971

Coming into Operation   16*th August* 1971

The Minister of Agriculture, Fisheries and Food and the Secretary of State, acting jointly, in exercise of the powers vested in them under sections 1(1), 11(vi) and (vii), 20(viii) and (ix), 50(1) and 85(1) of the Diseases of Animals Act 1950(a) (as read with the Transfer of Functions (Animal Health) Order 1955(b)) and all other powers enabling them in that behalf, hereby order as follows:—

Citation, extent and commencement

1. This order, which may be cited as the Diseases of Animals (Approved Disinfectants) (Amendment) Order 1971, shall apply to Great Britain and shall come into operation on 16th August 1971.

Interpretation

2. This order shall be construed as one with the Diseases of Animals (Approved Disinfectants) Order 1970(c) (hereinafter referred to as "the principal order").

Amendment of principal order

3. Parts I, II, III and IV of the Schedule to the principal order (which contain lists of disinfectants approved by the Minister of Agriculture, Fisheries and Food and the Secretary of State) are hereby deleted, and there shall be substituted therefor Parts I, II, III and IV of the Schedule set out at the end of this order.

Transitional Provisions

4. Notwithstanding the preceding provisions of this order, it shall be lawful for a period of 3 months from the date of coming into operation thereof to use for the purposes of any special disease order or general order in which a reference to a disinfectant or an approved disinfectant occurs any disinfectant listed in Part I, II, III or IV of the Schedule to the principal order which it was lawful to use for such purposes immediately before the coming into operation of this order.

(a) 1950 c. 36.   For change of title of the Minister see S.I. 1955/554 (1955 I, p. 1200).
(b) S.I. 1955/958 (1955 I, p. 1184).   (c) S.I. 1970/1372 (1970 III, p. 4599).

In Witness whereof the Official Seal of the Minister of Agriculture, Fisheries and Food is hereunto affixed on 30th July 1971.

(L.S.)

J. M. L. Prior,
Minister of Agriculture, Fisheries
and Food

Gordon Campbell,
3rd August 1971.   Secretary of State for Scotland.

SCHEDULE

PART I (Disinfectants approved by the Minister in respect of Foot-and-Mouth Disease Orders)

Column 1 Orders in respect of which disinfectant approved by the Minister	Column 2 Description of Disinfectant	Column 3 Dilution Rate
The Foot-and-Mouth Disease Order of 1928; as amended (a);	Action Approved Disinfectant	One part to 240 parts of water
	Agridyne	One part to 240 parts of water
	Anabac	One part to 240 parts of water
	Boots Lysol BP	One part to 9 parts of water
	Castrol Solvex ICD 109	One part to 50 parts of water
	Citric Acid BP	One part to 500 parts of water
	Combat	One part to 240 parts of water
	Compass Farm Fluid	One part to 50 parts of water
	Compass Lysol BP	One part to 9 parts of water
The Foot-and-Mouth Disease (Infected Areas Restrictions) Order of 1938(b), as amended (c)	Crown Special Detergent Disinfectant	One part to 240 parts of water
	Delta Farm Disinfectant	One part to 240 parts of water
	Disteola	One part to 240 parts of water
	Fakta Four Plus	One part to 300 parts of water
	FAM	One part to 240 parts of water
	Famosan	One part to 160 parts of water
	Famosan Mark II	One part to 139 parts of water
	Famosan Mark III	One part to 120 parts of water
	Farm Aid	One part to 240 parts of water
	Formalin BP (containing not less than 34% formaldehyde)	One part to 9 parts of water
	GR 250	One part to 10 parts of water
	Hygasan	One part to 20 parts of water
	Iodel X	One part to 130 parts of water

(a) S.R. & O. 1928/133, 1938/192 (Rev. II, p. 499: 1928 p. 94, 1938 I, p. 151): S.I. 1969/1444 (1969 III, p. 4661).
(b) S.R. & O. 1938/1434 (Rev. II, p. 528: 1938 I, p. 155).
(c) The relevant amending instrument is SI. 1969/1445 (1969 III, p. 4667).

PART I Continued

Column 1 Orders in respect of which disinfectant approved by the Minister	Column 2 Description of Disinfectant	Column 3 Dilution Rate
	Iodet	One part to 240 parts of water
	Iofarm	One part to 240 parts of water
	Iosan 4	One part to 240 parts of water
	Jeyes Farm Fluid	One part to 219 parts of water
	Ortho-phosphoric acid (Technical Grade)	One part to 330 parts of water
	Polykil	One part to 240 parts of water
	Professional No. 1	One part to 300 parts of water
	Resiguard F	One part to 80 parts of water
	Ropolik	One part to 240 parts of water
	Sani-Squad	One part to 5 parts of water
	Sanol FM	One part to 140 parts of water
	Sodium Carbonate (Decahydrate) Complying with BS 3764 of 1963	
	Steriguard	One part to 24 parts of water
	Sulphamic Acid	One part to 90 parts of water
		One part to 500 parts of water

PART II (Disinfectants approved by the Minister in respect of Fowl Pest Orders)

Column 1 Orders in respect of which disinfectant approved by the Minister	Column 2 Description of Disinfectant	Column 3 Dilution Rate
The Fowl Pest Order of 1936(a), as amended (b);	Absol Emulsion	One part to 30 parts of water
	Action Approved Disinfectant	One part to 80 parts of water
	Agridyne	One part to 80 parts of water
	Anabac	One part to 80 parts of water
	Basol 99	One part to 20 parts of water
	Boots Farm Disinfectant	One part to 30 parts of water
	Boots Lysol BP	One part to 39 parts of water
	Byro Disinfectant Fluid	One part to 30 part of water
	Combat	One part to 80 parts of water
	Compass Farm Fluid	One part to 100 parts of water
	Compass Lysol BP.	One part to 39 parts of water
The Fowl Pest (Infected Areas Restrictions) Order 1956(c), as amended (d):	Coopers Farm Disinfectant	One part to 29 parts of water
	Crown Special Detergent Disinfectant	One part to 80 parts of water
	Dellaphen General Purpose Soluble Disinfectant	One part to 60 parts of water
	Delta Farm Disinfectant	One part to 80 parts of water
	Disteola	One part to 80 parts of water
	Fakta Four Plus	One part to 80 parts of water
	FAM	One part to 80 parts of water
	Famosan Mark II	One part to 79 parts of water
	Famosan Mark III	One part to 59 parts of water
	Farm Aid	One part to 80 parts of water
	Gloquat S.D. Extra	One part to 50 parts of water
	Hygasan	One part to 60 parts of water
	Iodel X	One part to 49 parts of water
	Iodet	One part to 80 parts of water
	Iodicide	One part to 30 parts of water
	Iofarm	One part to 80 parts of water
	Iosan 4	One part to 80 parts of water

(a) S.R. & O. 1936/1297 (Rev. XVIII, p. 422: 1936 II, p. 2086).
(b) The relevant amending instrument is S.I. 1963/629 (1963 I, p. 760).
(c) S.I. 1956/1611 (1956 II, p. 1883).
(d) The amending order is not relevant to the subject matter of this order.

PART II continued

Column 1 Orders in respect of which disinfectant approved by the Minister	Column 2 Description of Disinfectant	Column 3 Dilution rate
	Izal Germicide	One part to 30 parts of water
	Izal Green Label Germicide	One part to 30 parts of water
	Jeyes Farm Fluid	One part to 39 parts of water
	Lysovet	One part to 49 parts of water
	Microl-Plus	One part to 60 parts of water
	Polykil	One part to 80 parts of water
	Professional No. 1	One part to 80 parts of water
	Ropolik	One part to 80 parts of water
	Steriguard	One part to 79 parts of water
	Sterilite Farm Disinfectant.	One part to 30 parts of water
	Sudol	One part to 60 parts of water
	Summit	One part to 30 parts of water
	Tekresol	One part to 90 parts of water
	White Cresanol	One part to 30 parts of water

PART III (Disinfectants approved by the Minister in respect of Tuberculosis Orders)

Column 1 Orders in respect of which disinfectant approved by the Minister	Column 2 Description of Disinfectant	Column 3 Dilution Rate
The Tuberculosis Order 1964(a)	Absol Emulsion	One part to 90 parts of water
	Action Approved Disinfectant	One part to 25 parts of water
	Agridyne	One part to 25 parts of water
	Anabac	One part to 25 parts of water
	Applied 8-57 White Disinfectant	One part to 49 parts of water
	Basol 99	One part to 20 parts of water
The Tuberculosis (Scotland) Order 1964(b)	Boots Farm Disinfectant	One part to 90 parts of water
	Boots Lysol BP	One part to 39 parts of water
	Byro Disinfectant Fluid	One part to 90 parts of water
	Combat	One part to 25 parts of water
	Compass Lysol BP	One part to 39 parts of water
	Coopers Farm Disinfectant	One part to 99 parts of water
	Crown Special Detergent Disinfectant	One part to 25 parts of water
	Dellaphen General Purpose Soluble Disinfectant	One part to 65 parts of water
	Delta Farm Disinfectant	One part to 25 parts of water
	Disteola	One part to 25 parts of water
	FAM	One part to 25 parts of water
	Farm Aid	One part to 25 parts of water
	Horton Extra Strong White Disinfectant Emulsion	One part to 105 parts of water
	Iodet	One part to 25 parts of water
	Iofarm	One part to 25 parts of water
	Iosan 4	One part to 15 parts of water
	Izal Germicide	One part to 90 parts of water
	Izal Green Label Germicide	One part to 80 parts of water
	Jeyes Farm Fluid	One part to 24 parts of water
	Lenfectant White Fluid	One part to 49 parts of water

(a) S.I. 1964/1151 (1964 II, p. 2634).
(b) S.I. 1964/1109 (1964 II, p. 2463).

PART III continued

Column 1 Orders in respect of which disinfectant approved by the Minister	Column 2 Description of Disinfectant	Column 3 Dilution Rate
	Microl-Plus	One part to 65 parts of water
	Polykil	One part to 25 parts of water
	Ropolik	One part to 25 parts of water
	Stericol	One part to 25 parts of water
	Sterilite Farm Disinfectant	One part to 90 parts of water
	Sterilite WD White Disinfectant	One part to 49 parts of water
	Sudol	One part to 65 parts of water
	Summit	One part to 90 parts of water
	Tekresol	One part to 80 parts of water
	Warden Black Disinfectant	One part to 160 parts of water
	White Cresanol	One part to 90 parts of water
	White Cyllin Disinfectant	One part to 49 parts of water
	White Zenos Disinfectant	One part to 49 parts of water
	Youngs White Septol 'B'	One part to 100 parts of water

PART IV (Disinfectants approved by the Minister in respect of general orders until further notice)

Column 1 Orders in respect of which disinfectant approved by the Minister	Column 2 Description of Disinfectant	Column 3 Dilution Rate
Any general order	Absol Emulsion	One part to 100 parts of water
	Action Approved Disinfectant	One part to 145 parts of water
	Agridyne	One part to 145 parts of water
	Applied 8-57 White Disinfectant	One part to 89 parts of water
	Basol 99	One part to 20 parts of water
	Boots Farm Disinfectant	One part to 100 parts of water
	Boot Lysol BP	One part to 49 parts of water
	Byro Disinfectant Fluid	One part to 100 parts of water
	Combat,	One part to 145 parts of water
	Compass Farm Fluid	One part to 100 parts of water
	Compass Lysol BP	One part to 49 parts of water
	Coopers Farm Disinfectant	One part to 99 parts of water
	Crown Special Detergent Disinfectant	One part to 145 parts of water
	Dellaphen General Purpose Soluble Disinfectant	One part to 70 parts of water
	Delta Farm Disinfectant	One part to 145 parts of water
	Dettol	One part to 20 parts of water
	Disteola	One part to 100 parts of water
	Fakta Four Plus	One part to 150 parts of water
	FAM	One part to 145 parts of water
	Famosan Mark III	One part to 59 parts of water
	Farm Aid	One part to 145 parts of water
	Horton Extra Strong White Disinfectant Emulsion	One part to 116 parts of water
	Iodet	One part to 145 parts of water
	Iofarm	One part to 145 parts of water
	Iosan 4	One part to 80 parts of water
	Izal Germicide	One part to 90 parts of water
	Izal Green Label Germicide	One part to 120 parts of water
	Jeyes Fluid	One part to 50 parts of water

PART IV Continued

Column 1 Orders in respect of which disinfectant Approved by the Minister	Column 2 Description of Disinfectant	Column 3 Dilution Rate
	Jeyes Farm Fluid	One part to 29 parts of water
	Kilcrobe W.O. Disinfectant Fluid Special Grade	One part to 99 parts of water
	Lenfectant White Fluid	One part to 89 parts of water
	Lysovet	One part to 49 parts of water
	Microl-Plus	One part to 70 parts of water
	Polykil	One part to 145 parts of water
	Professional No. 1	One part to 150 parts of water
	Ropolik	One part to 145 parts to water
	San Izal	One part to 16 parts of water
	Steriguard	One part to 49 parts of water
	Sterilite Farm Disinfectant	One part to 100 parts of water
	Sterilite WD White disinfectant	One part to 89 parts of water
	Sudol	One part to 70 parts of water
	Summit	One part to 100 parts of water
	Tekresol	One part to 135 parts of water
	White Cresanol	One part to 100 parts of water
	White Cyllin Disinfectant	One part to 89 parts of water
	White Zenos Disinfectant	One part to 89 parts of water
	Youngs White Septol 'B'	One part to 100 parts of water

EXPLANATORY NOTE

(This Note is not part of the Order.)

This order revokes and re-enacts with amendments the lists of disinfectants approved by the Minister and the Secretary of State in Parts I, II, III and IV of the Schedule to the Diseases of Animals (Approved Disinfectants) Order 1970.

These Parts of the Schedule contain lists of approved disinfectants in relation to orders under the Diseases of Animals Act 1950 dealing with Foot and Mouth Disease (Part I), Fowl Pest (Part II), Tuberculosis (Part III) and disinfectants approved until further notice in relation to other general orders under the Diseases of Animals Act (Part IV).

STATUTORY INSTRUMENTS

1971 No. 1288

CHILDREN AND YOUNG PERSONS

The Children and Young Persons (Designation of Isle of Man Order) Order 1971

Made - - -		*4th August* 1971
Coming into Operation		*16th August* 1971

In exercise of the powers conferred upon me by section 26(1) of the Children and Young Persons Act 1969(a), I hereby make the following Order :—

1. This Order may be cited as the Children and Young Persons (Designation of Isle of Man Order) Order 1971 and shall come into operation on 16th August 1971.

2. A care order made for the purpose of section 2 of the Children and Young Persons Act 1971 (an Act of Tynwald), being an order which satisfies the conditions set out in section 26(1) of the Children and Young Persons Act 1969 (transfers between England or Wales and the Channel Islands or Isle of Man), is hereby designated for the purposes of the said section 26.

R. Maudling,
One of Her Majesty's Principal
Secretaries of State.

Home Office,
Whitehall.
4th August 1971.

EXPLANATORY NOTE
(This Note is not part of the Order.)

This Order designates a care order made under the Children and Young Persons Act 1971 (an Act of the Isle of Man legislature) for the purposes of section 26 of the Children and Young Persons Act 1969.

This section enables the Secretary of State to authorise a local authority in England or Wales to receive into their care any person who is the subject of an order made by a court in the Isle of Man or any of the Channel Islands which is designated for the purposes of the section. Orders which may be so designated are orders which provide for the committal to the care of a public authority of a person under the age of eighteen and which appear to the Secretary of State to be of the same nature as a care order (other than an interim order) within the meaning of the 1969 Act.

(a) 1969 c. 54.

STATUTORY INSTRUMENTS

1971 No. 1290

HOUSING, ENGLAND AND WALES
HOUSING, SCOTLAND

The Housing Corporation Advances (Increase of Limit) Order 1971

Laid before the House of Commons in draft

Made - - - *4th August* 1971

Coming into Operation 18*th August* 1971

The Secretary of State for the Environment, the Secretary of State for Scotland and the Secretary of State for Wales, acting jointly in exercise of their powers under section 9(2) of the Housing Act 1964(a), and of all other powers enabling them in that behalf, hereby make the following order in the terms of a draft approved by resolution of the Commons House of Parliament :—

1. This order may be cited as the Housing Corporation Advances (Increase of Limit) Order 1971 and shall come into operation on 18th August 1971.

2. The Interpretation Act 1889(b) shall apply for the interpretation of this order as it applies for the interpretation of an Act of Parliament.

3. Advances made to the Housing Corporation under section 9(1) of the Housing Act 1964 shall not together exceed £100,000,000.

Peter Walker,
Secretary of State for the Environment.

30th July 1971.

Gordon Campbell,
Secretary of State for Scotland.

2nd August 1971.

Peter Thomas,
Secretary of State for Wales.

4th August 1971.

(a) 1964 c. 56.   (b) 1889 c. 63.

EXPLANATORY NOTE

(This Note is not part of the Order.)

Under section 9 of the Housing Act 1964 the three Secretaries of State respectively may make advances to the Housing Corporation to enable the Corporation to exercise and perform their functions. The total amount which may be advanced to the Corporation is limited to £50,000,000 or such greater sum, not exceeding £100,000,000, as the three Secretaries of State jointly may by order specify. This order specifies that the total amount which may be so advanced shall not exceed £100,000,000, and supersedes the Housing Corporation Advances (Increase of Limit) Order 1969 (S.I. 1969/518) which specifies £75,000,000 as the limit.

STATUTORY INSTRUMENTS

1971 No. 1291 (C.33)

SOCIAL SECURITY

The Social Security Act 1971 (Commencement No. 1) Order 1971

Made - - -	*5th August* 1971
Laid before Parliament	*13th August* 1971
Coming into Operation	*16th August* 1971

The Secretary of State for Social Services, in exercise of powers conferred upon him by section 11(4) of the Social Security Act 1971(a) and of all other powers enabling him in that behalf, hereby makes the following Order :—

Citation and Commencement

1. This Order may be cited as the Social Security Act 1971 (Commencement No. 1) Order 1971 and shall come into operation on 16th August 1971.

Appointed days

2.—(1) The day appointed for the coming into operation of section 7 of the Social Security Act 1971 (amendment of qualification for unemployment, sickness and injury benefit) and section 11(6) of the said Act (repeals) so far as it relates to Part II of Schedule 2 to the said Act shall be 16th August 1971.

(2) The day appointed for the coming into operation of section 8 of the said Act (increase of maximum fines for failure to pay contributions) shall be 6th September 1971.

Signed by authority of the Secretary of State for Social Services.

Michael Alison,
Parliamentary Under Secretary of State,
Department of Health and Social Security.

5th August 1971.

(a) 1971 c. 73.

STATUTORY INSTRUMENTS

1971 No. 1292 (L.33)

SUPREME COURT OF JUDICATURE, ENGLAND

The Crown Court Rules 1971

Made - - - - -	3rd August 1971
Laid before Parliament	16th August 1971
Coming into Operation	1st January 1972

ARRANGEMENT OF RULES

PART I

INTRODUCTION

PART II

JUSTICES AS JUDGES OF CROWN COURT

PART III

APPEALS TO THE CROWN COURT

PART IV

COSTS BETWEEN PARTIES IN CROWN COURT

Part V

Miscellaneous

We, the Crown Court rule committee, in exercise of the powers conferred upon us by sections 5(2) and (6), 7(4), 13(5), 14(1) and (2), 15, 34(3) and 50 of the Courts Act 1971(a), hereby make the following Rules:—

Part I

Introduction

Citation and commencement

1. These Rules may be cited as the Crown Court Rules 1971 and shall come into operation on 1st January 1972.

Interpretation

2.—(1) In these Rules, unless the context otherwise requires, any reference to a judge is a reference to a judge of the High Court or a Circuit judge or a Recorder ; "justice" means a justice of the peace ; and "Taxing Master" means a Master of the Supreme Court (Taxing Office).

(2) In these Rules any reference to a Rule or Schedule shall be construed as a reference to a Rule contained in these Rules or, as the case may be, to a Schedule thereto; and any reference in a Rule to a paragraph shall be construed as a reference to a paragraph of that Rule.

(3) The Interpretation Act 1889(b) shall apply to the interpretation of these Rules as it applies to the interpretation of an Act of Parliament.

Part II

Justices as Judges of Crown Court

Number and qualification of justices

3.—(1) Subject to the provisions of Rule 4 and to any directions under section 5(5) of the Courts Act 1971, on any proceedings to which a subsequent paragraph of this Rule applies, the number of justices sitting to hear the proceedings and the qualification of those justices shall be as specified in that paragraph.

(a) 1971 c. 23.   (b) 1889 c. 63.

(2) On the hearing of an appeal against a decision of licensing justices under the Licensing Act 1964(a) the Crown Court shall consist of a judge sitting with four justices, each of whom is a member of a licensing committee appointed under Schedule 1 to that Act and two (but not more than two) of whom are justices for the petty sessions area comprising the premises to which the appeal relates.

(3) On the hearing of an appeal against a decision of any authority under the Betting, Gaming and Lotteries Act 1963(b) or the Gaming Act 1968(c), the Crown Court shall consist of a judge sitting with four justices, two (but not more than two) of whom are justices for the petty sessions area comprising the premises to which the appeal relates.

(4) On the hearing of an appeal from a juvenile court or of proceedings on committal by a juvenile court to the Crown Court under section 28 of the Magistrates' Courts Act 1952(d) or section 67 of the Mental Health Act 1959(e) the Crown Court shall consist of a judge sitting with two justices each of whom is a member of a juvenile court panel and who are chosen so that the Court shall include a man and a woman.

Dispensations for special circumstances

4.—(1) The Crown Court may enter on any appeal or any proceedings on committal to the Court for sentence notwithstanding that the Court is not constituted as required by section 5(1) of the Courts Act 1971 or Rule 3 if it appears to the judge that the Court could not be so constituted without unreasonable delay and the Court includes—

> (*a*) in a case to which paragraph (2) of that Rule applies, at least two justices each of whom is a member of a committee specified in that paragraph, provided that the Court includes a justice for the petty sessions area so specified and a justice for some other area;
>
> (*b*) in a case to which paragraph (3) of that Rule applies, at least two justices including a justice for the petty sessions area so specified and a justice for some other area;
>
> (*c*) in a case to which paragraph (4) of that Rule applies, one justice who is a member of a juvenile court panel;
>
> (*d*) in any other case, one justice:

Provided that the judge may sit without one or both of the justices required by sub-paragraphs (*a*) and (*b*) above if the parties appearing at the hearing of the appeal agree.

(2) The Crown Court may at any stage continue with any proceedings with a Court from which any one or more of the justices initially comprising the Court has withdrawn, or is absent for any reason.

Disqualifications

5. A justice of the peace shall not sit in the Crown Court on the hearing of an appeal in a matter on which he adjudicated or of proceedings on committal of a person to the Court for sentence under section 28 or 29 of the Magistrates' Courts Act 1952 by a court of which he was a member.

(a) 1964 c. 26.　　　　　　　　　(b) 1963 c. 2.
(c) 1968 c. 65.　　　　　　　　　(d) 1952 c. 55.
(e) 1959 c. 72.

PART III

APPEALS TO THE CROWN COURT

Application of Part III

6.—(1) Subject to the following provisions of this Rule, this Part of these Rules shall apply to every appeal which by or under any enactment lies to the Crown Court from any court, tribunal or person.

(2) This Part of these Rules shall have effect subject to the provisions of the enactments listed in Part I of Schedule 1 (being enactments which make special procedural provisions in respect of certain appeals) which enactments shall be amended in accordance with Part II of that Schedule.

Notice of appeal

7.—(1) An appeal shall be commenced by the appellant's giving notice of appeal in accordance with the following provisions of this Rule.

(2) The notice required by the preceding paragraph shall be in writing and shall be given—

    (*a*) in a case where the appeal is against a decision of a magistrates' court, to the clerk of the magistrates' court ;

    (*b*) in any other case, to the appropriate officer of the Crown Court ; and

    (*c*) in any case, to any other party to the appeal.

(3) Notice of appeal shall be given within 21 days after the day on which the decision appealed against is given and, in the case of an appeal arising out of a conviction by a magistrates' court, shall state whether the appeal is against conviction or sentence or both.

(4) For the purposes of the preceding paragraph, the day on which a decision of a magistrates' court is given shall, where the court has adjourned the trial of an information after conviction, be the day on which the court sentences or otherwise deals with the offender.

(5) The time for giving notice of appeal may be extended, either before or after it expires, by the Crown Court, on an application made in accordance with paragraph (6).

(6) An application for an extension of time shall be made in writing, specifying the grounds of the application and sent to the appropriate officer of the Crown Court.

(7) Where the Crown Court extends the time for giving notice of appeal, the appropriate officer of the Crown Court shall give notice of the extension to the appellant and, in the case of an appeal from the decision of a magistrates' court, to the clerk of that court; and the appellant shall give notice of the extension to any other party to the appeal.

Entry of appeal and notice of hearing

8. On receiving notice of appeal, the appropriate officer of the Crown Court shall enter the appeal and give notice of the time and place of the hearing to the appellant, any other party to the appeal and, where the appeal is against a decision of a magistrates' court, to the clerk of the magistrates' court.

Abandonment of appeal

9.—(1) Without prejudice to the power of the Crown Court to give leave for an appeal to be abandoned, an appellant may abandon an appeal by giving notice in writing, in accordance with the following provisions of this Rule, not later than the third day before the day fixed for hearing the appeal.

(2) The notice required by the preceding paragraph shall be given—

    (*a*) in a case where the appeal is against a decision of a magistrates' court, to the clerk of the magistrates' court ;

    (*b*) in the case of an appeal under section 21 of the Licensing Act 1964, to the clerk to the licensing justices ;

    (*c*) in any other case, to the appropriate officer of the Crown Court ; and

    (*d*) in any case, to any other party to the appeal;

and, in the case of an appeal mentioned in sub-paragraph (*a*) or (*b*), the appellant shall send a copy of the notice to the appropriate officer of the Crown Court.

(3) For the purposes of determining whether notice of abandonment was given in time there shall be disregarded any Saturday, Sunday and any day which is, or is to be observed as, a bank holiday, or a holiday under the Bank Holidays Act 1871**(a)** or the Holidays Extension Act 1875**(b)**, in England and Wales.

Part IV

Costs between Parties in Crown Court

Jurisdiction to award costs

10.—(1) Subject to the provisions of section 85(2) of the Magistrates' Courts Act 1952 (power of magistrates' courts to award costs on abandonment of appeals from magistrates' courts) and section 22(4) of the Licensing Act 1964 (application of section 85(2) of the Act of 1952 to appeals under section 21 of the Act of 1964), no party shall be entitled to recover any costs of any proceedings in the Crown Court from any other party to the proceedings except under an order of the Court.

(2) Subject to section 48 of the Courts Act 1971 and to the following provisions of this Rule, the Crown Court may make such order for costs as it thinks just.

(3) In the case of an appeal under section 21 of the Licensing Act 1964—

    (*a*) no order for costs shall be made on the abandonment of an appeal by giving notice under Rule 9;

    (*b*) no order for costs shall be made against a person who appeared before the licensing justices and opposed the grant of the justices' licence unless he appeared at the hearing of the appeal and opposed the appeal;

    (*c*) if the appeal, not being an appeal against the grant of a justices' licence, is dismissed, the Court shall order the appellant to pay to the justices against whose decision he has appealed, or such person as those justices may appoint, such sum by way of costs as is, in the opinion of the Court, sufficient to indemnify the justices from all costs and charges to which they have been put in consequence of his having given notice of appeal.

(4) No order for costs shall be made on the abandonment of an appeal from a magistrates' court by giving notice under Rule 9.

    (a) 1871 c. 17.   **(b)** 1875 c. 13.

(5) Without prejudice to the generality of paragraph (2), the Crown Court may make an order for costs on dismissing an appeal where the appellant has failed to proceed with the appeal or on the abandonment of an appeal not being an appeal to which paragraph (3) or (4) applies.

Costs in proceedings from which appeal is brought

11. Where an appeal is brought to the Crown Court from the decision of a magistrates' court or a tribunal and the appeal is successful, the Crown Court may make any order as to the costs of the proceedings in the magistrates' court or tribunal which that court or tribunal had power to make.

Taxation

12.—(1) Where under these Rules the Crown Court has made an order for the costs of any proceedings to be paid by a party and the Court has not fixed a sum, the amount of the costs to be paid shall be ascertained as soon as practicable by the appropriate officer of the Crown Court (hereinafter referred to as the taxing authority).

(2) On a taxation under the preceding paragraph or under section 48(2) of the Courts Act 1971, there shall be allowed such sum as is reasonably sufficient to compensate the party for the expenses properly incurred by him.

Review by taxing authority

13.—(1) Any party dissatisfied with the taxation of any costs by the taxing authority under section 48(2) of the Courts Act 1971 or Rule 12 may apply to the taxing authority to review his decision.

(2) The application shall be made by giving notice to the taxing authority and to any other party to the taxation within 14 days of the taxation, specifying the items in respect of which the application is made and the grounds of objection.

(3) Any party to whom notice is given under the preceding paragraph may within 14 days of the service of the notice deliver to the taxing authority answers in writing to the objections specified in that notice to the taxing authority and, if he does, shall send copies to the applicant for the review and to any other party to the taxation.

(4) The taxing authority shall reconsider his taxation in the light of the objections and answers, if any, of the parties and any oral representations made by or on their behalf and shall notify them of the result of his review.

Further review by Taxing Master

14.—(1) Any party dissatisfied with the result of a review of taxation under Rule 13 may, within 14 days of receiving notification thereof, request the taxing authority to supply him with reasons in writing for his decision and may within 14 days of the receipt of such reasons apply to the Chief Taxing Master for a further review and shall, in that case, give notice of the application to the taxing authority and to any other party to the taxation, to whom he shall also give a copy of the reasons given by the taxing authority.

(2) Such application shall state whether the applicant wishes to appear or be represented, or whether he will accept a decision given in his absence and shall be accompanied by a copy of the notice given under Rule 13, of any answer which may have been given under paragraph (3) thereof and of the reasons given by the taxing authority for his decision, together with the bill of costs and full supporting documents.

(3) A party to the taxation who receives notice of an application under this Rule shall inform the Chief Taxing Master whether he wishes to appear or be represented at the further review, or whether he will accept a decision given in his absence.

(4) The further review shall be conducted by a Taxing Master and if the applicant or any other party to the taxation has given notice of his intention to appear or be represented, the Taxing Master shall inform the parties (or their agents) of the date on which the further review will take place.

(5) Before reaching his decision the Taxing Master may consult the judge who made the order for costs and the taxing authority and, unless the Taxing Master otherwise directs, no further evidence shall be received on the hearing of the further review ; and no ground of objection shall be valid which was not raised on the review under Rule 13.

(6) In making his review, the Taxing Master may alter the assessment of the taxing authority in respect of any sum allowed, whether by increase or decrease.

(7) The Taxing Master shall communicate the result of the further review to the parties and to the taxing authority.

Appeal to High Court judge

15.—(1) Any party dissatisfied with the result of a further review under Rule 14 may, within 14 days of receiving notification thereof, appeal by originating summons to a judge of the Queen's Bench Division of the High Court if, and only if, the Taxing Master certifies that the question to be decided involves a point of principle of general importance.

(2) On the hearing of the appeal the judge may reverse, affirm or amend the decision appealed against or make such other order as he thinks appropriate.

Supplementary provisions

16.—(1) On a further review or an appeal to a judge of the High Court the Taxing Master or judge may make such order as he thinks just in respect of the costs of the hearing of the further review or the appeal, as the case may be.

(2) The time prescribed by Rule 13, 14 or 15 may be extended by the taxing authority, Taxing Master or judge of the High Court on such terms as he thinks just.

PART V

MISCELLANEOUS

Applications to Crown Court for bail

17.—(1) This Rule applies where an application to the Crown Court for bail is made otherwise than during the hearing of proceedings in the Crown Court.

(2) Subject to paragraph (8), notice in writing of intention to apply to the Crown Court for bail shall be given to the prosecutor and to the Director of Public Prosecutions, if the prosecution is being carried on by him, at least 24 hours before the application is made.

(3) On receiving notice under paragraph (2), the prosecutor or Director of Public Prosecutions shall—

(a) notify the appropriate officer of the Crown Court and the applicant that he wishes to be represented at the hearing of the application; or

(b) notify the appropriate officer and the applicant that he does not oppose the application; or

(c) give to the appropriate officer, for the consideration of the Crown Court, a written statement of his reasons for opposing the application, at the same time sending a copy of the statement to the applicant.

(4) A notice under paragraph (2) shall be in the form prescribed in Schedule 2 or a form to the like effect, and the applicant shall give a copy of the notice to the appropriate officer of the Crown Court.

(5) The applicant shall not be entitled to be present on the hearing of his application unless the Crown Court gives him leave to be present.

(6) Where a person who desires to apply for bail has not been able to instruct a solicitor to apply on his behalf under the preceding paragraphs of this Rule, he may give notice in writing to the Crown Court of his desire to apply for bail, requesting that the Official Solicitor shall act for him in the application, and the Court may, if it thinks fit, assign the Official Solicitor to act for the applicant accordingly.

(7) Where the Official Solicitor has been so assigned the Crown Court may, if it thinks fit, dispense with the requirements of paragraph (2) and deal with the application in a summary manner.

Supplementary provisions about bail

18.—(1) Every applicant to the Crown Court for bail shall inform the Court of any earlier application to the High Court or the Crown Court for bail in the course of the same proceedings.

(2) On hearing an application for bail the Crown Court may order that the applicant shall be released from custody on entering into a recognizance, with or without sureties, or giving other security before—

(a) an officer of the Crown Court;

(b) a justice; or

(c) any other person authorised by virtue of section 95(1) of the Magistrates' Courts Act 1952 to take a recognizance where a magistrates' court having power to take the recognizance has, instead of taking it, fixed the amount in which the principal and his sureties, if any, are to be bound.

(3) A person who, in pursuance of an order made by the Crown Court under this Rule, proposes to enter into a recognizance or give other security before a justice or other person must, unless the Crown Court otherwise directs, give notice to the prosecutor at least 24 hours before he enters into the recognizance or gives security as aforesaid.

(4) Where, in pursuance of an order of the Crown Court, a recognizance is entered into or other security given before a justice or other person, it shall be his duty to cause the recognizance or, as the case may be, a statement of the other security given, to be transmitted forthwith to the appropriate officer of the Crown Court and, unless the recognizance is entered into at a prison, a copy of such recognizance or statement shall at the same time be sent to the governor of the prison in which the applicant is detained.

Time limits for beginning of trials

19. The periods prescribed for the purposes of paragraphs (*a*) and (*b*) of section 7(4) of the Courts Act 1971 shall be 14 days and 8 weeks respectively and accordingly the trial of a person committed by a magistrates' court—

> (*a*) shall not begin until the expiration of 14 days beginning with the date of his committal, except with his consent and the consent of the prosecution, and

> (*b*) shall, unless the Crown Court has otherwise ordered, begin not later than the expiration of 8 weeks beginning with the date of his committal.

Appeal against refusal to excuse from jury service

20.—(1) A person summoned under Part V of the Courts Act 1971 for jury service may appeal in accordance with the provisions of this Rule against any refusal of the appropriate officer to excuse him under section 34(2) of that Act.

(2) Subject to paragraph (3), an appeal under this Rule shall be heard by the Crown Court.

(3) Where the appellant is summoned under the said Part V to attend before the High Court or a county court and the appeal has not been decided by the Crown Court before the day on which the appellant is required by the summons to attend, the appeal shall be heard by the court before which he is summoned to attend.

(4) An appeal under this Rule shall be commenced by the appellant's giving notice of appeal to the appropriate officer of the Crown Court and such notice shall be in writing and shall specify the matters upon which the appellant relies as providing good reason why he should be excused from attending in pursuance of the summons.

(5) The Court shall not dismiss an appeal under this Rule unless the appellant has been given an opportunity of making representations.

(6) Where an appeal under this Rule is decided in the absence of the appellant, the appropriate officer of the Crown Court shall notify him of the decision without delay.

Application to Crown Court to state case

21.—(1) An application under section 10(3) of the Courts Act 1971 to the Crown Court to state a case for the opinion of the High Court shall be made in writing to the appropriate officer of the Crown Court within 14 days after the date of the decision in respect of which the application is made.

(2) The time for making such an application may be extended, either before or after it expires, by the Crown Court.

(3) If the Crown Court considers that the application is frivolous, it may refuse to state a case, and shall in that case, if the applicant so requires, cause a certificate stating the reasons for the refusal to be given to him.

(4) If the Crown Court so orders, the applicant shall, before the case is stated and delivered to him, enter before an officer of the Crown Court into a recognizance, with or without sureties and in such sum as the Crown Court considers proper, having regard to the means of the applicant, conditioned to prosecute the appeal without delay.

Business in chambers

22.—(1) The jurisdiction of the Crown Court specified in the following paragraph may be exercised by a judge of the Crown Court sitting in chambers.

(2) The said jurisdiction is—

    (*a*) hearing applications for bail;

    (*b*) issuing a summons or warrant;

    (*c*) hearing any application relating to procedural matters preliminary or incidental to proceedings in the Crown Court, including applications relating to legal aid but not including an application under section 7(3) of the Courts Act 1971 (application for direction varying the place of trial on indictment);

    (*d*) jurisdiction under Rule 7(7), 20 or 21.

Service of documents

23. Any notice or other document which is required by these Rules to be given to any person may be served personally on that person or sent to him by post at his usual or last known residence or place of business in England or Wales or, in the case of a company, at the company's registered office in England or Wales.

Repeal of enactments

24. The enactments specified in Schedule 3 (being enactments about appeals to the Crown Court or costs between party and party in the Crown Court which are superseded by the provisions of these Rules) are hereby repealed to the extent specified in the third column of that Schedule in their application to England and Wales.

Dated 3rd August 1971.

Hailsham of St. Marylebone, C.
Widgery, C. J.
Frederick Lawton, J.
George Bean, J.
D. R. Thompson
J. B. Edwards
Basil Wigoder
David Calcutt
A. Crawford Caffin
G. G. A. Whitehead

Rule 6   SCHEDULE 1

ENACTMENTS RELATING TO APPEALS TO CROWN COURT

PART I

ENACTMENTS MAKING SPECIAL PROVISIONS ABOUT PROCEDURE ON APPEALS TO CROWN COURT

Chapter	Act	Section or Schedule
1930 c. 44.	The Land Drainage Act 1930	Section 30.
1952 c. 68.	The Cinematograph Act 1952	Section 6.
1957 c. 56.	The Housing Act 1957	Section 14(5).
1963 c. 2.	The Betting, Gaming and Lotteries Act 1963	Schedule 1, paragraphs 21, 28. Schedule 2, paragraph 6. Schedule 3, paragraph 13. Schedule 6, paragraph 8. Schedule 7, paragraph 5.
1963 c. 33.	The London Government Act 1963	Schedule 12, paragraph 19(4).
1964 c. 26.	The Licensing Act 1964	Sections 22, 50, 146, 154.
1967 c. 9.	The General Rate Act 1967	Section 7(1).
1968 c. 27.	The Firearms Act 1968	Section 44. Schedule 5 Part II.
1968 c. 54.	The Theatres Act 1968	Section 14(4).
1968 c. 65.	The Gaming Act 1968	Schedule 2, paragraphs 29, 31, 45, 46, 50, 61. Schedule 3, paragraphs 12, 13, 15, 16. Schedule 7, paragraphs 11, 20. Schedule 9, paragraph 11.
1969 c. 54.	The Children and Young Persons Act 1969	Section 21(5).

PART II

AMENDMENTS

1. In section 14(5) of the Housing Act 1957 for the words "one month" there shall be substituted the words "twenty-one days".

2.—(1) In paragraph 21(1) of Schedule 1 to the Betting, Gaming and Lotteries Act 1963, for the words "fourteen days" there shall be substituted the words "twenty-one days".

(2) In paragraph 6 of Schedule 2 to that Act for the words "and he may appeal" to the end of the paragraph there shall be substituted the words "and within twenty-one days of being so notified he may by notice to the appropriate officer of the Crown Court and to the registering authority appeal against the refusal or revocation to the Crown Court".

(3) In paragraph 13(2) of Schedule 3 to that Act, for the words from "to the next" to the end of the paragraph there shall be substituted the words "to the Crown Court, and such appeal shall be commenced by giving notice to the appropriate officer of the Crown Court and to the licensing authority within twenty-one days of the holder's being notified of the revocation by the licensing authority".

(4) In paragraph 5 of Schedule 7 to that Act, for the words from "to the next practicable" to the end of the paragraph there shall be substituted the words "to the Crown Court and such appeal shall be commenced by giving notice to the appropriate officer of the Crown Court and to the local authority within twenty-one days of the day on which notice of the refusal or revocation is given to the society".

3. In section 22(1) of the Licensing Act 1964 for the words "fourteen days" there shall be substituted the words "twenty-one days".

4. In section 7(1) of the General Rate Act 1967(a) for the words "to the next practicable court of quarter sessions" there shall be substituted the words "to the Crown Court and such appeal shall be commenced by giving notice to the appropriate officer of the Crown Court within twenty-one days of—

(a) the date of publication of the rate under section 4 of this Act ; or

(b) the act or thing done by the rating authority ; or

(c) the giving of notice for the purposes of this section to the rating authority as to the neglect or omission concerned,

whichever is the latest".

5. In the Gaming Act 1968 for the words "fourteen days" where they occur in paragraph 29(1) of Schedule 2, paragraphs 12 and 15 of Schedule 3 and paragraphs 11 and 20 of Schedule 7 there shall be substituted the words "twenty-one days".

6. In section 3(8) of the Children and Young Persons Act 1969 for the words "fourteen days" there shall be substituted the words "twenty-one days".

SCHEDULE 2   Rule 17(4)

FORM OF NOTICE OF APPLICATION FOR BAIL

IN THE CROWN COURT

Application for Bail

Take notice that an application for bail will be made to the Crown Court at

      on   at   a.m./p.m.

(*see note below*) on behalf of

Full name: Forenames   Surname

(block letters)

_____

Crown Court reference number:—

_____

Place of detention:—

(if detained in prison,

give prison number)

_____

Particulars of proceedings

during which applicant was

committed to custody:—

_____

(a) 1967 c. 9.

SCHEDULE 2—*continued*

Details of any relevant previous
applications for bail:—

Grounds of application for bail.
(State fully facts relied upon and list
previous convictions (if any). Give
details of any proposed sureties and
answer any objections raised
previously.):—

Notes

The appropriate officer of the Crown Court should be consulted about the time and place
of the hearing before this Notice is sent to the prosecutor. A copy of this Notice should be
sent to the Crown Court.

Rule 24   **SCHEDULE 3**

REPEAL OF ENACTMENTS

Chapter	Short Title	Extent of repeal
35 & 36 Vict. c. 93.	The Pawnbrokers Act 1872.	In section 52 the words from "for the county or place" to the end of the section.
53 & 54 Vict. c. 59.	The Public Health Acts Amendment Act 1890.	In section 7 the words "in manner provided by the Summary Jurisdiction Acts".
61 & 62 Vict. c. 16.	The Canals Protection (London) Act 1898.	In section 5 the words "in manner provided by the Summary Jurisdiction Acts".
7 Edw. 7. c. 53.	The Public Health Acts (Amendment) Act 1907.	In section 7 the words "in manner provided by the Summary Jurisdiction Acts".
15 & 16 Geo. 5. c. 38.	The Performing Animals (Regulation) Act 1925.	In section 2(2) the words "in manner provided by the Summary Jurisdiction Acts".
15 & 16 Geo. 5. c. 50.	The Theatrical Employers Registration Act 1925.	In section 6(1) the words "in the manner prescribed by the Summary Jurisdiction Acts".
17 & 18 Geo. 5. c. 21.	The Moneylenders Act 1927.	In section 2(7) the words from "in manner" to the end of the subsection.
23 & 24 Geo. 5. c. 25.	The Pharmacy and Poisons Act 1933.	In section 21(2) the words "in accordance with rules made for the purposes of this section by the Secretary of State".
7 & 8 Eliz. 2. c. 25.	The Highways Act 1959.	Section 276.
1963 c. 2.	The Betting, Gaming and Lotteries Act 1963.	In Schedule 1, paragraph 22 and in paragragh 28(2) the words "22 or as the case may be".

SCHEDULE 3—*continued*

Chapter	Short Title	Extent of repeal
1964 c. 26.	The Licensing Act 1964.	In section 22(3) the words from "but no order" to the end of the subsection. Section 24. In section 25(1) the words "under section 24(2) of this Act".
1968 c. 27.	The Firearms Act 1968.	In Schedule 5, in paragraph 4 the words "and if he does so" to the end of the paragraph, and paragraphs 6 and 8.
1968 c. 65.	The Gaming Act 1968.	In Schedule 2, paragraph 30(1) and in paragraph 30(2) the words "under the preceding sub-paragraph". In Schedule 9, paragraph 14(1) and in paragraph 14(2) the words "under the preceding sub-paragraph".

EXPLANATORY NOTE
(This Note is not part of the Rules.)

The Courts Act 1971 establishes, with effect from 1st January 1972, a new court, the Crown Court, to try indictments and to exercise other jurisdiction previously exercised by courts of quarter sessions. These Rules regulate the procedure and practice of the Crown Court with regard to the matters specified in the Rules.

STATUTORY INSTRUMENTS

1971 No. 1295

SEA FISHERIES

The White Fish (Inshore Vessels) and Herring Subsidies (United Kingdom) Scheme 1971

Made - - -	*8th July* 1971
Laid before Parliament	*12th July* 1971
Coming into Operation	*1st August* 1971

The Minister of Agriculture, Fisheries and Food, and the Secretaries of State for Scotland and Wales (being the Secretaries of State respectively concerned with the sea fishing industry in Scotland and Wales) in exercise of the powers conferred upon them by section 49 of the Sea Fish Industry Act 1970(a) and of all other powers enabling them in that behalf, with the approval of the Treasury, hereby make the following scheme:—

Citation, extent, commencement and interpretation

1.—(1) This scheme, which may be cited as the White Fish (Inshore Vessels) and Herring Subsidies (United Kingdom) Scheme 1971, shall apply to the United Kingdom and shall come into operation on 1st August 1971.

(2) In this scheme, unless the context otherwise requires—
   "the appropriate Minister"—
   (a) in relation to England and Northern Ireland, means the Minister of Agriculture, Fisheries and Food;
   (b) in relation to Scotland, means the Secretary of State concerned with the sea fishing industry in Scotland;
   (c) in relation to Wales, means—
      (i) for the purpose of the actual making of any payment under this scheme, the Minister of Agriculture, Fisheries and Food, and
      (ii) for all the other purposes of this scheme, the said Minister and the Secretary of State concerned with the sea fishing industry in Wales acting jointly;
   "approved" means approved by the appropriate Minister;
   "gross proceeds" in relation to a voyage means the proceeds from the first hand sale of all fish (including white fish, herring, salmon, migratory trout and shellfish) taken by the vessel on that voyage less such deductions as may be determined by the appropriate Minister in respect of the part of such proceeds which forms the perquisite of the crew of the vessel on that voyage;

(a) 1970 c. 11.

"herring stonage payment" means any grant payable in accordance with the provisions of paragraph 3(1)(*c*);

"herring voyage payment" means any grant payable in accordance with the provisions of paragraph 3(1)(*d*);

"length" in relation to a vessel, means the length in relation to which its tonnage was calculated for the purposes of registration under Part IV of the Merchant Shipping Act 1894**(a)**;

"month" means a calendar month;

"paragraph" means a paragraph of this scheme;

"vessel" means a vessel registered in the United Kingdom as a fishing vessel;

"white fish" means fish of any kind found in the sea, except herring, salmon, migratory trout and shellfish;

"white fish stonage payment" means any grant payable in accordance with the provisions of paragraph 3(1)(*a*);

"white fish voyage payment" means any grant payable in accordance with the provisions of paragraph 3(1)(*b*).

(3) For the purpose of this scheme the trans-shipment of white fish or herring in a port in the United Kingdom or within the exclusive fishery limits of the British Islands other than the waters within the fishery limits of the British Islands which are adjacent to the Isle of Man or any of the Channel Islands shall be treated as the landing of white fish or herring in the United Kingdom.

(4) The Interpretation Act 1889**(b)** shall apply for the interpretation of this scheme as it applies for the interpretation of an Act of Parliament and as if this scheme and the schemes hereby revoked were Acts of Parliament.

Revocation of previous schemes

2. The White Fish and Herring Subsidies (United Kingdom) Scheme 1968**(c)** and the White Fish and Herring Subsidies (United Kingdom) (Amendment) Scheme 1969**(d)** are hereby revoked.

General conditions of grant

3.—(1) A grant may be paid in accordance with the following provisions of this scheme to the owner (or his agent) or, where there is a charter-party, to the charterer (or his agent), of a vessel, in respect of—

(a) white fish landed from the vessel in the United Kingdom during the period beginning with 1st August 1971 and ending with 31st July 1972;

(b) a voyage made by the vessel during the period last hereinbefore referred to for the purpose of catching white fish and landing them in the United Kingdom;

(c) herring landed from the vessel in the United Kingdom during the period beginning with 1st August 1971 and ending with 31st July 1972; or

(d) a voyage made by the vessel during the period last hereinbefore referred to for the purpose of catching herring and landing them in the United Kingdom:

Provided that no grant shall be payable by virtue of this sub-paragraph in any case where the white fish or herring are landed in the Isle of Man or Channel Islands.

(2) Whether or not a grant is payable by virtue of sub-paragraph (1) of this paragraph, a grant may be paid as aforesaid in respect of herring landed from the vessel in the United Kingdom during the period beginning with 1st August

---

(a) 1894 c. 60.

(b) 1889 c. 63.

(c) S.I. 1968/1235 (1968 II, p. 3336).

(d) S.I. 1969/471 (1969 I, p. 1349).

1971 and ending with 31st July 1972 and sold for conversion into oil, meal or other approved product, if the appropriate Minister is satisfied that the said herring could not have been sold for purposes other than such conversion:

Provided that no grant shall be payable by virtue of this sub-paragraph in respect of—

(i) herring landed at any port not specified in Part I of Schedule 1 to this scheme;

(ii) more than 20% of the total landings of herring in any month at any port specified as aforesaid or, where such port is comprised in any group of ports specified in Part II of the said Schedule, at any such group of ports, as the case may be.

4. The owner or charterer of a vessel (or his duly authorised agent) who applies for payment of a grant under this scheme or any person acting on behalf of such owner or charterer and appointed by him for the purpose shall, within such time in such form and for such period as may be specified by the appropriate Minister, supply such information and make such returns concerning fishing operations, costs and trading results as may be required by the appropriate Minister, including detailed accounts of the financial results of the operation of all vessels to which this scheme applies owned or chartered by such owner or charterer, and shall when required at any time during the period comprising the remainder of the calendar year current when an application for grant is made in respect of any such vessel and the two years immediately following that year, make any relevant books and records open to examination by any person authorised by the appropriate Minister.

5. Application for payment of a grant under this scheme shall be made by the owner or charterer (or his duly authorised agent) in such form as the appropriate Minister may from time to time require and shall be completed and certified in all respects as so required and shall be delivered to the appropriate Minister at such address as he may specify for the purpose.

6. Application for payment of a grant under this scheme shall be made not later than one month after the landing of the white fish or herring or the completion of the voyage, as the case may be, or such longer period as the appropriate Minister may allow.

7. Notice that a person is authorised to make application for and receive payment of grants under this scheme on behalf of an owner or charterer shall be given in writing signed by the owner or charterer in such form as the appropriate Minister may from time to time require and shall be sent to the address specified by the appropriate Minister for the purpose of paragraph 5:

Provided that not more than one person shall be authorised as aforesaid at any time at a port in respect of grants payable under either paragraph 3(1) or paragraph 3(2) in relation to a vessel.

8. Without prejudice to the discretion of the appropriate Minister in the payment of grants under this scheme—

(a) if any owner or charterer or any person acting on his behalf makes a statement or produces a document which is false in a material particular or fails, without reasonable cause, or refuses to supply any information, make any return or produce any document in respect of any of the matters required to be disclosed either in connection with an application for payment of grant under this scheme or in accordance with the provisions of paragraph 4; or

(b) if any of the conditions of grant or conditions relating to the payment of grants under this scheme are not complied with by any owner or charterer or any person acting on behalf of an owner or charterer,

payment of grants to that owner, charterer or person at any time may be refused.

9.—(1) For the purpose of determining the grant, if any, which may be paid under this scheme in the case of two or more vessels jointly operating the same gear, the weight of white fish or herring landed from the combined voyage, the proceeds from the sale of such white fish or herring and the gross proceeds of such voyage shall be deemed to be divided equally between the vessels concerned whether they are of the same length or of different lengths, and the grant, if any, shall be calculated separately for each vessel in accordance with the provisions of this scheme.

(2) Notwithstanding the provisions of paragraphs 10, 13 and 14 any grant under this scheme shall be paid, if at any time after 1st September 1963 any structural alteration shall have been made to any vessel which has increased or decreased its length, at the rate appropriate to the length of the vessel before such alteration unless in any such case the appropriate Minister is satisfied that the alteration was likely to be conducive to the increased fishing efficiency of the vessel.

Conditions relating to payments for voyages

10. Subject to the provisions of this scheme—

(a) a white fish voyage payment may be made in respect of each voyage made by a vessel falling within one of the categories specified in Part I of Schedule 2 to this scheme;

(b) a herring voyage payment may be made in respect of each voyage made by a vessel falling within one of the categories specified in Part II of Schedule 2 to this scheme,

such payment being, in each case, an amount equal to the appropriate rate of grant per day at sea set out in Part I, or as the case may be Part II, of Schedule 2 to this scheme multiplied by such number of days as the appropriate Minister is satisfied are to be taken into account for the purposes of this scheme as days at sea on that voyage.

11.—(1) Subject to sub-paragraph (2) of this paragraph, and without prejudice to the generality of the provisions of paragraph 10, in computing for the purposes of that paragraph the length of a voyage—

(a) the day of departure and the day of arrival of the vessel may each be reckoned as one day at sea so however that if the day of arrival is also the day of departure upon a subsequent voyage whether made for the catching and landing in the United Kingdom of white fish or of herring, then that day shall not be reckoned with the subsequent voyage;

(b) each period of 24 hours which is spent during a voyage in any port shall be excluded.

(2) Where reference is made in this scheme to a voyage made during a specified period the reference shall be construed, in the case of a voyage only part of which is made during that period, as a reference to that part.

12.—(1) In a case where, in respect of a voyage, both a white fish voyage payment and a herring voyage payment might otherwise have been made only one such payment shall be made, being, in a case where the proceeds from the sale of the white fish exceed the proceeds from the sale of the herring, a white fish voyage payment, and in a case where the proceeds from the sale of the herring exceed the proceeds from the sale of the white fish, a herring voyage payment.

(2) No white fish voyage payment or herring voyage payment shall be made if the proceeds from the sale of white fish and herring landed in consequence of the voyage, taken together, amount to less than half the gross proceeds of the voyage.

(3) Where by virtue of the last preceding sub-paragraph neither a white fish voyage payment nor a herring voyage payment may be made, a claim may be made for a white fish stonage payment or for a herring stonage payment or for both in respect of white fish or herring landed in consequence of the voyage, notwithstanding that the vessel falls within one of the categories specified in Part I or Part II of Schedule 2 to this scheme:

Provided that a payment made in pursuance of this sub-paragraph shall in no case exceed the payment which would have been made but for the operation of the last preceding sub-paragraph.

(4) In this paragraph "proceeds", in relation to the sale of white fish, or, as the case may be herring, means the total proceeds from the first-hand sale thereof.

Conditions relating to payments for white fish and herring landed

13.—(1) Subject to the provisions of this scheme a white fish stonage payment may be made in the case of a vessel under 60 feet in length, not being a vessel falling within Category A of Part I of Schedule 2 to this scheme, in respect of white fish landed and sold at first-hand otherwise than by retail, at the appropriate rate set out in Part I of Schedule 3 to this scheme.

(2) No white fish stonage payment shall be made—

(a) in respect of fish (other than filleted fish, wings of ray and skate, skinned dogfish and monkfish tails) landed without heads or tails or from which any portion of the head or tail has been removed; or

(b) in respect of fish which is determined by the appropriate Minister to form part of the perquisite of the crew of the vessel from which the fish were landed; or

(c) in respect of white fish which are subject to the prohibitions contained in section 1(1) of the Sea Fish (Conservation) Act 1967(a).

14.—(1) Subject to the provisions of this scheme a herring stonage payment may be made, in the case of a vessel under 40 feet in length, not being a vessel falling within Category C of Part II of Schedule 2 to this scheme, in respect of herring landed, at the rate set out in Part II of Schedule 3 to this scheme;

(2) Subject to the provisions of this scheme a grant may be paid at the rate set out in Part III of Schedule 3 to this scheme in respect of herring landed from a vessel and sold for conversion into oil, meal or other approved product.

15.—(1) For the purpose of computing the amount of a white fish stonage payment or a herring stonage payment which may be made under paragraphs

---

(a) 1967 c. 84.

13(1) and 14(1) of this scheme the weight of the white fish or herring, as the case may be, shall be the weight determined at the time of the first-hand sale.

(2) No white fish stonage payment shall be made in consequence of a voyage where a claim for a herring voyage payment is made in respect of the same voyage and no herring stonage payment shall be made in consequence of a voyage where a claim for a white fish voyage payment is made in respect of the same voyage.

(3) No white fish stonage payment shall be made in respect of white fish landed from a vessel where the voyage on which the fish was caught commences and terminates on one day, that day being also the day of arrival of the vessel from a voyage, or the day of the departure of the vessel upon a voyage, in respect of which a claim for a herring voyage payment is made.

In Witness whereof the official seal of the Minister of Agriculture, Fisheries and Food is hereunto affixed on 8th July 1971.

(L.S.)

> *J. M. L. Prior,*
> Minister of Agriculture,
> Fisheries and Food.

Given under the Seal of the Secretary of State for Scotland on 7th July 1971.

(L.S.)

> *Gordon Campbell,*
> Secretary of State for Scotland.

Given under my hand on 7th July 1971.

> *Peter Thomas,*
> Secretary of State for Wales.

Approved on 8th July 1971.

> *P. L. Hawkins,*
> *Bernard Weatherill,*
> Two of the Lords Commissioners of
> Her Majesty's Treasury.

Paragraph 3

SCHEDULE 1

PART I

Ports

Aberdeen	Girvan	Oban
Annalong	Gourock	Peterhead
Anstruther	Greenock	Portavogie
Arbroath	Grimsby	Portpatrick
Ardglass	Hartlepool	Scalloway
Ayr	Inverness	Scarborough
Berwick on Tweed	Kilkeel	Seahouses
Bridlington	Kyle of Lochalsh	Stornoway
Buckie	Leith	Tarbert (Harris)
Eyemouth	Lerwick	Tarbert (Loch Fyne)
Fleetwood	Lowestoft	Ullapool
Fort William	Mallaig	Whitby
Fraserburgh	Milford Haven	Whitehaven
Gairloch	Newhaven	Yarmouth
	North Shields	

PART II

Groups of Ports

1

Aberdeen
Fraserburgh
Peterhead

5

Berwick on Tweed
Hartlepool
North Shields
Seahouses

9

Kyle of Lochalsh
Mallaig
Oban

2

Anstruther
Arbroath
Eyemouth
Leith
Newhaven

6

Bridlington
Scarborough
Whitby

10

Lerwick
Scalloway

3

Annalong
Ardglass
Kilkeel
Portavogie

7

Gairloch
Stornoway
Tarbert (Harris)
Ullapool

11

Lowestoft
Yarmouth

4

Ayr
Girvan
Gourock
Greenock
Tarbert (Loch Fyne)

8

Fleetwood
Whitehaven

SCHEDULE 2
PART I

CATEGORIES OF VESSELS AND RATES OF GRANT IN RESPECT
OF VOYAGES FOR THE CATCHING AND LANDING OF WHITE FISH

Category A

Vessels of 35 feet in length or over but under 60 feet in length, provided, in relation to any such vessel registered in the United Kingdom as a fishing vessel before 1st January 1971 that the appropriate Minister is satisfied that the total of any grants payable in respect of:—

(*a*) white fish or herring landed from the vessel (not being grants in respect of herring landed and sold for conversion into oil, meal or other approved product), or

(*b*) voyages made by the vessel for the catching and landing of white fish or herring

amounted, or would but for special circumstances beyond the control of the owner or charterer have amounted, in the year 1970 to at least £250.

	Rate of grant per day at sea £p
Vessels of 35 feet in length or over but under 40 feet in length ...	3·85
Vessels of 40 feet in length or over but under 45 feet in length ...	4·15
Vessels of 45 feet in length or over but under 55 feet in length ...	4·60
Vessels of 55 feet in length or over but under 60 feet in length ...	4·90

Category B

Vessels of 60 feet in length or over but under 80 feet in length.

	Rate of grant per day at sea £p
Vessels of 60 feet in length or over but under 65 feet in length ...	4·90
Vessels of 65 feet in length or over but under 80 feet in length ...	5·80

PART II

CATEGORIES OF VESSELS AND RATES OF GRANT IN RESPECT
OF VOYAGES FOR THE CATCHING AND LANDING OF HERRING

Category C

Vessels of 35 feet in length or over but under 40 feet in length, provided, in relation to any such vessel registered in the United Kingdom as a fishing vessel before 1st January 1971, that the appropriate Minister is satisfied that the total of any grants payable in respect of:—

(*a*) white fish or herring landed from the vessel (not being grants in respect of herring landed and sold for conversion into oil, meal or other approved product), or

(*b*) voyages made by the vessel for the catching and landing of white fish or herring

amounted, or would but for special circumstances beyond the control of the owner or charterer have amounted, in the year 1970 to at least £250.

	Rate of grant per day at sea £p
Vessels of 35 feet in length or over but under 40 feet in length ...	3·50

Category D
Vessels of 40 feet in length or over.

	Rate of grant per day at sea £p
Vessels of 40 feet in length or over but under 60 feet in length ...	4·65
Vessels of 60 feet in length or over but under 80 feet in length ...	5·25
Vessels of 80 feet in length or over	6·50

Paragraph 13

SCHEDULE 3
PART I
RATES OF GRANT IN RESPECT OF WHITE FISH LANDED
Kind of Fish

	Rate of grant per stone p
All whole gutted white fish and filleted white fish of a kind normally sold for human consumption (including roes and chitlings), wings of ray and skate, skinned dogfish and monkfish tails	5
Ungutted bass, dogfish, eels, mackerel, mullet (red and grey) and pilchards	5
All other whole ungutted white fish, if the appropriate Minister is satisfied that such fish has been sold for human consumption ...	3·5
All other whole white fish	1

Paragraph 14

PART II
RATE OF GRANT IN RESPECT OF HERRING LANDED

	Rate of grant per stone p
Herring landed	1·5

Paragraph 14

PART III
RATE OF GRANT IN RESPECT OF HERRING LANDED AND SOLD FOR CONVERSION INTO OIL, MEAL OR OTHER APPROVED PRODUCT

	Rate of grant per cran £p
Herring landed from vessels and sold for conversion into oil, meal or other approved product...	1·10

EXPLANATORY NOTE

(This Note is not part of the Scheme.)

The Sea Fish Industry Act 1970 (c. 11) provides that schemes may be made for the payment of grants to the owners or charterers of fishing vessels engaged in catching and landing of white fish and herring.

This scheme provides for the payment of grants in respect of the catching and landing of white fish by vessels under 80 feet and of catching and landing of herring, such grants being calculated by reference either to voyages made by vessels or to fish landed from them. The period in respect of which grants are payable is from the 1st August 1971 to the 31st July 1972.

This scheme succeeds the White Fish (Inshore Vessels) and Herring Subsidies (United Kingdom) Scheme 1970 (S.I. 1970/1100).

STATUTORY INSTRUMENTS

1971 No. 1296 (S.165)

HOUSING, SCOTLAND

The Housing Subsidies (Representative Rates of Interest) (Scotland) Order 1971

Laid before the House of Commons in draft

Made - - -		*2nd August* 1971
Coming into Operation		*27th August* 1971

In exercise of the powers conferred upon me by section 2(2), (3) and (5) of the Housing (Financial Provisions) (Scotland) Act 1968(a) and of all other powers enabling me in that behalf and after consultation with certain recipient authorities and such associations of other recipient authorities as appeared to me to be concerned, I hereby make the following order in the terms of a draft which has been laid before the Commons House of Parliament and has been approved by resolution of that House :—

Citation, commencement and interpretation

1.—(1) This order may be cited as the Housing Subsidies (Representative Rates of Interest) (Scotland) Order 1971 and shall come into operation on 27th August 1971.

(2) The Interpretation Act 1889(b) shall apply for the interpretation of this order as it applies for the interpretation of an Act of Parliament.

Representative rates of interest

2. The rates of interest to be specified for the purposes of section 2(2) of the Housing (Financial Provisions) (Scotland) Act 1968 in respect of approved houses completed in the financial year commencing in 1971 shall be as follows :—

    (*a*) in relation to all local authorities and all housing associations (except the Scottish Special Housing Association)—8·48 per cent.;

    (*b*) in relation to the Scottish Special Housing Association—9·32 per cent.; and

    (*c*) in relation to all development corporations—9·19 per cent.

> *Gordon Campbell,*
> One of Her Majesty's Principal
> Secretaries of State.

St. Andrew's House,
Edinburgh.
2nd August 1971.

(a) 1968 c. 31.   (b) 1889 c. 63.

EXPLANATORY NOTE

(This Note is not part of the Order.)

This Order specifies the representative borrowing rates for the year 1971-72 applicable to the several bodies who receive housing subsidies under section 2 of the Housing (Financial Provisions) (Scotland) Act 1968. The subsidy meets the difference between the loan charges on the aggregate approved cost of houses completed in that year at the borrowing rate specified in the Order and the loan charges which would have been incurred at a fixed borrowing rate of 4 per cent.

STATUTORY INSTRUMENTS

1971 No. 1297

EDUCATION, ENGLAND AND WALES

The Awards (First Degree, etc. Courses) Regulations 1971

Made - - - -	4th August 1971
Laid before Parliament	19th August 1971
Coming into Operation	1st September 1971

The Secretary of State for Education and Science, in exercise of her powers under section 1 of the Education Act 1962(a), hereby makes the following regulations:—

PART I

GENERAL

Citation, commencement and interpretation

1.—(1) These regulations may be cited as the Awards (First Degree, etc. Courses) Regulations 1971 and shall come into operation on 1st September 1971.

(2) The Interpretation Act 1889(b) shall apply for the interpretation of these regulations as it applies for the interpretation of an Act of Parliament.

Definitions

2.—(1) In these regulations, unless the context otherwise requires—

"academic authority" means appropriate authority of an establishment;

"authority" means local education authority;

"award" includes an award bestowed under any regulations superseded by these regulations;

"designated course" has the meaning assigned to it by paragraph (2) below;

"establishment" means a university or establishment of further education;

"ordinarily resident" is to be construed in accordance with schedule 1 to the Education Act 1962;

"prescribed fraction" has the meaning assigned to it by paragraph 1 of schedule 4;

"prescribed qualification" means an educational qualification specified in, or prescribed under, regulation 6;

"sandwich year" has the meaning assigned to it by paragraph 1 of schedule 4;

"student" means a person upon whom an award has been bestowed under these regulations or under any regulations superseded by these regulations;

"university" means a university in the United Kingdom and includes a university college and a constituent college, school or hall of a university;

(a) 1962 c. 12. (b) 1889 c. 63.

"year" means the period of twelve months beginning on 1st January, 1st April or 1st September according as the academic year of the course in question begins in the spring, the summer or the autumn respectively; and

"first year" means first such year of a designated course.

(2) "Designated course" means a course prescribed by or under regulation 7 and any reference otherwise unqualified to a course shall as the context requires be construed as a reference to a designated course which the person in question attends or has applied to attend.

(3) For the purposes of these regulations a person's marriage is to be treated as having been terminated, not only by the death of the other spouse or the annulment or dissolution of the marriage by an order of a court of competent jurisdiction, but also by virtue of the parties to the marriage ceasing to live together, whether or not an order for their separation has been made by any court.

Revocations

3. The regulations specified in schedule 5 are hereby revoked.

PART II

AWARDS

Duty to bestow awards

4. Subject to and in accordance with these regulations, it shall be the duty of every authority to bestow an award on any person who—

(*a*) is ordinarily resident in their area; and

(*b*) possesses a prescribed qualification—

in respect of his attendance at a designated course beginning after 31st August 1971.

Modification of provisions for determining ordinary residence

5.—(1) This regulation shall have effect for modifying paragraph 2 of schedule 1 to the Education Act 1962 in the case of a person who, apart from this regulation, would be treated by virtue of that paragraph as having been ordinarily resident in the area of more than one authority within the period of twelve months ending with the date on which the course is due to begin.

(2) Any such person as is described in paragraph (1) above shall be treated as being ordinarily resident in the area of the authority in which he was so resident on the last day of the month of October, February or June preceding the beginning of the course according as the course begins in the spring, the summer or the autumn respectively.

Educational qualifications

6. The requisite educational qualifications shall be

(*a*) in relation to any course one of the following—

(i) a pass at advanced level in two subjects in the examination for the General Certificate of Education;

(ii) an Ordinary National Certificate or Diploma, in the examination for which the holder obtained either a mark of not less than 60 per cent. in any two final year subjects or an average mark of not less than 60 per cent. in any three final year subjects;

(iii) a pass in two principal subjects in the examination for the Higher School Certificate;

(iv) an Attestation of Fitness of the Scottish Universities Entrance Board;

(v) a pass in three subjects in the higher grade gained at not more than two sittings of the Scottish Universities Preliminary Examination, the Scottish Certificate of Education Examination or the examination for the Scottish Leaving Certificate;

(vi) a pass at advanced level in two subjects in the Northern Ireland General Certificate or Senior Certificate of Education Examination;

(vii) any other qualification for the time being prescribed by the Secretary of State for the purposes of these regulations; and

(b) in relation to a course for the Diploma in Art and Design—

(i) any qualification specified by, or prescribed under, sub-paragraph (a) above; or

(ii) the successful completion of, or exemption with the approval of the National Council for Diplomas in Art and Design from, a foundation course of at least one year's duration and a pass in the examination for the General Certificate of Education either in five subjects at ordinary level or in three subjects at ordinary level and one subject at advanced level.

For the purposes of this sub-paragraph a pass at Grade 1 level in a subject in an examination for the Certificate of Secondary Education shall be treated as a pass at the ordinary level in the corresponding subject in an examination for the General Certificate of Education.

Designated Courses

7. The following are prescribed as designated courses—

(a) a full-time course of study at a university or at an establishment of further education maintained or assisted out of public funds, being a course of study for a first degree (other than the degree of Bachelor of Education) of a university or for the degree of Bachelor of Medicine or an equivalent degree;

(b) a full-time course of study at an establishment of further education maintained or assisted out of public funds in preparation for a first degree of the Council for National Academic Awards;

(c) a full-time course of study of at least three years' duration at a university in preparation for a Certificate or Diploma;

(d) a sandwich course in preparation for any such degree, Certificate or Diploma as is mentioned in the three preceding paragraphs;

(e) any other full-time course for the time being prescribed by the Secretary of State for the purposes of these regulations.

Conditions

8.—(1) The duty of an authority to bestow an award shall be subject to the conditions that—

(*a*) an application in writing for the award reaches the authority before the date on which the course is due to begin; and

(*b*) the applicant gives the authority a written undertaking that, where any sum is paid in pursuance of the award before the end of the year in respect of which the sum is payable, he will if called upon to do so repay the amount by which the sums paid during the year exceed the grant payable in respect of that year.

(2) If the applicant is a minor, paragraph (1)(*b*) shall have effect, with the necessary modifications, as if the references to the applicant were references to the applicant or his parent.

Exception for non-residents, etc.

9. An authority shall not be under a duty to bestow an award upon—

(*a*) a person who has not been ordinarily resident in the United Kingdom for the three years immediately preceding the first year, unless the authority are satisfied that he has not been so resident only because he, his wife (or, in the case of a woman student, her husband) or his parent was for the time being employed outside the United Kingdom;

(*b*) a person who has, in the opinion of the authority, shown himself by his conduct to be unfitted to receive an award.

Other exceptions

10.—(1) An authority shall not be under a duty to bestow an award upon any person who—

(*a*) has attended a designated course;

(*b*) has attended a full-time course of initial training as a teacher or has successfully completed a part-time course of such training;

(*c*) has attended any full-time course of further education of not less than two years' duration (not being a course in preparation for a prescribed qualification) or a comparable course outside the United Kingdom;

(*d*) has successfully completed a part-time course of a kind described in paragraph (*a*) or (*b*) of schedule 1 to the Further Education Regulations 1969**(a)** (not being a course in preparation for a prescribed qualification) or a comparable course outside the United Kingdom.

(2) For the purposes of this regulation a person shall be deemed to have attended a course if he has attended any part of that course.

Transfer of awards

11.—(1) Subject to paragraph (2) below, an award shall be transferred by the authority so as to be held in respect of attendance at a course other than that in respect of which it was bestowed in any case where either—

(i) on the recommendation of the academic authority made before the expiry of two months after the end of the first year, the student commences to attend another course at the establishment; or

---

(a) S.I. 1969/403 (1969 I, p. 1138).

(ii) with the consent of the academic authority of both establishments concerned, given on educational grounds before the expiry of two months after the end of the first year, the student commences to attend a course at another establishment.

(2) The authority may, after consultation with the academic authority, refuse to transfer the award under paragraph (1) above if they are satisfied that when the student applied for it he did not intend to complete the course to which the application related.

Termination of awards

12.—(1) The award shall terminate on the expiry of the period ordinarily required for the completion of the course:

provided that—

(a) if the academic authority refuse to allow the student to complete the course, the authority shall terminate the award forthwith;

(b) if the student does not complete the course within the period ordinarily required, the authority

(i) may extend the award until the student has completed the course; and

(ii) shall extend it for a period equivalent to any period in respect of which they have made any payment under regulation 23 below.

(2) The authority may, after consultation with the academic authority, terminate the award if they are satisfied that the student has shown himself by his conduct to be unfitted to hold it.

Supplementary provisions

13. The authority may require the student to provide from time to time such information as they consider necessary for the exercise of their functions under this Part; and if in the case of any student the authority are satisfied that he has wilfully failed to comply with any such requirement, they may terminate the award or withhold any payments due under it as they see fit.

PART III

PAYMENTS

Ordinary Cases

Payments

14. Except in a case to which any of regulations 17 to 21 below inclusive applies the authority shall, subject to regulation 23 below, in respect of each year pay in pursuance of the award either the sum of £50 (in these regulations called "minimum payment") or a grant calculated in accordance with regulation 15, whichever is the greater.

Calculation of grant

15. The grant payable to the student in any year shall be the amount by which his resources fall short of his requirements, and for the purpose of ascertaining that amount—

(a) the requirements of any student shall be taken to be the aggregate of such of the amounts specified in schedule 1 as are applicable to his case;

(b) the resources of any student shall be taken to be the aggregate of his income for the year calculated in accordance with Part 1 of schedule 2 and any parental contribution applicable to his case by virtue of Part 2 of that schedule.

Assessment of requirements and resources

16. The requirements and resources of the student shall be assessed by the authority, and for the purpose of the exercise of their functions under this regulation the authority shall require the student to provide from time to time such information as they consider necessary as to the resources of any person whose means are relevant to the assessment of his requirements and resources.

Special Cases

Women Students

17. In pursuance of an award to a woman student (other than a woman student who is a member of a religious order) the authority shall pay in each year whichever is the greater of the minimum payment and a grant calculated in accordance with regulation 15 above as modified by virtue of schedule 3.

Sandwich courses

18. In the case of a sandwich course—

    (a) the authority shall—

        (i) in respect of a sandwich year, pay a grant calculated in accordance with regulation 15 above as modified by virtue of schedule 4; and

        (ii) in respect of a year in which there are no periods of experience within the meaning of paragraph 1 of schedule 4, make a payment in accordance with regulation 14 above; and

    (b) in respect of a year in which there are no periods of full-time study no payment shall be made.

Members of religious orders

19.—(1) Subject to paragraph (2) below, there shall in each year be paid in pursuance of an award to a student who is a member of a religious order the aggregate of the appropriate sum specified under paragraph (3) below and the sums specified by paragraphs 1 and 8 of schedule 1.

(2) As respects any sandwich year in which the period of full-time study does not exceed 30 weeks, paragraph (1) above shall have effect with the substitution for the reference to the appropriate sum specified under paragraph (3) below of a reference to the prescribed fraction of that sum.

(3) The sum referred to in paragraphs (1) and (2) above is—

if a student resides at his parent's home or in the house of a religious order £190

if the student resides elsewhere—

    in the case of a student attending a course at the university of Oxford or Cambridge, at an establishment within the area comprising the City of London and the Metropolitan Police District or an institution outside the United Kingdom £255

    in the case of a student attending a course elsewhere £235

Students whose parents have not been found

20. In the case of any student in respect of whom a grant would apart from this regulation be payable the authority may, if they see fit, pay the minimum payment instead of the grant if they are unable to assess the parental contribution because his parents have not been found but the authority are not satisfied that they cannot be found.

Assisted students

21. Notwithstanding anything in the preceding provisions of these regulations, no payment shall be made in any year to or in respect of a student—

    (*a*) who holds a state scholarship or any award from a government department or other public body or is in receipt of any other payment in respect of his attendance at the course; and

    (*b*) to, or in respect of, whom there is paid in pursuance of that scholarship, award or payment an amount which is not less than the aggregate of the requirements for fees and ordinary maintenance prescribed as applicable to his case by schedule 1.

General

Method of payment

22.—(1) The authority shall make any payment due under these regulations in such instalments (if any) and at such times as they consider appropriate; and in the exercise of their functions under this paragraph the authority may in particular make provisional payments pending the final calculation of the grant.

(2) Any payment in respect of such fees as are described in Part 1 of schedule 1 may be made to the academic authority but subject thereto all payments shall be made to the student.

Payments for special periods

23. In respect of any period during which the student repeats any part of the course, the authority shall pay in pursuance of the award such sums (if any) as they consider appropriate, being sums not exceeding the amount of any payment that would, apart from this regulation, be payable in respect of that period.

Suspension, etc., of payments

24.—(1) The authority may withhold any payment to or in respect of any student who is for the time being in default of any requirement to provide such information as is described in regulation 16:

Provided that, in the case of a student in respect of whom apart from this paragraph a grant (other than a grant in respect of a sandwich year) would be payable, the authority shall in respect of any year in which he remains in default pay a grant of a sum not less than the minimum payment.

(2) The authority shall reduce the payment otherwise due under these regulations by an amount equal to the sum specified by paragraph (3) below in respect of—

    (*a*) any period after the termination of the award; and

    (*b*) any period during which the student is excluded from attendance at the course by the academic authority or is absent without leave;

and in respect of any other period during which the student does not attend the course (other than a period of not more than 28 days due to his illness) they may reduce the payment by such amount not exceeding that sum as, having regard to all relevant circumstances, they consider appropriate.

(3) The sum referred to in paragraph (2) above is the aggregate of—

(a) fees otherwise due that are not payable by reason of the student not attending the course; and

(b) the appropriate proportion of the balance of the grant.

SCHEDULE I   Regulation 15(a)

REQUIREMENTS

PART I

FEES

1. The amount of the following fees—

(a) except in the case of a college to which sub-paragraph (b) applies, sessional or tuition fees, which in the case of a composition fee shall not include the element of the fee attributable to maintenance;

(b) so much of the fees as does not exceed £400, in respect of the sessional or tuition fees of a college of a university (other than a college of the university of Oxford or Cambridge) which is a college in respect of which no grant is paid out of moneys provided by Parliament to the university to which it belongs;

(c) special fees, including lecture fees, laboratory fees and any fees in respect of such courses as are described in Part 3 of this schedule;

(d) fees for admission or registration;

(e) fees for matriculation or matriculation exemption and graduation;

(f) fees for examinations taken as part of a course;

(g) at any university which is organised on a collegiate basis, university and college dues;

(h) where a sum representing the subscription to a students' union, junior common room or similar body is not included in the fee charged under sub-paragraph (a), (b) or (d) above—

    (i) the fees charged for such membership at the university of Durham, the university of Newcastle, any college of the universities of Oxford and Cambridge or any establishment designated by the Secretary of State as a Polytechnic;

    (ii) at any other establishment, the subscription to any one such body membership of which is obligatory by virtue of any requirement contained in, or having effect under, the instruments regulating the conduct of the establishment.

PART 2

ORDINARY MAINTENANCE

2.—(1) This Part shall apply for the ascertainment of the student's requirements for his maintenance in respect of his attendance at the course during term.

(2) The lower rate prescribed by paragraph 3(3) below shall be applicable in the case of—

(a) any student who resides at his parent's home, unless his case falls within sub-paragraph (3)(c) below; and

(b) any student whose case falls within the exception to sub-paragraph (3)(b) below.

(3) The appropriate higher rate prescribed by paragraph 3 below shall be applicable in the case of—

> (*a*) any student who, on the recommendation of the academic authority, resides in the establishment or in a hostel administered by the academic authority;

> (*b*) any other student who does not reside at his parent's home, unless he can in the opinion of the authority conveniently attend the course from his parent's home and the authority, after consultation with the academic authority, consider that in all the circumstances the lower rate would be appropriate; and

> (*c*) any student residing at his parent's home whose parents by reason of age, incapacity or otherwise cannot reasonably be expected to support him and in respect of whom the authority are satisfied that in all the circumstances the higher rate would be appropriate.

(4) In this Part of this schedule references to the parent's home include, in the case of a student whose spouse attends a full-time course in any establishment or college of education, the home of the parent of the student's spouse.

3.—(1) Higher rate for the university of Oxford, the university of Cambridge, the university of London and any other establishment within the city of London and the Metropolitan Police District £465

(2) Higher rate for any other establishment in the United Kingdom   .. £430

(3) Lower rate £345

(4) Higher rate for an institution outside the United Kingdom in respect of attendance (otherwise than on an exchange basis) required as part of a course   .. £465

PART 3

SUPPLEMENTARY MAINTENANCE, ETC.

4.—(1) For each additional fortnight or incomplete part of an additional fortnight in attendance at the course—

if the student resides at his parent's home   ..   .. £9·80

if the student does not reside at his parent's home—

> in the case of a student attending a course at an establishment within the area comprising the City of London and the Metropolitan Police District or at an institution outside the United Kingdom..   ..   .. £19·60

> in the case of a student attending a course elsewhere   ..   ..   .. £16·80

(2) For the purposes of this paragraph attendance at the course in any year is additional if it is in excess of 26 weeks at the university of Oxford or Cambridge or in excess of 31 weeks at any other establishment or an institution outside the United Kingdom.

5. Subject to paragraph 7, in the case of a student attending a course at an establishment which is not a university—

> (*a*) for each day in respect of vacation study on the recommendation, and under the guidance, of the academic authority—

>> if the student resides at his parent's home 70p

>> if the student does not reside at his parent's home—
>> in the case of study within the area comprising the City of London and the Metropolitan Police District or at an institution outside the United Kingdom   ..   .. £1·40

>> in any other case ..   .. £1·20

> (*b*) in respect of vacation study, undertaken on the recommendation of the academic authority by a student studying modern languages, in a country whose

language is a main language of the course, for each day on which he resides with a family approved for the purposes of this paragraph by the academic authority   .. .. £1·40

(c) for each day in respect of any additional expenditure on his maintenance incurred for the purpose of attending, as part of the course, a period of residential study during term away from the establishment .. .. so much of the expenditure as does not exceed £1·30.

6.—(1) Subject to paragraph 7, in respect of any expenditure which he is obliged to incur—

(a) within the United Kingdom for the purpose of attending the establishment;

(b) within or without the United Kingdom, for the purpose of attending any period of study to which paragraph 3(4) or 5 applies;

(c) on any other travel within the United Kingdom in connection with the course during term (but, in the case of a student attending a course at a university, excluding any travel for the purpose of attending a period of residential study away from the establishment)   .. ..

the amount by which the expenditure exceeds £15.

(2) In the case of a student whose home is for the time being outside the United Kingdom, in respect of expenditure necessarily incurred at the beginning and end of term on travel between his home and the establishment .. .. .. such sum (if any) as the authority consider appropriate.

7. Paragraphs 5(a), (c) and 6(1)(b) above shall apply in relation to a period of study or, as the case may be, travel outside the United Kingdom only where the academic authority certify that if the student did not attend or, as the case may be, did not travel he would not be eligible to complete the course; and where no such certificate is given the student's requirements shall be treated as such a sum (if any) not exceeding the amount specified in the relevant paragraph as the authority consider appropriate.

8. In respect of expenditure necessarily incurred on the purchase of special equipment for the course by a student attending a course in—

(a) medicine, veterinary science or medicine, architecture or ophthalmic optics;

(b) dentistry   .. ..

so much of the expenditure as does not during the course exceed (a) £20 and (b) £60 respectively.

9. In the case of any student who in the opinion of the authority would otherwise suffer undue hardship, in respect of any week during the vacation in respect of which no sum is prescribed by the preceding provisions of this Part . . . . . . such sum (if any) not exceeding £6·55 as, regard being had to the means of the student, the authority consider appropriate.

PART 4

MAINTENANCE OF DEPENDANTS

10.—(1) The requirements of a student to whom this paragraph applies for the maintenance of persons in the United Kingdom who are dependent on him shall be the amount by which the relevant sum specified in paragraph 11 exceeds the income of the dependant concerned.

(2) This paragraph applies to a student who married before the first year, being—

(a) any student who for any three years preceding the first year supported himself out of his earnings;

(b) a man who attained the age of 25 before that year; or

(c) a woman who attained the age of 21 before that year:

provided that, in their application to paragraphs 11(1)(*b*) and 12 below—

    (i) this sub-paragraph is to be read without the words "who married before the first year"; and

    (ii) sub-paragraph (2)(*c*) above shall be construed as a reference to a woman who attained the age of 25 before the first year.

(3) In this Part—

"income" means income (less income tax and national insurance contributions) for the year and in calculating that income there shall be disregarded, in the case of the spouse, the first £100 and a sum equivalent to any payment made by the student in pursuance of an obligation reasonably incurred by him before the first year and, in the case of any dependant, family allowances;

"child" includes a person adopted in pursuance of adoption proceedings and a stepchild.

11.—(1)(*a*) Wife (or, in the case of a woman student, incapacitated husband); or

    (*b*) one other adult dependant; or

    (*c*) the first child £250

(2) except where sub-paragraph (1)(*c*) above applies, the first child £105

(3) the second child £60

(4) any other child £55

12. The requirements of a student to whom paragraph 10 applies for the maintenance in the United Kingdom, at a place other than that at which he resides during the course, of a home for himself and any such dependant as is described in paragraph 11 shall be £90.

13. The requirements of—

    (*a*) a student to whom paragraph 10 applies, for the maintenance of any dependant outside the United Kingdom;

    (*b*) a student to whom paragraph 10 does not apply, for the maintenance of any dependant in the United Kingdom—

shall be such sum not exceeding the amount that would be treated as his requirements if his case fell within paragraph 10 as the authority, having regard to all the circumstances, consider reasonable.

PART 5

OLDER STUDENTS

14.—(1) The requirements of any student to whom this paragraph applies shall include the sum of £29 for every complete year not exceeding five by which his age at the beginning of the first year exceeds 25.

(2) This paragraph applies to any student—

    (*a*) who attained the age of 26 before the first year; and

    (*b*) whose gross earnings in any three of the six years immediately preceding that year amount to a sum which exceeded by not less than one quarter the aggregate of £430 and the amounts specified as his requirements by paragraph 10 and 13.

Note 1:—Any reference in this Schedule to a requirement, expenditure or attendance in respect of which no period of time is specified is to be construed as a reference to such a requirement, expenditure or attendance for the year.

Note 2:—The provisions of paragraphs 4, 5 and 9 of this Schedule are to be so applied that, unless in the case of any student the authority for special reasons determine otherwise, the number of weeks in respect of which his requirements for his maintenance are taken into account under this schedule does not exceed 48.

SCHEDULE 2   Regulation 15(*b*)

RESOURCES

PART 1

STUDENT'S INCOME

Calculation of student's income

1. In calculating the student's income there shall be taken into account his income (reduced by income tax and national insurance contributions) from all sources, but there shall be disregarded the following resources—

(*a*) the first £100 of income;

(*b*) in the case of a student who—

    (i) has no parent living; and

    (ii) is not such a person as is described in sub-paragraph (*a*), (*b*) or (*c*) of paragraph 3 below—

£200 of any such income as is described in paragraph 5(2) below: provided that the amount disregarded under this sub-paragraph shall not, together with the amount disregarded under sub-paragraph (*a*) above, exceed £200;

(*c*) any disability pension not subject to income tax;

(*d*) any bounty received as a Reservist with the Armed Forces;

(*e*) remuneration for work done in vacations;

(*f*) in the case of a student in respect of whom a parental contribution is by virtue of Part 2 of this schedule treated as forming part of his resources, any payment made under covenant by his parent;

(*g*) any payment made for a specific educational purpose not treated by schedule 1 as a requirement for the purposes of these regulations;

(*h*) family allowances;

(*i*) any benefit under the Ministry of Social Security Act 1966(a);

and in the case of any such student as is described in sub-paragraph (*a*), (*b*) and (*c*) of paragraph 3 below there shall be deducted a sum equivalent to any payment made by him in pursuance of an obligation reasonably incurred by him before the first year unless a deduction in respect of the payment has been made under paragraph 10(3) of schedule 1.

PART 2

PARENTAL CONTRIBUTION

Definitions

2. In this Part—

"child" includes a person adopted in pursuance of adoption proceedings but, except in paragraphs 4(2) and 6(12) below, does not include a child who holds a statutory award nor, except in sub-paragraph (1), (10) and (11) of paragraph 6 below, a stepchild; and "parent" shall be construed accordingly;

"gross income" has the meaning assigned to it by paragraph 5 below;

"income of the student's parent" means the total income of the parent from all sources computed as for income tax purposes, except that no deduction shall be made which is of a kind for which provision is made by paragraph 6 below;

"residual income" means the balance of gross income remaining in any year after the deductions specified in paragraph 6 below have been made;

"statutory award" means any award bestowed or grant paid under the Education Act 1962 or any analogous grant which is paid out of moneys provided by Parliament.

(a) 1966 c. 20.

Application of Part 2

3. A parental contribution ascertained in accordance with this Part shall be applicable in the case of every student except any of the following—

(a) a student who for any three years preceding the first year supported himself out of his earnings;

(b) a student who attained the age of 25 before that year;

(c) a woman who both married and attained the age of 21 before that year;

(d) a student in respect of whom the authority are satisfied that his parents cannot be found.

Parental contribution

4.—(1) Subject to sub-paragraph (2) below, the parental contribution shall be—

(a) in any case in which the residual income is not less than £1100 and not more than £1699, £30 with the addition of £1 for every complete £10 by which it exceeds £1100, and

(b) in any case in which the residual income is not less than £1700, £100 with the addition of £1 for every complete £10 by which it exceeds £1700;

and in any case in which the residual income is less than £1100 the parental contribution shall be nil.

(2) For any year in which more than one child of the parent holds a statutory award, the parental contribution for each student shall be such proportion of the parental contribution, ascertained in accordance with this Part, as the authority consider just.

Gross Income

5.—(1) Subject to the provisions of this paragraph "gross income" means the income of the student's parent in the financial year preceding the year in respect of which the resources of the student fall to be assessed; provided that, where the authority are satisfied that the income of the parent in the next succeeding financial year is likely to be not more than four-fifths of that income, they may for the purpose of calculating the parental contribution ascertain the gross income by reference to that next succeeding financial year; and in that case the above definition shall have effect accordingly both in relation to that year and, if the authority so determine, the year following that year and any subsequent year.

(2) Where trustees of property held in trust for a student or for any other person dependent on the parent pay, by virtue either of section 31(1) of the Trustee Act 1925(a) or of the trust instrument, any income of that property to the parent or otherwise apply it for or towards the maintenance, education or other benefit of the beneficiary the amount so paid or applied shall be treated as part of the gross income of the parent.

(3) Any dividends or interest paid or credited to the parent by a building society which has entered into arrangements with the Commissioners of Inland Revenue under section 343(1) of the Income and Corporation Taxes Act 1970(b) shall be deemed to have been received by him after deduction of income tax at the reduced rate determined under those arrangements for the year of assessment in which the dividends or interest are paid or credited; and the amount deemed to have been so deducted shall be treated as part of his gross income.

(4) There shall be treated as part of the gross income all income arising from an office or employment which by virtue of any enactment is as such exempt from tax.

(5) There shall be disregarded any income of the student which is treated as income of the parent in accordance with any provision of the Income Tax Acts relating to the aggregation of the income of unmarried minors not regularly working.

(6) Where the parents do not ordinarily live together the parental contribution shall

---

(a) 1925 c. 19.   (b) 1970 c. 10.

be ascertained by reference to the income of whichever parent the authority consider the more appropriate in the circumstances.

Deductions

6.—(1) In respect of any child dependent on the parent during the year for which the contribution falls to be ascertained . . . . . the amount by which £200 exceeds the child's income.

(2) In respect of any other person, other than a spouse, dependent on the parent during the year for which the contribution falls to be ascertained . . . . . the amount by which £200 exceeds the income of that person.

(3) The amount of any sums paid as interest (including interest on a mortgage) in respect of which relief is given under the Income Tax Acts or as interest under the option mortgage scheme.

(4) The amount of any contribution to a dependants' pension scheme being a contribution in respect of which relief is given under the Income Tax Acts.

(5) So much of the aggregate of the amount of any other contribution to a pension or superannuation fund or scheme (excluding national insurance and graduated pensions contributions) and any premium on a policy of life assurance being a contribution or premium in respect of which relief is given under the Income Tax Acts as does not exceed fifteen per cent. of the gross income.

(6) Where the parents are living together and are gainfully employed . . . . . the cost in wages of domestic assistance not exceeding whichever is the less of £200 and the emoluments of the parent who earns the less.

(7) Where the parents ordinarily live together and one of them is incapacitated . . . . . so much of the cost in wages of domestic assistance as does not exceed £200.

(8) Where a parent whose marriage has terminated either is gainfully employed or is incapacitated . . . . . so much of the cost in wages of domestic assistance as does not exceed £200.

(9) In respect of additional expenditure incurred by reason of the fact that the parent lives in a place where the cost of living is higher than that cost in the United Kingdom . . . . . such sum (if any) as the authority consider reasonable in all the circumstances.

(10) In respect of the fees paid and other expenditure incurred on the education of a child attending school . . . . . so much of the expenditure incurred as does not exceed £200.

(11) In respect of the cost incurred on the further training (including university education and vocational training) of a dependent child . . . . . so much of the expenditure incurred as does not exceed £350.

(12) In respect of any payment made under covenant otherwise than for the benefit of a child who holds a statutory award . . . . . so much of the gross amount as does not exceed £200.

(13) In the case of a parent who holds a statutory award . . . . . the amount by which the aggregate of his requirements for his ordinary maintenance and £100 exceeds the sum payable in pursuance of that award.

SCHEDULE 3 Regulation 17

Women Students

1. In its application to a woman student whose marriage terminates during the course, regulation 15 shall have effect subject to the proviso that the grant shall be payable to her after the termination of her marriage at a rate not lower than that at which it was payable before its termination.

2.—(1) Except in a case falling within sub-paragraph (2), Parts 2 and 3 of schedule 1 shall, in their application to a married woman who resides in the matrimonial home, have effect subject to the following modifications:—

(a) her requirements for ordinary maintenance shall be £275;

(b) her requirements under paragraph 4 shall be £9·80;

(c) the references in paragraph 5 to the parent's home shall be construed as references to the matrimonial home.

(2) If—

(a) her husband is incapacitated and dependent on her; or

(b) he attends a full-time course in any establishment or college of education—

Parts 2 and 3 of schedule 1 shall apply without modification.

3. If the student is a person in respect of whom any requirements are specified by paragraph 10 of schedule 1 as applicable and her marriage has terminated, whether before or during the course, then—

(a) the sum to be disregarded under paragraph 1(a) of schedule 2 shall be £200 instead of £100; or

(b) her requirements for the maintenance of persons dependent on her shall be treated as increased by the sum of £100; or

(c) in the case of a student to whom paragraph 14 of schedule 1 applies, her requirements shall be treated as including the sum specified by that paragraph—

whichever is the most favourable to her.

4. A woman whose marriage has terminated may elect that the sums specified as her requirements under Part 4 of schedule 1 shall be disregarded and that in lieu thereof there shall in calculating her income be disregarded £300 in respect of her first dependent child and £100 in respect of every other dependent child.

Regulation 18   **SCHEDULE 4**

SANDWICH COURSES

1. In this schedule—

(a) "sandwich course" means a course consisting of alternate periods of full-time study in an establishment and associated industrial, professional or commercial experience (in this schedule called "periods of experience") at a place outside the establishment so organised that, taking the course as a whole, the student attends the periods of full-time study for an average of not less than 19 weeks in each year; and for the purpose of calculating his attendance the course shall be treated as beginning with the first period of full-time study and ending with the last such period;

"periods of experience" does not include unpaid service in a hospital, with a local authority acting in the exercise of their functions relating to health, welfare or the care of children and young persons or with a voluntary organisation providing facilities or carrying out activities of a like nature, or unpaid research in an establishment;

"sandwich year" means, as respects any student, any year of a sandwich course which includes periods of both such study and such experience as are described above;

"prescribed fraction" means the fraction of which the denominator is 30 and the numerator is the number of weeks in the year for which the student in question attends the establishment;

"modified fraction" means the fraction of which the denominator is 52 and the numerator is the number of weeks in the year in which there are no periods of experience for the student in question; and (*b*) in the application of this schedule to women students, references to schedules 1 and 2 are to be construed as references to those schedules as modified in accordance with schedule 3.

2. The provisions of schedule 1 shall, as respects any sandwich year, have effect subject to the following modifications—

(*a*) where the period of full-time study does not exceed 31 weeks, the student's requirements for his maintenance shall be the prescribed fraction of the appropriate amount specified by Part 2;

(*b*) where the period of full-time study exceeds 31 weeks, the student's requirements for his maintenance shall be the aggregate of the appropriate amount specified in Part 2 and the appropriate amount specified by paragraph 4 of Part 3;

(*c*) the student's requirements for travelling expenses under paragraph 6(1) of Part 2 shall be the amount by which the expenditure incurred exceeds the prescribed fraction of £15;

(*d*) the student's requirements for the maintenance of a dependant shall be the modified fraction of the sum specified by Part 4; and

(*e*) if the student is a person to whom paragraph 14 of schedule 1 applies, his requirements under that paragraph shall be the prescribed fraction of the amount specified by it.

3. The provisions of schedule 2 shall, as respects any sandwich year, have effect subject to the following modifications—

(*a*) the sum to be disregarded under paragraph 1(*a*) shall be the prescribed fraction of £100 and the reference in the proviso to paragraph 1(*b*) to £200 shall be construed as a reference to the aggregate of £100 and that prescribed fraction;

(*b*) in calculating the student's income there shall be disregarded any payment made to him by his employer in respect of any period of experience; and

(*c*) the amount of the parental contribution applicable to his case shall be the prescribed fraction of the contribution ascertained in accordance with Part 2 of the schedule.

SCHEDULE 5   Regulation 3

REVOCATIONS

Regulations revoked	References
The Awards (First Degree, etc. Courses) Regulations 1970.	S.I. 1970/497 (1970 I, p. 1676).
The Awards (First Degree, etc. Courses) (Amendment) Regulations 1970.	S.I. 1970/867 (1970 II, p. 2800).
The Awards (First Degree, etc. Courses) (Amendment No. 2) Regulations 1970.	S.I. 1970/1266 (1970 II, p. 4111).
The Awards (First Degree, etc. Courses) (Amendment No. 3) Regulations 1970.	S.I. 1970/1686 (1970 III, p. 5572).
The Awards (First Degree, etc. Courses) (Amendment) Regulations 1971.	S.I. 1971/884 (1971 II, p. 2604).

Given under the Official Seal of the Secretary of State for Education and Science on 4th August 1971.

(L.S.)

Margaret H. Thatcher,
Secretary of State for Education and Science.

EXPLANATORY NOTE

(This Note is not part of the Regulations.)

Section 1 of the Education Act 1962 imposes on local education authorities a duty to make awards in order to enable students to attend designated courses at universities and establishments of further education.

These regulations consolidate with amendments the regulations, specified in schedule 5, which designate the courses and prescribe the conditions and exceptions to which the duty is subject, the educational qualifications requisite and the payments to be made in pursuance of awards. The principal amendments are the increases in the sums treated by schedule 1 as the student's requirements and the modification of the provisions of schedule 2 relating to the assessment of the parental contribution.

STATUTORY INSTRUMENTS

1971 No. 1298 (C.34)

CUSTOMS AND EXCISE

The Finance Act 1971 Schedule 1 (Customs Procedures etc.) (Commencement) Order 1971

Made - - - -   6th August 1971

The Commissioners of Customs and Excise in exercise of the powers conferred on them by section 11 of and paragraph 15 of Schedule 1 to the Finance Act 1971(a) hereby make the following Order:—

1. This Order may be cited as the Finance Act 1971 Schedule 1 (Customs Procedures etc.) (Commencement) Order 1971.ˈ

2. Paragraphs 1, 4, 5, 7 and 11 of Schedule 1 to the Finance Act 1971 shall come into operation on 25th October 1971.

6th August 1971.

J. M. Woolf,
Commissioner of Customs and Excise.

King's Beam House,
Mark Lane,
London, EC3.

EXPLANATORY NOTE

(This Note is not part of the Order.)

This Order brings into operation on 25th October 1971 certain provisions of Schedule 1 to the Finance Act 1971 which modify Customs procedures dealing with the documentation of goods for exportation.

(a) 1971 c. 68.

STATUTORY INSTRUMENTS

1971 No. 1299

CUSTOMS AND EXCISE

The Aircraft (Customs) Regulations 1971 (Amendment) Regulations 1971

Made - - - -	6th August 1971
Laid before Parliament	11th August 1971
Coming into Operation	25th October 1971

The Commissioners of Customs and Excise in exercise of the powers conferred on them by section 54(1) of the Customs and Excise Act 1952(a) as amended by section 11 of and paragraph 9 of Schedule 1 to the Finance Act 1971(b) and of all other powers enabling them in that behalf hereby make the following Regulations:—

1.—(1) These Regulations may be cited as the Aircraft (Customs) Regulations 1971 (Amendment) Regulations 1971 and shall come into operation on 25th October 1971.

(2) In these Regulations—

"freight container" means an article of transport equipment suitable for repeated use and specially designed for the carriage of goods by one or more means of transport without intermediate reloading, and includes a portable tank or cargo flat,

"vehicle" means a road vehicle, and includes a trailer or semi-trailer.

(3) The Interpretation Act 1889(c) shall apply for the interpretation of these Regulations as it applies for the interpretation of an Act of Parliament.

2. For paragraph (1) of Regulation 7 of the Aircraft (Customs) Regulations 1971(d) there shall be substituted the following paragraph:—

"(1) No person shall load on an aircraft about to depart on a flight to an eventual destination outside the United Kingdom goods for exportation or as stores—

(a) except at the examination station at a customs airport, or such other place as the Commissioners may permit,

(b) without the authority of the proper officer,

(c) save as permitted by the Commissioners, until, as respects goods to be loaded as cargo, the commander or owner of the aircraft or his agent either (i) has had communicated to him the number assigned pursuant to paragraph 3 of Schedule 1 to the Finance Act 1971 (register of exporters and assignment of identifying numbers) to a registered person concerned in the exportation of those goods,

---

(a) 1952 c. 44.
(c) 1889 c. 63.

(b) 1971 c. 68.
(d) S.I. 1971/848 (1971 II, p. 2455).

or (ii) is in possession of a copy, stamped on behalf of the Commissioners, of the entry outwards of those goods delivered pursuant to section 47 of the Customs and Excise Act 1952 or to paragraph 1 of Schedule 1 to the Finance Act 1971,

or (iii) in the case of goods consolidated for shipment, is in possession of a breakdown list for the consolidation showing in respect of each consignment or lot included in the consolidation,

    (A) the house waybill number;

    (B) the number of packages;

    (C) the description of the goods, and

    (D) either:—

        (1) the number assigned pursuant to paragraph 3 of Schedule 1 to the Finance Act 1971 to a registered person concerned in the exportation of those goods, or

        (2) the customs number on a copy, stamped on behalf of the Commissioners, of the entry outwards of those goods delivered pursuant to section 47 of the Customs and Excise Act 1952 or to paragraph 1 of Schedule 1 to the Finance Act 1971

and having attached thereto copies of any entries of which the numbers are shewn on the breakdown list for the consolidation in accordance with (D)(2) above.

or (iv) in the case of goods to be exported in a freight container or in a vehicle, is in possession of a manifest for the container or vehicle showing:—

    (*a*) the container or vehicle identification number, and

    (*b*) in respect of each consignment or lot of goods in the container or vehicle:—

        (i) the name of the consignor;

        (ii) the marks and numbers of the packages;

        (iii) the number and kind of packages;

        (iv) the description of the goods; and

        (v) either:—

            (A) the number assigned pursuant to paragraph 3 of Schedule 1 to the Finance Act 1971 to a registered person concerned in the exportation of those goods, or

            (B) the customs number on a copy, stamped on behalf of the Commissioners, of the entry outwards of those goods delivered pursuant to section 47 of the Customs and Excise Act 1952 or to paragraph 1 of Schedule 1 to the Finance Act 1971

and having attached thereto copies of any entries of which the numbers are shewn on the manifest in accordance with (*b*)(v)(B) above."

6th August 1971.   *J. M. Woolf*,
                                    Commissioner of Customs and Excise.
King's Beam House,
Mark Lane,
London EC3.

EXPLANATORY NOTE

(This Note is not part of the Regulations.)

These Regulations amend the Aircraft (Customs) Regulations 1971 so as to change the Customs requirements for the loading of cargo for exportation by air.

STATUTORY INSTRUMENTS

1971 No. 1300

CUSTOMS AND EXCISE

The Ship's Report, Importation and Exportation by Sea Regulations 1965 (Amendment) Regulations 1971

Made - - - -	*6th August* 1971
Laid before Parliament	*11th August* 1971
Coming into Operation	*25th October* 1971

The Commissioners of Customs and Excise, in exercise of the powers conferred on them by section 54(1) of the Customs and Excise Act 1952(a) as amended by section 11 of and paragraph 9 of Schedule 1 to the Finance Act 1971(b) and of all other powers enabling them in that behalf, hereby make the following Regulations:—

1. These Regulations may be cited as the Ship's Report, Importation and Exportation by Sea Regulations 1965 (Amendment) Regulations 1971 and shall come into operation on 25th October 1971.

2.—(1) In these Regulations—

(a) "the principal Regulations" means the Ship's Report, Importation and Exportation by Sea Regulations 1965(c),

(b) "freight container" means an article of transport equipment suitable for repeated use and specially designed for the carriage of goods by one or more means of transport without intermediate reloading, and includes a portable tank or cargo flat,

(c) "vehicle" means a road or rail vehicle, and includes a trailer or semi-trailer.

(2) The Interpretation Act 1889(d) shall apply for the interpretation of these Regulations as it applies for the interpretation of an Act of Parliament.

3. After Regulation 8 of the principal Regulations there shall be added the following:—

"8A. No person shall, save as is permitted by the Commissioners, load into a ship goods for exportation until the master or owner of that ship or his agent either

(1) has had communicated to him the number assigned pursuant to paragraph 3 of Schedule 1 to the Finance Act 1971 (register of exporters and assignment of identifying numbers) to a registered person concerned in the exportation of those goods,

or (2) is in possession of a copy, stamped on behalf of the Commissioners, of the entry outwards of those goods delivered pursuant to section 47 of the Customs and Excise Act 1952 or to paragraph 1 of Schedule 1 to the Finance Act 1971,

---

(a) 1952 c. 44.
(c) S.I. 1965/1993 (1965 III, p. 5873).
(b) 1971 c. 68.
(d) 1889 c. 63.

or (3) in the case of goods to be exported in a freight container, or in a vehicle, is in possession of a manifest for the container or vehicle showing:—

(*a*) the container or vehicle identification number, and

(*b*) in respect of each consignment or lot of goods in the container or vehicle:—

(i) the name of the consignor;

(ii) the marks and numbers of the packages;

(iii) the number and kind of packages;

(iv) the description of the goods; and

(v) either—

(A) the number assigned pursuant to paragraph 3 of Schedule 1 to the Finance Act 1971 to a registered person concerned in the exportation of those goods, or

(B) the Customs number on a copy, stamped on behalf of the Commissioners, of the entry outwards of those goods and delivered pursuant to section 47 of the Customs and Excise Act 1952 or to paragraph 1 of Schedule 1 to the Finance Act 1971

and having attached thereto copies of any entries of which the numbers are shown on the manifest in accordance with (*b*)(v)(B) above.".

4. For paragraph (*a*) of Regulation 9 of the principal Regulations there shall be substituted:—

"(*a*) deliver to the proper officer within 14 days after the clearance outwards of the ship a manifest containing such particulars as the Commissioners direct of all goods shipped as cargo, together with such other documents relating to the cargo as the Commissioners direct.".

6th August 1971.

J. M. Woolf,
Commissioner of Customs and Excise.

King's Beam House,
Mark Lane,
London, EC3.

EXPLANATORY NOTE

(*This Note is not part of the Regulations.*)

These Regulations amend the Ship's Report, Importation and Exportation by Sea Regulations 1965, so as to change the Customs requirements about the loading of goods for exportation by sea and about the delivery of ships' manifests.

STATUTORY INSTRUMENTS

1971 No. 1303

LAND DRAINAGE

The Land Drainage (Compensation) (Amendment) Regulations 1971

Made - - - -	5th August 1971
Laid before Parliament	16th August 1971
Coming into Operation	17th August 1971

The Minister of Agriculture, Fisheries and Food, in exercise of the power conferred on him by section 18(6) of the Land Drainage Act 1961(a), and of all other powers enabling him in that behalf, hereby makes the following regulations :—

Citation and commencement

1. These regulations may be cited as the Land Drainage (Compensation) (Amendment) Regulations 1971, and shall come into operation on 17th August 1971.

Interpretation

2.—(1) In these regulations, unless the context otherwise requires,—

"the principal regulations" means the Land Drainage (Compensation) Regulations 1964(b) ; and

"regulation" means regulation contained in the principal regulations.

(2) Unless the context otherwise requires, any reference in these regulations, or in the principal regulations as amended by these regulations, to the provisions of any enactment shall be construed as a reference to those provisions as amended or re-enacted by any subsequent enactment.

(3) The Interpretation Act 1889(c) shall apply for the interpretation of these regulations as it applies for the interpretation of an Act of Parliament.

Amendment of the principal regulations

3.—(1) In regulation 2(1) (which defines expressions used in the principal regulations)—

(a) in the definition of " accrued pension " and " accrued retiring allowance ", for the words " regulation 22(2) of these regulations " there shall be substituted the words " regulations 22(2) and 42 of these regulations " ;

(b) in paragraph (a) of the definition of "net emoluments", after the words " the annual rate " there shall be inserted the words " (subject to regulation 42 of these regulations) " ;

(c) for the definition of " local authority " there shall be substituted the following definition—

" " local authority " means the council of a county, county borough, metropolitan borough, London borough, county district, rural parish or borough included in a rural district, the Greater London Council, the Common Council of the City of London, the council of the Isles

---

(a) 1961 c. 48.   (b) S.I. 1964/1892 (1964 III, p. 4194).   (c) 1889 c. 63.

of Scilly, any two or more of those authorities acting jointly, and any joint committee, combined authority or joint board and a police authority for a county, a borough or a combined police area ; " ; and

(d) in the definition of " relevant employment ", after the word " means " there shall be inserted the words " subject to paragraph (1A) of this regulation ".

(2) In regulation 2, after paragraph (1) there shall be added the following paragraph—

" (1A) Except as provided in regulations 5(2) and 11(2) of these regulations, the expression " relevant employment " shall not include service in the armed forces of the Crown.".

4. For paragraph (a) of regulation 7(1) (which provides for calculation of the amount of resettlement compensation) there shall be substituted the following paragraph—

" (a) unemployment, sickness or injury benefit under any Act relating to National Insurance claimable by him in respect of such week (excluding any amount claimable by him in respect of any dependant) ; ".

5. In regulation 17(1), in proviso (iii), after the words " accrued incapacity pension " there shall be inserted the words " or accrued incapacity retiring allowance " and after the words " such pension " there shall be inserted the words " or retiring allowance ".

6. In regulation 18(1), in proviso (ii), for the words " determination of the claim " there shall be substituted the words " decision on the claim has been notified or, where the decision has been reviewed under regulation 32(3) of these regulations, not later than two years after the review or, if there has been more than one such review, after the latest ".

7. In regulation 19, for the words " Subject as hereinafter provided " there shall be substituted the words " Subject to the provisions of these regulations ".

8. In regulation 27—

(a) for paragraphs (1) and (2) there shall be substituted the following paragraphs—

" (1) Except in relation to any accrued pension, accrued retiring allowance, accrued incapacity pension or accrued incapacity retiring allowance attributable to service as a contributory employee or local Act contributor, the provisions of regulations 17, 18, 19 and 20 of these regulations shall not apply to a person who had been participating in a scheme associated with his employment for providing superannuation benefits by means of contracts or policies of insurance, and who, after the loss of his employment or the diminution of his emoluments, continued to participate in that scheme, or became entitled to a benefit or prospective benefit thereunder other than a return of contributions.

(2) If the claimant is such a person as is mentioned in paragraph (1) of this regulation who has lost his employment, the compensating authority may, if the relevant scheme so permits, make such payments to him, whether by way of the payment of premiums or otherwise, as will secure that his benefits under the scheme are increased to an extent actuarially equivalent to that by which similar amounts of retirement compensation could be increased under regulation 22(2) or (4) of these regulations." ; and

(b) in paragraph (3), after the word " benefits " there shall be inserted the words " under the scheme ".

9. The following regulation shall be inserted after regulation 30—

" *Deduction in respect of National Insurance benefits*

30A.—(1) Where in any week a person is entitled to long-term compensation for loss or diminution of emoluments and is also entitled to unemployment, sickness or injury benefit under any Act relating to National Insurance, other than a benefit claimable by him in respect of a dependant, there shall be deducted from the long-term compensation payable for that week a sum equal to the amount by which the aggregate of such National Insurance benefits claimable in respect of that week, the weekly rate at which the long-term compensation would be payable but for this regulation, and the weekly rate of any superannuation benefit taken into account for the purpose of regulation 14(4) of these regulations, exceeds two-thirds of the weekly rate of the net emoluments of the employment which he has lost or in which the emoluments have been diminished :

Provided that this paragraph shall not apply in relation to any such sickness or injury benefit in so far as an equivalent sum is deducted from the emoluments of his current employment and such deduction from those emoluments has not occasioned an increase in his long-term compensation.

(2) For the purposes of paragraph (1) of this regulation the expression " weekly rate " means seven three hundred and sixty-fifths of the relevant annual rate.".

10. For regulation 31 there shall be substituted the following regulation—

" 31. Where—

(a) a pensionable officer after suffering loss of employment or diminution of emoluments enters any employment referred to in regulation 21 of these regulations or becomes entitled to any superannuation benefit on ceasing to hold such employment, or

(b) a person entitled to long-term compensation enters employment the remuneration whereof is payable out of public funds, or ceases to hold such employment, or receives any increase in his remuneration in such employment, or

(c) a person entitled to retirement compensation enters employment in which the compensation is subject to reduction or suspension under regulation 30 of these regulations, or ceases to hold such employment, or receives any increase in his remuneration in such employment, or

(d) a person entitled to long-term compensation is receiving or starts to receive any benefit, any increase in benefit or any further benefit under any Act relating to National Insurance,

he shall forthwith inform the compensating authority in writing of that fact.".

11. In regulation 32 (which relates to the review of awards of compensation), in paragraph (7), for the words " regulation 29 or 30 " there shall be substituted the words " regulation 29, 30 or 30A ".

12. After regulation 41 there shall be added the following regulation—

" *Temporary variation of emoluments*

42. In calculating for the purposes of these regulations the amount of any emoluments lost or the amount by which any emoluments have been diminished, and in determining the net emoluments, the accrued pension or the accrued retiring allowance of any person who has suffered such a loss or diminution, no account shall be taken of any increase in the amount

of the person's emoluments which is attributable to any temporary allowance made in consequence of the making of any such order as is mentioned in regulation 4 of these regulations and which is made otherwise than in the ordinary course of his employment.".

In witness whereof the Official Seal of the Minister of Agriculture, Fisheries and Food is hereunto affixed on 5th August 1971.

(L.S.) *J. M. L. Prior,*

Minister of Agriculture, Fisheries and Food.

EXPLANATORY NOTE

(This Note is not part of the Regulations.)

These regulations amend the Land Drainage (Compensation) Regulations 1964 (" the principal regulations ") made under section 18(6) of the Land Drainage Act 1961.

The main amendments to the principal regulations are as follows—

(1)—(i) The expression " relevant employment " (which is defined in regulation 2(1) of the principal regulations and which affects qualification for compensation and calculation of the amount) is not to include service in the armed forces of the Crown other than certain national service which is expressly made relevant employment for determining whether a person is qualified to claim compensation (Regulation 3(1)(*d*)) ;

(ii) All National Insurance benefits (other than benefits payable in respect of dependants) are to be taken into account in assessing resettlement compensation and not only, as at present, benefits at the flat rate applicable to a single person (Regulation 4) ;

(iii) National Insurance benefits (other than benefits payable in respect of dependants) are to be deducted from long-term compensation to such extent as is necessary to ensure that the total of benefits and compensation received in any week does not exceed two-thirds of the emoluments for the loss or reduction of which compensation is payable. This was formerly secured by regulations under the National Insurance Acts (Regulation 9) ;

(2) Provision is made for the payment of retirement compensation to persons entitled under the regulations whose pension rights derive in part from statutory schemes and in part from schemes based on policies of insurance (Regulation 8) ;

(3) Persons claiming compensation are required to inform the compensating authority if they become entitled to pension benefits (Regulation 10) ;

(4) In assessing compensation no account is to be taken of any temporary increase of remuneration granted in connection with the reorganisation or other event which has led to the claim (Regulation 12).

A number of other minor amendments are made to bring the principal regulations generally in line with the Local Government (Compensation) Regulations 1963 as amended (S.I. 1963/999 as amended by S.I. 1965/571 and S.I. 1968/913).

The Regulations apply to England and Wales.

STATUTORY INSTRUMENTS

1971 No. 1309

MEDICINES

The Medicines (Exportation of Specified Veterinary Products) Order 1971

Made - - - -	*6th August* 1971
Laid before Parliament	*16th August* 1971
Coming into Operation	*31st August* 1971

Whereas it appears to the Minister of Agriculture, Fisheries and Food, the Secretary of State for Scotland (being the Secretary of State concerned with agriculture in Scotland) and the Minister of Agriculture for Northern Ireland (hereinafter called "the Ministers") to be requisite for securing that any exemption conferred by section 48(1) of the Medicines Act 1968(a) does not apply to medicinal products consisting wholly or partly of substances, the purity or potency of which cannot, in their opinion, be adequately tested by chemical means, that the following order shall be made:

Now, therefore the Ministers, acting jointly, in exercise of their powers under section 49 of the Medicines Act 1968, and of all other powers enabling them in that behalf, and after consulting such organisations as appear to them to be representative of interests likely to be substantially affected by this order, hereby order as follows:—

Citation and commencement

1. This order may be cited as the Medicines (Exportation of Specified Veterinary Products) Order 1971 and shall come into operation on 31st August 1971.

Interpretation

2.—(1) In this order, unless the context otherwise requires—

"the Act" means the Medicines Act 1968;

"antigens" are substances which on administration to a human being or animal are capable of eliciting a specific immunological response;

"antisera" are substances which consist wholly or partly of sera derived from animals which have been immunised against one or more micro-organisms, viruses or other antigens;

"antitoxins" are substances which consist wholly or partly of immuno-globulins of antisera derived from animals which have been immunised against one or more toxins whether detoxified or not;

(a) 1968 c. 67.

"corticotrophin" is a substance obtained from the anterior lobe of the pituitary gland and which contains the peptide hormone that increases the rate at which corticoid hormones are secreted by the adrenal gland;

"heparin" is a substance containing the sodium salt of a sulphated polysaccharide obtained from mammalian tissues which has the property of prolonging the clotting time of blood in human beings or animals;

"hyaluronidase" is a substance prepared from mammalian testicles or sperm or from other sources of the enzymes which diminish the viscosity of the hyaluronic acid present in mammalian tissues;

"insulin" is a preparation of the specific antidiabetic principle of the pancreas;

"plasma" means the fluid element of uncoagulated blood;

"preparations of the pituitary (posterior lobe)" include the active principles thereof (whether obtained by fractionation of the gland or by synthesis) and derivatives of those principles with the same specific biological action;

"sera" means the fluid element of coagulated blood;

"toxins" are substances used in the diagnosis, prevention or treatment of disease and consisting wholly or partly of poisonous substances derived from specific micro-organisms, plants or animals;

"vaccines" are substances which consist wholly or partly of—

(a) any micro-organisms, viruses or other organisms in any state,

(b) any toxins of microbial origin which have been detoxified, or

(c) any extracts or derivatives of any micro-organisms or of any viruses, being substances which, when administered to human beings or animals, are used for the prevention or treatment of specific diseases;

and other expressions have the same meaning as in the Act.

(2) The Interpretation Act 1889(a) shall apply to the interpretation of this order as it applies to the interpretation of an Act of Parliament.

Provisions in respect of the exporting of certain classes of medicinal products

3. There are hereby specified the following classes of medicinal products and substances in relation to which nothing in section 48(1) of the Act shall affect the operation of any of the provisions of sections 7 to 47 of the Act, that is to say:—

medicinal products and substances for use other than for human beings which consist wholly or partly of antigens, antisera, antitoxins, corticotrophin, heparin, hyaluronidase, insulin, plasma, preparations of the pituitary (posterior lobe), sera, toxins, vaccines and other medicinal products or substances derived from animals.

In Witness whereof the official seal of the Minister of Agriculture, Fisheries and Food is hereunto affixed on 26th July 1971.

(L.S.)

J. M. L. Prior,
Minister of Agriculture, Fisheries and Food.

Gordon Campbell,
30th July 1971.   Secretary of State for Scotland.

Given under my hand on 6th August 1971.

H. W. West,
Minister of Agriculture for Northern Ireland.

(a) 1889 c. 63.

EXPLANATORY NOTE

(This Note is not part of the Order.)

This order, made under section 49(1) of the Medicines Act 1968, excepts from the postponement of the operation of sections 7 to 47 of the Act, effected by section 48(1) of the Act, certain classes of veterinary medicinal products and substances the purity or potency of which cannot in the opinion of the Agriculture Ministers be adequately tested by chemical means.

STATUTORY INSTRUMENTS

1971 No. 1316

PENSIONS

The Pensions (Preservation of Increases) Order 1971

Made - - - -	9th August 1971
Coming into Operation -	1st September 1971

The Minister for the Civil Service by virtue of the powers conferred on him by section 6 of the Pensions (Increase) Act 1971(a) hereby makes the following Order:—

Citation and commencement

1.—(1) This order may be cited as the Pensions (Preservation of Increases) Order 1971.

(2) This order shall come into operation on 1st September 1971.

Construction

2.—(1) The Interpretation Act 1889(b) shall apply for the interpretation of this order as it applies for the interpretation of an Act of Parliament.

(2) In this order—

(a) " the 1971 Act " means the Pensions (Increase) Act 1971, " the 1944 Act " means the Pensions (Increase) Act 1944(c), and similarly with other expressions of the same kind;

(b) " average emoluments " and " final emoluments " mean, in relation to a pension payable in respect of a person's service in an office or employment, the average rate of the relevant emoluments over a period of service in the office or employment and the rate of the relevant emoluments in the office or employment received immediately before the pension begins, respectively;

(c) " averaging period ", in relation to a pension computed by reference to average emoluments, means the period of service by reference to which the average emoluments fall to be determined;

(d) " the supplement " means the addition to the 1971 rate which is dealt with by Article 9 of this order (in accordance with section 6(5) of the 1971 Act);

and (without prejudice to any further operation of section 31 of the Interpretation Act 1889) this order is to be construed in accordance with the definitions and other interpretative provisions repeated from the 1971 Act in Part I of Schedule 1 to this order.

(3) Any reference in this order to a rate of pension or emoluments is a reference to the annual rate.

(4) This order has effect subject to any provision made in the exercise of the powers conferred by section 5(3) of the 1971 Act.

(a) 1971 c. 56.	(b) 1889 c. 63.	(c) 1944 c. 21.

Interpretation and use of Tables

3.—(1) In the Tables annexed to this order the expression " up to ", where used with reference to a date, is to be read as including that date, but in a head or line preceded by one operating by reference to an earlier date as excluding the time up to that earlier date, except in any case to which the preceding head or line does not apply; and similarly where the expression " up to " is used with reference to a rate of pension.

(2) To find from the relevant Table the 1971 rate (with or without supplement) for any pension, the head or line to be used is that relevant to the date when the pension begins; and the basic rate or other rate on which the Table operates for that pension is to be multiplied by the figure given in the column headed by the multiplication sign, and to the result so obtained there is to be added any amount given in a column headed by the £ sign.

(3) The Tables giving the 1971 rate include in a separate division figures indicating, in terms of the basic rate of a pension to which the Table applies, where the 1971 rate (with or without supplement) or the 1969 standard is the higher; but this division is not to be treated as having operative effect, and the indications given are not applicable in cases where the comparison is affected either—

(*a*) by apportionment of any increase or of the supplement; or

(*b*) by a reduction in the 1971 rate on account of a war increase in the pension;

unless the apportionment or reduction affects only a 1944 element to be derived from another Table.

Except in cases where the comparison is so affected, in this division of any Table—

(i) a single figure indicates the basic rate up to which the 1971 rate, with or without supplement according to the column, would be used as being higher than the 1969 standard and above which the 1969 standard would be used;

(ii) a pair of figures indicates, for cases where the 1971 rate depends on variable factors other than the basic rate, by the lower figure the basic rate up to which the 1971 rate would be used in all cases, and by the higher figure the basic rate at or above which it would not be used;

(iii) the expression " nil " is accordingly used to indicate that the 1969 standard is always higher than the alternative, and the expression " not relevant " (or the abbreviation " n/r ") is used to indicate that the 1969 standard cannot be the higher;

(iv) a dash is used to indicate that variable factors prevent the giving of an indication;

(v) where in a pair of figures one figure is replaced by a dash, the figure given is to be treated as the higher or lower figure of a pair according to its position on the right or on the left.

Application of order, and revocation of superseded provisions

4.—(1) This order applies to the pensions specified in Schedule 2 to the order, except that it does not apply either—

(*a*) to any pension that qualified for an increase under the 1920 Act; or

(*b*) to any lump sum or gratuity other than a gratuity specified in section 9(8) of the 1971 Act (which is repeated in Part II of Schedule 1 to this order).

(2) Schedule 2 to this order notes for each description of pension the Act under or by reference to which increases dealt with by this order were first payable on pensions of that description, and references in this order to a pension being, or not being, within the 1944 Act or another Act of the series are to be construed as references to its being, or not being, noted in that Schedule as within the Act mentioned.

(3) In relation to pensions that are not within the 1944 Act, this order is to have effect as if provisions applying only to pensions beginning on or before 1st April 1947, or relating to a 1944 element, were omitted.

(4) This order does not apply to pensions other than those to which it is applied by paragraph (1) above, and in particular it does not apply to pensions which would not be noted in Schedule 2 as within the 1962 Act or an earlier Act (the 1969 standard for these pensions being in all cases higher than the 1971 rate and no supplement being payable).

(5) There is hereby revoked any order specified in Schedule 3 to this order, or so much of it as is there included (the provisions there included being provisions which are superseded by there being treated as relevant increases for purposes of section 6 of the 1971 Act and this order any increases of pension authorised by those provisions by reference to the relevant increases.)

Ascertainment of 1971 *rate*

5.—(1) Except as otherwise provided in this order, the 1971 rate of a pension (unless that rate is, in accordance with section 6(3) of the 1971 Act, to be taken to be the rate at which the pension is being paid on 31st August 1971) shall be ascertained in accordance with the following provisions of this Article from the Tables annexed to this order.

(2) For earnings-related pensions based on final emoluments, the Tables to be used are as follows:—

(*a*) for a pension beginning on or before 31st March 1952—

   (i) if it is based on emoluments of less than £1,365, Table I is to be used;

   (ii) if it is based on emoluments of £1,365 or over, Table II is to be used, but in the case of a pension beginning after 31st December 1947 and based on emoluments less than £1,500 is to be applied as if the basic rate were that appropriate to a pension based on emoluments of £1,500;

(*b*) for a pension beginning on or after 1st April 1952 (but not after 1st April 1961) Table IA and IIA is to be used.

For a pension beginning after 1st April 1961 the 1969 standard is in all cases higher than the 1971 rate, and accordingly a 1971 rate is not given.

(3) For earnings-related pensions based on average emoluments with an averaging period beginning on or before 1st January 1947, the Tables to be used are as given in sub-paragraphs (*a*) and (*b*) below, but in cases within paragraph (*c*) are to be applied as there mentioned:—

(*a*) for a pension beginning on or before 31st March 1952—

   (i) if it is based on average emoluments of less than £1,500, Table I is to be used, unless it begins after 1st January 1948 and sub-paragraph (iii) below applies;

(ii) if it is based on average emoluments of £1,500 or over, Table III is to be used;

(iii) if it is based on average emoluments less than £1,500 and begins after 1st January 1948, Table III is to be used, but to be applied as if the basic rate were that appropriate to a pension based on emoluments of £1,500, where the 1971 rate so obtained is less than under Table I (as will happen if the emoluments are over £1,365 multiplied by the figure represented in Table III by the symbol Q);

(*b*) for a pension beginning on or after 1st April 1952, Table IIIA and IVA is to be used, but the basic rate is to be treated as increased, as mentioned in the notes to the Table, according to the proportion of the averaging period falling before the time there indicated;

(*c*) in the case of pensions beginning on or after 1st April 1947, but with an averaging period beginning before 1st April 1946—

(i) if the pension begins on or before 31st March 1952, the rate given by Table I or III is to be increased by the addition of the adjusted 1944 element, if any, to be derived from Table V;

(ii) if the pension begins on or after 1st April 1952, the multiplier in Table IIIA and IVA is to be applied to the basic rate further increased (after the increase referred to in paragraph (*b*) above) by the adjusted 1944 element, if any, to be derived from Table V.

(4) For earnings-related pensions based on average emoluments with an averaging period beginning after 1st January 1947, the Tables to be used are as follows:—

(*a*) for a pension beginning on or before 31st March 1952—

(i) if it is based on average emoluments of less than £1,365, Table I is to be used;

(ii) if it is based on average emoluments of £1,365 or over, Table II is to be used, but in the case of a pension based on emoluments of less than £1,500 is to be applied as if the basic rate were that appropriate to a pension based on emoluments of £1,500;

(*b*) for a pension beginning on or after 1st April 1952—

(i) if it is based on average emoluments of less than £1,500, with an averaging period beginning on or before 1st April 1951, Table IIIA and IVA is to be used, but the basic rate is to be treated as increased, as mentioned in the notes to the Table, according to the proportion of the averaging period falling before the time there indicated;

(ii) otherwise Table IA and IIA is to be used, unless the pension begins after 1st April 1961.

For a pension beginning after 1st April 1961 (and not based on average emoluments of less than £1,500 with an averaging period beginning on or before 1st April 1951) the 1969 standard is in all cases higher than the 1971 rate, and accordingly a 1971 rate is not given in Table IA and IIA.

(5) For flat-rate pensions the Tables to be used are as follows:—

(*a*) for a pension which is not within the 1944 Act, or which became payable only on or after 1st January 1966—

(i) if it begins on or before 31st March 1952, Table I is to be used; and

(ii) if it begins on or after 1st April 1952 (but not after 1st April 1961) Table IA and IIA is to be used;

(*b*) for a pension which is within the 1944 Act and became payable on or before 31st December 1965—

    (i) if it begins on or before 31st March 1952, Table IV is to be used;

    (ii) if it begins on or after 1st April 1952, Table IIIA and IVA is to be used, but the multiplier is to be applied to the basic rate increased by the 1944 element or adjusted 1944 element to be derived from Table V.

For a pension beginning after 1st April 1961 and not within paragraph (*b*) above, the 1969 standard is in all cases higher than the 1971 rate, and accordingly a 1971 rate is not given in Table IA and IIA.

(6) In relation to any of the following, that is to say—

(*a*) pensions payable under the Police Pensions Act 1921(**a**);

(*b*) pensions payable under any provision repealed by the Police Pensions Act 1948(**b**) of the Police and Firemen (War Service) Act 1939(**c**) in respect of service which is treated as approved service in a police force; and

(*c*) pensions payable under the Police Pensions Act 1948 otherwise than in respect of overseas service within the meaning of the Police (Overseas Service) Act 1945(**d**);

paragraphs (2), (3) and (4) above shall have effect as if references to 1st January 1947 were references to 2nd July 1948, and references to 31st December 1947 and to 1st January 1948 were references to 1st July 1949, and as if paragraphs (2)(*a*) and (3)(*a*) each required Table I to be used for any pension beginning on or before 1st July 1949.

Effect on 1971 rate of war increases (Tables I, II and III)

6.—(1) Where a pension within the 1944 Act is based on final emoluments and begins on or before 1st April 1947, or is based on average emoluments and begins on or before 31st March 1947, and there has been a war increase in the basic rate of the pension, then the operation of Table I, II or III, if it applies in relation to the pension, shall be modified in accordance with the rules applicable to the case which are contained in the notes to Table V.

(2) For the purpose of the provisions of this order relating to pensions within the 1944 Act, "war increase" means any increase which may have resulted from an addition after 3rd September 1939 to the emoluments on which the pension is based, being an addition which the pension authority are satisfied was an addition by way of war bonus or other similar allowance.

Apportionments for 1971 rate in case of double pension (Tables I, II, III and IV)

7.—(1) Where a pensioner is in receipt of a pension within the 1944 Act, and—

(*a*) the pension—

    (i) is an earnings-related pension beginning on or before 1st April 1947 if it is based on final emoluments, or on or before 31st March 1947 if it is based on average emoluments; and

    (ii) is not one for which head 1 of Table I, II or III is excluded by the rules as to war increases contained in the notes to Table V; or

---

(**a**) 1921 c. 31.   (**b**) 1948 c. 24.   (**c**) 1939 c. 103.
(**d**) 1945 c. 17 (9 & 10 Geo. 6).

(*b*) the pension is an earnings-related pension based on average emoluments which begins after 31st March 1947 but on or before 31st March 1952, with an averaging period beginning before 1st April 1946, and is not one for which the adjusted 1944 element obtained from note 3 to Table V would be nil; or

(*c*) the pension is a flat-rate pension beginning on or before 31st March 1952 and became payable on or before 31st December 1965;

then, if the pensioner is in receipt also of another pension which is aggregable under paragraph (4) below, Table I, II, III or IV is not to be used to find the 1971 rate of the pension, but that rate shall be arrived at by adding together the adjusted 1944 element, if any, to be derived from Table V, the adjusted 1952 element to be derived from Table VI and the adjusted basic rate.

For this purpose the adjusted basic rate is 1·8887 times the basic rate or, if the basic rate is more than £1,000, is the sum of 1·7170 times the basic rate and £171·70, except for pensions within sub-paragraph (*b*) above which begin after 1st January 1948 and for which, but for this Article, Table III would be used to find the 1971 rate; and for those pensions the adjusted basic rate is the rate given by Table IIIA and IVA as the 1971 rate for a pension beginning on 1st April 1952 and not within the 1944 Act.

(2) Where a pensioner is in receipt of a pension beginning on or before 31st March 1952, and either—

(*a*) the pension is within the 1944 Act, but paragraph (1) above does not operate in relation to it; or

(*b*) the pension is within the 1952 Act;

then, if the pensioner is in receipt also of another aggregable pension, the 1971 rate given for the pension first referred to by Table I, II or III shall be reduced by the amount, if any, required by the rules contained in the notes to Table VI.

(3) For purposes of this Article a person for whose benefit a pension is payable shall be deemed to be in receipt of the pension notwithstanding that it is payable to some other person; and—

(*a*) where a man and his wife are in receipt, one of a substituted pension, and the other of the original pension, then in relation to the 1971 rate of either pension paragraph (1) or (2) above shall apply as if the one in receipt of the original pension were in receipt also of the substituted pension (instead of the one actually in receipt of it); and

(*b*) where a pensioner is in receipt of a pension described in paragraph (1) or (2) above and payable in respect of the services of the pensioner's deceased husband or wife, and another person is in receipt of a pension so described payable in respect of those services but payable for his benefit to that pensioner, then in relation to the 1971 rate of any of the pensions paragraph (1) or (2) above shall apply as if the person in receipt of it were in receipt also of any other of them; and

(*c*) where a pensioner is in receipt of a pension described in paragraph (1) above and payable in respect of the services of the pensioner's deceased husband, and a person under the age of 16 who is dependent on her is also in receipt of a pension so described payable in respect of those services (whether or not payable for his benefit to that pensioner), then in relation to the 1971 rate of any of the pensions paragraph (1) above shall apply as if the person in receipt of it were in receipt also of any other of them.

(4) The following pensions are aggregable for purposes of this Article:—

(*a*) any pension within the 1944 Act which either—

(i) is an earnings-related pension based on final emoluments that begins on or before 1st April 1947; or

(ii) is an earnings-related pension based on average emoluments, that either begins on or before 31st March 1947 or begins at any time before the year 1969 but with an averaging period beginning before 1st April 1946; or

(iii) is a flat rate pension that either begins on or before 1st April 1947 or became payable on or before 31st December 1965;

(*b*) subject to paragraph (6) below, any service pension of which the rate is increasable by an amount corresponding to the 1944 element;

(*c*) any pension in the case of which an increase is payable under any scheme (wherever in force and whether or not authorised by or under any enactment) which was determined for the corresponding purpose of the 1944 Act and 1947 Act to be similar to the provisions of those Acts.

(5) In relation to the 1952 element the following pensions are also aggregable for purposes of this Article:—

(*a*) any pension within the 1952 Act that begins on or before 31st March 1952;

(*b*) subject to paragraph (6) below, any service pension of which the rate is increasable by an amount corresponding to the 1952 element;

(*c*) any pension in the case of which an increase is payable under any scheme (wherever in force and whether or not authorised by or under any enactment) which was determined for the corresponding purpose of the 1952 Act to be similar to the provisions of that Act.

(6) In paragraphs (4) and (5) above " service pension " means a pension granted under any Order in Council, Royal Warrant or Order of Her Majesty in respect of service in Her Majesty's naval, military or air forces, whether that service has been rendered by the pensioner or by any other person; but there shall be disregarded—

(*a*) the whole of any service pension granted solely on account of death or disablement which is attributable to service in those forces, or granted partly on account of death or disablement which is so attributable but without any specific part of the pension being referable to the death or disablement; and

(*b*) so much as is specifically referable to the death or disablement of any other pension granted partly on account of death or disablement which is so attributable.

For purposes of sub-paragraphs (*a*) and (*b*) above a person's death or disablement shall be treated as attributable to service in Her Majesty's naval, military or air forces, if it is wholly or partly due to any wound, injury or disease which has been caused or aggravated by service in those forces.

(7) In the case of a pension aggregable by virtue of paragraph (4)(*c*) or (5)(*c*) above, account may be taken of it to such greater or less extent as was determined, by the determination there referred to, to have been appropriate for the corresponding purpose of the 1944 Act and 1947 Act or of the 1952 Act, as the case may be.

Adaptations for 1971 *rate for derivative pensions under*
Superannuation Acts 1965 *and* 1967

8.—(1) Where a pension payable under Part III or IV of the Superannuation Act 1965(a) enures for the benefit of more than one child or dependant, the pension shall be treated for the purpose of determining the 1971 rate (including any purpose of Article 7 of this order) as a number of separate pensions equal to the number of those children or dependants; and the amount of each pension shall be deemed for that purpose to be a sum ascertained—

(*a*) where the whole of the pension is paid to the same person, by dividing the amount of the pension by the number of children or dependants; and

(*b*) where different parts of the pension are paid to different persons, by dividing each part by the number of children or dependants for whose benefit that part is paid.

(2) Where two or more pensions are payable either—

(*a*) under Part III or IV of the Superannuation Act 1965 in respect of children or dependants of the same person; or

(*b*) in accordance with a warrant issued or having effect as issued under section 18 of that Act in respect of children of the same person;

and the pensions are paid to one person for the benefit of the pensioners but the case is not within Article 7(3)(*b*) of this order, that Article shall apply as if the same pensioner were in receipt of both or all those pensions.

Amount of supplement

9.—(1) Where a pension begins on or before 1st April 1961, and any qualifying condition is satisfied other than one of the conditions specified in section 3(3)(*b*), (*c*) and (*d*) of the 1971 Act (which relate to pensioners in receipt of derivative pensions while of an age less than 16 or receiving education or training) the addition to be made to the 1971 rate in accordance with section 6(5) of that Act shall, subject to paragraph (2) below, be of the amount which—

(*a*) is given by reference to the 1971 rate in Table VII annexed to this order; and

(*b*) is incorporated by reference to the basic rate in Tables I, II, IA and IIA, IV and IIIA and IVA for the pensions (or some of the pensions) to which those Tables apply.

(2) Where the supplement may be added to the 1971 rate of a pension, and the pensioner is in receipt also of another aggregable pension, then the amount of the supplement shall be reduced by the amount, if any, required by the rules contained in the notes to Table VII.

(3) For purposes of paragraph (2) above, a person for whose benefit a pension is payable shall be deemed to be in receipt of the pension notwithstanding that it is payable to some other person; and, where a man and his wife are in receipt, one of a substituted pension, and the other of the original pension, then in relation to the supplement payable on either pension paragraph (2) above shall apply as if the one in receipt of the original pension were in receipt also of the substituted pension (instead of the one actually in receipt of it).

(a) 1965 c. 74.

(4) The following pensions are aggregable for purposes of paragraph (2) above:—

(a) any pension in the case of which the supplement may be added to the 1971 rate;

(b) subject to paragraph (5) below, any service pension of which the rate is increasable by an amount corresponding to the supplement;

(c) any pension in the case of which an increase is payable under any scheme (wherever in force and whether or not authorised by any enactment) which was determined for the corresponding purpose of the 1962 Act to be similar to the provisions of that Act.

(5) Article 7(6) above shall apply for purposes of paragraph (4) of this Article as it applies for purposes of Article 7(4) and (5).

(6) In the case of a pension aggregable by virtue of paragraph (4)(c) above the provisions of this Article and of Table VII as to the reduction of the supplement where the pensioner is in receipt of more than one pension shall apply subject to the like modifications, if any, as were directed to have effect for the corresponding purpose of the Act of 1962.

Continuation for certain earnings-related pensions
of increases under 1944 Act and 1956 Act

10.—(1) In respect of any period beginning on or after 1st September 1971 the rate of an earnings-related pension based on average emoluments and beginning after the year 1968 may, if it falls within paragraph (2) or (3) below, be increased (in accordance with section 6(6) of the 1971 Act) by the amount indicated in that paragraph, and any increase under section 1 or 2 of the 1971 Act shall be calculated by reference to the rate of pension as so increased as if it were the basic rate.

(2) A pension within the 1944 Act, if the averaging period began on or before 1st April 1946, may be increased by the addition of the adjusted 1944 element, if any, to be derived from Table V by applying paragraph (1)(a) and (b) and paragraph (2) (but not paragraph (1)(c)) of note 3 to that Table.

(3) A pension within the 1956 Act or any earlier Act, if the averaging period began on or before the earlier relevant date, may be increased or further increased (after any increase authorised by paragraph (2) above) by the appropriate fraction of the basic rate or, if that is more than £1,000, by the appropriate fraction of £1,000, subject however to the restriction imposed by paragraph (5) below in the case of a pension based on average emoluments of less than £1,500.

The appropriate fraction for this purpose is one-tenth of the fraction that results from dividing by the total number of half-years in the averaging period the number of them ending on or before the later relevant date (any incomplete half-year at the end of the period being disregarded).

(4) The dates referred to in paragraph (3) above are as follows:—

(a) in relation to a pension based on average emoluments of £1,500 or over, the earlier relevant date is 1st January 1947 and the later relevant date is 31st December 1947;

(b) in relation to a pension based on average emoluments of less than £1,500, the earlier relevant date is 1st April 1951 and the later relevant date is 31st March 1952.

(5) A pension based on average emoluments of less than £1,500 is not to be increased under paragraph (2) above—

(a) if the averaging period began after 1st January 1947, by more than would raise its basic rate to that appropriate to a pension based on average emoluments of £1,500; or

(b) if the averaging period began on or before 1st January 1947, by more than would raise its basic rate to that appropriate to a pension based on average emoluments of £1,500 plus the addition that could be made to it under paragraph (2).

Given under the official seal of the Minister for the Civil Service on 9th August 1971.

J. E. Herbecq,

(L.S.)   Authorised by the Minister
                                          for the Civil Service.

Article 2   **SCHEDULE 1**

Provisions repeated from 1971 Act

Part I

Interpretative Provisions

Meaning of " pension " and " beginning "

8.—(1) For purposes of this Act "pension" includes (subject to section 9 below)*—

(*a*) any allowance or other benefit payable (either in respect of the services of the pensioner or in respect of the services of any other person) by virtue of any superannuation scheme, whether contained in an enactment or otherwise, including a superannuation scheme providing benefits in the case of injury or death; and

(*b*) any compensation payable in respect of retirement from an office or employment in pursuance of the provisions of an enactment, any compensation payable in respect of the loss, abolition or relinquishment of an office or employment occasioned by an alteration in the organisation of a department or service or by a transfer or other reorganisation of the functions of local authorities, and any compensation payable in respect of a diminution in the emoluments of an office or employment which has been occasioned as aforesaid.

(2) A pension shall be deemed for purposes of this Act to begin on the day following the last day of the service in respect of which the pension is payable (whenever the pension accrues or becomes payable), except that—

(*a*) an earnings-related pension based, directly or indirectly, on emoluments received for a period not ending with the last day of that service, other than a substituted pension, is to be deemed to begin on the day following the last day of that period; and

(*b*) a substituted pension is to be deemed to begin on the same day as the original pension, or, if earlier, on the day from which the surrender of the original pension takes effect.

* Section 9 relates to gratuities and lump sums—see Article 4(1)(*b*) of this Order.

Other definitions

17.—(1) For purposes of this Act, unless the context otherwise requires,—

" basic rate " means the annual rate of a pension apart from any increase under or by reference to this Act or any enactment repealed by this Act, or any corresponding increase made otherwise than under or by reference to this Act or an enactment repealed by it;

" derivative pension " and " principal pension " mean a pension which is not, and one which is, payable in respect of the pensioner's own services;

" earnings-related pension " means a pension computed by reference to a rate of emoluments (whether actual emoluments or not and whether final or average emoluments), or payable at alternative rates one of which is so computed, and includes a derivative pension computed by reference to the rate of an earnings-related pension;

" flat rate " means a rate fixed otherwise than by reference to a rate of emoluments or to the rate of another pension, and " flat-rate pension " means a pension payable at a flat rate only, but includes a derivative pension computed by reference to the rate of a flat-rate pension;

.   .   .   .

" substituted pension " means a pension granted in consideration of the surrender of the whole or part of another pension (" the original pension ").

PART II
GRATUITIES TO WHICH ORDER APPLIES

9.—(8) The gratuities to which subsection (7) above applies are—

(*a*) any gratuity granted by way of periodical payments under any of the following enactments:—

(i) section 23 of the Local Government and other Officers' Superannuation Act 1922(**a**);

(ii) paragraph 4 of Part I of Schedule 1 to the Local Government (Clerks) Act 1931(**b**);

(iii) section 11 of the Local Government Superannuation Act 1937(**c**) or of the Local Government Superannuation (Scotland) Act 1937(**d**);

(*b*) any gratuity granted by way of periodical payments or by way of an annuity under section 18 of the Local Government Superannuation Act 1953(**e**);

(*c*) any gratuity granted by way of periodical payments or by way of an annuity under any local Act (or provisional order confirmed by Parliament) corresponding to any of the enactments mentioned in paragraphs (*a*) and (*b*) above.

Any question whether a local Act or provisional order corresponds to any of the enactments mentioned in paragraphs (*a*) and (*b*) above shall be determined, in the event of dispute, by the Secretary of State.

SCHEDULE 2   Article 4
PENSIONS TO WHICH ORDER APPLIES

[NOTE: The paragraphs in this Schedule are numbered to match the corresponding paragraphs in Schedule 2 to the 1971 Act. They incorporate references to the 1944 Act, etc., and this indicates the Act " within " which the pensions are for purposes of this order.]

PART I
STATE PENSIONS
Ministerial and parliamentary

2. A pension payable under the Lord Chancellor's Pension Act 1832.(**f**) [1962 Act.]

3. A pension payable under Mr. Speaker Morrison's Retirement Act 1959.(**g**) [1962 Act.]

Civil service

4. A pension payable under the Superannuation Acts 1965 and 1967:—

(*a*) payable under Part III or IV of the Superannuation 1965. [1952 Act];

(*b*) payable otherwise than under Part III or IV of that Act. [1944 Act.]

Administration of justice

5. A pension payable under any of the following:—

(*a*) the Appellate Jurisdiction Act 1876(**h**) (Lords of Appeal);

(*b*) section 14 of the Supreme Court of Judicature (Consolidation) Act 1925(**i**) (higher judiciary in England and Wales);

(*c*) the Judges' Pensions (Scotland) Act 1808(**j**) (higher judiciary in Scotland);

(*d*) section 19 of the Supreme Court of Judicature Act (Ireland) 1877(**k**) (higher judiciary in Northern Ireland).
[1962 Act.]

(**a**) 1922 c. 59.	(**b**) 1931 c. 45.	(**c**) 1937 c. 68.	(**d**) 1937 c. 69.
(**e**) 1953 c. 25.	(**f**) 1832 c. 111.	(**g**) 1959 c. 1 (8 & 9 Eliz. 2).	
(**h**) 1876 c. 59.	(**i**) 1925 c. 49.	(**j**) 1808 c. 145.	(**k**) 1877 c. 57.

6. A pension payable out of the Consolidated Fund or out of moneys provided by Parliament under Part I of the Administration of Justice (Pensions) Act 1950(a) (widows and children of judges and senior officials in the legal system, including the Chairman and Deputy Chairman of the Monopolies Commission). [1952 Act.]

7. A pension payable under section 9 of the County Courts Act 1934(b) (county court judges). [1944 Act.]

8. A pension payable under section 20 of the Sheriff Courts (Scotland) Act 1907(c) (sheriffs and salaried sheriffs-substitute). [1944 Act.]

9. A pension payable under section 34(1) of the Courts-Martial (Appeals) Act 1951(d) (Judge Advocate General). [1959 Act.]

10. A pension payable under section 4(5) of the Criminal Justice Administration Act 1956(e) (Recorder of Manchester or Liverpool). [1962 Act.]

13. A pension payable under the Police Magistrates (Superannuation) Acts 1915 and 1929. [1944 Act.]

Police and firemen

14. A pension payable by a Secretary of State under the Police (Overseas Service) Act 1945(f) to a person who at the time of his retirement was engaged as mentioned in section 1(1) of the Act. [1952 Act.]

This paragraph includes a substituted pension not so payable if the original pension is so payable.

15. A pension payable by a Secretary of State under the Police Pensions Act 1948(g) to a person who at the time of his retirement was engaged as mentioned in section 1(1) of the Police (Overseas Service) Act 1945. [1944 Act].

This paragraph includes a substituted pension not so payable if the original pension is so payable.

16. A pension payable by a Secretary of State in accordance with a scheme in force under section 26 of the Fire Services Act 1947.(h) [1956 Act.]

This paragraph does not apply to a flat-rate pension, except where the rate depends on section 27(3) of that Act.

Teachers

17. A pension payable under the Elementary School Teachers (Superannuation) Acts 1898 to 1912. [1944 Act.]

18. A pension payable under the Teachers (Superannuation) Acts 1918 to 1956. [1944 Act.]

This paragraph does not include—

(a) a pension specified in paragraph 56 of this Schedule; or

(b) so much of any pension payable under the said Acts of 1918 to 1956 as would not have been payable apart from an election under section 10(1) of the Teachers (Superannuation) Act 1956.(i)

19. A pension payable under the Education (Scotland) Acts 1939 to 1967. [1944 Act.]

This paragraph does not include a pension granted under Regulation 45 of the Teachers (Superannuation) (Scotland) Regulations 1957.(j)

20. A pension payable under regulations made under section 1 of the Teachers' Superannuation Act 1967.(k) [1944 Act.]

21. A pension payable under the Teachers Superannuation (Scotland) Act 1968.(l) [1944 Act.]

(a) 1950 c. 11 (14 & 15 Geo. 6).   (b) 1934 c. 53.   (c) 1907 c. 51.
(d) 1951 c. 46.   (e) 1956 c. 34.   (f) 1945 c. 17 (9 & 10 Geo. 6).
(g) 1948 c. 24.   (h) 1947 c. 41.   (i) 1956 c. 53.
(j) S.I. 1957/356 (1957 I, p. 733).   (k) 1967 c. 12.   (l) 1968 c. 12.

National health service

22. A pension payable by a Secretary of State under or by virtue of any of the following:—

(a) section 6 of the National Health Service Act 1946(a) or of the National Health Service (Scotland) Act 1947(b) (former officers of voluntary hospitals). [1952 Act];

(b) section 67 or 68 of the National Health Service Act 1946 or section 66 or 67 of the National Health Service (Scotland) Act 1947 (former officers of hospital authorities and others engaged in health services). [1944 Act.]

23. A pension payable by a Secretary of State in consequence of any change affecting the National Health Service and payable in pursuance of an order under section 11(9) of the National Health Service Act 1946. [1959 Act].

National insurance

24. A pension payable by a Secretary of State in pursuance of regulations made under section 67 of the National Insurance Act 1946(c) (loss of employment or diminution of emoluments attributable to passing of that Act of former employees of approved societies etc.). [1952 Act.]

25. A pension payable in pursuance of rules made under section 3 of the Superannuation (Miscellaneous Provisions) Act 1948(d) (former employees of approved societies etc.). [1952 Act.]

This paragraph does not include a pension payable under the Superannuation Acts 1965 and 1967.

Diplomatic, colonial and overseas service

27. A pension payable under the Governors Pensions Acts 1957 and 1967 and beginning before 18th December 1947. [1944 Act.]

Any other pension payable under those Acts. [1952 Act.]

28. A pension payable under the Judges Pensions (India and Burma) Act 1948(e). [1944 Act.]

29. A pension payable under the Diplomatic Salaries &c. Act 1869(f). [1944 Act.]

Service in Ireland

30. A pension payable under Schedule 8 to the Government of Ireland Act 1920(g) (former Irish civil servants). [1944 Act.]

31. A pension payable to or in respect of an existing Irish officer within the meaning of the Government of Ireland Act 1920, under the Superannuation Acts 1834 to 1965. [1944 Act.]

32. A pension payable under the enactments relating to pensions of the Royal Irish Constabulary. [1944 Act.]

This paragraph does not include a pension payable under regulations made under section 1 of the Royal Irish Constabulary (Widows' Pensions) Act 1954(h).

Miscellaneous

34. A pension payable under the following (compensation to tax collectors and assessors for loss of employment)—

(a) section 29 of the Finance Act 1932(i) [1944 Act]; or

(b) section 60 of the Finance (No. 2) Act 1945(j) or section 62 of the Finance Act 1946(k). [1952 Act.]

36. A widow's pension payable by a Secretary of State in accordance with a scheme framed by the then Army Council under the Injuries in War (Compensation) Act 1914 (Session 2)(l) for established civil servants employed abroad within the sphere of military operations. [1944 Act.]

(a) 1946 c. 81.   (b) 1947 c. 27.   (c) 1946 c. 67.   (d) 1948 c. 33.
(e) 1948 c. 4 (12, 13 & 14 Geo. 6).   (f) 1869 c. 43.   (g) 1920 c. 67.
(h) 1954 c. 17.   (i) 1932 c. 25.   (j) 1945 c. 13 (9 & 10 Geo. 6).
(k) 1946 c. 64.   (l) 1914 c. 18 (5 & 6 Geo. 5).

Part II

Pensions out of Local Funds

Local government service

39. A pension payable by a local authority in respect of service ending with local government service. [1944 Act.]

This paragraph does not include—

(a) a pension payable, in respect of service as a member of a fire brigade, in accordance with a scheme in force under section 26 of the Fire Services Act 1947;

(b) a pension within paragraph 45 of this Schedule;

(c) a pension payable by a police authority under regulations made under section 60(2) of the Local Government Act 1958(a) or section 85(4) of the London Government Act 1963(b) (compensation for loss of employment or emoluments due to reorganisation of local government etc.).

Administration of justice

40. A pension payable under section 33 of the Justices of the Peace Act 1949(c) (stipendiary magistrates). [1959 Act.]

41. A pension payable by a local authority under Part I of the Administration of Justice (Pensions) Act 1950 (widows and children of stipendiary magistrates and of chairmen and deputy chairmen of London Sessions). [1959 Act.]

42. A pension payable under section 22 of the Administration of Justice (Pensions) Act 1950 (chairmen and deputy chairmen of London Sessions). [1962 Act.]

Police and firemen

43. A pension payable under any of the following:—

(a) the Police Pensions Act 1948, or any enactment repealed by that Act or by the Police Pensions Act 1921(d);

(b) section 34 of the Police Act 1964(e);

(c) section 26 of the Police (Scotland) Act 1967(f);

other than a pension within paragraph 14 or 15 above, or a pension payable by a Secretary of State under the Police Pensions Act 1948 to a person who at the time of his retirement was engaged in service in respect of which the provisions of section 5 of the Overseas Service Act 1958(g) had effect, or serving as an inspector or assistant inspector of constabulary under the Police Act 1964 or the Police (Scotland) Act 1967, or engaged in central service pursuant to section 43 of the Police Act 1964 or section 38 of the Police (Scotland) Act 1967, or a substituted pension of which the original pension is so payable. [1944 Act.]

This paragraph does not include a derivative pension other than a substituted pension, nor a substituted pension if the original pension was a derivative pension.

44. A pension payable by a local authority, in respect of service as a member of a fire brigade, in accordance with a scheme in force under section 26 of the Fire Services Act 1947:—

(a) payable in respect of whole-time service [1944 Act];

(b) payable in respect of part-time service ending on or after 10th July 1956, other than a derivative pension [1962 Act].

This paragraph does not apply to a flat-rate pension, except where the rate depends on section 27(3) of that Act.

45. A pension payable by a local authority in respect of—

(a) service as a professional fireman (as defined by the Fire Brigade Pensions Act 1925)(h); or

---

(a) 1958 c. 55.   (b) 1963 c. 33.   (c) 1949 c. 101.   (d) 1921 c. 31.
(e) 1964 c. 48.   (f) 1967 c. 77.   (g) 1958 c. 14.   (h) 1925 c. 47.

(*b*) service which, by or under any enactment, is treated as approved service in a fire brigade;

other than a pension payable in accordance with a scheme in force under section 26 of the Fire Services Act 1947.   [1944 Act.]

46. A derivative pension payable under the Police Pensions Act 1921 in respect of a person to whom the National Fire Service (Preservation of Pensions) (Police Firemen) Regulations 1941(a) applied at the time of that person's death or retirement. [1944 Act.]

Court and police staffs

47. A pension payable by a local authority in England or Wales under any enactment other than section 15(1) to (7) of the Superannuation (Miscellaneous Provisions) Act 1967(b) in respect of—

(*a*) service as a justices' clerk or as the employee of a justices' clerk [1944 Act]; or

(*b*) service as a person employed by a magistrates' courts committee to assist a justices' clerk.   [1956 Act.]

49. A pension payable by the Greater London Council under any enactment in respect of service in the employment of the standing joint committee for the county of London as clerk of the peace or deputy clerk of the peace or in any other capacity. [1944 Act.]

50. A pension payable under section 15(1) to (7) of the Superannuation (Miscellaneous Provisions) Act 1967 (metropolitan civil staffs).   [1944 Act.]

51. A pension payable by a local authority, or by a police authority in England or Wales other than a local authority, under any enactment other than section 15 of the Superannuation (Miscellaneous Provisions) Act 1967 in respect of service ending with—

(*a*) service as a civilian employed under section 10 of the Police Act 1964 by such a police authority; or

(*b*) service as a traffic warden employed by such a police authority under section 2 of the Road Traffic and Roads Improvement Act 1960(c) or section 81(9) of the Road Traffic Regulation Act 1967(d).

[1962 Act.]

Probation and after-care service

53. A pension payable in accordance with regulations under Schedule 4 to the Local Government Superannuation Act 1953 in respect of service as a probation officer or as a person appointed to assist a probation officer in the performance of his duties by a probation and after-care committee, by the Secretary of State or, before 1st July 1944, by a probation officer.   [1944 Act.]

54. A pension payable by a local authority in England and Wales in respect of service as a member of the staff of an approved probation home or an approved probation hostel.   [1956 Act.]

Teachers and school staff

56. A pension payable by a local authority under section 14(3)(*b*) of the Teachers (Superannuation) Act 1925(e).   [1944 Act.]

57. A pension payable by a local authority in England or Wales under any enactment in respect of service as an employee of the managers of a non-provided school within the meaning of the Education Act 1921(f) or a voluntary school within the meaning of the Education Act 1944(g).   [1944 Act.]

58. A pension payable by a local authority in England or Wales under any enactment in respect of service as an employee of the governing body of any school or educational institution (other than a public elementary school or a county or voluntary

---

(a) S.R. & O. 1941/1271 (1941 I, p. 328).   (b) 1967 c. 28.   (c) 1960 c. 63.
  (d) 1967 c. 76.   (e) 1925 c. 59.   (f) 1921 c. 51.   (g) 1944 c. 31.

school) if the whole cost of maintaining the school or educational institution after deducting such part of the cost (if any) as is met by the governing body fell or falls to be met by the local authority. [1944 Act.]

59. A pension payable by a local authority in respect of service as a member of the staff of an approved school. [1944 Act.]

Miscellaneous

60. A pension payable by a local authority under any enactment in respect of service as a registration officer as defined in section 40 of the Local Government Superannuation Act 1937 or section 34 of the Local Government Superannuation (Scotland) Act 1937. [1944 Act.]

61. A pension payable under section 6 of the Coroners (Amendment) Act 1926(**a**) (county and borough coroners.) [1944 Act.]

62. A pension payable by a local authority in respect of service as a clerk, officer or servant employed under section 47 of the Local Government Act 1948(**b**) or section 92 of the General Rate Act 1967(**c**) by a local valuation panel. [1952 Act.]

64. A pension payable by a local authority by way of such compensation as is mentioned in section 8(1)(*b*) of the 1971 Act. [1944 Act.]

PART III
OTHER PENSIONS

65. A pension payable by the trustees of a trustee savings bank or by the Inspection Committee of trustee savings banks. [1944 Act.]

66. A pension payable in respect of service with, or as compensation for loss of employment on the winding up of, the Raw Cotton Commission. [1952 Act.]

67. A pension payable by the Greater London Council or the council of a London borough under section 80(9) to (11) of the London Passenger Transport Act 1933(**d**). [1944 Act.]

68. A pension payable by the council of the London borough of Southwark in respect of employment in the borough market, Southwark. [1944 Act.]

Article 4(5)   SCHEDULE 3

PROVISIONS REVOKED

Trustee savings banks

Article 5 of the Trustee Savings Banks (Pensions) Order 1955(**e**).

The Trustee Savings Banks (Increase of Pensions) Order 1956(**f**).

The Trustee Savings Banks (Increase of Pensions) Order 1959(**g**).

The Trustee Savings Banks (Increase of Pensions) Order 1963(**h**).

Metropolitan civil staffs

The Metropolitan Police Staffs (Increase of Superannuation Allowances) Order 1956(**i**).

The Metropolitan Police Staffs (Increase of Superannuation Allowances) Order 1960(**j**).

The Metropolitan Police Staffs (Increase of Superannuation Allowances) Order 1963(**k**).

The Metropolitan Police Staffs (Increase of Superannuation Allowances) Order 1966(**l**).

(a) 1926 c. 59.   (b) 1948 c. 26.   (c) 1967 c. 9.   (d) 1933 c. 14.
(e) S.I. 1955/842 (1955 II, p. 2388).   (f) S.I. 1956/1456 (1956 II, p. 2197).
(g) S.I. 1959/1534 (1959 II, p. 2468).   (h) S.I. 1963/901 (1963 II, p. 1511).
(i) S.I. 1956/1901 (1956 I, p. 1210).   (j) S.I. 1960/1099 (1960 II, p. 2022).
(k) S.I. 1963/1979 (1963 III, p. 4167).   (l) S.I. 1966/810 (1966 II, p. 1874).

TABLE I

(1) 1971 rate

(2) Choice of 1969 standard or 1971 rate

1. Beginning up to 31st March/1st April 1947†

Basic rate	×	1. Without supplement £	2. With supplement £	Date of beginning (with 1969 factor)	Basic rate (£) 1. Without supplement	Basic rate (£) 2. With supplement
Up to £55·71 ...	3·3768*	—	27·376*	Up to 1944 (3·052) ...	93	120
Up to £100 ...	2·5755	44·643	72·019	1945 (2·583) ...	212	252
Up to £133·33 ...	1·8887	113·323	140·699	1946 (2·348) ...	321	381
Up to £200 ...	2·4038	44·643	72·019	1947 (2·327) ...	336	399
Over £200 ...	1·8887	147·664	175·040			

† 31st March for earnings-related pensions based on average emoluments, 1st April for other pensions.

* 31st March for basic rates below £36·32, the 1971 rate with supplement is 4·1306 times the basic rate.

2. Beginning up to 31st March 1948

Basic rate	×	1. Without supplement £	2. With supplement £	Date of beginning (with 1969 factor)	Basic rate (£) 1. Without supplement	Basic rate (£) 2. With supplement
Up to £78 ...	2·4611*	—	27·376*	Up to 1944 (3·052) ...	nil	nil
Over £78 ...	1·8887	44·643	72·019	1945 (2·583) ...	nil	103
				1946 (2·348) ...	97	156
				1947 (2·327) ...	101	164
				1948 (2·179) ...	153	248

* For basic rates below £49·83, the 1971 rate with supplement is 3·0104 times the basic rate.

3. Beginning up to 31st March 1949

Basic rate	×	1. Without supplement £	2. With supplement £	Date of beginning (with 1969 factor)	Basic rate (£) 1. Without supplement	Basic rate (£) 2. With supplement
Up to £63 ...	2·4611*	—	27·376*	1948 (2·179) ...	124	218
Over £63 ...	1·8887	36·057	63·433	1949 (2·119) ...	156	275

* For basic rates below £49·83, the 1971 rate with supplement is 3·0104 times the basic rate.

TABLE I - cont.

	(1) 1971 rate			(2) Choice of 1969 standard or 1971 rate		
Basic rate	£ 1. Without supplement		£ 2. With supplement	Date of beginning (with 1969 factor)	Basic rate (£) 1. Without supplement	2. With supplement

4. Beginning up to 31st March 1950

Basic rate	factor	1. Without supplement	2. With supplement
Up to £48	2·4611*	—	*
Over £48	1·8887*	27·472	54·848*

Date of beginning (with 1969 factor)	1. Without supplement	2. With supplement
1949 (2·119)	119	238
1950 (2·059)	161	322

* For basic rates up to £48, the 1971 rate with supplement is 3·0104 times the basic rate plus £50·39 (but above £48), it is 2·3103 times the basic rate plus £33·604.

5. Beginning up to 31st March 1951

Basic rate	factor	1. Without supplement	2. With supplement
Up to £33	2·4611*	—	*
Up to £1,000	1·8887*	18·887	46·263*
Over £1,000	1·7170	190·589	217·965

Date of beginning (with 1969 factor)	1. Without supplement	2. With supplement
1950 (2·059)	110	271
1951 (1·886)	1,127	1,289

* For basic rates up to £33, the 1971 rate with supplement is 3·0104 times the basic rate plus £54·94 (but above £33), it is 2·3103 times the basic rate plus £23·103.

6. Beginning up to 31st March 1952

Basic rate	factor	1. Without supplement	2. With supplement
Up to £18	2·4611*	—	*
Up to £1,000	1·8887*	10·302	37·678*
Over £1,000	1·7170	182·004	209·380

Date of beginning (with 1969 factor)	1. Without supplement	2. With supplement
1951 (1·886)	1,077	1,239
1952 (1·728)	not relevant	not relevant

* For basic rates up to £18, the 1971 rate with supplement is 3·0104 times the basic rate plus £59·48 (but above £18), it is 2·3103 times the basic rate plus £12·602.

NOTE:—

In the case of earnings-related pensions beginning on or after 1st April 1947, but with an averaging period beginning before 1st April 1946, there is to be added to the 1971 rate as given by heads 2 to 6 of this Table the adjusted 1944 element, if any, to be derived from Table V.

In these cases, the right-hand division of the Table does not apply; and (the 1944 element being variable) alternatives are not given. With the maximum 1944 element (taken on the basis of a continuous averaging period of 40 years), the entry in head 1 would apply also in head 2 for years up to 1947, the figures given above would be increased for 1948 by about £350, for 1949 by about £450 and for 1950 by about £600 and the 1969 standard becomes not relevant in 1951.

TABLE II

(1) 1971 rate — Basic rate

1. Beginning up to 31st March/1st April 1947†

	×	1. Without supplement £	2. With supplement £
Up to £55·71 ...	3·3768*	—	27·376*
Up to £100 ...	2·5755	44·643	72·019
Up to £133·33 ...	1·8887	113·323	140·699
Up to £200 ...	2·4038	44·643	72·019
Over £200 ...	1·8887	147·664	175·040

(2) Choice of 1969 standard or 1971 rate

Date of beginning (with 1969 factor)	Basic rate (£) 1. Without supplement	Basic rate (£) 2. With supplement
Up to 1944 (3·052) ...	93	120
1945 (2·583) ...	212	252
1946 (2·348) ...	321	381
1947 (2·327) ...	336	399

† 31st March for pensions based on average emoluments, 1st April for pensions based on final emoluments.

* For basic rates below £36·32, the 1971 rate with supplement is 4·1306 times the basic rate.

2. Beginning up to 1st January 1948/31st December 1947†

	×	1. Without supplement £	2. With supplement £
Up to £78 ...	2·4611*	—	27·376*
Over £78 ...	1·8887	44·643	72·019

Date of beginning (with 1969 factor)	Basic rate (£) 1. Without supplement	Basic rate (£) 2. With supplement
Up to 1944 (3·052) ...	Nil	Nil
1945 (2·583) ...	Nil	103
1946 (2·348) ...	97	156
1947 (2·327) ...	101	164
1948 (2·179) ...	153	248

† 1st January 1948 for pensions based on average emoluments, 31st December 1947 for pensions based on final emoluments.

* For basic rates below £49·83, the 1971 rate with supplement is 3·0104 times the basic rate.

3. Beginning up to 31st March 1948

	×	1. Without supplement £	2. With supplement £
Up to £78 ...	2·2894*	—	27·376*
Over £78 ...	1·7170	44·643	72·019

Date of beginning (with 1969 factor)	Basic rate (£) 1. Without supplement	Basic rate (£) 2. With supplement
1948 (2·179) ...	96	155

* For basic rates below £53·57, the 1971 rate with supplement is 2·8004 times the basic rate.

TABLE II - cont.

(1) 1971 rate		£	£		(2) Choice of 1969 standard or 1971 rate	
					Basic rate (£)	
Basic rate	×	1. Without supplement	2. With supplement	Date of beginning (with 1969 factor)	1. Without supplement	2. With supplement

4. Beginning up to 31st March 1949

Up to £63		2·2894*	—	1948 (2·179) ...	78	137
Over £63		1·7170*	36·057	27·376*		
				63·433	1949 (2·119) ...	89	157

* For basic rates below £53·57, the 1971 rate with supplement is 2·8004 times the basic rate.

5. Beginning up to 31st March 1950

Up to £48		2·2894*	—	*	1949 (2·119) ...	68	136
Over £48		1·7170*	27·472	54·848*	1950 (2·059) ...	80	160

* For basic rates up to £48, the 1971 rate with supplement is 2·8004 times the basic rate; for those below £55·43 (but above £48), it is 2·1003 times the basic rate plus £33·604.

6. Beginning up to 31st March 1951

Up to £33		2·2894*	—	*	1950 (2·059) ...	55	135
Over £33		1·7170*	18·887	46·263*	1951 (1·886) ...	111	273

* For basic rates up to £33, the 1971 rate with supplement is 2·8004 times the basic rate; for those below £60·43 (but above £33), it is 2·1003 times the basic rate plus £23·103.

7. Beginning up to 31st March 1952

Up to £18		2·2894*	—	*	1951 (1·886) ...	60	222
Over £18		1·7170*	10·302	37·678*	1952 (1·728) ...	938	3,431

* For basic rates up to £18, the 1971 rate with supplement is 2·8004 times the basic rate; for those below £65·43 (but above £18), it is 2·1003 times the basic rate plus £12·602.

TABLE IA AND IIA

A. WITH SUPPLEMENT

(1) 1971 rate			(2) Choice of 1969 standard or 1971 rate	
Basic rate	×	£	*Date of beginning (with 1969 factor)*	£
1. Beginning on 1st April 1952				
Up to £71·429	**2·1003**	—	1952 (1·728) 2,493	
Over £71·429	**1·7170**	**27·376**		
2. Beginning up to 1st April 1953				
Up to £72·727	**2·0628**	—	1952 (1·728) 657	
Over £72·727	**1·6864**	**27·376**	1953 ... not relevant.	
3. Beginning up to 1st April 1954				
Up to £74·074	**2·0253**	—	1953 (1·675) 1,418	
Over £74·074	**1·6557**	**27·376**	1954 ... not relevant.	
4. Beginning up to 1st April 1955				
Up to £75·472	**1·9878**	—	1954 (1·645) 1,371	
Over £75·472	**1·6250**	**27·376**	1955 ... not relevant.	
5. Beginning up to 1st July 1955				
Up to £76·923	**1·9503**	—	Not relevant.	
Over £76·923	**1·5944**	**27·376**		
6. Beginning up to 1st April 1956				
Up to £76·923	**1·9337**	—	Not relevant.	
Over £76·923	**1·5809**	**27·144**		
7. Beginning up to 1st July 1956				
Up to £66·667	**1·8689**	—	Not relevant.	
Over £66·667	**1·5228**	**23·072**		
8. Beginning up to 1st April 1957				
Up to £66·667	**1·8529**	—	Not relevant.	
Over £66·667	**1·5098**	**22·875**		
9. Beginning up to 1st July 1957				
Up to £56	**1·7588**	—	1957 (1·448) 934	
Over £56	**1·4282**	**18·514**		
10. Beginning up to 1st April 1958				
Up to £56	**1·7436**	—	1957 (1·448) 571	
Over £56	**1·4159**	**18·354**	1958 ... not relevant.	
11. Beginning up to 1st July 1958				
Up to £40	**1·6873**	—	1958 (1·404) 332	
Over £40	**1·3653**	**12·880**		
12. Beginning up to 1st April 1959				
Up to £40	**1·6726**	—	1958 (1·404) 252	
Over £40	**1·3534**	**12·768**	1959 (1·397) 292	
13. Beginning up to 1st July 1959				
Up to £28	**1·6177**	—	1959 (1·397) 94	
Over £28	**1·3042**	**8·778**		

TABLE IA AND IIA - *cont.*

A. With Supplement - *cont.*

(1) 1971 rate			(2) Choice of 1969 standard or 1971 rate	
Basic rate	×	£	*Date of beginning (with 1969 factor)*	£
14. Beginning up to 1st April 1960				
Up to £28	**1·6035**	—	1959 (1·397)	83
Over £28	**1·2927**	**8·701**	1960 (1·383)	96
15. Beginning up to 1st July 1960				
Up to £16	**1·5499**	—	1960 (1·383)	35
Over £16	**1·2448**	**4·882**		
16. Beginning up to 1st April 1961				
Up to £16	**1·5362**	—	1960 (1.383)	32
Over £16	**1·2338**	**4·838**	1961 (1·338)	46

B. WITHOUT SUPPLEMENT

In the cases given below the 1971 rate is to be used, and the 1969 standard is not relevant; in all other cases in this Table, the 1969 standard is to be used and the 1971 rate is not relevant.

Beginning (dates inclusive)							1971 rate ×
1st January 1953—1st April 1953	...	...	...	...	...	...	**1·6864**
1st January 1954—1st April 1954	...	...	...	...	...	...	**1·6557**
1st January 1955—1st April 1955	...	...	...	...	...	...	**1·6250**
2nd April 1955—1st July 1955	...	...	...	...	...	...	**1·5944**
2nd July 1955—1st April 1956	...	...	...	...	...	...	**1·5809**
2nd April 1956—1st July 1956	...	...	...	...	...	...	**1·5228**
2nd July 1956—1st April 1957	...	...	...	...	...	...	**1·5098**
1st January 1958—1st April 1958	...	...	...	...	...	...	**1·4159**

TABLE III

| (1) 1971 rate | | | | (2) Choice of 1969 standard or 1971 rate Basic rate (£) | | | |
Basic rate	×	£	Date of beginning (with 1969 factor)	(a) No 1944 element 1. Without supplement	(a) No 1944 element 2. With supplement	(b) With 1944 element 1. Without supplement	(b) With 1944 element 2. With supplement
1. Beginning up to 31st March 1947							
Up to £55·71 ...	3·3768	—	Up to 1944 (3·052)	.	.	93	120
Up to £100 ...	2·5755	44·643	1945 (2·583)	.	.	212	252
Up to £133·33 ...	1·8887	113·323	1946 (2·348)	.	.	321	381
Up to £200 ...	2·4038	44·643	1947 (2·327)	.	.	336	399
Over £200 ...	1·8887	147·664					
2. Beginning up to 1st January 1948							
Up to £78 ...	2·4611	—	Up to 1944 (3·052)	Nil	Nil		
Over £78 ...	1·8887	44·643	1945 (2·583)	Nil	103		
			1946 (2·348)	97	156		
			1947 (2·327)	101	164	101/331	164/394
			1948 (2·179)	153	248	153/500	248/595
3. Beginning up to 31st March 1948							
Up to £78 ...	0·5723+1·7170Q	—	1948 (2·179)	128/154	207/249	128/500	207/595
Over £78 ...	1·7170Q	44·643					
4. Beginning up to 31st March 1949							
Up to £63 ...	0·5723+1·7170Q	—	1948 (2·179)	95/124	168/217	95/458	168/552
Over £63 ...	1·7170Q	36·057	1949 (2·119)	108/154	190/271	108/571	190/688
5. Beginning up to 31st March 1950							
Up to £48 ...	0·5723+1·7170Q	—	1949 (2·119)	79/117	159/232	79/519	159/635
Over £48 ...	1·7170Q	27·472	1950 (2·059)	93/154	187/307	93/687	187/840

TABLE III - cont.

	(1) 1971 rate			(2) Choice of 1969 standard or 1971 rate			
				Basic rate (£)			
				(a) No 1944 element		(b) With 1944 element	
Basic rate	×	£	Date of beginning (with 1969 factor)	1. Without supplement	2. With supplement	1. Without supplement	2. With supplement
6. Beginning up to 31st March 1951							
Up to £33	$\dfrac{0\cdot5723+1\cdot7170Q}{1\cdot7170}$	—	1950 (2·059) ...	63/105	154/256	63/617	154/768
Up to £1,000	$\dfrac{1\cdot7170Q}{1\cdot7170}$	18·887	1951 (1·886) ...	144/1,052	353/1,214	144/1,601	353/1,763
Over £1,000		18·887+171·702q					
7. Beginning up to 31st March 1952							
Up to £18	$\dfrac{0\cdot5723+1\cdot7170Q}{1\cdot7170}$	—	1951 (1·886) ...	76/838	279/1,151	76/1,522	279/1,684
Up to £1,000	$\dfrac{1\cdot7170Q}{1\cdot7170}$	10·302	1952 (1·728) ...	3,781/—	6,274/—	3,781/—	6,274/—
Over £1,000		10·302+171·702q					

NOTES:—

Except in relation to pensions mentioned in Article 5(6) of this Order, symbol q represents the fraction that results from dividing by the total number of half-years in the averaging period the number of them ending on or before 31st December 1947; the symbol Q represents the number obtained by dividing by ten times the total number of half-years in the period the sum of ten times that number and the number ending on or before 31st December 1947 (or is 1+q/10). Any incomplete half-year at the end of the period is to be disregarded. In the application of head 5 or any later head of this Table to a pension mentioned in Article 5(6) of this Order (and beginning on or after 2nd July 1949), the symbols Q and q have a corresponding meaning, but 1st July 1949 is to be substituted for 31st December 1947.

The 1971 rate with supplement cannot be given in this Table; the amount of the supplement is £27·376 or, if the 1971 rate is less than £124·44, then seven-fiftieths of the 1971 rate.

The right-hand division of this Table assumes, for the higher figures, a continuous averaging period not longer than forty years. It does not apply to pensions based on average emoluments of less than £1,500, or to a pension mentioned in Article 5(6) of this Order.

TABLE IV

(1) 1971 rate

1. Beginning up to 31st March 1948

Basic rate	×	1. Without supplement £	2. With supplement £
Up to £55·71 ...	3·3768*	—	27·376*
Up to £100 ...	2·5755	44·643	72·019
Up to £133·33 ...	1·8887	113·323	140·699
Up to £200 ...	2·4038	44·643	72·019
Over £200 ...	1·8887	147·664	175·040

* For basic rates below £36·32, the 1971 rate with supplement is 4·1306 times the basic rate.

2. Beginning up to 31st March 1949

Basic rate	×	1. Without supplement £	2. With supplement £
Up to £45 ...	3·3768*	—	27·376*
Up to £100 ...	2·5755	36·057	63·433
Up to £133·33 ...	1·8887	104·738	132·114
Up to £200 ...	2·4038	36·057	63·433
Over £200 ...	1·8887	139·080	166·456

* For basic rates below £36·32, the 1971 rate with supplement is 4·1306 times the basic rate.

3. Beginning up to 31st March 1950

Basic rate	×	1. Without supplement £	2. With supplement £
Up to £34·28 ...	3·3768*	—	—*
Up to £100 ...	2·5755*	27·472	54·848*
Up to £133·33 ...	1·8887	96·153	123·529
Up to £200 ...	2·4038	27·472	54·848
Over £200 ...	1·8887	130·495	157·871

* For basic rates up to £34·28, the 1971 rate with supplement is 4·1306 times the basic rate; for those below £36·95 (but above £34·28), it is 3·1504 times the basic rate plus £33·604.

(2) Choice of 1969 standard or 1971 rate

Date of beginning (with 1969 factor)	Basic rate (£) 1. Without supplement	Basic rate (£) 2. With supplement
Up to 1944 (3·052) ...	93	120
1945 (2·583) ...	212	252
1946 (2·348) ...	321	381
1947 (2·327) ...	336	399
1948 (2·179) ...	508	603
1948 (2·179) ...	479	573
1949 (2·119) ...	603	722
1949 (2·119) ...	566	685
1950 (2·059) ...	766	927

TABLE IV - cont.

4. Beginning up to 31st March 1951

Up to £23·57	3·3768*	—	*
Up to £100	2·5755*	18·887	46·263*
Up to £133·33	1·8887	87·568	114·944
Up to £200	2·4038	18·887	46·263
Up to £1,000	1·8887	121·910	149·286
Over £1,000	1·7170	293·612	320·988

1950 (2·059)			715	876
1951 (1·886)			1,737	1,899

* For basic rates up to £23·57, the 1971 rate with supplement is 4·1306 times the basic rate; for those below £40·29 (but above £23·57), it is 3·1504 times the basic rate plus £23·103.

5. Beginning up to 31st March 1952

Up to £12·85	3·3768*	—	*
Up to £100	2·5755*	10·302	37·678*
Up to £133·33	1·8887	78·983	106·359
Up to £200	2·4038	10·302	37·678
Up to £1,000	1·8887	113·322	140·698
Over £1,000	1·7170	285·024	312·400

1951 (1·886)			1,686	1,848
1952 (1·728)			n/r	n/r

* For basic rates up to £12·85, the 1971 rate with supplement is 4·1306 times the basic rate; for those below £43·62 (but above £12·85), it is 3·1504 times the basic rate plus £12·602.

TABLE IIIA AND IVA

A: PENSIONS BEGINNING 1ST APRIL 1952 TO 1ST APRIL 1961

(1) 1971 rate and Supplement

Pensions beginning	(a) 1971 rate ×	(b) Supplement 1. Normal £	2. Small pensions 1971 rate (£)	×
On 1.4.52	1·7170	27·376	124·44	0·22
Up to 1.4.53	1·6864	27·376	124·44	0·22
Up to 1.4.54	1·6557	27·376	124·44	0·22
Up to 1.4.55	1·6250	27·376	124·44	0·22
Up to 1.7.55	1·5944	27·376	124·44	0·22
Up to 1.4.56	1·5809	27·144	123·38	0·22
Up to 1.7.56	1·5228	23·072	100·31	0·23
Up to 1.4.57	1·5098	22·875	99·46	0·23
Up to 1.7.57	1·4282	18·514	80·50	0·23
Up to 1.4.58	1·4159	18·354	79·80	0·23
Up to 1.7.58	1·3653	12·880	53·67	0·24
Up to 1.4.59	1·3534	12·768	53·20	0·24
Up to 1.7.59	1·3042	8·778	36·58	0·24
Up to 1.4.60	1·2927	8·701	36·25	0·24
Up to 1.7.60	1·2448	4·882	19·53	0·25
Up to 1.4.61	1·2338	4·838	19·35	0·25

NOTES:—

This part of the Table gives the 1971 rate for the classes of pension described below, by applying the multiplier not to the basic rate but to the adjusted rate specified for each class of pension.

The supplement is of the amount given in column 3, unless the 1971 rate is less than the amount given in the first division of column 4: it is then obtained by multiplying the 1971 rate by the factor given in the second division of that column. As to the choice of 1969 standard or 1971 rate, see the next division of the Table.

TABLE IIIA AND IVA - *cont.*

Relevant rate of pension

(a) For flat-rate pensions within the 1944 Act (which became payable on or before 31st December 1965), the rate to be used is the basic rate with the addition of the 1944 element to be derived from Table V: see note 1 to that Table (or, in a case of apportionment, note 5).

(b) For earnings-related pensions within the 1944 Act (based on average emoluments and with an averaging period beginning before 1st April 1946), the rate to be used is the basic rate with the addition both—

  (i) of the adjusted 1944 element to be derived from Table V: see note 3 to that Table (or, in a case of apportionment, note 4); and

  (ii) of the amount given by paragraph (c) or (d) below.

(c) For any earnings-related pension based on average emoluments of £1,500 or over and with an averaging period beginning on or before 1st January 1947, the rate to be used is the basic rate with the addition (further to the addition, if any, under paragraph (b) above) of the appropriate fraction of that rate or, if the rate is more than £1,000, of the appropriate fraction of £1,000; the appropriate fraction for this paragraph is one-tenth of the figure that results from dividing by the total number of half-years in the averaging period the number of them ending on or before 31st December 1947 (any incomplete half-year at the end of the period being disregarded). In relation to pensions mentioned in Article 5(6) of this Order, this paragraph applies with the substitution for 1st January 1947 and for 31st December 1947 of 2nd July 1948 and of 1st July 1949.

(d) For any earnings-related pension based on average emoluments of less than £1,500 and with an averaging period beginning on or before 1st April 1951, the rate to be used is the basic rate with the addition (further to the addition, if any, under paragraph (b) above) either of the appropriate fraction of the basic rate or, if it is less, of the amount that would raise the basic rate—

  (i) where the averaging period began on or before 1st January 1947, to the basic rate appropriate to a pension based on emoluments of £1,500 plus the addition that would be made to it under paragraph (c) above; or

  (ii) where the averaging period began after 1st January 1947, to the basic rate appropriate to a pension based on emoluments of £1,500; the appropriate fraction for this paragraph is one-tenth of the figure that results from dividing by the total number of half-years in the averaging period the number of them ending on or before 31st March 1952 (any incomplete half-year at the end of the period being disregarded). In relation to pensions mentioned in Article 5(6) of this Order, this paragraph applies with the substitution for 1st January 1947 of 2nd July 1948.

(2) Choice of 1969 standard or 1971 rate

Except for pensions beginning at the periods mentioned below in the central panel, 1971 rate is to be used, and the 1969 standard is not relevant. For earnings-related pensions the upper limits here given assume an averaging period of 40 years or less. Where the restriction in paragraph (d)(i) or (ii) above operates, this division of the Table does not apply (but for pensions not within the 1944 Act Table IA and IIA applied to the basic rate appropriate to emoluments of £1,500 will give the 1971 rate with or without supplement, and the choice between that rate and the 1969 standard).

Flat-rate		(a) Pensions within 1944 Act (basic rate)				Beginning (with 1969 factor): all pensions	(b) Pensions not within 1944 Act (basic rate)			
		Average earnings £1,500 or over		Average earnings less than £1,500			Average earnings £1,500 or over		Average earnings less than £1,500	
1. Without supplement	2. With supplement	1. Without	2. With supplement	1. Without	2. With supplement		1. Without	2. With supplement	1. Without	2. With supplement
n/r	n/r	2,838/—	5,326/—	n/r	n/r	On 1.4.52 (1·728)	2,838/—	5,326/—	n/r	n/r
2,430	3,087	1,225/—	1,332/	n/r	n/r	2.4.52 to 31.12.52 (1·728)		1,332/—	n/r	n/r
5,147	6,565	1,017/—	2,643/	n/r	n/r	2.4.53 to 31.12.53 (1·675)	—/7,400	2,643/8,818	n/r	n/r
4,885	6,256		2,389/	n/r	n/r	2.4.54 to 31.12.54 (1·645)	—/6,819	2,389/8,191	n/r	n/r
4,326	5,260	—/8,634	2,068/9,568	—	n/r	2.4.57 to 1.7.57 (1·448)	—/5,498	2,068/6,432	n/r	n/r
2,645	3,216	—/5,224	953/5,796	—	627/—	2.7.57 to 31.12.57 (1·448)	—/3,307	953/3,878	—	627/—
2,116	2,448	—/4,082	477/4,415	—	379/—	2.4.58 to 1.7.58 (1·404)	—/2,601	477/2,934	—	379/—
1,605	1,857	—/3,064	324/3,316	—	478/—	2.7.58 to 31.12.58 (1·404)	—/1,940	324/2,192	—	478/—
1,863	2,155	—/3,556	389/3,848	—	113/—	1.1.59 to 1.4.59 (1·397)	—/2,252	389/2,544	—	113/—
843	937	—/1,570	106/1,665	—	96/—	2.4.59 to 1.7.59 (1·397)	—/1,001	106/1,096	—	96/—
744	827	—/1,370	92/1,454	—	114/—	2.7.59 to 31.12.59 (1·397)	nil	92/631	—	114/—
859	955	—/1,583	107/1,679	—/924	39/—	1.1.60 to 1.4.60 (1·383)	—/1,003	107/1,099	nil	39/122
540	575	—/923	37/1,006	—	35/—	2.4.60 to 1.7.60 (1·383)	nil	37/93	nil	35/93
496	528	—/730	34/804	—	52/—	2.7.60 to 31.12.60 (1·383)	nil	34/75	nil	52/564
710	756	—/1,261	50/1,308			1.1.61 to 1.4.61 (1·338)	nil	50/232		

B: PENSIONS BEGINNING 2ND APRIL 1961 OR LATER

| Pensions beginning | (1) 1971 rate | | (2) Choice of 1969 standard or 1971 rate | | |
| | | | Pensions within 1944 Act (basic rate) | | |
	1971 rate ×	Beginning (with 1969 factor)	Flat-rate	Average earnings £1,500 or over	Average earnings less than £1,500
2.4.61 to 1.7.61	1·1872	1961(1·338)	472	—/618	—/739
Up to 1.4.62	1·1766	1961(1·338)	437	—/520	—/616
		1962(1·282)	669	—/1,145	—
Up to 1.7.62	1·1544	1962(1·282)	542	—/770	—/979
Up to 1.4.63	1·1440	1962(1·282)	497	—/620	—/768
		1963(1·258)	602	—/970	nil
Up to 1.7.63	1·1220	1963(1·258)	495	—/576	—/691
Up to 1.4.64	1·1016	1963(1·258)	422	—/421	—/488
		1964(1·218)	567	—/756	—/968
Up to 1.7.64	1·08	1964(1·218)	469	—/479	—/560
Up to 1.7.65	1·06	1964(1·218)	402	—/361	—/411
		1965(1·162)	623	—/853	—
Up to 1.7.66	1·04	1965(1·162)	511	—/506	—/617
		1966(1·118)	...	—/1,154	—
Up to 1.7.67	1·02	1966(1·118)	...	—/689	—/928
		1967(1·091)	...	—/1,186	—
Up to 31.12.68	1·00	1967(1·091)	...	—/696	—/958
		1968(1·042)	...	—	—

NOTES:—

This part of the Table gives (so far as relevant) the 1971 rate for the same classes of pension as the first part. No supplement is payable on pensions beginning after 1st April 1961; and (assuming for earnings-related pensions a continuous averaging period of 40 years or less) the 1969 standard will be higher than the 1971 rate for any pension not within the 1944 Act.

The rate of pension to be used in finding the 1971 rate is not the basic rate, but the rate given in paragraphs (a) to (d) under the heading " Relevant rate of pension," in the notes to the first division of the Table: where the restriction in paragraph (d)(i) or (ii) operates, the right-hand division here does not apply.

TABLE V

Rate of pension		×	£
Up to £100 ...	...	0·4	—
Up to £133·33	...	—	40
Up to £200 ...	...	0·3	—
Over £200 ...	...	—	60

Notes

1. The 1944 element for any pension, when it is to be ascertained in accordance with this Table, is to be obtained by applying the Table to the basic rate of the pension or, where the basic rate of an earnings-related pension includes a war increase, to the basic rate less the war increase (referred to in this Table as " the pre-war rate "); but, where an adjusted 1944 element is required, the amount so arrived at is to be dealt with in accordance with such of the following notes as is applicable.

A. War increases for earnings-related pensions
(effect on head 1 of Table I, II or III)

2.—(1) Where head 1 of Table I, II or III would, in accordance with Article 5 of this order, be used to find the 1971 rate of an earnings-related pension, but the basic rate includes a war increase equal to or greater than the 1944 element ascertained in accordance with note 1 above, then the Table applies as if head 1 were omitted.

(2) Where head 1 of Table I, II or III is to be used to find the 1971 rate of an earnings-related pension, and the basic rate includes a war increase less than the 1944 element ascertained in accordance with note 1 above, then the 1971 rate is to be obtained—

(a) by applying that head to the pre-war rate instead of the basic rate; and

(b) by adding to the resulting figure an amount equal to 0·1717 times the war increase.

In a case within this paragraph the 1971 rate with supplement is not to be taken from head 1 of Table I or II if the pre-war rate is less than £36·32, but is to be obtained by adding to the 1971 rate the amount given by Table VII (namely, £27·376 or, if the 1971 rate is less than £124·44, then eleven-fiftieths of the 1971 rate).

B. Adjusted 1944 element for earnings-related pensions with
averaging period partly before 1st April 1946

3.—(1) In the case of an earnings-related pension beginning on or after 1st April 1947 and based on average emoluments with an averaging period that begins but does not end before 1st April 1946, the adjusted 1944 element required to find the 1971 rate by using Table I, III or IIIA and IVA is to be obtained as follows, unless note 5 applies:—

(a) the 1944 element is to be ascertained in accordance with note 1 above, except that the Table is to be applied to the 1946 basic rate, reduced by any war increase included in it, if that rate as so reduced is less than £200;

(b) if the amount so obtained for the 1944 element is less than a war increase included in the 1946 basic rate, the adjusted 1944 element is nil, but otherwise the amount so obtained less the amount of any war increase so included shall be reduced in accordance with paragraph (2) below;

(c) the adjusted 1944 element—

(i) where it is to be added to a rate obtained by using Table I or III is 1·7170 times the reduced amount obtained under paragraph (2), with any addition which is to be made under paragraph (3) below;

(ii) where it is to be added to the basic rate in order to obtain the 1971 rate from Table IIIA and IVA is that reduced amount.

(2) The amount mentioned in paragraph (1)(*b*) above is to be reduced by multiplying it by the fraction that results from dividing by the total number of years in the averaging period the number of them beginning before 1st April 1946 (any incomplete year at the end of the period being disregarded).

(3) Where the adjusted 1944 element obtained under this note is to be dealt with as mentioned in paragraph (1)(*c*)(i) above, and the basic rate to which Table I or III is being applied is less than the £78, £63, £48, £33 or £18 mentioned in the first column in the relevant head of the Table, an amount equal to 0·5723 times the difference or, if less, to 0·5723 times the reduced amount given by paragraph (1)(*b*) above shall be added to the adjusted 1944 element as given by paragraph (1)(*c*).

(4) The 1946 basic rate of a pension is that at which the pension could have been granted if based on the average rate of emoluments for the years of the averaging period beginning before 1st April 1946.

C. *Adjusted 1944 element in cases of apportionment*

4.—(1) Where the adjusted 1944 element of a pension is required in order to find the 1971 rate in accordance with Article 7(1) of this order, then subject to paragraphs (2) and (3) below it is to be found as follows:—

(*a*) there shall be found in accordance with note 1 above the amount of the 1944 element for a pension of a basic rate (not containing any war increase) equal to the sum of the basic rates of the aggregable pensions;

(*b*) the amount so arrived at shall be apportioned between the aggregable pensions in proportion to their basic rates;

(*c*) the adjusted 1944 element for the pension in question—

(i) if it is an earnings-related pension and the basic rate contains a war increase equal to or greater than the amount apportioned to the pension, is nil;

(ii) if it is an earnings-related pension and the basic rate contains a war increase less than the amount apportioned to the pension, is 1·7170 times the difference between that amount and the war increase;

(iii) otherwise is 1·7170 times the amount apportioned to the pension.

(2) If the pension in question or another aggregable pension is one described in note 3(1) above, then in relation to it references in paragraph (1) above to the basic rate are references to the 1946 basic rate (as defined in note 3(4)); and if the pension in question is one so described, the amount arrived at under paragraph (1)(*c*)(ii) or (iii) shall be reduced in accordance with paragraph (2) of note 3.

(3) The pensions aggregable for this purpose are limited to those aggregable under Article 7(4), and there shall be disregarded any pension relevant by virtue only of Article 7(3)(*b*).

5. Where Table IIIA and IVA is to be used to obtain the 1971 rate of a pension, and the multiplier is to be applied to the basic rate increased by a 1944 element, then ifthe pensioner is, or would for purposes of Article 7 of this order be treated as being, in receipt also of another pension which for purposes of Article 7 is aggregable under Article 7(4), note 4 above shall apply as it applies where the adjusted 1944 element is required in order to find the 1971 rate in accordance with Article 7(1), except that the adjusted 1944 element under note 4(1)(*c*)(ii) or (iii) shall be the actual difference between the amount apportioned to the pension and the war increase or the actual amount apportioned to the pension, as the case may be, instead of 1·7170 times that difference or amount.

TABLE VI

1952 element

Pensions beginning				*1. Normal*	*2. Small pensions (minimum rate for normal increase)*
				£	£
Up to 31st March 1948	...	...	...	44·643	78
Up to 31st March 1949	...	...	...	36·057	63
Up to 31st March 1950	...	...	...	27·472	48
Up to 31st March 1951	...	...	...	18·887	33
Up to 31st March 1952	...	...	...	10·302	18

Notes

1.—(1) This Table gives the amount of the 1952 element for the purpose of apportioning increases under Article 7 of this order.

(2) Column 2 gives the full amount of the 1952 element for pensions beginning at the time stated in column 1, unless the relevant rate of pension is less than the figure given in column 3 of this Table; if it is less, the full amount of the 1952 element is obtained by multiplying the relevant rate by the figure 0·5723.

2.—(1) On an apportionment under Article 7 the 1952 element is to be reduced if, but only if, the full amounts of the 1952 elements that would be included in the aggregable pensions together exceed the sum given in column 2 of this Table for the period when they begin (or if they do not all begin in the same period, the earlier or earliest of the periods when any of them begins).

(2) On an apportionment under Article 7(1), if no reduction is to be made in the 1952 element that may be included in the pension in accordance with note 1 above, the full amount that may be so included shall be treated as the adjusted amount; but if a reduction is to be made, the adjusted amount is to be obtained by apportioning between the aggregable pensions the sum given in column 2 of this Table for the period mentioned in sub-paragraph (1) above, the apportionment being made according to the full amounts of the 1952 element which would be included in each pension if there were no reduction.

(3) Where the 1952 element is to be reduced on an apportionment under Article 7(2), the 1971 rate as obtained by use of Table I, II, III or IV shall be reduced by deducting from the aggregate amount of the 1952 elements that would be included in the aggregable pensions if there were no reduction the sum given in column 2 of this Table for the period mentioned in sub-paragraph (1) above, and reducing the rate by a proportionate part of the resulting figure, the apportionment being made on the same basis as under sub-paragraph (2) above.

3.—(1) In determining the adjusted 1952 element for any pension there shall be disregarded a pension relevant only by virtue of Article 7(3)(c) of this order.

(2) In these notes " relevant rate " means in relation to any pension, the basic rate increased by the appropriate 1944 element, if any; and the appropriate 1944 element for this purpose is—

(a) on an apportionment under Article 7(1), the adjusted 1944 element obtained under note 4 to Table V, before multiplication by any factor of 1·7170; and

(b) on an apportionment under Article 7(2), is the 1944 element as given by note 1 to that Table reduced by the amount of any war increase or, for a pension described in note 3 to that Table, the reduced amount obtained under paragraph (2) of that note.

(3) Where any of the aggregable pensions is not one to which this order applies these notes shall have effect in relation to it with the necessary adaptations of the expressions used as if it were such a pension.

TABLE VII

Pensions beginning			*1. Normal*	*2. Small pensions*	
			£	*1971 rate (£)*	×
Up to 1st July 1955 ...	...	...	27·376	124·44	0·22
Up to 1st April 1956	...	...	27·144	123·38	0·22
Up to 1st July 1956 ...	...	...	23·072	100·31	0·23
Up to 1st April 1957	...	...	22·875	99·46	0·23
Up to 1st July 1957 ...	...	...	18·514	80·50	0·23
Up to 1st April 1958	...	...	18·354	79·80	0·23
Up to 1st July 1958 ...	...	...	12·880	53·67	0·24
Up to 1st April 1959	...	...	12·768	53·20	0·24
Up to 1st July 1959 ...	...	...	8·778	36·58	0·24
Up to 1st April 1960	...	...	8·701	36·25	0·24
Up to 1st July 1960 ...	...	...	4·882	19·53	0·25
Up to 1st April 1961	...	...	4·838	19·35	0·25

Notes

1. Except for cases within note 2 below, column 2 of this Table gives the amount of the supplement for pensions beginning at the time stated in column 1, unless the 1971 rate is less than the figure given in the first division of column 3; if it is less, the amount of the supplement is obtained by multiplying the 1971 rate by the figure given in the second division of column 3.

2.—(1) If—

(*a*) the pensioner is, or is to be treated for purposes of Article 9(2) of this order as being, in receipt of another aggregable pension; and

(*b*) the supplements that would be payable on the pensions if note 1 applied together exceed the sum given in column 2 of this Table for the period when they begin (or if they do not all begin in the same period, the earlier or earliest of the periods when any of them begins);

then the amount of the supplement is to be obtained by apportioning between those pensions the sum given in column 3 of the Table for that period, the apportionment being made according to the amounts of the supplements that would be payable if note 1 applied.

(2) The 1971 rate with supplement included (as given in any of the other Tables) may be adjusted to give effect to sub-paragraph (1) above by deducting from the aggregate amount of the supplements that would be payable on the pensions if note 1 applied the sum to be apportioned under sub-paragraph (1), and reducing the rate by a proportionate part of the resulting figure, the apportionment being made on the same basis as under sub-paragraph (1).

(3) Where any of the aggregable pensions is not one to which this order applies, this note shall have effect in relation to it with the necessary adaptations of the expressions used as if it were such a pension.

EXPLANATORY NOTE

(*This Note is not part of the Order.*)

The Pensions (Increase) Act 1971 repealed the Pensions (Increase) Acts 1920 to 1969; but for pensions " beginning " before 1969 the increase under the 1971 Act is related to the higher of the following, namely—

(*a*) " the 1969 standard ", that is to say, the figure obtained by applying to the basic pension the appropriate multiplier given by the Act (and related to changes in purchasing power between the year in which the pension began and 1st April 1969); and

(*b*) " the 1971 rate ", with the supplement mentioned below where payable.

The 1971 rate for any pension is a rate that takes account of the cumulative effect of increases under the repealed Acts; and the supplement is the equivalent of the special increase payable to the over-70 under section 2 of the 1962 Act (but under the 1971 Act extended for the purpose of the comparison referred to above to any pension other than a dependant's pension that only qualifies for an increase because payable to a child or a person receiving education or training). Generally speaking, a pension " begins " the day after the end of the service for which it is payable, even if it is a frozen pension, a widow's pension or the like that does not become payable until later.

The main purpose of this Order is, in accordance with section 6 of the 1971 Act, to enable the pensions for which the 1971 rate and the supplement may be relevant, and the amount of the rate and supplement for any of those pensions, to be ascertained without reference to the repealed Acts. The effect of the Order is however liable to modification under the power given by section 5(3) of the 1971 Act (corresponding to powers given by the repealed Acts and used in particular in relation to pensions not based on earnings).

The Order does not apply to pensions qualifying for increases under the Pensions (Increase) Acts 1920 and 1924; for these the 1971 rate is always the rate in payment. And pensions beginning after 1st April 1961, with some exceptions, qualify only for the increases under the Acts of 1965 and 1969, and the 1971 rate is necessarily less than the 1969 standard; the Order accordingly makes no provision for these pensions.

Certain pensions beginning after 1st April 1961 and based on average earnings calculated over periods beginning before April 1951 (or an earlier date) continued to qualify for increases under the Act of 1944 or the Act of 1956, and this applies to pensions beginning after the year 1968 or in the future. The Order deals (so far as relevant) with the 1971 rate of these pensions where they begin before the year 1969, and for the continuance of the increases where they begin later.

STATUTORY INSTRUMENTS

1971 No. 1319

AGRICULTURE

The Price Stability of Imported Products (Rates of Levy) (Eggs) (No. 16) Order 1971

Made -	-	-	-	9th August 1971
Coming into Operation				10th August 1971

The Minister of Agriculture, Fisheries and Food, in exercise of the powers conferred upon him by section 1(2), (4), (5), (6) and (7) of the Agriculture and Horticulture Act 1964(a) and of all other powers enabling him in that behalf, hereby makes the following order:—

1. This order may be cited as the Price Stability of Imported Products (Rates of Levy) (Eggs) (No. 16) Order 1971, and shall come into operation on 10th August 1971.

2.—(1) In this order—

" the Principal Order " means the Price Stability of Imported Products (Levy Arrangements) (Eggs) Order 1970(b) as amended by any subsequent order, and if any such order is replaced by any subsequent order the expression shall be construed as a reference to such subsequent order;

AND other expressions have the same meaning as in the Principal Order.

(2) The Interpretation Act 1889(c) shall apply to the interpretation of this order as it applies to the interpretation of an Act of Parliament and as if this order and the order hereby revoked were Acts of Parliament.

3. In accordance with and subject to the provisions of the Principal Order (which provides for the charging of levies on imports of those eggs and egg products which are specified commodities for the purposes of the Agriculture and Horticulture Act 1964) the rate of general levy for such imports into the United Kingdom of any specified commodity as are described in column 2 of the Schedule to this order in relation to a tariff heading indicated in column 1 of that Schedule shall be the rate set forth in relation thereto in column 3 of that Schedule.

4. The Price Stability of Imported Products (Rates of Levy) (Eggs) (No. 15) Order 1971(d) is hereby revoked.

In Witness whereof the Official Seal of the Minister of Agriculture, Fisheries and Food is hereunto affixed on 9th August 1971.

(L.S.)

G. P. Jupe,
Assistant Secretary.

(a) 1964 c. 28.   (b) S.I. 1970/359 (1970 I, p. 1277).   (c) 1889 c. 63.
(d) S.I. 1971/1271(1971 II, p. 3661).

SCHEDULE

1. Tariff Heading	2. Description of Imports	3. Rate of General Levy
04.05	Imports of:—	
	Birds' eggs (*in shell or not in shell*), *fresh, dried or otherwise preserved, sweetened or not, other than egg yolks:*	(per 120 eggs)
	A. Eggs in shell:	p
	1. Not exceeding 11 lb. in weight per 120 ..	35
	2. Over 11 lb. but not exceeding 12½ lb. in weight per 120	40
	3. Over 12½ lb. but not exceeding 14 lb. in weight per 120	60
	4. Over 14 lb. but not exceeding 15½ lb. in weight per 120	60
	5. Over 15½ lb. but not exceeding 17 lb. in weight per 120	50
	6. Over 17 lb. in weight per 120	50
	B. Eggs not in shell:	(per ton)
	Whole dried	£110
	Whole frozen or liquid	£60

EXPLANATORY NOTE

(*This Note is not part of the Order.*)

This order, which comes into operation on 10th August 1971, supersedes the Price Stability of Imported Products (Rates of Levy) (Eggs) (No. 15) Order 1971. It—

(*a*) reduces the rates of general levy to be charged on imports of eggs in shell in the weight grades numbered 1 to 6 in the Schedule to the order; and

(*b*) reimposes unchanged the rates of general levy to be charged on imports of dried, frozen or liquid whole egg not in shell.

STATUTORY INSTRUMENTS

1971 No. 1326

MEDICINES

The Medicines (Importation of Medicinal Products for Re-exportation) Order 1971

Made - - - -	*9th August* 1971
Laid before Parliament	*18th August* 1971
Coming into Operation	*1st September* 1971

The Secretary of State for Social Services and the Secretary of State for Wales (being the Secretaries of State respectively concerned with health in England and in Wales), the Minister of Agriculture, Fisheries and Food, the Secretary of State for Scotland (being the Secretary of State concerned with health and with agriculture in Scotland), the Minister of Health and Social Services for Northern Ireland and the Minister of Agriculture for Northern Ireland, acting jointly, in exercise of their powers under section 13(2) and 13(3) of the Medicines Act 1968(a) as having effect subject to the provisions of article 2(2) of and Schedule 1 to the Transfer of Functions (Wales) Order 1969(b), and of all other powers enabling them in that behalf, and after consulting such organisations as appear to them to be representative of interests likely to be substantially affected by this order, hereby make the following order:—

Citation and commencement

1. This order may be cited as the Medicines (Importation of Medicinal Products for Re-exportation) Order 1971 and shall come into operation on 1st September 1971.

Interpretation

2.—(1) In this order, unless the context otherwise requires—

"the Act" means the Medicines Act 1968;

"antigens" are substances which on administration to a human being or animal are capable of eliciting a specific immunological response;

"antisera" are substances which consist wholly or partly of sera derived from animals which have been immunised against one or more micro-organisms, viruses or other antigens;

"antitoxins" are substances which consist wholly or partly of immuno-globulins of antisera derived from animals which have been immunised against one or more toxins whether detoxified or not;

"corticotrophin" is a substance obtained from the anterior lobe of the pituitary gland and which contains the peptide hormone that increases the rate at which corticoid hormones are secreted by the adrenal gland;

(a) 1968 c. 67.　　　　(b) S.I. 1969/388 (1969 I, p. 1070).

"heparin" is a substance containing the sodium salt of a sulphated poly-saccharide obtained from mammalian tissues which has the property of prolonging the clotting time of blood in human beings or animals;

"hyaluronidase" is a substance prepared from mammalian testicles or sperm or from other sources of the enzymes which diminish the viscosity of the hyaluronic acid present in mammalian tissues;

"insulin" is a preparation of the specific antidiabetic principle of the pancreas;

"plasma" means the fluid element of uncoagulated blood;

"preparations of the pituitary (posterior lobe)" include the active principles thereof (whether obtained by fractionation of the gland or by synthesis) and derivatives of those principles with the same specific biological action;

"sera" means the fluid element of coagulated blood;

"toxins" are substances used in the diagnosis, prevention or treatment of disease and consisting wholly or partly of poisonous substances derived from specific micro-organisms, plants or animals;

"vaccines" are substances which consist wholly or partly of—

(a) any micro-organisms, viruses or other organisms in any state,

(b) any toxins of microbial origin which have been detoxified, or

(c) any extracts or derivatives of any micro-organisms or of any viruses,

being substances which, when administered to human beings or animals, are used for the prevention or treatment of specific diseases;

and other expressions have the same meaning as in the Act.

(2) The Interpretation Act 1889(a) shall apply to the interpretation of this order as it applies to the interpretation of an Act of Parliament.

Removal of restriction on importation of certain medicinal products

3.—(1) The restriction imposed by section 7(3) of the Act (which prohibits the importation, except in accordance with a product licence, of medicinal products and of articles and substances in relation to which that subsection has effect) shall, subject to paragraph (2) of this article, not apply to the importation of the medicinal products, articles and substances referred to in Part I of the Schedule to this order, not being medicinal products or substances specified in Part II of the said Schedule.

(2) The exemption conferred by paragraph (1) of this article shall take effect only in relation to medicinal products, articles and substances which, having been imported, are to be exported—

(a) in the form in which they were imported, and

(b) without being assembled in a way different from the way in which they were assembled on being imported.

4th August 1971   *Keith Joseph,*
Secretary of State for Social Services.

(a) 1889 c. 63.

Given under my hand on 5th August 1971.

Peter Thomas,
Secretary of State for Wales.

In Witness whereof the official seal of the Minister of Agriculture, Fisheries and Food is hereunto affixed on 2nd August 1971.

(L.S.)

J. M. L. Prior,
Minister of Agriculture, Fisheries and Food.

Gordon Campbell,
3rd August 1971.   Secretary of State for Scotland.

Given under my hand on 9th August 1971.

W. K. Fitzsimmons,
Minister of Health and Social Services
for Northern Ireland.

Given under my hand on 6th August 1971.

H. W. West,
Minister of Agriculture for Northern Ireland.

Article 3.   SCHEDULE

PART I

Medicinal products, articles and substances (other than those specified in Part II of this Schedule) to the importation of which section 7(3) of the Act does not apply.

1. All medicinal products.

2. The substances to which the Medicines (Control of Substances for Manufacture) Order 1971(a) applies.

3. The articles and substances to which the Medicines (Surgical Materials) Order 1971(b) applies.

PART II

Medicinal products and substances to the importation of which section 7(3) of the Act continues to apply.

Medicinal products and substances, for use other than for human beings, and consisting wholly or partly of antigens, antisera, antitoxins, corticotrophin, heparin, hyaluronidase, insulin, plasma, preparations of the pituitary (posterior lobe), sera, toxins, vaccines or other medicinal products or substances derived from animals.

(a) S.I. 1971/1200 (1971 II, p. 3506).   (b) S.I. 1971/1267(1971 II, p. 3632).

EXPLANATORY NOTE

(This Note is not part of the Order.)

Section 7(3) of the Medicines Act 1968 prohibits the importation of medicinal products except in accordance with a product licence. The subsection also has effect in relation to such articles and substances to which it has been applied by orders made under sections 104 or 105 of the Act.

This order, made under section 13(2) of the Act, exempts from such prohibition the importation of medicinal products and the articles and substances which are the subject of orders under sections 104 and 105, other than certain specified medicinal products and substances for veterinary use. The exemption only takes effect where the medicinal products, articles and substances are to be re-exported without any change in their form or their manner of assembly.

STATUTORY INSTRUMENTS

1971 No. 1327

POLICE

The Police Pensions (Amendment) (No. 2) Regulations 1971

Made - - - -	9th August 1971
Laid before Parliament	19th August 1971
Coming into Operation	1st September 1971

In exercise of the powers conferred on me by sections 1 and 3 of the Police Pensions Act 1948(a) (read with Article 2(1) of the Minister for the Civil Service Order 1968(b)), as extended and amended by section 43 of the Reserve and Auxiliary Forces (Protection of Civil Interests) Act 1951(c), section 5(3) of the Overseas Service Act 1958(d) and Schedule 2 thereto, section 1(1) of the Police Pensions Act 1961(e), sections 40, 43(4), 45(4) and 63 of the Police Act 1964(f) and Schedules 6 and 9 thereto, sections 35 and 38(4) of the Police (Scotland) Act 1967(g), section 4(5) of the Police Act 1969(h) and section 14 of the Pensions (Increase) Act 1971(i), and after consultation with the Police Council for the United Kingdom, I hereby, with the consent of the Minister for the Civil Service, make the following Regulations, which contain only such provisions as appear to me to be necessary or expedient in connection with the passing of the said Act of 1971:—

1. These Regulations may be cited as the Police Pensions (Amendment) (No. 2) Regulations 1971.

2. These Regulations shall come into operation on 1st September 1971.

3. In these Regulations any reference to the principal Regulations is a reference to the Police Pensions Regulations 1971(j), as amended (k).

4. In Regulation 34(3)(b) of the principal Regulations (widow's award under former Acts) the words "(without taking into account any increase under the Pensions (Increase) Acts 1944 and 1947)" shall be omitted.

5. In Regulation 89(5) of the principal Regulations (awards to servicemen) the words "paragraph (3)(a) shall have effect as if it referred to a rate of not less than a twelfth of his average pensionable pay increased in accordance with Regulation 106, and" shall be omitted.

(a) 1948 c. 24.	(b) S.I. 1968/1656 (1968 III, p. 4485).
(c) 1951 c. 65.	(d) 1958 c. 14.
(e) 1961 c. 35.	(f) 1964 c. 48.
(g) 1967 c. 77.	(h) 1969 c. 63.
(i) 1971 c. 56.	
(j) S.I. 1971/232 (1971 I, p. 700).	
(k) The amending Regulations are not relevant to the subject matter of these Regulations.	

6. For Regulation 90(5) of the principal Regulations (awards on death of servicemen) there shall be substituted the following provision:—

"(5) The weekly amount of any pension payable under paragraph (4)(*a*) shall be £2·85.".

7. For Part XIII of the principal Regulations (application of Pensions (Increase) Acts) there shall be substituted the Part set out in the Schedule to these Regulations.

8. The following provisions of Schedule 2 to the principal Regulations (increases in the case of a person who retired before 1st July 1949), namely—

(*a*) paragraph 4 of Part I (ordinary pension);

(*b*) paragraph 5 of Part II (ill-health or short service pension), and

(*c*) paragraph 3 of Part VI (supplemental pension),

are hereby revoked.

9. For paragraphs 3 and 4 of Part I of Schedule 3 to the principal Regulations (widow's ordinary pension—standard rate) there shall be substituted the following provisions:—

"3.—(1) Where in respect of any period a widow so elects, then, subject to paragraph 4, the weekly amount of her ordinary pension in respect of that period shall be, if her husband at the time when he ceased to be a regular policeman—

(*a*) held a rank higher than that of inspector, £4·47;

(*b*) held the rank of inspector, £3·72;

(*c*) held a rank lower than that of inspector, £2·85.

(2) Where the husband held the rank of chief inspector in the City of London police force, the preceding sub-paragraph shall apply as though he had held a rank higher than that of inspector.

4. Where the husband was entitled to reckon at least 10 years' pensionable service the weekly amount of a widow's ordinary pension calculated in accordance with paragraph 3 shall be increased by 20p.".

10.—(1) For paragraph 1 of Scheme I of Part II of Schedule 3 to the principal Regulations (widow's ordinary pension—preserved rate) there shall be substituted the following provision:—

"1. Subject to paragraphs 2 and 3 of this Scheme, the weekly amount of a widow's ordinary pension shall be, if her husband at the time when he ceased to be a regular policeman—

(*a*) held a rank higher than that of inspector, £4·47;

(*b*) held the rank of inspector, £3·72;

(*c*) held a rank lower than that of inspector, £2·85.".

(2) Paragraph 4 shall be omitted from the said Scheme I.

11. For paragraph 2 of Part IV of Schedule 3 to the principal Regulations (widow's augmented special pension) there shall be substituted the following provision:—

"2. The weekly amount calculated in accordance with paragraph 1 shall be increased in accordance with Part XIII of these Regulations so, however, that the notional pension referred to in Regulation 106 shall not be treated as having begun for the purposes of the said Part XIII and the Pensions (Increase) Act 1971 earlier than 1st April 1952.".

12.—(1) For the Table in paragraph 1 of Part I of Schedule 4 to the principal Regulations (child's ordinary allowance) there shall be substituted the following Table:—

"TABLE

Parent's Rank	Weekly Amount
Higher than Inspector	£1·17
Inspector	£0·95
Lower than Inspector	£0·80"

(2) For the Table in paragraph 2 of the said Part I there shall be substituted the following Table:—

"TABLE

Parent's Rank	Weekly Amount
Higher than Inspector	£1·75
Inspector	£1·41
Lower than Inspector	£1·18"

13. For the Table in paragraph 1(1)(*a*) of Part III of Schedule 4 to the principal Regulations (discretionary increase in child's allowance) there shall be substituted the following Table:—

"TABLE

Parent's Rank	Increased Amount
Higher than Inspector	£2·33
Inspector	£1·87
Lower than Inspector	£1·56"

R. Maudling,
One of Her Majesty's Principal
Secretaries of State.

9th August 1971.

Consent of the Minister for the Civil Service given under his Official Seal on 9th August 1971.

(L.S.)

J. E. Herbecq,
Authorised by the
Minister for the Civil Service.

SCHEDULE

Part Substituted for Part XIII of the Principal Regulations

PART XIII

Application of Pensions (Increase) Act 1971

Increase by reference to Pensions (Increase) Act 1971

106. Where it is provided in these Regulations that, for the purpose of calculating an award (hereafter referred to in this Part of these Regulations as the "relevant award"), an amount shall be increased in accordance with this Part of these Regulations it shall be increased by the amount, if any, by which a pension, within the meaning of the Pensions (Increase) Act 1971, of the amount first mentioned would from time to time be increased under sections 1 and 6(1), or under an order made under section 2, of that Act if—

(a) the person concerned were in receipt of such a pension (hereinafter referred to in this Part of these Regulations as the "notional pension");

(b) the notional pension were one of the pensions which are specified in paragraph 43 of Part II of Schedule 2 to that Act;

(c) the notional pension were subject to any regulations under section 5(3) of that Act applicable to a pension so specified, and

(d) save as otherwise provided in these Regulations, the notional pension began, within the meaning of that Act, on the day on which the relevant award so began.

Preservation for certain purposes of benefit of previous increases

107.—(1) For the purpose of determining an increase under Regulation 106 by reference to section 6(1) of the said Act of 1971, the 1971 rate of the notional pension shall be ascertained in accordance with this Regulation and, save as hereinafter provided, the provisions of section 6(2), (3), (4) and (5) shall not have effect.

(2) Where the relevant award is a widow's pension granted under the former Acts on or before 16th August 1920 which falls to be calculated in accordance with Regulation 34(3)(b), the 1971 rate of the notional pension shall be taken to be the annual rate at which the relevant award was payable on 31st August 1971, or, if on that date it was payable at a rate increased by reference to Scheme I of Part II of Schedule 3, the rate at which it would have been payable on that date had it been payable at a rate which included relevant increases; and, in determining for the purposes hereof the rate at which the relevant award was, or would have been, payable on 31st August 1971, account shall be taken of any increase which was or, as the case may be, would have been payable under the Pensions (Increase) Act 1920(a).

(3) Where the relevant award does not fall within paragraph (2) and was being paid on 31st August 1971 at a rate which included relevant increases, the 1971 rate of the notional pension shall be taken to be the amount first mentioned in Regulation 106, together with the relevant increases, as calculated at that date and expressed as an annual rate, unless it is shown that that rate should have been revised or that there is a change of circumstances that would affect the 1971 rate if ascertained under paragraph (4).

(4) Where the relevant award does not fall within paragraph (2), the 1971 rate of the notional pension shall, unless paragraph (3) applies, be ascertained in accordance with section 6(4) and (5) of the said Act of 1971 as if it were one of the pensions which are specified in paragraph 43 of Part II of Schedule 2 to that Act.

(5) Where the relevant award is a widow's pension which began within the meaning of the said Act of 1971 on or before 1st April 1961 and paragraph (3) applies, then, unless

(a) 1920 c. 36.

the pensioner had attained the age of 70 on or before 31st August 1971, there shall be added to the 1971 rate of the notional pension ascertained under paragraph (3) an amount prescribed by order of the Minister for the Civil Service under section 6(5) of that Act, in the case of a pension specified in paragraph 43 of Part II of Schedule 2 to the said Act of 1971, as corresponding to the increase provided for by section 2 of the Pensions (Increase) Act 1962(a).

(6) In this Regulation any reference to relevant increases is a reference to increases in accordance with this Part of these Regulations as originally made.

Duration of increase in child's allowance

108. Where it is provided in these Regulations that for the purposes of calculating a child's allowance an amount shall be increased in accordance with this Part of these Regulations, then that amount shall be increased so long as the allowance is payable, and accordingly Regulation 106 shall have effect for the said purpose as if section 3(3) were omitted from the Pensions (Increase) Act 1971 (which provision would otherwise govern the duration of the increase).

EXPLANATORY NOTE

(*This Note is not part of the Regulations.*)

These Regulations contain amendments to the Police Pensions Regulations 1971 which appear necessary or expedient in connection with the passing of the Pensions (Increase) Act 1971 and come into operation on 1st September 1971 (the date from which increases authorised by that Act are payable).

The principal changes are described below.

The 1971 Regulations contain provisions for the increase of widows' pensions and children's allowances (other than flat-rate awards), in accordance with Part XIII thereof, by reference to Pensions (Increase) Acts which are repealed and replaced by that of 1971. The present Regulations substitute a new Part XIII providing for increases by reference to the Pensions (Increase) Act 1971 (Regulation 7 and the Schedule).

The 1971 Regulations also contain provisions for the increase of pensions payable to policemen who retired before 1st July 1949 (or ceased to serve in the armed forces before 1st January 1952), in accordance with Regulation 106 thereof, by reference to the Pensions (Increase) Acts 1944(c. 21) and 1947(c. 7).

These pensions will qualify for increases under the Pensions (Increase) Act 1971 which replace, *inter alia*, increases in accordance with the Acts of 1944 and 1947 and the present Regulations revoke the provisions of the 1971 Regulations described above (Regulations 5 and 8).

Under the 1971 Regulations the amounts of certain widows' pensions and children's allowances are determined by reference to specified flat rates. The present Regulations increase these flat rates (Regulations 6, 9, 10, 12 and 13).

(a) 1962 c. 2 (11 & 12 Eliz. 2).

STATUTORY INSTRUMENTS

1971 No. 1328

POLICE

The Special Constables (Pensions) (Amendment) (No. 2) Regulations 1971

Made - - - -	9th *August* 1971
Laid before Parliament	19th *August* 1971
Coming into Operation	1st *September* 1971

In exercise of the powers conferred on me by section 34 of the Police Act 1964(a) (read with section 1(2) of the Police Pensions Act 1961(b)), I hereby make the following Regulations:—

1. These Regulations may be cited as the Special Constables (Pensions) (Amendment) (No. 2) Regulations 1971 and shall come into operation on 1st September 1971.

2. In these Regulations any reference to the Instrument of 1971 is a reference to the Special Constables (Pensions) Regulations 1971(c), as amended (d).

3.—(1) In the application of the Police Pensions Regulations 1971(e) to the calculation of an award to or in respect of a special constable under the Instrument of 1971, those Regulations shall apply as amended by the Police Pensions (Amendment) (No. 2) Regulations 1971(f) (amendments necessary or expedient in connection with the passing of the Pensions (Increase) Act 1971(g)).

(2) In accordance with paragraph (1) of this Regulation, for Regulation 3(1) of the Instrument of 1971 (which, as set out in the Special Constables (Pensions) (Amendment) Regulations 1971(h), defines the expression "the principal Regulations") there shall be substituted the following paragraph:—

"(1) In these Regulations the expression "the principal Regulations" means the Police Pensions Regulations 1971, as amended by the Police Pensions (Amendment) Regulations 1971(i) and the Police Pensions (Amendment) (No. 2) Regulations 1971.".

4. In Regulation 4(2) of the Instrument of 1971 (special constable's supplemental pension) the reference to Regulation 106 of the principal Regulations shall be omitted and, accordingly, for the words "67 and 106" there shall be substituted the words "and 67".

(a) 1964 c. 48.
(b) 1961 c. 35.
(c) S.I. 1971/233 (1971 I, p. 802).
(d) S.I. 1971/584 (1971 I, p. 1576).
(e) S.I. 1971/232 (1971 I, p. 700).
(f) S.I. 1971/1327.
(g) 1971 c. 56.
(h) S.I. 1971/584 (1971 I, p. 1576).
(i) S.I. 1971/583 (1971 I, p. 1573).

5. Regulation 12 of the Instrument of 1971 (limitation on application of Regulation 106 of the principal Regulations) is hereby revoked.

R. Maudling,
One of Her Majesty's Principal
Secretaries of State.

Home Office,
Whitehall.
9th August 1971.

EXPLANATORY NOTE

(This Note is not part of the Regulations.)

These Regulations amend the Special Constables (Pensions) Regulations 1971 which give to special constables and their dependants certain pension benefits for which members of police forces and their dependants are eligible under the Police Pensions Regulations 1971.

The Police Pensions (Amendment) (No. 2) Regulations 1971 contain amendments to the Police Pensions Regulations 1971 which appear necessary or expedient in connection with the passing of the Pensions (Increase) Act 1971 and come into operation on 1st September 1971 (the date from which increases authorised by the 1971 Act are payable).

These Regulations, which come into operation on the same date, make similar provision in connection with the passing of the 1971 Act as respects the benefits payable to or in respect of special constables.

STATUTORY INSTRUMENTS

1971 No. 1329

FIRE SERVICES

The Firemen's Pension Scheme (Amendment) Order 1971

Made - - -	*9th August* 1971
Laid before Parliament	*19th August* 1971
Coming into Operation	*1st September* 1971

In exercise of the powers conferred on me by section 26 of the Fire Services Act 1947(a), (read with Article 2(1) of the Minister for the Civil Service Order 1968(b)), as amended and extended by section 42 of the Reserve and Auxiliary Forces (Protection of Civil Interests) Act 1951(c) and section 15 of the Pensions (Increase) Act 1971(d), I hereby, with the approval of the Minister for the Civil Service and after consultation with the Central Fire Brigades Advisory Council and the Scottish Central Fire Brigades Advisory Council, make the following Order, which contains only such provisions as appear to me to be necessary or expedient in connection with the passing of the said Act of 1971:—

PART I

CITATION, OPERATION AND INTERPRETATION

1. This Order may be cited as the Firemen's Pension Scheme (Amendment) Order 1971.

2. This Order shall come into operation on 1st September 1971.

3. In this Order the following expressions have the meanings hereby respectively assigned to them, that is to say:—

"the Scheme of 1971" means the Firemen's Pension Scheme 1971, set out in Appendix 2 to the Firemen's Pension Scheme Order 1971(e);

"the Scheme of 1966" means the Firemen's Pension Scheme 1966, set out in Appendix 2 to the Firemen's Pension Scheme Order 1966(f), as amended(g) and in so far as it continues to have effect(h);

"the Scheme of 1964" means the Firemen's Pension Scheme 1964, set out in Appendix 2 to the Firemen's Pension Scheme Order 1964(i), as amended(j) and in so far as it continues to have effect(k);

(a) 1947 c. 41.
(b) S.I. 1968/1656 (1968 III, p. 4485).
(c) 1951 c. 65.
(d) 1971 c. 56.
(e) S.I. 1971/145 (1971 I, p. 320).
(f) S.I. 1966/1045 (1966 II, p. 2504).
(g) The relevant amending instruments are S.I. 1968/157, 1969/1001 (1968 I, p. 386; 1969 II, p. 2945).
(h) *See* S.I. 1971/145 (1971 I, p. 320).
(i) S.I. 1964/1148 (1964 II, p. 2574).
(j) The amending instruments are not relevant to the subject matter of this Order.
(k) *See* 1966/1045 (1966 II, p. 2504).

"the Scheme of 1956" means the Firemen's Pension Scheme 1956, set out in the Appendix to the Firemen's Pension Scheme Order 1956(a), as amended(b) and in so far as it continues to have effect(c);

"the Scheme of 1952" means the Firemen's Pension Scheme 1952, set out in Appendix 1 to the Firemen's Pension Scheme Order 1952(d), as amended(e) and in so far as it continues to have effect(f), and

"the Scheme of 1948" means the Firemen's Pension Scheme 1948, set out in the Appendix to the Firemen's Pension Scheme Order 1948(g), as amended(h) and in so far as it continues to have effect(i).

PART II
AMENDMENTS OF ARTICLES RELATING TO INTERPRETATION

4.—(1) This Article shall have effect for the purposes of the amendment of the following provisions, namely:—

Article 8(1) of the Scheme of 1971;

Article 82(1) of the Scheme of 1966;

Article 80(1) of the Scheme of 1964.

(2) The definition of the expression "relevant Pensions (Increase) Acts" shall be omitted from each of the said provisions.

PART III
AMENDMENTS OF ARTICLES RELATING TO WIDOWS' ORDINARY PENSIONS

5.—(1) This Article shall have effect for the purposes of the amendment of the following provisions, namely:—

Article 21(2)(b) of the Scheme of 1971;

Article 10(2)(b) of the Scheme of 1966;

Article 10(2) of the Scheme of 1964.

(2) The words "subject however to Schedule 4" shall be omitted from each of the said provisions.

6. In Article 10(1) of the Scheme of 1956 the words "and the Fourth Schedule" shall be omitted.

7.—(1) This Article shall have effect for the purposes of the amendment of the following provisions, namely:—

Article 4(1) of the Scheme of 1952;

Article 4(1) of the Scheme of 1948.

(2) For the words "and Sixteenth Schedules", in both of the said provisions, there shall be substituted the word "Schedule".

(a) S.I. 1956/1022 (1956 I, p. 953).
(b) The relevant amending instruments are S.I. 1956/2014, 1959/802, 1962/729 (1956 I, p. 994; 1959 I, p. 1282; 1962 I, p. 744).
(c) See 1964/1148 (1964 II, p. 2574).
(d) S.I. 1952/944 (1952 I, p. 1003).
(e) The relevant amending instruments are S.I. 1952/1447, 1952/2166, 1954/1663 (1952 I, p. 1046; 1952 I, p. 1047; 1954 I, p. 909).
(f) See S.I. 1956/1022 (1956 I, p. 953).
(g) S.I. 1948/604 (1948 I, p. 1091).
(h) The relevant amending instrument is S.I. 1952/2166 (1952 I, p. 1047).
(i) See S.I. 1952/944 (1952 I, p. 1003).

PART IV

AMENDMENTS OF ARTICLES RELATING TO WIDOWS' SPECIAL PENSIONS

8.—(1) This Article shall have effect for the purposes of the amendment of the following provisions, namely:—

Article 22(2) of the Scheme of 1971;

Article 11(2) of the Scheme of 1966;

Article 11 of the Scheme of 1964.

(2) The words "subject however to Schedule 4" shall be omitted from each of the said provisions.

9. In Article 11 of the Scheme of 1956 the words "and the Fourth Schedule" shall be omitted.

10.—(1) This Article shall have effect for the purposes of the amendment of the following provisions, namely:—

Article 7(2) of the Scheme of 1952;

Article 7(2) of the Scheme of 1948.

(2) For the words "and Sixteenth Schedules", in both of the said provisions, there shall be substituted the word "Schedule".

PART V

AMENDMENTS OF ARTICLES RELATING TO WIDOWS' AUGMENTED AWARDS

11.—(1) This Article shall have effect for the purposes of the amendment of the following provisions, namely:—

Article 23(2) of the Scheme of 1971;

Article 11A(2) of the Scheme of 1966.

(2) The words "subject however, in either case, to Schedule 4" shall be omitted from both the said provisions.

PART VI

AMENDMENT OF ARTICLE RELATING TO CHILDREN'S ORDINARY ALLOWANCES

12. In Article 5(1) of the Scheme of 1952 the words "and of the Sixteenth Schedule to this Scheme" shall be omitted.

PART VII

AMENDMENTS OF ARTICLES RELATING TO CHILDREN'S SPECIAL ALLOWANCES

13.—(1) This Article shall have effect for the purposes of the amendment of the following provisions, namely:—

Article 29 of the Scheme of 1971;

Article 17 of the Scheme of 1966;

Article 17 of the Scheme of 1964.

(2) The words "and to Schedule 4" shall be omitted from each of the said provisions.

14. In Article 17 of the Scheme of 1956 the words "and the Fourth Schedule" shall be omitted.

2aa

15. In Article 8(2) of the Scheme of 1952 the words "and of the Sixteenth Schedule to this Scheme" shall be omitted.

PART VIII
AMENDMENTS OF ARTICLES RELATING TO AWARDS ON DEATH OF SERVICEMEN

16.—(1) This Article shall have effect for the purposes of the amendment of the following Articles, namely:—

Article 65 of the Scheme of 1971;

Article 53 of the Scheme of 1966;

Article 51 of the Scheme of 1964;

Article 46 of the Scheme of 1956.

(2) For paragraph (4)(*a*) of each of the said Articles there shall be substituted the following provision:—

"(*a*) pay to the widow, in lieu of a gratuity, a pension at the rate of £148·27 a year, and".

(3) Each of the said Articles shall end with the words "qualifying injury" in paragraph (4)(*b*) and, accordingly, any words or provisions following those words are hereby revoked.

17.—(1) This Article shall have effect for the purposes of the amendment of the following Articles, namely:—

Article 37B of the Scheme of 1952;

Article 37B of the Scheme of 1948.

(2) For paragraph (4)(*a*) of each of the said Articles there shall be substituted the following provision:—

"(*a*) pay to the widow, in lieu of a gratuity, a pension at the rate of £111·20 a year, and".

(3) In paragraph (4)(*b*) of each of the said provisions the words following the words "qualifying injury" shall be omitted.

18.—(1) This Article shall have effect for the purposes of the amendment of the following Articles, namely:—

Article 10 of the Scheme of 1952;

Article 10 of the Scheme of 1948.

(2) For the proviso to paragraph (2)(i) of each of the said Articles there shall be substituted the following proviso:—

"Provided that where the said pension, after taking account of any increase provided for by or under the Pensions (Increase) Act 1971, is payable at a rate less than that of £111·20 a year, it shall be paid at the rate of £111·20 a year;".

(3) The provisos or proviso following paragraph (2)(iii) of each of the said Articles shall be omitted.

(4) At the end of each of the said Articles there shall be added the following paragraph:—

"(5) Save as provided in paragraph (2)(i) of this Article, for the purposes of this Article no account shall be taken of any increase provided for by or under the Pensions (Increase) Act 1971 so, however, that nothing in this paragraph shall be construed as precluding such an increase in a rate determined in accordance with this Article (otherwise than in accordance with the proviso to paragraph (2)(i)).".

PART IX

AMENDMENTS OF ARTICLES RELATING TO AWARDS IN RESPECT OF WHOLE-TIME FIREMEN WHO ARE NOT REGULAR FIREMEN

19.—(1) This Article shall have effect for the purposes of the amendment of the following provisions, namely:—

Article 72(3) of the Scheme of 1971;

Article 60(3) of the Scheme of 1966;

Article 58(3) of the Scheme of 1964.

(2) The words "any increase in accordance with Schedule 4 being ignored" shall be omitted from each of the said provisions.

20. In Article 53(3) of the Scheme of 1956 the words "any increase in accordance with the Fourth Schedule to this Scheme being ignored" shall be omitted.

21. In Article 24(3) of the Scheme of 1952 the words "ignoring any increase in accordance with the provisions of the Sixteenth Schedule to this Scheme" shall be omitted from the proviso.

22. The following provisions, namely:—

Article 72(4) of the Scheme of 1971;

Article 60(4) of the Scheme of 1966;

Article 58(4) of the Scheme of 1964;

Article 53(4) of the Scheme of 1956;

Article 24(4) of the Scheme of 1952;

Article 24(4) of the Scheme of 1948,

are hereby revoked.

PART X

AMENDMENT OF ARTICLES RELATING TO AWARDS TO OR IN RESPECT OF PART-TIME FIREMEN

23.—(1) This Article shall have effect for the purposes of the amendment of the following provisions, namely:—

Article 55(3) of the Scheme of 1956;

Article 23A(2) of the Scheme of 1952.

(2) For the rates specified in sub-paragraphs (*a*) and (*b*) of each of the said provisions there shall be substituted, respectively, the rates of £5·51 a week and of £3·70 a week.

(3) For the rate specified in sub-paragraph (*c*) of Article 55(3) of the Scheme of 1956 there shall be substituted the rate of £2·88 a week.

24.—(1) This Article shall have effect for the purposes of the amendment of the following provisions, namely:—

Article 75(3) of the Scheme of 1971;

Article 63(3) of the Scheme of 1966;

Article 61(3) of the Scheme of 1964;

Article 56(1) of the Scheme of 1956;

Article 23B(1) of the Scheme of 1952.

(2) For the rates specified in sub-paragraphs (*a*), (*b*) and (*c*) of each of the said provisions there shall be substituted, respectively, the rates of £2·04 a week, £3·06 a week and £4·61 a week.

(3) The proviso to Article 23B(1) of the Scheme of 1952 shall be omitted.

25.—(1) This Article shall have effect for the purposes of the amendment of the following provisions, namely:—

Article 76(3) of the Scheme of 1971;

Article 64(3) of the Scheme of 1966;

Article 62(3) of the Scheme of 1964;

Article 57(1) of the Scheme of 1956.

(2) For the rate specified in sub-paragraph (*a*) of each of the said provisions there shall be substituted the rate of £1·10 a week.

(3) For the rates first and last specified in sub-paragraph (*b*) of each of the said provisions there shall be substituted, respectively, the rates of £0·83 a week and of £1·10 a week.

26. For the rate specified in Article 23C(1) of the Scheme of 1952 there shall be substituted the rate of £1·10 a week.

27. The following provisions, namely:—

Article 77(3) of the Scheme of 1971;

Article 65(3) of the Scheme of 1966;

Article 63(3) of the Scheme of 1964,

are hereby revoked.

PART XI

AMENDMENTS OF SCHEDULES RELATING TO WIDOWS' ORDINARY PENSIONS

28.—(1) This Article shall have effect for the purposes of the amendment of the following provisions, namely:—

Part I of Schedule 2 to the Scheme of 1971;

Part I of Schedule 2 to the Scheme of 1966.

(2) For paragraph 2 of each of the said provisions there shall be substituted the following paragraph:—

"2.—(1) Subject to sub-paragraph (2), where in respect of any period a widow so elects, her ordinary pension in respect of that period shall be of such amount that the rate of payment is—

(*a*) where the husband's last rank was not higher than that of sub-officer, £148·27 a year;

(*b*) where the husband's last rank was higher than that of sub-officer but not higher than that of divisional officer (Grade I), £193·62 a year;

(*c*) where the husband's last rank was higher than that of divisional officer (Grade I), £233·03 a year.

(2) Where the husband was entitled to reckon at least 10 years' pensionable service, the preceding sub-paragraph shall have effect as if for the rates of £148·27, £193·62 and £233·03 a year there were substituted, respectively, the rates of £158·27, £203·62 and £243·03 a year.".

29.—(1) This Article shall have effect for the purposes of the amendment of the following provisions, namely:—

Part II of Schedule 2 to the Scheme of 1971;

Part II of Schedule 2 to the Scheme of 1966;

Part I of Schedule 2 to the Scheme of 1964;

Part I of Schedule 2 to the Scheme of 1956.

(2) The first sentence of each of the said provisions shall end with the words "the higher pension" and, accordingly, any words following those words shall be omitted from the said sentence.

(3) For Scheme I of each of the said provisions there shall be substituted the following Scheme:—

"SCHEME I

The pension shall be of such amount that the rate of payment is—

(a) where the husband's last rank was not higher than that of sub-officer, £148·27 a year;

(b) where the husband's last rank was higher than that of sub-officer but not higher than that of divisional officer (Grade I), £193·62 a year;

(c) where the husband's last rank was higher than that of divisional officer (Grade I), £233·03 a year.".

(4) In Scheme II of each of the said provisions paragraph 2 shall be omitted.

30.—(1) This Article shall have effect for the purposes of the amendment of the following Schedules, namely:—

Schedule 3 to the Scheme of 1952;

Schedule 3 to the Scheme of 1948.

(2) The words "after taking into account the increase, if any, conferred by virtue of the Pensions (Increase) Acts, 1944 and 1947" shall be omitted from the first sentence of each of the said Schedules.

(3) Subject in the case of the Scheme of 1948 to the following paragraph, for Scheme I of each of the said Schedules there shall be substituted the following Scheme:—

"SCHEME I

The pension shall be of such amount that the rate of payment is—

(a) where the husband's last rank was not higher than that of sub-officer, £111·20 a year;

(b) where the husband's last rank was higher than that of sub-officer but not higher than that of divisional officer (Grade I), £145·22 a year;

(c) where the husband's last rank was higher than that of divisional officer (Grade I), £178·27 a year.".

(4) At the end of Scheme I of Schedule 3 to the Scheme of 1948, as set out in the preceding paragraph there shall be added the following proviso:—

"Provided that where the husband died before 5th July 1948 or the widow is not entitled in right of her husband's insurance to widow's benefit or a retirement pension under the National Insurance Act 1965**(a)** but would have

---

(a) 1965 c. 51.

been so entitled had her husband not failed to satisfy the contribution conditions therefor (otherwise than by defaulting in the payment of contributions), this Scheme shall have effect as if for the rates of £111·20, £145·22 and £178·27 a year there were substituted, respectively, the rates of £148·27, £193·62 and £233·03.".

(5) The proviso to paragraph 1 of Scheme II of each of the said Schedules shall be omitted.

PART XII

AMENDMENTS OF SCHEDULES RELATING TO WIDOWS' SPECIAL PENSIONS

31.—(1) This Article shall have effect for the purposes of the amendment of the following provisions, namely:—

Part IV of Schedule 2 to the Scheme of 1971;

Part V of Schedule 2 to the Scheme of 1971;

Part IV of Schedule 2 to the Scheme of 1966;

Part VI of Schedule 2 to the Scheme of 1966;

Part III of Schedule 2 to the Scheme of 1964;

Part III of Schedule 2 to the Scheme of 1956;

Schedule 7 to the Scheme of 1952;

Schedule 7 to the Scheme of 1948.

(2) Paragraph 2 shall be omitted from each of the said provisions.

PART XIII

AMENDMENTS OF SCHEDULES RELATING TO CHILDREN'S ALLOWANCES

32.—(1) For each of the following provisions, namely:—

Part I of Schedule 3 to the Scheme of 1971;

Part I of Schedule 3 to the Scheme of 1966;

Part I of Schedule 3 to the Scheme of 1964;

Part I of Schedule 3 to the Scheme of 1956;

Part I of Schedule 5 to the Scheme of 1952,

there shall be substituted the provisions set out in the following paragraph.

(2) Subject in the case of the Scheme of 1952 to the following paragraph, the provisions referred to in the preceding paragraph shall be as follows:—

"PART I

CHILD'S ORDINARY ALLOWANCE

1. Subject to Part III of this Schedule, where the mother of the child is alive the child's ordinary allowance shall be of such amount that the rate of payments is—

(a) where the father's last rank was not higher than that of sub-officer, £41·26 a year;

(b) where the father's last rank was higher than that of sub-officer but not higher than that of divisional officer (Grade I), £49·26 a year;

(c) where the father's last rank was higher than that of divisional officer (Grade I), £60·96 a year.

2. Subject to Part III of this Schedule, where the father was the only surviving parent or in respect of the period after the death of the mother, the child's ordinary allowance shall be of such amount that the rate of payment is—

(a) where the father's last rank was not higher than that of sub-officer, £61·58 a year or such higher rate not exceeding £81·28 as the fire authority may from time to time determine;

(b) where the father's last rank was higher than sub-officer but not higher than that of divisional officer (Grade I), £73·27 a year or such higher rate not exceeding £97·29 as the fire authority may from time to time determine, or

(c) where the father's last rank was higher than that of divisional officer (Grade I), £91·13 a year or such higher rate not exceeding £121·30 as the fire authority may from time to time determine.".

(3) In Part I of Schedule 5 to the Scheme of 1952, as set out in the preceding paragraph, for the words "Part III of this Schedule", in both places where they occur, there shall be substituted the words "Schedule 8A to this Scheme".

33. Part II of Schedule 5 to the Scheme of 1952 is hereby revoked.

34.—(1) For each of the following provisions, namely:—

Part III of Schedule 3 to the Scheme of 1971;

Part III of Schedule 3 to the Scheme of 1966;

Part III of Schedule 3 to the Scheme of 1964;

Part III of Schedule 3 to the Scheme of 1956,

there shall be substituted the provisions set out in the following paragraph.

(2) The provisions referred to in the preceding paragraph shall be as follows:—

"PART III

VARIATION OF CHILD'S ALLOWANCE

1.—(1) Subject as hereinafter provided, where under any enactment specified in the first column of the following Table a payment specified in the second column is made to the recipient mentioned in the third column thereof, a child's ordinary or special allowance shall be reduced by so much as is necessary to reduce the allowance or, in the case of a special allowance, the increased allowance, by the weekly amount specified in the fourth column, and where that reduction is greater than the allowance determined under the preceding provisions of this Schedule, that allowance shall not be payable.

In this sub-paragraph the expression "increased allowance" in relation to a child's special allowance means the amount which would be payable in respect thereof by virtue of this Scheme and the Pensions (Increase) Act 1971, if this paragraph were not in force.

TABLE

1 Enactment	2 Type of Payment	3 Recipient	4 Weekly Reduction
National Insurance Act 1965, s. 27	Widowed mother's allowance	Child's mother	37p
National Insurance Act 1965, s. 29	Guardian's allowance in respect of the child ...	Child's guardian	60p
National Insurance Act 1965, s. 40	Increased widow's allowance	Child's mother	37p
National Insurance Act 1965, s. 40	Increased retirement pension	Child's mother	37p
Family Allowances Act 1965 (a)	Family allowance in respect of the child ..	Any person	25p
National Insurance (Industrial Injuries) Act 1965(b), s. 21	Death benefit in respect of the deceased's child at the higher weekly rate prescribed by that section..	Any person	37p

(2) Where a woman has 2 or more children who would apart from the provisions of this paragraph be entitled to a child's allowance, only the allowance of the elder or eldest of those children shall be reduced in respect of the payment to her of a widowed mother's allowance, increased widow's allowance or increased retirement pension.

(3) Where the child's allowance is an ordinary allowance, it shall not be reduced in respect of the payment of death benefit.".

35.—(1) This Article shall have effect for the purposes of the amendment of Schedule 8 to the Scheme of 1952.

(2) In paragraph 1 of Part I of the said Schedule after the words "Subject as hereinafter provided" there shall be inserted the words "and to Schedule 8A to this Scheme".

(3) Part II of the said Schedule is hereby revoked.

36. After Schedule 8 to the Scheme of 1952 there shall be inserted as Schedule 8A the provisions set out in Article 34(2) of this Order.

PART XIV

REVOCATION OF SCHEDULES RELATING TO INCREASES BY REFERENCE TO THE PENSIONS (INCREASE) ACT 1952

37. The following provisions are hereby revoked, namely:—

Schedule 4 to the Scheme of 1971;
Schedule 4 to the Scheme of 1966;
Schedule 4 to the Scheme of 1964;
Schedule 4 to the Scheme of 1956;
Schedule 16 to the Scheme of 1952;
Schedule 16 to the Scheme of 1948.

(a) 1965 c. 53. (b) 1965 c. 52.

PART XV

AMENDMENT OF SCHEDULES RELATING TO FIREMEN SERVING
ON 10TH JULY 1956

38.—(1) This Article shall have effect for the purposes of the amendment of the following provisions, namely:—

Schedule 10 to the Scheme of 1971;

Schedule 10 to the Scheme of 1966;

Schedule 9 to the Scheme of 1964;

Schedule 8 to the Scheme of 1956.

(2) For sub-paragraphs (*a*) and (*b*) of paragraph 5 of each of the said provisions there shall be substituted the words "in paragraph (4)(*a*) for the words "£148·27 a year" there shall be substituted the words "£111·20 a year".".

(3) For the last three paragraphs of each of the said provisions (numbered either 9, 10 and 11, or 8, 9 and 10) there shall, subject in the case of the Schemes of 1964 and 1956 to the following paragraph of this Article, be substituted the two following paragraphs:—

"9. For Scheme I of Part II of Schedule 2 there shall be substituted the following Scheme:—

"SCHEME I

1. The pension shall be of such amount that the rate of payment is—

(*a*) where the husband's last rank was not higher than that of sub-officer, £111·20 a year;

(*b*) where the husband's last rank was higher than that of sub-officer but not higher than that of divisional officer (Grade I), £145·22 a year; or

(*c*) where the husband's last rank was higher than that of divisional officer (Grade I), £178·27 a year.".

10. For Part I of Schedule 3 there shall be substituted the following Part:—

"PART I

1. Subject to Part III of this Schedule, where the mother of the child is alive the child's ordinary allowance shall be payable at the following rate:—

(*a*) where the father's last rank was not higher than that of sub-officer, £41·26 a year;

(*b*) where the father's last rank was higher than that of sub-officer but not higher than that of divisional officer (Grade I), £49·26 a year; or

(*c*) where the father's last rank was higher than that of divisional officer (Grade I), £60·96 a year.

2. Subject to Part III of this Schedule, where the father was the child's only surviving parent or in respect of the period after the death of the mother, the child's ordinary allowance shall be payable at the following rate:—

(*a*) where the father's last rank was not higher than that of sub-officer, £61·58 a year or such higher rate not exceeding £81·28 a year as the fire authority may from time to time determine;

(*b*) where the father's last rank was higher than that of sub-officer but not higher than that of divisional officer (Grade I), £73·27 a year or such higher rate not exceeding £97·29 a year as the fire authority may from time to time determine; or

(c) where the father's last rank was higher than that of divisional officer (Grade I), £91·13 a year, or such rate not exceeding £121·30 a year as the fire authority may from time to time determine.".".

(4) In paragraph 9 of Schedule 9 to the Scheme of 1964 and in paragraph 9 of Schedule 8 to the Scheme of 1956, in both cases as set out in the preceding paragraph, for the words "For Scheme I of Part II" there shall be substituted the words "For Scheme I of Part I".

R. Maudling,
One of Her Majesty's Principal
Secretaries of State.

9th August 1971.

Approval of the Minister for the Civil Service given under his Official Seal on 9th August 1971.

(L.S.)

J. E. Herbecq,
Authorised by the
Minister for the Civil Service.

EXPLANATORY NOTE
(This Note is not part of the Order.)

This Order contains amendments to the Firemen's Pension Schemes of 1971, 1966, 1964, 1956, 1952 and 1948 which appear necessary or expedient in connection with the passing of the Pensions (Increase) Act 1971. It comes into operation on 1st September 1971 (the date from which increases authorised by the Act of 1971 are payable).

The principal changes are described below.

The Schemes contain provisions for the increase of certain earnings related widows' and children's awards by reference to the Pensions (Increase) Act 1952 (c. 45). These awards will qualify for increases under the Pensions (Increase) Act 1971 which replace, *inter alia*, increases in accordance with the Act of 1952 and the Order revokes the provisions of the Schemes described above (Articles 5 to 15, 22, 31 and 37).

Under the Schemes the amounts of certain awards are determined by reference to specified flat-rates which, in some cases, are subject to provisions for their increase by reference to the Pensions (Increase) Act 1952. These awards do not qualify for increases under the Pensions (Increase) Act 1971. The Order increases these flat-rates and revokes the provisions of the Schemes described above (Articles 16, 17, 18, 23 to 26, 28 to 30, 32 and 38).

1971 No. 1330

PENSIONS

The Increase of Pensions (Police and Fire Services) Regulations 1971

Made - - - -	*9th August* 1971
Laid before Parliament	*19th August* 1971
Coming into Operation	*1st September* 1971

In exercise of the powers conferred on me by section 5(3) of the Pensions (Increase) Act 1971(a), I hereby, with the consent of the Minister for the Civil Service, make the following Regulations:—

Citation

1. These Regulations may be cited as the Increase of Pensions (Police and Fire Services) Regulations 1971.

Operation

2. These Regulations shall come into operation on 1st September 1971.

Interpretation

3.—(1) Any reference in these Regulations to any enactment or instrument shall be construed as including a reference to that enactment or instrument as amended by or under any other enactment or instrument.

(2) Any reference in any of these Regulations to a paragraph or to a Regulation shall be construed, unless the context otherwise requires, as a reference to a paragraph of that Regulation or, as the case may be, to a Regulation contained in these Regulations.

(3) In these Regulations the following expressions have the meanings hereby respectively assigned to them, that is to say:—

"the Firemen's Pension Scheme" means a scheme from time to time in force under section 26 of the Fire Services Act 1947(b);

"pension" includes an allowance;

"the Police Pensions Regulations" means the Regulations from time to time in force under the Police Pensions Act 1948(c);

(a) 1971 c. 56.   (b) 1947 c. 41.
(c) 1948 c. 24.

"the Police Cadets (Pensions) Regulations" means the Regulations from time to time in force under section 35 of the Police Act 1964(a) or under section 27 of the Police (Scotland) Act 1967(b);

"the principal Act" means the Pensions (Increase) Act 1971;

"the Special Constables (Pensions) Regulations" means the Regulations from time to time in force under section 34 of the Police Act 1964 or section 26 of the Police (Scotland) Act 1967.

Pensions reduced on account of additional benefit

4.—(1) This Regulation shall apply to a pension payable in accordance with—

(*a*) the Police Pensions Regulations;

(*b*) the Special Constables (Pensions) Regulations;

(*c*) the Police Cadets (Pensions) Regulations, or

(*d*) the Firemen's Pension Scheme,

which is reduced in amount or is not payable on account of the payment of some additional benefit.

(2) Subject to paragraphs (6) and (7), in relation to a pension to which this Regulation applies, the basic rate, the 1969 standard and the 1971 rate shall be calculated (where Regulation 5 applies, having regard to paragraphs (3) and (4) thereof) as if no additional benefit were payable and there shall be construed accordingly—

(*a*) the reference to the annual rate on 31st August 1971 in section 6(3) of the principal Act, and

(*b*) the reference to the annual rate in the definition of the expression "basic rate" in section 17(1) of the principal Act.

(3) Subject to paragraphs (6) and (7), where the permitted reduction in the amount of a pension to which this Regulation applies exceeds—

(*a*) the 1969 standard or the 1971 rate, whichever is the greater, in the case of a pension which began before the year 1969, or

(*b*) the basic rate of the pension in any other case,

(having regard to the provisions of these Regulations and, in particular, to paragraph (5)) section 1 of the principal Act shall have effect as if it were provided therein that the increase payable thereunder should be reduced by the excess.

(4) Subject to paragraph (6), where the permitted reduction in the amount of a pension to which this Regulation applies exceeds the basic rate of the pension as authorised to be increased as mentioned in subsection (6) of section 2 of the principal Act (having regard to the provisions of these Regulations and, in particular, to paragraph (5)) the said section 2 shall have effect as if it were provided therein that any increase provided for by an order thereunder should be reduced by the excess.

(a) 1964 c. 48.   (b) 1967 c. 77.

(5) For the purposes of paragraphs (3) and (4), without prejudice to paragraph (2), in determining the 1971 rate of the pension and in determining the basic rate of the pension as authorised to be increased as mentioned in paragraph (4) (in so far as that rate depends upon the 1971 rate) there shall be disregarded—

(a) any relevant increase (within the meaning of section 6 of the principal Act) payable to the pensioner on 31st August 1971 by reason that he had attained the age of 70 on or before that date, and

(b) the provisions of section 6(5) of the principal Act.

(6) If the modifications of the principal Act contained in paragraph (3) or, as the case may be, in paragraph (4) (in either case read with paragraphs (2) and (5)) would result in the increase of a pension under section 1, or the increase of a pension provided for by an order under section 2, being less than it would have been but for the modifications in question, then, for the purpose of calculating that increase, the said modifications shall not apply.

(7) If, in the case of a pension to which this Regulation applies, increases were in payment under the Pensions (Increase) Act 1956(a) or the Pensions (Increase) Act 1959(b) on 31st August 1971 and the increase of that pension under section 1 of the principal Act is less than those increases, the said section 1 shall, notwithstanding anything in the preceding provisions of this Regulation, have effect subject to such modifications as will secure that the increase thereunder is not less than those which would have been payable under the said Acts of 1956 and 1959 had the principal Act not been enacted.

(8) In this Regulation the expression "additional benefit" means—

(a) any benefit payable under the National Insurance Act 1965(c) together with any supplement thereto payable under section 2 of the National Insurance Act 1966(d);

(b) any benefit payable under the National Insurance (Industrial Injuries) Act 1965(e) together with any supplement payable therewith under the said section 2;

(c) any armed forces pension payable in pursuance of any Royal Warrant or other instrument;

(d) any family allowances payable under the Family Allowances Act 1965(f); or

(e) any payment of whatever nature, other than a pension payable as mentioned in paragraph (1) of this Regulation, which is made to the pensioner by a fire authority, by any other local authority or by a Minister of the Crown,

and the expression "permitted reduction" means the amount (expressed as an annual rate) by which a pension would fall to be reduced on account of the payment of additional benefit if the reduction were not limited by the size of the pension.

Police, special constabulary and police cadet supplemental pensions

5.—(1) This Regulation shall apply where a supplemental pension is payable in accordance with—

(a) the Police Pensions Regulations;

(b) the Special Constables (Pensions) Regulations; or

(c) the Police Cadets (Pensions) Regulations

(a) 1956 c. 39.   (b) 1959 c. 50.
(c) 1965 c. 51.   (d) 1966 c. 6.
(e) 1965 c. 52.   (f) 1965 c. 53.

whether or not the pension is reduced in amount or is not payable on account of the payment of some additional benefit within the meaning of Regulation 4.

(2) Section 3(2) of the principal Act shall have effect in relation to such a supplemental pension as if the pensioner had retired on account of physical or mental infirmity.

(3) Where, in accordance with the Regulations mentioned in paragraph (1)(*a*) or (*c*), the pensioner is entitled to some other pension, notwithstanding anything in those Regulations, the provisions of the principal Act and of Regulation 4 shall have effect (where paragraph (4) applies, subject to the provisions thereof) as if the supplemental pension and the other pension constituted separate awards.

(4) Where, in accordance with the Regulations mentioned in paragraph (1)(*a*), the pensioner is entitled to some other pension, for the purpose of ascertaining the 1971 rates of the supplemental and of the other pension under section 6 of the principal Act, the 1971 rate of the other pension shall be ascertained without regard to the supplemental pension but the difference between that rate and the 1971 rate of the combined pensions (where Regulation 4 applies to the supplemental pension, having regard to paragraph (2) thereof) shall be treated as the 1971 rate of the supplemental pension.

Flat-rate fire service pensions

6.—(1) This Regulation shall apply to a flat-rate pension which began, within the meaning of the principal Act, after the year 1943 and which is payable in accordance with—

(*a*) the Firemen's Pension Scheme, where in relation to the pension that Scheme is subject to the modifications set out in section 27(3) of the Fire Services Act 1947;

(*b*) the Fire Brigades Pensions Act 1925(**a**);

(*c*) the Police Pensions Act 1921(**b**)—

    (i) in respect of a person to whom the National Fire Service (Preservation of Pensions) (Police Firemen) Regulations 1941(**c**) applied at the time of his death or retirement; or

    (ii) as applied by the Leicester Fire Brigade Provisional Order Confirmation Act 1925(**d**); or

    (iii) as applied by section 80 of the Birmingham Corporation Act 1922(**e**);

(*d*) the Police Act 1890(**f**)—

    (i) as applied by section 13 of the Salford Improvement Act 1893(**g**); or

    (ii) as applied by section 63 of the Bolton Tramways and Improvement Act 1897(**h**); or

    (iii) as applied by section 187 of the Derby Corporation Act 1901(**i**); or

    (iv) as applied by section 50 of the Leicester Corporation Act 1908(**j**); or

    (v) as applied by section 46 of the Birmingham Corporation Act 1914(**k**);

(**a**) 1925 c. 47.   (**b**) 1921 c. 31.
(**c**) S.R. & O. 1941/1271 (1941 I, p. 328); and *see* S.R. & O. 1945/1649 (1945 I, p. 389).
(**d**) 1925 c. lxxvi.   (**e**) 1922 c. lxxvi.
(**f**) 1890 c. 45.   (**g**) 1893 c. xxxi.
(**h**) 1897 c. cxxxiv.   (**i**) 1901 c. cclxvii.
(**j**) 1908 c. lvi.   (**k**) 1914 c. cvi.

(e) regulations made under section 8 of the Metropolitan Fire Brigade Act 1865(a);

(f) regulations made under section 88 of the West Ham Corporation Act 1925(b).

(2) In relation to a pension to which this Regulation applies, section 8(2) of the principal Act shall have effect as if it provided that the pension should be deemed to have begun during the year 1943.

Fire service widows' and children's augmented awards

7.—(1) This Regulation shall apply to a gratuity payable in accordance with the Firemen's Pension Scheme which is comprised in a widow's augmented award or a child's special gratuity and, in either case, is computed, directly or indirectly, by reference to a rate of emoluments as at the date of the husband's or father's death.

(2) In relation to a gratuity to which this Regulation applies, where the husband or father had ceased to serve before he died, sections 8(2) and 9(2)(a) of the principal Act shall have effect as if they provided that the gratuity should be deemed to have begun on the day of his death.

R. Maudling,
One of Her Majesty's Principal
Secretaries of State.

9th August 1971.

Consent of the Minister for the Civil Service given under his Official Seal on 9th August 1971.

J. E. Herbecq,
Authorised by the
Minister for the Civil Service.

(L.S.)

EXPLANATORY NOTE

(This Note is not part of the Regulations.)

These Regulations provide that the provisions of the Pensions (Increase) Act 1971 shall apply in relation to certain police, special constabulary, police cadet and fire service pensions subject to modifications and adaptations.

Regulation 4 provides that in calculating the basic rate, the 1969 standard and the 1971 rate of a pension (by reference to which the amount of an increase under section 1, or under an order under section 2, of the Act of 1971 is determined)

(a) 1865 c. 90.   (b) 1925 c. cxii.

no account shall be taken of reductions in the pension made on account of the payment of certain national insurance and other additional benefits but that, in certain cases, the increase is to be abated on account of such payment.

Regulation 5 provides that where a police or police cadet award comprises a supplemental and some other pension, those pensions are to be increased separately.

Regulation 6 relates to certain flat-rate fire service pensions which are payable at basic rates laid down at various dates before 1944; it provides that they shall be treated (for the purpose of determining entitlement to, and the amount of, increases) as having begun in 1943.

Regulation 7 relates to certain widows' and children's gratuities computed by reference to a rate of emoluments at the date of the husband's or father's death; it provides that they shall be treated (for the like purpose) as having begun on the day of his death.

STATUTORY   INSTRUMENTS

1971 No. 1331

SOCIAL SECURITY

The Supplementary Benefit (Claims and Payments)
Amendment Regulations 1971

Made - - - -	11th August 1971
Laid before Parliament	20th August 1971
Coming into Operation	20th September 1971

The Secretary of State for Social Services, in exercise of the powers conferred
by paragraph 2(3) of Schedule 2 to the Ministry of Social Security Act 1966(a),
as modified by regulation 2(2) of the Supplementary Benefit (Decimalisation of
the Currency) Regulations 1970(b), and all other powers enabling him in that
behalf, hereby makes the following regulations:—

Citation, interpretation and commencement

1. These regulations, which may be cited as the Supplementary Benefit
(Claims and Payments) Amendment Regulations 1971, shall be read as one with
the Supplementary Benefit (Claims and Payments) Regulations 1966(c), as
amended (d) (hereinafter referred to as "the principal regulations"), and shall
come into operation on 20th September 1971.

Regulation substituted for regulation 12 of the principal regulations

2. For regulation 12 of the principal regulations there shall be substituted
the following regulation—

"12.—(1) For the purposes of paragraph 2(3) of Schedule 2 to the Act
(aggregation of benefit and such other payments as may be prescribed by the
Secretary of State), the other payments there referred to shall be payments
under the National Insurance Act 1965(e) of unemployment benefit and the
benefits mentioned in sub-paragraph (5) of this regulation (hereinafter
referred to as "the relevant benefits") and the said paragraph 2(3) shall
apply in the following circumstances—

(*a*) where the Secretary of State has arranged for the unemployment
benefit and the benefit under the Act to be paid together whether in
cash or by instrument of payment; or

(*b*) subject to the following provisions of this regulation, where the
Secretary of State has arranged, or the Commission are satisfied that
he will as soon as practicable arrange, for any of the relevant benefits
to be so paid together with benefit under the Act.

(a) 1966 c. 20.　　　　　　　　　　(b) S.I. 1970/1784 (1970 III, p. 5793).
(c) S.I. 1966/1067 (1966 II, p. 2622).
(d) The relevant amending instruments are S.I. 1967/422, 1969/1169, 1970/1784 (1967 I,
　　p. 1362; 1969 II, p. 3438; 1970 III, p. 5793).
(e) 1965 c. 51.

(2) Where any one or more of the relevant benefits and any benefit under the Act were being paid separately to a beneficiary immediately before the date on which sub-paragraph (b) of the foregoing paragraph would otherwise apply in his case, that sub-paragraph shall not apply unless or until the determination with respect to the amount of his benefit under the Act is reviewed.

(3) Where the said sub-paragraph (b) applies in the case of a beneficiary and by reason of an election by him or otherwise his relevant benefit or benefits and his benefit under the Act cease to be paid together, the said sub-paragraph shall continue to apply in his case unless or until the determination with respect to the amount of the benefit under the Act is reviewed.

(4) The said sub-paragraph (b) shall not apply to any case where the Commission are satisfied that there are exceptional circumstances which make its application inappropriate.

(5) For the purposes of this regulation "relevant benefits" means the following benefits under the National Insurance Act 1965—

  (a) retirement pension;

  (b) age addition;

  (c) attendance allowance."

Regulations revoked

3. The Supplementary Benefit (Claims and Payments) Amendment Regulations 1967(a) are hereby revoked.

Signed by authority of the Secretary of State for Social Services.

Paul Dean,
Parliamentary Under Secretary of State,
Department of Health and Social Security.

11th August 1971.

EXPLANATORY NOTE

(This Note is not part of the Regulations.)

These Regulations amend the Supplementary Benefit (Claims and Payments) Regulations 1966. They add age addition and attendance allowance to unemployment benefit and retirement pension as payments which are to be aggregated with benefit under the Ministry of Social Security Act 1966 for the purpose of rounding the latter to the nearest 5p. The Supplementary Benefit (Claims and Payments) Amendment Regulations 1967 are revoked.

(a) S.I. 1967/422 (1967 I, p. 1362).

STATUTORY INSTRUMENTS

1971 No. 1332 (C.34)

SOCIAL SECURITY

The National Insurance Act 1971 (Commencement No. 2)
Order 1971

Made - - -	11*th August* 1971
Laid before Parliament	19*th August* 1971
Coming into Operation	23*rd August* 1971

The Secretary of State for Social Services in exercise of powers conferred by
section 16(3) of and paragraph 1 of Schedule 6 to the National Insurance Act
1971**(a)** and of all other powers enabling him in that behalf, hereby makes the
following Order:—

Citation and commencement

1. This Order may be cited as the National Insurance Act 1971 (Commencement No. 2) Order 1971 and shall come into operation on 23rd August 1971.

Appointed day

2. The day appointed for the coming into force of paragraphs (*a*) and (*b*)
of section 16(1) (citation with certain other Acts) of the National Insurance
Act 1971 shall be 23rd August 1971.

Signed by authority of the Secretary of State for Social Services.

Paul Dean,
Parliamentary Under Secretary of State,
Department of Health and Social Security.

11th August 1971.

(a) 1971 c. 50.

STATUTORY INSTRUMENTS

1971 No. 1333

DISTRESS

The Distress for Rent (Amendment) Rules 1971

Made - - - -	6*th August* 1971
Coming into Operation	1*st September* 1971

The Lord Chancellor, in the exercise of the powers conferred on him by section 8 of the Law of Distress Amendment Act 1888(a), hereby makes the following Rules:—

1.—(1) These Rules may be cited as the Distress for Rent (Amendment) Rules 1971 and shall come into operation on 1st September 1971.

(2) Rule 2 of these Rules shall not apply in respect of a distress levied before the coming into operation of these Rules.

(3) The Interpretation Act 1889(b) shall apply to the interpretation of these Rules as it applies to the interpretation of an Act of Parliament.

2. The Distress for Rent Rules 1953(c) shall be amended by deleting Appendix I and Form 5 (Back) in Appendix II and substituting Appendix 1 and Form 5 (Back) set out in the Schedule to these Rules.

Dated 6th August 1971.

Hailsham of St. Marylebone, C.

SCHEDULE

APPENDIX 1

TABLE OF FEES CHARGES AND EXPENSES

1. For levying distress—

    (i) where the sum demanded and due does not exceed £20 ...   75p

    (ii) where the sum demanded and due exceeds £20 ... ...   5% on the first £100, 2½% on the next £400, 1½% on any additional sum.

(a) 1888 c. 21.
(b) 1889 c. 63.
(c) S.I. 1953/1702 (1953 I, p. 574).

2. For taking possession—

    (i) where a man is left in physical possession ... ... £1 per day

    (ii) where walking possession is taken ... ... 25p per day

Notes: The charge for walking possession is payable only if a walking possession agreement in Form 6 has been signed by the tenant.

A man left in possession must provide his own board in every case.

The possession fee is payable in respect of the day on which the distress is levied, but a fee for physical possession must not be charged where a walking possession agreement is signed at the time when the distress is levied.

3. For appraisement, where the tenant or owner of the goods by writing requires such appraisement to be made, 5p on every £2 of the value as appraised, whether by one broker or more, with a minimum fee of £1 for each broker; the costs of the appraisement are to be borne by the tenant or owner requiring it.

4. For removal, the reasonable costs and charges attending the removal; the costs and charges are subject to taxation under Rule 20.

5. For sale—

    (i) where the sale is held on the auctioneer's premises, for commission to the auctioneer, an inclusive charge to include all out-of-pocket expenses except costs of removal:—

        on the first £100 ... ... £15·00 per cent.
        on the next £900 ... ... £12·50 per cent.
        above £1,000 ... ... £10·00 per cent.

    (ii) where the sale is held on the debtor's premises, for commission to the auctioneer, in addition to out-of-pocket expenses actually and reasonably incurred, $7\frac{1}{2}$ per cent, on the sum realised.

6. Reasonable fees, charges and expenses, where distress is withdrawn or where no sale takes place, and for negotiations between landlord and tenant respecting the distress, subject to taxation under Rule 20.

7. For the purpose of calculating any percentage charges a fraction of £1 will be reckoned as £1 but any fraction of a penny in the total amount of the fee so calculated shall be disregarded.

APPENDIX 2

FORMS

FORM 5 (*Back*)

Scale of Fees

A bailiff authorised to levy a distress for rent is entitled to the following fees, charges and expenses:

1. For levying distress—

    (i) where the sum demanded and due does not exceed £20 ... 75p

    (ii) where the sum demanded and due exceeds £20 ... ... 5% on the first £100, $2\frac{1}{2}$% on the next £400, $1\frac{1}{2}$% on any additional sum.

2. For taking possession of the goods—
  (i) where a man is left in physical possession ... ... £1 per day
  (ii) where walking possession is taken ... ... 25p per day

Note: The charge for walking possession is payable only if a walking possession agreement has been signed by the tenant.

A man left in possession must provide his own board in every case.

The possession fee is payable in respect of the day on which the distress is levied, but a fee for physical possession must not be charged where a walking possession agreement is signed at the time when the distress is levied.

3. In addition the following fees, charges and expenses may become payable by you if the goods are removed from the premises or sold:—

  (*a*) for appraisement, where the tenant or owner of the goods by writing requires such appraisement to be made, 5p on every £2 of the value as appraised, whether by one broker or more, with a minimum fee of £1 for each broker;

  (*b*) for removal, the reasonable costs and charges attending the removal;

  (*c*) for sale:—

    (i) where the sale is held on the auctioneer's premises, for commission to the auctioneer, an inclusive charge to include all out-of-pocket expenses except costs of removal:—

      on the first £100 ... ... £15·00 per cent.
      on the next £900 ... ... £12·50 per cent.
      above £1,000 ... ... £10·00 per cent.

    (ii) where the sale is held on the debtor's premises, for commission to the auctioneer, in addition to out-of-pocket expenses actually and reasonably incurred, 7½ per cent. on the sum realised:

  (*d*) reasonable fees, charges and expenses, where distress is withdrawn or where no sale takes place, and for negotiations between landlord and tenant respecting the distress.

Note: For the purpose of calculating any percentage charges a fraction of £1 will be reckoned as £1 but any fraction of a penny in the total amount of the fee so calculated shall be disregarded.

EXPLANATORY NOTE

(This Note is not part of the Rules.)

These Rules amend the fees, charges and expenses recoverable in respect of the levying of distress for rent under the Distress for Rent Rules 1953. Revised fees are prescribed and a single scale replaces the two separate scales for amounts not exceeding and exceeding £20.

STATUTORY INSTRUMENTS

1971 No. 1335 (C. 35)

ROAD TRAFFIC

The Road Traffic Act 1962 (Commencement No. 7) Order 1971

Made - - - *10th August* 1971

The Secretary of State for the Environment, in exercise of his powers under section 52(3) of the Road Traffic Act 1962(a) and of all other enabling powers, hereby makes the following Order:—

1. Section 41 of the Road Traffic Act 1962 shall come into operation on 1st October 1971.

2. This Order may be cited as the Road Traffic Act 1962 (Commencement No. 7) Order 1971.

Signed by authority of
the Secretary of State.
10th August 1971.

L. E. Dale,
An Under Secretary in the
Department of the Environment.

EXPLANATORY NOTE

(*This Note is not part of the Order.*)

This Order brings into operation on 1st October 1971 section 41 of the Road Traffic Act 1962 which empowers the Secretary of State for the Environment to make regulations requiring, subject to any exceptions specified in the Regulations, persons driving or riding (otherwise than in side-cars) on motor cycles to wear protective headgear.

(a) 1962 c. 59.

STATUTORY INSTRUMENTS

1971 No. 1348

CUSTOMS AND EXCISE

The Anti-Dumping (Provisional Charge to Duty) (No. 3) (Amendment) Order 1971

Made - - -	12*th August* 1971
Laid before the House of Commons	19*th August* 1971
Coming into Operation	20*th August* 1971

The Secretary of State, in exercise of the powers conferred upon him by sections 1, 2, 8, 9(3) and 15(4) of the Customs Duties (Dumping and Subsidies) Act 1969(**a**), hereby makes the following Order :—

1. This Order may be cited as the Anti-Dumping (Provisional Charge to Duty) (No. 3) (Amendment) Order 1971 and shall come into operation on 20th August 1971.

2. The Anti-Dumping (Provisional Charge to Duty) (No. 3) Order 1971(**b**) shall have effect as if in the Schedule thereto—

    (*a*) for the words "Wood chipboard without surface lamination" there were substituted "Wood chipboard without surface lamination of a thickness exceeding 8 millimetres, other than integrally tongued and grooved chipboard (whether or not rebated) of a thickness not less than 18 millimetres and not more than 22 millimetres" ; and

    (*b*) after paragraph (*f*) there were added—

"(*g*) originating in Portugal and being a product of Joao Marques Pinto & Cia Lda or Sociadade de Iniciativa e Approveitamentos Florestais SARL.	£2·00 per cubic metre".

Anthony Grant,
Parliamentary Under Secretary of State,
Department of Trade and Industry.

12th August 1971.

(**a**) 1969 c. 16.   (**b**) S.I. 1971/1075 (1971 II, p. 3206).

EXPLANATORY NOTE

(This Note is not part of the Order.)

This Order amends the Anti-Dumping (Provisional Charge to Duty) (No. 3) Order 1971, which imposed a provisional charge in respect of an anti-dumping duty on the import of wood chipboard without surface lamination of various origins.

The provisional charge imposed by that Order will now only apply to wood chipboard of the description mentioned in Article 2(*a*) of this Order, but it will also apply to wood chipboard of that description originating in Portugal and produced by the companies mentioned in Article 2(*b*).

STATUTORY INSTRUMENTS

1971 No. 1352
MERCHANT SHIPPING
SAFETY

The Merchant Shipping (Load Lines) (Fees) (Amendment No. 2) Regulations 1971

Made - - - -	10th August 1971
Laid before Parliament	17th August 1971
Coming into Operation	18th August 1971

The Secretary of State, with the approval of the Treasury and in exercise of his powers under section 26 of the Merchant Shipping (Load Lines) Act 1967(a) and of all other powers enabling him in that behalf, hereby makes the following Regulations :—

1.—(1) These Regulations may be cited as the Merchant Shipping (Load Lines) (Fees) (Amendment No. 2) Regulations 1971 and shall come into operation on 18th August 1971.

(2) The Interpretation Act 1889(b) shall apply to the interpretation of these Regulations as it applies to the interpretation of an Act of Parliament.

2.—(1) The Merchant Shipping (Load Lines) (Fees) Regulations 1968(c), as amended(d), shall have effect subject to the further amendment that except as provided in paragraph (2) of this Regulation the fee payable in respect of a survey or periodical inspection of a ship shall be one half of that payable in respect of that service immediately before the coming into operation of these Regulations.

(2) Paragraph (1) of this Regulation shall not apply in relation to—

(a) any survey or inspection started before 1st May 1971, or

(b) any additional fee payable by virtue of paragraph 5 or paragraph 6 of Part II of the Schedule to the Merchant Shipping (Load Lines) (Fees) Regulations 1968 as so amended.

Anthony Grant,
Parliamentary Under Secretary of State,
Department of Trade and Industry.

9th August 1971.

We approve the making of these Regulations.

Walter Clegg,
P. L. Hawkins,
Two of the Lords Commissioners of
Her Majesty's Treasury.

10th August 1971.

(a) 1967 c. 27.
(b) 1889 c. 63.
(c) S.I. 1968/1117 (1968 II, p. 3072).
(d) S.I. 1971/644 (1971 I, p. 1706).

EXPLANATORY NOTE

(This Note is not part of the Regulations.)

These Regulations amend the Merchant Shipping (Load Lines) (Fees) Regulations 1968, as amended by the Merchant Shipping (Load Lines) (Fees) (Amendment) Regulations 1971. With specified exceptions, the fees payable under the 1968 Regulations as so amended for surveys and inspections carried out in pursuance of the Merchant Shipping (Load Lines) Act 1967 and the Rules made thereunder are reduced by one half.

STATUTORY INSTRUMENTS

1971 No. 1353

MERCHANT SHIPPING

The Merchant Shipping (Fees) (Amendment No. 2) Regulations 1971

Made - - - -	10*th August* 1971
Laid before Parliament	17*th August* 1971
Coming into Operation	18*th August* 1971

The Secretary of State, with the approval of the Treasury and in exercise of his powers under section 33 of the Merchant Shipping (Safety Convention) Act 1949(**a**) as extended by section 2(4) of the Merchant Shipping Act 1964(**b**) and of all other powers enabling him in that behalf, hereby makes the following Regulations:—

1.—(1) These Regulations may be cited as the Merchant Shipping (Fees) (Amendment No. 2) Regulations 1971 and shall come into operation on 18th August 1971.

(2) The Interpretation Act 1889(**c**) shall apply to the interpretation of these Regulations as it applies to the interpretation of an Act of Parliament.

2. The Merchant Shipping (Fees) Regulations 1971(**d**), as amended(**e**), shall have effect subject to the further amendment that, except in a case to which paragraph (3) of Regulation 2 thereof applies, the fee or maximum fee, as the case may be, payable in respect of any service specified in Parts 1 to 6, 8 to 11 and 21 of the Schedule thereto shall be one half of that payable in respect of the service immediately before the coming into operation of these Regulations.

Anthony Grant,
Parliamentary Under Secretary of State,
Department of Trade and Industry.

9th August 1971.

We approve the making of these Regulations.

Walter Clegg,
P. L. Hawkins,
Two of the Lords Commissioners
of Her Majesty's Treasury.

10th August 1971.

(a) 1949 c. 43.   (b) 1964 c. 47.   (c) 1889 c. 63.
(d) S.I. 1971/643 (1971 I, p. 1686).   (e) S.I. 1971/1003 (1971 II, p. 2947).

EXPLANATORY NOTE

(This Note is not part of the Regulations.)

These Regulations amend the Merchant Shipping (Fees) Regulations 1971 as amended. They reduce by one half the amount of fees payable under those Regulations for surveys, inspections and the issue of certificates for safety purposes and for tonnage measurement.

STATUTORY INSTRUMENTS

1971 No. 1354

REGISTRATION OF BIRTHS, DEATHS, MARRIAGES, ETC.

ENGLAND AND WALES

The Removal of Bodies (Amendment) Regulations 1971

Made - - - *12th August* 1971

Coming into Operation *1st October* 1971

The Secretary of State for Social Services, in exercise of his powers under section 9 of the Births and Deaths Registration Act 1926(**a**), and of all other powers enabling him in that behalf, with the concurrence of the Secretary of State for the Home Department, hereby makes the following regulations :—

Title and commencement

1. These regulations may be cited as the Removal of Bodies (Amendment) Regulations 1971 and shall come into operation on 1st October 1971.

Interpretation

2.—(1) In these regulations the expression "the principal regulations" means the Removal of Bodies Regulations 1954(**b**).

(2) The Interpretation Act 1889(**c**), applies to the interpretation of these regulations as it applies to the interpretation of an Act of Parliament.

Endorsement of certificate for cremation

3. For regulation 5(2) of the principal regulations (which provides for the coroner's endorsement of the certificate for cremation where notice is given of intention to cremate the body in Scotland or the Channel Islands) there shall be substituted the following paragraph :—

"(2) Any coroner's order for burial or certificate for cremation sent to the coroner under regulation 4 of these regulations shall be retained by him unless he is notified in writing by the person wishing to remove the body out of England that it is intended that the body shall be cremated in Scotland, Northern Ireland, the Channel Islands or the Isle of Man, in which case the coroner shall endorse the certificate with words to the effect that it shall henceforth be valid only for cremation in Scotland, Northern Ireland, the Channel Islands or the Isle of Man, as the case may be, and return it to the person receiving the acknowledgement of the receipt of notice under sub-paragraph (*a*) of paragraph (1) of this regulation."

(**a**) 1926 c. 48.   (**b**) S.I. 1954/448 (1954 II, p. 1915).   (**c**) 1889 c. 63.

Notice of intention to remove a body out of England

4. For the first schedule to the principal regulations (which sets out the form of notice of intention to remove a body out of England) there shall be substituted the following schedule :—

FIRST SCHEDULE

FORM OF NOTICE TO A CORONER OF INTENTION TO REMOVE A BODY OUT OF ENGLAND

To the Coroner for ....

....

I/We ....

of (full postal address)...

....

in pursuance of section 4 of the Births and Deaths Registration Act 1926, hereby give you notice that I/we intend to remove out of England the body, now lying within your jurisdiction at ....

....

(Here state address or place where body is lying)

of .... deceased, who

died at (or whose body was found at) ....

.... on ....

— and I/we deliver herewith the certificate for disposal given by the registrar of births and deaths.*

— and I/we deliver herewith the coroner's order for burial or certificate for cremation of the deceased.*

— and I/we declare that it is intended to remove the body to Scotland/Northern Ireland/the Channel Islands/the Isle of Man and to cremate it there.*

— and I/we declare that to the best of my/our knowledge and belief no certificate for disposal has been given by a registrar of births and deaths in England or Wales and no coroner's order for burial or certificate for cremation has been issued.*

— and I/we declare that the death took place out of England and Wales.*

† You are requested to send any communication regarding this notice to:—

    (Name) ....

    Full postal address ....

    Signature of person giving notice ....

    Date......................

---

*Delete where inapplicable.

†This paragraph is for use only where the person giving notice desires the coroner's acknowledgment to be sent to some other person.

Signed by authority of the Secretary of State for Social Services.

Aberdare,
Minister of State,
Department of Health and Social Security.

6th August 1971.

I concur,

R. Maudling,
Secretary of State for the Home Department.

12th August 1971.

EXPLANATORY NOTE

(This Note is not part of the Regulations.)

The principal regulations require notice to be given to a coroner by a person intending to remove a body out of England and require the coroner to endorse a cremation certificate to make it valid for cremation in Scotland or the Channel Islands. These regulations provide for a coroner to make a cremation certificate valid for cremation in Northern Ireland or the Isle of Man. They also provide that the notice shall state to which country it is intended to remove the body.

STATUTORY INSTRUMENTS

1971 No. 1356

CUSTOMS AND EXCISE

The Temporary Importation (Magnetic Tapes) Regulations 1971

Made - - -	16th *August* 1971
Laid before Parliament	23rd *August* 1971
Coming into Operation	1st *September* 1971

The Commissioners of Customs and Excise, in exercise of the powers conferred upon them by section 40 of the Customs and Excise Act 1952(a) and of all other powers enabling them in that behalf, hereby make the following Regulations :—

1. These Regulations may be cited as the Temporary Importation (Magnetic Tapes) Regulations 1971 and shall come into operation on the 1st September 1971.

2.—(1) In these Regulations "officer" means the proper officer of Customs and Excise.

(2) The Interpretation Act 1889(b) applies for the interpretation of these Regulations as it applies for the interpretation of an Act of Parliament.

3.—(1) Subject to paragraph (2) of this Regulation, the goods to which these Regulations apply are magnetic recording media, which consist essentially of material with magnetic properties, with or without mechanical carrying or supporting material not having magnetic properties, and which are designed for the retention thereon, and recognition therefrom, of a magnetic record, and are such that any magnetic record thereon can be amended or erased at will.

(2) The goods to which these Regulations apply may carry recordings or not as the case may be, but any goods carrying recordings of sound or visual phenomena shall not be entitled to relief if such goods are of a kind produced in quantity for general sale as so recorded.

4. If any goods to which these Regulations apply are imported into the United Kingdom and the importer satisfies the Commissioners that—

(*a*) the goods are being imported only temporarily for use, for recording, or for any recording thereon to be amended or erased ;

(*b*) the goods will thereafter be exported in the same state, fair wear and tear excepted, as they were in when imported, the making, amendment or erasure of any recording thereon being disregarded in this connection ; and

---

(**a**) 1952 c. 44.   (**b**) 1889 c. 63.

(c) the following provisions of these Regulations will be complied with, the goods may be delivered without payment of duty, and duty shall not be payable so long as the Commissioners continue to be so satisfied.

5. The importer shall at the time of importation—

(a) produce the goods to the officer for examination, and

(b) deposit such sum of money or give such other security as the officer may require to secure the duty and compliance with these Regulations.

6. Goods delivered without payment of duty under these Regulations shall not be, nor be offered to be, sold or otherwise disposed of to a person in the United Kingdom.

7. The importer or other person having charge of the goods shall—

(a) keep such records relating to the goods and their use in the United Kingdom as the officer may require, and

(b) at any time furnish to the officer such information relating to the goods as the officer may require, and produce all such records as he may have been required to keep and such other documents relating to the goods as the officer may require.

8. The goods shall be exported from the United Kingdom not later than three months from the date of their importation, or within such further period as the Commissioners may in any particular case allow.

Provided that, upon prior application being made to them by the importer, the Commissioners may, subject to such conditions as they see fit to impose, permit the goods to be disposed of otherwise than by exportation.

16th August 1971.

C. H. Blake,
Commissioner of Customs and Excise.

King's Beam House,
Mark Lane,
London, E.C.3. 7H.E.

EXPLANATORY NOTE

(*This Note is not part of the Regulations.*)

These Regulations provide for the temporary importation without payment of customs duty of certain magnetic tapes and other similar magnetic recording media, whether carrying recordings or not.

STATUTORY INSTRUMENTS

1971 No. 1357

CUSTOMS AND EXCISE

The Anti-Dumping (Provisional Charge to Duty) (No. 4) Order 1971

Made - - - -	16*th August* 1971
Laid before the	
House of Commons	23*rd August* 1971
Coming into Operation	24*th August* 1971

The Secretary of State, in exercise of the powers conferred upon him by sections 1, 2, 8 and 9(3) of the Customs Duties (Dumping and Subsidies) Act 1969(**a**), hereby makes the following Order: —

1. This Order may be cited as the Anti-Dumping (Provisional Charge to Duty) (No. 4) Order 1971 and shall come into operation on 24th August 1971.

2. Goods of the description set out in the Schedule hereto (being goods classified in the Customs Tariff 1959(**b**) under the heading mentioned in the first column of that Schedule) shall be subject to a provisional charge to duty in respect of a duty of customs at the rate set out in the third column of that Schedule.

3. Section 2 of the Customs Duties (Dumping and Subsidies) Act 1969 (which allows relief to be given where goods are shown not to have been dumped or where the margin of dumping is less than the provisional charge) shall apply to the provisional charge imposed by this Order.

> *Michael Noble,*
> Minister for Trade,
> Department of Trade and Industry.

16th August 1971.

SCHEDULE

Relevant Tariff Heading	Description of Goods	Relevant Rate
Ex 28.21(B)	Chromic anhydride (CrO_3) originating in the Union of Soviet Socialist Republics.	£50 per ton

(**a**) 1969 c. 16.   (**b**) See S.I. 1970/1522 (1970 III, p. 4935).

EXPLANATORY NOTE

(This Note is not part of the Order.)

This Order imposes a provisional charge in respect of an anti-dumping duty on imports of chromic anhydride (also known as chromium trioxide or chromic acid) originating in the Union of Soviet Socialist Republics.

The making of the Order enables the Commissioners of Customs and Excise to require security for the payment of any anti-dumping duty which may be imposed retrospectively on such imports. A retrospective duty may only be imposed on goods imported while the Order is in force, and its rate may not exceed the rate mentioned in the Schedule.

The Order expires automatically after three months unless previously revoked or extended (for not more than three months) by a further Order.

STATUTORY INSTRUMENTS

1971 No. 1358

IRON AND STEEL

The Iron and Steel (Pension Schemes) (Transfer) Regulations 1971

Made - - -	16*th August* 1971
Laid before Parliament	24*th August* 1971
Coming into Operation	1*st September* 1971

The Secretary of State in exercise of his powers under section 40 of the Iron and Steel Act 1949(a), as revived and amended by section 31 of the Iron and Steel Act 1967(b), and all other powers in that behalf enabling him, after consultation with the British Steel Corporation and such organisations as appear to him to be representative of persons concerned, hereby makes the following regulations:—

Citation and commencement

1.—(1) These regulations may be cited as the Iron and Steel (Pension Schemes) (Transfer) Regulations 1971, shall come into operation on 1st September 1971 and, subject to paragraph (2) hereof, shall have effect from that date.

(2) Regulation 5 shall have effect from 1st May 1970 in respect of the Schemes specified in Part 1 of the Schedule hereto and from 1st July 1970 in respect of the Schemes specified in Part 2 of that Schedule.

2.—(1) In these regulations—

"pension" has the meaning assigned thereto by the Iron and Steel Act 1949;

"pension fund" in relation to a scheduled scheme means all investments and moneys which, or the income from which, can be applied at the date of the coming into operation of these regulations for the purposes of paying pensions;

"pension rights" has the meaning assigned thereto by the Iron and Steel Act 1949;

"the principal scheme" means the British Steel Corporation Staff Superannuation Scheme approved by the Minister of Power on 7th July 1969;

"scheduled scheme" means a pension scheme specified in the Schedule hereto.

(2) The Interpretation Act 1889(c) shall apply to the interpretation of these regulations as it applies to the interpretation of an Act of Parliament.

Transfer of Pension Funds of, and Policies of Assurance relating to scheduled schemes

3.—(1) The pension fund of each of the scheduled schemes, and every right of trustees of a scheduled scheme to receive moneys on the occurrence of certain events by virtue of a policy of assurance held for the purposes of that scheme together with every obligation of the trustees under that policy, shall on these

---

(a) 1949 c. 72.   (b) 1967 c. 17.   (c) 1889 c. 63.

regulations coming into operation be transferred by virtue of these regulations and without further assurance to the trustees of the principal scheme.

(2) The pension funds aforesaid and the moneys received in respect of the said rights together with the pension fund constituted under the principal scheme shall be invested and managed as one fund in accordance with the provisions of the principal scheme relating to the investment and management of the pension fund established under the principal scheme.

4.—(1) A certificate, signed by a trustee of the principal scheme and by any person in whom the pension fund or any part thereof or a right as aforesaid transferred by these regulations was vested, that the pension fund or that part or that right was so transferred, or a copy of the said certificate certified by a trustee of the principal scheme to be a true copy thereof, shall be received by all persons responsible for the registration or inscription of the title to the pension fund or that part thereof or by the assurers, as the case may be, as evidence that it was transferred as aforesaid.

(2) Every person in whom was vested the pension fund or any part thereof or a right transferred as aforesaid shall do all things necessary, or which the trustees of the principal scheme may require to be done, for the purpose of ensuring—

(a) the due registration or inscription of the title of the trustees of the principal scheme to the pension fund or transfer of the right, as the case may be;

(b) the delivery to the said trustees of any document constituting evidence of the said registration, inscription or transfer; and

(c) the receipt by the said trustees of all dividends or interest in respect of the pension fund so transferred due for payment after the date of the coming into operation of these regulations.

Provisions of scheduled schemes

5.—(1) The provisions of a scheduled scheme which relate to eligibility for the payment of benefits and which provide for the payment of contributions shall continue in effect, except that all payments of benefits due under those provisions (including those outstanding immediately before 1st May 1970 in the case of the Schemes specified in Part 1 of the Schedule hereto and those outstanding immediately before 1st July 1970 in the case of the Schemes specified in Part 2 of that Schedule) shall be made by the trustees of the principal scheme from the fund constituted by regulation 3 and all contributions due under those provisions (including those outstanding immediately before 1st May 1970 in the case of the Schemes specified in Part 1 of the Schedule hereto and those outstanding immediately before 1st July 1970 in the case of the Schemes specified in Part 2 of that Schedule) shall be made to the said trustees for payment into the said fund.

(2) Any power or discretion to pay a benefit conferred by the provisions of a scheduled scheme on any person shall be exercisable by the trustees of the principal scheme in place of the person invested with that power or discretion by the scheduled scheme.

(3) Any trustee of a scheduled scheme who would but for the operation of these regulations have been entitled to payment of a sum by way of an indemnity from the pension fund of that scheme shall be so entitled from the fund constituted by regulation 3, and the trustees of the principal scheme shall accordingly pay him that sum.

(4) Except as provided by this regulation the provisions of a scheduled scheme shall cease to have effect.

Elections under principal scheme

6.—(1) This regulation applies to an election made by a member of a scheduled scheme under a provision of the principal scheme to receive benefits provided for in the principal scheme instead of benefits provided for in the scheduled scheme.

(2) The trustees of the principal scheme shall ensure that an election to which this regulation applies shall not operate so as to place any person (other than the person exercising the election) having pension rights under the scheduled scheme in any worse position by reason of the exercise of the election, and the said trustee shall make such payments to that person as may be necessary to secure that result.

Dated 16th August 1971.

John Eden,
Minister for Industry,
Department of Trade and Industry.

<hr>

SCHEDULE

Regulation 2(1)

PART 1

William Robertson Limited Staff Pension Fund and Life Assurance Scheme (1956)
William Robertson Limited Staff Pension and Life Assurance Scheme (1944)

PART 2

Lancashire Steel Corporation and Associated Companies Pension Scheme

Lancashire Steel Corporation and Associated Companies Supplementary Pension Scheme.

Lancashire Steel Corporation Limited and Associated Companies Widows' Pension Scheme

Lancashire Steel Corporation Limited Staff Life Insurance and Pension Scheme

Whitecross Company Limited Staff Life Insurance and Pension Scheme

Rylands Brothers Limited Staff Life Insurance and Pension Scheme

Pearson and Knowles Engineering Company Limited Staff Life Insurance and Pension Scheme

Wigan Coal Corporation Limited Staff Life Insurance and Pension Scheme

Penfold Fencing and Engineering Company Limited Staff Life Insurance and Pension Scheme

John Summers and Sons Limited and Subsidiary Companies Staff Pension Fund and Assurance Scheme (Male)

John Summers and Sons Limited and Subsidiary Companies Staff Pension and Assurance Scheme (Female)

John Summers and Sons and Subsidiary Companies Pension and Assurance Scheme (1936)

Wolverhampton Corrugated Iron Company Limited Pension and Assurance Scheme (1936)

Pension Scheme of Shelton Iron, Steel and Coal Company Limited and its Subsidiaries (1936)

Staff Pension Scheme of the Staffordshire Chemical Company (1917) Limited

John Summers and Sons Limited and Subsidiaries Senior Executives Staff Pension and Assurance Scheme (1962)

John Summers and Sons Limited Special Staff Pension and Assurance Scheme

John Summers and Sons Limited Supplementary Pension and Life Assurance Scheme for Executive Officials and Salaried Directors (1946)

John Summers and Sons Limited Additional Pension and Assurance Scheme for Executive Officials and Salaried Directors (1949)

EXPLANATORY NOTE

(This Note is not part of the Regulations.)

These regulations provide for the transfer to the Trustees of the British Steel Corporation Staff Superannuation Scheme of the assets and liabilities of those pension schemes listed in the Schedule.

All the pension funds relating to the scheduled schemes, and the rights of the Trustees to receive payments under assurance policies held for the purposes of the schemes, are to be transferred to the Trustees of the Corporation's scheme and the pension funds and monies received under those policies, together with the Corporation's scheme pension fund, are to be administered as one fund (regulation 3). Transfer certificates are to be given to those responsible for effecting the transfers and all documents relating to the scheduled schemes are to be delivered to the Trustees of the Corporation's scheme (regulation 4). The provisions of the scheduled schemes which relate to eligibility for the payment of benefits and contributions are, with the exceptions specified, to continue to have effect from 1st May 1970 in the case of those schemes listed in Part 1 of the Schedule and from 1st July 1970 in the case of those schemes listed in Part 2 thereof, but the other provisions are to cease to have effect from those dates (regulation 5). A member of a scheduled scheme may elect to receive benefits provided under the Corporation's scheme instead of those provided under his old scheme. The Trustees of the Corporation's scheme are required to ensure that no person other than the member making such an election is placed in a worse position as a result of that election (regulation 6).

STATUTORY INSTRUMENTS

1971 No. 1366

TAXES

The Capital Gains Tax (Exempt Gilt-edged Securities) (No. 2) Order 1971

Made -   -   -   -   16*th August* 1971

The Treasury, in exercise of the powers conferred on them by section 41(2) of the Finance Act 1969(a), hereby make the following Order:—

1. This Order may be cited as the Capital Gains Tax (Exempt Gilt-edged Securities) (No. 2) Order 1971.

2. The Interpretation Act 1889(b) shall apply for the interpretation of this Order as it applies for the interpretation of an Act of Parliament.

3. The following security, being a stock denominated in sterling and issued after 15th April 1969 under section 12 of the National Loans Act 1968(c), is hereby specified for the purposes of section 41 of the Finance Act 1969 (gilt-edged securities exempt from tax on capital gains if held for more than 12 months):—

6 per cent Treasury Stock 1975.

Walter Clegg,
P. L. Hawkins,
Two of the Lords Commissioners
of Her Majesty's Treasury.

16th August 1971.

EXPLANATORY NOTE

(*This Note is not part of the Order.*)

This Order adds the following gilt-edged security to the category of stocks and bonds which are exempt from tax on capital gains if held for more than 12 months:—

6 per cent Treasury Stock 1975.

(a) 1969 c. 32.	(b) 1889 c. 63.	(c) 1968 c. 13.

STATUTORY INSTRUMENTS

1971 No. 1368

EDUCATION, ENGLAND AND WALES

The Provision of Milk and Meals (Amendment No. 2) Regulations 1971

Made - - - -	17th *August* 1971
Laid before Parliament	25th *August* 1971
Coming into Operation	1st *September* 1971

The Secretary of State for Education and Science and the Secretary of State for Wales, in joint exercise of their powers under section 49 of the Education Act 1944(a) and section 1 of the Education (Milk) Act 1971(b), hereby make the following regulations:—

Citation, commencement and interpretation

1.—(1) These regulations may be cited as the Provision of Milk and Meals (Amendment No. 2) Regulations 1971 and shall be included among the regulations which may be cited together as the Provision of Milk and Meals Regulations 1969 to 1971.

(2) These regulations shall come into operation on 1st September 1971.

(3) The Interpretation Act 1889(c) shall apply for the interpretation of these regulations as it applies for the interpretation of an Act of Parliament.

Amendment of Regulations

2. Regulations 4 and 10 of, and schedule 1 to, the Provision of Milk and Meals Regulations 1969(d) as amended (e) shall have effect subject to the amendments specified in Part A of the schedule and, in accordance with those provisions, shall have effect as set out in Part B of the schedule.

Regulation 2   SCHEDULE

PART A

AMENDMENT OF PROVISIONS OF 1969 REGULATIONS
Regulation 4

1. In paragraph (1) there shall be substituted for everything after the words "provided for" the following:—

"(*a*) every pupil in every special school;

(*b*) every pupil in every primary school until the end of the summer term ending next after the date on which he attains the age of seven; and

---

(a) 1944 c. 31.   (b) 1971 c. 74.
(c) 1889 c. 63.   (d) S.I. 1969/483 (1969 I, p. 1382).
(e) S.I. 1970/339, 511, 1417, 1971/169 (1970 I, p. 1225; I, p. 1715; III, p. 4667; 1971 I, p. 520).

(c) every other pupil in a primary school, and every junior pupil in an all-age school or a middle school, in respect of whom there is for the time being in force a certificate given by a medical officer of the authority stating that his health requires that he should be provided with milk at school."

2. After paragraph (2) there shall be inserted as a new paragraph—

"(3) On any school day milk may be provided for any pupil in any school whether or not milk is provided for him under paragraph (1) or (2) above."

3. At the end of the regulation there shall be added as a new paragraph—

"(6) In these regulations—

"primary school" means a school for providing primary education;

"all-age school" means a school which is deemed to be a primary school by virtue only of section 114(3) of the Education Act 1944;

"middle school" means a school which is deemed to be a primary school or a secondary school by virtue of an order under section 1(2) of the Education Act 1964(a)."

Regulation 10

4. After paragraph (1) there shall be inserted as a new paragraph—

"(2) The authority shall make arrangements for securing that the expense of providing milk under regulation 4(3) is defrayed by the pupil or his parent."

5. In paragraph (2)(a) after the word "in" there shall be inserted the words "a nursery school or".

6. In paragraph (3) for the reference to paragraph (2) there shall be substituted a reference to paragraph (3) and after the word "charge" there shall be inserted the words "under sub-paragraphs (a) and (b)".

7. In paragraph (4) for the reference to paragraph (3) there shall be substituted a reference to paragraph (4); after the words "Ministry of Social Security Act 1966" there shall be inserted the words "or a benefit under the Family Income Supplements Act 1970(b)"; and for the reference to paragraph (2)(a) there shall be substituted a reference to paragraph (3)(a).

SCHEDULE 1

8. In paragraph 1 for the table and the first note there shall be substituted the following table and note.

PART A   PART B

Size of family	Net weekly income in £p					
	1	2	3	4	5	6
1	13·25					
2	16·35	15·75				
3	19·45	18·85	18·25			
4	22·55	21·95	21·35	20·75		
5	25·65	25·05	24·45	23·85	23·25	
6	28·75	28·15	27·55	26·95	26·35	25·75

(a) 1964 c. 82.   (b) 1970 c. 55.

For larger families, in respect of each child—

(a) £3·10 is to be added at each incremental point in every additional line.

(b) £0·60 is to be subtracted at each incremental point in every additional column.

9. In paragraph (3), sub-paragraph (2)(f) shall be omitted.

10. For the references to 40s. in paragraph 3(1), (2), (3) and (9) there shall be substituted references to £2.

11. For the references to 20s. in paragraph 3(2) and 3(4) there shall be substituted references to £1.

12. For the reference to 25s. in paragraph 3(8) there shall be substituted a reference to £1·25.

13. In paragraph 3(12) for everything before the words "received as a contribution" there shall be substituted the words "Any income".

14. In paragraph 4(6) for the reference to 12s. 6d. there shall be substituted a reference to 75p.

PART B

TEXT OF PROVISIONS AS AMENDED

Regulation 4

Provision of milk

4.—(1) On every school day one third of a pint of milk shall be provided for—

(a) every pupil in every special school;

(b) every pupil in every primary school until the end of the summer term ending next after the date on which he attains the age of seven; and

(c) every other pupil in a primary school, and every junior pupil in an all-age school or a middle school, in respect of whom there is for the time being in force a certificate given by a medical officer of the authority stating that his health requires that he should be provided with milk at school.

(2) On any school day a further third of a pint of milk may be provided in any special school for any delicate pupil within the meaning of the Handicapped Pupils and Special Schools Regulations 1959(a) as amended (b).

(3) On any school day milk may be provided for any pupil in any school whether or not milk is provided for him under paragraph (1) or (2) above.

(4) The authority shall provide milk—

(d) which is pasteurised or ultra heat treated or, if no such milk is obtainable, designated for sale as untreated; and

(b) from sources and of a quality approved for the purposes of these regulations by the medical officer of health for the area of the authority after consultation with the medical officer of health for any county district concerned and the school medical officer.

(a) S.I. 1959/365 (1959 I, p. 1024).
(b) The amending Regulations are not relevant to the subject matter of these Regulations.

(5) If it is not reasonably practicable for the authority to comply with the requirements of paragraph (4)(*b*) above, they shall provide full-cream dried milk prepared for drinking or milk tablets.

(6) In these regulations—

"primary school" means a school for providing primary education;

"all-age school" means a school which is deemed to be a primary school by virtue only of section 114(3) of the Education Act 1944;

"middle school" means a school which is deemed to be a primary school or a secondary school by virtue of an order under section 1(2) of the Education Act 1964(**a**).

Regulation 10

Expenses

10.—(1) Subject to the provisions of this regulation, the expense incurred in providing milk, meals and other refreshment under these regulations shall be defrayed by the authority.

(2) The authority shall make arrangements for securing that the expense of providing milk under regulation 4(3) is defrayed by the pupil or his parent.

(3) The authority shall make arrangements for the payment by the parent of—

(*a*) a charge of 12p. for every meal provided in a nursery school or a county or voluntary school under regulation 5(1);

(*b*) such a charge (if any) as they consider appropriate for any meal provided in a special school under regulation 5(1); and

(*c*) such charges as they consider appropriate for meals and refreshment provided under regulation 5(2).

(4) The arrangements made by the authority under paragraph (3) above shall include provision for the remission of the charge under sub-paragraphs (*a*) and (*b*) in the case of any parent who satisfies them that he is unable to pay it without hardship.

(5) For the purposes of paragraph (4) above, a parent who is in receipt of a supplementary pension or a supplementary allowance under section 4 of the Ministry of Social Security Act 1966(**b**) or a benefit under the Family Income Supplements Act 1970(**c**) shall be treated as unable to pay the charge without hardship; and in the case of the charge under paragraph (3)(*a*) above, the question whether any parent not in receipt of such benefit is so unable to pay shall be determined in accordance with schedule 1.

SCHEDULE 1   Regulation 10(5)

DETERMINATION OF FINANCIAL HARDSHIP

Net income scale

1. Where the net weekly income of the parent of a family of any size specified in Part A of the following table is less than any amount shown in the corresponding entry in Part B, the number of children in respect of whom the charge

(a) 1964 c. 82.   (b) 1966 c. 20.
(c) 1970 c. 55.

shall be remitted is the number at the head of the column in Part B in which there appears the lowest amount in that entry which exceeds his income.

PART A   PART B

Size of Family	Net weekly income in £p					
	1	2	3	4	5	6
1	13·25					
2	16·35	15·75				
3	19·45	18·85	18·25			
4	22·55	21·95	21·35	20·75		
5	25·65	25·05	24·45	23·85	23·25	
6	28·75	28·15	27·55	26·95	26·35	25·75

For larger families, in respect of each child—

(a) £3·10 is to be added at each incremental point in every additional line.

(b) £0·60 is to be subtracted at each incremental point in every additional column.

For the purposes of this paragraph the expression "size of family" means the number of dependent children in the family who have not attained the age of 19.

Calculation of net income

2. In calculating the net income of the parent there shall be taken into account his income (reduced by income tax and national insurance contributions but including any benefit in kind other than a dwelling) from all sources, but there shall be disregarded the resources specified in paragraph 3 below and a deduction shall be made in respect of the expenses specified in paragraph 4 below.

Resources to be disregarded

3.—(1) £2 of the income consisting of any one or more of the following—

(a) workmen's compensation;

(b) disablement benefit;

(c) disability pension;

(d) the amount by which—

(i) a war widow's pension;

(ii) a widow's pension under section 19(3) of the National Insurance (Industrial Injuries) Act 1965(a) or an analogous payment—

exceeds the rate of pension payable under schedule 3 of the National Insurance Act 1965(b).

(2) £1 of any income other than any earnings or any of the following—

(a) benefit under the National Insurance Acts 1965 and 1966(c);

(a) 1965 c. 52.   (b) 1965 c. 51.
(c) 1965 c. 51; 1966 c. 6.

(*b*) industrial injury benefit under the National Insurance (Industrial Injuries) Acts 1965 and 1966;

(*c*) family allowances;

(*d*) payments for maintenance (including any marriage allowance);

(*e*) any rent received in respect of accommodation whether let furnished or unfurnished:

provided that the amount disregarded under this sub-paragraph shall not, together with the amount disregarded under sub-paragraph (1) above, exceed £2.

(3) £2 of the earnings of a mother or female guardian.

(4) £1 of the casual earnings of an unemployed father or male guardian.

(5) Any maternity grant under section 23 of the National Insurance Act 1965.

(6) Any death grant under section 39 of the National Insurance Act 1965.

(7) Any payment in respect of a pupil under the Regulations for Scholarships and Other Benefits 1945(a) as amended (b).

(8) £1·25 of any income if one parent is blind.

(9) £2 of any income if both parents are blind.

(10) One-tenth of the rent received in respect of accommodation let unfurnished.

(11) One-quarter of the rent received in respect of accommodation let furnished.

(12) Any income received as a contribution towards the expenses of the household from any other member of, or person living with, the family.

Expenses to be deducted

4.—(1) The amount of any premium on a policy of assurance on the life of either parent.

(2) Any expenses reasonably incurred in the provision of necessary household assistance and necessary day care for a child below compulsory school age where—

(*a*) the parent is widowed, divorced or permanently separated from the other party to the marriage;

(*b*) either parent is incapacitated;

(*c*) the parent is an unmarried woman.

(3) Any expenses necessarily incurred in the course of the parent's employment, including travelling expenses, trade union subscriptions and superannuation contributions.

(4) The amount of any rent, general and water rates and mortgage payments in respect of the home and of any hire purchase payments in respect of any caravan or houseboat which is the permanent home of the family.

(a) S.R. & O. 1945/666 (Rev. VI, p. 378: 1945 I, p. 340).
(b) S.I. 1948/688, 2223 (Rev. VI, p. 378: 1948 I, p. 754; 1948 I, p. 755), S.I. 1964/1294 (1964 II, p. 2974).

(5) Any payment made—

(a) for the maintenance of a former wife or her child;

(b) under an affiliation order;

(c) under a contribution order in respect of a child in the care of a local authority.

(6) 75p. of the cost of any special diet prescribed by a registered medical practitioner.

Given under the Official Seal of the Secretary of State for Education and Science on 16th August 1971.

(L.S.)   *Margaret Thatcher,*
Secretary of State for Education
and Science.

Given under my hand on 17th August 1971.

Peter Thomas,
Secretary of State for Wales.

EXPLANATORY NOTE

(This Note is not part of the Regulations.)

These regulations amend those parts of the Provision of Milk and Meals Regulations 1969 to 1971 which regulate the supply of milk, and the arrangements for defraying the expenses of providing milk and meals, for pupils attending schools maintained by local education authorities. The changes relating to milk give effect to section 1 of the Education (Milk) Act 1971. The principal change relating to the arrangements for the defraying of expenditure is the amendment of the provisions for the calculation of a parent's income for the purpose of determining his entitlement to remission of the charge for school dinner.

The text of the amended provisions is set out in Part B of the schedule to the regulations.

STATUTORY INSTRUMENTS

1971 No. 1369

WAGES COUNCILS

The Wages Regulation (Aerated Waters) (Scotland)
Order 1971

Made - - - -   17th August 1971

Coming into Operation   13th September 1971

Whereas the Secretary of State has received from the Aerated Waters Wages Council (Scotland) the wages regulation proposals set out in the Schedule hereto;

Now, therefore, the Secretary of State in exercise of his powers under section 11 of the Wages Councils Act 1959(a), and of all other powers enabling him in that behalf, hereby makes the following Order:—

1. This Order may be cited as the Wages Regulation (Aerated Waters) (Scotland) Order 1971.

2.—(1) In this Order the expression "the specified date" means the 13th September 1971, provided that where, as respects any worker who is paid wages at intervals not exceeding seven days, that date does not correspond with the beginning of the period for which the wages are paid, the expression "the specified date" means, as respects that worker, the beginning of the next such period following that date.

(2) The Interpretation Act 1889(b) shall apply to the interpretation of this Order as it applies to the interpretation of an Act of Parliament and as if this Order and the Order hereby revoked were Acts of Parliament.

3. The wages regulation proposals set out in the Schedule hereto shall have effect as from the specified date and as from that date the Wages Regulation (Aerated Waters) (Scotland) Order 1970(c) shall cease to have effect.

Signed by order of the Secretary of State.

17th August 1971.

J. R. Lloyd Davies,
Assistant Secretary,
Department of Employment.

(a) 1959 c. 69.   (b) 1889 c. 63.
(c) S.I. 1970/1409 (1970 III, p. 4653).

Article 3
SCHEDULE

The following minimum remuneration shall be substituted for the statutory minimum remuneration fixed by the Wages Regulation (Aerated Waters) (Scotland) Order 1970 (Order A.S. (72)).

STATUTORY MINIMUM REMUNERATION
PART I
GENERAL

1. The minimum remuneration payable to a worker to whom this Schedule applies for all work except work to which a minimum overtime rate applies under Part III, is—

(1) in the case of a time worker, the hourly general minimum time rate payable to the worker under Part II of this Schedule;

(2) in the case of a worker employed on piece work, piece rates each of which would yield, in the circumstances of the case, to an ordinary worker at least the same amount of money as the hourly general minimum time rate which would be payable to the worker under Part II of this Schedule if he were a time worker.

PART II
GENERAL MINIMUM TIME RATES

2. The general minimum time rates payable to all male and female workers are as follows:—

	Per hour p	Per week of 40 hours £
(1) Male workers aged 19 years or over—		
(a) Up to and including 30th September 1971		
Aged:—		
21 years or over	35·00	14·00
20 and under 21 years	31·83	12·73
19 „ „ 20 „	29·25	11·70
(b) From 1st October 1971 up to and including 31st March 1972		
Aged:—		
20 years or over	35·00	14·00
19 and under 20 years	29·25	11·70
(c) On and after 1st April 1972		
Aged 19 years or over	35·00	14·00
(2) Female workers aged 19 years or over—		
(a) Up to and including 30th September 1972... ...	29·25	11·70
(b) From 1st October 1972 up to and including 31st March 1973	30·70	12·28
(c) From 1st April 1973 up to and including 30th September 1973	32·13	12·85
(d) From 1st October 1973 up to and including 31st March 1974	33·56	13·42
(e) From 1st April 1974 up to and including 30th September 1974	34·28	13·71
(f) On and after 1st October 1974	35·00	14·00

		Per hour	Per week of 40 hours
		p	£
(3) All workers aged—			
18 and under 19 years		25·07	10·03
17 „ „ 18 „		21·36	8·54
16 „ „ 17 „		17·64	7·06
Under 16 years		14·40	5·76

PART III

OVERTIME AND WAITING TIME

MINIMUM OVERTIME RATES

3.—(1) Minimum overtime rates are payable to a worker to whom this Schedule applies as follows:—

    (a) on a Sunday or a customary holiday, for all time worked ... ... **DOUBLE TIME**

    (b) in any week, exclusive of any time in respect of which an overtime rate is payable under the provisions of (a) of this sub-paragraph, for all time worked in excess of 40 hours ... ... **TIME-AND-A-HALF**

(2) In this Part of this Schedule—

    (a) the expressions "time-and-a-half" and "double time" mean respectively:—

        (i) in the case of a time worker, one and a half times and twice the hourly general minimum time rate otherwise payable to the worker;

        (ii) in the case of a worker employed on piece work, one and a half times and twice the piece rates otherwise payable to the worker under paragraph 1(2);

    (b) the expression "customary holiday" means—

1st and 2nd January (or, if either of these days falls on a Sunday, 3rd January shall be substituted for such day); the local Spring holiday, the local Summer holiday and the local Autumn holiday, each to be allowed on a Monday fixed by the employer and notified to the worker not less than three weeks before the holiday; and Christmas Day (or, if Christmas Day falls on a Sunday, 26th December shall be substituted).

WAITING TIME

4.—(1) A worker is entitled to payment of the minimum remuneration specified in this Schedule for all time during which he is present on the premises of his employer unless he is present thereon in any of the following circumstances:—

    (a) without the employer's consent, express or implied;

    (b) for some purpose unconnected with his work and other than that of waiting for work to be given to him to perform;

    (c) by reason only of the fact that he is resident thereon;

    (d) during normal meal times in a room or place in which no work is being done, and he is not waiting for work to be given to him to perform.

(2) The minimum remuneration payable under sub-paragraph (1) of this paragraph to a piece worker when not engaged on piece work is that which would be applicable if he were a time worker.

PART IV

APPLICABILITY OF STATUTORY MINIMUM REMUNERATION

5. This Schedule applies to workers in relation to whom the Aerated Waters Wages Council (Scotland) operates, that is to say, workers employed in Scotland in the trade specified in the Schedule to the Trade Boards (Aerated Waters Trade, Scotland) (Constitution and Proceedings) Regulations 1939(a), namely:—

The manufacture, wherever carried on, of mineral or aerated waters, non-alcoholic cordials, flavoured syrups, unfermented sweet drinks, and other similar beverages, and the manufacture in unlicensed premises of brewed liquors, including:—

(a) the operations of bottle washing, bottling and filling, and all other operations preparatory to the sale of any of the aforesaid liquors in bottles, jars, syphons, casks, or other similar receptacles;

and including also:—

(b) the operations of bottle washing, bottling and filling, and all subsidiary operations preparatory to the sale in bottles, jars or other similar receptacles of cider, ale, stout, porter and other alcoholic beers, where all or any of such last-mentioned operations are, or is, conducted or carried on in association with or in conjunction with all or any of the operations specified under (a) above so as to form a common or interchangeable form of employment for workers, and whether the two sets of operations or any of them are, or is, carried on simultaneously or not.

EXPLANATORY NOTE

(This Note is not part of the Order.)

This Order, which has effect from 13th September 1971, sets out the statutory minimum remuneration payable in substitution for that fixed by the Wages Regulation (Aerated Waters) (Scotland) Order 1970 (Order A.S. (72)), which Order is revoked.

New provisions are printed in italics.

(a) S.R. & O. 1939/1367 (1939 II, p. 3178).

1971 No. 1370

EXCHANGE CONTROL

The Exchange Control (Authorised Dealers and Depositaries) (Amendment) (No. 2) Order 1971

Made - - - - *14th August* 1971
Coming into Operation *2nd September* 1971

The Treasury, in exercise of the powers conferred upon them by sections 36(5) and 42(1) of the Exchange Control Act 1947(a), hereby make the following Order:—

1.—(1) This Order may be cited as the Exchange Control (Authorised Dealers and Depositaries) (Amendment) (No. 2) Order 1971, and shall come into operation on 2nd September 1971.

(2) The Interpretation Act 1889(b) shall apply for the interpretation of this Order as it applies for the interpretation of an Act of Parliament.

2. Schedule 2 to the Exchange Control (Authorised Dealers and Depositaries) Order 1971(c), as amended (d), shall be further amended as follows:—

(*a*) by deleting the words "Australia and New Zealand Bank Ltd.";

(*b*) by inserting the words "Banco do Brasil S.A." after the words "Banco de Bilbao.";

(*c*) by inserting the words "Bank of America Ltd." after the words "Bank of Adelaide.";

(*d*) by deleting the words "British Linen Bank.";

(*e*) by deleting the words "Co-operative Wholesale Society Ltd." and substituting the words "Co-operative Bank Ltd.";

(*f*) by deleting the words "Crocker-Citizens National Bank." and substituting the words "Crocker National Bank.";

(*g*) by deleting the words "English, Scottish and Australian Bank, Ltd.";

(*h*) by inserting the words "Gray Dawes & Co. Ltd." after the words "Girard Trust Bank.";

(*i*) by inserting the words "London Interstate Bank Ltd." after the words "Lloyds Bank Ltd.";

(*j*) by inserting the words "Nordic Bank Ltd." after the words "Nippon Kangyo Bank Ltd., The.";

(*k*) by inserting the words "Orion Bank Ltd." after the words "Northern Trust Company, The."; and

(a) 1947 c. 14.   (b) 1889 c. 63.
(c) S.I. 1971/477 (1971 I, p. 1425).   (d) S.I. 1971/1028 (1971 II, p. 3009).

(*l*) by inserting the words "Standard and Chartered Banking Group Ltd." after the words "Société Générale pour favoriser le développement du Commerce et de l'Industrie en France."

3. This Order shall extend to the Channel Islands, and any reference in this Order to the Exchange Control Act 1947 includes a reference to that Act as extended by the Exchange Control (Channel Islands) Order 1947**(a)**.

Walter Clegg,
P. L. Hawkins,
Two of the Lords Commissioners
of Her Majesty's Treasury.

14th August 1971.

EXPLANATORY NOTE

(This Note is not part of the Order.)

This Order amends the list of persons authorised by the Treasury under the Exchange Control Act 1947 to act as dealers in gold and foreign currencies and as depositaries for the purpose of the deposit of securities.

(a) S.R. & O. 1947/2034 (Rev. VI, p. 1001: 1947 I, p. 660).

STATUTORY INSTRUMENTS

1971 No. 1377

MINES AND QUARRIES
The Mines and Quarries (Tips) Regulations 1971

Made - - - -	*17th August* 1971
Laid before Parliament	*26th August* 1971
Coming into Operation	*1st October* 1971

Whereas in pursuance of Part I of Schedule 2 to the Mines and Quarries Act 1954(a) the Secretary of State has published notice of his intention to make the following regulations and has not received any objection to the draft thereof in respect to which he is required to refer the draft regulations for inquiry and report :

Now, therefore, the Secretary of State in exercise of his powers under sections 141 and 143 of the Mines and Quarries Act 1954 and sections 1 and 4 to 8 of the Mines and Quarries (Tips) Act 1969(b) and all other powers in that behalf enabling him hereby makes the following regulations:—

PART I

GENERAL

Citation and commencement

1. These regulations may be cited as the Mines and Quarries (Tips) Regulations 1971 and shall come into operation on 1st October 1971.

Interpretation

2.—(1) In these regulations—

"the 1954 Act" means the Mines and Quarries Act 1954;

"the 1969 Act" means the Mines and Quarries (Tips) Act 1969;

"classified tip" means a tip to which Part I of the 1969 Act applies, being a tip of any of the following classes—

  (*a*) the tip consists of refuse accumulated or deposited wholly or mainly in a solid state and not in solution or suspension and—

    (i) the superficial area of the land covered by the refuse exceeds 10,000 square metres; or

    (ii) the height of the tip exceeds 15 metres; or

    (iii) the average gradient of the land covered by the refuse exceeds 1 in 12;

  (*b*) the tip consists of refuse accumulated or deposited wholly or mainly in solution or suspension and—

    (i) any part of the tip (other than any wall or other structure retaining or confining it but including any liquid in it) is more than 4 metres above the level of any part of the neighbouring land within 50 metres of the perimeter of the tip; or

---

(a) 1954 c. 70.   (b) 1969 c. 10.

(ii) the volume of the tip (other than any wall or other structure retaining or confining it but including any liquid in it) exceeds 10,000 cubic metres:

Provided that for the purposes of determining whether refuse has been accumulated or deposited wholly or mainly in a solid state or wholly or mainly in solution or suspension any wall or other structure retaining or confining the tip shall be excluded

And in these regulations "active classified tip" and "closed classified tip" shall be construed accordingly;

"dangerous occurrence" in relation to a tip means any occurrence in which any movement of material or any fire or any other event indicates that the tip is, or is likely to become, insecure;

"height" in relation to a tip means the vertical distance between the horizontal planes passing through the lowest and highest points of the tip;

"the person having responsibility for a tip" means—

(a) in the case of a tip which is associated with a quarry, the owner of the quarry; and

(b) in the case of an active tip which is associated with a mine, the manager of the mine; and

(c) in the case of a closed tip which is associated with a mine, the owner of the mine;

"watercourse" includes all rivers, streams, ditches, drains, sewers, culverts, cuts, dykes, sluices and passages, through which water flows.

(2) Expressions to which meanings are assigned by the Mines and Quarries Acts 1954 and 1969 or by these regulations shall (unless the contrary intention appears) have the same meanings in any document issued under the provisions of these regulations.

(3) The Interpretation Act 1889(a) shall apply to the interpretation of these regulations as it applies to the interpretation of an Act of Parliament.

Exemptions

3. An inspector may by notice served on the person having responsibility for a tip exempt—

(a) in the case of an active tip, the mine or quarry with which the tip is associated or any part thereof including the tip; or

(b) in the case of a closed tip, the tip or any part thereof

from the application of any of the provisions of these regulations if he is satisfied that the application of that provision is inappropriate in relation to the mine or quarry as the case may be or any part thereof or the closed tip or any part thereof or that the security of the tip will not be prejudiced in consequence of the granting of the exemption.

PART II

GENERAL PROVISIONS RELATING TO TIPS

Drainage of Tips

4.—(1) Tipping operations from every mine and quarry shall be carried out in such a way as to secure that the operations and the tip resulting from them

(a) 1889 c. 63.

do not cause an accumulation of water in under or near the tip which may make the tip insecure.

(2) Every active and closed tip shall be kept efficiently drained.

Supervision of Tips

5.—(1) For every active tip there shall be appointed by the person having responsibility for the tip a competent person to supervise or effect the carrying out of tipping operations on the tip.

(2) For every active and closed tip there shall be appointed by the person having responsibility for the tip a competent person to supervise or effect—

(*a*) any provision of a system of drainage for the tip;

(*b*) the maintenance in proper order of the drainage of the tip; and

(*c*) the making and keeping of the tip secure.

(3) For every active and closed tip other than a classified tip there shall be appointed by the person having responsibility for the tip a competent person to supervise or effect the regular inspection of the tip and of the premises on which it is situated and to the best of his ability of its drainage.

(4) Every competent person so appointed under this regulation shall record in a book provided for that purpose by the owner of the mine or quarry with which the tip is associated a report of every defect revealed by any inspection of the tip, the premises on which it is situated and its drainage in pursuance of this regulation.

(5) The person having responsibility for a tip shall record in a book provided for that purpose by the owner of the mine or quarry with which the tip is associated the action taken to remedy any defect revealed by any inspection of the tip, the premises on which it is situated and its drainage in pursuance of this regulation.

6.—(1) It shall be the duty of the owner and, without prejudice to the provisions of section 14 of the 1954 Act, of the manager of every mine and of the owner of every quarry to ensure to the best of his ability that every person appointed by him in pursuance of these regulations to carry out supervision or inspections understands the nature and scope of any duties which fall to be performed by that person by virtue of these regulations.

(2) It shall be the duty of the owner of every mine and quarry with which is associated a closed tip, with respect to each report, record or other item of information on or relating to the tip which, in pursuance of any provision of the Mines and Quarries Acts 1954 and 1969 or regulations, is entered in a book which by or by virtue of those Acts is required to be provided by him for that purpose, to secure that there is promptly brought—

(*a*) to his notice; or

(*b*) to the notice of any person to whom written instructions have been given by the owner in pursuance of section 1 of the 1954 Act specifying as, or including amongst, the matters with respect to which that person is charged with securing the fulfilment in relation to the tip of statutory responsibilities of the owner, matters of the class to which the provision relates

any matter disclosed by the report, record or other item of information which either is of an abnormal or unusual nature as regards the tip or, not being of such a nature, is of a kind which will or may necessitate the taking of any steps by the owner or any other person.

Notification of beginning and ending of Tipping Operations

7. Every class and description of mines and quarries are hereby prescribed for the purposes of section 4(1) and (2) of the 1969 Act.

Notification of intention whether to begin a Classified Tip

8.—(1) If at any time tipping operations from a mine or quarry are to be begun on premises which at that time are not the site of a tip to which Part I of the 1969 Act applies, the owner of the mine or quarry shall, in addition to the notice required to be given under section 4 of the 1969 Act, give notice to the inspector for the district stating whether it is intended that the resulting tip is or is not to be a classified tip not less than thirty days, or such shorter period as the inspector may permit, before the beginning of the operations.

(2) Where an owner of a mine or quarry has given notice as aforesaid that it is intended that the resulting tip is not to be a classified tip an inspector may at any time before tipping operations are begun for the purpose of ensuring the security of the resulting tip or for securing that the land on which the tipping operations are to be carried out is satisfactory for the purpose by notice served on the owner direct that the resulting tip shall be treated for the purposes of these regulations as a classified tip, and any such notice shall, if it is so specified therein, become operative forthwith.

(3) The provisions of Part XV of the 1954 Act with respect to references upon notices served by inspectors shall apply to a notice served by an inspector under the last preceding paragraph, and the relevant ground of objection shall be that compliance with the notice is unnecessary for the purpose of ensuring the security of the resulting tip or for securing that the land on which the tipping operations are to be carried out is satisfactory for the purpose.

(4) Where an owner of a mine or quarry has given notice as aforesaid that it is intended that the resulting tip is to be a classified tip, the tip shall be treated for the purposes of these regulations as being a classified tip.

Part III

Provisions relating to Active Classified Tips

Procedure before beginning Tipping Operations

9.—(1) If at any time before tipping operations from a mine or quarry are begun on premises which at that time are not the site of a tip to which Part I of the 1969 Act applies an owner of a mine or quarry gives notice pursuant to regulation 8(1) that it is intended that the resulting tip is to be a classified tip or an inspector gives a direction pursuant to regulation 8(2) that the resulting tip shall be treated for the purposes of these regulations as a classified tip, then the owner shall, not less than thirty days, or such shorter period as the inspector may permit, before the beginning of the tipping operations, obtain or make and thereafter keep, until the premises become the site of an active classified tip (in relation to which regulation 13 applies to impose a like duty on the manager of the mine or the owner of the quarry), at the office at the mine or quarry or at such other place as may be approved by an inspector—

   (*a*) a geological map of the district in which it is intended that the tip shall be situated, being a map on the scale of 1/10,000 or, if a map on so large a scale is not available, a map on the nearest scale which shows the boundaries of the premises on which it is intended that the tip shall be situated and the neighbouring land within 250 metres of the said boundaries;

(*b*) such accurate sections on a scale of not less than 1/1250 of the strata underlying the intended tip as may be necessary to show any variation in the thickness or character of the strata, which may affect the security of the tip, and to show, so far as it can be ascertained, the position of any known fault which may affect the security of the tip;

(*c*) an accurate plan of the premises on which it is intended that the tip shall be situated and of the neighbouring land within 250 metres of the boundaries of the said premises being a plan—

    (i) on a scale of not less than 1/2500 contoured and orientated to and correlated with the Ordnance Survey National Grid and marked with squares corresponding to the 100 metre squares shown on Ordnance Survey sheets on the scale of 1/2500; and

    (ii) showing all mine workings (whether abandoned or not), previous landslips, springs, artesian wells, watercourses and other natural and other topographical features which might affect the security of the intended tip or might be relevant for determining whether the land on which the tipping operations are to be carried out is satisfactory for the purpose.

(2) If at any time before tipping operations from a mine or quarry are begun on premises which at that time are not the site of a tip to which Part I of the 1969 Act applies an owner of a mine or quarry gives notice pursuant to regulation 8(1) that it is intended that the resulting tip is to be a classified tip or an inspector gives a direction pursuant to regulation 8(2) that the resulting tip shall be treated for the purposes of these regulations as a classified tip, tipping operations shall not be begun until the following conditions have been satisfied—

(*a*) the owner of the mine or quarry has obtained a report from a person competent to make the report on the method of carrying out the intended tipping operations and on every other matter which might affect the security of the tip or might be relevant for determining whether the land on which the tipping operations are to be carried out is satisfactory for the purpose containing in particular—

    (i) the designed total amount of the refuse to be deposited and average amount per week;

    (ii) an account of any surveys, tests, boreholes and ground water measurements made for the purposes of the report and the results thereof;

    (iii) details of the site preparation, drainage and foundations of the intended tip;

    (iv) accurate plans on a scale of not less than 1/2500 and sections on a scale of not less than 1/1250 of the intended tip or on such larger scale as an inspector may direct in either case by notice served on the owner of the mine or quarry, recording the design of the tip including in particular the superficial area of the land to be covered by the refuse, the gradients in respect of any such land, the designed height of the tip, the designed contours and boundaries of the tip, the designed position and nature of construction of any wall or other structure retaining or confining the tip and the nature and location of the types of refuse to be deposited;

    (v) a specification of the intended tip showing the method of depositing and (where necessary) compacting the refuse;

    (vi) the nature and extent of inspection, supervision and safety measures that in the opinion of the person making the report are necessary to be carried out during the tipping operations to ensure the security of the intended tip;

(b) the owner of the mine or quarry has given notice to the inspector for the district that he has obtained the said report and any supplementary report required to be obtained under paragraph (3) hereof;

(c) the owner of the mine or quarry has preserved the said reports at the office at the mine or quarry or at such other place as may be approved by an inspector; and

(d) a period of thirty days has expired beginning with the date on which the last of the notices referred to in this regulation became operative or such shorter period as the inspector for the district may permit.

(3) If an inspector is of opinion that additional surveys, tests, boreholes or ground water measurements ought to be made before tipping operations are begun or that provision ought to have been made in any report under this regulation for any matter for which provision was not made in the report or that different provision ought to have been made in the report, he may serve on the owner of the mine or quarry a notice stating that he is of that opinion, specifying the additional surveys, tests, boreholes or ground water measurements which in his opinion ought to be made or the matter for which, in his opinion, provision or, as the case may be, different provision ought to have been made in the report and the nature of the provision which, in his opinion, ought to be made, and requiring the owner to make additional surveys, tests, boreholes or ground water measurements and to obtain a supplementary report from the person who made any previous report under this regulation or from some other person competent to make the report in accordance with the tenor of the notice, and any such notice shall, if it is so specified therein, become operative forthwith.

(4) The provisions of Part XV of the 1954 Act with respect to references upon notices served by inspectors shall apply to a notice served under the last preceding paragraph, and the relevant ground of objection shall be that adequate surveys, tests, boreholes or ground water measurements have already been made or that adequate provision is already made in the report for ensuring the security of the intended tip or for determining whether the land on which the tipping operations are to be carried out is satisfactory for the purpose.

Tipping Rules

10.—(1) In the case of any mine or quarry with which is associated an active classified tip, the manager of the mine or, as the case may be, the owner of the quarry shall make tipping rules with respect to tipping operations on that tip and the nature of the refuse to be deposited on that tip and such rules shall in particular specify the following matters—

(a) the manner in which tipping operations on that tip are to be carried out;

(b) the nature and extent of supervision of such tipping operations and the precautions to be taken in carrying out such tipping operations in order to avoid a dangerous occurrence in relation to the tip and in order to keep the tip secure and which of the persons employed at the mine or quarry has been appointed under regulation 5(1) to carry out that supervision and which of them are to take those precautions;

(c) the nature and frequency of inspections of the tip and of the premises on which it is situated and of the drainage of the tip that in the opinion of the person making the rules are necessary to be carried out during such tipping operations to ensure the security of the tip, additional to the inspections required by other provisions of these regulations, and which of the persons employed at the mine or quarry are to carry out those inspections;

(*d*) the action to be taken in respect of any defect revealed by any of those inspections.

(2) Where after the coming into operation of these regulations tipping operations are begun on premises which at that time are not the site of a tip to which Part I of the 1969 Act applies, the tipping rules shall be made upon the beginning of the operations.

Inspections

11. In the case of any mine or quarry with which is associated an active classified tip—

(*a*) the manager of the mine or, as the case may be, the owner of the quarry shall make and ensure the efficient carrying out of arrangements whereby a competent person appointed for that purpose by the manager of the mine, or, as the case may be, by the owner of the quarry shall inspect weekly every such tip and the premises on which it is situated and to the best of his ability inspect the drainage of the tip and shall carry out such other inspections as are required by tipping rules;

(*b*) a person who has carried out an inspection in pursuance of this regulation shall forthwith make and sign a full and accurate report of the inspection, and every such report, or a copy of such report, shall, until the expiration of three years after such inspection, be kept at the office at the mine or quarry or at such other place as may be approved by an inspector and be open to inspection by, or by a person authorised in that behalf in writing by, any person employed at that mine or quarry;

(*c*) a person who has carried out an inspection in pursuance of this regulation shall forthwith record in a book provided for that purpose by the owner of the mine or quarry a report of every defect revealed by the inspection;

(*d*) the person having responsibility for a tip shall record in a book provided for that purpose by the owner of the mine or quarry the action taken to remedy any defect revealed by any inspection carried out in pursuance of this regulation.

Reports

12.—(1) In the case of any mine or quarry with which is associated an active classified tip it shall not be lawful (subject to paragraph (3) below) for tipping operations to be carried out at that tip unless a report has been obtained in the last two preceding years from a person competent to make the report on the tip and on every matter which might affect the security of the tip.

(2) A special supplementary report on the tip and on every matter which might affect the security of the tip shall be obtained from a person competent to make the report as soon as practicable after a dangerous occurrence has occurred in relation to the tip, or after such a change in the design of the tip or in the nature or location of the types of refuse deposited or such a variation to or departure from its specification, as might affect its security, has been made.

(3) Where after the coming into operation of these regulations tipping operations are begun on premises which at that time are not the site of a tip to which Part I of the 1969 Act applies, the first report (other than a special

supplementary report) for the purposes of this regulation shall be obtained not more than two years after the date on which the tipping operations begin.

(4) Every report obtained for the purposes of this regulation shall contain in particular—

(a) an opinion whether the tip is secure;

(b) an opinion whether, so far as the person making the report can ascertain, there have been any changes in the design of the tip or in the nature or location of the types of refuse deposited or any variation to or departure from the specification since the original design and specification (other than those noted in a previous report under these regulations) with details of them;

(c) an opinion whether, so far as the person making the report can ascertain, there has occurred or is likely to occur any subsidence or other surface movement which may affect the security of the tip with details of the subsidence or other surface movement and its effect or probable effect on the security of the tip;

(d) an account of any surveys, tests, boreholes and ground water measurements made for the purposes of the report and the results thereof;

(e) the nature and extent of inspection, supervision and safety measures that in the opinion of the person making the report are necessary to be carried out during tipping operations to ensure the security of the tip.

Reports, Plans and Sections of Tips and Geological Map

13. In the case of any mine or quarry with which is associated an active classified tip it shall be the duty of the manager of the mine or, as the case may be, of the owner of the quarry to keep at the office at the mine or quarry or at such other place as may be approved by an inspector—

(a) any report on or relating to every such tip obtained under these regulations;

(b) any directions relating to every such tip made by an inspector or the Secretary of State under or by virtue of the Mines and Quarries Acts 1954 and 1969;

(c) accurate plans and sections of every such tip showing clearly and accurately the extent of the tip up to a date not more than fifteen months past or such other date as an inspector may require in any particular case, accurate plans of the premises on which every such tip is situated and of the neighbouring land within 250 metres of the boundaries of the said premises and such accurate sections of the strata underlying every such tip as may be necessary to show any variation in the thickness or character of the strata which may affect the security of the tip;

(d) a geological map of the district in which every such tip is situated, being a map on the scale of 1/10,000 or, if a map on so large a scale is not available, a map on the nearest scale which shows the boundaries of the premises on which the tip is situated and the neighbouring land within 250 metres of the said boundaries.

Records of Refuse tipped

14. In the case of any mine or quarry with which is associated an active classified tip—

(a) it shall be the duty of the manager of the mine or, as the case may be, of the owner of the quarry to make and ensure the efficient carrying out of arrangements whereby a weekly record of the nature, quantity and location of the types of refuse deposited at every such tip is entered by a competent person appointed by him in a book provided for that purpose by the owner of the mine or quarry;

(b) it shall be the duty of the manager of the mine or, as the case may be, of the owner of the quarry to make and ensure the efficient carrying out of arrangements whereby an annual record of the nature, quantity and location of the types of refuse deposited at every such tip is made by a competent person appointed by him, and every such record, or a copy of such record, shall, until the tip ceases to be an active classified tip, be kept at the office at the mine or quarry or at such other place as may be approved by an inspector and be open to inspection by, or by a person authorised in that behalf in writing by, any person employed at that mine or quarry.

Notification of change in design or specification of tips

15. Where such a change in the design of an active classified tip or in the nature or location of the types of refuse deposited or such a variation to or departure from its specification, as might affect its security, has been made, it shall be the duty of the manager of the mine or of the owner of the quarry with which the tip is associated to give notice forthwith of the change, variation or departure to the inspector for the district.

Transitional provisions for existing tips

16. Regulations 10(1), 11 (in so far as it refers to tipping rules), 12(1) and 13(c) and (d) shall not apply in relation to any tip which is an active classified tip at the date of the coming into operation of these regulations until twelve months after the said date.

PART IV

PROVISIONS RELATING TO CLOSED CLASSIFIED TIPS

Inspections

17.—(1) In the case of any mine or quarry with which is associated a closed classified tip the owner of the mine or quarry shall make and ensure the efficient carrying out of arrangements whereby a competent person appointed for that purpose by the owner shall inspect every such tip and the premises on which it is situated and to the best of his ability inspect the drainage of the tip—

(a) where the tip consists of refuse accumulated or deposited wholly or mainly in solution or suspension, at intervals not exceeding six months;

(b) where the tip consists of refuse accumulated or deposited wholly or mainly in a solid state and not in solution or suspension, at intervals not exceeding twelve months.

(2) A person who has carried out an inspection in pursuance of this regulation shall forthwith make and sign a full and accurate report of the inspection, and every such report, or a copy of such report, shall, until the expiration of three years after such inspection, be kept at the office at the mine or quarry or at such other place as may be approved by an inspector and be open to inspection by, or by a person authorised in that behalf in writing by, any person employed at that mine or quarry.

(3) A person who has carried out an inspection in pursuance of this regulation shall forthwith record in a book provided for that purpose by the owner of the mine or quarry a report of every defect revealed by the inspection.

(4) The person having responsibility for a tip shall record in a book provided for that purpose by the owner of the mine or quarry the action taken to remedy any defect revealed by any inspection carried out in pursuance of this regulation.

(5) Every entry made in any such book as aforesaid or a copy of that entry shall be preserved—

(a) where the tip consists of refuse accumulated or deposited wholly or mainly in solution or suspension, until the expiration of five years after the date on which it was made or until a report has been obtained for the purposes of regulation 18, whichever is the earlier;

(b) where the tip consists of refuse accumulated or deposited wholly or mainly in a solid state and not in solution or suspension, until the expiration of ten years after the date on which it was made or until a report has been obtained as aforesaid, whichever is the earlier.

Reports

18.—(1) In the case of any mine or quarry with which is associated a closed classified tip the owner of the mine or quarry shall obtain—

(a) a report from a person competent to make the report on the tip and on every matter which might affect the security of the tip—

(i) where the tip consists of refuse accumulated or deposited wholly or mainly in solution or suspension, at intervals not exceeding five years;

(ii) where the tip consists of refuse accumulated or deposited wholly or mainly in a solid state and not in solution or suspension, at intervals not exceeding ten years; and

(b) a special supplementary report on the tip and on every matter which might affect the security of the tip from a person competent to make the report as soon as practicable after a dangerous occurrence has occurred in relation to the tip.

(2) Every report obtained for the purposes of this regulation shall contain in particular—

(a) an opinion whether the tip is secure;

(b) details of any subsidence or other surface movement that has occurred which may affect the security of the tip;

(c) an account of any surveys, tests, boreholes and ground water measurements made for the purposes of the report and the results thereof;

(d) the nature and extent of inspection, supervision and safety measures that in the opinion of the person making the report are necessary to be carried out to ensure the security of the tip.

(3) The owner shall obtain the first report under sub-paragraph (a) of paragraph (1) of this regulation—

(a) where no report has been obtained from a person competent to make the report on the tip under any other provisions of these regulations— within two years after the tip becomes a classified tip or, in the case of a tip which is a classified tip at the date of the coming into operation of these regulations, within two years after the said date;

(b) where a report has been obtained from a person competent to make the report on the tip under any other provisions of these regulations and the tip consists of refuse accumulated or deposited wholly or mainly in solution or suspension—within five years after the report has been obtained;

(c) where a report has been obtained as aforesaid and the tip consists of refuse accumulated or deposited wholly or mainly in a solid state and not in solution or suspension—within ten years after the report has been obtained.

Reports, Plans and Sections of Tips and Geological Maps

19.—(1) In the case of any mine or quarry with which is associated a closed classified tip, it shall be the duty of the owner of the mine or quarry to make and ensure the efficient carrying out of arrangements whereby correct particulars of any operations carried out at every such tip which might affect its security are recorded by a competent person appointed by him in a book provided by him for that purpose and (where necessary) on plans, drawings and sections attached thereto.

(2) For the purposes of this regulation "operations" includes surveys and tests as well as building, engineering, mining and other operations.

20.—(1) In the case of any mine or quarry with which is associated a closed classified tip it shall be the duty of the owner of the mine or quarry to keep at the office at the mine or quarry or at such other place as may be approved by an inspector—

(a) any reports on or relating to every such tip obtained under these regulations;

(b) any directions relating to every such tip made by an inspector or the Secretary of State under or by virtue of the Mines and Quarries Acts 1954 and 1969;

(c) accurate plans and sections of every such tip showing clearly and accurately the extent of the tip up to the date on which it ceased to be used for the deposit of refuse from the mine or quarry, accurate plans of the premises on which every such tip is situated and of the neighbouring land within 250 metres of the boundaries of the said premises and such accurate sections of the strata underlying every such tip as may be necessary to show any variation in the thickness or character of the strata which may affect the security of the tip;

(d) a geological map of the district in which every such tip is situated, being a map on the scale of 1/10,000 or, if a map on so large a scale is not available, a map on the nearest scale which shows the boundaries of the premises on which the tip is situated and the neighbouring land within 250 metres of the said boundaries;

(e) all records (or copies thereof) of refuse deposited at every such tip made pursuant to regulation 14(b);

(f) all records of operations carried out at every such tip made pursuant to regulation 19.

(2) In the case of any tip which is a closed classified tip at the date of the coming into operation of these regulations, sub-paragraphs (c) and (d) of paragraph (1) of this regulation shall not apply until two years after the said date, and in the case of any tip which becomes a closed classified tip after the said date by virtue of a direction given by an inspector under these regulations, the said sub-paragraphs of paragraph (1) of this regulation shall not apply until two years after the direction becomes operative.

Part V

Resumption of Tipping Operations at Closed Tips

Procedure before resumption

21.—(1) If at any time tipping operations from a mine or quarry are to be resumed at a tip which at that time is a closed tip but not a classified tip, the owner of the mine or quarry shall, in addition to the notice required to be given under section 4 of the 1969 Act, give notice to the inspector for the district stating whether it is intended that the tip is or is not to become a classified tip not less than thirty days or such shorter period as the inspector may permit, before the resumption of the operations.

(2) The provisions of paragraphs (2) to (4) of regulation 8 shall apply in relation to such a notice as they apply in relation to a notice under regulation 8(1) as if the references in the said paragraphs to the resulting tip were a reference to the closed tip and as if the reference in regulation 8(2) to the beginning of tipping operations were a reference to the resumption of tipping operations.

22.—(1) If at any time tipping operations from a mine or quarry are to be resumed at a tip which at that time is a closed classified tip or if an owner of a mine or quarry with which is associated a closed tip, at which tipping operations are to be resumed but which is not a classified tip, gives notice pursuant to regulation 21(1) that it is intended that the tip is to become a classified tip, or if an inspector before tipping operations from a mine or quarry are resumed at a closed tip which is not a classified tip gives a direction by virtue of regulation 21(2) that the tip shall be treated for the purposes of these regulations as a classified tip—

> (*a*) the owner of the mine or quarry, with which the tip is associated, shall, not less than thirty days, or such shorter period as the inspector may permit, before the resumption of tipping operations at that tip from the mine or quarry, obtain or make and thereafter keep, until the premises become the site of an active classified tip, at the office at the mine or quarry or at such other place as may be approved by an inspector such maps, sections and plans as are required to be obtained or made and kept by regulation 9(1);

> (*b*) tipping operations shall not be resumed at that tip from the mine or quarry until such conditions are satisfied as are specified in regulation 9(2); but nothing in this sub-paragraph shall require the owner to obtain a report within two years of any report already obtained on the tip and on every matter which might affect the security of the tip under the provisions of regulations 9(2)(*a*), 9(3) and 12(1), unless such a change in the design of the tip or in the nature or location of the types of refuse deposited or such a variation to or departure from its specification, as might affect its security, has been made.

(2) The provisions of regulation 9(3) and (4) shall apply as if the reference in regulation 9(3) to the reports under that regulation were a reference to the reports required to be obtained by virtue of sub-paragraph (*b*) of paragraph (1) of this regulation and as if the reference in regulation 9(3) to the beginning of tipping operations were a reference to their resumption.

Tipping Rules

23. Where after the coming into operation of these regulations tipping operations are resumed at a tip which at that time is a closed classified tip tipping rules shall be made upon the resumption of the operations.

PART VI

MISCELLANEOUS PROVISIONS

Transmission of plans etc relating to tips ceasing to be associated with a mine or quarry

24. In the event of the abandonment of a mine or quarry, the owner of the mine or quarry shall within three months thereafter send to the inspector for the district—

(a) all such plans, drawings and sections relating to tips associated with the mine or quarry as were required to be kept by virtue of section 6 of the 1969 Act;

(b) all such other plans relating to tips associated with the mine or quarry as were required to be kept under these regulations;

(c) all such reports or records relating to tips associated with the mine or quarry as were required to be kept by virtue of regulations 13, 14(b) and 20.

25. Before an owner of a mine or quarry with which is associated a tip to which Part I of the 1969 Act applies parts with the exclusive occupation of the whole of the premises on which the tip is situated, he shall send to the inspector for the district all such plans, drawings, sections, reports and records relating to the tip as are referred to in regulation 24 or an accurate copy thereof.

Directions

26.—(1) An inspector may at any time not already provided for in these regulations by notice served on the person having responsibility for a tip which is not a classified tip for the purpose of ensuring the security of the tip direct that the tip shall be treated for the purposes of all or any of these regulations as a classified tip and any such notice shall, if it is so specified therein, become operative forthwith.

(2) The provisions of Part XV of the 1954 Act with respect to references upon notices served by inspectors shall apply to a notice served by an inspector under the last preceding paragraph, and the relevant ground of objection shall be that compliance with the notice is wholly, or to a particular extent, unnecessary for the purpose of ensuring the security of the tip.

Conduct of employees

27.—(1) Without prejudice to the generality of section 3(3) of the 1954 Act, every person employed at a tip to which Part I of the 1969 Act applies shall obey any instruction given to him by any person upon whom duties are laid by these regulations, being an instruction given by that person for the purpose of the performance of those duties.

(2) No person so employed shall impede or obstruct any other person in the performance of such duties.

(3) Regulation 2(1) of the Coal and Other Mines (General Duties and Conduct) Regulations 1956(a) shall not apply to any such instruction and regulation 2(2) of those regulations shall not apply to such duties.

Application of other regulations

28. Any reference in any other regulations to the 1954 Act shall, except where the context otherwise requires, include a reference to Part I of the 1969 Act

---

(a) S.I. 1956/1761 (1956 I, p. 1256).

where such a reference is appropriate for the purpose of ensuring the security of tips to which the said Part I applies.

Revocation

29. The Mines and Quarries (Notification of Tipping Operations) Regulations 1969(a) are hereby revoked.

Dated 17th August 1971.

John Eden,
Minister for Industry,
Department of Trade and Industry.

EXPLANATORY NOTE

(This Note is not part of the Regulations.)

These regulations made under the Mines and Quarries Acts 1954 and 1969 set out general requirements (regulations 4-8) notably in relation to responsibility for the drainage, supervision, maintenance and inspection of all existing and new tips to which Part I of the Mines and Quarries (Tips) Act 1969 applies. They revoke (regulation 29) the Mines and Quarries (Notification of Tipping Operations) Regulations 1969 and incorporate their substance (regulation 7). More detailed provisions applicable to "classified tips", i.e. tips which because of their size or location are more likely to present a potential hazard, are set out in regulations 9-26. "Classified tips" are defined in regulation 2.

Regulation 27 deals with the conduct of employees.

Regulation 28 defines the extent to which existing regulations, made under the Mines and Quarries Act 1954, are applicable to matters covered by Part I of the Mines and Quarries (Tips) Act 1969.

(a) S.I. 1969/1141 (1969 II, p. 3401).

STATUTORY INSTRUMENTS

1971 No. 1378

MINES AND QUARRIES

The Mines and Quarries (Tipping Plans) Rules 1971

Made - - -	*17th August* 1971
Laid before Parliament	*26th August* 1971
Coming into Operation	*1st October* 1971

The Secretary of State in exercise of his powers under section 6(2) of the Mines and Quarries (Tips) Act 1969(**a**) and all other powers in that behalf enabling him hereby makes the following rules :—

Citation and commencement

1. These rules may be cited as the Mines and Quarries (Tipping Plans) Rules 1971 and shall come into operation on 1st October 1971.

Interpretation

2. The Interpretation Act 1889(**b**) shall apply to the interpretation of these rules as it applies to the interpretation of an Act of Parliament.

Application

3. The provisions of these rules shall apply to all such plans and sections of active or closed tips associated with mines and quarries and to all such sections of the strata underlying these tips as are required to be kept in pursuance of regulations 13(*c*) and 20(1)(*c*) of the Mines and Quarries (Tips) Regulations 1971(**c**).

Scale of plans and sections

4. Every such plan shall be on a scale of not less than 1/2500 and every such section shall be on a scale of not less than 1/1250.

Correlation with Grid

5. Every such plan shall be orientated to and correlated with the Ordnance Survey National Grid and marked with squares corresponding to the 100 metre squares shown on Ordnance Survey sheets on the scale of 1/2500.

Contour Lines, Gradient and Faults

6.—(1) Every such plan shall be marked with contour lines showing vertical variations from Ordnance Datum at intervals not exceeding five metres.

(2) In every case the vertical variation represented by any consecutive contour lines marked on every such plan shall be the same throughout the plan and the lines shall be marked with the height relative to the Ordnance Datum.

(**a**) 1969 c. 10. (**b**) 1889 c. 63.

(**c**) S.I. 1971/1377(1971 II, p. 3857).

(3) Every such plan shall show the general direction and rate of dip of the strata underlying the tip.

(4) Every such plan and section shall show, so far as it can be ascertained, the position of any known fault which may affect the security of the tip.

Topographical features

7. Every such plan shall show all mine workings (whether abandoned or not), previous landslips, springs, artesian wells, watercourses and other natural and other topographical features which might affect the security of the tip or might be relevant for determining whether the land on which tipping operations are to be carried out is satisfactory for the purpose.

Design etc.

8. Every such plan and section shall show the land covered or to be covered by the refuse to be deposited, the designed height for the time being of the tip, the designed contours and boundaries for the time being of the tip and the nature and location of the types of refuse deposited at the tip up to a date not more than fifteen months past or such other date as an inspector may require in any particular case.

Correlation

9. Every such plan shall indicate—

(*a*) the direction of the National Grid North ;

(*b*) the date on which it was made ; and

(*c*) the date on which it was last revised.

Dated 17th August 1971.

John Eden,
Minister for Industry,
Department of Trade and Industry.

EXPLANATORY NOTE

(This Note is not part of the Rules.)

These rules, made under section 6(2) of the Mines and Quarries (Tips) Act 1969, lay down the scales, orientation, correlation with the National Grid and other requirements affecting the plans and sections of tips associated with mines and quarries and of the strata underlying the tips which the Mines and Quarries (Tips) Regulations 1971 require to be kept.

STATUTORY INSTRUMENTS

1971 No. 1380

PENSIONS

The Superannuation (Teaching and Police) Interchange Rules 1971

Made - - -	17*th August* 1971
Laid before Parliament	27*th August* 1971
Coming into Operation	31*st August* 1971

The Secretary of State for Education and Science, with the consent of the Minister for the Civil Service, in exercise of the powers conferred on her by sections 2 and 15 of the Superannuation (Miscellaneous Provisions) Act 1948(**a**), as amended by section 11 of the Superannuation (Miscellaneous Provisions) Act 1967(**b**) and as read with the Minister for the Civil Service Order 1968(**c**), hereby makes the following Rules :—

PART I

GENERAL

1. These Rules may be cited as the Superannuation (Teaching and Police) Interchange Rules 1971 and shall come into operation on 31st August 1971.

Interpretation

2.—(1) In these Rules, unless the context otherwise requires—

"the Act of 1948" means the Superannuation (Miscellaneous Provisions) Act 1948 ;

"national service" means, in relation to any person, compulsory national service and service which is relevant service within the meaning of the Reserve and Auxiliary Forces (Protection of Civil Interests) Act 1951(**d**) and any similar service immediately following such service entered into with the consent of the body or person by whom he was last employed before undertaking the service ;

"operative date" means the date of the coming into operation of these Rules ;

"pension" has the meaning assigned to it by the Act of 1948 ;

"police authority" means—

(*a*) in relation to a person who has become or becomes a policeman after ceasing to be employed in teaching service, the authority which on the day on which these Rules become applicable to him is for the purposes of the Police Pensions Regulations the police authority in relation to him ; and

---

(**a**) 1948 c. 33. (**b**) 1967 c. 28.
(**c**) S.I. 1968/1656 (1968 III, p. 4485). (**d**) 1951 c. 65.

(b) in relation to a person who has become or becomes employed in teaching service after ceasing to be a policeman, the authority which last was or is treated for the purposes of the Police Pensions Regulations as the police authority in relation to him ;

"policeman" means a regular policeman within the meaning of the Police Pensions Regulations ;

"Police Pensions Regulations" means the Police Pensions Regulations 1971(a) ;

"prescribed period" has the meaning assigned to it by rule 3 ;

"reckonable service" means reckonable service within the meaning of the Teachers' Superannuation Act 1967(b) ;

"the Secretary of State" means the Secretary of State for Education and Science ;

"the Teachers' Regulations" means the Teachers' Superannuation Regulations 1967 to 1971 ; and "the principal Teachers' Regulations" means the Teachers' Superannuation Regulations 1967(c) ;

"teaching service" means—

(a) reckonable service ; and

(b) service which for the purposes of the Teachers' Regulations is service as an organiser, a teacher in an admitted school, a services civilian teacher, a services education officer or a part-time teacher ;

"the Transfer Value Regulations" means the Local Government Superannuation (Transfer Value) Regulations 1954(d) ;

"voluntary contributions" means—

(a) in relation to employment in teaching service, additional contributions being paid under section 19 of the Teachers (Superannuation) Act 1956(e) or regulation 32 of the principal Teachers' Regulations in respect of a period of previous employment within the meaning of those provisions and any other contributions being paid by virtue of other rules made under section 2 of the Act as a condition of—

(i) making reckonable a period of service not otherwise reckonable;

(ii) increasing the length at which a period of service would otherwise be reckonable ; or

(iii) service being increased by the addition thereto of a period ; and

(b) in relation to service as a policeman, sums being paid in accordance with Schedule 5 to the Police Pensions Regulations.

(2) Other expressions which have meanings assigned to them by the Teachers' Regulations or the Police Pensions Regulations shall, unless the context otherwise requires, have the same respective meanings for the purposes of these Rules.

(3) Any reference in these Rules to any enactment, rules, regulations or other instrument or to provisions thereof shall, unless the context otherwise requires, be construed as a reference to such enactment, rules, regulations or other instrument or to those provisions as amended, modified, extended, applied, or re-placed by any subsequent enactment, rules, regulations or instrument.

(a) S.I. 1971/232 (1971 I, p. 700). (b) 1967 c. 12.
(c) S.I. 1967/489 (1967 I, p. 1562).
(d) S.I. 1954/1212 (1954 II, p. 1723). (e) 1956 c. 53.

(4) Any reference in these Rules to a rule, Part or paragraph shall, unless the context otherwise requires, be construed as a reference to that rule or Part of these Rules or to that paragraph of the rule in which the reference occurs, as the case may be.

(5) The Interpretation Act 1889(a) shall apply for the interpretation of these Rules as it applies for the interpretation of an Act of Parliament.

Prescribed Period

3.—(1) For the purposes of these Rules, subject as hereafter in this rule provided, the expression "prescribed period" shall mean a period of twelve months.

(2) The Secretary of State in the case of a person becoming employed in teaching service and the police authority in the case of a person becoming a policeman may, with the agreement of the other, in any particular case extend the period of twelve months specified in paragraph (1).

(3) In the case of a person who in his new employment is in teaching service—

(*a*) the period of twelve months specified in paragraph (1) shall be deemed not to expire until six months after the termination of national service in which he became engaged immediately after ceasing to be a policeman ; and

(*b*) no account shall be taken of any period spent by him on a course of study or training undertaken after ceasing to be a policeman if—

(i) before so ceasing (or, if between so ceasing and undertaking the said course he was engaged in national service, before the termination of that service) he gave notice in writing to the police authority of his intention to undertake the said course ; and

(ii) the Secretary of State is satisfied that by reason of his having undertaken the said course he is better fitted for employment in teaching service.

PART II

TRANSFER FROM TEACHING SERVICE TO POLICE SERVICE

Application

4. Except as hereinafter provided, this Part shall apply to a person who—

(*a*) becomes, or before the operative date became, a policeman within the prescribed period after ceasing to be employed in teaching service ;

(*b*) within three months after becoming a policeman or within six months after the operative date, whichever period shall last expire, or within such longer period as the police authority may with the agreement of the Secretary of State in any particular case allow, gives notice in writing to the police authority that he desires this Part to apply to him and furnishes that authority with particulars in writing of his teaching service and of any national service in which he was engaged after ceasing to be employed in teaching service ; and

---

(a) 1889 c. 63.

(c) pays to the police authority in accordance with regulation 55(1)(e) of the Police Pensions Regulations a sum equal to the amount, if any, by which the transfer value payable in respect of him under rule 6 falls to be reduced on account of any sum paid to him by way of repayment of contributions.

Excepted Cases

5. This Part shall not apply to a person who—

(a) has received payment of any pension (other than repayment of contributions) under the Teachers (Superannuation) Acts 1918 to 1956 or the Teachers' Regulations ; or

(b) last ceased to be employed in teaching service before the operative date, unless—

(i) he is a policeman on the operative date or becomes a policeman after that date and within the prescribed period ; and

(ii) the Secretary of State and the police authority agree that this Part shall apply to him.

Transfer Value

6.—(1) In respect of a person to whom this Part applies the Secretary of State shall, out of moneys provided by Parliament, pay to the police authority a transfer value of an amount calculated in accordance with the following provisions of this rule.

(2) Subject as hereafter in this rule provided, the amount of the transfer value shall be an amount equal to that which would have been payable under the Transfer Value Regulations if the person, at the date when he ceased to be employed in teaching service, had ceased to be a contributory employee under one local authority and had become such an employee under another local authority and had been entitled to reckon as contributing service his reckonable service and his service reckonable for the purposes of Part VII, IX, and X of the principal Teachers' Regulations at the length at which it is so reckonable.

(3) For the purposes of paragraph (2) service which is reckoned as contributing service shall be deemed to have been affected or modified in accordance with regulations applicable to contributing service made under section 110 of the National Insurance Act 1965(a) in like manner and to the like extent, as nearly as may be, as it was affected or modified by other such regulations.

(4) In calculating the amount of a transfer value there shall be excluded—

(a) any period of war service within the meaning of the Teachers Superannuation (War Service) Act 1939(b) and of national service within the meaning of the Teachers Superannuation (National Service) Rules 1949(c) in respect of which, at the time the transfer value is paid, the contributions remain unpaid ; and

(b) any period in respect of which the person was immediately before ceasing to be employed in teaching service paying voluntary contributions and in respect of which, at the time the transfer value is paid, he has not elected to continue to pay such contributions.

(a) 1965 c. 51.　　　　　　　　　(h) 1939 c. 95.
(c) S.I. 1949/468 (1949 I, p. 1533).

(5) The amount of transfer value payable in respect of a person shall be calculated by reference to his age—

    (a) on the operative date if, having ceased to be employed in teaching service more than twelve months before that date, he became a policeman before that date ; or

    (b) on the date on which he became a policeman if that date is on or after the operative date and more than twelve months after that on which he ceased to be employed in teaching service.

(6) In a case in which the prescribed period exceeds one year the amount of the transfer value payable in respect of any person shall be reduced by an amount equal to the compound interest calculated as in paragraph (7) provided on any sum (including any sum deducted therefrom by reason of liability to income tax arising on its payment) paid to him after he last ceased to be employed in teaching service by way of repayment of contributions (other than voluntary contributions and contributions made for the purpose of securing benefits for his widow, children or other dependants).

(7) For the purposes of paragraph (6)—

    (a) compound interest shall be calculated on the sum therein mentioned at three per cent. per annum with half-yearly rests from the day one year after that on which the person ceased to be employed in teaching service or from the day on which contributions were repaid to him, whichever shall be the later, to the day on which he gave notice to the police authority in accordance with Rule 4(b) ; and

    (b) if the amount of compound interest calculated as aforesaid exceeds a sum equal to one-half of the difference between the amount of the transfer value payable under this rule apart from paragraph (6) and the amount of the transfer value which would have been so payable if calculated by reference to the person's age on ceasing to be employed in teaching service, it shall be reduced to that sum.

Benefits under the Teachers' Regulations

7.—(1) Subject to the provisions of Part III and of interchange rules no payment of any pension shall be made under the Teachers' Regulations to or in respect of any person in respect of any service which is taken into account in calculating the amount of a transfer value under rule 6 other than a payment by way of return of voluntary contributions.

(2) In this rule "interchange rules" means rules made under section 2 of the Act of 1948 and includes provisions similar to those of such rules contained in any instrument made under any other Act.

PART III

TRANSFER FROM POLICE SERVICE TO TEACHING SERVICE

Application

8.—(1) Except as hereinafter provided, this Part shall apply to a person who—

    (a) becomes, or before the operative date became, employed in teaching service within the prescribed period after ceasing to be a policeman ;

(b) within three months after becoming employed in teaching service or within six months after the operative date, whichever period shall last expire, or within such longer period as the Secretary of State may with the agreement of the police authority in any particular case allow, gives notice in writing to the Secretary of State that he desires this Part to apply to him and furnishes the Secretary of State with particulars in writing of his service which is pensionable service for the purposes of the Police Pensions Regulations and of any national service in which he was engaged after ceasing to be a policeman ;

(c) is a person in respect of whom the Secretary of State receives from the police authority a transfer value calculated in accordance with Schedule 9 to the Police Pensions Regulations ; and

(d) within three months after becoming employed in teaching service or within six months after the operative date, whichever period shall last expire, or within such longer period as the Secretary of State may in any particular case allow, pays to the Secretary of State a sum equal to the amount, if any, by which the said transfer value falls to be reduced under paragraph 5 of the said Schedule 9.

Excepted Cases

9. This Part shall not apply to a person who last ceased to be a policeman before the operative date unless he is employed on that date in teaching service or the Secretary of State agrees that this Part shall apply to him.

Reckoning of Service

10.—(1) Subject as in paragraph (2) and rule 11 provided, the pensionable service reckonable for the purposes of the Police Pensions Regulations by a person to whom this Part applies immediately before he ceased to be a policeman, increased by one-third, shall be reckoned as reckonable service.

(2) For the purposes of this rule pensionable service reckonable for the purposes of the Police Pensions Regulations shall not include service so reckonable by reason of the payment of voluntary contributions or an undertaking to pay such contributions.

Average Salary

11. For the purpose of calculating under section 4(3) of the Teachers' Superannuation Act 1967 the average salary of a person to whom this Part applies whose teaching service after ceasing to be a policeman amounts to less than three years—

(a) such period immediately prior to his ceasing to be a policeman as, together with the period of teaching service, amounts to three years shall be reckoned as teaching service ; and

(b) his salary during any period so reckoned shall be his pensionable pay within the meaning of the Police Pensions Regulations for that period.

Voluntary Contributions

12.—(1) A person to whom this Part applies may, within three months of becoming employed in teaching service or within such longer period as the Secretary of State may in any particular case allow, elect to continue to pay voluntary contributions being paid by him immediately before ceasing to be a policeman.

(2) In relation to a person who elects as aforesaid and thereafter pays to the Secretary of State any amounts outstanding in respect of such voluntary contributions at the time at which they would have been payable if he had remained a policeman rule 10 shall have effect as if paragraph (2) thereof were omitted.

(3) The provisions of paragraphs (5)(*b*), (6), (7), (8) and (12) of regulation 32 and of regulation 38 of the principal Teachers' Regulations shall apply to voluntary contributions payable under this rule as if they were additional contributions payable in respect of previous employment within the meaning of those Regulations.

(4) If a person does not elect as aforesaid or if voluntary contributions are repaid to him under regulation 38 of the principal Teachers' Regulations as applied by this rule—

(*a*) the period to which such contributions related shall be reckoned for the purposes of the Teachers' Regulations only to the extent, if any, to which it would have been so reckoned if no such contributions had been made in respect thereof ; and

(*b*) the Secretary of State shall repay to the police authority the amount by which the transfer value paid in respect of him was under the Police Pensions Regulations enhanced by reason of the payment by him when a policeman of such contributions.

Commencement of Employment

13. For the purposes of regulation 41(1)(*a*)(ii) of the principal Teachers' Regulations the date on which a person to whom this Part applies became a policeman shall be deemed to be a date on which he became employed in teaching service.

Return of Contributions

14.—(1) Where a person to whom this Part applies ceases to be employed in teaching service or dies, then, to any sum to which he or his personal representatives shall be entitled under the Teachers' Regulations by way of repayment of contributions there shall be added—

(*a*) if pension contributions under the Police Pensions Regulations were related to either 5 per cent. or 4·5 per cent. of pensionable pay, a sum equal to the amount of the aggregate contributions within the meaning of those Regulations ; or

(*b*) if pension contributions under the Police Pensions Regulations were related to 6·25 per cent. of pensionable pay, a sum equal to the amount of the aggregate contributions within the meaning of those Regulations which he would have paid had he paid pension contributions related to 5 per cent. of pensionable pay.

(2) The sum to be added under paragraph (1) to that to which a person or his personal representatives shall be entitled shall be—

(*a*) reduced by a sum equal to any sum paid under Regulation 38 of the principal Teachers' Regulations as applied by rule 12 by way of repayment of voluntary contributions made while a policeman ; and

(*b*) increased by compound interest on the amount thereof after any such reduction as aforesaid.

(3) For the purposes of paragraph (2) compound interest shall be calculated in accordance with the provisions of Part IV of the principal Teachers' Regulations from the date on which the person became employed in teaching service.

Modification of Contributions and Benefits by reason of National Insurance

15.—(1) In relation to a person to whom this Part applies—

(*a*) the following paragraphs of Schedule 5 to the principal Teachers' Regulations, that is to say—

paragraph 2 (which provides for the reduction of contributions),

paragraph 4 (which provides for the reduction of pensions by fixed annual amounts specified therein) and

paragraph 5 (which provides for the reduction of pensions in accordance with a table contained therein specifying ages at a given date and annual amounts)

shall not apply if any pension payable to him under the Police Pensions Regulations would not have been subject to any reduction by virtue of paragraph 1(2) of Part III of Schedule 2 to those Regulations ;

(*b*) paragraphs 2 and 5 of the said Schedule 5 shall apply if any pension payable to him under the Police Pensions Regulations would have been subject to reduction under paragraph 1(3) of Part III of Schedule 2 to those Regulations ; and

(*c*) paragraphs 2 and 4 of the said Schedule 5 shall apply in any other case.

(2) Where, by virtue of paragraph (1)(*b*), paragraph 5 of Schedule 5 to the principal Teachers' Regulations applies to a person the date of modification for the purposes of the latter paragraph shall be the date which was in relation to him the appropriate date within the meaning of paragraph 1(3) of Part III of Schedule 2 to the Police Pensions Regulations.

Given under the Official Seal of the Secretary of State for Education and Science on 16th August 1971.

(L.S.)
          Margaret Thatcher,
          Secretary of State for Education
          and Science.

Consent of the Minister for the Civil Service given under his Official Seal on 17th August 1971.

(L.S.)
          J. E. Herbecq,
          Authorised by the Minister for
          the Civil Service.

EXPLANATORY NOTE

(This Note is not part of the Rules.)

These Rules relate to the superannuation of persons who transfer from service pensionable under the Teachers' Superannuation Regulations 1967 to 1971 to pensionable service as a policeman, or vice versa. A policeman becoming a teacher is enabled, if a transfer value is paid to the Secretary of State, to aggregate his service as a policeman (increased by one-third) with his later service as a teacher so that he will receive a single superannuation allowance based on his total service. In the case of a teacher becoming a policeman provision is made for the payment of a transfer value by the Secretary of State to the appropriate police authority so that a single pension may be paid under the Police Pensions Regulations 1971.

The Rules may have retrospective effect in certain cases under the express powers of, and subject to the safeguards required by, section 2(5) of the Superannuation (Miscellaneous Provisions) Act 1948.

STATUTORY INSTRUMENTS

1971 No. 1381

WAGES COUNCILS

The Wages Regulation (Fur) Order 1971

Made - - - -	18*th August* 1971
Coming into Operation	13*th September* 1971

Whereas the Secretary of State has received from the Fur Wages Council (Great Britain) the wages regulation proposals set out in the Schedules hereto;

Now, therefore, the Secretary of State in exercise of his powers under section 11 of the Wages Councils Act 1959(a) and of all other powers enabling him in that behalf, hereby makes the following Order:—

1. This Order may be cited as the Wages Regulation (Fur) Order 1971.

2.—(1) In this Order the expression "the specified date" means the 13th September 1971, provided that where, as respects any worker who is paid wages at intervals not exceeding seven days, that date does not correspond with the beginning of the period for which the wages are paid, the expression "the specified date" means, as respects that worker, the beginning of the next such period following that date.

(2) The Interpretation Act 1889(b) shall apply to the interpretation of this Order as it applies to the interpretation of an Act of Parliament and as if this Order and the Order hereby revoked were Acts of Parliament.

3. The wages regulation proposals set out in the Schedules hereto shall have effect as from the specified date and as from that date the Wages Regulation (Fur) Order 1970(c) shall cease to have effect.

Signed by order of the Secretary of State.

18th August 1971.

J. R. Lloyd Davies,
Assistant Secretary,
Department of Employment.

(a) 1959 c. 69.   (b) 1889 c. 63.
(c) S.I. 1970/809 (1970 II, p. 2620).

SCHEDULE 1 Article 3

The following minimum remuneration shall be substituted for the statutory minimum remuneration fixed by the Wages Regulation (Fur) Order 1970 (Order Z. (89)).

STATUTORY MINIMUM REMUNERATION

PART I

APPLICATION

1.—(1) Subject to the provisions of Part III of this Schedule, the minimum remuneration payable to a worker to whom this Schedule applies for all work except work to which a minimum overtime rate applies under Part IV is—

(a) in the case of a time worker, the hourly general minimum time rate payable to the worker under the provisions of this Schedule;

(b) in the case of a worker employed on piece work (other than an apprentice in the Dressers' and Dyers' Section of the trade to whom paragraph 10 applies):

(i) where a general minimum piece rate applies under Part VI, that rate;

(ii) where no general minimum piece rate applies, piece rates each of which would yield, in the circumstances of the case, to an ordinary worker at least the same amount of money as the piece work basis time rate applicable to the worker or, where no piece work basis time rate applies, at least the same amount of money as the hourly general minimum time rate which would be payable if the worker were a time worker, or

(c) in the case of an apprentice in the Dressers' and Dyers' Section of the trade who is employed on piece work and to whom paragraph 10 applies, the piece rates specified in that paragraph:

Provided that where an hourly guaranteed time rate is applicable to the worker and his minimum remuneration calculated on a time work basis at that rate exceeds the minimum remuneration calculated at the said piece rates the worker shall be paid not less than that guaranteed time rate.

(2) In this Schedule the expressions "hourly general minimum time rate" and "hourly guaranteed time rate" mean respectively the general minimum time rate and the guaranteed time rate applicable to the worker under Part II of this Schedule divided in either case by 40.

2. This Schedule applies to workers in relation to whom the Fur Wages Council (Great Britain) operates, that is to say, workers employed in Great Britain in the trade specified in the Regulations made by the Minister and dated 25th October 1919(a), with respect to the Constitution and Proceedings of the Trade Board for the Fur Trade (Great Britain), namely:—

The dressing, dyeing and making up of furs or of skins for furriers' purposes including:—

(1) The dressing or dyeing or general preparation of furs or skins;

(2) The manufacture of furs or skins into garments, rugs, or other articles;

(3) The remaking, repairing or cleaning of articles made from furs or skins where carried on by fur dressers or fur manufacturers;

(a) S.R. & O. 1919/1634 (Rev. XXIII, p. 474: 1919 II, p. 549).

(4) The lining with fur of coats, cloaks, mantles, capes, gloves or similar articles where carried out by fur manufacturers;

(5) Bundling, packing, warehousing and other operations carried on by fur skin merchants, fur dressers, fur dyers or fur manufacturers;

but excluding:—

(a) The making up of fur toys, purses, boots, shoes or slippers;

(b) The making of fur hats when carried on in association with or in conjunction with the making or trimming of men's, women's or children's headgear from other materials;

(c) Warehousing, packing and other similar operations carried on in shops wholly, mainly, or substantially engaged in the retail distribution of articles of any description that are not made on the premises.

PART II

GENERAL MINIMUM, GUARANTEED AND PIECE WORK BASIS

TIME RATES

CUTTING AND NAILING BRANCH OF THE FURRIERS' SECTION
GENERAL MINIMUM TIME RATES

3. Subject to the provisions of this Schedule, the general minimum time rates per week of 40 hours applicable to workers in the cutting and nailing branch of the Furriers' Section are as follows:—

£

(1) CUTTERS who, having worked in the said branch for six years or, in the case of workers who were apprentices, for five years, have subsequently worked as cutters for—

    (a) not less than one year   ...   .   15·00

    (b) less than one year   ...   .   13·50

(2) NAILERS who, having worked in the said branch for six years or, in the case of workers who were apprentices, for five years, have subsequently worked as nailers for—

    (a) not less than one year   ...   .   14·00

    (b) less than one year   ...   .   13·00

Provided that where a nailer performs also the work of a cutter the rate applicable to him in respect of that work shall be that which would be applicable if he were a cutter.

(3)(a) APPRENTICES to cutting and nailing, whose employment complies with the provisions of paragraph 18, during the following years of apprenticeship;

(b) LEARNERS to cutting and nailing, whose employment complies with the conditions specified in paragraph 21, during the following years of employment; and

(c) ALL OTHER WORKERS employed in cutting and nailing or in either of such operations, during the following years of employment—

	Workers aged 18 years or over	All Other Workers
	£	£
The first year	8·50	5·50
The second year	9·00	6·50
The third year	9·70	7·70
The fourth year	10·70	
The fifth year	12·00	

£

(4) MALE WORKERS aged 21 years or over and engaged in CLEAN-ING by any method, fur skins or articles manufactured from fur...   12·50

PIECE WORK BASIS TIME RATES—CUTTERS OR NAILERS

4. The piece work basis time rate applicable to a cutter or nailer specified in sub-paragraph (1) or sub-paragraph (2) of paragraph 3 when employed on piece work is a rate equal to one-and-one-third times the hourly general minimum time rate which would be applicable if the worker were employed on time work.

MACHINING, LINING, FINISHING AND HAND FUR SEWING BRANCH OF THE FURRIERS' SECTION

GENERAL MINIMUM TIME RATES

5. Subject to the provisions of this Schedule, the general minimum time rates per week of 40 hours applicable to female workers in the machining, lining, finishing and hand fur sewing branch of the Furriers' Section are as follows:—

£

(1) FUR MACHINISTS who have worked for five years in the said branch ... ...   10·60

(2) LINERS, FINISHERS, HAND FUR SEWERS OR MACHIN-ISTS (other than fur machinists) who have worked for five years in the said branch ... ...   10·10

(3)(a) LEARNERS to machining, lining, finishing or hand fur sewing, or to two or more of such operations, whose employment complies with the conditions specified in paragraph 22, during the following years of employment; and

(b) **ALL OTHER WORKERS** employed in the said branch, during the following periods of employment—

	Workers aged 18 years or over	All Other Workers
	£	£
The first year	7·00	5·50
The second year	7·70	6·50
The third year	8·50	6·70
The fourth year	8·70	
The fifth year	9·50	

PIECE WORK BASIS TIME RATES

6. The piece work basis time rate applicable to a female worker specified in sub-paragraph (1) or sub-paragraph (2) of paragraph 5 when employed on piece work is a rate equal to one-and-one-third times the hourly general minimum time rate which would be applicable if she were employed on time work.

RECKONING OF EMPLOYMENT IN THE FURRIERS' SECTION

7.—(1) A worker (not being an apprentice) who enters, or has entered, the Furriers' Section at or over the age of 18 years shall be treated for the purpose of this Part of this Schedule as though he had, at the date of his entry, completed the following period of learnership or other employment, as the case may be, in the branch in which he is employed—

(a) in the case of a worker in the cutting and nailing branch aged at the date of his entry in the said section—

(i) 18 and under 19 years ... ... 1 year

(ii) 19 and under 20 years ... ... 2 years

(iii) 20 years or over ... ... 3 years

(b) in the case of a worker in the machining, lining, finishing and hand fur sewing branch ... ... 1 year

(2) For the purpose of calculating any period of employment in the Furriers' Section, any employment in the machining, lining, finishing and hand fur sewing branch shall count as employment in the cutting and nailing branch and any employment in the cutting and nailing branch shall count as employment in the machining, lining, finishing and hand fur sewing branch.

FUR SORTERS' SECTION

GENERAL MINIMUM TIME RATES

8. The general minimum time rates per week of 40 hours applicable to workers employed in the Fur Sorters' Section in merchants' or brokers' warehouses are as follows:—

£

(1) MALE FUR SORTERS aged 21 years or over ...   .   14·00

(2) MALE WORKERS aged 21 years or over and employed in a FUR SORTING department under the supervision of a male fur sorter or as COUNTERS, STRIPERS or SIZERS ...   .   13·00

(3) ALL OTHER MALE WORKERS employed in the Fur Sorters' Section (except male skin packers), being aged—

	£
18 years or over, after six months	13·00
18 „ „ „ , during first six months	10·50
16 and under 18 years	8·00
Under 16 years	6·00

(4) FEMALE WORKERS employed as FUR SORTERS, ASSISTANTS TO FUR SORTERS, COUNTERS, STRIPERS or SIZERS, being aged—

	£
18 years or over	9·50
16 and under 18 years	7·50
Under 16 years	6·50

DRESSERS' AND DYERS' SECTION

GENERAL MINIMUM TIME RATES FOR WORKERS OTHER THAN APPRENTICES

9. The general minimum time rates per week of 40 hours applicable to workers (other than the apprentices to whom paragraph 10 applies) in the Dressers' and Dyers' Section are as follows:—

£

(1) MALE TUBBERS ... ...   12·70

(2) WORKERS EMPLOYED AS ROLLER FLESHING MACHINE OPERATORS (other than shaving machine operators)—

	£
(a) Male workers	12·70
(b) Female workers	8·50

(3) WORKERS EMPLOYED AS HAND FLESHERS OR ROTARY FLESHING MACHINE OPERATORS—

	£
(a) Male workers	16·50
(b) Female workers	11·20

(4) ALL OTHER MALE WORKERS employed in the Dressers' and Dyers' Section (except the apprentices to whom paragraph 10 applies), being aged—

	£
19 years or over	10·90
17 and under 19 years	8·50
Under 17 years	5·70

(5) ALL OTHER FEMALE WORKERS employed in the Dressers'
and Dyers' Section (except the apprentices to whom paragraph 10
applies), being aged—

18 years or over	7·70
Under 18 years	5·80

MINIMUM RATES FOR APPRENTICES

10.—(1) The general minimum time rates specified in Column 2 of the next following
table are applicable during the first six months of apprenticeship to apprentices
employed, in accordance with the conditions specified in paragraph 19, on time work
in the Dressers' and Dyers' Section, and the piece rates and guaranteed time rates
specified in Columns 3 and 4 respectively are applicable to such workers when employed
in accordance with the said conditions on piece work during the remainder of their
apprenticeship.

Column 1	Column 2	Column 3	Column 4
Period of Apprenticeship	General Minimum Time Rates	Piece Rates	Guaranteed Time Rates
The first six months	A rate equal to the general minimum time rate applicable to a worker of the same age and sex under sub-paragraph (4) or sub-paragraph (5) of paragraph 9.	—	—
The second six months	—	One-quarter of the piece rates specified in sub-paragraph (2) of this paragraph.	A rate equal to the general minimum time rate applicable to a worker of the same age and sex under sub-paragraph (4) or sub-paragraph (5) of paragraph 9.
The second year	—	One-half of the piece rates specified in sub-paragraph (2) of this paragraph.	
The third year	—	Three-quarters of the piece rates specified in sub-paragraph (2) of this paragraph.	—
The fourth year	—	The piece rates specified in sub-paragraph (2) of this paragraph.	—

(2) The piece rates referred to in Column 3 of the said table are the general minimum
piece rates specified in Part VI of this Schedule or, where no piece rate is so specified,
piece rates each of which would yield, in the circumstances of the case, to an ordinary
worker of the same sex at least the same amount of money as the general minimum
time rate applicable under sub-paragraph (3) of paragraph 9 to a worker employed
as a hand flesher or rotary fleshing machine operator.

PIECE WORK BASIS TIME RATES

ROLLER FLESHING MACHINE OPERATORS

11. The piece work basis time rates per week of 40 hours applicable to male or female workers employed in the Dressers' and Dyers' Section as roller fleshing machine operators (other than shaving machine operators) are as follows:—

		£
(1)	Male workers	14·40
(2)	Female workers	10·20

ALL SECTIONS OF THE TRADE

GENERAL MINIMUM TIME RATES

12. The general minimum time rates per week of 40 hours applicable to all workers to whom the foregoing provisions of this Part of this Schedule do not apply, are as follows:—

(1) MALE SKIN PACKERS being aged—

	£
18 years or over, after six months	12·50
18 „ „ „ , during first six months	10·50

(2) ALL OTHER MALE WORKERS, being aged—

	£
19 years or over	11·00
17 and under 19 years	8·70
Under 17 years	5·80

(3) ALL FEMALE WORKERS, being aged—

	£
18 years or over	8·00
Under 18 years	6·20

DEFINITIONS

13. For the purposes of this Part of this Schedule—

"CUTTER" means a person engaged, wholly or mainly, in cutting furs or skins in connection with manufacture, remodelling, alterations or repairing, including any preparation of furs or skins actually performed by such person for such cutting but not including nailing by a worker engaged, wholly or mainly, in nailing;

"FUR SORTER" means a worker who assumes sole responsibility for the proper grading of skins;

"NAILER" means a person engaged, wholly or mainly, in nailing;

"SKIN PACKER" means a worker engaged in and responsible for baling or packing skins for transport;

"TUBBER" means a worker in the Dressers' and Dyers' Section who has at least five years' experience therein and is capable of handling in an expert manner most varieties of fur skins from the raw stage through the various processes (except fleshing) to the finished article.

Part III

NIGHT WORKERS IN ALL SECTIONS OF THE TRADE

14.—(1) Notwithstanding anything contained in this Schedule, a night worker shall be paid for any work between the hours of 7 p.m. on any day and 7 a.m. on the next succeeding day one-and-one-third times the appropriate minimum rate: Provided that this provision shall not apply to a time worker in respect of any overtime.

(2) For the purposes of this paragraph—

"APPROPRIATE MINIMUM RATE" means, in the case of a time worker, the hourly general minimum time rate otherwise applicable to the worker or, in the case of a worker employed on piece work, the minimum rate which would be applicable if he were not a night worker;

"NIGHT WORKER" means a worker whose usual hours of work (exclusive of overtime) include at least 4 hours a night between 7 p.m. and 7 a.m.: Provided that a worker who is usually so employed during part only of the week shall be treated as a night worker in respect of that part of the week;

"OVERTIME" means, in the case of a time worker, any time in respect of which a minimum overtime rate applies or, in the case of a worker employed on piece work, any time in respect of which such a rate would apply if he were a time worker.

PART IV

OVERTIME AND WAITING TIME

MINIMUM OVERTIME RATES

15.—(1) Subject to the provisions of this paragraph, minimum overtime rates are payable to ANY TIME WORKER as follows:—

(a) On any day other than a Saturday, Sunday or a customary holiday, for all time worked in excess of 8 hours—Time-and-a-half:

Provided that where the employer normally requires the worker's attendance only from Monday to Friday (inclusive) the said rate shall be payable after 8¼ hours on two of those days and after 8½ hours on the remaining three days;

(b) On a Saturday, not being a customary holiday, for all time worked in excess of 4 hours—Time-and-a-half:

Provided that where the employer normally requires the worker's attendance only from Monday to Friday (inclusive) the said rate shall be payable for all time worked on a Saturday;

(c) On a Sunday or a customary holiday, for all time worked—Double time.

(d) In any week exclusive of any time in respect of which a minimum overtime rate is payable under the provisions of (a), (b) or (c) above—
For all time worked in excess of 40 hours—Time-and-a-half.

(2) For the purpose of calculating the number of hours worked by a worker on any day, regard shall be had to the whole of the worker's turn of duty and, where that turn extends beyond midnight, it shall be regarded as having been worked wholly on the day upon which it commences:

Provided that

(a) this provision shall not apply in respect of any time worked between midnight on Saturday and midnight on Sunday and for that time double time shall be payable as provided in sub-paragraph (1)(c) of this paragraph;

(b) all time worked on a Monday morning as part of a turn of duty normally commencing on Sunday shall be treated as though it were worked on the previous Saturday and included in a turn of duty which commenced on that day.

(3) Where the worker is normally employed on Sunday instead of Saturday and, in the case of a woman or young person, such substitution is not unlawful—

(a) for the purposes of sub-paragraph (1) of this paragraph, Saturday shall be treated as a Sunday and Sunday as a Saturday;

(b) for the purposes of sub-paragraph (2) of this paragraph, Saturday shall be treated as a Friday, Sunday as a Saturday and Monday as a Sunday.

16. In this Part of this Schedule—

(1) "TIME-AND-A-HALF" and "DOUBLE TIME" mean respectively,

(*a*) in the case of a worker other than a night worker, one-and-a-half times and twice the hourly general minimum time rate otherwise payable to the worker;

(*b*) in the case of a night worker, one-and-a-half times and twice the hourly general minimum time rate which would be payable if the worker were not a night worker and a minimum overtime rate did not apply.

(2) "CUSTOMARY HOLIDAY" means—

(*a*) In England and Wales—

Christmas Day (or, if Christmas Day falls on a Sunday, such weekday as may be appointed by national proclamation, or, if none is so appointed, the next following Tuesday), Boxing Day, Good Friday, Easter Monday, Whit Monday (or, where another day is substituted therefor by national proclamation, that day) and August Bank Holiday;

(*b*) In Scotland—

New Year's Day (or, if New Year's Day falls on a Sunday, the following Monday);

the local Spring holiday;

the local Autumn holiday; and

three other days (being days on which the worker normally works) in the course of a calendar year, to be fixed by the employer and notified to the worker not less than four weeks before the holiday; or

(*c*) in the case of each of the said days (other than a day fixed by the employer in Scotland and notified to the worker as aforesaid) a day substituted therefor, being either a day recognised by local custom as a day of holiday in substitution for the said day or a day fixed by agreement between the employer and the worker or his representative.

(3) "NIGHT WORKER" has the same meaning as in paragraph 14.

WAITING TIME

17.—(1) A worker is entitled to payment of the minimum remuneration specified in this Schedule for all time during which he is present on the premises of his employer unless he is present thereon in any of the following circumstances:—

(*a*) without the employer's consent, express or implied;

(*b*) for some purpose unconnected with his work and other than that of waiting for work to be given to him to perform;

(*c*) by reason only of the fact that he is resident thereon;

(*d*) during normal meal times in a room or place in which no work is being done, and he is not waiting for work to be given to him to perform.

(2) The minimum remuneration payable under sub-paragraph (1) of this paragraph to a piece worker when not engaged on piece work is that which would be payable if he were a time worker.

PART V

CONDITIONS AS TO APPRENTICES AND LEARNERS

APPRENTICES TO CUTTING AND NAILING

18.—(1) Subject to the provisions of this Schedule, the general minimum time rates specified in paragraph 3(3) apply only to an apprentice to cutting and nailing in whose case the conditions following are fulfilled—

(a) the apprentice shall be employed during the whole of his time for a period of five years as an apprentice to cutting and nailing under a written contract of apprenticeship which has been duly executed and which includes the following provisions, which the Wages Council considers necessary for securing the effective instruction of the apprentice, or provisions substantially to the same effect and no provisions contrary thereto:—

(i) the apprentice of his own free will and with the consent of the guardian binds himself to serve the employer as his apprentice in his trade of furrier for a term of five years;

(ii) the employer shall keep the worker as his apprentice during the said term, and to the best of his power, skill and knowledge instruct the apprentice or cause him to be instructed in cutting and nailing in the Furriers' Section of the fur trade;

(iii) the employer shall keep the apprentice under his own supervision or place him under one or more fully qualified journeymen;

(iv) during the first three years of apprenticeship the employer shall not require the apprentice to work any time in respect of which any minimum overtime rates would apply under Part IV of this Schedule to a worker employed on time work;

(v) during the first two years of apprenticeship the employer shall not require the apprentice to do any piece work;

(b) in the establishment in which the apprentice is employed the number of apprentices to cutting and nailing shall be limited in proportion to the number of journeymen employed in the cutting and nailing branch at the time of the engagement of the apprentice as follows—

Number of Journeymen	Number of Apprentices
5 or under	1
From 6 to 10	2
From 11 to 15	3
From 16 to 20	4
From 21 to 25	5

and thereafter in the proportion of one additional apprentice to each five additional journeymen, any number of journeymen in excess of an exact multiple of five being treated as five;

(c) the apprentice shall be the holder of a certificate of registration of apprenticeship issued by the Wages Council or shall have made an application for such a certificate which has been acknowledged and is still under consideration:

Provided that the certification of an apprentice may be cancelled by the Wages Council if the other conditions of apprenticeship are not complied with.

(2) For the purpose of determining the proportion of apprentices to journeymen in accordance with the last preceding sub-paragraph, "journeyman" means a male or female worker other than an apprentice or a learner, and an employer who employs no journeymen but personally instructs an apprentice shall be treated as a journeyman.

APPRENTICES IN THE DRESSERS' AND DYERS' SECTION

19.—(1) Subject to the provisions of this Schedule, the minimum remuneration specified in paragraph 10 applies only to an apprentice to dressing and dyeing in whose case the conditions following are fulfilled:—

(a) the apprentice shall be employed during the whole of his time for a period of four years as an apprentice to dressing and dyeing under a written contract of apprenticeship, entered into on or after his sixteenth birthday, which is duly executed and which includes the following provisions which the Wages Council considers necessary for securing the effective instruction of the apprentice or provisions substantially to the same effect and no provisions contrary thereto:—

(i) the apprentice of his own free will and with the consent of the guardian binds himself to serve the employer as his apprentice in his trade of fur dressing and dyeing for a term of four years;

(ii) the apprentice shall during the period of service attend at his own expense or that of his guardian such classes outside the factory as his employer may from time to time recommend;

(iii) the employer shall keep the worker as his apprentice during the said term and to the best of his power, skill and knowledge instruct the apprentice or cause him to be instructed in hand fleshing or rotary machine fleshing or shaving or unhairing, and during the first six months of service shall give the apprentice opportunity for spending a proportion of his time on work in all sections in the dressing and dyeing shop as carried on by the employer;

(iv) the employer shall keep the apprentice under his own supervision or place him under a fully qualified journeyman;

(v) during the first six months of service the employer shall not put the apprentice on piece work;

(b) in the establishment in which the apprentice is employed the number of apprentices to dressing and dyeing shall be limited in proportion to the number of journeymen in the service of the employer in the Dressers' and Dyers' Section at the time of the engagement of the apprentice as follows:—

Number of Journeymen	Number of Apprentices
5 or under	1
From 6 to 10	2
From 11 to 15	3
From 16 to 20	4
From 21 to 25	5

and thereafter in the proportion of one additional apprentice to each additional five journeymen, any number of journeymen in excess of an exact multiple of five being treated as five;

(c) the apprentice shall be the holder of a certificate of registration of apprenticeship issued by the Wages Council or shall have made application jointly with the employer to the Wages Council for such a certificate which has been acknowledged and is still under consideration:

Provided that the certification of an apprentice may be cancelled by the Wages Council if the other conditions of apprenticeship are not complied with.

(2) For the purpose of determining the proportion of apprentices to journeymen in accordance with the provisions of the last preceding sub-paragraph, "journeyman" means a worker employed as a hand flesher, rotary machine flesher, shaver or unhairer to whom there apply the general minimum piece rates for fleshers, shavers or unhairers specified in Part VI of this Schedule or the general minimum time rates for such workers specified in paragraph 9, and an employer who employs no journeymen but personally instructs the apprentice shall be treated as a journeyman.

PROSPECTIVE APPRENTICES

20. Notwithstanding the foregoing provisions of this Schedule, where an employer employs a worker as a prospective apprentice for a probationary period not exceeding four weeks and all the appropriate conditions as to apprenticeship other than those with regard to employment under a written contract of apprenticeship and certification by the Wages Council are fulfilled, the minimum remuneration applicable to that worker during the said period shall be that applicable to an apprentice employed in accordance with the conditions specified in paragraph 18 or paragraph 19 as the case may be and, in the event of the worker being continued thereafter at his employment as an apprentice, the said probationary period shall for the purpose of this Schedule be treated as part of the period of apprenticeship, whether or not it is included therein.

LEARNERS TO CUTTING AND NAILING

21. The general minimum time rates specified in sub-paragraph (4) of paragraph 3 apply to a learner to cutting and nailing who (not being an apprentice to whom the minimum rates in sub-paragraph (3) of that paragraph apply) is employed during the whole or a substantial part of his time for a period not exceeding five years in learning cutting and nailing by an employer who provides him with reasonable facilities for such learning.

LEARNERS TO MACHINING, LINING, FINISHING OR HAND FUR SEWING

22. The minimum rates specified in sub-paragraph (3) of paragraph 5 apply to a learner to machining, lining, finishing or hand fur sewing, or to two or more of such operations, who is employed during the whole or a substantial part of her time for a period not exceeding five years in learning machining, lining, finishing or hand fur sewing, or two or more of such operations, by an employer who provides her with reasonable facilities for such learning.

PART VI

GENERAL MINIMUM PIECE RATES

HAND OR MACHINE FLESHING

23. The general minimum piece rates applicable to workers employed on piece work (other than apprentices to whom paragraph 10 applies, during the first three years of their apprenticeship) in any of the operations specified in Columns 2, 3 and 4 of Table 1 or Columns 2 and 3 of Table II of this paragraph, are as follows:—

TABLE I

Skin (of any size except where otherwise stated) Column 1	Hand Fleshing (per 100 skins) Column 2	Machine Fleshing (per 100 skins) Column 3	Paring out all over from Pickle or Leather by hand or machine (per 100 skins) Column 4
	£	£	£
Anteater	33·10	24·83	16·85
Antelope Furriers (hand or machine)	2·10	2·10	2·10
„ Cow or large Furriers (hand or machine)	3·15	3·15	3·15
Badger	6·60	4·95	2·40
Baranduki	1·05	0·79	—
Bears, Black...	41·50	31·13	—
„ „ Cub	21·05	15·79	—
„ Brown	48·95	36·71	—
„ „ Cub	24·05	18·04	—
„ Grizzly	69·85	52·39	—
„ „ Cub...	34·30	25·72	—
„ Green	139·70	104·77	36·10
„ „ Cub...	69·80	52·35	17·45
„ Indian	69·80	52·35	17·45
„ „ Cub...	34·90	26·17	—
„ Polar...	104·65	78·49	27·05
„ „ Cub...	51·70	38·77	—
Beaver	16·55	12·41	16·55
„ Cub	10·40	7·80	5·10
Buffalo	124·50	93·38	61·35
Bullock	124·50	93·38	61·35
Cat, Biscution	4·80	3·60	—
„ Bush	7·25	5·44	—
„ Civet	1·50	1·13	—
„ Dutch	3·00	2·25	—
„ House	2·90	2·18	—
„ Leopard (hand or machine) ...	7·50	7·50	7·50
„ Luke	9·30	6·98	—
„ Lynx	12·50	9·38	—
„ Ocelot (hand or machine) ...	4·40	4·40	4·40
„ Serval	6·90	5·18	—
Cheetah	27·65	20·74	13·85
Chinchilla	5·00	3·75	—
Cow	124·50	93·38	61·35
Calf (English)	69·85	52·39	34·90
„ (English stillborn)	18·65	13·99	6·05
„ Other types	13·80	10·35	—
Coyote	8·45	6·34	—
Deer, Antelope	46·90	35·18	23·45
„ Dik Dik	5·70	4·28	2·85
„ Duiker...	7·25	5·44	3·60
„ Elk	41·50	31·13	20·75
„ Fawn	8·70	6·53	4·35
„ Gazelle	12·65	9·49	6·90
„ Hartbeest	34·30	25·73	17·15
„ Park	21·00	15·75	10·50
„ Reindeer	21·00	15·75	10·50
„ Springbok	13·25	9·94	6·60
„ Waterbuck	41·80	31·55	20·90
Dogs, Furriers	11·45	8·59	—
„ Odd skins	23·45	17·59	—
Donkey	124·50	93·38	61·35
Ermine (including Solongoi) ...	1·25	0·94	—
Fischer	12·60	9·45	6·35
Fitch, Open	1·85	1·39	—
„ (extra if opened by flesher)...	0·25	0·25	—
„ Cased	2·10	1·58	—

TABLE I—*continued*

Skin (of any size except where otherwise stated) Column 1	Hand Fleshing (per 100 skins) Column 2	Machine Fleshing (per 100 skins) Column 3	Paring out all over from Pickle or Leather by hand or machine (per 100 skins) Column 4
	£	£	£
Flying Fox	4·20	3·15	—
Flying Squirrel	4·20	3·15	—
Fox, Black	17·50	13·13	—
„ Blue	17·50	13·13	—
„ Cross	17·50	13·13	—
„ Silver	17·50	13·13	—
„ Platina	17·50	13·13	—
„ Kamchatka	17·50	13·13	—
„ Russian	9·20	6·90	—
„ Canadian	9·20	6·90	—
„ American & European ...	9·20	6·90	—
„ Australian	7·50	5·63	—
„ Persian	7·50	5·63	—
„ English	7·50	5·63	—
„ S. American (other than Kit)	7·50	5·63	—
„ Cape	7·50	5·63	—
„ All Kits	5·40	4·05	—
„ Indian	5·40	4·05	—
„ King	5·40	4·05	—
„ White	12·50	9·38	—
„ Boning paws (per 100 pairs) „ Boning and/or Fleshing tails (per 100)	2·20	—	—
Gazelle, Furriers	1·80	1·35	—
Goats	12·65	9·49	—
„ Kid	4·20	3·15	—
Hamster	1·00	0·75	—
Hare	2·30	1·73	—
Horse	132·00	99·00	66·00
„ Pony (British)	132·00	99·00	66·00
„ Foals for furrier purposes ...	12·65	9·49	6·30
Hyena	25·25	18·94	12·65
Hyrax	2·40	1·80	—
Jackal (all types)	6·30	4·73	—
„ Boning paws (Per 100 paws)	1·20	—	—
Jaguar	33·10	24·82	16·85
Jap Mink	1·875	1·406	—
Kangaroo, Large	10·85	8·13	5·40
„ Medium	8·30	6·23	4·15
„ Small	5·40	4·05	2·70
Kolinsky	1·875	1·406	—
„ (extra if opened by flesher)	0·20	0·20	—
Lambs, Indian	4·20	3·15	—
„ Persian	6·60	4·95	—
Leopard	30·70	23·02	17·15
„ Snow	32·50	24·37	18·05
Lion	65·00	48·75	32·50
Lioness	43·30	32·48	21·65
Llama	25·25	18·94	—
Lynx	19·85	14·89	10·80
Marmot	2·05	1·54	—
„ Kansu	3·15	2·36	—
„ Kotel	1·45	1·088	—
„ Mindel	1·35	1·013	—
Marten (All species, including Canadian Sable) (hand or machine) ...	3·35	3·35	3·35
Mink (blubbering)	5·00	—	—
„ Wild (hand or machine) ...	2·90	2·90	2·90

TABLE I—*continued*

Skin (of any size except where otherwise stated) Column 1	Hand Fleshing (per 100 skins) Column 2	Machine Fleshing (per 100 skins) Column 3	Paring out all over from Pickle or Leather by hand or machine (per 100 skins) Column 4
	£	£	£
Mink Farm (hand or machine) ...	2·60	2·60	2·60
Mole	0·60	0·45	—
„ South African	1·05	0·788	—
Monkey	6·30	4·73	3·15
Musquash, Natural Black	1·875	1·406	0·935
„ Western...	1·20	0·90	0·575
„ Southern	1·20	0·90	0·575
„ French, Finnish and Czech	1·20	0·90	0·575
„ Russian (clean scraped only)	0·975	0·732	0·525
„ Chinese...	1·25	0·937	0·575
„ Kit and Mice	1·00	0·75	—
Nutria (large and medium) ...	4·15	3·11	—
„ (small)	3·85	2·89	—
Ocelot (proper) (hand or machine)	5·40	5·40	8·45
Opossum, American	1·90	1·42	—
„ Australian	2·20	1·65	—
„ Ringtail	1·85	1·39	—
„ Tasmanian	3·10	2·33	—
„ Victorian...	3·10	2·33	—
„ New Zealand	3·10	2·33	—
Otter, Open	12·60	9·45	—
„ Cased...	16·55	12·41	8·40
„ Sea	41·80	31·35	20·90
„ Cub	20·75	15·56	10·25
Pahmi	1·45	1·088	0·75
Panther	25·25	18·94	12·65
Peschaniki	1·20	0·90	0·40
Platypus	4·20	3·15	—
Puma...	25·25	18·94	12·65
Rabbit, Wild...	1·05	0·788	—
„ Battery	1·25	0·938	—
„ (extra if opened by flesher)	0·15	0·15	—
Rabbit English Dutch German Swiss (Price to include cutting open by the Flesher)	2·50	1·875	—
Rabbit Entredeux	1·65	1·238	—
„ Clapier	2·20	1·65	—
„ Fortes	2·45	1·837	—
Racoon	7·10	5·32	—
„ Russian	8·75	6·56	8·75
Sable, Russian (hand or machine)...	5·00	5·00	5·00

	Unhairing			
Seal (Fur)		—	—	—
„ Wig ...	1·49 per skin	—	—	—
„ Middling ...	1·06 „	—	—	—
„ Small ...	0·806 „	—	—	—
„ Large Pup...	0·577 „	—	—	—
„ Middling Pup	0·493 „	—	—	—

Sheep (odd skins)	21·05	15·79	—
„ Furriers	10·85	8·14	—
Skunk	2·40	1·80	1·20
Squirrel, Canadian	0·875	0·656	—
„ all other types	1·125	0·844	—
Susliki	1·25	0·937	—

TABLE I—*continued*

Skin (of any size except where otherwise stated) Column 1	Hand Fleshing (per 100 skins) Column 2	Machine Fleshing (per 100 skins) Column 3	Paring out all over from Pickle or Leather by hand or machine (per 100 skins) Column 4
	£	£	£
Tiger	41·50	31·13	20·75
,, Cub	20·75	15·56	14·45
Vicuna	16·85	12·64	8·45
Guanaco	16·85	12·64	8·45
Viscasha	3·45	2·59	—
Wallaby, Large	6·25	4·69	2·40
,, Medium	4·15	3·11	1·80
,, Small	3·35	2·51	1·20
Weasel and Stoat	1·25	0·938	—
Weasel Chinese	1·875	1·406	—
Wolf, Russian and Large Timber...	26·25	19·69	—
,, Other types	13·15	9·86	—
Wolverine	13·15	9·86	—
Wombat	6·30	4·73	—
Zebra...	332·00	249·00	86·60

TABLE II

HAND BEAM WORK ONLY

Skin Column 1	Cutting down (per skin) Column 2	Shaving (per skin) Column 3
	p	p
Bears, Black	42	14
,, ,, Cub	21	7
,, Brown	47	22
,, ,, Cub	25	11
,, Grizzly	72	36
,, ,, Cub	36	18
,, Green	140	36
,, ,, Cub	70	18
,, Indian	72	36
,, ,, Cub	36	18
,, Polar	90	54
,, ,, Cub	52	20
Bullock	144	72
Cheetah	36	18
Cow	144	72
Donkey	144	72
Horse	216	72
Jaguar	36	22
Leopard	36	18
,, Snow	36	18
Lion	72	54
Lioness	54	36
Puma	36	18
Tiger	54	36
Zebra	332	87

24.—(1) The general minimum piece rate for paring out all over from pickle or leather, where no piece rate is specified in Column 4 of Table I of paragraph 23, shall be an amount equal to one-third of the appropriate general minimum piece rate for hand fleshing or machine fleshing applicable to the worker under the provisions of paragraph 23.

(2) The general minimum piece rate for tubbing shall be an amount equal to the appropriate general minimum piece rate for hand fleshing (excluding extras) applicable to the worker under the provisions of paragraph 23.

25. In this Part of this Schedule,

(1) "BEAM WORK" means—

(a) such damping as may be required on all skins (except beaver, hair or fur seals) after liquoring by tubber has been completed; and

(b) cutting down and shaving, or either of these operations;

(2) "HAND FLESHING" means—

(a) fleshing throughout after all liquoring and damping has been completed for the fleshers;

(b) cleaning off afterwards where imperfect fleshing has been done in the initial stages; and

(c) cutting open and pulling over or either of such operations in the raw state before or after fleshing or damping;

(3) "FLESHING THROUGHOUT" does not include boning of fleshing tails, shaving, paring out, thinning edges, boning paws or burring ears (that is to say, taking shells completely out) where separate piece rates are specified for those operations in this Part of this Schedule, but includes, in the case of hand fleshing, any damping of completed skins performed by the flesher at his own option;

(4) "MACHINE FLESHING" means—

(a) fleshing throughout on a rotary or banjo machine;

(b) cleaning off afterwards where imperfect fleshing has been done in the initial stages; and

(c) cutting open and pulling over or either of such operations in the raw state before or after fleshing or damping;

(5) "PARING OUT" means shaving, paring out, thinning edges;

(6) "PULLING" means removing upper portion of hair;

(7) "TUBBING" means—

(a) preparing skins for the flesher and after fleshing leathering them in a tub and completing the dressing, or

(b) preparing skins for the flesher and after fleshing preparing them and putting them through the machine for leathering and completing the dressing;

(8) "UNHAIRING" means preparing skins by soaking and heating and removing hair.

2dd

Article 3

SCHEDULE 2

HOLIDAYS AND HOLIDAY REMUNERATION

The Wages Regulation (Fur) (Holidays) Order 1970(a) (Order Z. (90)) shall have effect as if in the Schedule thereto for the definition of "one day's holiday pay" in paragraph 11 there were substituted the following definition:—

" 'one day's holiday pay' means—

(1) the appropriate proportion of the remuneration which the worker would be entitled to receive from his employer at the date of the annual holiday, or at the termination of the employment, as the case may require, for one week's work if working his normal working week and the number of daily hours normally worked by him (exclusive of overtime)—

     (a) in the case of a time worker, under the arrangement current immediately prior to the holiday;

     (b) in the case of a piece worker other than a flesher, shaver and unhairer, if he were employed as a time worker at a time rate equal to the piece work basis time rate of statutory minimum remuneration then applicable to him as a piece worker or where no piece work basis time rate is applicable, at the appropriate hourly general minimum time rate of statutory minimum remuneration;

(2) in the case of piece workers employed as fleshers, shavers and unhairers

Males	Females
£3·30	£2·24

In this definition 'appropriate proportion' means—

where the worker's normal working week is six days ...	one-sixth
where the worker's normal working week is five days ...	one-fifth
where the worker's normal working week is four days ...	one-quarter
where the worker's normal working week is three days ...	one-third
where the worker's normal working week is two days ...	one-half."

EXPLANATORY NOTE

(*This Note is not part of the Order.*)

This Order has effect from 13th September 1971. Schedule 1 sets out the statutory minimum remuneration payable in substitution for that fixed by the Wages Regulation (Fur) Order 1970 (Order Z. (89)), which order is revoked. Schedule 2 amends the Wages Regulation (Fur) (Holidays) Order 1970 (Order Z. (90)) by providing for increased holiday remuneration for certain piece-workers.

New provisions are printed in italics.

(a) S.I. 1970/810 (1970 II, p. 2640).

STATUTORY INSTRUMENTS

1971 No. 1387

CUSTOMS AND EXCISE

The Import Duties (General) (No. 6) Order 1971

Made - - - -	20th August 1971
Laid before the	
House of Commons	26th August 1971
Coming into Operation	2nd September 1971

The Lords Commissioners of Her Majesty's Treasury, by virtue of the powers conferred on them by sections 1, 2 and 13 of the Import Duties Act 1958(a) and of all other powers enabling them in that behalf, on the recommendation of the Secretary of State hereby make the following Order:—

1.—(1) This Order may be cited as the Import Duties (General) (No. 6) Order 1971.

(2) The Interpretation Act 1889(b) shall apply for the interpretation of this Order as it applies for the interpretation of an Act of Parliament.

(3) This Order shall come into operation on 2nd September 1971.

2.—(1) Schedule 1 to the Import Duties (General) (No. 7) Order 1970(c) (which by reference to the Customs Tariff 1959 sets out the import duties chargeable under the Import Duties Act 1958) shall be amended by omitting any rate of duty specified in column 3 (in relation to goods of Convention area origin) in the following places—

(a) in sub-heading (C) (the residual sub-heading) of heading 08.05 (nuts other than those falling within 08.01);

(b) in sub-heading (F) (the residual sub-heading) of heading 11.08 (starches; inulin);

(c) in sub-headings (A)(1) and (2) (fondants, etc.) of heading 17.04 (sugar confectionery, not containing cocoa); and

(d) in heading 22.10 (vinegar and substitutes for vinegar).

(2) The rate of import duty applicable to goods of Convention area origin falling within sub-heading (A)(1) of heading 09.01 (coffee unmixed, roasted or ground) of the Customs Tariff 1959 shall be the same as that applicable in the case of goods qualifying for Commonwealth preference, and accordingly the said Schedule 1 shall be amended by substituting for column 3 of that sub-heading the following:—

C and E £0·2350 per cwt.

(a) 1958 c. 6.   (b) 1889 c. 63.   (c) S.I. 1970/1522 (1970 III, p 4935).

(3) In paragraphs (1) and (2) above " Convention area origin " has the same meaning as in the European Free Trade Association Act 1960(a).

Walter Clegg,

P. L. Hawkins,

Two of the Lords Commissioners of Her Majesty's Treasury.

20th August 1971.

EXPLANATORY NOTE

(This Note is not part of the Order.)

This Order reduces or removes the E.F.T.A. rates of import duty on certain agricultural products which have not previously been subject to E.F.T.A. duty reductions.

(a) 1960 c. 19.

STATUTORY INSTRUMENTS

1971 No. 1388

CUSTOMS AND EXCISE

The Import Duties (Temporary Exemptions) (No. 6) Order 1971

Made - - - -	20th August 1971
Laid before the House of Commons	26th August 1971
Coming into Operation	2nd September 1971

The Lords Commissioners of Her Majesty's Treasury, by virtue of the powers conferred on them by sections 3(6) and 13 of the Import Duties Act 1958(a), and of all other powers enabling them in that behalf, on the recommendation of the Secretary of State, hereby make the following Order:—

1.—(1) This Order may be cited as the Import Duties (Temporary Exemptions) (No. 6) Order 1971.

(2) The Interpretation Act 1889(b) shall apply for the interpretation of this Order as it applies for the interpretation of an Act of Parliament.

(3) This Order shall come into operation on 2nd September 1971.

2.—(1) Until the beginning of 1st January 1972 or, in the case of goods in relation to which an earlier day is specified in Schedule 1 to this Order, until the beginning of that day, any import duty which is for the time being chargeable on goods of a heading of the Customs Tariff 1959 specified in that Schedule shall not be chargeable in respect of goods of any description there specified in relation to that heading.

(2) The period for which goods of the headings of the Customs Tariff 1959 and descriptions specified in Schedule 2 to this Order are exempt from import duty shall be extended until the beginning of 1st January 1972 or, in the case of goods in relation to which an earlier day is specified in that Schedule, until the beginning of that day.

(3) Any entry in column 2 in Schedule 1 or Schedule 2 to this Order is to be taken to comprise all goods which would be classified under an entry in the same terms constituting a subheading (other than the final subheading) in the relevant heading in the Customs Tariff 1959.

(4) For the purposes of classification under the Customs Tariff 1959, in so far as that depends on the rate of duty, any goods to which paragraph (1) or paragraph (2) above applies shall be treated as chargeable with the same duty as if this Order had not been made.

Walter Clegg,

P. L. Hawkins,

Two of the Lords Commissioners
of Her Majesty's Treasury.

20th August 1971.

(a) 1958 c. 6.   (b) 1889 c. 63.

SCHEDULE 1

GOODS TEMPORARILY EXEMPT FROM IMPORT DUTY

Tariff Heading	Description
28.43	Mercuric cyanide
29.06	4-Ethylphenol
29.14	2-Ethylhexyl acrylate (until 4th November 1971)
29.16	3-Hydroxy-2,2-dimethylpropyl 3-hydroxydimethylpropionate
29.19	*trans*-2-Chloro-1-(2,4,5-trichlorophenyl)vinyl dimethyl phosphate
29.22	2-Nitroaniline
29.31	Dapsone
	Dithio-oxamide

29.35
Adenosine 5'-(dipotassium dihydrogen triphosphate)
Adenosine 5'-(sodium dihydrogen pyrophosphate)
2-Chloro-4-(1-cyano-1-methylethylamino)-6-ethylamino-1,3,5-triazine
7-Chloro-1-(2-diethylaminoethyl)-5-(2-fluorophenyl)-1,3-dihydrobenzo-1,4-diazepin-2-one dihydrochloride
7-Chloro-1-(2-diethylaminoethyl)-5-(2-fluorophenyl)-1,3-dihydrobenzo-1,4-diazepin-2-one *mono*hydrochloride
Coenzyme A, trilithium salt
3,4,5,6,7,8,9,10,11,12-Decahydro-7,14,16-trihydroxy-3-methyl-2-benzoxacyclotetradecin-1-one
2'-Deoxyadenosine 5'-(disodium dihydrogen triphosphate)
2'-Deoxycytidine 5'-(sodium trihydrogen triphosphate)
2'-Deoxyguanosine 5'-(tetrasodium triphosphate)
2,6-Dichloro-3,5-dicyano-4-phenylpyridine
Thymidine 5'-(trisodium hydrogen triphosphate)
4-(Triphenylmethyl)morpholine

29.39	$6\alpha,7\alpha$-Difluoromethylene-6β-fluoro-17α-hydroxypregna-1,4-diene-3,20-dione acetate
29.43	*di*Magnesium hydrogen D-ribose 5-phosphate 1-pyrophosphate
38.03	Acid-activated montmorillonite which, when examined by X-ray powder diffraction, shows four principal lines corresponding to crystal interplanar spacings (*d* values) of 0·44, 0·40, 0·33 and 0·25 nanometres, the line corresponding to 0·40 nanometre being the most intense
38.15	Mixtures consisting of *N-tert*butylbenzothiazole-2-sulphenamide and *N*-cyclohexanesulphenylphthalimide and containing not less than 45 per cent. by weight of each constituent
44.09	Cleft pales, stub-pointed, not less than 914 millimetres nor more than 1·83 metres in length, split from stems or branches of sweet chestnut of not less than 101 millimetres girth
48.03	Genuine vegetable parchment paper of a substance not exceeding 75 grammes per square metre
58.02	" Synthetic Grass " being a knitted pile fabric with a pile of green polyamide strip of not less than 350 decitex of heading No. 51.02 and a ground of polyester and polyamide man-made fibres (until 4th November 1971)
68.13	Asbestos paper, rubber impregnated, in rolls, being not less than 0·55 millimetre and not more than 0·85 millimetre in thickness, weighing not less than 500 grammes and not more than 780 grammes per square metre, and having a loss on ignition at 1,000° centigrade of not less than 24 per cent. by weight and not more than 32 per cent. by weight

Tariff Heading   *Description*

85.18   Tantalum capacitors greater than 12 microfarads in capacitance of a
         working voltage of not less than 4 volts, of a kind for incorporation
         in deaf aids, with a maximum length not exceeding 8 millimetres
         exclusive of leads with a transverse cross section having a circumfer-
         ence not exceeding 13 millimetres

85.21   Bases for packaging electronic microcircuits, such bases consisting
         of a square or rectangular sheet of single or multi-layer alumina
         ceramic furnished with a central metal circuit pad and metal or
         ceramic square or circular sealing frame, and with printed refractory
         metal conductor paths which terminate as leads at one edge of the
         ceramic or are bonded to metal alloy lead frames along two opposite
         or all four edges, all exposed and unglazed metal surfaces being
         gold-plated

SCHEDULE 2

GOODS FOR WHICH EXEMPTION FROM IMPORT DUTY IS EXTENDED

Tariff Heading   *Description*

29.02   Vinyl chloride (until 4th November 1971)

29.06   Sodium biphenyl-2-yloxide
         3,5-Xylenol (until 4th November 1971)

29.07   2,2-Di-(3,5-dibromo-4-hydroxyphenyl)propane
         4,6-Dinitro-*o*-cresol (-OH at 1), ammonium salt

29.14   Methyl chloroacetate
         Undec-10-enoic acid (until 4th November 1971)

29.22   4-Nitroaniline (until 4th November 1971)

29.25   *N*-(3-Chloro-4-methoxyphenyl)-*N'N'*-dimethylurea
         3,4,4'-Trichloro-*NN'*-diphenylurea (until 4th November 1971)

29.31   Diethyl sulphide (until 4th November 1971)

29.35   Menaphthone hydrogen bisulphite-2-hydroxy-4,6-dimethylpyrimidine
         complex

29.42   Theobromine

39.01   Nylon 6 in the forms covered by Note 3(*b*) of Chapter 39, containing
         not more than 2 per cent. by weight of titanium dioxide and not
         more than 2·5 per cent. by weight of carbon black, but not otherwise
         compounded (until 4th November 1971)

39.03   Regenerated cellulose in the form of sheets not exceeding 430 milli-
         metres by 1,020 millimetres in size, 18 grammes per square metre in
         weight or 12 micrometres in thickness

70.20   Glass fibre continuous filament yarn of low alkali borosilicate glass
         (E glass)

73.14   Iron-nickel alloy wire, copper-clad and nickel-plated, having an overall
         diameter of not less than 400 microns and not more than 450 microns,
         the nickel plating being not less than 2 microns and not more than
         15 microns in thickness; the whole containing not less than 20 per
         cent. by weight of copper, not less than 25 per cent. by weight of
         nickel and not less than 40 per cent. by weight of iron, and having,
         when measured on an 0·20 metre length, a percentage elongation
         not less than 18 and not more than 25, and a tensile strength not
         less than 430 newtons per square millimetre and not more than
         530 newtons per square millimetre, the rate of straining being 50
         millimetres per minute

Tariff Heading	Description

81.04   Chromium electrolytic, in the form of cathode chips, which contains not more than $0 \cdot 10$ per cent. by weight of total oxygen, not more than $0 \cdot 015$ per cent. by weight of total aluminium, and not more than $0 \cdot 001$ per cent. by weight of aluminium compounds insoluble in boiling 5N hydrochloric acid and in boiling fuming perchloric acid, and estimated as Al

83.13   Tinplate caps for sealing jars, of an internal diameter on the rim of not less than $1 \cdot 580$ inches and not more than $1 \cdot 610$ inches and a maximum depth of not less than $0 \cdot 415$ inch and not more than $0 \cdot 425$ inch stamped from tinplate of nominal thickness of $0 \cdot 0055$ inch or of $0 \cdot 0066$ inch, with an internal curl, a vinyl coating applied to the internal surface and a plasticised lining compound deposited on the internal side wall and top sealing panel to form a sealing gasket

85.18   Tantalum capacitors greater than 10 microfarads in capacitance, of a kind for incorporation in deaf aids, with a maximum length not exceeding 7 millimetres exclusive of leads and with a transverse cross section having a circumference not exceeding 14 millimetres
Tantalum capacitors, of a kind for incorporation in deaf aids, with a maximum length not exceeding 7 millimetres exclusive of leads and with a transverse cross section having a circumference not exceeding 10 millimetres (until 4th November 1971)

90.01   Lenses, prisms, mirrors and other optical elements not optically worked, of barium fluoride
Lenses, prisms, mirrors and other optical elements, not optically worked, of thallium bromide-iodide
Optical windows of zinc sulphide, unmounted

EXPLANATORY NOTE

(This Note is not part of the Order.)

This Order provides that the goods listed in Schedule 1 shall be temporarily exempt from import duty, and those listed in Schedule 2 shall continue to be exempt from import duty, both until 1st January 1972, except for items for which an earlier day is specified.

STATUTORY INSTRUMENTS

1971 No. 1392

INDUSTRIAL TRAINING

The Industrial Training Levy (Furniture and Timber) Order 1971

Made - - - -	*19th August* 1971
Laid before Parliament	*31st August* 1971
Coming into Operation	*3rd September* 1971

The Secretary of State after approving proposals submitted by the Furniture and Timber Industry Training Board for the imposition of a further levy on employers in the furniture and timber industry and in exercise of his powers under section 4 of the Industrial Training Act 1964(a) and of all other powers enabling him in that behalf hereby makes the following Order:—

Title and commencement

1. This Order may be cited as the Industrial Training Levy (Furniture and Timber) Order 1971 and shall come into operation on 3rd September 1971.

Interpretation

2.—(1) In this Order unless the context otherwise requires:—

(a) "agriculture" has the same meaning as in section 109(3) of the Agriculture Act 1947(b) or, in relation to Scotland, as in section 86(3) of the Agriculture (Scotland) Act 1948(c);

(b) "an appeal tribunal" means an industrial tribunal established under section 12 of the Industrial Training Act 1964;

(c) "assessment" means an assessment of an employer to the levy;

(d) "the Board" means the Furniture and Timber Industry Training Board;

(e) "business" means any activities of industry or commerce;

(f) "charity" has the same meaning as in section 360 of the Income and Corporation Taxes Act 1970(d);

(g) "dock work" and "registered dock worker" have the same meanings as in the Docks and Harbours Act 1966(e);

(h) "emoluments" means all emoluments assessable to income tax under Schedule E (other than pensions), being emoluments from which tax under that Schedule is deductible, whether or not tax in fact falls to be deducted from any particular payment thereof;

(a) 1964 c. 16.	(b) 1947 c. 48.
(c) 1948 c. 45.	(d) 1970 c. 10.
(e) 1966 c. 28.	

(*i*) "employer" means a person who is an employer in the furniture and timber industry at any time in the fifth levy period;

(*j*) "the fifth base period" means the period of twelve months that commenced on 6th April 1970;

(*k*) "the fifth levy period" means the period commencing with the day upon which this Order comes into operation and ending on 5th April 1972;

(*l*) "furniture and timber establishment" means an establishment in Great Britain engaged in the fifth base period wholly or mainly in the furniture and timber industry for a total of twenty-seven or more weeks or, being an establishment that commenced to carry on business in the fifth base period, for a total number of weeks exceeding one half of the number of weeks in the part of the said period commencing with the day on which business was commenced and ending on the last day thereof;

(*m*) "the furniture and timber industry" means any one or more of the activities which, subject to the provisions of paragraph 2 of the Schedule to the industrial training order, are specified in paragraph 1 of that Schedule as the activities of the furniture and timber industry;

(*n*) "the industrial training order" means the Industrial Training (Furniture and Timber Industry Board) Order 1969**(a)** as amended by the Industrial Training (Furniture and Timber Industry Board) Order 1969 (Amendment) Order 1970**(b)**;

(*o*) "the levy" means the levy imposed by the Board in respect of the fifth levy period;

(*p*) "notice" means a notice in writing.

(2) In the case where a furniture and timber establishment is taken over (whether directly or indirectly) by an employer in succession to, or jointly with, another person, a person employed at any time in the fifth base period at or from the establishment shall be deemed, for the purposes of this Order, to have been so employed by the employer carrying on the said establishment on the day upon which this Order comes into operation, and any reference in this Order to persons employed by an employer at or from a furniture and timber establishment in the fifth base period shall be construed accordingly.

(3) Any reference in this Order to an establishment that commences to carry on business or that ceases to carry on business shall not be taken to apply where the location of the establishment is changed but its business is continued wholly or mainly at or from the new location, or where the suspension of activities is of a temporary or seasonal nature.

(4) The Interpretation Act 1889**(c)** shall apply to the interpretation of this Order as it applies to the interpretation of an Act of Parliament.

Imposition of the Levy

3.—(1) The levy to be imposed by the Board on employers in respect of the fifth levy period shall be assessed in accordance with the provisions of this Article.

(2) The levy shall be assessed by the Board separately in respect of each furniture and timber establishment of an employer (not being an employer who is exempt from the levy by virtue of paragraph (5) of this Article) but in agreement with the employer one assessment may be made in respect of any number of such establishments, in which case those establishments shall be deemed for the purposes of that assessment to constitute one establishment.

(**a**) S.I. 1969/1290 (1969 III, p. 3820).   (**b**) S.I. 1970/1634 (1970 III, p. 5372).
(**c**) 1889 c. 63.

(3) Subject to the provisions of this Article, the levy assessed in respect of a furniture and timber establishment of an employer shall be an amount equal to—

   (a) 0·75 per cent. of the sum of the emoluments of all the persons employed by the employer at or from the establishment in the fifth base period or of the first £10,000 of that sum where it exceeds £10,000;

   (b) 1·0 per cent. of the amount (if any) of the said sum of emoluments in excess of £10,000 but not exceeding £20,000; and

   (c) 1·25 per cent. of the amount (if any) of the said sum of emoluments in excess of £20,000.

(4) The amount of the levy imposed in respect of an establishment that ceases to carry on business in the fifth levy period shall be in the same proportion to the amount that would otherwise be due under paragraph (3) of this Article as the number of days between the commencement of the said levy period and the date of cessation of business (both dates inclusive) bears to the number of days in the said levy period.

(5) There shall be exempt from the levy—

   (a) an employer in whose case the sum of the emoluments of all the persons employed by him in the fifth base period at or from the furniture and timber establishment or establishments of the employer is less than £7,500;

   (b) a charity.

(6) For the purposes of this Article no regard shall be had to the emoluments of any person wholly employed—

   (a) in agriculture;

   (b) as a registered dock worker in dock work; or

   (c) in the supply of food or drink for immediate consumption.

Assessment Notices

4.—(1) The Board shall serve an assessment notice on every employer assessed to the levy, but one notice may comprise two or more assessments.

(2) An assessment notice shall state the amount (rounded down, where necessary to the nearest £1) of the levy payable thereunder, and where the notice comprises two or more assessments the said amount shall, before any such rounding down, be equal to the total amount of the levy assessed by the Board under Article 3 of this Order in respect of each establishment included in the notice.

(3) An assessment notice shall state the Board's address for the service of a notice of appeal or of an application for an extension of time for appealing.

(4) An assessment notice may be served on the person assessed to the levy either by delivering it to him personally or by leaving it, or sending it to him by post, at his last known address or place of business in the United Kingdom or, if that person is a corporation, by leaving it, or sending it by post to the corporation, at such address or place of business or at its registered or principal office.

Payment of Levy

5.—(1) Subject to the provisions of this Article and of Articles 6 and 7, the amount of the levy payable under an assessment notice served by the Board shall be payable to the Board in two instalments equal respectively to one-fifth and four-fifths of the said amount, and the first such instalment shall be due one month after the date of the notice and the second on 1st January 1972 except where the date of the assessment notice is later than 1st October 1971 in which case the second instalment shall be due three months after the date of the notice.

(2) The amount of an instalment mentioned in the last foregoing paragraph may be rounded up or down by the Board to a convenient figure, but so that the aggregate amount of both instalments shall be equal to the amount of the levy stated in the assessment notice in accordance with Article 4(2) of this Order.

(3) An instalment of an assessment shall not be recoverable by the Board until there has expired the time allowed for appealing against the assessment by Article 7(1) of this Order and any further period or periods of time that the Board or an appeal tribunal may have allowed for appealing under paragraph (2) or (3) of that Article or, where an appeal is brought, until the appeal is decided or withdrawn.

Withdrawal of Assessment

6.—(1) The Board may, by a notice served on the person assessed to the levy in the same manner as an assessment notice, withdraw an assessment if that person has appealed against that assessment under the provisions of Article 7 of this Order and the appeal has not been entered in the Register of Appeals kept under the appropriate Regulations specified in paragraph (5) of that Article.

(2) The withdrawal of an assessment shall be without prejudice—

> (*a*) to the power of the Board to serve a further assessment notice in respect of any establishment to which that assessment related and, where the withdrawal is made by reason of the fact that an establishment has ceased to carry on business in the fifth levy period, the said notice may provide that the whole amount payable thereunder in respect of the establishment shall be due one month after the date of the notice;

> (*b*) to any other assessment included in the original assessment notice, and such notice shall thereupon have effect as if any assessment withdrawn by the Board had not been included therein.

Appeals

7.—(1) A person assessed to the levy may appeal to an appeal tribunal against the assessment within one month from the date of the service of the assessment notice or within any further period or periods of time that may be allowed by the Board or an appeal tribunal under the following provisions of this Article.

(2) The Board by notice may for good cause allow a person assessed to the levy to appeal to an appeal tribunal against the assessment at any time within the period of four months from the date of the service of the assessment notice or within such further period or periods as the Board may allow before such time as may then be limited for appealing has expired.

(3) If the Board shall not allow an application for extension of time for appealing, an appeal tribunal shall upon application made to the tribunal by the person assessed to the levy have the like powers as the Board under the last foregoing paragraph.

(4) In the case of an establishment that ceases to carry on business in the fifth levy period on any day after the date of the service of the relevant assessment notice the foregoing provisions of this Article shall have effect as if for the period of four months from the date of the service of the assessment notice mentioned in paragraph (2) of this Article there were substituted the period of six months from the date of the cessation of business.

(5) An appeal or an application to an appeal tribunal under this Article shall be made in accordance with the Industrial Tribunals (England and Wales) Regulations 1965(a) as amended by the Industrial Tribunals (England and Wales) (Amendment) Regulations 1967(b) except where the establishment to which the relevant assessment relates is wholly in Scotland in which case the appeal or application shall be made in accordance with the Industrial Tribunals (Scotland) Regulations 1965(c) as amended by the Industrial Tribunals (Scotland) (Amendment) Regulations 1967(d).

(6) The powers of an appeal tribunal under paragraph (3) of this Article may be exercised by the President of the Industrial Tribunals (England and Wales) or by the President of the Industrial Tribunals (Scotland) as the case may be.

Evidence

8.—(1) Upon the discharge by a person assessed to the levy of his liability under an assessment the Board shall if so requested issue to him a certificate to that effect.

(2) The production in any proceedings of a document purporting to be certified by the Secretary of the Board to be a true copy of an assessment or other notice issued by the Board or purporting to be a certificate such as is mentioned in the foregoing paragraph of this Article shall, unless the contrary is proved, be sufficient evidence of the document and of the facts stated therein.

Signed by order of the Secretary of State.

19th August 1971.

Paul Bryan,
Minister of State,
Department of Employment.

EXPLANATORY NOTE

(This Note is not part of the Order.)

This Order gives effect to proposals submitted to the Secretary of State for Employment by the Furniture and Timber Industry Training Board for the imposition of a further levy upon employers in the furniture and timber industry for the purpose of raising money towards the expenses of the Board.

The levy is to be imposed in respect of the fifth levy period commencing with the day upon which this Order comes into operation and ending on 5th April 1972. The levy will be assessed by the Board and there will be a right of appeal against an assessment to an industrial tribunal.

(a) S.I. 1965/1101 (1965 II, p. 2805).   (b) S.I. 1967/301 (1967 I, p. 1040).
(c) S.I. 1965/1157 (1965 II, p. 3266).   (d) S.I. 1967/302 (1967 I, p. 1050).

STATUTORY INSTRUMENTS

1971 No. 1393

WAGES COUNCILS

The Wages Regulation (Toy Manufacturing) Order 1971

Made - - - -	19*th August* 1971
Coming into Operation	13*th September* 1971

Whereas the Secretary of State has received from the Toy Manufacturing Wages Council (Great Britain) the wages regulation proposals set out in the Schedule hereto;

Now, therefore, the Secretary of State in exercise of his powers under section 11 of the Wages Councils Act 1959(a), and of all other powers enabling him in that behalf, hereby makes the following Order:—

1. This Order may be cited as the Wages Regulation (Toy Manufacturing) Order 1971.

2.—(1) In this Order the expression "the specified date" means the 13th September 1971, provided that where, as respects any worker who is paid wages at intervals not exceeding seven days, that date does not correspond with the beginning of the period for which the wages are paid, the expression "the specified date" means, as respects that worker, the beginning of the next such period following that date.

(2) The Interpretation Act 1889(b) shall apply to the interpretation of this Order as it applies to the interpretation of an Act of Parliament and as if this Order and the Order hereby revoked were Acts of Parliament.

3. The wages regulation proposals set out in the Schedule hereto shall have effect as from the specified date and as from that date the Wages Regulation (Toy Manufacturing) Order 1970(c) shall cease to have effect.

Signed by order of the Secretary of State.
19th August 1971.

J. R. Lloyd Davies,
Assistant Secretary,
Department of Employment.

(a) 1959 c. 69.   (b) 1889 c. 63.
(c) S.I. 1970/498 (1970 I, p. 1692).

Article 3

SCHEDULE

The following minimum remuneration shall be substituted for the statutory minimum remuneration fixed by the Wages Regulation (Toy Manufacturing) Order 1970 (Order Y. (83)).

STATUTORY MINIMUM REMUNERATION

PART I

GENERAL

1. The minimum remuneration payable to a worker to whom this Schedule applies is:—

(1) for all work except work to which a minimum overtime rate applies under Part III of this Schedule—

    (*a*) in the case of a time worker, the general minimum time rate payable to the worker under Part II of this Schedule;

    (*b*) in the case of a worker employed on piece work, piece rates each of which would yield, in the circumstances of the case, to an ordinary worker at least the same amount of money as the piece work basis time rate applicable to the worker under Part II of this Schedule;

(2) for all work to which a minimum overtime rate applies under Part III of this Schedule, that rate;

(3) any additional remuneration payable to the worker under Part IV of this Schedule.

PART II

GENERAL MINIMUM TIME RATES

MALE OR FEMALE WOOD-CUTTING MACHINISTS OR WOOD BODY MAKERS

2. The following general minimum time rates are payable to male or female workers aged 21 years or over:—

	Per hour	
	Up to and including 31st October 1971	On and after 1st November 1971
(1) WOOD-CUTTING MACHINISTS as follows:—		
(*a*) Workers employed on wood-cutting machines who are required to set up, take down and sharpen cutters and to keep in order their machines	*p*	*p*
	34·0	*34·5*
(*b*) Workers who have had not less than 12 months' experience in any trade on any wood-working machine and who are employed on any such machine (except boring, sanding or dowelling machines) but do not sharpen their own tools	*33·3*	*33·8*
(*c*) Other workers employed, wholly or mainly, on wood-cutting machines	*32·4*	*32·9*
(2) WOOD BODY MAKERS, that is to say, workers employed in wood-working operations which necessitate the use of hand wood-cutting tools, such operations being performed in connection with the construction of bodies of toy perambulators which are not capable of carrying a child or of toy motor cars which are capable of carrying, and of being pedal driven by, a child ...	*33·3*	*33·8*

MALE WORKERS

3. The following general minimum time rates are payable to male workers to whom paragraph 2 does not apply:—

	Per hour	
	Up to and including 31st October 1971	On and after 1st November 1971
(1) BODY PAINTERS, aged 21 years or over, that is to say, workers employed on body colour painting by hand with brush (excluding priming and spraying) of bodies of toy perambulators which are not capable of carrying a child or of toy motor cars which are capable of carrying, and of being pedal driven by, a child	p	p
	32·1	32·6
(2) OTHER WORKERS		
(a) Workers aged 21 years or over	31·5	32·0
(b) Workers aged under 21 years whose employment is not of a casual, seasonal or temporary nature and who are employed under conditions which, in the circumstances of the case, afford a reasonable prospect of advancement to a minimum rate of *31·5p* per hour, *up to and including 31st October 1971, and 32·0p per hour on and after 1st November 1971*, being aged		
20 and under 21 years	27·1	27·5
19 „ „ 20 „	24·1	24·5
18 „ „ 19 „	22·0	22·4
17 „ „ 18 „	19·6	20·0
16 „ „ 17 „	16·7	17·0
under 16 years	13·5	13·8
(c) All other workers aged under 21 years ...	31·0	31·5

FEMALE WORKERS

4. The following general minimum time rates are payable to female workers to whom paragraph 2 does not apply:—

	Per hour	
	Up to and including 31st October 1971	On and after 1st November 1971
	p	p
(1) Workers aged 20 years or over	26·5	27·0
(2) Workers aged under 20 years whose employment is not of a casual, seasonal or temporary nature and who are employed under conditions which, in the circumstances of the case, afford a reasonable proposect of advancement to a minimum rate of *26·5p* per hour, *up to and including 31st October 1971, and 27·0p per hour on and after 1st November 1971*, being aged		
19 and under 20 years	23·4	23·8
18 „ „ 19 „	22·0	22·4
17 „ „ 18 „	19·6	20·0
16 „ „ 17 „	16·7	17·0
under 16 years	13·5	13·8
(3) All other workers aged under 20 years ...	25·9	26·4

MALE OR FEMALE WORKERS

LATE ENTRANTS

5. Notwithstanding the foregoing provisions of this Part of this Schedule, the general minimum time rate payable to a male or female worker whose employment is not of a casual, seasonal or temporary nature and who enters the trade for the first time at or over the age of 16 years and cannot suitably be employed on piece work shall, until the expiry of two months' employment in the trade, be a rate equal to three quarters of the general minimum time rate appropriate to the worker's age under paragraph 3 or 4.

PIECE WORK BASIS TIME RATE

6. The piece work basis time rate applicable to any worker, male or female, employed on piece work shall be a rate equal to the general minimum time rate which would be payable to the worker, if he were a time worker, increased by 10 per cent.

PART III

OVERTIME AND WAITING TIME

MINIMUM OVERTIME RATES

7.—(1) Minimum overtime rates are payable to a worker to whom this Schedule applies as follows:—

(a) On any day other than a Saturday, Sunday or a customary holiday—

(i) for the first 2 hours worked in excess of $7\frac{1}{2}$ hours ...   time-and-a-quarter

(ii) thereafter   ...   .   time-and-a-half

Provided that where the employer normally requires the worker's attendance on 5 days only in the week, the foregoing minimum overtime rates of time-and-a-quarter and time-and-a-half shall be payable after 8 and 10 hours' work respectively.

(b) On a Saturday not being a customary holiday—

for all time worked in excess of $2\frac{1}{2}$ hours ...   .   time-and-a-half

Provided that the said overtime rate of time-and-a-half shall be payable in respect of all time worked on Saturday by a worker who is normally required by the employer to attend on 5 days only in the week if that worker has worked for the employer for at least 40 hours during the 5 days immediately preceding the Saturday, and for the purposes of this provision the worker shall be treated as though he had worked for the employer for any normal working hours in the said 5 days during which he is absent from work with the permission of the employer or on account of his proved sickness or accident to him or the allowance of a holiday under a wages regulation order.

(c) On a Sunday or a customary holiday—

for all time worked   ...   .   double time

(d) In any week exclusive of any time in respect of which a minimum overtime rate is payable under the preceding provisions of this sub-paragraph—

for all time worked in excess of 40 hours...   ...   ...   time-and-a-quarter

(2) Where the employer normally requires the worker's attendance on Sunday instead of Saturday, for the purposes of this Part of this Schedule (except where in the case of a woman or young person such attendance on Sunday is unlawful) Saturday shall be treated as a Sunday and Sunday as a Saturday.

8. In this Part of this Schedule—

(1) the expression "customary holiday" means:—

(a) (i) in England and Wales—

Christmas Day (or, if Christmas Day falls on a Sunday, such weekday as may be appointed by national proclamation, or, if none is so appointed, the next following Tuesday), Boxing Day, Good Friday, Easter Monday, Whit Monday (or where another day is substituted therefor by national proclamation, that day) and August Bank Holiday;

(ii) in Scotland—

New Year's Day (or, if New Year's Day falls on a Sunday, the following Monday);

the local Spring holiday;

the local Autumn holiday; and

three other days (being days on which the worker normally works for the employer) in the course of a calendar year to be fixed by the employer and notified to the worker not less than three weeks before the holiday;

or (b) in the case of each of the said days (other than a day fixed by the employer in Scotland and notified to the worker as aforesaid) a day substituted by the employer therefor, being a day recognised by local custom as a day of holiday in substitution for the said day.

(2) the expressions "time-and-a-quarter", "time-and-a-half" and "double time" mean respectively:—

(a) in the case of a time worker one and a quarter times, one and a half times and twice the general minimum time rate otherwise applicable to the worker;

(b) in the case of a worker employed on piece work:—

(i) a time rate equal respectively to one quarter, one half and the whole of the general minimum time rate which would be applicable to the worker if he were a time worker and a minimum overtime rate did not apply, and, in addition thereto,

(ii) piece rates each of which would yield, in the circumstances of the case, to an ordinary worker at least the same amount of money as the piece work basis time rate otherwise applicable to the worker.

WAITING TIME

9.—(1) A worker is entitled to payment of the minimum remuneration specified in this Schedule for all time during which he is present on the premises of his employer unless he is present thereon in any of the following circumstances:—

(a) without the employer's consent, express or implied;

(b) for some purpose unconnected with his work and other than that of waiting for work to be given to him to perform;

(c) by reason only of the fact that he is resident thereon; or

(d) during normal meal times in a room or place in which no work is being done, and he is not waiting for work to be given to him to perform.

(2) The minimum remuneration payable under sub-paragraph (1) of this paragraph to a piece worker when not engaged on piece work is that which would be payable if he were a time worker.

PART IV

ADDITIONAL MINIMUM REMUNERATION

NIGHT WORK

10. A worker shall be paid for all time worked between 10.0 p.m. and 7.0 a.m. the minimum remuneration to which he is entitled under the foregoing provisions of this

Schedule with the addition of an amount equal to one quarter of the general minimum time rate applicable to the worker under Part II of this Schedule or which would be applicable to the worker if he were a time worker:

Provided that this paragraph shall not apply to a shift worker whose shift commences at 6.0 a.m. or between 6.0 a.m. and 7.0 a.m.

PART V

APPLICABILITY OF STATUTORY MINIMUM REMUNERATION

11. This Schedule does not apply to workers who are persons registered as handicapped by disablement in pursuance of the Disabled Persons (Employment) Acts 1944 and 1958(a), in respect of their employment by Remploy Limited, but save as aforesaid, applies to workers in relation to whom the Toy Manufacturing Wages Council (Great Britain) operates, that is to say, workers employed in Great Britain in the trade specified in the Schedule to the Trade Boards (Toy Manufacturing Trade, Great Britain) (Constitution and Proceedings) Regulations 1935(b), as varied by the exclusion therefrom of operations specified in the Appendix to the Trade Boards (Rubber Manufacturing) Order 1938(c). The Schedule to the said Regulations is as follows:—

1. Except as hereinafter provided the Toy Manufacturing Trade shall consist of all work in connection with the making of children's toys and carnival novelties when performed:—

   (a) in a toy making establishment or a perambulator making establishment, or

   (b) in any other establishment by a worker who during the whole time that he works in any week in such other establishment is wholly employed on such work, or

   (c) by a home worker.

2. For the purposes of this Schedule the following expressions shall have the meanings hereby respectively assigned to them, that is to say:—

   "Carnival novelties" includes carnival hats or caps, carnival noise makers, folly sticks and favours, fancy paper costumes, confetti, paper garlands, streamers and any other articles which are known in the trade as carnival novelties (whether intended for children or otherwise, and whether made from paper or other materials); or parts of such articles.

   "Children's toys" includes children's novelties such as Christmas stockings, miniature shops, snowballs, lucky dips, surprise packets, dabs, suckers and other similar novelties and any parts of such toys or novelties.

   "Home worker" means a worker who works in his or her own home or any other place not under the control or management of the employer.

   "Making" includes:—

   (a) the assembling of parts of articles, and

   (b) the filling of articles with sweets or toys.

   "Perambulator making establishment" means an establishment, branch or department in which the principal business carried on is the trade specified in the Trade Boards (Perambulator and Invalid Carriage) Order 1926(d), or any amendment or variation thereof.

   "Toy making establishment" means an establishment, branch or department in which work in connection with the making of children's toys and/or carnival novelties is the principal business carried on.

   "Work in connection with the making of children's toys and carnival novelties" including all operations of sweeping up in any part of an establishment, branch or department, mainly engaged upon work in connection

---

(a) 1944 c. 10 and 1958 c. 33. (b) S.R. & O. 1935/399 (1935, p. 1684).
(c) S.R. & O. 1938/1159 (1938 II, p. 3229). (d) S.R. & O. 1926/23 (1926, p. 1332).

with the making of such articles, and packing, warehousing, despatching, stock taking and any other such work in connection with children's toys or carnival novelties when carried on in association or in conjunction with the making of such articles.

3. Notwithstanding any of the foregoing provisions of this Schedule, but without prejudice to the construction of any expression contained in those provisions, there shall not be deemed to be included in the Toy Manufacturing Trade any of the following operations, that is to say:—

   (a) the making of sports requisites;

   (b) the making from ceramic materials of dolls or dolls' parts, dolls' china, marbles or similar articles, when carried on in association with or in conjunction with the manufacture of other pottery;

   (c) operations included in the trades specified in the Orders hereinafter mentioned or any amendments or variations thereof, that is to say:—

   The Trade Boards (Brush and Broom) Order 1919**(a)**.

   The Trade Boards (Hat, Cap and Millinery) Order 1919**(b)**.

   The Trade Boards (Hollow-ware Making) Order 1928**(c)**.

   The Trade Boards (Paper Box) Order 1925**(d)**.

   The Trade Boards (Sugar Confectionery and Food Preserving) Order 1913**(e)**.

   The Trade Boards (Tailoring) Order 1919**(f)**.

   The Trade Boards (Women's Clothing) Order 1919**(g)**.

EXPLANATORY NOTE

(This Note is not part of the Order.)

This Order, which has effect from 13th September 1971, sets out the statutory minimum remuneration payable in substitution for that fixed by the Wages Regulation (Toy Manufacturing) Order 1970 (Order Y. (83)), which Order is revoked.

New provisions are printed in italics.

(a) S.R. & O. 1919/610 (1919 II, p. 505).   (b) S.R. & O. 1919/1262 (1919 II, p. 515).
(c) S.R. & O. 1928/842 (1928, p. 1258).   (d) S.R. & O. 1925/1126 (1925, p. 1613).
(e) Confirmed by 3 & 4 Geo. 5. c. clxii.   (f) S.R. & O. 1919/1201 (1919 II, p. 528).
(g) S.R. & O. 1919/1263 (1919 II, p. 531).

STATUTORY INSTRUMENTS

1971 No. 1394

WAGES COUNCILS

The Wages Regulation (Toy Manufacturing) (Holidays) Order 1971

Made - - - -	*19th August* 1971
Coming into Operation	*13th September* 1971

Whereas the Secretary of State has received from the Toy Manufacturing Wages Council (Great Britain) the wages regulation proposals set out in the Schedule hereto;

Now, therefore, the Secretary of State in exercise of his powers under section 11 of the Wages Councils Act 1959(a), and of all other powers enabling him in that behalf, hereby makes the following Order:—

1. This Order may be cited as the Wages Regulation (Toy Manufacturing) (Holidays) Order 1971.

2.—(1) In this Order the expression "the specified date" means the 13th September 1971, provided that where, as respects any worker who is paid wages at intervals not exceeding seven days, that date does not correspond with the beginning of the period for which the wages are paid, the expression "the specified date" means, as respects that worker, the beginning of the next such period following that date.

(2) The Interpretation Act 1889(b) shall apply to the interpretation of this Order as it applies to the interpretation of an Act of Parliament and as if this Order and the Order hereby revoked were Acts of Parliament.

3. The wages regulation proposals set out in the Schedule hereto shall have effect as from the specified date and as from that date the Wages Regulation (Toy Manufacturing) (Holidays) Order 1970(c) shall cease to have effect.

Signed by order of the Secretary of State.

19th August 1971.

J. R. Lloyd Davies,
Assistant Secretary,
Department of Employment.

(a) 1959 c. 69.   (b) 1889 c. 63.
(c) S.I. 1970/499 (1970 I, p. 1699).

Article 3   SCHEDULE

The following provisions as to holidays and holiday remuneration shall be sub-
stituted for the provisions as to holidays and holiday remuneration set out in the Wages
Regulation (Toy Manufacturing) (Holidays) Order 1970 (hereinafter referred to as
"Order Y. (84)").

PART I

APPLICATION

1. This Schedule applies to every worker (other than a home worker) for whom
statutory minimum remuneration has been fixed.

PART II

CUSTOMARY HOLIDAYS

2.—(1) An employer shall allow to every worker to whom this Schedule applies
a holiday (hereinafter referred to as a "customary holiday") in each year on the days
specified in the following sub-paragraph, provided that the worker has worked for the
employer throughout the last working day on which work was available to him prior
to the holiday (unless excused by the employer or absent by reason of the proved illness
of, or accident to, the worker).

(2) The said customary hoidays are:—

(a) (i) in England and Wales—

Christmas Day (or, if Christmas Day falls on a Sunday, such weekday as
may be appointed by national proclamation, or, if none is so appointed, the
next following Tuesday), Boxing Day, Good Friday, Easter Monday, Whit
Monday (or where another day is substituted therefor by national proclamation, that day) and August Bank Holiday;

(ii) in Scotland—

New Year's Day (or, if New Year's Day falls on a Sunday, the following
Monday);

the local Spring holiday;

the local Autumn holiday; and

three other days (being days on which the worker normally works for the
employer) in the course of a calendar year to be fixed by the employer and
notified to the worker not less than three weeks before the holiday;

or (b) in the case of each of the said days (other than a day fixed by the employer in
Scotland and notified to the worker as aforesaid) a day substituted by the
employer therefor, being a day recognised by local custom as a day of holiday
in substitution for the said day.

(3) Notwithstanding the preceding provisions of this paragraph, an employer
may (except where in the case of a woman or young person such a requirement would
be unlawful) require a worker who is otherwise entitled to any customary holiday
under the foregoing provisions of this Schedule to work thereon, and, in lieu of any
customary holiday on which he so works, the employer shall allow to the worker a
day's holiday (hereinafter referred to as a "holiday in lieu of a customary holiday")
on a weekday on which he would normally work for the employer within the period
of four weeks next ensuing.

(4) A worker who is required to work on a customary holiday shall be paid:—

(a) for all time worked thereon at the minimum rate then appropriate to the worker
for work on a customary holiday; and

(b) in respect of the holiday in lieu of the customary holiday, holiday remuneration in accordance with paragraph 6.

PART III
ANNUAL HOLIDAYS

3.—(1) Subject to the provisions of paragraph 4, in addition to the holidays specified in Part II of this Schedule an employer shall between the date on which this Schedule becomes effective and 31st October 1971, and in each succeeding year between 1st April and 31st October, allow a holiday (hereinafter referred to as an "annual holiday") to every worker in his employment to whom this Schedule applies who has been employed by him during the 12 months immediately preceding the commencement of the holiday season for any of the periods of employment (calculated in accordance with the provisions of paragraph 10) set out in the table below and the duration of the annual holiday shall, in the case of each such worker, be related to his period of employment during that 12 months as follows:—

| Period of employment | Duration of annual holiday for workers with a normal working week of— | | | |
| | Six days | Five days | Four days | Three days or less |
Column 1	Column 2	Column 3	Column 4	Column 5
At least 48 weeks	18 days	15 days	12 days	9 days
„ „ 47 „	17 „	14 „	11 „	8 „
„ „ 46 „	17 „	14 „	11 „	8 „
„ „ 45 „	16 „	14 „	11 „	8 „
„ „ 44 „	16 „	13 „	11 „	8 „
„ „ 43 „	16 „	13 „	10 „	8 „
„ „ 42 „	15 „	13 „	10 „	7 „
„ „ 41 „	15 „	12 „	10 „	7 „
„ „ 40 „	15 „	12 „	10 „	7 „
„ „ 39 „	14 „	12 „	9 „	7 „
„ „ 38 „	14 „	11 „	9 „	7 „
„ „ 37 „	13 „	11 „	9 „	6 „
„ „ 36 „	13 „	11 „	9 „	6 „
„ „ 35 „	13 „	10 „	8 „	6 „
„ „ 34 „	12 „	10 „	8 „	6 „
„ „ 33 „	12 „	10 „	8 „	6 „
„ „ 32 „	12 „	10 „	8 „	6 „
„ „ 31 „	11 „	9 „	7 „	5 „
„ „ 30 „	11 „	9 „	7 „	5 „
„ „ 29 „	10 „	9 „	7 „	5 „
„ „ 28 „	10 „	8 „	7 „	5 „
„ „ 27 „	10 „	8 „	6 „	5 „
„ „ 26 „	9 „	8 „	6 „	4 „
„ „ 25 „	9 „	7 „	6 „	4 „
„ „ 24 „	9 „	7 „	6 „	4 „
„ „ 23 „	8 „	7 „	5 „	4 „
„ „ 22 „	8 „	6 „	5 „	4 „
„ „ 21 „	7 „	6 „	5 „	3 „
„ „ 20 „	7 „	6 „	5 „	3 „
„ „ 19 „	7 „	5 „	4 „	3 „
„ „ 18 „	6 „	5 „	4 „	3 „
„ „ 17 „	6 „	5 „	4 „	3 „
„ „ 16 „	6 „	5 „	4 „	3 „
„ „ 15 „	5 „	4 „	3 „	2 „
„ „ 14 „	5 „	4 „	3 „	2 „
„ „ 13 „	4 „	4 „	3 „	2 „
„ „ 12 „	4 „	3 „	3 „	2 „
„ „ 11 „	4 „	3 „	2 „	2 „
„ „ 10 „	3 „	3 „	2 „	1 day
„ „ 9 „	3 „	2 „	2 „	1 „
„ „ 8 „	3 „	2 „	2 „	1 „
„ „ 7 „	2 „	2 „	1 day	1 „
„ „ 6 „	2 „	1 day	1 „	1 „
„ „ 5 „	1 day	1 „	1 „	—
„ „ 4 „	1 „	1 „	1 „	—

(2) Notwithstanding the provisions of sub-paragraph (1) of this paragraph the number of days of annual holiday which an employer is required to allow to a worker in the holiday season 1st April 1971 to 31st October 1971 and in each succeeding year between 1st April and 31st October shall not exceed in the aggregate *three times* the number of days constituting the worker's normal working week.

(3) The duration of the worker's annual holiday in the holiday season ending on 31st October 1971, shall be reduced by any days of annual holiday duly allowed to him by the employer under the provisions of Order Y. (84) between 1st April 1971, and the date on which the provisions of this Schedule become effective.

(4) In this Schedule the expression "holiday season" means in relation to an annual holiday during the year 1971, the period commencing on 1st April 1971, and ending on 31st October 1971, and in relation to each subsequent year, the period commencing on 1st April and ending on 31st October in that year.

4.—(1) Subject to the provisions of this paragraph, an annual holiday shall be allowed on consecutive working days, being days on which the worker is normally called upon to work for the employer.

(2)(*a*) Where the number of days of annual holiday for which a worker has qualified exceeds the number of days constituting his normal working week but does not exceed twice that number, the holiday may be allowed in two periods of consecutive working days or, in the circumstances specified in sub-paragraph (4) of this paragraph, in more than two periods; so however that when a holiday is so allowed, one of the periods shall consist of a number of consecutive working days not less than the number of days constituting the worker's normal working week.

(*b*) Where the number of days of annual holiday for which a worker has qualified exceeds twice the number of days constituting his normal working week, the holiday may be allowed as follows:—

(i) as to two periods of consecutive working days, each such period not being less than the period constituting the worker's normal working week, during the holiday season; and

(ii) as to the additional days, on working days which need not be consecutive, to be fixed by the employer, either during the holiday season or before the beginning of the next following holiday season and notified to the worker not less than three weeks before the holiday.

(3) For the purposes of this paragraph, days of annual holiday shall be treated as consecutive notwithstanding that a day of holiday allowed to a worker under Part II of this Schedule or a Sunday intervenes.

(4) Where a day of holiday allowed to a worker under Part II of this Schedule immediately precedes a period of annual holiday or occurs during such a period then, notwithstanding the foregoing provisions of this paragraph, the duration of that period of annual holiday may be reduced by one day and in such a case one day of annual holiday may be allowed on any working day (not being the worker's weekly short day) in the holiday season.

(5) Subject to the provisions of sub-paragraph (1) of this paragraph, any day of annual holiday under this Schedule may be allowed on a day on which the worker is entitled to a day of holiday or to a half-holiday under any enactment other than the Wages Councils Act 1959.

5. Subject to the provisions of paragraph 4, an employer shall give to a worker reasonable notice of the commencing date or dates and duration of the period of periods of his annual holiday. Such notice may be given individually to the worker or by the posting of a notice in the place where the worker is employed.

PART IV

HOLIDAY REMUNERATION

A.—CUSTOMARY HOLIDAYS AND HOLIDAYS IN LIEU OF CUSTOMARY HOLIDAYS

6.—(1) Subject to the provisions of this paragraph, for each day of holiday to which a worker is entitled under Part II of this Schedule he shall be paid by the employer holiday remuneration equal to the amount which he would have been entitled to receive from the employer under the arrangement current immediately prior to the holiday if the day had not been a day of holiday and he had worked thereon for the number of hours usually worked by him excluding overtime on that day of the week:

Provided that payment of the said holiday remuneration is subject to the condition that the worker presents himself for employment on the first working day following the holiday or, if he fails to do so, failure is by reason of the proved illness of, or accident to, the worker or with the consent of the employer.

(2) In relation to a piece worker, a worker remunerated by a system of payment by results or a worker in receipt of a bonus the amount of which fluctuates according to output the provisions of sub-paragraph (1) of this paragraph shall have effect as if for the words "under the arrangement current immediately prior to the holiday" there were substituted the words "if he had been employed as a time worker at the general minimum time rate then applicable to him increased by 20 per cent. and".

(3) Holiday remuneration in respect of any holiday allowed under Part II of the Schedule shall be paid to the worker not later than on the pay day on which the wages for the pay week including the first working day following the holiday are paid:

Provided that the said payment shall be made immediately upon the termination of the worker's employment in the case where he ceases to be employed before being allowed a holiday in lieu of a customary holiday to which he is entitled, and in that case the proviso to sub-paragrah (1) of this paragraph shall not apply.

B.—ANNUAL HOLIDAY

7.—(1) Subject to the provisions of paragraph 8, a worker qualified to be allowed an annual holiday under this Schedule shall be paid by his employer in respect thereof, on the last pay day preceding such annual holiday, one day's holiday pay (as defined in paragraph 11 of this Schedule) in respect of each day thereof.

(2) Where under the provisions of paragraph 4 an annual holiday is allowed in more than one period, the holiday remuneration shall be apportioned accordingly.

8. Where any accrued holiday remuneration has been paid by the employer to the worker (in accordance with paragraph 9 of this Schedule or under Order Y. (84)) in respect of employment during any of the periods referred to in that paragraph or that Order respectively, the amount of holiday remuneration payable by the employer in respect of any annual holiday for which the worker has qualified by reason of employment during the said period shall be reduced by the amount of the said accrued holiday remuneration unless that remuneration has been deducted from a previous payment of holiday remuneration made under the provisions of this Schedule or of Order Y. (84).

ACCRUED HOLIDAY REMUNERATION PAYABLE ON TERMINATION OF EMPLOYMENT

9. Where a worker ceases to be employed by an employer after the provisions of this Schedule become effective, the employer shall, immediately on the termination of the employment, pay to the worker as accrued holiday remuneration:—

(1) in respect of employment in the 12 months up to and including the 31st day of the preceding March, a sum equal to the holiday remuneration for any days of annual holiday for which he has qualified, except days of annual holiday which

he has been allowed or has become entitled to be allowed before leaving the employment; and

(2) in respect of any employment since the 31st day of the preceding March, a sum equal to the holiday remuneration which would have been payable to him if he could have been allowed an annual holiday in respect of that employment at the time of leaving it.

PART V

GENERAL

10. For the purpose of calculating any period of employment qualifying a worker for an annual holiday or for any accrued holiday remuneration under this Schedule, the worker shall be treated:—

(1) as if he were employed for a week in respect of any week in which—

(a) he has worked for the employer for not less than 20 hours and has performed some work for which statutory minimum remuneration is payable; or

(b) (i) he has been absent throughout the week, or

(ii) he has worked for the employer for less than 20 hours
solely by reason of the proved illness of, or accident to, the worker:

Provided that the number of weeks which may be treated as weeks of employment for such reasons shall not exceed six in the aggregate in the period of 12 months immediately preceding the commencement of the holiday season; or

(c) he is absent from work owing to suspension due to shortage of work:

Provided that the number of weeks which may be treated as weeks of employment for such reason shall not exceed eight in the aggregate in any such period as aforesaid; and

(2) as if he were employed on any day of holiday allowed under the provisions of this Schedule, or of Order Y. (84), and for the purposes of the provisions of sub-paragraph (1) of this paragraph, a worker who is absent on such a holiday shall be treated as having worked thereon for the employer for the number of hours ordinarily worked by him on that day of the week on work for which statutory minimum remuneration is payable.

11. In this Schedule, unless the context otherwise requires, the following expressions have the meanings hereby respectively assigned to them, that is to say:—

"home worker" means a worker who works in his or her own home or any other place not under the control or management of the employer.

"normal working week" means the number of days on which it has been usual for the worker to work in a week in the employment of the employer in the 12 months immediately preceding the commencement of the holiday season or, where under paragraph 9 accrued holiday remuneration is payable on the termination of the employment, in the 12 months immediately preceding the date of the termination of the employment:

Provided that—

(1) part of a day shall count as a day;

(2) no account shall be taken of any week in which the worker did not perform any work for which statutory minimum remuneration has been fixed.

"one day's holiday pay" means the appropriate proportion of the amount which the worker would be entitled to receive from his employer at the date of the annual holiday (or where the holiday is allowed in more than one period at the date of each period) or at the termination date as the case may require for a week's work if working his normal working week and the number of daily hours usually worked by him (exclusive of overtime) and if he were paid:—

(a) where the worker is employed as a piece worker, is remunerated by a system of payment by results or is in receipt of a bonus, the amount of which fluctuates according to output, the general minimum time rate then applicable to the worker, increased by 20 per cent;

(*b*) in the case of any other worker, the total remuneration which the worker would be entitled to receive from the employer under the arrangement current at the date of the annual holiday (or where the holiday is allowed in more than one period at the date of each period) or at the termination date as the case may require.

and in this definition "appropriate proportion" means:—

Where the worker's normal working week is six days   ...   one-sixth
Where the worker's normal working week is five days   ...   one-fifth
Where the worker's normal working week is four days   ...   one-quarter
Where the worker's normal working week is three days or less...   one-third.

"statutory minimum remuneration" means minimum remuneration (other than holiday remuneration) fixed by a wages regulation order made by the Secretary of State to give effect to proposals submitted to him by the Toy Manufacturing Wages Council (Great Britain).

"total remuneration" means all payments paid or payable to the worker under his contract of employment for time worked, any long service or other bonus payable to the worker on a weekly, fortnightly or monthly basis and merit payments so payable but does not include any other payments.

"week" in paragraphs 3 and 10 means "pay week".

12. The provisions of this Schedule are without prejudice to any agreement for the allowance of any further holidays with pay or for the payment of additional holiday remuneration.

EXPLANATORY NOTE

(This Note is not part of the Order.)

This Order, which has effect from 13th September 1971, sets out the holidays which an employer is required to allow to workers and the remuneration payable for those holidays in substitution for the holidays and holiday remuneration fixed by the Wages Regulation (Toy Manufacturing) (Holidays) Order 1970 (Order Y. (84)) which Order is revoked.

New provisions are printed in italics.

STATUTORY INSTRUMENTS

1971 No. 1398

THERAPEUTIC SUBSTANCES

The Therapeutic Substances (Supply of Zinc Bacitracin for Agricultural Purposes) Regulations 1971

Made - - - -	*23rd August* 1971
Laid before Parliament	*31st August* 1971
Coming into Operation	*1st September* 1971

The Secretary of State for Social Services, the Secretary of State for Wales, the Secretary of State for Scotland and the Minister of Health and Social Services for Northern Ireland, jointly, in exercise of their powers under section 9 of the Therapeutic Substances Act 1956(a), as amended by the Transfer of Functions (Wales) Order 1969(b), and as having effect subject to the provisions of the Ministries (Transfer of Functions) (No. 2) Order (Northern Ireland) 1964(c) and of the Ministries (Transfer of Functions) (Northern Ireland) Order 1965(d), and of all other powers enabling them in that behalf, after consultation with the Medical Research Council and the Agricultural Research Council, hereby make the following regulations:—

Title and commencement

1. These regulations may be cited as the Therapeutic Substances (Supply of Zinc Bacitracin for Agricultural Purposes) Regulations 1971, and shall come into operation on 1st September 1971.

Interpretation

2.—(1) In these regulations, unless the context otherwise requires—

"the appropriate Minister" means—

(*a*) as respects preparations sold or supplied in England and Wales, the Minister of Agriculture, Fisheries and Food,

(*b*) as respects preparations sold or supplied in Scotland, the Secretary of State for Scotland,

(*c*) as respects preparations sold or supplied in Northern Ireland, the Minister of Agriculture for Northern Ireland;

"approved" means—

(*a*) as respects preparations manufactured in England, or sold or supplied in England after importation into the United Kingdom, approved by the Secretary of State for Social Services,

---

(a) 1956 c. 25.
(c) S.R. & O. (N.I.) 1964 No. 205.
(b) S.I. 1969/388 (1969 I, p. 1070).
(d) S.R. & O. (N.I.) 1965 No. 13.

(b) as respects preparations manufactured in Wales, or sold or supplied in Wales after importation into the United Kingdom, approved by the Secretary of State for Wales,

(c) as respects preparations manufactured in Scotland, or sold or supplied in Scotland after importation into the United Kingdom, approved by the Secretary of State for Scotland,

(d) as respects preparations manufactured in Northern Ireland, or sold or supplied in Northern Ireland after importation into the United Kingdom, approved by the Minister of Health and Social Services for Northern Ireland;

"calf" means the young of a domestic bovine animal up to six months of age;

"lamb" means the young of a sheep up to six months of age;

"feeding stuffs containing zinc bacitracin" means calf, lamb, pig or poultry food to which zinc bacitracin supplement has been added;

"poultry" means domestic fowls, turkeys, geese, ducks, guinea-fowls, pigeons, pheasants and partridges;

"zinc bacitracin" means the zinc complex of bacitracin;

"zinc bacitracin supplement" means a dilute preparation of zinc bacitracin prepared by an approved method and with the use of an approved diluent.

(2) The Interpretation Act 1889(a) shall apply to the interpretation of these regulations as it applies to the interpretation of an Act of Parliament.

Sale or supply without prescription

3. Section 9(1) of the Therapeutic Substances Act 1956 (which controls the sale and supply of substances to which Part II of the Act applies) shall not apply to the sale or supply of animal feeding stuffs containing zinc bacitracin or to zinc bacitracin supplement when sold or supplied in accordance with the conditions set out in the succeeding provisions of these regulations.

4.—(1) The amount of zinc bacitracin contained in each ton of feeding stuffs shall not exceed the equivalent of 5,250,000 international units of bacitracin when sold or supplied for feeding to calves, lambs, pigs or poultry.

(2) The amount of zinc bacitracin contained in any one pound weight of zinc bacitracin supplement shall not exceed the equivalent of 2,100,000 international units of bacitracin.

5. When a concentrated animal feeding stuff containing zinc bacitracin is mixed with another animal feeding stuff before being fed the concentrated animal feeding stuff shall not contain a greater number of international units of bacitracin in each ton of feeding stuff than that found by the formula $n \left(\frac{f}{c} + 1 \right)$ where c represents the number of units of weight of a concentrated feeding stuff, f represents the number of units of weight of the other feeding stuff and n represents 5,250,000 international units, provided that $\frac{f}{c} + 1$ in the foregoing formula shall not exceed 20.

(a) 1889 c. 63.

6. Any feeding stuff containing zinc bacitracin shall have printed on the container or have affixed thereto, or inserted therein, or the container shall be accompanied by a label showing in such manner as the appropriate Minister may require such particulars as the appropriate Minister may require with respect to—

(*a*) a statement that the feeding stuff contains zinc bacitracin,

(*b*) the number of international units of bacitracin to which the zinc bacitracin contained in a given weight of the feeding stuff is equivalent,

(*c*) whether or not the feeding stuff is in concentrated form,

(*d*) conditions of storage and use of the feeding stuff,

(*e*) considerations of safety,

(*f*) the gross or net weight of the feeding stuff,

(*g*) the amount of concentrated feeding stuff to be added to other feeding stuffs for different purposes:

Provided that when the feeding stuff is supplied unpackaged in bulk the supplier shall furnish the purchaser, on delivery, with a statement in writing containing the particulars mentioned in items (*a*) to (*g*) of this paragraph.

7.—(1) Zinc bacitracin supplement shall be packed in containers suitable for preserving the potency of the contents up to the date at which the contents may be expected to retain such potency.

(2) Any zinc bacitracin supplement shall have printed on the container or have affixed thereto or inserted therein, or the container shall be accompanied by a label showing in such manner as the appropriate Minister may require, such particulars as the appropriate Minister may require with respect to the following information—

(*a*) a statement that the supplement contains zinc bacitracin,

(*b*) the weight of the contents, and the number of international units of bacitracin to which the quantity of zinc bacitracin contained in any one pound of the contents is equivalent,

(*c*) the date up to which the contents may be expected to retain potency,

(*d*) the nature of the diluent,

(*e*) conditions of storage and use of the supplement,

(*f*) considerations of safety.

Revocation of the Therapeutic Substances (Supply of Zinc Bacitracin for Agricultural Purposes) Regulations 1970

8. The Therapeutic Substances (Supply of Zinc Bacitracin for Agricultural Purposes) Regulations 1970**(a)** are hereby revoked.

(a) S.I. 1970/475 (1970 I, p. 1579).

Signed by authority of the Secretary of State for Social Services.

Paul Dean,
Parliamentary Under Secretary of State.

12th August 1971.

Peter Thomas,
Secretary of State for Wales.

18th August 1971.

Gordon Campbell,
Secretary of State for Scotland.

23rd August 1971.

W. K. Fitzsimmons,
Minister of Health and Social Services
for Northern Ireland.

16th August 1971.

EXPLANATORY NOTE

(This Note is not part of the Regulations.)

These regulations made under section 9(1) of the Therapeutic Substances Act 1956 legalise the sale or supply without prescription of feeding stuffs for young calves, young lambs, pigs and poultry, containing zinc bacitracin or of zinc bacitracin supplement in accordance with conditions laid down. They revoke and replace regulations previously in force.

STATUTORY INSTRUMENTS

1971 No. 1401

AGRICULTURE

The Price Stability of Imported Products (Rates of Levy) (Eggs) (No. 17) Order 1971

Made - - - 23rd August 1971

Coming into Operation 24th August 1971

The Minister of Agriculture, Fisheries and Food, in exercise of the powers conferred upon him by section 1(2), (4), (5), (6) and (7) of the Agriculture and Horticulture Act 1964 (a) and of all other powers enabling him in that behalf, hereby makes the following order:—

1. This order may be cited as the Price Stability of Imported Products (Rates of Levy) (Eggs) (No. 17) Order 1971, and shall come into operation on 24th August 1971.

2.—(1) In this order—

" the Principal Order " means the Price Stability of Imported Products (Levy Arrangements) (Eggs) Order 1970 (b) as amended by any subsequent order, and if any such order is replaced by any subsequent order the expression shall be construed as a reference to such subsequent order

AND other expressions have the same meaning as in the Principal Order;

(2) The Interpretation Act 1889 (c) shall apply to the interpretation of this order as it applies to the interpretation of an Act of Parliament and as if this order and the order hereby revoked were Acts of Parliament.

3. In accordance with and subject to the provisions of the Principal Order (which provides for the charging of levies on imports of those eggs and egg products which are specified commodities for the purposes of the Agriculture and Horticulture Act 1964) the rate of general levy for such imports into the United Kingdom of any specified commodity as are described in column 2 of the Schedule to this order in relation to a tariff heading indicated in column 1 of that Schedule shall be the rate set forth in relation thereto in column 3 of that Schedule.

4. The Price Stability of Imported Products (Rates of Levy) (Eggs) (No. 16) Order 1971 (d) is hereby revoked.

In Witness whereof the Official Seal of the Minister of Agriculture, Fisheries and Food is hereunto affixed on 23rd August 1971.

(L.S.)

G. P. Jupe,
Assistant Secretary.

(a) 1964 c. 28.   (b) S.I. 1970/359 (1970 I, p. 1277).   (c) 1889 c. 63.
(d) S.I. 1971/1319 (1971 II, p. 3788).

STATUTORY   INSTRUMENTS

1971 No. 1401

AGRICULTURE

The Price Stability of Imported Products (Rates of Levy) (Eggs) (No. 17) Order 1971

Made - - - *23rd August* 1971

Coming into Operation 24th August 1971

The Minister of Agriculture, Fisheries and Food, in exercise of the powers conferred upon him by section 1(2), (4), (5), (6) and (7) of the Agriculture and Horticulture Act 1964 (a) and of all other powers enabling him in that behalf, hereby makes the following order:—

1. This order may be cited as the Price Stability of Imported Products (Rates of Levy) (Eggs) (No. 17) Order 1971, and shall come into operation on 24th August 1971.

2.—(1) In this order—

" the Principal Order " means the Price Stability of Imported Products (Levy Arrangements) (Eggs) Order 1970 (b) as amended by any subsequent order, and if any such order is replaced by any subsequent order the expression shall be construed as a reference to such subsequent order

AND other expressions have the same meaning as in the Principal Order;

(2) The Interpretation Act 1889 (c) shall apply to the interpretation of this order as it applies to the interpretation of an Act of Parliament and as if this order and the order hereby revoked were Acts of Parliament.

3. In accordance with and subject to the provisions of the Principal Order (which provides for the charging of levies on imports of those eggs and egg products which are specified commodities for the purposes of the Agriculture and Horticulture Act 1964) the rate of general levy for such imports into the United Kingdom of any specified commodity as are described in column 2 of the Schedule to this order in relation to a tariff heading indicated in column 1 of that Schedule shall be the rate set forth in relation thereto in column 3 of that Schedule.

4. The Price Stability of Imported Products (Rates of Levy) (Eggs) (No. 16) Order 1971 (d) is hereby revoked.

In Witness whereof the Official Seal of the Minister of Agriculture, Fisheries and Food is hereunto affixed on 23rd August 1971.

(L.S.)

G. P. Jupe,
Assistant Secretary.

(a) 1964 c. 28.   (b) S.I. 1970/359 (1970 I, p. 1277).   (c) 1889 c. 63.
(d) S.I. 1971/1319 (1971 II, p. 3788).

STATUTORY INSTRUMENTS

1971 No. 1402 (S.168)

POLICE

The Special Constables (Pensions) (Scotland) Amendment (No. 2) Regulations 1971

Made - - - -	*21st August* 1971
Laid before Parliament	*31st August* 1971
Coming into Operation	*1st September* 1971

In exercise of the powers conferred on me by section 26 of the Police (Scotland) Act 1967(a) (as read with section 1(2) of the Police Pensions Act 1961(b)), and of all other powers enabling me in that behalf, and after consultation with the Joint Central Committee and such bodies and associations as are mentioned in section 26(9)(*b*) of the said Act of 1967, I hereby make the following regulations:—

1. These regulations may be cited as the Special Constables (Pensions) (Scotland) Amendment (No. 2) Regulations 1971 and shall come into operation on 1st September 1971.

2. In these regulations any reference to the Instrument of 1971 is a reference to the Special Constables (Pensions) (Scotland) Regulations 1971(c), as amended (d).

3.—(1) In the application of the Police Pensions Regulations 1971(e) to the calculation of an award to or in respect of a special constable under the Instrument of 1971, those regulations shall apply as amended by the Police Pensions (Amendment) (No. 2) Regulations 1971(f) (amendments necessary or expedient in connection with the passing of the Pensions (Increase) Act 1971(g)).

(2) In accordance with paragraph 1 of this regulation, for regulation 3(1) of the Instrument of 1971 (which, as set out in the Special Constables (Pensions) (Scotland) Amendment Regulations 1971(h), defines the expression "the principal regulations") there shall be substituted the following paragraph:—

"(1) In these regulations the expression "the principal regulations" means the Police Pensions Regulations 1971 as amended by the Police Pensions (Amendment) Regulations 1971(i) and the Police Pensions (Amendment) (No. 2) Regulations 1971.".

4. In regulation 4(2) of the Instrument of 1971 (special constables' supplemental pension) the reference to regulation 106 of the principal regulations shall be omitted and, accordingly, for the words "67 and 106" there shall be substituted the words "and 67".

(a) 1967 c. 77.
(b) 1961 c. 35.
(c) S.I. 1971/234 (1971 I, p. 864).
(d) S.I. 1971/585 (1971 I, p. 1578).
(e) S.I. 1971/232 (1971 I, p. 690).
(f) S.I. 1971/1327 (1971 II, p. 3794).
(g) 1971 c. 56.
(h) S.I. 1971/585 (1971 I, p. 1578).
(i) S.I. 1971/583 (1971 I, p. 1573).

5. Regulation 12 of the Instrument of 1971 (limitation on application of regulation 106 of the principal regulations) is hereby revoked.

Gordon Campbell,
One of Her Majesty's Principal
Secretaries of State.

St. Andrew's House,
Edinburgh.
21st August 1971.

EXPLANATORY NOTE

(This Note is not part of the Regulations.)

These regulations amend the Special Constables (Pensions) (Scotland) Regulations 1971 which give to special constables and their dependants certain pension benefits for which members of police forces and their dependants are eligible under the Police Pensions Regulations 1971.

The Police Pensions (Amendment) (No. 2) Regulations 1971 contain amendments to the Police Pensions Regulations 1971 which appear necessary or expedient in connection with the passing of the Pensions (Increase) Act 1971 and come into operation on 1st September 1971 (the date from which increases authorised by the 1971 Act are payable).

These regulations, which come into operation on the same date, make similar provision in connection with the passing of the 1971 Act as respects the benefits payable to or in respect of special constables.

STATUTORY INSTRUMENTS

1971 No. 1403 (S.169)

NATIONAL HEALTH SERVICE, SCOTLAND

The Scottish Hospital Trust (Administration) Regulations 1971

Made - - - -	*23rd August* 1971
Laid before Parliament	*31st August* 1971
Coming into Operation	*1st September* 1971

In exercise of the powers conferred on me by section 8(2) of the Hospital Endowments (Scotland) Act 1971(a), and of all other powers enabling me in that behalf, I hereby make the following regulations:—

PART I

General

1. These regulations may be cited as the Scottish Hospital Trust (Administration) Regulations 1971 and shall come into operation on 1st September 1971.

2. In these regulations:—

"the Act" means the Hospital Endowments (Scotland) Act 1971;

"the Trust" means the Scottish Hospital Trust constituted by and in accordance with section 1(1) of and the Schedule to the Act;

"the appointed day" and "relevant endowment" have the same meanings respectively as in the Act.

3. The Interpretation Act 1889(b) shall apply for the interpretation of these regulations as it applies for the interpretation of an Act of Parliament.

PART II

Term of office of members of the Trust, filling of vacancies, etc.

4.—(1) The first chairman of the Trust shall hold office until the first day of September 1977.

(2) Of the members of the Trust, other than the chairman, one-third, or as near as may be, shall retire on the first day of September 1973, one-third, or as near as may be, on the first day of September 1975, and the remainder on the first day of September 1977.

(a) 1971 c. 8.   (b) 1889 c. 63.

(3) Subject to the provisions of this regulation the term of office of the members of the Trust shall be six years:

Provided that at the expiration of his term of office a member of the Trust shall be eligible for re-appointment.

5.—(1) A member of the Trust who desires to resign his membership shall give written intimation of his resignation to the Secretary of State.

(2) If the Secretary of State is satisfied that a member of the Trust—

(*a*) has, without reasonable cause, not attended a meeting of the Trust or of any committee of the Trust throughout a period of twelve consecutive months;

(*b*) has become incapacitated by physical or mental illness; or

(*c*) has granted a trust deed for behoof of his creditors or has had his estates sequestrated in Scotland or has been adjudged bankrupt elsewhere than in Scotland,

the Secretary of State may declare that such member has ceased to be a member of the Trust.

6. If a vacancy occurs in the membership of the Trust (other than by retiral in rotation in accordance with Regulation 4(2) of these Regulations), the Secretary of State may, if he sees fit, fill the vacancy, and any person so appointed shall hold office for the remainder of the term of office of the person in whose place he is appointed.

PART III

Appointments, etc. of officers of the Trust

7.—(1) The Trust shall appoint a secretary whose duties may also include those of investment adviser. The secretary may be a body corporate.

(2) The Trust may in addition appoint such other officers and servants as it may from time to time consider necessary for the efficient administration of the Trust.

(3) The Trust out of the funds under its charge—

(*a*) shall pay to the secretary and to any other officers and servants of the Trust remuneration at such rates as it thinks fit and shall apply to such secretary and to the other officers and servants such conditions of service as it thinks fit; and

(*b*) may make such contributions as it thinks fit in respect of super-annuation of the secretary and of any other officers and servants of the Trust.

PART IV

Procedure

8. The Trust shall hold such meetings as are required for the discharge of their functions under the Act:

Provided that the Trust shall hold a meeting after the close of each financial year for the purpose of adopting the accounts of the Trust in respect of that year and preparing an annual report of its proceedings in accordance with the provisions of section 1(5) of the Act.

9.—(1) At any meeting of the Trust a majority of the members thereof for the time being shall form a quorum.

(2) Any meeting of the Trust may be adjourned to any other day, hour and place.

10.—(1) At every meeting of the Trust the chairman, if present, shall preside.

(2) If the chairman is absent from any meeting, the members present at the meeting shall elect from among themselves a person to act as chairman for that meeting.

(3) All acts of, and all questions coming or arising before, the Trust shall be done and decided by a majority of the members of the Trust present and voting at a meeting of the Trust and, in the event of an equality of votes, the person presiding at the meeting shall give a casting vote.

11.—(1) Minute books shall be kept by the secretary containing a record of the proceedings of the Trust and of any committee of the Trust.

(2) All minutes of the Trust and of any committee of the Trust shall be submitted to the next ensuing meeting of the Trust for approval and shall be signed by the person presiding at that meeting.

12. The Trust may make such standing orders as it considers necessary or expedient for the regulation of its business and may vary and revoke the same.

13.—(1) The Trust may appoint committees of its own number for the exercise of such functions as the Trust think fit and may appoint conveners of such committees.

(2) The Trust shall fix the number of members of such a committee which shall form a quorum.

PART V

Payment of expenses

14. The Trust may, out of the funds under its charge, make to the members thereof payments at rates determined by the Secretary of State in respect of loss of earnings which they would otherwise have made or any additional expenses (including travelling and subsistence expenses) to which they would not otherwise have been subject, being loss or expenses necessarily incurred by them for the purpose of enabling them to perform duties as members of the Trust.

Gordon Campbell,
One of Her Majesty's Principal
Secretaries of State.

St. Andrew's House,
Edinburgh.
23rd August 1971.

EXPLANATORY NOTE

(This Note is not part of the Regulations.)

These Regulations made under section 8 of the Hospital Endowments (Scotland) Act 1971 make provision in respect of the term of office of members of the Scottish Hospital Trust constituted under the Act and in respect of the appointment of officers of the Trust and of the procedure of the Trust.

STATUTORY INSTRUMENTS

1971 No. 1404

NATIONAL ASSISTANCE SERVICES

The National Assistance (Charges for Accommodation) Regulations 1971

Made - - -	*23rd August* 1971
Laid before Parliament	*31st August* 1971
Coming into Operation	*20th September* 1971

The Secretary of State for Social Services, in exercise of his powers under section 22 of the National Assistance Act 1948(a), and of all other powers enabling him in that behalf, hereby makes the following regulations :—

Citation and commencement

1. These regulations may be cited as the National Assistance (Charges for Accommodation) Regulations 1971, and shall come into operation on 20th September 1971.

Interpretation

2.—(1) In these regulations unless the context otherwise requires—

"the Act of 1948" means the National Assistance Act 1948 ;

"the Act of 1970" means the National Insurance (Old Persons' and Widows' Pensions and Attendance Allowance) Act 1970(b) ;

"Personal Injuries Scheme", "Service Pensions Instrument" and "1914-18 War Injuries Scheme" have the same meanings as in the National Insurance (Overlapping Benefits) Regulations 1948(c) (as amended) (d).

(2) The Interpretation Act 1889(e) applies to the interpretation of these regulations as it applies to the interpretation of an Act of Parliament and as if these regulations and the regulations hereby revoked were Acts of Parliament.

Revocation of existing regulations

3. The National Assistance (Charges for Accommodation) Regulations 1969(f) are hereby revoked.

(a) 11 & 12 Geo. 6. c. 29.   (b) 1970 c. 51.
(c) S.I. 1948/2711 (Rev. XVI, p. 196: 1948 I, p. 2657).
(d) The amending regulations are not relevant to the subject matter of these regulations.
(e) 1889 c. 63.   (f) S.I. 1969/1265 (1969 III, p. 3784).

Prescription of minimum charges

4. For the purposes of section 22(3) of the Act of 1948 (which relates to charges to be made for accommodation provided under Part III of the Act) the liability of a person to pay for accommodation provided in premises managed by a local authority shall in no case be reduced below the sum of £4·80 per week.

5. Where accommodation is provided for a child accompanied by a person over the age of 16, the liability of that person under section 22(7) of the Act of 1948 to pay for the accommodation of that child shall in no case be reduced below such one of the following sums as is appropriate, that is to say :—

(*a*) in respect of a child under 5 years of age, the sum of £1·70 per week ;

(*b*) in respect of a child aged 5 years or over but less than 11 years, the sum of £2 per week ;

(*c*) in respect of a child aged 11 years or over but less than 13 years, the sum of £2·45 per week ;

(*d*) in respect of a child aged 13 years or over but less than 16 years, the sum of £3 per week.

Prescription of sum needed for personal requirements

6. For the purposes of section 22(4) of the Act of 1948 a local authority shall assume that a person to whom subsection (3) of that section applies will need for his personal requirements the sum of £1·20 per week :

Provided that if that person is someone to whom there is payable attendance allowance under the provisions of section 4(2) of the Act of 1970 or constant attendance allowance under any Personal Injuries Scheme, Service Pensions Instrument or any 1914-18 War Injuries Scheme, the aforementioned sum assumed to be needed for his personal requirements shall be increased by the amount of such attendance allowance or constant attendance allowance.

Signed by authority of the Secretary of State for Social Services.

Paul Dean,
Parliamentary Under Secretary of State,
Department of Health and Social Security.

23rd August 1971.

EXPLANATORY NOTE

(This Note is not part of the Regulations.)

These regulations replace the National Assistance (Charges for Accommodation) Regulations 1969. The minimum weekly amount which a person is required to pay for accommodation managed by a local authority under Part III of the National Assistance Act 1948 is increased from 80s. to £4·80. Where a person is accompanied by a child the weekly amounts payable in respect of the child are increased from 28 shillings to £1·70 when the child is under 5 years, from 33 shillings to £2 when the child is aged 5 years or over but less than 11 years, from 41 shillings to £2·45 when the child is aged 11 years or over but less than 13 years and from 44 shillings to £3 when the child is aged 13 years or over but less than 16 years. The weekly sum for personal requirements which (unless in special circumstances the local authority considers a different sum appropriate) the local authority shall allow in assessing a person's ability to pay for accommodation is increased from 20 shillings to £1·20 but if the person is one to whom there is payable attendance allowance under the Act of 1970 or constant attendance allowance under any Personal Injuries Scheme, Service Pensions Instrument or any 1914-18 War Injuries Scheme, the weekly sum for personal requirements shall be increased by that amount.

STATUTORY INSTRUMENTS

1971 No. 1405

THERAPEUTIC SUBSTANCES

The Therapeutic Substances (Supply of Antibiotics and Chemotherapeutic Substances for Agricultural Purposes) (Amendment) Regulations 1971

Made - - - -	*24th August* 1971
Laid before Parliament	*31st August* 1971
Coming into Operation	*1st September* 1971

The Secretary of State for Social Services, the Secretary of State for Wales, the Secretary of State for Scotland and the Minister of Health and Social Services for Northern Ireland, jointly, in exercise of their powers under section 9 of the Therapeutic Substances Act 1956(a), as amended by the Transfer of Functions (Wales) Order 1969(b), and as having effect subject to the provisions of the Ministries (Transfer of Functions) (No. 2) Order (Northern Ireland) 1964(c) and of the Ministries (Transfer of Functions) (Northern Ireland) Order 1965(d), and of all other powers enabling them in that behalf, after consultation with the Medical Research Council and the Agricultural Research Council, hereby make the following regulations:—

Title and commencement

1. These regulations may be cited as the Therapeutic Substances (Supply of Antibiotics and Chemotherapeutic Substances for Agricultural Purposes) (Amendment) Regulations 1971, and shall come into operation on 1st September 1971.

Interpretation

2. The Interpretation Act 1889(e) shall apply to the interpretation of these regulations as it applies to the interpretation of an Act of Parliament.

Amendment of the Therapeutic Substances (Supply of Antibiotics and Chemotherapeutic Substances for Agricultural Purposes) Regulations 1971.

3. The Therapeutic Substances (Supply of Antibiotics and Chemotherapeutic Substances for Agricultural Purposes) Regulations 1971(f) shall be amended as follows:—

(a) 1956 c. 25.	(b) S.I. 1969/388 (1969 I, p. 1070).
(c) S.R. & O. (N.I.) 1964 No. 205.	(d) S.R. & O. (N.I.) 1965 No. 13.
(e) 1889 c. 63.	(f) S.I. 1971/304 (1971 I, p. 1024).

In column (2) of Schedule 1 in place of the number 75 (which indicates the maximum number of parts of sulphaquinoxaline to one million parts of feeding stuff) there shall be substituted the number 156.

Signed by authority of the Secretary of State for Social Services.

Paul Dean,
Parliamentary Under Secretary of State,
Department of Health and Social Security.

24th August 1971.

Signed by authority of the Secretary of State for Wales.

J. D. Gibson-Watt,
Minister of State,
Welsh Office.

24th August 1971.

Gordon Campbell,
Secretary of State for Scotland.

24th August 1971.

W. K. Fitzsimmons,
Minister of Health and Social
Services for Northern Ireland.

23rd August 1971.

EXPLANATORY NOTE

(This Note is not part of the Regulations.)

These Regulations amend Schedule I of the Therapeutic Substances (Supply of Antibiotics and Chemotherapeutic Substances for Agricultural Purposes) Regulations 1971 by increasing the maximum number of parts of sulphaquinoxaline that may be contained in one million parts of poultry feeding stuff when sold or supplied.

STATUTORY INSTRUMENTS

1971 No. 1406

EXCHANGE CONTROL

The Exchange Control (Scheduled Territories) (Amendment) Order 1971

Made - - -	*24th August* 1971
Laid before Parliament	*1st September* 1971
Coming into Operation	*2nd September* 1971

The Treasury, in exercise of the powers conferred upon them by sections 1(3)(*b*) and 36(5) of the Exchange Control Act 1947(**a**). hereby make the following Order:—

1.—(1) This Order may be cited as the Exchange Control (Scheduled Territories) (Amendment) Order 1971, and shall come into operation on 2nd September 1971.

(2) The Interpretation Act 1889(**b**) shall apply for the interpretation of this Order as it applies for the interpretation of an Act of Parliament.

2. Schedule 1 to the Exchange Control Act 1947, as amended by the Exchange Control (Scheduled Territories) Order 1967(**c**) and as further amended (**d**), shall be further amended by inserting after paragraph 2 the following paragraph:—

"2A.   Bahrain, the State of."

3. This Order shall extend to the Channel Islands, and any reference in this Order to the Exchange Control Act 1947 includes a reference to that Act as extended by the Exchange Control (Channel Islands) Order 1947(**e**).

Walter Clegg,
V. H. Goodhew,
Two of the Lords Commissioners
of Her Majesty's Treasury.

24th August 1971.

(**a**) 1947 c. 14.　　　　　　　　　　(**b**) 1889 c. 63.
(**c**) S.I. 1967/1767 (1967 III, p. 4736).
(**d**) S.I. 1968/333, 1399, 1970/748, 1455 (1968 I, p. 971; II, p. 4047; 1970 II, p. 2343; III, p. 4785).
(**e**) S.R. & O. 1947/2034 (Rev. VI, p. 1001: 1947 I, p. 660).

EXPLANATORY NOTE

(This Note is not part of the Order.)

Bahrain has ceased to be a protected state, and is no longer covered by that description in the list of scheduled territories contained in Schedule 1 to the Exchange Control Act 1947. This Order amends that list by the inclusion of the State of Bahrain by name.

STATUTORY INSTRUMENTS

1971 No. 1410

MEDICINES

The Medicines (Exemption from Licences) (Foods and Cosmetics) Order 1971

Made - - - -	23rd August 1971
Laid before Parliament	3rd September 1971
Coming into Operation	6th September 1971

The Secretaries of State respectively concerned with health in England, in Wales and in Scotland and the Minister of Health and Social Services for Northern Ireland, acting jointly, in exercise of their powers under section 15(1) of the Medicines Act 1968(a) (as having effect subject to the provisions of Article 2(2) of and Schedule 1 to the Transfer of Functions (Wales) Order 1969(b)) and of all other powers enabling them in that behalf, after consulting such organisations as appear to them to be representative of interests likely to be substantially affected by the following order, hereby make the following order:—

Citation, commencement and interpretation

1.—(1) This order may be cited as the Medicines (Exemption from Licences) (Foods and Cosmetics) Order 1971 and shall come into operation on 6th September 1971.

(2) In this order, unless the context otherwise requires—

"the Act" means the Medicines Act 1968;

"cosmetic" means any substance or preparation intended to be applied to the various surfaces of the human body including epidermis, pilary system and hair, nails, lips and external genital organs, or the teeth and buccal mucosa wholly or mainly for the purpose of perfuming them, cleansing them, protecting them, caring for them or keeping them in condition, modifying their appearance (whether for aesthetic purposes or otherwise) or combating body odours or normal body perspiration;

"food" includes beverages, confectionery and articles and substances as ingredients in the preparation of food and includes any manufactured substance to which there has been added any vitamin and which is advertised (within the meaning of Section 92 of the Act) as available and for sale to the general public as a dietary supplement;

(a) 1968 c. 67. (b) S.I. 1969/388 (1969 I, p. 1070).

"medicinal product" includes articles or substance specified in orders made under section 104 or section 105 of the Act which are for the time being in force and which direct that Part II of the Act shall have effect in relation to such articles or substances as that Part has effect in relation to medicinal products within the meaning of the Act;

"mineral salts" means salts of any one or more of the following, iron, iodine, calcium, phosphorus, fluorine, copper, potassium, manganese, magnesium or zinc;

"vitamin preparation" means any medicinal product the active ingredients of which consist only of vitamins or vitamins and mineral salts;

"vitamins" means any one or more of the following, vitamins A, B1, B2, B6, C, D and E, biotin, nicotinamide, nicotinic acid, pantothenic acid and its salts, biflavonoids, inositol, choline, para-aminobenzoic acid, cyanocobalamin or folic acid;

and other expressions have the same meaning as in the Act.

(3) Except in so far as the context otherwise requires, any reference in this order to any enactment shall be construed as a reference to that enactment as amended, extended or re-enacted by any other enactment.

(4) The Interpretation Act 1889(a) applies for the purpose of the interpretation of this order as it applies for the purpose of the interpretation of an Act of Parliament.

Exemption from licences for certain foods and cosmetics

2.—(1) Subject to the provisions of paragraph (2) of this Article, the restrictions imposed by sections 7 and 8 of the Act (licences for dealings in and manufacture of medicinal products) shall not apply to anything done in relation to a medicinal product which is wholly or mainly for use by being administered to one or more human beings and which is or is to be for sale either for oral administration as a food or for external use as a cosmetic.

(2) The exemption conferred by the preceding paragraph of this Article does not apply to a medicinal product as aforesaid which—

(*a*) is or is to be sold with, accompanied by or having in relation to it, any particulars in writing specifying that product's curative or remedial function in relation to a disease specified or the use of that product for such curative or remedial purposes, or

(*b*) being a product for oral administration as a food as aforesaid, comes within any of the descriptions contained in the Schedule to this order, or

(*c*) being a product for external use as a cosmetic as aforesaid contains any antibiotic or any hormone in a proportion in excess of 0·4 per cent or resorcinol in a proportion in excess of 1 per cent (the said proportions calculated on the weight of the medicinal product), or

(a) 1889 c. 63.

(*d*) being neither a vitamin preparation nor a substance coming within the description in paragraph 3 of the said Schedule, is or is to be sold with, accompanied by or having in relation to it any particulars in writing specifying the dosage relevant to that product's medicinal purpose.

Signed by authority of the Secretary of State for Social Services.

Paul Dean,
Parliamentary Under Secretary of State,
Department of Health and Social Security.

13th August 1971.

Peter Thomas,
Secretary of State for Wales.

18th August 1971.

Gordon Campbell,
Secretary of State for Scotland.

23rd August 1971.

W. K. Fitzsimmons,
Minister of Health and Social Services
for Northern Ireland.

16th August 1971.

| SCHEDULE | Article 2(2)(*b*) |

Description of certain medicinal product foods which are not exempt from licences

1. Any vitamin preparation in relation to which there are no written particulars or directions as to dosage.

2. Any vitamin preparation in relation to which there are written particulars or directions as to dosage specifying a recommended daily dosage for adults which involves a daily intake in excess of—

   (i) the equivalent of 2,500 Units (within the meaning of the 1968 edition of the British Pharmacopoeia) of vitamin A activity, or

   (ii) the equivalent of 250 Units (within the meaning of the 1968 edition of the British Pharmacopoeia) of antirachitic activity, or

   (iii) 25 micrograms of folic acid, or

   (iv) 5 micrograms of cyanocobalamin.

3. Any medicinal product, not being a vitamin preparation, to which one or more of the ingredients vitamin A or D, folic acid or cyanocobalamin has been added and in relation to which product there are written particulars or directions as to recommended use of that substance which involves a daily intake in excess of the quantities and ingredients specified in the preceding paragraph.

EXPLANATORY NOTE

(This Note is not part of the Order.)

This Order exempts from the restrictions imposed by Part II of the Medicines Act 1968 as to dealings in and manufacture of medicinal products except in accordance with a licence granted under that Act, certain medicinal products which are for oral administration as foods or which are for external use as cosmetics.

STATUTORY INSTRUMENTS

1971 No. 1411 (S.170)

HOUSING, SCOTLAND

The Housing (Amount of Improvement Grant) (Scotland) Regulations 1971

Made - - -	*24th August* 1971
Laid before Parliament	*1st September* 1971
Coming into Operation	*2nd September* 1971

In exercise of the powers conferred upon me by section 29(1)(*bb*) of the Housing (Financial Provisions) (Scotland) Act 1968(**a**), as read with section 54 of that Act and with section 3(5) of the Housing Act 1971(**b**), and of all other powers enabling me in that behalf, I hereby, with the consent of the Treasury, make the following regulations :—

1.—(1) These regulations may be cited as the Housing (Amount of Improvement Grant) (Scotland) Regulations 1971 and shall come into operation on 2nd September 1971.

(2) The Interpretation Act 1889(**c**) shall apply for the interpretation of these regulations as it applies for the interpretation of an Act of Parliament.

2.—In respect of any works eligible for financial assistance to which section 29(1)(*bb*) of the said Act of 1968 (which determines the maximum amount of improvement grant) and the said Act of 1971 apply, there shall be substituted in the said section 29(1)(*bb*) for the sum of twelve hundred pounds, the sum of eighteen hundred pounds.

Gordon Campbell,
One of Her Majesty's Principal
Secretaries of State.

St. Andrew's House,
EDINBURGH 1.
16th August 1971.

We consent.
24th August 1971.

Walter Clegg,
V. H. Goodhew,
Two of the Lords Commissioners of
Her Majesty's Treasury.

(**a**) 1968 c. 31.   (**b**) 1971 c. 76.   (**c**) 1889 c. 63.

EXPLANATORY NOTE

(This Note is not part of the Regulations.)

These Regulations increase from £1,200 to £1,800 per dwelling the limit on the amount of improvement grant which may be paid by a local authority in Scotland to an applicant for financial assistance under section 27 of the Housing (Financial Provisions) (Scotland) Act 1968.

Financial assistance may be given under that section for the improvement of dwellings, or for the provision of dwellings by the conversion of houses or other buildings. The limit on the amount of grant applies to each dwelling improved or, as the case may be, each dwelling provided by conversion.

The increase in the limit on the amount of grant applies only where the Housing Act 1971 applies—that is, where the works have not been begun before 23rd June 1971, and the works are completed before 23rd June 1973 ; and where the local government area is wholly or partly within a development or intermediate area on 23rd June 1971, or comes wholly or partly within such an area before 23rd June 1973. At 23rd June 1971 all local government areas in Scotland were within a development area or intermediate area.

STATUTORY INSTRUMENTS

1971 No. 1413 (S.171)

PRIVATE LEGISLATION PROCEDURE, SCOTLAND
The Private Legislation Procedure (Scotland)
General Order 1971

Made - - -	*24th August* 1971
Laid before Parliament	*2nd September* 1971
Coming into Operation	*1st November* 1971

We, the Chairman of Committees of the House of Lords and the Chairman of Ways and Means in the House of Commons, acting jointly with the Secretary of State, in exercise of the powers vested in us by section 15 of the Private Legislation Procedure (Scotland) Act 1936(a), hereby make the following order :—

1. This order may be cited as the Private Legislation Procedure (Scotland) General Order 1971 and shall come into operation on 1st November 1971.

2. The Private Legislation Procedure (Scotland) General Orders 1946(b) as amended (c) shall be amended as follows :—

(1) In General Order 22, for "Postmaster General" there shall be substituted "Post Office".

(2) In General Order 28(3), for "Ministry of Agriculture, Fisheries and Food" there shall be substituted "Department of the Environment".

(3) In General Order 29, for "Ministry of Transport" there shall be substituted "Department of the Environment" ; and for "Ministry" there shall be substituted "Department".

(4) In General Order 30, for "Ministry of Power" there shall be substituted "Department of Trade and Industry".

(5) In General Order 32, for "Ministry of Transport" there shall be substituted "Department of Trade and Industry, the Office of the Crown Estate Commissioners".

(6) In General Order 35, for "Ministry of Transport" there shall be substituted "Department of the Environment".

(7) In General Order 39, for that part to the end of sub-paragraph (1) there shall be substituted :—

"On or before the Fourth day of April, or the Fourth day of December, as the case may be, printed copies shall be deposited—

(1) of every draft Provisional Order, two at the Department of

---

(a) 1936 c. 52.
(b) S.R. & O. 1946/2157 (Rev. XVIII, p. 719: 1946 I, p. 1415).
(c) The relevant amending instruments are S.R. & O. 1947/2347 (Rev. XVIII, p. 719: 1947 I, p. 1891); S.I. 1949/331, 1950/1748, 1952/656, 1954/1141, 1957/465, 1964/1840 (1949 I, p. 3541; 1950 II, p. 439; 1952 III, p. 2693; 1954 II, 1841; 1957 II, p. 1924; 1964 III, p. 4004).

the Environment and at the Ministry of Posts and Tele-
communications ; and one at the Department of Health and
Social Security, the Treasury, the Department of Trade and
Industry, the Ministry of Agriculture, Fisheries and Food,
the Civil Service Department, the Ministry of Defence, the
Department of Employment, the Office of the Crown Estate
Commissioners and the Office of the Commissioners of
Inland Revenue";

in sub-paragraph (2) after "line" where that word occurs for the
second time there shall be inserted "one"; sub-paragraph (3) shall be
omitted; in sub-paragraph (4) the words "which relates to the erection,
improvement, repair, maintenance or regulation of any market or
market place at which cattle are exposed for sale, or" shall be
omitted, after "Scotland" there shall be inserted "one" and for "Ministry of Agriculture, Fisheries and Food" there shall be substituted
"Department of the Environment"; in sub-paragraph (5) after "Commissioners" where that word occurs for the second time there shall be
inserted "one"; and in sub-paragraph (6) after "deposited" there shall
be inserted "one".

(8) In General Order 43(3) for "pier or works of any description on the
foreshore" there shall be substituted "or pier"; and for "Ministry of
Transport" there shall be substituted "Department of the Environment".

(9) In General Order 69(1), after "Examiners" there shall be inserted "and
signed by those parties or their Agents"; and after "General Orders"
where those words occur for the second time there shall be inserted
"or his Agent".

(10) In General Order 70, after the word "Examiners" where that word
first occurs there shall be inserted "and signed by him or his Agent".

(11) In General Order 70A, for "by the Agent who deposited such
Memorial" there shall be substituted "his Agent"; for "signed by
more than one person" there shall be substituted "deposited by or on
behalf of more than one person"; and for "person signing the Memorial" there shall be substituted "of those persons".

(12) In General Order 78A, in the first paragraph at the beginning there
shall be inserted "(1)"; for "by the Agent who deposited the Petition"
there shall be substituted "his Agent"; for "signed by more than one
person" there shall be substituted "deposited by or on behalf of more
than one person" ; and for "person signing the Petition" there shall be
substituted "of those persons".

(13) In General Order 93(3), the words "the Admiralty and the Board of
Trade" shall be omitted.

(14) In General Order 97(1), the words "provided that it shall not be
necessary to make such deposit at the Air Ministry unless so required
by the Secretary of State for Air" shall be omitted.

(15) In General Order 99, for "Minister of Transport" there shall be substituted "Secretary of State for the Environment"; for "Ministry of
Transport" there shall be substituted "Department of the Environment"; for "Secretary of State and the Minister" there shall be substituted "Secretary of State for Scotland and the Secretary of State
for the Environment" and for "and the Ministry" there shall be
substituted "and the Department of the Environment".

(16) General Order 100 shall be omitted.

(17) General Order 103 shall be omitted.

(18) In General Order 106, for "Minister of Transport" on each occasion where these words appear there shall be substituted "Secretary of State for the Environment".

(19) In General Order 107, for "Board of Trade, the Secretary of State or the Minister of Transport" there shall be substituted "Secretary of State for Trade and Industry, the Secretary of State for Scotland or the Secretary of State for the Environment"; for "Board or Secretary of State or Minister" there shall be substituted "Secretary of State".

(20) In General Order 123, in sub-paragraph (1) for "[The above fees to be increased by one-third when the money to be raised or expended exceeds £100,000 and does not exceed £250,000 and to be doubled" there shall be substituted "[The above fees shall each be increased to £33 when the money to be raised or expended exceeds £100,000 and does not exceed £250,000 and to £50"; and for sub-paragraph (3) there shall be substituted:—

"General:—

For each witness to whom an oath or affirmation is administered at a local inquiry before Commissioners,—payable by the Promoters, Opponents, or other party calling such witness.   50p
For each order for the attendance of witnesses or for the production of books, papers, plans or documents,—payable by the applicants for such order.   50p"

(21) For General Order 124 there shall be substituted:-

"124. The following scale of fees shall be a General Order:-

SCALE OF FEES ON TAXATION OF COSTS UNDER SECTION 6(6) OF THE PRIVATE LEGISLATION PRO-CEDURE (SCOTLAND) ACT, 1936

For every application to the Auditor of the Court of Session for the Taxation of a Bill of Costs   £1

£1 per cent. upon the amount of the Bill as sent in for taxation, or added to in taxation

For every certificate which shall be signed by the Auditor of the Court of Session   £1

For copies of any Documents in the office of the Auditor of the Court of Session, per folio of 72 words $2\frac{1}{2}$p"

Listowel,
Chairman of Committees of
the House of Lords.

5th August 1971.

R. Grant-Ferris,
Chairman of Ways and Means in
the House of Commons.

5th August 1971.

Gordon Campbell,
One of Her Majesty's Principal
Secretaries of State.

24th August 1971.

EXPLANATORY NOTE

(This Note is not part of the Order.)

The Order amends the General Orders made under Section 15 of the Private Legislation Procedure (Scotland) Act, 1936, which regulate the procedure for obtaining Parliamentary powers by way of Provisional Order in matters affecting Scotland.

Most of the amendments correspond to amendments which have been made to the Standing Orders of the House of Lords and House of Commons.

STATUTORY INSTRUMENTS

1971 No. 1415

WAGES COUNCILS

The Wages Regulation (Flax and Hemp) Order 1971

Made - - - -	26th August 1971
Coming into Operation	20th September 1971

Whereas the Secretary of State has received from the Flax and Hemp Wages Council (Great Britain) the wages regulation proposals set out in the Schedule hereto;

Now, therefore, the Secretary of State in exercise of his powers under section 11 of the Wages Councils Act 1959(a), and of all other powers enabling him in that behalf, hereby make the following Order:—

1. This Order may be cited as the Wages Regulation (Flax and Hemp) Order 1971.

2.—(1) In this Order the expression "the specified date" means the 20th September 1971, provided that where, as respects any worker who is paid wages at intervals not exceeding seven days, that date does not correspond with the beginning of the period for which the wages are paid, the expression "the specified date" means, as respects that worker, the beginning of the next such period following that date.

(2) The Interpretation Act 1889(b) shall apply to the interpretation of this Order as it applies to the interpretation of an Act of Parliament and as if this Order and the Order hereby revoked were Acts of Parliament.

3. The wages regulation proposals set out in the Schedule hereto shall have effect as from the specified date and as from that date the Wages Regulation (Flax and Hemp) Order 1970(c) shall cease to have effect.

Signed by order of the Secretary of State.
26th August 1971.

J. R. Lloyd Davies,
Assistant Secretary,
Department of Employment.

Article 3
SCHEDULE

The following minimum remuneration shall be substituted for the statutory minimum remuneration fixed by the Wages Regulation (Flax and Hemp) Order 1970 (Order F.H. (125)).

(a) 1959 c. 69.   (b) 1889 c. 63.
(c) S.I. 1970/1281 (1970 II, p. 4175).

STATUTORY MINIMUM REMUNERATION

Part I

GENERAL

1.—(1) The minimum remuneration payable to a worker to whom this Schedule applies for all work except work to which a minimum overtime rate applies under Part IV of this Schedule is:—

(a) in the case of a time worker, the hourly general minimum time rate applicable to the worker under the provisions of this Schedule;

(b) in the case of a worker employed on piece work, piece rates each of which would yield, in the circumstances of the case, to an ordinary worker (that is to say, a worker of ordinary skill and experience in the work) at least the same amount of money as the hourly piece work basis time rate applicable to the worker or, where no such rate applies, at least the same amount of money as the hourly general minimum time rate which would be applicable if the worker were a time worker:

Provided that where an hourly guaranteed time rate is applicable to a piece worker under paragraph 5 or under paragraph 9 and the remuneration calculated on a time work basis at that rate exceeds the remuneration calculated on the basis of the said piece rates, the worker shall be paid not less than that guaranteed time rate.

(2) In this Schedule, the expressions "hourly general minimum time rate", "hourly guaranteed time rate" and "hourly piece work basis time rate" mean respectively the general minimum time rate, the guaranteed time rate and the piece work basis time rate applicable to a worker under Part II or Part III of this Schedule divided in each case by 40.

Part II

FEMALE WORKERS

GENERAL MINIMUM TIME RATES

Per week
of 40 hours
£

2.—(1) The following general minimum time rates are applicable to female workers:—

(a) Spinners aged 18 years or over	11·13
(b) Spinners aged under 18 years who have completed two years' employment (including any period of learnership) in some or all of the processes of bobbin carrying, doffing, piecing, or assisting at spinning frame, and who are in charge of a frame	10·76
(c) Card-cutters aged 18 years or over	11·13
(d) Weavers, winders, reelers and warpers aged 18 years or over ...	11·13

(e) All other workers (except learners to whom the minimum rates specified in paragraph 3(1) apply)—

Aged 18 or over	10·67
„ 17½ years and under 18 years	9·58
„ 17 „ „ „ 17½ „	8·75
„ 16½ „ „ „ 17 „	8·14
„ 16 „ „ „ 16½ „	7·59
„ 15½ „ „ „ 16 „	7·11
„ under 15½ years	6·73

(2) For the purposes of this paragraph a winder is a worker (other than a bit or beating winder) who is employed wholly or mainly on winding from the reel, hank or bobbin.

LEARNERS AND WEAVING TEACHERS

3.—(1) The following general minimum time rates are applicable to female learners:—

Per week
of 40 hours
£

(a) Learners employed in weaving, warping, winding, reeling or spinning for one period of learnership not exceeding six months where such learnership is commenced—

(i) At 16 years of age or over ... ... 7·59
(ii) At 15½ years and under 16 years of age ... ... 7·11
(iii) Under 15½ years of age ... ... 6·73

(b) Learners employed in card-cutting for one period of learnership not exceeding 12 months where such learnership is commenced—

(i) At 16 years of age or over ... ... 7·59
(ii) At 15½ years and under 16 years of age ... ... 7·11
(iii) Under 15½ years of age ... ... 6·73

(2) For the purposes of this paragraph a learner is a female worker who is employed during the whole or a substantial part of her time in learning weaving, warping, winding, reeling, spinning or card-cutting by an employer who ensures that she receives reasonable and proper facilities for such learning and, in the case of a learner employed in weaving, is placed under a competent worker to be taught.

(3) Notwithstanding the provisions of paragraph 2, the weekly remuneration applicable to a worker who is employed in teaching a learner weaving shall not be less than the sum of the following amounts, that is to say—

(a) the amount obtained by multiplying the worker's average hourly earnings during the previous eight weeks (exclusive of any week during which she was teaching a learner) by the number of hours constituting the worker's normal working week while teaching the learner;

(b) the amount (if any) by which the piece work basis time rate in paragraph 4 exceeds the piece work basis time rate which was applicable at the end of the period of eight weeks specified in (a); and

(c) 60p a week.

PIECE WORK BASIS TIME RATE

Per week
of 40 hours
£

4. The piece work basis time rate applicable to female workers employed on piece work is ... ... 11·21

GUARANTEED TIME RATES FOR PIECE WORKERS

5. The guaranteed time rates applicable to female workers employed on piece work (except learners to whom the minimum rates specified in paragraph 3(1) apply) are as follows:—

Per week
of 40 hours
£

Aged 18 years or over ... ... 10·67
„ 17½ years and under 18 years ... ... 9·58
„ 17 „ „ „ 17½ „ ... ... 8·75
„ 16½ „ „ „ 17 „ ... ... 8·14
„ 16 „ „ „ 16½ „ ... ... 7·59
„ 15½ „ „ „ 16 „ ... ... 7·11
„ under 15½ years ... ... 6·73

Part III

MALE WORKERS

GENERAL MINIMUM TIME RATES

Per week
of 40 hours
£

6. The following general minimum time rates are applicable to male workers:—

(1) Tenters aged 21 years or over	*15·51*
(2) Under-tenters aged 20 years or over	*14·52*
(3) Dressers, mounters, card-cutters and hacklers (hand-dressers) aged 20 years or over	*15·03*
(4) Hemp-rollers on non-reciprocating machines and hemp-breakers aged 20 years or over...	*15·19*

(5) Day Shift spinners—

Aged 19 years or over	*14·09*
„ 18 years and under 19 years	*10·76*
„ 17½ „ „ „ 18 „	*9·58*
„ 17 „ „ „ 17½ „	*8·75*

(6) Night Shift spinners—

Aged 19 years or over	*16·44*
„ 18 years and under 19 years	*12·55*

(7) Weavers aged 19 years or over—

(a) During the first six months of employment as a weaver at or after the age of 19 years	*14·09*
(b) Thereafter	*14·52*

(8) All other workers (except the apprentices and improvers to tenting or dressing to whom paragraph 7 applies)

Aged 19 years or over	*14·03*
„ 18 years and under 19 years	*10·67*
„ 17½ „ „ „ 18 „	*9·58*
„ 17 „ „ „ 17½ „	*8·75*
„ 16½ „ „ „ 17 „	*8·14*
„ 16 „ „ „ 16½ „	*7·59*
„ 15½ „ „ „ 16 „	*7·11*
„ under 15½ years	*6·73*

APPRENTICES AND IMPROVERS TO TENTING OR DRESSING

Per week
of 40 hours
£

7.—(1) The following general minimum time rates are applicable to male workers:—

(a) Apprentices to tenting, aged 16 years or over, whose employment complies with the provisions of Part V of this Schedule—

During the—

1st six months of apprenticeship	*7·59*
2nd „ „ „ „	*8·14*
3rd „ „ „ „	*8·75*
4th „ „ „ „	*9·58*
3rd year of apprenticeship	*10·67*
4th „ „ „	*14·09*

(b) Improvers to tenting—

During one year of employment as an improver	*14·80*

(c) Apprentices to dressing aged 16 years or over, whose employment complies with the provisions of Part V of this Schedule—

During the—

1st six months of apprenticeship	7·59
2nd ,, ,, ,, ,, ...	8·14
3rd ,, ,, ,, ,, ...	8·75
4th ,, ,, ,, ,, ...	9·58
3rd year of apprenticeship	10·67

(d) Improvers to dressing—

During one year of employment as an improver	14·09

(2) For the purposes of this paragraph:—

(a) an improver to tenting is a male worker who having completed four years' apprenticeship to tenting in accordance with the provisions of Part V of this Schedule has had thereafter less than two years' employment in tenting and is the holder of a certificate of registration as an improver to tenting issued by, or on behalf of, the Wages Council or has made application for such certificate which has been acknowledged and is still under consideration;

(b) an improver to dressing is a male worker who having completed three years' apprenticeship to dressing in accordance with the provisions of Part V of this Schedule has had thereafter less than one year's employment in dressing.

PIECE WORK BASIS TIME RATE
HOSE-PIPE WEAVERS

Per week
of 40 hours
£

8. The piece work basis time rate applicable to male hose-pipe weavers employed on piece work on power or hand looms is ... ...   *14·95*

GUARANTEED TIME RATE FOR PIECE WORKERS
WEAVERS

Per week
of 40 hours
£

9. The guaranteed time rates applicable to male weavers employed on piece work are as follows:—

(1) During the first six months of employment as a weaver at or after the age of 19 years ... ...   *14·09*

(2) Thereafter ... ...   *14·52*

PART IV

OVERTIME AND WAITING TIME

MINIMUM OVERTIME RATES—ALL WORKERS

10.—(1) Subject to the provisions of this paragraph, minimum overtime rates are payable to any worker as follows:—

(a) on any day other than a Saturday, Sunday or a customary holiday—

(i) for the first two hours worked in excess of 8¼ hours ... ... time-and-a-quarter

(ii) thereafter ... ... time-and-a-half

Provided that where the worker normally attends on five days only in the week or on five shifts in the case of a shift worker the said minimum overtime rates of time-and-a-quarter and time-and-a-half shall be payable after 9 and 11 hours' work respectively.

(b) on a Saturday, not being a customary holiday—
for all time worked in excess of 3¾ hours ... time-and-a-half

Provided that where the worker normally attends on five days only in the week or on five shifts in the case of a shift worker the said minimum overtime rate of time-and-a-half shall be payable for all time worked on Saturday.

(c) on a Sunday or a customary holiday—
for all time worked ... ... double time

(2) Subject to the provisions of sub-paragraph (3) of this paragraph, where the employer and the worker by agreement in writing fix in respect of each week-day or shift the number of hours after which a minimum overtime rate shall be payable and the total number of such hours amounts to 40 weekly, the following minimum overtime rates shall be payable in substitution for those set out in sub-paragraph (1) of this paragraph—

(a) on any day other than a Saturday, Sunday or a customary holiday—
    (i) for the first two hours worked in excess of the
        agreed number of hours ... ... time-and-a-quarter
    (ii) thereafter ... ... time-and-a-half

(b) on a Saturday, not being a customary holiday—
for all time worked in excess of the agreed number of
hours ... ... time-and-a-half

Provided that where the said agreement provides that Saturday shall not normally be a working day, the said minimum overtime rate of time-and-a-half shall be payable for all time worked on Saturday.

(c) on a Sunday or a customary holiday—
for all time worked ... ... double time

(3) Where a worker is employed on a turn of duty which commences on one day and extends into the following day, the whole of that turn of duty shall, for the purposes of this paragraph, be treated as occurring on the day on which the worker was required to commence such turn of duty:

Provided that where the worker is employed on regular night shifts for five nights in the week, and by agreement between the worker and his employer commences a turn of duty on Sunday, then the whole of that turn of duty shall be treated as occurring on Monday.

11. In this Part of this Schedule:—

(1) The expression "customary holiday" means—

(a) (i) In England and Wales—

Christmas Day (or, if Christmas Day falls on a Sunday, such week-day as may be appointed by national proclamation, or, if none is so appointed, the next following Tuesday), Boxing Day, Good Friday, Easter Monday, Whit Monday (or, where another day is substituted therefor by national proclamation, that day) and August Bank Holiday:

Provided that in the case of workers who normally work on each week-day except Saturday if Christmas Day falls on a Saturday the holiday shall be the next following Tuesday;

(ii) In Scotland—

New Year's Day and the following day:

Provided that if New Year's Day falls on a Sunday, the holidays shall be the following Monday and Tuesday; if New Year's Day falls on a Saturday then in the case of workers who normally work on each week-day except Saturday the holidays shall be the following Monday and Tuesday and in the case of all other workers, New Year's Day and the following Monday;

the local Spring holiday;

the local Autumn holiday;

and two other days (being days on which the worker normally works for the employer) in the course of a calendar year, to be fixed by the employer in consultation with the worker or his representative and notified to the worker not less than three weeks before the holiday;

or

(b) in the case of each of the said days (other than a day fixed by the employer in Scotland and notified to the worker as aforesaid) a day substituted by the employer therefor, being a day recognised by local custom as a day of holiday in substitution for the said day.

(2) The expressions "time-and-a-quarter", "time-and-a-half" and "double time" mean respectively:—

(a) in the case of a time worker, one and a quarter times, one and a half times and twice the hourly general minimum time rate otherwise applicable to the worker;

(b) in the case of a female worker employed on piece work:—

(i) a time rate equal respectively to one quarter, one half and the whole of the hourly piece work basis time rate otherwise applicable to the worker, and, in addition thereto,

(ii) the minimum remuneration otherwise applicable to the worker under paragraph 1(1)(b);

(c) in the case of a male hose-pipe weaver employed on piece work:—

(i) a time rate equal respectively to one quarter, one half and the whole of the hourly piece work basis time rate otherwise applicable to the worker, and, in addition thereto,

(ii) the minimum remuneration otherwise applicable to the worker under paragraph 1(1)(b);

(d) in the case of any other male worker employed on piece work:—

(i) a time rate equal respectively to one quarter, one half and the whole of the hourly general minimum time rate which would be applicable to the worker if he were a time worker and a minimum overtime rate did not apply, and, in addition thereto,

(ii) the minimum remuneration otherwise applicable to the worker under paragraph 1(1)(b).

WAITING TIME

12.—(1) A worker is entitled to payment of the minimum remuneration specified in this Schedule for all the time during which he is present on the premises of the employer, unless he is present thereon in any of the following circumstances, that is to say—

(a) without the employer's consent, express or implied;

(b) for some purpose unconnected with his work and other than that of waiting for work to be given to him to perform;

(c) by reason only of the fact that he is resident thereon; or

(d) during normal meal times in a room or place in which no work is being done, and he is not waiting for work to be given to him to perform.

(2) The minimum remuneration payable under sub-paragraph (1) of this paragraph to a piece worker when not engaged on piece work is that which would be applicable to him if he were employed as a time worker.

PART V

CONDITIONS AS TO RATES FOR MALE APPRENTICES AND PROSPECTIVE APPRENTICES TO TENTING OR DRESSING

13. Subject to the provisions of this Part of this Schedule, the general minimum time rates applicable to apprentices to tenting or dressing under paragraph 7 apply only where the following conditions are fulfilled:—

(1) The apprentice shall be employed during the whole of his time under a written contract of apprenticeship, for a period of four years in the case of an apprenticeship to tenting or three years in the case of an apprenticeship to dressing, which has been duly executed and which contains the following provisions, or provisions substantially to the same effect, and no provisions contrary thereto:—

(a) the apprentice of his own free will and with the consent of the guardian binds himself to serve the employer as his apprentice in his trade for the term of three or four years as aforesaid;

(b) the employer will employ the apprentice as his apprentice during the said term, and to the best of his power, skill and knowledge instruct the apprentice, or cause him to be instructed, in tenting or dressing as the case may be;

(c) the employer will keep the apprentice under his own supervision or place him under the supervision of one or more fully qualified journeymen;

and

(d) the employer will, during the term of the apprenticeship, afford the apprentice reasonable facilities, during working hours if necessary, to attend classes at which technical instruction in the principles of the operation being taught is given, or, if at any time no such class exists in the district in which the apprentice is employed, the employer will place the apprentice under the charge of one of his own workers who need not be a journeyman mentioned in (c) of this sub-paragraph, but is competent to instruct the apprentice in the elementary principles of the operation being taught.

(2) The apprentice shall be the holder of a certificate of registration of apprenticeship issued by, or on behalf of, the Wages Council or shall have made application for such certificate which has been duly acknowledged and is still under consideration:

Provided that the Wages Council may decline to issue a certificate in any case where it is not satisfied that the said conditions have been complied with at the date of the application therefor, and the Wages Council may at any time thereafter cancel the certificate, if, in its opinion, any of the said conditions have not been complied with.

PROSPECTIVE APPRENTICES

14. Notwithstanding the foregoing provisions of this Schedule, where an employer employs a worker as a prospective apprentice to tenting or dressing for a probationary period not exceeding 12 weeks and all the conditions specified in the foregoing paragraph other than those with regard to employment under a written contract of apprenticeship and certification by the Wages Council are fulfilled, the minimum remuneration

applicable to that worker during the said period shall be that applicable to an apprentice employed in accordance with the conditions specified in the said paragraph, and in the event of the worker being continued thereafter at his employment as an apprentice, the probationary period shall for the purposes of this Schedule be treated as part of the period of apprenticeship, whether or not it is included therein:

Provided that where the employer does not on or before the last day of the said probationary period enter into with the worker such a contract of apprenticeship as is mentioned in the said paragraph, the employer shall pay to the worker a sum equal to the difference between the minimum remuneration payable to him as a prospective apprentice and the amount that would have been payable to him had the provisions of this paragraph not applied.

PART VI

APPLICABILITY OF STATUTORY MINIMUM REMUNERATION

15. This Schedule applies to the workers in relation to whom the Wages Council operates, that is to say, workers employed in Great Britain in the trade specified in the Schedule to the Trade Boards (Flax and Hemp Trade, Great Britain) (Constitution and Proceedings) Regulations 1940(a), that is to say:—

The preparing, spinning, and weaving (a) of scutched flax, (b) of hemp, (c) of a mixture of scutched flax and any other fibre, or (d) of a mixture of hemp and any other fibre;

including:—

(1) The preparing and spinning of waste reclaimed at any stage; and

(2) All packing, despatching, warehousing, storing or other operations incidental to or appertaining to any of the above-mentioned work;

but excluding:—

(1) The calendering, bleaching, dyeing or finishing of any of the above-mentioned materials; and

(2) The preparing or spinning of materials required for the making or re-making of (a) rope (including driving rope and banding), (b) cord (including blind and window cord, but excluding silk, worsted and other fancy cords), (c) core for wire ropes, (d) lines, (e) twine (including binder and trawl twine), (f) lanyards, (g) net and similar articles when such spinning or preparing is carried on in the same factory or workshop as the said making or re-making; and

(3) The making or repair of sacks or bags; and also

(4) The weaving of carpets, rugs and mats.

EXPLANATORY NOTE

(*This Note is not part of the Order.*)

This Order, which has effect from 20th September 1971, sets out the statutory minimum remuneration payable in substitution for that fixed by the Wages Regulation (Flax and Hemp) Order 1970 (Order F.H. (125)), which Order is revoked.

New provisions are printed in italics.

(a) S.R. & O. 1940/1886 (1940 I, p. 1031).

STATUTORY INSTRUMENTS

1971 No. 1419

SOCIAL SECURITY

The National Insurance (Miscellaneous Amendments) Regulations 1971

Made - - - -	*26th August* 1971
Laid before Parliament	*3rd September* 1971
Coming into Operation—	
for all purposes except invalidity benefit -	*20th September* 1971
for the purposes of invalidity benefit -	*23rd September* 1971

ARRANGEMENT OF REGULATIONS

SCHEDULES

SCHEDULE 1— Provisions Conferring Powers Exercised in Making these Regulations

SCHEDULE 2— Provisions to be substituted for Part I of Schedule 1 to the National Insurance (Claims and Payments) Regulations 1971

The National Insurance Joint Authority and the Secretary of State for Social Services, in exercise of the powers conferred by the provisions of the National Insurance Acts set out respectively in Parts I and II of Schedule 1 to this instrument, and in each case in exercise of all other powers enabling them in that behalf and in conjunction with the Treasury so far as relates to matters with regard to which they have so directed, hereby make the following regulations, which are made in consequence of the National Insurance Act 1971(a) and contain no provisions other than such as are so made, and which accordingly by virtue of section 16 of and paragraph 2(2)(a) of Schedule 6 to that Act, are exempt from the requirements of section 107(1) of the National Insurance Act 1965(b) (no regulations to be made wholly or partly by virtue of the provisions of section 22(4), 100 or 102 of that Act unless a draft of the regulations has been approved by resolution of each House of Parliament) and by virtue of section 16 of and paragraph 2(1)(a) of Schedule 6 to the said Act of 1971, are exempt from the requirements of section 108 of the said Act of 1965 (reference to the National Insurance Advisory Committee):—

Citation, commencement and interpretation

1.—(1) These regulations may be cited as the National Insurance (Miscellaneous Amendments) Regulations 1971.

(2) Except for the purposes of invalidity benefit under the National Insurance Act 1965, these regulations shall come into operation on 20th September 1971 and for the purposes of the said invalidity benefit they shall come into operation on 23rd September 1971.

(3) Each provision of these regulations which amends other regulations shall be construed as one with the regulations which it amends.

Amendment of the National Insurance (Widow's Benefit and Retirement Pensions) Regulations 1948

2. In regulation 11 of the National Insurance (Widow's Benefit and Retirement Pensions) Regulations 1948(c) (unemployment and sickness benefit in certain cases of persons over pensionable age after an election), as amended (d), there shall be added at the end the following paragraph—

"(4) This regulation shall apply for the purposes of the provisions of section 3 of the National Insurance Act 1971 (invalidity benefit) in relation to invalidity pension as it applies for the purposes of the said section 26 in relation to sickness benefit."

Amendment of the National Insurance (Residence and Persons Abroad) Regulations 1948

3.—(1) The National Insurance (Residence and Persons Abroad) Regulations 1948(e), as amended(f), shall be further amended in accordance with the following provisions of this regulation.

(a) 1971 c. 50.   (b) 1965 c. 51.
(c) S.I. 1948/1261 (Rev. XVI, p. 207: 1948 I, p. 2704).
(d) Regulation inserted by S.I. 1957/1309 (1957 I, p. 1615) and amended by S.I. 1970/1580 (1970 III, p. 5325).
(e) S.I. 1948/1275 (Rev. XVI, p. 88: 1948 I, p. 2864).
(f) The relevant amending instrument is S.I. 1967/828 (1967 II, p. 2474).

(2) In regulation 7 (modification of the Act in relation to payment of benefit abroad)—

(*a*) in paragraphs (1) and (1A), after the words "sickness benefit" there shall be inserted the words "or invalidity benefit";

(*b*) after paragraph (2) there shall be inserted the following paragraphs—

"(2A) A person shall not be disqualified for receiving age addition by reason of being absent from Great Britain if—

(*a*) he is ordinarily resident in Great Britain; or

(*b*) he was ordinarily resident in Great Britain and was entitled to age addition before he ceased to be ordinarily so resident; or

(*c*) in the case of a person who ceased to be ordinarily resident in Great Britain before 20th September 1971, he is entitled to a retirement pension and, by virtue of an Order in Council made under section 105 of the National Insurance Act 1965, he is not disqualified for receiving that pension at a higher rate than was applicable in his case when he was last ordinarily resident in Great Britain; or

(*d*) in the case of a person who ceased to be ordinarily resident in Great Britain on or after 20th September 1971, he is entitled to a retirement pension, and had he ceased to be ordinarily resident in Great Britain before that date, by virtue of an Order in Council made under section 105 of the National Insurance Act 1965 he would not have been disqualified for receiving that pension at a higher rate after that date than before it.

(2B) A person shall not be disqualified for receiving invalidity benefit by reason of being absent from Great Britain if by virtue of an Order in Council made under section 105 of the National Insurance Act 1965 he would not be disqualified for receiving sickness benefit."

(3) After regulation 7 there shall be inserted the following regulations—

"*Modifications of the rate of age addition for certain persons who are or have been outside Great Britain*

7A. Where a person is entitled to a retirement pension at a rate which is calculated by reference to any period completed by that person in some territory outside Great Britain while insured under the Act, any age addition to which he may be entitled shall be calculated as if it were an increase in that pension.

Modifications of the Act in relation to title to invalidity benefit

7B. A person who is or has been outside Great Britain while insured under the Act and who by virtue of an Order in Council made under section 105 of the National Insurance Act 1965 would but for the provisions of section 3 of the National Insurance Act 1971 have been entitled to sickness benefit in respect of any period, shall be entitled to invalidity pension for that period."

Amendment of the National Insurance (Sickness Benefit, Maternity Benefit and Miscellaneous Provisions) (Transitional) Regulations 1948

4.—(1) The National Insurance (Sickness Benefit, Maternity Benefit and

Miscellaneous Provisions) (Transitional) Regulations 1948(a), as amended(b), shall be further amended in accordance with the provisions of this regulation.

(2) In regulation 3(1) (insurance and contributions under the Health Insurance Acts to be taken into account for the purposes of the Act)—

(*a*) after the words "sickness benefit," in the first and second places where they occur there shall be inserted the words "invalidity pension,";

(*b*) in sub-paragraph (*a*)(ii) there shall be added at the end the words "and of section 3(2) of the National Insurance Act 1971 (which relates to invalidity pension)".

(3) For regulation 6 (avoidance of exhaustion of sickness benefit in certain cases) there shall be substituted the following regulation—

"*Avoidance of exhaustion of sickness benefit and provision relating to invalidity pension in certain cases*

6. Where, in the case of an existing contributor, since his entry into insurance under the Health Insurance Acts one hundred and four weeks have elapsed and one hundred and four weekly contributions have been paid by or in respect of him under those Acts, or have under regulation 2(2) of the National Health Insurance and Contributory Pensions (Navy, Army and Air Force Emergency Provisions) Regulations, 1945, been treated as paid—

(*a*) section 21(2) of the National Insurance Act 1965 shall not apply to any claim by him for sickness benefit under that Act ; and

(*b*) section 3(2) of the National Insurance Act 1971 shall not apply to any claim by him for invalidity pension under the said section 3."

Amendment of the National Insurance (Airmen) Regulations 1948

5. The National Insurance (Airmen) Regulations 1948(c), as amended(d), shall be further amended by inserting the words "or invalidity benefit" after the words "sickness benefit" in regulations 4(1) and (2) (removal of disqualification for benefit in the case of airmen absent from Great Britain) and 7 (evidence of incapacity).

Amendment of the National Insurance (Married Women) Regulations 1948

6. Regulation 8A of the National Insurance (Married Women) Regulations 1948(e) (modifications, in relation to widows, of provisions relating to certain benefits), as amended(f), shall be further amended as follows—

(*a*) in paragraph (1)(*f*) there shall be added at the end the words "or an invalidity pension";

(*b*) in paragraph (4)(*b*) for the words "or sickness benefit" there shall be substituted the words "sickness benefit or invalidity benefit";

(*c*) in paragraph (5), for the words from the beginning of the paragraph to but not including the words "which would not be payable" there shall be substituted the words "Where a woman is entitled to a widow's basic pension, the provisions of regulation 2(3A) of the Overlapping Benefits Regulations (limitation on adjustment) shall not apply where the other personal benefit in question is unemployment benefit, sickness benefit or invalidity pension";

(a) S.I. 1948/1276 (Rev. XVI, p. 49: 1948 I, p. 2639).
(b) There is no amendment which relates expressly to the subject matter of these regulations.
(c) S.I. 1948/1466 (Rev. XVI, p. 108: 1948 I, p. 2616).
(d) S.I. 1958/1238 (1958 II, p. 1577).
(e) S.I. 1948/1470 (Rev. XVI, p. 123: 1948 I, p. 2795).
(f) S.I. 1956/2108 (1956 I, p. 1681).

(d) in paragraph (6) there shall be inserted at the beginning the words "For the purposes of a retirement pension";

(e) in paragraph (9) for the words "or sickness benefit" there shall be substituted the words "sickness benefit or invalidity pension".

Amendment of the National Insurance (Overlapping Benefits) Regulations 1948

7.—(1) The National Insurance (Overlapping Benefits) Regulations 1948(a), as amended(b), shall be further amended in accordance with the following provisions of this regulation.

(2) In regulation 2 (adjustment of personal benefit under that Act where other personal benefit is payable)—

(a) in paragraph (1)—

(i) after the words "any other personal benefit" there shall be inserted the words "(whether of the same or a different description)",

(ii) in sub-paragraph (a) for the words "paragraph (2)" there shall be substituted the words "paragraphs (2) and (3A)",

(iii) in sub-paragraph (b) for the words "paragraph (3)" there shall be substituted the words "paragraphs (3) and (3A)";

(b) after paragraph (3) there shall be inserted the following paragraph—

"(3A) Where an adjustment falls to be made in accordance with the provisions of paragraph (2) or (3) of this regulation and either—

(a) one of the benefits in question is widow's basic pension payable to a widow by virtue of the insurance of her husband who died before 5th July 1951, and the other is unemployment benefit, sickness benefit, invalidity benefit or maternity benefit or a specified benefit other than a personal death benefit; or

(b) one of the benefits in question is a widow's basic pension or a contributory old age pension and the other is a supplement on account of unemployability payable under the Industrial Injuries Act, any Personal Injuries Scheme, any Service Pensions Instrument or any 1914-1918 War Injuries Scheme, or any Pneumoconiosis and Byssinosis Benefit Scheme,

any such adjustment shall not reduce the aggregate amount payable in respect of the benefits in question to less than the aggregate amount of any invalidity allowance to which the beneficiary may be entitled and the sums which would have been payable in respect of the other benefits had they been calculated at the respective rates appropriate to the period immediately before 20th September 1971 (or in the case of invalidity pension had it been calculated at the rate appropriate to sickness benefit for that period) and had no adjustment fallen to be made under this regulation.";

(c) in paragraph (4) after sub-paragraph (b) there shall be inserted the following sub-paragraph—

"(bb) any personal benefit under any Personal Injuries Scheme or Service Pensions Instrument or any 1914-1918 War Injuries Scheme

---

(a) S.I. 1948/2711 (Rev. XVI, p. 196: 1948 I, p. 2657).
(b) S.I. 1952/526, 1954/189, 1957/2077, 1961/557, 1962/12, 1966/920, 1971/621 (1952 II, p. 2196; 1954 I, p. 1387; 1957 I, p. 1556; 1961 I, p. 1228; 1962 I, p. 10; 1966 II, p. 2340; 1971 I, p. 1623).

being an additional allowance payable only to a beneficiary who is entitled to a supplement on account of unemployability;".

(3) In regulation 8 (construction of Part II of the regulations) after paragraph (*a*) there shall be inserted the following paragraph—

"(*aa*) that any personal benefit by way of age addition shall be adjusted except by reference to another age addition; or".

(4) In regulation 12 (provisions for adjusting benefit for part of a week)—

(*a*) in paragraph (1), in the proviso—

(i) for the words "or sickness benefit" there shall be substituted the words "sickness benefit or invalidity benefit";

(ii) for the words from and including the words "paragraph (*d*) of subsection (2)" to the end of the paragraph there shall be substituted the words "section 20(1)(*e*) of the National Insurance Act 1965 (Sunday or some other prescribed day to be disregarded for the purpose of unemployment, sickness and invalidity benefit) is a day other than Sunday, the first reference in this paragraph to Sunday shall be construed as a reference to that other day";

(*b*) for paragraph (3) there shall be substituted the following paragraph—

"(3) In this regulation, the word "benefit" (except in the expressions "unemployment benefit", "sickness benefit" and "invalidity benefit") includes any pension or allowances (whether under the Act or otherwise)."

(5) In the Schedule (benefits not to be adjusted by reference to other named benefits)—

(*a*) for paragraph (1) of column 2, there shall be substituted the following paragraph—

"(1) Invalidity allowance or any increase of unemployability supplement payable by virtue of section 13A of the National Insurance (Industrial Injuries) Act 1965";

(*b*) for paragraph (3) of column 1, there shall be substituted the following paragraph— "(3) Invalidity allowance";

(*c*) in paragraph (5) of column 1 the words "widow's basic pension or contributory old age pension" shall be omitted;

(*d*) after the words "sickness benefit" where they occur in paragraphs (6) and (13) of column 1 and paragraph (12) of column 2 there shall be inserted the words "invalidity benefit";

(*e*) in paragraph (6) of column 1 there shall be added at the end the words—
"or
(*c*) in so far as it does not consist of a retirement pension payable by virtue of section 1(1) of the National Insurance (Old persons' and widows' pensions and attendance allowance) Act 1970(**a**) or of section 5(1) of the National Insurance Act 1971(**b**)";

(*f*) at the end there shall be added the following paragraphs—

(i) in   column 1—

"(14) Invalidity pension in so far as it does not consist of a sum calculated by reference to section 3(6) of the National Insurance Act 1971

(**a**) 1970 c. 51.   (**b**) 1971 c. 50.

(15) Invalidity allowance

(16) Any personal benefit under the Act other than invalidity allowance" and

(ii) in column 2 opposite to those paragraphs respectively—

"(14) Invalidity allowance

(15) Invalidity pension in so far as it does not consist of a sum calculated by reference to section 3(6) of the National Insurance Act 1971

(16) Any allowance to which regulation 2(4)(*bb*) of these regulations refers".

Amendment of the National Insurance (*Hospital In-Patients*) *Regulations* 1949

8.—(1) The National Insurance (Hospital In-Patients) Regulations 1949**(a)**, as amended**(b)**, shall be further amended in accordance with the following provisions of these regulations.

(2) In regulation 3(1) (adjustment of personal benefit)—

(*a*) after the words "sickness benefit" there shall be inserted the words "invalidity benefit";

(*b*) after the words "widow's pension" there shall be inserted the words "age addition";

(*c*) at the end there shall be added the words "so however that in the case of a person to whom two or more such personal benefits (being benefits by way of retirement pension, age addition or both), or to whom invalidity pension and invalidity allowance, are payable the weekly rate referred to in this paragraph shall be the aggregate of the weekly rates of those benefits".

(3) In regulation 5(4)(*d*) (adjustment where beneficiary is married)—

(*a*) after the words "sickness benefit" there shall be inserted the words "invalidity benefit";

(*b*) after the words "by way of ", in the second place where they occur, there shall be inserted the words "invalidity benefit or";

(*c*) after the words "Provided that" there shall be inserted the words "the provisions of head (i) of this sub-paragraph shall not apply in the case of a beneficiary who is a woman and who is receiving an increase of invalidity pension in respect of her husband and".

(4) After regulation 5 there shall be inserted the following regulation—

"*Special provisions for certain persons entitled to widow's basic pension*

5A. Where a beneficiary is entitled to a widow's basic pension by virtue of the insurance of her husband who died before 5th July 1951 and to some other benefit to which regulation 3(1) of these regulations relates—

(*a*) regulation 4 or 5(2) of these regulations shall not require a greater reduction in those benefits than would reduce the aggregate amount payable in respect of them to a sum equal to the aggregate amount which would have been payable in respect of them had they been calculated—

(i) in the case of any benefit other than an invalidity benefit, at the rate appropriate to that beneficiary for the period immediately before 20th September 1971, and

---

(a) S.I. 1949/1461 (1949 I, p. 2718).

(b) S.I. 1952/2179, 1957/1849, 2077 (1952 II, p. 2147; 1957 I, p. 1546, 1556).

(ii) in the case of invalidity pension, at the rate appropriate to that beneficiary for sickness benefit for that period, and

(iii) in the case of invalidity allowance, at the rate at which it is payable; and

had they been adjusted under these regulations as in force on 19th September 1971 (invalidity pension and invalidity allowance as so calculated being for this purpose aggregated and treated as sickness benefit);

(b) regulation 5(1) of these regulations shall not operate to permit the aggregate amount payable in respect of those benefits in the case of a tuberculosis patient to exceed £2·50, and in any other case to exceed £2·00."

(5) In regulation 6C(1)(a) (adjustment or further adjustment of benefit in certain cases), after the words "sickness benefit" there shall be inserted the words "invalidity benefit".

(6) In regulation 8 (persons constituting "dependants")—

(a) after paragraph (d) there shall be inserted the words—
"or

(e) in the case of a man to whom a retirement pension is payable by virtue of section 5(1) of the National Insurance Act 1971(a) (which relates to retirement pension for persons over 80)—

(i) he is married and is residing with his wife, or
(ii) he has a child or children in his family; or

(f) in the case of a woman to whom a retirement pension is payable by virtue of the said section 5(1)—

(i) she is married and is residing with her husband and he is in receipt of a retirement pension, or

(ii) she has a child or children in her family;"

(b) after the words "those purposes, be regarded as a dependant" there shall be inserted the words "and, in relation to a beneficiary who is regarded as having a dependant by virtue of the provisions of paragraph (e) or (f) of this regulation, the spouse, child or children shall, for those purposes, be regarded as a dependant or dependants".

(7) After regulation 13 there shall be inserted the following regulation—

"Treatment of age addition in certain cases

13A. In a case where age addition would, but for the provisions of this regulation, be payable to a person to whom a retirement pension is not payable, regulations 3, 4 and 5 of these regulations shall not apply so as to reduce that age addition, but where that person is receiving or has received free in-patient treatment continuously for a period exceeding 52 weeks, age addition shall not be payable to that person for any part of that period which falls after the first 52 weeks thereof, and during which that person has not a child or children in his or her family or a wife who resides with him."

Amendment of the National Insurance (Increase of Benefit, Re-entry into Regular Employment and Miscellaneous Provisions) Regulations 1951

9. In paragraph (3) of regulation 11 of the National Insurance (Increase of Benefit, Re-entry into Regular Employment and Miscellaneous Provisions)

(a) 1971 c. 50.

Regulations 1951**(a)** (special provision relating to the effect of election by certain persons who have elected to be treated as retired), as amended**(b)**,—

(a) for sub-paragraph (b) there shall be substituted the following sub-paragraph—

"(b) no increase of unemployment benefit, sickness benefit or invalidity pension shall be payable to the husband under section 43 or 43A of the National Insurance Act 1965 (which relate to increases of benefit for adult dependants) whether in respect of her or any other person;"

(b) in sub-paragraph (d), after the words "sickness benefit" there shall be inserted the words "or invalidity pension".

Amendment of the National Insurance (Unemployment and Sickness Benefit) Regulations 1967

10.—(1) The National Insurance (Unemployment and Sickness Benefit) Regulations 1967**(c)**, as amended**(d)**, shall be further amended in accordance with the following provisions of these regulations.

(2) In regulation 4 (special provisions for day substituted for Sunday), in paragraphs (1) and (3) after the words "sickness benefit" there shall be inserted the words "or invalidity benefit".

(3) In regulation 5 (night workers)—

(a) in paragraph (1), for the words "and sickness benefit" there shall be substituted the words "sickness benefit and invalidity benefit";

(b) in paragraphs (3) and (4) after the words "sickness benefit" there shall be inserted the words "or invalidity benefit".

(4) In regulation 7 (days not to be treated as days of incapacity for work)-

(a) in paragraph (1) for the words "unemployment and sickness benefit" there shall be substituted the words "unemployment, sickness and invalidity benefit";

(b) in paragraph (1)(d) after the words "sickness benefit" there shall be inserted the words "or invalidity benefit";

(c) after paragraph (2) there shall be added the following paragraph—

"(3) For the purposes of invalidity pension, a day shall not be treated as a day of incapacity for work if it is a day in respect of which a person who is over pensionable age would not be entitled to a retirement pension if he had retired from regular employment on attaining that age and made the necessary claim."

(5) After regulation 7 there shall be inserted the following regulation—

"*Days to be treated as days of incapacity for work for the purposes of invalidity allowance*

7A.—(1) For the purpose only of ascertaining days of incapacity for work for the purposes of section 3(5) of the National Insurance Act 1971 (which relates to invalidity allowance) the days specified in paragraph (2) of this regulation shall be treated as days of incapacity for work if they are days in

---

(a) S.I. 1951/1232 (1951 I, p. 1457).
(b) There is no amendment which relates expressly to the subject matter of these regulations.
(c) S.I. 1967/330 (1967 I, p. 1131).
(d) There is no amendment which relates expressly to the subject matter of these regulations.

respect of which the person concerned would have had a right to sickness or invalidity benefit—

  (*a*) if he had claimed it; and

  (*b*) in a case to which regulation 8 of the National Insurance (Members of the Forces) Regulations 1968**(a)**, as amended**(b)**, applies, if that regulation did not apply; and

  (*c*) in a case to which paragraph (2)(*c*) of this regulation applies and in which the widow had not satisfied the contribution conditions set out in paragraph 1 of Schedule 2 to the Act, if she had satisfied them.

(2) The said days are—

  (*a*) in the case of a person who was a serving member of the forces within the meaning of the National Insurance (Members of the Forces) Regulations 1968, days when he was serving as such a member; and

  (*b*) in the case of a person who entered into an undertaking with his employer to refrain from claiming sickness, invalidity or injury benefit or maternity allowance in consideration of his drawing unabated sick pay, days in respect of which such an undertaking is in force, so however that this sub-paragraph shall apply only where the undertaking is approved for the purposes of this regulation by the Secretary of State in his discretion;

  (*c*) in the case of a widow who was entitled to widow's allowance, days during the period between the date of her husband's death and the date on which she ceased to be so entitled;

  (*d*) in the case of a widow entitled to widow's pension or widowed mother's allowance, days before 23rd September 1972 being days in respect of which she is so entitled at the rate specified in relation to that pension or allowance, as the case may be, in Schedule 3 to the Act."

(6) In regulation 10(2) (special provision relating to delay or failure in claiming or giving notice for earnings-related supplement), for the words "or sickness benefit" there shall be substituted the words "sickness benefit or invalidity benefit".

(7) In regulation 11(1) (disqualifications for sickness benefit) after the words "sickness benefit" there shall be inserted the words "and invalidity benefit".

(8) In regulation 12 (increase of benefit for dependent relative and further conditions applicable)—

  (*a*) in paragraph (2)(*a*)(ii), for the words "column 6" there shall be substituted the words "column 5 of Part II";

  (*b*) after paragraph (2) there shall be added the following paragraph—
    "(3) The provisions of this regulation shall apply for the purposes of section 43A(7) of the Act (increase of invalidity pension) as if the reference in paragraph (2)(*d*) to "sickness benefit" were a reference to "invalidity pension"."

(9) In regulation 14—

  (*a*) after the words "persons over pensionable age)" there shall be inserted the words "or of the provisions of section 3(4) of the National Insurance Act 1971 (invalidity pension for persons over pensionable age)";

(a) S.I. 1968/827 (1968 II, p. 2228).
(b) The relevant amending instrument is the National Insurance (Miscellaneous Amendments) Regulations 1971 (S.I. 1971/1419).

(b) after the words "or sickness benefit" in each place where they occur, there shall be inserted the words "or invalidity pension";

(c) after the words "or (2)(c)" there shall be inserted the words "or 43A(1) or (4)".

Amendment of the National Insurance (Medical Certification) Regulations 1967

11. In regulation 2(1) of the National Insurance (Medical Certification) Regulations 1967**(a)** (evidence of incapacity for sickness benefit purposes), after the words "sickness benefit" there shall be inserted the words "or invalidity benefit".

Amendment of the National Insurance (Determination of Claims and Questions) (No. 2) Regulations 1967

12. In regulation 15 of the National Insurance (Determination of Claims and Questions) (No. 2) Regulations 1967**(b)** (decisions involving payment of or increase in benefit), as amended**(c)**,—

(a) in paragraph (1)(b), after the words "sickness benefit" there shall be inserted the words "or invalidity benefit"; and

(b) in paragraph (1)(c), for the words "and a retirement pension" there shall be substituted the words "a retirement pension and an age addition"; and

(c) for paragraph (2)(a) there shall be substituted the following sub-paragraph—

"(a) Subject to the provisions of sub-paragraph (d) of this paragraph, except where it is certified by the decision on review that the original decision was revised by reason only of one or more of the following—

(i) a matter specified in section 64(1)(a) of the Act (contributions), or

(ii) a matter specified in section 2(9) of the National Insurance Act 1966**(d)** (determination of reckonable earnings), or

(iii) a matter relating to the number of days in respect of which the claimant has been entitled to sickness benefit,

the proviso to paragraph (1) of this regulation shall apply subject to the condition that no sum on account of benefit shall be paid to any person in respect of any part of the period referred to in that proviso earlier than twelve months before the date on which the application for the review was made."

Amendment of the National Insurance (Computation of Earnings) Regulations 1967

13.—(1) The National Insurance (Computation of Earnings) Regulations 1967**(e)** shall be amended in accordance with the following provisions of these regulations.

(2) In regulation 4(2) (payments to be disregarded in calculating earnings), for the words "and 43" there shall be substituted the words ", 43 and 43A".

(a) S.I. 1967/520 (1967 I, p. 1702).   (b) S.I. 1967/1570 (1967 III, p. 4350).
(c) S.I. 1969/290, 1971/621 (1969 I, p. 792; 1971 I, p. 1623).   (d) 1966 c. 6.
(e) S.I. 1967/760 (1967 II, p. 2266).

(3) In regulation 6 (calculation of earnings of certain retirement pensioners and adult dependants)—

(a) for the words "an adult dependant thereof" there shall be substituted the words "an adult dependant of such a pensioner or of an invalidity pensioner" ;

(b) for the words "and 43" there shall be substituted the words ", 43 and 43A".

(4) In regulation 7 (interim payments)—

(a) in paragraph (1) after the words "any increase thereof", in each place where they occur, there shall be inserted the words "or any increase of an invalidity pension" ;

(b) in paragraph (3), after the word "retirement" in each place where it occurs there shall be inserted the words "or invalidity" and at the end of the paragraph there shall be added the words "as the case may be".

(5) In regulation 8 (calculation of earnings from boarders and lodgers in the case of certain retirement pensioners and adult dependants)—

(a) after the words "adult dependant thereof" there shall be inserted the words "or of an invalidity pensioner" ;

(b) for the words "and 43" there shall be substituted the words ", 43 and 43A".

(6) For regulation 9 (earnings of a wife of a retirement pensioner) there shall be substituted the following regulation—

"Earnings of dependant of retirement or invalidity pensioner

9. In calculating under the foregoing provisions of these regulations the weekly earnings of any dependant of a beneficiary for the purposes of section 43A of the Act (increases of retirement or invalidity pension for adult dependants) the week by reference to which such earnings shall be calculated shall be the calendar week ending last before any week for which the beneficiary is entitled to a retirement pension or before any day for which he is entitled to invalidity pension as the case may be."

Amendment of the National Insurance (Members of the Forces) Regulations 1968

14. In regulation 8 of the National Insurance (Members of the Forces) Regulations 1968(a) (serving members of the forces not entitled to unemployment or sickness benefit), as amended (b), for the words "or sickness benefit" there shall be substituted the words ", sickness benefit or invalidity benefit".

Amendment of the National Insurance (Old Persons' Pensions) Regulations 1970

15.—(1) The National Insurance (Old Persons' Pensions) Regulations 1970(c), as amended (d), shall be further amended in accordance with the following provisions of this regulation.

(2) In regulation 1(2), after the definition of "the Act of 1970" there shall be inserted the following—

" 'the Act of 1971' means the National Insurance Act 1971".

(a) S.I. 1968/827 (1968 II, p. 2228).
(b) There is no amendment relevant to the subject matter of these regulations.
(c) S.I. 1970/1280 (1970 II, p. 4168).
(d) The relevant amending instrument is S.I. 1970/1580 (1970 III, p. 5325).

(3) After regulation 2, there shall be inserted the following regulation—

"Conditions for entitlement to retirement pension by virtue of s.5(1) of the Act of 1971

2A.—(1) The conditions specified in the following paragraph of this regulation shall be the conditions for entitlement to a retirement pension by virtue of section 5(1) of the Act of 1971 (which relates to retirement pension for persons over 80 years of age).

(2) The said conditions are that the person concerned—

(a) has been resident in Great Britain for a period of 10 years in the period of 20 years ending on 19th September 1971 or the day before he attained 80 years of age whichever is the later ; and

(b) was ordinarily resident in Great Britain on—

(i) 20th September 1971 or on the day he attained 80 years of age whichever is the later ; or

(ii) if he was not ordinarily resident in Great Britain on either of those days and the date of his claim for the said pension was later than both of those days, on the date of that claim, so however that where a person has satisfied this condition under this head he shall be deemed to have satisfied it on the date that he became ordinarily so resident."

(4) In regulation 7 (rates of benefit and increases for adult dependants)—

(a) paragraph (2) shall be omitted ;

(b) in paragraph (3), for the words "section 1(1) of the Act of 1970" there shall be inserted the words "these regulations" ;

(c) in paragraph (4), the words "first and last" shall be omitted.

(5) In regulation 8 (adjustment of rates of benefit in cases of overlapping benefits)—

(a) in paragraph (1), after the words "Act of 1970" there shall be inserted the words "or section 5(1) of the Act of 1971" and after the words "section 1(1)", in the second place where they occur, there shall be inserted the words "or 5(1), as the case may be," ;

(b) paragraph (3) shall be omitted.

(6) Regulation 11 (provision as to claims for benefit) shall be renumbered 11(1) and the following paragraph shall be added at the end—

"(2) Retirement pension under section 5(1) of the Act of 1971 may be paid without a claim being made for it in the case of a person—

(a) who was ordinarily resident in Great Britain on 20th September 1971 or on the day on which he attained 80 years of age, whichever is the later ; and

(b) to whom another retirement pension is payable."

(7) In regulation 12 (provision as to payment of benefit), after the words "Act of 1970" there shall be inserted the words "or section 5(1) of the Act of 1971" and for the words "1948, as amended" there shall be substituted the words "1971(a)".

(a) S.I. 1971/707 (1971 I, p. 1908).

Amendment of the National Insurance (General Benefit) Regulations 1970

16.—(1) The National Insurance (General Benefit) Regulations 1970(**a**), as amended (**b**), shall be further amended in accordance with the provisions of this regulation.

(2) In regulation 4(1) (increase of benefit for wife), for the words "or a retirement pension under section 43" there shall be substituted the words "invalidity pension or a retirement pension under section 43 or 43A as the case may be".

(3) In regulation 5 (increase of benefit for female person having care of child)—

(*a*) the words "and (4)", the words "or (4)", in each place where they occur, and the words "or retirement pension" shall be omitted ;

(*b*) after the words "unemployment benefit" there shall be inserted the word "or" ;

(*c*) for the words "column 6", in each place where they occur, there shall be substituted the words "column 5 of Part II".

(4) After regulation 5 there shall be inserted the following regulation—

"Increase of pension for female person having care of child

5A.—(1) Section 43A(4) of the Act (which provides for increases of retirement and invalidity pensions in respect of a female person having the care of a child or children of the beneficiary's family) shall not apply in any case where—

(*a*) the beneficiary neither is entitled to an increase of retirement pension or invalidity pension, as the case may be, in respect of a child or children of his family or of a child or children treated as such for the purposes of section 40 of the Act (which relates to increases of benefit in respect of children), nor would be so entitled but for the provisions of any regulations for the time being in force under the Act relating to overlapping benefits ; or

(*b*) the said female person is not residing with him unless either—

(i) she is employed by him in an employment in respect of which the weekly expenses incurred by the beneficiary are not less than the amount specified in relation to the benefit in question in column 5 of Part II of Schedule 3 to the Act and was so employed by him before he became unemployed or incapable of work or retired from regular employment, as the case may be, subject to the qualification that the condition of employment before that event shall not apply in a case where the necessity for her employment first arose thereafter, or

(ii) the beneficiary is contributing to her maintenance at a weekly rate not less than that specified in relation to the benefit in question in column 5 of Part II of Schedule 3 to the Act and her earnings from any gainful occupation in which she is engaged (other than her employment, if any, by the beneficiary in caring for a child or children of his family) do not exceed the amount of the increase specified in the said column 5 ; or

(*c*) the said female person is undergoing imprisonment or detention in legal custody ; or

---

(**a**) S.I. 1970/1981 (1970 III, p. 6461).
(**b**) There is no amendment relevant to the subject matter of these regulations.

(*d*) the said female person is absent from Great Britain, except for any period during which she is residing with the beneficiary outside Great Britain and for which, by virtue of the provisions of regulation 7 of the National Insurance (Residence and Persons Abroad) Regulations 1948(**a**), as amended (**b**), the beneficiary is not disqualified for receiving that benefit.

(2) In a case to which section 43A(4) of the Act applies and in which the female person is residing with the beneficiary and the earnings of the female person (excluding her earnings, if any, from her employment by the beneficiary in caring for a child or children of his family) for the calendar week ending last before any week for which the beneficiary is entitled to benefit exceeded £9·50, the weekly rate of the increase of benefit under the said section 43A(4) shall for the last-mentioned week be reduced—

(*a*) where the excess is less than £2·00, by 5 new pence for each complete 10 new pence of the excess, and

(*b*) where the excess is not less than £2·00, by 5 new pence for each complete 10 new pence of the excess up to £2·00 and by 5 new pence for each complete 5 new pence of any further excess."

(5) In regulation 7 (contributions to maintenance of adult dependants)—

(*a*) after the words "section 43(1)", in each place where they occur, there shall be inserted the words "or 43A(1)";

(*b*) after the words "sickness benefit" there shall be inserted the words "invalidity benefit";

(*c*) for the words "column 6" there shall be substituted the words "column 5 of Part II".

(6) In regulation 8 (children treated as included in a family for increase of certain benefits)—

(*a*) after the words "sickness benefit" there shall be inserted the words "invalidity pension";

(*b*) for the words "in column 5" there shall be substituted the words "in relation to unemployment or sickness benefit in column 4 of Part II";

(*c*) the words "in relation to the benefit in question" shall be omitted.

(7) In regulation 9(2) (contributions towards cost of maintaining child), after the words "sickness benefit" there shall be inserted the words "invalidity benefit".

(8) In regulation 11(3) (exceptions from disqualification for imprisonment etc)—

(*a*) after the words "sickness benefit" there shall be inserted the words "invalidity benefit";

(*b*) for the words "or retirement pension" there shall be substituted the words "retirement pension or age addition".

(9) In regulation 13 (interim payments, arrears and repayments)—

(*a*) in paragraph (2)(*b*), for the words "or a retirement pension" there shall be substituted the words "retirement pension or age addition";

(*b*) in paragraph (10), after the words "sickness benefit" there shall be inserted the words "invalidity benefit".

Amendment of the National Insurance (Claims and Payments) Regulations 1971

17.—(1) The National Insurance (Claims and Payments) Regulations 1971(**c**) shall be amended in accordance with the following provisions of this regulation.

(**a**) S.I. 1948/1275 (Rev. XVI, p. 88: 1948 I, p. 2864).
(**b**) The relevant amending instrument is S.I. 1955/983 (1955 I, p. 1624).
(**c**) S.I. 1971/707 (1971 I, p. 1908).

(2) In regulation 9 (time and manner of payment of certain benefits), after the words "sickness benefit," there shall be inserted the words "invalidity benefit,".

(3) After regulation 15, there shall be inserted the following regulation—

"Payment of benefit to third party

15A. For any period during which benefit is payable to a beneficiary in respect of another person only if the beneficiary is contributing at not less than a certain weekly rate to the maintenance of, or to the cost of providing for, that other person, then if it appears to the Secretary of State to be necessary for protecting the interests of the beneficiary or of the other person, or if the beneficiary so requests the Secretary of State, the Secretary of State may direct that the whole or part of the benefit payable to the beneficiary (whether or not benefit payable in respect of the other person) shall be paid to another person on behalf of the beneficiary."

(4) In Schedule 1 (claims for one benefit treated as claims for another)—

(*a*) for the provisions of Part I there shall be substituted the provisions set out in Schedule 2 to these regulations ;

(*b*) in column 2 of Part II—

  (i) after the words "Sickness benefit" in the first place where they occur there shall be inserted the words "or invalidity benefit",

  (ii) after the words "sickness benefit" in the second place where they occur there shall be inserted the words "or of invalidity pension".

(5) In column 1 of Schedule 2 (time for claiming benefit and disqualifications for late claim)—

(*a*) in paragraph 2, after the word "Sickness", in the first place where it occurs, there shall be inserted the words "or invalidity" ;

(*b*) in paragraph 6, after the word "benefit" there shall be added the words "or invalidity pension".

(6) In Schedule 3 (special provisions), after the word "sickness", in each place where it occurs in paragraphs 2(1) and 3, there shall be inserted the words "or invalidity".

Signed by authority of the Secretary of State for Social Services.

Mildred Riddelsdell,
Second Permanent Secretary,
Department of Health and Social Security.

25th August 1971.

Given under the Official Seal of the National Insurance Joint Authority.

(L.S.)

25th August 1971.

D. G. Kelly,
Secretary,
National Insurance Joint Authority.

Walter Clegg,
Bernard Weatherill,
Two of the Lords Commissioners
of Her Majesty's Treasury.

26th August 1971.

SCHEDULE 1

PROVISIONS CONFERRING POWERS EXERCISED IN MAKING THESE REGULATIONS

PART I

PROVISIONS CONFERRING POWERS EXERCISED BY THE NATIONAL INSURANCE JOINT
AUTHORITY

Enactment	Relevant Provisions	Relevant Amending Enactments
The National Insurance Act 1965(a)	Section 20(1) and (2)(a)	—
	Section 21(4)	
	Section 22(3)	
	Section 43(2)(c)	—
	Section 49	—
	Section 50	—
	Section 99	The National Insurance Act 1966(b) section 1(1) and Schedule 1 paragraph 9
	Section 114(5)	—
	Schedule 11 paragraph 17	—

(a) 1965 c. 51.   (b) 1966 c. 6.

SCHEDULE 1 (*Contd.*)

PART II

PROVISIONS CONFERRING POWERS EXERCISED BY THE SECRETARY OF STATE FOR SOCIAL SERVICES

Enactment	Relevant Provisions	Relevant Amending Enactments
The National Insurance Act 1965	Section 22(4)	—
	Section 35	—
	Section 41(3)	—
	Section 43A(5) and (6)	The National Insurance Act 1971(a) section 4
	Section 48	The National Insurance (Old persons' and widows' pensions and attendance allowance) Act 1970(b) section 9(1) and Schedule 2 Part I, paragraph 4
	Section 49	—
	Section 52	The National Insurance &c. Act 1969(c) section 2(1) and the Post Office Act 1969(d) section 141(1) and Schedule 11 Part II
	Section 73	—
	Section 75(2)	—
	Section 81(3) and (4)	—
	Section 100	—
	Section 102	—
	Section 103	—
	Section 114(3)	—
The National Insurance Act 1966	Section 2(8)(*a*)	—
The National Insurance (Old persons' and widows' pensions and attendance allowance) Act 1970	Section 1(1)	—
	Section 8(7)	—
The National Insurance Act 1971	Section 5(1)	—
	Schedule 5 paragraph 13(1)	—

(a) 1971 c. 50.   (b) 1970 c. 51.
(c) 1969 c. 4.   (d) 1969 c. 48.

Regulation 17 SCHEDULE 2

PROVISIONS TO BE SUBSTITUTED FOR PART I OF SCHEDULE 1 TO THE NATIONAL INSURANCE
(CLAIMS AND PAYMENTS) REGULATIONS 1971

Benefit claimed and benefit for which the claim may be treated as a claim in the alternative

Benefit claimed (1)	Alternative Benefit (2)
Sickness benefit	Invalidity benefit
Invalidity benefit	Sickness benefit
Unemployment benefit	Sickness benefit or invalidity benefit
An increase of unemployment benefit	An increase of sickness benefit or of invalidity pension
Sickness benefit for a woman	Maternity allowance
Invalidity benefit for a woman	Maternity allowance
Maternity allowance	Sickness benefit or invalidity benefit
Retirement pension for a woman by virtue of her husband's insurance	Widow's benefit

EXPLANATORY NOTE
(This Note is not part of the Regulations.)

These Regulations are made in consequence of the National Insurance Act 1971 and accordingly, by virtue of paragraph 2(1) of Schedule 6 to that Act, are exempt from reference to the National Insurance Advisory Committee and no such reference has been made.

The regulations contain provisions relating to invalidity benefit for the chronic sick, age addition for retirement pensioners who have attained the age of 80, retirement pensions for certain persons who have attained that age and provisions relating to increases of retirement and invalidity pensions in respect of female persons having the care of the pensioner's children. The various regulations amended are set out in the 'Arrangement of Regulations'.

Generally, the provisions relating to invalidity benefit correspond to those relating to sickness benefit, except in relation to increases for adult dependants where they correspond to those relating to retirement pensions : those relating to age addition correspond to those relating to retirement pensions : those relating to retirement pensions for persons over 80 correspond to those for retirement pensions under the National Insurance (Old persons' and widows' pensions and attendance allowance) Act 1970. In relation to the increase of retirement and invalidity pensions in respect of female persons having the care of the beneficiary's children the regulations provide that such increases in respect of female persons residing with the pensioner are to be subject to the same earnings rule as was introduced by the National Insurance Act 1971 in respect of wives. They also prescribe the cases in which no increases are payable ; these latter provisions correspond to those previously in force in relation to persons having the care of retirement pensioners' children.

The regulations also contain minor and consequential provisions.

STATUTORY INSTRUMENTS

1971 No. 1420

SOCIAL SECURITY

The National Insurance (Mariners) Amendment Regulations 1971

Made - - -	*26th August* 1971
Laid before Parliament	*3rd September* 1971
Coming into Operation—	
Regulation 2	*23rd September* 1971
Remainder	*21st September* 1971

The National Insurance Joint Authority in exercise of powers conferred by section 20 of the National Insurance Act 1965(**a**), and the Secretary of State for Social Services in exercise of his powers under sections 4(4), 4(7), 14(1)(*a*), 22(4), 49, 75(2) and 100 of that Act, and in each case in exercise of all other powers enabling them in that behalf, and in conjunction with the Treasury so far as relates to matters with regard to which they have so directed, hereby make the following regulations, which contain no provisions other than such as are made in consequence of the National Insurance Act 1971(**b**) and which accordingly by virtue of section 16(3) of and paragraph 2(1)(*a*) of Schedule 6 to that Act are exempt from the requirements of section 108 of the said Act of 1965 (reference to the National Insurance Advisory Committee), and which are made in consequence of the said Act of 1971 and which accordingly by virtue of section 16(3) of and paragraph 2(2)(*a*) of Schedule 6 to that Act are exempt from the requirements of section 107(1) of the said Act of 1965 (no regulations to be made wholly or partly by virtue of the provisions of section 22(4) or 100 of that Act unless a draft of the regulations has been approved by resolution of each House of Parliament): —

Citation, interpretation and commencement

1. These regulations, which may be cited as the National Insurance (Mariners) Amendment Regulations 1971, shall be read as one with the National Insurance (Mariners) Regulations 1967(**c**), as amended (**d**) (hereinafter referred to as "the principal regulations"), and shall come into operation in the case of regulation 2 on 23rd September 1971, and in the case of the remainder of the regulations on 21st September 1971.

Application of invalidity benefit to mariners

2.—(1) In regulations 10(*a*), 13(2) and 14(2) of the principal regulations, after the word "sickness" there shall be inserted the words "or invalidity".

(2) In regulations 10(*b*) and 13(1) of the principal regulations, for the words "or sickness" there shall be substituted the words ", sickness or invalidity".

(**a**) 1965 c. 51. (**b**) 1971 c. 50.
(**c**) S.I. 1967/386 (1967 I, p. 1294).
(**d**) S.I. 1967/594, 1969/1277, 1970/46, 507, 977 (1967 I, p. 1801; 1969 III, p. 3811; 1970 I, p. 243, 1713; II, p. 3089).

Amendment of regulation 18(7) *of, and Schedules* 5 *and* 6 *to, the principal regulations*

3.—(1) Regulation 18(7) of, and Schedules 5 and 6 to, the principal regulations (seaman's liability for graduated contributions and their assessment) shall be amended in accordance with the following provisions of this regulation.

(2) In the proviso to the said regulation 18(7), for the proportions "4¾ per cent., 4¼ per cent., 3¼ per cent., 2¾ per cent. and ½ per cent." there shall be substituted the proportions "4·75 per cent., 4·35 per cent., 4·25 per cent., 3·85 per cent., 3·25 per cent., 2·75 per cent., 1·6 per cent., 1·1 per cent., 0·5 per cent. and 0·4 per cent." and for the words "as amended by section 1(2) of the National Insurance Act 1969" there shall be substituted the words "as from time to time in force".

(3) After the said proviso there shall be added the following proviso :—

"And provided that under paragraph (7) of this regulation no amount shall be payable which is in excess of the maximum weekly or, as the case may be, monthly amount specified in column (2) of the appropriate Schedule, or, in a case to which paragraph (4) of this regulation applies and in which the employer is liable to pay more than one weekly employer's contribution in respect of the employment of the seaman for the relevant voyage period or pay period, of a sum equal to the said maximum weekly amount multiplied by the number of contributions the employer is so liable to pay".

(4) For the tables set out in the said Schedules 5 and 6 there shall be substituted the tables set out in the Schedule to these regulations.

Amendment of regulation 20(2) *of, and revocation of Schedule* 7 *to, the principal regulations*

4.—(1) For paragraph (2) of regulation 20 (separate additional overtime payments) of the principal regulations there shall be substituted the following paragraph :—

"(2) Where remuneration for overtime work as a seaman earned in any of the last 6 days of a voyage is not included in the terminal payment, then, in respect of any subsequent payment on account of that remuneration (not being a payment of less than one pound) and subject to regulations 19 and 22, the employer and the seaman shall each be liable to pay a graduated contribution of the difference (if any) between the following amounts, that is to say—

(*a*) the amount which he would, in accordance with the provisions of regulation 18 but disregarding the provisions of this regulation, have been liable to pay in respect of the terminal payment if it had included the remuneration for the said overtime work ; and

(*b*) the amount which he is or was liable to pay in accordance with regulation 18 in respect of the terminal payment."

(2) Schedule 7 to the principal regulations is hereby revoked.

Amendment of regulation 21(2)(a) *of the principal regulations*

5. In regulation 21(2)(*a*) of the principal regulations (annual maximum) the words "or after" in sub-head (vi) shall be omitted and after the said sub-head (vi) there shall be added the following sub-heads :—

"(vii) which ends on 5th April 1972 shall, if the graduated contributions so paid in that year amount to £62·81 or more, be £62·31 ;

(viii) which ends on or after 5th April 1973 shall, if the graduated contributions so paid in that year amount to £78·41 or more, be £77·91 ;".

Transitory provisions

6. Notwithstanding the provisions of regulation 3 of these regulations, the graduated contributions payable in respect of any payment of remuneration—

(a) in respect of a voyage commencing before 21st September 1971, which ends before 21st December 1971, or in respect of any period of leave on pay immediately following such a voyage ; or

(b) in respect of such part of a voyage ending on or after 21st December 1971 as occurs before 21st September 1971 ;

shall not be increased but shall be calculated as if these regulations had not been made.

Signed by Authority of the Secretary of State for Social Services.

Paul Dean,
Parliamentary Under Secretary of State,
Department of Health and Social Security.

23rd August 1971.

Given under the Official Seal of the National Insurance Joint Authority.

(L.S.)
D. G. Kelly,
Secretary,
National Insurance Joint Authority.

24th August 1971.

Walter Clegg,
Bernard Weatherill,
Two of the Lords Commissioners of
Her Majesty's Treasury.

26th August 1971.

Regulation 3   SCHEDULE

1. Schedule to be substituted for Schedule 5 to the principal regulations.

Regulation 18   SCHEDULE 5

Employment which is not a non-participating employment

PART I

Scale for pay period of a week or for a voyage period for which no or one weekly
employer's contribution is payable

Amount of payment	Amount of contribution
(1)	(2)
£	£
9·01	0·01
9·25	0·02
9·50	0·04
10·00	0·06
10·50	0·08
11·00	0·11
11·50	0·13
12·00	0·15
12·50	0·18
13·00	0·20
13·50	0·23
14·00	0·25
14·50	0·27
15·00	0·30
15·50	0·32
16·00	0·34
16·50	0·37
17·00	0·39
17·50	0·42
18·00	0·45
19·00	0·49
20·00	0·54
21·00	0·58
22·00	0·62
23·00	0·67
24·00	0·71
25·00	0·75
26·00	0·80
27·00	0·84
28·00	0·88
29·00	0·93

SCHEDULE (contd.)

SCHEDULE 5

PART I (contd.)

Amount of payment (1)	Amount of contribution (2)
£	£
30·00	0·97
31·00	1·01
32·00	1·06
33·00	1·10
34·00	1·15
35·00	1·19
36·00	1·23
37·00	1·28
38·00	1·32
39·00	1·36
40·00	1·41
41·00	1·45
42·00 or more	1·47

PART II

Scale for pay period of one month

Amount of payment (1)	Amount of contribution (2)
£	£
39·02	0·02
40·00	0·09
42·00	0·19
44·00	0·28
46·00	0·38
48·00	0·47
50·00	0·57
52·00	0·66
54·00	0·76
56·00	0·85
58·00	0·95
60·00	1·04
62·00	1·14
64·00	1·23
66·00	1·33
68·00	1·42

SCHEDULE (contd.)

SCHEDULE 5

Part II (contd.)

Amount of payment (1)	Amount of contribution (2)
£	£
70·00	1·52
72·00	1·61
74·00	1·71
76·00	1·80
78·00	1·94
82·00	2·11
86·00	2·29
90·00	2·46
94·00	2·64
98·00	2·81
102·00	2·98
106·00	3·16
110·00	3·33
114·00	3·51
118·00	3·68
122·00	3·85
126·00	4·03
130·00	4·20
134·00	4·38
138·00	4·55
142·00	4·72
146·00	4·90
150·00	5·07
154·00	5·25
158·00	5·42
162·00	5·59
166·00	5·77
170·00	5·94
174·00	6·12
178·00	6·29
182·00 or more	6·38

SCHEDULE (contd.)

2. Schedule to be substituted for Schedule 6 to the principal regulations.

SCHEDULE 6   Regulation 18

Non-participating employment

PART I

Scale for pay period of a week or for a voyage period for which no or one weekly employer's contribution is payable

Amount of payment (1)	Amount of contribution (2)
£	£
9·01	0·01
12·00	0·02
15·00	0·04
18·00	0·07
19·00	0·11
20·00	0·15
21·00	0·20
22·00	0·24
23·00	0·28
24·00	0·33
25·00	0·37
26·00	0·41
27·00	0·46
28·00	0·50
29·00	0·55
30·00	0·59
31·00	0·63
32·00	0·68
33·00	0·72
34·00	0·76
35·00	0·81
36·00	0·85
37·00	0·89
38·00	0·94
39·00	0·98
40·00	1·02
41·00	1·07
42·00 or more	1·08

SCHEDULE (contd.)

SCHEDULE 6 (contd.)

PART II

Scale for pay period of one month

Amount of payment (1)	Amount of contribution (2)
£	£
39·01	0·01
40·00	0·03
50·00	0·08
60·00	0·13
70·00	0·17
78·00	0·28
82·00	0·46
86·00	0·63
90·00	0·80
94·00	0·98
98·00	1·15
102·00	1·33
106·00	1·50
110·00	1·67
114·00	1·85
118·00	2·02
122·00	2·20
126·00	2·37
130·00	2·54
134·00	2·72
138·00	2·89
142·00	3·07
146·00	3·24
150·00	3·41
154·00	3·59
158·00	3·76
162·00	3·94
166·00	4·11
170·00	4·28
174·00	4·46
178·00	4·63
182·00 or more	4·72

EXPLANATORY NOTE

(This Note is not part of the Regulations.)

These regulations contain no provisions other than such as are made in consequence of the National Insurance Act 1971 and accordingly, by virtue of paragraph 2 of Schedule 6 to that Act, no reference of them has been made to the National Insurance Advisory Committee, nor has a draft of the regulations been laid before Parliament for approval by resolution of each House.

The regulations amend the provisions of the National Insurance (Mariners) Regulations 1967 relating to sickness benefit (so that they relate also to invalidity benefit) (regulation 2) ; relating to seamen's liability for graduated contributions and their assessment and calculation (regulations 3, 4 and 6 and the Schedule) ; and relating to the annual maximum amount payable by way of graduated contributions (regulation 5).

STATUTORY INSTRUMENTS

1971 No. 1421

SOCIAL SECURITY

The National Insurance and Industrial Injuries (Classification, Contributions and Collection of Contributions) Amendment Regulations 1971

Made - - -	*26th August* 1971
Laid before Parliament	*3rd September* 1971
Coming into Operation—	
Regulations 1 and 3(4)	*6th September* 1971
Regulations 2 and 4	*20th September* 1971
Regulation 3(2)	*27th September* 1971
Remainder	*23rd September* 1971

The Secretary of State for Social Services in exercise of his powers under sections 1(3), 8(5) and 10(1) (as amended by section 1(4)(*b*) of the National Insurance Act 1971**(a)**) of the National Insurance Act 1965**(b)** and section 3(3)(*b*) of the National Insurance (Industrial Injuries) Act 1965**(c)** and of all other powers enabling him in that behalf and in conjunction with the Treasury so far as relates to matters with regard to which they have so directed, hereby makes the following regulations which contain no provisions other than such as either are made in consequence of the said Act of 1971 or operate with reference to the amount of a person's earnings and which accordingly by virtue of section 16 of and paragraph 2(1)(*a*) and (*b*) of Schedule 6 to that Act are exempt from the requirements of section 108 of the said National Insurance Act 1965 and section 62(2) of the said National Insurance (Industrial Injuries) Act 1965 (reference to the National Insurance Advisory Committee and the Industrial Injuries Advisory Council):—

Citation, commencement and interpretation

1.—(1) These regulations may be cited as the National Insurance and Industrial Injuries (Classification, Contributions and Collection of Contributions) Amendment Regulations 1971 and shall come into operation in the case of this regulation and regulation 3(4) on 6th September 1971, in the case of regulations 2 and 4 on 20th September 1971, in the case of regulation 3(2) on 27th September 1971 and in the case of the remainder of the regulations on 23rd September 1971.

(2) Each provision of these regulations which amends other regulations shall, unless the context otherwise requires, be read as one with the regulations which it amends.

(a) 1971 c. 50.   (b) 1965 c. 51.   (c) 1965 c. 52.

Amendment of the National Insurance (Classification) Regulations 1948

2. In Schedule 1 to the National Insurance (Classification) Regulations 1948**(a)**, as amended**(b)**, (classification of insured persons)—

(*a*) for the sum "£4" in paragraphs 8 of column (B), 11 of columns (A) and (B), 32, 34 to 44A and 46 to 53 of column (B) there shall be substituted the sum "£5·00", and

(*b*) for the sum "£2·00" in paragraph 17 of column (A) there shall be substituted the sum "£4·00".

Amendment of the National Insurance (Contributions) Regulations 1969

3.—(1) The National Insurance (Contributions) Regulations 1969**(c)**, as amended**(d)**, shall be amended in accordance with the following paragraphs of this regulation.

(2) In regulation 3 (incapacity for work)—

(*a*) for paragraph (2) there shall be substituted the following:—

"(2) Notwithstanding anything contained in the foregoing provisions of this regulation—

(*a*) where industrial injury benefit is payable to an insured person under the Industrial Injuries Act in respect of a week of incapacity for work, that person shall be excepted from liability to pay a contribution under the Act, and a contribution as an employed person shall be credited to him for that week;

(*b*) subject to the proviso to this sub-paragraph, an insured person shall be excepted from liability to pay a contribution under the Act for any week which is a week of incapacity for work and in respect of which invalidity benefit is payable and a contribution shall be credited to him for that week as follows:—

(i) as an employed person if, in respect of the last week which was a week of incapacity for work and in which he was entitled to sickness benefit, he was entitled to be credited with a contribution as an employed person;

(ii) in any other case, as a self-employed person:

Provided that, if in respect of any week for which invalidity benefit is payable to an insured person that person would but for the foregoing provisions of this sub-paragraph have been credited under paragraph (1) of this regulation with a contribution as an employed person, he shall, notwithstanding the provisions of head (ii) of this sub-paragraph, be credited with such contribution for that week.".

(*b*) in paragraph (3) after the words "sickness benefit" there shall be added the words "or invalidity benefit".

(3) In regulation 5 (determination of days of unemployment or incapacity for work)—

(a) S.I. 1948/1425 (Rev. XVI, p. 95: 1948 I, p. 2738).
(b) The relevant amending instruments are S.I. 1950/830, 1957/2175, 1969/1135, 1362 (1950 II, p. 12; 1957 I, p. 1623; 1969 II, p. 3371; III, p. 4069).
(c) S.I. 1969/1696 (1969 III, p. 5323).
(d) There is no amendment which relates expressly to the subject matter of these regulations.

(a) for the words "unemployment benefit and sickness benefit" in paragraph (3)(a) there shall be substituted the words "unemployment benefit, sickness benefit and invalidity benefit";

(b) for the words "or sickness benefit" in paragraph (3)(c)(i) there shall be substituted the words "sickness or invalidity benefit";

(c) for the words "either such benefit" in paragraph (3)(c)(ii) there shall be substituted the words "unemployment, sickness, or as the case may be, invalidity benefit";

(d) for the words "or sickness benefit" in paragraph (3)(c)(iii) there shall be substituted the words "sickness benefit or invalidity benefit".

(4) In regulation 15(3) (small income exception) for the words from the beginning of the paragraph to and including the words "but any such person" there shall be substituted the words "Any person in respect of whom a certificate of exception has been granted and" and the word "nevertheless" shall be omitted.

(5) In regulation 25 (late paid contributions)—

(a) for the words "or sickness" in the heading and in paragraph (1) there shall be substituted the words "sickness or invalidity", and

(b) for the word "aforesaid" in paragraph (2) there shall be substituted the words "of unemployment or sickness benefit".

(6) In the Arrangement of Regulations, for the words "or sickness" in the description of the said regulation 25 there shall be substituted the words "sickness or invalidity".

Amendment of the National Insurance and Industrial Injuries (Collection of Contributions) Regulations 1948

4. In regulation 10A of the National Insurance and Industrial Injuries (Collection of Contributions) Regulations 1948**(a)**, as amended**(b)**, (contributions when no services are rendered) and in the proviso to regulation 11 of those Regulations (contributions during holidays) for the sum "£4" there shall be substituted the sum "£5·00".

Signed by authority of the Secretary of State for Social Services.

Mildred Riddelsdell,
Second Permanent Secretary,
Department of Health and Social Security.

25th August 1971.

Walter Clegg,
Bernard Weatherill,
Two of the Lords Commissioners
of Her Majesty's Treasury.

26th August 1971.

(a) S.I. 1948/1274 (Rev. XVI, p. 148: 1948 I, p. 3037).
(b) The relevant amending instruments are S.I. 1959/207, 1969/1362 (1959 II, p. 1893; 1969 III, p. 4069).

EXPLANATORY NOTE

(This Note is not part of the Regulations.)

By virtue of section 16 of and paragraph 2(1)(*a*) and (*b*) of Schedule 6 to the National Insurance Act 1971 these Regulations are exempt from reference to the National Insurance Advisory Committee and to the Industrial Injuries Advisory Council, and no such references have been made.

These Regulations, by amending various paragraphs of Schedule 1 to the National Insurance (Classification) Regulations 1948 and regulations 10A and 11 of the National Insurance and Industrial Injuries (Collection of Contributions) Regulations 1948, raise the figure of weekly earnings in the case of certain insured persons in specified employments where classification is modified or where liability for contributions is determined by reference to their earnings.

The Regulations also, by amending regulation 3(2) of the National Insurance (Contributions) Regulations 1969, provide for an insured person to be excepted from liability to pay a contribution for any week which is a week of incapacity for work and in respect of which invalidity benefit is payable and to be credited with a contribution as an employed person or, as the case might be, as a self-employed person for that week. They also amend regulation 5 of those Regulations by making the provisions therein contained determining days of incapacity for work apply for the purposes of such exception and credit. They also, by amending regulation 25 of those Regulations, provide for the treatment for the purposes of invalidity benefit of late paid contributions.

These Regulations also amend regulation 15(3) of the National Insurance (Contributions) Regulations 1969 by removing the general bar against the crediting of contributions to persons while a certificate remains in force excepting them on account of low income from liability to pay contributions.

The remaining provisions are of a minor character.

STATUTORY INSTRUMENTS

1971 No. 1422

SOCIAL SECURITY

The National Insurance (Members of the Forces) Amendment Regulations 1971

Made - - -	*26th August* 1971
Laid before Parliament	*3rd September* 1971
Coming into Operation—	
Regulations 1, 2(1)	*20th September* 1971
Regulation 2(2)	*21st September* 1971

The Secretary of State for Social Services, in exercise of his powers under sections 4(6) and (7) of the National Insurance Act 1965(a), and the National Insurance Joint Authority, in conjunction with the Treasury. in exercise of the powers conferred by section 99 of that Act (as extended by section 1(1) of and paragraph 9 of Schedule 1 to the National Insurance Act 1966(b)), in each case in exercise of all other powers enabling him or them in that behalf, hereby make the following regulations, which contain no provisions other than such as are made in consequence of the National Insurance Act 1971(c) and which accordingly by virtue of section 16(3) of and paragraph 2(1)(*a*) of Schedule 6 to that Act are exempt from the requirements of section 108 of the said Act of 1965 (reference to the National Insurance Advisory Committee) :—

Citation, interpretation and commencement

1. These regulations, which may be cited as the National Insurance (Members of the Forces) Amendment Regulations 1971, shall be read as one with the National Insurance (Members of the Forces) Regulations 1968(d), as amended (e) (hereinafter referred to as "the principal regulations"), and shall come into operation in the case of regulations 1 and 2(1) on 20th September 1971 and in the case of regulation 2(2) on 21st September 1971.

Amendment of Schedules 3, 4, 5 and 5A to the principal regulations

2.—(1) For the table set out in Schedule 3 (reduction of weekly rates of flat-rate contributions) to the principal regulations there shall be substituted the table set out in Schedule A to these regulations.

(2) For the tables set out in Schedules 4 (statutory provisions applying to graduated contributions which are modified in their application to employment as a serving member of the forces), 5 (scale of graduated contributions in respect of employment which is not a non-participating employment) and 5A (scale of graduated contributions in respect of non-participating employ-

---

(a) 1965 c. 51. (b) 1966 c. 6.
(c) 1971 c. 50. (d) S.I. 1968/827 (1968 II, p. 2228).
(e) S.I. 1969/1508, 1970/46, 977 (1969 III, p. 4898; 1970 I, p. 243; II, p. 3089).

ment) to the principal regulations there shall be substituted the tables set out in Schedules B, C and D respectively to these regulations.

Signed by authority of the Secretary of State for Social Services.

Mildred Riddelsdell,
Second Permanent Secretary,
Department of Health and Social Security.

25th August 1971.

Given under the Official Seal of the National Insurance Joint Authority.

(L.S.)

D. G. Kelly,
Secretary,
National Insurance Joint Authority.

25th August 1971.

Walter Clegg,
Bernard Weatherill,
Two of the Lords Commissioners of
Her Majesty's Treasury.

26th August 1971.

Regulation 2   **SCHEDULE A**

Schedule to be substituted for Schedule 3 to the principal regulations

Regulation 4   **SCHEDULE 3**

Reduction of Weekly Rates of Contributions

	Reduction of weekly rate of contribution	
Description of employed persons who are serving members of the forces	Employed person	Employer
1	2	3
	£	£
Men over the age of 18	0·09	0·097
Women over the age of 18	0·07	0·071
Boys under the age of 18	0·05	0·06
Girls under the age of 18	0·04	0·04

SCHEDULE B   Regulation 2

Schedule to be substituted for Schedule 4 to the principal regulations

SCHEDULE 4   Regulation 5

Statutory Provisions applying to Graduated Contributions which are modified in their application to employment as a serving member of the Forces

(1) Provision	(2) Subject matter	(3) Modifications
National Insurance Act 1965 Section 4(1) (as amended by section 1(2) of the National Insurance Act 1969(a) and by section 1(3) of the National Insurance Act 1971)	Graduated contributions by employed persons and employers	For paragraph (*c*), there shall be substituted the following paragraphs:— "(*c*) except where the employment is at the time of the payment a non-participating employment, the amount of the graduated contribution payable by each of them shall be the aggregate of— (i) 4·25 per cent. of any amount, up to £9, by which that payment exceeds £9 (or of the equivalent amount for remuneration not paid weekly); and (ii) 3·35 per cent. of any amount, up to £24, by which that payment exceeds £18 (or of the equivalent amount for remuneration not paid weekly); and

(a) 1969 c. 44.

SCHEDULE B (contd.)

(1) Provision	(2) Subject matter	(3) Modifications
		(d) where the employment is at the time of the payment a non-partici-pating employment, the amount of the graduated contribution payable by each of them shall be 3·35 per cent. of any amount, up to £24, by which that payment exceeds £18 (or the equivalent amount for re-muneration not paid weekly)."
National Insurance (Assessment of Grad-uated Contributions) Regulations 1967(a) Regulation 2(2) (as amended by regula-tion 2 of the Nat-ional Insurance (Assessment of Graduated Contri-butions) Amend-ment Regulations 1969(b) and by regu-lation 2 of the Nat-ional Insurance (Assessment of Graduated Contri-butions) Amend-ment Regulations 1971(c))	Equivalent amounts	For sub-paragraph (a), there shall be sub-stituted the following sub-paragraph:— "(a) where the graduated contribu-tion period is a week: (i) in the case where the employ-ment is not at the time of the payment a non-participating employment, £9 and the amount, up to £9, by which the payment exceeds £9, and the amount, up to £24, by which the payment exceeds £18; (ii) in the case where the employ-ment is at the time of the pay-ment a non-participating em-ployment, £18 and the amount, up to £24, by which the pay-ment exceeds £18;" For sub-paragraph (c), there shall be substituted the following sub-paragraph:— "(c) where the graduated contribution period is a month: (i) in the case where the employ-ment is not at the time of the payment a non-participating employment, £39 and the amount, up to £39, by which the payment exceeds £39, and the amount, up to £104, by which the payment exceeds £78; (ii) in the case where the employ-ment is at the time of the pay-ment a non-participating em-ployment, £78 and the amount, up to £104, by which the pay-ment exceeds £78;".

(a) S.I. 1967/844 (1967 II, p. 2513).   (b) S.I. 1969/1133 (1969 II, p. 3363).
(c) S.I. 1971/1202 (1971 II, p. 3522).

SCHEDULE B (contd.)

(1) Provision	(2) Subject matter	(3) Modifications
Regulation 3 (as amended by regulation 17(4) of the Family Allowances, National Insurance, Industrial Injuries and Miscellaneous Provisions (Decimalisation of the Currency) Regulations 1970(a) and by regulation 3 of the National Insurance (Assessment of Graduated Contributions) Amendment Regulations 1971)	Calculation of graduated contributions	For the first proviso to paragraph (3) there shall be substituted the following proviso:— "Provided that 4·25 per cent., 3·35 per cent., 2·50 per cent., 0·90 per cent. and 0·85 per cent. of any amount (other than the amount of the graduated contribution), or of any equivalent amount, referred to in the provisions substituted for section 4(1)(c) of the Act (as amended) by the first entry in column (3) of Schedule 4 to the National Insurance (Members of the Forces) Regulations 1968 (as amended by the National Insurance (Members of the Forces) amendment Regulations 1971), or of the total of more than any one such amount or equivalent amount, may be calculated to the nearest £0·01, any amount of £0·005 being disregarded." For paragraph (4) there shall be substituted the following paragraph:— "(4) In this regulation 'appropriate Schedule' means Schedule 5 to the National Insurance (Members of the Forces) Regulations 1968 (as amended by the National Insurance (Members of the Forces) Amendment Regulations 1971) in the case of an employment which is not a non-participating employment and means Schedule 5A to those regulations in the case of a non-participating employment."

(a) S.I. 1970/46 (1970 I, p. 243).

SCHEDULE C

Regulation 2

Schedule to be substituted for Schedule 5 to the principal regulations

SCHEDULE 5

Regulation 5

Employment which is not a non-participating employment

PART I

Weekly Scale

Amount of payment	Amount of contribution
£	£
9·01	0·01
9·25	0·02
9·50	0·03
10·00	0·05
10·50	0·07
11·00	0·10
11·50	0·12
12·00	0·14
12·50	0·16
13·00	0·18
13·50	0·20
14·00	0·22
14·50	0·24
15·00	0·27
15·50	0·29
16·00	0·31
16·50	0·33
17·00	0·35
17·50	0·37
18·00	0·40
19·00	0·43
20·00	0·47
21·00	0·50
22·00	0·53
23·00	0·57
24·00	0·60
25·00	0·63
26·00	0·67
27·00	0·70
28·00	0·73
29·00	0·77
30·00	0·80
31·00	0·83
32·00	0·87
33·00	0·90
34·00	0·94
35·00	0·97
36·00	1.00
37·00	1·04
38·00	1·07
39·00	1·10
40·00	1·14
41·00	1·17
42·00	1·19
or more	

PART II

Monthly scale

Amount of payment	Amount of contribution
£	£
39·02	0·02
40·00	0·08
42·00	0·17
44·00	0·25
46·00	0·34
48·00	0·42
50·00	0·51
52·00	0·59
54·00	0·68
56·00	0·76
58·00	0 85
60·00	0·93
62·00	1·02
64·00	1·10
66·00	1·19
68·00	1·27
70·00	1·36
72·00	1·44
74·00	1·53
76·00	1·61
78·00	1·72
82·00	1·86
86·00	1·99
90·00	2·13
94·00	2·26
98·00	2·39
102·00	2·53
106·00	2·66
110·00	2·80
114·00	2·93
118·00	3·06
122·00	3·20
126·00	3·33
130·00	3·47
134·00	3·60
138·00	3·73
142.00	3·87
146·00	4·00
150·00	4·14
154·00	4·27
158·00	4·40
162·00	4·54
166·00	4·67
170·00	4·81
174·00	4·94
178·00	5·07
182·00	5·14
or more	

SCHEDULE D Regulation 2

Schedule to be substituted for Schedule 5A to the principal regulations

SCHEDULE 5A Regulation 5

Non-participating employment

PART I

Weekly scale

Amount of payment	Amount of contribution
£	£
18·01	0·02
19·00	0·05
20·00	0·08
21·00	0·12
22·00	0·15
23·00	0·18
24·00	0·22
25·00	0·25
26·00	0·28
27·00	0·32
28·00	0·35
29·00	0·39
30·00	0·42
31·00	0·45
32·00	0·49
33·00	0·52
34·00	0·55
35·00	0·59
36·00	0·62
37·00	0·65
38·00	0·69
39·00	0·72
40·00	0·75
41·00	0·79
42·00 or more	0·80

Part II

Monthly scale

Amount of payment	Amount of contribution
£	£
78·05	0·07
82·00	0·20
86·00	0·33
90·00	0·47
94·00	0·60
98·00	0·74
102·00	0·87
106·00	1·00
110·00	1·14
114·00	1·27
118·00	1·41
122·00	1·54
126·00	1·67
130·00	1·81
134·00	1·94
138·00	2·08
142·00	2·21
146·00	2·34
150·00	2·48
154·00	2·61
158·00	2·75
162·00	2·88
166·00	3·01
170·00	3·15
174·00	3·28
178·00	3·42
182·00	3·48
or more	

EXPLANATORY NOTE

(This Note is not part of the Regulations.)

These Regulations contain no provisions other than such as are made in consequence of the National Insurance Act 1971 and accordingly they are, by virtue of section 16(3) of and paragraph 2 of Schedule 6 to that Act, exempt from reference to the National Insurance Advisory Committee and no such reference has been made.

The Regulations amend the provisions of the National Insurance (Members of the Forces) Regulations 1968 relating to flat-rate and graduated contributions payable by serving members of the forces and substitute new tables prescribing the rates of graduated contributions payable from 21st September 1971 and the reduction in the flat-rate contributions payable from 20th September 1971.

STATUTORY INSTRUMENTS

1971 No. 1423 (C.36)

MERCHANT SHIPPING

The Merchant Shipping (Oil Pollution) Act 1971 (Commencement) Order 1971

Made - - - *26th August* 1971

The Secretary of State in exercise of the powers conferred on him by section 21(3) of the Merchant Shipping (Oil Pollution) Act 1971(a) hereby orders as follows :—

1. This Order may be cited as the Merchant Shipping (Oil Pollution) Act 1971 (Commencement) Order 1971.

2. The provisions of the Merchant Shipping (Oil Pollution) Act 1971 specified in the Schedule to this Order shall come into operation on 9th September 1971.

Anthony Grant,
Parliamentary Under Secretary of State,
Department of Trade and Industry.

26th August 1971.

SCHEDULE

Provisions of the Act	Subject matter of provisions
Section 1 excluding subsection (2) ..	Liability for oil pollution damage in the United Kingdom.
Section 2	Exceptions from liability under section 1.
Section 3	Restriction of liability for oil pollution damage.
Section 9	Extinguishment of claims arising under section 1 after specified period.
Section 13 subsection (1)	Jurisdiction of courts over claims arising under section 1.
Section 14 subsection (1)	Government ships.

(a) 1971 c. 59.

Provisions of the Act	Subject matter of provisions
Section 15	Liability for cost of preventive measures where section 1 does not apply.
Section 16	Recourse actions.
Sections 17, 18, 20 and 21	Miscellaneous provisions.

EXPLANATORY NOTE

(This Note is not part of the Order.)

This Order brings into force the provisions of the Merchant Shipping (Oil Pollution) Act 1971 specified in the Schedule. These impose strict liability on the owners of ships carrying persistent oil in bulk as cargo for oil pollution damage caused by oil from their ships. They also deal with liability for the cost of preventive measures taken to prevent or reduce oil pollution damage in cases where section 1 does not apply, extinguishment of liability under section 1, jurisdiction in relation to claims under section 1 and miscellaneous provisions.

STATUTORY INSTRUMENTS

1971 No. 1426

EDUCATION, ENGLAND AND WALES

The Remuneration of Teachers (Further Education) (Amendment) Order 1971

Made - - -	*27th August* 1971	
Coming into Operation	*28th August* 1971	

Whereas—

(1) in pursuance of section 2(2) of the Remuneration of Teachers Act 1965(a) (hereinafter referred to as "the Act") the Committee constituted under section 1 of the Act for the purpose of considering the remuneration payable to teachers in establishments for further education (other than farm institutes) maintained by local education authorities (hereinafter referred to as "the Committee") have transmitted to the Secretary of State for Education and Science (hereinafter referred to as "the Secretary of State") recommendations agreed on by them with respect to the remuneration of such teachers ;

(2) there are in force orders made under section 2 of the Act with respect to the remuneration of such teachers, namely, the Remuneration of Teachers (Further Education) Order 1969(b) and the Remuneration of Teachers (Further Education) (Amendment) Order 1970(c) ;

(3) it appears to the Secretary of State that effect can more conveniently be given to the recommendations of the Committee by amending the scales and other provisions set out in the document referred to in the said Orders, namely, the document published by Her Majesty's Stationery Office on 28th November 1969 under the title "SCALES OF SALARIES FOR TEACHERS IN ESTABLISHMENTS FOR FURTHER EDUCATION, ENGLAND AND WALES, 1969" (hereinafter referred to as "the Document") ;

(4) in pursuance of section 2(5) of the Act the Secretary of State has prepared a draft Order setting out the amendments of the scales and other provisions set out in the Document which, in her opinion, are requisite for giving effect to the recommendations of the Committee ; and

(5) the Secretary of State, as required by section 2(6) of the Act, has consulted the Committee with respect to the draft Order and the Committee have made no representations with respect thereto.

Now therefore the Secretary of State, in pursuance of section 2(6) of the Act, hereby orders as follows—

Citation and Commencement

1. This Order may be cited as the Remuneration of Teachers (Further Education) (Amendment) Order 1971 and shall come into operation on 28th August 1971.

(a) 1965 c. 3.	(b) S.I. 1969/1713 (1969 III, p. 5387).
(c) S.I. 1970/741 (1970 II, p. 2331).	

Interpretation

2. The Interpretation Act 1889(**a**) shall apply for the interpretation of this Order as it applies for the interpretation of an Act of Parliament.

Amendment of Document

3. The scales and other provisions set out in the Document are hereby amended—

(*a*) with effect from 1st April 1969, in the manner specified in Schedule 1 to this Order ; and

(*b*) with effect from 1st November 1970, in the manner specified in Schedule 2 to this Order.

SCHEDULE 1

AMENDMENTS EFFECTIVE FROM 1ST APRIL 1969

1. In Appendix 1 of the Document (which specifies the qualifications entitling assistant lecturers and lecturers grade 1 to be placed in Group II or Group III)—

(*a*) the following qualification shall be substituted for that specified in paragraph 42 of Part B : —

"42. Council of Engineering Institutions—

(*a*) the passing of Parts 1 and 2 of the Council's examination ; or

(*b*) the passing of Part 2 of the Council's examination and an examination accepted by the Council as giving exemption from Part 1 thereof." ; and

(*b*) the following qualification shall be added after that specified in paragraph 71 of Part B : —

"71A. The Diploma of Licentiate of the College of Preceptors obtained by examination under the regulations of the College introduced in 1963."

2. In Appendix VI of the Document (which specifies the qualifications entitling assistant lecturers and lecturers grade 1 to receive an addition to the appropriate salary scale)—

(*a*) the following qualifications shall be added to paragraph 2 of Part A : —

"Durham   Diploma in Advanced Studies in Education

London   Diploma in Linguistics and English Teaching" ; and

(*b*) the following paragraph shall be substituted for paragraph 8 of Part A : —

"8. The Diploma of Licentiate of the College of Preceptors obtained by examination, provided that the teacher is not placed in Group II by virtue thereof."

(**a**) 1889 c. 63

SCHEDULE 2

AMENDMENT EFFECTIVE FROM 1ST NOVEMBER 1970

In paragraph 1 of Section M of the Document (which provides that there shall be an additional annual payment for teachers serving in the London Area) for the sum of £85 there shall be substituted the sum of £118.

Given under the Official Seal of the Secretary of State for Education and Science on 27th August 1971.

(L.S.)

Margaret H. Thatcher,
Secretary of State for Education and Science.

EXPLANATORY NOTE

(This Note is not part of the Order.)

In accordance with recommendations made by the Committee for the consideration of the remuneration of teachers in establishments for further education (other than farm institutes) this Order makes minor changes in, and additions to, the qualifications entitling teachers to be paid at a higher rate and increases the additional payment to teachers in the London area by £33 a year.

The Order has retrospective effect by virtue of section 7(3) of the Remuneration of Teachers Act 1965.

STATUTORY INSTRUMENTS

1971 No. 1427

EDUCATION, ENGLAND AND WALES

The Remuneration of Teachers (Primary and Secondary Schools) (Amendment No. 2) Order 1971

Made - - - -	*27th August* 1971
Coming into Operation	*28th August* 1971

Whereas—

(1) in pursuance of section 3(1) of the Remuneration of Teachers Act 1965**(a)** (hereinafter referred to as "the Act") certain matters in respect of which agreement had not been reached in the Committee constituted under section 1 of the Act for the purpose of considering the remuneration payable to teachers in primary and secondary schools maintained by local education authorities (hereinafter referred to as "the Committee") were referred to arbitration;

(2) in pursuance of section 2(2) of the Act the Committee have transmitted to the Secretary of State for Education and Science (hereinafter referred to as "the Secretary of State") recommendations agreed on by them with respect to certain other matters affecting the remuneration of such teachers;

(3) there are in force with respect to the remuneration of such teachers the orders made under section 2 of the Act specified in Schedule 1 to this order;

(4) it appears to the Secretary of State that effect can more conveniently be given to certain of the recommendations of the arbitrators and to the recommendations of the Committee by further amending the scales and other provisions set out in the document referred to in the said Order, namely, the document published by Her Majesty's Stationery Office on 28th April 1969 under the title "SCALES OF SALARIES FOR TEACHERS IN PRIMARY AND SECONDARY SCHOOLS, ENGLAND AND WALES, 1969" (hereinafter referred to as "the Document");

(5) in pursuance of sections 2(5) and 4(1) of the Act the Secretary of State has prepared a draft order setting out the amendments of the scales and other provisions set out in the Document which, in her opinion, are requisite for giving effect to the said recommendations of the arbitrators and the Committee; and

(6) the Secretary of State, as required by sections 2(6) and 4(1) of the Act, has consulted the Committee with respect to the draft Order and the Committee have made no representations with respect thereto.

(a) 1965 c. 3.

Now therefore the Secretary of State, in pursuance of sections 2(6) and 4(1) of the Act, hereby orders as follows:—

Citation and Commencement

1. This Order may be cited as the Remuneration of Teachers (Primary and Secondary Schools) (Amendment No. 2) Order 1971 and shall come into operation on 28th August 1971.

Interpretation

2. The Interpretation Act 1889(a) shall apply for the interpretation of this Order as it applies for the interpretation of an Act of Parliament.

Amendment of Document

3. The scales and other provisions contained in the Document are hereby amended—

    (*a*) with effect from 1st April 1969, in the manner specified in Schedule 2 to this Order; and

    (*b*) with effect from 1st November 1970, in the manner specified in Schedule 3 to this Order.

SCHEDULE 1

Orders	References
The Remuneration of Teachers (Primary and Secondary Schools) Order 1969	S.I. 1969/618 (1969 I, p. 1725).
The Remuneration of Teachers (Primary and Secondary Schools) (Amendment) Order 1970	S.I. 1970/28 (1970 I, p. 222).
The Remuneration of Teachers (Primary and Secondary Schools) (Amendment No. 2) Order 1970	S.I. 1970/251 (1970 I, p. 981).
The Remuneration of Teachers (Primary and Secondary Schools) (Amendment No. 3) Order 1970	S.I. 1970/739 (1970 II, p. 2327).
The Remuneration of Teachers (Primary and Secondary Schools) (Amendment) Order 1971	S.I. 1971/437 (1971 I, p. 1255).

SCHEDULE 2

AMENDMENTS EFFECTIVE FROM 1ST APRIL 1969

1. In Appendix I of the Document (which specifies the qualifications entitling a qualified assistant teacher to be placed in Group II or Group III)—

    (*a*) the following qualification shall be substituted for that specified in paragraph 42 of Part B:—

      "42. Council of Engineering Institutions—

        (*a*) the passing of Parts 1 and 2 of the Council's examination; or

---

(a) 1889 c. 63.

Now therefore the Secretary of State, in pursuance of sections 2(6) and 4(1) of the Act, hereby orders as follows:—

Citation and Commencement

1. This Order may be cited as the Remuneration of Teachers (Primary and Secondary Schools) (Amendment No. 2) Order 1971 and shall come into operation on 28th August 1971.

Interpretation

2. The Interpretation Act 1889(a) shall apply for the interpretation of this Order as it applies for the interpretation of an Act of Parliament.

Amendment of Document

3. The scales and other provisions contained in the Document are hereby amended—

(*a*) with effect from 1st April 1969, in the manner specified in Schedule 2 to this Order; and

(*b*) with effect from 1st November 1970, in the manner specified in Schedule 3 to this Order.

SCHEDULE 1

Orders	References
The Remuneration of Teachers (Primary and Secondary Schools) Order 1969	S.I. 1969/618 (1969 I, p. 1725).
The Remuneration of Teachers (Primary and Secondary Schools) (Amendment) Order 1970	S.I. 1970/28 (1970 I, p. 222).
The Remuneration of Teachers (Primary and Secondary Schools) (Amendment No. 2) Order 1970	S.I. 1970/251 (1970 I, p. 981).
The Remuneration of Teachers (Primary and Secondary Schools) (Amendment No. 3) Order 1970	S.I. 1970/739 (1970 II, p. 2327).
The Remuneration of Teachers (Primary and Secondary Schools) (Amendment) Order 1971	S.I. 1971/437 (1971 I, p. 1255).

SCHEDULE 2

Amendments Effective from 1st April 1969

1. In Appendix I of the Document (which specifies the qualifications entitling a qualified assistant teacher to be placed in Group II or Group III)—

(*a*) the following qualification shall be substituted for that specified in paragraph 42 of Part B:—

"42. Council of Engineering Institutions—

(*a*) the passing of Parts 1 and 2 of the Council's examination; or

---

(a) 1889 c. 63.

STATUTORY INSTRUMENTS

1971 No. 1429

AGRICULTURE

The Price Stability of Imported Products (Rates of Levy) (Cereals) (No. 3) Order 1971

Made - - - - *27th August* 1971

Coming into Operation *1st September* 1971

The Minister of Agriculture, Fisheries and Food, in exercise of the powers conferred upon him by section 1(2), (4), (5), (6) and (7) of the Agriculture and Horticulture Act 1964(a) and of all other powers enabling him in that behalf, hereby makes the following order:—

1. This order may be cited as the Price Stability of Imported Products (Rates of Levy) (Cereals) (No. 3) Order 1971, and shall come into operation on 1st September 1971.

2.—(1) In this order—

" the Principal Order " means the Price Stability of Imported Products (Levy Arrangements) (Cereals) Order 1971(b), as amended by any subsequent order and if any such order is replaced by any subsequent order the expression shall be construed as a reference to such subsequent order;

AND other expressions have the same meaning as in the Principal Order.

(2) The Interpretation Act 1889(c) shall apply to the interpretation of this order as it applies to the interpretation of an Act of Parliament.

3. In accordance with and subject to the provisions of Part II of the Principal Order (which provides for the charging of levies on imports of certain specified commodities) the rate of levy for such imports into the United Kingdom of any specified commodity as are described in column 2 of the Schedule to this order in relation to a tariff heading indicated in column 1 of that Schedule shall be the rate set forth in relation thereto in column 3 of that Schedule.

4. The Price Stability of Imported Products (Rates of Levy) (Cereals) (No. 2) Order 1971(d) is hereby revoked.

In Witness whereof the Official Seal of the Minister of Agriculture, Fisheries and Food is hereunto affixed on 27th August, 1971.

(L.S.)

K. W. Wilkes,
Assistant Secretary.

(a) 1964 c. 28.   (b) S.I. 1971/631 (1971 I, p. 1660).   (c) 1889 c. 63.
(d) S.I. 1971/1264 (1971 II, p. 3628).

SCHEDULE

1. Tariff Heading	2. Description of Imports	3. Rate of Levy
	Imports of:—	per ton £
10.01	Wheat (other than denatured wheat)..	3·25
11.01	Wheat flours not containing chalk and containing not more than 1 per cent. by weight of fibre at the prescribed standard moisture content	4·25

EXPLANATORY NOTE

(This Note is not part of the Order.)

This order, which comes into operation on 1st September 1971, supersedes the Price Stability of Imported Products (Rates of Levy) (Cereals) (No. 2) Order 1971. It—

(*a*) increases to £3·25 per ton the rate of levy on imports of wheat (other than denatured wheat); and

(*b*) reimposes unchanged the rate of levy in force immediately before the commencement of the order in relation to certain specified wheat flours.

STATUTORY INSTRUMENTS

1971 No. 1430 (S.172)

PENSIONS

The Superannuation (Teaching and National Health Service) Interchange (Scotland) Rules 1971

Made - - -	*26th August* 1971
Laid before Parliament	*7th September* 1971
Coming into Operation	*10th September* 1971

ARRANGEMENT OF RULES

In exercise of the powers conferred upon me by sections 2 and 15 of the Superannuation (Miscellaneous Provisions) Act 1948(**a**), as amended by section 11 of the Superannuation (Miscellaneous Provisions) Act 1967(**b**) and as read with the Minister for the Civil Service Order 1968(**c**), and of all other powers enabling me in that behalf, and with the consent of the Minister for the Civil Service, I hereby make the following rules :—

PART I

GENERAL

Citation and Commencement

1. These rules may be cited as the Superannuation (Teaching and National Health Service) Interchange (Scotland) Rules 1971 and shall come into operation on 10th September 1971.

Interpretation

2.—(1) In these rules, unless the context otherwise requires—

"the Act of 1948" means the Superannuation (Miscellaneous Provisions) Act 1948 ;

"the Act of 1968" means the Teachers Superannuation (Scotland) Act 1968(**d**) ;

"employing authority" has the same meaning as in the Health Service Regulations ;

"employment as an officer" means employment which is or is treated as employment by an employing authority as an officer entitled to participate in superannuation benefits under the Health Service Regulations ;

"Health Service Regulations" means the National Health Service (Superannuation) (Scotland) Regulations 1961 and 1966(**e**) ; and the "principal Health Service Regulations" means the former regulations ;

"national service" means, in relation to any person, service which is relevant service within the meaning of the Reserve and Auxiliary Forces (Protection of Civil Interests) Act 1951(**f**) and any similar service immediately following relevant service entered into with the consent of the body or person by whom he was last employed before undertaking the service ;

"operative date" means the date of the coming into operation of these rules ;

"prescribed period" has the meaning assigned to that expression by rule 4 ;

"reckonable service" means such service as is by virtue of the Teachers Regulations of 1969 reckonable service for all the purposes of Part I of the Act of 1968 ;

(**a**) 1948 c. 33.   (**b**) 1967 c. 28.
(**c**) S.I. 1968/1656 (1968 III, p. 4485).   (**d**) 1968 c. 12.
(**e**) S.I. 1961/1398, 1966/1522 (1961 II, p. 2697; 1966 III, p. 4268).
(**f**) 1951 c. 65.

"the Teachers Regulations of 1957" means the Teachers (Superannuation) (Scotland) Regulations 1957(a) as amended (b) ;

"the Teachers Regulations of 1969" means the Teachers Superannuation (Scotland) Regulations 1969(c) as amended (d) ;

"the Teachers Schemes" means the Superannuation Scheme for Teachers in Scotland dated 5th June 1919(e), the Superannuation Scheme for Teachers (Scotland) 1926(f) and the Superannuation Scheme for Teachers (Scotland) 1952(g) ;

"teaching service" means—

(a) reckonable service ; and

(b) service which for the purposes of the Teachers Regulations of 1969 is service as an organiser ;

"teachers superannuation account" means the account kept under section 5 of the Act of 1968 ;

"voluntary contributions" means—

(a) in relation to employment in teaching service, additional contributions paid or being paid under regulation 31 of the Teachers Regulations of 1969 in respect of a period of previous employment and any contributions being paid as a condition of any other period (not being a period of war service within the meaning of the Education (Scotland) (War Service Superannuation) Act 1939(h) or of national service) being reckoned as reckonable service ; and

(b) in relation to employment as an officer, additional contributory payments within the meaning of the Health Service Regulations and payments in respect of added years within the meaning of those regulations.

(2) Any reference in these rules to the provisions of any enactment, rules, regulations or other instrument shall, unless the context otherwise requires, be construed as a reference to those provisions as amended, modified, affected, or re-enacted by any subsequent enactment, rules, regulations or instrument.

(3) Any reference in these rules to a rule or to a Part shall, unless the context otherwise requires, be construed as a reference to a rule or to a Part of these rules, as the case may be.

(4) The Interpretation Act 1889(i) shall apply for the interpretation of these rules as it applies for the interpretation of an Act of Parliament.

Amendment of Health Service Regulations

3.—(1) The provisions of the principal Health Service Regulations specified in Part I of the Schedule to these rules shall have effect subject to the amendments set out in that Part.

(a) S.I. 1957/356 (1957 I, p. 733).
(b) S.I. 1958/1595, 1963/2111, 1965/1166, 1966/1229, 1967/1736 (1958 I, p. 1077; 1963 III, p. 4685; 1965 II, p. 3284; 1966 III, p. 3295; 1967 III, p. 4657).
(c) S.I. 1969/77 (1969 I, p. 133).
(d) S.I. 1969/659 (1969 II, p. 1820).
(e) S.R. & O. 1919/1105 (1919 I, p. 688).
(f) S.R. & O. 1926/363 (1926 p. 449).
(g) S.I. 1952/464 (1952 I, p. 873).   (h) 1939 c. 96.
(i) 1889 c. 63.

(2) The provisions of the regulations specified in Part II of the said Schedule, being regulations relating to National Health Service superannuation, are hereby revoked.

Prescribed Period

4.—(1) For the purposes of these rules, subject as hereafter in this rule provided, the expression "prescribed period" shall mean—

   (*a*) in the case of a person who immediately after leaving his employment in teaching service or as an officer became engaged in national service, a period of six months after the date of termination of the national service ;

   (*b*) in the case of a person who within twelve months of leaving his employment in teaching service—

      (i) did not enter employment as an officer ; and

      (ii) became employed in external service within the meaning of the Teachers Regulations of 1969,

   a period of twelve months after the date of the termination of such external service, if the Secretary of State agrees ;

   (*c*) in the case of a person who after leaving his employment as an officer—

      (i) entered employment approved by the Secretary of State for the purposes of regulation 77 of the principal Health Service Regulations ; and

      (ii) within twelve months of leaving his employment as an officer did not become employed in teaching service,

   a period of twelve months after the date of the termination of the employment approved as aforesaid, if the Secretary of State agrees ; and

   (*d*) in the case of any other person, a period of twelve months after the date of the termination of his employment in teaching service or as an officer.

(2) In reckoning the periods of six months and twelve months mentioned in paragraph (1) of this rule no account shall be taken of any period spent by a person on a course of study or training which he undertook after leaving his former employment—

   (*a*) in the case of a person whose new employment is as an officer, if the Secretary of State agrees ; or

   (*b*) in the case of a person whose new employment is teaching service, if the said course was approved by the Secretary of State and if the Secretary of State is satisfied that by reason of his having undertaken it he is better fitted for the duties of his new employment.

PART II

TRANSFER FROM TEACHING SERVICE TO NATIONAL HEALTH SERVICE

Application

5.—(1) Subject as provided in paragraph (3) of this rule, this Part shall apply to a person who—

   (*a*) on or after the operative date enters employment as an officer within the prescribed period after ceasing to be employed in teaching service ; and (*b*) within three months after entering employment as an officer, or within such longer period as the Secretary of State may in any particular case allow—

> (i) gives notice in writing to his employing authority that he desires this Part to apply to him and furnishes that authority with particulars of his teaching service ; and

> (ii) pays to his employing authority an amount determined in accordance with paragraph (2) of this rule.

(2) The amount to be paid by an officer to his employing authority under paragraph (1)(*b*)(ii) of this rule shall be the aggregate of—

> (*a*) any sum paid to him after he last ceased to be employed in teaching service by way of repayment of contributions (other than voluntary contributions and contributions made or deemed to be made for the purpose of securing benefits for his widow, children or other dependants), together with any interest included therein, and not since repaid by him to the Secretary of State ; and

> (*b*) any sum deducted from such payment as aforesaid in respect of liability to income tax arising by reason of its payment.

(3) This Part shall not apply to a person who has become entitled to any benefit (other than repayment of contributions) under any of the Teachers Schemes, or under the Teachers Regulations of 1957, or under the Teachers Regulations of 1969, unless the Secretary of State consents.

Transfer Value

6.—(1) In respect of a person to whom this Part applies there shall be included as expenditure in the teachers superannuation account such a sum by way of transfer value as shall be calculated in accordance with the following provisions of this rule.

(2) Subject as hereafter in this rule provided, the transfer value shall be an amount equal to the transfer value which would have been payable under the Local Government Superannuation (Transfer Value) (Scotland) Regulations 1954(**a**) if the person, at the date when he ceased to be employed in teaching service, had ceased to be a contributory employee under one local authority and had become such an employee under another local authority and had been entitled to reckon as contributing service his reckonable service and his service reckonable for the purposes of Part VII of the Teachers Regulations of 1969.

(3) For the purposes of paragraph (2) of this rule service which is reckoned as contributing service shall be deemed to have been affected or modified in accordance with regulations applicable to contributing service made under section 110 of the National Insurance Act 1965(**b**), or under any provision corresponding thereto contained in an enactment repealed by that Act, in like manner and to the like extent. as nearly as may be. as it was affected or modified by other such regulations.

(**a**) S.I. 1954/1256 (1954 II, p. 1736).   (**b**) 1965 c. 51.

(4) In calculating the amount of the transfer value there shall be excluded—

(*a*) any period of war service within the meaning of the Education (Scotland) (War Service Superannuation) Act 1939 and of national service within the meaning of the Teachers' Pensions (National Service) (Scotland) Rules 1952(**a**) in respect of which, at the time the transfer value is paid, the contributions remain unpaid ; and

(*b*) any period in respect of which the person was immediately before ceasing to be employed in teaching service paying voluntary contributions and in respect of which, at the time the transfer value is paid, he has not elected to continue to pay such contributions.

(5) In respect of a person who—

(*a*) after ceasing to be employed in teaching service and before entering employment as an officer, has undergone a course of study or training and to whom rule 4(2) applies ; or

(*b*) has entered employment as an officer more than twelve months after ceasing to be employed in teaching service and to whom rule 4(1)(*b*) applies,

the amount of the transfer value shall be calculated by reference to the person's age at the date on which he entered employment as an officer.

(6) In this rule "contributory employee" and "contributing service" have the same respective meanings as in the Local Government Superannuation (Scotland) Act 1937(**b**).

Benefits under Teachers Regulations of 1969

7. Subject to the provisions of Part III and any provisions similar thereto contained in other rules made under the Act of 1948, no payment of any benefit shall be made under the Teachers Regulations of 1969 to any person or his personal representatives in respect of any service which is taken into account in calculating the amount of a transfer value under rule 6.

PART III

TRANSFER FROM NATIONAL HEALTH SERVICE TO TEACHING SERVICE

Application

8.—(1) Subject as provided in paragraph (2) of this rule, this Part shall apply to a person who—

(*a*) on or after the operative date becomes employed in teaching service within the prescribed period after leaving employment as an officer ; and

(*b*) within three months of becoming employed in teaching service, or within such longer period as the Secretary of State may in any particular case allow—

(i) gives notice in writing to the Secretary of State that he desires this Part to apply to him and furnishes the Secretary of State with particulars of his employment reckonable as service for the purposes of the Health Service Regulations ; and

---

(**a**) S.I. 1952/518 (1952 I, p. 928).   (**b**) 1937 c. 69.

    (ii) pays to the Secretary of State an amount equal to any sum paid to him by way of return of contributions (other than voluntary contributions) and not already repaid by him to the Secretary of State on or after he last left employment as an officer, together with an amount equal to any sum deducted therefrom in respect of income tax.

(2) This Part shall not apply to a person who—

    (a) has become entitled to any benefit (other than repayment of contributions) under the Health Service Regulations, unless the Secretary of State consents ; or

    (b) in consequence of an offence of a fraudulent character or of grave misconduct, has forfeited under regulation 54 of the principal Health Service Regulations all claim to superannuation benefits.

Transfer Value

9.—(1) In respect of a person to whom this Part applies there shall be included as revenue in the teachers superannuation account such a sum by way of transfer value as is equal to the transfer value which would, subject as in paragraph (2) of this rule provided, have been payable under regulation 80 of the principal Health Service Regulations if the person, at the date when he left employment as an officer, had become a contributory employee within the meaning of the Local Government Superannuation (Scotland) Act 1937.

(2) In respect of a person who, after leaving employment as an officer and before becoming employed in teaching service—

    (a) entered employment approved by the Secretary of State for the purposes of regulation 77 of the principal Health Service Regulations and to whom rule 4(1)(c) applies ; or

    (b) underwent a course of study or training and to whom rule 4(2) applies,

the amount of the transfer value shall be calculated by reference to the person's age at the date on which he became employed in teaching service.

Reckoning of Service

10.—(1) Any period of service of a person to whom this Part applies shall—

    (a) if treated as contributing service within the meaning of the Health Service Regulations for the purpose of calculating under rule 9 the amount of the transfer value, be reckoned as reckonable service ; and

    (b) if treated as non-contributing service within the meaning of the Health Service Regulations for the said purpose, be reckoned as to one-half thereof as reckonable service.

(2) Any period of service of a person to whom this Part applies which was non-contributing service for the purposes of the Health Service Regulations shall, to such extent as it is not reckoned under paragraph (1) of this rule as reckonable service, be class C external service for the purposes of the Teachers Regulations of 1969.

(3) Any other period of service which a person to whom this Part applies was entitled to reckon under the Health Service Regulations solely for the purpose of determining whether he was entitled to any benefit under those regulations shall be similarly reckoned for the purposes of the Teachers Regulations of 1969.

(4) The salary of a person to whom this Part applies during any period reckoned as reckonable service under paragraph (1) of this rule shall, for the purpose of determining his average salary under section 4(3) of the Act of 1968, be such remuneration as would be taken under regulation 35 of the principal Health Service Regulations into account for the purpose of calculating the annual average of his remuneration during that period.

Voluntary Contributions

11.—(1) A person to whom this Part applies may, within three months of becoming employed in teaching service or within such longer period as the Secretary of State may in any particular case allow, elect to continue to pay voluntary contributions being paid by him immediately before leaving employment as an officer.

(2) If a person elects as aforesaid and—

   (a) within three months of becoming employed in teaching service, or within such longer period as the Secretary of State may in any particular case allow, pays to the Secretary of State a sum equal to the aggregate of any sum paid to him by way of return of voluntary contributions on or after his leaving his employment as an officer, any interest added thereto and any amount deducted therefrom in respect of liability to income tax by reason of the payment ; and

   (b) thereafter pays to the Secretary of State any amounts outstanding in respect of such voluntary contributions at the times at which they would have been payable if he had remained in employment as an officer,

his teaching service shall be affected in the same manner, as nearly as may be, as his service reckonable for the purposes of the Health Service Regulations would have been affected if he had completed the payment thereof before leaving employment as an officer.

(3) The provisions of regulation 31(5)(b), (6), (7) and (10) and of regulation 37 of the Teachers Regulations of 1969 shall apply to voluntary contributions payable under this rule as if they were additional contributions payable in respect of previous employment within the meaning of those regulations.

(4) If a person does not elect as aforesaid or if his voluntary contributions are repaid under regulation 37 of the Teachers Regulations of 1969, as applied by this rule, the period in respect of which such contributions were paid shall be reckoned for the purposes of the Teachers Regulations of 1969 only to the extent, if any, to which it would have been so reckoned if no such payments or contributions had been made in respect thereof.

Commencement of Employment as an Officer

12. For the purposes of regulation 40(1)(*a*)(ii) of the Teachers Regulations of 1969 the date on which a person to whom this Part applies became employed in service taken into account for the purpose of calculating under rule 9 of these rules the amount of a transfer value shall be deemed to be a date on which he became employed in teaching service.

Return of Contributions

13.—(1) Where a person to whom this Part applies ceases to be employed in teaching service or dies, then, in computing the sum to which he or his personal representatives shall be entitled under the Teachers Regulations of 1969, there shall be included a sum in respect of contributions paid by him in respect of service which by virtue of these rules is reckoned as reckonable service and, in the case of a person who has elected in pursuance of rule 11 to continue paying voluntary contributions, in respect also of voluntary contributions paid by him before becoming employed in teaching service which have either not been returned to him or, if returned, have been paid to the Secretary of State under rule 11(1) and have not subsequently been again returned.

(2) In computing the amount of the sum so included for the purposes of this rule compound interest shall be calculated—

(*a*) as respects the period ending immediately before the date on which the person became employed in teaching service, in the manner in which such interest, if any, would have been calculated if the occasion for making the calculation had occurred immediately before that date ; and

(*b*) as respects the period beginning with that date. in accordance with the provisions of Part IV of the Teachers Regulations of 1969.

Modification of Contributions and Benefits by reason of National Insurance

14.—(1) In relation to a person to whom this Part applies—

(*a*) paragraph 3 of Schedule 5 of the Teachers Regulations of 1969 (which paragraph provides for the reduction of contributions payable under sub-sections (3) and (4) of section 3 of the Act of 1968) shall apply if paragraph (2) of regulation 51 of the principal Health Service Regulations applied to him immediately before he left employment as an officer ;

(*b*) paragraph 6 of Schedule 5 to the Teachers Regulations of 1969 (which paragraph provides for the reduction of annual superannuation allowances in the case of certain persons in employment before the beginning of July 1948) shall apply if either paragraph (3)(*a*) or (3)(*b*) of regulation 51 of the principal Health Service Regulations would have applied to him if he had become entitled to a pension under those regulations ; and

(*c*) paragraph 5 of Schedule 5 to the Teachers Regulations of 1969 (which paragraph provides for the reduction of annual superannuation allowances in the case of other persons) shall apply if paragraph (3)(*c*) of regulation 51 of the principal Health Service Regulations would have applied to him if he had become entitled to any benefit under those regulations.

(2) Where, by virtue of paragraph (1)(*b*) of this rule, paragraph 6 of Schedule 5 to the Teachers Regulations of 1969 applies to a person the date of modification for the purposes of the latter paragraph shall be—

(*a*) in a case to which paragraph (3)(*a*) of regulation 51 of the principal Health Service Regulations would have applied, the date which was in relation to him the material date for the purposes of that paragraph ; and

(*b*) in a case to which paragraph (3)(*b*) of the said regulation would have applied, 5th July 1948 or the date on which he entered employment as an officer, whichever was the later.

Gordon Campbell,
One of Her Majesty's
Principal Secretaries of State.

St. Andrew's House,
Edinburgh.
17th August 1971.

Consent of the Minister for the Civil Service given under his Official Seal on 26th August 1971.

(L.S.)

A. W. Wyatt,
Authorised by the Minister for
the Civil Service.

Rule 3

SCHEDULE

PART I

Amendments to the Principal Health Service Regulations

1. In regulation 2(2) (which contains definitions)—

(*a*) after the definition "the Teachers Superannuation Regulations" there shall be inserted the following definition—

"the Teachers Regulations of 1969" means the Teachers Superannuation (Scotland) Regulations 1969(**a**) as amended (**b**) ;

(*b*) in the definition of "added years"(*) for item (*d*) there shall be substituted the following words—

"or (*d*) regulation 15 of the Teachers Regulations of 1969" ;

(*c*) after the definition of "short service gratuity" there shall be inserted the following definition—

" 'teaching service' has the same meaning as in the Superannuation (Teaching and National Health Service) Interchange (Scotland) Rules 1971".

(**a**) S.I. 1969/77 (1969 I, p. 133).   (**b**) S.I. 1969/659 (1969 II, p. 1820).
(*) as amended by regulation 26 of S.I. 1966/1522 (1966 III, p. 4268).

2. In regulation 19(1) (which relates to the reckoning as service of previous periods of employment) for proviso (*b*) there shall be substituted the following proviso—

"(*b*) in the case of a person who, before entering the employment in which he is an officer, was employed in teaching service—

(i) there shall not be reckonable as service under these regulations, except for the sole purpose of determining whether he is entitled to any benefit hereunder, any period of external service within the meaning of the Teachers Regulations of 1969 ; and

(ii) any period of employment which was qualifying service within the meaning of the Teachers Regulations of 1969 shall be disregarded ;".

3. In regulation 19(3) for paragraph (*c*) there shall be substituted the following paragraph—

"(*c*) employment in teaching service ;".

4. In regulation 30(1) (which relates to the reckoning of contributing service) for sub-paragraph (*b*)(ii) there shall be substituted the following sub-paragraph—

"(ii) teaching service ; or".

5. In regulation 51 (which effects modifications in connection with National Insurance)—

(*a*) in paragraph (3)(*a*), for the words "subject to the Teachers Superannuation Regulations as a person in first class service," there shall be substituted the words "in teaching service or subject to" ;

(*b*) in paragraphs (3)(*a*) and (*b*), (8), (9) and (12)(*a*), for the words "in first class service under the Teachers Superannuation Regulations" wherever these words occur there shall be substituted the words "in teaching service";

(*c*) in paragraph (12)(*b*), for the words "such a person in first class service under the Teachers Superannuation Regulations as aforesaid" there shall be substituted the words "in teaching service".

6. In regulation 58(2) (which relates to accounts) for the words "as a person in first class service under the Teachers Superannuation Regulations" there shall be substituted the words "in teaching service".

PART II

Revocations

In the principal Health Service Regulations—

1. In regulation 75, in the heading the words "or teaching service", in paragraph (1), the words "or a person in first class service under the Teachers Superannuation Regulations", in paragraph (1)(*a*) the words "or first class service, as the case may be", in paragraph (1)(*b*) the words "or as third class service for the purposes of the Teachers Superannuation Regulations", in proviso (i) the words "or a person in first class service under the Teachers Superannuation Regulations", the words "or if he is a person in first class service under the Teachers Superannuation Regulations" ; and paragraph (3) ; and

2. In Schedule 2, in paragraph 3(*d*)(ii) the words "enters employment in first class service under the Teachers Superannuation Regulations, as is mentioned in sub-paragraph (*c*) of paragraph (3) of regulation 19, or", the words "the Secretary of State or", the words "as the case may be,", and the words "Secretary of State or".

EXPLANATORY NOTE

(This Note is not part of the Rules.)

These Rules maintain existing arrangements for preservation of teachers superannuation rights on transfer of employment to or from the National Health Service in Scotland.

Provision for this purpose has, since 1948, been included in National Health Service (Superannuation) (Scotland) Regulations made under section 66 of the National Health Service (Scotland) Act 1947. The present Rules, like other similar Rules affecting teachers, are made under section 2 of the Superannuation (Miscellaneous Provisions) Act 1948 and follow from the revision of the law relating to teachers superannuation by the Teachers Superannuation (Scotland) Act 1968 and the Teachers Superannuation (Scotland) Regulations 1969. Consequential amendments are made to the Regulations relating to National Health Service superannuation.

A minor change in the previous arrangements enables superannuation rights to be transferred where the interval between leaving teaching and entering National Health Service has been spent in certain kinds of "approved" service ; also the time within which application for transfer of rights must be made is extended.

1971 No. 770

PARLIAMENT

Resolution of the House of Commons dated 4th May 1971, passed in pursuance of the House of Commons Members' Fund Act 1948, s. 3 (11 and 12 Geo. 6. c. 36)

Resolved,

That, in pursuance of the provisions of section 3 of the House of Commons Members' Fund Act 1948 (a), the maximum annual amounts of the periodical payments which may be made out of the House of Commons Members' Fund under the House of Commons Members' Fund Act 1939(b) as amended by the said Act of 1948 and by the Resolutions of the House of 17th November 1955(c), 7th March 1957(d), 17th May 1961(e) and 9th March 1965(f), be varied as from 1st May 1971 as follows :—

(a) for paragraph 1 of Schedule 1 to the said Act of 1939, as so amended, there shall be substituted the following paragraph :—

'1. The annual amount of any periodical payment made to any person by virtue of his past membership of the House of Commons shall not exceed £600 or such sum as, in the opinion of the trustees, will bring his income up to £850 per annum, whichever is the less :

Provided that if, having regard to length of service and need, the trustees think fit, they may make a larger payment not exceeding £1,080 or such sum as, in their opinion, will bring his income up to £1,330 per annum, whichever is the less' ;

(b) for paragraph 2 of the said Schedule there shall be substituted the following paragraph :—

'2. The annual amount of any periodical payment to any person by virtue of her being a widow of a past Member of the House of Commons shall not exceed £360 or such sum as, in the opinion of the trustees, will bring her income up to £610 per annum, whichever is the less :

Provided that if, having regard to her husband's length of service or to her need, the trustees think fit, they may make a larger payment not exceeding £540 or such sum as, in the opinion of the trustees, will bring her income up to £790 per annum, whichever is the less' ;

(c) in paragraph 2A of the said Schedule for the words 'the annual amount of any periodical payment' to the end of paragraph, there shall be substituted the words—

'the annual amount of any periodical payment made to any such widower shall not exceed £360 or such sum as, in the opinion of the trustees, will bring his income up to £610 per annum, whichever is the less :

Provided that if, having regard to his wife's length of service or to his needs, the trustees think fit, they may make a larger payment not exceeding £540 or such sum as, in the opinion of the trustees, will bring his income up to £790 per annum, whichever is the less'.

(a) 1948 c.36. (b) 2 & 3 Geo. 6. c.49.
(c) S.I. 1956/1668 (1956 II, p. 2993). (d) S.I. 1957/388 (1957 II, p. 3068).
(e) S.I. 1961/958 (1961 II, p. 3348). (f) S.I. 1965/718 (1965 I, p. 2567).

APPENDIX OF CERTAIN INSTRUMENTS NOT REGISTERED AS S.I.

Orders in Council, Letters Patent and Royal Instructions

relating to the Constitutions etc. of Overseas Territories or to appeals to the Judicial Committee,

Royal Proclamations, etc.

PACIFIC ISLANDS

The Gilbert and Ellice Islands Colony (Entitled Officers) Order 1971

At the Court at Buckingham Palace, the 25th day of May 1971

Present,

The Queen's Most Excellent Majesty in Council

Her Majesty, by virtue and in exercise of all the powers in Her Majesty vested, is pleased, by and with the advice of Her Privy Council, to order, and it is hereby ordered, as follows: —

Citation and Commencement

1.—(1) This Order may be cited as the Gilbert and Ellice Islands Colony (Entitled Officers) Order 1971.

(2) This Order shall come into operation on 2nd June 1971.

Interpretation

2.—(1) In this Order " the scheme " means the scheme providing for pecuniary benefits for members of Her Majesty's Overseas Civil Service or Her Majesty's Overseas Judiciary serving in the Western Pacific.

(2) The Interpretation Act 1889(a) shall apply, with the necessary adaptations, for the purpose of interpreting this Order and otherwise in relation thereto as it applies for the purpose of interpreting, and in relation to, Acts of Parliament of the United Kingdom.

Application of Schedule

3. The provisions contained in the Schedule to this Order shall have effect within the Gilbert and Ellice Islands Colony.

Resident Commissioner need not consult Executive Council

4. To the extent to which functions under the Schedule to this Order may be assigned to him by the High Commissioner, the Resident Commissioner may exercise those functions without consulting the Executive Council of the Gilbert and Ellice Islands Colony.

Transitional provisions

5. Where the High Commissioner, any officer or authority has before the commencement of this Order in pursuance of any provision of the

(a) 1889 c. 63.

scheme, made any application, given any notice, permission, consent or undertaking or granted any benefit or made any payment or done any other thing, as the case may be, for the purposes of that scheme, that application, notice, permission, consent, undertaking, benefit, payment or other thing shall be deemed to have been made, given, granted or done, as the case may be, under the corresponding provision of the Schedule to this Order, and the provisions of that Schedule shall have effect accordingly.

N. E. Leigh

SCHEDULE

PECUNIARY BENEFITS FOR CERTAIN OFFICERS IN THE PUBLIC SERVICE OF THE GILBERT AND ELLICE ISLANDS COLONY

Interpretation

1.—(1) In this Schedule, unless the context otherwise requires—

" appropriate law " in relation to an officer in the public service means the law in force in the Colony that governs the grant of pensions, gratuities and other like benefits in respect of the service of that officer in the public service ;

" Colony " means the Gilbert and Ellice Islands Colony ;

" dollar " means the dollar which under the Currency Ordinance of the Colony(a) is legal tender in the Colony ;

" entitled officer " means an officer in the public service who on the operative date has not attained the age of fifty-five years and who—

(a) was immediately before the operative date the substantive holder of an office that was at that date a pensionable office for the purposes of the appropriate law ; and

(b) is a member of Her Majesty's Overseas Civil Service and a designated officer for the purposes of the Overseas Service (Gilbert and Ellice Islands Colony) Agreement 1961 ; and

(c) has, under paragraph 2 of this Schedule, been given permission by the High Commissioner to become a participant in the scheme ; and

(d) has since the operative date been the substantive holder of an office service in which may during his tenure thereof be taken into account in computing his pension under the appropriate law ; and

(e) has been confirmed in his appointment, where his appointment is subject to confirmation ;

" General Orders " means the General Orders of the Government ;

" Government " means the Government of the Colony ;

" operative date " means 1st April 1969 ;

" pecuniary benefit " means the amount to which an officer is entitled under paragraph 4 of this Schedule ;

" pensionable emoluments " means emoluments that may be taken into account in computing the pension of an officer under the appropriate law ;

" pensionable service " means the aggregate amount of service that may be taken into account for the purpose of computing the pension of an officer under the appropriate law ;

" public service " means the public service of the Colony ;

" substantive holder " in relation to any office includes a person serving in that office on probation but does not include a person (other than a person serving under a probationary agreement) serving in that office for a specified term under a contract ;

(a) Cap. 54 of the Revised Laws of the Gilbert and Ellice Islands 1952 and Ordinance No. 6/66.

" vacation leave " has the meaning assigned to it by the General Orders in force on the operative date.

(2) For the purposes of this Schedule—

(a) a person shall not be regarded as holding any office on the operative date if on that date he was on leave of absence pending his retirement otherwise than under this Schedule ;

(b) a person whose office has been abolished and who retires in consequence of the abolition of his office shall be deemed to be the substantive holder of that office during the period between the date on which the office was abolished and the date of expiration of any leave of absence granted to him pending his retirement ;

(c) when an officer on probation is required to retire—

    (i) under paragraph 6 of this Schedule ;

    (ii) in consequence of injury or ill-health ;

    (iii) in consequence of the abolition of his office or for the purpose of facilitating improvements in the organisation of that part of the public service to which he belongs by which greater economy or efficiency may be effected ; or

    (iv) on the grounds of age in accordance with the provisions of the appropriate law,

he shall be deemed to have been confirmed in his appointment immediately before the operative date ;

(d) subject to the provisions of head (a) of this sub-paragraph, an officer who satisfies the conditions specified in heads (a), (b), (c) and (e) of the definition of " entitled officer " in sub-paragraph (1) of this paragraph, and who has, before the date of the commencement of this Order retired or died, shall be deemed to have become entitled to a pecuniary benefit under paragraph 4 of this Schedule and the provisions of this Schedule shall have effect in relation to such officer as if he were an entitled officer immediately before such retirement or death.

(3) For the purpose of calculating the pecuniary benefit to which an officer is entitled under this Schedule, where the officer is seconded to the service of another government or authority on the date in relation to which the assessment is made he shall be deemed to have such annual pensionable emoluments on that date as he would have had on that date if he had not been so seconded but had continued until that date to hold the office in the public service that he was holding immediately before his secondment and had been granted all increments and other increases of salary for which he would thus have been eligible.

(4) Where an entitled officer transfers to the public service of the British Solomon Islands or to the British Service of the New Hebrides the provisions set out in paragraph 1 of the First Annex to this Schedule shall apply to that officer ; and where a person who is an entitled officer under the British Solomon Islands Protectorate (Entitled Officers) Order 1971(a) or the New Hebrides (British Service) (Entitled Officers) Order 1971(b) transfers to the public service. the provision set out in paragraph 2 of the First Annex to this Schedule shall apply to that officer.

(5) In this Schedule references to the Pensions Ordinance or Pension Rules or to any Part, section or Rule thereof, shall, unless it is otherwise stated, include references to any Ordinance, Rules, Part, section or Rule amending or replacing the same.

Permission to join the scheme

2.—(1) Subject to the provision of sub-paragraph (2) of this paragraph, if an officer who satisfies the conditions specified in heads (a), (b), (d) and (e) of the definition of " entitled officer " in paragraph 1(1) of this Schedule, applies to

(a) S.I. 1971/870 (1971 II, p. 2545).   (b) S.I. 1971/871 (1971 II, p. 2562).

the High Commissioner within a period of three months of the operative date for permission to become a participant in the scheme, the High Commissioner shall give that officer such permission:

Provided that the High Commissioner may in respect of a particular officer extend the period during which application for permission may be made.

(2) The High Commissioner shall not grant such permission—

(a) if the officer has not undertaken, in the form prescribed by the High Commissioner, that he will, to such extent as may be required, continue to serve in an office in the public service (service in which may during his tenure thereof be taken into account in computing his pension under the appropriate law) until—

(i) in the case of an officer who on the operative date has not attained the age of fifty years, 1st April 1979 or in the case of an officer who attains that age on a date between 1st April 1972 and 1st April 1979, that date, and

(ii) in the case of an officer who on or before the operative date has attained that age, 1st April 1972 or the date on which he attains the age of fifty-five years, whichever is the earlier ;

(b) if disciplinary proceedings are being taken or are about to be taken against the officer which might lead to his dismissal.

(3) Where disciplinary proceedings are being taken or are about to be taken against such an officer then if those proceedings are not taken or do not lead to his dismissal, the High Commissioner shall, if such officer has given the undertaking referred to in paragraph (a) of sub-paragraph (2) of this paragraph, give such officer permission to become a participant in the scheme.

Penalty for breach of undertaking

3.—(1) This paragraph shall not apply to an entitled officer to whom paragraph 9 or paragraph 10 of this Schedule applies.

(2) If an entitled officer to whom this paragraph applies ceases to serve in accordance with the undertaking given by him for the purposes of paragraph 2 of this Schedule, otherwise than with the consent of the High Commissioner or by reason of his death or his retirement in circumstances described in paragraph 11(1) of this Schedule, he shall cease to be an entitled officer and shall not be entitled as from the date on which he ceases to serve to any benefit or pension under this Schedule or the appropriate law.

Entitlement to pecuniary benefit

4.—(1) Subject to the provisions of this Schedule, every entitled officer shall be entitled to a pecuniary benefit which shall be assessed in accordance with the provisions of this paragraph and at each assessment shall be calculated by multiplying the amount of the full annual pensionable emoluments enjoyed by him on the date in relation to which the assessment is made by the appropriate factor and the resulting amount or twenty-one thousand, four hundred and thirty dollars, whichever is the less, shall be the amount to which he is entitled.

(2) The pecuniary benefit of each entitled officer under this paragraph shall, if it has not already been provisionally assessed, be provisionally assessed as soon as is reasonably practicable after the commencement of this Order and for that purpose the date in relation to which the assessment is to be made shall be the operative date.

(3) The pecuniary benefit of each entitled officer under this paragraph shall be provisionally re-assessed upon each anniversary of the operative date and shall be finally assessed upon the expiration of the period for which he has undertaken in pursuance of paragraph 2 of this Schedule to continue to serve or upon his retirement under this Schedule or death whichever is the earlier ; and for the purposes of this sub-paragraph the date in relation to which the

assessment is to be made shall be such date (not being earlier than the operative date or later than the date upon which his pecuniary benefit is provisionally re-assessed or finally assessed, as the case may be) as is most advantageous in relation to the officer.

(4) When the pecuniary benefit of any entitled officer is provisionally assessed or re-assessed or is finally assessed, he (or, in the case of an officer who has died, his personal representatives) shall thereupon be given a statement showing the amount of the pecuniary benefit to which, in accordance with that provisional assessment or re-assessment or final assessment, he is entitled.

(5) In this paragraph " the appropriate factor " in relation to an officer means the factor obtained from Table I of the Second Annex to this Schedule that is appropriate to the age and pensionable service of that officer on the date in relation to which the assessment is to be made in completed years and months or, if it is more favourable to the officer, reckoned in completed years without regard to parts of a year.

Payment of pecuniary benefits

5.—(1) When the pecuniary benefit of an entitled officer has been provisionally assessed a first payment shall be made to that officer on 1st April 1970, or, in the case of an officer who retires under paragraph 6 or paragraph 7 of this Schedule, on the date on which his leave pending retirement expires, whichever is the earlier, which shall be an amount equal to the amount of the pecuniary benefit as so assessed or if that amount exceeds two thousand, one hundred and forty-three dollars then one-sixth of the amount of the pecuniary benefit or two thousand, one hundred and forty-three dollars, whichever is the greater.

(2) Subject to the provisions of paragraph 13 of this Schedule, a further payment shall be made to every entitled officer upon each anniversary of the date of the first payment which—

(a) in the case of a payment upon the first, second, third or fourth anniversary shall be an amount equal to the appropriate fraction of the balance of the pecuniary benefit then outstanding ; and

(b) in the case of a payment made upon the fifth or any later anniversary shall be an amount equal to the balance of the pecuniary benefit then outstanding :

Provided that—

(i) where the balance of the pecuniary benefit outstanding upon the first, second, third or fourth anniversary exceeds one thousand and seventy-one dollars, an amount equal to the appropriate fraction of the balance or eight hundred and fifty-seven dollars, whichever is the greater, shall be paid ;

(ii) where the balance so outstanding is less than one thousand and seventy-one dollars an amount equal to that balance shall be paid.

(3) In this section " the appropriate fraction "—

(a) in relation to an assessment made upon the first anniversary, means one-fifth ;

(b) in relation to an assessment made upon the second anniversary, means one quarter ;

(c) in relation to an assessment made upon the third anniversary, means one third ; and

(d) in relation to an assessment made upon the fourth anniversary, means one half.

Compulsory retirement

6.—(1) The High Commissioner may by notice require an entitled officer to retire from the public service and such officer shall retire from the public service on the expiration of the leave of absence for which he is eligible.

(2) The period of the notice to be given under sub-paragraph (1) of this paragraph shall be such as the High Commissioner considers appropriate in any particular case:

Provided that where notice is to be given to an officer who is not on vacation leave having completed a tour of residential service—

(a) the period of the notice shall not be less than a period of six months residential service or such shorter period as the High Commissioner may, with the consent of the officer, determine ; and

(b) if the notice is to be given to the officer within three months of the commencement of his tour of residential service, the period of the notice shall commence to run on the day following the completion of the first three months of such tour.

Voluntary retirement

7.—(1) Where an entitled officer who is on vacation leave having completed a tour of residential service desires to retire, he may, whether or not he has fulfilled the undertaking he gave for the purposes of paragraph 2 of this Schedule, give notice to the High Commissioner of his desire to retire and, if the High Commissioner gives his consent to his retirement, that officer shall retire from the public service on the expiration of the vacation leave for which he is eligible:

Provided that the High Commissioner may make his consent to the officer's retirement conditional on the officer returning to the Colony after the expiration of his vacation leave for a period of six months residential service, in which event the officer shall retire from the public service on the expiration of the vacation leave for which he may be eligible on completing that period of six months residential service.

(2) In any other case, an officer desiring to retire shall give six months notice to the High Commissioner of his desire to retire and shall retire from the public service on the expiration of any vacation leave for which he may be eligible on the expiration of such notice:

Provided that—

(a) in the case of an officer who has not fulfilled the undertaking he gave for the purposes of paragraph 2 of this Schedule, he may not retire without the consent of the High Commissioner ;

(b) the officer may give such shorter period of notice as the High Commissioner may, with the agreement of the officer, determine ;

(c) if within six months from the date on which the officer has given notice, he will have completed a tour of thirty-six months residential service or if the officer has, before the date on which he gave notice, been given leave to proceed on vacation leave within the period of notice, then the period of the notice shall terminate on the date on which the officer will have completed thirty-six months residential service or the date on which he is to proceed on vacation leave, as the case may be ;

(d) if the officer gives notice to retire within three months of the commencement of his tour of residential service, the period of notice shall commence to run on the day following the completion of the first three months of such tour.

(3) An entitled officer, who has given notice to retire under this paragraph may, with the consent of the High Commissioner, withdraw the notice.

Special gratuity on the death of certain officers

8.—(1) Where an entitled officer dies while in the public service and it is lawful under the provisions of the appropriate law for a gratuity to be granted to his personal representatives, there shall be granted to his personal representatives either that gratuity or a gratuity equal to the maximum gratuity that could have been granted to that officer under the provisions of paragraph 11 of this Schedule if he had retired under this Schedule at the date of his death, whichever is the greater:

Provided that, in the case of an officer to whom Part III of the Pensions Rules of the Colony applied, in respect of that proportion of the pension for which he would have been eligible, if he had retired under this Schedule at the date of his death and which is attributable to his pensionable service otherwise than in a public service in the Western Pacific, the provisions of paragraph 11(2)(*b*) of this Schedule shall apply but the permitted fraction referred to in that paragraph shall not be less than three-quarters.

(2) For the purposes of the proviso to sub-paragraph (1) of this paragraph the proportion of a pension which is attributable to the pensionable service of an officer otherwise than in a public service in the Western Pacific shall be that proportion of the pension for which the officer would have been eligible if his pensionable service had been wholly in a public service in the Western Pacific as the aggregate amount of his pensionable emoluments during his pensionable service otherwise than in a public service in the Western Pacific bears to the aggregate amount of his pensionable emoluments throughout his pensionable service.

(3) The High Commissioner may direct that, instead of being paid to the personal representatives, any gratuity payable under this paragraph shall be paid to one of the dependants of the deceased or two or more of those dependants in such proportions as the High Commissioner may think fit.

(4) In this paragraph, " in a public service in the Western Pacific " means in the public service of the British Solomon Islands Protectorate or in the public service of the Gilbert and Ellice Islands or in the British Service of the New Hebrides.

Officers re-appointed to United Kingdom service

9.—(1) This paragraph applies to an entitled officer who has retired under this Schedule and—

(*a*) who was transferred to the public service from pensionable employment under the Government of the United Kingdom in a public office as defined by the Superannuation Act 1892(a) ; and

(*b*) who not later than twelve months after he retired has (other than as the result of a competition conducted by the Civil Service Commissioners of the United Kingdom) returned to such pensionable employment.

(2) A person to whom this paragraph applies shall cease to be entitled to a pecuniary benefit under paragraph 4 of this Schedule, but shall be entitled to a pecuniary benefit of an amount equal to one-half of the amount he would receive if he were entitled to a pecuniary benefit under paragraph 4 of this Schedule.

(3) If the provisions of this paragraph become applicable to any person, his pecuniary benefit shall forthwith be re-assessed, and

(*a*) if the amount of the pecuniary benefit as so re-assessed exceeds the amount he has already received under this Schedule, the balance of the pecuniary benefit then outstanding shall be paid, together with any unpaid interest that has accrued under this Schedule before the re-assessment, in the manner prescribed by paragraph 5 of this Schedule for the payment of a pecuniary benefit assessed under paragraph 4 of this Schedule ; or

(*b*) if the amount of the pecuniary benefit he has already received under this Schedule exceeds the amount of the pecuniary benefit to which he is entitled under this paragraph, the excess shall forthwith become repayable, but in any such case any interest received on account of such excess shall not be repayable.

Transfer to other public service

10.—(1) This paragraph applies to an entitled officer who is transferred from the public service—

(*a*) to the service of a government or authority that is a Scheduled Government for the purposes of Part III of the Pensions Rules of the Colony in

(a) 1892 c. 40.

circumstances in which he remains eligible for the grant of a pension under the appropriate law upon his eventual retirement ;

(b) to service in the office of Governor in such circumstances that he is or may become eligible for a pension under the Governors' Pensions Act 1957(**a**) :

Provided that—

(i) it does not apply to an officer to whom paragraph 9 of this Schedule applies or who is transferred to the service of the British Solomon Islands or to the British Service of the New Hebrides or who has completed the period during which he has undertaken in pursuance of paragraph 2 of this Schedule to continue to serve ;

(ii) it applies to any officer who transfers to pensionable employment under the Government of the United Kingdom in a public office as defined in the Superannuation Act 1892.

(2) An officer to whom this paragraph applies shall cease to be an entitled officer and shall not be entitled to any pecuniary benefit or pension under this Schedule ; and any instalments of the pecuniary benefit to which he was entitled and which have been paid to him under paragraph 5 of this Schedule shall forthwith become repayable.

Grant of pension and gratuities

11.—(1) This paragraph shall apply to an entitled officer who—

(a) retires or is required to retire under this Schedule ;

(b) is permitted to retire by reason of injury or ill-health ;

(c) is required to retire in consequence of the abolition of his office or for the purpose of facilitating improvements in that part of the organisation of the public service to which he belongs by which greater economy or efficiency may be effected ;

(d) is required to retire in the public interest ;

(e) retires on or after the termination of the period during which he has undertaken, in accordance with paragraph 2 of this Schedule, to continue to serve ; or

(f) in the case of a woman, is required to retire on her marriage.

(2) Subject to the provisions of paragraph 19 of this Schedule, an entitled officer, on his retirement under this Schedule may be granted at his option (such option to be exercised in accordance with the provisions of Rule 25 of the Gilbert and Ellice Islands Colony Pensions Rules) either—

(a) a pension of such amount as may be granted under the appropriate law ; or

(b) a reduced pension equal to such fraction as he may desire of the pension that may be granted under the appropriate law (not being less than the permitted fraction) together with a gratuity equal to the annual amount of the remaining fraction of that pension multiplied by the appropriate factor.

(3) For the purposes of this paragraph an officer shall be deemed to be eligible for the grant of a pension under the appropriate law—

(a) notwithstanding that he may have retired before attaining the age specified in the appropriate law as qualifying him for the grant of a pension ; and

(b) notwithstanding that he may not have completed at the date of his retirement the period of qualifying service required by the appropriate law to render him eligible for the grant of a pension.

(4) Where an officer retires by reason of injury or ill-health in circumstances in which he could under the appropriate law be granted an additional pension the provisions of this paragraph shall have effect in relation to that officer as if

---

(**a**) 1957 c. 62.

references to the pension that may be granted under the appropriate law included references to that additional pension.

(5) Where an officer to whom this paragraph applies retires in consequence of the abolition of his office or for the purpose of facilitating improvements in the organisation of the part of the public service to which he belongs by which greater economy or efficiency may be effected in circumstances in which he could under the appropriate law be granted an additional pension, the provisions of this paragraph shall have effect in relation to that officer as if references to the pension that may be granted under the appropriate law did not include references to that additional pension.

(6) For the purposes of this paragraph the amount of the pension or gratuity that an officer who is required to retire under paragraph 6 of this Schedule may be granted under the appropriate law shall be calculated by reference to the full annual pensionable emoluments enjoyed by him on the date immediately prior to his retirement.

(7) If an officer has not exercised the option conferred upon him by sub-paragraph (2) of this paragraph within the period in which it is required to be exercised he shall be deemed to have opted for the grant of a pension of such amount as may be granted under the appropriate law.

(8) In this paragraph—

" the appropriate factor " in relation to an officer means the factor obtained from Table II of the Second Annex to this Schedule that is appropriate to the age of that officer on the date immediately prior to his retirement reckoned in completed years and completed months ;

" the permitted fraction "—

(a) in relation to an officer who retires within one year of the operative date, means three-quarters ; and

(b) in relation to an officer who retires within not less than one year of the operative date, means such fraction as is obtained by subtracting one-sixteenth for each complete year of his pensionable service, but not exceeding four years, after the operative date from three-quarters :

Provided that in reckoning for the purposes of this sub-paragraph the years of pensionable service of an officer who is granted leave of absence pending his retirement, leave of absence granted in respect of service prior to the operative date the enjoyment of which had on the operative date been deferred shall not be taken into account.

Special gratuity for certain officers

12.—(1) Subject to the provisions of paragraph 19 of this Schedule, where any entitled officer to whom Part III of the Pensions Rules of the Colony applies retires under this Schedule and is granted by any government or other authority that is a Scheduled Government for the purposes of that Part both a pension and a gratuity, having elected to receive that pension and that gratuity in lieu of a pension of greater amount, he may be granted (in addition to any gratuity that may be granted to him under paragraph 11 of this Schedule) a gratuity equal to the amount (if any) by which the amount produced by—

(i) subtracting the annual amount of the pension granted to him by the Scheduled Government from the annual amount of the pension that would have been granted to him by that Government had he not elected to receive the gratuity granted to him by the Scheduled Government ; and

(ii) multiplying the resulting amount by the appropriate factor,

exceeds the amount of the gratuity granted to him by the Scheduled Government.

(2) In this paragraph " the appropriate factor " has the same meaning as in paragraph 11 of this Schedule.

Special provisions as to payment of pecuniary benefits

13.—(1) Whenever an entitled officer who has not already received the whole of the pecuniary benefit to which he is entitled—

(a) completes the period during which he has undertaken, in pursuance of paragraph 2 of this Schedule, to continue to serve or dies before completing that period ; or

(b) is required to retire under paragraph 6 of this Schedule or retires in the circumstances described in paragraph 11(1)(b), (c) or (d) of this Schedule,

the balance of the pecuniary benefit to which he is entitled shall be paid to him or, if he is dead, to his personal representatives.

(2) The High Commissioner may direct that instead of any payment being made to the personal representatives of a deceased person payment shall be made to one of the dependants of the deceased or two or more of those dependants in such proportions as the High Commissioner may think fit.

(3) Whenever any instalment of a pecuniary benefit becomes due under this Schedule interest at the rate of five per centum per annum shall accrue from day to day—

(a) in cases where the pecuniary benefit has not been finally assessed, during the period between the date on which the amount of the pecuniary benefit was last due to be assessed and the date on which the next following assessment is to be made ;

(b) in cases where the pecuniary benefit has been finally assessed, during the period between the date on which that instalment of the pecuniary benefit became due and the date on which the next following instalment of the pecuniary benefit will become due,

upon any part of the pecuniary benefit that did not then become payable and that interest shall become payable at the end of the period during which it accrued :

Provided that, for the purpose of calculating interest under this sub-paragraph the pecuniary benefit to which the officer is entitled shall be deemed to have been provisionally assessed, and the first instalment thereof paid to the officer, on the operative date.

(4) When the pecuniary benefit of an entitled officer is finally assessed under paragraph 4(3) of this Schedule upon his retirement, in addition to the interest payable under sub-paragraph (3) of this paragraph that officer shall be paid a sum equal to the interest that would, if the balance of the pecuniary benefit due to him on the date of his retirement had not been paid and provision had been made for interest at the rate of five per centum per annum to accrue from day to day on that balance, have accrued upon that balance during the period between the date of his retirement and the next anniversary of the operative date.

Leave and subsistence allowance

14.—(1) This paragraph shall apply to an entitled officer who is required to retire under paragraph 6 of this Schedule.

(2) An officer to whom this paragraph applies who is on vacation leave after completing a tour of residential service when he is required to retire shall—

(a) if the period of vacation leave for which he is eligible on the date upon which he is given notice requiring him to retire is less than six months, be granted such additional vacation leave as will bring the aggregate period of such vacation leave from that date up to six months ;

(b) if with the consent of the High Commissioner he returns to the Colony to settle his affairs, he shall be paid a subsistence allowance at the rate prescribed by General Orders for the period of his stay in the Colony or twenty-one days, whichever is the less.

(3) An officer to whom this paragraph applies who is not on vacation leave after completing a tour of residential service when he is required to retire shall, if the period of vacation leave for which he is eligible on the date of his departure

from the Colony is less than six months, be granted such additional vacation leave as will bring the aggregate period of such vacation leave from that date up to six months.

Option to forgo leave

15. An entitled officer—

(*a*) to whom paragraph 11 of this Schedule applies who is not on vacation leave having completed a tour of residential service, may at any time before the end of his tour of residential service, or

(*b*) who returns to the Colony in accordance with a condition laid down by the High Commissioner under the proviso to paragraph 7(2) of this Schedule or to whom paragraph 14(2)(*b*) of this Schedule applies, may within three days of his return,

elect to forgo all leave for which he would be eligible on his departure from the Colony ; and to receive in lieu of such leave a terminal payment equal to the aggregate amount of the emoluments which he would have received during the leave for which he was eligible if he had taken it :

Provided that such terminal payment shall not form part of the pensionable emoluments of the officer.

Passages and baggage facilities

16.—(1) In the case of an entitled officer on vacation leave having completed a tour of residential service, in respect of whom the High Commissioner has granted his consent to his retirement under paragraph 7 of this Schedule, if he returns to the Colony after the expiration of his vacation leave at the requirement of the High Commissioner for a period of six months residential service, he shall be provided with appropriate passages and appropriate baggage facilities for himself and his family in respect of his and their return journey to the Colony and in respect of his and their journey from the Colony consequential upon his retirement ; and in any other case (whether or not he returns to the Colony) he shall be provided with appropriate baggage facilities for himself and his family for the purpose of removing his and their effects from the Colony.

(2) In the case of an entitled officer on vacation leave after completing a tour of residential service being required to retire under paragraph 6 of this Schedule he shall, if the High Commissioner considers that it would be reasonable for him to return to the Colony to settle his affairs and he returns, be provided with appropriate passages in respect of his return journey to the Colony and his subsequent journey from the Colony ; and in any case (whether or not he returns to the Colony) he shall be provided with appropriate baggage facilities for himself and his family for the purpose of removing his and their effects from the Colony.

(3) In the case of an entitled officer who is not on vacation leave after completing a tour of residential service and who is required to retire under paragraph 6 of this Schedule, or who retires under paragraph 7(2) of this Schedule, he shall be provided with appropriate passages for himself and his family in respect of his and their journey from the Colony (if any) consequential upon his retirement ; and in any case (whether or not such passages are provided) he shall be provided with appropriate baggage facilities for himself and his family for the purpose of removing his and their effects from the Colony.

(4) In this paragraph " appropriate passages " and " appropriate baggage facilities ", in relation to an entitled officer or, as the case may be, to the family of an entitled officer, mean respectively such passages and such baggage facilities as an officer of his status is entitled to under General Orders for the purpose of travelling to the Colony in order to begin a tour of residential service or, as the case may be, for the purpose of travelling from the Colony when retiring from the public service, having attained the age of fifty-five years and having completed such a tour.

Disciplinary proceedings

17.—(1) When disciplinary proceedings are taken, or are about to be taken, against any person who is serving as an entitled officer and those proceedings might lead to his dismissal, the payment of any pecuniary benefit under this Schedule and interest thereon shall be withheld pending the determination of those proceedings.

(2) Where any person who is serving as an entitled officer is dismissed, any pecuniary benefit that he has not already received may, on the discretion of the High Commissioner, be withheld.

(3) The provisions of section 5(2) of the Pension Ordinance of the Colony(a) shall apply in relation to any pecuniary benefit to which a person may be entitled under this Schedule as they apply in relation to any pension, gratuity or other allowance to which a person may be eligible under that Ordinance.

Place of payment and rate of exchange

18. Any pecuniary benefit, gratuity or interest payable under this Schedule to an officer or to his personal representatives or dependants shall be paid, in accordance with any request made from time to time by such officer, his personal representatives or his dependants, as the case may be, in any of the following countries—

(a) in the United Kingdom ;

(b) in the Colony, the British Solomon Islands or the New Hebrides ;

(c) in the country from which the officer was recruited or where he intends to reside ;

(d) in the case of payment to the personal representatives of an officer or his dependants, in the country in which the personal representatives or the dependants, as the case may be, reside ; or

(e) in such other country as the officer or his personal representatives or dependants may, with the concurrence of the High Commissioner, select,

in the currency of the country in which payment is to be made ; and, where payment is to be made in a country other than the Colony, the amount of the payment shall be such as would produce, at the official rate of exchange prevailing at the date of payment, the amount in sterling of the pecuniary benefit, gratuity or interest as calculated at the official rate of exchange prevailing on the operative date.

Application of appropriate law

19. The provisions of the appropriate law shall, subject to the provisions of this Schedule, apply in relation to the grant of any pension or gratuity under this Schedule and to any pension or gratuity granted thereunder as they apply in relation to the grant of a pension or gratuity, and to any pension or gratuity granted, under the appropriate law ;

Provided that section 11 of the Pensions Ordinance of the Colony or any law amending or replacing that section shall not apply in relation to any pension granted under the provisions of this Schedule.

Exemption from tax

20. Any pecuniary benefit or gratuity payable under any of the provisions of this Schedule shall be exempt from tax under any law in force in the Colony or the British Solomon Islands relating to the taxation of incomes or imposing any other form of taxation.

Exercise of options

21. Any option exerciseable by any person for the purposes of this Schedule—

(a) shall be irrevocable after the end of the period within which it is to be exercised ;

(a) Cap. 10 of the Revised Laws of the Gilbert and Ellice Islands Colony 1952.

(*b*) shall be exercised by notice in writing to the High Commissioner ;

(*c*) shall be deemed to have been exercised on the date on which the notice is received:

Provided that the High Commissioner may, if he thinks fit, generally or in respect of a particular person and subject or not to conditions, extend the period for the exercise of an option.

FIRST ANNEX

Schedule paragraph 1(4)

OFFICERS TRANSFERRING TO OR FROM THE BRITISH SOLOMON ISLANDS OR THE NEW HEBRIDES

1. Where an entitled officer is transferred to the public service of the British Solomon Islands or to the British Service of the New Hebrides—

(*a*) so long as he continues to serve in either of those services in an office service in which may during his tenure thereof be taken into account in computing his pension under the pension laws of the service, such service shall for the purposes of paragraphs 1 and 3 of this Schedule be deemed to be service in an office in accordance with the undertaking given by the officer for the purposes of paragraph 2 of this Schedule ;

(*b*) if he has not already received the whole of the pecuniary benefit to which he is entitled, he shall cease to be entitled under paragraph 5 of this Schedule to any further payments of that pecuniary benefit ;

(*c*) if he retires from either of those services in circumstances in which he is permitted under the appropriate Order to retire on pension, in calculating the pension or gratuity for which he is eligible under the appropriate law, the provisions of paragraph 11 of this Schedule shall be applied.

2. Where a person who is an entitled officer for the purposes of the appropriate Order is transfered from an office in the service of the British Solomon Islands or in the British Service of the New Hebrides, service in which may during his tenure thereof be taken into account in computing his pension under the pension law of the service, to an office in the public service, service in which may during his tenure thereof be taken into account in computing his pension under the appropriate law—

(*a*) the provisions of this Schedule other than paragraphs 2 and 3 shall apply to him as if he were an entitled officer:

Provided that—

(i) any payments of a pecuniary benefit paid to the officer under the British Solomon Islands Protectorate (Entitled Officers) Order 1971 or the New Hebrides (British Service) (Entitled Officers) Order 1971, as the case may be, shall be deemed to be payments of a pecuniary benefit paid to the officer under and in accordance with the provisions of this Schedule,

(ii) the proviso to paragraph 8(1) of this Schedule shall not apply in .relation to an officer who dies while in the public service ;

(*b*) if he ceases, otherwise than with the consent of the High Commissioner or by reason of his death or his retirement in circumstances described in paragraph 11 of this Schedule, to serve in such an office in the public service before the termination of the period for which he had undertaken under the appropriate Order to serve in an office in the public service of the British Solomon Islands or in the British Service in the New Hebrides, as the case may be, the provisions of this Schedule shall cease to apply to him and he shall not be entitled to any pension or other benefit under this Schedule or the appropriate law.

3. In this Annex " appropriate Order "—

(a) in the case of an officer in the public service of the British Solomon Islands Protectorate, means the British Solomon Islands Protectorate (Entitled Officers) Order 1971 ; and

(b) in the case of an officer in the British Service of the New Hebrides, means the New Hebrides (British Service) (Entitled Officers) Order 1971.

SECOND ANNEX

INSTRUCTIONS FOR OBTAINING THE APPROPRIATE FACTOR FROM TABLE I (OFFICERS)

I. Read off from the table the factors for the officer's age at his last birthday and his : —

(a) completed years of service,

(b) completed years of service plus one year.

II. Subtract I(a) from I(b), divide the difference by twelve and multiply the result by the number of completed months of service, if any, in excess of the completed years of service.

III. Add I(a) and II.

IV. Repeat steps to III for the officer's age at his next birthday.

V. Divide the difference between III and IV by twelve and multiply by the number of completed months of age, if any, since the officer's last birthday.

VI. If IV is greater than III, add V to III.

If IV is less than III, subtract V from III.

VI is the factor required.

INSTRUCTIONS FOR OBTAINING THE APPROPRIATE FACTOR FROM TABLE II (COMMUTATION)

I. Read off from the table the factors for the officer's age : —

(a) at his last birthday ;

(b) at his next birthday.

II. Divide the difference between I(a) and I(b) by twelve and multiply by the number of completed months of age since the last birthday.

III. If I(b) is greater than I(a), add II to I(a).

If I(b) is less than I(a), subtract II from I(a).

III is the factor required.

In calculating factors by interpolation in respect of tables I and II calculation should be rounded off to two decimal points and where this results in a difference of point nought one in either direction, such difference should be ignored.

TABLE I   Schedule paragraph 4(5)

OFFICERS WITH RETIREMENT AGE OF 55

Age of Officer	Factor where length of service is							
	3 years	4 years	5 years	6 years	7 years	8 years	9 years	10 years or more
25 ...	·26	·35	·44	·53	·62			
26 ...	·30	·40	·50	·59	·69	·79		
27 ...	·33	·44	·56	·67	·78	·89	1·00	
28 ...	·38	·50	·63	·76	·88	1·01	1·13	1·26
29 ...	·43	·57	·72	·86	1·00	1·14	1·29	1·43
30 ...	·49	·65	·82	·98	1·14	1·31	1·47	1·63
31 ...	·56	·75	·93	1·12	1·31	1·50	1·68	1·87
32 ...	·64	·85	1·06	1·28	1·49	1·70	1·92	2·13
33 ...	·72	·96	1·20	1·43	1·67	1·91	2·15	2·39
34 ...	·80	1·06	1·33	1·60	1·86	2·13	2·39	2·66
35 ...	·88	1·17	1·46	1·75	2·04	2·34	2·63	2·92
36 ...	·95	1·27	1·58	1·90	2·22	2·54	2·85	3·17
37 ...	1·01	1·35	1·69	2·03	2·37	2·70	3·04	3·38
38 ...	1·06	1·42	1·78	2·13	2·48	2·84	3·19	3·55
39 ...	1·10	1·46	1·83	2·20	2·56	2·93	3·29	3·66
40 ...	1·11	1·48	1·85	2·22	2·59	2·96	3·33	3·70
41 ...	1·10	1·47	1·84	2·21	2·58	2·94	3·31	3·68
42 ...	1·08	1·44	1·80	2·16	2·52	2·88	3·24	3·60
43 ...	1·04	1·38	1·73	2·07	2·42	2·77	3·11	3·46
44 ...	·99	1·32	1·64	1·97	2·30	2·63	2·96	3·29
45 ...	·93	1·24	1·54	1·85	2·16	2·47	2·78	3·09
46 ...	·86	1·15	1·44	1·72	2·01	2·30	2·58	2·87
47 ...	·79	1·05	1·31	1·58	1·84	2·10	2·37	2·63
48 ...	·72	·96	1·20	1·44	1·68	1·92	2·16	2·40
49 ...	·65	·87	1·08	1·30	1·52	1·74	1·95	2·17
50 ...	·58	·77	·96	1·16	1·35	1·54	1·74	1·93
51 ...	·50	·67	·84	1·01	1·18	1·34	1·51	1·68
52 ...	·43	·57	·71	·85	·99	1·14	1·28	1·42
53 ...	·30	·40	·50	·60	·70	·80	·90	1·00
54 ...	·15	·20	·25	·30	·35	·40	·45	·50
55 and over	Nil	Nil	Nil	Nil	Nil	Nil	Nil	Nil

NOTE: The factor corresponding to the officer's age and service in years and completed months should be obtained by interpolation.

TABLE II   Schedule paragraph 11(8)

COMMUTATION OF PENSION

Table showing the lump sum to be paid for the commutation of each $1 p.a. of pension.

Age of Officer					Factor
25	...	...	...	...	17·08
26	...	...	...	...	16·97
27	...	...	...	...	16·86
28	...	...	...	...	16·74
29	...	...	...	...	16·62
30	...	...	...	...	16·50
31	...	...	...	...	16·38
32	...	...	...	...	16·25
33	...	...	...	...	16·12
34	...	...	...	...	15·98
35	...	...	...	...	15·84
36	...	...	...	...	15·70
37	...	...	...	...	15·55
38	...	...	...	...	15·40
39	...	...	...	...	15·24
40	...	...	...	...	15·07
41	...	...	...	...	14·90
42	...	...	...	...	14·73
43	...	...	...	...	14·55
44	...	...	...	...	14·36
45	...	...	...	...	14·17
46	...	...	...	...	13·97
47	...	...	...	...	13·76
48	...	...	...	...	13·54
49	...	...	...	...	13·32
50	...	...	...	...	13·08
51	...	...	...	...	12·84
52	...	...	...	...	12·59
53	...	...	...	...	12·50
54	...	...	...	...	12·50
55 and over	...	...	...		12·50

NOTE: The factors corresponding to the officer's age in years and completed months should be obtained by interpolation.

EXPLANATORY NOTE

(This Note is not part of the Order.)

This Order makes provision for certain officers in the public service of the Gilbert and Ellice Islands Colony to participate in a scheme whereby, in return for undertaking to continue to serve in that public service for a specified period, the officers receive certain pecuniary benefits.

BY THE QUEEN

A PROCLAMATION

ALTERING THE DAY APPOINTED FOR THE AUGUST BANK HOLIDAY
IN ENGLAND AND WALES IN THE YEAR 1971

ELIZABETH R.

Whereas We consider it inexpedient that the first Monday in August should be a bank holiday in England and Wales in the year 1971 :

Now, therefore, We, in exercise of the powers conferred on Us by section 5 of the Bank Holidays Act 1871(**a**), section 3 of the Holidays Extension Act 1875(**b**) and section 3(3) of the Customs and Excise Act 1952(**c**), do hereby, by and with the advice of Our Privy Council, declare and appoint that in England and Wales in the year 1971 the first Monday in August shall not be a bank holiday, a public holiday in the Inland Revenue Offices or a holiday in the Customs and Excise, and instead the thirtieth day of August shall be a bank holiday, a public holiday in the Inland Revenue Offices and a holiday in the Customs and Excise.

Given at Our Court at Buckingham Palace, this twenty-third day of June in the year of Our Lord one thousand nine hundred and seventy-one, and in the twentieth year of Our Reign.

GOD SAVE THE QUEEN

(**a**) 1871 c. 17.   (**b**) 1875 c. 13.   (**c**) 1952 c. 44.

BY THE QUEEN

A PROCLAMATION

DIRECTING THAT CERTAIN COINS OF THE OLD CURRENCY
SHALL BE TREATED AS COINS OF THE NEW CURRENCY

ELIZABETH R.

Whereas under section 11 of the Coinage Act 1870(**a**), as extended by section 15(5) of the Decimal Currency Act 1969(**b**), We have power, with the advice of Our Privy Council, by Proclamation to direct that cupro-nickel or silver coins of the old currency issued by Our Mint before the fifteenth day of February One thousand nine hundred and seventy-one shall be treated as coins of the new currency and as being of such denomination of that currency as may be specified in the Proclamation:

We, therefore, in pursuance of section 11 of the Coinage Act 1870, as extended by section 15(5) of the Decimal Currency Act 1969, and of all other powers enabling Us in that behalf, do hereby, by and with the advice of Our Privy Council, proclaim, direct and ordain as follows:—

Cupro-nickel or silver coins issued by Our Mint before the fifteenth day of February One thousand nine hundred and seventy-one in accordance with the Coinage Acts 1870 to 1946, being coins of the denominations of the crown, the double-florin, the florin, the shilling, and the sixpence, shall, after the coming into force of this Proclamation, be treated as coins of the new currency made by Our Mint in accordance with section 2 of the Decimal Currency Act 1967 and as being of the denominations respectively of twenty-five, twenty, ten, five, and two and a half new pence.

This Proclamation shall come into force on the thirtieth day of August One thousand nine hundred and seventy-one.

Given at Our Court at Buckingham Palace, this twenty-eighth day of July in the year of our Lord One thousand nine hundred and seventy-one and in the twentieth year of Our Reign.

GOD SAVE THE QUEEN

(**a**) 1870 c. 10. (**b**) 1969 c. 19.

Modifications to Legislation

Year and Number (or date)	Act or Instrument	How affected
1857	Probates and Letters of Administration Act (Ireland) 1857 (c. 79)	s. 63 **am.**, 1971/875
1859	Court of Probate Act (Ireland) 1859 (c. 31)	s. 8 **r.**, 1971/875
1870	Common Law Procedure Amendment Act (Ireland) 1870 (c. 109)	**r.**, 1971/875
1872	Pawnbrokers Act 1872 (c. 93)	s. 52 **am.**, 1971/1292
1874	Civil Bill Courts (Ireland) Act 1874 (c. 66)	**r.**, 1971/875
1877	County Officers and Courts (Ireland) Act 1877 (c. 56)	ss. 35, 36, 51, 52, 57, 58 **r.**, 1971/875
	Supreme Court of Judicature Act (Ireland) 1877 (c. 57)	s. 60 **r.**, 1971/875
1890	Public Health Acts Amendment Act 1890 (c. 59)	s. 7 **am.**, 1971/1292
1898	Canals Protection (London) Act 1898 (c. 16)	s. 5 **am.**, 1971/1292
1907	Limited Partnerships Act 1907 (c. 24) Sheriff Courts (S.) Act 1907 (c. 51)	s. 4(2) **mod.**, 1971/782 sch. 1 rule 5 **am.**, 15B **inserted**, 1971/1214
	Public Health Acts (Amendment) Act 1907 (c. 53)	s. 7 **am.**, 1971/1292
1909 *Instrt. not S.I.* 10 Aug.	Hong Kong (Appeal to Privy Council) O. in C. 1909 (Rev. XI, p. 374)	**am.**, 1971/1239
1912 69	Irish Land (Finance) Rules 1912 (1912 p. 405)	**am.**, 1971/860

Year and Number (or date)	Act or Instrument	How affected
1915	Indictments Act 1915 (c. 90)	sch. **am.,** 1971/1253
1916 282	Indictment Rules 1916 (Rev. V, p. 331)	**r.,** 1971/1253
323	Indictment (Criminal Informations and Inquisitions) Rules 1916 (Rev. V, p. 335)	**r.,** 1971/1253
1920 581	Writs of Fieri Facias, sheriffs' or sheriffs' officers' fees—O. 1920 (Rev. XX, p. 734)	**am.,** 1971/808
1921 352	Anthrax, control of imports—O. in C. 1921 (1921, p. 38)	**r.,** 1971/1234
622	Fees for certificates of Savings Bank Rules, Awards, etc.—Warrant 1921 (Rev. XX, p. 606)	**am.,** 1971/981
827	Sheriffs' and sheriffs' officers' fees— O. 1921 (Rev. XX, p. 736)	**am.,** 1971/808
1923 1364	Indictment Rules 1923 (Rev. V, p. 336)	**r.,** 1971/1253
1925	Performing Animals (Regulation) Act 1925 (15 & 16 Geo. 5. c. 38)	s. 2(2) **am.,** 1971/1292
	Theatrical Employers Registration Act 1925 (15 & 16 Geo. 5. c. 50)	s. 6(1) **am.,** 1971/1292
1093	Land Registration Rules 1925 (Rev. XII, p. 81)	**am.,** 1971/1197
1927	Moneylenders Act 1927 (17 & 18 Geo. 5. c. 21)	s. 2(7) **am.,** 1971/1292
1933	Pharmacy and Poisons Act 1933 (23 & 24 Geo. 5. c. 25)	s. 21(2) **am.,** 1971/1292
48	Sheriffs' ordinary and small debt. cts.— forms of procedure—A.S. 1933 (Rev. XX, p. 829)	**am.,** 1971/1164
1934 *Instrt. not S.I.* 26 Nov.	Rules of the Salford Hundred Ct. of Record 1935*	**am.,** 1971/798

* Not included in Annual Volume of S.R. & O. Copies obtainable from the Registrar of the Court.

Year and Number (or date)	Act or Instrument	How affected
1935		
488	Sheriff Ct., solicitors', etc. fees—A.S. 1935 (Rev. XX, p. 880)	**am.,** 1971/904
1936		
626	County Ct. Rules 1936 (1936 I, p. 282)	**am.,** 1971/781, 836
1317	Administration Order Rules 1936 (Rev. V, p. 164)	**r.,** 1971/1095
1937		
993	Methylated Spirits (Sale by Retail) (S.) O. 1937 (Rev. XXI, p. 474)	**am.,** 1971/813
1217	Indian Civil Service Family Pension Fund Rules 1937 (Rev. X, p. 715)	**am.,** 1971/823
1225	Superior Services (India) Family Pension Fund Rules 1937 (Rev. X, p. 597)	**am.,** 1971/825
1226	Indian Military Service Family Pension Fund Rules 1937 (Rev. X, p. 632)	**am.,** 1971/822
1227	Indian Military Widows' and Orphans' Fund Rules 1937 (Rev. X, p. 662)	**am.,** 1971/824
1939	Marriage (S.) Act 1939 (c. 34) ...	sch. 1 **replaced** 1971/1159
	House of Commons Members' Funds Act 1939 (c. 49)	sch. 1 **am.,** 1971/770
1942	Supreme Court (N.I.) Act 1942 (6 & 7 Geo. 6. c. 2)	s. 1(1)(2) **r.,** 1971/875
1946		
1708	Pensions Appeal Tribunals (E. and W.) Rules 1946 (Rev. XVII, p. 733)	**r.,** 1971/769
2157	Private Legislation Procedure (S.) General O. 1946 (Rev. XVIII, p. 719)	**am.,** 1971/1413
1947	Exchange Control Act 1947 (c. 14) ...	sch. 1 **am.,** 1971/1406
	Statistics of Trade Act 1947 (c. 39) ...	s. 17(3) **replaced** 1971/719
	Industrial Organisation and Development Act 1947 (c. 40)	s. 1(2) **am.,** 1971/719
	Crown Proceedings Act 1947 (c. 44)	s. 20(2) **am.,** 1971/875
1948		
55	National Insurance (Pensions, Existing Beneficiaries and other Persons) (Transitional) Regs. 1948 (Rev. XVI, p. 36)	**am.,** 1971/1220
226	Electricity (Pension Schemes) Regs. 1948 (Rev. VI, p. 917)	**am.,** 1971/936

Year and Number (or date)	Act or Instrument	How affected
1948		
604	Firemen's Pension Scheme O. 1948 (1948 I, p. 1091)	**am.**, 1971/1329
612	National Insurance (Pensions, Existing Contributors) (Transitional) Regs. 1948 (Rev. XVI, p. 18)	**am.**, 1971/1220
714	Local Govt. (Payment of Accounts) (S.) Regs. 1948 (Rev. XII, p. 624)	**am.**, 1971/767
1261	National Insurance (Widow's Benefit and Retirement Pensions) Regs. 1948 (Rev. XVI, p. 207)	**am.**, 1971/1220, 1419
1274	National Insurance and Industrial Injuries (Collection of Contributions) Regs. 1948 (Rev. XVI, p. 148)	**am.**, 1971/993, 1421
1275	National Insurance (Residence and Persons Abroad) Regs. 1948 (Rev. XVI, p. 88)	**am.**, 1971/1419
1276	National Insurance (Sickness Benefit, Maternity Benefit and Miscellaneous Provns.) (Transitional) Regs. 1948 (Rev. XVI, p. 49)	**am.**, 1971/1419
1425	National Insurance (Classification) Regs. 1948 (Rev. XVI, p. 95)	**am.**, 1971/1421
1466	National Insurance (Airmen) Regs. 1948 (Rev. XVI, p. 108)	**am.**, 1971/1419
1470	National Insurance (Married Women) Regs. 1948 (Rev. XVI, p. 123)	**am.**, 1971/906, 1419
2172	Electricity (Pension Rights) Regs. 1948 (Rev. VI, p. 918)	**am.**, 1971/936
2361	Air Corporations (General Staff Pensions) Regs. 1948 (Rev. I, p. 1275)	**am.**, 1971/927
2711	National Insurance (Overlapping Benefits) Regs. 1948 (Rev. XVI, p. 196)	**am.**, 1971/1419
1949	Special Roads Act 1949 (c. 32) ...	sch. 2 **am.**, 1971/1211
	Patents Act 1949 (c. 87)	s. 18 **am.**, 1971/719
352	National Insurance (New Entrants Transitional) Regs. 1949 (1949 I, p. 2737)	**am.**, 1971/1220
744	Gas (Pension Scheme) Regs. 1949 (1949 I, p. 1997)	**am.**, 1971/915
1461	National Insurance (Hospital In-Patients) Regs. 1949 (1949 I, p. 2718)	**am.**, 1971/1220, 1419
2105	Pensions Appeal Tribunals (E. and W.) (Amdt.) Rules 1949 (1949 I, p. 3008)	**r.**, 1971/769
2275	Administration Order (Amdt.) Rules 1949 (1949 I, p. 1200)	**r.**, 1971/1095

Year and Number (or date)	Act or Instrument	How affected
1950		
376	Coal Industry Nationalisation (Superannuation) Regs. 1950 (1950 I, p. 356)	am., 1971/914
1195	Double Taxation Relief (Taxes on Income) (Denmark) O. 1950 (1950 I, p. 1019)	am., 1971/717
1206	Gas (Pension Rights) Regs. 1950 (1950 I, p. 814)	am., 1971/915
1539	Superannuation (Transfers between the Civil Service and Public Bds.) Rules 1950 (1950 II, p. 291)	am., 1971/752
1951		
1232	National Insurance (Increase of Benefit, Re-entry into Regular Employment and Miscellaneous Provns.) Regs. 1951 (1951 I, p. 1457)	am., 1971/1419
1952	Customs and Excise Act 1952 (c. 44) ...	s. 88(4) **am.**, 1971/1033
60	Injury Warrant 1952 (1952 II, p. 2400)	am., 1971/1209
944	Firemen's Pension Scheme O. 1952 (1952 I, p. 1003)	am., 1971/1329
1869	Marriage (Authorised Persons) Regs. 1952 (1952 II, p. 1691)	am., 1971/1216
2228	Aircraft (Customs) Regs. 1952 (1952 I, p. 669)	r., 1971/848
1953		
130	Pensions Appeal Tribunals (E. and W.) (Amdt.) Rules 1953 (1953 II, p. 1544)	r., 1971/769
1702	Distress for Rent Rules 1953 (1953 I, p. 574)	am., 1971/1333
1709	Ecclesiastical Officers Remuneration O., No. 2 1953 (1953 I, p. 598)	am., 1971/1130
1954		
189	National Insurance (Maternity Benefit and Miscellaneous Provns.) Regs. 1954 (1954 I, p. 1387)	am., 1971/1220
448	Removal of Bodies Regs. 1954 (1954 II, p. 1915)	am., 1971/1354
1955		
346	Town and Country Planning (Minerals) (S.) Regs. 1955 (1955 II, p. 2665)	r., 1971/778
842	Trustee Savings Banks (Pensions) O. 1955 (1955 II, p. 2388)	am., 1971/1316

Year and Number (or date)	Act or Instrument	How affected
1956		
630	Bd. of Inquiry (Army) Rules 1956 (1956 I, p. 207)	**am.**, 1971/1257
894	Schools (S.) Code 1956 (1956 I, p. 735)	**am.**, 1971/1079
1022	Firemen's Pension Scheme O. 1956 (1956 I, p. 953)	**am.**, 1971/1329
1456	Trustee Savings Banks (Increase of Pensions) O. 1956 (1956 II, p. 2197)	**r.**, 1971/1316
1901	Metropolitan Police Staffs (Increase of Superannuation Allowances) O. 1956 (1956 I, p. 1210)	**r.**, 1971/1316
1957	House of Commons Disqualification Act 1957 (c. 20)	sch. 2 **am.**, 1971/719 sch. 1 Pt. II **am.**, 1971/1175
	Housing Act 1957 (c. 56)	s. 14(5) **am.**, 1971/1292
87	Airways Corporations (General Staff, Pilots and Officers Pensions) (Amdt.) Regs. 1957 (1957 I, p. 395)	**am.**, 1971/927
669	Indictment Rules 1957 (1957 I, p. 533)	**r.**, 1971/1253
1074	Motor Vehicles (International Circulation) O. 1957 (1957 II, p. 2154)	**am.**, 1971/869
1421	Town and Country Planning (Minerals) (Amdt.) (S.) Regs. 1957 (1957 II, p. 2574)	**r.**, 1971/778
1800	Local Govt. (Allowances for Attendance at Road Safety Conferences) Regs. 1957 (1957 I, p. 1328)	**r.**, 1971/753
1827	Pensions Appeal Tribunals (E. and W.) (Amdt.) Rules 1957 (1957 II, p. 1833)	**r.**, 1971/769
1958	Adoption Act 1958 (7 & 8 Eliz. 2. c. 5)	sch. 2 **replaced**, 1971/1160
	Land Powers (Defence) Act 1958 (c. 30)	ss. 7, 8(1), 10(1) **am.**, 10(8) **r.**, 11(1) sch. 3 para. 1 **am.**, 1971/719
	Defence Contracts Act 1958 (c. 38) ...	s. 6(1) **am.**, 1971/719
787	Savings Bank (Fees) (Amdt.) Warrant 1958 (1958 II, p. 2123)	**r.**, 1971/981
1959	Highways Act 1959 (c. 25)	s. 276 **r.**, 1971/1292 sch. 4 **am.**, 1971/1156
3	Magistrates Cts. (Maintenance Orders Act 1958) Rules 1959 (1959 I, p. 1646)	**am.**, 1971/809
763	A.S. Adoption of Children 1959 (1959 I, p. 649)	**am.**, 1971/1163

Year and Number (or date)	Act or Instrument	How affected
1959		
1147	Motorways Traffic Regs. 1959 (1959 II, p. 2507)	am., 1971/1087
1262	County Ct. Fees O. 1959 (1959 I, p. 803)	am., 1971/1083
1340	Pensions Appeal Tribunals (E. and W.) (Amdt.) Rules 1959 (1959 II, p. 2068)	r., 1971/769
1534	Trustee Savings Bank (Increase of Pensions) O. 1959 (1959 II, p. 2468)	r., 1971/1316
Instrt. not S.I. 22 Dec.	Montserrat L.P. 1959 (1959 II, p. 3386)	am., 1971/873
1960	Road Traffic Act 1960 (c. 16)	s. 117(3) am., 1971/1142
1099	Metropolitan Police Staffs (Increase of Superannuation Allowances) O. 1960 (1960 II, p. 2022)	r., 1971/1316
1961		
153	Tribunals and Inquiries (Air Operators' Certificates) O. 1961	r., 1971/831
243	Food (Meat Inspection) (S.) Regs. 1961	am., 1971/1196
251	Financial Statements (Parishes) Regs. 1961	r., 1971/819
1071	Cereals (Protection of Guarantees) (Amdt.) O. 1961	r., 1971/290
1210	Special Roads (Classes of Traffic) O. 1961	r., 1971/1156
1398	National Health Service (Superannuation) (S.) Regs. 1961	am., 1971/1430
1506	Western Pacific (Courts) O. in C. 1961	am., 1971/715
2040	Anthrax Prevention (Goat Hair and Shaving Brushes) O. 1961	r., 1971/1234
1962	Health Visiting and Social Work (Training) Act 1962 (c. 33)	sch. 1 am., 1971/1241
1532	Preservatives in Food Regs. 1962 ...	am., 1971/882
1614	Pensions Appeal Tribunals (E. and W.) (Amdt.) Rules 1962	r., 1971/769
1926	Preservatives in Food (S.) Regs. 1962 ...	am., 1971/988
2758	British Transport Reorganisation (Pensions of Employees) (No. 3) O. 1962	am., 1971/1128
1963	Betting, Gaming and Lotteries Act 1963 (c. 2)	sch. 1 paras. 21(1) am., 22 r., 28(2) am., sch. 2 para. 6 am., sch. 3 para. 13(2) am., sch. 7 para. 5 am., 1971/1292

Year and Number (or date)	Act or Instrument	How affected
1963		
	Purchase Tax Act 1963 (c. 9)	sch. 1 Pt. I **gen. am.,** 1971/1145
		sch. 1 Pt. I Group 28 **am.,** 1971/731
		sch. 1 Pt. I Group 11, 12 **am.,** 1971/1078
		sch. 1 Pt. I Group 33 **am.,** 1971/1166
901	Trustee Savings Banks (Increase of Pensions) O. 1963	**r.,** 1971/1316
1064	Superannuation (Teaching and N.I. Local Govt.) Interchange Rules 1963	**r.** (saving), 1971/907
1221	Town and Country Planning (Minerals) Regs. 1963	**r.,** 1971/756
1229	Meat Inspection Regs. 1963	**am.,** 1971/1179
1979	Metropolitan Police Staffs (Increase of Superannuation Allowances) O. 1963	**r.,** 1971/1316
1964	Licensing Act 1964 (c. 26)	s. 22(1) (3) **am.,** 1971/1292
	Shipping Contracts and Commercial Documents Act 1964 (c. 87)	s. 2(1) **am.,** 2(2) **r.,** 1971/719
	Ministers of the Crown Act 1964 (c. 98)	sch. 1 para. 5–7 **mod.,** sch. 2 **am.,** 1971/719
73	National Insurance (Industrial Injuries) (Claims and Payments) Regs. 1964	**am.,** 1971/1201
463	Fatstock (Guarantee Payments) O. 1964	**am.,** 1971/801
504	National Insurance (Industrial Injuries) (Benefit) Regs. 1964	**am.,** 1971/1019, 1201
711	Building (Forms) (S.) Regs. 1964 ...	**r.,** 1971/747
712	Building (S.) Act 1959 (Procedure) Regs. 1964	**r.,** 1971/746
814	Price Stabilisation Levies (Supplementary Provns.) Regs. 1964	**am.,** 1971/1033
840	Cereals (Guarantee Payments) O. 1964	**r.,** 1971/289
1033	Legal Officers Fees O. 1964	**am.,** 1971/1130
1071	Civil Aviation (Navigation Services Charges) Regs. 1964	**r.,** 1971/1135
1084	Special Roads (Classes of Traffic) (S.) O. 1964	**r.,** 1971/1211
1148	Firemen's Pension Scheme O. 1964 ...	**am.,** 1971/1329
1410	Act of Adj. (Criminal Legal Aid Fees) 1964	**am.,** 1971/926
1892	Land Drainage (Compensation) Regs. 1964	**am.,** 1971/1303
2077	Personal Injuries (Civilians) Scheme 1964	**am.,** 1971/1178
1965	Science and Technology Act 1965 (c. 4)	s. 5(1) **am.,** 1971/719
	Ministerial Salaries Consolidation Act 1965 (c. 58)	sch. 1 **am.,** 1971/719

Year and Number (or date)	Act or Instrument	How affected
1965		
273	Pensions Appeal Tribunals (E. and W.) (Amdt.) Rules 1965	r., 1971/769
283	Justices of the Peace Act 1949 (Compensation) Regs. 1965	am., 1971/1119
321	A.S. (Rules of Ct., consolidation and amdt.) 1965	am., 1971/1161, 1162, 1215
329	Motor Vehicles (International Circulation) Regs. 1965	r., 1971/937
517	Clerks of the Peace and Justices' Clerks (Compensation) Regs. 1965	am., 1971/1122
563	Fire Services (Compensation) Regs. 1965	am., 1971/1121
620	Probation (Compensation) Regs. 1965	am., 1971/1120
654	London Govt. O. 1965	am., 1971/753
901	Administration Orders (Amdt.) Rules 1965	r., 1971/1095
1046	Merchant Shipping (Pilot Ladders) Rules 1965	am., 1971/724
1343	Wages Regulation (Stamped or Pressed Metal Wares) (Holidays) O. 1965	r., 1971/1089
1412	Milk (N.I.) O. 1965	r., 1971/1037
1421	Superannuation (Teaching and Belfast Corporation) Interchange Rules 1965	r. (saving), 1971/907
1734	British Commonwealth and Foreign Parcel Post Regs. 1965	r., Post Office Scheme 15/6/71*
1735	British Commonwealth and Foreign Post Regs. 1965	r., Post Office Scheme 15/6/71†
1776	Rules of the Supreme Court 1965 ...	am., 1971/835, 1132, 1269
1839	Registration of Births, Still Births, Deaths and Marriages (Prescription of Forms) (S.) Regs. 1965	am., 1971/1158
1841	Registration of Births, Deaths and Marriages (Adopted Children Register) (S.) Regs. 1965	r., 1971/1160
1843	Registration of Births, Deaths and Marriages (Civil Marriage Schedule) (S.) Regs. 1965	r., 1971/1159
1993	Ship's Report, Importation and Exportation by Sea Regs. 1965	am., 1971/1300
1966	Ministry of Social Security Act 1966 (c. 20)	sch. 2 Pt. II para. 9–11 replaced, 12A added 13, 14, 17 am., 1971/1054
164	Pneumoconiosis, Byssinosis and Miscellaneous Diseases Benefit Scheme 1966	am., 1971/1222

* Not S.I. *see* London Gazette 30.6.71 p. 26S.
† Not S.I. *see* London Gazette 30.6.71 p. 14S.

Year and Number (or date)	Act or Instrument	How affected
1966		
165	Workmen's Compensation (Supplementation) Scheme 1966	am., 1971/1223
224	Road Vehicles (Excise) Prescribed Particulars) Regs. 1966	am., 1971/1284
465	Civil Aviation (Navigation Services Charges) (Amdt.) Regs. 1966	r., 1971/1135
484	Cereals (Guarantee Payments) (Amdt.) O. 1966	r., 1971/289
485	Cereals (Protection of Guarantees) (Amdt.) O. 1966	r., 1971/290
505	Therapeutic Substances (Manufacture of Antibiotics) Regs. 1966	am., 1971/888
530	Motorways Traffic (E.) (Amdt.) Regs. 1966	r., 1971/1087
810	Metropolitan Police Staffs (Increase of Superannuation Allowances) O. 1966	r., 1971/1316
898	Petroleum (Production) Regs. 1966 ...	am., 1971/814
1045	Firemen's Pension Scheme O. 1966 ...	am., 1971/1329
1067	Supplementary Benefit (Claims and Payments) Regs. 1966	am., 1971/1331
1143	Alkali &c. Works O. 1966	am., 1971/960
1305	London Govt. O. 1966	am., 1971/753
1421	Pension Appeal Tribunals (E. and W.) (Amdt.) Rules 1966	r., 1971/769
1547	County Cts. (Admiralty Jurisdiction) O. 1966	r., 1971/1152
1967	General Rate Act 1967 (c. 9)	s. 7(1) am., 1971/1292
	Parliamentary Commissioner Act 1967 (c. 13)	sch. 2 am., 1971/719
	Decimal Currency Act 1967 (c. 47) ...	s. 4(2) r., 1971/1175
25	Double Taxation Relief (Taxes on Income) (Federal Republic of Germany) O. 1967	am., 1971/874
226	Dominica Constitution O. 1967 ...	am., 1971/714
330	National Insurance (Unemployment and Sickness Benefit) Regs. 1967	am., 1971/807, 1220, 1419
372	Fishing Vessels (Acquisition and Improvement) (Grants) Scheme 1967	am., 1971/797
386	National Insurance (Mariners) Regs. 1967	am., 1971/1420
422	Supplementary Benefit (Claims and Payments) (Amdt.) Regs. 1967	r., 1971/1331
455	Milk (G.B.) O. 1967	r., 1971/1038
471	Virgin Islands (Constitution) O. 1967	am., 1971/1240
520	National Insurance (Medical Certification) Regs. 1967	am., 1971/1419

Year and Number (or date)	Act or Instrument	How affected
1967		
599	Veterinary Surgeons (Examination of Commonwealth and Foreign Candidates) Regs. 1967	am., 1971/749
601	Valuation (Water Undertakings) (S.) (No. 1) O. 1967	am., 1971/1212
646	Wages Regulation (Retail Bespoke Tailoring) (S.) O. 1967	r., 1971/934
760	National Insurance (Computation of Earnings) Regs. 1967	am., 1971/1419
815	Commonwealth Countries and Republic of Ireland (Immunities) (No. 2) O. 1967	r., 1971/1237
844	National Insurance (Assessment of Graduated Contributions) Regs. 1967	am., 1971/1202
876	Injury Warrant 1967	am., 1971/1209
937	National Health Service (General Dental Services) Regs. 1967	am., 1971/984
1021	Police (Discipline) (S.) Regs. 1967 ...	am., 1971/843
1082	Iron and Steel (Pension Schemes) Regs. 1967	am., 1971/916
1162	Teachers (Education Training and Registration) (S.) Regs. 1967	am., 1971/903
1164	Valuation (Scottish Gas Bd.) (S.) O. 1967	r., 1971/1213
1265	National Insurance (Increase of Benefit and Miscellaneous Provns.) Regs. 1967	am., 1971/1220
1555	Beef Cow (E. and W.) Scheme 1967 ...	am., 1971/1025
1570	National Insurance (Determination of Claims and Questions) (No. 2) Regs. 1967	am., 1971/1419
1659	Magistrates' Cts. (Attachment of Earnings) Rules 1967	r., 1971/809
1861	Building Societies (Special Advances) O. 1967	r. (saving), 1971/1067
1870	Hill Sheep Subsidy Payment (E. and W.) O. 1967	am., 1971/945
1976	Beef Cow (N.I.) Scheme 1967 ...	am., 1971/942
1968	Firearms Act 1968 (c. 27)	s. 24 r., 25(1) am., sch. 5 para. 4 am., 6, 8 r., 1971/1292
	Housing (Financial Provns.) (S.) Act 1968 (c. 31)	s. 29(1) (*bb*) am., 1971/1411
	Gaming Act 1968 (c. 65)	sch. 2 para. 29(1) am., 30(1) r., 30(2) am., sch. 3 para. 12, 15 am., sch. 7 para. 11, 20 am., sch. 9 para. 14(1) r., 14(2) am., 1971/1292

Year and Number (or date)	Act or Instrument	How affected
1968		
	Transport Act 1968 (c. 73)	ss. 96(2)-(4) (6) (7), 103 **am.**, 1971/818
25	Police Cadets Regs. 1968	**am.**, 1971/804
208	Police Cadets (S.) Regs. 1968	**am.**, 1971/810
219	Matrimonial Causes Rules 1968 ...	**r.**, (saving), 1971/953
281	Matrimonial Causes (Costs) Rules 1968	**r.**, 1971/987
423	Civil Aviation (Navigation Service Charges) (Second Amdt.) Regs. 1968	**r.**, 1971/1135
464	Commonwealth Countries and Republic of Ireland (Immunities) (Amdt.) O. 1968	**r.**, 1971/1237
570	Petroleum (Inflammable Liquids) O. 1968	**r.**, 1971/1040
619	Plant Breeders' Rights (Fees) Regs. 1968	**am.**, 1971/1102
710	Domestic Water Rate Product (S.) Rules 1968	**am.**, 1971/416
716	Police (S.) Regs. 1968	**am.**, 1971/1203
767	Cereals (Guarantee Payments) (Amdt.) O. 1968	**r.**, 1971/289
827	National Insurance (Members of the Forces) Regs. 1968	**am.**, 1971/1419, 1422
831	Hill Sheep Subsidy Payment (N.I.) O. 1968	**am.**, 1971/946
892	Continental Shelf (Jurisdiction) O. 1968	**am.**, 1971/721
927	Inflammable Liquids (Conveyance by Road) Regs. 1968	**r.**, 1971/1061
928	Inflammable Substances (Conveyance by Road) (Labelling) Regs. 1968	**r.**, 1971/1062
981	Hill Cattle (S.) Scheme 1968	**am.**, 1971/1187
1077	Cinematograph Films (Collection of Levy) Regs. 1968	**am.**, 1971/1206
1117	Merchant Shipping (Load Lines) (Fees) Regs. 1968	**am.**, 1971/1352
1235	White Fish and Herring Subsidies (U.K.) Scheme 1968	**r.**, 1971/1295
1253	Inland Postal Regs. 1968	**am.**, Post Office Scheme 15.6.71*
1374	Commonwealth Countries and Republic of Ireland (Immunities) (Amdt.) (No. 2) O. 1968	**r.**, 1971/1237
1389	Patents Rules 1968	**am.**, 1971/263
1869	Double Taxation Relief (Taxes on Income) (France) O. 1968	**am.**, 1971/718
1966	Special Roads (Classes of Traffic) (E. and W.) O. 1968	**r.**, 1971/1156
1982	Special Roads (Classes of Traffic) (S.) O. 1968	**r.**, 1971/1211

* Not S.I. *see* London Gazette 30.6.71 p. 27S.

Year and Number (or date)	Act or Instrument	How affected
1968		
2011	British Transport (Pensions of Employees) (No. 1) O. 1968	am., 1971/1128
2049	Registration of Births, Deaths, and Marriages Regs. 1968	am., 1971/1218
1969	Children and Young Persons Act 1969 (c. 54)	s. 3(8) am., 1971/1292
142	Commonwealth Countries and Republic of Ireland (Immunities) (Amdt.) O. 1969	r., 1971/1237
321	Motor Vehicles (Construction and Use) Regs. 1969	am., 1971/979
344	Motor Vehicles (Authorisation of Special Types) General O. 1969	am., 1971/980
371	Anguilla (Temporary Provn.) O. 1969	r., 1971/1235
471	White Fish and Herring Subsidies (U.K.) (Amdt.) Scheme 1969	r., 1971/1295
481	Designs (Amdt.) Rules 1969	r., 1971/262
483	Provision of Milk and Meals Regs. 1969	am., 1971/1368
510	Civil Aviation (Navigation Services Charges) (Third Amdt.) Regs. 1969	r., 1971/1135
519	Companies (Bd. of Trade) Fees O. 1969	am., 1971/1020
522	Trade Marks (Amdt.) Rules 1969 ...	r., 1971/261
610	Wages Regulation (Coffin Furniture and Cerement-Making) O. 1969	r., 1971/922
611	Wages Regulation (Coffin Furniture and Cerement-Making) (Holidays) O. 1969	r., 1971/923
628	Fishing Nets (Northwest Atlantic) O. 1969	r., 1971/1172
667	Motor Vehicles (International Circulation) (Amdt.) Regs. 1969	r., 1971/937
668	Motor Vehicles (International Motor Insurance Card) Regs. 1969	r., 1971/792
672	Cereals (Guarantee Payments) (Amdt.) O. 1969	r., 1971/289
763	Matrimonial Causes (Amdt.) Rules 1969	r. (saving), 1971/953
903	Heavy Goods Vehicles (Drivers' Licences) Regs. 1969	am., 1971/736
915	Equine Animals (Importation) O. 1969	am., 1971/1137
931	Pensions Appeal Tribunals (E. and W.) (Amdt.) Rules 1969	r., 1971/769
972	Milk (G.B.) (Amdt.) O. 1969	r., 1971/1038
973	Milk (N.I.) (Amdt.) O. 1969	r., 1971/1037
1021	Plant Breeders' Rights Regs. 1969 ...	am., 1971/1094
1024	Plant Breeders' Rights (Trees, Shrubs and Woody Climbers) Scheme 1969	am., 1971/1093
1141	Mines and Quarries (Notification of Tipping Operations) Regs. 1969	r., 1971/1377

Year and Number (or date)	Act or Instrument	How affected
1969		
1265	National Assistance (Charges for Accommodation) Regs. 1969	r., 1971/1404
1307	Control of Hiring O. 1969	r., 1971/1146
1308	Hire Purchase and Credit Sale Agreements (Control) O. 1969	r., 1971/1147
1399	Postal Packets (Customs and Excise) Regs. 1969	r., 1971/1057
1633	Fees of Appointed Factory Doctors O. 1969	r., 1971/1060
1696	National Insurance (Contributions) Regs. 1969	am., 1971/1421
1823	Fishing Nets (North East Atlantic) O. 1969	r., 1971/1171
1970		
16	County Ct. Districts O. 1970	am., 1971/1081
29	Matrimonial Causes (Amdt.) Rules 1970	r. (saving), 1971/953
60	Wages Regulation (Retail Drapery, Outfitting and Footwear) O. 1970	r., 1971/845
123	Drivers' Hours (Goods Vehicles) (Keeping of Records) Regs. 1970	am., 1971/847
163	Pensions Appeal Tribunals (E. and W.) (Amdt.) Rules 1970	r., 1971/769
231	Justices' Clerks Rules 1970	am., 1971/809
257	Drivers' Hours (Goods Vehicles) (Modifications) O. 1970	am., 1971/818
283	Wages Regulation (Hairdressing) O. 1970	r., 1971/1136
296	Wages Regulation (Stamped or Pressed Metal-Wares) O. 1970	r., 1971/1088
311	Wages Regulation (Pin, Hook and Eye, and Snap Fastener) O. 1970	r., 1971/868
348	Wool Textile Industry (Export Promotion Levy) O. 1970	am., 1971/880
349	Wool Textile Industry (Scientific Research Levy) O. 1970	am., 1971/881
356	Drivers' Hours (Passenger Vehicles) (Modifications) O. 1970	r., 1971/818
359	Price Stability of Imported Products (Levy Arrangements) (Eggs) O. 1970	am., 1971/947
364	Purchase Tax (No. 1) O. 1970 ...	r., 1971/1166
376	National Insurance (Industrial Injuries) (Colliery Workers Supplementary Scheme) Amdt. and Consolidation O. 1970	am., 1971/1263
428	Wages Regulation (Retail Food) (S.) O. 1970	r., 1971/1023

Year and Number (or date)	Act or Instrument	How affected
1970		
475	Therapeutic Substances (Supply of Zinc Bacitracin for Agricultural Purposes) Regs. 1970	**r.,** 1971/1398
497	Awards (First Degree, etc. Courses) Regs. 1970	**r.,** 1971/1297
498	Wages Regulation (Toy Manufacturing) O. 1970	**r.,** 1971/1393
499	Wages Regulation (Toy Manufacturing) (Holidays) O. 1970	**r.,** 1971/1394
557	Land Registration Fee O. 1970 ...	**am.,** 1971/1082
573	Wages Regulation (Retail Bread and Flour Confectionery) (E. and W.) O. 1970	**r.,** 1971/1058
617	Wages Regulation (Retail Food) (E. and W.) O. 1970	**r.,** 1971/990
656	Wages Regulation (Brush and Broom) O. 1970	**r.,** 1971/859
702	Wages Regulation (Keg and Drum) O. 1970	**r.,** 1971/885
703	Wages Regulation (Keg and Drum) (Holidays) O. 1970	**am.,** 1971/885
783	Wages Regulation (Retail Bespoke Tailoring) (E. and W.) O. 1970	**r.,** 1971/830
798	Poisons Rules 1970	**r.,** 1971/726
809	Wages Regulation (Fur) O. 1970 ...	**r.,** 1971/1381
810	Wages Regulation (Fur) (Holidays) O. 1970	**am.,** 1971/1381
860	Wages Regulation (Retail Food) (S.) (Amdt.) O. 1970	**r.,** 1971/1023
867	Awards (First Degree, etc. Courses) (Amdt.) Regs. 1970	**r.,** 1971/1297
877	Hill Cattle (Breeding Herds) (E. and W.) (Amdt.) Scheme 1970	**am.,** 1971/940
878	Hill Cattle Subsidy (Breeding Herds) (E. and W.) Payment O. 1970	**am.,** 1971/941
883	Wages Regulation (Hat, Cap and Millinery) O. 1970	**r.,** 1971/1022
978	Wages Regulation (Rope, Twine and Net) O. 1970	**r.,** 1971/750
1005	Wages Regulation (Licensed Non-residential Establishment) O. 1970	**r.,** 1971/991
1078	Milk (G.B.) (Amdt.) O. 1970	**r.,** 1971/1038
1079	Milk (N.I.) (Amdt.) O. 1970	**r.,** 1971/1037
1085	Air Navigation (Fees) Regs. 1970 ...	**am.,** 1971/1105
1106	Wages Regulation (Licensed Non-residential Establishment) (Managers and Club Stewards) O. 1970	**r.,** 1971/992
1137	Building Standards (S.) (Consolidation) Regs. 1970	**am.,** 1971/748, 1032

Year and Number (or date)	Act or Instrument	How affected
1970		
1160	Matrimonial Causes (Costs) (Amdt.) Rules 1970	r., 1971/987
1161	Matrimonial Causes (Amdt. No. 2) Rules 1970	r. (saving), 1971/953
1227	Wages Regulation (Made-up Textiles) O. 1970	r., 1971/1280
1266	Awards (First Degree, etc. Courses) (Amdt. No. 2) Regs. 1970	r., 1971/1297
1280	National Insurance (Old Persons' Pensions) Regs. 1970	am., 1971/1220, 1419
1281	Wages Regulation (Flax and Hemp) O. 1970	r., 1971/1415
1301	Wages Regulation (Retail Bread and Flour Confectionery) (E. and W.) (Amdt.) O. 1970	r., 1971/1058
1349	Matrimonial Causes (Amdt. No. 3) Rules 1970	r. (saving), 1971/953
1372	Diseases of Animals (Approved Disinfectants) O. 1970	am., 1971/1287
1409	Wages Regulation (Aerated Waters) (S.) O. 1970	r., 1971/1369
1445	Hill Cattle Subsidy (Breeding Herds) (N.I.) Payment O. 1970	am., 1971/944
1446	Beef Cow Subsidy Payment (N.I.) O. 1970	am., 1971/943
1459	Brucellosis (Payments for Cows in Accredited Herds) (S.) Scheme 1970	am., 1971/1072
1522	Import Duties (General) (No. 7) O. 1970	am. (*temp.*), 1971/1012, 1013, 1388 am., 1971/851, 856, 858, 1056, 1075, 1357, 1387
1537	Secretary of State for Trade and Industry O. 1970	am., 1971/716
1650	Beef Cow (S.) (Amdt.) Scheme 1970 ...	am., 1971/1189
1686	Awards (First Degree, etc. Courses) (Amdt. No. 3) Regs. 1970	r., 1971/1297
1712	Cubic Measures (Sand, Ballast and Agricultural Materials) Regs. 1970	am., 1971/827
1759	Farm Capital Grant Scheme 1970 ...	am., 1971/1077
1805	Farm Capital Grant (S.) Scheme 1970	am., 1971/1076
1853	Superannuation (Local Govt. and Approved Employment) Interchange (S.) Rules 1970	am., 1971/1031
1863	Irish Land (Finance) (Amdt.) (No. 2) Rules 1970	r., 1971/860
1865	Matrimonial Causes (Costs) (Amdt. No. 2) Rules 1970	r., 1971/987

Year and Number (or date)	Act or Instrument	How affected
1970		
1870	Supreme Ct. Fees O. 1970	**am.,** 1971/1245
1981	National Insurance (General Benefit) Regs. 1970	**am.,** 1971/1018, 1419
2007	Bankruptcy Fees O. 1970	**am.,** 1971/1017
2024	Beef Cow Subsidy Payment (E. and W.) O. 1970	**am.,** 1971/1026
1971		
7	Price Stability of Imported Products (Rates of Levy) (Eggs) (No. 1) O. 1971	**r.,** 1971/37
29	Wages Regulation (Licensed Non-residential Establishment) (Amdt.) O. 1971	**r.,** 1971/991
30	Wages Regulation (Licensed Non-residential Establishment) (Managers and Club Stewards) (Amdt.) O. 1971	**r.,** 1971/992
37	Price Stability of Imported Products (Rates of Levy) (Eggs) (No. 2) O. 1971	**r.,** 1971/166
64	Acquisition of Land (Rate of Interest after Entry) Regs. 1971	**r.,** 1971/673
65	Acquisition of Land (Rate of Interest after Entry) (S.) Regs. 1971	**r.,** 1971/675
66	A.S. (Rules of Ct. Amdt. No. 1) 1971	**am.,** 1971/201
76	National Insurance and Industrial Injuries (Collection of Contributions) Amdt. Provnl. Regs. 1971	**r.,** 1971/993
77	Welfare Foods (Amdt.) O. 1971 ...	**r.,** 1971/457
107	Witnesses' Allowances Regs. 1971 ...	**am.,** 1971/1259
108	Coroners (Fees and Allowances) Rules 1971	**am.,** 1971/1260
126	A.S. (Citation of Witnesses) 1971 ...	**expired** 8.3.71
127	A.S. (Citation of Jurors) 1971 ...	**expired** 8.3.71
129	Registration of Marriages (Welsh Language) Regs. 1971	**am.,** 1971/1217
145	Firemen's Pension Scheme O. 1971 ...	**am.,** 1971/1329
156	Police Regs. 1971	**am.,** 1971/659, 1141
166	Price Stability of Imported Products (Rates of Levy) (Eggs) (No. 3) O. 1971	**r.,** 1971/192
167	A.S. (Citation of Defencers in the Sheriff Ct.) 1971	**expired** 8.3.71
192	Price Stability of Imported Products (Rates of Levy) (Eggs.) (No 4) O. 1971	**r.,** 1971/327
209	Lands Tribunal (Temporary Provns.) Rules 1971	**expired** 5.4.71

Year and Number (or date)	Act or Instrument	How affected
1971		
214	Judicial Ctee. (Medical Rules) O. 1971	**r.,** 1971/393
232	Police Pensions Regs. 1971	**am.,** 1971/583, 1327
233	Special Constables (Pensions) Regs. 1971	**am.,** 1971/1328
234	Special Constables (Pensions) (S.) Regs. 1971	**am.,** 1971/585, 1402
273	Import Duties (Temporary Exemptions) (No. 2) O. 1971	**am.,** 1971/499
274	Import Duty Drawbacks (No. 1) O. 1971	**am.,** 1971/1186
288	Legal Aid (S.) (Children) Regs. 1971...	**am.,** 1971/554
303	Therapeutic Substances (Control of Sale and Supply) Regs. 1971	**r.,** 1971/459
304	Therapeutic Substances (Supply of Antibiotics and Chemotherapeutic Substances for Agricultural Purposes) Regs. 1971	**am.,** 1971/1405
311	Live Poultry (Restrictions) O. 1971 ...	**am.,** 1971/1036
327	Price Stability of Imported Products (Rates of Levy) (Eggs) (No. 5) O. 1971	**r.,** 1971/603
356	A.S. (Extension of Prescribed Time) 1971	**expired** 8.3.71
357	A.S. (Removal Notices) 1971	**expired** 8.3.71
364	Anti-Dumping (Provisional Charge to Duty) O. 1971	**r.,** 1971/518
450	Road Vehicles (Registration and Licensing) Regs. 1971	**am.,** 1971/1285
460	Industrial Training Levy (Knitting, Lace and Net) O. 1971	**am.,** 1971/1070
477	Exchange Control (Authorised Dealers and Depositaries) O. 1971	**am.,** 1971/1028, 1370
519	Anti-Dumping (Provisional Charge to Duty) (No. 2) O. 1971	**r.,** 1971/1048
603	Price Stability of Imported Products (Rates of Levy) (Eggs) (No. 6) O. 1971	**r.,** 1971/684
621	National Insurance (Attendance Allowance) Regs. 1971	**am.,** 1971/707
643	Merchant Shipping (Fees) Regs. 1971...	**am.,** 1971/1003, 1353
684	Price Stability of Imported Products (Rates of Levy) (Eggs) (No. 7) O. 1971	**r.,** 1971/773
707	National Insurance (Claims and Payments) Regs. 1971	**am.,** 1971/1219, 1419
773	Price Stability of Imported Products (Rates of Levy) (Eggs) (No. 8) O. 1971	**r.,** 1971/817

Year and Number (or date)	Act or Instrument	How affected
1971		
817	Price Stability of Imported Products (Rates of Levy) (Eggs) (No. 9) O. 1971	**r.,** 1971/912
848	Aircraft Customs Regs. 1971	**am.,** 1971/1299
884	Awards (First Degree, etc., Courses) (Amdt.) Regs. 1971	**r.,** 1971/1297
912	Price Stability of Imported Products (Rates of Levy) (Eggs) (No. 10) O. 1971	**r.,** 1971/952
952	Price Stability of Imported Products (Rates of Levy) (Eggs) (No. 11) O. 1971	**r.,** 1971/985
985	Price Stability of Imported Products (Rates of Levy) (Eggs) (No. 12) O. 1971	**r.,** 1971/1027
1022	Hydrocarbon Oil Duties (Drawback) (No. 1) O. 1971	**r.,** 1971/1233
1027	Price Stability of Imported Products (Rates of Levy) (Eggs) (No. 13) O. 1971	**r.,** 1971/1157
1069	Price Stability of Imported Products (Rates of Levy) (Cereals) (No. 1) O. 1971	**r.,** 1971/1264
1075	Anti-Dumping (Provisional Charge to Duty) (No. 3) O. 1971	**am.,** 1971/1348
1157	Price Stability of Imported Products (Rates of Levy) (Eggs) (No. 14) O. 1971	**r.,** 1971/1271
1264	Price Stability of Imported Products (Rates of Levy) (Cereals) (No. 2) O. 1971	**r.,** 1971/1429
1271	Price Stability of Imported Products (Rates of Levy) (Eggs) (No. 15) O. 1971	**r.,** 1971/1319
1319	Price Stability of Imported Products (Rates of Levy) (Eggs) (No. 16) O. 1971	**r.,** 1971/1401

Index to Parts I and II

SBN 11 840090 8*